A PLUME BOOK

THE FILMMAKER'S HANDBOOK

STEVEN ASCHER is an Oscar-nominated filmmaker whose films include *Troublesome Creek*, *So Much So Fast*, and *Raising Renee* (trilogy codirected with his wife, Jeanne Jordan). He has taught filmmaking at Harvard University and the Massachusetts Institute of Technology, and in workshops around the world. His awards include the Sundance Grand Jury Prize and Audience Award, the Prix Italia, a George Foster Peabody Award, and an Emmy Award, and he was nominated for a Directors Guild of America Award. His website is www.WestCityFilms.com.

EDWARD PINCUS's pioneering work in personal documentary led to *Diaries (1971–76)*. He codirected *Black Natchez*, *One Step Away*, *Panola*, *Portrait of a McCarthy Supporter*, and *The Axe in the Attic*. He founded the Film Section at the Massachusetts Institute of Technology and later taught filmmaking at Harvard. He has received a Guggenheim Fellowship and National Endowment for the Arts grants. He is author of the widely used *Guide to Filmmaking* and grows cut flowers commercially in northern New England.

Pincus and Ascher also codirected *Life and Other Anxieties*.

THE FILMMAKER'S HANDBOOK

A COMPREHENSIVE GUIDE FOR THE DIGITAL AGE

FOURTH EDITION

Steven Ascher & Edward Pincus

Drawings by Carol Keller and Robert Brun
Original Photographs by Ted Spagna
and Stephen McCarthy

Completely Revised and Updated by Steven Ascher
With Contributions by David Leitner

A PLUME BOOK

PLUME
Published by the Penguin Group
Penguin Group (USA) Inc., 375 Hudson Street, New York, New York 10014, U.S.A. • Penguin Group (Canada), 90 Eglinton Avenue East, Suite 700, Toronto, Ontario, Canada M4P 2Y3 (a division of Pearson Penguin Canada Inc.) • Penguin Books Ltd., 80 Strand, London WC2R 0RL, England • Penguin Ireland, 25 St. Stephen's Green, Dublin 2, Ireland (a division of Penguin Books Ltd.) • Penguin Group (Australia), 707 Collins Street, Melbourne, Victoria 3008, Australia (a division of Pearson Australia Group Pty. Ltd.) • Penguin Books India Pvt. Ltd., 11 Community Centre, Panchsheel Park, New Delhi – 110 017, India • Penguin Group (NZ), 67 Apollo Drive, Rosedale, Auckland 0632, New Zealand (a division of Pearson New Zealand Ltd.) • Penguin Books, Rosebank Office Park, 181 Jan Smuts Avenue, Parktown North 2193, South Africa • Penguin China, B7 Jaiming Center, 27 East Third Ring Road North, Chaoyang District, Beijing 100020, China

Penguin Books Ltd., Registered Offices: 80 Strand, London WC2R 0RL, England

First published by Plume, a member of Penguin Group (USA) Inc.

First Printing, June 1984
First printing (second edition), March 1999
First printing (third edition), August 2007
First printing (fourth edition), December 2012
20 19 18 17 16 15 14 13 12

Copyright © Edward Pincus and Steven Ascher, 1984, 1999
Copyright © Steven Ascher, 2007, 2012
Drawings and photographs copyright © Steven Ascher, 1999, 2007, 2012
Drawings copyright © Carol Keller, 1999
Drawings copyright © Robert Brun, 1999
Photographs copyright © Ted Spagna, 1983
All rights reserved

 REGISTERED TRADEMARK—MARCA REGISTRADA

CIP data is available.
ISBN 978-0-452-29728-9

Printed in the United States of America

ALWAYS LEARNING   PEARSON

For Jordan

For Jane

CONTENTS

If you look at how storytelling in movies changes over time, you can see moments when new technology has made new kinds of narratives possible. Sometimes it's a seismic shift. The introduction of sound in the 1920s transformed scriptwriting, film acting, and editing. Or it may be more gradual, but just as dramatic, like the way digital has led to documentary and fiction films that would have been technically or financially impossible before.

As a filmmaker, you find that changes come so fast these days that it's really daunting to try to tell stories while having to learn and master so much about your craft. This book, which is for beginners and for working professionals, can help you. Inevitably, some parts won't be as current as the latest information on the Web, but the book offers something most websites can't: a view of the entire filmmaking process from beginning to end. It will give you the foundation and language to understand new developments as they come along.

The Filmmaker's Handbook started out almost thirty years ago, and through the editions it's become a stockpot of ingredients added and removed. In 1984 Ed and I wrote the first edition about working with celluloid film. After that, Ed bowed out of working on the book and in 1999 I wrote an expanded second edition to include analog video; in 2007 I did another major expansion to introduce digital, doubling the size of the original book. David Leitner—a talented filmmaker and explorer of technology—contributed his expertise to that third edition and to this fourth edition. As of this edition, I've had to jettison a lot of material about once-proud film, which is painful. But digital is the future and the book is already a doorstop (or the e-book equivalent).

The world of moviemaking is really made up of many separate but related worlds. I've tried to address the needs of fiction and documentary filmmakers, who may be creating work on their own or as part of a large organization, to be shown in any number of ways, for profit or not.

In a sense, all moviemakers start out as independents. More often than not, beginners must become versed in all aspects of production—shooting, sound recording, editing, raising money, distribution—simply because there's no one else to perform these tasks. Learning all the facets of filmmaking has advantages no matter what your future career is in movies. In fact, with shrinking budgets and the growing power of technology, professional moviemakers are often expected to have a range of skills that go well beyond traditional job categories. This book is written with the assumption that you may be performing all the tasks of making a movie, or that you'll at least want to understand them. And of course, it's a reference: so read what concerns you and skip the sections that don't.

For help along the way, thanks go to Mark Abbate, Benjamin Bergery, Richard Bock, David Brown, Michael Callahan, Elvin Carini, Claude Chelli, Frank Coakley, Victoria Garvin Davis, Bob Doyle, Stefan Forbes, Sandra Forman, Patrick Gaspar, Len Gittleman, Alfred Guzzetti, Arnie Harchik, Bruce Jacobs, Sam Kauffmann, Rudolph Kingslake, Dennis Kitsz, Mark Lipman, Julie Mallozzi, Greg McCleary, Ross McElwee, Matt McMakin, Eric Menninger, Robb Moss, Graeme Nattress, Michael Phillips, Sami Pincus, Adam Schatten, Moe Shore, Tim Spitzer, and Serena Steuart.

Thanks to Ted Spagna, Stephen McCarthy, Ned Johnston, and Andy Young for photographs, to Carol Keller and Rob Brun for illustrations, and to researchers Joshua Weinstein and Luke Gasbarro.

Thanks also to the many people, too numerous to mention, who graciously provided assistance, information, or pictures.

Particular thanks to David Leitner for his deep knowledge and precise mind.

Jeanne Jordan, my filmmaking partner and wife, and our son, Jordan Ascher, both contributed to the book, my work, and my life in more ways than I can express or possibly thank them for.

Steven Ascher

May 2012

THE
FILMMAKER'S
HANDBOOK

CHAPTER 1

Introduction to Digital and Film Systems

This book is about making movies, whether they are dramatic features, documentaries, music videos, corporate videos, multimedia projects, TV programs, commercials, webisodes, or home videos. Actually, "movie" isn't the right term to describe all types of productions; no single word is. You could call them "motion pictures," but that has echoes of Hollywood hype (especially when preceded by "major"). Sometimes the name we use for a production has to do with how it's made. For example, if you say you're making a "video," people will probably assume you're shooting with a video camera, not a film camera. But often the name has more to do with how the end product is distributed. A documentary shown in a theater might be a "film," but if you saw the same thing on television you might call it a "show" or a "program." A two-hour drama may begin life as a "picture," be called a "feature" when shown at a festival, a "release" in theaters, a "movie" when broadcast on television or streamed on the Internet, and a "DVD" or "Blu-ray" at a retail store.

This confusion about names reflects how diverse the many forms of production and distribution have become. There was a time when a "film" was photographed on celluloid film, edited on film, and shown on film. Though that is still possible, today a digital production will most likely be shot in high definition video, or in a 2K or 4K digital file format using a digital cinematography camera; then it will be digitally edited and released in a wide variety of digital media including professional tape cassette, DVD, Blu-ray, and hard disk drives containing digital media files for Internet streaming and downloading, digital broadcast and cable, and digital theater projection.

Because movies are now created, manipulated, and shown in all sorts of new ways, the old, hard distinctions between filmmakers, videomakers, and digital video artists no longer apply. In the wake of the digital video revolution, all approaches now pass through a computer. This is why the term *workflow*, borrowed from IT (information technology) to describe the careful step-by-step management of a complex project, is now used by filmmakers to talk about strategies for managing digital production, editing, and finishing.

The first edition of *The Filmmaker's Handbook* was about film only. The second and third editions added analog, then digital video. In this fourth edition, the focus is shifted even further toward digital technologies. This is not because film is dead— it isn't yet, though its future is increasingly limited. Equipment manufacturers are no longer making film cameras, and theaters are steadily converting to digital. Nevertheless, some of the largest and smallest productions are still being done with film. This book is written from the point of view that media makers will reach for whatever tools suit them best to record, edit, and display their work. Their toolset can include digital and film technologies in any number of configurations.

Which brings us back to the problem of names. Given the expansiveness of the media-making process, what shall we call the work being produced? As this is *The Filmmaker's Handbook*, we'll call the end product a "film" or a "movie." This is for convenience only and is not meant to suggest any limitations in terms of the media, formats, or equipment used to make or distribute the production.

This first chapter is intended as an overview of the moviemaking process, an outline of techniques and equipment.

Making a Movie

The technical, creative, financial, and social aspects of filmmaking are tightly interwoven, perhaps more so than in any other art form. The more you understand about all these aspects of production, the better prepared you'll be for the challenges of making a movie and getting it seen.

Movie production ranges from multimillion-dollar, big-screen Hollywood epics to a home video of a child's birthday. Although movies vary widely in terms of budgets, number of personnel, and intended audiences, many of the processes used to create movies are similar for all types of productions. Moviemaking tasks can be divided chronologically into *development, preproduction, production, postproduction,* and *distribution* periods.

Fig. 1-1. Moviemaking is a collaborative art.

The development phase is when an idea grows into a project that can be produced. A topic is chosen; research is done. For fiction projects, a *treatment* may be written in preparation for a *script*. Documentaries may start as a written proposal outlining what is to be filmed. The producer draws up a *budget* of the movie's estimated cost and arranges for financing. For higher-budget projects, this usually involves soliciting investors, distributors, grants, or a television contract. Low-budget projects are often self-financed, often with the hope of recouping costs after the movie is finished.

During the preproduction period, preparations are made for shooting. The *crew* is assembled and *locations* (the sites where the movie will be shot) are scouted. For fiction films, *casting* is done to choose actors, and all the elements of production design including sets, props, and wardrobe are determined.

The production period essentially begins when the camera rolls. This is sometimes called the start of *principal photography*. Since movie equipment can be expensive, it is often rented for the duration of production, or only on the days it is needed. Lower-priced gear may be purchased outright. *Additional photography* or *pickup shots* are scenes filmed separately from the main production or after the principal shooting is done. The material that's been filmed may be viewed during production, on set, or elsewhere. The traditional film term for the footage recorded by the camera is *rushes* or *dailies*, because the film is processed and printed at the lab as fast as possible for daily viewing (these terms can also be used for digital video, which may or may not need processing before viewing). Rushes are unedited, though often not all the footage that was shot gets printed, copied, or viewed.

The postproduction period (often just called *post*, as in, "We're scheduled for eight weeks of post") generally begins once the principal shooting is completed. On many films, the editor works during production, cutting as soon as each scene is shot, which can give the director and crew feedback in time to make corrections. On other projects, editing starts after the shooting stops. Editing is done to condense what is typically many hours' worth of raw film or digital footage into a watchable movie. It is usually in the editing room that the project can be seen in its entirety for the first time. Movies are often substantially rearranged and reworked during editing. Documentaries often find their structure and shape in the editing room, not from a preplanned script. The first edited version of a movie is the *assembly* or *string-out* (all the scenes in order). The assembly is condensed into a *rough cut*, which is then honed to a *fine cut*. When a satisfactory version is complete (called *picture lock*), the various stages of *finishing* take place. This may include *scoring* with original music or adding prerecorded music; *sound editing* (to clean up and enhance the sound track); *sound mix* (to balance and perfect the sound); and creating titles and any visual effects that weren't done earlier.

When a movie that was shot on film is finished, 35mm *prints* can be made if the movie is intended for theatrical release. A movie shot digitally and intended for theaters can also be transferred to 35mm film; this process is sometimes called a *film-out*. Whether originated on film or digital media, movies meant for theatrical release are also converted to a *Digital Cinema Package* (*DCP*), a file format standardized by Hollywood for digital projection of feature films. (Whether or not a DCP is made, all movies, regardless of whether they were shot on film or digitally, are eventually distributed in some digital form.)

Finally, the movie is *released* or *distributed*—sent out into the world to find its audience. There are many types of distribution, aimed at different markets. *Theatri-*

cal release is the goal of most feature films. A theatrical run may take place in *first-run movie houses* or smaller, specialized *art houses*, which are often part of a *specialty chain*. *Television distribution* may include traditional broadcast television, cable TV, or satellite. *Educational* or *AV (audiovisual)* distribution usually implies selling or renting DVDs or Blu-ray Discs or digitally streaming movies to schools and libraries. *Home video* release is selling or renting movies either directly to consumers or through retail outlets. *Video-on-demand (VOD)* and *pay-per-view (PPV)* are cable distribution methods that bridge the gap between television and home video sales by allowing viewers to select and/or pay individually for programming when they want it. Distribution over the Internet—including streaming and downloading of movie files to laptops, tablets, smartphones, and Web-connected TVs—is becoming a dominant form of movie distribution. Consumers and distributors both like the fact that no physical disc need be purchased or shipped; movies are following the model of music downloading, which decimated the sales of music CDs.

A given project may be distributed through all of these channels or in various combinations; moreover, because movies are increasingly distributed in a global marketplace, issues of multiple languages, technologies, and venues must be dealt with. Many decisions you make while you're producing a movie affect what kind of distribution is possible, and you must try to anticipate distribution goals from the very start of your project.

The Moving Image

A video or film camera has a lens that focuses an image of the world onto a light-sensitive electronic sensor (see Fig. 1-4) or a piece of light-sensitive film (see Fig. 1-31). This part of the process is much like a still camera. But how do we capture *movement*? The impression of continuous movement in a motion picture is really an illusion. A film or video camera records a sequence of still images (frames) in rapid succession (see Fig. 1-2). In film, the standard frame rate is 24 *frames per second*, written 24 *fps*. When the images are then displayed one after another on a screen (for example, a theater screen or a TV), if the frames in the sequence change from one to the next quickly enough and the differences between them are not too great, the brain perceives smooth, realistic motion. This effect brings the magic of motion to film, video, and flip books.

Fig. 1-2. All motion pictures—in video or film—are made up of a series of still images that appear to move when shown rapidly, one after the other. (Steven Ascher)

Traditionally, this illusion has been explained by something called *persistence of vision*, which is based on the idea that the eye retains an impression of each frame slightly longer than it is actually exposed to it. According to this theory, when each new frame is displayed, the eye blends it with the afterimage of the previous frame, creating a smooth transition between them. There are many problems with this explanation (for example, afterimages move with your eyes if you look left or right; they don't stay in place on the screen). A perceptual illusion called *beta movement* describes one situation in which viewers interpret successive still images as motion. A static shot of a ball is flashed on the left side of a screen, then on the right side, and viewers see it as moving from left to right. Think of a lighted ticker tape–style sign in a store, on which messages seem to scroll from right to left across the display as the lights flash on and off.

The full picture of how the brain and eye actually perceive motion is still under investigation. What we do know is that for a realistic viewing experience we need to create the illusion of both smooth motion and consistent illumination. If the images change too slowly from one to the next, the illusion falls apart. Instead of smooth motion you see jerky, stop-start motion, and instead of continuous illumination, the screen may appear to *flicker* (get brighter and darker as the images change). For more on this, see Judder or Strobing, p. 393.

Fig. 1-3. Sony PMW-F3 camcorder. Has a Super 35 sensor and records XDCAM EX internally and other formats to external recorders. Shown with Zacuto external viewfinder and follow-focus control. (Zacuto USA)

DIGITAL VIDEO SYSTEMS

Camera and Recorder Basics

We've just seen that the concept behind motion picture recording is to capture a series of still images and then play them back. Let's look at how this is done in digital video.

The video camera focuses its image on the flat surface of a solid-state electronic chip that is sensitive to light. This chip is the camera's *sensor* or *imager*. There are two types of sensor chips: *CCD* (*charge-coupled device*) and *CMOS* (*complementary metal oxide semiconductor*). CMOS is now the most common chip used in video cameras because of its versatility and lower cost and power consumption. The surface of a sensor is divided into a very fine grid of light-sensitive sites called *pixels* (from "picture elements") or *photosites*. Each photosite in the chip acts in some ways like a tiny light meter that reads the brightness of the light at that spot. When a photosite is struck by light, it creates and stores an electric charge. The more light that strikes it, the more charge builds up (this process can be compared to a bucket filling with rainwater; see Fig. 5-25). A given sensor may have millions of pixels in a chip that is less than an inch across. To capture the whole picture, the charge at each pixel in the grid is read out at an instant in time and the output from all the pixels taken together is reassembled into the *video frame*.

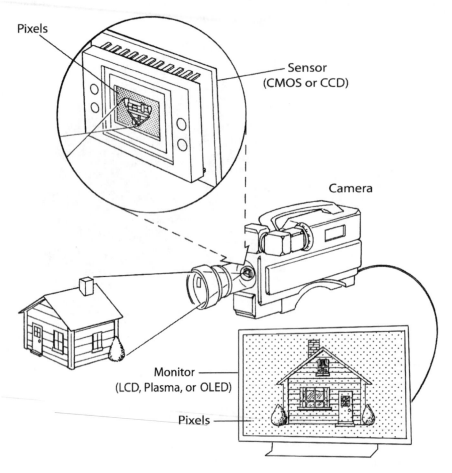

Fig. 1-4. Video camera and monitor. The camera's lens focuses an image of the world onto the sensor, which contains light-sensitive pixels. The camera converts the image into a digital video signal, which can be displayed on a monitor. The monitor's surface is made up of pixels that emit light. (Robert Brun)

In the earliest days of television, the only way to preserve the image from a live TV camera was to record it on black-and-white film using a *kinescope*, basically a 16mm camera aimed at a TV. In 1956 the *videotape recorder (VTR)* was introduced, which records on magnetic tape. VTRs are sometimes called *tape decks, video decks*, or just *decks*. Later tape decks used tape in cassettes, although the term *videocassette recorder (VCR)* was usually reserved for machines used in the home. These days, video recording is also done to solid-state flash memory media, to hard disk drives, and to recordable optical discs. When a camera and recorder are combined in one unit, it's called a *camcorder*. Today, devices capable of recording video include mobile phones, tablets, and *DSLRs (digital single-lens reflex* cameras), which are also called *HDSLRs (high definition single-lens reflex* cameras). DSLRs were originally designed to shoot still images, but like many devices these days they can now shoot both stills and motion video.

Video can be viewed on a display called a *monitor*. Types of flat-screen monitors include *LCD (liquid crystal display)*, which is what many computers use, *OLED (organic light-emitting diode)*, and *plasma*. Video can also be digitally projected onto a large screen using a number of technologies. The traditional analog TV was based on the *cathode ray tube*, or *CRT*, which is no longer made. For more on monitors, see p. 216.

Fig. 1-5. Videotape recorder, or VTR. Panasonic AJ-HD1400 plays and records high definition DVCPRO HD. Can also play standard definition DVCPRO, DVCAM, and DV. (Panasonic Broadcast)

Analog Versus Digital

Until the 1980s, video and audio production was done with analog equipment. In analog tape recorders, continuously changing video or audio signals are recorded as continuously changing amounts of magnetism on tape. In today's digital recorders, the video or audio signal is *digitized*—converted to a set of numbers that can then be stored in various ways (for more on how digital works, see p. 227).

Though most countries have already or will soon stop broadcasting analog TV, echoes of these obsolete, standard definition analog broadcast standards survive into the digital era. They include the NTSC (National Television System Committee) standard, which was used for broadcasts in North America and parts of Asia, including Japan, South Korea, and Taiwan, and the PAL (Phase Alternating Line) standard used in the UK, western Europe, Australia, and parts of Asia and South America.[1]

---

1. In France and Russia, video was produced in PAL but broadcast in SECAM (*Séquentiel Couleur à Mémoire*), which has the same frame rate and number of lines.

Fig. 1-6. Digital single-lens reflex (DSLR). The Canon EOS 5D Mark II played a key role in sparking the use of DSLRs for filmmaking. (Canon U.S.A., Inc.)

As we'll see below, various aspects of digital video formats depend on whether you're in a former NTSC country or a country that used PAL. It's worth noting that the terms "NTSC" and "PAL" properly refer only to analog formats, not digital formats that have similar frame size, even though many people use the terms loosely to mean either analog or digital.

Ironically, digital video equipment often includes analog components, such as CCD or CMOS sensors (yes, they're analog) or analog microphone inputs on a digital audio recorder. It's common to convert sounds and images back and forth between analog and digital forms when needed, though there is some quality loss each time you do.[2] Ideally, once the video and audio are in digital form, they should remain digital for as much of the production process as possible.

THE VIDEO FORMAT

Video format refers to how many lines or pixels form an image, the basic shape of the picture, how a signal is processed or compressed along the way, what medium it's recorded onto, what broadcast standard is used, and a host of other technical aspects of how video is captured, transmitted, or reproduced. There are many formats in use today—so many that even professionals get confused trying to keep track of them all. Though video formats are defined by their key differences, they all have a lot in common. Let's look at the ways that video formats capture images and sounds.

How Many Pixels: Standard Definition, High Definition, and Beyond

A digital video image is formed by a rectangular grid of pixels (see Fig. 5-26). Each pixel represents the brightness (and color, if any) of that part of the image. The *frame* is all the pixels that can be seen in the picture (these are known as *active pixels*). It helps to visualize the pixel grid as a set of horizontal lines stacked on top of one another, since that's how the picture information is processed. Each horizontal line, or *scan line*, is a row of horizontal pixels, and the total pattern of all the lines stacked together is called the *raster*.

---

2. There can also be quality loss when converting between different digital formats.

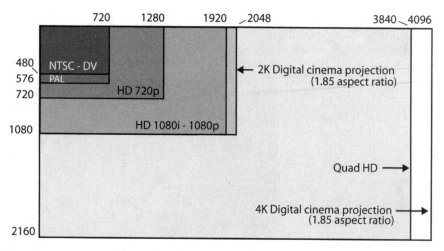

Fig. 1-7. Pixel counts in different digital formats. This shows the number of pixels in standard definition 480i (NTSC countries) and 576i (PAL countries), high definition 720p and 1080i/p, digital cinema projection in 2K and 4K, and Quad HD. Note that the number of pixels in a digital recording format is not the same as the physical size of the sensor (see Fig. 2-7). For example, if you have an HD camera and an SD camera, the sensor on the HD camera could have a smaller surface area, even though the HD recording format has more pixels (it depends on the camera). As shown here, NTSC- and PAL-based formats have different pixel counts, but when viewed on screen, the shape of their frames is actually the same (which is accomplished by using different-shaped pixels). (Steven Ascher)

Video formats differ in how many pixels and how many lines they have (see Fig. 1-7).

Standard-definition television (also called *SDTV, SD,* or *standard def*) has the smallest number of pixels of the broadcast formats. As a legacy of the analog era, there are two flavors of digital SD used in different parts of the world (see above for the specific countries).

In NTSC territories, today's digital standard definition frame is a rectangle of about 480 horizontal lines, each 720 pixels wide (this is often indicated as 720 x 480 and pronounced "720 by 480"). In former PAL countries, the digital SD picture has 576 horizontal lines, also 720 pixels wide.

High-definition television (*HDTV, HD,* or *high def*) uses more pixels per frame. How many more? There are also two sizes of HD. The larger HD format, sometimes called *Full HD*, is 1920 x 1080 (1080 horizontal lines, each 1920 pixels wide). This format has a total of around 2 million pixels, or two megapixels (Mpx). A smaller HD format, usually referred to as *720p*, is 1280 x 720, which is a little less than 1 Mpx. Both of these formats are worldwide standards used in both former NTSC and former PAL countries.

Why do we care about the number of pixels? As the pixel count goes up, so does the ability to record fine detail in the image, allowing for a clearer, sharper picture. Formats that have more pixels are considered higher *resolution* (there are other factors that contribute to resolution, as well). On a very small screen, you might not be able to see a big difference between SD and HD. But the larger the screen size, the worse

SD looks: there may be an overall fuzziness or lack of detail and you may see the individual pixels, which makes the picture look "digital" and not natural. High definition formats allow you to display the image on a bigger screen while still maintaining sharpness and clarity. Bigger screens give a more cinemalike viewing experience.

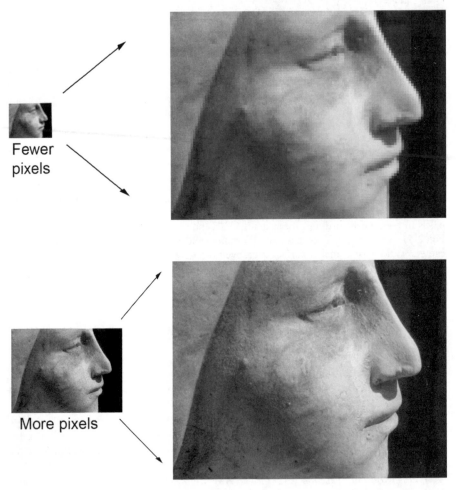

Fewer pixels

More pixels

Fig. 1-8. (top) When you enlarge a low-resolution image, it starts to look unsharp. You may begin to see individual pixels and unwanted artifacts like the jagged line on the edge of the nose. (bottom) When a higher-resolution image is enlarged, it retains more of its sharpness and clarity. This is one reason why high definition video looks better than standard definition, especially on a big screen. (Steven Ascher)

When it comes to an *actual* cinema experience—widescreen projection in a large theater—there are digital motion picture formats that use higher pixel counts than HD video. Many theaters are equipped with *digital cinema* projectors that can display a *2K* (2048 x 1080) or *4K* (4096 x 2160) image. At these resolutions, digital images rival or surpass the resolution of projected 35mm film. Cameras that can record 2K, 4K, and other resolutions higher than HD are increasingly affordable and are sought after by filmmakers who want to create images that will maintain clarity and detail on a big screen.

A 4K format gaining traction is *Quad HD*, also called *Ultra HD 4K* or *Ultra High Definition TV* (*UHDTV*). The frame is 3840 x 2160; you can think of it as four 1920 x 1080 Full HD frames put together. (Some call this *4K2K*, though others use *4K2K* to mean the digital cinema 4K frame size, which is just a little wider; see Fig. 1-7.) There is even an 8K UHD format on the horizon.

Many feel that Ultra HD will make HD obsolete, just as HD has done to SD. As discussed later, the benefits of very high resolution formats (including advantages for 3D) have to be weighed against the increase in data, equipment costs, focus challenges in shooting, and questions about how much resolution provides the best viewer experience (more is not necessarily visibly better on smaller screens). Even so, some people are shooting projects in 4K or 6K so they'll be ready for the future, even if they finish the movie in HD today.

Converting between formats that have different pixel counts is sometimes called *scaling* or *rescaling*. Going from low resolution to high resolution is *upconverting*, *upscaling*, or *up-resing* (pronounced "up-rezzing" and sometimes spelled with *zs*). Going the other way is *downconverting*, *downscaling*, or *down-resing*. When material shot in high definition is downconverted to standard definition, the footage will generally look better than material that was originally shot in SD (though results depend on the footage and the method of downscaling). Standard definition footage that is upscaled to HD will never look as good as material that originated in high def.

A NOTE ABOUT FRAME AND SENSOR SIZE. We've been talking about how different digital formats have different numbers of pixels (that is, different frame sizes). Keep in mind that the number of pixels recorded by a digital video format (as shown in Fig. 1-7) is different from the number of light-sensitive photosites on the surface of the camera's sensor that capture the image (see Fig. 1-13). Confusingly, people usually refer to those photosites as pixels, even though with most cameras, the signals from several photosites are combined to form one pixel in the final recorded image. And to add another ingredient to the mix, when people talk about sensor size, they're often referring to the physical dimensions of the sensor itself, not the number of pixels (see Fig. 2-7).

As an example, a compact video camera might capture 1920 x 1080 Full HD (frame size) using a very small 2 megapixel sensor (photosites/pixels) that's only ¼ inch across (physical size), while a DSLR might capture the same HD format with a 21 megapixel sensor that's six times as large—almost 1½ inches across. (And with a simple switch in the menu, both of those cameras are likely capable of recording in a variety of others frame sizes as well, such as 720 x 480 SD or 1280 x 720 HD.) For more on the importance of sensor size, see p. 66.

Progressive and Interlace Scanning

Many digital cameras are capable of recording using either *progressive* or *interlace scanning* (though the choice may not be available at all frame rates). When a camera uses progressive scanning, all the pixels of each frame are captured at the same in-

Fig. 1-9. With the lens removed, you can clearly see the camera's sensor. The Super 35–sized sensor in this Sony NEX-FS100 is the same as the sensor in the Sony F3. (Steven Ascher)

stant in time (or nearly so). Progressive scanning is similar to the way a film camera exposes an entire frame at once, then moves on to the next frame. Processing one whole frame at a time is very simple, very clean.

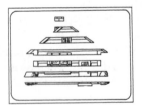  

Fig. 1-10. Interlace. Each field contains half the horizontal video lines. When the two fields are shown rapidly one after the other, the eye integrates them into one complete frame with all the lines. As seen in Fig. 1-11, actual lines are much thinner than shown here. (Robert Brun)

Interlace scanning is an earlier method, still in wide use. Interlace dates back to the first days of NTSC when television systems were too slow to capture and transmit an entire frame at once. With interlace, only half the frame is recorded at a time.[3] The camera starts at the top of the picture and works its way down, capturing

---

3. If you think about it, broadcasting half frames to cut bandwidth in half was the original form of video compression.

odd-numbered lines (1, 3, 5, 7 . . .), while skipping the lines in between. This is the *upper field* (also called the *odd field*). It then returns to the second line from the top and records the other half, the even-numbered lines (2, 4, 6, 8 . . .), all the way to the bottom. This is the *lower* or *even field*.[4] The two fields follow each other rapidly and together they make one frame. Since there are two fields for every frame, 30 frames per second interlace can also be thought of as 60 fields per second.

Though some producers and broadcasters still use interlace, and television viewers are accustomed to it, working in progressive scan can produce superior results.

The problems with interlace include, for starters, that you're seeing only half the lines at a time, which means lower resolution.[5] Interlace also creates various *artifacts* (flaws or irregularities in the image). For example, diagonal lines in a scene can end up looking like jagged stair steps on TV (see Fig. 1-11). This is called *stair-step aliasing*.[6] Another artifact, called *twitter*, happens when thin horizontal lines appear

Fig. 1-11. Interlace artifacts. Each interlace field contains only half of the horizontal lines. In this image you're seeing both fields together. Notice how the man in the foreground has moved between the two fields. You can see how each field has half the resolution, with obvious *edge tear* or *combing* along the edge of his shirt. The diagonal line behind the man in the background reveals an undesirable stair-step pattern called *aliasing* or "jaggies" (which may also occur, to a lesser extent, with progressive formats). See also Fig. 5-17. (Stephen McCarthy)

---

4. In many formats, like DV, the lower fields are recorded first. See Interlace and Field Order, p. 600.

5. Though only half the pixels are seen at once, the resolution isn't cut in half—it's slightly better than that (about 70 percent of the full progressive resolution).

6. The term *aliasing* may also be used to mean any kind of distortion caused by not having enough digital samples to accurately record picture or sound.

to vibrate or flicker as they move up or down in the frame. This is often visible in the text of a credit roll at the end of a movie.

Because interlace involves capturing the first half of each frame (first field) a split second earlier than the second half (second field), you can get motion artifacts when the two halves are shown together. Figure 1-11 shows both interlace fields together as one frame. Notice how the man in the foreground has moved between the first field and the second, causing the edge of his body to have a torn, jagged look (this is called *edge tear* or *combing*). Edge tear doesn't happen if neither the camera nor the subject moves, but when there is movement, edge tear can reduce resolution when the video is playing at normal speed, and if the video is slowed down (say, for sports replays) or frozen (for still images), edge tear can become much more bothersome.

Today we watch video on digital monitors and projectors, all of which are progressive. So interlaced material must be converted to progressive (called *deinterlacing*) in order to watch it. The monitor may do the deinterlacing, or it may take place at an earlier stage. Deinterlacing involves creating a single progressive frame by blending two fields together or sometimes just discarding one field and doubling the other. Deinterlacing can result in lower resolution, and artifacts like edge tear can be a real problem with some material (for more on deinterlacing, see p. 213).

With progressive formats, on the other hand, most of the problems with interlace aren't seen at all and stair-step aliasing is minimized. Footage shot with a progressive camera plays nicely on monitors and projectors and can be posted to the Web or converted to film or converted to still images with no deinterlacing necessary. Today, digital video is distributed in many different ways, often requiring the picture to be resized, repositioned, or converted to different formats. These tasks are much easier to do at high quality if you're working with progressive.

For all these reasons, shooting in progressive is highly recommended. As a rule, if you capture video in progressive, it's easy to convert to interlace later if needed. It's harder to convert interlace to progressive with good results.

Since there is still a lot of interlace video equipment around—though this is changing fast—working in progressive can require finding ways to be compatible with interlace. As an example, a common technique for recording a progressive-scan image is to embed it in an interlace pattern that can be played on interlace decks (for more on this, see Working with 24p and Pulldown, p. 601).

When all digital video is progressive (as it should be), interlace will not be missed.

The Frame Rate

The number of frames recorded each second is the frame rate, which affects how motion appears on screen. Modern digital cameras offer a choice of frame rates, although the legacy of analog broadcast systems has imposed certain standard frame rates among the choices.

The NTSC system used in North America and Japan was designed to run at 60 fields per second because the electric power in wall outlets in these countries runs at 60 Hz. The original analog, black-and-white TV signal was 60 interlaced fields, or 30 frames, every second.

In 1953, NTSC color TV was introduced, and because the color components of the new broadcast signal caused interference at 60 fields per second, the existing 30 fps frame rate was adjusted downward by 0.1 percent to reduce the problem. This made NTSC's *actual* frame rate 29.97 fps, which is often used today for digital productions. For simplicity's sake, when people talk about this rate they often round it up to 30. In NTSC countries, whenever you see a video scanning rate expressed in a whole number, that's for convenience, and the actual rate is 0.1 percent lower. That is, 30 fps really means 29.97 fps and 60 fields per second really means 59.94 fields.

The frame rate 24 fps is a special case. When most digital video cameras in NTSC territories are set to record at 24 fps they are actually recording at 23.976 fps (often written 23.98 fps). Unfortunately, there *are* times when 24 fps really does mean *exactly* 24 fps (such as when shooting with film cameras or with digital cinematography cameras, see p. 28). To avoid confusion, it helps to be as precise as you can when talking about frame rates with members of the production team.

In the rest of the world where PAL once ruled, electric power runs at 50 Hz; the standard frame rate of 25 fps (50 interlaced fields per second) was adopted for analog video and continues to be used on many productions in the digital age. Happily, this is *exactly* 25 fps with no monkey business.

For more on the look of different frame rates and choosing one for your production, see Frame Rate and Scanning Choices, p. 81.

The Shape of the Video Frame

Aspect ratio is a term used to describe the shape of the picture, the ratio of the frame's width to its height (see Fig. 1-12).

Traditional standard definition television has an aspect ratio of 4:3, which means four units wide by three units high. In video this is pronounced "four by three" and is sometimes written 4 x 3. In film, and increasingly with digital, the same thing is described as 1.33, the quotient of 4 divided by 3.

Widescreen video is 16:9, pronounced "sixteen by nine" or written as 16 x 9. Standard definition video can be either 4:3 or 16:9. All forms of HD are 16:9 (which can also be described as 1.78). Some digital productions are done at wider aspect

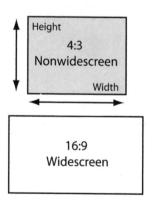

Fig. 1-12. The aspect ratio is the width of the frame divided by its height. Nonwidescreen video has an aspect ratio of 4:3, and widescreen is 16:9.

ratios to match cinema standards of 1.85 or 2.40 (see Fig. 1-35). Digital cinema projection in 2K or 4K is often done at 1.85 aspect ratio (roughly 17:9), which is also the shape of the 4K2K format.

For more on aspect ratio, see pp. 41 and 74.

How Color Is Recorded

Inside your eyeballs are retinal cones, natural sensors that allow you to see color. One type of cone is sensitive to red light, another to blue light, and the third to green. When you look around a room, every color you see is a mix of red, green, and blue light in different proportions.

The sensors in a video camera also measure the relative amounts of red, green, and blue light in the image. Actually, a CCD or CMOS chip "sees" only in black-and-white (it measures only brightness) but it can be tricked into reading color. One method, used in single-chip color cameras, is to place tiny red, green, and blue filters over individual pixels (see Fig. 1-13). In three-chip color cameras, a beam-splitting prism behind the lens divides the incoming image into separate red, green, and blue (RGB) components and sends each to a separate sensor dedicated to that color (see Fig. 1-14).

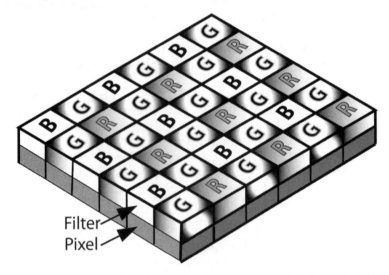

Filter
Pixel

Fig. 1-13. In single-chip cameras, tiny colored filters are positioned over individual photosites (pixels) so that each one records either red, green, or blue light. In the commonly used Bayer pattern shown here, there are twice as many green pixels as either red or blue. The pixels are a bit like tiles in a mosaic, and prior to viewing the image, the data from the sensor must be "demosaicked" (also called "debayered") to calculate full RGB color values for each pixel. For more on this, see p. 203. (Steven Ascher)

RGB, COMPONENT, AND COMPOSITE COLOR. Capturing digital video in color sounds like an easy process—just digitize and store the separate red (R), green (G), and blue (B) signals produced by the camera's sensor. Indeed, when computers create video for, say, *computer-generated imagery* (*CGI*) special effects, they work in *RGB color*, in which signals representing each of the three colors are processed along three separate paths (see Fig. 5-14). Some digital cinema cameras can record RGB color (see below).

Most digital video cameras use a different method of capturing color, one that originated back in the analog era. Black-and-white TV used a single brightness signal called *luminance*. When color was introduced, two color-based signals, called *chrominance* (or "color difference"), were added. This technique of encoding the camera's original RGB signals into one luminance

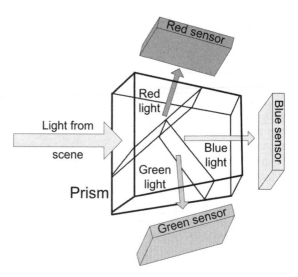

Fig. 1-14. In a three-chip camera, light entering through the lens strikes a prism that divides it into its red, green, and blue components. Each is captured by a separate sensor. (Steven Ascher)

(brightness) and two chrominance (color) signals still defines digital video and digital video cameras (as distinct from digital cinema cameras and their true RGB formats). The three encoded signals are called *component* signals; and video recording formats, whether analog or digital, that maintain separation of these signals are called *component video*. Digital component video formats include DV, DVCAM, DVCPRO, XDCAM, AVCHD, and HDCAM.

Both RGB and component video process color information in *separate* streams; this allows the cleanest color and highest-quality image. Digital broadcast, cable, and satellite all use component signals.

In *composite video*, formerly the basis of analog NTSC and PAL broadcasting, the three video components are joined or encoded into *one* signal that can travel on a single path. Composite can be thought of as "video soup," since all the color and brightness information, as well as audio and sync signals, are mixed together into a single electronic signal. Many digital cameras and monitors still offer composite video inputs and outputs for convenience, but using composite results in a marked loss of image quality.

See p. 207 for more on component and composite systems.

REDUCING COLOR DATA. In high-end digital cinema cameras, all of the color information captured by the camera's sensor is recorded and displayed. Sony's F35 and ARRI's Alexa, for example, can output uncompressed RGB signals with no color data reduction or encoding of any kind. This is sometimes referred to as *RGB 4:4:4 color*.

The drawback of RGB is that it creates an enormous amount of data to be processed and stored. To reduce the amount of data, digital video cameras make use of the fact that when looking at fine details, the human eye is much more sensitive to brightness than to color.[7] High-end component digital video cameras routinely throw away half of their color pixels (which reduces the color detail by half compared to luminance) and most viewers can't see that anything's missing—this is how we're used to looking at digital video.

This technique of throwing away half the color information, called *color sampling* or *color subsampling*, is notated as *4:2:2*. The numbers indicate that all of the video camera's luminance signal is recorded (represented by "4") while only half of each of the chrominance signals ("2" and "2") is preserved. Formats with 4:2:2 color are the highest-quality digital video achievable (RGB 4:4:4 is not considered traditional video).

In order to reduce data (and cost) even further, formats designated 4:1:1 or 4:2:0 record only one-quarter as much information about color as brightness. This economical method is used in many formats, including DV, DVCAM, DVCPRO, HDV, AVCHD, and XDCAM EX. Again, in a typical viewing experience most people can't see the difference. To be clear, the range of color values (the *color gamut*) in these formats is the same as in 4:2:2 video; there's just less color information in the fine details. Greater color subsampling, however, can sometimes make it more difficult to do special effects like green-screen work (see p. 211).

For more on color sampling see p. 209.

What Do You Call That Format?

As you've noticed, an awful lot of numbers and letters get thrown around when talking about video. It's easy to get confused, and the situation isn't helped by the fact that different people use different letters and numbers to talk about the same thing.

These days, the most common notation used to describe a format is:

- the vertical size of the frame (say, 1080 or 480 lines),
- followed by *p* or *i* (for progressive or interlace),
- followed by the number of scans per second (the frame rate or field rate).

So, a format indicated as *1080p/24* tells us that the frame is 1080 pixels high, scanned at 24 progressive frames per second. The digital version of PAL video is sometimes called *576i/25* (576 lines high, interlaced, at 25 fps).

However, with interlaced formats, often it's the *field rate*, not the frame rate, that's indicated (remember, there are two fields for every interlaced frame). So the same PAL format can be written 576i/50. This is the convention you'll find in this book (using the frame rate for progressive and the field rate for interlace). The digital version of NTSC video would be written 480i/60.[8]

In ads, articles, and equipment manuals, notation varies in small and large ways. For example, 1080p/24 may be written 1080/24p.

---

7. The eye registers most picture detail in the green part of the color spectrum, and green makes up over 70 percent of the luminance signal.

8. As mentioned on p. 15, in NTSC countries whole number frame rates are used for convenience, but the actual rate is .01 percent slower. So 60 fields per second is really 59.94.

Sometimes people don't indicate the frame or field rate at all. PAL may be called just 576i, since people know it runs at 25 frames per second. Or they'll refer to Full HD as 1080i or 1080p when they want to denote the frame size without getting into questions of frame rate. Sometimes when people are talking about the motion and look of video they'll just refer to the frame or field rate *without* the frame size, such as 24p or 60i.

As noted earlier, NTSC and PAL were analog formats. To talk about *digital* NTSC or PAL doesn't really make sense. However, for convenience many people use these terms to refer to digital video that has roughly the same frame size and frame rate. So you'll hear people refer to NTSC DV when they mean digital video that's 720 x 480 at 29.97 fps.

One more usage note: the term "digital video" is used in different ways. There are many video formats that are digital and there is a particular standard definition format called DV that uses ¼-inch videotape in MiniDV cassettes along with a type of digital compression also called DV. In this book, the generic term "digital video" is used to refer to *all* digital formats, and DV means that particular format.

No one said this stuff is simple, and don't feel bad if you're confused! Believe it or not, these terms will sort themselves out as you use them.

Fig. 1-15. Devices like the Steadicam Merlin can bring a gliding smoothness to camera moves. (The Tiffen Company)

WHAT IS COMPRESSION?

As time goes on, consumers and content providers expect ever-higher quality and definition from their video systems. The problem is that high definition video in its native state involves lots and lots of digital data that has to be captured, stored, and transmitted. Working with all that data can be expensive because it calls for big storage devices, fast computers, and high-speed connections for broadcasting or Internet distribution.

At the same time, consumers and content providers want formats that are afford-able, easy to work with, and flexible enough to display on screens big and small.

To balance these two needs we have *digital compression.*

The goal of compression is to shrink digital video and audio data down to a smaller size while maintaining picture and sound quality. After images and sound have been compressed, they take up less storage space on computer disks or tape. This allows us to use smaller, cheaper camcorders (production), load more footage into an editing system (postproduction), or fit a longer movie onto a disc for play-back at home (distribution).

A crude analogy to compressed video is instant coffee, which is made by taking brewed coffee and removing the water to make a powder that's compact and easy to store. To drink it, you have to add the water back, restoring the coffee to some-thing close to its original form and (hopefully) taste.

With digital compression, video and audio signals are compressed into a smaller package for storage and transmission. When it's time to view or listen to them, they must be decompressed (expanded). The intent is that the decompressed video will resemble the original as closely as possible. Compression schemes are called *codecs* (from *co*mpressor/*deco*mpressor or *co*der/*deco*der).[9]

There are many different codecs in use. Some are designed to maintain the highest picture quality, others to shrink the amount of data as much as possible. Most try to do both to some extent. If you've ever downloaded music from the Internet you've worked with an audio codec such as *MP3* or the superior *AAC*. These codecs shrink the size of the original music file to speed up downloading and allow you to store more songs on your music player. As codecs evolve, engineers are finding ways to make files smaller while maintaining better quality.

One way to compare video formats is to look at how much data they create (the *data rate* or *bit rate*). This is often measured in *megabits per second* (*Mbps* or *Mb/s*). For example, to record or play back uncompressed standard definition video requires about 172 Mbps, while the compressed DV format uses only about 36 Mbps.[10]

The amount of compression is often indicated as a ratio between the original size of the video/audio data and its compressed size. DV, as described above, is con-sidered 5:1. The DigiBeta format uses 2:1 compression (cutting the data rate in half) for a bit rate of about 90 Mbps. HDV uses a compression ratio of about 40:1.

People often assume that the greater the compression (and thus the lower the data rate), the worse the material will look or sound after it's decompressed. But there has been remarkable progress in recent years and some codecs that are very compressed—called *lossy*—are capable of astonishingly high picture and sound quality. The MPEG-2 compression that makes possible the 40:1 ratio of HDV also makes possible DVDs, Blu-rays, digital TV broadcasting, and cable, while newer, more efficient MPEG-4 codecs like H.264 are widely used in Internet streaming, in AVCHD recording, and in most DSLRs.

With some digital video codecs—called *visually lossless*—a side-by-side compari-

---

9. Sometimes a codec is a software-only mathematical formula called an *algorithm*, and sometimes the algorithm resides in a computer chip.

10. Most people think DV uses a bit rate of 25 Mbps, but this represents only video data. A full DV stream also includes audio, timecode, and other data.

son of uncompressed video and the same material after it has been compressed and decompressed by the codec shows no detectable difference. Examples of these high-quality codecs include Sony's HDCAM SR compression (MPEG-4), Avid's DNxHD 220, and Apple ProRes 422 HQ.

Codecs that employ a high degree of compression may require a lot of computing power to get the job done, which can make working with them slow, depending on your equipment. It's important to understand compression and have a feel for the codecs currently being used because compression plays a key role in what video format you choose to work in, what camera you use, how you edit, and how you distribute your movie.

For more on compression and individual codecs, see p. 245.

COMPARING VIDEO FORMATS

This section will serve as an outline of common video formats. For more on choosing a format and a camera to work with, see Chapter 2. If any of the terms below are unfamiliar, see earlier in this chapter and check the index.

THE EVOLUTION OF FORMATS. Like buying a computer that may be outdated a few months after you get it, when you invest in a digital video format (either because you're purchasing gear or you're simply using it to shoot a project) you need to remember that a new, better format may be just around the corner. The upside is that video systems keep getting smaller, cheaper, and more powerful. The downside is that formats and equipment become obsolete. The movie you shoot today may need to be transferred to another format in several years when you can no longer find playback equipment or editing software in the old format.

Fig. 1-16. Consumer HD camera. Panasonic SD800K records 1080p in AVCHD. Uses three ¼-inch CMOS sensors. (Panasonic)

At one time, format choices were few, and camera choices centered on what size tape they recorded to. Nowadays, a single camera will offer a choice of formats, or different flavors of a given format, and may record to hard drives or memory cards. All this makes it hard to talk about formats in a simple way, and it's not helped by the fact that by the time you finish reading this paragraph, new cameras and formats will have been introduced.

HIGH END VS. LOW END. When manufacturers design and market a piece of equipment they generally try to target a certain type of user. The user categories are not exact, but in descending order of quality and sophistication they are: digital cinema, broadcast, professional/industrial, "prosumer," home/consumer. The assumption is that professionals will pay top prices and can handle complexity, while consumers want something cheap and easy to use. Revolutions have been made, particularly by independent filmmakers, in seizing tools intended for the lower end of the market and showing that they can produce professional-quality work. Footage shot with an inexpensive camcorder or DSLR can look surprisingly like footage from a $100,000 professional rig if it's well shot and lit and the sound is good. On the other hand, it's often true that you get what you pay for, and a high-end camera can provide more control and a better image. It's not uncommon for high- and low-end cameras to be used on the same production for different scenes or situations.

Fig. 1-17. Sony FS100 records AVCHD to memory cards and/or an SSD. Super 35 sensor (see Fig. 1-9).

When comparing formats, take a look at the data rate. Generally speaking, formats that are more compressed (i.e., that have a low data rate) are more affordable. The cameras are smaller and less expensive; you can store more material on a memory card, hard drive, or tape. The highest-quality formats tend to use the least compression (and thus have high data rates) and are often preferred when the footage will be shown on a big screen. However, when deciding on a format, bear in mind that some formats that operate at a high data rate may be within your budget and, by the same token, formats that are less expensive and more compressed may still have excellent sound and picture quality. In this flexible age, you may have several compression options since many cameras offer a choice of higher and lower data rates, and some, such as those with HDMI or HD-SDI output, can output an uncompressed digital signal, allowing you to record to a separate device with yet more compression possibilities. For more on how data rates and formats relate to camera choices and image quality, see Thinking About Camera Choices, Compression, and Workflow, p. 94.

As you'll see in the following section, there's a lot of competition between formats to look best "by the numbers" because filmmakers want the most resolution, the least compression, etc. The competition is fanned by manufacturers trying to market their products. The truth of the matter is that a lot of formats these days look astoundingly good and the differences between some of them may seem noticeable on paper but not to audiences watching them on screen.

STANDARD DEF VS. HIGH DEF. Today broadcasters require that programming be shot in widescreen 16:9 high definition, even if they continue to broadcast some programs in standard definition. If you want to keep the most options open for showing your finished work on television, shooting HD is mandatory. If your work is intended for theaters, you could shoot HD or, if you can afford it, consider shooting at higher resolution like 4K with a digital cinema camera.

That said, many websites stream video in standard definition (or smaller frame sizes) and video-enabled devices like smartphones display video on tiny screens, some of which can't display high definition. So if your work is intended for these outlets, you might choose to shoot HD and downconvert to a smaller frame size in postproduction, or you might even shoot SD. Many high definition camcorders offer a choice of recording in standard definition or they can downconvert internally from HD to SD. Thanks to oversampling, an HD camera will usually produce a better-looking SD image than the image made by a comparable SD camera.

Fig. 1-18. Canon XF305 camcorder records MPEG-2 to CompactFlash cards. Three ⅓-inch chips with 4:2:2 color. (Canon U.S.A., Inc.)

HIGH DEFINITION DIGITAL FORMATS

As of this writing there are two common types of high definition used for broadcasting and cable: 1080i (1920 x 1080 pixels, interlaced) and 720p (1280 x 720 pixels, progressive). However, 1080p, which is at a higher quality level and data rate, is used for a great deal of production, especially at lower frame rates of 24 (23.98), 25, and 30 (29.97) frames per second. 1080p can easily be converted to 1080i or 720p for broadcast if necessary.

1920 x 1080 is also called Full HD since this is the largest HD frame. However, several HD formats with 1080 lines actually record less than 1920 pixels across; 1080i HDCAM and HDV camcorders, for instance, record only 1440 pixels across instead of the standard 1920.[11] This is one of several techniques used to squeeze huge HD signals into small files and onto small-gauge tape formats.

Many consumer and professional SD and HD cameras record digital video with 8 bits of precision (also called bit depth). Some higher-end cameras can record at 10 or 12 bits, which can extend dynamic range and improve image quality, but this increases the amount of data to be processed and stored. See p. 230 for more on bit depth, and Digital Compression, p. 245, for more on the compression methods mentioned below.

All HD cameras shoot in 16:9 widescreen aspect ratio.

Fig. 1-19. DSLRs provide affordable, compact HD recording, usually with some compromises in audio quality and sometimes artifacts in the recorded picture. Shown here with slider for side-to-side movements. (Cinevate)

---

11. These formats record using nonsquare pixels that are expanded to standard square pixels on playback, filling out the 1920 width.

DSLRs and HDSLRs

Digital single-lens reflex cameras that also record video, dubbed *DSLRs* or *HD-SLRs*, typically record in a variety of formats. Common options include Full HD 1920 x 1080 at 30p, 25p, and 24p; 1280 x 720 HD at 60p and 50p; and standard definition 640 x 480 at 60p and 50p. When shooting stills, higher-end DSLRs generally offer the choice of capturing in the uncompressed RAW format (large, unprocessed RGB files at the highest quality, see p. 203) or the compressed JPEG format (smaller file sizes, lower quality). RAW video files are too big to be recorded by the current crop of DLSRs, so compression is required to reduce demands on processing and storage. Codecs such as AVCHD (H.264/MPEG-4 AVC: see below) are used in a number of cameras and some use M-JPEG (motion JPEG). Many filmmakers choose to transcode to a less compressed codec for editing (see p. 558). Already there are DSLRs capable of recording in higher bit rate formats for improved image quality (including versions of H.264 that use intraframe compression only, see p. 246), and filmmakers are clamoring for DSLRs capable of outputting uncompressed RAW, RGB, or component video that can be recorded externally.

HDV

When the DV format was introduced in the mid-1990s, it provided an affordable way to record compressed, standard definition video to a small MiniDV tape cassette. Ten years later *HDV (High Definition Video)* was introduced, using the same MiniDV cassettes as DV, with a signal small enough to be sent through the same FireWire as DV. What made this possible was the use of more efficient MPEG-2 compression instead of DV compression. HDV uses 4:2:0 color sampling, in which only a quarter of the original color samples are preserved. Manufacturers have developed HDV in different ways. Sony and Canon offer recording at 1440 x 1080 at 60i, 30p, and 24p with a data rate of 25 Mbps. Progressive recording is done with pulldown (see p. 601). Some cameras will also record to *CompactFlash (CF)* media cards.

JVC's line of ProHD cameras shoot 1280 x 720 at 24p, 25p, 30p, and 60p with a video data rate of 19 Mbps. They can also shoot 1440 x 1080 at 50i/60i with a data rate of 25 Mbps. (The new line of ProHD cameras can also record in other formats.)

HDV is capable of very good image quality, but due to its relatively heavy video compression at 19 Mbps and 25 Mbps, the industry is moving toward formats with higher data rates or more efficient AVCHD codecs.

Fig. 1-20. Sony HVR-V1U. Records HDV as well as DVCAM and DV to tape cassettes and an optional external hard drive. Three ¼-inch CMOS sensors. (Sony Electronics, Inc.)

AVC and AVCHD

AVC (Advanced Video Coding) is a family of codecs that uses H.264/MPEG-4 AVC compression, which is newer than MPEG-2 and twice as efficient. With MPEG-4 you need less data to achieve the same or better image quality as MPEG-2, which means longer recording times on a disc, media card, or hard drive. Both professional and consumer camcorders use AVC, which in some cameras is called *AVCHD*.

As an example of AVCHD's versatility, Sony's professional NXCAM line of camcorders offers a range of format choices including Full HD 1920 x 1080 at 60p, 24p, and 30p, and 1280 x 720 at 60p, with a maximum bit rate of 28 Mbps for highest quality (see Fig. 1-17). There is also an HDV-like 1440 x 1080 format at 60i. (Compared to HDV's 25 Mbps video data rate, the AVCHD version of 1440 x 1080 is only 9 Mbps.) Like HDV, AVCHD color sampling is 4:2:0.

Panasonic's professional AVCCAM line of camcorders also use AVCHD. At highest quality, they can record full raster 1920 x 1080 at a maximum bit rate of 24 Mbps.

Fig. 1-21. Panasonic AG-HPX500 can record DVCPRO HD and standard definition DVCPRO 50, DVCPRO, and DV to P2 memory cards. Relatively large, shoulder-mount camcorders are popular with broadcast news organizations. (Panasonic Broadcast)

AVC-Intra and AVC Ultra

Other Panasonic professional cameras record what Panasonic calls *AVC-Intra*. Unlike AVCHD's long-GOP interframe compression, AVC-Intra uses only intraframe compression (see p. 246), which makes editing and processing simpler and can improve image quality. AVC-Intra provides highly efficient 10-bit encoding with quality comparable to DVCPRO HD at half the data rate, so you can get twice as much material on a P2 card. The AVC-Intra codec has two modes: 100 Mbps with 4:2:2 chrominance sampling (very high quality, comparable to D-5 HD) and 50 Mbps with 4:2:0 sampling for high quality at a lower data rate.

At the pinnacle of AVC codecs is Panasonic's AVC Ultra, for visually lossless 4:4:4 recording of 1080p, 2K, and 4K at data rates up to 450 Mbps.

XDCAM HD and XDCAM EX

Sony's XDCAM HD cameras record to Blu-ray–based "Professional Discs," which in the era of tapeless acquisition offer the advantage of a physical disc that can be archived. Formats include 1920 x 1080; 1440 x 1080 for reduced data rate; and 1280 x 720. XDCAM employs MPEG-2 at a choice of three data rates: 18 Mbps (variable bit rate), 25 Mbps (constant bit rate, functionally equivalent to HDV), and 35 Mbps (variable bit rate). The higher data rates provide best quality. Color sampling is 4:2:0. The top-of-the-line XDCAM HD422 format records full raster 1920 x 1080 with 4:2:2 color. XDCAM HD camcorders are fairly compact and economical yet Sony includes them in its high-end CineAlta HD camera family.

XDCAM EX cameras are more affordable and record to SxS memory cards instead of Blu-ray Discs (See Fig. 1-27).

Fig. 1-22. Blue-laser disc cartridge used by Sony XDCAM and XDCAM HD cameras. (Sony Electronics, Inc.)

DVCPRO HD

Panasonic's DVCPRO HD format is a 100 Mbps high definition format with 4:2:2 color and 6.7:1 compression. It uses DV *intraframe* compression, meaning that each frame is individually compressed for simplified editing and postproduction (see p. 246).

DVCPRO HD was the original format of Panasonic's VariCam camcorders, which used the same-sized ¼-inch tape cassettes as standard def DVCPRO camcorders. More recent Panasonic camcorders capture DVCPRO HD to P2 flash memory cards instead of to tape.

HDCAM and HDCAM SR

Sony's HDCAM records 1440 x 1080 HD on ½-inch tape in both interlace and progressive formats. HDCAM color is subsampled at a unique 3:1:1, using 7:1

compression for a data rate of 140 Mbps. Sony's CineAlta family of HDCAM cameras, camcorders, and decks can record at true 24p, useful for transfer to 35mm film. They can also record at 23.98 fps for HD compatibility. Other frame rates include 25p, 30p, 50i, and 60i.

HDCAM SR (superior resolution) is Sony's highest-quality codec—recording RGB or 4:2:2 HD at 880, 440, or 220 Mbps to tape or flash memory using mild, lossless MPEG-4 compression. Like Panasonic's AVC Ultra, HDCAM SR doubles as an HD, 2K, and 4K mastering format in post (see Fig. 14-35).

D-5 HD

D-5 HD, based on ½-inch tape cassettes, is Panasonic's highest-quality HD mastering format with data rates up to 235 Mbps. D-5 HD accommodates all 1080-line HD formats, as well as 720-line HD formats. D-5 has been an industry workhorse tape format.

DIGITAL CINEMATOGRAPHY SYSTEMS

Broadcast television has evolved from the standard definition analog systems of the twentieth century to today's high definition digital TV. Because of this history, what we call "video" today has inherited a set of standards for things like pixel counts and frame rates, along with a number of technical compromises.

To sidestep those standards and compromises, a newer generation of digital motion picture cameras, called *digital cinematography* or *digital cinema cameras*, has pushed beyond the limits of HD to achieve higher resolutions, higher frame rates, greater dynamic range, wider aspect ratios, and a wider range of colors. Some can be used for shooting high-resolution 3D.

Fig. 1-23. ARRI Alexa digital cinema camera. Single Super 35 sensor. Accepts standard PL-mount 35mm cine lenses. Can record RAW data, RGB 4:4:4, and other formats including ProRes. One of the most popular cameras for feature film production. (ARRI, Inc.)

Digital cinematography refers to high-quality acquisition, often in the 2K and 4K formats, for productions that previously would have been shot on 35mm film. Digital cinematography projects are often shot at 24p or 25p for transfer to film (also known as *film-out*) or transcoding to DCP for digital theatrical projection.

At the high end of cost and quality, digital cinema cameras like the Sony F35, Sony F65, Panavision Genesis, and ARRI Alexa emulate the size, look, and feel of 35mm motion picture cameras. These cameras contain a single large CCD or CMOS sensor identical in size to a Super 35mm film frame. Employing a Super 35–sized sensor permits the use of standard 35mm motion picture lenses for a traditional feature film look.

At the other end of the cost scale, consumer DSLRs also have large sensors and with modification can often accept 35mm motion picture lenses, which has had a significant impact on the digital cinema world.

In the middle are compact digital cinema cameras, often modular in build, also featuring Super 35–sized sensors. ARRI's Alexa has one foot in this camp too, since it is entirely modular and can be reconfigured in several ways. The RED One camera is similar in size and modularity to Alexa, while Sony's F3, not as modular, is lighter and considerably more affordable. Even smaller are the RED Epic and RED Scarlet, true 4K cameras about the size of a view camera for stills. Epic has been a runaway hit with those shooting 3D, who need small cameras to reduce the size and weight of 3D rigs.

Digital cinema cameras capture images in high-data-rate formats such as RAW and *RGB 4:4:4 log*. Neither RAW nor log output is intended for direct viewing—the images look flat and the color is desaturated. Instead, these formats are used as a "digital negative" to provide a great deal of flexibility in post for creating different looks. Motion images in 2K and 4K RAW are comparable to the unprocessed, direct-from-sensor still images captured by DSLRs in RAW mode (however, the motion images are recorded at 24 times a second). Examples include the Alexa's 2K ARRIRAW and RED's 4K REDCODE format (which is slightly compressed). In 4:4:4 log, the 10-bit RGB tonal values are mapped to a *logarithmic curve* that better approximates the eye's response to highlight detail. A popular example is the *S-Log* recording offered in Sony's CineAlta line of cameras. Both RAW and 4:4:4 log are capable of capturing an enormous range of brightness from dark to light—some cameras can handle fourteen stops of dynamic range. For more on RAW and log recording, see p. 203.

Some digital cinema cameras have smaller sensors, such as Sony's F23, which uses three $\frac{2}{3}$-inch progressive-scan CCDs to capture 1080p RGB images, or Silicon Imaging's SI-2K Mini, which uses a single $\frac{2}{3}$-inch progressive-scan CMOS to capture 2K or 1080p RGB.

The Blackmagic Cinema Camera by Blackmagic Design is as small as a DSLR and similarly priced. It can record uncompressed 2.5K RAW in the Adobe *CinemaDNG* file format, as well as compressed HD in Apple ProRes or Avid DNxHD.

As technology improves and inexpensive digital video cameras are sporting larger sensors, distinctions break down between "standard" video cameras and those that are appropriate for digital cinema productions. High-end cameras offer power, flexibility, and reliability for high-budget productions, but many feature films also employ lower-end cameras for certain looks or scenes. It's worth noting that 1080p

Fig. 1-24. RED's Epic DSMC (Digital Still and Motion Camera) has a 5K, Super 35 sensor. Acquisition formats include RAW and RGB 4:4:4. Can capture up to eighteen stops dynamic range with HDRx recording. Popular for features and adapts well to 3D. (RED)

HD (which is available on many affordable cameras) is only 6 percent smaller in terms of total pixels than the 2K image projected in many cinemas today—a difference in resolution that may not be perceptible to the audience (see p. 70).

STANDARD DEFINITION DIGITAL FORMATS

Standard definition was once the only form of video, and there is still a lot of SD equipment in the world (some of it being used, a lot of it sitting on shelves). While there are some legitimate reasons to produce in SD, the future belongs to HD and larger frame sizes. Below are some standard def formats you may choose to work in, or may encounter when you want to include archival SD material in an HD production.

In former NTSC territories like North America and Japan, digital SD is 720 x 480 pixels, interlaced.[12] This can be notated as 480i.

In former PAL territories like Europe, Australia, and parts of Asia, standard definition means 720 x 576 pixels, interlaced, which is called 576i.

Some cameras can embed a progressive scan image in an interlace stream (see How 24p Is Recorded, p. 84).

All SD cameras record in 4:3 aspect ratio and many can shoot in widescreen 16:9 as well.

12. ITU-R 601 video, used for conventional NTSC broadcast, is 720 x 486.

DV, DVCAM, and DVCPRO

DV (Digital Video) records a component digital image on a very small sette. Introduced in the mid-1990s, DV revolutionized independent and multimedia production.

The basic DV codec (also called DV25 for its 25 Mbps video data rate) uses 5:1 compression with 4:1:1 color sampling (the PAL version is 4:2:0). The quality of the DV picture can be very good, but it depends a lot on the particular camera. When shown on large screens, DV material may show artifacts caused in part by the compression. Also, if you plan to do a lot of visual effects, the 4:1:1 or 4:2:0 color subsampling is not ideal, since it represents a loss of picture detail.

The consumer version is usually referred to as *MiniDV*. For broadcast and professional use, there are Sony's DVCAM and Panasonic's DVCPRO. Both of these formats use the same codec as MiniDV but have certain professional enhancements. The tape goes through the camcorder faster, reducing the chance of *dropouts* (momentary loss of recording). DVCAM and DVCPRO cameras accommodate MiniDV-sized tape cassettes and many accept a full-sized cassette shell that's several inches larger and can hold more tape (see Fig. 2-18). Newer cameras can record these codecs to file on a memory card instead of tape. All of these formats can be copied and edited with simple FireWire connections.

Fig. 1-25. Standard definition Panasonic DVX100B camcorder. Records to MiniDV tape. (Panasonic Broadcast)

DVCPRO50 and D-9

Panasonic makes camcorders that combine two 25 Mbps DV codecs to record in DVCPRO50 (sometimes called DV50), a 50 Mbps format with superior 4:2:2 color sampling and an image quality that rivals Digital Betacam but at lower cost. Compression is 3.3:1.

Digital Betacam

Sony's *Digital Betacam* (also called *DigiBeta* or *D-Beta*) is a high-quality ½-inch tape format. DigiBeta records with 4:2:2 color sampling, which makes it good for effects work, and uses 2:1 lossless compression (about 90 Mbps). Most people can't see the difference between 2:1 and uncompressed video. DigiBeta has been used widely around the world for both production and postproduction. Often projects shot on lower-resolution SD formats are finished on DigiBeta.

STANDARD DEFINITION ANALOG FORMATS

All of these are obsolete, but there are countless hours of material recorded on them, some of which will get transferred to digital.

2-inch Quad and 1-inch Type-C

In 1956, Ampex videotape machines running 2-inch-wide tape on open reels successfully made the first electronic recordings of live broadcast TV. In 1976, 1-inch Type-C videotape format replaced 2-inch. It remained an industry workhorse into the late 1990s.

¾-inch U-matic, Betamax, and VHS

The *¾-inch* professional videotape cassette format called *U-matic* by Sony was widely used for viewing film dailies and for doing offline editing. It was introduced as a consumer format but, like *Betamax*, a ½-inch videotape version, it failed with consumers. However, the *VHS* (*Video Home System*) format, which used ½-inch tape cassettes, launched the worldwide home video market. (For years, when people talked about "videos" VHS is what they meant.)

Video8 and Hi8

In the mid-1980s, *8mm* tape was introduced. Despite smaller tape cassettes and camcorders, Video8's image quality matched VHS's. In the late 1980s, *Hi8* (*high-band* Video8) brought enhanced resolution. *Digital 8* cameras were hybrids, capable of playing analog Hi8 tapes and recording in DV.

Betacam and Betacam SP

For many years, Sony's *Betacam* camcorders were the tool of choice for *ENG* (*electronic news gathering*). Introduced in 1982, the original Betacam format used a ½-inch cassette to record an analog component video signal. *Betacam SP* (superior performance) came along in 1986, improving horizontal resolution.

RECORDING TO MEMORY CARDS, DRIVES, AND DISCS

The job of a digital video camera is to turn light into digital data. How do we record and store that data? Traditionally, video was recorded to videotape only. Now other options are more widely used.

Flash Memory Cards

Many newer cameras and audio recorders are capable of recording to flash memory cards, which are reusable, solid-state storage with no moving parts. Popular types of flash memory cards include *CompactFlash* (*CF*), *Secure Digital* (*SD*), and

SDHC (*High Capacity*); Sony's *Memory Stick* and *SxS*; and Panasonic's *P2 cards*. Flash memory cards are small, require less power than a hard drive or tape mechanism, and are more resistant to the physical shocks and dirt of a challenging location environment.

Fig. 1-26. Secure Digital High Capacity (SDHC) flash memory card. When buying cards, be sure the read/write speed is sufficient for the video format you're recording. This card is rated at 30 MB per second. (Steven Ascher)

To record to a card, you insert it (or several cards) in the camera or audio recorder. When a card is full, you remove it and download to a hard drive or other storage device. The card can then be erased and reused.

Like recording directly to hard drives, using flash memory allows you to move quickly from shooting to editing. Cards can be inserted in a laptop's card slot, or easily connected to any computer with an adapter. Files can be copied to the computer or in some cases editing is done right off the cards. For more on working with memory cards, see p. 90.

Hard Drives and Solid-State Drives

A *hard disk drive recorder* (*HDD*) is a portable hard drive system for recording video. Some HDDs are lightweight and can be mounted on a camera. *Solid-state drives* (*SSDs*) are similar but use flash memory instead of a spinning disk to store data. HDDs and SSDs can be set up to capture video and audio in the format used by your nonlinear editing system. The files can then be imported into the editing system much faster than tape, saving time in the editing room. This method is sometimes called *direct-to-edit* (*DTE*) recording.

In some cases, recording to an external drive may allow longer recording times, or recording at a higher resolution than permitted by a camera's internal tape or media drive. You also may be able to record one format in camera and another to the external unit.

HDDs are also used in the home to record TV programming from cable or other sources. Another name for this is *digital video recorder (DVR)*. DVRs generally record compressed video, using MPEG-2 or other codecs. TiVo is a well-known example.

For more on the use of HDDs and SSDs in shooting, see p. 90 and p. 115. For more on the use of hard drives in editing, see p. 238.

Fig. 1-27. Sony EX3 camcorder records XDCAM EX to internal memory cards, but can record less compressed formats when used with an external recorder such as the nanoFlash unit pictured here. In this shot, a high-capacity V-mount battery is mounted between the camera and the recorder. (George T. Griswold; Convergent Design)

DVDs and Blu-ray Discs

Digital video discs (DVDs) were introduced in the mid-1990s as a format for watching videos at home. Using MPEG-2 compression, DVDs offer component color and multiple sound tracks, and they quickly became the format of choice for distributing standard definition videos. DVDs play only standard definition video.[13]

The newer *Blu-ray Disc* (or *BD*) format can record and play both high and standard definition. Blu-ray Discs support 1920 x 1080 HD (50i, 60i, and 24p); 1280 x 720 HD (50p, 60p, and 24p); and SD at 720 x 576/480 (50i or 60i). They can handle a number of codecs: MPEG-2, MPEG-4 (H.264), and VC-1. Single-layer Blu-ray Discs can hold 25 gigabytes (GB) and dual-layer discs can record 50 GB, which is about five to ten times the capacity of a standard DVD. Larger capacities are expected.

Most people think of DVDs and Blu-rays as simply a handy way to watch movies. For filmmakers, these disc formats serve multiple functions. Camcorders that record directly to discs range from consumer models to Sony's XDCAM HD camcorders that record to blue-laser disc cartridges (technically not Blu-rays but similar). Filmmakers often *burn* (record) video to DVDs for distribution, and also use them as a storage medium for video, audio, still images, or text. Blu-rays are increasingly popular as a low-cost HD screening format at film festivals.

13. It is possible to put an HD video file on a DVD, but not for playback in a typical DVD player.

SOUND RECORDING FOR VIDEO

Most video sound recording is done right in the camera—the sound is recorded with the picture to flash memory, tape, or disc. Different cameras and video formats have different configurations of audio channels. Most formats allow for two; some formats allow you to record four or more separate tracks. For some productions, having multiple tracks can provide great flexibility, since you can assign different microphones to different channels. When it comes to distribution, having four tracks allows you to send out a movie for international use in two different versions (for example, a version with narration and one without). Regardless of what format you use to shoot your movie, postproduction almost always involves transfer to different formats for finishing. So even if you shoot your film with a two-channel camera, you could release in various 5.1-channel formats (see p. 669).

Fig. 1-28. Documentary crew. The sound recordist carries a boom microphone and a mic mixer, shown here connected to the camera by a cable. (Bob Corkey)

Most camcorders have a microphone (also called a *mic*—pronounced "mike") built into the camera or mounted on it. On-camera mics are simple and convenient, but often result in poor sound, since the microphone is typically too far from the sound source for optimal recording. Professionals generally use separate mics, which can be placed nearer the subject. The audio from the mic may be fed to the camcorder through a cable or by using a wireless transmitter. When there's a sound recordist on the crew, microphones are usually fed first to a mixer, which allows easy monitoring of sound levels and blending of multiple mics. Recording sound in the camera along with the picture is called *single system recording*.

Sound may also be recorded *double system* (sometimes called *dual system*), which means using a separate audio recorder. This may be done for a feature or concert film to achieve the highest quality, or because multiple audio tracks are needed. Sometimes this is done because the camera or format has poor recording capability—many DSLRs, for example, record much lower quality audio than video, so a separate recorder can make a big difference. Before you can work with the footage, sound from the audio recorder has to be married to the picture and synchronized (synced up). This is usually done in the editing system prior to editing.

See p. 417 for more on audio for video camcorders.

VIDEO EDITING

Digital Nonlinear Editing

Virtually all video and film editing today is done with a *nonlinear editing* system (*NLE*). A nonlinear editor is computer software that allows you to edit and manipulate video much like the way a word processing program allows you to write, cut, paste, and format text. In nonlinear editing, video and audio data is stored on hard drives for instant access. A nonlinear editing system includes a computer, hard drives for storage, and often an external monitor for viewing. It can also include a video deck if material was recorded on tape in the field. NLEs range from professional systems, with all the bells and whistles that cost thousands of dollars, to simple programs like Apple's iMovie, which consumers can run on a basic laptop.

Fig. 1-29. Nonlinear editing. Most NLEs can be run on a laptop pretty much anywhere. (Avid Technology, Inc.)

Nonlinear editing gets its name because it is unlike older tape editing systems that forced you to start at the first shot of the movie and edit in a straight line (linearly) to the end. With nonlinear systems you can work on any scene at any time, with the freedom to expand, shorten, or change it as you like. Nonlinear systems make it easy to do complex sound editing and processing. In fact, there are nonlinear systems specifically designed for sound work, which are called *digital audio workstations*, or *DAWs*.

Compared to traditional tape or film editing, nonlinear editors make it much easier to try ideas and incorporate complex graphics and effects. The downside is that indecisive moviemakers may get trapped in a morass of endless possibilities.

WORKING WITH AN NLE. To begin editing on an NLE, you load the footage from the camera onto the editing system's hard drives. If the camera you used in the field recorded to file-based media like CompactFlash, SD cards, or hard drives, then loading that material into the NLE is called *ingesting, importing*, or *transferring*. If the camera recorded to a digital tape format, then loading that material into the NLE is called *capturing*. Any video or audio material recorded to analog tape has to be converted to digital form before it can be stored on the NLE; in this case bringing in the footage is called *digitizing*.[14]

Sometimes the total amount of footage you shot exceeds the storage capacity of your system's computer drives. When this happens, you can work on material in smaller chunks. Another approach is to import the footage at a lower resolution, which sacrifices image quality but increases the system's storage capacity. Some systems can work with *proxy images*, which are of very low resolution.

How you work with an NLE depends in part on the resolution of your original footage, how powerful your editing system is, and what you plan to do with the finished movie.

For example, if you're working on a school project, you might shoot with a DSLR camera and do all your editing on a low-cost NLE. Even basic NLEs can do video effects, create titles, and do some degree of sound balancing or mixing. A finished movie can then be exported from the system as a file for the Web, burned to a DVD or Blu-ray, or recorded to tape.

However, if you're doing a project for broadcast, you might do the majority of your editing on a midpowered NLE, then finish the project on a high-end NLE that's better equipped for color correction, graphics, and output to high-quality tape formats if needed. This way of working is known as an *offline/online* workflow. The offline NLE is used to find the movie's structure and put the shots in their proper order. Fine-tuning the color and sound are usually not top priority during the offline edit. After the offline is done, you move the project to a post facility with an online NLE that has all the scopes, monitors, and decks needed to do the final polish.

The audio may be sent to yet another system for mixing (usually a DAW in a specialized sound studio), then brought into the online system or recorded directly to the final file or tape.

Another situation that calls for an offline/online approach is when you're work-

---

14. Not all nonlinear editing systems are set up to digitize analog material.

Fig. 1-30. An online editing suite in a post house includes an NLE and external video monitors and scopes. Avid Symphony high-end system. (Avid Technology, Inc.)

ing in a high-resolution format that exceeds the capabilities of your NLE: for example, if you've shot in a 4K RAW format and your NLE lacks the storage capacity or processing power to handle such large files. In this case, you might downconvert to a lower-data-rate file format such as Apple ProRes or Avid DNxHD to do your offline edit. After you complete the offline edit, you then move to an online system with fast drives and conform the 4K material to the edit you created in the offline.

Editing on Tape

For many years, all video cameras recorded to videotape, and video editing was done by rerecording from one piece of tape to another. Traditional tape editing has now been replaced by the nonlinear editing systems just discussed. Nevertheless, tape is still used for shooting and it is also used after editing to store the finished movie. Many terms and concepts of nonlinear editing come from tape editing, so it's helpful to understand a little about it.

The idea of tape editing is based on using two tape machines. One is a player, in which you put the footage from the camera. Using an edit controller—a device with frame-accurate control of both decks—you find the first shot you want to use. You then play it on the play deck while rerecording it on the record deck, which contains the editing master tape. Once that's recorded, you move on to the next shot. This way, you build up the movie on the master tape, *linearly*, one shot at a time.

The concept of offline/online editing got its start with tape editing but with tape it's done differently than with nonlinear. The early computer-controlled ("online") editing systems used expensive, high-quality tape machines—too expensive for long-form projects. So, to first do an offline tape edit, the source tapes are dubbed (copied) to a lower-cost format. These offline tapes are called the *worktapes*, which are then edited with cheaper, lower-quality offline tape decks.

When you've structured the movie in the offline edit, the system generates a list of every shot you used. This is called an *edit decision list*, or *EDL*. The EDL is brought from the offline system to the online system, where the movie you created in the offline edit is reconstructed using the high-quality original camera tapes.

Tape-to-tape editing is rare today, but editing from an NLE to a tape machine is still common: for example, when outputting the finished movie from an NLE to create a master tape for later duplication.

For more on nonlinear and tape editing, see Chapter 14.

FILM SYSTEMS

The Camera and Projector

As discussed earlier in this chapter, the principle behind motion pictures is to record a series of still frames rapidly—one after another—and then display them on a screen rapidly, one after another (see p. 4).

The film camera works by focusing light from the scene being photographed onto a small rectangular area of photographic film. After each rectangle (*frame*) is exposed to light, a *shutter* blocks off the light. The camera's *claw* then pulls more unexposed film into position and holds it in place. The shutter opens again, allowing light to strike the fresh frame of film. This stop-start process is called the camera's *intermittent movement*. The camera is loaded with a roll of film that may be 50 to 1,000 feet long. Each *camera roll* records thousands of frames.

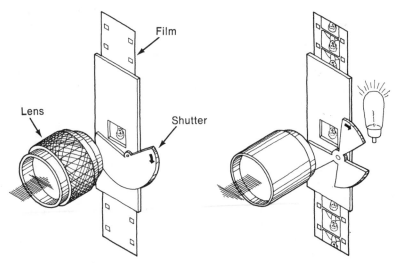

Fig. 1-31. The camera and the projector. The camera (left) draws in light to capture an image of the world on film; the projector (right) throws the image back onto a screen. (Carol Keller)

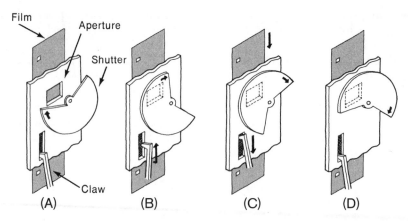

Fig. 1-32. The shutter and intermittent movement. (A) The claw holds the film in place during exposure. (B, C) The shutter rotates to block light from the film while the claw moves up to pull down the next frame. (D) The claw freezes in position to hold the next frame steady for exposure. (Carol Keller)

The film projector operates on the same principle, but rather than focusing light from the original scene onto the unexposed film, it projects the developed image onto a white screen using a bright lamp placed behind the film frame. As long as the projector runs at the same speed as the camera, motion will appear normal. Sometimes cameras are run at a higher speed so that motion will appear slowed down (*slow motion*) in projection. See p. 257 for more on camera speeds.

The Film Format

While all film cameras expose images in essentially the same way, the size and shape of the images produced vary with the camera type. The first movies, made in the 1890s by Thomas Edison, were shot on cellulose nitrate–based film that was about 35mm wide. Nitrate film is highly flammable and can become explosive as it deteriorates with age. Much of the first version of Robert Flaherty's *Nanook of the North* was destroyed by a fire (though the fire's cause is debated). Nitrate was replaced in the early 1950s by the more stable cellulose acetate, or "safety film," which

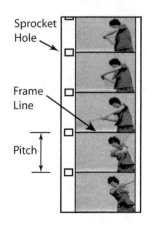

Fig. 1-33. Each still image on the film is called a *frame*. Successive frames are divided by a *frame line*. The claw advances the film by engaging a sprocket hole, or perforation (perf). The *pitch* is the distance between perfs. Various formats have a different number of perfs in different positions.

today has been somewhat replaced by indestructible polyester. The 35mm gauge remains the most commonly used in theatrical filmmaking.

In the 1920s, 16mm film was introduced as an amateur format. The area of the 16mm frame is only one-quarter that of the 35mm frame and when they're projected side by side, it looks grainier and less sharp. By the 1960s, 16mm became widely used in professional filmmaking. In the 1970s, *Super 16* was developed. Unlike regular 16mm, Super 16 has only one row of perforations. By extending the image almost to the edge of the film into the area formerly occupied by the second set of perforations, Super 16 allows a 40 percent larger image to be recorded for each frame (see Fig. 1-39).

In 1932, 8mm cameras were introduced that recorded an image half the width of 16mm, on film that had twice as many perforations (*Double 8mm* or *Regular 8mm*). In 1965 Kodak introduced *Super 8* film that was 8mm wide, but with smaller, repositioned sprocket holes that made room for an image 50 percent larger than regular 8mm. Super 8 was preloaded into easy-to-use cartridges. Once the prime format for home movies, Super 8 now has limited use among artists and music video producers.

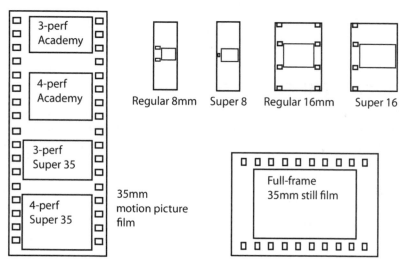

Fig. 1-34. Comparison of film formats. At left are different formats that can be recorded on 35mm motion picture film. With 35mm still film (shown at right) the width of the frame runs along the length of the film, instead of across it as it does with movie film. This is why the "full-frame" 35mm SLR and DSLR image format is larger than 35mm motion picture formats. With both Super 8 and Super 16, a different configuration of sprocket holes allows a larger recording area than their "regular" counterparts.

Aspect Ratio and Film

A film's *format* refers to the width of the film material itself (the film *gauge*), as well as the size and shape of the image that's recorded on it. The 16mm and Super 16 formats use film of the same gauge (16mm), but the size and shape of their frames are different. The shape of the frame is described by the proportions of its rectangle: the width of the frame divided by the height is the *aspect ratio* (see Fig. 1-12). A rectangle four units wide and three units high is the standard for several formats (including regular 8mm, Super 8, 16mm, and traditional standard definition video). This aspect ratio is 4:3 ("four by three"). In the film world, that ratio is expressed as 1.33:1 and spoken as "one three three to one" (often written 1.33 and spoken as "one three three").

In 35mm, the full frame for sound film has an aspect ratio of about 1.33:1 and is called *Academy aperture*, named for the Academy of Motion Picture Arts and Sciences, which defined it. Though the Academy frame was standard for feature films in the early twentieth century, it is no longer used for films shown in theaters. Theatrical features are generally widescreen, with an aspect ratio of at least 1.85:1 and often as wide as 2.40:1.

For more on aspect ratio and widescreen formats, see p. 74.

| 1.33:1 | 1.85:1 | 2.40:1 |

Fig. 1-35. Some common film aspect ratios (also used in digital productions). Different aspect ratios call for different approaches to image composition.

COMPARING FILM FORMATS

As a rule of thumb, as the size of the format increases, so do the cost, the image quality, and the size and weight of the camera. When a large area of film emulsion is used for each exposure, the grain and imperfections of the film detract less from the image. In the 35mm camera, about 12 square inches of film are exposed each second; in 16mm only about 2½ square inches are used.[15] When a 16mm frame is projected on a modest eight-by-ten–foot screen, it must be enlarged about 100,000 times. To fill a screen of the same size, a Super 8 frame must be magnified more than 300,000 times. This is why theatrical features that are not shot digitally are usually shot on 35mm or 65mm film. For more on how format size affects picture quality, see p. 60.

The film image is affected not only by the format but also, in order of increasing importance, by the particular camera being used, the lenses, and the choice of camera negative (called *film stock* or *raw stock*). A film camera will produce vastly different results depending on choice of both film stock and processing.

Color negative film stocks are used for most professional productions shot in film. Upon developing, negative stocks render a scene with reversed tonalities and colors; that is, what was light in reality is dark on the negative, what was green in reality is magenta on the negative (see Fig. 7-2). When the *camera original* (the film that actually went through the camera) is negative, it must be printed on *positive* film stock to be viewable in a projector. Much less commonly, films can be shot with

15. This is comparing 35mm Academy frame to regular 16mm. Standard 1.85 aspect ratio 35mm film exposes about 9 square inches each second.

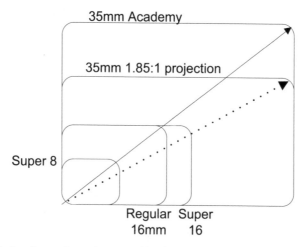

Fig. 1-36. Relative frame sizes of various film formats. The solid diagonal line shows that three of the formats have the same aspect ratio. The dotted line shows that Super 16 and 35mm 1.85 projection have nearly the same aspect ratio.

reversal film stocks. Like slides in still photography—also reversal—they show a normal image as soon as they're developed.

As noted earlier, most productions that are shot on film are scanned to a digital format (called a *digital intermediate*, or *D.I.*) from which digital files and film prints can be made for distribution and screening.

Super 8

Super 8 is becoming obsolete and most equipment is only available secondhand. The people still shooting on Super 8 are students, enthusiasts who relish the particular look and feel of Super 8, and sometimes filmmakers who use it to test film stocks prior to shooting in a larger format. Super 8 footage has found its way into music videos, commercials, and feature films. Sometimes a rough, grainy image is desired, perhaps as a stylistic touch or to simulate the look of old movies. Instead of

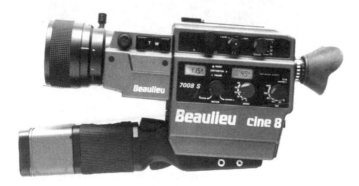

Fig. 1-37. Beaulieu Super 8 sync-sound camera. (Pro8mm, Inc.)

trying to degrade a 16mm or 35mm image, filmmakers may shoot on one of the grainier, more contrasty Super 8 stocks.

Traditionally, Super 8 shooting was done with reversal Ektachrome or the now-discontinued Kodachrome, both of which could be projected directly without making a print. Pro8mm in Los Angeles has created a line of color and black-and-white negative and reversal stocks by using a film-cutting machine to load professional 35mm film emulsions into Super 8 cartridges.

Rather than edit or distribute films in Super 8, most people transfer to video and/or blow up (enlarge) to 35mm.

16mm and Super 16

During its life span, 16mm has gone through enormous changes. Starting as an amateur format (once considered "spaghetti" by pros), the portability of 16mm cameras made them the tool of choice for TV news and documentaries and later for low-budget features, animation, and avant-garde films. Today, standard 16mm is pretty much dead, but Super 16 is still used for some higher-budget documentaries, made-for-TV movies, and low-budget features. With newer, technically advanced color negatives, Super 16 is capable of a rich image that rivals 35mm.

As a distribution format, 16mm has pretty much disappeared. Films that originate on Super 16 are transferred to digital or are blown up to 35mm for distribution. The Super 16 frame has an aspect ratio of 1.67:1, which is very close to widescreen video's 16:9, so a transfer to HD or widescreen SD formats can be done with negligible cropping (see Fig. 1-39). When blowing up to 35mm, you can create prints at 1.66:1 or the much more common 1.85:1. For more on blowups from 16mm and Super 16, see p. 708.

Fig. 1-38. Aaton Xterà Super 16 camera. Versatile and well balanced for handheld work. (AbelCine)

35mm

35mm dates back to a collaboration between Thomas Edison's laboratory and George Eastman's Kodak in the early 1890s. Early 35mm motion picture cameras were hand-cranked and relatively compact. As late as the Vietnam War, wind-up 35mm Bell & Howell Eyemos with 100-foot loads found favor with combat cameramen.

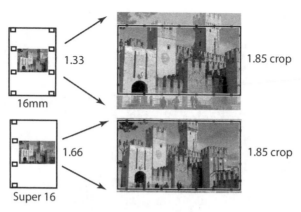

Fig. 1-39. Blowing up 16mm film to 35mm. (top) When regular 16mm is blown up to 35mm, the image must be significantly cropped, losing the top and/or bottom of the frame. (bottom) By using the area normally reserved for the optical sound track, the Super 16 frame closely approximates the 1.85:1 widescreen aspect ratio. Very little of the Super 16 image is lost when a blowup or transfer to HD is done. (Steven Ascher)

Motorization and larger 400-foot and 1,000-foot loads, along with heavy sound dampening, produced generations of large, heavy 35mm cameras. Added bulk includes weighty PL or Panavision mount lenses, video assists, and many attachments.

As a result, traditional 35mm cameras have been cumbersome and expensive. These cameras are usually supported on tripods or dollies because of their considerable size and also the importance of having a steady image on a large theater screen. The newer generation of lighter, hand-holdable sync-sound 35mm cameras like Aaton's Penelope (see Fig. 2-20) and ARRI's Arricam Lite, along with stabilization devices like Steadicam (which enables the operator to carry the camera smoothly; see Fig. 9-48), provides greater mobility and allows more nimble filming techniques to be used in feature films. (Steadicams are also used with digital camera systems.)

In general, the highest-quality equipment, techniques, and lab services have been available for 35mm production, for which film budgets usually run in the millions. Due to the bulkiness of the equipment and the complexity of projects done in 35mm, crews of about eight to more than a hundred persons are employed.

The standard 35mm frame is four perforations high. In the days of silent cinema, a boxy 1.33:1 image occupied all the available space between the perforations along each side. With the advent of sound in the early 1930s, the Academy of Motion Picture Arts and Sciences standardized a slightly scaled-down frame of the same shape, which it offset to the right in order to accommodate a sound-on-film track along the left edge. This reduced frame became known as the common "Academy" format, prevalent until the arrival of widescreen formats (see Fig. 1-34).

All 35mm motion picture formats position or squeeze their image between the right row of perfs and the protected sound track area to the left, with one exception—Super 35. Super 35 was "created" in the 1980s in order to take back the sound track area for the purposes of exposing a 32 percent larger image. It is, in effect, the original silent image reclaimed. As such, it is only a production format. There are no Super 35 projectors. Super 35 must be scanned digitally, then either recorded

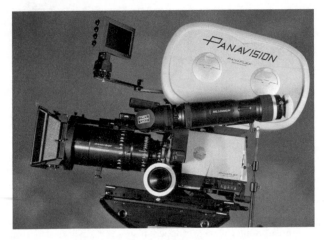

Fig. 1-40. 35mm camera. Panaflex Millennium. (Panavision, Inc.)

back to film as a scaled-down frame, making room for the standard sound track of conventional film projection, or output to a DCP (Digital Cinema Package).

Some 35mm cameras are set up for the *three-perf* 35mm format, which uses a frame that is only three perforations high. Because less film is needed for each frame, this results in a 25 percent savings in the cost of film stock and processing. This format is well suited to 1.78:1 (16:9) capture and is popular for production of TV series. Three-perf looks the same as four-perf when transferred to 16:9 digital formats and can be printed to the standard four-perf format for film distribution at the conventional 1.85:1 aspect ratio.

Less common is *two-perf* 35mm. Two-perf was introduced as the *Techniscope* format in the early 1960s. This was done because the anamorphic lenses needed to horizontally squeeze a panoramic 2.40:1 frame (also called CinemaScope, or 'Scope) into a squarish four-perf 35mm frame are much heavier and optically slower than conventional lenses for 35mm cameras. Why not instead use a regular 35mm format lens, shoot on a two-perf 35mm frame that has half the normal height and a 2.40 aspect ratio to begin with? The result could be printed and projected as conventional CinemaScope. Benefits include a 50 percent cost savings in film stock and processing and mags that last twice as long. Not bad.

A number of classic films were shot in two-perf, including George Lucas's *American Graffiti* and spaghetti Westerns such as *The Good, the Bad, and the Ugly*. Today the digital intermediate process makes it a snap to scan a two-perf original 35mm negative, then record it back out to a squeezed four-perf 35mm negative. Aaton's *Penelope*, mentioned above, switches easily between three- and two-perf pulldown.

Large Formats

There are a number of widescreen formats used primarily for feature films. Some high-budget films are shot in 65mm, which is then shown in theaters using 70mm prints (the added width is used for sound tracks). *Lawrence of Arabia* and *2001: A Space Odyssey* demonstrate the stunning detail and rich image of this format. The 65mm negative is reduced to 35mm for smaller theaters.

Even larger are the IMAX and OMNIMAX formats, which run 65mm film *horizontally* through the camera, creating an image that spans fifteen perforations per frame instead of 65mm's five. These are shown on huge, enveloping screens in specially constructed theaters. (OMNIMAX is designed for domed screens.) The image is spectacular.

SOUND RECORDING FOR FILM

Virtually all films have sound tracks; even silent films were intended to be shown with musical accompaniment. Unlike video cameras, which typically record audio right in the camcorder, today's film cameras do not record sound. Instead, a separate audio recorder is used that captures audio to memory cards or hard drives. As noted earlier, using a separate audio recorder is called double system or dual system.

Fig. 1-41. Recordist's sound cart including mic mixer and digislate. (Pawel Wdowczak/ Denecke, Inc.)

Before portable recording equipment became available, most sound films were made in the studio under controlled conditions. The soundstage was acoustically isolated from distracting noises. When it was necessary to film on location, there was usually no attempt made to record a high-quality sound track. Instead, the film would be *looped* afterward in the sound studio. Looping, sometimes called *dubbing*, involved cutting scenes into short, endless loops that the actors watch while re-speaking their lines. Today, dialogue replacement may be done to fix sound that was badly recorded, or when the dialogue is to be rerecorded in another language. *ADR* (*automatic dialogue replacement*) is now done with more sophisticated digital equipment.

In the 1950s, advances in magnetic tape recorders made it practical to record sound on location. From the 1960s through the 1980s, classic portable ¼-inch reel-to-reel recorders made by Nagra and Stellavox were the rule. By the 1990s, lightweight *DAT* (*digital audiotape*) cassette recorders were in common use on film sets. Today, all double-system sound is recorded using digital *file-based recorders* that capture audio to flash memory cards or hard drives.

The smallest, least expensive film cameras are noisy and are intended for shooting without sound (though sound can be added later). These cameras are sometimes called *MOS* (see p. 258), or *wild cameras*. Confusingly, the term *silent camera* is sometimes used to mean an MOS camera, and sometimes means one that is quiet enough to be used for sound filmmaking. Audible camera noise on the sound track can be disastrous, especially in nondocumentary projects. Most good sound cameras are extremely quiet.

Synchronous or *sync* sound, also known as *lip sync*, matches the picture in the way you are used to hearing it: when the actor's lips move on the screen, you hear the words simultaneously. *Nonsynchronous* or *wild sound* is not in sync, or matched to the picture, in this way. Some films use wild sound exclusively, such as those that have only narration and a musical background.

Because sync sound requires precise alignment of sound and picture, only film cameras equipped for sync-sound work can be used. Sync-sound cameras are crystal controlled (*crystal sync*) to operate at a precisely fixed speed (usually 24 fps). In the days of analog tape recorders, only specially equipped recorders like the Nagra could be used for sync filming, but with today's digital audio recorders "sync drift" is usually not an issue.

In double-system recording, the camera and sound recorder are generally not attached to each other, so the microphone can be positioned close to the sound source for good recording, regardless of where the camera is. See Chapters 10 and 11 for more on sound recording.

FILM EDITING

From the beginning of filmmaking, movies were edited by cutting rolls of film into pieces (individual shots), arranging the shots in the desired order and length, and reattaching them into rolls. Celluloid film was literally cut and spliced back together, which is why editing is also called *cutting*.

In the 1990s, a sea change took place in the way films are edited. Instead of cutting on film—using film editing equipment—filmmakers today transfer their film footage to a digital format and do their editing with computer-based, nonlinear editing systems (NLEs; see p. 36 and p. 544). Nonlinear video editing has myriad advantages over editing on film: you have much more control; you can try out visual effects, create titles, do more sophisticated sound editing, and easily output video copies of the edit when you need them.

Given the benefits of digital editing, why would anyone still cut on film? Film schools may encourage cutting on film to learn film craft. If you're making a movie that will be shown on film in theaters, working with film may give you a better sense of what it will eventually look like on screen; however, this argument is weakening with the growing prevalence of digital distribution.

Digital Film Editing

When a production is to be shot on film and edited in a digital system, there are many options and technologies available. The process can be fairly simple or quite complex depending on what route you choose.

During the production of the movie, the film that actually went through the camera—called *camera original film*, or *original camera negative* (*OCN*)—is sent to the laboratory to be processed and then transferred to digital. When the transfer comes back, it is called *digital dailies*, *video dailies*, or *rushes* (because on big productions it's rushed back and viewed every day; small films may not get such good service).

Sound recorded in the field must be combined with the picture, and lined up properly so that the sound and picture are in sync (called *synchronizing the rushes* or *syncing up*). Syncing may take place when the dailies are transferred to video or afterward in the editing system.

Once the dailies are loaded into the NLE and the sound is in sync, editing can begin. Working with an NLE to edit a movie that was shot on film involves most of the same procedures as editing a movie shot on video. There may be certain differences stemming from the frame rate, how the audio is handled, and how the project will be finished.

When you're done editing, there are several options for finishing and distributing the movie—depending on whether the original camera negative was transferred by telecine or film scanner, and to which format.

- The project may be finished in HD and distributed solely as video (broadcast TV, cable, Internet, DVD, Blu-ray). In this case, though film was used for shooting, the movie becomes essentially a video production.
- It may be finished in HD and then recorded to 35mm film (called film-out) or transcoded to a DCP for projection in theaters.
- It may be finished by scanning the original negative to a 2K or 4K digital file format in order to create a digital intermediate (D.I.; see p. 685). This option is expensive but offers a lot of control over the image. From the finished D.I., either a new 35mm film negative and prints are made or a DCP is generated.
- Instead of making a D.I., the project may be finished in the traditional way by cutting the original film negative and making film prints (see below).

Traditional Film Editing

Even though few projects today are edited the traditional way and once-iconic film editing equipment is relegated to museums, it's useful for filmmakers to understand something about conventional film editing, since most of the concepts—developed over a century of filmmaking—are still employed, even if in digital form. An understanding of the basic process of classic film postproduction will also help you appreciate what went into the making of every classic film you admire.

In traditional film production, the camera original footage is sent to the lab for processing and then a *workprint* is made—that is, a positive print of the original negative. The workprint is sent back to the production as dailies; this prevents damage to the original, which is stored at the lab.

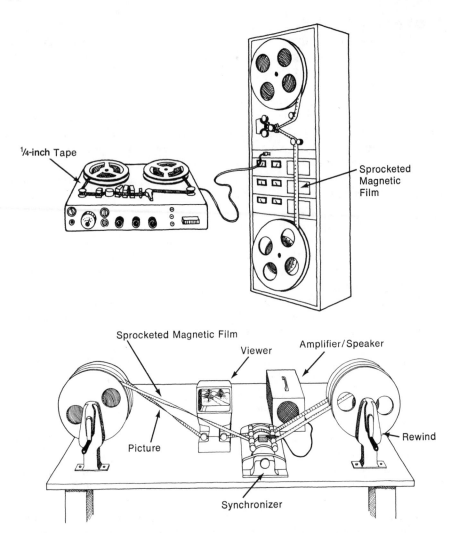

Fig. 1-42. Traditional film editing. (top) Sound recorded in the field (represented here with a ¼-inch tape deck) is transferred to sprocketed magnetic film for editing. (bottom) The mag film can then be edited with the picture in frame-for-frame correspondence. Most of the equipment shown here is now rarely used. (Carol Keller)

In preparation for editing, the sound recorded in the field is rerecorded or transferred to *magnetic film*, also called *mag*, *mag stock*, *stripe* (in 35mm), or, in some cases, *fullcoat*. Mag has the same dimensions and sprocket holes as 16mm or 35mm picture film, but it has a magnetic oxide like that used in sound recording tape. Editing is then done with two strands of material (picture and sound) that are both sprocketed and can be lined up, frame for frame. Before editing, the dailies must be synced up. This is usually done by cutting and placing the mag alongside its corresponding workprint. Once the rushes are in sync, the two strands are then *edge coded* by mechanically printing the same *ink numbers* on the edge of each strand. Edge code allows pieces of sound and picture to be quickly identified and put back in sync at any point in the editing process.

During editing, sound and picture can be freely cut and combined. Multitrack editing machines can play two or more sound tracks in sync with the picture. After editing is complete and the picture is locked, a sound mix is done to rerecord all the various sound tracks onto one final track. The pristine camera original is cut to match the edited workprint (called *negative matching* or *conforming*). Prints can then be made directly from the original negative or from a *duplicate negative* (*dupe neg*).

Simple image transitions are done while making the print—such as *dissolves* (where one image melds into another) or *fades* (where the image appears from or disappears into darkness). Today, more complex effects are done digitally, and a new piece of film with the effect is edited into the film. Traditionally, these effects were called *opticals* and were done in a separate step using an *optical printer*. Color correction (also called *grading*) is done by a *color timer* (or *grader*), who views each scene in the film and estimates the correct printer settings for red, green, and blue exposure.

Typically, lab personnel do the color corrections and then the director and/or director of photography views them in the *first answer print*. Any adjustments are then made and *corrected prints* are struck. After all the adjustments are done, a *release print* is made. The sound track is now combined with the picture; prints with sound tracks are called *composite* or *married prints*.

For more on working with film in postproduction, see Chapter 16.

SHOOTING DIGITAL VERSUS SHOOTING FILM

Many younger filmmakers know the convenience of digital and have never experienced film, so perhaps the question should be: what are the reasons *not* to shoot digital?

One of the key reasons would be that you like the look of film. This is discussed more in later chapters. Film has a distinctive feel, with a rich history of associations. While high-end digital cinema cameras like the ARRI Alexa can capture much of that look, there are still differences (and many digital cameras perform far worse than those top-of-the line models). Film stocks capture a tonal range that easily surpasses many digital cameras.

On a per-minute basis, film can be a lot more expensive than digital. That is, a hard drive that can store an hour of HD direct from the camera costs far less than sixty minutes of film, especially when you add up the costs of film stock, processing, and transferring the film to digital for editing. However, when you consider the whole budget, film isn't *always* much more expensive. For example, on a per-day basis, you may be able to rent a film rig for much less than a high-end digital cinema camera. So if your production will take place over many days, there may be savings in equipment rentals if you shoot film. Similarly, if you can be frugal in how much footage you shoot (say, restricting yourself to only a few takes for each shot in a drama), the higher cost of film won't be as much of a problem. Students can get a lot of benefit from the discipline of shooting film, and the planning and control it requires—skills you may not get if you shoot only digital (for more, see The Shooting Ratio, p. 360).

On some shoots, film cameras can have an advantage for being a simpler technology that may hold up better in extreme conditions. They're less susceptible to overheating, generally consume less power, and don't require data management in the field.

Another consideration is that film is a firmly established technology that hasn't fundamentally changed in years. Digital, on the other hand, has been going through a period of explosive growth, and today's hot formats are likely to be obsolete before long. One argument for shooting film is that a production shot on celluloid may have better shelf life and adapt better to new digital technologies as they come along. When it comes to long-term archival storage, it's hard to guess how many years in the future any particular digital recording—whether it is stored on video-tape, hard drive, or disc—will still be playable. That said, different film stocks age better than others, and the storage environment plays a key role in film preservation.

Of course, as this is being written, film labs are dropping like flies, and the survival of even major film manufacturers is in question. So, by the time you read this, shooting in film may not be a viable option. A very sad thought after such an astonishing history of work.

Fig. 1-43. The digital present looks out over the analog past. (RED)

CHAPTER 2

Before You Begin Production

This chapter is an attempt to corral in one place some of the production and technical questions to consider before you even begin your movie. The discussion that follows ties together topics that are addressed separately and often in more detail in later chapters; use the index if any terms are unfamiliar.

Particularly in moviemaking, we live in a transitional time with enormous changes between how things used to be done, how they're done now, and how they'll be done in the near future. Knowing the history, staying alert to current developments, and keeping an eye to "future proofing" your production are all important parts of planning your path.

Before you begin a project, you have to make some fundamental choices about what methods and equipment you'll use. The number of options in terms of financing, formats, camera settings, editing procedures, software, and distribution can be oppressive, and many people feel bewildered by them. Some of these choices can affect how the movie gets made, how it looks, its cost, and where you can show it when you're done. But keep in mind that the technical and media landscape today is so advanced and so flexible that even if you go with a less-than-optimal choice or set a switch on your camera the wrong way, you'll probably be fine in the long run.

GETTING YOUR MOVIE OFF THE GROUND

Germinating the Idea

You have a great idea for a movie, be it fiction or documentary. Perhaps there's an article, story, or novel you think would make a great film. Or maybe you have a personal relationship to something or someone interesting, or special access to unfolding or historical events.

How do you turn your dream of a movie into a reality? There is no set route, and getting a film made involves plenty of detours, dead ends, rejections, and successes. Depending on your ambitions and your means, you may need a lot of money and a large organization, or you may be working in the DIY (do-it-yourself) mode, made increasingly feasible by low-cost HD equipment. Even for large-scale productions, producers often have to do a lot on their own before getting support for a project.

A narrative film may begin with an idea or a treatment, which outlines the characters and plot. You may need to write a *spec script* (speculative—written before any deal is in place) as a way to get the project going. If you want to base a screenplay on an existing novel or short story, you need to *option* the story from the rights holder (see p. 742).

A documentary might begin with research, a written proposal, and often some preliminary footage (more on this below). Documentaries may also involve securing rights to books, or getting permission from individuals, institutions, or government agencies before filming.

It's important to write about your idea, in part to clarify in your own mind what you're trying to do. Make yourself answer the tough questions and get specific about your vision—that specificity can help you communicate with and inspire collaborators. Create a full, detailed proposal or treatment of the project, which you'll need for various types of fundraising. Then condense it into a short, engaging version (no more than a few pages) for busy readers with short attention spans. See Developing the Project, p. 718, for more.

Work up a one- or two-sentence *logline* that captures the story in an intriguing way (do a Web search on "logline" to see many good and bad examples). Practice an *elevator pitch* that can get someone interested in less than a minute. This forces you to be clear and succinct, both of which are essential. Practice a longer pitch you might give an executive if you had ten minutes on the phone or in person.

Some people like to blog, create websites, post videos, tweet, or do other types of online promotion at the early stages of a project. Others guard their ideas until the production's really under way. It's up to you to decide when publicity might help.

Working Backward from Distribution

Some people create movies for their private use, but for most filmmakers, the goal is not just to make a film but to get it *seen*. How that happens depends in part on the choices you make: aesthetic, practical, technical, and commercial. There are many gatekeepers along the way who will decide whether to finance, buy, or show your movie. Depending on your goals, these may include funders, festivals, distributors, theater bookers, broadcasters, galleries, businesses, or school systems. Each will have certain expectations that influence whether they accept or reject your project. So when you're starting out, it helps to consider the end product you're aiming for.

Perhaps the single most important question you can ask is: Who is your core audience? Who is going to be most interested in your project and support it when you're making it and when it's done? Who is going to forward your emails, join your Twitter feed, share links to your blog, or help you crowdfund on sites like Kickstarter (see Chapter 17)? If you can identify your audience and engage them, you're on your way.

Educate yourself about the world you want to work in. Research what projects have been successful recently in whatever area of filmmaking you're interested in. Read case study articles ("how we made our movie") to learn about what kinds of financing, technology, or production methods were used. Go to festivals and theaters to see what's current. Visit museums and galleries. Watch TV. Get a sense of production values of successful films and how audiences respond. Read the "trades"—industry papers, magazines, and websites—to find out about what kinds of projects are getting produced and distributed.

The point is not to imitate what's successful at the moment (though Hollywood has made an industry of that). Hopefully, you'll make your film as fresh and original as you can. In fact, people who pattern their work too closely on recently successful films often find that the public and the gatekeepers are looking for something completely different by the time their film comes out. Short-term trends about what's hot can prove meaningless because for most projects there's a delay of months or years between when you plan the movie, when (if ever) you get funding, when it's completed, and when (if ever) it finds distribution. Entire genres go through cycles from hot to not ("What, another vampire film?" or "There were two docs on solar power already this year."). Look for things that inspire you and give you ideas, then take your best guess about what the world will be like when you make and finish your film.

The world is a global marketplace, so find ways that your project can appeal to audiences outside your own country. This might influence how you approach the story, the actors you cast, where you film, or what festivals you apply to.

Achieving theatrical distribution has been a mark of success for fiction films and many documentaries as well, but the theatrical marketplace, particularly for independent films, is in turmoil. High marketing costs and low fees have driven many indie distributors and filmmakers out of business. A theatrical rollout can get you reviews in major papers and media outlets, which can be great, but there are lots of expenses for HD masters or film prints, ads, and sometimes an indie film will even need to guarantee a rental fee to the theater. So even if you're aiming for theaters, you should focus just as much on other distribution channels, which may ultimately contribute more to your bank account. Again, knowing your core audience and engaging them is crucial to making money in the new distribution models.

When it comes to technology, there are a lot of options to choose from. If you're planning for a particular type of distribution (say, cable or broadcast television) there will be criteria about what formats are acceptable and certain technical specs that must be met. Many broadcasters have websites with production requirements and things like standard program lengths.[1]

Are there long-term technical trends that might affect your film? For example, broadcasters such as PBS in the U.S. now require that all submissions be in HD (though they will still accept some SD material upconverted to HD). Even if you shoot in HD, various broadcasters may have strict rules about which cameras and formats they'll accept and which they consider subpar. If you hope to sell your movie, you'll want to be prepared.

New forms of distribution create new markets and income streams. Keep an ear to the ground for what's coming so you can take advantage. Distribution contracts

---

1. Such as the PBS *Red Book* in the United States, available online, which details policies and deliverables.

sometimes refer to "formats now known or hereafter devised" as a way to lay claim to developments yet to come. In theory, the Internet can fully democratize distribution, removing the gatekeepers altogether. However, while posting your film on a website may make it available to viewers, there are still the hurdles of attracting an audience and trying to make a living from your work.[2] Some things don't change, and whenever money is involved, the gatekeepers are never far behind; filmmakers will always need to find a way to work with them.

WORKING IN 3D. Along with a third dimension, 3D adds a host of further challenges and concerns. All realms—aesthetic, practical, technical, and commercial—are touched by the decision to fashion a story, whether dramatic or documentary, low-budget or Hollywood summer tent pole, in 3D space. Advances in digital cinema like smaller, more affordable cameras are making 3D production accessible in ways never before imagined. As consumers purchase more 3D camcorders and TVs, 3D is reaching into the mainstream. For a serious filmmaker, shooting in 3D means a lot more than simply using two cameras instead of one—there's a lot to learn about the basics of 3D perception and good stereoscopy. These subjects can easily fill a book and so will be touched upon lightly in this one. See p. 396 for more on filming and exhibiting in 3D.

Finding Funding and Support

Many nonfilmmakers fantasize that the filmmaker's life is one of endless creativity, with satisfying days filled with one artistic experience after another. There may be a few filmmakers who live like that, but for most, moviemaking involves seemingly short periods of real creative work and seemingly endless amounts of *business*. And when it comes to business, the biggest item is often finding money for the next project.

"Independent filmmaking" is usually defined as working outside a studio or other large organization that bankrolls and controls your work. But even if you're on salary with a large corporation, you'll probably still need to convince others to fund your project. Raising money can be one of the most arduous and painful parts of making a movie.

How you go about finding money depends on the type of project. Generally, the more elements of the project you can set in place before going to a funder, the better it will look. This is especially important if you don't have a track record.

Fiction films benefit enormously from having recognizable names in the cast and crew. Getting a well-known actor to commit to a role or getting a successful filmmaker to sign on as executive producer can help you draw in other talented people and increase interest in the film. To lure a key actor, create a juicy role that will let that actor show his or her range. It may take months or even years to get a known actor to read a script that has no money behind it, but if you're offering a brilliant role, you have something of real value.

---

2. And even on the Internet there are gatekeepers. As discussed in Chapter 17, with distribution such as iTunes, Netflix, and VOD, it's very hard for a filmmaker to make a deal directly without first going through an aggregator (middleman).

Fig. 2-1. Small video crew. Including, at right, videographer, assistant, and dolly grip. (From the *Better & Better* series with Elizabeth Hepburn. Photo by Arledge Armenaki.)

Documentarians sometimes seek out endorsements from well-known people or sign up a group of advisers or consultants to lend credibility to the proposed project.

Funders—be they film studios, broadcasters, or foundations—love nothing more than sure bets. They want to minimize their risk by putting money into projects that seem likely to offer a return on their investment (in the case of a foundation, return may be measured not in dollars but in visibility or community outreach). This is why money tends to go to established producers or to fund projects that resemble previously successful projects (hence the production of *Hit Film: The Sequel*). If you're new to the business, or trying to do something new, you'll have an uphill battle. In this case, you may find that funders will support you only after the project is fairly far along or has received other backing ("first money" is always the riskiest).

Sometimes you can obtain seed or development money to develop the proposal or script, begin serious fundraising, or do other preproduction work. Be aware that in some situations when you receive development funds you may be required to give up some or all ownership or control of the project.

If it's feasible to shoot selected scenes of a drama or documentary, you can improve your chances a lot by preparing a short *trailer* (coming-attractions promo) or sample reel. Some people put together short excerpts with narration, to describe the project and pique interest. For a drama, sometimes a slick theatrical trailer is made to give investors a sense of how the film might be marketed. Another approach is simply to edit together a few scenes, which may better indicate the movie's style and the director's ability. For a documentary, you can go a long way with a few scenes that show emotion, conflict, and compelling characters. Increasingly, broadcasters and funders insist on seeing footage or a sample reel from the project before they'll put down money, particularly for documentaries.

One of the biggest questions is when to share the project. Though you may have a clear idea of what the movie will look like and how great it will be, funders can be stunningly unimaginative when it comes to sharing that vision. Examples are legion of successful movies that collected a thick pile of rejection letters along the rocky road to completion. Often, the same funding sources have to be approached more than once before they say yes. But before you approach any potential funder or investor, think hard about whether the script or project is *really* ready. Surely there are movies that have been bankrolled by distributors on the basis of an unpolished rough cut; but there are probably far more examples of projects that were shown before they were presentable and ended up turning off the very people the filmmakers hoped to entice. Everyone in the business has a stack of scripts, proposals, and sample reels to look at. In a crowded marketplace, you often have only *one* shot at many potential backers, so be sure you're taking your best shot.

Working Backward from the Budget

As you move toward actually producing the project, you'll need an *estimated budget* that states how much money you need and details how you plan to spend it. For fiction films, an experienced producer or production manager creates a budget based on the script. Documentaries can sometimes be hard to predict, especially if you're filming ongoing events (your main character is trying to stop oil drilling in a nature preserve—how long will that take?). For all types of films, the initial budget is based on estimating the number of shooting days, salaries for crew (and actors, if any), locations, travel, editing time, special effects, and so on.

You can think of the estimated budget as a tool for fundraising and a tool for planning the production. But there's an ongoing dynamic that often follows this sequence: (1) you determine how much money you need to do the project; (2) you go out and discover that the amount you can raise is less—often a lot less; (3) you reconfigure your plan so you can get it done on a smaller budget.

You can help yourself from the outset by looking closely at every element in the script or plan and asking what can be cut without deeply compromising the film. Can you reduce the number of scenes, characters, or locations (some films, like *Reservoir Dogs*, restrict the action mostly to one setting)? Can you be creative with art direction and make the same location work for several unrelated scenes? Can you take a *walk-and-talk* dialogue scene in which characters wander through a busy mall and restage it in an empty park or a doorway so it can be done faster and with a smaller crew? Look for ways you can leverage things you own or have access to (cars, props, locations) by writing them into the script.

While some independent films, both fiction and documentary, have been impressive for accomplishing a slick, high-budget look with very little money, far more have been successful by embracing a no-frills, low-budget aesthetic and focusing on storytelling and characters. If you're operating with limited resources, put them into crafting a compelling, well-told story and don't be overly concerned with "production value."

With experience you'll learn where it makes sense to scrimp and where it doesn't. Many filmmakers have learned the hard way the true costs of not taking enough time on the set to get good lighting; not trying to fix poor audio on the spot (which

Fig. 2-2. A small camera provides a lot of flexibility for run-and-gun shooting. (Jonathan Weyland/Small HD)

may be unfixable later); or using nonprofessional equipment that creates problems in postproduction.

Often, movies are started with less than the full budget in hand, with hopes of raising the rest later. Filmmakers figure they'll get something *in the can* (that is, through production but not necessarily all the way through postproduction) and worry about finishing funds later. This may be the only way to get into production, and if done responsibly it can be a smart strategy. Particularly if you don't have a strong track record (but even if you do), it allows you to show backers, distributors, and broadcasters something concrete before they commit to a project.

Nevertheless, there can be pitfalls to this approach. Filmmakers may have the strategy of paying the minimum for things out of pocket with the hope of getting a distributor to pick up finishing costs at the end. Keep in mind that most expenses that are "paid" by the distributor are usually deducted from your share of the film's revenue (often with interest charges tacked on), so you're really choosing between paying now or being paid less later.

Avoid the temptation to finance your project on credit cards. The press may love stories of films that started on credit cards and went on to success, but no one talks about the far greater number of projects that left their makers with crippling debt when they went unsold.

For more on budgeting, fundraising, and distribution, see Chapter 17.

FORMATS FOR THE BIG SCREEN AND THE SMALL(ER) SCREEN

The past sixty years have seen a war of technology between the big screen (theaters) and the small screen (TV). When television started stealing audiences from the theaters in the 1950s, cinema fought back with widescreen formats (see below), 3D, and multichannel surround sound. Now widescreen TV is common, 3D TV is gaining ground, and flat-screen TVs have increased in size to the point that some can provide a more cinemalike viewing experience in the home. Even a blockbuster Hollywood film will be seen by far more people sitting on couches at home than by audiences in theater seats. Even so, only the theater offers the communal experience of watching a movie with a large group, on an enveloping screen in a dark room, away from the distractions of daily life.

The term "small screen" used to be understood as meaning broadcast television typically viewed on a modest-sized box in the living room. Now screens for personal viewing range from enormous wall-mounted displays to 10-inch tablets to inch-wide cell phones. The source of the programming can be OTA (over the air), satellite, cable, DVD, Blu-ray, hard drives, the Web, or any number of other storage and transmission technologies. For a filmmaker, it's hard to know where or how your work will be seen or how you should prepare for that. The coming years will no doubt see new types of displays and viewing habits, and even if you're producing mainly for one, you'll want to take other viewing technologies into account.

Though it may be possible to work in one format exclusively, today it's more common to shoot in one or more formats, edit in another, and release the movie in several others. It helps to consider the three stages of the filmmaking process separately, while also keeping in mind the whole.

1. *Acquisition.* How will you record picture and sound? Will you shoot video or film? Which format(s); which camera?
2. *Postproduction.* How will you edit? What kinds of picture or sound manipulations will you need to do? What technologies will you use?
3. *Distribution.* Where do you want to show the movie? What kind of steps do you need to take *in advance* to be sure the movie is suitable for these outlets?

Theatrical Exhibition

Projection on a large screen puts great demands on the image because any defects, shakiness, or lack of focus will be greatly enlarged and have the potential to disturb the viewing experience. Traditionally feature films for theaters were shot in 35mm film. For the feature film industry, this has meant that many of the tools and techniques of production and postproduction were geared toward 35mm (or even larger film formats).

Historically speaking, the 35mm standard has played an important role for audiences worldwide. Even if they can't describe why the picture looks the way it does, people have associated Hollywood movies with the feel of 35mm in terms of the tonal range, clarity of the image, frame rate, lenses, and other aspects (see The "Look" of the Movie, below). Obviously, films shot in 35mm can look very different from one another and may employ a variety of film stocks, lenses, or filters in order to achieve different looks. But there are certain qualities in common—qualities that have been deeply intertwined with our collective experience of seeing fictional movies in theaters. It's worth noting that the 35mm film image has various characteristics that aren't by definition "good"—things like graininess, unsteady projection, and motion artifacts (jerkiness during fast pans or wagon wheels that appear to spin backward).

Fig. 2-3. Large-screen projection puts particular demands on image and sound quality. (Film-Tech.com)

Today, more and more features are shot digitally, and our visual and cultural reference points are evolving. Not very long ago, audiences could easily recognize when a production was shot on video, but with many of today's digital cameras, audiences and even professionals often don't know if the movie they're watching originated in digital or on film. Professional digital cinema cameras employ sensors the same size as 35mm film cameras (see below) and use the same lenses. Moreover, digital image quality is highly adjustable and can take on many different looks. Of course, not all digital cameras and recording formats are equal, and some digital movies, especially when shown on large screens, do reveal artifacts or flaws in the image.

From an artistic point of view, this is not to say that film, or the 35mm look, is *better* than other formats. The films of John Cassavetes that were shot with a handheld 16mm camera would not be better if shot in 35mm. The look of a lowresolution cell phone camera may be perfectly suited to a scene or movie you're shooting. Some people who shoot in digital have no interest in emulating Hollywood styles, or they may be seeking the unique possibilities of digital media. At the same time, as Hollywood moves toward digital, the grain and feel of the film image can sometimes seem almost old-fashioned compared to the latest digital cinema formats.

Whether you choose to shoot in digital or film, another set of issues arise when the movie is sent out for theatrical release. Traditionally most theaters showed features using 35mm film projectors. This meant that productions shot in 16mm had to be blown up to 35mm, and productions shot in video had to be transferred to 35mm film via the film-out process. For a low-budget production, this blowup or film-out often represented a significant portion of the budget. Today all Hollywood productions shot on 35mm film go through a digital intermediate (D.I.) process and undergo a film-out if 35mm prints are needed, so the film-out process may be involved regardless of what format you shoot in.

However, digital projection, also called *digital cinema* or *D-cinema*, is rapidly replacing 35mm print projection in theaters. Digital projectors operate at 2K and 4K resolution and offer theaters and producers lots of advantages, such as no longer needing to make heavy film prints to ship around the world. Digital projection is rock-steady and you'll never sit through a screening with a scratched print. And of course there would be no rebirth of 3D in Hollywood without digital projection.

For filmmakers who shoot digital, being able to project digitally means not having to do an expensive film-out to 35mm. However, there are costs in preparing a Digital Cinema Package (DCP), which is the standardized set of encrypted files (impossible to pirate) for digital projection, which is distributed on a hard drive. Sometimes smaller theaters may instead project using Blu-ray players, which bring down costs for both the exhibitor and the producer. See p. 625 for more on DCPs, and p. 747 for their impact on distribution.

If you're producing for theatrical exhibition, plan on an aspect ratio that's at least 16:9 or wider (see p. 74). Theatrical projection, whether on film or digital, is standardized at 24 fps.

Digital Television

In 2009, American television switched from analog to digital broadcasting. Much of the rest of the world has already switched or will eventually convert to digital. *Digital television (DTV)* offers advantages to both consumers and broadcasters. Unlike analog TV, which is susceptible to ghosting and multiple images, DTV reception is crystal clear. (With digital broadcasting, the signal is either cleanly displayed or nothing is displayed—though occasionally digital errors do creep in.) DTV, like digital cable TV, is capable of transmitting a high definition channel and multiple standard definition channels in the same signal space, or bandwidth, as a single conventional analog TV channel. So broadcasters can offer several programs at the same time.

It's important to remember that DTV does not necessarily mean high definition. As of this writing, broadcasters are offering both SD and HD channels, and millions of consumers are still using SD televisions with digital conversion boxes.

In the United States, the digital broadcast television standards are known as *ATSC* (after *Advanced Television Systems Committee*). As you can see in Fig. 2-4, ATSC standards include a variety of resolutions and frame rates in 4:3 and 16:9 aspect ratios. ATSC uses MPEG-2 video compression (the same codec used in DVDs, satellite, and digital cable TV) and Dolby Digital audio compression, capable of 5.1 audio channels (see Chapter 16).

ATSC FORMATS

Resolution	Frame Rates	Aspect Ratio	Pixel Format
HIGH DEFINITION			
1920 x 1080	24p, 30p, 60i	16:9	square
1280 x 720	24p, 30p, 60p	16:9	square
STANDARD DEFINITION			
704 x 480	24p, 30p, 60i, 60p	4:3	nonsquare
704 x 480	24p, 30p, 60i, 60p	16:9	nonsquare
640 x 480	24p, 30p, 60i, 60p	4:3	square

Fig. 2-4. ATSC formats. Digital television broadcast in the United States includes these formats; 60i means 30 fps, interlaced. In former PAL countries, such as in Europe and Asia, HD frame sizes are the same, frame rates are 25p and 50i, and SD frame sizes conform to PAL standards (including 720 x 576).

American broadcasters have chosen different HD formats. For example, as of this writing, CBS, NBC, and HBO use 1080i for their high definition programming, while ABC, ESPN, and Fox use 720p. After undergoing MPEG-2 compression and broadcast compromises, it's unlikely that home viewers can see a lot of difference between the two formats for most types of programming.

Meanwhile, 1080p at 24 and 30 fps is supported by some satellite services (like Dish Network and DirecTV), on-demand services (like Hulu), and devices like Blu-ray players, PlayStation, and Xbox. ESPN has announced sports programming in 1080p at 60 fps. In the future, it's inevitable that 1080p will gain a greater foothold in broadcast.

For filmmakers, if you shoot in either 1080p or 720p formats, you should be in a good position to deliver for any type of broadcast, but be sure to explore individual broadcasters' submission requirements.

Europe, Australia, and parts of Asia have adopted the DVB (Digital Video Broadcasting) set of standards. DVB-T (terrestrial) uses MPEG-2 compression, but also includes H.264 (MPEG-4 AVC) for delivery of both standard and high definition. For HD broadcasting, DVB offers the same common image formats (CIFs) as ATSC—1080i, 1080p, and 720p; however, in former PAL countries the field and frame rates are typically 50 and 25 instead of ATSC's 60 and 30.

Web and Mobile Delivery

Not very many years ago, people watched television only via over-the-air broadcasts. Then came cable TV, which could bring more channels to your home on a wire, and satellite TV, which could beam them down from space. With the Internet, we gained the ability to watch content from websites worldwide. In the early stages, we did this while sitting at our computers.

Now we have devices that can deliver programming from the Internet to the widescreen TV in our living room. These include Web-enabled televisions, Blu-ray players, and dedicated devices like Apple TV that can stream movies and TV shows purchased or rented from a wide range of providers. This form of distribution is sometimes called "over-the-top TV" since it often comes into your house on the same cable furnished by a cable TV operator, but it effectively rides over that company's programming and allows you to choose your own.

Fig. 2-5. Mobile video. In *Sunset Boulevard*, silent film star Norma Desmond says, "I *am* big; it's the pictures that got small." This is a lot smaller.

In a related development, movies and television can also be delivered to mobile phones and tablets, further fragmenting the way media are consumed. To take one example in the U.S., with a Netflix subscription you can stream part of a movie to your phone, go home, turn on your TV, and continue watching where you left off. Watching a movie on a phone, a tablet, or a laptop is a very different experience than seeing it in a theater or even on a big TV. Texture and details are lost, and scale and proportion are completely different. On the other hand, especially when using headphones, there can be a particular immediacy with a movie playing in your hand. Filmmakers tend to fall into two camps about mobile video: those who are horrified by the idea of people watching their work on a tiny screen amid the distractions of the street or a gym, and those who are thrilled about the potential of more distribution channels and revenue streams.

Over-the-top and on-demand services have the potential to seriously disrupt established modes of producing and consuming television and movies. For more on the financial implications for filmmakers, see Chapter 17.

DVD and Blu-ray Discs

VHS cassettes created a revolution in the 1970s by allowing consumers to watch movies at home on their own schedule. DVDs upped the ante in the mid-1990s with far better picture and sound quality, multiple languages, and extras—which killed off VHS. DVDs became a huge revenue source for films and TV shows.

DVDs are standard definition only and were joined, in 2006, by Blu-ray Discs

(BDs) designed to handle both SD and HD content. When Blu-ray was introduced, many expected another explosion of revenue as consumers converted to the new high definition technology. But the convenience and quality of streaming video, coupled with consumer satisfaction with "good enough" DVD quality, slowed Blu-ray adoption and computer manufacturers hesitated to adapt costlier BD drives to laptops. As of this writing, DVDs and BDs maintain an 80/20 split in home distribution of movies on optical disc, with Blu-ray increasingly gaining share. Further gains for Blu-ray are expected as prices fall, disc capacities increase, and Blu-ray 3D grows popular.

THE "LOOK" OF THE MOVIE

How a movie looks has an enormous impact on what the movie means to the audience. As Marshall McLuhan said, "The medium is the message," and without a doubt the medium itself plays a large part in how we understand a movie's content and experience its emotional impact. There are cultural traditions that associate certain technologies and styles with certain types of movies. As discussed above, the dramas we're used to seeing in theaters have been closely associated with the look of 35mm film (even if many of them are now produced digitally). Hollywood films are typically shot with a large crew, careful lighting, and sophisticated dollies and other equipment to move the camera smoothly. In contrast, television news stories typically have the look of handheld video, often shot with harsh, camera-mounted lights. Clearly, there is a noticeable difference in terms of the emotional feel and texture of the two formats/looks.

In a simplistic way, the crisp, bright video look makes news and sports feel "real." But the same look can make TV dramas (like soap operas) seem "fake"—that is, instead of allowing the audience to enter into the dramatic world the show is trying to create, the video image makes us aware of the "reality" of a bunch of actors walking around on sets. Higher-budget dramas were traditionally shot on film in order to capture a richer, softer feel that allows viewers to "suspend disbelief" and enter into the fictional world of the movie. Today, productions done with digital cameras that are well lit and carefully shot can capture a very similar rich look.

Over time, certain looks and styles can become clichés. At one time, so many documentaries were shot using grainy 16mm film and shaky handheld camerawork that their look became associated with "documentary." When fiction films try to simulate a documentary look they often resort to shaky handheld camerawork and bad lighting. Meanwhile, documentary forms have evolved, and many nonfiction films have beautiful lighting and fluid, elegant camerawork.

Styles are continually being borrowed and traded between different genres of filmmaking. As technologies and tastes develop, an ever wider range of looks and styles become possible. How audiences interpret those looks and styles keeps changing too, as new films explore different combinations.

As a filmmaker, you have at your disposal many techniques and tools to create different looks and moods. The most important by far for the success of the movie are all the things that take place in front of the camera, including direction, performances, lighting, sets, and costumes. Then there are choices about how the movie is recorded (such as what camera, which lenses, what format) and the things done in postproduction (including editing, sound work, color correction, and music). Of course, for some filmmakers, the concerns of story, content, cost, and convenience are so much more pressing than the look or visual style that they'll shoot with whatever they can get their hands on, and they pay as little attention as possible to technique.

Quality is important. Many movies have been dragged down by inattention to the technical aspects of filmmaking. But for most audiences, the story comes first. If viewers feel emotionally or intellectually involved in a film, or simply find it entertaining, they can be very forgiving of an imperfect image. But if they're not interested in the film, style alone won't make them love it. For some films—experimental films, for example—style and texture can be especially important; even so, as you make stylistic choices, be sure they serve the film, not the other way around.

Let's examine some of the factors that go into particular looks. Some of these things can be experimented with or changed on a shot-by-shot or scene-by-scene basis. Others you may need to commit to before you start shooting, and stick with that choice to the end.

THE IMPACT OF SENSOR SIZE AND FILM GAUGE

As we saw in Chapter 1, a digital video camera focuses the image that comes through the lens onto an electronic sensor (see Figs. 1-4, 1-9, and 2-6). Similarly, a film camera focuses the image on a piece of film (see Fig. 1-31). The size of that sensor or the gauge of the film can affect the recorded image in a number of ways.

Fig. 2-6. DSLR sensor from a Nikon D5100. The sensor size is Nikon DX, which is one of the APS-C formats. (Nikon, Inc.)

Digital video cameras are available in a wide range of sensor sizes (see Fig. 2-7). Some compact consumer or prosumer video cameras have sensors as small as ¼ inch or ⅓ inch.[3] Many cameras used for news or television production have ½-inch or ⅔-inch chips (the latter has been a professional standard for years). DSLRs and digital cinema cameras have much larger sensors, including Four Thirds, APS-C, and full-frame 35mm, the same size as an image captured on film by traditional 35mm still cameras. Sensors in most digital cinema cameras are nearly identical in size to Super 35 motion picture film.

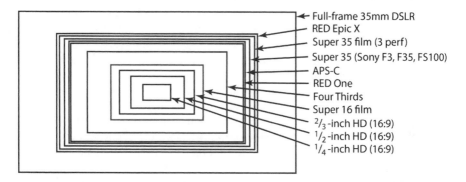

Fig. 2-7. Comparison of different sensor sizes. This diagram represents the physical area of the sensor when recording in a 16:9 format (and is enlarged for clarity). A number of digital cameras have sensors roughly the size of Super 35 film (in this chart, the Super 35 group loosely includes everything from the RED Epic X to APS-C and RED One). As of this writing, only certain DSLRs have "full-frame" 35mm sensors (including the Canon EOS 5D Mark II and EOS-1D X). Some cameras use only part of their sensor for some recording formats. Don't confuse the physical recording area of the sensor with the number of pixels in a given digital format, which is shown in Fig. 1-7. (Steven Ascher)

There is a relationship between sensor size and pixels: for any given resolution—say, 1280 x 720—the smaller the sensor, the smaller the pixels need to be fit on it. If you envision each pixel (photosite) on the sensor as a tiny bucket that collects light, the bigger the sensor, the bigger each bucket can be. Bigger buckets have three advantages: they're more sensitive (so you need less light to shoot), they have better dynamic range (they can handle scenes with greater range from dark to light), and they produce an image with less noise.

The sensor size also affects the relationship between a given lens and the recorded image. For any focal length lens (say, 50mm), a larger sensor will produce a wider angle of view (see Figs. 4-6 and 4-7). Another way of saying the same thing is that for the same angle of view, the camera with the larger sensor will require a lens with a longer focal length, which can result in shallower depth of field (more on this below and in Chapter 4). In terms of lenses, a large sensor may or may not be an advantage, depending on what you're trying to do. In the case of film cameras, a larger-gauge film like 35mm will always have better image quality than a smaller-

3. Sensor sizes indicated as fractions of an inch are a *diagonal measurement* that comes from analog days when the target sensor fit inside a glass cylinder of that diagonal, so the sensor is slightly smaller than the stated size.

gauge like 16mm, due to less grain and image defects. However, sensitivity will be the same if the same film emulsion is used. The relationship just described between lenses and sensor size applies to film gauges as well.

These topics are described in more depth below and in later chapters.

COLOR AND SENSITIVITY TO LIGHT

Digital and film cameras are tools for capturing an image of the world that can then be displayed on a screen. That screen image may look a lot like the scene as it appeared in real life, or it may look very different, depending in part on the camera, the way it is adjusted, and other factors. Many digital cameras are highly adjustable in terms of color and contrast; you can opt for more muted, pastel tones or go for more vibrant, saturated hues.

While it's best to choose an overall look for a production or for a scene before you shoot, it is often not advisable to "bake in" anything too extreme. You'll always have much better control over color in postproduction, and leaving camera settings fairly neutral allows you more flexibility in post. If you're shooting film, different stocks are known for their palettes and inherent contrast. But again, fine-tuning color is best done in post.

Color and the response to light are complex topics and are discussed more in Chapters 5, 7, and 8. But it's worth thinking about these things when deciding on the camera system you'll use to shoot your movie. ("Camera system" in this sense is meant to include the whole package, including the camera, its internal adjustments, its lens, and the recording format or, for a movie camera, the film stock.)

Low-Light Shooting

Digital and film camera systems vary widely in their sensitivity to light. Some can record an acceptable image using the light level of a normal home or office; others require much brighter movie lights. The camera's ability to handle low light can have a big impact on your production style and budget. If you can shoot with available light (whether it's daylight or artificial) or a minimal amount of movie lights, you'll be able to work faster, more efficiently, and more freely. Low-light sensitivity can make a huge difference if you need to shoot outdoors in the evening or on the street at night. Anytime you're filming real people going about their lives, it's far preferable to not *have* to light them. There are many times you'll want to add lights for artistic reasons (more on this below), but if your camera can get enough basic exposure without a lot of added lighting, your shoot will be easier and you'll have the option of capturing the natural feel of the locations where you shoot.

When you're choosing a camera or a film stock, look into its low-light performance. Talk with knowledgeable people who have worked with it. As a rule of thumb, digital video cameras with larger sensors have better sensitivity than those with smaller chips. A video camera's sensitivity depends in part on the frame rate (slower rate requires less light) and also whether you're shooting progressive or interlace (interlace usually requires less light for the same frame rate). The camera manual or advertising may list the minimum amount of light needed (this may be indicated in light units called *lux*), or the camera may have an ISO rating (see

p. 133). But ads and generalities aside, it's worth doing tests to see how the camera actually performs.

Most video cameras have a *gain* setting that can increase low-light sensitivity; a little gain boost can often help, but too much gain can introduce electronic *noise* to the image. Similarly, there are high-speed film stocks designed for low-light shooting that tend to be grainier than other stocks. You may or may not object to the graininess.

With cameras that have detachable lenses, the choice of lens can make a big difference in how much light you need to shoot (see p. 168).

Handling High Contrast

Pay attention not just to the *minimum* amount of light the camera needs, but also to its ability to handle a wide *range* of brightness in a scene. Most scenes you'll want to shoot contain areas that are much brighter or darker than other parts of the scene. All camera systems are significantly more limited than your eyes in being able to see details in both bright areas and shadows at the same time (see Fig. 7-16). Camera systems also vary in their ability to handle these high-contrast scenes. A film stock that can capture detail in shadows and bright areas at the same time is said to have wide *latitude* or *exposure range*. In video, the same thing can be described by saying the camera can handle a large *dynamic range*. In the past, film cameras had much greater range than video cameras. One of the giveaways that something is shot on video can be that the *highlights* (bright areas of the scene) are burned out, leaving bleached-out white areas. Today's high-end digital cinema cameras are capable of tremendous dynamic range; some claim fourteen stops or more, which exceeds many film stocks.

Many digital cameras allow you to create customized picture profiles, in which you can adjust *gamma* and *knee settings* that affect how the camera captures highlights or shadow detail (see p. 198). Experiment with different settings to create different looks.

Wide dynamic range can make as much difference to the overall quality of the image as high resolution; look carefully at a camera's dynamic range when buying or renting. The better your camera handles high-contrast scenes, the faster you'll be able to work and the less lighting you'll need. If the range of brightness in a scene is too great for your camera, there are a number of steps you can take (see p. 512).

It's worth noting here that careful lighting can work wonders to elevate the image produced by a low-end camera, and poor lighting will look bad even with the priciest camera. For more on lighting (and the use of light from natural sources), see Chapter 12.

Color Versus Black-and-White

Today's audiences expect color and may think of black-and-white as old-fashioned. However, because black-and-white is now relatively unusual, it can also command attention and feel stylish. Black-and-white films made in the "color era" have a unique place; for example, Martin Scorsese's *Raging Bull*. Distribution for black-and-white movies is generally more difficult.

Part of the aesthetic challenge of black-and-white is to render the world through the range of gray tones from black to white. Lighting tends to be more difficult because there is no color contrast to give snap to the image. For example, in black-and-white, a green leaf and red apple may appear as the same gray tone, whereas in color they would be strongly differentiated.[4] The Hollywood lighting style for black-and-white includes strong backlighting, or a rim light, to separate the subject from the background (see Chapter 12). On the other hand, one advantage when lighting a scene for black-and-white is you don't need to worry about matching the color of your lighting sources.

Black-and-white movies made today are mostly shot in color (*always* in the case of digital) and then made monochrome in postproduction. For shooting the genuine item—black-and-white film—there is Kodak Double-X Negative for 35mm and 16mm and Tri-X Reversal for 35mm, 16mm, and Super 8mm.

Fig. 2-8. The GoPro Hero2 is a small, waterproof HD camera that can be mounted on a surfboard, helmet, or vehicle for action scenes. (GoPro)

SHARPNESS AND FOCUS

The word "resolution" can have different meanings, but it's often used to talk about how much *information* a format can record. In a high-resolution image, fine details appear sharp and distinct; in a low-resolution image they may be blurred or

---

4. When shooting digital, different color tones can be separated in post during the conversion to black-and-white.

not visible due to digital artifacts in the picture (see Fig. 1-8). Different video and film formats vary in their resolution. High-resolution formats—like 35mm film, digital cinema 2K and 4K, and HD video—can capture details in a scene with sharpness and clarity. Certain types of shots or subject matter reveal differences in resolution more than others. For example, a wide shot of a landscape with a lot of detail will look dramatically better in high definition, while a close-up of a face might look more similar in either standard or high definition.

High resolution can make images look better, and because of the benefits of "oversampling," when you capture images in high resolution, it can improve their look even when they're shown on displays of lower resolution. If you've ever seen a black-and-white Ansel Adams photograph reproduced in a magazine, itself not capable of matching the fine detail or tonal scale of the original print, it's likely you nevertheless felt the superior image quality of the original.

However, as digital technology gets more sophisticated, a kind of arms race has developed between makers of cameras and TVs, all touting the advantages of their new, higher-res gear. Aside from the fact that the numbers claimed are sometimes fudged, it's worth taking this battle with a grain or two of salt.

First, there's a lot of debate about how much resolution a typical viewer in a typical living room watching a typical TV can even perceive. As noted earlier, many people can't see the difference between 720p and 1080p at typical viewing distances. Look at Figure 5-26: these images are very low resolution, but when viewed from far enough away, they begin to look sharp. The smaller the screen (and the larger the distance between the viewer and the screen) the less benefit you get from high-resolution cameras and TVs.

In a theatrical setting, screens are bigger and viewers may sit proportionally closer or farther from the screen than viewers at home. A digital cinema production shot in a 4K format and projected in 4K may look great, but many digital theaters project in 2K. Will shooting with a more affordable 1080p HD camera put you at a disadvantage compared to shooting 2K? The difference in total pixels is only about 6 percent, which many would argue is not perceptible.[5]

Even so, the resolution race ignores a key fact about vision that's perhaps more important: *sharpness*, which is our sensation of how crisp and in focus an image looks, has less to do with seeing fine details (determined by resolution) and more to do with there being bold contrast between black and white in the image (see Fig. 5-5C). By adjusting contrast you can often make a low-res image look sharper or a high-res image appear softer.

It would seem logical to assume that more sharpness is a good thing—and it often is—but the effect of sharpness on the look of your movie is something to consider closely. First of all, it's quite possible for the image to be *too* sharp. With

5. Meanwhile, manufacturers of 4K cameras argue that shooting 4K and downconverting to 2K or HD is noticeably better than shooting those lower-res formats. If so, then you need to weigh whether it's enough better to justify the increased data and cost. As noted earlier, some theaters project from Blu-ray players, which are at HD resolution. One advantage of shooting at higher resolution than you plan to deliver (for example, shooting 4K for distribution in HD) is that you can enlarge or reposition the image in post without loss of quality. In general, HD and higher-res formats allow you to do things like zoom in 25 percent or more during editing, sometimes including the zoom as a move on screen, which isn't possible in SD without noticeable softening.

very high resolution you may see things you don't want to—like every blemish on an actor's face, or the telltale imperfections that let the audience know your sets are just sets. Sometimes the picture just looks *too* crisp. On many dramas, diffusion filters (see p. 315), smoke, and other techniques are used to soften the image, to make things feel a little less real and create some mood. Romantic scenes and historical dramas are often made to look more gauzy than sharp. In these cases, filmmakers working in high definition formats are deliberately throwing away some resolution.

With some formats, particularly ones that aren't high resolution, certain tricks are used to boost the apparent resolution. Since increasing contrast can make an image seem sharper than it really is, many video cameras have a *detail* or *enhancement* circuit that can put a thin light or dark edge around people and objects to get them to pop out more in the picture (see Fig. 3-18). Particularly with low-end cameras, the detail setting may be too high, and the image takes on a very electric, videolike look. This can work fine for things like sports, but may look cheap if you're trying to achieve a more subtle feel. If possible, find a camera with user-adjustable detail settings and experiment with the look you like (see Chapter 3). Many TVs also have a detail or sharpness adjustment, which is generally set too high at the factory to create a vivid look.

LENS QUALITY. Experienced filmmakers know that lens quality is paramount. The image can't be any better than the lens is. No matter what format you work in, if your camera accepts detachable lenses, keep in mind that using a higher-quality lens will noticeably improve the image. You may want to rent or borrow a good lens (or set of lenses) for your shoot.

While SD zooms costing tens of thousands of dollars are often considered insufficiently sharp to shoot HD with its demands for higher resolution and superior contrast, this may not necessarily be the case. Moreover, the explosive popularity of DSLRs has put a new range of SLR still camera lenses into play, of widely varying quality. There is no better advice than to test, test, test when it comes to considering any type of lens for your movie.

Depth of Field

Many dramas aim for a look that has very shallow depth of field (see Figs. 2-9 and 4-9). Depth of field is discussed in Chapter 4, but the effect of shallow depth of field is that you can easily set up shots in which the subject is sharp but the background and/or foreground is out of focus. Isolating people from their surroundings this way can be a powerful tool, useful in both fiction and documentary. It can both create a mood and allow the filmmaker to use *selective focus* to draw the audience's attention to different elements in the frame. This is one of the key factors that characterizes the look of the classic 35mm feature film.

Many factors go into controlling depth of field, some of which can be adjusted shot by shot while you are filming. But your choice of camera is also important. The larger the film format, or for digital cameras, the larger the sensor, the easier it is to achieve shots with shallow depth of field. So, for example, if you shoot with a DSLR that has a full-frame sensor, you'll find it much easier to create shots with shallow depth of field than if you use a video camera with a ⅓-inch chip. However, despite

Fig. 2-9. Shallow depth of field. This shot from *Capote* is in focus on Philip Seymour Hoffman's eyes and nose, while his shoulders and the background are soft, which lends a certain mood and intimacy. (Sony Pictures Classics)

the claims of some camera ads, while a large sensor *facilitates* shooting with shallow depth of field, individual shots may actually have very large depth of field, depending on the particular lens and settings.

For video cameras with small sensors (like ⅓ inch and ½ inch) there are cine lens adapters that allow you to use PL-mount lenses or SLR still camera lenses to deliver the same depth of field and angle of view that a 35mm motion picture camera would, although often at a cost of several stops of exposure (see Fig. 2-10). These adapters are especially popular for use with MiniDV and HDV camcorders. The best known are made by P+S Technik, Redrock Microsystems, and Kinomatik.

Fig. 2-10. Redrock Micro M3 cinema lens adapter allows you to mount cine lenses on a variety of small-format video cameras to achieve the angle of view and depth of field of a 35mm film camera. (Redrock Micro)

The excitement about DSLRs is due in part to the ability to shoot with shallow depth of field, like "real" movies. But not all films and scenes benefit from this look. It's one thing if you're filming actors who hit their marks and you have an assistant pulling focus; it's entirely different if you're filming an uncontrolled documentary scene with several characters rushing around in different directions. Even if you get a person in focus, he may quickly move out of focus. Having the subject sharp and the background soft can look sexy; simply having the subject out of focus usually doesn't. For unplanned, active scenes, having great depth of field can be a huge benefit, and that's easier to do with a smaller sensor. Ironically, it was considered a major stylistic advance when Gregg Toland used wide-angle lenses, bright lights, and fast film stocks to overcome the shallow depth of field of typical 35mm movies to achieve his famous deep-focus look on *Citizen Kane* back in 1941 (see Fig. 9-10).

With HD, if your subject's out of focus, you're *really* going to notice it. Thankfully many camcorders have a "magnify" or "focus assist" or "expanded focus" button that momentarily enlarges the viewfinder image for more precise focusing. Nevertheless, if possible bring a good-sized, high definition monitor to check focus on any HD production.

ASPECT RATIO CHOICES

See the discussions of aspect ratio on p. 15 and p. 41 before reading this section.

For many years, both in film and in video, the shape of the frame was a rectangle, four units wide by three units high. In the film world this shape was expressed as a ratio, 1.33:1 (4 divided by 3). In the video world, the same thing was expressed as 4:3. Today, it's often called *nonwidescreen*.

Cinema was first to move to a wider screen image. In *widescreen* formats, the screen's horizontal dimension extends to nearly twice its height or more (see Fig. 1-35).

Many movies viewed in American theaters are made to be shown at the widescreen aspect ratio of 1.85:1, introduced in the early 1950s. European theatrical films may be made for projection at the not-quite-as-wide 1.66:1 (5 divided by 3). In HD video, widescreen means 16:9, which is the equivalent of 1.78:1, making it just slightly less wide than the cinema standard 1.85 for the same screen height. Some very widescreen theatrical films are shot at 2.39:1 (sometimes written 2.39, 2.35, or 2.40), popularly known as CinemaScope or 'Scope.

Different aspect ratios call for different approaches to composing your shots, which can affect your choice of locations, the way you move the camera, art direction, and blocking of action (see p. 80).

Though 4:3 is still used to broadcast standard def television, all HD formats are 16:9 and TV sets are now configured to this proportion. You should shoot 16:9 widescreen if you're producing for TV, and you may consider either 16:9 or a wider aspect ratio for theatrical release. Before you start shooting you need to decide which aspect ratio you want to work in, and how you're going to achieve that. Depending on the camera and the format, there are various alternatives that can affect the resolution of the image, the postproduction workflow, and the way the movie is shown.

Widescreen Options for Digital Cameras

Many if not most HD cameras have 16:9 sensors, so it's 16:9 widescreen from start to finish. DSLRs and some digital cinema cameras have boxier-shaped sensors that are taller than 16:9 (they have additional pixels on top and bottom). In their case, the 16:9 widescreen image is extracted from the sensor by ignoring the unneeded pixels top and bottom (using only part of the sensor is called *windowing*). So, for example, the same DSLR can shoot stills at around 1.5:1 and produce HD video at the wider 1.78:1 (which is 16:9).

With any camera, you can create a wider aspect ratio by masking off the top and bottom of the frame in postproduction. George Lucas shot some of the *Star Wars* films with HD cameras that natively capture 16:9, but he extracted a 2.39 widescreen image by cropping the top and bottom.

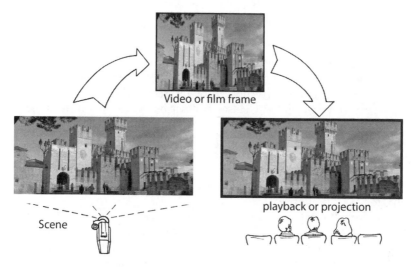

Video or film frame

playback or projection

Scene

Fig. 2-11. A widescreen image can be *squeezed* (compressed horizontally) to record it on a nonwidescreen video or film format. It is then *unsqueezed* for widescreen viewing. In film, the squeezing process is done with anamorphic lenses on the camera and projector. In video, normal or anamorphic lenses are used (depending on the aspect ratio and the recording format) and the image is compressed electronically. (Robert Brun)

ANAMORPHIC LENSES. Another approach to getting wider aspect ratios than 16:9 is to use anamorphic lenses—a technology originally developed for film but now used on both digital and film cameras. Anamorphic lenses use a special lens element that optically squeezes a superwide frame horizontally, so it can be recorded in a frame that is not as wide. The anamorphic image looks squished horizontally—people look too tall and skinny and circles become vertical ovals (see Fig. 2-11). To view the picture properly, you need to unsqueeze (stretch) the image horizontally. Unsqueezing may be done by a camera viewfinder or a monitor to view the image properly while you're shooting. In postproduction, the image can be unsqueezed electronically or optically so it can be viewed with conventional equipment. For theatrical film exhibition, lenses in the projector do the unsqueezing. Anamorphic systems are called 'Scope (for CinemaScope). Normal, nonanamorphic lenses are called *spherical* and nonanamorphic film prints are called *flat*.

Traditional 'Scope lenses squeeze the image by a factor of 2, so you can capture a 2.39 widescreen image on a conventional 35mm film negative or a digital cinema camera like the ARRI Alexa Studio that has a 4:3 sensor. For digital cameras with 16:9 sensors, you can shoot the same widescreen format using Hawk anamorphic lenses that have a 1.3 squeeze factor.

Anamorphic lenses are more challenging to use than spherical lenses. Horizontal angle of view is doubled by the added "anamorphosing" lens element. (Vertical angle of view, however, is not affected.) To obtain the same horizontal angle of view you would get with a nonanamorphic lens, you have to use an anamorphic lens of twice the focal length—which means depth of field is proportionately less, so anamorphic lenses require very accurate focus pulling. Most of these lenses aren't fast, either, so more lighting is needed. Anamorphic lenses are also larger and heavier.

STANDARD DEFINITION VIDEO. While standard definition video has a native 4:3 aspect ratio, there are a number of ways to create a 16:9 image in SD. The best way is to use a camera with 16:9 sensor and record the image anamorphically. This doesn't involve anamorphic lenses as described above, but instead the image is electronically squeezed by the camera in recording and unsqueezed by the monitor in playback. This method is called *full-height anamorphic (FHA)* or sometimes *full-height, squeezed* (see Fig. 2-12F). Shooting full-height anamorphic with a 16:9 sensor is the most professional way to record widescreen in SD. Similarly, in postproduction, delivering a widescreen program to a broadcaster in full-height anamorphic format is preferred.

With older SD cameras that have 4:3 sensors, you can create 16:9 by masking off the top and bottom of the sensor and either recording that as a letterbox with black bars on top and bottom (see Fig. 2-12E) or by digitally stretching the image in the vertical axis in camera so it becomes anamorphic (sometimes called *squeeze mode* or *digital stretch*). These options result in a 25 percent loss of resolution, which in SD can be a real problem.

Widescreen Options for Film Cameras

As you can see in Fig. 1-36, the original frame of motion pictures is 1.33:1 (which is the same as 4:3). This includes Super 8, 16mm, and 35mm.

If you're working in 16mm, avoid standard 16mm when possible. Super 16 is the obvious choice for widescreen productions, theatrical or TV, since its native 1.67 aspect ratio is a virtual match to 16:9. Some people shoot Super 16 with Hawk anamorphic lenses for a wider-screen look.

In 35mm, there are several options for widescreen. Before reading this, you may want to review different 35mm formats on p. 44.

The most common method is to expose the entire 1.33 frame, but use a viewfinder marked with 1.85 frame lines (see Fig. 6-6). When the film is projected or transferred to digital, the area outside the 1.85 central letterbox is masked out or removed. This technique once had the advantage that it provided a separate 4:3 version of a theatrical film for TV broadcast (which cinematographers disliked because it ignored their precise 1.85 widescreen compositions). With the adoption of 16:9 broadcasting, separate 4:3 versions are usually not needed or desirable.

As discussed above, anamorphic lenses can be used to record a 2.39 'Scope image to the full 35mm film frame minus the area reserved for the sound track. Because this anamorphic format uses the largest area of any four-perf 35mm format, the grain is tightest, projection is brightest (no masking in projector gate), and the result is glorious on the big screen.

However, because of the unique production challenges posed by anamorphic lenses, three alternative methods have been developed to achieve a 2.39 aspect ratio using conventional spherical lenses, which, as discussed above, are always faster, sharper, and cheaper than anamorphic lenses.

Super 35 is a four-perforation format that uses the entire width of the camera negative area from one row of perfs to the other—basically it's the original 1.33 silent film frame. During digital intermediate finishing, a 16:9 or 1.85 image is produced by cropping the top and bottom of the full 1.33 image, from which conventional four-perf prints or a DCP file can be made. Alternatively, the full 1.33 frame can be greatly cropped to 2.39, then digitally squeezed and exposed into the area of a 35mm negative used for ordinary anamorphic images. Again, conventional 2.39 squeezed prints can be struck, or a 2.39 DCP file can be made.

The latest 35mm cameras can shoot a three-perf-high frame that, like Super 35, occupies the entire width of the negative from one row of perfs to the other, but which results in an image virtually identical in aspect ratio to 16:9. Not only does this new format save 25 percent in camera film costs, but it provides an ideal framing for HD. Three-perf negatives must be scanned into digital files, since no three-perf projection format exists.

If you look at the narrow 2.39 image on a Super 35mm negative, you'll realize how much of the four-perf "real estate" is wasted. In fact, the 2.39 frame would fit nicely on a frame only two perfs high, while cutting film costs in half. With the advent of D.I., two-perf has achieved a new popularity for economical production of 2.39 images using conventional spherical lenses.

Converting from One Aspect Ratio to Another

Whether you work in video or film, widescreen or nonwidescreen, there will be situations in which you have to accommodate other aspect ratios. For example, your widescreen movie may be seen on nonwidescreen TVs. Or you may want to incorporate 4:3 footage into a 16:9 production. Different forms of distribution call for different aspect ratios, and if you're converting from one to another it pays to think ahead. This discussion will address 4:3 and 16:9 but the same principles apply to other widescreen formats as well.

FROM WIDESCREEN TO NONWIDESCREEN. Because many people still own 4:3 televisions, if you make a movie in 16:9 you may need to prepare a version that can be shown on a 4:3 screen. Converting from 16:9 to 4:3 can be done in a number of ways.

Letterboxing means showing the entire 16:9 image inside of the 4:3 screen, with black bars on the top and bottom (see Fig. 2-12E). If the original was 16:9, letterboxing involves scaling down the 16:9 image to fit within the 4:3 screen. Letterbox-

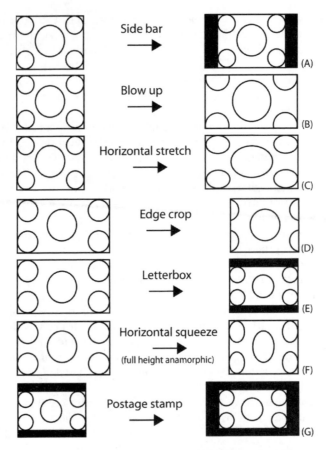

Fig. 2-12. Converting from one aspect ratio to another. When going from a nonwidescreen format to a widescreen format: (A) you can place the nonwidescreen frame within the widescreen frame with bars on either side; (B) you can enlarge the smaller frame, cropping the top and/or bottom edges and sacrificing some resolution; or (C) you can stretch it horizontally, causing a distorted picture. When converting from a widescreen format to a nonwidescreen format, you can: (D) crop the left and/or right sides; (E) letterbox the shot, preserving the whole frame but making it smaller; or (F) squeeze the image horizontally. Horizontal squeeze is commonly used to record widescreen images anamorphically on nonwidescreen video and film formats (the full-height anamorphic picture is later unsqueezed to restore the original widescreen frame). (G) If a letterboxed frame is displayed in a widescreen format using side bars, you get a postage stamp—a small image with black all around.

ing has become widely accepted, and it is perhaps the best solution to creating a 4:3 version of a 16:9 original because it preserves the original image composition.

Another approach is called *edge crop* or sometimes *center crop*. Here, a 4:3 rectangle is cut out of the center of the frame (see Fig. 2-12D). Edge crop may arbitrarily cut off important action—someone talking on the edge of the widescreen frame may not even be visible on screen. To reduce this problem, *pan and scan* may be used. With pan and scan, the position of the 4:3 crop is adjusted on a shot-by-shot basis or even within a shot so you can keep key action on screen. This is done during editing or post and may introduce artificial "camera" movements that the director or cinematographer never intended. At the very least, it is time-consuming if not also expensive.

The third method, sometimes called *squeeze mode*, is to squeeze the picture horizontally, creating an anamorphically distorted picture in which people look tall and skinny and circles become vertical ovals (see Fig. 2-12F). Squeeze mode can be useful for outputting a full-height anamorphic SD image from a widescreen HD master, or directly from an HD camera, but only if it will later be unsqueezed for viewing (see above). Squeeze mode is *not* a good way to watch a program.

FROM NONWIDESCREEN TO WIDESCREEN. Say you have a movie or some footage shot in 4:3 standard definition and want to convert it to 16:9, either as part of an upconvert to HD, or for display in SD on a widescreen monitor. There are several options; none is ideal.

One approach is to center the 4:3 picture within the 16:9 frame with black bars on either side. This is variously called *pillarbox*, *curtained*, or *sidebarred* (see Fig. 2-12A). The advantage of pillarbox is that the entire 4:3 frame is preserved, with no loss of resolution or added distortion. There are, however, a few disadvantages. For one, the picture may seem too small since it doesn't fill the frame. Some broadcasters won't allow pillarbox. Another issue with pillarboxing is that some widescreen TVs are set to recognize the black bars and then stretch the image horizontally, distorting it (see Fig. 2-12C). Sometimes instead of black bars, a background of some sort is put behind the 4:3 image in editing or post to fill out the frame and create the sense that the whole frame is being used. One such technique involves placing an enlarged, out-of-focus version of the image itself into the background in order to fill in the empty sides.

Another approach for converting 4:3 to 16:9 is to enlarge the 4:3 image so that it matches the width of the 16:9 frame (see Fig. 2-12B). While this is perhaps the most common technique, it means cropping the top and/or bottom of the picture and results in a 25 percent loss of resolution. If this is done during an editing session, you can move individual shots up or down to avoid cropping out important details. This is much like pan and scan and is sometimes called *tilt and scan*. Widescreen TVs typically have a *zoom mode* to scale up 4:3 material, which results in cropping and softening.

Another approach is to stretch the 4:3 image horizontally by 33 percent (the opposite of squeeze mode described above). The resulting anamorphic distortion makes circles look like horizontal ovals and people look heavier than they are (see Fig. 2-12C). Widescreen TVs usually offer this as an option, and some consumers prefer it because it seems to "fill the screen," but filmmakers who have carefully crafted their images may find the distortion disturbing. Some TVs apply more distortion to the edges of the frame than the center (called *panorama mode*) in hopes of disguising it a bit. It's common to see programming stretched on airport or restaurant TVs, and many people probably aren't even aware of it.

In the course of converting material between 4:3 and 16:9, it can happen that letterboxed footage later gets pillarboxed, or vice versa. Either way, that footage can end up as a small rectangle with black bars on *all* sides; called *postage stamp* or *win-dowbox*, it's something to avoid (see Fig. 2-12G).

How Aspect Ratio Affects Your Shooting

All this discussion of aspect ratios is to prepare you to think about how your choices affect the production from start to finish, and particularly to help you while you're shooting. Let's look at that part now.

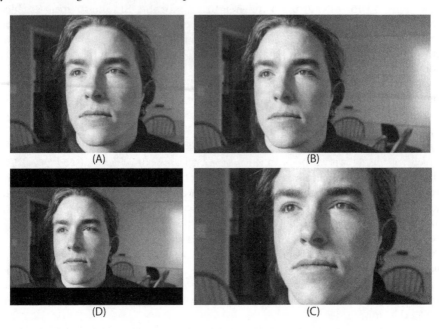

Fig. 2-13. Composition and aspect ratio. (A) The 4:3 nonwidescreen frame is well suited to a close-up of a face. (B) Shooting the same subject at the same size in 16:9 widescreen includes a lot more of the background, which needs to be taken into account. (C) If you shoot tighter to show the same amount of background as in A, the frame crops out the forehead and chin. (D) When B is letterboxed, the framing doesn't change, but everything looks smaller. (Stephen McCarthy/Steven Ascher)

One thing you can say for nonwidescreen 4:3, it's well suited to the proportions of the human face. A close-up of a person talking can fill the frame nicely (see Fig. 2-13). If you shoot a close-up of a face in 16:9, you have a choice between cutting off the forehead or shooting wider and seeing a lot more of the background. When you're shooting widescreen, you need to pay more attention to positioning the person in the space of the room and to the other things that are visible around and behind the person. When you're selecting locations, *dressing* them (place objects or props), and choosing your camera angles, be sure you're making good use of the widescreen frame. If you're filming a single character, you'll often want to counterbalance the person with objects or perhaps with lighting elsewhere in the frame.

Widescreen formats are well suited to wide shots with more than one character or where landscape is featured. Widescreen formats work well in the cinema because even things that are relatively small are easy to see when enlarged on the big screen. When widescreen films are shown on smaller displays, details may disappear. The shot from *Lawrence of Arabia* in which a camel rider appears as a speck on a vast expanse of desert and comes toward us is suspenseful and glorious when shown in the theatrical Super Panavision 70mm prints at 2.20:1 aspect ratio. The same shot letterboxed on a small TV may leave you wondering for a while what (if anything) is going on.

If you anticipate releasing a version of your movie in a different aspect ratio, keep that in mind when framing shots and blocking action. How you adjust depends on what format you're shooting and what kind of conversion you'll do. Again, though this discussion addresses 16:9 and 4:3, the same principles apply to conversions between other aspect ratios.

If you're shooting widescreen 16:9 and plan to make a letterboxed 4:3, you know the entire frame will be visible in the 4:3 version, but everything will be smaller. If there's some element that's crucial for the audience to see or read in the scene, make sure it's big enough in the frame to still be legible when scaled down in the letterbox.

If you're shooting 16:9 and will be making a 4:3 version by doing edge crop, be careful not to position important elements too close to the left and right edges of the screen (or, if you're doing pan and scan, you can use one edge or the other but not *both* at the same time). For example, it often looks good in 16:9 to have one character on the far left and one on the far right. Once converted to 4:3, one of them will probably be cut off. A classic problem occurs when someone enters frame from the left or right of the 16:9 version and on the 4:3 version you hear them before they enter the 4:3 frame.

When doing edge crop, the frames of the 16:9 and 4:3 version share a "common top and bottom," so the *headroom*—the distance from the top of someone's head to the top of the frame—is the same for both. But the sides are different. You can't be expected to put all the action in the center of the frame, but bear in mind the cropping that may happen later. Some broadcasters ask that when shooting 16:9 you *protect* for 14:9, a compromise that forces you to keep the action a little closer to the middle. Broadcasters may also require that graphics in a 16:9 production stay within an even narrower 4:3 safe area.

When shooting in a 4:3 format that you plan to convert later to 16:9, the two versions will share "common sides" but you need be concerned with the cropping of the top and bottom of the frame. If you're converting to 16:9 by enlarging the image (see Fig. 2-12B), you'll be cutting out the top and/or bottom of the picture. This means when shooting you should leave enough room above and below the action so you don't lose key details after the conversion.

FRAME RATE AND SCANNING CHOICES

Not that many years ago, choosing the basic frame rate for your movie was a no-brainer. If you were shooting film, you shot at 24 frames per second. If you were shooting video in North America, it was NTSC 60i (30 frames per second, interlaced) and in the UK, Asia, and Europe it was PAL 50i (25 frames per second, interlaced). Though these are still widely used frame rates, things have gotten a lot more complicated. You have more choices about frame rates and whether to shoot interlace or progressive. These choices can have a big impact on the look of your movie, your shooting style, and your postproduction and distribution options. Before reading this section, see pp. 11–15 in Chapter 1, and keep in mind that in the following discussion, we're talking about the base frame rate for a project, not the use of high and low frame rates to create slow motion and sped-up motion (that's discussed on p. 389).

Let's look now at the standard frame rates in ascending order of speed.

24 fps Film and Digital

In the silent era, early film cameras were hand-cranked at about 16 frames per second (but theater owners projected them faster so they could get more showings per day—hence the classic, sped-up look). Movies used to be called *flickers* (later *flicks*) because the image on the screen flickered (got brighter and darker). When talkies were introduced in the late 1920s, film cameras and projectors were motorized, and the speed was standardized to 24 fps to accommodate sound. This reduced flicker, but even at 24 fps the light would appear to flash on and off if projectors weren't equipped with extra blades (see Fig. 16-15). The projector essentially flashes each frame on the screen two or three times, with an instant of darkness between. This gives an apparent "flash rate" of 48 to 72 flashes per second, which is fast enough so we perceive the illumination as continuous and not flickering.

Over the years, we've come to associate 24 fps with the cinema experience. The look of Hollywood feature films is integrally tied to that frame rate. But shooting only 24 frames each second is a relatively slow "sample rate" in terms of the slices of time that are recorded. This reveals itself in several ways.

First, when a camera runs at 24 fps, the standard amount of time that each frame is exposed to light is $\frac{1}{48}$ second. This is slow enough that when a person moves across the frame quickly, he will be blurred while he is in motion (see Fig. 2-14). Audiences are used to this particular *motion blur*; they may even like it—it's part of the "film" look.

Fig. 2-14. Motion blur. (left) When the subject or camera moves quickly, there is motion blur within each frame that looks natural in video or film footage. (right) Shooting with a higher shutter speed reduces motion blur, which allows you to grab sharper still frames but can make motion seem choppy at some frame rates. (Steven Ascher)

Another result of shooting 24 fps is that motion isn't perfectly continuous. There's a characteristic unsmoothness that you may not be consciously aware of (until you see a side-by-side comparison with footage shot at a higher frame rate). However, you can become *very* aware of it if the camera pans (pivots horizontally) across a landscape too quickly: the objects in the landscape will not appear to move smoothly across the screen, but instead seem to jump or stutter from one position to the next. This is called *judder, skipping,* or *strobing.* It happens when camera or subject movement is too fast, and it destroys the illusion of continuous movement (and gives viewers a headache). There are shooting techniques that help minimize strobing, such as throwing the background out of focus, tracking with a moving subject, and not panning too fast (for more on judder, see p. 393).

The first 24p HD video camcorder was developed by Sony in response to a 1977 request from George Lucas, who was in the early planning stages of *Star Wars.* Today many if not most HD video and digital cinematography cameras can shoot at 24 fps, progressive. Many digital filmmakers like 24p because motion feels more filmlike. For digital acquisition of footage that will ultimately be transferred to film, 24p is particularly useful (it's a very clean transfer, one progressive video frame per film frame) and it's popular for movies that will remain digital from start to finish.

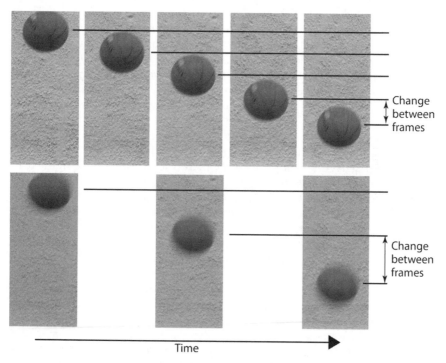

Change between frames

Change between frames

Time

Fig. 2-15. Frame rate and the smoothness of motion. (top) Consecutive frames of a basket-ball falling. (bottom) The same action shot at a slower frame rate: now there are fewer frames in the same amount of time, and the ball moves farther between frames, which can increase the chance of choppy motion or judder. Note also that the slower frame rate typically has a slower shutter speed—resulting in more motion blur in each frame—which can help make the increase in judder less noticeable. (Steven Ascher)

With its relatively long exposure time, 24p is better than faster frame rates for shooting in low light.

In terms of motion, 24p digital comes with many of the advantages and disadvantages of 24 fps film. When shot at the standard shutter speed of ¹⁄₄₈ second, it has the same motion blur of film. It may have somewhat worse strobing problems, however. This is because judder is most noticeable on parts of the frame that are sharply in focus, and with many digital cameras it's harder to work at shallow depth of field, where you can throw the background out of focus (though large-sensor DSLRs and digital cinema cameras are an exception). Also, video monitors are typically brighter than film projectors, which exacerbates judder and flicker.

So, while many digital filmmakers like 24p because of its look and because it's progressive, keep in mind that in terms of its *temporal* (time) qualities, it's a relatively slow frame rate that may cause the motion artifacts just discussed, which is why a lot of people shooting digital *don't* prefer it.

HOW 24p IS RECORDED. HD cameras use a variety of techniques to record 24p to file or to tape. Some HD cameras can record 24 fps "natively," which means simply recording 24 progressively scanned frames each second in a digital file format to media like memory cards or hard drives. In Panasonic cameras, 24p native is sometimes indicated as "24pN."

Cameras that record 24p to tape divide each progressively scanned frame into two fields—first all the odd lines, then all the even lines—which in some ways resembles recording interlace at 48 fields per second. However, unlike normal interlace, since both fields *originate from the same frame*, that is, they are created during the same ¹⁄₄₈-second exposure, they can be recombined upon playback into a single, clean progressive frame. This method is known as *progressive segmented frame* (*PsF*).

Both 24p native and PsF allow you to record 20 percent more material on a drive or a tape compared to the pulldown methods described below.

Because 24p arrived on the scene after there was already 60i equipment in wide use, manufacturers felt that 24p would be most useful if it could be played on existing decks and monitors. Many digital cameras therefore use a technique of embedding the 24p stream in a 60i recording that can be viewed and edited on any 60i-compatible equipment. This is done using a process called *2:3 pulldown* (also called *3:2 pulldown*). For every four progressive frames that the camera captures, it splits them into five interlaced frames that are recorded as standard 60i to tape or to file. Using 2:3 pulldown, the speed of the movie doesn't change and the resulting video can be edited like any other 60i video. If you want to edit or finish in 24p, the pulldown process can be reversed during postproduction to recover the original 24p stream.

There are a few variations on pulldown. Panasonic also developed a system in which 24p and other frame rates are recorded into a 60p stream. This method is found on many cameras that record 720p HD. Panasonic developed another technique, called 24p Advanced pulldown (24pA), that offers some benefits when you shoot DV material for editing at 24 fps.

For more on all of these methods, see Working with 24p and Pulldown on p. 601.

WHEN 24p ISN'T QUITE 24 fps. As discussed on p. 14, frame rates for digital video cameras in formerly NTSC countries are usually not the whole numbers they appear to be. So digital video cameras running at 30 fps are really running at 29.97 fps and those set to 24 fps are generally recording at 23.976 fps (sometimes written 23.98 fps). A few high-end digital cinema cameras can run at *precisely* 24 fps, which is done primarily for feature films aimed for theaters. Material shot at true 24 fps can be converted to 23.976 when necessary, and vice versa. For more on the implications for audio recording, see p. 690.

25p Digital

If you live in a former PAL country, 25p can be an effective frame rate choice. It is very similar to 24 fps film in terms of how motion is rendered. Indeed, made-for-television productions shot on film in these countries are often shot at 25 fps.[6] You can easily convert 25p to 50i for broadcast with good quality.

30p Digital

People living in former NTSC countries may choose 30p because it's progressive, works well for video posted to the Web, and converts easily to 60i if needed for broadcast. Being a little faster than 24p, it handles motion with less objectionable judder. In many ways, 30p can feel like a fairly neutral frame rate, with no obvious flavor. If you're shooting progressive HD and plan to intercut standard def NTSC material in the project, 30p allows the SD footage to be used without any frame rate conversion. One caveat about shooting 30p: if you plan to distribute your movie in formerly PAL territories, transferring from 30p to 25p or 50i may not result in the smoothest motion. For this kind of distribution, shooting 24p might be the better choice.

50i/60i Digital

As noted above, in formerly PAL countries, 50i (25 fps, interlaced) is the legacy frame rate still widely used for broadcast and for lots of different video equipment. In formerly NTSC countries, the equivalent is 60i (30 fps, interlaced). Interlace has the disadvantages discussed on p. 11. However, in terms of motion, since scanning takes place at 50 or 60 fields per second, there's less judder than with frame rates like 24p, so things can move in the frame and the camera itself can pan more quickly without risk of strobing. In some sense, the look of 50i and 60i is more "realistic"— it's closer to the way we normally perceive motion. It's also the scanning rate many people have grown accustomed to from years of television, including sports, news, documentary, and corporate videos. Because of these associations, dramas shot at 50i and 60i may sometimes look less like "movies" and more like TV.

48p/50p/60p Digital and Beyond

Compared to 24p, motion looks much smoother when you shoot 48p for cinema or 50p or 60p for HD television. You get less motion blur when the camera or objects in the frame move (because the exposure time is much shorter), which can be

6. Or they're shot on film at 24 fps and then sped up by 4 percent to 25 fps when transferred to video.

a benefit for sports and other material where you want to capture all the action and be able to get good slow motion and crisp freeze frames. Like 50i and 60i, you get less judder than at slower frame rates but, being progressive, 48p, 50p, and 60p avoid edge tearing and other interlace weirdness.

Visual effects pioneer Douglas Trumbull and James Cameron, among other filmmakers, have talked about how immersive and real the image feels at high frame rates, and how the increase in *temporal resolution* you get as the frame rate increases can be more exciting than the *spatial resolution* of simply increasing the number of pixels in the frame. Shooting at 48p, 50p, and 60p (and displaying at the same frame rates so that motion is rendered in real time) is a step in that direction.

You can shoot HD at 1280 x 720 pixels at 60 fps (the format commonly known as 720p) and a number of networks broadcast in this format (see p. 63). A growing number of 1080-line HD and 2K digital cinema cameras can record at 48p, 50p, and 60p, and some monitors can display these frame rates directly—but as of this writing, corresponding theatrical and TV formats are not yet common for distribution or broadcast because of the high data rates.

Big-screen 3D productions can be particularly enhanced by high frame rates. Peter Jackson's *Hobbit* films were shot in 3D at 48p. There is talk of future standards of 72 or even 144 fps. For some dramas, high frame rates may look too realistic, as discussed earlier.

Delivering Different Frame Rates

Your choice of frame rate should be based mostly on the look you hope to achieve. Before you go into production, shoot some tests. You may find, for example, that the judder you get when panning at 24p bothers you, or that you need to adjust your shooting to minimize it.

Bear in mind that we often see frame rates displayed in something other than their "pure" form. In NTSC countries most digital systems apply pulldown to 24p, as described above, so that by the time you see it on a screen you're really looking at 24p converted to 60p (or *first* 60i then 60p). That footage will still look different from material originally shot at 60i, but it's not the same as, say, watching a 24 fps film in a movie theater.

As noted earlier, how the picture looks depends in part on how many frames are recorded each second, and also by how many times each frame is flashed on screen. In video, this is determined by the monitor or projector *refresh rate*. If you display video that was recorded at 30p on a monitor that has a 60 Hz refresh rate, each frame gets shown twice. Newer monitor technologies, such as screens that refresh at 120 or 240 Hz, repeat each frame more often and may make motion look smoother and reduce flicker. However, while you're shooting, when you look in your camera viewfinder or on a monitor that has a slower refresh rate, the same footage may look choppier.[7] For more, see p. 221.

---

7. ARRI describes the stuttering you may see in the Alexa camera viewfinder when doing quick pans at low frame rates as a "worst-case scenario," since the effect will be much less apparent on external monitors or projectors. When recording to file at 24 fps, the Alexa offers a *smooth mode* to feed a 48 fps image at the same shutter speed to the viewfinder (to reduce apparent judder for the camera operator).

As discussed earlier in the chapter, the frame rate you shoot in is often different from the frame rate the movie is ultimately broadcast or distributed in. These days many editing programs or software apps can do frame rate conversions—some better than others. In the past, dedicated hardware systems provided the highest-quality conversions, but today there are both hardware tools and sophisticated software apps that can convert pretty much anything to anything and do it well. For example, if you shoot 60i, it's fairly easy to convert to 50i for distribution in formerly PAL countries. Some people prefer to shoot digital at 24p (or transfer from film to 24p) to create a "universal master" from which 24p, 25p, 50i, and 60i can be relatively easily created for different distribution outlets.[8] In general, shooting progressive is preferable since you can easily convert to interlace if necessary, but going the other way may result in lowered quality.

Before choosing a frame rate, talk with post facilities and others with experience in the kind of project you're doing. For more on frame rates, see Chapters 9 and 16; for more on frame rate conversions, see p. 598.

CHOOSING A CAMERA

Before you can choose a camera (or cameras) for your production, you have to make some basic decisions about whether you're shooting digital or film and in what format or gauge. Chapter 1 and this chapter discuss those options. Then you'll look at individual cameras and lenses for their capabilities. The next five chapters can serve as a reference for those choices. Below is an outline of things to consider.

DIGITAL FORMATS. As you've seen, many things go into what might be called the "format," including the type of compression (the codec), the amount of compression (or data rate, often user selectable), the frame size, the frame rate, and whether you're shooting interlace or progressive. It may seem like a long list, but it's less complicated than it looks. Seek advice, and remember that a format isn't just a format, it's the recipe of all these choices together. In the end you'll decide on a recipe that you'll follow for your movie and then get equipment that can deliver it. Or you'll pick a recipe based on what your camera can handle. The truth of the matter is that movies have been made with wildly different format recipes and audiences for the most part don't know or care.

DIGITAL RECORDING MEDIA. Will you record to flash memory cards, hard drives, videotape, or some combination? More on this below.

SIZE OF SENSOR OR FILM GAUGE. As discussed on p. 66, a digital camera's sensor size or the width of the film gauge can affect your choice of lenses and make it easier or more difficult to shoot either with shallow depth of field or deep

---

8. However, going from 24p to 25 fps PAL often involves a change in speed and pitch (see p. 69).

focus (other factors affect these things too). Sensor size also affects sensitivity and the size of the camera. This is a key factor in picking a camera.

LENS OPTIONS. A camera that accepts detachable lenses will give you more options for choosing the right one for a scene or shot. Cameras with fixed lenses are sometimes more affordable and compact. The lens mount and sensor size can affect the range of available lenses in terms of focal length, speed, and cost. There's a good argument for spending more on high-quality glass (which can last for years) than on the camera (which may soon be outdated).

ABILITY TO HANDLE LOW LIGHT AND HIGH CONTRAST. See Color and Sensitivity to Light, p. 68. Remember that dynamic range and color may depend on how you adjust internal menus, so a camera may not look its best straight out of the box.

CAMERA SIZE AND SHAPE. Camera size is a key consideration. The cost of a production is often closely tied to the size of the camera. If you're shooting with a 35mm Panavision camera, you'll need a sizable crew to lug it around. If you're working with a DSLR, on the other hand, you might need only a cameraperson. If you're shooting alone or with a small crew, a small camera that can be tossed into a shoulder bag and carried onboard an airplane can be a big asset.

The size of a camera affects how people respond to the production. In documentary shooting, big cameras often draw attention ("What TV station will this be on?") or may make subjects uncomfortable. A small camera that looks like a consumer model (or *is* a consumer model) sometimes helps you fly under the radar and avoid raising suspicions. Sometimes people ignore a DSLR because they assume you're shooting stills, although the video capability of these cameras is no longer a secret.

On a feature film, a small camera may make some people think it isn't a "real" (that is, Hollywood) film. At times this can be a help—for example, if people can see you're working with a small budget, they may be more understanding when you can't pay them a lot. At other times, you might not be taken as seriously. As technology develops, small is often seen as cool.

From the cameraperson's standpoint, small cameras have advantages and disadvantages. Small, prosumer, or consumer cameras may not have the features or accept the accessories that professionals rely on to do their job. You may find your creativity hampered by the lack of manual controls, or, with DSLRs, the need to mount external viewfinders, monitors, audio recorders, and power sources that might otherwise be built into a dedicated video camera.

For handheld shooting, some people love to work with a little camera that can be cradled in the hands, floated above the ground, or fit into small spaces. But when you hold a small camera up to your eye, all the weight is on your right arm, which can make steadiness difficult and be very tiring after a few hours. A heavier, longer camera that balances on the shoulder may be easier to work with. But beware of a camera that has a shoulder rest or brace but doesn't really *balance* on the shoulder— your arm still has to hold it up. Some camerapeople like to wear a body brace for handheld work; others find that cumbersome. Once you trick out a DSLR with a

(A)

(B)

(C)

(D)

Fig. 2-16. (A) A small handheld camera is light and portable but can be hard to hold steady. (B) This camera perches on the shoulder, which increases steadiness, but a lot of the weight is on your right arm, which can get tiring. (C) A shoulder-mount camera that balances on the shoulder can be steadier and sometimes more comfortable for handheld work, even if it's heavier. (D) Some shoulder braces for small cameras place batteries or counterweights behind the back to help balance the camera. (Panasonic Broadcast; Redrock Micro)

full shoulder brace to adapt it for handheld work (and add the matte box, external viewfinder, and other attachments) it's no longer really a small camera.

THE LATEST THING? In choosing a camera or format, some filmmakers like to work at the cutting edge of technology (often thought of as the "bleeding edge" for the problems you may encounter). Other filmmakers feel more comfortable with the tried and true. In exploring equipment or methods that are new to the market, be sure to look at the implications for shooting, editing, repairs, and so on. It usually takes some months or years for all the kinks to be worked out.

STAYING FLEXIBLE. You may decide to use one camera system as your A camera to record the majority of the project and then have one or more other systems around for specialized shots, tight quarters, two-camera shooting, or whatever. The image from an inexpensive DSLR may show artifacts such as moiré (see p. 213) that a more expensive video camera might not, but it may be right for your purposes and budget (as either an A camera or B camera). Many successful films have combined high- and low-end gear in the same movie.

PLANNING YOUR WORKFLOW

As noted in Chapter 1, *workflow* is a term used in the digital video era to describe the sequence of steps or tasks needed to accomplish a goal in production, editing, or finishing. For example, if you shoot HDV and record on tape, your postproduction workflow will include capturing the video from the tape to a hard drive before you can start editing. However, if you record directly to a hard drive in the field, your workflow is simplified and you may be able to start editing immediately.

Particularly now that there are so many technologies and ways of doing things, it's important to plan out your workflow in advance. Often, choices you make at the beginning commit you to a certain workflow later on. The best workflow choices harmonize the steps of production, editing, and finishing, so you save time and don't waste money fixing mistakes in post.

Perhaps the best way to prepare a project workflow is to talk to people at each step of the production process and find out before you start how they like to work and what they need to do their jobs. If you're shooting film, visit the film lab, meet the telecine colorist, and ask his or her advice about using the latest film stocks. If you're shooting video or film, ask the people at the postproduction facility how they want material delivered, what kind of timecode they need, or if they have any particular audio requirements. Discuss strategies of online conforming and color correction with your editor and your post house. The value of talking to people in advance cannot be overstated! Don't go blindly into decisions that may leave you regretting them later.

MANAGING DATA IN PRODUCTION AND POST

Digital video creates a lot of data to be recorded, processed, and stored. From the get-go, you need to consider which technologies and techniques you'll use, as they affect many aspects of production and postproduction.

Choosing Media for Recording and Storage

Not too many years ago, a typical video camcorder recorded only one format onto a particular size tape cassette—end of story. Today, many cameras offer a variety of formats and ways to record them.

When thinking about digital video recording, it helps to remember that digital video is just a form of computer data stored in files, whether on a tape, a hard disk drive (HDD), an optical disc, or a solid-state memory card like SD, Sony Memory Stick, CompactFlash, or Panasonic P2. Video files are a whole lot bigger than text files, but the basic operations of storing, copying, and moving them aren't so different from what you might do with word processing files on your home computer.

Fig. 2-17. (left) P2 card. These flash memory cards are about the size of a credit card and are available in various storage capacities. (right) The Panasonic AG-MSU10 unit can transfer the contents of a P2 card (in the upper slot) to a removable hard drive or SSD (in the tray below). Allows you to download cards in the field without a computer. (Panasonic Broadcast)

SHOOT WITH TAPE OR GO TAPELESS? Videotape originated in the analog era and continues to be a useful medium for recording digital video. Tape cassettes are cheap, they can be quickly loaded and unloaded from a camera, and they can be used for long-term storage. Unlike a hard drive, a tape cassette is not a piece of "equipment"; so, for example, if you shoot footage for a client, you can give the client the tape and not be concerned about getting the drive back later.

Tape continues to be used for some high-end digital cameras (such as Sony's CineAlta cameras, which record to HDCAM SR) and for some lower-end cameras (like HDV models). However, the majority of new cameras no longer use tape; instead they record files to memory cards, hard drives, and discs.

Fig. 2-18. DVCAM tape cassettes. The small cassette is MiniDV size. The larger shell holds more tape and can be used with larger professional cameras. (Sony Electronics, Inc.)

The advantages of file-based, tapeless recording are numerous. Cameras no longer need a delicate tape transport and spinning head drum assembly, so they're cheaper, there's little or no mechanism to break, and they're more robust in challenging shooting environments. Perhaps most important, any given camcorder can record to several different formats, even at different frame rates, which wasn't possible in the old days of tape. File-based recording makes it easy to check takes in the field, mark them with comments, or get started editing.

To get the best of both worlds, some people record simultaneously to both tape and either a hard disk drive (HDD) or solid-state drive (SSD). The HDD or SSD gets them editing faster and the tape goes to long-term storage in the archive. Sony HDV camcorders, for one example, can record HDV internally to a MiniDV cassette and simultaneously output the same HDV signal via FireWire to an external HDD or SSD controlled by the camera for dual starts and stops. This is called *dual recording*. Dual recording is also available in cameras that record to solid-state media. Some Sony AVCHD camcorders, for instance, that primarily record to SD cards or Memory Sticks can simultaneously record to an optional SSD, which has more than ten times the capacity of the smaller memory cards.

PROTECTING DIGITAL DATA. While file-based recording has lots of benefits, it does introduce a new set of tasks and challenges during the shoot; namely, managing all the data produced by the camera. If you can afford enough flash memory cards, you can shoot all day and deal with downloading after the shoot. If not, you have to stop shooting when your cards fill up, and manage the process on set or location. Similarly, some cameras record to internal or external hard drives that need to be downloaded when they're full.

While flash memory continues to drop in price, many still consider it too expensive for long-term storage. The long-term stability of flash memory is also unproven. So when a flash memory card or drive fills up, most people download it to a hard drive or optical disc.

Downloading can be done with a laptop; alternatively, there are several stand-alone portable hard drive solutions that can automatically download from a card to one or more drives, complete with verifying the data. Before you wipe forever clean the memory card so you can put it back in the camera, you want to be absolutely sure that you have copied intact working files to the backup device, because your footage is costly if not impossible to replace. Often this means that someone is assigned the

Fig. 2-19. The Atomos Ninja recorder can record, monitor, and play back Apple ProRes 422. Stores files on a removable hard drive or SSD. Can be used as an external recorder with cameras that can output uncompressed video via HDMI, allowing you to bypass the camera's native codec and record high-quality 10-bit ProRes files. The ProRes files are ready for editing, usually with little or no conversion necessary. The Atomos Samurai adds Avid DNxHD recording and has HD/SD-SDI inputs. (Atomos)

responsibility of first playing back and inspecting the copied files before the card is recycled. All this takes time and equipment. Anyone who has feverishly downloaded cards under pressure from a crew waiting to get back to work with those cards may look back wistfully to the days when you could simply pop a recorded tape out of the camera and pop in a fresh one.

Files can get corrupted and hard drives are susceptible to failure, so download-ing precious footage to a single drive doesn't make it safe. Some productions follow a "three by two by two" rule: download files to three storage devices (using at least two different technologies; see below) and store them in at least two dif-ferent locations in case of a fire or other disaster. On some shoots, hard drives are given to different members of the production team to bring home in separate cars or flights.

As of this writing, optical disc recording is limited mostly to professional cam-corder systems like Sony's XDCAM HD (Blu-ray based). The disc drive is integral to the camcorder and play/record decks. The "professional discs" can then be used for archiving.

SAVING TIME IN EDITING. With videotape, you can't start editing until you "capture" the material onto the hard drive of the editing system, which involves playing each tape in real time (an hour tape takes at least an hour to capture). One of the selling points of file-based recording is that you can start editing more quickly. However, not all tapeless systems are equal in this regard.

Some systems are truly direct-to-edit. For example, the high-end ARRI Alexa can record to Apple's ProRes codec, as can a variety of lower-end cameras using devices like AJA's Ki Pro external recorder (see Fig. 5-11) or the Atomos Ninja (see Fig. 2-19). You can attach a drive with your ProRes files to a Final Cut Pro editing system and get right to work.

Not all workflows are this seamless. DSLRs, for example, record in MPEG-4 file formats that must sometimes be converted before you can edit with them. (As native editing of mixed codecs becomes the norm in leading nonlinear editing sys-tems, such conversions will become a thing of the past.) For various reasons, you may choose to transcode to a different codec for editing or finishing (more on this below). Although such conversions can usually be done faster than real time, the process is far from instantaneous.

Also, regardless of what technology you use, there is still the time-consuming step of logging: the task of breaking down and labeling clips before you edit.

LONG-TERM STORAGE. Not unlike the nuclear power industry, which keeps churning out nuclear waste without a good solution for storing it, digital video producers keep recording terabyte after terabyte of data without any good, long-term, archival storage system.

Memory cards may still be too expensive to put on the shelf, issues of archival stability aside. Hard drives are a medium-term solution, but costs add up when you have a lot of data to store. Some filmmakers buy "bare" SATA drives cheaply on the Internet without any cables or housing. Bare drives can be mounted in a removable enclosure or a drive tray in a Mac Pro or HP workstation. Once you've uploaded your data, you take the bare drive out of the enclosure and store it. Since all hard drive mechanisms are destined to fail over time, some people recommend starting up your drives at least once a year, and after a few years transferring the data to another drive.

Another solution is an *LTO* (*Linear Tape—Open*) drive, which accepts LTO tape cassettes. LTO is a linear tape format that uses simple, fixed magnetic heads instead of the complex spinning heads used in video recording. It provides high storage capacity and is considered archival. (Many industries use LTO for backup, including banks and financial institutions.) The latest LTO format, called LTO-5, which can store 1.5 terabytes per cassette, is sometimes used to archive video. In 2010 a new file system was announced for LTO tapes called *Linear Tape File System* (*LTFS*) that will allow an LTO tape drive to appear on a computer's desktop as if it were just another hard drive. LTFS was created with video storage in mind. While LTO tapes are relatively cheap, as of this writing the drives aren't. There is, of course, the irony that, thanks to progress, our cameras no longer use magnetic tape, but if we want to archive footage from these cameras, we may need . . . magnetic tape.

A DVD can store 4.7GB and a Blu-ray Disc can store considerably more, depending upon number of recording layers: 25GB, 50GB, up to 128GB. The archival longevity of these discs, particularly DVDs, is questionable. Like color film, most DVDs rely on organic dyes that fade due to aging and temperature. Sony, however, claims its Professional Discs, based on Blu-ray technology, have an archival life of fifty years.

Of course, with any archiving system, you need to make basic decisions about whether you'll save everything from a project or you'll weed out bad takes, outtakes, or other material to reduce storage requirements.

For more, see Recording to Cards, Drives, and Optical Discs, p. 115.

Cloud-based Workflows

Various online services allow you to upload your video files to their servers over the Internet ("cloud storage"). Web-based systems can be used throughout the production process, including uploading high resolution camera footage, transcoding to editing formats and web-friendly viewing formats, archival storage, and collaborative tools that enable members of the production team to watch, label, and even edit material from wherever they are. For more, see www.aframe.com, www.sampledigital.com, and www.wevideo.com.

Thinking About Camera Choices, Compression, and Workflow

See the discussion of compression on p. 20 before reading this; for more on color systems, see p. 16.

We've seen that shooting digital video involves processing a lot of digital data. The more resolution the camera is capable of, the more data you've got to deal with, which drives up costs. Compression reduces the amount of data, and is done at several stages between the sensor that captures the image and the device that will eventually display it. Let's look at the different stages and the implications for workflow and choices you might make about cameras and postproduction.

Fig. 2-20. Blackmagic Production Camera 4K. Shoots wide dynamic range Ultra HD 4K, recording in RAW (CinemaDNG) or ProRes 422 (HQ) at surprisingly low cost. The similar Blackmagic Cinema Camera shoots 2.5K. Both feature built-in SSD recorders. (Blackmagic Design)

If you're using a large single-sensor camera to record in a RAW format, or to record RGB 4:4:4 in a log format like Sony S-Log, you've chosen the least-processed, most data-intensive type of recording. RAW files, for instance, come right off the sensor and allow maximum flexibility for adjusting color and tonal scale in postproduction. Uncompressed RAW recording requires a lot of fast storage. (The RED One and Epic get around this by compressing their RAW output.) During the shoot, processing is needed to convert RAW to something you can view properly on a monitor (see p. 203).

RGB 4:4:4 also has a very high data rate, and it can be recorded with only a fast drive array or other high-throughput recording system. It's worth noting that because neither RAW nor RGB 4:4:4 can be recorded and broadcast with typical video equipment, many people don't consider them "video"; instead, they're digital motion picture formats. All the formats discussed below are video.

Most video cameras further process the RGB signal into component color (4:2:2), which involves throwing away some of the color resolution and reducing the data rate (see p. 209). This 4:2:2 component signal is also extremely high quality even though the data rate is lower than for RAW or RGB. Uncompressed 4:2:2 still requires so much storage that it isn't practical for most productions and may not provide much benefit (that is, you may not see any difference in the picture between working in uncompressed and using some compression).

To reduce storage needs more, most video cameras compress the 4:2:2 signal using one of the formats and codecs discussed in Chapter 1 (see High Definition Digital Formats, p. 23); for example, AVCHD or DVCPRO HD. Compression levels vary from light to heavy depending on the format and the options selected. Many codecs throw away even more color resolution; HDV and Sony's XDCAM EX, for instance, are 4:2:0. For the vast majority of productions, these varieties of compressed video provide ample quality.

One reason manufacturers offer so many different systems is that productions vary considerably in their relative priorities of quality, convenience, and cost. If you

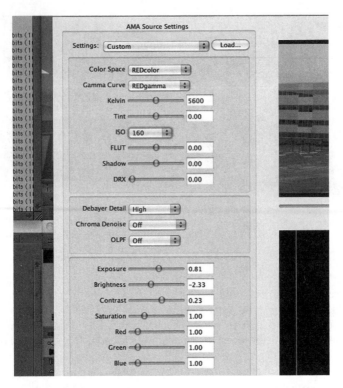

Fig. 2-21. RAW files allow you to adjust many aspects of the image in postproduction, including exposure, color temperature, ISO, and color balance. Some NLEs, such as Avid Media Composer (shown here with settings for REDCODE files) and Adobe Premiere Pro, can work with RAW files natively, allowing you to make adjustments as you edit, without "baking in" a look beforehand. Not all systems can handle large RAW files with adequate performance for editing. (Avid Technology, Inc.)

can afford it, there are advantages to shooting with as little compression as possible. On the other hand, a highly compressed system may suit your needs very well. As time goes on and codecs improve, you can work at lower data rates (more compressed) without sacrificing quality.

Some cameras may offer various options for compression. If you're able to work with an external recorder you may have even more. For example, some cameras can only record highly compressed video within the camera, but can output uncompressed HD via an HD-SDI link or an HDMI cable to a flash memory recorder or hard drive.

As you move into postproduction, you have more options about compression. If you shot in a relatively uncompressed, high-data-rate format and want to edit in that format, you'll need a lot of storage and a powerful, fast hard drive array. On many productions, to save money and storage, footage is downconverted or compressed prior to editing. For example, HD material might be compressed to a low-data-rate file that's easy to store and edit. After offline editing, the original, full-res files are linked to the edited sequence, and the movie can be output in its highest-quality form (see Fig. 14-9).

In another type of postproduction workflow, camera footage is made *less* compressed before editing (making the files larger). Since the H.264 compression used in some DSLRs can create issues in editing, filmmakers may prefer to decompress or transcode footage to a less compressed codec like ProRes 422 or DNxHD 145 prior to editing (for more on compression and editing, see p. 554).

Fig. 2-22. Most DSLRs create small, highly compressed video files that are easy to store, but are sometimes easier to work with when converted to a less compressed format prior to editing. (Ally Shore/SmallHD)

In finishing your project, you'll face yet more considerations about what format to create the master in, and how to manage up- or downconversions from that master for distribution (see Chapter 14).

Workflow decisions about compression through the production chain have a whole array of pros and cons that you can best evaluate by talking with people and doing research on the Internet.

THE IMPORTANCE OF SOUND

In filmmaking, *sound quality is often more important than picture quality.* This may seem counterintuitive, but you can test it yourself. First watch a scene that's well lit and in focus but has distant, scratchy, rumbling sound with dialogue that's hard to understand. Then watch a scene that's very underexposed and maybe a little out of focus, but has pristine audio with crystal-clear voices. After a minute or two, the first scene becomes truly irritating; the second one, though not ideal, is at least watchable.

On many productions a misguided priority is placed on image over sound. For example, the director of photography may be given hours to light the set; then, at the last minute, the sound recordist is told to slide a microphone in wherever there's room—as long as it doesn't cast any shadows. Or a filmmaker may spend thousands to get a high-resolution camera, only to shoot with a cheap on-camera mic.

For a fiction film, sound recorded poorly on the set can be remedied by rerecording the dialogue later in a studio (called *ADR—automatic dialogue replacement*). Even on an otherwise well-recorded movie, ADR may be necessary for scenes shot in noisy locations or where mics are impractical. ADR, of course, takes money and time.

On a documentary, ADR is not done (even if it could be, most would argue it *shouldn't* be). Many a great documentary scene has been abandoned on the cutting room floor because of unintelligible sound.

Sound recording and editing is discussed in Chapters 10, 11, and 16. But there are several aspects to sound that you should consider before you begin production.

Microphones

When it comes to recording the human voice, there's no substitute for getting close to the source. Miking from a few feet away usually allows you to capture the voice clearly, without too much competing background sound.

Professional sound recordists often use a microphone at the end of a boom, which can be positioned close to the person talking. This may be a directional mic that reduces background noise (see Chapter 10). Another solution is to put a wireless mic on the main person(s) talking; a wireless lapel mic can be hidden under clothing or, for some documentaries, clipped on a tie or shirt.

With video camcorders and DSLRs there's a temptation to use the mic that is built in or mounted on the camera. On-camera mics can be useful for run-and-gun situations, or when the subject is very close to the camera. However, if you plan to shoot your movie mostly with an on-camera mic, be aware that there will be many situations where you'll get bad sound. The camera is usually farther from the subject than is optimal for audio, and it's often pointed at something other than the sound source. Also, built-in mics often pick up camera or handling noise. Avoid them when you can! Even if you're filming alone, a wireless mic or sometimes a handheld mic can be a big improvement.

The Recording System

As discussed in Chapter 1, film is always shot double system. When shooting digital video, sound is recorded in the camera and it may also be recorded double system with a separate audio recorder. When choosing a camcorder, look into its sound recording capabilities. Few if any camcorders record audio that is the equal of high-quality professional sound recorders because professional recorders have expensive preamps and processing optimized for first-rate audio. But many camcorders record sound that is almost as good, typically 48 kHz, 16-bit digital audio, the same as many other digital recorders. Many indie features and documentaries have been successfully made with in-camera audio.

Sometimes a particular camcorder or digital video format results in audio that is of lower quality. For example, DSLRs often have cheap preamps and inferior audio capabilities. Many filmmakers, especially those making dramatic feature films, prefer instead to use portable flash- or disc-based recorders to record uncompressed audio while shooting with DSLRs. Generally, audio is recorded in camera as well, to assist in syncing up (see p. 589).

Talk to audio recordists or postproduction mixers to get advice about your setup. For professional results, you may decide to use different camera settings, a different camera, or a separate audio recorder. When you shoot video double system, you gain a certain flexibility, but there may be added complexity on the shoot and you also need to allow some time to sync the sound and picture during editing.

Music

Music is a powerful force in movies. It can have a huge impact on the audience's emotions and energy. It can also have a huge impact on your budget. Filmmakers often plan scenes around their favorite song or find themselves shooting a scene in which a cool tune is playing in the background. Unless you have deep pockets, beware!

If a character in your film plays or sings a song, you'll need to clear the rights to it with the song's publisher. To use a prerecorded song by a popular artist (whether it's playing in the scene or added in editing) you'll need to license it from both the publisher and the record company. This can cost thousands or tens of thousands of dollars. Never commit yourself to using a song (for example, by having a character perform it) without finding out first if you can clear and afford it (and leave several months for the process). Even a tune as ubiquitous as "Happy Birthday" is copyrighted and needs to be licensed.

If you're shooting a documentary, it's generally a good idea to avoid radios or other music sources while you're filming. Turn them off when possible. (It also makes cutting easier if no continuous music exists in the background.) There is an exception, however, which applies mostly to documentaries. The legal concept of copyright includes the idea of "fair use," which permits limited use of unlicensed audio and video materials under specific circumstances.

There's more on music editing in Chapter 16 and on the legal aspects of clearing music and fair use in Chapter 17.

The Sound Mix

Early sound recordings were monophonic—just one audio channel. Then stereo (two channels) became standard. Now some sound systems have five or more channels. Having a multichannel sound mix can enhance your distribution opportunities (or be required by a broadcaster or distributor), but it adds complexity and cost to finishing the film. If you want or need a multichannel mix, budget for it and plan ahead (particularly in editing, but even in shooting). See Chapter 16 for more on mixing.

COPING WITH TECHNOLOGY

Surviving the Onslaught of Technology

So, you're setting out to make a movie, and you have to decide about equipment, formats, frame rates, perhaps even how many dimensions. As we've seen, there are many ways to go—too many, really. Your choices will be somewhat limited by the equipment you have or can afford. You may face difficult trade-offs that force you to sacrifice one option for another. And when you ask for advice, be prepared to hear different people argue passionately for or against any given choice. Some of these people will actually know what they're talking about and others will be equally as sure of themselves.

Fig. 2-23. A format is rarely just a format. This image was shot in 16mm film, transferred to DigiBeta, dubbed to DVCAM, exported as a TIFF file, up-resed and deinterlaced in Photoshop, then printed in black-and-white. A lot of film and video footage goes through a similarly complex path from acquisition to display. You can go crazy trying to control how each stage changes the picture. (Stephen McCarthy)

It would seem that any disagreements about formats and settings could be settled by a simple test to see which looks best. But it's often not that simple. Say you like the look of a certain movie and want to emulate it on your production. Well, as we've seen, there are lots of things that contribute to what you're seeing: the direction, the subject, art direction (for a drama), lighting, camera, lenses, format, frame rate, the monitor or projector.

As if all these considerations weren't enough, there's also the simple truth that the exact same technical specs can look good when shot and displayed with well-designed professional equipment and appear a lot worse with cheap consumer gear. It can seem overwhelming to account for so many factors. But to understand what you're doing and why, you need to be a critical thinker and try to examine one factor at a time. For example, using just one camera and one monitor, experiment with different frame rates. Get to know the different feels they produce. Then, when you see the output of another camera, you'll have a sense of whether it looks the way it does thanks to the frame rate or some other factor. And when you find something you like, try watching it in different environments—on small screens and large—to see how it holds up.

It's easy to get caught up in numbers. Filmmakers and consumers always want to know which is the "best" format, camera, or TV. Preferably, they'd like a simple numbered scale or ranking to compare "A" to "B." As we've seen, there are many numbers used to quantify different things, but the numbers are sometimes more misleading than helpful. What your eye perceives can't be boiled down to a meaningful number. Sometimes an image that "should" look inferior according to the numbers actually looks great. People develop prejudices based on old assumptions or how much something costs and then are shocked by a new technology that performs better than anything before in its price range. A format or camera may be just fine for your purposes even if another is technically "superior."

In the end, it's not the numbers that matter, it's what you see and hear. Over time you'll learn to interpret why something looks and sounds the way it does, so you can decide if it's right for you, or what you might do differently.

The Cost of Independence

As digital technology becomes more sophisticated, filmmakers are expected to understand and work with some really complex tools. These tools put a great deal of power in your hands, but require a lot of attention when you might rather concentrate on other things.

As digital equipment and software become more affordable, it becomes technically possible for one person to shoot and edit a movie, do the color correction and sound mix, create the titles, effects, and everything else. Working this way can be a real boon: it saves time, money, and hassle and gives the filmmaker unprecedented creative control. But it entails some losses. When you're no longer interacting with the professionals who would have otherwise done the sound mix, color correction, graphic layout, and such, you lose the benefit of their expertise. Technology can be democratizing, but it can be isolating too.

CHAPTER 3

The Video Camcorder

This chapter is about the basic operation of video cameras and recorders used in production. Before reading this, see the overview of digital video systems in Chapter 1. The use of lenses is discussed in Chapter 4 and a more detailed discussion of video recording is in Chapter 5. See Chapters 10 and 11 for microphones and audio recording for video.

Overview of the Digital Camcorder

Devices that can record video range from dedicated video cameras designed for professionals and consumers to mobile phones, tablet computers, and digital still cameras including DSLRs and point-and-shoot models. Obviously there are big differences between them, but they all share things in common. The idea of a camcorder comes from the days when video cameras recorded to videotape, and the camcorder combined a camera and videotape recorder (VTR) in one convenient

On-camera mic

Lens

Viewfinder
(eyepiece)

Memory
card slots

Battery

Flip-out LCD monitor

Fig. 3-1. Video camcorder. (Panasonic Broadcast)

unit. Today most camcorders record directly to flash memory cards, disk drives, or optical discs, but videotape is still used on some productions, either within a camcorder or when recording to a separate VTR. All camcorders have these elements:

1. *The lens.* Forms an image of the scene on the camera's sensor(s). Most lenses have controls for the focus of the image, the brightness of the image (using the *iris diaphragm*), and—with zoom lenses—the magnification of the image (using the zoom to change focal length). On some cameras the lens is built into the camera; on others it is detachable and different lenses can be used.

2. *The sensor.* Light-sensitive electronic chip that converts the image formed by the light coming through the lens into a grid of electrical charges. Either a CMOS or CCD type of imager. See Figs. 1-9 and 2-6.

3. *Digital signal processor.* A microprocessor that digitizes the electrical charges from the sensor and converts them into a digital video signal. Other tasks for these complex chips may include adjusting color and tonal reproduction, setting frame rate and length of exposure (using the *shutter*), and adjusting the sensitivity of the sensor (using the *gain* control), plus managing and storing a range of complex parameters.

4. *The viewfinder.* A small video monitor viewed through an eyepiece that allows you to see what you're shooting or playing back. Most camcorders also provide a separate fold-out LCD screen for external viewing.

5. *The recording system.* Stores the video signal on flash media, hard drive, tape, or disc.

6. *Audio recording.* Most camcorders have built-in or attached microphones and provisions to plug in external mics. Professional camcorders offer full manual control of audio input and recording (see Chapters 10 and 11).

7. *The power supply.* Camcorders can be run on rechargeable batteries or by plugging them into an AC power supply.

8. *Timecode.* An hour:minute:second:frame timestamp for each frame of video, critical for many aspects of postproduction (see p. 223). All professional camcorders have full timecode capability, while nonprofessional camcorders provide a limited type of timecode that is nonetheless useful when timecode is required.

Many consumer cameras are designed for the "point-and-shoot" user and are highly automated. Since control of focus, exposure, and color is part of the creative process of shooting, it's often not an advantage to have these things set automatically. Professional camcorders are generally not as automatic and always provide manual overrides. If you hope to capture high-quality images and sound, it's important to know when it's best to make adjustments manually and, when using automatic settings, which automatic settings can be trusted.

Before you can start shooting, you need to set up the camera to capture the picture and sound properly. Some of the settings, such the format and basic frame rate, can be thought of as "project settings"—once set, you may not change them much at all for an entire movie. Other settings are picture controls, such as exposure, which you'll probably adjust on every shot. Then there are the tasks of managing your recording (how to handle the digital data being recorded to memory cards, drives, or tape) and managing your power supply (batteries or AC).

INITIAL SETTINGS

Here are some items to set up before you shoot; some of these you may change later for individual scenes or shots.

FORMAT. Most camcorders can shoot in more than one format, so you will need to make choices about resolution (say, 1080p or 480i), type of compression ("codec"), data rate, and choice of progressive or interlace scanning. These options are discussed in Chapters 1 and 2. Your options will be determined by your camera, and some choices may not be available (for example, a given resolution may not be available at all frame rates). Typically, you'll use one format for the entire production. On some cameras, selecting the "recording format" is a single menu choice that sets a host of things at once. An example from one Sony camera: by choosing the "1080/60i FX" format you will record 1920 x 1080 HD at 30 fps interlace in the AVCHD codec at 24 Mbps data rate.

FRAME RATE. Before starting production, choose a base frame rate for the project. See p. 81 for options. As just noted, some formats are limited to certain frame rates; for example, PAL 576i is always 25 fps. Having a project frame rate doesn't prevent you from shooting some footage at higher or lower frame rates for slow- or fast-motion footage if your camera has that capability (see p. 389). At the same time, if you want to include footage in your production that was shot at other frame rates (such as archival material or shots from other cameras), you can usually convert the frame rate if you want that footage to appear at normal speed in the movie.

SHUTTER SPEED. With traditional video cameras, you won't usually need to make a shutter speed choice to start shooting. Shutter speed is usually by default about half the frame rate. For example, if you're shooting at 30 fps, the default shutter speed will typically be $\frac{1}{60}$ second. With professional cameras and many consumer models, you can manually select higher or lower shutter speeds if you want them for different effects.

With DSLRs and some newer cameras, unless you put them into an automatic mode you'll need to select the shutter speed prior to shooting. As a starting point, it's safe to set the speed for about half the frame rate ($\frac{1}{50}$ second for 24p, 25p, or 50i; $\frac{1}{50}$ or $\frac{1}{60}$ second for 30p; $\frac{1}{60}$ second for 60i or 60p). For more on shutter speed see p. 135.

GAIN AND ISO SPEED. Traditional video cameras have a gain adjustment to boost the video signal for dark scenes. Gain should normally be set at 0 dB, and increased only when you can't get enough exposure otherwise, because increasing gain will add electronic noise to the image. DSLRs and some video cameras have an *ISO speed* setting that is much like gain. The camera manufacturer may recommend a particular ISO as a starting point, which you can adjust up and down for individual shots. Like gain, if you set ISO too high, the image may be noisy. With a DSLR, you normally want to start with one of the lower ISO numbers if there's enough light to shoot. For more on gain and ISO, see Camera Sensitivity, p. 133.

ASPECT RATIO. If you're shooting HD, the aspect ratio is by default 16:9. If you're shooting SD, you'll have a choice between 4:3 and 16:9 (though not all SD cameras can shoot 16:9). Wider aspect ratios are available with digital cinema cameras and with HD cameras using anamorphic lenses or other means. For more, see Aspect Ratio Choices, p. 74.

VIEWFINDER AND MONITOR SETUP

To see the video image, we use a *monitor*. The viewfinder is a miniature monitor mounted on the camera that allows you to see the image you're shooting through a magnifying eyepiece. Professionals often work with a larger, separate monitor as well, which permits others to watch too. Many camcorders have both an eyepiece-style viewfinder and a fold-out LCD screen (see Fig. 3-1). Fold-out LCD screens allow you to hold the camera away from your face and in positions that would be difficult with a viewfinder. But they can drain the battery faster and may be hard to see in bright daylight. DSLRs and some video cameras can be difficult to operate with the camera's LCD unless a magnifying loupe is attached to the screen. Many people prefer an external *electronic viewfinder (EVF)*, as shown in Figures 1-3 and 3-2.

Fig. 3-2. An adjustable LCD screen allows you to see the picture from a variety of angles. (left) Nikon D5100 with pivoting screen. (right) SmallHD external LCD monitor with magnifying loupe eyepiece, which also blocks stray light from striking the screen. (Nikon, Inc.; Angel De Armas/SmallHD)

Viewfinders and other types of monitors are essential for checking how the shot is framed and if the focus, exposure, and color are correct. However, it takes experience to learn when you can trust the picture and when you should take what you're seeing in the viewfinder with a grain of salt. Some examples:

- When you're shooting, viewfinders and monitors show you the video as it comes out of the camera, but they don't tell you what is actually being recorded. So if there are problems with the recording device or tape, you'll find out only when you stop recording and watch playback.
- The edges of the frame that you see in the viewfinder or monitor may be different from what the audience will see. See p. 327 for discussion of TV cutoff and aspect ratio.
- Exposure, color contrast, and various image defects (such as moiré) may look quite different in the viewfinder compared to what is actually being recorded. LCD-based viewfinders and monitors in particular are poor at accurately displaying dark details, often "plugging up" shadows and not revealing the camera's full latitude.

The more you work with any given camera or monitor, the better you'll be able to translate what you see in the viewfinder to what's really being recorded. The ultimate picture reference is a high-quality studio monitor in a dimly lit room.

Camera viewfinders can be set to display information about things like battery power, timecode, audio levels, and recording time remaining (see Fig. 3-3). This info is very useful, but sometimes having all that text on the screen is distracting. Also, there's a natural tendency when shooting to avoid positioning things in the frame where they're hidden by the data displays. (Later on, when you see the image on a monitor with no data overlays you may wonder why parts of the picture look empty.) Most cameras allow you to turn off all viewfinder data when you want to, usually with the quick press of a button.

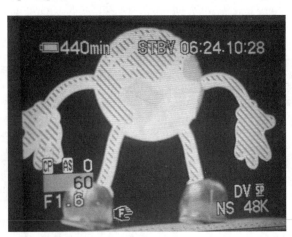

Fig. 3-3. Data in the viewfinder. You can choose to display lots of information about battery level, timecode, lens settings, and menu choices. Sometimes all the clutter blocks what you want to see. The zebras (stripes) shown here indicate overexposure.

Adjusting the Viewfinder

With the exception of some consumer cameras, most viewfinders and monitors have adjustments for brightness, contrast, and color. Adjustments made to the viewfinder or monitor affect only what you see in the monitor itself—they have no effect on the video that's being recorded. However, if the monitor is not "set up" properly, you won't be able to evaluate the image correctly and this may lead you to make other changes (in exposure, lighting, focus) that *will* affect the actual recorded video. It's very important to set up a camera viewfinder or LCD screen *before* you shoot by adjusting the brightness, contrast, and color so that what you see is what you get (WYSIWYG). See Appendix A for instructions.

Some viewfinders have a *peaking* or *detail* adjustment that helps you focus by adding a fine white or colored edge around things that are sharply in focus. If you set the peaking level high and turn the focus ring on the lens, objects will really pop in the viewfinder when you've got them in focus.[1] However, a problem with setting the peaking very high is that the white edges can make it harder to judge the lighting and exposure. Often a medium setting is a good compromise.

Some cameras allow you to quickly magnify the center of the image as a focusing aid. This can be particularly helpful in HD, where focus is especially critical. Many cameras have a *zebra indicator* that highlights areas in the frame that may be overexposed (see Fig. 3-3). For more on use of zebras, see The Digital Video Camera's Response to Light, p. 185.

VIEWFINDER FOCUS. If your camera is equipped with a typical eyepiece (tubelike viewfinder), you must focus the viewfinder for your eye before shooting. This is done with the focus or *diopter* adjustment on the viewfinder. This has no effect on the focus of the image being recorded through the camera lens; rather, it allows you to make the tiny monitor screen in the viewfinder as sharp as possible for your eye. Everyone's eyes are different and you should reset the viewfinder focus anytime someone else has been using the camera.

With the camera on, turn or slide the viewfinder focus adjustment until the picture or printed characters on the screen are sharp. If your camera generates bars (a test signal), they provide a sharp image to look at while focusing the eyepiece. It is important that your eye be relaxed and not straining to focus.

Modern video viewfinders are very wide in diameter (they have a large "exit pupil"), so you can easily wear glasses while hand-holding. On some cameras you can flip the magnifying lens out of the way, which some people who wear glasses find more comfortable. If the camera's diopter won't compensate for your vision, try switching to contact lenses.

PICTURE CONTROLS

Setting the Exposure

Once you've selected overall settings for frame rate, shutter speed, and ISO or gain, you can manually control the moment-to-moment exposure of a scene by adjusting the iris (see p. 151), which regulates how much light comes through the

---

1. This can be especially helpful when you're working with a camera that has its internal detail set low; see p. 138.

lens. On some cameras you must turn the iris ring on the lens to do this (turn to-ward the lower *f*-numbers to increase exposure; see *F*-stops on p. 151). On other cameras there is no mechanical iris ring to turn; instead you control the lens iris with a knob or button on the camera body, which activates the iris electronically. It's an advantage to use a camera that allows you to adjust the iris smoothly up or down; avoid cameras that have clicks or detents in the setting, which can make for jarring changes during a shot.

How should you set the exposure? The simplistic answer is: so the picture looks good. With too much exposure, the scene will look very bright and washed out. The brightest parts will have no detail at all—just blown-out areas of undifferentiated white. With too little exposure, the scene will be murky and dark—the darkest parts of the scene will appear as masses of undifferentiated black (see Fig. 5-2).

To start, make sure the viewfinder or monitor is properly adjusted (see Appendix A). Then set the exposure so the balance between light and dark is as pleasing as possible. The most important elements of the scene—often people's faces—should have sufficient detail and be neither washed out nor murky. Overexposure can be a particular problem with video. Washed-out areas of the frame often look objection-able and may "bloom" or spread into other parts of the frame. Even so, sometimes you have to let a bright sky or window burn out if you hope to see detail in darker parts of the frame.

In some situations there may not be enough light to get a good exposure, in which case you might increase the camera's sensitivity by raising the gain/ISO set-ting, or in some cases by lowering the shutter speed (see below).

If there's too much light even when the lens is stopped down, use a neutral den-sity filter (see p. 134). Sometimes the overall exposure seems okay, but there's too great a range between the bright and dark parts of the scene to get a pleasing image (see Fig. 7-16). For all of these exposure problems, there are several solutions, in-cluding using lights or repositioning or adjusting the camera. As a rule of thumb, scenes that are slightly underexposed are easier to fix in post than scenes that are grossly overexposed, so it's usually best to slightly underexpose rather than overex-pose when shooting digital video.

This discussion of exposure is deliberately simplified. For more precise and specific ways to adjust exposure, see Forming the Video Image, p. 185.

AUTOMATIC EXPOSURE CONTROL. Many video cameras (and some film cameras) have the ability to set the exposure automatically. *Autoexposure* (*AE*) can be helpful in some situations, particularly for fast-moving documentary scenes. But though many beginners prefer the supposed security of AE, professionals usu-ally avoid it because even small shifts in light and dark tones within a scene can cause the auto-iris to fluctuate in an undesirable way. This sort of inconstant expo-sure is a hallmark of amateur shooting.

The camera's autoexposure system works by measuring the brightness of the scene through the lens and guessing an appropriate iris setting. Depending on the particu-lar camera, its settings, and the amount of light, the AE system may also try to adjust the gain/ISO speed (see p. 133) and/or the shutter (see p. 135). Changes to each of these can affect not only the exposure, but other aspects such as noise and how motion looks. More advanced cameras permit you to select which of these functions to make automatic. For example, there may be a setting that allows you to use just *auto-iris control* or *auto-gain control* (*AGC*). If you want to experiment with automatic exposure, it's a good idea to start by setting the gain and shutter manually, and then see the effect of auto-iris alone (on some DSLRs this is called *shutter-priority mode*).

The central drawback of automatic exposure is that the AE system doesn't know which part of the scene you're interested in; it assumes the center zone. Dark or light backgrounds can be a particular problem. If you shoot someone against a bright background or with backlighting, the camera reads all that brightness and closes down the iris, darkening the scene and often throwing your subject into silhouette. Some cameras have a *backlight feature* that compensates by increasing the exposure a stop or more or an *AE shift* setting to increase or decrease exposure a set amount. (See Fig. 7-17 for more on backlight.) Some cameras allow you to select a section or portion of the frame on which to base the automatic exposure, and this can help in getting the exposure you want.

AE systems often make exposure adjustments when none is needed. Say you're shooting your subject and a person with a dark sweater crosses the frame close to the camera, between you and the subject. Normally you would want the exposure to remain constant—you don't want the exposure of the subject and background to change when the person walks by. AE, however, may open the iris momentarily as the dark sweater passes through the frame. Similarly, if you pan the camera (turn it horizontally) across a group of dark and light objects, the brightness of the background may change unnaturally as the camera passes the various objects.

Automatic exposure control works best in scenes that are front lit (where the light comes from behind the camera position), that have relatively uniform backgrounds, and where the subject and background are neither excessively bright nor dark. AE can be of enormous help in run-and-gun documentary situations when your subject changes locations rapidly, and it can work acceptably in scenes where the lighting is even.

Autoexposure will generally prevent you from overexposing, so some camera operators let the auto-iris initially set the exposure, then lock the setting in place by switching to manual control. Some camcorders have an "iris lock" or "exposure lock" button on the side that toggles the auto-iris on and off—when you press the button, auto-iris is on; when you press a second time, the iris is locked at that exposure. Professional cameras with ⅔-inch sensors use zoom lenses with a similar button on the lens handgrip that momentarily enables auto-iris for as long as it is held down. Using this function, you might, for instance, let auto-iris get a reading of a wide shot of the scene, or you might zoom in on the most important part of the frame. In either case, let the iris adjust, lock it in place, then set the zoom where you want.

Setting the White Balance

Video and film cameras need to compensate for the color of light falling on a scene so that the image doesn't come out with an unintended blue or yellow color cast. When shooting video, adjusting the camera to the color of the light is called *setting the white balance*.[2] Before reading this section, please see the discussion of color temperature on p. 308.

---

2. In film, the similar issue of the suitability of a film stock for certain lighting conditions is usually talked about in terms of *color temperature* or *color balance*. For example, a particular Kodak or Fuji color negative film will be described as daylight- or tungsten-balanced.

Most places you go, your eye and brain adjust to the available lighting to make the overall color of light appear white. But in actuality, every different lighting environment, indoors and out, has a different color balance. For example, daylight is relatively blue, while incandescent bulbs used in the home as well as in professional tungsten movie lights are by comparison yellow/red. Most cameras have a 3200°K white balance setting for tungsten movie lights. If all you did was shoot under studio lighting, the 3200°K setting would be all you needed. But if you go outside to shoot in daylight, which has a higher color temperature than tungsten, the picture will look blue; skin tones and anything red in the scene will look cold and unnatural.

So we need a way to adjust the camera's white balance to different types of lighting. When white balance is adjusted normally, white objects will look white on screen. Most video cameras give you three ways to set white balance: by using presets; by adjusting the white balance manually; or by letting it set itself automatically. Before manually setting white balance, be sure that your monitor or color viewfinder is properly set up (see Appendix A).

USING WHITE BALANCE PRESETS. Most cameras have a white balance switch with a "preset" position for 3200°K, which may be labeled "tungsten" or "indoors." Many cameras also have a daylight preset at 5600°K.

On most ⅔-inch sensor cameras, to shoot in daylight you use the 3200°K preset along with a built-in filter wheel that, in the "5600K" position, inserts an orange filter to warm up the light coming through the lens before it reaches the sensor. (This filter is similar to the 85 filter used for tungsten-balanced films. It cuts down the light intensity by about two-thirds of a stop; see p. 309.)

Using presets is fast and convenient and many pros use them routinely. If you're shooting in lighting that's exactly 3200°K or 5600°K, you should get a true white. If your lighting situation varies from those two standards, you can usually correct the resulting off-balance color in post-production—or you may not want to. For more, see Fine-Tuning White Balance, p. 112.

On some professional video cameras and DSLRs, you can also dial in a white balance preset for an exact color temperature in Kelvin degrees, usually in increments of one hundred degrees. This setting can be recalled as needed.

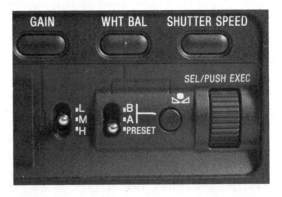

Fig. 3-4. Some image controls on a Sony FS100. (lower left) Gain control: three-position toggle switch; the amount of gain at each position is set in the menu. (center) White balance toggle with preset and two user-settable memory positions. The buttons in the top row switch the gain, white balance, and shutter speed settings between manual and automatic control.

MANUAL WHITE BALANCE. Many professionals prefer to reset the white balance by hand for every new lighting condition. For example, scenes lit by household bulbs, tungsten movie lights, fluorescents, sunlight, or shade (no direct sun, just skylight) will all have a different color balance. Whenever the lighting changes they "do a white balance" by holding a white card or piece of white paper in the same light as the subject, zooming in so the card fills most of the frame, then pushing the camera's white balance button.[3]

On some DSLRs, a manual white balance setting is obtained by taking a still image of a white card or a transluscent white lens cap and using that to set a custom white balance, which can be recalled as needed when shooting. To set a custom white balance, check the manual of your particular DSLR for instructions. (DSLRs are designed primarily for taking stills in an instant of time, and many photographers rely on instantaneous auto white balance, called AUTO or AWB, over standard color balance presets. Presetting a custom color balance is not standardized as it is on video cameras.)

When white-balancing, the camera's circuits adjust the relative strength of the red, green, and blue signals coming from the sensor(s) until the white card looks white on video (if white objects look white, then the other colors will look natural too). It does no good if the white card isn't reflecting back the same light that's falling on the subject, so be aware of light sources that hit the subject but not the card, or vice versa. Also make sure you're exposed properly for the scene before doing the white balance. If you're not sure about your exposure, switch the lens into auto-iris mode and let the camera decide exposure. If the camera doesn't have enough light to white-balance properly, it will indicate this in the viewfinder.

It's okay if the white paper has black text as long as, when you zoom in on it, the white predominates. In documentary situations, any white object in the prevailing light of the scene will do—for instance, a white shirt or a white wall. A neutral gray card will also work or even a truly gray object in a pinch.

Professional video cameras can memorize two white balances, and they have a button or switch to choose one or the other. Maybe you're shooting a documentary and one room is lit with dim reddish tungsten bulbs, while another is lit with greenish cool white fluorescents. Once you've done a white balance in each room, a flip of the switch is all it takes to toggle between the two.

As noted above, some cameras use a filter wheel for balancing in daylight. Normally you would dial in the filter before doing a manual white balance, unless there's not enough light.

AUTOMATIC WHITE BALANCE. All consumer camcorders and DSLRs and many professional camcorders have the ability to set the white balance continuously and automatically with no user input. This is called *auto white balance* or *auto tracing white balance* (*ATW*).

On some video cameras and DSLRs, auto white balance works surprisingly well. Experiment with yours to see how you like it. In run-and-gun situations, having quick, automated white balance can be very convenient. However, there are reasons why pros generally don't leave the white balance on auto. Usually the

---

3. Confusingly, on some cameras the button that performs a manual white balance is labeled "auto white balance." This should not be mistaken for settings that continuously and automatically alter the balance (see Automatic White Balance, above).

Fig. 3-5. Iconix camera and control unit. The camera head is a little bigger than a golf ball and can be used for hard-to-reach camera angles and point-of-view shots as well as stereoscopic 3D applications. Outputs 2K and most flavors of HD. (Iconix Video)

auto feature needs a few seconds after a lighting change to make its adjustment. Some systems get confused by very bright light or by discontinuous-spectrum light sources such as fluorescent or mercury vapor. But even if the automatic feature is working perfectly you can end up with inconsistent results. Say you're shooting a person in tungsten light, then change position to shoot the same person from a different angle that reveals a window in the background. The auto white balance will try to compensate for the bluer window, making the skin tone warmer in the second shot. With the change in the skin tone, the two shots may not cut together well. If a noticeable color shift takes place in the middle of a continuous shot, it's difficult if not impossible to fix it in post.

Color balance is a creative element in shooting and when possible it's best to control it yourself.

FINE-TUNING WHITE BALANCE. Other than when shooting with professional tungsten studio lights, almost every lighting situation varies a little or a lot from the preset "standards." Household bulbs can be warmer or cooler than 3200°K, and 5600°K is only a crude average of the actual color temperature you'll find at any given moment outdoors (think of all of the variations of yellow sun, blue sky, amber sunset, gray cloud cover, etc.). What does that mean for the filmmaker?

One of the arguments for using presets is that every scene doesn't *need* to be corrected for identical whites. In the world, white is rarely simply white. Think of a white linen tablecloth under candlelight. It should be warm, not pure white. Look at figurative paintings and you'll rarely see white applied as colorless white. The tinting of white has graphic and emotional power. If you shoot video under candlelight with 3200°K preset, whites will indeed look warm and yellowish. However, if you do a manual white balance, white will be rendered white but the warmth and mood will be removed.

So, by using presets as a creative tool, the whites may be "off" but the color balance can still serve the scene you're shooting. Some cameras allow you to easily tweak the color warmer or cooler to your liking or, as mentioned above, to dial in a specific color temperature by Kelvin number.

If you prefer a neutral color balance and don't want to have to fix it in post, then do a manual white balance. But sometimes even after white-balancing, the overall balance seems too cool or too warm. This could be a problem with the way the monitor is adjusted or it may be simply the way the camera's electronics work. For example, some cameras have a tendency to balance on the cool side. In general, skin tone looks better if slightly too warm rather than too blue.

A simple, low-tech trick is to "fool" the camera by doing a white balance on a nonwhite object. If you balance on a piece of pale blue paper, the camera will try to make the blue appear white, which will warm the entire image (alternatively, you could do the white balance with a blue filter over the lens). Vortex Media (www .warmcards.com) and other manufacturers make sets of cards of different shades of blue and green; by white-balancing on them you can warm or cool the image for a more pleasing look.

Another approach is to use screw-on filters or a matte box (see Fig. 8-10). An 81B filter adds a mild amount of warming and an 812 warms a bit more. Remember you must put the filter on *after* you do the white balance; otherwise the camera will try to remove the warming effect of the filter.

If you're using lighting, you can do a normal balance using white light, then put colored warming gels on the lights (see Chapter 12). For shooting a scene that has light sources of different color temperature, see Mixed Lighting, p. 514.

BLACK BALANCE. Professional video cameras have a black balance feature, which ensures that black is truly black with no color cast. A black balance should be done if the camera is new, if it hasn't been used for a while, if it was just used by someone else, or if it has experienced a dramatic temperature change. On some cameras it's recommended to black-balance after changing shutter speed or switching between progressive and interlace recording. To black-balance, press the black-balance control button. If your camera doesn't automatically close the iris before black balancing, cap the lens or close down the iris all the way to "C" (if it closes all the way to "C," that is). Afterward, do a new white balance.

Setting the Focus

Before you shoot, you need to focus the camera's lens on what you're shooting. This is discussed in Focusing the Image, p. 153. Most professional cameras allow you to focus manually by turning the focus ring on the lens. As discussed in Adjusting the Viewfinder, p. 106, some cameras have a peaking feature in the viewfinder to assist you in seeing proper focus. Some cameras also allow you to magnify the viewfinder image so you can see the focus more clearly.

AUTOFOCUS. Many camcorders have autofocus capability, notably consumer camcorders that rely on autofocus and as a result can be tricky or impossible to focus manually. There are several types of autofocus. Passive autofocus, the most common, works either by (1) analyzing the image and adjusting the lens to maximize fine-detail contrast and therefore sharpness in the center of the image or (2) dividing a small sample of incoming light into pairs of images, then comparing them to determine object distances. Video cameras typically use the former; DSLRs use the latter. A less-used technique, active autofocus, involves emitting and sensing the reflection of an infrared beam in order to gauge object distance. Passive auto-focus can focus through windows but gets confused by underexposed or low-contrast scenes. Active autofocus can't focus through glass (it reflects the infrared beam) but works fine with dark scenes.

Some autofocus systems work quite well and can be handy in various situations, including times when you can't look through the viewfinder or when focusing is difficult. Many cameras offer three focus modes: full manual; full automatic (with continuous autofocus adjustment); and manual with instant focus readjustment when you push and hold a button (similar to iris lock). This last mode can be very useful, especially with LCD viewfinders in which it may be hard to see precise focus. Point the camera at the subject, press the focus button, and let the camera lock focus at that point. Then you can frame the shot as you like. This method can result in very accurate focus, particularly when the camera and subject aren't moving.

However, using the camera in continuous autofocus mode can produce unwanted results, particularly in scenes where there's movement or unusual framing. One problem is that the autofocus system may not focus on the things you want to be in focus. Say you're shooting a man close to the camera who's looking at a mountain in the distance. Normally, the filmmaker should control whether the man or the mountain is in better focus. Using autofocus, however, the camera will usually choose whichever part of the scene is centered in the frame. Sometimes there's nothing of interest in the center. Say you're positioned at the head of a table, shooting a person on the left side of the table talking to a person on the right side. Autofocus may

Fig. 3-6. Panasonic AG-AF100. Four Thirds CMOS sensor. Records AVCCAM internally to SDXC cards. Can output uncompressed 4:2:2 via HDMI for external recording. (Panasonic Broadcast)

try to focus on the wall behind them. Some newer cameras have face-recognition ability that can help keep the focus on a person. When the camera and/or subject are moving, autofocus can sometimes track the action better than you can manually, but other times it will make focus changes when none is called for.

Autofocus systems do a certain amount of "hunting" to find proper focus, though recent cameras respond a lot faster than older models; small-sensor cameras with lightweight lenses are the fastest. Situations that may throw off autofocus include low light, low contrast, shooting through glass or other material (like a scrim or a fence), bright backlight, and horizontal stripes.

Because focus is one of the key creative controls in shooting, continuous autofocus should be used only if absolutely necessary.

RECORDING TO CARDS, DRIVES, AND OPTICAL DISCS

The latest digital video camcorders record to nonlinear media like flash memory cards, solid-state drives, hard disk drives, and optical discs instead of linear videotape (discussed below). This provides flexibility during shooting that includes instant playback of takes in any order, longer record times, recording at higher data rates and resolutions, and a choice of frame rates. Sometimes today's camcorders even record to two types of media at once (tape included) for instant backup. In postproduction, recording to nonlinear media saves time while ingesting clips into an editing system.

These camcorders vary in terms of available codecs, file formats, and other factors. See p. 21 for an overview of these systems, and p. 90 for considerations of working with them.

TYPES OF MEDIA

Solid-State Media

There are several types of solid-state media cards (also called flash memory media), including *CompactFlash* (*CF*); *Secure Digital* (*SD*); *Secure Digital High Capacity* (*SDHC*); *Secure Digital Extended Capacity* (*SDXC*); Sony's *SxS* (pronounced "S by S"); Panasonic's *P2*; and Sony's *Memory Stick*. Check your camera manual for recommended cards. You'll need a card that can store data fast enough to keep up with the format you're shooting, so be sure to check the *sustained* read/write rate of the particular card, which is often expressed in megabytes per second (MB/s).[4] Keep in mind that shooting at a higher frame rate or larger frame size on the same camera may require a higher data transfer rate. If you're shooting with a DSLR, be aware that video requires a high transfer rate, so slower cards suitable for stills may not work for video.

Some people buy cards with the most storage capacity they can afford, so they can shoot as long as possible without downloading. Others prefer smaller cards, so that if one gets lost or corrupted, they don't lose as much material at once. Get name-brand cards—this is not a place to skimp on quality.

Each memory card should be formatted before first use or when you want to wipe all the data to reuse it. To avoid possible errors, format the card on the same camera you're going to be using it with. Insert cards carefully into the camera's card slots and never try to remove a card or power down while the camera is formatting, reading, or writing data (often indicated by a red light near the card slot).

There are many external devices that record on flash media and connect to

---

4. The data rate of camera codecs is often expressed in mega*bits* per second (Mb/s). To convert from megabits to megabytes, divide by 8 (so, for example, if the camera generates 24 Mb/s that's about 3 MB/s).

Fig. 3-7. This Nexto DI portable backup device can transfer the contents of a P2, SxS, or CompactFlash card to two hard drives simultaneously, with error checking. Allows previewing files and downloading in the field without a computer. (Nexto DI Co., Ltd.)

the camera via HDMI, HD-SDI, or other cabling, such as AJA's Ki Pro series, Convergent Design's nanoFlash, and Cinedeck's Extreme. Some of these allow you to insert flash media cards in the device; others use their own internal solid-state drive storage (see below). Use the device's menu to select format, codec, and data rate, if applicable. Different editing systems use different container file formats, or "wrappers," to package the video/audio data (see p. 242); the recorder may offer file choices such as AVI, MOV, or MXF. Check to make sure you're using the right file format for your editing system. If the proper format isn't supported you'll need to do the extra step of converting the files while transferring them into the editing system before you edit.

With some camera/drive combinations, you can slave the drive to the camera, so it starts and stops when you press the camera trigger.

Hard Disk Drives

Compared to flash memory media, HDDs are heavier and more fragile and need more power, so they're used less often for direct recording (they're still essential for backing up in the field, however). High-end digital cinema cameras may require direct-to-disk video recorders (such as systems made by S.two or Codex Digital) or a RAID (redundant array of independent disks) to handle the high data rates of uncompressed video and provide bulletproof data protection (see p. 240). At the low-budget end, some people record directly to a laptop, using their NLE's capture function. Some small external recorders are available with HDD or SDD options (see Fig. 2-19).

Solid-State Drives

Solid-state drives, or SSDs, are literally a cross between flash memory and hard disk drives. Think of them as hard disk drives with the disk removed and stuffed instead with flash memory. This means they function as exact replacements for hard disk drives, with the same SATA multipin connections. They are silent, have no moving parts and no heads to crash, and take no seek time—all of which equals less power usage and near-instant access to data. In terms of capacity, they leave flash memory cards in the dust. Unfortunately, their lone drawback is that they still cost considerably more than hard disk drives.

SSDs have rapidly replaced HDDs for field recording of video and digital cinema. Increasingly they're found slotted directly into cameras (including the Sony NEX-FS100, RED Epic, and Aaton Delta-Penelope), as well as affordable field recorders from Cinedeck, Convergent Design, Atomos, Blackmagic Design, and

Ikegami. The most popular sizes are 128GB and 256GB, but Sony has introduced a family of SRMemory cards including 512GB and 1TB capacities, along with a portable SR-R1 portable field recorder for use with high-end Sony cameras that previously required HDCAM SR tape recorders.

Optical Discs

As of this writing, camcorders recording to optical discs include a few consumer models and Sony's XDCAM HD family of products, which use Sony's Professional Disc media based on Blu-ray technology housed in a cartridge shell (see Fig. 1-22). Present capacities of Professional Disc media are 50GB (dual layer, rewritable) for camcorders and 128GB (quad layer, write once) for editing and archival purposes. Optical discs combine the benefits of a digital, nonlinear file-based workflow with a physical object that can be saved and archived. Sony's Professional Disc format claims an estimated archival life of fifty years, while hard disk drives and flash memory are deemed not archival in any sense. As a consequence, Sony's optical disc format, being the only existing archival nonlinear medium, remains popular with television networks, reality show productions, and independent producers concerned with preserving extensive volumes of work.

MANAGING DATA ON THE SHOOT

To safely navigate from the shoot through postproduction, you need to be *extremely* careful with the data recorded in the field. This means planning your workflow in advance so the data is safely stored, in a well-organized way, with plenty of backups in case any files or storage systems get corrupted. You should create a system that's clearly understood and coordinated with everyone on the production and postproduction team. Even if you're working alone, it's not uncommon in postproduction to need to return to the original camera data, so you want to make sure files can be easily located and reused as necessary. Being organized also includes logging and managing the metadata that will help you find and work with your files (see Importing and Organizing Your Material, p. 562).

Different people use different systems to label, organize, and process their data. It depends in part on the production, your equipment, and your preferences. Below are some suggestions that may or may not be appropriate for your workflow.

Recording

If you're using flash memory cards, label the outside of each card with a unique number, such as F1, F2, etc. ("F" for flash, or whatever letter you like). If more than one camera is on the shoot, you could use a name like C2F3. If you're using paper labels, put them only in the space provided on the card. This number identifies the physical card.

Once you've filled up the card and are ready to download its contents to a folder on a hard drive, you need a system to identify the contents of each card. Different productions use different systems. In some productions, the contents of each card download is assigned a reel number, with the numbers advancing consecutively throughout the entire project, much as you would assign a tape number to a videotape when you recorded on it. The folder on the hard drive should be given that reel number, along with the project name (such as OCEAN-002). You can also include the number of the physical card (such as OCEAN-002-F3), which helps you stay organized and can help identify the source of any data problems later. Some people prefer a system that includes the date, with reel numbers starting at 1 each day, such as OCEAN-120610-02. Come up with a system that works for you and keep it consistent for the production.

Each time you press the button to start recording, the camera creates a new clip or file, which represents that shot (actually, often more than one file is produced for each clip). Some cameras automatically name clips with a multidigit number (which helps ensure that no two clips have the same number). On higher-end cameras you can assign a clip name. As an example, RED cameras use a naming scheme that includes the camera letter, reel number, the date, and a random two-digit number. So the file name A004_C010_0612K5_001.RDM tells us that this is the tenth clip recorded on the A camera's fourth card on June 12.

If a clip exceeds the capacity of one card, some cameras with multiple card slots will allow a clip to span to a second card. This creates two *spanned clips*, which can be rejoined when ingested into the editing system. Often the editing system will do this automatically.

When a card fills up, store the card safely until it can be downloaded and backed up. Use a dedicated memory card case, Ziploc bag, or area in your camera case for your cards—they're small and easy to lose! Some people like to slide the write-protect tab on the card (if there is one) to prevent erasure or changes to the files; others prefer to simply mark full cards with a piece of tape or store them in a place or holder reserved for full cards. With some equipment you can download directly from the device via cable without removing the card; this may be helpful with microSD cards, which are particularly easy to misplace.

It goes without saying that you can't be too careful or attentive when recording to solid-state media. Why? Well, there's no sound of tape or film traveling through the camera. How do you know anything is being recorded? You don't unless you watch the timecode counter, check takes in playback, keep an eye on media usage, and generally respect the fact that a camcorder is an image-capture computer. As with all computers, glitches happen.

Downloading and Backing Up

On some productions, there are enough cards so that downloading (also called offloading) can be done at the end of the day, in the comfort of the production office or editing room. On other shoots, downloading takes place on location, while shooting is ongoing. If this is the case, set up a downloading station in a safe, quiet spot away from distractions whenever possible. Regardless of how and when downloading is done, the goal is to make sure the transfer from the memory card to the storage drive(s) is done without any data errors. Multiple backups should be made as quickly as possible for protection.

One approach for location work is to use a device that transfers data from the memory card to an internal SSD or hard drive. For example, Nexto DI makes handheld units that can accept various types of media cards and automatically

Fig. 3-8. This setup for downloading camera files is well organized and placed away from other activities. Under the laptop is the Mobile Rocket by Maxx Digital, containing the RED ROCKET card, for accelerated processing of RED R3D files (including debayering, color correction, and downscaling). (David Kruta)

download them to an internal drive (see Fig. 3-7). Once you have the data in the unit, you can connect the Nexto DI device to a laptop or desktop computer to transfer files for backup and editing. Panasonic makes units that download P2 cards to a removable hard drive that can later be connected to a computer (see Fig. 2-17). The advantage of transfer units is that they are easy to carry in the field, the transfer is relatively quick, and many systems employ error checking to verify that data is transferred accurately. Field transfer devices can often play back video so you can visually check clips, using either built-in screens or by connecting to a monitor.

Another approach is to use a laptop computer with either a built-in memory card slot or an external card reader connected by USB or other connection. One or two external drives are connected to the laptop, if possible using a fast connection such as FireWire, eSATA, or Thunderbolt.

Transferring files from cards can be done manually, using the Finder (for Macs) or Windows Explorer, but there are a number of dedicated applications that offer advantages. For example, ShotPut Pro can copy files to more than one destination at the same time. It also allows you to define how you want folders to be named and can print out a report of where files are stored. Synk and other applications can streamline syncing and backing up from one drive to another. Programs that use a verified transfer or *checksum verification* are preferable to simple copying with the Finder or Windows Explorer in order to ensure data integrity.

When transferring files from a card, it's not a bad idea to slide the record-inhibit tab on the memory card to prevent any files from being added or deleted during the transfer process.

FOLDER MANAGEMENT. It's essential that you organize the data properly when you store it. The postproduction team may have their own system—if so, use it. Here is one organizational method that you can modify as appropriate for your production. For this example, we'll call the project "Ocean" and assume you've shot with flash memory cards, which you're downloading to a laptop that's connected to an external drive.

- First decide what type of external hard disk drive is appropriate to your needs. Are you shooting at a relatively low data rate like AVCHD, HDV, or XDCAM EX, or higher data rate like ProRes 422 HQ or even uncompressed? Are you just parking the files for later ingest into an NLE, or do you wish to play back the files for visual inspection from the hard drive? Bear in mind that 5400 rpm drives are slower; 7200 rpm drives are faster. USB 2.0 is slower; FireWire 800 is faster; Thunderbolt is fastest (for more, see p. 237).
- Create a folder for all of the project's media on the external drive. Give it a clear name, such as "OCEAN Source Media." Depending on the production, there may be a production number or episode number, which you can include in the folder name.
- Open that folder and create a subfolder within it. This will be the session folder for the day's shoot. Name it using the date, the location, and/or other information, such as the cameraperson's initials. For example, the folder might be named "120610-Harbor Exteriors-RD." If you use a date format that begins with the year (such as YYMMDD), it's easier to sort the files.
- Open that folder and create a subfolder within it for each card download. Name it with whatever system the production is using, as described above. For example, this might be the consecutive reel number system (such as OCEAN-002-F3) or the method that uses the project title, date, and card number for that day (such as OCEAN-120610-02-F3). Whatever method you use, be sure that each download folder has a unique name that is not repeated.
- Insert the card into the card reader. When the card's icon appears on the desktop, double-click it to open the card. Select the *entire* contents of the

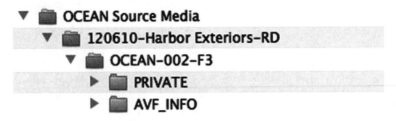

Fig. 3-9. A possible folder structure for organizing downloads of memory cards from the camera (see text). Note that camera cards typically contain a variety of subfolders and files (such as the "PRIVATE" and "AVF_INFO" folders here). Though the specific names of these subfolders and files vary by camera system and shoot, be sure to copy *all* of them into the folder you make for each card download (in this illustration, the folder for this card is named "OCEAN-002-F3").

card and drag or copy it to the card folder you just made—don't leave out files just because you don't know what they are. Don't rename any files or change the directory structure in any way. Simply copy everything as it is from the card to the folder. Don't download the contents of more than one card into the folder.

- Always check after each download that it has been completed properly. The quickest way to do this is to examine the size in megabytes or gigabytes of the folder or folders contained in the card's icon, and compare them directly to the copied folder or folders. They do not have to match exactly but they should be virtually the same size. If there is an obvious difference in size, you have a problem.

After Downloading

After the card has been downloaded, immediately back up the data to a second drive if at all possible. Do you really want to rely on only a single copy of the camera's files, once the flash memory card has been erased for reuse?

Which brings up a commonsense suggestion: don't wipe or erase flash memory cards or SSDs until the last minute, when they're actually needed for reuse. If you can get through a day using other cards, then the cards you've filled serve as additional backups. As they say, you can't be too rich or too thin—or have too many backups.

On many productions, each clip is visually checked to ensure that it has been safely downloaded. This may be done using nonlinear editing software (discussed in Chapter 14). Some camera manufacturers make stand-alone applications for viewing media from their cameras.

One more time: before erasing the card, work out a protocol so you're *absolutely sure* it has been downloaded, checked, and backed up. It's a good idea to assign one crew member to be responsible for managing cards and getting them back to the camera department for reuse.

RECORDING TO DIGITAL TAPE

This section is for those using a camcorder that records to tape. For the basic principles of recording to tape, see the discussion of audio on p. 405 and video on p. 227.

The Tape Path

When you insert a tape cassette into the videotape recorder (VTR), a mechanism inside the machine opens the front of the cassette, pulls the tape out, and wraps it around the *head drum*, which is a fast-spinning cylinder containing *magnetic heads* for recording, playback, and erasure (see Fig. 3-10). Other *fixed* (stationary) heads for audio and control tracks may be positioned inside the VTR along the edge of the tape path. A *capstan* and *pinch wheel* actually pull the tape along.

During recording, each head sweeps a diagonal path across the tape, magnetiz-

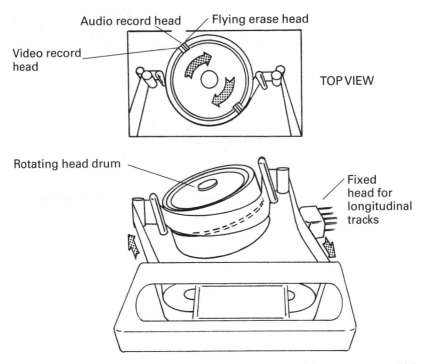

Audio record head · Flying erase head

Video record head

TOP VIEW

Rotating head drum

Fixed head for longitudinal tracks

Fig. 3-10. Simplified view of the tape path and heads. Video formats vary widely in the configuration of the heads and the tape path. (Robert Brun)

ing a short swath (called a *helical scan*). In the case of MiniDV, DVCAM, and DVCPRO, for instance, ten diagonal tracks equals one frame of video. Each of the tracks also includes a section for audio, for timecode, and for timing (control) of tracks. Some formats also have tracks running along the edge of the videotape called *longitudinal* or *linear* tracks (see Fig. 3-11).

The VTRs for different video formats differ widely in the way the heads are arranged and in many other aspects of the system.

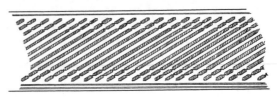

Fig. 3-11. Digital videotape track layout. Individual formats differ in the number, type, and position of tracks. (Robert Brun)

The Power Switch

Professional tape-based camcorders have a two- or three-position power switch to allow you to put the camera in different states of readiness. In one state, power is supplied to the camera so you can see through it, but the tape is not threaded in the VTR. This is sometimes called "save" mode. In another state, the tape is threaded, the heads are spinning, and the tape will start recording immediately when you push the trigger (sometimes called "standby" or "operate" mode). The names vary, and not all camcorders have a true "save" mode.

"Standby" mode should be used when recording is imminent. It allows you to roll tape instantly and generally ensures a clean transition from one shot to the next. However, when you are paused between shots, going to "save" mode disengages the tape and stops the heads from spinning. This conserves power and cuts down wear and tear, but when you're ready to shoot, the camera takes a few seconds to come up to speed. If there is fast-breaking action, it's probably best to leave the camera in "standby." If you know it will be several minutes between shots, switch to "save" or power down the camera completely.

Clean Cuts from Shot to Shot

Tape-based digital camcorders provide seamless transitions between shots. If you press stop at the end of one shot, then press start again, the new shot begins without a glitch. However, you may get a brief breakup in the image (and break in timecode) between shots if you power the camera down, switch to "save" mode, take the tape out of the camera, or play back a shot to check it. If you do any of these things, you can still ensure a glitch-free transition. Some cameras have an "end search" button (professional cameras often have a return button marked "RET"); these will pause the camera at the very end of the last shot, ready to begin the new shot with continuous control track. On consumer cameras, often if you just play to the end of the last recorded shot and press stop while still on the shot, the camera can pick up from there, recording smoothly into the next shot.

To avoid potential problems in editing, it's a good idea to let the camera roll for five seconds or so after pressing start before beginning shooting or calling "action." This *preroll* time ensures that the recording has fully stabilized. Similarly, it's prudent to wait a few seconds after the scene stops before stopping the camera.

Tape Recording Problems

If the heads encounter tape particles or dirt, they won't make good contact with the tape, which can cause dropouts. In DV this can appear as a sudden "hit" of little checkerboard patterns of image breakup. What you are viewing is highly sophisticated digital error correction attempting to compensate for the dropout. Dropout in HDV, which uses MPEG-2 compression, is rarely seen because of its advanced error correction. Dropout with MPEG-4 formats like AVCHD is even more uncommon. If dropout is severe, however, entire sections of a frame of MPEG-2 or MPEG-4 can get blocky or even freeze for several seconds.

If you think you need to clean the record or playback heads of a camcorder, get a head-cleaning cassette for that video format and read the instructions for its use. Typically, it is run like an ordinary tape through the machine for five or ten seconds. Never rewind or reuse the head cleaner. Some people clean the heads on a regular basis; others only when the heads are obviously dirty (as indicated by bad recordings).

Fig. 3-12. Sony HVR-V1U. Records HDV, including 1080/24p, to MiniDV tape. Also records DV and DVCAM (to DVCAM tape). Three ¼-inch CMOS sensors and HDMI output. (Sony Electronics, Inc.)

Protecting and Labeling Material

If you decide to go back and check something you just shot for performance or technical reasons, be *very* careful to make sure you return to the end of the recorded section of the tape before recording again. Hearts have been broken by cuing to the wrong spot and unintentionally burning a good take. Some cinematographers refuse to rewind on set for that reason (though without checks you then run the risk of being unaware of a head clog or other problem).

When you've finished recording a tape, remove it from the VTR and immediately slide the record lock on the cassette to prevent erasure. Label all tapes before shooting or immediately after. On the tape cassette itself, indicate the name of the project, the production company, the date, the tape number, and be sure to write "Camera Original" or apply the manufacturer's premade sticker.[5] Put the same information on the tape box label. On the box, include a line or two about the content; you may want to note the starting timecode (if any) as well.

Tape Stock

Videotape is composed of a *base* or backing material (polyester) and a thinner, magnetically sensitive layer that actually records the video signal. Manufacturers make a variety of formulations for the magnetic layer, ranging from various oxides to higher-quality "metal" tapes.

Metal tapes come in two varieties: metal particle (MP) and metal evaporated (ME). All digital formats today use one or the other. The format determines which type of metal tape is required. For instance, MiniDV and HDV require ME tape, while Panasonic's DVCPRO formats use MP tape and Sony's DVCAM format uses ME tape. It is important not to use MP tapes in devices designed for ME tapes, as it can damage the recording heads through wear.

Today's video formats record a lot of data on narrow tapes, and the quality of the tape stock is critical. A higher-quality tape will have fewer defects and allow you to record with fewer dropouts. Talk to people and check online user groups for sug-

---

5. *Never* label a cassette using masking tape or other tape. It can easily jam in a deck.

gestions on picking a brand of tape. Some manufacturers offer "mastering" stocks for top quality (at a top price). If you're renting a camera, the rental house will often have a preference. Many people recommend finding one brand you like and staying with it (or at least cleaning the heads between brands).

Cassettes come loaded with different-length tapes. Often, longer tapes are less expensive per minute of running time, and allow you to make fewer tape changes while shooting. On the other hand, sometimes long-playing cassettes contain tape stock with a thinner base, which may be more vulnerable to stretching. One consideration on cassette length: if a tape gets lost or damaged, the longer it is, the more you suffer. Losing a half hour of footage is bad enough; losing three hours is a whole lot worse.

Though tape stock is reusable, each pass through the VTR adds to the likelihood of dropouts or other defects. Professionals generally only use fresh, virgin tapes for critical camera recordings but if you need to reuse a tape don't lose sleep over it. Relative to all the costs of production, tape is usually very cheap. Don't scrimp. You can find good prices online and save by buying in lots of ten or more.

STORING TAPE STOCK. Improperly stored videotape can deteriorate in various ways, including becoming brittle or losing its magnetic charge. Keep tapes away from any magnetic fields (including electric motors). Store them in spaces that would be comfortable for humans—Sony recommends medium humidity (neither very dry nor very moist) at temperatures from 59° to 77°F (15° to 25°C). Tapes should be fully wound or rewound and stored upright. Since all tape formats eventually become obsolete, it's a good idea to transfer important archive masters to a new format—or possibly to a hard drive—every several years.

OPERATING THE CAMCORDER

Shooting Checklist
Some things to review before shooting:

- Charge and/or check the batteries (see below).
- Review or adjust initial settings such as format, frame rate, shutter speed, and gain (see p. 104).
- Set the timecode, if any (see Timecode, p. 223).
- For information on audio recording, see Audio in the Video Camera, p. 417, as well as Chapters 10 and 11. We'll assume here that audio is ready to go.
- Insert a formatted memory card or a fresh tape cassette.
- Make sure the viewfinder is focused for your eye and adjusted for color and brightness.
- When you're ready to shoot, check or set the white balance, exposure, and lens focus (see pp. 107–114).

See Chapter 9 for on-set procedures and other production considerations. For logging, see Chapters 9, 13, and 14.

Fig. 3-13. Canon EOS C300 camera. Has a Super 35 sensor and records HD using the XF codec (MPEG-2, long GOP, 4:2:2 color) to CF cards. Supports HD-SDI output to external recorders or monitors. Available in Canon EF lens mount and PL-mount versions. (Canon U.S.A., Inc.)

The Camera Trigger

All cameras have a trigger to start and stop the recording device (push once to go into "record" mode; push again to stop). Get in the habit of glancing up to check the record indicator in the viewfinder to make sure that you're *actually* rolling when you think you are. It's surprisingly easy to get off cycle, and push the button thinking you're starting the camera when actually you're stopping it (and when you check later, you're shocked to find you've recorded none of the takes you wanted, just lots of nothingness in between). This horrifying mistake is particularly easy to make when recording to flash memory since the camera is equally quiet when it's recording or not.

The red *tally light* in the viewfinder indicates when you're recording or, for a switched, multicamera shoot, when the camera is being selected ("taken"). There is usually a tally light on the outside of the camera so everyone knows when you're recording. For documentary work, many filmmakers turn it off or put a piece of tape over it.

Temperature and Humidity

In winter, when bringing a cold camera into a warm house, allow it to warm up in a sealed plastic bag to avoid condensation. When shooting in cold weather, try to keep the camera warm. Frozen tapes should be warmed before use. A hair dryer on low heat or air setting is sometimes used to warm or dehumidify equipment. Don't store the camera or media in a closed car in hot, sunny weather. Since humidity can cause recording problems, avoid steamy locations when possible.

Some digital cinema and HD cameras and certain DSLRs are prone to overheating even when used in moderate temperatures. Give the camera time to cool down if it feels very hot or displays a warning light. When possible, carry a spare DLSR body and switch bodies when one overheats.

See below for the effect of temperature on batteries.

Bars and Tone

Since the analog era, it has been a professional practice to record 30 seconds of color bars and audio reference tone at the start of every camera tape, using the camera's color bar generator and an audio test tone from the camera or the sound mixer (see Appendix A and Reference Tone, p. 452). The idea was to roll far enough into the tape to avoid any dirt and also to provide bars and tone for video and audio calibration later on.

In digital video, levels are encoded into the digital stream and can't be adjusted during copying or cloning, so recorded bars and tone are not that useful. However, if there's an analog step—perhaps you're using a video monitor connected through an analog video input—bars and tone can help with setup. For instance, you may want to put bars on at least some cassettes to help in adjusting picture monitors on location or in the NLE.[6]

In the working world you may, however, encounter editors or producers who expect or demand bars and tone, regardless of their actual value. Many who cut their teeth in the analog world are reluctant to part with what they consider professional practices.

Lastly, when recording to digital tape, some people think it's a good idea to record at least ten seconds of *something* at the head of each tape—why not bars and tone?—to avoid potential dropouts. But it's common practice among cinema verité filmmakers, for instance, to eject a spent cassette and immediately load another, without a break, to continue shooting an ongoing scene. They don't seem to complain much about tape dropouts.

BATTERIES AND POWER SUPPLIES

All electronic gear needs power to run. For a shoot to go smoothly, you must have power when you need it.

AC Power Supplies

For interior work, you can use an *AC power supply*, which is plugged into the wall. (In the UK, wall current is called the "mains.") With AC (alternating current), you never run out of juice, but your mobility is limited by the cable. When shooting in a foreign country, keep in mind that different countries have different types of power (see Electric Power, p. 518). The AC power may be supplied at 120 or 240 volts at a line frequency of 50 or 60 Hz. In some remote places what comes out of the wall isn't AC at all. Fortunately, many power supplies and battery chargers can accommodate different types of power (either automatically or with a switch). In

---

6. When it comes to postproduction, bars and tone are still considered essential when making finished master tapes of the edited movie.

some cases, you have to convert the power to a different standard before plugging in (see p. 519). Check the manual that came with your equipment.

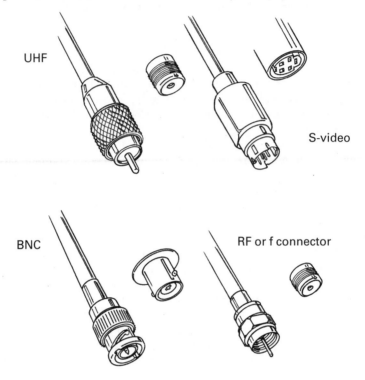

UHF

S-video

BNC

RF or f connector

Fig. 3-14. Common video connectors. Also see Figs. 5-29, 10-13, and 10-32 for other connectors used for video and audio. (Robert Brun)

Battery Power

For shooting in the field, and when portability is important, rechargeable batteries are used to power the camera. Most camcorders and film cameras use *onboard* camera-mounted batteries that range from several ounces to a few pounds. *Battery belts* and *packs* can also be used, especially for larger cameras.

There are several types of rechargeable batteries. *Nickel-cadmium* (*NiCad*) is a widely used type of professional camera battery that has improved a lot in recent years and is well suited to high power demands. Newer battery formulations that are more expensive and lighter weight include *nickel–metal hydride* (*NiMH*) and *lithium-ion* (*Li-Ion*). NiMH is somewhat heavier than lithium for the same power output, but has no travel restrictions (see below). *Lead acid* batteries (what nonelectric cars use) are heavy for the amount of power they supply. These may be used for powering lights directly or sometimes for camera power, using a car's interior accessory outlet. Batteries with the same chemistry can vary a lot in terms of power output and life depending on how they're made. Beware of cheap, poor-quality cells.

When getting a battery to use for your gear, first make sure that the voltage it delivers is compatible with your camera (check the manual). Some cameras specify a particular voltage, like 7.9 volts; others can accept a range, such as 11 to 17 volts. Keep in mind that every battery has a rated ("nominal") voltage, but will typically deliver somewhat more than this when fully charged and less as it discharges. For example, a 12-volt nominal battery might start out at 14 volts and drop to 10 volts after a couple of hours of shooting. Since many professional cameras require at least 10.5 or 11 volts to operate, Anton/Bauer, maker of widely used battery systems, recommends using a battery rated 13.2 volts for a 12-volt camera, since it will deliver at least 11 volts before running out of juice.

To estimate how long a battery will last, look in the camera manual for how much power the camera consumes, which is usually indicated in *watts*. Batteries are often rated in *watt-hours*. If the camera consumes 26 watts and the battery supplies 52 watt-hours of power, that should give you about two hours of use, which is a reasonable minimum for most shooting situations.[7]

Actually, estimating how much power you'll need for a day of shooting can be tricky because video cameras consume varying amounts of power depending on whether you're using a built-in LCD monitor, a viewfinder, or both. Also, digital recorders use power whether they're actually recording or merely standing by with the circuits on, so you could spend hours rehearsing actors with the gear on, then run out of power just before you start to record. It's better to be safe than sorry, so bring plenty of batteries, a charger, and an AC power unit if you can. You can nurse batteries along by powering down the camera when not recording. With tape-based cameras, you can save battery power by switching to "save" mode when not rolling (but don't bother for less than a few minutes' break) and avoid rewinding tapes.

With small-format camcorders, it's usually a good idea to use larger, *extended batteries* instead of the small ones that usually come with the camera. DSLRs can drain batteries quickly; consider a battery grip that contains extra cells, which can also help in holding the camera.

With larger, professional cameras you may have a choice between a heavy, high-capacity *brick* or smaller battery packs. The lighter batteries won't run as long, but if you'll be hand-holding the camera, they may save your back. On the other hand, sometimes large batteries balance a shoulder-mounted camera better. Pro batteries are available with various camera mounts; two of the most common are the *V-mount* (see Fig. 1-27) and Anton/Bauer's *Gold Mount*.

Estimating your battery needs with a film camera is more straightforward. Check the manual to determine how much film your camera will shoot per battery. If you know how much film you plan to shoot, you know how many charged batteries you need for the day.

Newer cameras and batteries often have a display that indicates how many more minutes of use the battery has in it. Bear in mind that most rechargeable batteries will maintain a working voltage for a time, then drop sharply when depleted, so battery checks while shooting don't always give much prior warning of when you'll run out. Batteries should be checked under load (with the camera running) if possible.

---

7. This assumes you're using a battery with a high enough nominal voltage, as described above.

Batteries put out much less power when they're cold. For cold-weather shooting, keep the battery warm until you're ready for it or get an extension power cable so you can keep the battery inside your coat while shooting.

Camera-mounted lights (and video taps on film cameras) consume a lot of power. It's always safer to run them off their own battery (separate from the camera's) to be sure you can keep the camera going even if the other systems run out of juice. A battery belt or battery pack makes a good auxiliary supply. On an expedition where normal battery charging is difficult, consider a solar-powered charger or a high-capacity, nonrechargeable lithium *expedition battery*.

For many types of smaller equipment that consume less power (including audio recorders, microphones, and wireless transmitters), you can get high-capacity rechargeable batteries in AA, AAA, and 9-volt form. Nonrechargeable batteries are available in different chemistries: alkaline cells provide more power than standard cells. Lithium and other expensive types are better yet. When replacing any battery, be sure the polarity is correct (that is, the plus-minus orientation of each cell). If the equipment uses several batteries together, never replace less than a full set. Reversed or dead cells will drain the others.

Fig. 3-15. DSLR (Olympus E-5) with Redrock Micro shoulder mount. (Redrock Micro)

Battery Charging and Maintenance

There are many types of batteries and chargers, so be sure to read the manual that comes with your gear. Most rechargeable camera batteries have a number of individual cells inside wired together. NiCads often charge faster than NiMH or Li-Ion. Always use a charger designed for the batteries you're using and don't mix different battery chemistries on the same charger unless the charger is specifically designed for it.

Generally, the more power a battery puts out, the more time it needs to charge. Some chargers are designed to switch off when the battery is fully charged. With others, you must unplug the battery when done. Overcharging a battery can destroy it. If the charger isn't one that automatically shuts off, unplug a battery if it feels hot.

Proper battery charging is surprisingly complex and the best chargers use microprocessors to quickly supply the initial charge, then go into *equalize mode* to top off and balance all the cells without overheating them. With many chargers, a light will go on or off when the battery is mostly charged, but more time is needed to charge the final 10 or 20 percent. For example, with some of its chargers, Sony recommends leaving the battery on for an hour after the charge light goes off to allow for topping off. Avoid old-fashioned slow chargers that can take up to sixteen hours depending on the system. Fast chargers may work in as little as an hour, and that can make all the difference for recharging during a shoot or when you're on the road.

After you take a battery off the charger, it will lose some charge over time (called *self-discharge*). Batteries retain their charge best in a cool place: 32° to 50°F (0° to 10°C) is ideal. Li-Ion batteries hold their charge longer than NiCad or NiMH. If a battery has been off the charger for some time, be sure to check it and recharge if necessary just before a shoot. Some chargers are designed so you can leave the battery on charge indefinitely without harm. However, avoid low-end chargers that supply a constant *trickle charge*, which may reduce capacity and battery life. If you're storing a battery for weeks or months between uses, discharge it, put it in a plastic bag, and put it in a refrigerator for maximum life (especially with Li-Ion).

Never charge a cold or frozen battery. Warm it up to the manufacturer's recommended minimum temperature first (room temperature is always safe). As noted above, batteries output less power when cold. Don't charge batteries if the temperature is above 110°F (43°C).

Overdischarging can harm a battery as much as overcharging. Most video cameras will shut off before overdischarging a battery, but a lighting fixture or a "deep discharger" may drain it past the safety point. A 12-volt battery should never be allowed to go below 9 or 10 volts. If you're getting a low-battery indication from your equipment, replace the battery with a fresh one.

There's a lot of debate about the concept of battery memory. Some people claim that if a NiCad or NiMH battery is repeatedly discharged only partway and recharged, it will eventually lose its ability to store a full charge. According to Anton/Bauer this is a myth, and an apparent loss of capacity over time is not a memory effect but due to the use of trickle chargers and batteries that are of too low nominal voltage for the camera.[8]

Even so, rotating through your batteries may have benefits and causes no harm. Shoot with each battery until you get the low-battery warning on the camera, put it on the charger, and continue shooting with the next one. As you go through the rotation over the course of days, each one will get fully charged and discharged.

Some chargers double as AC power supplies for the camera—very handy when all your batteries are dead and you don't have time to recharge.

Rechargeable batteries have a limited life in terms of both age and the number

8. For more, see the Video Battery Handbook at www.antonbauer.com.

of discharge/charge cycles. You should expect to get around 400 to 600 cycles from a NiCad or NiMH battery and around 1,000 cycles from a NiMH before the battery won't hold a full charge. Larger batteries tend to last longer than smaller ones when used with the same equipment. You may be able to replace just the cells in a professional battery pack, saving the cost of buying a whole new battery. Both heat and physical shocks can destroy a battery or lessen its life.

Fig. 3-16. A fitted foam insert in a hard-shell case protects and organizes your gear. Zacuto makes a variety of precut inserts. (Zacuto USA)

Travel Restrictions

Airlines restrict the size and number of lithium batteries you can fly with due to fire hazard. The following are the U.S. Department of Transportation's policies: No spare lithium batteries are allowed in checked baggage (spares are ones not installed in equipment). For carry-on baggage, there is generally no restriction on the number of smaller spare batteries; this includes cell phone batteries and AA and AAA cells, as well as most standard laptop computer batteries. As for the larger batteries often used with professional cameras, you are allowed one larger lithium-ion battery installed in a device (such as a brick battery rated between 100 and 300 watt-hours (8 to 25 grams of lithium content), plus up to two spares, but the spares must be carried on and not checked. For more information, see http://safetravel.dot.gov.

International rules may be more restrictive. The International Air Transport Association (IATA) currently prohibits you from flying with lithium-ion batteries above 160 watt-hours.

CAMERA SENSITIVITY

Digital cameras have improved greatly in their sensitivity to light, particularly as large-sensor cameras, which are inherently more sensitive than small-sensor cameras, have become more common.

Your camera's sensor—whatever the size—can capture images formed by only a certain range of light levels; the scene you want to shoot may be within that range or it may be too dark or too bright. To expand this range, you can increase the camera's sensitivity for dark scenes or insert a dark neutral density filter in front of the sensor when there's too much light.

Setting the Gain or ISO Speed

Most cameras have a *gain* or *sensitivity* switch that can brighten the image for low-light shooting. The trade-off is that increasing the gain also increases noise in the image, which looks a bit like graininess in film. Video gain is measured in dB (decibels). A typical gain switch might include settings for 0, 3, 6, 9, and 18 dB. Boosting gain by 6 dB doubles sensitivity, equivalent to opening up one stop. (This is like doubling the ISO or, when processing film, pushing one stop.) Switching to 18 dB is like opening up three stops. Usually, small increases in gain can improve the image in low-light situations without introducing too many image defects, but higher increases may show noticeable noise and should be used only if necessary (such as the *hypergain* setting in some cameras that can look like a snowstorm of noise). However, some newer cameras can be gained over 20 dB with a very clean image. Increasing gain may allow you to shoot at a higher *f*-stop to increase depth of field or to use less lighting.

DSLRs and some digital cameras have an *ISO speed* setting, which is functionally equivalent to gain. The ISO scale used in digital cameras is akin to the system used for rating the speed of still and motion picture film (see p. 275). Doubling the ISO number doubles sensitivity, like opening up one stop or increasing gain by 6 dB. As in the case of increased gain, a higher ISO speed will add noise to the image, so many people tend to shoot with the lowest possible ISO given the amount of light and other settings. However, cameras are optimized for a particular ISO, and lowest may not be best. Check the manual and do tests to see which setting has the cleanest image.

One thing to keep in mind about increasing gain and ISO speed is that neither truly increases the *sensitivity* of the sensor. Instead, they boost the signal after it leaves the sensor. So when you're shooting a very dark scene that registers down near the noise level of the sensor, if you increase the gain or ISO, you're boosting the noise along with the picture. If the scene is so bright that the highlights are clipped at the sensor, reducing the ISO will make the highlights look darker, but they'll still be clipped. Though it's a little counterintuitive (especially to anyone who has shot film), reducing the ISO or gain can actually *reduce* the camera's dynamic range in terms of its ability to handle bright highlights. For example, according to Canon, the EOS C300 camera has a native ISO of 850, at which setting "the dynamic range, especially in highlight areas, reaches its maximum. At lower ISO settings, the dynamic range tends to shift more toward shadow detail." For more on this, see p. 205.

For extremely dark scenes, some cameras can record *infrared* (and may be equipped with an infrared on-camera "light"; see Fig. 2-16A). Infrared responds to heat, not visible light, and the image looks unnatural; but with it, you can shoot scenes too dark to shoot otherwise. You may like the weirdness of the look. Sony calls its consumer infrared system *NightShot*.

THE ISO STANDARD. In still photography, each film manufacturer is required to rate its film products based on an ISO standard. A photographer may choose to rate a particular film emulsion higher, but the relationship between ISO rating and film sensitivity is the same from one manufacturer to the next.

With digital cameras, the relationship between sensitivity and ISO is much more complicated. Manufacturers of digital still cameras use two types of ISO ratings: an arbitrary Recommended Exposure Index, which can be anything the manufacturer decides, or a Standard Output Specification, which specifies a standard output level corresponding to 18 percent gray (middle of the gray scale) when the camera is exposed at the declared ISO rating.

Unlike ISO ratings for still photography, which apply to the film and not the camera, digital ISO ratings apply to the digital camera system as a whole, not to individual components such as sensors, which have no separate sensitivity rating.

The ISO Standard Output Specification does not apply to digital cinema images, only to compressed digital still images like JPEG encoded to sRGB color space (a web standard)—not to RAW images captured directly off the sensor. In the case of RAW images, only the arbitrary Recommended Exposure Index can be used.

So don't *assume* that the ISO rating of a particular digital camera system or image is necessarily applicable to any other in terms of overall sensitivity until verifying it.

Neutral Density Filters for Digital Cameras

In sunlit scenes, there's often too much light for the camera. Even with the lens iris closed down to a minimum aperture, the image may be overexposed. Most professional digital video cameras are equipped with internal *neutral density filters* that cut down the amount of light coming through the lens (see Neutral Density Filters, p. 312). For example, a camera might have a neutral density filter dial with three positions: (1) ¼, or one-quarter the amount of light, equal to two stops and created by a 0.6 ND filter; (2) ⅟₁₆, or one-sixteenth the amount of light, equal to four stops and created by a 1.2 ND; and (3) ⅟₆₄, or one sixty-fourth the amount of light, equal to six stops and created by a very dark 1.8 ND.

Some professional digital video cameras also provide a second filter wheel on the same axis as the ND wheel to permit selection of different levels of ND in combination with an orange filter for warming up daylight (the orange filter further cuts light intensity by almost half; see p. 309).

With some digital video cameras there is no internal ND filter wheel; instead you must use glass ND filters that either screw on the lens or fit in a matte box.

You can also buy *variable ND filters* that can be adjusted for different amounts of darkening (see Fig. 8-6). Be sure to get a high-quality variable ND or you risk softening the image.

Neutral density filters can be helpful when you want to shoot at a wider iris for shallower depth of field (see p. 156) or when you want to avoid shooting at high *f*-stops, which reduce sharpness due to diffraction (see Lens Sharpness, p. 173). Adjusting the ISO speed can help in these situations too.

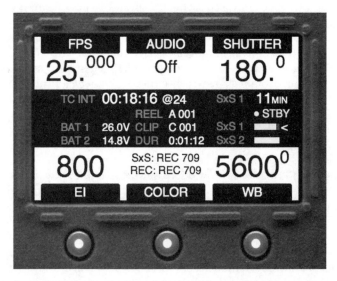

Fig. 3-17. This panel on the ARRI Alexa displays key camera settings. Starting in the lower right and moving clockwise, you can see the white balance is set to 5600 degrees kelvin; the EI (same as ISO) is set to 800; the frame rate is set to 25 fps; and the shutter angle is set to 180 degrees. Shutter angle is simply another way of expressing the shutter speed; a 180-degree shutter is open for half of each frame, so the shutter speed at 25 fps is 1/50 second. (ARRI, Inc.)

Shutter Speed

If you've done much still photography, you know that still cameras have a *shutter speed adjustment* that controls how long the film or digital chip is exposed to light when you press the trigger. You might use a high shutter speed (short exposure time) for shooting sports when you want to freeze fast-moving action (see Fig. 2-14). You might use a slow shutter speed (long exposure time) in a dark scene when you need to collect as much light as possible to get enough exposure on the digital sensor or film.

Most video cameras also have a shutter speed adjustment; it controls not how many frames are taken each second (that's the frame rate; see p. 81) but the length of time the sensor collects light while each frame is being captured. The standard shutter speed is determined in part by the frame rate; as noted on p. 104, the standard shutter speed is generally about half the frame rate.

There are times when you might want to use a higher shutter speed. Some cameras are capable of shutter speeds up to 1/10,000 second or more (the faster the shutter speed, the shorter the exposure). Why use a higher shutter speed? In a normal video or film image, any motion in the frame (whether caused by the camera or the subject movement) will cause a certain amount of blur (see Fig. 2-14). This blur looks natural at normal playback speed, but if you plan to extract still frames or slow the footage down with pixel estimation software for digital slow motion, you will want to make each frame crisper by using a higher shutter speed of at least 1/500 second or more. High shutter speeds are also useful in analyzing footage from sporting events. For more on slow motion, see p. 389.

Using high shutter speeds may cause certain image problems, particularly if there's a lot of camera or subject movement (see Judder or Strobing, p. 393). High shutter speeds are sometimes used to create a deliberately choppy feel, which cinematographer Janusz Kaminski famously employed in *Saving Private Ryan* to add a jittery, electric atmosphere to battle sequences.

Because high shutter speeds cut down the exposure, if you increase the shutter speed you'll need to compensate by opening the iris, by increasing the gain or ISO speed, or by adding more light. Very high shutter speeds are usually feasible only in bright light. In a situation where you deliberately want to reduce exposure so you can open the iris to achieve shallow depth of field (see p. 153), you might increase the shutter speed, but be aware that this may affect the way motion looks, as noted above. Because changing shutter speed affects motion, if you're using a DSLR on autoexposure, you'll usually want to prevent the AE from changing the shutter speed.

Slower shutter speeds produce more motion blur and are sometimes used for a more gentle, dreamy effect. Some cameras have a *slow shutter mode* that allows you to select shutter speeds that are longer than one frame or field: for example, 1/15-, 1/8-, and 1/4-second shutter speeds when shooting 60i. This causes a single exposure to effectively stretch across multiple frames. Any camera or subject movement will result in blurring and highlight trails. You might like this as a special effect, but if not, use a good tripod and avoid any camera or subject movement. In static shots you can use a slow shutter speed to get more exposure when there isn't enough light to shoot otherwise.

Some digital cameras can indicate shutter speed in terms of the shutter angles cinematographers are familiar with from shooting film (see p. 255). A shutter angle of about 180 degrees results in a shutter speed that's about half the frame rate (for example, 1/50-second shutter speed when shooting at 24 fps).

Shooting computer and video monitors can be challenging if the *refresh rate* (scanning rate) of the monitor doesn't match the frame rate of the camera, which will result in a rolling frame bar or uneven screen illumination (flicker). Some cameras have a special shutter control that allows you to dial the shutter speed up or down in small increments to match the scanning rate of the camera to the monitor. Sony and Canon call it Clear Scan; Panasonic calls its system Synchro Scan. See Chapter 9 for more on shooting monitors.

Flicker may also occur when shooting with any pulsed lighting source, such as HMIs or fluorescents. See HMI Bulbs, p. 481, for recommended shutter speeds.

Camera Sensors

For background on sensors, see Digital Video Systems, p. 5, and Forming the Video Image, p. 185.

It used to be the case that video cameras with three sensors (one each for red, green, and blue) produced better images than single-chip cameras. In a three-chip camera, an internal prism splits the light into the three primary color components (see Fig. 1-14). Some three-chip cameras also use a *pixel shift* technique to increase apparent resolution by offsetting the red and blue sensors by half a pixel from the green sensor to effectively double the number of discrete image samples.

While three-chip digital video cameras provide advantages in light sensitivity and full pixel counts for each color component, today both the highest-end cameras and the lowest-end cameras are single-chip, not to mention DSLRs. Such cameras typically use a *Bayer pattern* filter on the front surface of the sensor to create separate red, green, and blue pixels (see Fig. 1-13). To accomplish this, a Bayer filter contains microscopic red, green, and blue filters that cover exactly one pixel each. The result is always that 50 percent of pixels are covered by a green filter, and 25 percent each by a red or blue filter. This pattern is sometimes called RGBG.

A three-chip video camera requires a beam-splitting prism behind the lens, and you must use a lens specifically designed for that type of prism. With single-chip cameras there is no prism, which simplifies the optical path and, in the case of large sensors, allows the use of high-quality PL-mount film lenses designed for 16mm and 35mm film cameras as well as a universe of lenses designed for SLR and DSLR cameras.

It's imperative to keep a single sensor free of dust. Always put a cap on the camera if you remove the lens and try not to change lenses in a dusty environment. Dust may appear in the viewfinder without impairing the recorded image; but if you see dark specs in the image and on the sensor, it may need cleaning. The sensor is *extremely* delicate; it's easy to damage in cleaning, and, if you're cleaning a DSLR sensor, it's easy to damage the mirror too. Some sensors are self-cleaning. Others can be blown clean gently with a rubber squeeze blower. Follow instructions in your camera's manual or consider having it done by a professional.

Since focused sunlight can damage the sensor, don't point the camera at the sun for extended periods. Similarly, direct sunlight focused through a camera's viewfinder can damage the monitor screen if left for too long.

Camera Setup

Numerous adjustments and settings provided by a camera's digital signal processing affect the color, contrast, and sharpness of the image. These settings are user-adjustable, although some people prefer to leave them to the expertise of a *digital imaging technician (DIT)*. When you get a new professional or semiprofessional camera, it's a good idea to have a knowledgeable person explain the internal image settings to you. Many people, including experienced operators, choose to leave such settings alone, relying instead on the default or factory settings.

If you elect to fine-tune the image, some cameras offer a *scene file* or *picture profile* capability to store settings for different looks as defined by adjustments to color phase and intensity, white balance tint, tonal scale reproduction (selectable gamma curves) and black stretch, and other image parameters including sharpness. On many cameras you can store these scene files on a memory card, which you can bring from shoot to shoot to re-create that look when you use the exact same type of camera, or to ensure consistency on a multicamera shoot, again when you use the same type of camera (though different lenses may cause differences between cameras).

GAMMA. In video, *gamma* determines the apparent contrast of the image, particularly in the midtones. Gamma has a big impact on the feel of the image and whether details are visible in shadows or highlights. Many prosumer and professional cameras offer a choice of gamma settings. Options may include settings that look vibrant and contrasty; other settings are more muted and "cinelike." For more on gamma and contrast, and choosing a gamma setting, see p. 193.

Fig. 3-18. Detail or enhancement. (top) A shot made with the detail set to minimum. (bottom) Detail set to maximum. Notice the artificial white edge around the numbers on the clock and other objects. (Steven Ascher)

DETAIL. Before reading this, see Sharpness and Focus on p. 70. *Detail* (sometimes called *enhancement, edge enhancement, sharpness,* or *aperture correction*) is a setting that affects the apparent sharpness of a video image (see Fig. 3-18). Many cameras have a menu setting for detail (this is for the recorded image, *not* a viewfinder adjustment). When image detail is set too high, a crisp, clear outline appears around objects, making them stand out boldly with a kind of electric "ringing" effect.[9] When detail is set very low, the image may seem soft or unsharp. (You cannot truly add sharpness that doesn't exist to an image. When detail is low or turned off, that is, in fact, the true resolution of the video image.)

With small-sensor cameras, increasing the detail to a high setting feels "videolike," while setting the detail lower appears more "filmlike." An example of the first is TV news footage, which is often shot with a crisp, enhanced look. Shots made with a low detail setting can sometimes look mushy, but your eye gets used to the mellower, subtler look.

Depending on your small-sensor camera, what you're shooting, and your preferences, you may like more or less detail, but overuse of enhancement should be avoided, particularly with HD, which has inherently more resolution and looks sharper without any extra help. If you use Photoshop, play around with the Sharpen or Unsharp Mask filters on a still image to get an idea of what setting the detail circuit too high does to a digital video image.

In the case of large-sensor digital video cameras, any detail circuit should be turned off. In most cases, this is the factory default setting anyway. Detail enhancement is an electronic cheat that large-sensor cameras, with their native ability to capture and reproduce true fine detail, no longer require.

Likewise with small-sensor cameras: when in doubt, less detail is safer than more, since it can be added later but can't be removed. Be aware that what looks good on a small monitor may look very different when projected big. Always experiment first with the detail setting if you're planning to project the final results on a big screen.

CHROMA. The *chroma* setting affects how saturated colors are. High chroma means bright, deep colors; low chroma means pale, desaturated colors. Very saturated colors may look appealing on a small monitor, but are sometimes too vibrant on a bigger screen. Your choice of gamma setting will also have an effect on chroma. For more on color, see p. 304.

If you're not a video tech or a DIT with experience in adjusting color matrix parameters, it's prudent to avoid toying with internal color settings. The camera's default settings will usually produce attractive images, and hue, saturation, and the like can be easily adjusted in postproduction, when ideally you will have access to a large, calibrated monitor in a controlled visual environment.

OTHER CAMERA FEATURES

Prerecord Cache

Some digital video cameras have a *prerecord cache* (also called *loop* or *retroloop*) system that continually stores about five to ten seconds of material when the camera's on but not rolling. Then, when you hit the trigger to record, the shot begins

---

9. The detail setting doesn't actually improve the ability to see fine details. It doesn't increase resolution, it just makes shapes pop out more—which fools the eye into seeing things as sharper.

five to ten seconds *before* you pressed start. This can be particularly useful in unpredictable documentary situations—say, if you're waiting for an animal to emerge from a nest. Some external HDD or flash memory recorders can add this capability to cameras that lack it.

Image Stabilization

Small-sensor video cameras often feature internal optical or electronic *image stabilization* to counteract camera shake or jostling and make it less noticeable when hand-holding the camera. Experiment with yours to see if you like the effect. Many people leave the stabilization on routinely. Image stabilization is also available to DSLR users when built in to individual lenses. See Chapter 9 for devices, such as Steadicams, that can stabilize large and small cameras.

Digital Tricks

Professional video cameras have a *skin detail* function that can target skin tones and soften facial textures for a more flattering look while leaving the rest of the image sharp. Some cameras can capture a previously recorded image and superimpose it in the viewfinder, helping you to re-create a setup recorded earlier. Some cameras can adjust the hue of a specific color, leaving other colors unaffected.

Consumer video cameras typically offer a range of in-camera visual effects, including titles, fades and dissolves, in-camera editing, colorizing, posterizing, and other image distortions. Consult your camera's manual for details. In general, it is far better to do these effects in postproduction than in the camera.

Cameras that record to nonlinear media are generally capable of interval recording or shooting individual frames, allowing you to do time-lapse or animation work (see p. 392).

Like DSLRs—obviously designed to shoot stills more than video—many digital video cameras can now capture high-quality stills, some while simultaneously recording video. If your camera doesn't have a dedicated still capture mode, you may be able to get frame grabs from the video footage (easy to do by exporting from an NLE). This works best with progressive formats, of HD or higher resolution. Since they are made from one field only, SD cameras generally produce stills of low quality, and stills from interlaced HD formats are only somewhat better.

CHAPTER 4

The Lens

This chapter is about lenses for both digital and film cameras. To create the kinds of images you want it's necessary to understand the basic characteristics of lenses and how they control light to form images.

Camera lenses gather light rays reflected from a scene in front of the camera and bend or "focus" them into a tiny image on the surface of a frame of film or a camera's sensor. If you think about the fact that you can project a sharp, colorful image created by the puny ⅓-inch sensor of an HD camcorder onto a screen twenty feet across, as routinely happens at film festivals, you'll realize the level of performance required of even an inexpensive zoom lens.

All photographic lenses are complex assemblies of simpler lenses called *elements*, which are akin to the lens in a magnifying glass. Some of these elements are cemented together to form *compound elements.* The elements are mounted in groups inside the lens *barrel* (housing).

Generally speaking, motion picture film cameras, DSLRs, shoulder-mount camcorders, and some smaller digital video cameras accept interchangeable lenses, allowing you to select the best lens for a given situation. Lower-end video cameras, however, have fixed lenses, so your choice of camera will be based partly on its lens.

FOCAL LENGTH AND PERSPECTIVE

Focal Length

If we aim a simple lens at a light source at infinity distance—a star will work fine, but anything at a great distance can serve as "infinity"—the lens will focus the incoming rays at a point behind the lens equal in distance to the *focal length* of the lens. This point falls on the *focal plane* (see Fig. 4-1). In a digital camera, the CMOS or CCD sensor is positioned at the focal plane; in a film camera, the film rests in the focal plane when exposed. (Because most lens concepts are identical for digital and film, in this chapter the terms "sensor" and "film" are used interchangeably to mean the surface where the image is formed.)

Focal length is a measure of the power of a lens to bend light rays coming from the subject. The shorter the focal length, the greater the bending power and the

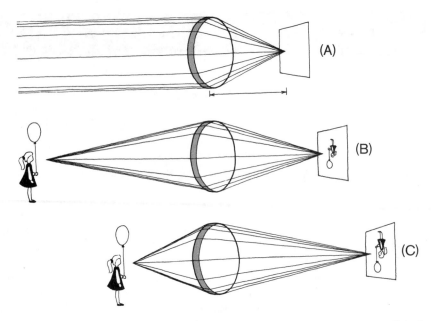

Fig. 4-1. Focal length. (A) The rays from a point source of light at infinity are parallel when they strike the lens. The distance from the lens to the focal plane (where the rays are brought back to a point) is the *focal length*. (B) The photographic lens forms an upside-down image flipped from left to right. (C) The closer an object is to the lens, the farther from the lens the rays converge and the larger the object appears on the film. (Carol Keller)

closer the focal plane is to the rear of the lens.[1] Lenses are identified by their focal length. *Prime lenses* (also called *fixed focal length lenses*) have only one focal length. *Zoom lenses* have a range of focal lengths, allowing you to change focal length during a shot. Focal length is expressed in millimeters.

For each shot, the cinematographer decides how large the subject should be in the frame. For example, should the shot include the whole body or should the face fill the frame? There are two ways to increase the size of the subject in the frame: you can either move the camera closer to the subject or use a longer focal length lens (see Fig. 4-2). If we view a scene with two lenses, the lens with the longer focal length will reveal less of the scene and make any object in its field of view appear larger. This lens "sees" the scene through a narrower angle—the longer the focal length, the narrower this *angle of view* (also called *field of view*).

The size that an object appears in a digital or film image is directly proportional to lens focal length. If we double the focal length (keeping the distance to the subject constant), the subject will appear twice as large. Also, the size of the object is inversely proportional to its distance from the camera—that is, if we double the distance, we halve the size of the subject on film (see Fig. 4-3). At 10 feet, a 50mm lens yields the same size subject as a 25mm lens does at 5 feet.

1. Technically, the focal length of a lens is defined as the distance from the *nodal point* (optical center) of the lens to the focal plane when the lens is focused at infinity.

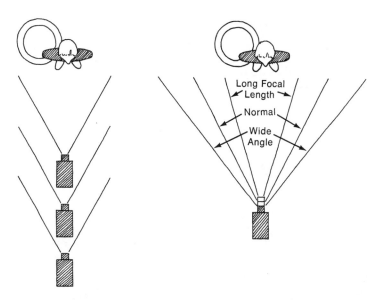

Fig. 4-2. Angle of view and focal length. (left) Keeping the angle of view constant, moving closer to the man (dollying in), makes him appear larger. (right) Keeping the camera in the same position while using increasingly longer focal lengths also makes the man larger but decreases the angle of view. See the results in Fig. 4-3. (Carol Keller)

Perspective

As just discussed, there are two ways to control the size of an object in the image: change the focal length or change the distance between camera and subject. Does it make a difference if you move the camera closer to the subject rather than use a longer focal length lens? Figure 4-3 illustrates that it does. When you change focal length to enlarge part of a scene, it's like magnifying the original image. Both foreground and background objects become larger to the same relative extent. In other words, if the focal length is doubled, all the objects in the frame double in size.

On the other hand, as the camera is moved closer, the relative size of foreground and background objects increase at different rates. Objects closer to the camera increase in size more than objects farther from the camera. In the first set of photographs in Fig. 4-3, the camera is moved closer to the subject. The building in the background does not increase in size nearly as much as the man in the foreground. If you move twice as close to an object, the object doubles in size on film, but objects in the background increase by less than that.

Perspective may be thought of as the rate at which objects become larger the closer they are to the camera. In Fig. 4-3, as the camera moves in toward the subject, the man increases in size at a rate faster than that of the building, increasing the feeling of depth and making the man appear relatively far from the building. However, in the other set of pictures we can see that if we change only the focal length and don't move the camera, the perspective doesn't change. Although the image is magnified, the relationship between the man and the building remains the same. By

Fig. 4-3. Zooming compared to dollying. When you start at the same position (top), you can move the camera closer (the two photos at left) or zoom in (the two photos at right). In the zoom, everything gets proportionally larger—the man and the building double in size. In the dolly shot, at left, the man doubles in size but the building stays about the same size. (Compare how many windows are visible in the bottom pair of photographs.) (Ted Spagna)

cropping out closer objects, the space appears flatter and the foreground and background seem compressed.

By altering both focal length and camera-to-subject distance, the cinematographer can control perspective. Coming in closer and using a wide-angle lens exaggerates distances, while moving back and using a lens with a long focal length compresses distances. An image is said to have natural perspective when the perspective appears similar to what one would see if standing at the camera position. A medium focal length lens that produces a natural perspective is termed "normal" (for more, see What's a Normal Lens?, p. 151).

Lenses of appreciably shorter-than-normal focal length are called *wide-angle* or *short focal length lenses*. A rough rule of thumb is that wide-angle lenses are about half the focal length of normal lenses (50 percent), while lenses below about 35 percent of normal are *extreme wide angle*. Lenses with a focal length appreciably longer than normal are called *long focal length* or *telephoto lenses*. Lenses longer than about 150 percent of normal focal length are considered telephoto.

Perspective Effects

As discussed above, the farther the camera is from the subject, the flatter or more compressed the perspective; that is, objects of different distances from the camera do not appear greatly different in size on film. With a long focal length lens, distant objects do not appear as small as you might expect (see Fig. 4-4). This effect is easily observed when a race is filmed head-on with a long focal length lens. The runners seem to be closer to one another than they actually are, and although they seem to be running hard, they don't appear to be making much progress. This illusion occurs because of the great distance to the subject and the use of a long focal length lens. A very long lens can make the world seem almost flat or two-dimensional.

Wide-angle lenses are apt to exaggerate depth; the distance between foreground and background seems greater than you would expect, objects far from the camera seeming too small in relation to the objects closer up. This phenomenon is sometimes called *wide-angle lens distortion* or *perspective distortion*. Although you may not find exaggerated perspective pleasing, it is, in fact, not "distorted," and if you view the image on screen from up close, the perspective seems natural. As you get even closer to the screen, the perspective flattens. If you tend to sit close to a movie or TV screen (and not because you're nearsighted), you probably prefer compressed perspective; if you sit far from the screen, it may be because you prefer more depth in the image.

You can use a wide-angle lens to make a room seem larger. However, if someone is near the camera and moves toward it, he will appear to move unnaturally fast. In general, use a wide-angle lens to exaggerate the speed of any movement toward or away from the camera. A wide-angle lens on a moving vehicle pointed in the direction of the movement strongly suggests speed, especially if objects sweep past near the lens. Use a wide-angle lens to emphasize heights; for example, shoot down from the top of a building or shoot a person from below. Perspective effects are accentuated when there are objects in both the close foreground and the distant background. A distant landscape or seascape with nothing in the foreground will show perspective less.

Fig. 4-4. Compression and exaggeration of depth. (top) The long focal length lens makes the foreground and background appear close together. The cars look flat, packed together, and close to the distant sign. (bottom) In this still from *Citizen Kane*, a feeling of deep space is created, in part, by using a short focal length lens. (Ted Spagna; RKO General)

PERSPECTIVE IN THE CLOSE-UP. When you shoot a head-and-shoulder close-up with a wide-angle lens, the camera must be fairly close, which exaggerates depth. If you get very close, the nose will seem too large, and the ears too small and too far from the front of the face. Such close-ups are often used for comic or eerie effect. A hand movement in the direction of the camera seems too fast, the hand itself too large. Faces in profile and motion perpendicular to the lens's axis show this exaggeration of perspective less.

Figure 4-5 was shot with a DSLR that has a full-frame 35mm sensor. The image on the left was shot with a 28mm lens from about 8 inches away; the one on the right was shot with an 85mm lens at 4 feet. As photographer Bill Wadman notes, it wasn't the choice of lenses but the distance from the subject that created the different perspective between the two shots (however, the longer focal length in the image on the right does make the subject larger, so her face is the same size, despite the greater distance).

Fig. 4-5. Close-ups with different focal length lenses. (left) A head-and-shoulder close-up shot with a wide-angle lens from very close to the subject results in distorted facial features—the forehead and nose can appear too large and the face too wide. (right) A medium-length lens from a middle distance gives a feeling of dimensionality without looking unflattering. For details, see text. (Bill Wadman)

If you film at the most common filming distances—about 5 feet or more from the subject—you don't have to worry about exaggerating facial features. For close-ups of faces, it's generally better to err on the side of flatter perspective (a longer focal length lens at a greater distance). However, when perspective is too flat, intimacy can be lost and the viewer may feel distant from the subject.

Focal Length and Format

With experience, cinematographers learn which focal lengths will achieve the effect they're looking for. For example, when shooting a typical interview with an HD camera that has a ⅔-inch sensor, a range of focal lengths from about 10mm to 50mm will allow everything from a medium shot of the subject to a close-up of the face. Or, for a compressed-perspective shot of a stream of people flowing down a sidewalk, you could shoot from far away with a 150mm lens. Once you get comfortable shooting in any format, you'll begin to have an instinctive feel for roughly what length lens you need in various situations, and what angle of view each focal length provides.

When you shoot with different digital or film formats, keep in mind that the angle of view associated with any particular focal length becomes larger or smaller according to the actual size of your camera's sensor or film format.

Figure 4-6 shows that when using the same focal length lens, a camera with a larger sensor captures a wider angle of view than a camera with a smaller sensor. In Figure 4-7 you can see the results. The lens projects a circular image on the sensor, and a larger sensor (outer frame) captures a wider angle of view than a smaller sensor (inner frame). If we display the images from these two sensors on the same-sized monitor or screen, the smaller sensor's image will look magnified, as if we had filmed with a longer focal length lens (as though we had zoomed in).

Comparing two cameras with different-sized sensors, if you want the same angle of view from both of them, you'd need to use a wider-angle lens (shorter focal length) on the camera with the smaller sensor. To get a sense of the relationship of angle of view, focal length, and sensor or film format size, look at Appendix E. It

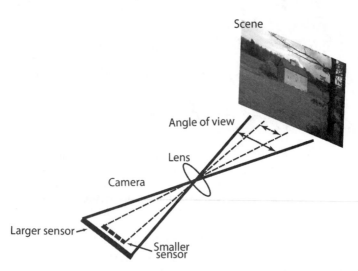

Fig. 4-6. Angle of view and sensor size. If two cameras have the same focal length lens, the camera with the smaller sensor will see the scene with a narrower angle of view than the camera with a larger sensor. With film cameras, the same principle applies to wider and narrower film formats. See the results in Fig. 4-7. (Steven Ascher)

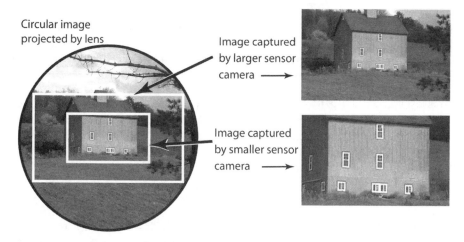

Fig. 4-7. The lens projects a circular image onto the sensor. If we were to record the image with two different sensors, the larger sensor would capture more of the picture than the smaller sensor. When the image from each sensor is shown on a monitor, the larger-sensor image shows a wider angle of view, and the smaller-sensor image looks enlarged or zoomed in, as though it had been shot with a longer focal length lens. So if you want the same angle of view from two cameras that have different sensor sizes, you need to use a wider-angle lens with the smaller-sensor camera. (Steven Ascher)

indicates the focal length needed to achieve an identical 40-degree angle of view in cameras of various formats.

What does this mean for your filmmaking? First of all, for any particular shot (say, a head-and-shoulders close-up of an actor filmed from across a table), if you shoot with a large-sensor digital camera (like a DSLR with a full-frame sensor) or a film format with a large recording area, you'll use a longer focal length lens than if you were shooting the same shot from the same position with a smaller-sensor camera. This will result in less depth of field behind the subject, making it easier to throw the background out of focus with the large-sensor camera.[2] A shot taken with a digital camera with a ⅔-inch sensor will have roughly half the depth of field of a shot taken with a camera with a ⅓-inch sensor that has the same angle of view and f-stop.[3]

Another consideration relates to shooting with a wide angle of view, which is often desirable, for example, when shooting in tight quarters or when filming a large group. If you shoot with a small-sensor camera, you'll need a lens with a quite short focal length. With small-sensor cameras, at times there simply may not be a short enough lens to shoot very wide angle. For example, when shooting with a digital camera like the Sony F3 that has a Super 35–sized sensor, an 18mm lens can produce a nice wide-angle shot; for the same shot with a ⅓-inch sensor you'd need a 4mm lens, which is typically not available (though wide-angle adapters can help).

---

2. In theory, you could get similarly shallow depth of field with a small-format film or video sensor, but you'd need a very wide aperture (low f-number) and many lenses just aren't fast enough.

3. This is a rule of thumb; other factors come into play.

On the other hand, a smaller sensor helps if you want to shoot a tight shot over great distance with a telephoto lens (often an advantage for sports or nature shooting). For any given focal length lens, you'll get a more enlarged image (narrower angle of view) using a camera with a smaller sensor. And the smaller-sensor camera makes it easier to shoot deep-focus shots with great depth of field.

MOVING BETWEEN FORMATS. Once you learn how various focal lengths look in one format, you can translate those numbers when working in another format. At www.abelcine.com you'll find an excellent "Field of View Comparator" that shows the relationship of focal length to angle of view in various formats; there are apps for mobile devices as well that determine focal length for any format and angle of view (see the Bibliography).

Comparing the angle of view of different lenses and formats is sometimes talked about in terms of a *crop factor* relative to a full-frame 35mm SLR or DSLR image (Canon 5D Mark II, for example). Looking at Appendix E, if we take the Canon 5D with its full-frame 35mm sensor as a reference (which measures 36mm in width in HD movie mode), then a camera like the Canon 7D with its smaller APS-C sensor (22.3mm width) would have a crop factor of about 0.6x. To match the angle of view produced by a 50mm lens on a Canon 5D when shooting with the Canon 7D, we'd multiply by 0.6 to find the equivalent, which is a 32mm lens. This concept is also called *focal length multiplier*. Crop factors, when available, can be used to compare lenses on any two formats, not just relative to full-frame 35mm.

One thing to keep in mind when using lenses with different formats: if you use a lens designed for a smaller format on a camera with a larger sensor (or film gauge) it may not project a large enough image to cover the entire frame of a larger format. Or it may cover the frame, but produce vignetting (darkening) around the edges. There are special devices, however, to adapt lenses designed for smaller formats like ⅔ inch to larger format cameras like Super 35 by means of a tube that contains additional optical elements. When using these adapters, there is a light loss of several stops, but the resulting image is sharp, with no vignetting. There are also special devices to adapt PL-mount lenses to ⅔-inch sensor cameras, which maintain the angle of view of the larger format. These adapters often flip the image in the process, so the ⅔-inch camera must be capable of flipping the image back. Both types of adapters are usually considered rental items.

WHEN ONLY PART OF THE SENSOR IS USED. Cameras that can shoot in more than one format sometimes use only part of the sensor to capture a particular format (called windowing). If the window is narrower than the full width of the sensor, this reduces the angle of view (think of the inner and outer boxes in Figure 4-7 as being on the same sensor).

Video cameras that have a 16:9-shaped sensor will have a 25 percent narrower angle of view when switched to 4:3 mode, which crops the right and left edges (it will look as though you zoomed in slightly). A similar thing happens when you extract a 4:3 image from the center of a 16:9 HD shot using edge crop (see Fig. 2-12D). In either situation, what *was* your widest angle lens when working in 16:9 will appear less wide (narrower angle of view) in 4:3—you lose the edges of the shot.

Changing the recording resolution may also have an effect on field of view. With cameras like the RED Epic or RED Scarlet-X, the full width of the sensor is active when shooting at 5K resolution, but when shooting at lower resolutions, like 2K or 1080p, the active image area of the sensor is not as wide (fewer pixels are used), resulting in a narrower angle of view. However, not all cameras behave this way. Many cameras use the full width of the sensor regardless of the resolution, and then scale the image upon output to the selected frame size.

WHAT'S A NORMAL LENS? As noted above, for any given format, a lens of medium focal length that yields an image with natural perspective is called "normal." In still photography, 50mm is considered normal for 35mm SLR and full-frame DSLRs. Used with these formats, a 50mm lens provides about a 40-degree horizontal angle of view.

It's interesting that in cinema, a narrower angle of view defines a normal lens. The classic Academy 35mm motion picture format, for instance, occupies four perforations of 35mm film compared to the eight perforations of an SLR frame, making it a little more than half the size. When a 50mm lens is used, this results in a smaller 24-degree horizontal angle of view, yet a 50mm lens is also considered normal for Academy 35mm. The equivalent horizontal angle of view in standard 16mm film is a 25mm lens. As "normal" benchmarks for film lenses, it's easy to remember 50mm and 25mm.

Why the difference between stills and motion pictures in what is considered a normal lens? It's based on the effects of screen distance on perspective as seen by the audience. Traditionally motion pictures were viewed in a movie theater, with the average distance between the audience and the screen about twice the screen diagonal, whereas we usually look at photographs from a much closer distance, say arm's length. Today your work may be shown on a big screen, a flat-panel TV, a laptop, a tablet, or a phone and viewed from far away, across the room, or close up—so no one approach to what is a normal lens will work for all.

It's probably safe to say that any lens with a horizontal angle of view between 40 and 24 degrees will fit within the range of normal perspective in any format. In the end, however, it's best not to get too hung up on this, since what feels normal is ultimately subjective, and "normal" may not be your goal anyway.

THE LIGHT-GATHERING POWER OF THE LENS

F-stops

The lens gathers light from the subject and projects its image on the film or on the digital camera's sensor. The maximum light-gathering efficiency of the lens is called the *speed* of the lens. It is expressed as an *f-number* (*f-stop* or *relative aperture*), which is the ratio between the focal length of the lens and its diameter (maximum aperture):

$$f\text{-number} = \frac{\text{focal length}}{\text{lens diameter}}$$

The *f*-number essentially tells us the light-passing power of a lens. As the lens diameter increases, so does the amount of light that passes through the lens. As the focal length increases, the light is dispersed over a greater area and the amount of light available for exposure to the film or video sensor decreases. The *faster* a lens, the more light it lets through; the *slower* a lens, the less light. Lenses of about *f*/2 (that is, the diameter of the lens is one-half the focal length) are usually considered fast.

Inside most lenses is the *iris diaphragm*, which can close down to control the amount of light that the lens lets through. The iris is a mechanical device, usually made of overlapping blades (see Fig. 4-8), that can be set to form a large or small hole or *aperture* (*lens aperture*). It functions similarly to the iris in the eye. In dim light, the eye's iris opens to admit more light, and in bright light it closes down to let less light pass through.

f/16   f/8   f/2.8

Fig. 4-8. Iris diaphragm. As the blades of the iris open, more light passes through the lens.

A formula similar to the one that describes the speed of the lens is used to express the light-gathering power of the lens at any iris diaphragm opening. The *f*-number, or *f*-stop, is the focal length of the lens divided by the diameter of the aperture. The standard series of *f*-stops, or *f*-numbers, is:

$$1, 1.4, 2, 2.8, 4, 5.6, 8, 11, 16, 22, 32$$

The distance between consecutive numbers is called a *stop*. On most professional cine (movie) lenses, the *f*-stops are engraved on a ring on the lens barrel. Each stop represents the halving (or doubling) of the amount of light that the lens passes. At high *f*-numbers, the iris is more closed and less light passes through. As the ring is turned toward the lower numbers (*opening up*), the iris opens; conversely, as the ring is turned to the higher numbers (*stopping down* or *closing down*), the iris closes. For a lens set at *f*/4, for instance, opening up a stop would mean setting the lens at *f*/2.8 (which doubles the amount of light for exposure), and closing down two stops from *f*/4 would mean setting the lens at *f*/8. Remember, opening the lens three stops lets eight—not six—times more light in (each stop doubles the previous amount). See Fig. 7-14 for intermediate *f*-stops.

Lens manufacturers generally engrave the focal length, serial number, and speed of the lens (widest relative aperture) near the front element. The speed is sometimes written as a ratio; 1:1.4 would be an *f*/1.4 lens.

A standard technique for setting the iris is to open the lens wider than the *f*-stop you want, then stop down to the selected opening without passing it. This avoids any play in the iris that, in some lenses, can cause errors at the smaller apertures.

On some digital cameras, the iris is not adjusted on the lens itself but through controls in the camera. With certain cameras, the iris adjustment is made in discrete steps instead of continuously, which is a real disadvantage when making changes during a shot (adjustments are sudden, not smooth).

T-stops

Particularly when using a light meter to calculate exposure (either for film or digital), it's important to know how much light is *actually* passing through the lens to the film or sensor. The *f*-stop is a geometric relationship between focal length and aperture and doesn't take into account how much light is lost within a lens. Each air-to-glass surface within the lens reflects some light. A zoom lens may have more than fifteen elements and can lose a significant amount of light to internal scatter. A *T-stop* accounts for this loss (*T* is for "true" stop or "transmission"). A T-stop is defined as the equivalent to an *f*-stop of a perfect lens (a perfect lens transmits all the light it gathers with no internal losses). Thus, on a perfect lens, the *f*-stop and T-stop are identical. On a zoom lens that loses a full stop internally (that is, a 50 percent loss), setting the lens to *f*/8 would result in the same exposure as T11. Note that the T-stop is always a higher number than the *f*-stop.

Some cine lenses are calibrated in both *f*-stops and T-stops (sometimes the *f*-stop in white on one side of the iris diaphragm ring and the T-stop in red on the other side). Many lenses are marked only in T-stops; others only in *f*-stops. Be sure to check the lens you're using. With prime lenses, the difference between *f*-stops and T-stops is usually less than one-quarter stop—not enough to upset exposure calculations. With zoom lenses, the difference is usually greater. One zoom might have the widest aperture marked as *f*/2, but the T-stop could be T2.5, which means this lens loses two-thirds stop in transmission.

If the lens is marked with T-stops, use them to calculate film exposures even though the light meter is marked in *f*-numbers (see Chapter 7). For depth of field calculations (see below), use *f*-stops.

FOCUSING THE IMAGE

Depth of Field

On most lenses, you turn the lens barrel to focus. Many lenses have distance markings on them to aid accurate focusing. When shooting a portrait of a woman ten feet from the camera, you can set the focus mark on the lens barrel to 10 feet and she will be brought into sharp focus.

In an ideal (theoretical) lens, there is only one subject plane in focus—everything in front of or behind this plane is out of focus. In the case of the portrait, if the woman's eyes were exactly ten feet from the camera, her nose and ears would be out of focus. Fortunately, with real lenses the area that looks in focus is more generous. A zone (called the *depth of field*, or *DOF*) extends from in front of the subject to behind the subject, delineating the area of acceptable sharpness (see Fig. 4-9). In other words, the depth of field is the zone, measured in terms of near distance and far distance from the camera, where the image appears acceptably sharp.

Fig. 4-9. Depth of field. In both shots, the camera is focused on the girls. (top) This shot has enough depth of field so that the foreground and the background are both in focus. (bottom) This shot has shallower depth of field, and only the girls are in sharp focus. It's easier to create a shot with shallow DOF using a digital camera with a large sensor, or a film camera with a large film gauge like 35mm. See also Fig. 2-9. (Ned Johnston)

Depth of field is not an absolute. There is no clear demarcation between parts of the image that are sharp and those that are blurry and out of focus. Instead, there is a gradual transition between the two. Even the idea of "acceptable sharpness" is relative. It depends on many factors, including the digital or film format, the use of lens filters, and lighting. For more on how depth of field varies with different formats, see p. 72.

What "In Focus" Means

To understand depth of field, it helps to understand what being "in focus" or "out of focus" actually means. A point in the subject or scene is considered in *critical focus* when it registers as a point on video or film (see Fig. 4-10). All of the points in the subject that are in critical focus make up the *plane of critical focus* (also called the *plane of primary focus*). Any point that is nearer or farther from the camera than this plane registers as a circle instead of a point in the image. This circle is the *circle of confusion* (*CoC*).

When circles are sufficiently small or far enough away, they appear to the eye as points (you can check this by making a circle on a piece of paper and viewing it from a distance). The depth of field is determined by the region on either side of the plane of critical focus where points in the subject are circles so small that they appear to the viewer as points (and thus appear to be in sharp focus).

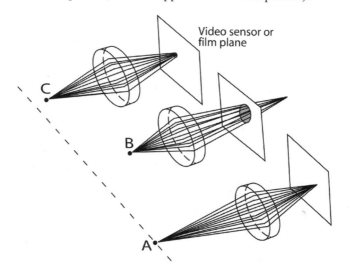

Video sensor or film plane

Fig. 4-10. Depth of field. All three lenses are focused at the dashed line. (bottom) Point A is on the line and the rays of light converge to a point at the video sensor. This is in sharp focus. (middle) Point B is closer to the lens so the rays of light form a circle (*circle of confusion*) where they hit the sensor. This is out of focus. (top) The rays of light from point C also form a circle, but it's small enough to appear as a point to the eye. This seems in focus to the viewer and thus C is within the depth of field. The same principle applies for a film camera; substitute the film for the sensor in the description above. (Steven Ascher)

We use depth of field to define what parts of the subject are acceptably sharp, but as noted above, "acceptable sharpness" depends on many things. In part, the eye perceives sharpness in a relative way. For example, if you shoot with a low-resolution format (or use a diffusion filter to soften the image), the apparent depth of field is greater since *nothing* is particularly sharp. High definition video formats tend to have less depth of field than standard definition formats because they are capable of producing a very sharp image.

One of the key considerations in focusing and depth of field is how much the

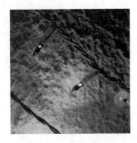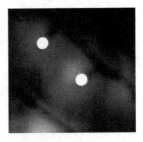

Fig. 4-11. In focus and out of focus. Point sources of light appear as circles when they're out of focus. The quality of the blurred image, which depends on the lens and its settings, is sometimes referred to as the boke or bokeh. A lens's boke is most noticeable around highlights and light sources. (Steven Ascher)

image is magnified (points start to look like circles when you enlarge them). Something that looks sharp on a small TV screen may look out of focus when the same image is projected on a large theater screen. Depth of field will seem smaller on the big screen.

In general, the more you magnify an image, the softer (less sharp) it looks (see Fig. 1-8).

Controlling Depth of Field

There are two ways to control depth of field: change the size an object appears in the image (*image reproduction ratio*) or change the *f*-stop.[4] The larger an object is reproduced, the less the depth of field. You can make an object appear larger by moving the camera closer and/or by using a longer focal length lens (if you're using a zoom lens, zoom in). You might want to decrease depth of field for a portrait in order to throw the background out of focus. You might want to increase depth of field for a large group portrait, in which case you move the camera farther away from the subject and/or use a wider-angle lens.

Stopping down the *f*-stop (using a smaller aperture) increases depth of field (see Fig. 4-12). The iris can be stopped down if you add light to the subject, increase video gain or ISO speed (see Chapter 3), or use a faster film (see Chapter 7). You can open the iris when there is less light on the subject, when you use a neutral density filter (see Chapter 8), when you increase shutter speed (see Chapters 3 and 6), or when you use a slower film.

To minimize depth of field, open the iris, move closer, or use a longer focal length lens. To increase depth of field, stop down, move farther away, or use a wide-angle lens (also see Split-Field Diopters, p. 171). Long focal length lenses at close focusing distances and with wide apertures (for example, at *f*/2) yield the least depth of field, whereas wide-angle lenses at far distances and stopped down (for example, at *f*/16) give maximum depth of field. A 25mm lens set at *f*/2 when focused at 4 feet has a total depth of field of 7 inches (about half a foot).[5] At *f*/11, total depth is 6 feet.

---

4. Some consumer or prosumer camcorders don't have *f*-stop markings on the iris, but adjusting the iris still means changing the *f*-stop.

5. With a $\frac{1}{1000}$-inch circle of confusion.

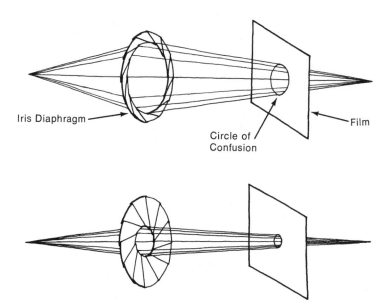

Fig. 4-12. Stopping down the lens increases depth of field. (top) Circle of confusion at wide aperture. (bottom) As the iris diaphragm closes, the diameter of the cone of light gets smaller and so the circle of confusion is smaller. (Carol Keller)

If the same lens were set at *f/2* but focused at 10 feet, total depth of field would be more than 5 feet. In other words, moving farther back, stopping down, or doing both increases depth of field dramatically.

It's true that wide-angle lenses have more depth of field than longer focal length lenses. However, at relatively close distances it's not as much as cinematographers tend to think. Say you're filming something nearby and you find you don't have enough depth of field to keep your subject in proper focus, so you consider going to a wider-angle lens and getting closer to the subject, with the goal of keeping the subject the same size in the frame. For example, you change from a 50mm lens at 10 feet to a 25mm at 5 feet. Will the wider-angle lens give you more depth of field? With these lenses, at close distances like this, the difference is negligible, and you will not improve the situation. However, for the zone *outside* the depth of field, the wider-angle lens will make the background less blurry than the longer focal length lens. For this reason, when cinematographers want to throw a background out of focus, they reach for their long focal length lenses.

Different lenses produce a different blurry look in areas that are out of focus. The Japanese term *boke* (pronounced and sometimes spelled "bokeh") is used to talk about the particular quality and amount of blurring, which can vary depending on lens design, iris shape and setting, and focal length. Some people feel that a lens iris with many blades—which produces a more circular aperture and therefore a smoother, more circular boke—is more pleasing (see Fig. 4-11).

Although depth of field increases as the iris is closed down, small iris openings don't produce the sharpest images because diffraction can cause an overall softening (see Lens Sharpness, p. 173).

Focusing the Lens

For feature films and other controlled filming situations with large crews, setting the lens focus is often done by measuring the camera-to-subject distance with a tape and then adjusting the lens using the distance markings on the lens barrel. For documentary or other uncontrolled shooting, focus setting is generally done by eye, looking through the viewfinder to determine proper focus. Some digital cameras have provisions for automatic focus control (see Setting the Focus, p. 113).

WHERE TO FOCUS. Focus is one of the creative aspects of image making. You can use focus to draw the viewer's attention where you want. However, if something important is out of focus, the viewer may feel annoyed or uncomfortable. Generally, when someone is speaking, he or she should be in focus, unless another person's reaction is more important. For close shots, a rule of thumb is to focus on the subject's eyes.

A properly constructed lens focuses on a plane perpendicular to the direction of the lens. For example, suppose you want to focus on a group of people for a portrait and want them as sharp as possible at 10 feet from the camera. Should they be lined up along the arc of a circle, so that they are all 10 feet from the lens? No, only the person directly on line with the lens should be 10 feet away. All the others should be in the same plane, perpendicular to the axis of the lens.

If you are focused on a subject, you will have roughly twice as much depth of field behind the subject as in front of it. Thus, if two objects are at different distances from the camera, focusing at a point halfway between them will not render the two objects equally sharp. Instead, a rule of thumb is to focus on a point one-third the distance from the closer to the farther object (see Fig. 4-13). If one object is at 10 feet and the other at 40 feet, the split focus distance is 20 feet (that is, 10 feet in front and 20 feet behind). This rule is not exact, and the proportion of the in-focus area that's in front of the focus point versus behind it varies with focal length and distance from the camera. For a shot in which the camera and/or the actors' movements are planned (blocked out), you should rehearse focus changes (*follow*

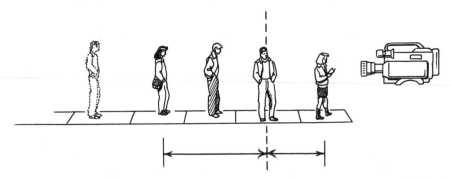

Fig. 4-13. Split focus. As a rule of thumb, depth of field extends roughly twice as far behind the plane at which the lens is focused as in front. (Robert Brun)

focus). A camera assistant or focus puller often changes (*pulls*) focus during the shot. Follow-focus devices (sometimes remotely controlled) are available to make it easier to pull focus and repeat moves precisely (see Figs. 4-15 and 1-3). Place tape or make chalk marks on the floor to cue the actors or the focus puller. Put tape on the lens distance scale and mark settings with a Sharpie for a homemade follow-focus device.

TAPE FOCUS. On some productions—dramas, for instance—and for some shots like product shots in commercials, an assistant measures critical distances for focusing with a 50-foot tape or electronic measuring device. Sometimes measurements are made to near and far points that must be kept in focus at the same time, in order to determine a distance setting that keeps everything sharp. If there is adequate depth of field, this split focus distance can be calculated and the focus set accordingly.

As a general rule for wide-angle lenses, tape focusing is often more accurate than eye focus. This is because it can be hard to discern fine degrees of focus in a small viewfinder when depth of field is so deep. When later shown on a big screen, however, the smallest degrees of focus will be terribly obvious.

In film cameras, the distance is measured from the film plane, which is marked on film cameras by an engraved Φ on the camera housing and sometimes also by a small knob on which you can conveniently

Fig. 4-14. Some cameras have a hook to attach a tape measure when doing tape focus. The Φ indicates the position of the sensor (or the film plane in a film camera). (Steven Ascher)

hook the end of the measuring tape. The focus scales on cine lenses are large and finely calibrated so that you can easily and accurately focus near or far.

Video lenses, particularly zooms, work somewhat differently. They are meant to be focused primarily by eye, so focus scales are smaller and less detailed. Their focus scales presume a focus measurement *from the front element of the lens*, not from the sensor's focal plane. This mostly makes a difference in focusing very close objects, in that if you tape-measure from the focal plane inside the camera body instead of the front surface of the lens, your focus will be off.

Similarly SLR and DSLR lenses are small with narrow barrels and comparatively crude focus markings. They also are meant to be focused by eye, not tape.

With the advent of digital cinema and video cameras with large sensors, particularly those that accept film-style PL-mount lenses, digital focusing principles have aligned with film-style practice, not video. The Sony NEX-FS100, for instance, is a video camcorder with a Super 35–sized sensor that features both an engraved Φ to mark the focal plane on the camera body and also a steel pin on which to hook a measuring tape (see Fig. 4-14). If you use a film-style PL-mount lens on a DSLR by means of an adapter, you will want to measure focus from the sensor's focal plane.

Tape focus doesn't work, of course, if your lens doesn't have distance markings, and the lens must be properly collimated for the focusing scale to be accurate (see Depth of Focus, p. 180).

FOCUS IN THE VIEWFINDER. In many shooting situations, focusing by eye through the viewfinder is preferable to tape focus. With small crews or when the action is uncontrolled, it may be impossible to use a tape. Eye focus is often faster and usually more accurate with long focal length lenses or in other situations where depth of field is shallow.

Be sure the viewfinder's diopter is adjusted properly to your vision before focusing either a video camera (see Chapter 3) or a film camera (see Chapter 6). To focus the camera lens, rotate the focus ring or other focus control until the subject is brought into sharpest focus. If the camera is not running, "go through" focus once or twice—that is, rotate the focus ring past the point where the image is sharpest, stop, and then rotate back to the point of sharpest focus.

Professional camcorders also allow you to enhance the detail in the viewfinder (often called "peaking"), or to magnify portions of it, which can be a big help in seeing focus (see p. 107). You may also want to use the camera's autofocus to find focus (but don't leave it on auto; see p. 113).

To see the image pop in and out of focus better, it always helps to focus a lens at the widest aperture. With video camcorders, you can use built-in ND filters for focusing (before you then stop down to the proper *f*-stop for the actual shot).

Fig. 4-15. The follow-focus device has a geared wheel that engages a toothed ring on the lens. If the lens has no gear ring, or the teeth are the wrong size, a ring can usually be added. Also see Fig. 1-3. (Zacuto USA)

When focusing a film or video zoom lens, remember that depth of field will be minimized at the longest focal length (zoomed in). To focus a film or video zoom lens, zoom all the way in, set focus, then zoom out to whatever focal length you like. (If, instead, you were to focus first at a wider focal length—where depth of field is greater—the subject will usually go out of focus when you zoom in.) While shooting, if the image is sharp at wide angle but goes out of focus when zoomed in, it probably means you didn't focus at the longest focal length as you should have. If the image becomes seriously out of focus when zooming out from long focal length to wide angle, it may mean the lens is not properly seated (see The Lens Mount, p. 176).

Note that when the subject is too close to the camera, closer than the zoom's *minimum object distance* (*MOD*), this method doesn't work, because when you zoom in, focus is not achievable. (See Minimum Focus Distance, p. 166.)

Focusing a zoom lens made for an SLR or DSLR is somewhat different and more difficult than with film or video zooms because these zooms don't necessarily maintain exact focus through their zoom range while being zoomed.[6] Why? Because they're designed for taking still photos (a still photographer using a zoom adjusts the framing of a shot before focusing and clicking the shutter, refocusing for each shot either manually or using autofocus). Therefore when using SLR or DSLR zooms, it's always a good idea to check and recheck focus by eye whenever focal length has changed. Using image magnification in the viewfinder is ideal for this.

When pulling focus during a shot, you obviously shouldn't do too much "going through" focus as described above. If an unrehearsed focus pull must be done while the camera is rolling, documentary filmmakers often zoom in quickly, refocus, and zoom back to the new selected focal length. This "focusing zoom" is generally edited out. With some video cameras and digitally controlled zooms, you can preprogram zoom and focus and exposure settings and have the camera automatically transition from one to the other for very fluid moves, including very slow moves that are hard to do manually. (Sony calls this camcorder feature Shot Transition.)

Whenever you're shooting, always have a general idea of how much depth of field you're working with. For example, if you're using a wide-angle lens stopped down to a high *f*-number, you know you have a lot of depth of field, so focusing is less critical. Using the hyperfocal distance (see below) can help you estimate when refocusing is necessary.

Because of the increased sharpness of HD compared to SD, focus is particularly critical when shooting HD. When shooting with digital cameras, focus and depth of field can be judged in the viewfinder or monitor (and a large, sharp monitor can help a lot). When using film cameras, some viewfinders provide a better sense of focus and depth of field than others (see p. 258). In general, any small video or film viewfinder image tends to exaggerate depth of field. If something looks out of focus in the viewfinder, it will be out of focus when recorded on film or video. But a sharp viewfinder image is not a guarantee that the picture will look sharp on screen.

---

6. Lenses that shift focus as the zoom (magnification) changes are called *varifocal lenses*. Most true video and film lenses hold focus across the zoom range and are *parfocal lenses*.

Depth of Field Charts

Depth of field charts and calculators give an estimate of the depth of field. For a given focal length lens, you cross-reference the distance the lens is focused at, the lens aperture (*f*-stop), and the circle of confusion (CoC) to find the near and far extent of depth of field. You can also get depth of field apps for mobile devices (DOFMaster and pCAM are popular), and some lenses have rough depth of field guides engraved opposite the *f*-stop ring. Remember to use only *f*-stops, not T-stops, in depth of field calculations.

Charts and calculators are designed for a "generic" reading of depth of field. In practice, the performance of your lens, the exact size of your film format or video sensor, and the amount of enlargement upon viewing can result in actual depth of field that is as much as 15 to 20 percent different, possibly throwing off readings at close focusing distances. So don't think of depth of field—or DOF charts—as an absolute. Think of DOF charts and apps as useful guides that are necessary but not infallible.

To provide a reference point for sharpness, a permissible *maximum* circle of confusion is chosen for different formats (sometimes called the *circle of least confusion*). To use a depth of field chart, you need to choose what circle of confusion you want to work with. For example, the 1986 edition of the *American Cinematographer Manual* recommends a 0.025mm (0.001 inch) permissible circle of confusion for 35mm film and a 0.015mm (0.0006 inch) CoC for 16mm.

For a chart and more on circle of confusion, see Appendix C.

The Hyperfocal Distance

For any lens at a particular focal length and *f*-stop, the closest distance setting such that the far limit of depth of field extends to infinity is called the *hyperfocal distance* (see Appendix D). When the lens is set at the hyperfocal distance, depth of field extends from half that distance to infinity (infinity may be written ∞ on lenses and charts). For example, a 25mm lens at *f*/8 has a hyperfocal distance of 10 feet.[7] When the lens is focused at 10 feet, the depth of field extends from 5 feet to infinity. The hyperfocal distance is also the near limit of depth of field when the lens is focused at infinity.

The hyperfocal distance setting is quite handy when focusing is difficult. If you set the lens at the hyperfocal distance, you don't need to worry about focus unless the subject comes closer than one-half the hyperfocal distance. Of course, the remarks about depth of field not being an absolute apply here as well, and to use the hyperfocal distance chart you must choose an appropriate circle of confusion for your work.

Some very wide-angle lenses (and some very cheap lenses) have no provisions for focusing. These lenses are usually prefocused at the hyperfocal distance of the widest aperture. Consult the manufacturer's data sheet to find the closest focusing distances at the various *f*-stops.

---

7. Based on a 1/1000-inch circle of confusion.

CHOOSING A ZOOM LENS

The *zoom lens* offers a continuous range of focal lengths in one lens. Focal length may be smoothly adjusted during a shot (*zooming*) or between shots. Zoom lenses are optically and mechanically more complex than fixed focal length (prime) lenses. Because of this, they are larger, heavier, more delicate, and more prone to flare and distortion compared to primes. On the other hand, today's zoom designs have improved to the point that some high-quality zoom lenses are virtually as sharp as primes. This section is about choices in zoom lenses. For techniques of shooting with zooms, see p. 330.

In documentary, regardless of digital or film capture, the zoom reigns supreme. It is usually the only lens used on a production, so the choice of which one you use is critical. Whatever type of shoot you are considering, when selecting a zoom lens (or camera/zoom combination) there are various criteria to take into account.

Zoom Range

Zoom lenses vary widely in their range of focal lengths. By convention, zooms designed for film are typically designated by their zoom range (for example, 10–100mm), while zooms designed for video are designated by their widest focal length times a magnification factor (for example, 10 x 9.5, which is the same as 9.5–95mm).

Because the angle of view afforded by any particular focal length lens depends on the video or film format you're shooting, you need to know which sensor size or film gauge your camera has in order to evaluate what the range of focal lengths really means visually (see Focal Length and Format, p. 148). Often the manufacturer of a lens will list its focal lengths in terms of the full-frame 35mm SLR/DSLR equivalents.

Having a good wide-angle lens can make a big difference in many shooting situations, particularly in documentary work or whenever you're shooting in close quarters or want to capture wide vistas or deep-focus shots. To take the example of a 16mm film camera or digital camera with a ⅔-inch sensor (similar in size to 16mm), having a lens that zooms out to under 9mm opens up a whole range of possible shots (and ways that the camera can interact with the film subjects) that can't be done if your lens reaches only 10mm or 12mm. Shooting people in cars or around a dinner table often requires a really wide lens (even 5.5mm or 6mm can be helpful). A difference of a couple of millimeters at long focal

Fig. 4-16. Video-style zoom lenses like this that have an attached zoom motor and a built-in 2x range extender are often used with ⅔-inch or ½-inch chip video cameras that accept detachable lenses. (Fujinon, Inc.)

Fig. 4-17. Cine-style zooms (also called cinema-or film-style zooms) typically offer manual zoom, focus, and iris control, and have large geared teeth to accept an external zoom motor and/or a follow-focus device if desired. (Fujinon, Inc.)

lengths is trivial, but at short focal lengths it is very noticeable (a 9.5mm lens is about 25 percent wider than a 12mm). Many lower-end digital cameras with small sensors are really deficient in the short focal lengths and need to be used with a wide-angle adapter (see below).

Long focal lengths allow you to capture small details in the landscape or create shots with highly compressed perspective. Shooting at long focal lengths requires that the camera be very steady on a tripod (see Telephoto Lenses, p. 169). Having both long and short focal lengths in one lens gives you tremendous flexibility and allows for extreme zoom shots that range from a tight close-up to a distant, wide view in one shot. Some video cameras have a *digital zoom* feature that magnifies the image beyond the range of what the lens does optically. This is like enlarging the pixels using a digital video effect. It lowers the resolution and should generally be avoided.

CHANGING THE ZOOM RANGE. Some zoom lenses can be fitted with a wide-angle attachment over the front element to convert to a zoom range of shorter

Fig. 4-18. Zooms designed for SLR or DSLR still cameras usually provide autofocus and auto-iris control through the camera (depending on the lens/camera combination). Manual overrides may be available, but the lens itself may have no manual iris control. Zooming is done manually. Some lens/camera combinations offer image stabilization. Often there are no distance markings on the lens for focus. (Nikon, Inc.)

focal lengths. For example, a 0.8x wide-angle converter could be used with a 12–120mm zoom to make it 9.6–96mm. As a rule, these "zoom-through" attachments don't affect aperture or focus settings and may not significantly impair the image. Converters that do not maintain focus through the zoom range—you have to refocus each time you adjust focal length—are lighter, more compact, and less expensive, but much less useful.

Rear-mounted lens attachments, such as *range extenders*, change the relative aperture and reduce the speed of the lens. For example, a 2x range extender converts a 12–120mm zoom range to a 24–240mm one and changes an $f/2.2$ aperture to an $f/4.4$. Aberrations are also magnified and may make the image unacceptable. Stopping down does minimize most of the aberrations, but stopping down to $f/8$ is the equivalent of $f/16$ when using a 2x extender.

Many pro video zooms of the type used in newsgathering have a built-in 1.5x or 2x range extender that can be set by switching a lever (see Fig. 4-16). Doing so provides longer focal lengths, but sacrifices some image quality and lens speed. Front-mounted range extenders don't change relative aperture, but sometimes they vignette at the shorter focal lengths. Range extenders are also used with prime lenses.

Fig. 4-19. Century Double Aspheric 0.6x wide-angle adapter mounts on the front of the lens. With this adapter you can't zoom during shots, but other Century adapters do permit full zooming. (Fletcher Chicago/Schneider Optics)

Zoom Lens Speed

The widest-aperture f-stop and T-stop are an important part of zoom lens designations. Faster lenses allow you to shoot in lower light. (Using very wide apertures limits depth of field and lens sharpness; see Depth of Field, p. 153, and Lens Sharpness, p. 173.)

The Angenieux Optimo $f/2.6$, 16–42mm T2.8 designation tells us this lens is *f*/2.6 at its widest aperture. Its equivalent T-stop is T2.8 (it loses less than one-third of a stop); thus, it is a relatively fast zoom lens with a limited zoom range of 16–44mm (2.7 x 16 tells us its magnification factor is only 2.7).

In order to claim higher speeds, some zoom lenses are designated with a fast aperture that is maintained only at wide angle. As you zoom in with the iris wide open, these lenses lose or *ramp* f-stop, which causes the image to darken. For example, the Fujinon 20 x 6.4 zoom (6.4–128mm) is a very fast *f*/1.4 from 6.4mm to 90mm but ramps to *f*/2 at 128mm. This means that if you were to shoot wide open at *f*/1.4 at 50mm and then zoom to 128mm, you'd lose a full stop of light at the long focal length. Generally, it's undesirable to zoom across a range that loses more than one-third of a stop. When this lens is stopped down to *f*/2, the f-stop is constant across the zoom range and there are no problems. Some lenses have special detents on the T-stop ring that prevent zooming at focal lengths that will change the f-stop.

Minimum Focus Distance

Being able to focus on a subject that's close to the camera can have a big impact on your shooting style. There are many situations where you want to get in very close to the subject; a common one is shooting the driver of a car from the passenger seat. The need to get close is particularly an issue in documentary work, where the relative position of camera and subject is often not under your control. The minimum object distance (MOD) is the closest an object can be to the lens and be in focus. Some zooms focus down to 2 feet, some even down to their front element. Others focus only to 6 feet or more and need close-up diopters or must be switched into macro mode for close focusing (see p. 170 for more on these items). To give you greater flexibility in shooting, ideally a zoom should focus to around a couple of feet or less with no additional attachments or adjustments.

Front Element and Barrel

The diameter of the front element of the zoom affects what size filters, lens shade, or matte box you can use (see Chapter 8). Particularly when you're using more than one lens, it helps if both lenses accept the same size attachments (you may need adapter rings).

On some zooms, the entire front part of the lens barrel rotates for focusing and moves in and out depending upon the focusing distance. The front element can crash into a matte box or filter if they are not mounted with adequate separation from the lens.

On other zooms, called "internal focusing," the outermost part of the front of the lens remains fixed, which is important when mounting polarizing or graduated filters that should not be rotated once they are positioned. If you are using a matte box, this is not an issue (see Chapter 8). Most cine zooms today are internal focusing. Many video zooms are not.

There are differences between cine-style zooms, video zooms, and zooms designed for still cameras in terms of handling. The focus ring may turn in different directions, which is irritating when you're used to one style of lens. The same holds true for the iris ring (if there is one—many autofocusing still zoom lenses don't have them). 35mm-style cine zooms are designed with wide barrels, and focus rings that rotate through a wide swing with large, evenly spaced focus marks for fine, critical focusing. Video zooms tend to be narrow-barreled for light weight, and electronic still zooms sometimes have no markings at all besides focal length. Gear teeth for focusing or zooming are spaced differently on film and video zooms, which is a concern when using external follow-focus devices or motors. Some video and still zooms can be modified by attaching rubber rings with cine-style teeth.

DSLRs, Four Thirds, and Super 35 digital camcorders have opened the flood-gates to use of zooms designed for still cameras, and it would take an entire chapter to explore this subject adequately. Suffice it to say that zoom lenses for DSLRs are designed for both the professional and advanced consumer markets. Having a broad market helps keep prices down; however, these lenses often lack capabilities cinema-tographers rely on. As noted on p. 161, a still photography zoom may not hold perfect focus through its zoom range. Another issue is that certain still photography zooms extend in length when zooming. Their front section literally telescopes out-ward, sometimes almost doubling their length, making matte boxes and mounting rods useless. In documentary situations, this makes it quite obvious to your subjects when you're zooming in on them, which is usually not what you want.

Fig. 4-20. Extreme wide angle shot taken with Century 0.55x Super Fisheye adapter. Note barrel distortion causing trees to appear curved. (Fletcher Chicago/Schneider Optics)

Zoom Lens Problems

Some zooms, notably those with front focusing elements that turn, change image magnification noticeably when you rack (pull) focus. The effect is called *focus breathing* or *pumping*, and you can see it through the viewfinder. This is more com-mon with video and still lenses than cine lenses. Avoid these lenses if you can.

Check zoom lenses for vignetting with the lens wide open, at the shortest focal length and the distance scale at infinity (see Chapter 8). The lens shade or matte box should also be checked with the lens set at the closest focusing distance.

Before you use a mechanical zoom lens, it's a good idea to zoom back and forth several times to distribute the lubrication in the mechanism. Some manual lenses have "zoom creep"—the lens zooms by itself, sometimes due to the effect of gravity on internal elements. In this case, bring the lens to a technician for repair, but a temporary solution is to fit a wide rubber band, not too loose or too tight, around the zoom ring and barrel to create a little friction.

Zoom lenses, due to their optical complexity, often have less depth of field than primes of equivalent focal length, which can be an issue at close focusing distances.

PRIME LENSES

Fast Lenses

Due to their fewer elements, prime lenses in general are faster than zoom lenses. For low-light shooting, there are even "high-speed" primes optimized for shooting at their widest aperture. For ⅔-inch HD cameras, for example, nothing tops Zeiss DigiPrime lenses, which are mostly T1.6 (about a third of a stop slower than *f*/1.4) and come in several focal lengths, including an extremely wide 3.9mm. Though not inexpensive, DigiPrimes are true "diffraction-limited" lenses—sharpest when they're wide open.

Depth of field at common camera-to-subject distances can be very shallow when using fast lenses at full aperture. As a result, focusing can be difficult. One solution when shooting at night is to use wide-angle high-speed primes, because of the great depth of field of wide-angle lenses at common filming distances.

Fig. 4-21. Canon 85mm cinema prime lens, T1.3, EF mount. Cine-style lenses usually have wide barrels and focus rings with clear, well-spaced marks for focusing. Note the large-sized teeth on the focus ring. (Canon U.S.A., Inc.)

Telephoto Lenses

Telephoto lenses (also called *tele-lenses*) are, loosely speaking, about 50 percent longer-than-normal lenses for the format; for example, a lens greater than about 12mm for a ⅓-inch sensor camera or greater than about 70mm for a camera with a Super 35 sensor would be considered telephoto.

Telephoto lenses render the subject large even at great distances, providing extreme compression of perspective. The camera crew can be unobtrusive and can work a safe distance from dangerous events. Since they have little depth of field, telephotos are useful for throwing a distracting background out of focus or doing a dramatic focus pull.

You can simulate a moving camera shot by using a telephoto to track a subject moving laterally to the lens (that is, pan with the subject from far away). The tracking pan keeps the subject's size constant in the frame and makes it appear that the camera is dollying. Akira Kurosawa often used these tracking pans in his samurai movies to simulate the movement through space usually achieved with a dolly—the longer the focal length, the more sustained the effect.

Telephotos are extremely vulnerable to camera vibration. A camera may function perfectly well with shorter focal lengths but reveal vibrations with a 300mm lens. You should use a lens support or cradle with long telephotos to minimize vibration and to avoid straining the lens mount; use a very steady tripod and do not hand-hold the camera (but see Image Stabilization Devices, p. 387). Heat waves often show up in landscape telephoto shots, which can be avoided by shooting in the morning before the ground has heated up. Distant scenes may be overexposed due to atmospheric haze; use a haze filter and stop the lens down one-half to one full stop. Tele-extenders may be used to increase focal length, but keep in mind the limitations discussed in Changing the Zoom Range, p. 164.

Fig. 4-22. Panavision Primo prime lens family. (Panavision)

CLOSE FOCUSING

Some zoom lenses focus no closer than 3 feet from the subject. Prime lenses usually focus closer. Specialized *macro lenses* allow you to bring very close objects into focus. Often macro lenses can yield an image reproduction ratio of 1:1, that is, the image size is the same as the subject size—a thumbtack would fill the frame. Many video lenses have a built-in macro mechanism, which allows for close focusing but may cause the focus to shift while zooming.

Many lenses can be extended farther from the film plane by the use of *extension bellows* or *extension tubes*. Bellows permit a wider range of focusing distances and greater magnification and are faster to adjust than tubes. Extension tubes and bellows work best with normal or slightly long focal length lenses. If they are used with a zoom lens, the zoom will not remain in focus across its range, and the results are often not sharp. You may need to increase exposure to compensate for light loss, and lighting can be a challenge at very close distances.

Close-Up Diopters

Close-up diopters or *plus diopters* are supplementary lenses screwed into the front of a lens like a filter. Also called *Proxars* (actually a brand name), these permit closer focusing with all lenses and require no exposure compensation. They are simple lenses with a single thin element, like a magnifying glass.

Diopters come in varying strengths (+½, +1, +2, etc.). They are intended to be used on a lens that has been focused to infinity. When the host lens is focused to infinity, the diopter will bring an image into focus at a distance in meters equal to the reciprocal of its diopter number. A +½ diopter, for instance, will bring an image into focus at a distance of 2 meters. A +1 diopter will focus an image at 1 meter. A +2 diopter will focus an image at ½ meter. The higher the number of a plus diopter, the closer you can focus.

As the diopter power increases, however, the quality of the image deteriorates. It's better to use a longer focal length lens with a less powerful diopter than a shorter focal length with a more powerful diopter. For best results, close down the lens a few stops to curtail aberrations.

You can also use a close-up diopter on a lens that is not focused to infinity, but the focus scale on the lens will not be accurate, nor will the diopter cause the lens to focus at a reciprocal of its diopter strength. You'll have to experiment and focus by eye through the viewfinder.

If the diopter has a flat side and a convex side, usually the convex (curved) side of the diopter should face the subject. If an arrow is marked on the diopter mount, face it toward the subject. Diopters may be combined to increase power. Place the higher-power diopter closer to the lens, and make sure the glass surfaces of the diopters don't touch. A +2 diopter combined with a +3 diopter has the same power as a +5 diopter. If you're going to stack diopters, it's a good idea to obtain diopters with antireflective coatings to protect image contrast. They cost more than uncoated diopters, but they're worth it.

Split-Field Diopters

Split-field diopters are usually half clear glass and half close-up diopter. These diopters allow half the frame to be focused on far distances and half to be focused at close distances. Frame the distant objects through the clear glass, the close ones through the plus diopter. The area between the two parts of the diopter will be out of focus and, for the shot to be successful, should be an indeterminate field. Carefully compose the shot on a tripod. If the diopter is used in a matte box, it may be positioned so that an area greater or less than half the frame is covered by the plus diopter.

LENS QUALITY AND CONDITION

At the start of production on a feature film, lens tests were traditionally shot on film, printed, and projected to ensure that the lenses being used were sharp, working properly, and well matched to one another. Today with many feature films shot digitally, procedures have changed. It's easy to place the lenses in question on the digital cinema camera to be used, then scrutinize their performance directly on a high-resolution monitor or project the picture onto a large screen.

Lens testing at rental facilities is available to all productions, large and small, usually for free.

Many rental facilities make available lens test projectors that throw a super-high-resolution test chart backward through the lens and onto a screen. Any aberration or mechanical flaw in the lens can be seen immediately, even by a nontechnician. Lens test projectors are invaluable for testing any type of lens, prime or zoom, video or film, even DSLR.

Even expensive lenses vary in quality, which can be readily seen on a lens test projector. When you purchase a costly lens, if possible examine it first on a lens test projector with a technician on hand to answer any questions. Small bubbles, which are often visible in a lens element, usually do not affect quality. Small surface scratches on used lenses do not affect performance unless they are fairly numerous, in which case they lower image contrast. A chip in a lens element can severely impair the image by scattering light. All the parts of a lens should move smoothly, and nothing should rattle when you shake the lens. There should be no play in the iris diaphragm.

Zooms for standard definition video cameras were generally made to lower standards than cine lenses for film cameras. Since then, HD video cameras have placed significantly higher demands on lens design because of the need for four to five times the resolution of SD on the same-sized sensor. This is why it is not a good idea to attach a standard definition zoom to an HD camera, even if it fits the camera.

High-quality, professional HD lenses often cost as much if not more than the camera, and this is not going to change. There is no lens equivalent to Moore's Law, by which computer processors increase in power while decreasing in cost every couple of years. If anything, the trend is in the opposite direction, as demand for optical performance rises and lens costs skyrocket. For better or worse, with lenses you get what you pay for. For this reason, DSLR lenses may seem like an extreme

Fig. 4-23. Tilt-focus or *perspective control* (*PC*) lens. Tilt-shift lenses are sometimes used when shooting architecture to adjust perspective lines that appear to recede too fast. By tilting the lens axis, you can position the plane of focus at an angle to the camera instead of perpendicular to it. Tilting, shifting, and/or rotating the plane of focus allow you to bring an angled subject into even focus or create an out-of-focus effect (see Fig. 4-21). (Nikon, Inc.)

bargain compared to cine lenses, but cine lenses have advantages that become apparent in the intensity of production. Even if the optics are superior, it's very difficult to accurately focus-pull a DSLR lens—which is why a cottage industry exists of rebarreling the best DSLR optics into slightly more expensive lenses that can pass muster on a film set. Zeiss Compact Primes are a good example of DSLR lenses adapted to digital cinema use, in this case, by the manufacturers themselves.

LENS ABERRATIONS. Centuries before the invention of lenses, painters used a *camera obscura* (literally, "dark room"), which is a dark room with a small hole in one wall that looks out onto an exterior landscape. The landscape is

Fig. 4-24. With a tilt-focus lens, the in-focus part of the image can be manipulated to create interesting effects. The lens sometimes makes real-world scenes look like miniatures. This effect can also be simulated in post for footage shot normally.

projected on the opposite wall, flipped and upside down. Reduced in size, this concept is the *pinhole* (lensless) *camera*. Using a lens in a camera increases brightness and sharpness, but introduces aberrations in the image. Lens aberrations are distortions in the formation of the two-dimensional image by the lens. Common aberrations include *spherical aberration* (rays enter the outer edges of the lens and focus at different points than rays close to the lens axis, creating subtle ghosting and loss of contrast); *chromatic aberration* (rays of different colors bend at different angles, adding a color fringe to image detail and decreasing sharpness); *curvature of field* (if the lens is perpendicular to a wall, either the edges or the center of the frame will be sharp but not both); and *astigmatism* (vertical lines focus in a different plane than horizontal lines). *Geometric distortions* are most apparent when a grid is photographed. *Barrel distortion* causes the grid lines to bow away from the center; *pincushion distortion* will make them appear bowed in.

Nearly all aberrations, except geometric distortion, are most apparent when the lens iris is wide open or nearly so, and they limit lens sharpness. As the iris is stopped down, the effect of the aberrations becomes less pronounced as the iris blocks those rays bent at the outer edges of the lens. Some professional digital video cameras have a menu option to electronically correct for chromatic aberration when certain zooms are used.

VIGNETTING. *Vignetting* is an optical phenomenon in which less light reaches the edge of the image than the center. Vignetting, in the loose sense, refers to any darkening toward the edges of the frame. This often occurs when lenses from a smaller format are used in a larger format (for example, some still lenses designed for an APS-C sensor may vignette when mounted on a camera with a full-frame 35 sensor). Vignetting is most apparent when the lens is wide open and the distance scale is set at infinity (and, in the case of zoom lenses, at the widest angle). If a lens shade or matte box cuts off picture area, it too is said to "vignette."

LENS SHARPNESS. Defining lens sharpness presents the same problems as defining digital and film sharpness, which are discussed in Chapters 5 and 7. Resolution, contrast, acutance, and modulation transfer function (MTF) are all terms related to lens sharpness (see p. 233).

Diffraction occurs when light passing through a small hole bends around the edges of the hole and scatters, rendering the image less sharp. When an iris diameter is sufficiently large, as in the case of an $f/1.4$ aperture in any of the formats popular in film or digital cameras, diffraction is of little concern. However, as you close down the aperture, and the size of the hole becomes very small, the softening effect of diffraction becomes more noticeable. At which f-stop this effect takes place depends on the focal length. While long focal length lenses may stop down to $f/32$ without problems, some wide-angle lenses will only close down to $f/11$ to prevent loss of sharpness at the smallest openings.

The reason for this can be seen in the formula for f-stops on p. 151. Another way of stating the formula is that the diameter of the iris opening equals the focal length divided by the f-number. So for any given f-number, the shorter the focal length of your lens, the smaller the physical hole in the iris for the light to pass through. At $f/8$, the iris diameter of a 60mm lens is 7.5mm, while that of a 6mm lens is 0.75mm.

Because of this relationship, the effect of diffraction depends in part on what digital or film format you're shooting. As explained in Focal Length and Format (p. 148), the larger the sensor or film format, the longer focal length lenses you'll typically be using. As a result, diffraction becomes less of a problem the larger your sensor size. With 35mm or Super 35 cameras, digital or film, even $f/16$ or $f/22$ is typically usable. However, when using a camera with a ¼-inch or ⅓-inch sensor, closing the iris beyond $f/8$ may noticeably soften the image. With 16mm or ⅔-inch video cameras, $f/8$ is usable, although it's advisable to avoid $f/11$ or smaller.

In lens design, diffraction is the only true limit to perfection. In fact, an ideal lens design is called *diffraction-limited*, meaning that it is free of aberrations and limited in performance only by the physics of diffraction.

Traditionally it's been said that lenses are sharpest when stopped down two to three stops from their widest aperture. That's because optical aberrations that degrade the image are most evident at the widest apertures, and stopping down a couple of stops masks the most visible effects of these aberrations. The best lenses, however, are those *designed* to be used at their widest aperture, like $f/1.4$ or $f/2$. That's because these are diffraction-limited designs, which are never the cheapest.

Because lens sharpness is limited at the wide apertures by aberrations and at the very smallest apertures by diffraction, you should try to shoot at middle apertures when using a lens you are concerned about or unfamiliar with. (Exceptions to this prudent practice are ⅓-inch and ¼-inch sensor cameras, which if in good condition are optically sharpest at their widest apertures due to diffraction.) To avoid shooting at the smallest apertures, use a neutral density filter (or a slower film stock) so you can open the iris a few stops. Some people think there is a contradiction in the idea that sharpness decreases at small f-stops while depth of field increases. Sharpness, however, refers to how clear the image can be, whereas depth of field tells us the relative sharpness of objects at different distances from the camera.

To get the most out of a sharp lens, you need to use a high-resolution digital format or a sharp film stock. However, particularly in video, a sharp lens can often vastly improve the look of a format that is lower resolution than the lens (cheap lenses make any format look bad). By the same token, HD cameras require very sharp (and expensive) lenses to capture the resolution they are capable of. As you can imagine, much of lens evaluation is subjective. The cinematographer may just like the look of a particular lens or favor a lens and format combination. In small-format digital and film cameras the tendency is to maximize image sharpness, but in larger formats that can achieve great sharpness, many cinematographers prefer a softer, more diffuse image.

FLARE. Lenses are made of multiple glass elements. The more elements, the more reflections take place within the lens, which can create a wash of light that adds exposure to the image and lowers contrast. Zoom lenses are particularly vulnerable. This is particularly noticeable when a light source is in the image; for example, when someone is standing in front of a bright window. This type of *flare* diffuses the image, lightens the blacks, increases the appearance of grain, decreases sharpness, and often softens the edges of backlit figures.

Nearly all modern lenses have multiple antireflective coatings on their elements

Fig. 4-25. *Vivre sa vie* (*My Life to Live*), Godard's 1962 film. Anna Karina is backlit with window light. Note how the extensive flare obscures the border between her hair and the window. (Corinth)

to suppress internal reflections. One rule of thumb for checking coatings is that the more colors you can see reflected in the front elements of the lens, the more efficient the coating will be.

The front element of a lens often picks up stray light from bright objects or other light sources even when the light source is not in the frame. This may cause flare and internal reflections of the iris diaphragm to appear in the image as bright spots in the shape of the iris opening. If the front element of the lens is viewed from in front of the camera and you can see reflections from light sources, there will be some flare in the image. The solution is to use a deeper lens shade or matte box or to flag the light source (see Chapter 12). Since flare adds exposure to the film, it sometimes affects the exposure calculation (see Chapter 7).

Flare is generally considered a phenomenon that deteriorates the quality of the image, a form of system noise. On the other hand, you may like the effects of flare. It was considered an artistic breakthrough when Jean-Luc Godard's cameraman, Raoul Coutard, in the early 1960s, pointed the camera lens into large café windows in interior shots and "degraded the image with flare" (see Fig. 4-25).

THE LENS MOUNT

Most professional cameras accept interchangeable lenses. The *lens mount* is the system that allows the lens to be attached to a camera. There are lens mounting systems that require a lens to be screwed in by threads (C mount), inserted and locked with a twist like a bayonet (SLRs, DSLRs, Sony E-mount, ARRI bayonet), or clamped down by a locking ring (ARRI PL, Aaton, Panavision, Sony F3, or B4 mount for ⅔-inch video cameras).

In addition to a locking mechanism, all lens mount systems provide ultraprecise surfaces for the camera and lens to meet, plus a standard *flange focal distance* measured from the surface where the camera and lens meet to the focal plane of the sensor or film emulsion. This distance, sometimes called the *register* or *flange back distance*, must be precisely set and maintained in order for focusing marks to be accurate. (For more, see below.)

Many lens mounts accept adapters to other lens mount systems in order to join otherwise incompatible lenses and cameras. If a camera's lens mount has a relatively shallow flange focal distance, such as the Micro Four Thirds mount, it may be able to accommodate—using an adapter—a wide range of lenses with mounts designed for greater flange focal distance. But if the camera's mount has a relatively large flange focal distance, you can't really use lenses that have mounts designed for less depth.

Another concern is that the lens needs to project a large enough image to cover the sensor or film area of the format you're using (see Fig. 4-7). For example, a lens designed for a small-sensor camera may not work with a camera that has a larger sensor, or it may show darkening (vignetting) or softening around the edges of the frame.

Consumer camcorders have permanently mounted zoom lenses. This prohibits the use of other lenses but eliminates the possibility of lens mounting errors.

Whenever changing lenses or using lens adapters, be sure the lens is properly seated before shooting. *Collimation* is a professional technique for checking camera flange focal distance and the seating of the lens in film and digital cinema cameras (see p. 180).

Mounts for Film Cameras

The *C mount* was at one time the most common 16mm lens mount. It is a simple screw mount, an inch in diameter, that is not particularly strong and therefore not ideal for zooms or heavy lenses. There are adapters to fit lenses from virtually any other type of mounting system, including ARRI PL, onto a camera that accepts C mounts, but you cannot adapt a C-mount lens to a modern 16mm film camera with a spinning mirror, for example, an Arriflex or Aaton.

The Bolex RX mount is a variant of the C mount. It has the same dimensions as an ordinary C mount and looks the same, but it has a longer flange focal distance to accommodate the change in back focus created by the behind-the-lens viewfinder prism in the Bolex H16 and later reflex models. Lenses intended for an RX mount should be used only on these reflex Bolexes and not on other C-mount cameras. (All RX lenses have "RX" inscribed on the barrel. If you have a C-mount lens that is not marked RX, it isn't.)

Arriflex 16mm and 35mm lens mounts have evolved over decades. The original *standard* mount from the 1930s was replaced by the *bayonet* ("Arri bayo") in the 1960s, which was replaced by the modern *PL (positive lock)* mount in the 1980s. With adapters, the earlier mounts can be used on PL-equipped cameras, but PL lenses

Fig. 4-26. Panasonic Lumix GH1 with PL to Micro Four Thirds lens adapter. Allows use of PL-mount lenses on some Olympus and Panasonic cameras, including the AF100. (MTF Services, Ltd.)

will not fit on cameras equipped with the earlier mounts. With the advent of digital cinema cameras with Super 35–sized sensors, the ARRI PL mount has exploded in popularity. In addition to digital cinema cameras from ARRI, the PL mount is found on large-sensor cameras from RED, Sony, P+S Technik, Vision Research, and Aaton, and various DSLRs including popular Canon models, which sometimes require physical modification to accept a PL mount.

Some recent PL mounts have tiny built-in electrical contacts that transmit lens data (focus setting, T-stop, depth of field) from the lens to the camera during recording. What's required is an "intelligent" lens than can transmit its own data and a camera that can record it. The two lens-data systems common in PL mounts are the Cooke Optics */i Technology* and the ARRI *LDS* (*Lens Data System*). Lens data is useful in re-creating shots exactly at a later date and serves myriad functions in post and special effects.

Many other film camera manufacturers have their own mounts, including Aaton, Mitchell, Cinema Products (CP), and Eclair. Panavision lenses can be used on Panavision cameras and on Arriflex and other cameras modified for the Panavision PV mount.

Mounts for Digital Cameras

Most professional video cameras accept detachable zoom lenses. As noted above, the lenses used must be appropriate to the size of the sensor. For example, a lens for a ⅔-inch chip needs to cover a larger area than one designed for a ½-inch chip. All three-chip video cameras (⅔ inch, ½ inch, ⅓ inch, ¼ inch) employ a beam-splitter prism assembly behind the lens, and zooms made for three-chip cameras are optically compensated for this prism in their design. A zoom designed for a three-chip camera cannot be used on a one-chip camera of identical sensor size that lacks a prism, unless you want chromatic aberration, uneven sharpness, and an incorrect focus scale. The bottom line is, video zooms should be used only with the type of camera for which they were designed.[8]

All video lenses for ⅔-inch sensors, whether three-chip or one-chip, use a locking-ring mount called a B4 mount, with three flanges instead of the four flanges typical of film lens mounts like the ARRI PL. A reduced-size version of the B4 is used on interchangeable-lens camcorders with ½-inch and ⅓-inch sensors. Examples of ⅓-inch camcorders using this smaller mount include the Sony HVR-Z7 and all JVC shoulder-mount camcorders.

There are compact, viewfinderless "box" or "cube" cameras and point-of-view cameras (all of which can resemble security cameras) that typically feature a C mount. On occasion a manufacturer will introduce a new mount like the wide-throated, locking-ring mount that Sony debuted on the PMW-EX3 and repeated as a "neutral" mount on the PMW-F3.

As mentioned in the preceding section, ARRI's PL mount has been universally adopted for digital cinema cameras with Super 35–sized sensors. (All large-sensor

---

8. Professional video zooms typically have coded names that indicate the format they were designed for. Take the example of the Fujinon A22x7.8BERM-28. *A* indicates this is for a ⅔-inch sensor, *B* indicates camera manufacturer, *E* indicates internal range extender, *R* means servo zoom, *M* means manual focus, and *28* indicates camera type. Different manufacturers use different code letters.

cameras are single-chip.) The PL-mount lens data systems from Cooke Optics and ARRI described above also function with certain digital cinema cameras.[9]

Image converters such as the P+S Technik Mini35 allow the use of 35mm cine and still lenses on ⅓-inch HD camcorders. There are various makes and designs for cameras that accept detachable lenses and for small-format video cameras that have permanently mounted lenses (see Fig. 2-10). These can provide the angle of view and depth of field associated with the lens as it would appear on a 35mm film camera, even though the camcorder has a much smaller sensor area.

DSLRs from Canon, Nikon, Panasonic, and others use the compact, bayonet-type mounts their manufacturers have developed for still photography. Those capable of capturing HD video are typically recent models optimized for autofocus lenses. They tend to lack the mechanical linkages between the lens and camera that typified SLRs of an earlier era. The Canon 5D Mark II, for instance, accepts only electronically driven EF-mount lenses. Earlier Canon lenses with the mechanical Canon FD mount are incompatible.

Sony's E-mount is a DSLR-type bayonet mount dedicated to its NEX line of HD-capable still cameras and large-sensor camcorders with APS-C– or Super 35–sized sensors. Notable is the extremely shallow 18mm flange focal distance, which means that just about any lens can be adapted to an E-mount camera with the proper mechanical adapter. For the NEX-FS100 camcorder (same sensor as in the Sony F3), there are lens adapters for Nikon, Canon, Zeiss, Leica, Sony Alpha, and PL-mount lenses. The same holds true for the shallow (20mm flange focal distance) Micro Four Thirds mount adopted by Panasonic for its AG-AF100 large-sensor camcorder.

Fig. 4-27. Sony Alpha to E-mount adapter. Allows use of A-mount lenses on Sony's NEX line of cameras, including the FS100 and FS700. In general, lens adapters vary in terms of communication between the lens and the camera for control of focus and iris (if any). Research your particular lens/adapter/camera combination before purchasing one.

Fortunately, older-style mechanical SLR lenses like those with a Canon FD mount or Nikon F mount are ideal for mechanical lens adapters.

---

9. Some professional camcorders communicate with their zoom lenses and display lens data in the viewfinder. Some can save lens data files to flash memory cards. But no standardized system yet exists to capture or exploit this data.

LENS SEATING PROBLEMS

Depth of Focus

Never confuse depth of focus with depth of field. *Depth of focus* is a zone of focus *behind* the lens (inside the camera) where the video or film camera's sensor can record an acceptably sharp image. In a sense, it's like a miniature depth of field surrounding the focal plane.

The greater the depth of focus, the more leeway you have for a lens that is mounted slightly too close or too far from the sensor or film. Like depth of field, depth of focus increases as the iris is stopped down. However, unlike depth of field, it is least in wide-angle lenses and when shooting objects far from the camera. This means that a fast wide-angle lens needs to be very accurately mounted. On some lenses, even tiny pieces of dirt on the mount can throw off focus.

If a prime lens is not properly seated, its focus scale will not be accurate and a tape-measured focus setting will be inaccurate. Although focusing through the viewfinder will correct this error, an improperly seated lens might not be able to focus to infinity.

If a zoom lens is not properly seated, it will go out of focus as it is zoomed out to wide angle. The lens may focus well at long focal lengths where depth of focus is considerable (although there is little depth of field), but as the lens is zoomed to wide angle, tolerances become more critical and the picture may go out of focus. If the image goes out of focus when zooming in from wide to telephoto, it means you probably didn't focus properly. If it goes out of focus when zooming out from telephoto to wide angle, it probably means the lens is out of collimation.

In an emergency, an improperly seated zoom can still be used as a variable focal length lens (that is, for changing focal lengths between shots), especially at the longer focal lengths and when the lens is stopped down.

Flange Focal Distance and Back Focus

Proper lens mounting is critical, and as noted above, each lens mount system has a specified *flange focal distance*, measured from the surface on the mount where the camera and lens join to the sensor or film emulsion. This distance must be precisely set and rigorously maintained. If the flange focal distance is set correctly, you should be able to use many different lenses, assuming they are set up to specs, without focus problems.

Mass-market cameras with interchangeable lenses like DSLRs have no provision for fine adjustment of flange focal distance, but professional 16mm and 35mm film cameras do, as do large-sensor digital cinema cameras such as the RED One, RED Epic, and ARRI Alexa.

Why would the flange focal distance need to be adjusted? Usually it doesn't. But perhaps a camera with a heavy lens attached has been dropped. Or the flange focal adjustment in the camera has loosened. Some people feel that temperature extremes can cause a mount to expand or contract, making focus scales unreliable.

The larger the film or sensor format is (that is, the larger the circle of confusion), the more mechanical tolerance is permissible. Full-frame 35mm (still) and Super 35 (motion) are vastly more forgiving of errors in flange focal distance than cameras with ⅔-inch sensors and smaller, where tolerances are minute.

In film cameras, adjustments to the flange focal distance are made with ultrathin

Fig. 4-28. Focus chart. Get a full-sized chart or use this one in a pinch. (Schneider Optics)

metal spacers called shims. A technician must perform this operation, typically using a device called a *collimator*—an optical instrument that projects tiny test patterns through the lens and onto the surface of the film or sensor. When a film lens is mounted improperly, it's said to be "out of collimation."

Video lenses are adjusted differently. *Back focus* is the distance from the rear element of the lens to the sensor's focal plane. When a video lens is mounted improperly, people say "the back focus is off." Video lenses typically have a small ring behind the iris ring that adjusts back focus by shifting the rear element of the lens closer to or farther away from the sensor. Adjusting a lens's back focus affects only that individual lens, not the lens mount.

Back focus is so critical in small-sensor cameras that camcorders with ¼-inch sensors are only made with fixed, noninterchangeable lenses. Some Sony cameras with ⅓-inch and ½-inch sensors have an automated electronic "flange back" or back focus adjustment, which can be found in the camera's menu.[10]

10. The use of the term "flange back" here is a confusing mix of "flange focal distance" and "back focus." As discussed above, these are related but different concepts. This electronic lens adjustment only affects back focus.

Adjusting Back Focus—Video Cameras

With small-sensor video cameras (from⅓ inch to ⅔ inch) that have interchangeable lenses, back focus can usually be checked or adjusted in the field when needed.

Put the camera on a tripod and view the image with the sharpest, biggest monitor you can find. Pin a large Siemens star to the wall, or sharply display one on your laptop (see Fig. 4-28). Position it at least seven to ten feet away. Use only enough light (or use filters) so that you can set the iris to wide open. Zoom in on the chart and focus the lens, then zoom out to the widest angle. Loosen the small, knurled retaining knob on the back focus ring and turn the ring until the image is as sharp as possible. Touching *only* the zoom control, zoom in all the way. If the image is not sharp, refocus the lens using the front focus ring, *not* the back focus adjustment. Zoom out and reset the back focus again if necessary. Repeat this process until one lens focus setting produces a sharp image at both telephoto and wide angle, then gently tighten down the knurled retaining knob, making sure not to nudge the back focus ring in the process. Ideally this should be close to the dot or other marking for the standard position on the back focus adjustment.

Adjusting Flange Focal Distance or Back Focus— Digital Cinema Cameras

With large-sensor digital cinema cameras, the adjustment of lens back focus or camera flange focal distance varies with make and model. The ARRI Alexa uses the same PL lens mount shimming technique used for ARRI film cameras. The RED One uses an adjustable ring, located behind the PL-mount locking ring, to adjust flange focal distance of its PL mount. The flange focal distance of DSLRs can't be adjusted, but their PL-mount adapters often can.

A host of precision devices are made for adjusting the flange focal distance or back focus in the field. Some of them use the principle of the collimator—projecting an illuminated test pattern to test the lens/camera combination. An example of this approach is the Zeiss Sharp Max, meant for ⅔-inch three-chip cameras. Another approach is for the test device to fit into the PL mount like a lens and project an illuminated Siemens star focused precisely at 52mm, the flange focal depth of the PL mount, which you can observe on a monitor while adjusting the flange focal depth. This is the principle behind uniQoptics' diascope and RED's own RED Focus. A third approach is a device that fits into the PL mount and projects a series of lines on the sensor, which the user, viewing the monitor, must align by turning the device.

Checking Collimation—Film Cameras

In the past, film camera assistants would pin a dollar bill, lens resolution chart, or Siemens star to the wall, light it for the widest aperture of the lens in question, and shoot focus tests at various distances. The film then had to be processed, printed, and projected. Today, with the pressures of time and loss of film labs, this is impractical.

Most camera rental facilities have lens test devices that can be used for instant checks of lens performance by nontechnicians. A lens technician with an autocollimator can quickly spot-check whether the lens set at infinity focus is focusing sharply on a piece of test film running through the camera.

CARE OF THE LENS

When possible, remove lenses from the camera when shipping and pack them in fitted, foam-lined cases (see Fig. 3-16). Shocks, prolonged vibration, and extreme heat can loosen a lens element. Keep the lens mount clean, especially the surface of the metal flanges where the lens mount meets the camera's mounting surface. Both camera and lens mating parts must be free of dirt and dust to ensure proper seating of the lens, especially in the case of zoom and wide-angle lenses. If necessary, clean the mount with a soft cloth.

When a lens is not in use—even if it's still on the camera—cover the front element with a lens cap to protect it from dust, fingerprints, rain, ocean spray, etc. Use a rear element cap when the lens is not on the camera. Some people like to keep a clear or UV filter in place at all times to protect the front element (see Chapter 8), although professionals usually abstain from this practice to avoid reducing contrast.

Dust on the Lens

Dust on the lens can lower contrast. It may be blown off with a rubber syringe or squeeze-bulb air blower available at any pharmacy or photo store, or with a small container of compressed air (like Dust-Off). If using a can of compressed air, keep the can upright so that air and not propellant is deposited onto the lens surface. Tip the lens down when blowing dust off so that the dust falls downward. Some cinematographers use their breath to remove dust, but take care not to blow saliva on the element, since it is harder to remove than dust.

If air doesn't remove all the dust, use a clean camelhair brush, reserved for the sole purpose of lens cleaning. Avoid touching the bristles, since oil from the hand will transfer to and remain on them. An alternate method is to fold photographic lens tissue over itself several times, then tear off an edge and lightly brush the element with the torn edge. Don't rub a dry element with the lens tissue; you may damage the lens coating.

Fingerprints on the Lens

Oil and fingerprints are more difficult to remove and, if left on the lens, can etch themselves into the coating; remove them as soon as possible. First, remove dust from the lens as described above. Use a wetted photographic tissue or Q-tip—not an eyeglass or silicone-coated tissue, which may damage the coating. The tissue or Q-tip must be perfectly clean, not previously used. Never rub a dry tissue or Q-tip on a dry lens.

To remove the oil of fingerprints, apply a drop of lens-cleaning solution (pros favor Pancro lens-cleaning fluid) or isopropyl alcohol (available at most drugstores) to the tissue or tip of the Q-tip—in other words, *not* directly to the lens. Take care that liquid does not come into contact with the area where the element meets the barrel, as it may loosen the element. After moistening the element, rub the wetted tissue or Q-tip as gently as possible, using a circular motion combined with a rolling motion to lift any dirt off the element. To avoid grinding grit into the coating, continually use a clean portion of the tissue or additional unsoiled Q-tips. As you do this, the liquid will slowly dry, leaving a clean area on the lens surface. If Q-tips are used, blow off any remaining cotton fibers with a rubber air blower. (Cotton swabs on wooden sticks made for hobbyists shed fewer fibers and are preferable to Q-tips if available.)

If need be, you can breathe on the lens to cause condensation. When the condensation evaporates, breathe on the lens again. Condensed breath will remove only what water can dissolve, not the oil of fingerprints.

CHAPTER 5

The Video Image

This chapter provides more technical information about digital video recording in production and postproduction. For the basics of video formats, cameras, and editing, see Chapters 1, 2, 3, and 14.

FORMING THE VIDEO IMAGE

THE DIGITAL VIDEO CAMERA'S RESPONSE TO LIGHT

You'll find simplified instructions for setting the exposure of a video camera on p. 107. Let's look more closely at how the camera responds to light so you'll have a better understanding of exposure and how to achieve the look you want from your images.

The camera's sensor converts an image made of light into an electrical signal (see p. 5). Generally speaking, the more light that strikes the sensor, the higher the level of the signal. To look more closely at the relationship between light and the resulting video level, we can draw a simplified graph like the one in Fig. 5-1. The amount of light striking the sensor increases as we move from left to right.[1] The vertical axis shows the resulting video signal level.

This relationship between light input and video signal output is called a sensor's *transfer characteristic*. It resembles a characteristic curve for film (see Fig. 7-3, with the exception that it is a straight line: both CCD and CMOS sensors produce signals directly proportional to the light falling on them.

Look at the line marked "A." Note that below a certain amount of light (the far left side of the graph), the system doesn't respond at all. These are dark shadow areas; the light here is so dim that the photons (light energy) that strike the sensor from these areas simply disappear into the noise of the sensor. Then, as the amount of light increases, there is a corresponding increase in the video level. Above a certain amount

---

1. By the "amount of light" we mean *exposure*, which is determined by the amount of light in the scene, the setting of the lens iris, the filters being used, and the setting of the electronic shutter.

of exposure, the system again stops responding. This is the *white clip* level. You can keep adding light, but the video level won't get any higher. Video signals have a fixed upper limit, which is restricted by legacy broadcast standards, despite the fact that sensors today can deliver significantly more stops of highlight detail than in the past.

When the exposure for any part of the scene is too low, that area in the image will be undifferentiated black shadows. And anything higher than the white clip will be flat and washed-out white. For objects in the scene to be rendered with some detail, they need to be exposed between the two.

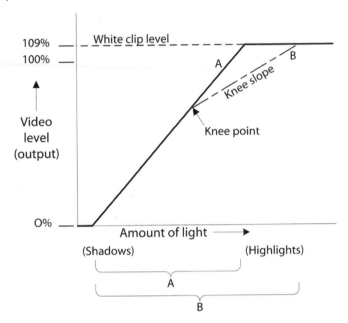

Fig. 5-1. The video sensor's response to light. The horizontal axis represents increasing exposure (light) from the scene. The vertical axis is the level of the resulting video signal that the camera produces. Line A shows that as the light increases, so does the video level—until the white clip is reached, at which point increases in light produce no further increase in video level (the line becomes horizontal). With some cameras, a knee point can be introduced that creates a less steep knee slope to the right of that point (Line B). Note how this extends the camera's ability to capture bright highlights compared to A. This graph is deliberately simplified. (Steven Ascher)

The limits of the video signal help explain why the world looks very different to the naked eye than it does through a video camera. Your eye is more sensitive to low light levels than most video cameras are—with a little time to adjust, you can see detail outdoors at night or in other situations that may be too dark for a camera. Also, your eye can accommodate an enormous *range* of brightness. For example, you can stand inside a house and, in a single glance, see detail in the relatively dark interior and the relatively bright exterior. By some estimates, if you include that our pupils open and close for changing light, our eyes can see a range of about twenty-four *f*-stops.

Digital video and film are both much more limited in the range of usable detail they can capture from bright to dark (called the *exposure range* or *dynamic range*). When shooting, you may have to choose between showing good detail in the dark areas or showing detail in the bright areas, but not *both* at the same time (see Fig. 7-16). Kodak estimates that many of its color negative film stocks can capture about a ten-stop range of brightness (a contrast ratio of about 1,000:1 between the brightest and darkest value), although color negative's S-shaped characteristic curve can accommodate several additional stops of information at either end of the curve.[2] Historically, analog video cameras were able to handle a much more limited range, sometimes as low as about five stops (40:1), but new high-end digital cameras capture an exposure range of around ten stops, and the latest digital cinematography cameras like the ARRI Alexa and Sony F65 claim fourteen stops. RED says its Epic camera can capture eighteen stops when using its high dynamic range function.

The image in Fig. 7-17 was shot with film; the middle shot shows a "compromise" exposure that balances the bright exterior and dark interior. With typical video cameras it is often harder to find a compromise that can capture both; instead you may need to expose for one or the other (more on this below).

To truly evaluate exposure range we need to look at the film or video system as a whole, which includes the camera, the recording format, and the monitor or projection system—all of which play a part. For example, a digital camera's sensor may be capable of capturing a greater range than can be recorded on tape or in a digital file, and what is recorded may have a greater range than can be displayed by a particular monitor.

Measuring Digital Video Levels

We've seen that the digital video camera records a range of video levels from darkest black to brightest white. This range is determined in part by what is considered "legal" by broadcast standards. We can think of the darkest legal black as 0 percent digital video level and the brightest legal white as 100 percent (sometimes called *full white* or *peak white*).

The actual range a digital video camera is capable of capturing always goes beyond what is broadcast legal. On most cameras today, the point at which bright whites are clipped off is 109 percent. The range above 100 is called *super white* or *illegal white* and can be useful for recording bright values as long as they're brought down before the finished video is broadcast. If you're not broadcasting—say, you're creating a short for YouTube or doing a film-out—you don't need to bring the super white levels down at all.

Professional video cameras have a viewfinder display called a *zebra indicator* (or just "zebra" or "zebras") that superimposes a striped pattern on the picture wherever the video signal exceeds a preset level (see Fig. 3-3). A zebra set to 100 percent will show you where video levels are close to or above maximum and may be clipped. Some people like to set the zebra lower (at 85 to 90 percent) to give some warning before highlights reach 100 percent. If you use the zebra on a camera that's not your own, always check what level it's set for.[3]

---

2. A Kodak test of 5245 color negative film once measured seventeen stops of latitude.
3. The default zebra level on many cameras may be closer to 70 percent.

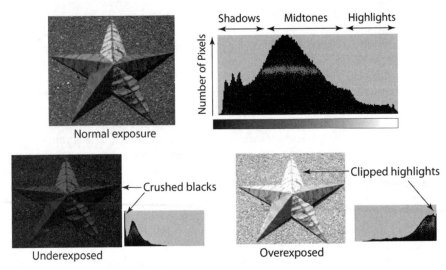

Fig. 5-2. Histograms. The normally exposed shot (top) produces a histogram with pixels distributed from dark tones to light. In this case, the distribution is a "mountain in the middle," with the most pixels in the midtones, and relatively few in the darkest shadows or brightest highlights. The underexposed shot (bottom left) creates a histogram with the pixels piled up against the left side, showing that blacks are being crushed and shadow detail is lost. The overexposed shot (bottom right) shows pixels concentrated in the bright tones on the right, with details lost due to clipped highlights. (Steven Ascher)

Many newer digital cameras and all DSLRs use a *histogram* to display the distribution of brightness levels in the image (see Fig. 5-2). A histogram is a dynamically changing bar graph that displays video levels from 0 to 100 percent along the horizontal axis and a pixel count along the vertical axis. In a dark scene, the histogram will show a cluster of tall bars toward the left, which represents a high number of dark pixels in the image. A bright highlight will cause a tall bar to appear on the right side. By opening and closing the iris, the distribution of pixels will shift right or left. For typical scenes, some people use the "mountain in the middle" approach, which keeps the majority of the pixels safely in the middle and away from the sides where they may be clipped.

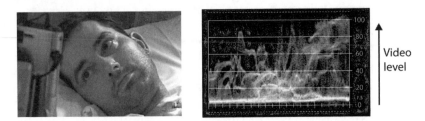

Fig. 5-3. A waveform monitor displays video levels in the image. In this case, you can see that the brightest parts of the bed sheet on the right side of the frame are exceeding 100 percent video level. (Steven Ascher)

A *waveform monitor* gives a more complete picture of video levels (see Fig. 5-3). On waveform monitors used for digital video formats, 0 percent represents absolute black and, at the top of the scale, 100 percent represents peak legal white level. (For analog video, waveform monitors were marked in *IRE*—from Institute of Radio Engineers—units of measurement. Absolute black was 0 IRE units and peak white was 100 IRE units. The units of percentage used for today's digital video signal directly parallel the old system of IRE units.)

Waveform monitors are commonly used in postproduction to ensure that video levels are legal. But a waveform monitor is also a valuable tool on any shoot. With a waveform monitor, unlike a histogram, if there is a shiny nose or forehead creating highlights above 100 percent signal level, you'll notice it easily—and know what's causing it (when a subject in a close-up moves from left to right, you can see the signal levels shift left to right on the waveform monitor). It's like having a light meter that can read every point in a scene simultaneously. Some picture monitors and camera viewfinders can display a waveform monitor on screen.

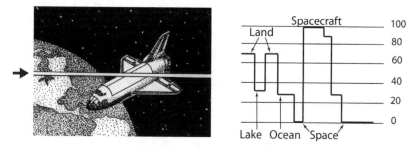

Fig. 5-4. By looking at the waveform display of a single horizontal line of pixels, you can more clearly see how luminance values in the image are represented in the waveform monitor. (Robert Brun)

USING A LIGHT METER. Some cinematographers like to use a handheld light meter when shooting digital, much as they would when shooting film. For any particular camera it will take some experimentation to find the best ISO setting for the meter (with digital video cameras that have ISO settings, you can't assume those will match the meter's ISO). Point the camera at a standard 18 percent gray card (see p. 307) and make sure the card fills most of the frame. Lock the shutter speed and the gain or ISO, and set the camera's auto-iris so it sets the *f*-stop automatically (shutter priority in DSLRs). Note the *f*-stop of the lens. Now, with the light meter, take a reflected reading of the gray card (or an incident reading in the same light) and adjust the meter's ISO until it has the same *f*-stop. If you have a waveform monitor, and are using a manual iris, set the iris so the gray card reads about 50 percent video level.

The fact is, in a digital video camera, no aspect of the digital video signal goes unprocessed (with such adjustments as gamma, black stretch, and so on) so there isn't an easily measured sensitivity, as there is for film or digital cinema cameras capturing RAW files directly from the sensor. For this reason, experienced video camera operators rarely use light meters to set exposure. They may, however, use light meters to speed up lighting, particularly if they know the light levels best suited to a particular scene and how to adjust key-to-fill ratios with a light meter alone.

Setting Exposure—Revisited

See Setting the Exposure on p. 107 before reading this. Setting exposure by eye—that is, by the way the picture looks in the viewfinder or monitor—is the primary way many videographers operate. But to be able to trust what you're seeing, you need a good monitor, properly set up, and there shouldn't be too much ambient light falling on the screen (see Appendix A).

By using the camera's zebra indicator, a histogram, or a waveform monitor (described above) you can get more precise information to help you set the level.

The goal is to adjust the iris so the picture is as pleasing as possible, with good detail in the most important parts of the frame. If you close the iris too much, the picture will look too dark and blacks will be *crushed* and show no detail. If you open the iris too much, the highlights will be *compressed* and the brightest parts of the scene will be blown out (see Fig. 5-2). As noted above, there is a white clip circuit that prevents the signal from going above about 109 percent on many cameras.[4] Say you were shooting a landscape, and exposing the sky around 100 percent. If a bright cloud, which would otherwise read at 140 percent, came by, the white clip will cut off (clip) the brightness level of the cloud somewhere between 100 and 109 percent, making it nearly indistinguishable from the sky. In Fig. 5-8A, the edge of the white chair is being clipped.

In most video productions, you have an opportunity to try to correct for picture exposure in postproduction when doing color correction. Given the choice, it's better to underexpose slightly than overexpose when shooting since it's easier in post to brighten and get more detail out of underexposed video than to try to reclaim images that were overexposed on the shoot. Once details are blown out, you can't recover them.

One method for setting exposure is to use the zebra indicator to protect against overexposing. If you have the zebra set at 100 percent, you'll know that any areas where the zebra stripes appear are being clipped or are right on the edge. You might open the iris until the zebra stripes appear in the brightest areas and then close it slightly until the stripes just disappear. In this way, you are basing the exposure on the highlights (ensuring that they're not overexposed) and letting the exposure of other parts of the frame fall where it may. If you're shooting a close-up of a face, as a general rule no part of the face should read above 100 percent (or even close) or else the skin in those areas will appear washed out in a harsh, unflattering way.

When using a camera with a histogram, you can do a similar thing by opening the iris until the pixels pile over to the right side of the display, then close it until they are better centered or at least so there isn't a large spike of pixels at the right-hand edge (see Fig. 5-2).

Even so, sometimes to get proper exposure on an important part of the scene you must allow highlights elsewhere in the frame to be clipped. If you're exposing properly for a face, the window in the background may be "hot." The zebra stripes warn you where you're losing detail. In this situation you may be able to "cheat" the

---

4. How highlights get clipped varies by camera and by gamma and knee settings; see below.

facial tones a little darker, or you may need to add light (a lot of it) or shade the window (see Fig. 7-17). Or, if seeing into shadow areas is important, you may want to ensure they're not too dark (because they may look noisy) and let other parts of the frame overexpose somewhat.

It's an old cliché of "video lighting" that it's necessary to expose flesh tones consistently from shot to shot, for example at 65–70 percent on a waveform monitor. This approach is outmoded (if not racist). First, skin tone varies a lot from person to person, from pale white to dark black. If you use auto-iris on close-ups of people's faces, it will tend to expose everyone the same. However, "average" white skin—which is a stop brighter than the 18 percent gray card that auto-iris circuits aim for—may end up looking too dark, and black skin may end up too light. (See Understanding the Reflected Reading, p. 292.) But, even more important, exposure should serve the needs of dramatic or graphic expression. The reality is that people move through scenes, in and out of lighting, and the exposure of skin tones changes as they do. In a nighttime scene, for instance, having faces exposed barely above shadow level may be exactly the look you want (See Fig. 5-10). For sit-down interviews with light-skinned people, a video level of 50–55 percent on a waveform monitor is usually a safe bet. Momentary use of auto-iris is always a good way to spot-check what the camera thinks the best average exposure should be, but don't neglect to use your eyes and creative common sense too.

As a rule of thumb when using a standard video gamma alone (see below for more on gamma), changing the exposure of a scene by a stop will cause the digital video level of a midtone to rise or fall by about 20 percent. If a digital video signal is defined by a range of 0 to 100 percent, does this imply that the latitude of broadcast video is five stops? It would seem so, but through the use of special gammas, digital video cameras can actually pack many more stops of scene detail into the fixed container that is the video signal. With today's digital video cameras, you have around ten stops of dynamic range. Use 'em.

For inspiration regarding the creative limits to which digital video exposure—particularly HD—can be pushed these days, watch the newest dramatic series on network or cable television for the latest trends in lighting. You may be in for some surprises.

UNDERSTANDING AND CONTROLLING CONTRAST

As we've seen, the world is naturally a very contrasty place—often too contrasty to be captured fully in a single video exposure. For moviemakers, contrast is a key concern, and it comes into play in two main areas:

- *Shooting.* Can you record pictures that have good detail in important parts of the frame? Are some parts so dark they're lost in the shadows and other parts so bright that details are blown out? This depends in part on the range of brightness in the scene, the exposure range of the camera, and how the exposure is set during recording.

Fig. 5-5. Thinking about contrast. (A) This image was captured with enough latitude or dynamic range to bring out details in the shadow areas (under the roadway) and in the highlights like the water. (B) This image has compressed shadow areas (crushed blacks), which can happen when you set the exposure for the highlights and your camera has insufficient dynamic range to reach into the shadows. (C) This shot has increased overall contrast; shadows are crushed and the highlights are compressed (note that details in the water are blown out). Notice also the greater separation of midtones (the two types of paving stones in the sidewalk look more similar in B and more different in C). Though increasing the contrast may result in loss of detail in dark and/or light areas, it can also make images look bolder or sharper. (D) If we display image C without a bright white or dark black, it will seem murky and flat despite its high original contrast. Thus the overall feeling of contrast depends both on how the image is captured and how it is displayed. (Steven Ascher)

- *Display.* When the recorded pictures are played back on a monitor or on a screen, does the range of tonalities reproduce the important details? Does the tonal range express the visual "feel" you're trying to convey? This depends in part on how the video was recorded, any contrast adjustments that were made during postproduction, and the settings and capabilities of the display device.[5]

Contrast is important because it's both about *information* (are the details visible?) and *emotion* (high-contrast images have a very different feel and mood than low-contrast images). Contrast can be thought of as the separation of tones (lights and

5. One key aspect of the display device is its contrast ratio; see p. 222.

darks) in an image. Tonal values range from the dark shadow areas to the bright highlights, with the *midtones* in the middle. The greater the contrast, the greater the separation between the tones.

Low-contrast images—images without good tonal separation—are called *flat* or *soft* (*soft* is also used to mean "not sharp" and often low-contrast images look unsharp as well, even if they're in focus). Low-contrast images are sometimes described as "mellow." High-contrast images are called *contrasty* or *hard*. An image with good contrast range is sometimes called *snappy*.

Contrast is determined partly by the scene itself and partly by how the camera records the image and how you compose your shots. For example, if you compose your shots so that everything in the frame is within a narrow tonal scale, the image can sometimes look murky or flat. When shooting a dark night shot, say, it can help to have *something* bright in the picture (a streetlight, a streak of moonlight) to provide the eye with a range of brightness that, in this case, can actually make the darks look darker (see Fig. 5-10).

Let's look at some of the factors that affect contrast and how you can work with them.

WHAT IS GAMMA?

Gamma in Film and Analog Video

In photography and motion picture film, gamma (γ) is a number that expresses the contrast of a recorded image as compared to the actual scene. A photographic image that perfectly matches its original scene in contrast is said to have 1:1 contrast or a "unity" gamma equal to 1.

A film negative's gamma is the slope of the straight line section of its characteristic curve (see Fig. 7-3). The steeper the characteristic curve, the greater the increase in density with each successive unit of exposure, and the greater the resulting image contrast. Actually, a negative and the print made from that negative each has its own separate gamma value, which when multiplied together yield the gamma of the final image. The average gamma for motion picture color negatives is 0.55 (which is why they're so flat looking), while the gamma for print film is far higher, closer to four.[6] When these two gamma values are multiplied (for example, 0.55 × 3.8 = 2), the result is an image projected on the screen with a contrast twice that of nature. We perceive this enhanced contrast as looking normal, however, because viewing conditions in a dark theater are anything but normal, and in the dark our visual system requires additional contrast for the *sensation* of normal contrast.

In analog video, the term "gamma" has a different meaning. This has caused endless confusion among those who shoot both film and video, which continues in today's digital era.

TV was designed to be watched in living rooms, not in dark theaters, and there-

6. Due to the complexity of developing color negative and print film, their respective gammas are fixed. With black-and-white motion picture film it was a different story, and throughout the black-and-white era, gamma was used as a creative tool to be adjusted during developing, often scene by scene, at the behest of the cinematographer.

fore there was no need to create any unnatural contrast in the final image. Video images are meant to reproduce a 1:1 contrast ratio compared to the real world. But the cathode ray tubes (CRTs; see Fig. 5-6) used for decades in TVs were incapable of *linear* image reproduction (in which output brightness is a straight line that's *directly proportional* to input signal level). Instead, a *gamma correction* was needed so that shadow detail wouldn't appear too dark and bright areas wouldn't wash out (see Fig. 5-7).[7]

In analog video, "gamma" is shorthand for this gamma correction needed to offset the distortions of an analog CRT display. When a gamma-corrected signal from an analog video camera is displayed on a CRT, the resulting image has a gamma of 1 and looks normal.

Fig. 5-6. For decades analog CRTs were the *only* kind of TV. Now no one makes them, though many are still in use. CRT monitors are recognizable because they're big and boxy (definitely *not* flat panel). (Sony Electronics, Inc.)

Digital Video Gamma

CRTs are a thing of the past. The video images you shoot will be viewed on plasma, LCD, LCOS, OLED, or laser displays or projectors that are not affected by the nonlinearity of CRT vacuum tubes. So why do digital video cameras still need gamma correction?

In theory we could create a digital camcorder and TV each with a gamma of 1. In fact, as shown in Fig. 5-1, digital video sensors natively produce a straight line response, and digital TVs and displays are capable of reproducing the image in a linear way, with output directly proportional to input. The problem is that this equipment would be incompatible with millions of existing televisions and cameras. So, new cameras and displays are stuck with gamma correction—let's return to the

---

7. Typically a CRT would have a 2.2 gamma value and a camera would have a gamma correction value of 1/2.2, or 0.45. In the real world, however, CRT gamma values varied from 2.2 to 2.6. Higher gamma values would give CRT images a slightly more contrasty appearance, which was often considered appealing.

shorthand "gamma"—as a legacy of the analog era. However, in today's professional digital video cameras, gamma curves can be used as a creative tool to capture a greater range of scene brightness than was possible in analog.

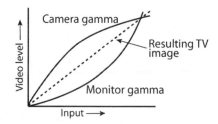

Altering the gamma has a noticeable effect on which parts of the scene show detail and on the overall mood and feel of the picture. A high gamma setting can create an image that looks crisp and harsh by compressing the highlights (crushing the detail in the bright areas), stretching the blacks, and rendering colors that appear more saturated and intense (see Fig. 5-8A). A low gamma setting can create a picture that looks flat and muted, allowing you to see more gradations and detail in the bright areas that would otherwise overex-

Fig. 5-7. Gamma correction. CRT monitors have a response curve that bows downward (darkening shadows and midtones), so cameras were designed to compensate by applying a gamma correction that bows upward. When we combine the camera's gamma-corrected video signal with the monitor's gamma, we get a straight line (linear) response, which appears to the TV viewer as normal contrast.

pose, while compressing shadow detail and desaturating colors (see Fig. 5-8D).

Some people choose to use various gamma settings on location, while others prefer to alter the look of the image in post under more controlled conditions. If contrast can be fully adjusted in post, why bother with gamma correction in the camera at all? When you adjust gamma in a camera—or any picture parameter, such as color or sharpness—what is being adjusted is the full video signal in the camera's DSP (digital signal processing) section prior to any compression. If you adjust the image after it's been compressed and recorded with typical camera codecs, quality can suffer (which is why some people go to the trouble of using external recorders with little or no compression).

Gamma or contrast adjustments in post can achieve only so much. Whether you record compressed or uncompressed, if you didn't capture adequate highlight detail in the first place by using an appropriate gamma (see the next section) you're out of luck. There is no way in post to invent missing highlight detail.

GAMMA OPTIONS WHEN SHOOTING

Standard Gamma

All digital video cameras out of the box offer a default or "factory setting" gamma meant to make that camera look good. In some cameras this is called standard gamma. In professional cameras, a camera's standard gamma will be the *internationally standardized* gamma for that video format. In high definition, the international standard for gamma is the ITU-R 709 video standard (also known as Rec. 709, CCIR 709, or just 709). Standard definition's international standard is ITU-R 601. The 709 and 601 standards apply to both gamma (contrast) and the range of legal colors (the color *gamut*), and they look quite similar to each other in these respects.

Fig. 5-8. Picture profiles. Many cameras offer a variety of preset or user-adjustable settings for gamma and other types of image control. (A) Standard gamma. (B) By adding a knee point (here at 82 percent) highlight detail can be captured without affecting other tonalities—note increased detail in the bright edge of the chair. (C) Some cameras offer a profile that emulates the look of a film print stock, with darker shadows for added contrast (note crushed blacks and loss of detail in dark areas like the woman's hair). You might use this setting if you like the look and aren't planning to do color correction in post. However, if you shoot with a standard gamma like A, it's very easy to achieve the look of C in post, and you don't risk throwing away shadow detail that can't be reclaimed later. (D) Some cameras can produce an extended dynamic range image that contains greater detail in highlights and shadows but looks too dark and flat for direct viewing. Different cameras may accomplish this kind of look using a cine gamma, or log or RAW capture. The flat image can be corrected to normal contrast in post, while retaining more detail in bright and dark areas than if it had been shot with standard gamma. All the images here are for illustration; your particular camera or settings may produce different results. (Steven Ascher)

ITU-R 709 and ITU-R 601 are designed to reproduce well without much correction in postproduction. They produce an overall bright, intense feel with relatively rich, saturated colors. For sports and news, this traditional video look makes for a vibrant image. At the same time, these are relatively high gammas that also result in a limited exposure range—extreme highlight detail is lost. These standardized gammas used alone don't allow you to capture all the dynamic range your camera is capable of, or that a high-quality professional monitor or projector can display.

The curve marked "Standard" in Figure 5-9 is not precisely Rec. 709, but it shares a basic shape. Notice that it rises quickly in the shadows, providing good separation of tones (good detail) in the dark parts of the scene. However, it rises at such a steep slope that it reaches 109 percent quite quickly compared to the other curves; thus it captures a more limited range of brightness in the scene.

Standard gammas like Rec. 709, which are based on the characteristics of conventional TV displays, not only limit dynamic range, they also fall short of the wider color gamut found in today's digital cinema projectors. To address this fact, some digital video cameras offer a gamma that incorporates DCI P3 (also called SMPTE 431-2), a new color standard established by Hollywood's Digital Cinema Initiatives for commercial digital video projectors. As a camera gamma, DCI P3 combines the dynamic range of Rec. 709 with an expanded color gamut modeled after 35mm print film. The advantage of using DCI P3 gamma is that what you see in the field will closely resemble what you see on the big screen. Note that LCD monitors must be DCI P3 compliant to accurately view color when using this gamma.

Standard Gamma with Knee Correction

As we've just seen, using a standardized gamma produces a snappy, fairly contrasty image at the expense of highlight detail. When the camera's sensitivity reaches maximum white, highlights are clipped. But there is a way to extend a camera's dynamic range to improve the handling of highlight detail when using Rec. 709 or Rec. 601.

On a professional digital video camera, you can manually introduce a *knee point* to the sensor's transfer characteristic (see Fig. 5-1). Normally, with no knee, the camera's response curve is a relatively straight line that clips abruptly at 100 or 109 percent. However, using menu settings, if you add a knee point at, say, 85 percent, the straight line can be made to bend at that point, sloping more gently and intersecting the white clip level further to the right along the horizontal axis, which corresponds to higher exposure values. This technique compresses highlights above 85 percent (in this example), so that parts of the scene that would otherwise be overexposed can be retained with some detail.[8]

When highlights are compressed by use of a knee point, their contrast and sharpness are compressed as well. They can appear less saturated. To correct for this, professional cameras also offer menu settings for "knee aperture" (to boost sharpness and contrast in highlights) and "knee saturation level" (to adjust color saturation in highlights). These are usually located next to the knee point settings in the camera's menu tree.

It is possible to set the knee point too low, say below 80 percent, where the *knee slope* can become too flat, with the result that highlights may seem too compressed, normally bright whites may seem dull, and light-skin faces may look pasty.

In addition to a knee point setting, most professional video cameras have an *automatic knee* function that, when engaged, introduces highlight compression on the fly. When no extreme highlights exist, this function places the knee point near the white clip level, but when highlights exceed the white clip level, it automatically lowers the knee point to accommodate the intensity of the brightest levels. Called

---

8. Technically speaking, the higher exposure values have been remapped along the "knee slope" to fit into the video signal's fixed 0–100 percent or 0–109 percent dynamic range. This is done in the camera's digital signal processing section.

Dynamic Contrast Control (DCC) in Sony cameras and Dynamic Range Stretch (DRS) in Panasonic cameras, automatic knee helps to preserve highlight details in high-contrast images, although sometimes the outcome is subtle to the eye. Some camera operators leave it on all the time; others feel that the manual knee is preferable. As with all knee point functions, you can experiment by shooting a high-contrast image and inspecting the results on a professional monitor. Everything you need to know will be visible on the screen.

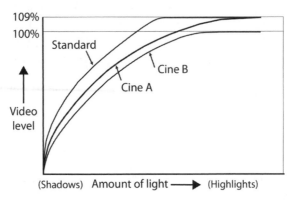

Fig. 5-9. Gamma curves. Standard gamma rises quickly in the shadows, creates relatively bright midtones, and reaches the white clip level relatively soon. By comparison, the Cine A curve provides darker shadows and midtones but continues to rise to the right of the point at which the standard curve has stopped responding, so it's able to capture brighter highlights. The Cine B curve is similar to Cine A, but tops out at 100 percent video level, so the picture is legal for broadcast without correction in post. These curves are for illustration only; the names and specific gamma curves in your camera may be different. (Steven Ascher)

"Cine" Gamma in Video Cameras

The technique just discussed of setting a knee point to control highlight reproduction has been with us for a while. Today's digital video cameras accomplish a similar but more sophisticated effect using special "cine" gamma curves that remap the sensor's output to better fit the limited dynamic range of the video signal.

All professional digital video cameras offer reduced gamma modes said to simulate the look of film negative or film print. These gamma curves typically darken midtones and compress highlight contrast, thereby extending reproducible dynamic range and allowing you to capture detail in extremely bright areas that would otherwise overexpose. The goal is to capture highlights more like the soft shoulder of a film negative's characteristic curve does. The cine curves in Fig. 5-9 represent such filmlike video gammas. Note that they continue to rise to the right of the standard video gamma curve, capturing bright highlights where the standard gamma has stopped responding.

The principle of most cine gammas is similar, but they come in two categories: (1) display cine gammas, whose images are meant to be viewed directly on a video monitor, and (2) intermediate cine gammas not meant for direct viewing, whose dark, contrast-flattened images need to be corrected in post.

Examples of the first type include Panasonic's CineGamma (called Cine-Like and Film-Like in some camcorders), Sony's CinemaTone (found in low-cost pro cameras), Canon's Cine, and JVC's Cinema gamma. Typically they come in gradations like Canon's Cine 1 and 2 or Sony's CinemaTone 1 and 2.[9] A more sophisticated cine gamma called HyperGamma, which extends the camera's dynamic range without the use of a knee point, is found in high-end Sony CineAlta cameras (it's also called CINE gamma in some Sony cameras, although it's exactly the same thing). HyperGamma features a parabolic curve and comes in four gradations.

Some of these cine gammas cut off at 100 percent, and keep the level legal for broadcast. Some reach up to 109 percent, which extends the ability to capture extreme highlights, but the maximum level must be brought down if the video will be televised.[10]

The second type of cine gammas are the intermediate gammas including Panasonic's FILM-REC (found in VariCams) and JVC's Film Out gamma. Both produce flat-contrast images with extended dynamic range, which need to be punched up in post for normal viewing. Both were a product of the 2000s, a decade in which independent filmmakers sometimes shot low-cost digital video for transfer to 35mm film for the film festival circuit.

Camcorder manuals invariably do a poor job describing what each cine gamma actually does, and the charts, if there are any, often use different scales (making them hard to compare) or are fudged. Cine gammas can be confusing if not misleading because their very name implies a result equal to film. Color negative film possesses a very wide dynamic range (up to sixteen stops), while digital video signals must fall inside a fixed range of 0–100 percent (for broadcast) or 0–109 percent (for everything else). Cine gamma curves must shoehorn several additional stops of highlight detail into these strict signal limits, regardless of the sensor's inherent dynamic range. It's no easy task.

Some people prefer cine gamma settings; others think that display cine gammas look disagreeably flat and desaturated. (In some cases, whites don't look very bright.) Many who do use cine gammas add contrast correction in postproduction to achieve a more normal-looking scene. At the end of the day, the main advantage to using a cine gamma is that you can capture extended highlights that would be unavailable in post if you hadn't.

As in the case of adding a knee point, you can experiment with cine gammas by shooting a variety of scenes and inspecting the results on a professional monitor or calibrated computer screen like an Apple Cinema Display. Watch the image on the monitor as you open the iris. Highlight areas that might otherwise clearly overexpose may take on a flat, compressed look as you increase the exposure. You may wish to underexpose by a half stop or more to further protect these areas. You may also

9. CinemaTone 1, for example, emulates the look of color negative transferred on a telecine to video, with characteristic open shadow detail. CinemaTone 2 emulates the look of film print transferred to video, with darker midtones and plugged-up shadow detail.

10. Why avoid use of a knee point in capturing highlight detail? Adding a knee point can affect the red, green, and blue signals differently, with a resulting color shift in highlights captured along the knee slope. Advanced cine gammas like HyperGamma are designed to handle R, G, and B signals equally, with no color shift. Sony's CinemaTone is an example of a cine gamma that does use a knee point to extend dynamic range, sometimes at the cost of false color in the highlights. When this occurs, one way to correct for it is to desaturate the highlights.

want to experiment with contrast and color correction in post in order to discover what impact a cine gamma has on dark detail and low-light noise levels.

In summary, most cine gammas attempt to capture the look of film for viewing on a video monitor or TV. To attempt to capture the latitude of film from a digital sensor requires something beyond the conventional video signal. To do this requires a more extreme approach, even a new kind of signal, which we will discuss next.

Fig. 5-10. This shot might be considered underexposed, but as a night shot it feels appropriate. The lights in the background accentuate the cigarette smoke and create a range of contrast that helps the scene feel natural by giving the eye a bright reference point that can make the blacks seem darker. (Steven Ascher)

Log and RAW Capture in Digital Cinema Cameras

High-end digital cinematography cameras offer two methods of capturing a much larger dynamic range, allowing you to record details in deeper shadows and brighter highlights.

LOG CAPTURE. *Logarithmic transfer characteristic*, or *log* for short, is one way to extract even more of a sensor's dynamic range from an uncompressed RGB video signal. Think of it as a super gamma curve.

In a typical linear scale, each increment represents adding a fixed amount (for example, 1, 2, 3, 4, 5 . . .). Along a logarithmic scale, however, each point is related by a *ratio*. In other words, each point on a logarithmic scale, although an equal distance apart, might be twice the value of the preceding point (for example, 1, 2, 4, 8, 16, 32).

Digital video is intrinsically linear, from sensors to signals (before gamma is applied), while both film and human vision capture values of light logarithmically.[11]

---

11. This is why an 18 percent gray card looks halfway between black and white. If the human visual system were linear·in its response to light, a 50 percent gray card would instead appear halfway.

So, for example, imagine you had a light fixture with thirty-two lightbulbs; you might think that turning on all the bulbs would appear to the eye thirty-two times as bright as one bulb. However, following a logarithmic scale, the eye only sees that as five times as bright (five steps along the 1, 2, 4, 8, 16, 32 progression).[12] At low light levels, the eye is very sensitive to small increases in light. At high light levels, the same small increases are imperceptible. The change in brightness you see when you go from one light to two lights (a one-light difference) is the same as going from sixteen lights to thirty-two lights (a sixteen-light difference).

Where the sampling of digital images is concerned, the advantage of a nonlinear logarithmic scale is that many more samples, and therefore bits, can be assigned to the gradations of image brightness we perceive best—namely, dark tones—and fewer bits to brightness levels we are less sensitive to, meaning whites and bright tones. Digital video with its linear capture of brightness levels can't do this; it assigns the same number of samples and precious digital bits to highlights as to shadows, without distinction. This is particularly disadvantageous in postproduction, where vastly more samples are needed in the dark half of the tonal scale for clean image manipulation.

The logarithmic mapping of image brightness levels originated in film scanning for effects and digital intermediate work using full-bandwidth RGB signals (no color subsampling or component video encoding), 10-bit quantization for 1024 bits per sample (compared to 8-bit quantization and 256 bits per sample of most digital video), and capture to an RGB bitmap file format pioneered by Kodak known as *DPX* (*Digital Picture Exchange*).

One of the first digital cinematography cameras to output a log transfer characteristic was Panavision's Genesis, a PL-mount, single-CCD camera introduced in 2005. Panavision was motivated to use what it called *PANALOG* because standard Rec. 709 gamma for HD could accommodate only 17 percent of the CCD's *saturation level* (the maximum exposure a sensor can handle). By dramatically remapping the video signal using a 10-bit log function to preserve the CCD's entire highlight range, a filmlike latitude of ten stops was achieved.[13]

PANALOG is output as uncompressed RGB (4:4:4) via dual-link HD-SDI cables and typically recorded to a Sony SSR-1 solid-state recorder or an HDCAM SR tape using a portable Sony field recorder.[14]

The equipment needed to capture and record uncompressed 10-bit log signals is expensive. The data flow is enormous: nearly 200 mega*bytes* (not bits) per second at 24 fps. Cameras must be capable of dual-link HD-SDI output. Hard-disk recording systems used on location must incorporate a lot of bandwidth and fast RAID

12. Note how this parallels the relationship between lens stops. Opening the iris one stop doubles the amount of light that passes through the lens. Opening five stops lets in thirty-two times as much light.

13. Put another way, with use of a log transfer characteristic, Genesis could capture five *f*-stops above 18 percent neutral gray, for a dynamic range equivalent to 600 percent in video signal terms. Same for Sony's F23, F35, and other digital cinematography cameras that can output an uncompressed log signal.

14. Interestingly, the HDCAM SR format itself uses compression to record the uncompressed 4:4:4 output of a digital cinematography camera. Namely, intraframe MPEG-4 Studio Profile at a lossless 4.2:1 compression ratio.

performance. Don't forget you have to transfer it all, and back it up at some point too.

For its F35, F23, and F3 digital cinematography cameras, Sony has its own version of log output, called *S-Log*. ARRI's Alexa uses a third type of log output, a SMPTE standard called *Log C*.[15] Each company might boast that its version contains the best secret sauce, but in fact with the proper LUT (lookup table), it's relatively easy to convert S-Log to Log C or PANALOG, or the other way around. In other words, they're easily intercut, just as they're also easily captured to standard 10-bit DPX files on hard disks.

Because a log transfer characteristic radically remaps the brightness values generated by the sensor, the video image that results is flat, milky, and virtually unwatchable in its raw state. In effect, you've committed your production to extensive D.I.-like color correction of every scene in post. On the upside, you'll obtain a video image that comes closest to film negative in its latitude and handling of color grading without quality loss. Don't forget, not only is there no color subsampling (full 4:4:4), but 10-bit log sampling of the individual RGB components also better captures the wide color gamut produced by the sensor, which is not reproducible by conventional video. All of this favors more accurate keying and pulling of mattes in effects work. With some cameras, such as the Sony F3, it is also possible to record log in 4:2:2 at a lower data rate internally or to more affordable external recorders such as the Ki Pro Mini or Atomos Ninja (see Figs. 2-19 and 5-11).

Each camera capable of log output has its own solution for displaying usable contrast in its viewfinder, as well as for providing viewing LUTs for monitoring the image on location. LUTs, simply put, convert the log image into something that looks normal. They are *nondestructive*, meaning they translate only the image for viewing but don't change the image in any way. LUTs created and used on

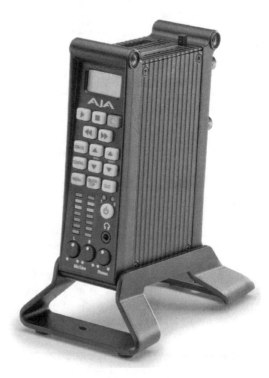

Fig. 5-11. The AJA Ki Pro Mini field recorder can be mounted on a camera. Records 10-bit HD and SD Apple ProRes files to CF cards. Inputs include SDI, HD-SDI, and HDMI. Files are ready to edit without transcoding. (AJA Video Systems)

15. Actually, Log C is more of a family. ARRI uses a slightly different one for each ISO setting.

location can be stored and sent to color correction as guides to a DP's or director's intent. When shooting log, it's recommended to not underexpose.

Canon's EOS C300 brings a new wrinkle to log output, an 8-bit gamma curve called *Canon Log*. (Echoes of the Technicolor CineStyle gamma curves found in Canon DSLRs.) This high-dynamic-range gamma is invoked when the C300 is switched into "cinema lock" mode. A built-in LUT permits viewing of normal contrast in the C300's LCD screen only. (Unavailable over HDMI or HD-SDI outputs—so you can't see it on an external monitor.) Since the C300 records compressed 50 Mbps, long-GOP MPEG-2 to CF cards and outputs uncompressed HD from a single HD-SDI connection—both only 8 bit, 4:2:2—it does not belong in the same class as the digital cinematography cameras described above.

RAW CAPTURE. For those who need the utmost in dynamic range from a digital cinematography camera, recording RAW files is the alternative to using a log transfer characteristic. RAW files are signals captured directly from a single CMOS sensor that uses a Bayer pattern filter to interpret color (see Fig. 1-13). Before being captured directly to disk, flash memory, or solid-state drive, the sensor's analog signals are first digitized—yes, linearly—but no other processing takes place, including video encoding or gamma curves. As a result, RAW is not video. Nor is it standardized.

RAW recording first gained popularity among professional still photographers, because it provides them with a "digital negative" that can be endlessly manipulated. As a result, it is the gold standard in that world. RAW recording of motion pictures works the same way, only at 24 frames per second.

It's called RAW for a reason. Upon recording, each frame has to be demosaicked or "debayered." Among CMOS sensors with Bayer filters, there are different types of relationships between the number of pixels that make up the final image (for instance, 1920 x 1080) and the number of photosites on that sensor that gather light for each individual pixel. The simplest arrangement is 1:1, where each photosite equals one pixel. In this case, a Bayer filter means that there will be twice as many green pixels/photosites as either red and blue. In the final image, the color of each pixel is represented by a full RGB value (a combination of red, green, and blue signals) but each photosite on the sensor captures only *one* of those signals (either red, green, or blue). Debayering involves averaging together (interpolating) the color values of neighboring photosites to essentially invent the missing data for each pixel. It's more art than science.

Next a transfer characteristic or gamma curve must be applied; otherwise, the image would appear flat and milky. White balance, color correction, sharpening—every image adjustment is made in postproduction. All of this consumes time, personnel, and computer processing power and storage, and none of it will satisfy those with a need for instant gratification. But the ultimate images can be glorious. It's like having a film lab and video post house in your video editing workstation.

RED pioneered the recording and use of RAW motion picture images with the RED One camera and its clever if proprietary *REDCODE RAW*, a file format for recording of compressed 4K Bayer images (compression ratios from 8:1 to 12:1). In this instance 4K means true 4K, an image with the digital cinema standard of 4,096 pixels across, like a film scan (instead of 3,840 pixels, sometimes called Quad HD by the video industry). REDCODE's wavelet compression enables instant viewing of lower-resolution images in Final Cut Pro and other NLEs by use of a Quick-Time component, and full resolution playback or transcoding when using the RED ROCKET card (see Fig. 3-8).

Both ARRI's D-21 and Alexa can output uncompressed *2K ARRIRAW* by dual-link HD-SDI, usually to a Codex Digital or S.two disk recorder. Uniquely, it is 12 bit and log encoded. ARRI says that 12-bit log is the best way to transport the Alexa's wide dynamic range. Actually, an ARRIRAW image is captured at 2,880 pixels across and remains that size until downscaled to 2,048 pixels (2K) upon postproduction and completion of effects.

The Sony F65 digital cinema camera captures 4K, 16-bit linear RAW with a unique 8K sensor (20 million photosites) that provides each 4K pixel with a unique RGB sample—no interpolation needed. Onboard demosaicking provides real-time RGB output files to a small docking SRMASTER field recorder that carries one-terabyte SRMemory cards.

More within reach for independent filmmakers is Silicon Imaging's SI-2K Mini with its ⅔-inch sensor and 2K RAW output captured using the *CineForm RAW* codec, a lossless wavelet compression similar to REDCODE. The Blackmagic Cinema Camera is an even-more affordable option (see p. 29).

Like video cameras that provide log output, motion picture cameras that output RAW files let you monitor a viewable image during production. By means of a LUT, they typically output an image close to standard ITU-R 709 gamma so you can get a rough sense of how the image will look after processing.

A wide latitude is always more flexible and forgiving. A side benefit to the film-like latitude provided by cameras with log and RAW output is that DPs can once again use their light meters for setting scene exposure, just as in film, using the camera's ISO rating.

Other Ways to Extend Dynamic Range

When you go into the world with a camera, you're constantly dealing with situations in which the contrast range is too great. You're shooting in the shade of a tree, and the sunlit building in the background is just too bright. You're shooting someone in a car, and the windows are so blown out you can't see the street. When the lighting contrast of a scene exceeds the camera's ability to capture it, there are a number of things you can do (see Controlling Lighting Contrast, p. 512).

Altering the gamma and adjusting the knee point and slope as discussed above are important tools in allowing you to capture greater dynamic range. Here are some other methods or factors.

USE MORE BITS, LESS COMPRESSION. When you can record video using 10 bits or 12 bits instead of the 8 bits common to consumer and many professional camcorders, you will be able to capture greater dynamic range and subtler differences between tones. With greater bit depth comes a more robust image better able to withstand color and contrast adjustment in postproduction. Often an external recording device is the answer. Convergent Design's nanoFlash records uncompressed HD to CompactFlash cards using Sony XDCAM HD422 compression up to 280 Mbps (see Fig. 1-27). The Atomos Ninja records uncompressed HD to a bare solid-state drive (SSD) via HDMI using 10-bit ProRes (see Fig. 2-19). For no compression, Convergent Design's Gemini 4:4:4 recorder records uncompressed HD and 2K via HD-SDI, and Blackmagic Design's HyperDeck Shuttle records 10-bit uncompressed HD, both to SSDs (see Fig. 5-30).

HIGHLIGHTS AND ISO. Video sensors have a fixed sensitivity, and changing the ISO or gain doesn't make the sensor more or less sensitive, it only affects how the image is processed after the sensor. Changing the ISO when shooting effectively rebalances how much dynamic range extends above and below middle gray. If you shoot with a high ISO (essentially underexposing the sensor), there's more potential latitude above middle gray, so you actually increase the camera's ability to capture highlights. If you decrease the ISO (overexposing), dynamic range below neutral gray increases, so you improve the camera's ability to reach into shadows. This is counterintuitive for anyone familiar with film, where using a faster, more sensitive stock usually means curtailing highlights (because a faster negative is genuinely more light sensitive).

HIGH DYNAMIC RANGE MODE. The RED Epic camera has a mode called *HDRx* (*high dynamic range*) in which it essentially captures two exposures of each frame, one exposed normally and one with a much shorter exposure time to capture highlights that would otherwise be overexposed. The two image streams can be combined in the camera or stored separately and mixed together in post. This extends the camera's latitude up to eighteen stops, allowing you to capture very dark and very bright areas in the same shot.

Black Level

The level of the darkest tones in the image is called the *black level*. The darkest black the camera puts out when the lens cap is on is known as *reference black*. Black level is important because it anchors the bottom of the contrast range. If the black level is elevated, instead of a rich black you may get a milky, grayish tone (see Fig. 5-5D).[16] Without a good black, the overall contrast of the image is diminished and the picture may lack snap. Having a dark black can also contribute to the apparent focus—without it, sometimes images don't look as sharp. In some scenes, blacks are intentionally elevated, for example, by the use of a smoke or fog machine. In some scenes, nothing even approaches black to begin with (for example, a close shot of a blank piece of white paper).

In all digital video, the world over, reference black is 0 percent video, also known as *zero setup*.[17] When you're recording digitally, or transferring from one digital format to another, the nominal (standard) black level is zero. Some systems can create black levels below the legal minimum, known as *super blacks*.

16. If you turn the brightness control up on a monitor you can see the effect of elevated blacks.

17. In analog NTSC video, black level was raised to 7.5 IRE units. Called *setup* or *pedestal*, the 7.5 IRE black level applied *only* to analog NTSC video used in North America, the Caribbean, parts of South America, Asia, and the Pacific. If you have archival NTSC analog videotape and want to transfer it to digital, the setup needs to be removed, to bring the black levels down from 7.5 IRE to 0. This is a menu option on professional decks.

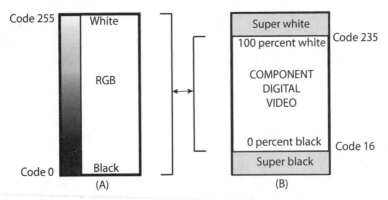

(A)   (B)

Fig. 5-12. Video levels in RGB and component color systems. (A) In RGB color, used in computer systems, digital still cameras, and some digital cinema cameras, the darkest black is represented by digital code 0 and the brightest white by code 255 (this is for an 8-bit system). (B) In component digital video (also called $Y'C_BC_R$ or YUV), used in most digital video cameras, 100 percent white is at code 235. Video levels higher than 100 percent are considered "super white"; these levels can be used to capture bright highlights in shooting and are acceptable for nonbroadcast distribution (for example, on the Web), but the maximum level must be brought down to 100 percent for television. Darkest legal black is at 0 percent level, represented by code 16. RGB has a wider range of digital codes from white to black and can display a wider range of tonal values than component. Problems can sometimes result when translating between the two systems. For example, bright tones or vibrant colors that look fine in an RGB graphics application like Photoshop may be too bright or saturated when imported to component video. Or video footage that looks fine in component may appear dull or dark when displayed on an RGB computer monitor or converted to RGB for the Web. Fortunately, when moving between RGB and component, some systems automatically remap tonal values (by adjusting white and black levels and tweaking gamma for midtones).

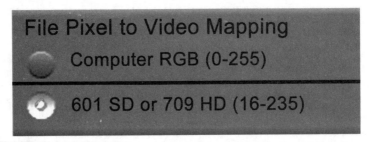

Fig. 5-13. Most editing systems operate in component video color space. When you import a file, the system needs to know if the source is an RGB file that needs to be converted to component, or one that is already component (either standard definition Rec. 601 or high definition Rec. 709). Shown here, some options in Avid Media Composer. Compare the code numbers here and in Fig. 5-12. (Avid Technology, Inc.)

BLACK STRETCH/COMPRESS. Some cameras have a *black stretch* adjustment that can be set to increase or decrease contrast in the shadow areas. Increasing the black stretch a little brings out details in the shadows and softens overall contrast. On some cameras, the darkest black can be a bit noisy, and adding some black stretch helps elevate dark areas up out of the noise. Some cameras also provide a *black compress* setting, which you can use to darken and crush shadow areas. Since stretching or compressing blacks alters the shape of the gamma curve, some cameras simply call these settings *black gamma.*

Because you can always crush blacks in post, it's a good idea not to throw away shadow detail in shooting.

Storing Picture Settings for Reuse

Professional cameras provide extensive preset and user-adjustable settings for gamma and many other types of image control. Generally, after you turn off a digital camera, your latest settings are retained in memory, available again when the camera is powered up.

Most cameras permit gathering together various image-control settings and storing them internally, to be called up as needed. These collections of settings are called scene files in Panasonic cameras, picture profiles in Sony cameras, custom picture files in Canon cameras, and camera process in JVC cameras. Typically you are able to store five to eight of these preprogrammed collections.

Many cameras also permit convenient storage of your settings on setup cards (usually inexpensive SD cards), allowing you to transfer settings from one camera to another or later restore the same settings for different scenes. These settings pertain only to the exact same model of camera.

Scene files or picture profiles make it easy to experiment with different looks. If you want to experiment with a particular gamma, for instance, hook up your digital video camera to a large video monitor (set to display standard color and brightness) and look carefully at how the image changes as you adjust various parameters of that gamma. Aim the camera at bright scenes with harsh contrast and also low-key scenes with underexposed areas. Inspect extremes of highlight and shadow detail. Often one size doesn't fit all, but with the ability to save and instantly call up several collections of settings, you can determine what works best for you before you shoot. It's a great way to get to know a digital video camera intimately.

VIDEO COLOR SYSTEMS

Color Systems

Be sure to read How Color Is Recorded, p. 16, and Thinking About Camera Choices, Compression, and Workflow, p. 94, before reading this section.

All digital camcorders accomplish the same basic set of tasks: (1) capture an image to a sensor; (2) measure the amounts of red, green, and blue light at photosites across the sensor; (3) process and store that data; and (4) provide a means to play back the recording, re-creating the relative values of red, green, and blue so a monitor can display the image.

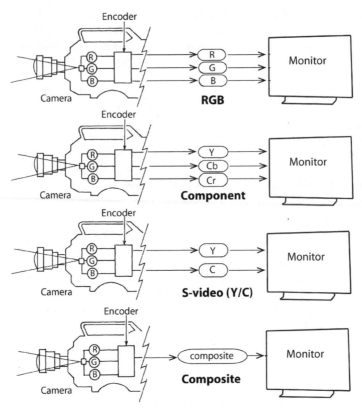

Fig. 5-14. RGB, component, S-video, and composite video systems vary in the paths they use to convey the video signal from one piece of equipment to another. For systems that use multiple paths, the signal is sometimes sent on multiple cables, but often the various paths are part of one cable. See text. (Robert Brun)

Different cameras use different methods, particularly when it comes to steps 2 and 3. As noted earlier, each photosite in a digital camera sensor can measure only brightness, but we can create color values in the image by placing a microscopic red, green, or blue filter over individual photosites (a technique used for single-sensor cameras; see Fig. 1-13) or by splitting the light from the lens into three paths using a prism and recording with three sensors (the technique used in three-chip cameras; see Fig. 1-14).

Let's briefly review how digital cameras acquire and process color; one or more of these methods may be employed by your camera.

RGB. All digital cameras internally process raw data from the sensor(s) to generate three distinct color signals—red, green, and blue (RGB). RGB (also called 4:4:4; see below) is a full-bandwidth, uncompressed signal that offers a wide gamut of hues and is capable of very high image quality. RGB output can be found in high-end cameras, including some digital cinematography cameras, and is usually recorded to a high-end format like HDCAM SR. RGB requires high bandwidth and storage space; it is particularly useful for visual effects. RGB handles brightness values differently than component video, so there may be translation issues, for instance, when moving between the RGB color of a computer graphics program and the component color of a video editing program (see Fig. 5-12).[18]

COMPONENT VIDEO. Most digital cameras today record *component video*. They acquire the three RGB signals from the sensor(s), digitize them, process them, then throw away either half or three-quarters of the color data to make a video signal that's easier to store and transmit. Prior to output, the three color signals (R, G, and B) are *encoded* into a monochrome *luminance* (sometimes called *luma*) signal, represented with the letter Y', which corresponds to the brightness of the picture, as well as two "color difference" signals (R minus Y, B minus Y), which are called *chrominance* (or sometimes *chroma*). Your color TV later decodes the luma and chroma signals and reconstructs the original RGB signals. Prominent examples of this type of video are the world standards for standard definition, ITU-R 601, and high definition, ITU-R 709.

Shorthand for component video is variously $Y'C_BC_R$, $YCbCr$, or $Y,B-Y,R-Y$. Though historically inaccurate, it's also widely referred to as YUV. Analog component is $Y'P_BP_R$.

S-VIDEO. *S-video* (*separate video*) is also called *Y/C*. This is for analog video only, and it's not so much a video system as a two-path method of routing the luminance signal separately from the two chrominance signals. It provides poorer color and detail than true component video, but is noticeably better than composite. If a camera or monitor has an S-video input or output, this is a superior choice over a composite input or output.

COMPOSITE VIDEO. Analog television, the original form of video, was broadcast as a single signal. What was uploaded to the airwaves was *composite video*, in which the luminance and two chrominance signals were encoded together. As a result, composite video could be sent down any single path, such as an RCA cable. Many different types of gear today still have analog composite inputs and outputs, often labeled simply "video in" and "video out" (see Fig. 14-13). These can be handy for, say, monitoring a camera on a shoot. Composite video was used for decades for analog broadcast PAL and NTSC, but it delivered the lowest-quality image of all the color systems, with many sacrifices in color reproduction due to technical compromises. No digital cameras today record composite video.

Color Sampling

See Reducing Color Data, p. 17, before reading this.

When we look at the world or a picture, our eyes (assuming we have good eyesight) can perceive subtle distinctions in brightness in small details. However, the

18. Particular attention has to be paid to the way bright values are treated (RGB allows for brighter whites than component) and which colors are legal (some RGB brightness levels and saturated colors are not legal in component broadcast video). Many graphics and compositing applications allow you to limit color selection to legal broadcast values.

eye is much less sensitive to color gradations in those same fine details. Because of this, smart engineers realized that if a video system records less information about color than brightness, the picture can still look very good, while cutting down the amount of data. This can be thought of as a form of compression.

As discussed above, most digital camcorders record component color. In this system there are three components: Y' (luma) and C_B and C_R (both chroma). When the signal from the camera's sensor is processed, some of the color resolution is thrown away in a step called *subsampling* or *chroma subsampling*; how much depends on the format.

To see how this works, look at a small group of pixels, four across (see Fig. 5-15). In a *4:4:4* ("four-four-four") digital video system there are four pixels each of Y', C_B, and C_R. This provides full-color resolution. Component 4:4:4 is used mostly in high-end video systems like film scanners. (RGB video, described above, is always 4:4:4, meaning that each pixel is fully represented by red, green, and blue signals.)[19]

In 4:2:2 systems, a pair of adjacent C_B pixels is averaged together and a pair of C_R pixels is averaged together. This results in half as much resolution in color as brightness. Many high-quality component digital formats in both standard and high definition are 4:2:2. This reduction in color information is virtually undetectable to the eye.

Some formats reduce the color sampling even further. In a 4:1:1 system, there are four luma samples for every C_B and C_R, resulting in one-quarter the color resolution. This is used in the NTSC version of DV. While the color rendering of 4:1:1 is technically inferior to 4:2:2, and the difference may sometimes be detectable in side-by-side comparisons, the typical viewer may see little or no difference. Another type of chroma sampling is 4:2:0, used in HDV and PAL DV. Here, the resolution of the chroma samples is reduced both horizontally and vertically. Like 4:1:1, the color resolution in 4:2:0 is one-quarter that of brightness.

Some people get very wrapped up in comparing cameras and formats in terms of chroma sampling, praising one system for having a higher resolution than another. Take these numbers with a grain of salt: the proof is in how the picture looks. Even low numbers may look very good. Also, bear in mind that chroma sampling applies only to resolution. The actual color gamut—the range of colors—is not affected.

The main problems with 4:1:1 and 4:2:0 formats have to do with the fact that after we've thrown away resolution to record the image, we then have to re-create the full 4:4:4 pixel array when we want to view the picture. During playback this involves *interpolating* between the recorded pixels (essentially averaging two or more together) to fill in pixels that weren't recorded. As a result, previously sharp borders between colored areas can become somewhat fuzzy or diffuse. This makes 4:1:1 and 4:2:0 less than ideal for titles and graphics, special effects, and blue- or green-screen work (though many people successful do green-screen work with 4:2:0 HD formats). Often projects that are shot in a 4:1:1 format like DV are finished on a 4:2:2 system that has less compression.

---

19. In postproduction, you may encounter codecs indicated 4:4:4:4 because they also include an alpha channel (see p. 590).

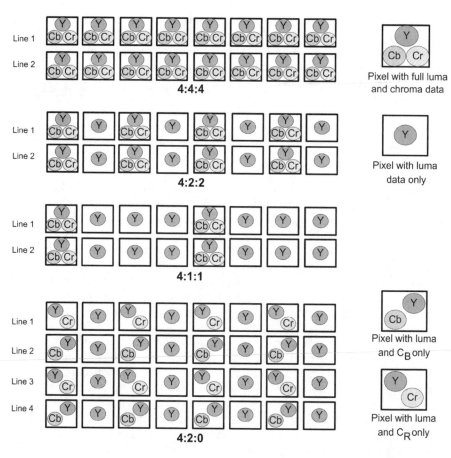

Fig. 5-15. Color sampling. In a 4:4:4 system, every pixel contains a full set of data about brightness (Y') and color (C_B and C_R). In 4:2:2 and 4:1:1 systems, increasing amounts of color data are thrown away, resulting in more pixels that have only brightness (luma) information. In 4:2:0 systems, pixels with Y' and C_R alternate on adjacent lines with ones that have Y' and C_B (shown here is PAL DV; other 4:2:0 systems use slightly different layouts).

SOME IMAGE MANIPULATIONS AND ARTIFACTS

Green Screen and Chroma Keys

There are digital graphic images, and scenes in movies and TV shows, that involve placing a person or object over a graphic background or a scene shot elsewhere. A common example is a weather forecaster who appears on TV in front of a weather map. This is done by shooting the forecaster in front of a special green background, called a *green screen*. A *chroma key* is used to target areas in the frame that have that particular green and "key them out"—make them transparent—

which leaves the person on a transparent background. The forecaster, minus the background, is then layered (*composited*) over a digital weather map. The green color is a special hue not otherwise found in nature, so you don't accidentally key out, say, a green tie. In some cases a blue background is used instead, which may work better with subjects that are green; blue is also used for traditional film opticals.

This technique is called a green-screen or blue-screen shot or, more generically, a *process* or *matte shot*. For situations other than live television, the chroma key is usually done in postproduction, and the keyer is part of the editing system. Ulti-matte is a common professional chroma key system and is available as a plug-in for various applications.

Green-screen shots are not hard to do, but they need to be lit and framed care-fully. Green background material is available in several forms, including cloth that can be hung on a frame, pop-up panels for close shots, and paint for covering a large background wall. When using a small screen, keep the camera back and shoot with a long lens to maximize coverage. It's important that the green background be evenly lit with no dark shadows or creases in the material, though some keying programs are more forgiving than others of background irregularities. For typical green-screen work shot on video, lighting the background with tungsten-balanced light should work fine, but for film and blue-screen work, filters or bulbs better matched to the screen color are often used. Don't underexpose the background, since you want the color to be vivid.

Avoid getting any of the green background color on the subject, since that may become transparent after the key. Keep as much separation as possible between the subject and the background and avoid green light from the background reflecting on the subject (called *spill*—most keying software includes some spill suppression). If you see green tones in someone's skin, reposition him or set a flag. If objects are reflecting the background, try dulling spray or soap. Fine details, like frizzy hair, feathers, and anything with small holes can sometimes be hard to key. Make sure your subject isn't wearing green (or blue for a blue screen) or jewelry or shiny fab-rics that may pick up the background. Don't use smoke or diffusion that would soften edges. Using a backlight to put a bright rim on the subject can help define his edges.

The Chromatte system uses a special screen that reflects back light from an LED light ring around the lens. This is fast to set up (since you don't need other light for the background) and works in situations where the subject is very close to the screen (but keep the camera back). Get your white balance before turning up the light ring.

Locked-down shots with no camera movement are the easiest to do. You can put actors on a treadmill, stationary bike, or turntable to simulate camera or sub-ject movement. Footage shot to be superimposed behind the subject is called a *background plate*. If the camera moves you'll want the background to move also, which may require motion tracking. Orange tape marks are put on the green screen for reference points for tracking. Do digital mockups or storyboards to plan your shots.

As a rule, keys work best with HD and with 4:2:2 color sampling (or even better, 4:4:4). That said, many successful keys have been done in SD, and even with formats like DV that are 4:1:1 or 4:2:0 (for more, see the previous section). Make sure the detail/enhancement on the camera isn't set too high. Bring a laptop with keying software to the set to see how the chroma key looks.

Fig. 5-16. Chroma key. The subject is shot in front of a green or blue background, which is then keyed out. The subject can then be composited on any background. NLEs usually include a chroma key effect or you may get better results with specialized software or plug-ins such as this Serious Magic product. (Serious Magic)

Deinterlacing

See Progressive and Interlace Scanning on p. 11 before reading this section.

It's very easy to convert from progressive to interlace. One frame is simply divided into two fields (this is PsF; see p. 602). This is done when you've shot using a progressive format but are distributing the movie in an interlaced one, such as 50i or 60i.

Creating progressive footage from interlace is more complex. This may be done when distributing interlaced material on the Web, for example, or when extracting still frames. Static images aren't a problem—you can just combine the two fields. But when there's any movement between fields they will show edge tear when you combine them (see Figs. 1-11 and 5-17). Some deinterlacing methods just throw away one of the fields and double the other (*line doubling*), which lowers resolution and can result in unsmooth motion. Some use *field blending* to interpolate between the two fields (averaging them), which may also lower resolution. "Smart" deinterlacers can do field blending when there's motion between two fields but leave static images unchanged. For more, see p. 600.

Moiré

In terms of video, *moiré* (pronounced "mwa-ray") is a type of visual artifact that can appear as weird rippling lines or unnatural color fringes. Sometimes you'll see moiré in video when people wear clothing that has a finely spaced checked, striped, or herringbone pattern. Moiré patterns often show up on brick walls, along with odd-colored areas that may seem to move. When you convert from a higher definition format to a lower definition one, various types of aliasing can result, including moiré and "jaggies" (stair steps on diagonal lines).

With the explosion of DSLRs, moiré is often showing up in scenes that would look fine if shot with traditional video cameras. Even hair, or clothing that has no visible pattern, may end up with moiré when shot with a DSLR. This happens in

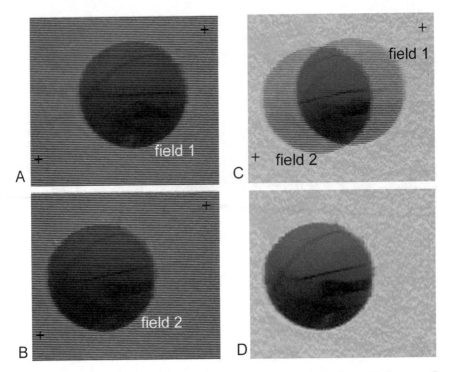

Fig. 5-17. Interlace and deinterlace. (A, B) Two consecutive fields from 60i footage of a basketball being thrown. (C) Here we see both fields together as one frame. You can clearly see that each field has half the resolution (half the horizontal lines), and that the ball has moved between the two fields. Makes for an ugly frame. (D) This deinterlaced frame was made by deleting the first field and filling in the gap it left. We can create new pixels for the gap by "interpolating" (essentially averaging) the lines on either side of each missing line. Though this creates a single frame that could be used for a progressive display, it's not as clean or sharp as true progressive footage shot in a progressive format. Deinterlacing works best when there's relatively little camera or subject movement. See also Fig. 1-11.

part because the DSLR's sensor is designed to shoot stills at a much higher resolution than HD or SD video. To create the video image, instead of doing a high-quality downconversion, as you might do in postproduction with specialized software or hardware, many DSLRs simply skip some of the sensor's horizontal lines of pixels. The resulting image forces together pixels that should have been separated by some distance, causing artifacts.

Though it may seem counterintuitive, the way to minimize this problem is essentially to lower the resolution of the picture at the sensor. With a DSLR, be sure that any sharpness settings are turned down. The camera may have a picture profile for a softer, mellower look. Sometimes you have to shoot a shot slightly out of focus to get rid of a particularly bothersome pattern. True video cameras avoid moiré by using an *optical low pass filter* (*OLPF*), which softens the image, removing very fine details that can cause artifacts (if you're shooting with a Canon EOS 5D Mark II DSLR, you could use Mosaic Engineering's VAF-5D2 Optical Anti-Aliasing filter).

Higher-end cameras that shoot both stills and video, like the RED Epic, avoid artifacts by not doing line skipping when they downconvert.

If you're on a shoot and you're seeing moiré in the viewfinder, it may be in the image or it may just be in the viewfinder. Try a different monitor to check. If it's in the image, to minimize the artifacts try shooting from a different angle and not moving the camera. You may also need to change wardrobe or other items that are causing issues.

Footage that has moiré in it can be massaged in post to try to soften the most objectionable parts, but it's a cumbersome process that usually delivers mixed results. Along with poor audio, moiré is one of the chief drawbacks of shooting with DSLRs.

Fig. 5-18. Moiré. The metal gate on the storefront has only horizontal slats, but this video image shot with a DSLR (Canon EOS 5D Mark II with full-frame sensor) shows a fan pattern of moving dark lines. This is one of several types of moiré that can occur in video, particularly with footage from DSLRs. (David Leitner)

Rolling Shutter

As described on p. 11, interlace involves scanning the picture from top to bottom, capturing each frame in two parts: one field (half of the frame) first, and the second field fractions of a second later. Progressive formats, on the other hand, capture the entire frame at the same instant in time.

Actually, the part about progressive is not entirely true. CCD sensors *can* capture an entire progressive frame at once, as can CMOS cameras equipped with *global shutters*. However, many CMOS cameras have *rolling shutters*, which scan from top to bottom. There's still only one field—it's truly progressive—but the scan starts at the top of the frame and takes a certain amount of time to get to the bottom. The result is that fast pans and movements can seem to wobble or distort. Straight vertical lines may seem to bend during a fast pan (sometimes called *skew*; see Fig. 5-19). Some people call the overall effect "jello-cam."

Some sensors scan faster than others, so you may not have a problem. To avoid rolling shutter issues, do relatively slow camera movements. Avoid whip pans. Keep in mind that fast events, like a strobe light, lightning, or photographer's flash may happen faster than the sensor's scan, leaving the top or the bottom of the frame dark.

Various software solutions minimize rolling shutter artifacts in postproduction, including Adobe After Effects, the Foundry's RollingShutter plug-in, and Core-Melt's Lock & Load.

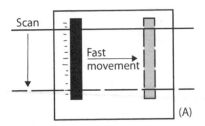 

Fig. 5-19. Rolling shutter and skew. (A) On cameras that have a rolling shutter, the sensor scans from top to bottom. If the camera or an object moves quickly, the top of an object may be in one part of the frame at the beginning of the scan, with the bottom of the object in a different place by the time the scan finishes. (B) The recorded frame shows the object tilted or skewed, even though it was in fact vertical. The slower a particular camera scans, the worse the problem.

Video Noise

As discussed elsewhere, different types of video noise can become apparent in the image when it is underexposed, enlarged, processed at a low bit depth, etc. Sometimes you can reduce the appearance of noise simply by darkening blacks in postproduction. Various types of noise-reducing software are available either as part of your NLE or as a plug-in, such as Neat Video.

VIDEO MONITORS AND PROJECTORS

See Camera and Recorder Basics, p. 5, and Viewfinder and Monitor Setup, p. 105, before reading this section.

On many productions, a lot of attention and money go into finding the best camera, doing good lighting, creating artful production design, etc. All in the service of creating a picture that looks great and captures the intent of the filmmakers.

But when showing the work in video, all that care can be undone by a display device that's not up to the task. There are numerous reasons why a given monitor or projector may not show the picture the way it should (see below). As a moviemaker, you can control some aspects of the viewing experience (such as what type of equipment you use yourself and how you set it up). In screening situations, always do a "tech check" beforehand to make sure anything adjustable is set correctly. Unfortunately, once your movie goes out into the world, you have no control over how it looks and viewers will see something that may or may not look the way you intended it.

Types of Displays

These days, video displays are everywhere and there are many different types. The following are some of the main varieties available. Many of these technologies come in different forms: as flat-panel screens (except CRT) and video projectors (which shine on a screen like a film projector). CRTs are analog; the rest are digital.

Fig. 5-20. Sony's Luma series of professional LCD video monitors. (Sony Electronics, Inc.)

CRT. Cathode ray tube (CRT) technology is what's behind the traditional TV set dating back to the beginning of broadcasting (see Fig. 5-6). For decades CRTs were the only game in town; now they're no longer made. Even so, high-quality CRTs continue to offer some of the best color and contrast reproduction of any monitors. Color and brightness are formed by a coating of phosphors on the inside of the tube that glows when struck from behind by a scanning electron beam. CRTs, as a result, are a direct light source.

LCD. Liquid crystal display (LCD) monitors use a fluorescent or LED back-light to project through a screen of liquid crystal molecules sandwiched together with tiny RGB filters. The brightness of a pixel is controlled by sending a voltage to it, which darkens it to prevent light from shining through. LCDs are very thin and can offer good color reproduction; good blacks are a problem, though, and shadow detail may be crushed. Contrast, however, is constantly improving and major broadcast manufacturers are beginning to introduce reference-quality LCD video monitors (see below).

LCDs are often limited in their viewing angle: if you sit *off axis* (to the side, above, or below) the image may grow lighter or darker. LCDs have no burn-in ef-fect (see Plasma, below).

PLASMA. Plasma screens are flat-panel displays that use tiny red, green, and blue pixels filled with a rare gas that gives off light when excited with electricity (similar to fluorescent light). Plasma screens can be very large, with a wide viewing angle. They have good contrast, color, and black levels. They use the same types of phos-phors as CRTs and share a similar color reproduction. They are heavier than LCDs.

Some plasmas can suffer from *screen burn-in*, which causes the screen to retain brightness values from static images held for a long time.

OLED. Organic light-emitting diode (OLED) displays are another newer thin-film display technology that may someday replace LCDs. When an electrical current is applied, OLEDs phosphoresce (glow), providing their own illumination. They offer excellent color and contrast and have perfect blacks, since black is simply the absence of illumination. (Nothing is backlit.) Their image-forming surface is paper-thin, and they can be remarkably light in weight.

DLP. Digital light processing (DLP) displays use millions of microscopic mirrors to direct light through colored filters. The mirrors switch on and off thousands of times a second. DLP projectors are capable of excellent color, contrast, and resolution; some are very affordable and compact. Many digital cinema projectors in commercial theaters are DLP.

Fig. 5-21. Panasonic 3D home theater projector with 1080p resolution. The PT-AE7000U uses transparent LCD panel technology. (Panasonic Broadcast)

OTHERS. LCOS (liquid crystal on silicon) is similar to LCD technology and is used for video projectors as well as camera viewfinders. JVC calls its version D-ILA and Sony calls its SXRD. LCOS eliminates the *screen door effect* created by visible pixels. (On some LCDs, the pixel grid is obvious in the image, as though viewing through a screen door.) Sony has a 4K SXRD projector popular for digital cinema use. Laser-based projectors are under development.

Computer and Video Monitors

Clearly there are numerous display technologies in use. As a moviemaker, you need to be aware that, even within one type of technology, all monitors are not created equal and you need the right type for the job you're doing.

Computer monitors are designed to show the output of a laptop or desktop computer. Depending on the system, computer monitors may be connected with a DVI (Digital Video Interface) cable, DisplayPort cable, Thunderbolt cable, or HDMI cable (see p. 237 for more on these connections). You'll be using a computer monitor as part of your nonlinear editing system (either built into a laptop or connected to a desktop). Computer monitors operate in RGB color space (see above) and are fine for viewing the editing interface and controls. However, when it comes to evaluating the color and contrast of the actual video you're making, other considerations come into play. Almost all broadcast video formats produced by HD and SD cameras are in component video color space (also called $Y'C_BC_R$ or YUV; see p. 209). So if you edit your movie with an NLE and output the component signal to a typical computer monitor, the picture will often look flat (low contrast) and too dark, because the color and tonal values are not properly converted from component to RGB (see Fig. 5-12). This problem can be addressed in a number of ways.

Fig. 5-22. When editing video, it's important that tonal values be correctly translated from the editing system any built-in or external monitors. Shown here, Avid Nitris DX input/output and monitoring interface. (Avid Technology, Inc.)

First, if you're producing something that will be seen *only* on the Web, cell phones, iPods, or computer monitors, then your computer monitor can serve as a picture reference, since your audience will be watching on RGB screens themselves. If you're using a good-quality monitor and the picture looks okay to you, it will hopefully look somewhat similar for your viewers. You may need to color-correct your material in the NLE for proper contrast and color.

However, if you're doing something for television or distribution in video (for example, on DVD or Blu-ray), you need to view the picture with proper component color values (for HD, the monitor should be compliant with Rec. 709). This is usually done with a monitor designed and calibrated for video use. A *broadcast monitor* is essentially a professional-quality video monitor capable of reproducing the full range of color to meet broadcast standards, with the kinds of controls and settings necessary to adjust the image properly. One particularly helpful control is the *blue-only* switch for accurate color adjustments (see Appendix A). Consumer TVs generally do not deliver consistent, controlled results; only with a broadcast monitor can you make the most realistic and accurate assessment of what the picture actually looks like. When doing critical tasks like color correction, a high-end *reference monitor* is even better.

You can feed a video monitor with the output from a camera, a deck, or a computer input/output (I/O) device. For example, you can output component video from an NLE using products such as Blackmagic Design's DeckLink or Intensity cards, AJA's Kona cards or Io boxes (see Fig. 14-4), or Matrox's MXO2 I/O devices (see Fig. 5-23). Some of these can be used with a desktop computer via a PCI card, or connected to a laptop via Thunderbolt or ExpressCard. The MXO2 units have a calibration utility that can help you set up a consumer TV that lacks the ability to display color bars with blue-only (see Appendix A). This utility also allows you to calibrate an RGB computer monitor to emulate the look of a YUV video monitor. Matrox promotes this as an affordable alternative to a broadcast monitor for HD color correction.

Newer versions of some NLEs, such as Adobe Premiere Pro CS6, claim to display HD video properly on the NLE's computer monitor (the desktop), so you may be able to view the picture with correct tonalities for TV without the need of an I/O device. However, I/O devices with dedicated video monitors may still offer better motion or quality, as well as larger full-screen playback.

Maddeningly, even if everything is set up correctly, you'll find that your video often looks quite different on different systems.

Some Monitor Issues

RESOLUTION AND SCANNING. Flat-panel displays have a fixed number of pixels, which is their *native resolution*, and they are at their best when playing video that has the same number of pixels (sometimes called *pixel-for-pixel*, or 1:1): for example, a 720p monitor displaying a 720p picture from a Blu-ray player. Check your monitor's manual for its native resolution; when working in HD, try to get one capable of "Full HD" (1920 x 1080).

If the video source has fewer pixels than the monitor, the picture may be displayed pixel-for-pixel, using only part of the screen and appearing as a smaller box within the frame. Or the monitor may scale up (enlarge) the picture to the monitor's size. Sometimes you have to do this manually (by pressing the zoom button on the remote). Scaling up an image will result in a less sharp picture.

If the video source has a higher resolution (more pixels), some detail will be lost and some of the picture area may actually be cut off. There are various devices that can convert from one format or resolution to another for monitoring. For example, if you're editing HD video and only have an SD monitor, you can use capture cards or external boxes that can downconvert to SD in real time (see p. 550), though editing HD in SD is not optimal.

Flat-panel displays and digital projectors are progressive by nature. If you input interlaced video, the player or monitor will deinterlace, which may cause artifacts (see above). The other side of that coin is that if you shoot in an interlaced format, there can be interlace artifacts (such as twitter), or errors in field order (due to mismatched cameras or improper NLE setups) that appear *only* on an interlaced CRT display. So if you have only a progressive LCD or plasma screen there could be image issues *you* won't see but others with CRTs may.

Newer flat-panel displays may offer high scanning rates, such as 120 Hz or 240 Hz in NTSC countries, which may reduce motion artifacts (see p. 86). Be aware that sometimes these have settings that create new, interpolated frames between existing frames (essentially increasing the frame rate), which can change the look of the video.

COLOR. Getting accurate color reproduction is one of the trickiest aspects of monitors and projectors. There are two aspects you need to be concerned with. One is *hue*, technically called *phase*, which is like dialing into place all the colors on a color wheel. The other aspect is *saturation*—how pale or rich the colors are—which is controlled by the chroma setting. See Appendix A for setup.

If you're working in HD, you'll want the monitor set up to Rec. 709 standards for color and contrast (see p. 195). Many consumer monitors come from the factory set too bright and with oversaturated colors because consumers are thought to like a punchy image. In some types of video or connections there is no need for phase adjustments, such as when using HDMI, HD-SDI, component analog RGB, or PAL. However, small errors in hue adjustment will throw off analog NTSC colors in a big way. Also, when using an NTSC standard definition monitor to display HD downconverted to SD, phase should be adjusted.

Some devices, such as the Matrox MXO2 boxes, can help you calibrate a monitor, especially helpful with a consumer monitor that lacks a blue-only mode.

Some newer, high-end digital reference monitors claim to be able to reproduce

Fig. 5-23. Matrox's MXO2 family offers a range of input/output (I/O) and monitoring options to use with editing apps like Adobe Premiere Pro, Apple Final Cut Pro, and Avid Media Composer. Various models offer I/O via HDMI (RGB or $Y'C_BC_R$), HD-SDI, SDI, and other connectors. The HDMI calibration utility lets an RGB monitor perform like a broadcast HD video monitor with proper display of Rec. 709 component color space so it can be used for color grading. (Matrox Electronic Systems, Ltd.)

colors accurately and consistently over time and from monitor to monitor without adjustment. The need for this kind of standardization can't be overstated. As things stand now, many monitors and projectors you encounter will be poorly adjusted, and many aren't even capable of reproducing all the colors in your video. But until the world is brimming with perfect digital monitors, keep those color bars handy.

CONTRAST RATIO. The range from the darkest black to the brightest white that a monitor can reproduce is critical (see Understanding and Controlling Contrast, p. 191). Manufacturers express this as a *contrast ratio*, such as 800:1. The higher the better, but be skeptical of the numbers in the ads; they are often fudged.

Be sure to set black level (brightness) and contrast as described in Appendix A. The screening environment also plays a role in contrast. If there's too much light in the room (and on the screen), you won't get a good black. If the room is *totally* dark, contrast may seem harsh. A dim ambient light often works best with consumer monitors.

ASPECT RATIO. Playing widescreen video on a nonwidescreen monitor, and vice versa, can cause issues. This is affected by the monitor and how the video itself is prepared (see p. 74). Another consideration is whether the video and the monitor both use square or nonsquare pixels (see p. 232). Sometimes consumers choose to stretch the width of an SD 4:3 image on an HD 16:9 monitor, so it "fills the frame," but this results in a distorted picture. Don't do it!

CONNECTIONS. Often video recorders and players offer a variety of output options through different connectors. For example, a player might have both composite and component outputs. Always use the highest-quality signal path possible. See Video Color Systems, p. 207, for a ranking of some of the options you may have. If the monitor has digital inputs, it's preferable to go digital out from the player to the monitor rather than using analog connections. For example, use a DVI connection or an HDMI connection, which supports uncompressed video and audio between player and monitor or other gear. However, with some equipment, direct digital connections are not available. See p. 237 for more on digital connections.

Professional monitors often allow you to *loop through* the signal—going into the monitor and out to another monitor or recorder.

Fig. 5-24. Timecode. Shown here burned in on screen (also called a window burn).

TIMECODE

The idea of timecode is simple: to assign a timestamp to every frame of picture or sound. Timecode is a running twenty-four-hour "clock" that counts hours, minutes, seconds, and frames (see Fig. 5-24). Timecode enables many different aspects of production and postproduction and is pretty much essential for serious video and audio work. Timecode comes in a few different flavors, which can sometimes be confusing.

Types of Timecode

In all types of video timecode the frame count depends on the frame rate you're working in.

For example, when shooting at 30 fps (either 30p or 60i), timecode can advance as high as 23:59:59:29 (twenty-three hours, fifty-nine minutes, fifty-nine seconds, and twenty-nine frames). One frame later it returns to 00:00:00:00. Note that since there are 30 frames per second, the frame counter only goes up to :29. This timecode system is called *SMPTE nondrop timecode*. Many people just refer to it as SMPTE (pronounced "simpty") or *nondrop* (often written *ND* or *NDF*). This is the standard, basic timecode often used in North America and places where NTSC has been standard.

In Europe and other parts of the world where PAL video has been standard, video is often shot at 25 fps (25p or 50i). Here, *EBU timecode* is used, which has a similar twenty-four-hour clock, except the frame counter runs up to :24 instead of :29.

DROP FRAME TIMECODE. One of the joys of video in NTSC countries is that with several formats, the frame rate is just slightly slower than what you might think it is (by 0.1 percent). For example, 30 fps video is actually 29.97 fps (which is to say, 60i is really 59.94i). When you shoot 24p video, that usually means 23.976p. This is described on p. 14.

You can't see the 0.1 percent reduction in speed, but it affects the overall running time of the video. Say you watch a movie shot at 29.97 fps that has nondrop timecode, and click a stopwatch just as it begins. If you stop the stopwatch when the video timecode indicates one hour, you'd see that actually one hour and 3.6 seconds has gone by. The nondrop timecode is not keeping real time. This discrepancy is no big deal if the movie is not intended for broadcast. Nondrop timecode is often used for production.

Because broadcasters need to know program length very exactly, *drop frame (DF)* timecode was developed. This system drops two timecode numbers every minute so that the timecode reflects real time.[20] A program that finishes at one hour drop frame timecode is indeed exactly one hour long. With drop frame timecode, no actual frames of video are dropped and the frame rate doesn't change. The only thing that's affected is the way the frames are counted (numbered). This is a point that confuses many people. Switching a camera from ND to DF has no affect on

---

20. The :00 and :01 frames are dropped every minute, unless the minute is a multiple of 10 (no frames are dropped at 10 min., 20 min., etc.). Thus, the number following 00:04:59:29 is 00:05:00:02. But the number following 00:09:59:29 is 00:10:00:00.

the picture or on the number of frames that are recorded every second. The only thing that changes is the way the digits in the timecode counter advance over time.

Television-bound programs in NTSC countries are usually shot with DF code (though see note about 24p below). Even if you shot NDF you can edit in DF (most editing systems can display whichever you choose) and broadcasters will require that you deliver in DF because program length must be precise. DF timecode is usually indicated with semicolons instead of colons between the numbers (00;14;25;15) or with a semicolon just before the frame count (01:22:16;04).

24p TIMECODE. If you're shooting and editing at 24p frame rate, you may be using 24-frame timecode (the frame counter goes up to :23).

When shooting, you generally want to avoid drop frame timecode in 24p mode because the dropped timecode numbers can make it harder to do pulldown removal in the editing system. Cameras that use pulldown to achieve 24p often will not record DF for this reason.

How Timecode Is Recorded

Most digital video cameras generate timecode in some form. The timecode may be embedded in the video recording, or it may be included with the digital video file as metadata (see p. 242).

One way to record timecode is to embed the data in each video frame, outside the picture area. This is *vertical interval timecode* (*VITC*, pronounced "vit-see"). One advantage of VITC for tape recording is that it can be read by the VTR even when the tape is not moving (useful for editing). VITC does not use up any audio tracks but must be recorded at the same time as the video and cannot be added later (except during dubbing to another tape).

On some videotape formats, there is a *longitudinal track* (*LTC*) just for timecode. With some video decks, the LTC is readable during high-speed shuttle but VITC isn't. Some formats allow you to record timecode on one of the audio tracks.

Timecode in Consumer Camcorders

Consumer digital camcorders don't offer professional SMPTE timecode but they do record a nondrop record run (see below) HOUR:MINUTE:SECONDS:FRAME for each frame of video, located in the data section of video tracks on tape or as metadata in the case of files. Fortunately, NLEs can read and manipulate this timecode as if it were SMPTE timecode. Mostly there is no way to preset anything. In the case of tape, like HDV, timecode in a consumer camcorder resets to 00:00:00:00 whenever a tape is changed or ejected. In the case of file recording, run a few tests with your consumer camcorder and import them into your NLE. It's the only way to know if the native timecode is adequate to your needs.

Late-model DSLRs popular for HD work may also have timecode capabilities.

Using Timecode in Production

While digital consumer cameras offer no control over timecode, all professional cameras and many prosumer models allow you to preset the starting code and may offer a choice of timecode options. Different productions call for different choices, and methods can be somewhat different with tape-based or file-based recording.

RECORD RUN MODE. The simplest timecode mode is called *record run*, which advances whenever the camera is recording. When shooting in record run mode, you can stop and start the camera as much as you want, but the code should advance on the tape or memory card uninterrupted from beginning to end.[21]

On most professional and prosumer cameras you can *preset timecode* to select the starting code. If you are using tapes or memory cards that store less than an hour of material, you might start the first at one hour (1:00:00:00), then start the second at two hours (2:00:00:00), and so on until you reach hour twenty, then start at hour one again. That way, the timecode on each tape and card is different, which helps keep things organized in editing. However, as long as you keep track of each tape or memory card, having two with the same code isn't a big problem (and it's un-avoidable if you shoot a lot of material on a project). Many cameras allow you to set *user bits* (*U-bits*), which are a separate set of data recorded with the timecode and can be used to identify camera roll numbers, the date, or other information. It helps to use U-bits if the timecode on any two tapes is the same.

TIME-OF-DAY AND FREE RUN MODES. On some cameras, you can shoot with a *time-of-day* (*TOD*) clock recorded as timecode. TOD code can be use-ful if you need to identify when things were filmed or when more than one camera is shooting at the same time. A similar system is sometimes called *free run mode*, which advances every second whether the camera is running or not, but can be set to start at whatever number you preset.

TOD code can create a number of issues, which are explained below in Avoiding Timecode Problems. One issue is that TOD code is discontinuous whenever you stop the camera (because when you start up again, it will jump to the new time of day). Another problem can occur if you're shooting tape and you record the same tape on different days. Say you finish the first day at four in the afternoon (16:00:00:00 code). You start the next day at eleven in the morning (11:00:00:00 code). When you edit this tape, the edit controller will find the lower code number after the high number, causing problems. Using TOD code will likely result in several tapes having the same code numbers, so try to put the date or tape number in the U-bits. You can avoid some of these problems with camcorders that have a *real time mode* that puts the time of day in the user bits (if you need it for reference) but uses record run mode for the regular timecode.

RED cameras can record two independent timecode tracks: "edge code" is SMPTE code that starts at 1:00:00 at the first frame of each piece of digital media (and is continuous between clips); "time code" is TOD code (or external free run code from another source) that is discontinuous between clips.

DOUBLE-SYSTEM AND MULTICAMERA SHOOTS. On productions when a separate audio recorder is being used, it will facilitate editing if the camera and recorder have the same timecode. For more on this, see p. 464.

On shoots when more than one video camera is being used at the same time, it's also helpful if they're operating with the same timecode. With cameras that can

21. Powering down, rewinding a tape, removing a tape, or replacing a tape may cause timecode breaks or discontinuities; see p. 226.

generate and accept an external timecode source, one technique is to run a cable from the timecode-out connector of one camera (the master) to the timecode-in on the second camera (the slave). Some cameras can import timecode via the FireWire connector. The master camera should be started first, then the slave. Make sure the two are running identical code before starting the take. Usually TOD code is used.

If you don't want the cameras wired together, you may be able to *jam-sync* one camera with the code from another or from a separate timecode source (such as Ambient's *Lockit box* or Denecke's *Syncbox*; see Fig. 11-20). The cameras are then used in free run mode and should maintain the same timecode. However, timecode may drift slightly over time, so you may need to rejam the cameras every few hours to keep their timecode identical.

Even with the same timecode, two or more cameras may not be perfectly in sync with each other for editing or live switching. For perfectly matched editing from one to the other, the cameras should be *genlocked* together. This can be done on professional cameras by running a cable from the video-out connector on one camera (or from a separate sync source) to the genlock-in connector on the other. With HD cameras, genlock is properly called *trilevel sync*. There are Lockit boxes and Syncboxes that can generate trilevel sync and timecode, to permit genlocked shooting with cameras not tethered by a wire.

Avoiding Timecode Problems

You can think of timecode as an organizational tool for keeping track of your material and locating it later. If you plan to do any editing, timecode is more than that: it's a crucial part of how the editing system retrieves video and audio data when needed. When using a camera that records to videotape, there are certain ground rules to follow (that are not an issue with file-based cameras).

REPEATING TIMECODE. You never want to have a situation in which the same timecode number occurs on a single tape in more than one place. A common way this can happen is with some DV and HDV cameras that reset the code to 00:00:00:00 every time you remove or insert a tape. You shoot part of a tape, take it out, then put it back in to finish recording it. When you're later searching for that great shot of a guitar player that starts at timecode 00:12:12:00, you find instead a shot of a drummer with the same code. This can create nightmares in editing.

With most tape camcorders you can avoid this whenever there's an interruption in code by rewinding the tape into the last previously recorded shot and playing to the end of it (*record review* or *end search* on the camera may do this automatically). Then when you start the new recording it will pick up where the timecode ended before (see Operating the Camcorder, p. 125). Some cameras have a *regen (regenerate) timecode* setting; this will continue the timecode already recorded on tape (as opposed to using "preset," which will usually start where you have it set). Regen should be used when shooting with a tape that was partially recorded before.

TIMECODE BREAKS. As discussed above, if you shoot carefully in record run mode you can record a whole tape with continuous, ascending timecode. However, wherever there are breaks in the timecode, when you bring the material into the editing system a new clip will be created at the break (see p. 571). When using time-of-day code, timecode breaks happen whenever you stop the camera (because the timecode jumps to a new time when you start recording again). Another way to cause a break is if you aren't careful and leave a gap after, say, rewinding the tape to check a take.

Timecode breaks aren't necessarily a big problem, but they can be annoying, especially if you're shooting a lot of short shots. If you know there's a break in code, be sure to leave five to ten seconds of preroll time after you start recording before calling "action." One solution for a tape that has timecode breaks or many short shots is to dub it to a new tape with continuous timecode before editing.

TIMECODE OUT OF ORDER. You want to avoid a situation in which a higher number timecode precedes a lower number on the same tape. This can happen when using time-of-day code (see above) or if you preset the code for an hour tape to start at 23:30:00:00 (because it would finish at 00:30:00:00). Editing systems expect the numbers on a tape to be *ascending* and get confused if a high number comes before a low number.

If you absolutely can't avoid this happening, make sure you note it carefully on the tape box or in the log for later reference.

DIGITAL VIDEO RECORDING— HOW IT WORKS

The Basic Idea

Before digital recording existed, there was analog. In analog recording, changes in light or sound are represented by a changing electrical signal. When a singer holds a microphone and starts to sing louder, the electrical voltage in the wire coming from the microphone increases. We can say that changes in the electrical signal are analogous to changes in the sound. If we use an analog tape deck to record the singer, those electrical changes are translated yet again into changes in magnetism on the tape. All these translations introduce small distortions and reduce the quality of the recording. When you copy an analog recording (and then make a copy of the copy) yet more distortions are introduced and the quality is reduced further.

The idea of digital recording is to express changes in light or sound as a set of binary numbers, ones and zeros, that represent those changes as precisely as possible. We can then transmit, record, and copy those basic digits with no translation errors. The copy is then a perfect clone of the original.

As a very simplistic idea of how digital transmission can be superior to analog, think of the "telephone" game kids sometimes play. A group of people sit in a circle and the first person whispers a phrase to the person on the right. Then that person whispers it to the next, and so on around the circle. Say, in this particular game, we use a musical tone instead: A woman plays a note on a piano, a B flat. The man next to her hears it, then tries to hum it to the next person. His pitch isn't perfect and neither is the next person's, and by the time you get around the circle the note sounds a lot different from what came out of the piano. This is the "analog" version of the game.

In the "digital" version, the woman doesn't play the note, but writes "B flat" on a piece of paper. The man copies what she's written (and checks that it's the same as the original); then the guy next to him copies and checks it again; and so on down the line. By passing along this written version of the note, when it comes fully around the circle, we can still know exactly what that note is and play it again on the piano.

Digital recording works by sampling the audio or video signal at regular intervals of time; each sample is a measurement of the voltage at that one slice in time. That measurement is converted to a number that can be recorded on tape or on disk (converting the voltage to a number is called *quantizing*). Once the number is recorded, we can pass it along, much like the written B flat in the game, and reproduce it exactly even after many copies have been made.

In digital systems, all numbers are expressed in binary code, which uses a series of ones and zeros. (The number 5 would be 101 in binary.) Each digit in a binary number is a bit (101 is thus a three-bit number). By convention, eight bits together make a byte. The entire process of converting a video or audio signal to digital form is called digitizing and is done by an analog-to-digital (A/D) converter, which is usually an internal chip or card. To view the picture or hear the sound, we need to convert it back from digital to analog form using a digital-to-analog (D/A) converter, because our eyes and ears are analog, not digital.

The process of digitally recording video shares a lot with digitally recording audio, but there are differences. Let's look at video first. Digital audio recording is described on p. 405.

Digital Video Recording—With Buckets

See Camera and Recorder Basics, p. 5, before reading this section.

Let's look at how a digital video camera converts light to a digital recording. The camera's sensor is a grid of thousands or millions of photosites that are sensitive to light. We'll assume here that each photosite equals one pixel, or picture element in the image (which is not always the case). For the rest of this discussion, we'll use the more common term, pixels, instead of photosites.

Each pixel is a receptor that collects light (*photons*) when the camera shutter is open. To use a simple analogy, we can think of each pixel as a tiny bucket that collects raindrops (see Fig. 5-25). We put out a large number of buckets in a grid and uncover them (opening the shutter), and rain falls into the buckets. Then we cover them again (close the shutter) and measure exactly how much fell into each bucket.

In the actual camera sensor, each pixel gets a different amount of light depending on whether it's in a bright area of the picture or in shadow. The *sampling* aspect of digital video takes place both in *space* (light is measured only where the pixels are) and in *time* (light is collected only during the time the shutter is open).

Returning to the water buckets, let's imagine that along the side of each one there's a numbered scale, with 0 at the bottom and 4 at the top. We can walk from bucket to bucket, writing down the water level in each according to that scale: for a half-full bucket we'd record a number 2; a full bucket would be a 4. We now have a list of numbers that describes how much water is in every bucket in this large array of buckets. We've converted the pattern of rainfall to numbers. This is quantizing.

If we wanted to, we could set up an identical set of buckets somewhere else, fill

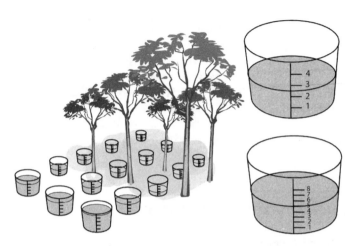

Fig. 5-25. Digital video recording—the bucket version. (left) Buckets placed on the ground in a grid pattern collect different amounts of rainwater depending on where they are in the scene. This is akin to how pixels in the camera's sensor collect different amounts of electric charge after being struck by light from the scene. (right) These two buckets have the same amount of water. The measurement scale on the upper bucket has only four levels, so the water level would be considered either 2 or 3, introducing a half-unit error (there's no such thing as 2½ in digital). The scale on the lower bucket has eight levels, so we can say the water level is precisely 5 units with no error. In the digital equivalent, the scale on the lower bucket can be thought of as having greater *bit depth* or *precision*. (Steven Ascher)

them with water according to our list of numbers, and reproduce the original pattern of rain.

This is essentially how digital imaging works. The pixels are struck by different amounts of light and respond by creating different amounts of electrical charge. The A/D converter measures the charge at each pixel and converts it to a number.[22] That digital number (after a lot of digital signal processing) can then be sent to a video monitor and converted back into light.

For a high-fidelity recording, we want to be able to reproduce the original scene as closely as possible. One key factor is how many pixels (buckets) we use; more on that below. Another factor is how precisely we measure the level of each one. In our rainwater example, the scale on the side of each bucket has four levels. But what if the level of water in one bucket were exactly halfway between level 2 and level 3? In digital systems, you can only record whole numbers, so we'd have to score what was actually a 2½ as either a 2 or a 3—introducing a rounding error that makes our recording inaccurate (see Figs. 5-25 and 10-3). In technical terms, this is a *quantizing error*.

For more precision, we could use buckets that had a finer scale, say from 0 to 8. Now we could score that same water level as precisely a 5, with no error. This is the

22. The sensor's job of translating light energy to electrical energy is an analog process (even in a digital camera). With a CCD chip, the sensor downloads the charge from one row of pixels at a time, sending the signal to the A/D converter. In a CMOS chip, every pixel does its own A/D conversion and the data comes off the chip already digitized.

concept of *bit depth* or *precision*. A two-bit system gives us four levels on the scale; a three-bit system gives us eight levels. The more levels (bits) we have, the more precisely and accurately we can measure the water in each bucket.

It's also important to think about what happens with buckets if they get too little or too much rain. If only a few drops fall in a bucket we can't measure it, because it's below our lowest level on the scale. In digital terms, that amount of light will be lost in the noise. And if too much rain falls, our bucket will overflow and stop collecting rain. When a pixel has absorbed all the photons it can handle, it becomes overexposed and stops responding. This is what happens when the sensor becomes saturated, and the light exceeds the exposure range of the camera (see p. 185).

PIXELS AND RESOLUTION

The Pixel Array

The digital video frame is made up of a lattice or grid of pixels. As discussed in Chapter 1, video formats differ in their number of pixels and in the number of horizontal lines the pixels are arranged in (see p. 8). Take a look at Fig. 5-26. The top image is divided into a lattice of fairly large pixels in relatively few horizontal lines. The middle image has far more pixels in the same area and more horizontal lines. The middle image is capable of capturing finer detail—its *resolution* is higher.

If the number of pixels is too low, the image will look unsharp, and other artifacts may be introduced. One such defect is aliasing, which can produce a moiré pattern (see Fig. 5-18) or cause diagonal lines in the frame to look like jagged stair steps (see Fig. 1-11).

If the number of pixels is high enough, the eye can't even discern that the image is divided into pixels at all. Compare Fig. 12-33, which is the same image with yet more (and smaller) pixels. HD video formats have higher resolution than SD formats in part because they have more horizontal lines and more pixels.

Interestingly, our ability to judge resolution in an image is directly related to how large the image appears. You can hold Fig. 12-33 fairly close to your face and it looks fine. With Fig. 5-26, which is a lower-resolution version, it looks pretty bad from close up, but if you view it from several feet away, it looks sharper. As you step back, the pixels start to disappear and the image begins to look continuous. In the ongoing debate about how much resolution we really need in our cameras and video formats, key questions are: How big is the screen? From how far away are you viewing it? For example, many people argue that in typical living room viewing conditions consumers can't see the difference between 1080p (1920 x 1080 pixels) and 720p (1280 x 720 pixels). When it comes to theatrical distribution, people debate how much difference audiences can detect between 1080p, 2K (about 2048 x 1080), and 4K (4096 x 2160); for more, see p. 71. It depends on screen size and how far back you sit in the theater.

Bit Depth or Precision

We've seen that resolution can be increased by increasing the number of pixels. We can also improve resolution by measuring the brightness of each pixel more

Fig. 5-26. (top) A relatively low number of pixels forms a coarse, low-resolution image. (middle) Using more pixels in a finer grid produces a higher-resolution image. (bottom) This image has the same number of pixels as the middle image but the bit depth is only three bits per pixel instead of eight. Note the discontinuous tonalities. Try viewing these images from a distance to see how they appear sharper. Compare with Fig. 12-33. Also see Fig. 1-8.

precisely. Remember the buckets and how we could measure the water level more precisely with a finer scale?

Eight-bit video systems can distinguish between 256 different brightness values for each pixel—which really means, if you think about it, 256 different shades of red, 256 different shades of green, and 256 shades of blue. For a total number of color combinations of 256^3. In the millions.

Sixteen-bit systems yield 65,536 gradations of each color. Or $65,536^3$ combinations of colors. That's a lot more colors. In the millions of millions.

The more gradations, the finer the detail you can render. Greater bit depth particularly facilitates any manipulation like color correction or recovering shadow detail that involves stretching image tones.

In Fig. 5-26, the middle image uses 8 bits, while the bottom image (which has the same number of pixels) has only 3 bits per pixel. Notice how the shading on the wall and on the man's face is relatively continuous in the middle picture and is blocky and discontinuous in the lower picture (this discontinuity is called *banding* or *posterization*).

The bottom image in Fig. 5-26 has no more than eight levels of brightness from black to white—you can actually count each level on the wall. Clearly, this is very unlike the way the scene appeared in reality. Unsurprisingly, you won't find any 3-bit camcorders on the market.

Many video formats use 8 bits, a few have 10- or 12-bit precision, and some high-quality HD systems use 16 bits. Increasing the number of bits beyond a certain point isn't necessarily directly visible to the eye. However, there are various types of digital processing (such as effects work and color correction) where any errors get multiplied, so having more precision helps prevent visible artifacts. The downside of using more bits is that it means more data to process, store, and transmit.

Pixel Shape

Not all pixels are created equal: the shape (proportions) depends on the format. The pixels in computer video systems and most HD video formats are square (see Fig. 5-27). However, the pixels used in SD video formats, and in 1080 HDV (but not 720p HDV), are rectangular (nonsquare). NTSC 601 nonwidescreen video uses pixels that are slightly taller than they are wide. PAL 601 nonwidescreen video has pixels that are slightly wider than they are tall.

Pixel shape can be described as a number: the *pixel aspect ratio (PAR)*. It's the ratio of pixel width to height, like the way display aspect ratio is expressed (see Fig. 1-12). Nonwidescreen 601 and NTSC DV have a pixel aspect ratio of 0.9; for wide-screen it's 1.2. PAL nonwidescreen is 1.066; widescreen is 1.42. Both 1080 HDV and DVCPRO HD are 1.33.

If you work in only one format, pixel aspect ratio is usually not a major concern. Most editing systems make the necessary adjustments when you input video from the camera. However, if you are working with a mix of formats that have different PARs, or you're creating graphics in an application like Photoshop, you need to be aware of it. Figure 5-27 shows that a ball originating in a square pixel format looks horizontally squished when shown in a format with narrower pixels. Similarly, if you create titles in a graphics program and import them into your SD video they could

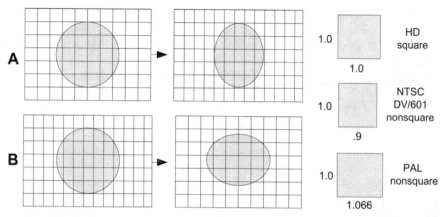

Fig. 5-27. Pixel aspect ratio. When converting between formats or systems that have different-shaped pixels, the image can become distorted if adjustments aren't made. (A) An image created in a square pixel format (such as HD or any computer graphics application) can look horizontally squeezed when imported into standard definition NTSC-based formats, which use tall, nonsquare pixels. (B) An image created in an NTSC-based format can look horizontally stretched when shown on a computer monitor (which displays square pixels) or imported into a computer graphics application. Note that settings vary, and some apps compensate automatically, so your results may not be distorted or may be distorted in different ways. The NTSC and PAL pixel aspect ratios indicated on the right are for nonwidescreen formats.

become distorted if not built and converted correctly. To avoid image distortions, consult the manuals of your graphics and editing software when combining material with different pixel aspect ratios.

Resolution and Sharpness

The *resolution* of a video image refers to its ability to reproduce fine detail. When fine detail is rendered clearly, an image will often look sharp to the eye. But sharpness is a complicated topic. There are many factors that play a part in apparent sharpness. These include the measurable fine detail of the image (resolution), the contrast of the picture (higher-contrast images tend to look sharper than low), and the distance from which we are viewing it (the farther away and smaller an image is, the sharper it looks). In the end, audiences care about the subjective perception of sharpness and not about resolution per se.

Particularly when comparing video formats or cameras, people look for numerical ways to express resolution and sharpness. All of them are useful to some extent, but none of them perfectly correlates to the actual experience of *looking* at video footage. If camera X has 10 percent better numbers than camera Y, it won't necessarily look that way on screen.[23]

23. Not to mention that manufacturers sometimes claim numbers that can be misleading. For example, a camera with a single 4K sensor cannot produce a 4K image (since with a Bayer pattern, once it is demosaicked, you only have about 80 percent of the original resolution; see RAW Capture, p. 203).

When talking about resolution, the first thing to consider is the frame size, particularly the number of horizontal lines. Standard definition DV has 480 horizontal lines of pixels; high definition HDCAM has 1080. HDCAM is thus a higher resolution format. Even so, you could have two formats that have the same number of lines, but different resolution due to one being interlaced and the other progressive (the latter is higher resolution). Bit depth or precision plays a part too: a 10-bit format has a higher resolution than an 8-bit format with the same pixel count. When comparing two cameras that record the same frame size, there can be differences in resolution due to the particular sensor, compression, or lens, or factors like frame rate (higher frame rates look sharper due to less motion blur).

Various methods are used to evaluate images.

One technique is to look closely at a test pattern of finely spaced vertical lines. The higher the resolution of the format, the smaller and more tightly packed the lines can be and still be distinguishable. If you were shooting a picket fence, how small could the fence be and still have individual slats visible? This can be measured in *TV lines per picture height* (*TVL/ph*). "Per picture height" means that instead of counting lines all the way across the frame, we measure only the same distance as the height of the picture. This allows comparisons between widescreen and non-widescreen images.

Don't confuse TV lines with the horizontal scan lines described above, or with the line-pairs-per-millimeter measurement used to evaluate film stocks. If someone says, "DV has a resolution of 500 lines," that person is referring to TV lines per picture height. TV lines are a rather inexact, simplified way to discuss resolution.

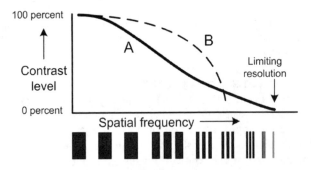

Fig. 5-28. An MTF (modulation transfer function) chart shows how well an imaging device (such as a lens) or a combined system (such as a lens plus a video camera, or a lens plus a film stock) can reproduce the contrast between black and white bars. On the left, the bars are far apart and the contrast is 100 percent. As we move to the right, the bars are thinner and more closely spaced; eventually they appear to blend together into gray (0 percent contrast). This point is the limiting resolution. System A can distinguish finer details than System B and has higher resolving power. However, B has better contrast in the middle range, which, for audiences viewing images from a distance, may make it look sharper.

A perhaps more useful measurement system is *MTF* (*modulation transfer function*), which looks at contrast as well as resolution. MTF examines a pattern of alternating black and white lines, specifically measuring the contrast between them. While TV lines per picture height measures only the *top limit* of resolution (which represents fine details that may not be that critical when images are viewed from far away), MTF looks at how the image holds up across a whole *range* of lines, from thick, widely spaced bars (low frequencies) to the finest lines (high frequencies). When the lines are relatively wide, any video system can recognize that the black lines are deep black and the white lines are bright white. (This is high contrast or "100 percent modulation.") But as the lines get very narrow, blurring across the borders between the lines makes the black bars lighter and the white bars darker, which reduces contrast. If the lines are so narrow that they exceed the resolution of the system (this is the TVL/ph limit) they all appear as gray. MTF can be used to compare lenses, cameras, film stocks, recording format, displays, or all together as a complete imaging system.

Bear in mind that even if a format or camera is theoretically capable of a certain resolution, many things can conspire to reduce resolution, including a low-quality lens, poor focus, or an unsharp monitor. Also note that sometimes a *less* sharp image looks better than an apparently sharp one (see p. 71).

Still Images and Video

If you're familiar with digital still photography or printing still images, you probably have a number of concepts in your head that *don't apply* to digital video. For example, the idea of talking about an image file's resolution in terms of *dots per inch* (DPI) or *pixels per inch* (PPI), which refer to the relationship of a digital image to how large it will eventually be printed on paper. This is irrelevant in digital video or images used on the Web.[24] In video, the size of the picture is simply its dimensions in pixels: how many pixels wide by how many pixels high. Sometimes people talk about video having a "resolution of 72 PPI," but that's merely a way to estimate how large an image will look on a monitor using numbers some people are familiar with.

Say you want to have a shot in your movie in which you zoom in on a still image. When you go to import the digital still or scan a photograph, all you care about is its dimensions in pixels. PPI or DPI numbers, which you may see in Photoshop or in a digital file's metadata, mean nothing in this context.[25] A still image with a lot of pixels relative to the video format you're working in may allow you to move in close and see details; an image with relatively fewer pixels will usually look soft or reveal individual pixels if you go in too close. If the image is too small to do a zoom with high quality, you can sometimes help yourself a little by scaling up the image to a larger size with a high-quality scaler (even so, you can't truly add resolution). Experiment with resizing settings in Photoshop or an application like PhotoZoom Pro that has sophisticated scaling algorithms. Sometimes sharpening the image helps too. For more on using stills in your movie, see p. 594.

24. DPI and PPI are sometimes used to talk about the spacing of pixels in a video monitor, but don't apply to the resolution of image files.

25. If you know the size of an image in inches and its DPI, you can calculate the size in pixels, which is what you need. One situation in which DPI *is* relevant is when scanning a still photograph, because a higher DPI setting in the *scanner* will result in more pixels in the resulting image file.

WORKING WITH DIGITAL DATA

While movies are about characters and stories, the tools of moviemaking are increasingly about creating, moving, and storing digital data. Even if you don't consider yourself a computer wiz, a little knowledge of basic concepts and common equipment can help you navigate this world.

You can think of digital audio and video as a stream of digits: ones and zeros. Different formats create different-sized streams. If data were water, imagine that the data stream produced by standard definition DV could flow through a thin garden hose. By comparison, uncompressed high definition 1080p might need a thick fire hose to move the data fast enough. The amount of information flowing every second is the *data rate*. The term *bandwidth* is also used to talk about data rate. Bandwidth is like the diameter of the hose. A high bandwidth connection can pass a lot of data quickly (high-speed Internet connections are called *broadband*). A connection with low bandwidth, or low *throughput*, has a relatively narrow hose.

In Appendix B, you can see a comparison of different formats and how much data they generate. Data rates are often expressed in megabits per second (Mbps). You will also see them as megabytes per second (MBps—note the capital *B*). There are eight bits in a byte, so a megabyte is eight times bigger. To review basic digital quantities: a kilobyte (KB) is 1,000 bytes; a megabyte (MB) is 1,000 KB and is often referred to as a "meg"; a gigabyte (GB) is 1,000 MB and is called a "gig"; and a terabyte (TB) is 1,000 GB.

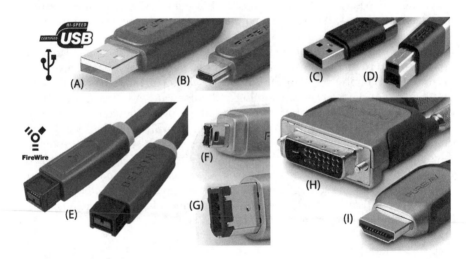

Fig. 5-29. Data and video connectors. (A) USB 2.0 male A connector. (B) USB 2.0 Mini B connector. (C) USB 3.0 male A connector (USB 3.0 is faster than 2.0 but this connector is backward compatible with 2.0 ports). (D) USB 3.0 male B connector. (E) FireWire 800 (IEEE 1394). (F) FireWire 400 four-pin connector. (G) FireWire 400 six-pin (the two extra pins supply power). (H) DVI connector. (I) HDMI connector. For other common connectors see Figs. 3-14, 10-13, and 10-32. (Belkin Corporation)

DIGITAL CONNECTIONS

When you work with cameras, monitors, computers, and editing systems you'll have many situations where you need to connect pieces of gear together. You may have several options depending on the equipment, the video format, and what you're trying to do. It's easy to get confused when talking about these connections because several factors can be involved:

- The original recording itself: what format it's in and the data rate being used.
- The output and input options of the equipment you're using: an HD camera, for example, might be able to output your recording as digital HD via an HDMI cable or as analog NTSC via a composite cable.
- The actual cables and connectors between machines: in some cases, one type of connector can carry only one of the options; in others, the same cable might be used for different formats.

As for the first item, you'll find a listing of some widely used formats starting on p. 21. For the second item, you find the video color systems and how they compare on p. 207. Regarding number three, here are the main types of connection technologies.

USB. *Universal Serial Bus* is a common, low-cost connector found on all computers. USB 2.0, with data rates up to 480 Mbps, has some video uses (like backing up data) but is usually not fast enough for video editing. Newer USB 3.0 connectors support data transfer up to about 3 to 5 Gbps, though not all machines have them, and not all are compatible with one another.

FIREWIRE (ALSO CALLED IEEE 1394 OR i.LINK). FireWire connections have been a mainstay of many consumer and prosumer cameras and computers since the late 1990s. FireWire is an Apple term for what's defined officially as *IEEE 1394*. Sony's name for the same thing is *i.Link*. Avid calls it simply *1394*.

People originally used FireWire cables to connect DV equipment, but many other formats can be used with FireWire, including HDV, DVCPRO HD, and uncompressed SD. The original FireWire system is capable of 400 Mbps and is called FW400. FW800 is twice as fast and is found on many computers and hard drives. FW400 connectors come in four-pin and six-pin styles (the six-pin has two pins to carry power); the FW800 connector has nine pins. FireWire devices can be *daisy-chained* and with the right cable or adapter you can connect FW400 devices to FW800 devices. However, if you do this the speed of all devices on that bus will only be 400 Mbps.

THUNDERBOLT. Apple and Intel have introduced an exciting connection technology called *Thunderbolt* that supports two channels of data transfer on the same connector, each up to 10 Gbps. It has the potential to make many other types of high-speed connections obsolete. Thunderbolt is compatible with PCI Express and DisplayPort devices and allows monitors, computers, drives, and other devices to be daisy-chained from one to another. Thunderbolt uses a small connector (see Fig.

14-5) and can supply power to hard drives. As of this writing, Thunderbolt exists on late-model Apple computers and a growing number of hard drives, RAIDs, monitors, and peripherals from various manufacturers. Converters, like AJA's T-Tap, allow you to output video from a Thunderbolt port to a monitor's HDMI or SDI input.

HDMI. *High Definition Multimedia Interface* is a single-cable connection technology for uncompressed high definition, including audio and metadata, that is finding wide use in connecting cameras, monitors, Blu-ray players, and many other devices (see Fig. 5-29). HDMI version 1.3 supports all HDTV standards as well as RGB 4:4:4, and eight channels of audio at up to 10 Gbps. The newer HDMI 1.4 version also supports 3D formats and digital cinema 4K formats. Some Sony cameras like the NEX-FS100 can embed 30p or 24p SMPTE timecode along with 2:3 pulldown markers in HDMI 1.3.

SDI, HD-SDI, AND DUAL LINK. *Serial Digital Interface (SDI)* is used widely in professional video equipment. SDI can carry 8- and 10-bit 4:2:2 standard definition video with up to eight channels of digital audio. Sometimes referred to as *SMPTE 259M*, this connection is capable of a data rate up to 270 Mbps and uses BNC cables (see Fig. 3-14).

HD-SDI is a faster version, up to 1.485 Gbps, capable of carrying component HD video. Also known as *SMPTE 292M.*

For higher speeds, both SDI and HD-SDI can be used in *dual-link* configurations (sometimes with two cables but there is a dual-link 3 Gbps HD-SDI standard that uses one cable). When a Sony F35 outputs uncompressed 4:4:4 high definition video, it uses a dual-link HD-SDI connection to a HDCAM-SRW1 field recorder, as does an ARRI Alexa when it outputs RAW to a Codex Digital or S.two digital disk recorder.

When you require SDI or HD-SDI, use real SDI cables, and not standard coax composite cables that also use BNC connectors and look similar. This is especially important for long cable runs.

ETHERNET. Some recorders and playback decks have the ability to communicate and send files over the Internet through direct *Ethernet* connections to a camera or computer. If you have a wired computer network in your home, you're probably familiar with the Cat. 5 Ethernet cable and connector. Some cameras have a *gigabit Ethernet* connection that can handle data rates up to 1,000 Mbps.

HARD DRIVE STORAGE

There are lots of ways to store digital data, including flash memory cards, SSDs (solid-state drives that use a form of flash memory), hard drives, videotape, optical discs (like DVDs and Blu-rays), and LTO linear tape cassettes. The choice between them depends on cost, speed, convenience, and other considerations. Memory card, tape, and drive systems used primarily for shooting and archiving are discussed in earlier chapters. In postproduction and editing, hard drive storage systems are most commonly used, though SSDs (much more expensive) are gaining popularity due to their high data transfer speed and robustness.

Fig. 5-30. Blackmagic Design's HyperDeck Shuttle is a compact video recorder that can capture uncompressed 10-bit HD or SD files to removable flash media SSDs. Connects to a camera via HDMI, HD-SDI, or SDI. Uncompressed files in a QuickTime wrapper are compatible with most editing systems, and material can be edited directly from the SSD. (Blackmagic Design)

Though editing can be done on a computer with only one drive (such as a laptop), it's generally recommended that video and audio media not be stored on the same physical hard drive on which the OS (operating system) and NLE application are installed.[26] If your computer has open bays, you can add additional internal drives, which provide fast data flow. External drives have the advantage that you can bring them from system to system as needed.

Hard drive systems vary in terms of the type of interface between the drive and the computer, and in terms of how the drives are configured: Are they independent disks or grouped together into RAIDs? Are they part of a shared-storage network? Do they provide redundancy in case some of the data is lost or corrupted?

As we've seen, video formats vary widely in their data rates. When you choose a hard drive system, make sure it's up to your needs in terms of throughput (data transfer rate) and *seek time* (how fast data can be accessed). A utility or application on your computer can show you how fast data is being written and read from the drive. In editing, hard drives should be able to handle not just the basic data rate of the format you're working in, but multiple streams of video for situations when you're compositing more than one image at a time (see Appendix B for data rates).

When buying individual hard drives, check their rotational speed (faster is better for video, usually at least 7200 rpm). Some drives are formatted for Mac systems, others for Windows. You can easily reformat a drive to work on your system (use Drive Utility in Macs; use Disk Management in Windows).

Be sure to consult knowledgeable people before choosing drives or setting up a system.

Hard Drive Interfaces

Hard drives can be installed in or attached to a computer using various technologies. The *interface* or *bus* that connects the drive(s) and the computer determines in part how fast the connection is, how long cables can be, and how many

26. This may not be necessary with an SSD.

drives can be grouped together. The following are some of the main interface types as of this writing.

- **SATA.** *Serial ATA* (*SATA*) drives are used widely in computers and make for affordable internal storage (within the computer case). Larger computer cases have room for additional SATA drives inside. When SATA drives are used in an external enclosure, an *eSATA* interface can be used to connect the drives to an eSATA adapter in the computer. SATA version 3.0 can transfer data at up to 6 Gbps.
- **FireWire drives.** A *FireWire drive* is simply a SATA drive with a FireWire "bridge" board mounted in a single hard drive enclosure. They are easy to set up and relatively inexpensive. As discussed above, FireWire connections come in FW400 and FW800 versions. Although FireWire allows devices to be daisy-chained, you'll get better performance (fewer dropped frames) if the media drives are on a different bus—digital signal path— than the deck or camera. Adding another FireWire controller card (set of FireWire connectors) to the PCI Express slot at the back of your computer isn't hard.
- **Fibre channel** combines high data rates several orders faster than FireWire with the ability to network many drives or devices together, with long cables between computer and drives. Fibre channel systems can be expensive.
- **SCSI** (pronounced "scuzzy") drives offer high performance and can be grouped together in high-capacity configurations. SCSI drives, once common, are used rarely for video today. They are more complex and more expensive than FireWire.

RAIDs

Several drives can be operated together as a single unit in a *RAID* (*redundant array of independent disks*). RAIDs can be made up of hard drives or SSD flash memory drives. Drives can be configured in different types of RAIDs for different purposes. Whichever type of RAID is used, the drives work together and are treated as one giant drive or "volume" by the computer.

- A set of drives in the RAID-0 configuration spreads data across multiple drives (called *striping*). RAID-0 both multiplies disk space and increases the data transfer rate, which may be needed for high definition and uncompressed formats. With striping, the system alternates between more than one disk at a time when writing and reading data, avoiding bottlenecks.
- RAID-1 configures drives for *mirroring*, in which the same data is placed on two or more drives at once for full redundancy.
- RAID-3 further protects against drive failures or corrupt data by using a technique called *parity*, which involves placing a reference copy of the data on a dedicated disk to safeguard against errors.
- RAID-5 is popular for video editing with Macs and uses a combination of striping for speed and parity for safety (if a drive goes down, data can be re-

built after the damaged drive is replaced). Since some storage space is used for this level of protection, four 1 TB drives in a RAID 5 configuration give you 3 TB of storage.

- RAID-6 is fast and provides maximum protection (some say it's for the paranoid).

A RAID system can be controlled with just software, or with a dedicated hardware controller attached to the computer. The latter is faster and reduces the load on the CPU. Be sure to get a RAID designed specifically to handle video.

Sometimes several drives are housed in the same enclosure, but are independent and not in a RAID configuration, so the computer just sees them as separate drives. They may be called JBOD—Just a Bunch of Disks.

Fig. 5-31. A RAID is several drives grouped together to improve performance and/or data security. In the rear view of this Mercury Elite Pro Qx2 unit you can see four hot-swappable hard drive bays. (Other World Computing)

Networks

There are many situations in which it's helpful for several users to access stored video and audio from different workstations or locations. For example, in a postproduction facility, an editor could be cutting a movie while special effects work is done on the same files, while the sound editor is using the same material to prep for the mix.

Many technologies are used to network computers and storage devices together. A *local area network* (*LAN*) can be used to transfer files between systems, and sometimes it's fast enough for editing. A *storage area network* (*SAN*) is a more versatile and expensive solution that allows multiple users to work from the same files. Apple's Xsan and Avid's Unity systems both use fibre channel and are complex systems requiring expert setup.

The least expensive but often sufficient method is to physically carry portable drives (such as FireWire drives) from machine to machine as needed. This low-tech solution is known affectionately as "sneakernet."

Hard Drive Storage Tips

When estimating how much hard drive storage you'll need during production, consult Appendix B to see the storage requirements per hour of material for the format you're working in (AJA makes a handy calculator, which can be found at AJA.com and as a mobile app). Don't forget to include extra drives for backup storage. If you're just starting a project and trying to estimate your future storage needs, you could multiply the number of shooting days by how much material you plan to shoot each day or you could guess based on the length of the finished piece and the shooting ratio (see p. 360).

When estimating how much storage you'll need during editing and postproduction, don't forget to include space for graphics, music, and other files you'll add during editing (such as outputs of the movie for the Web or finishing) and for the render files and timeline archiving that the NLE will create on its own.

Keep in mind that due to hard drive formatting and the way binary numbers are counted, you get less storage on a drive than the advertised capacity suggests (for example, a "1 TB" drive usually only has about 930 GB available storage). Also, many people feel you should leave 10 to 25 percent of a drive unused (filling a drive too full can result in slow data transfer).

Cleaning up unneeded files and doing maintenance can make a big difference. When using a Mac system, DiskWarrior is highly recommended to rebuild directories on a regular basis, which can help with performance and prevent crashes and data loss.

Generally speaking, all hard drives crash eventually. Your data is not secure if it's on only one drive. Back up your data and don't leave your backups in one location (see pp. 92 and 117).

FILE FORMATS AND DATA EXCHANGE

The digital systems we use to make movies involve lots of data. To exchange files between different systems, the data has to be packaged so it can be correctly interpreted. For example, when a digital video camera makes a recording, it doesn't just record the pixels that make up each frame, but also lots of data about things like the frame rate, timecode, audio, and sampling rate. As another example, a digital editing system doesn't simply play one shot after another, but works with all sorts of associated information, including how to transition from one shot to the next, how loud to play the audio, and what shape the frame should be.

We can divide all this information into two groups. The pictures and sounds themselves are the *media* (sometimes called the *essence*). The *metadata* is all the other information about how to play or edit the media, including things like the name of the file and the date it was created. Metadata is data about data. If making a movie were like baking a cake, the media files would be the ingredients and the metadata would be the nutrition label and/or the recipe.

To make movies, we need ways to transfer both the media and the metadata from a camera to an editing system, from one editing system to another, or from a disc to a video player. There are several file formats that serve as *containers* (also called *wrappers*) to bundle the media and metadata together and describe how they're stored, which makes it easier to work with them (see Fig. 5-32).

When you shoot video with a digital camera, the video is compressed with a codec (see Digital Compression, p. 245). For example, you might record using the AVCHD or DV codecs. The audio may be uncompressed or recorded with a different codec (for example, Dolby Digital). The movie file your camera records to a memory card or hard drive is made by wrapping the video and audio and metadata inside a container file format.

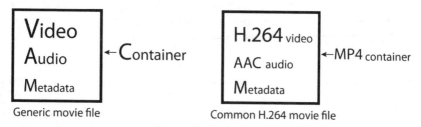

Generic movie file   Common H.264 movie file

Fig. 5-32. A digital movie file is made up of video, audio, and metadata packaged inside a container or wrapper. The video may be uncompressed or it may be compressed with one of many possible codecs (such as H.264, DV, DVCPRO HD, etc.). Similarly, the audio may be uncompressed (PCM) or compressed with a codec such as Dolby Digital, MP3, AAC, and so on. Common container formats include QuickTime (.mov), MXF (.mxf), and MPEG-4 (.mp4). When sharing files, it's important to know the video and audio codecs (if any) as well as the container format.

Container formats vary. Some are designed to be open exchange formats, allowing you to conveniently transfer media and metadata from one platform to another. Other wrappers are proprietary and work only on certain systems or with certain applications. In some cases, you might have video wrapped in one format, and you need to unwrap it and convert it to another wrapper format in order to work with it on your system.

File name extensions including .mov, .avi, .mxf, .flv, and .f4v are container formats that may contain different audio, video, or image formats. Your NLE may be able to import a given container file, but to work with the data it contains, the NLE needs to have installed the codec(s) that were used to compress the video and audio when the file was made.

This issue often comes up when people share footage or a movie that they're working on. When exchanging files, keep in mind that it's not just the container that matters. If someone says, "I sent you a QuickTime of the scene," you need to know what codec she used to make the QuickTime file, because if you don't have that codec on your machine, you may not be able to play the file. All of the wrappers listed below can contain a wide range of codecs. Often, instead of directly passing files back and forth, a production team will share material by posting to a website or a video-sharing site like YouTube or Vimeo. This has several advantages, including not having to exchange large files and usually not having to worry about whether the person you're sharing with can handle a particular codec or wrapper, since the sharing site will convert to commonly used formats. For more on making a movie file to share, see Exporting a File, p. 614.

Wrappers are used in both production and postproduction. In an ideal world, projects could be edited on any system in any format, then have the video, audio, and metadata wrapped so that the project could be transferred to any other system for display or for further work. That level of universal, seamless interchange is not yet here.

Some Common Wrappers

QUICKTIME. QuickTime was developed by Apple and is supported by a wide range of applications. Software from Apple is available for compatibility in Windows, though not all codecs may be supported. QuickTime files normally have the extension .mov.

MPEG-4. The newer MPEG-4 container file format (.mp4 or .m4v extension) was adapted from QuickTime. (Creating an .mp4 file from your video may still be called "QuickTime conversion.") What can get confusing is that while MPEG-4 is a container format, there are also codecs that are part of the MPEG-4 family. An MP4 file, for example, can contain MPEG-4 video in the form of H.264, but it can also contain MPEG-2 video. You have to open it up to find out what's inside.

WINDOWS MEDIA. Microsoft's container format has evolved and had various names, including Video for Windows and Windows Media. Like Apple, Microsoft has built a large media creation and distribution system around Windows Media formats and wrappers. Some files have the extension .wmv.

MXF. *MXF* (*Material Exchange Format*) is a wrapper used in cameras and editing systems to facilitate transfer of a wide range of media files and metadata from one system to another. It can be used at all stages of content creation, including acquisition, editing, and distribution. As one example, Sony's XDCAM EX wraps MPEG-2 files in the MXF format and offers the potential to include such metadata as voice notes from the cameraperson, or GPS location information.

AAF AND OMF. *AAF* (*Advanced Authoring Format*) shares many aspects of MXF and is also an open format for exchanging media and metadata between different applications or systems. AAF grew out of an Avid format called *OMFI* (*Open Media Framework Interchange*), which is often referred to just as *OMF*.

AAF is often used in postproduction as a way to transfer project elements such as video, audio, graphics, animation, and effects from one application to another. For example, AAF can be used to export sound files from a nonlinear editing system to a digital audio workstation in preparation for a sound mix. For more on this process, see Chapters 14 and 15.

XML. The *XML Interchange Format* is not a wrapper or a way to move media exactly, but it's a tool used to describe data in one application using plain text so it can easily be understood by another. As one example, XML is sometimes used to transfer an editing project from one NLE to another, and it provides information about the sequence, the video and audio settings, and so on. One NLE translates the project from its proprietary system into XML and the other reads the XML and translates that to its own proprietary system. Often, not *all* aspects of the project survive the translation. XML can be used to generate other types of files, like OMFs or AAFs, which help move files from one app to another.

DPX. *Digital Picture Exchange* is a nonproprietary container file for uncompressed images; it was originally derived from the Cineon (.cin) files of Kodak motion picture film scanners. DPX supports multiple resolutions—HD, 2K, 4K—as well as timecode, metadata, and embedded audio. Files can be log or linear, and restored on a per-frame basis to reduce the amount of storage required when conforming. DPX is used extensively in Hollywood for effects work.

DIGITAL COMPRESSION

See What Is Compression?, p. 19, before reading this section.

Though digital compression is a complex topic, the idea behind it is simple: take some video or audio, use a codec to compress it into a smaller package, then decompress it again when you want to view or hear it. Ideally, after going through this process, the material looks and sounds as good as it did originally.

Starting from the camera's sensor, there is a long chain of events from recording to editing to broadcast. Forms of compression can happen at every stage.[27] One of the first things that happens in most cameras is that the RGB data from the sensor is processed into component video, reducing the color information in a way that normally isn't noticeable to the viewer (see Video Color Systems, p. 207). Different formats throw away different amounts of color data.

At this point, we have what's called *uncompressed video*.[28] Uncompressed video uses a lot of data; how much depends on the format (see Appendix B). Uncompressed is the top quality the format is capable of. However, uncompressed video requires so much storage and processing power that it just isn't practical in most digital cameras. Uncompressed video is often used in editing and finishing, however.

To compress the video prior to recording, a codec (compression/decompression algorithm) is used. Some codecs are standardized for an entire format. For example, the DV codec is employed in all DV cameras; no matter which manufacturer made your camera, the video it records should be playable with DV from other cameras (even so, some cameras do a better job of compressing than others). Other codecs are proprietary to one company or a group of companies and, if they're good codecs, are intended to get you to buy that company's gear (for example, you won't find Panasonic's DVCPRO HD on a Sony camera). Codecs can be hardware—a chip, for example—or they can exist wholly in software.

Some codecs don't degrade the image at all. With *lossless compression*, you can decompress the video and get a picture that has perfect fidelity to the original before you compressed it. *Lossy compression*, on the other hand, throws away information that can never be restored. In practical use, almost all codecs are lossy but can still look great to viewers. Some codecs can be used at different levels of compression, so the same codec could look very good at a light compression setting, and worse with heavier compression. If you've worked with digital stills, you may

27. The word "compression" can have several meanings in film, video, and audio. The digital data compression being discussed here should not be confused with compressing audio levels (see p. 454) or video levels (see pp. 185–207).

28. Note that what is called "uncompressed" video has really already been compressed somewhat in the conversion from RGB to component color space, which discards some of the chroma information.

be familiar with the JPEG file format (with the file name extension .jpg), which allows you to select how much compression you want: the greater the compression, the smaller the file, and the lower the quality. Several video codecs are based on JPEG.

COMPRESSION METHODS

Different codecs use different techniques to compress video. These are some of the main methods.

Compressing Within a Frame

All codecs compress individual frames. In other words, they take each video frame one at a time, and delete some of the data while trying to preserve image quality.[29] This is called *intraframe compression* or *spatial compression*. Intraframe means "within the frame."

Many intraframe codecs use a process called *DCT* (*discrete cosine transform*). Versions of DCT are used in DV, DigiBeta, HDCAM, and other formats. Basically, DCT involves analyzing the picture in 8 x 8 blocks of pixels called *macroblocks*. It then uses sophisticated formulas to delete repetitive information and compact the data.

Another intraframe compression process, called *wavelet*, used for both video and audio, is gaining popularity. Hollywood's Digital Cinema Initiatives adopted wavelet-based JPEG 2000 for theatrical distribution partly because any dropouts cause the affected area to turn soft in focus instead of blocky, as DCT codecs do.

Different codecs compress the data by different amounts. For example, standard definition DigiBeta compresses about 2:1; DV uses heavier compression, about 5:1. The more compression, the greater the chance of artifacts, such as the "mosquito noise" that can sometimes be seen in DV images as dark or light pixels around sharp edges and text.

With intraframe compression, each frame stands on its own, independent of the others. This speeds up the compression/decompression process and makes editing much simpler. Apple's ProRes and Avid's DNxHD editing codecs are examples of this idea. However, intraframe compression alone creates files that are larger than if interframe compression is also used (see below).

Compressing a Group of Frames

Video images can be thought of as existing in the horizontal and vertical dimensions of the frame, as well as another dimension: time. The intraframe compression we just looked at compresses data in the first two dimensions. *Interframe compression* analyzes a string of frames over time and finds ways to delete repetitive information from one to the next (interframe meaning "between frames"). This method is also called *temporal* (relating to time) *compression*.

To get the idea of interframe compression, try looking at some video footage in

---

29. With interlaced formats, this may be done on a field-by-field instead of a frame-by-frame basis. DV uses adaptive *interfield* compression: if little difference is detected between two interlaced fields in a frame, the DV codec will compress them together as if they were progressive to save bits.

slow motion. You'll notice that very often, not much changes from frame to frame. An extreme example is a "locked off" (nonmoving) shot of an empty, windowless room. You could shoot for an hour and the first frame you recorded and the thousands that follow would be identical. Rather than record each of these individually, we could save a lot of space if we could somehow record just one frame with instructions to keep repeating it for an hour.

Obviously, most video footage has some movement, and some has a great deal, so we can't just repeat frames. However, codecs that use interframe compression look for anything that stays the same from frame to frame—even if it moves somewhat—and finds ways to reuse the data it already has stored rather than trying to store a whole new frame every time. Interframe compression works by looking at a group of frames together (referred to as a *group of pictures*, or *GOP*). The first frame in the group is recorded normally. But for several of the frames that follow, instead of storing a whole picture, the codec only records the *differences* between the frame and its neighboring frames. Recording only the differences between frames takes a lot less data than recording the actual frames themselves.

Interframe codecs are used for an impressive number of production, distribution, and transmission systems, including formats used in cameras, DVDs, and cable, satellite, and broadcast TV. Interframe codecs include those based on MPEG-2, such as HDV, XDCAM, and XDCAM HD, and those based on MPEG-4, such as AVCHD and H.264 used in DSLRs. In these codecs, each GOP has three types of frames (see Fig. 5-33).

- *I-frames (intraframes)* are independent frames that get fully recorded. I-frames are compressed using intraframe compression as described above. I-frames can be thought of as solid anchors that begin each GOP. They can be reproduced by themselves without reference to any other frames.
- *P-frames (predicted frames)* have about half as much information as I-frames. The P-frame contains only the differences between itself and the previous I-frame or P-frame. In playback, the codec uses those instructions to rebuild what the P-frame should look like.
- *B-frames (bidirectionally predicted frames)* have about one-fourth the information of I-frames. Each B-frame is made up of the differences between I- or P-frames that come before *and* after it (sometimes B-frames are called "between frames"). This is done by storing a group of frames in memory, making all the calculations, then outputting the frames and instructions in proper order.

Different interframe formats use a different-length GOP. The length of the GOP affects how the compressor handles motion and complexity: the longer the GOP, the more you can compress the data, but that means more processing power is needed to keep up with the calculations. The 720p version of HDV, for instance, uses a 6-frame GOP; the 1080i version uses a longer, 15-frame GOP.

As a filmmaker, what does all this mean for you? Well, the upside of interframe compression is that it results in more efficient compression and more convenient storage. It makes low-cost HD formats like XDCAM and AVCHD possible in the first place.

The downside is that it can create problems in shooting, editing, and distribution. Different versions of MPEG-2, MPEG-4, and other codecs that use interframe compression behave differently, so these problems may or may not apply to the system you're using. But it helps to understand some of the potential underlying issues, discussed below.

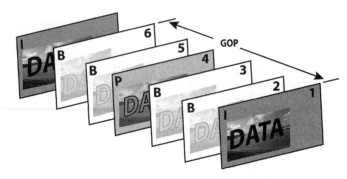

Fig. 5-33. Interframe compression means compressing several frames in a group (a group of pictures, or GOP). Only the I-frame is independently and completely stored; the P- and B-frames are calculated based on neighboring frames. The P-frame has about half as much data as the I-frame and the B-frames have one-quarter; compared to I-frames, they require more computing time to generate or view them. Pictured here is a 6-frame GOP used in the 720p version of HDV. The 1080i version uses a 15-frame "long GOP." The longer the GOP, the greater the compression, and the more computing time and power that's required to work with the material.

SHOOTING AND EDITING WITH INTERFRAME CODECS. In shooting, problems may result from the way interframe codecs handle footage that has a lot of complexity or action. As discussed, the codec is always looking for redundancy (repetition) between frames. When things don't change much (remember the locked-off shot of the room?) the codec has very little to do. But when things change a lot, the compressor can get overwhelmed by all the data (the more change, the harder it is for the codec to generate all those P- and B-frames). A shot that has a lot of detail and motion—for example, a tree branch with fluttering leaves or a panning wide shot of a stadium full of cheering fans—could cause the picture to momentarily break up: MPEG-2 may break into blocky, noisy artifacts; MPEG-4 may create less conspicuous artifacts because it uses smaller macroblocks than MPEG-2. On the whole, though, both codecs make excellent HD images with few obvious flaws.

In editing, a long GOP creates other challenges. In a certain sense, the P- and B-frames don't fully exist (at least they aren't completely stored); they have to be generated every time you want to look at one. This puts a lot of demand on the editing system when you view or edit individual frames. If you make a cut *within* a group of pictures, the system has to insert a new I-frame and build a new sequence of I-, P-, and B-frames before the footage can be output (you can't start a GOP with just P- and B-frames; you always need an I-frame to begin the group).

While editing long-GOP formats is not as straightforward as intraframe formats like DV, most professional and prosumer NLEs, including Final Cut and Avid, can handle them well as long as you have a reasonably fast computer. If you plan to do a lot of effects or have many streams of video, the system can slow down. With some NLEs, you can choose to edit natively with the interframe codec from your camera, but let the system create any effects with an intraframe codec like ProRes or DNxHD.

Another issue arises when you've edited the movie and you're ready to export it from the NLE to a file or on tape. To export an HDV sequence, for example, the NLE must first reestablish the 15-frame GOP structure along the entire length of the project. Depending upon the muscle of your computer's CPU and the amount of RAM you have, this begins a rendering process (also called *conforming*) that can take hours (or much longer if the work is feature length or contains many effects layers). Heaven forbid you have a crash in the meantime.

There are a few workarounds to this obstacle. One is to convert all your material to an intraframe codec either while importing it into the NLE or before editing. Many filmmakers shooting with DSLRs will transcode their H.264 camera files to ProRes or DNxHD when ingesting to the NLE. The transcoded files are then used from that point forward. This increases storage requirements, but working with ProRes or DNxHD often makes the NLE more responsive and can help maintain image quality.

Another possibility when editing HDV with Final Cut Pro is to use one of Matrox's MXO2 family of devices (see Fig. 5-23) or their Mojito card. These can accelerate HDV playback without requiring conforming. Several Matrox products are available with MAX technology that can accelerate the creation of H.264 files, which may allow you to encode H.264 files in real time when using compatible software.

Compared to HDV, the intraframe compressions used in formats such as DV and DigiBeta are very simple and straightforward. They only have I-frames, and their codecs make no attempt to take into account what happens before or after each frame. They're also longer in the tooth, dating back further in time. MPEG codecs are more sophisticated and therefore more efficient. So is there a way to have our cake and eat it too? The answer is that there are indeed forms of MPEG-2 (including Sony's 50 Mbps MPEG IMX) and MPEG-4 (such as Panasonic's AVC-Intra for P2) that use a one-frame GOP, which is sometimes called *I-frame only*. The advantages of I-frame only include fewer artifacts and much simpler editing and processing. H.264, part of the MPEG-4 standard, is considered to be twice as efficient as MPEG-2, taking up half the storage for the same quality of image, even in I-frame-only mode (see AVC-Intra and AVC Ultra, p. 26).

Constant and Variable Bit Rates

We've seen that shots with a lot of detail or motion require more data to process than ones that are relatively simple or static. With some codecs, the same amount of data is recorded for every frame, regardless of how complex it is. For example, the data rate of DV is 36 Mbps no matter what you're recording. This is a *constant bit rate* (*CBR*) format.

Some formats, however, allow for a higher data rate on shots that are complex or active, and reduce the data rate for scenes that are less demanding. These are *variable bit rate* (*VBR*) formats. VBR encoding is more efficient: it provides more data when you need it, less when you don't. It can result in fewer artifacts and smaller file sizes. The problem with VBR is that it requires more processing power and time to accomplish. In postproduction (for example, when creating DVDs) VBR compression is often done in a two-pass process: in the first pass, the system analyzes the entire movie to gauge where high and low data rates are called for; in the second pass the codec actually does the compressing.

An interesting example of a camcorder design that exploits both CBR and VBR is found in Sony's XDCAM HD camcorders, the PDW-F330 and PDW-F350, which record 1080i/60 and 1080p/24 using long-GOP MPEG-2 with a choice of 18 Mbps (variable), 25 Mbps (constant, functionally equivalent to HDV), and 35 Mbps (variable).

A FEW COMMON CODECS

There are numerous codecs, and new ones are always being developed. Some are employed in camera formats, some are used primarily in editing, and others are used mostly for distribution. Some codecs are used in all three areas.

See Comparing Video Formats, p. 21, for camera formats and the codecs they employ, including DV, DVCPRO, DVCPRO HD, H.264, and others. Below are just a few other codecs used in video production and postproduction.

MPEG-2

MPEG-2 has been around since the early 1990s and is widely used. (See Compressing a Group of Frames, above, for a basic idea of how MPEG-2 compression works.) MPEG-2 provides superb picture quality, all the way up to HD, and supports widescreen. It comes in a number of flavors (there are different *profiles*, each of which have various *levels*), which may behave differently and may not be compatible (a system that can play one may not be able to play another). As mentioned above, it is the codec used in standard definition DVDs and it's also one of the codecs used with Blu-ray. It is the basis for ATSC digital broadcasting in the U.S. and DBV digital broadcasting in Europe, as well as cable and satellite transmission.

Many professional camcorder systems use MPEG-2 to record HD, particularly Sony camcorders. Sony HDV cameras record MPEG-2 at 25 Mbps (constant bit rate) and Sony XDCAM EX cameras record up to 35 Mbps (variable bit rate), while XDCAM HD cameras record up to 50 Mbps (CBR).

One aspect of MPEG-2 that is generally misunderstood—and this goes equally for MPEG-4 codecs like H.264 below—is that although the decompression algorithms are standardized, the compression algorithms are not. What this means is that while any device that can play back MPEG-2 or MPEG-4 is expecting a standard type of video essence, how the camera gets there in creating a compressed recording is left up to the camera and codec designers. This has huge implications. It means that even though MPEG-2 has been around since the early 1990s, the MPEG-2 codecs of today are vastly superior and will continue to improve. It also means that even though two camcorders from difference manufacturers claim to use the same MPEG-2 or H.264 compression, the results can be quite different depending on the performance capabilities of the particular codec in each camera.

H.264

Versatile H.264 is found extensively in today's consumer camcorders and DSLRs under the brand name AVCHD. It's also used in postproduction and across the Web for streaming, for example in YouTube HD videos. Also known as AVC and MPEG-4, Part 10, this codec is twice as efficient as MPEG-2 (which means you can get the same quality with as little as half the data). H.264 is very scalable, which means you can use the same codec for high-quality needs like HD projection and for very low-resolution cell phones. Like MPEG-2, H.264 has several profiles; higher profiles offer better quality at smaller file sizes, take longer to encode, and need more processing to decode in real time. Because of the considerable processing power needed to encode and decode H.264, it can sometimes create bottlenecks when editing on an NLE.

H.264 is supported by many newer systems, including European digital broadcasting and Apple's QuickTime. It is the basis of Sony's HDCAM SR and also one of the three mandatory codecs for Blu-ray. To simplify editing while taking advantage of H.264's great efficiency, Panasonic created an I-frame-only version, which it calls AVC-Intra, for use with its P2 cards (see p. 26).

The successor to H.264, called *High Efficiency Video Coding* (*HEVC*) or *H.265*, is already on the horizon. H.265 is said to achieve the same or better image quality as H.264 at half the data rate.

Windows Media Video

Microsoft's WMV (Windows Media Video) is a competitor of MPEG-4 and offers many of the same advantages. Like MPEG-4, it has different profiles that can be used for high- and low-quality applications. WMV is sometimes called VC-1. As of this writing, Windows Media 9 is the most recent version and one of the three mandatory codecs for Blu-ray.

Apple ProRes

Apple introduced ProRes compression for editing with Final Cut Pro, originally positioning it as a kind of universal codec into which many other formats can be converted for editing and finishing. It has been so popular, and offers such good quality, that cameras like the ARRI Alexa and external digital recorders like the AJA Ki Pro and Atomos Ninja offer it as a recording codec, allowing you to go directly to editing with no transcoding or processing necessary (see Figs. 2-19 and 5-11). ProRes is stored in a QuickTime container (files have the extension .mov) and can be edited with Final Cut or NLEs made by other companies.

ProRes is really a family of codecs, all of which are I-frame only (intraframe compression) and offer fast encoding and decoding at data rates much lower than uncompressed video. All ProRes versions use variable bit rate (VBR) encoding.

ProRes 422 supports SD and full-resolution HD (both 1920 x 1080 and 1280 x 720) at 4:2:2 color sampling with 10-bit precision. Normal quality is targeted at 145 Mbps, and there is the high-quality ProRes 422 (HQ) version at 220 Mbps. To streamline editing of interframe codecs like H.264 and HDV you can transcode to

ProRes, which increases file sizes but can speed up processing while maintaining quality.

For projects such as news or sports that require smaller file sizes at broadcast quality, there is ProRes 4:2:2 (LT). For very small file sizes, ProRes 422 (Proxy) can be used for offline editing, followed by online editing with another ProRes version or another codec. At the top end of the quality scale, there is ProRes 4:4:4:4, which is 12 bit and uses 4:4:4 chroma sampling and includes support for an alpha channel (see p. 59).

An older format that can be used for similar purposes is Apple Intermediate Codec (AIC); this is sometimes used with systems that don't support ProRes.

Avid DNxHD

DNxHD is much like ProRes, but designed by Avid.[30] It works seamlessly with the Avid family of products and is also intended as an open standard to be used with applications and equipment by different manufacturers. DNxHD is I-frame only and typically stored in an MXF container, but it can be wrapped in QuickTime as well.

Like ProRes, it has different levels of compression. There is a 220 Mbps version at 10 or 8 bits as well as 8-bit versions at 145 and 36 Mbps. DNxHD 36 is often used for offline editing. DNxHD supports all common SD and HD frame sizes.

JPEG 2000

As noted above, JPEG 2000 is based on wavelet compression and used by Hollywood's Digital Cinema Initiatives for theatrical projection. It's scalable and capable of a very high-quality image.

CineForm

CineForm makes a range of compression products based on its wavelet-based CineForm codec. Silicon Imaging's SI-2K Mini records 2K RAW files to CineForm's RAW codec. Mostly, however, CineForm's workflow is based on transcoding any camera format, including AVCHD, XDCAM, P2, or large 2K or 4K RAW files, to CineForm as an "intermediate codec" used for editing, finishing, and archiving. It offers high image quality up to 12-bit precision in various color spaces and wrappers. CineForm can be used with Windows or Mac NLEs and applications; you don't need any particular NLE installed to take advantage of it.

Cineform is owned by GoPro and can be used in the postproduction workflow for footage from GoPro cameras (see Fig. 2-8).

---

30. Unlike many naming schemes in video in which the "x" is pronounced as "by," here the "x" is pronounced simply as x.

CHAPTER 6

The Film Camera

An Overview of the Camera

The motion picture camera has the following components:

Fig. 6-1. Arriflex 16mm BL. The film chamber door and magazine lid are open to reveal the film path. The feed roll is 400 feet of core-loaded film. The pressure plate is open to show the film gate. The camera has a mirror shutter for reflex viewing. (ARRI, Inc.)

- *The lens:* focuses light from the world onto the film.
- *The lens mount:* receptacle where the lens is attached to the camera (see Chapter 4 for the lens and lens mount).
- *The viewfinder:* allows the camera operator to see what image is being recorded on film.

- *The film chamber:* a light-tight compartment that holds the film before and after it is exposed to light. Many cameras use a detachable magazine to hold the film.
- *The motor:* supplies the power to run the film past the lens for exposure.
- *The film gate and claw:* The claw pulls down each frame of film for exposure and holds it steady in the film gate during exposure.
- *The shutter:* blocks light from the film when it is moving between successive exposures.

The unexposed film (*raw stock*) is loaded into the camera from the *supply* or *feed reel*. The film passes through the film gate for exposure and is spooled on the *take-up reel*.

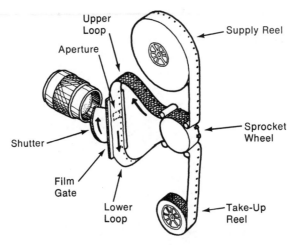

Fig. 6-2. Simplified camera. (Carol Keller)

THE FILM GATE AND SHUTTER

The Film Gate

In the *film gate*, the raw stock is exposed to light that comes through the lens. The gate is composed of two plates that sandwich the film. The plate between the lens and the film is the *aperture plate*. The *aperture* itself is a rectangle cut out of the aperture plate, through which light from the lens shines. The aperture's edges define the border of the image on the film. The base of the film rests on the other half of the gate, the *pressure plate*, which holds the film flat during exposure. Super 8 cartridges and some quick-change magazines (see Camera Film Capacity, p. 262) have a built-in pressure plate that is not part of the camera's body.

THE CLAW. Most cameras and projectors have a *claw* or *shuttle* that advances the film, frame by frame, in the gate. The claw engages a perforation in the film and

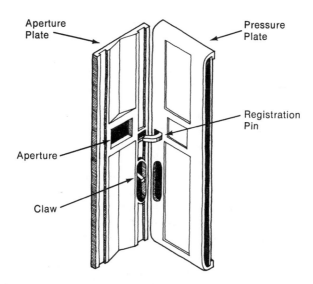

Fig. 6-3. Film gate with open pressure plate. Not all cameras use registration pins. (Carol Keller)

pulls the film forward one frame (the *pulldown*). After exposure, the claw engages the next frame and pulls it down (see Fig. 1-32).

It's critical that the film be held *absolutely* steady in the gate or else the image will not be steady when projected on screen. Some cameras have a *registration pin* to help ensure steadiness during exposure. The pin enters a perforation while the film is stopped in the gate and holds it motionless.

THE INTERMITTENT. The claw is on an *intermittent* (that is, a noncontinuous or stop-start) movement that allows the film alternately to stop in front of the aperture and then to move on. Since the film roll is moving continuously through the camera, there must be some slack between the intermittent claw and the constantly moving feed and take-up reels to prevent the film from tearing. On most cameras and projectors, *loops* are formed between the film gate and the *sprocket wheel*—which drives the film—to provide the needed slack.

Loops must be accurately formed. If they're too small, the film may tear or chatter. When a camera jams, it usually "loses its loop." If the loops are too large, they may rub against the camera housing and scratch the film. See your camera's manual for proper loop size.

The Shutter

After each frame of film is exposed to light coming through the lens, the shutter must close to block the light while the next frame moves into position in the gate. The film must be completely at rest before the shutter opens again for the next exposure. If the shutter does not block the light when the film is moving, the image will be blurred. The simplest kind of shutter is a rotating disc with a section removed.

A circle may be represented by 360 degrees. The shutter opening is the number of degrees open in the disc. The 180-degree shutter, a half-moon in shape, is used in many cameras, particularly in 16mm.

SHUTTER SPEED AND EXPOSURE. *Exposure* is determined by two elements: the intensity of light that passes through the lens and the time each frame is exposed to the light. The reciprocity law simply says: Exposure = Intensity × Time. Doubling exposure time is equivalent to doubling intensity. The halving and doubling of light intensity are measured in *stops* (see Chapter 4). If you close down the lens by one stop, you must double the time of exposure to keep exposure constant.

Standard film speed is 24 frames per second. A camera with a 180-degree shutter admits light to the film half the time (the disc is half open) so the exposure time (the shutter speed) is $\frac{1}{24} \times \frac{1}{2} = \frac{1}{48}$ second (which we usually round off to $\frac{1}{50}$ second). As a rule of thumb, most film cameras have a shutter speed of about $\frac{1}{50}$ second when operated at 24 fps, but check your camera to determine the angle of its shutter opening. The general formula for any shutter opening and camera speed is:

$$\text{Exposure time (shutter speed)} = \left(\frac{1}{\text{speed in fps}} \right) \times \left(\frac{\text{angle of shutter opening}}{360} \right)$$

For shutter openings less than 180 degrees, the shutter speed is faster than $\frac{1}{50}$ second. For example, a 135-degree shutter at 24 fps yields a shutter speed of $\frac{1}{24} \times$ 135/360 = $\frac{1}{64}$ (approximately $\frac{1}{65}$ second).

In general, longer exposure times have advantages: they decrease the possibility of judder (see p. 393) and they mean that less light is needed for proper exposure. However, if the exposure time is very long, there will be excessive motion blur in the image (see Fig. 2-14).

THE VARIABLE SHUTTER. On cameras equipped with a *variable shutter*, the shutter angle can be narrowed to change the shutter speed. Narrowing the angle reduces exposure time. A 90-degree shutter, for example, gives a shutter speed of about $\frac{1}{100}$ second at 24 fps. Closing the shutter reduces the exposure, allowing high-speed film to be used outdoors or allowing the lens to be opened to decrease depth of field or to shoot at a selected *f*-stop (see Chapter 4).

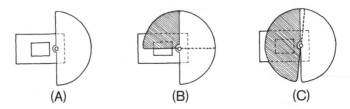

(A)   (B)   (C)

Fig. 6-4. Variable shutter. (A) A 180-degree shutter shown fully open. The small rectangle represents the aperture. (B) To close the shutter, an adjustable disc (shaded) swings out; shown here, it forms a 90-degree opening. (C) The shutter is almost completely closed. (Carol Keller)

A variable shutter that can be closed down while the camera is running allows exposure changes in the middle of a shot. For example, when the camera moves from a sunlit to a shaded area within a shot, it's often necessary to change exposure. If variable shutters are used for exposure control, you risk judder in the image if there is a great deal of camera or subject movement (see p. 393). On cameras with a variable shutter, always check that the shutter is properly set before every day's shooting. If someone else has used the camera, the shutter opening may have been narrowed.

CAMERA SPEED AND MOTORS

The first cameras were cranked by hand. The camera operator would hum a popular song of an appropriate tempo to approximate the filming speed. On modern cameras, either a spring-wound or electric motor drives the film through the camera and controls the rate at which the film moves.

Standard Speed

Standard worldwide theatrical film projection speed is 24 fps, and unless special effects are desired, it is assumed that the standard running speed of a film camera is also 24 fps (also known as *sound speed*). However, there are certain situations in which 24 fps is not used as the basic speed.

1. In Europe and other places where PAL video has been standard, film footage intended primarily for television is shot at 25 fps (see Chapter 16). Even theatrical films may be filmed at 25 fps to simplify postproduction; however, European theatrical film projection is typically 24 fps.
2. Film is sometimes shot at 23.976 fps. This is 0.1 percent slower than standard 24 fps and matches the video "24p" rate in formerly NTSC countries. This may be used to simplify video postproduction on a film project, or when the film footage needs to keep sync with a video camera, or sometimes when filming music videos to maintain sync with prerecorded music (see p. 456).
3. In NTSC countries, film is sometimes shot at 29.97 fps when filming video monitors.
4. Certain camera speeds can cause problems with some HMI, fluorescent, and other discharge-type lighting (see p. 481).

When the *camera speed* (or *frame rate*) matches the projection speed, movement on the screen looks natural. When the camera speed increases, more frames are filmed each second. When film shot at high speed (say, 40 fps) is projected at the normal speed (24 fps), action is slowed down (*slow motion*). Conversely, if you film at a slower speed, say 8 fps, and then project at normal speed, movement is sped up—in this case, three times as fast.

When you change camera speed, you need to make an exposure compensation, since the exposure time is different. Consult a frame-rate/exposure chart or use the formula for shutter speed specified above. In general, if you double the frame rate, you lose a stop of exposure, so compensate by opening the lens one stop. If you cut the frame rate in half, close the lens by a stop.

For a discussion of slow motion and time-lapse shooting, see p. 389.

Camera Motors

Most cameras today have electric motors powered primarily by rechargeable batteries (see Batteries and Power Supplies, p. 127). In order to be used for sync-sound filming (see p. 464), the speed of the camera must be very precisely controlled. Most modern cameras used for sound work are equipped with crystal-controlled motors, which use a very stable crystal oscillator to ensure accuracy. Some cameras are not intended for sound work. Sometimes called MOS or *wild cameras*, nonsync cameras may have variable-speed motors or governor motors. These cameras are often small, light, and noisy. Some nonsync cameras use spring-wound motors, like Bolexes, that are wound by hand prior to the shot.

Fig. 6-5. Bolex H16 Reflex 16mm camera. Beam-splitter reflex with nondivergent lens turret. Spring-wound motor capable of single-frame operation. This camera accepts 100-foot internal loads or an external magazine. It has a 135-degree variable shutter. (Bolex)

VIEWING SYSTEMS

The *viewfinder* allows you to see what is being recorded on film. Most modern cameras use a *reflex viewfinder*, which allows you to see through the lens (the *taking* lens). Some older or lower-cost cameras employ a *nonreflex viewfinder* that is separate from the taking lens.

THE REFLEX VIEWFINDER

Modern reflex cameras divert light coming through the lens to a viewfinder, where the image is projected on a *viewing screen*. Many newer cameras have *fiber-optic viewing screens*, which are bright and allow you to see if the image is properly focused across the whole image. By comparison, center-focusing viewfinders have disadvantages: they give no impression of depth of field, and you may need to focus on a point that is not in the center of the frame, so changing focus in the middle of a shot can be difficult.

Composition in the Viewfinder

The relationship between what you see in the viewfinder and the frame that will ultimately be seen by the audience depends on the camera and format you're shooting. Some viewfinder screens are marked with more than one frame line. For example, a 16mm viewfinder may show markings for the full 1:33 *camera aperture*, the 1.85:1 widescreen frame, and a TV safe action area (see Fig. 6-6). See p. 327 for more on TV cutoff and working with widescreen formats. Some viewfinders display an area that is even larger than the camera aperture and give you advance warning when objects, such as the microphone boom, are about to enter the frame, which is very helpful.

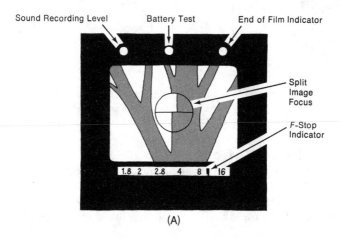

Fig. 6-6. Ground glass viewfinder screen typical of 16mm cameras. Note the safe viewing area, which provides warning of things just outside the frame. Horizontal marks near the edge of the frame indicate top and bottom frame lines when shooting for 1.85:1 widescreen aspect ratio. On some 35mm cameras, the viewfinder includes a magnification system to enlarge the frame for critical focusing, and a lens to unsqueeze an anamorphic image. (Carol Keller)

The Mirror Shutter

In some cameras, light is diverted from the lens to the viewfinder screen by a *mirror shutter*. The mirror, either part of the shutter or rotating in sync with it, alternately allows all the light to hit the film, and then, when the shutter is closed, all the light to go to the viewfinder (see Fig. 6-7). One advantage of a mirror shutter is that when each frame of film is exposed, no light is lost to the viewfinder, so in critical low-light situations you have as much exposure as possible. A disadvantage of mirror shutters is that when the camera is running, the viewfinder image flickers, since light goes to the viewfinder only about half the time.

One paradox of the mirror shutter is that you see an image in the viewfinder when the shutter is closed, but the viewfinder image goes dark when each frame of film is actually exposed. In some situations this can be misleading. For example, if you film a gunshot and see the flash of the gun in the viewfinder, it may not actually appear on film. Systems are available to synchronize gun triggers to the camera shutter.

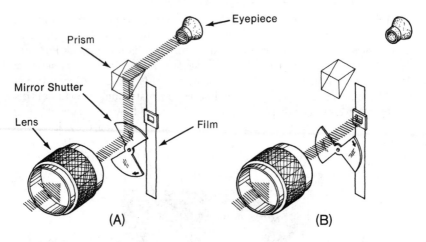

Fig. 6-7. Mirror shutter. (A) With the shutter closed, all the light is diverted to the viewfinder. (B) With the shutter open, all the light strikes the film and exposes it. Compare with Fig. 6-8. (Carol Keller)

Beam-Splitter Reflex

In an alternate design for reflex viewing, a partially reflecting mirror (*pellicule*) or a prism (*beam-splitter*) in the light path diverts some of the light to the viewfinder, letting the balance hit the film (see Fig. 6-8). This system is used in most Super 8 cameras. Anywhere from one-third of a stop to a full stop of light (depending on

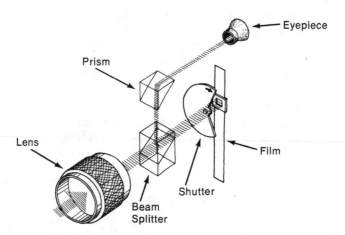

Fig. 6-8. Beam-splitter reflex. Some light is always diverted to the viewfinder, making it unavailable for exposing the film. (Carol Keller)

the camera) goes to the finder and does not contribute to exposing the film. The exposure loss can be serious in low-light filming. If the prism is in the camera body, an exposure compensation for the light loss is usually made by altering the shutter speed used for exposure calculation. For example, some 16mm Bolex cameras have 135-degree shutters ($\frac{1}{65}$ second at 24 fps), but the Bolex manual suggests that an exposure compensation be made by using an "effective" shutter speed of $\frac{1}{80}$ second with your light meter.

The Diopter Adjustment

The viewfinder eyepiece on reflex cameras can correct for the cameraperson's near- or farsightedness. Make sure the *diopter* adjustment on the eyepiece is adjusted every time someone new uses the camera. The diopter does not affect the actual focus of the image on film, but it does affect your ability to see if the image is in focus. For most 16mm and 35mm cameras, adjust the diopter as follows: Remove the lens or open the iris diaphragm on the lens. Point the camera at a bright area; the sky or a bright wall will do. (If viewing through a lens, throw the image out of focus as much as possible.) Adjust the eyepiece *diopter adjustment* until the grains of the ground glass (on fiber-optic screens use the etched frame line) are as sharp as possible. Lock the setting in place.

If you wear eyeglasses while shooting, adjust the diopter with your glasses on. Wearing eyeglasses during shooting makes it difficult, if not impossible, to see the whole viewfinder image. If possible, adjust the diopter for your eyes without glasses or wear contact lenses. If the camera's diopter adjustment is not strong enough to correct your eyesight, a correction lens can be mounted in some eyepieces.

The Eyepiece

With video cameras, it doesn't matter if your eye is near the viewfinder. With many film cameras, if your eye isn't pressed up against the eyepiece, stray light can enter, travel through the reflex system in reverse, and fog the film. When you are filming without looking through the eyepiece, close the viewfinder light trap or place something against the eyepiece. On some cameras, the light trap can be set so that it opens when you press your eye up against the eyepiece and closes when you pull your head away.

Some cameras have illuminated viewfinders that highlight the frame line, which can be a boon for shooting dark scenes. Condensation from your breath on a cold day can be a real problem. Some cameras offer heated viewfinders. Some people apply a little anticondensation coating to the viewfinder (never use this on the taking lens).

The eyepiece is usually fitted with a rubber eyecup that cushions the eye (or eyeglasses) and helps seal out stray light. A foam or chamois cover will make it more comfortable.

For tripod- or dolly-mounted cameras, use a viewfinder that extends to the back of the camera. For shoulder-mounted camera rigs, the ideal position of the viewfinder is close to the film plane, since this allows the camera to be better balanced. Cameras used in both tripod and handheld work should ideally have interchangeable finders.

Fig. 6-9. ARRI 416 camera. Super 16 format, quick-change magazines, video assist, 1 to 75 fps (though a high-speed model runs up to 150 fps). (ARRI, Inc.)

CAMERA FILM CAPACITY

Magazines

Some small cameras are designed to be used with film loaded on spools that mount inside the camera body. But most cameras use *magazines* (*mags*), which are detachable film chambers (see Figs. 6-1 and 6-10). The standard 16mm magazine is 400 feet, which runs 11 minutes at 24 fps (36 feet per minute). Some 16mm cameras accommodate 200- or 1,200-foot mags. Aaton makes an 800-foot mag that accommodates 800-foot film rolls. In 35mm, a 1,000-foot mag holds about 10 minutes of film (35mm runs at 96 feet per minute). Some 35mm cameras have 200-foot, 400-foot, 500-foot, or other size magazines. Large-capacity mags weigh more but allow more shooting between reloads.

Some magazines, like Mitchell mags, mount on top of the camera and are made up of a feed compartment in front of a take-up compartment. A variant of this is called a displacement magazine, like the 400-foot mag for the Arriflex 16 BL (see Fig. 6-1). Here the feed and take-up are together in one smaller chamber. *Coaxial magazines* often mount behind the camera body and have the feed and take-up chambers side by side (see Fig. 6-9). Coaxial mags have the advantage of being lower profile for shooting in tight spaces and they don't change the camera's balance as the load moves through the camera, which can be an advantage for Steadicam work. Generally, if the magazine has separate compartments for feed and take-up, this facilitates threading, unloading partial rolls, and dealing with problems.

In *quick-change magazines*, such as all Aaton mags and ARRI 16SR and 416 mags, much of the camera mechanism and the pressure plate are part of the magazine itself. This makes each mag more expensive and heavier, but it has the tremendous advantage that once magazines are loaded with film, they can be clipped on the camera with no additional threading. This can make all the difference in pressure-

Fig. 6-10. Magazine for Aaton 35-III camera is open, showing feed and take-up in same compartment. (AbelCine)

filled situations, especially in documentary shooting when the action won't wait for you to reload.

Loading Magazines

Magazines may be loaded with film prior to the day's shoot and then reloaded as necessary. Feature filmmakers may have a photographic darkroom available in either a studio or a truck. More typically, mags are changed using a *changing bag*, which is a lightproof, double-layered, double-zippered fabric bag (see Fig. 6-11). Look for a clean, dry place to work, with subdued light. Some people like to work on a table or flat surface. You can work on the floor, but this may introduce dirt. Some changing bags have a kind of tentlike design that gives you room to work with big mags. Some people prefer to load 16mm mags on their lap; your legs help keep things from sliding around. Also, a lap is good for many locations (like outdoors) where a good, clean surface may not be available. Cleanliness is essential, because any dirt on the film may lodge in the gate (see Checking the Gate, p. 268). Some people like to blow mags clean with a can of compressed air (like Dust-Off), a tank of nitrogen, or even a rubber bulb syringe. Be careful with any compressed gas: avoid blowing dirt into cavities in the mag or camera; also, the cold, expanding gas can damage mirror shutters. Some people prefer to clean mags with a paintbrush reserved for this purpose. You can also grab bits of dirt with a piece of tape, sticky side out, wrapped around a finger.

Before loading, the changing bag should be examined for rips or tears. If you find one, do a temporary repair with gaffer's tape or discard the bag. Turn the bag inside out and brush it clean with your hand. When not in use, zipper the bag closed and, if possible, keep it in a cover. When you're in the bag, bring the sleeves above the elbows to avoid light leaks and don't work in direct sunlight: find some shade or go inside.

Develop a standard operating procedure for loading mags so you won't get

Fig. 6-11. A changing bag functions as a portable darkroom. (Ted Spagna)

confused under pressure. Remove the moistureproof tape from around the film can before putting it in the changing bag. Hold the can closed and put it in the bag; you can put the can under the mag to make sure it doesn't accidentally open while you're closing up the bag.

Once you've zipped up the changing bag with the film and clean mag inside, and gotten your hands in, you can open the film can. The end of the film will usually be taped down. Don't lose track of this tape! It might end up jamming the camera. If you stick it on the inside of the can you'll know where it is. You can reuse it to tape up the film after it is exposed.

On some magazines, you just have to slip the film into the feed side in the dark and then you can do most of the threading outside the bag with the lights on. Be sure the feed roll pulls out smoothly. If the roll fights you or makes noise when pulled, it's probably not seated properly. Never pull hard on any film roll or you might cause cinch marks.

Nearly all raw stocks are supplied with the emulsion facing in (see Fig. 7-8). Some magazines take up with the emulsion facing in and others, emulsion out.

Many mags have a post to accept a standard 2-inch plastic core. When film is taken up on a core, attach it as shown in Fig. 6-12. Wind the film around the core several times in the direction it takes up, and make sure there is no bump where the film fits into the slot on the core (you

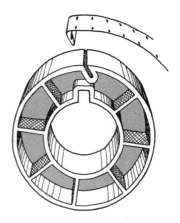

Fig. 6-12. Attaching the film to take-up core. Fold the film over itself and insert it in the slot. Position the slot as illustrated—angled against the direction of the take-up to keep the film from slipping out. Rotate the core to wind up several turns of film. Some magazines take up with emulsion facing in and others face out. (Carol Keller)

may have to refold it). Generally, the camera gate should be brushed or blown clean before attaching the fresh mag. Make sure all loops are the right size (you can count the frames and some mags have markings to help measure the loops) and be sure they are centered properly so they don't bind or rub. You should check the gate every time you change mags or more often.

Some mags use a "core adapter," which is a mechanical core that clamps shut on the film when you slide a lever. These have two disadvantages: it's easy to accidentally leave them in the film when unloading; and many labs prefer that film be delivered with a core in it.

Run a few feet of film through the camera to make sure everything is running smoothly. If you hear a fast ticking sound, your loops may be off. If you hear a low, slow rubbing sound, the film roll may have dished in the feed side, and needs to be gently pressed flat. Sometimes a firm slap with the palm of your hand on the side of the mag (take it off the camera first) will stop a roll from rubbing. With mags that have separate feed and take-up compartments, you can run the camera with the take-up side open to see if everything is okay, and check that the film is not being scratched (see p. 269 for a scratch test).

Labeling and Managing Magazines

After the mag is loaded, a piece of tape should be put across the latches to prevent accidental opening. The edges of the magazine covers are sometimes a source of light leaks that may fog film, especially with old equipment. Taping the magazine with camera tape along the length of the lid ensures against leaks (see p. 269 for a light leak test).

The magazine should be labeled with a piece of tape or a sticker to identify its contents:

1. The type of film (e.g., 7219).
2. The emulsion and roll number from the film can's label (see Fig. 7-7); this is useful if there are problems later.
3. The length of the roll (e.g., 400 feet).
4. The camera roll number (e.g., CR 55); this should be marked only *after* the mag is on the camera.
5. The mag's number or serial number (useful if scratches are found later).
6. The date.

In documentary shooting you may not have time to get everything down. Items 1, 3, and 4 are essential. Some people use color-coded tape for different types of stock. Never label two camera rolls with the same number!

Have on hand spare cores, cans, and black bags for *short ends* (the unshot portion of a partially filmed roll).

When the mag is put on the camera, each roll of film is normally slated at the head by shooting a card or clapper board with production name and company, camera roll number, date, and so on for a few seconds.

UNLOADING MAGAZINES. When unloading exposed film, tape up the end of the roll and be sure the black bag is neatly folded before closing and retaping the can. If the roll is a little loose, don't pull on the end to tighten it—you could scratch the emulsion or cause static discharge. Be sure to mark the can clearly as exposed. See Chapter 17 for labeling the can after the film is exposed and Chapter 7 for handling, storing, and shipping film stock.

When magazines are reloaded during a shoot, some people prefer to unload the exposed film, remove it from the changing bag, and then go back in with the fresh stock. This avoids any confusion. With mags that have separate feed and take-up compartments, it's faster to clean the empty feed side, put the mag and fresh stock in the changing bag, load the feed side, and—while you're still in the bag—unload the exposed film into the can you just emptied.

Magazines are often emptied at the end of the day's shooting and should be emptied before air travel. When unexposed film is put back in a can (*recanned*), it should be labeled as noted above, except without the camera roll and mag numbers. Mark "Unexposed/Recan" and put the name of the person unloading in case there are questions later.

SPARE MAGAZINES. Have at least one extra magazine. This lets you change mags if problems develop and allows you to load the next roll before it's needed, saving time at what might be a crucial moment. When you use two different raw stocks (for example, a slow-speed film for interiors and a high-speed for exteriors), the extra magazine makes both immediately available. On a feature film it is common to have five or more mags. Some documentary crews load up a lot of film at the beginning of a day's shoot so they can do without a magazine changer and keep the crew size to a minimum.

Daylight Spools

Film in 16mm and 35mm is supplied on cores (*darkroom load*) or *daylight spools* (see Fig. 6-13). You don't need a changing bag for daylight spools, but load them in subdued light since bright light could fog the edges of the film. Integral head and tail leaders and the way the unexposed film is wound on the spool help prevent stray light from penetrating to the inner layers. After shooting, the film is not as protected.

Most 16mm magazines have both core and spool adapters (sometimes you remove the core adapter to mount a spool). Though most magazines will accept daylight spools of up to 400 feet, spools are heavier than darkroom loads and may scrape against the side of the magazine, creating an annoying noise.

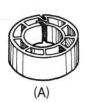  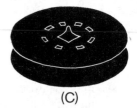

(A)   (B)   (C)

Fig. 6-13. Cores and daylight spool. (A) 16mm core. (B) 35mm core. (C) 16mm, 100-foot daylight spool. (Carol Keller)

Super 8 Cartridges

Super 8 Cartridges are lightproof, but you should still avoid exposing them to direct sunlight. Don't break the cartridge's moistureproof foil until you load the camera. A notch in the plastic cartridge automatically sets the ASA number on many Super 8 cameras with automatic exposure. When using Pro8 negative stocks, it may be necessary to manually carve out the notch for proper ASA and filter settings on certain cameras. On many cameras, the footage counter resets to zero when the film compartment door is opened. Be sure to write down the footage if you open the door to check the gate or change film in the middle of a cartridge.

OTHER CAMERA FEATURES

Video Assist

A *video assist* (also called a *video tap*) diverts some light from the film camera to an attached small video camera that allows you to watch the image on a monitor and/or record it on video. Video taps can be valuable for allowing the director or others to see the shot, for reviewing takes, and for logging or even editing footage prior to processing. A video assist can be crucial for Steadicam, crane, or car shots in which the operator can't look through the camera. However, there can be some drawbacks. The image is an approximation of what is being recorded on film and often misrepresents what the image will eventually look like. Since you're not actually seeing the film, you can't know about a host of film problems, including scratches or even a run-out.

Sound Dampening

Camera noise on the sound track can be annoying in a documentary or disastrous in a fiction film. Even when filming without sound, a noisy camera can be disruptive. Noise calls attention to the camera and can distract subjects or alter animal behavior when doing nature filming.

High-end 16mm and 35mm cameras designed for sync-sound work are usually very quiet. Camera noise can be dampened with a *barney*, which is a soft cover, sometimes made of lead foam. Barneys may cover the whole camera or just the magazine. In a pinch, a heavy coat or a sound blanket (see Chapter 11) can serve as a makeshift barney. White barneys can be used to reflect sunlight and keep the film cooler in hot weather. The *heater barney* keeps the camera warm when filming in very cold weather.

In-Camera Timecode

Timecode can be very useful in production and postproduction. Some film cameras can expose timecode along the edge of the film, which can be read after the film is developed (see Fig. 6-14). The Aaton/Panavision system uses both Arabic numerals (human readable) and a matrix of dots (machine readable). The Arriflex system uses a bar code instead.

Many cameras are not equipped for internal timecode but can still employ timecode using timecode slates. See Chapter 11 for use of timecode during shooting and Chapter 16 for timecode in film-to-video transfers.

Fig. 6-14. In-camera timecode. The camera exposes the timecode along the edge of the film. The AatonCode system uses both human-readable numbers and a machine-readable matrix of dots. (AbelCine)

Multiple-Format Cameras

Some cameras are capable of shooting more than one format. For example, suitably equipped Aaton and ARRI 16mm cameras can shoot either 16mm or Super 16. The camera must have a Super 16 gate and the proper viewfinder screen, and the lens must be shifted over (recentered on the frame) when changing between formats. Many 35mm cameras have a number of interchangeable gates and viewing screens for different aspect ratios and formats. Bear in mind that a lens designed for one format won't necessarily cover the full frame of a wider screen format. For example, Super 16 lenses will cover the 16mm frame, but the reverse is not necessarily true (see Chapters 1, 2, and 16 for more on 16mm and Super 16).

CAMERA TESTS AND MAINTENANCE

Of the following tests, checking the gate is done regularly while shooting. The other tests are often done before a shoot, when checking out a camera from a rental house or other equipment supplier.

CHECKING THE GATE. Dirt or bits of emulsion often lodge in the camera aperture and are exposed as dark lines or shapes at the edge of the picture ("hairs in the gate"). A good way to check the gate is to remove the lens and, from in front of the camera, examine the edges of the aperture with a lighted magnifier. You need to manually inch the motor forward so that the mirror shutter is open, giving you a clear view of the aperture and the film behind it. Some people prefer to check the gate through the lens. This takes practice and works well only with long lenses. Open the iris all the way, focus to infinity, and set a zoom to telephoto. Use a small flashlight to look around the edge of the frame. The advantage of this method is you're less likely to introduce dirt while checking the gate (in a dusty location, for example). However, if there's dirt you still have to take the lens off.

To clean the gate, carefully insert an *orangewood stick* (sold as cuticle sticks for nail care in drugstores) and lift the dirt out of the frame. Never insert anything metal and don't touch the mirror shutter or any of the optics. Compressed air may damage the mirror. Don't forget to inch the motor forward after cleaning to close the shutter and return the mirror to viewing position. You can inch the film forward a few frames or run it a bit and check again to be sure the dirt is really gone.

How often should you check the gate? The answer depends on the camera, the cinematographer, and the project. On a feature, the gate should be checked whenever a new film roll is begun and *at least* before the camera is moved from one setup to another. Some people check the gate after every good take (circle takes). Once you find a hair, you have the unpleasant task of trying to guess how long it's been there, so the more often you check, the safer you are. On a documentary, you may only have time to check once a roll. Hairs are more critical in 16mm—where the edge of the gate forms the edge of the image—than in some 35mm formats where the full Academy gate may give you some extra clearance from the part of the frame you're actually using. The gates on some cameras seem to naturally stay fairly hair-free, such as many Aaton and Panavision cameras. Dirty locations and soft film emulsions require more attention to the gate. Do everything you can when loading and cleaning magazines to avoid or remove dirt that might otherwise end up in the gate.

SCRATCH TEST. Run a few feet of film through the camera, and remove the film from the take-up reel. Examine the footage for surface scratches by holding the film obliquely toward a light source. To locate the cause of a scratch, mark the frame in the aperture; unload the film and mark where the scratch begins; then thread the film with the first marked frame in the aperture, and note the location where the scratch begins. Then clean the gate, rollers, or other possible scratching surfaces. Test for scratches whenever checking out a camera or magazine for the first time, and check occasionally during use. Keep some short ends around for scratch testing, but use only film that hasn't run through a camera gate before.

FRAMING CHART. At the start of a production, it's standard practice to shoot a framing chart to establish the framing and format you intend. Get a test chart that has frame outlines of different aspect ratios (charts are available from film labs and are downloadable from the Web). Shoot it head-on, at the same height as the camera, perpendicular to lens axis. Match up the lines on the chart to the frame lines of the viewfinder screen. Once developed, this becomes a framing leader that the lab, telecine operator, and postproduction team can use to match their systems to the framing of the particular widescreen or full-frame format that you're shooting, ensuring that the compositions intended by the cinematographer are maintained. This also checks the accuracy of the viewfinder.

LIGHT LEAK TEST. Light leaks show up on developed camera original as uneven fogging extending outside the picture area. If you detect light leak in your footage, it may come from poor handling when loading or unloading the magazines. To check a camera for light leaks, load it with unexposed raw stock and mark or expose the frame in the aperture. Move a bright light source (held a few inches from the camera) around from every angle, then develop the film and check for edge fogging. If edge fog is found, reload the footage, placing the marked frame in the aperture. Edge fog at any point locates the source of the light leak. When shooting, it's generally good practice to tape the edges of a magazine to reduce the chance of light leak.

OTHER TESTS. See Chapter 4 for lens focusing tests that may discover faults in the camera viewfinder or the adjustment of the lens mounting. Always check rushes for any defects (see Chapter 16) and immediately search for the problem. An image with total vertical blurring is a sign of a lost loop in the camera. Partial vertical blurring is a sign of a shutter timing error: the frame has been exposed while moving. The whole image moving in and out of focus (*breathing in the gate*) usually calls for pressure plate adjustment. Investigate any image flicker or unevenness in exposure.

Camera Care

Keep the camera clean. Don't blow compressed air into the aperture or places where dirt can become lodged. Never use metal to scrape emulsion from the gate. You can use alcohol on a cotton swab to remove emulsion deposits, but take care not to leave any cotton fibers. Acetone damages some plastics. Use magazine covers, lens socket caps, and body caps to keep dust out of camera openings.

Don't run a camera without film at speeds higher than 24 fps.

Hand-carry a camera on a plane if you can rather than checking it as baggage. When shipping, use rugged shipping cases, and detach the lens before shipping. Place all delicate equipment in foam-lined and fitted cases. Secure the camera on a car seat rather than leaving it loose on the car floor or in the trunk, where it will be subject to more vibration.

When you use a battery belt connected to the camera by a cable, be careful not to rest the camera on a surface and walk away, pulling the camera along behind you (sounds like obvious advice, but you'd be surprised how often it's been done). Use a coiled cable to minimize the risk. When you rest the camera on a table, don't let the lens extend over the edge where it may be hit by an unwary passerby.

Obtain the manufacturer's operation and maintenance manual for special information on oiling and overhaul instructions for your camera. Try to assemble a group of tools and spare parts for field repairs.

Shooter's Ditty Bag

Typical items in a cinematographer's (or assistant's) bag:

Changing bag	Camera tape (white and black)
Camelhair brush	Magnifying lens with light
Compressed air in a can	Orangewood sticks
Clean paintbrush	Lens tissue
Spare cores, cans, black bags	Lens cleaning fluid
Depth of field calculator or app	Small flashlight
Light meter(s)	Slate with color chip chart
Marking pens (Sharpies)	Swiss Army knife
50-foot measuring tape	Small video monitor
Grease pencil	Chalk
Screwdrivers	Needle-nose pliers
Jeweler's screwdrivers	Set of Allen wrenches
Adjustable wrench	Tweezers
Electrical multimeter	Soldering iron, wire
Crocus cloth for removing burrs	Camera oil or grease

CHAPTER 7

The Film Image

Unexposed film is called *raw stock*. After you choose the film gauge—Super 8, 16mm, or 35mm—the raw stock determines much of the look of the film. This chapter is about film stocks, exposure control, and dealing the film lab during production.

PROPERTIES OF THE FILM STOCK

Developing the Image

The top layer of the raw stock, the *emulsion*, consists of light-sensitive material, *silver halide crystals*, suspended in gelatin. The crystals vary in size, the larger ones being more sensitive to light. Exposure to light forms a *latent image* in the emulsion. The latent image becomes visible when the film goes through the *developer*, a liquid solution that reacts chemically with those silver halide crystals that have been exposed and reduces them to *metallic silver*, which is opaque to light. At a later stage, crystals that have not been exposed to light are removed by another solution, the *hypo* or *fixer*.

The areas of the emulsion most exposed to light end up with the greatest concentration of metallic silver. These are the densest, most opaque areas; they appear dark when you project light through them. Conversely, areas that receive little light

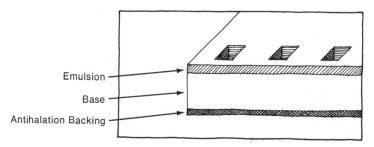

Emulsion

Base

Antihalation Backing

Fig. 7-1. A cross section of film. The antihalation backing, which on some stocks is between the emulsion and base, is removed during processing. (Carol Keller)

end up with less metallic silver and are relatively transparent. This is a *negative film* (see Fig. 7-2). On the negative, all the brightness values in the original scene are reversed: what was dark in the scene becomes light (transparent), and what was light becomes dark (dense).

The emulsion rests on a firm, flexible support material, the *base*. All currently manufactured stocks have a *safety base*, usually of cellulose triacetate (*acetate*) or a synthetic polyester base, such as Kodak's ESTAR, which is thinner and stronger than acetate. Release prints and intermediates (see Chapter 17) made on polyester can withstand rougher handling and take up less storage space.

Bright light can pass through the emulsion, scatter in the base, reflect off the back of the film, and reexpose the emulsion; this is known as *halation*. Most camera stocks have an *antihalation backing* to minimize these unwanted light rays.

The Negative-Positive Process

In the process discussed above, the exposed raw stock became a negative image of the photographed scene after development. If you make a print from the negative, using essentially the same process to reverse the tonalities again, you end up with a *positive* of the original scene. In the positive, bright areas of the scene end up light (transparent) and dark areas end up dense, which looks normal. The negative-positive process is the standard for film development in 16mm and 35mm filmmaking.

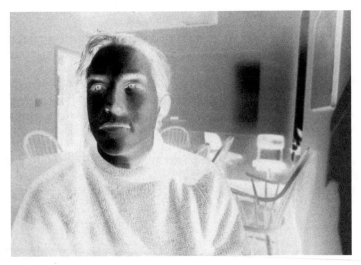

Fig. 7-2. The negative. Fig. 12-33 shows the positive image. (Stephen McCarthy)

The Reversal Process

Reversal film yields a positive image that can be directly projected without the need of a print (like a slide in still photography). Reversal was once the standard process in Super 8 and 16mm, though negative film is now used much more often.

The key to the reversal process lies in the development of the image. The film is exposed to light in the camera to form a latent image. As in the negative process, the developer reduces the silver halide of the latent image into metallic silver. In reversal development, instead of washing away the remaining (unexposed) silver halide crystals, the metallic silver is removed, leaving the unexposed silver halide crystals (which are still light sensitive) in the emulsion. The film is then uniformly exposed to light (or immersed in a fogging agent), exposing the remaining silver halide, and developed again. Thus, the reversal process maintains the relative brightness values of the original scene (light areas in the subject end up transparent and dark subject areas are more opaque).

The Characteristic Curve

A basic knowledge of characteristic curves will help you understand the practical aspects of exposure, which are discussed in detail later. The *characteristic curve* for a film stock is a graph that shows the relation between the amount of light that exposes the film and the corresponding density built up in the film. To plot the curve, the film is exposed to progressively greater amounts of light in constant increments. The film is then developed, and the densities are measured. For negative stocks, the greater the exposure, the greater the density, whereas for reversal, the greater the exposure, the less the density. Exposure is plotted along the horizontal axis and density along the vertical axis (see Fig. 7-3).

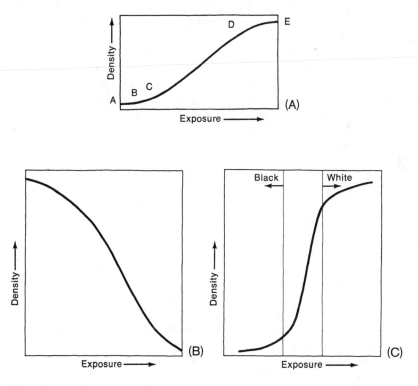

Fig. 7-3. Characteristic curves. (A) A simplified characteristic curve for black-and-white negative film: point A is the base-plus-fog density; B to C is the toe; C to D is the straight line portion; D to E is the shoulder. (B) Characteristic curve for reversal film. The greater steepness of the curve shows the higher contrast of reversal stock. (C) A very high-contrast black-and-white negative stock used for titles. (Carol Keller)

Even when the film receives no exposure, *some* density is built up. The base itself has some density (it absorbs some of the projected light), and the development process adds an overall light *fog* to the film. This is the minimum density of the film, also called *D-min*.

In the negative process, increases in exposure don't start to increase the density until the *threshold* of the emulsion, the point where the curve starts to rise, is reached (point B in Fig. 7-3A). Even though a dark area in the scene emits some light, if it falls below the threshold, it won't produce any change in the density. So, deep shadows appear in a positive print as undifferentiated black with no detail.[1]

The *straight line section* of the curve (point C to point D in Fig. 7-3A) is the portion where a given change in exposure produces a constant change in the density. This is normally where we want to expose as much of the scene as possible.

The *toe* of the curve (point B to point C) is the area of lowest densities—usually the darkest shadows that show some detail—where constant increases in the exposure do not lead to proportional increases in density. The densities here increase more gradually than they do in the straight line section; the slope in the toe is thus less steep (slower rising) than in the straight line section. The *shoulder* (point D to point E), like the toe, is a flatter curve than the straight line section. Again, constant increases in exposure do not lead to constant increases in density. At point E, increases in exposure do not cause any increase in density. This is the maximum density (*D-max*) possible in this film.[2]

If an area of the subject gets exposed high on the shoulder, differences in brightness will not be recorded as significant differences in density. For example, a white wall may be three times as bright as a face, but if both expose high on the shoulder, the difference in their densities will be insignificant (highlights are *compressed*). In a positive print, this area will appear as an undifferentiated white (*blocking of the highlights*).

Shadows will show no detail if they fall near the film's threshold, and highlights will show no detail if they fall too high on the shoulder. Generally, for correct exposure, the important parts of the subject that should show good tonal separation must fall on the straight line section. Shadow and highlight values may fall on the toe and shoulder, respectively, but, if you want some detail, they should not be too close to the outer limits. When you are filming, there are many ways to control exposure in order to control where on the characteristic curve parts of the subject will fall (see below).

Characteristic Curves for Color Film

Modern color film stocks are composed of three emulsion layers; each layer is similar to a black-and-white film emulsion. The top layer is sensitive to only blue light (and records the blue *record*, or blue part, of the scene). The second layer records the green record; the bottom, the red record. All the colors rendered by the film are created from a combination of the record of these three *primaries* (see Chapter 8 for more on primaries).

---

1. In video, the equivalent concept is that any dark areas that fall below the black clip level won't be visible (blacks are crushed).

2. The video equivalent is the white clip level.

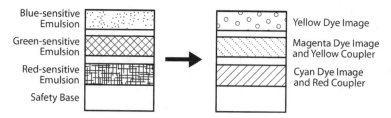

Fig. 7-4. Color negative before (left) and after processing. Yellow and red couplers are found in the green- and red-sensitive emulsions to compensate for deficiencies in color absorption of the magenta and cyan dyes.

Incorporated into each of the three emulsion layers is a group of *dye couplers* that release dyes of the appropriate color during development (see Fig. 7-4). The more exposure a particular emulsion layer receives, the more color dye that remains after development. The three color layers will be recorded with the dye color of each layer's complementary color; thus the blue, green, and red colors in the scene will be recorded with dyes colored yellow, magenta, and cyan, respectively.

Because of imperfections in the absorption of color dyes in negative stocks, an orange *masking* is added to compensate. Reversal films have no need for color masking.

Film Speed and ISO

The *speed* of a stock is a measure of its sensitivity to light. The "faster" a film stock, the less light it needs to produce an acceptable exposure. The *exposure index* (*EI*) expresses the speed as a number that can be used with light meters to help determine proper exposure. The film manufacturer recommends an exposure index for each stock that is usually given in the form of an *ISO number* (from a variant name of the International Organization for Standardization). The ISO number is an updated form of the *ASA number* and many people use ISO and ASA interchangeably. The *DIN number* is a similar speed-rating system developed in Germany and is marked with a degree sign. On the label for Eastman Kodak stocks you will find the exposure index indicated with both an ISO and a DIN number (see Fig. 7-7). EI 500/28° means ISO 500, DIN 28.

A medium-speed emulsion will be rated around ISO 100. ISO speeds below 50 are usually considered slow. Fast or high-speed emulsions are rated ISO 200 or higher. Doubling the ISO number means that the film will be twice as sensitive to light. A film rated at ISO 100 needs only half the exposure (that is, one stop less) than a film rated ISO 50. The faster film can be used in conditions with less light or to allow a smaller iris opening on the lens.

Black-and-white emulsions are sometimes rated by two exposure indexes, one for tungsten illumination and the other for daylight. The tungsten rating is generally about one-third of a stop slower than the daylight rating, representing the emulsion's lower sensitivity to the red end of the spectrum.

Color film stocks are also rated with one EI for tungsten light and one for daylight. Here the implication is that you will use a filter for one type of light, and some light will be absorbed by the filter. For example, a tungsten-balanced stock rated ISO 500 will be rated ISO 320 for use in daylight with an 85 filter (see p. 309).

The manufacturer's recommended exposure index is intended as a starting point. It is not unusual for cinematographers to rate the film at a slightly different ISO (see The Light Meter and Exposure Control, p. 286, for more on varying the EI).

CONTRAST OF THE IMAGE

Contrast measures the separation of tones (lights and darks) in an image. The higher the contrast, the greater the separation between tones (see Fig. 7-5). See Understanding and Controlling Contrast, p. 191, for an overview, and for how contrast and gamma apply to digital images. In film, many of the concepts are very similar, though gamma is defined differently.

Contrast and Gamma

Low-contrast images are called "flat." High-contrast images—with good tonal separation—are called "contrasty" or "hard." An image with good contrast range has "snap."

To visualize the idea of tonal separation, imagine two parts of a scene that have somewhat different brightness (say, the bright side of the man's face and the shadowed side in Fig. 7-5). With low contrast (left image) the dark and light tones are close together; with high contrast (right image) the tones are much more different, there's more separation between the dark and the light. Also see Fig. 5-5.

Fig. 7-5. Varying degrees of contrast. (left) Low-contrast image looks flat and dull. Note muddy blacks and lack of bright whites. (center) Normal contrast. (right) High-contrast image has bright whites and deep blacks but lacks midtones. Note loss of detail on bright side of face and dark sweater. (Stephen McCarthy)

The steepness of the film's characteristic curve (mathematically, the *slope*) indicates the amount of contrast at any point on the curve. The steeper the curve, the higher the contrast, and thus the greater the separation of tones. *Gamma* (γ, defined as the slope) is a measure of the steepness of the straight line section of the characteristic curve. Increasing gamma means increasing the contrast of tonalities that fall on the straight line section.

The straight line section is steeper than either the toe or the shoulder portion, so areas of the subject that are exposed on the straight line section will show more tonal separation (contrast) than areas that fall on the toe or shoulder.[3]

With video systems, "gamma" refers particularly to the contrast of the midtones. Video gamma curves have a different shape than film curves, resulting from the different ways the two systems respond to light (see Figs. 5-7 and 5-9).

FORCE PROCESSING AND GAMMA. Gamma depends on both the nature of the particular film stock and the way it's developed at the lab. Increasing gamma also increases the sensitivity of the film to light (it effectively raises the ISO number; see p. 275); when done for this purpose, it's called *force processing* or *pushing*.

Force processing may be used when there is insufficient light to shoot. For example, a film rated ISO 100 is exposed as though it were rated ISO 200 to effectively double its sensitivity. The lab is then instructed to "push one stop" to compensate for the underexposure by increasing development time. Some stocks can be pushed one to three stops, but force development increases graininess, sometimes to a degree that makes the image unacceptable.

When you're force processing, change the ISO/ASA speed on the light meter for exposure calculations. When pushing one stop, double the ISO number; when pushing two stops, multiply it by four.

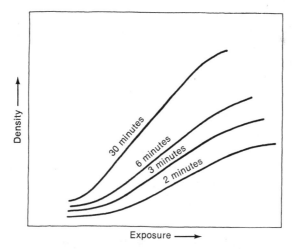

Fig. 7-6. Force processing. As the development time increases, the characteristic curve becomes steeper (contrast increases)—because the brighter parts of the scene (right side of graph) respond more to increased development than the darker parts. Fog level also increases with development time. (Carol Keller)

3. The tonalities in the straight line section are "stretched" and those in the toe and the shoulder are "compressed."

Pushing increases contrast because areas in the scene that fall on the straight line section and the shoulder increase in density more than those on the toe (see Fig. 7-6). Middle tones in the scene that would have otherwise been underexposed can get a significant boost from pushing.

However, pushing does not generally raise the threshold of the film, so pushing will not result in much more detail in the shadows. When we are concerned with "seeing into the shadows," stocks with long flat curves do best; pushing helps little. When reversal stocks are pushed, the blacks often become muddy and look grayish (a lower D-max).

Bleach Bypass

Another way to increase contrast in development is to use the *bleach bypass process* (sometimes called *skip bleach*). The film is processed without the bleach that would normally cause the silver grains to be removed. Metallic silver is left in the emulsion along with the colored dyes. The result is increased contrast, desaturated colors, and washed-out highlights. Some cinematographers use this to create a special look. This should be undertaken with tests only and the lab may not guarantee the results. If you are transferring to digital and then making a D.I. or film-out (see Chapter 17), you may be able to achieve these effects digitally without doing bleach bypass in processing.

Reducing Contrast in the Film Stock

Gamma can be increased via force processing, which affects the rendering of bright areas in the scene more than it does the dark areas. Gamma can be lowered by *underdeveloping* (*pulling*) the film in the lab. Pulling reduces film speed, grain, and contrast. If this is planned, the film is overexposed during shooting, then underdeveloped to the same degree. For example, you might rate the film at half its normal ISO (use ISO 50 for a film normally rated at ISO 100), then instruct the lab to pull by one stop. With some stocks, pulling can result in a rich image with subtle shading. Be sure to check with the lab first; not all stocks can be successfully pulled and the lab may not perform this service. Pulling is sometimes done for footage that is accidentally overexposed in shooting.

Another way to reduce contrast is by *flashing*, a process in which the film is uniformly exposed to a dim light either before (*preflashing*) or after (*postflashing*) the scene is photographed. This exposure increases the exposure of shadow areas, but it has little effect on the bright areas. It thus lowers the contrast and may also bring out some shadow detail.

You may not like the way flashing increases graininess, desaturates colors, and imparts a milkiness to the image, especially in the shadow areas. Be sure to consult your lab and make tests before flashing footage. This effect may be achievable—at least in part—in digital post without requiring changes in shooting or processing.

SHARPNESS

Definition, or *sharpness*, expresses the degree of clarity in an image. There are several physical measurements that more or less correspond to the viewer's sensation of sharpness.

Resolution and MTF

Resolution, or *resolving power*, is the ability to record fine detail in the image. Resolution in film is measured by photographing a test chart with sets of parallel lines in which the space between the lines is equal to the thickness of the lines, the thickness progressively diminishing. The image is then examined under a microscope to determine the greatest number of lines per millimeter that can be distinguished. Resolving power is of limited use for predicting the viewer's evaluations of sharpness, since those perceptions are highly dependent on the contrast in the image—the higher the contrast, the sharper the image appears. An image may have a very high resolution, say 100 lines/mm, but will not appear to be sharp if the contrast is excessively low. Modulation transfer function (MTF) measures contrast and is a better indicator of perceived sharpness. For more on MTF, see p. 234.

Graininess and Granularity

The photographic image is composed of small grains of metallic silver, or, in the case of color films, masses of dye that create a roughness in the image. The viewer's perception of this roughness is called *graininess*, and the objective measurement that attempts to quantify it is known as *granularity*. Graininess is usually considered to be an undesirable element but some grain structures may look beautiful, while others merely impair the image.

In general, faster films are made up of larger silver halide crystals and thus appear grainier. Fine-grain emulsions are usually found in slower film stocks. Generally, slightly overexposing color negative film results in less graininess, whereas in black-and-white overexposure causes an increase in graininess. Graininess varies with subject matter. A blue sky that is not overexposed will show more graininess than a landscape.

CHOOSING A RAW STOCK

As you prepare to shoot a movie, you select which stock or stocks to use for the project. Seek advice, do tests, and find out what stocks were used for movies that have a look you like. For the latest listing of available stocks, check the manufacturers' websites.

Every film stock has a particular *palette*, or range of colors or tones it creates on screen. How film stock will ultimately perform depends on the choice of stock, the exposure, the processing, and the filters used, among other things. Different laboratories may make the same stock appear quite different in terms of color, grain, and sharpness. Kodak's Look Manager System is a digital tool that can help previsualize various choices on a laptop using test stills shot with a digital camera.

Some movies are still printed the old-fashioned way, from the camera original film to print stock. However, today most movies shot on film are transferred to digital and all subsequent distribution comes from digital masters (see Chapter 16). Working in digital opens up many opportunities to change the look of the image in postproduction, which you should factor into the choices you make during the shoot.

Negative Versus Reversal

Most movies are made with negative stocks and if you're thinking of starting a project in 16mm or 35mm, think first of negative. There are more stocks available in negative than in reversal. Negative can handle a greater range of lighting conditions and is more forgiving of exposure errors. If you want to minimize costs, you can shoot reversal and project or edit it without making a print; however, this puts the original at great risk of scratching and should not be done for important projects. The traditional Super 8 home movie is reversal original (though negative Super 8 is available) and some people like the look. If you plan to edit and distribute digitally, you might just as well start with negative.

Film Speed

Film speed is often the key element in the selection of the raw stock. In general, the faster the speed, the more flexibility you have. Not only is it easier to shoot in available light, but supplementary lighting need not be as bright, cutting lighting costs and creating a better environment for the actors or subjects. High-speed film stock allows the lens to be stopped down to increase depth of field. On the other hand, high-speed films may produce a poorer-quality image, with more grain and less sharpness (though there are exceptions). As a rule of thumb, select the slowest film that allows you either to shoot at a preferred f-stop or to get an adequate exposure in situations where you can't use lights (important in documentaries). At this time, the range of standard color negative films extends from ISO 50 to 500. Documentary cinematographers who shoot in unpredictable available light situations often look for the fastest film of acceptable quality. On many productions, two or more stocks are used: a slow speed for exteriors and higher speeds for interiors or night work. Often, two different stocks are used for the same movie, but they look too different to be intercut in the same scene.

PUSHING. Film sensitivity can be increased with forced processing (also called *pushing*, see p. 277). Some stocks can be pushed a stop or more with acceptable results; others show objectionable graininess when pushed even one stop.

Daylight Balance Versus Tungsten

For a discussion of color balance and film stocks, see Chapter 8.

Film stocks are generally made to be used without a filter with either tungsten illumination (professional lighting at 3200°K) *or* daylight. Eastman Kodak uses the letter *T* or *D* after the ISO number to indicate the type (100T film is ISO 100, tungsten). Fuji uses a similar system. Films balanced for tungsten light can be used in daylight with an 85 filter. Similarly, films balanced for daylight can be used in tungsten light with an 80A filter.

If you plan to shoot *exclusively* in daylight (either outdoors or in a window-lit interior), then it makes sense to use daylight-balanced film. However, because the 80A filter cuts out two stops of light, this can cause problems when you shoot indoors with tungsten illumination. Two stops are a lot to lose when you're lighting a scene—you need four times as much light to compensate. (Of course, you could use daylight-balanced lighting units such as HMIs.)

For most filming situations, it's generally a better idea to order tungsten-balanced film. This allows you to shoot indoors with a minimum amount of artificial light (since no light is lost to the filter). When you shoot outside, the two-thirds stop lost by the 85 filter is usually not a problem. In fact, often you need additional ND filters to cut the light level down even more. In some situations you can shoot tungsten-balanced film outdoors with no filter (see Chapter 8).

Contrast and Film Stocks

Compared to high-contrast film stocks, low-contrast stocks have a longer, more gently sloped characteristic curve and can handle a greater range of brightness in the scene (they have greater exposure range or latitude; see p. 296). Generally, the slower a stock is, the greater its latitude will be—but not always. Negative stocks have greater latitude than reversal. Higher-contrast stocks often tend toward deeper, more saturated color.

Some stocks are designed especially for direct transfer to digital. These feature low contrast (great exposure range) and color rendering that is well matched to the telecine. In fact, one of the key benefits of shooting in film versus digital is that many film stocks can handle greater contrast range than traditional video cameras, allowing you to capture details in both highlights and shadows that can be brought out in the digital transfer. See Chapter 16 for more.

PACKAGING, HANDLING, AND PURCHASING

Most cameras use *core-mounted* film. The film roll is wound around a plastic hub (the core) and must be handled only in darkness (see Fig. 6-13). Some cameras accept *daylight spools*, which are solid metal reels that allow the film to be loaded in light. See Camera Film Capacity, p. 262, for a detailed discussion of roll lengths and camera loading procedures.

Film stocks have a multidigit identification number (see Fig. 7-7). The Kodak film in the illustration has the number 5279 184 1704. The film type is 5279; the "52" tells us this is a 35mm stock. If it were 16mm, it would start with "72" instead (7279). Experienced filmmakers often refer to stocks only with the second two digits, as in, "give me two rolls of 79." The remaining parts of the ID number are the emulsion batch number and the roll number from which this piece of film was cut. It's a good idea to note the entire number as a check against potential problems (see p. 265).

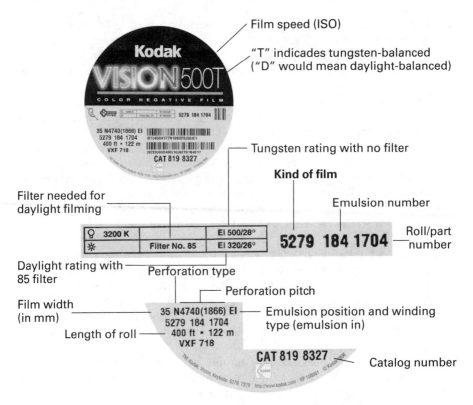

Fig. 7-7. Film label and enlarged details. This label is for Kodak 5279 color negative film, also called Vision 500T (now discontinued). The newer version is 5219 (Vision3 500T). (Eastman Kodak Company)

Perforations

Super 8 film is perforated on one side (*single-perforated*, or *single-perf*), while 35mm film is perforated on both sides (*double-perforated*, or *double-perf*). Film in 16mm may be single- or double-perforated (see Fig. 1-34). Double-perf film can be used in any camera and has a slight advantage over single-perf when cement-splicing the original. When shooting Super 16 you must use single-perf. The standard 35mm frame spans four perfs, but there are also three-perf and two-perf 35mm formats (see Chapter 1), which all use identical 35mm film stock.

Windings

16mm raw stock perforated on one edge and wound with the emulsion side in has two possible windings, designated *winding A* and *winding B* (see Fig. 7-8). Camera original is almost invariably in winding B. Stock in winding A is generally used only by labs for printing.

There's another laboratory use of these terms that often leads to confusion: *A-wind* and *B-wind* are used to distinguish whether the picture "reads correctly" (that is, not flipped left to right) when viewed facing the emulsion side (A-wind) or when

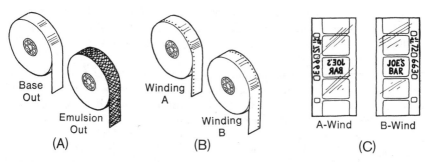

Fig. 7-8. Emulsion position and winds. (A) Film can be wound base out or emulsion out. (B) Single-perforated film in 16mm, wound base out, can be winding A or winding B, depending on the position of the perforations as shown. (C) With the base facing you, B-wind film reads properly through the base, while A-wind film will be reversed or flipped. Note that the key numbers usually read the same as the image. Compare with Fig. 16-12. (Carol Keller)

viewed facing the base (B-wind). An easy way to remember this is that *B*-wind film reads correctly through the *base*. B-wind is also called *camera original position*.

Key Numbers and Edge Identification

Along the edge of 16mm and 35mm film, the manufacturer exposes a latent image with information such as the name of the manufacturer, the film identification number, and a running footage count. This information is readable after the film is processed, and it can be printed from the negative to another piece of film. The numbers that track the footage are called *key numbers* or *latent edge numbers*. Key numbers allow each frame of film to be identified by number and are indispensable for conforming the original.

Most film stocks also have a machine-readable bar code version of the key number. This is generically called *keycode* (Kodak calls its system Eastman Keykode; Fuji calls its MR Code). When editing film digitally, keycode is tremendously useful because it allows the telecine and other machines to automatically identify and find each frame of film.

In 16mm, key numbers are printed every half foot (20 frames). When counting frames in 16mm there is a dot at the beginning of the number, which is the *zero-frame reference mark*. In Fig. 7-9, you can see the dot to the left of the "M" in the key

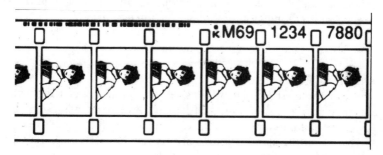

Fig. 7-9. 16mm key numbers and Keykode. (Eastman Kodak Company)

number M69 1234 7880. This is the frame that should be considered exactly 7880. The next frame going toward the tail (in the direction of 7881) would be 7880 + 1. The frame on the other side of the mark going toward the head (in the direction of 7879) would be 7879 + 19.

In 35mm, key numbers are printed every foot (16 frames for standard four-perf cameras). There is also a midfoot key number to help identify short pieces of film; this is located thirty-two perforations from the main number. When counting frames in 35mm, the zero-frame reference dot immediately follows the last four digits of the key number. Thus, for the key number KJ 23 1234 5677, the frame where the dot falls is 5677. The next frame going toward the tail (in the direction of 5678) would be 5677 + 1. The frame on the other side of dot (going toward the head) would be 5676 + 15.

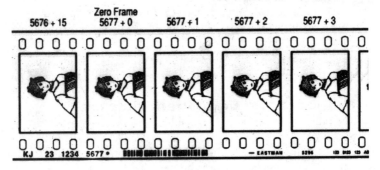

Fig. 7-10. 35mm key numbers and Keykode. (Eastman Kodak Company)

There are so many types of coding and numbering schemes in filmmaking that the names (and concepts) can be easily confused. Here are some things that key numbers and keycode are *not*:

1. *Ink edge numbers* (sometimes also called *edge code*, *Acmade numbers*, or just *edge numbers*). Generated by a machine that stamps an ink number on film workprint and mag sound to aid in synchronizing.
2. *In-camera timecode.* Generated by some cameras and exposed on the edge of the film during shooting (see Fig. 6-14).
3. *Video (telecine) timecode.* Generated during the film-to-digital transfer for use in video editing; not printed on the film (see p. 692).

For more on telecines, key numbers, and timecode, see Chapter 16.

Handling Film Stock

Over time, unprocessed film may lose speed and contrast and may shift in color. Aged film may shrink and become brittle. Kodak recommends using raw stock within six months of purchase. Avoid heat when storing film. The lower the temperature, the slower the aging process. An automobile left in the sun can heat up above 140°F (60°C), and film in the car can undergo significant changes in a matter of hours.

If storing film for up to three months before use, keep it below 55°F (13°C) at relative humidity of 60 percent or lower. Put it in a refrigerator when possible. Whenever storing film for more than three months, put it in a freezer, ideally at 0° to –10°F (–18° to –23°C). Pack film in plastic freezer bags to control humidity. After you remove the stock from cold storage, allow it to come to room temperature before breaking the moistureproof seal.

Once the seal is broken, expose the film as soon as possible, and then, after exposure, have it processed as soon as possible. If processing must be delayed, avoid high temperature and humidity. If the cans are resealed with the moisture-proof tape, a household refrigerator may be used to store the film, although a freezer at 0°F is preferred. Though not recommended, we have found that some exposed stocks maintained an excellent image when frozen for more than a year prior to processing. Store processed film in a cool, dry place, at 70°F (21°C) or lower.

AIR TRAVEL. When traveling through airports, beware of X-ray machines! Unprocessed film can tolerate some X-ray exposure, but excessive amounts will increase the fog level and grain. X-ray machines used for carry-on baggage shouldn't cause noticeable damage to most films. X-ray exposure is cumulative, so repeated X-ray inspections are most problematic, especially for high-speed films. Sometimes you do best by hand-carrying the film and asking for a hand inspection at the gate. However, some inspectors will demand to look inside the film cans! Bring a changing bag in case. Sometimes you can contact the airport manager in advance to get a manual inspection.

In the past, one solution was to pack the film in a cooler lined with lead foil and send it as baggage. However, newer baggage X-ray machines are far more powerful (and damaging to the film) than the ones used to inspect hand-carried items. Kodak recommends never shipping unprocessed film as checked baggage on commercial airlines. Check the X-ray policies of commercial couriers such as FedEx and UPS to see if they scan packages for domestic or international flights. Consider using an export company or customs broker to ship the film and do all the paperwork. Another possibility is to process the film in the area or country where you're shooting. Be sure to label film ("Photographic Materials—No X-ray"). Normal X-ray inspection shouldn't damage film that's already been processed, audio- or videotapes, or digital memory.

Purchasing Raw Stock

Order raw stock from the manufacturer's catalog by catalog number and stock name. For example, ordering Kodak Vision3 500T film allows numerous further possibilities, but the catalog number, 8738304, identifies the stock as 5219, 35mm, 400 feet on core, emulsion in, standard perforations.

Use fresh raw stock. Order it to arrive a week or so before it is needed rather than months in advance. If you encounter a raw stock of an unknown age, the manufacturer can tell from the emulsion number when it was manufactured. Of course, this tells you nothing about its past storage conditions. There are businesses that sell previously owned, unexposed stock including *short ends* (parts of complete rolls) for a discount. Test a roll by sending twenty feet of unexposed stock to the lab to be developed and checked for increased fog, which, if present, is a sign of poor storage or possible exposure to airport X-ray machines.

THE LIGHT METER
AND EXPOSURE CONTROL

Many of the ideas in this section build on concepts introduced in Properties of the Film Stock, p. 271.

Exposure

When you're filming a scene, there is no single "correct" exposure. We might say that a scene is properly exposed when the image on film looks pleasing to the eye and important elements in the scene are shown with sufficient detail. If a close-up of a person's face is significantly overexposed (that is, too much light is allowed to strike the film), the face on screen will look too bright and facial details will be washed out. If the shot is seriously underexposed, the image will look very dark and muddy. In both cases, facial details are lost—either because they are washed out or because they are indistinguishable from parts of the emulsion that have received no exposure at all.

When shooting negative film, the negative is exposed in the camera and then a positive print or video transfer is made to view the image. Compare the negative image in Fig. 7-2 with the positive in Fig. 12-33. You can see that the dark parts of the positive image (the man's sweater and the doorway on the left side) are quite thin and transparent on the negative. The light parts of the scene (the bright side of his face and the splash of sun on the back wall) show up in the negative as dark and relatively dense (thick or opaque). For an area in the scene to be rendered with good detail, that area in the negative needs to be sufficiently dense and detailed. Areas where the negative is too thin and transparent will have relatively little detail in the positive print or on video. In this image, the sweater or the doorway might be considered "underexposed" in the sense that they show up in the positive image as very dark and lacking much detail. However, in the context of the whole picture, this lack of detail seems natural. The most important part of this scene is the man's face, and as long as his skin tone appears naturally bright and rendered with good detail, other parts of the scene can be allowed to go brighter or darker. Thus, "correct" exposure means identifying what's important in the scene and exposing that properly.

If important details are visible on the film after processing, shots that are slightly too bright or too dark can be corrected when the film is printed or transferred to digital. When shooting with color negative stocks, you want to avoid significant *under*exposure because the resulting negative will be thin and without detail. When shooting reversal stocks, significant *over*exposure will result in the film being thin and lacking in detail. With both negative and reversal, the goal is to expose in the *middle* of the range, to capture detail in both the bright areas (the highlights) and the dark ones (shadows), so the overall exposure seems natural and pleasing.

LIGHT METERS

Meter Types

Light meters (also called *exposure meters*) allow us to measure light intensity so we can control exposure of the film stock. There are two types: *incident meters* measure the amount of light falling on the subject and *reflected meters* measure the amount of light reflected by the subject. Some meters can take *both* incident and reflected readings, though some are designed primarily for one type of reading and are inferior for the other.

Fig. 7-11. (left) The reflected meter is pointed at the subject from the direction of the camera. (right) The incident meter is held in the same light as the subject and pointed toward the camera. (Carol Keller)

The most useful meters give you a direct reading of *f*-stops when you push a button (see Fig. 7-12). Less useful are meters that require you to find the *f*-stop using a calculator dial on the meter (see Fig. 7-13)—time is precious when shooting. Most modern meters have a digital readout and use batteries.

Reading the Meter

In controlling exposure, you are regulating the amount of light that strikes each frame of film. The amount of light is determined by how long the shutter is open (the shutter speed, determined by the shutter angle and the camera speed) and how much light passes through the lens during this time (affected by the iris diaphragm setting, the filters in use, light loss in the lens, and light loss in the viewfinder optics). Usually the meter is set to compensate for all the other factors, then the light reading is used to determine the proper iris setting (that is, the *f*-number) for a particular shot.

Fig. 7-12. Sekonic digital meters that can take both incident and reflected readings. (left) L-758DR. (right) L-308DC. (Sekonic)

For typical film cameras, the shutter angle is about 180 degrees and, when run at sound speed (24 fps), the shutter speed is about ¹⁄₅₀ second. The shutter speed for any camera can be found in its instruction manual or can be easily calculated if you know the shutter angle (see Chapter 6). If you change the camera speed (for example, to produce slow-motion effects), you will alter the shutter speed.

The meter must be set to the proper film speed (ISO) for the film stock you are using. Remember to compensate for filters you may be using (for example—when shooting in daylight with tungsten-balanced color film—see Chapter 8). Cameras with built-in meters usually compensate for filters automatically and, in Super 8, the ISO and shutter speed may be set automatically as well. With direct-reading meters, the shutter speed is also set on the meter so that f-stops can be read directly when the trigger is depressed.

On meters with calculator dials, the indicator needle is read against a numbered scale (see Fig. 7-13). Set this number on the calculator dial. You will find the shutter speed on the *shutter speed scale* (sometimes labeled *time* or *zeit*), which is marked in fractions of a second ('60, '30, etc.). You can then read the f-stop opposite the proper shutter speed. With cameras equipped with 175- or 180-degree shutters, you may find it easier to read from the *cine scale*. This is marked in frames per second (64 fps, 32, 16, etc.) and usually has a bold mark at 24 fps, corresponding to ¹⁄₅₀-second shutter speed. After you have thus determined the f-number, you can set the lens's iris accordingly.

In most circumstances, it doesn't pay to be more precise than about one-third of

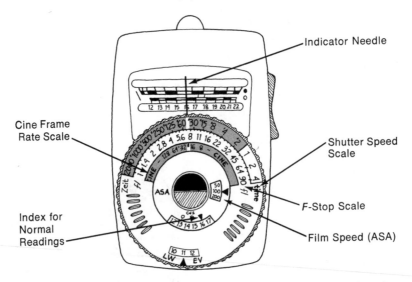

Fig. 7-13. Calculator dial found on Gossen Luna-Pro meter. The film speed window indicates that the meter is set for ASA 100 film. The light reading (16) is set opposite the triangle in the window just below the ASA setting. A camera with a 180-degree shutter run at 24 fps has a shutter speed of ¹⁄₅₀ second (50 can be found on the time scale between '60 and '30). The f-stop is read opposite this point. Alternatively, the f-stop could be read opposite the 24 fps mark on the cine scale (found between 32 and 16). The meter indicates a reading between f/5.6 and f/8. (Carol Keller)

a stop when calculating exposures; few meters are accurate enough and few film stocks (especially negative stocks) will show the difference.

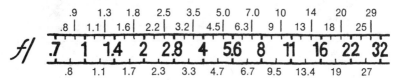

Fig. 7-14. Intermediate values on the *f*-stop scale. Above the scale are one-third stop increments; below the scale are half-stop increments. (Carol Keller)

VIEWFINDER OPTICS. With cameras that have internal beam-splitter viewfinders (for example, most Super 8 cameras and the 16mm Bolex), some light is diverted from the film to the viewfinder (see Fig. 6-8). When you use a *handheld light meter* rather than a built-in one, do not set it to the *actual* shutter speed (based on shutter angle and frame rate); instead, use an *effective* shutter speed that compensates for light lost in the viewfinder. The effective speed is always faster. On some Bolexes at 24 fps, actual speed is ¹⁄₆₅ second, effective is ¹⁄₈₀. Your camera's manual should indicate the proper setting.

F-STOPS AND T-STOPS. *F*-stops do not take into account light lost internally in a lens, whereas T-stops do (see p. 153). When you use a professional lens marked in T-stops (sometimes a red scale on the opposite side of the iris ring from the *f*-stops), use the T-stops instead of the *f*-stops for all exposure calculations. Ignore the fact that light meters are marked in *f*-stops. T-stops should also be used whenever you are filming with more than one lens.

The Angle of Acceptance

All meters built into still and movie cameras are of the reflected type. Built-in, through-the-lens meters may average together the light from the entire frame (called *averaging meters*), they may read only the light from objects in the center of the frame (*spot meters*; see Fig. 7-15), or they may read the whole frame, giving more emphasis to the center (*center-weighted meters*). Consult your camera manual to find out what part of the frame your meter reads.

Handheld reflected meters have a window over the photocell that allows light to enter from an *angle of acceptance* (usually between 15 and 60 degrees). Some meters are designed to simulate the angle of view of a "normal" lens, but the meter may read a wider or narrower area than the lens you are using. All the light reflected by objects within the angle of acceptance is averaged together, so if you are trying to read the light from an individual object, it is necessary to get close to it. Handheld spot meters are simply reflected meters that have a very narrow angle of acceptance, often 1 degree or less. They can be used to read the light from small areas at a greater distance.

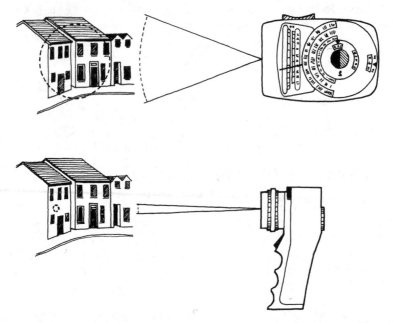

Fig. 7-15. (top) A typical reflected light meter has a wide angle of acceptance (about 40 degrees here) and averages areas of differing brightness. (bottom) A spot meter (pictured here with a 5-degree angle of acceptance) can isolate a small area in the subject. (Carol Keller)

TAKING READINGS

Exposure and Incident Light

The exposure of an object on film is related to the amount of light *falling on the object*—that is, the *incident light*. Incident light can be measured with an incident light meter that has a translucent plastic hemisphere (or *hemispherical diffuser*), which simulates the light-gathering ability of a typical three-dimensional subject—specifically, the human head. The incident meter is held at the position of the subject (or in the same light) and is *pointed in the direction of the camera*. The meter averages together the light coming from the front, the sides, and, to a lesser extent, the back of the subject. Be sure not to block the light with your body when you take a reading.

Many cinematographers use incident meters almost exclusively. Incident light readings are quick and easy to do, and they usually result in proper exposure of facial skin tones. Faces, especially in close-ups and medium shots, are often the most important element in the frame.

Incident meters are preferred when studio lighting is used because they conveniently indicate how much light is contributed by each light source. In this case, the hemispherical diffuser may be replaced with a *flat disc diffuser* that can more easily be aimed at one light at a time.

Incident meters are often advantageous in those situations in which it is difficult to approach the subject to take a reading. If the subject is fairly far away outdoors, you can take an incident reading from the camera position (assuming it is in the same light), and—unlike a reflected reading—it won't be thrown off by large expanses of sky or other extraneous elements. Unlike the reflected meter, the incident meter is useless when you film something that emits light (like a television screen), when you film through something that filters light (for example, a tinted car windshield), or whenever the meter cannot be placed in the same light as the subject.

INCIDENT METERS AND CONTRASTY SCENES. Some scenes contain a great range of incident light and the incident reading must be interpreted and not used directly. Consider the example of filming people by a building on a sunny day. If you take an incident reading near the people in the shadows, and then set the exposure accordingly, the people in the sun are likely to be drastically overexposed. Conversely, if the incident reading is taken in the sun, the people in the shadows will be underexposed. This can happen to varying degrees with all film stocks. The reason is that the range of brightness in the scene (the lighting contrast; see p. 476) exceeds the film's sensitivity range (latitude or exposure range; see p. 296).

Fig. 7-16. A scene with high lighting contrast. (left) If you take a light meter reading in the sunlit area and expose accordingly, the shadow area is underexposed. (right) If you take your reading in the shadows, the sunlit area is overexposed. (center) A compromise exposure, slightly underexposing the figures in the shadows. Film stocks vary in their ability to handle high-contrast scenes. (Steven Ascher)

In Fig. 7-16, the figures in the foreground are lit by direct sun and the figures in the background above them are in shadow. Had you witnessed this scene with your naked eye (and a dramatic scene it was), you would have had no problem seeing detail in both the shadow and sunlit areas. This is because the eye's retina has a great range of sensitivity and your iris constantly adjusts the amount of light that strikes it. Film stocks, however, have a much narrower range of sensitivity. The image on the left is exposed for the sun. The image on the right is exposed for the shadows. The image in the center is a compromise exposure that attempts to split the difference.

Other approaches to this contrast problem include adding light to the shadow areas to reduce contrast or using a lower-contrast film stock that has greater latitude.

Exposure and Reflected Light

The incident reading tells us how much light is falling on the subject, but the subject's exposure on film actually results from the *total amount of light reflected by the object* in the direction of the camera's lens, which depends on what percentage of the incident light is reflected by the object (that is, its *reflectance*). Subject reflectance is determined by color and surface texture; a dark-colored, textured object reflects less light than a light-colored, smooth one does. For example, a dark wool sweater in the sun (low reflectance, high incident light) might produce the same amount of exposure as a bright white car in the shade (high reflectance, low incident light). That is to say, their *brightness* (*luminance* or *intensity*) is the same.

To see how reflectance relates to incident light, look at the middle image in Fig. 7-16. Of the figures in the background, the tiger and the figure in the middle receive equal amounts of incident light, but the white, reflectant tiger produces more exposure than the dark clothes of the man next to him.

The amount of light reflected by the subject can be measured with a reflected light meter. This meter can give more precise readings than the incident meter, especially for subjects whose reflectance is not near that of facial skin tones, but it requires more care to use properly. It can also be used in certain situations, like filming through a window, where the incident meter would be useless. The reflected meter is *pointed at the subject* from the camera position (or closer). The reflected reading must always be interpreted and never taken at face value.

UNDERSTANDING THE REFLECTED READING. When film is exposed, developed, and then projected on a screen or transferred to video, it can produce a range of tonalities from dark black (where the dense film holds back the light) to bright white (where most of the light shines through). The tone in the middle of this range is called *middle gray*. Reflected light meters are designed so that if you take a reading of any uniform object and then expose the film accordingly, the object will appear as middle gray on film. So, if you take a reading of an "average" subject, it will appear in the middle of the tonal range on screen and it will look natural. But what if the subject isn't average? Say you take a reflected reading of a black cat. This will result in the cat appearing on screen as middle gray—which means the cat will be unnaturally bright and other objects in the scene will probably be very overexposed. If you want dark objects to appear dark, you must give them less exposure than the reflected meter reading of the object would indicate. Similarly, for light objects to appear light, they must be given more exposure than the meter suggests.

A *gray card*, or neutral test card, is a piece of dull gray cardboard that reflects 18 percent of the light that strikes it. This card is intended to represent an indoors object of "average" reflectance. If you take a reading of the gray card and expose the film accordingly, the tonality of objects in the scene will usually look natural on film—neither too light nor too dark.

Gray cards are available at photographic or film supply stores. It's a good idea to carry one. Keep it protected in an envelope. As an experiment, set up a gray card facing the camera from several feet away. Use an incident meter to take a light reading at the card (remembering to point the meter toward the camera). Now take a reading of the card with a reflected meter (pointing it toward the card from a few feet away). The two readings should be the same.

Since "average" Caucasian skin is about twice as reflectant as the gray card—having about 35 percent reflectance—you could just as well base an exposure on a reading of that skin tone, as long as you remember to give the film twice as much exposure as the meter indicates. This is normally done by opening the iris diaphragm one stop (see below for other types of skin).

Taking Reflected Readings

Many people are familiar with the idea of reflected readings from doing still photography with cameras equipped with built-in meters. Still cameras often have averaging meters or center-weighted meters. You take a reading of the whole scene, set the exposure, and shoot. This kind of reflected reading can work fine for "average" subjects, particularly if they are front lit (the light coming from behind the camera). But a single reflected reading of the whole scene may cause the subject to be poorly exposed if the subject or the background is particularly light or dark, or if the light is coming from behind the subject. For movies, there is the added factor that the framing of the picture may change significantly *during* the shot.

Whenever you use a reflected meter, always ask yourself if the area of the scene that you're pointing the meter at is important. Base the exposure on the most important areas, and use readings of other areas to give you a sense of the overall range of brightness in the scene. Also ask yourself how you want the area you're reading to look on film. As discussed above, the reflected reading of an object will cause that object to appear on film in the middle of the tonal range. If you're reading an object that's near to average reflectance (like the 18 percent gray card), then the meter reading will result in that object looking natural on film. But if the object you're reading should look relatively dark on film, you need to give it less exposure than the meter indicates (usually by closing down the iris—that is, using a higher *f*-stop than the one indicated on the meter).

CLOSE-UPS AND MEDIUM SHOTS. In medium shots and close-ups of people (see Fig. 9-2), it's important that facial skin tones be exposed correctly. To take readings directly from the subject's face, put the meter close enough so that other areas are excluded from the meter's field of view. Be careful not to block the light or cast shadows with your body or the meter. If your skin tone is similar to your subject's, you can read the back of your hand instead, as long as it is in the same light. Since Caucasian skin is about twice as reflective as the gray card, you must give it about twice as much exposure as the meter indicates to render it appropriately light on film. Thus if the meter reads *f*/8, open up the iris to *f*/5.6. Black skin is usually less reflective than the gray card. You might stop down the iris a half stop for medium black skin or a full stop for darker black skin (a meter reading of *f*/8 would then be exposed at *f*/11).

Faces are normally lit so that part of the face is bright and part is in shadow. In general, if compensations are made as above, the exposure should be based on a reading of the brighter side. However, if the light comes from the side, more than half the face may be in shadow. You may want the dark side to remain dark. But if it's important to see more detail in the shadows, you might increase the exposure a half to one stop from the exposure used for the bright side.

WIDE SHOTS. In wide shots—landscapes and scenes where people do not figure prominently—instead of basing the exposure on skin tone, it's often better to take a reading of the average amount of reflected light in the scene. To do this, point the meter at the scene from the camera position. If you are shooting outside, a bright sky will tend to throw off the reading; angle the meter downward somewhat to avoid reading too much of the sky. In general, you should avoid pointing the meter at light sources. An averaging meter with a wide angle of acceptance can take in the whole scene and give you an average just by pressing the button. A spot meter, on the other hand, will fluctuate wildly as you scan it across highlight and shadow areas, so you will need to calculate the average. Some meters will store readings in memory, helping you to find the average.

One approach is to take readings of the brightest and darkest areas where you want to see detail and base your exposure on the average between them. When calculating the average between readings of bright and dark areas, you are not looking for the mathematical average, but one that is expressed in *f*-stops. Thus, the average of two readings (say, *f*/2 and *f*/16) is the stop halfway between the two (*f*/5.6), not the mathematical average (2 + 16) / 2 = 9. Some meters indicate light readings on a numbered scale, which can be averaged in the familiar way and then converted to *f*-stops.

Backlight

Light that comes from behind the subject in the direction of the camera is called *backlight*. Backlighting is often encountered outdoors when shooting in the direction of the sun or when shooting people in cars, or indoors when the subject is positioned in front of a window. Usually when you expose a backlit subject, it is desirable for the shaded side of the subject to appear *slightly* dark, which it is, but not so dark that the person appears in silhouette with no facial detail (see Fig. 7-17).

If you base the exposure on a typical reflected light meter reading from the camera position, the meter's angle of acceptance will include a great deal of the background. The meter then assumes that the subject is very light; it indicates that you should stop down quite far, throwing the person into silhouette. A rule of thumb to prevent silhouetting in this case is to open the iris one and a half stops above what the meter indicates (for example, open from *f*/8 to halfway between *f*/4 and *f*/5.6). Some film and video cameras have a backlight button that does just that.

In backlit settings, it is common to have one exposure for wide shots that include a lot of the bright background and another for closer shots where shadow detail may be more important. The latter might be opened up a half stop or so more than the former.

If you're filming in the direction of a strong light source that's shining directly into the lens you may pick up lens flare from light that reflects within the lens (see Fig. 4-25). Zoom lenses are prone to severe flare. Flare tends to fog the film, desatu-

Fig. 7-17. A backlighting problem when shooting toward a window. (top) Exposed for the interior, the outside is overexposed. (bottom) Exposed for outside, the woman is silhouetted. (middle) A compromise exposure, slightly underexposing the woman. (Stephen McCarthy)

rating colors and increasing overall exposure. If there's no way to block this light with a lens shade, a French flag, or your hand, keep in mind that flare can increase exposure a half stop or more. When flare is severe in backlit situations, you may want to close the iris a half stop in addition to the correction you made for backlighting.

Special Exposure Conditions

Setting exposure may involve a series of compromises, especially when areas in the scene vary greatly in their brightness. If you're interested in seeing detail in bright areas you may want to "bias" or "weight" the exposure by closing the iris a half to one stop from the incident reading; if detail in shaded areas is important, open up the same amount. You may also decide to adjust the exposure for creative purposes; for example, if you want a person lurking in the shadows to look dark, close the iris from an incident reading taken in the shadow.

NIGHT SCENES. As long as some bright highlights, such as street signs, storefronts, or narrow areas of streetlight, are visible, large areas of the frame can be rendered dark in night scenes. Similarly, if there are bright facial highlights recorded on the film, then the general exposure of the face can be lower than normal. (See Fig. 5-10.)

DISTANT LANDSCAPES. Haze, which may not be apparent to the eye, increases the exposure of distant objects on film (see Fig. 9-26). In hazy conditions, use a skylight or haze filter on the camera. Use a spot meter to average distant highlight and shadow areas, or, with an incident meter, decrease the exposure a half stop for front-lit scenes, or about a stop for side-lit scenes.

SUNRISE AND SUNSET. For sunrise or sunset shots in which the foreground scene is mostly silhouetted, take a reflected reading of the sky but not the sun directly. Closing down the iris from this reading may deepen the color of the sun, but it will also make the landscape darker. When possible, bracket exposures by using the reading you think is correct, then shoot with a half to one stop more, then the same amount less. If scenes are front lit by a red rising or setting sun, no 85 filter need be used with tungsten-balanced color film. Backlit scenes may look blue without it.

EXPOSURE AND FILM STOCKS

Beginners usually think about exposure on the basic level of "Did the picture come out?" In some ways, that question never goes away, but experienced cinematographers understand that exposure offers opportunities to create a wide range of effects on film.

Exposure Range

Perhaps the biggest challenge when exposing either film or video is accommodating the fact that the range of brightness in many scenes exceeds the camera's ability to faithfully record it. A common example is shooting an interior scene with bright windows visible in the background. You might have to choose between exposing for either the interior or the exterior, but you can't count on both being rendered with detail (see Fig. 7-17).

Stocks that can accommodate a great range in scene brightness are said to have great *latitude* or *exposure range*. A stock's latitude is determined by the length of the straight line portion of the film's characteristic curve (see p. 273). You can determine the exposure range of a stock by shooting tests, asking the lab, or checking the manufacturer's website. Most color negative stocks have about a ten- to twelve-stop range; most reversal films have closer to six stops. Traditionally, video cameras have had a more limited exposure range than negative stocks, but some high-end digital cameras have fourteen stops or more.

With a reflected light meter, you can check the difference in *f*-stops between important light and dark areas in the frame. If the brightness range of the scene is too great for the film stock, it may be necessary to recompose the shot, add light, flash the film, change an actor's costume or makeup, or redecorate the set (see Controlling Lighting Contrast, p. 512).

Exposure Error

Cinematographers always want to know, "How much can I be off in my exposure and still get an acceptable image?" The answer depends in part on the latitude or exposure range of the stock. However, the amount of acceptable error also depends on what you're shooting: the higher the lighting contrast in the scene, the less leeway you have. As an example, imagine shooting an outdoor scene with areas of bright sun and deep shadow. With proper exposure, you might just be able to capture detail in the brightest areas and the shadows. But if the exposure were increased even slightly, the highlights might be pushed into the shoulder of the characteristic curve and lose detail. Similarly, if the exposure were decreased, the dark areas would now fall on the toe of the curve and no longer show detail.

Now imagine shooting the same scene on a cloudy day. The contrast range between highlights and shadow is now much smaller, so all the areas of the image fall on the straight line portion of the curve, far from the toe or shoulder. You might be able to increase or decrease exposure a few stops without losing detail.

With an average subject, color negative stocks might allow one to one and a half stops of underexposure or two or more stops of overexposure. A color reversal film might have only a stop or less leeway at either end. Some degree of exposure error can be corrected during video transfer and/or printing.

Confusingly, the word "latitude" is used to mean both the total exposure range and the degree of acceptable error (in the latter case, it is sometimes called *exposure latitude*). If someone says, "This stock has a latitude of ten stops," she means the total exposure range the stock is capable of. If she says, "You have two stops of latitude on the overexposure side," she's talking about exposure error.[4]

---

4. As discussed above, latitude as a measure of acceptable exposure error depends not only on the exposure range of the stock, but also on the contrast of the particular scene.

Exposure and Image Quality

As a rule of thumb, slight overexposure of negative film stocks results in less apparent grain, more saturated color, richer blacks, and increased contrast. Some cinematographers routinely overexpose color negative about a half stop or so. Underexposure can result in more grain, smoky blacks, and less perceived sharpness. If faces have sufficient exposure (and thus are dense enough on the negative), then in printing a bright printer light can be used that will produce a rich black in the shadows and help suppress grain. This is why it's important in night scenes, for example, to have *some* bright highlights in the frame. If the highlights are properly exposed, then you can make the dark parts of the frame look dark and clean. But if *everything* is dark and underexposed in shooting, the printed image will be murky and grainy, and color will be muted.

When shooting color negative specifically for digital transfer, bear in mind that while overexposure decreases grain, it requires a higher video gain in the telecine, which increases noise (and noise can look a lot like grain!). When shooting 35mm negative for transfer, overexposure may not be recommended. However, 16mm can still be overexposed up to a stop.

Gross over- or underexposure should be avoided. "Printing down" when the lab makes a print from overexposed negative *may* yield a bright white and a rich black, but it will usually not restore much detail in the highlights.

Exposure Control

In brief, you have the following means of controlling exposure at your disposal.

1. *Film speed.* Aside from the choice of raw stocks, film speed can be altered via force development (pushing) and sometimes via underdevelopment (pulling). A film that is properly exposed in the highlights but contains areas of underexposed shadow can sometimes be helped with flashing.

2. *The lens.* The iris diaphragm is the primary means of exposure control. Neutral density filters can be used to avoid overexposure or for opening the iris to a selected *f*-stop (to control depth of field or maximize lens sharpness). Polarizing filters and, in black-and-white, contrast filters can be used to alter the exposure of various elements in the scene (see Chapter 8).

3. *Shutter speed.* Cameras equipped with variable shutters can be set to increase and decrease exposure time, but this may affect the smoothness of motion. Changing the camera speed (frame rate) affects exposure time, but it also affects the speed of motion (see Chapter 6).

4. *Ambient light.* Light on the scene, or on selected parts, can be increased with artificial lighting fixtures or with reflectors that reflect sunlight. Neutral density and colored filters can be placed over lights and windows, and lightweight cloth nets can be used to cut down the amount of light falling on a subject (see Chapter 12).

THE FILM LAB DURING PRODUCTION

Shooting Tests

After a lab has been selected, tests are sometimes made of camera, sets, actors (*screen tests*), costumes, and makeup. Particularly important are tests of film stock and processing. The production team should evaluate the tests, and the cinematographer should discuss with the lab any adjustments that need to be made in processing, video transfer, or printing.

Fig. 7-18. Film processing machine. (DuArt Film and Video)

Processing the Original

Deliver the film to the lab as soon as possible after it is exposed. Pack core-wound film in its black bag and tape down the end so the film does not unravel in transit. Prominently mark "EXPOSED" on the can, so no one mistakes it for unexposed stock. See p. 265 for unloading magazines and preparing cans for the lab. See p. 284 for general considerations in handling unprocessed film. Each film shipment to the lab should include the following information (labs will often supply a form for these items or use a camera report). The first ten items should be marked on each can of unprocessed camera original.[5] Normally, a letter or purchase order accompanies the shipment.

1. The production company name.
2. The working title of the production. Don't change the title in midproduction or the lab may lose your materials.
3. The date.

---

5. As discussed on p. 265, you will normally write some of this information on a piece of tape or a label when you load the camera magazine, and you can move the label to the can when you unload the magazine.

4. Both the common name of the film stock (for example, Vision 500T) and the emulsion number (such as 7219). See Fig. 7-7.

5. The amount of footage and the gauge. Mark if Super 16.

6. Special processing instructions, including force developing (for example, push one, push two), pulling (underdevelopment to compensate for overexposure), or flashing. Discuss any special processing with the lab before ordering the work.

7. The camera roll number. Never repeat a camera roll number.

8. The approximate location of footage where any camera jams or torn perfs occurred. The lab will do a hand inspection to see that no problems will occur in the processing machines that could ruin your footage and possibly footage from another production.

9. Any tests; for example, 15-foot tail exposure test.

10. For a daylight spool on which you wish to save a run-out shot or a darkroom (core) load, mark "OPEN ONLY IN DARK." If the core has popped out, mark "NO CORE" or "AIR WIND."

11. Tell the lab what it should do with the processed original. "HOLD ORIGINAL" means it should be stored in the lab's vault.

12. The name, address, and telephone number of the person to contact in case of questions (or the name of the cinematographer or director, if applicable).

THE LAB REPORT. Many laboratories supply a *lab report* (also called a *negative report*) with the rushes. The lab report lists gross camera errors and damage to the film. If you can't view the rushes on a daily basis, try to get the lab to include information about bad focus, dirt in the gate, flicker, poor image registration, or other problems.

STORING THE NEGATIVE. If you don't have a cool, safe place with low humidity to store the original, have the lab store it until it is conformed or transferred to video. Find out if the lab charges for this service, and get a tour of the lab's vaults—a romantic name for what may be a dusty back room. There are also warehouses that specialize in film storage where film can be kept in temperature- and humidity-controlled spaces for an added charge.

SCREENING THE RUSHES

Today, most productions that are shot on film are edited digitally, and immediately after processing, the camera original film is transferred to digital video for viewing and editing. In the many decades before digital editing existed, camera original would be *workprinted* after processing. *Workprint* is film—a protection copy of the original negative—used for editing.

The unedited footage from the camera, whether in digital form or workprint, is called *rushes*, or *dailies*, because the lab turns them out quickly. The lab processes the dailies overnight and the filmmakers view them the following day (small labs may not deliver this fast). When a lab provides same-day service for rushes this is sometimes called *daylighting*.

The cinematographer and director should look at the rushes as soon as possible after shooting. If working with video dailies, use a high-quality, large broadcast monitor whenever possible. If viewing workprint, be sure to project on a good-sized screen, since editing systems may hide errors such as image flicker, slight softness of focus, and bad registration.

Digital dailies have improved a great deal, as have color management systems that standardize color reproduction on different monitors. Nevertheless, it's sometimes difficult to evaluate rushes when transferred to video, as monitors can be inconsistent. Also, the video may not reveal subtleties that the cinematographer needs to see to evaluate lighting and shooting choices. On some feature films, the first few days of shooting are workprinted to confirm that things look good; then the rest of the rushes are done digitally.

Preparing digital dailies and other issues of digital transfer are discussed in Chapter 16.

Ordering Workprint

When ordering workprint, there are three basic types of color correction that can be ordered—one-light, best-light, and scene-to-scene.

A *one-light* or *one-lite* print (also called an *untimed print*) is made with the same printing light for the entire camera roll; no compensations are made for exposure or color differences from one shot to the next (labs usually refer to shots as "scenes"). A one-light print is sometimes made with a *standard light*, which is around the middle of the printer's scale. For example, many printers have a range of lights from 1 to 50 points, the lab's standard light being around 25. Cinematographers may work with the lab to establish a standard light for the entire project, which makes any errors in exposure or color balance immediately apparent.

Another method, sometimes called a *best-light print*, bases the exposure on the first few scenes on the roll and stays consistent for the rest of the roll. If there are gross variations in exposure, sometimes the lab will make a few corrections.

For a *timed workprint* (also called a *graded* or *color-balanced workprint*), the lab makes *scene-to-scene corrections*, choosing the best light for each take. There may be a surcharge of 30 percent or more for this service. Don't expect these corrections to be as accurate as those on an answer print (see p. 710). A timed print may be beyond your budget; however, if sections of a one-light workprint are badly timed, it may be worthwhile to have them reprinted, since the workprint is often viewed by many people.

LAB INSTRUCTIONS. Indicate in your workprint order:

1. One-light print? Standard light? Timed and color-corrected?
2. (For 16mm only): single- or double-perforated? Double perf is more versatile.
3. Request print-through key numbers.
4. For returning workprint: Pickup? Shipped? Insurance?

5. Special instructions; for example, day-for-night scenes or unusual color balance.

6. In 35mm, make sure the camera report details which takes are to be printed.

Troubleshooting Errors

The following are possible problems that may be evident when screening video dailies or projected workprint. Some may be problems with the original camera negative, others may be due to the workprint or video transfer.

SCRATCHES OR CINCH MARKS. If you see a scratch during the screening, check immediately for its source. The lab report may note whether the scratch is on the emulsion or base (*cell scratch*). If there's no notation on the lab report, and you're screening workprint, stop the projector and hold the scratched film at an angle to a light source so that you can see the reflection of the light on the film. Twist the film in relation to the reflection to see if the scratch is actually on the film. If it's not on the workprint, the scratch is on the original.

Most scratches on original come from the camera, although some come from laboratory or manufacturer errors. A scratch test (see p. 269) prior to filming will usually show a camera scratch. If a scratch is precise with no wobble or if it has a slight fuzziness on the edge of the scratch (a sign of a preprocessing scratch), it is probably a camera scratch.

Further questions to help detect the origin of scratches are: Does the camera scratch now? Do only those rolls shot in a particular mag show the scratch? Did an inexperienced person load the camera? *Cinch marks* appear as discontinuous oblique scratches usually caused by poor film handling, such as pulling unraveled film tight or squeezing dished, core-wound film back into place. Liquid gate printing (see p. 689) and buffing often hide base scratches, some minor emulsion scratches, and cinch marks on the base.

DIRT. Dust or dirt that shows black on the screen is less noticeable than when it is white. Dirt on reversal film shows up as black, while dirt on a processed negative original will appear white (called sparkle). If a workprint itself is dirty, the dirt shows up black. If the dirt is on the original, it may be due to lab handling or dirty changing bags, mags, or cameras. Dirt and hairs may be in the camera gate or the projector gate, extending out into the image, often from the top or bottom edge.

EDGE FOG. *Edge fog* is caused by a light leak that fogs the film before processing. Edge fog lowers contrast and it changes as the camera moves in relation to the light source. The effect is similar to lens flare, but, unlike lens flare, edge fog appears on camera original outside the image area. Light leaks can be caused by a loose magazine lid, a loose camera door, a hole in the changing bag, not packing core-wound film in the black bag, or opening a can of unprocessed film. Edge fog at the head or tail of spool-wound film is to be expected. See Light Leak Test, p. 269.

PROCESSING ERRORS AND RAW STOCK DEFECTS. Processing errors can result in mottling, streaking, or uneven tonalities. Consult the lab immediately if you suspect an error. In the event of lab error, most labs will replace only stock and refund the cost of processing. Defects in the raw stock are often difficult to distinguish from processing errors. The manufacturer will usually replace defective stock and sometimes pay processing costs.

CAMERA DEFECTS. For bad registration, lost loop, timing errors, and breathing in the gate, see Chapter 6. Flicker in the image may be a camera motor defect or a problem with lighting, particularly HMIs or other pulsed lights (see Chapter 12). See Chapter 4 for lens problems.

CHAPTER 8

Color and Filters

The first part of this chapter is about the basic principles of color for both digital and film systems. The second part is about color- and image-control filters.

COLOR

Primary Colors and Complementaries

If a red light, a blue light, and a green light all shine on the same spot, the spot will appear white. You can think of white light as made up of these three colors, called the *additive primaries*, and expressed as:

$$\text{red} + \text{blue} + \text{green} = \text{white}[1]$$

Red and blue light together yield a purple-red color called magenta. Blue and green light produce a green-blue color called cyan, and red and green light together produce yellow.

$$\text{red} + \text{blue} = \text{magenta}$$
$$\text{blue} + \text{green} = \text{cyan}$$
$$\text{red} + \text{green} = \text{yellow}$$

Cyan, magenta, and yellow are the *subtractive primaries*; that is, they are made by subtracting one of the additive primaries from white light. For example, if the red component is taken away from white light, cyan (blue + green) is left:

$$\text{cyan} = \text{blue} + \text{green} = \text{white} - \text{red}$$

Similarly,

$$\text{magenta} = \text{blue} + \text{red} = \text{white} - \text{green}$$
$$\text{yellow} = \text{red} + \text{green} = \text{white} - \text{blue}$$

---

1. People familiar with painting may think of the primary colors as red, blue, and yellow. This is a different color system. Mixing all colors in paint produces black. Mixing lights of all colors produces white.

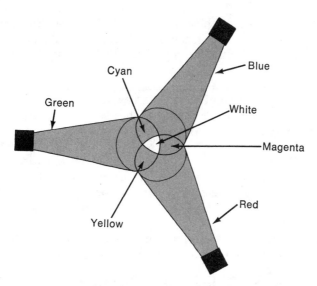

Fig. 8-1. Additive color. Spotlights of the additive primaries—red, green, and blue—form white light where all three overlap. Where any two overlap, the subtractive primaries are formed. (Carol Keller)

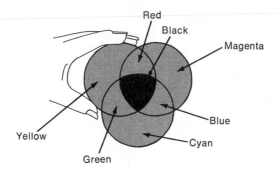

Fig. 8-2. Subtractive color. If you view white light through yellow, cyan, and magenta filters, you get the additive primaries where any two overlap and black where all three overlap. (Carol Keller)

Each additive primary has a *complementary color*, a color that when added to it produces white. From the above three equations, you can see that cyan is the complement of red, magenta the complement of green, and yellow the complement of blue. A filter works by passing the components of its own color and absorbing its complement. A yellow filter thus passes its components (red and green) and absorbs its complement (blue).

The eye is more sensitive to the green portion of the light spectrum than to the red or blue parts. To create light that appears white, the three colors are not mixed in equal proportion. In video, a signal that is a mixture of 72 percent green,

21 percent red, and 7 percent blue will appear white on screen.[2] Because more visual information is conveyed in the green component, the green sensor in a three-chip video camera, or the green light in a film printing report, is of special importance.

Color in Video and Film Systems

We use various terms to describe colors. The *hue* is the base color (such as red, green, etc.). *Saturation* describes how pure the color is. Saturation can be thought of as the absence of white; the more saturated a color is, the less white it has in it. Very saturated colors are intense and vivid. Desaturated colors are pale; very desaturated colors are almost monochrome (black-and-white). Experiment with a video monitor or TV to get a sense of changing color values. A TV's "hue" or "tint" control changes the base color, and the "color" control varies the saturation (see Appendix A).

Many factors influence our perception of color. For example, the same color will seem more saturated when surrounded by a black border than a white border.

Standardizing Color Reproduction

There are many opportunities for color values to change (intentionally or not) between the time you shoot a scene and the time that scene appears in a finished video or film print. Whenever digital material is transferred from one format to another, or film is printed, the color may change either because someone adjusted it or because of the inherent nature of the system.[3]

There are various ways to measure color and to try to keep it consistent.

In video, standardized *color bars* can be recorded at the head of a tape or file and used to adjust color reproduction on monitors when the program is played back (see Appendix A). With digital formats, the color should remain unchanged when cloning tapes, copying files, or capturing to an editing system, regardless of bars.

To measure color values, a *vectorscope* is used (see Fig. 8-3). A color's hue is indicated by the position of the signal around the circular face of the vectorscope. The saturation (chrominance level) is indicated by the distance from the center (closer to the edge means higher chroma). There are various other types of scopes used in editing and finishing systems (see Chapter 14).

Color scales (chip charts) are sometimes filmed along with the slate to aid in timing (color balancing) film or video dailies. Perhaps more useful is to shoot an 18 percent gray card (see p. 292). A patch of bright white and dark black next to the gray can help too. By adjusting the picture in post so that the gray card is reproduced at proper exposure without any color cast, all the other colors fall into place in terms of hue (see Fig. 8-4).

Sometimes you shoot with nonstandard lighting to create a certain effect. For example, you might use colored gels for a firelight effect or a nightclub scene. If you

---

2. This is for high definition ITU-709 color space; standard def NTSC ITU-601 is about 59 percent green, 30 percent red, and 11 percent blue.

3. Analog NTSC (sometimes called "Never Twice the Same Color") video was particularly notorious for shifting color values.

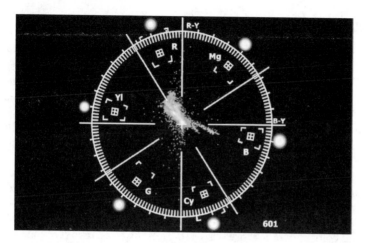

Fig. 8-3. The vectorscope shows color information. This scope, part of Adobe Premiere Pro, is displaying standard definition (Rec. 601) video. (Adobe Systems, Inc.)

shoot the gray card under standard (uncolored) tungsten light, and *then* turn on the gelled lights, you have a better chance of getting the color you're looking for in the workprint or video dailies. Increasingly, DPs use digital stills and digital color control systems to indicate to the postproduction team how color and effects are intended to look.

Often a LUT (lookup table) is applied to a digital image to create a particular palette of colors and contrast. When starting a production, you might choose a particular LUT or camera picture profile to achieve the look you want.

Fig. 8-4. Shooting a gray card helps in adjusting the color balance and exposure in post. A patch of white is also helpful. (AbelCine)

COLOR TEMPERATURE

The human eye adjusts to most lighting situations so that the color of the light source appears to be white. However, a light source will appear colored if it's strongly deficient in one or more of the primaries. Daylight looks bluer than tungsten light when the two are seen together. For example, if you stand outside on an overcast day and look through a store window into a space lit by tungsten or halogen bulbs, the interior light will seem relatively yellow compared to the bluer daylight. However, if you go in the store, your eye will adjust so that the interior light appears white.

Although the eye accepts a broad range of light sources as white, different light sources are, in fact, composed of unequal amounts of the primaries. The reddish cast of sunset and the blue of an overcast winter day occur when one of the components of white light clearly predominates. Unlike the human eye, digital camera sensors and color film stocks are designed for light of a *particular* color balance. If the light source differs in its color balance (the proportions of the primaries), the digital camera or film stock will not provide natural rendition of color—unless compensations are made electronically or by using filters. In order to judge how much compensation is needed, we need a way of measuring the color components of the light source.

If a piece of metal is heated, it first becomes red in color ("red hot"). Heated to a higher temperature, the metal starts to become blue and then white ("white hot"). You can correlate the temperature of an ideal substance, called a *black body*, with the color of the light it radiates when it is heated to different temperatures. This color temperature is usually measured using the *Kelvin* temperature scale.

Standard tungsten studio lamps have a color temperature of 3200°K (read "degrees kelvin"; actually, in contemporary scientific usage it would just be "3200 kelvin" or "3200 K" and written without the degree sign, but since many equipment manufacturers use the old convention, it's used here for clarity).

A lower color temperature light source has a larger red component, while a higher color temperature source has a larger blue component. Light sources and images are thought of as being warm or warmer as they move toward red (think of red in fire), and cold or colder as they move toward blue (think of the icy blue light of an overcast winter day). Some people get confused by the fact that *colder* blue light reads higher (*hotter*) on the Kelvin temperature scale.

In terms of the light you're likely to encounter when filming, there are a few benchmarks worth memorizing. As just noted, studio tungsten lights are 3200°K. Studio HMI lights and "nominal" daylight are around 5600°K (though daylight, which is made up of both warmer direct sunlight and bluer light from the sky, can vary a lot by conditions). It used to be the case that typical home interiors were lit with tungsten incandescent bulbs that are warmer than studio lights, often around 2800°K. Now many homes are lit with *compact fluorescent lamps* (*CFLs*), which are available in various color temperatures ranging from a warm white that is close to tungsten up to daylight (though manufacturers may be inconsistent in their labeling). Actually, typical fluorescents have a discontinuous spectrum and don't have a true color temperature; the temperature indicated is a rough equivalent. However, there are fluorescents made expressly for video and film use, such as Kino Flo lamps, available in true 3200°K and 5500°K versions.

Some scenes contain a great range of color temperatures. For example, when shooting indoors with illumination coming from both tungsten lights and windows (see Mixed Lighting, p. 514).

Differences in color temperature are more significant at the lower color temperatures. The difference between 3000°K and 3200°K is noticeable, while the difference between 5400°K and 5600°K is not very significant.

APPROXIMATE COLOR TEMPERATURES
OF COMMON LIGHT SOURCES

Light Source	Degrees Kelvin
Match flame	1700
Candle flame	1850–2000
Sunrise or sunset	2000
100- to 200-watt household bulbs	2900
Studio tungsten lights	3200
Photofloods and reflector floods	3200–3400
Fluorescent warm white tubes	3500
Sunlight one hour after sunrise or one hour before sunset	3500
Early-morning or late-afternoon sunlight	4300
Fluorescent daylight tubes	4300
Summer sunlight, noon, Washington, DC	5400
Xenon arc projector	5400
Nominal photographic "daylight"	5500
Average daylight (sunlight and blue sky)	5500–6500
HMI lamps	5600
Overcast sky	6000–7500
Summer shade	8000
Summer sunlight with no sun	9500–30,000

Digital Cameras and Color Temperature
With video cameras, adjusting the camera for light of different color temperatures is called *white-balancing*. This is discussed in Setting the White Balance, p. 109.

Film Cameras and Color Temperature
When a color film emulsion is manufactured, it is balanced for a light of a particular color temperature. The color temperature of the light source should approximately match the film in order to reproduce natural color; otherwise, a color conversion filter can be used.

TUNGSTEN BALANCE. Film stocks balanced for 3200°K are called tungsten-balanced, or Type B tungsten. When tungsten-balanced films are shot with daylight illumination, the excess blue in daylight can overexpose the blue layer in the emulsion, giving a bleached-out, bluish look to the film. So you will want to warm up the daylight to match tungsten illumination using an 85 filter (this is the Kodak Wratten filter number). An 85 filter (sometimes called a *straight 85*) is used for typical 3200°K color negative; it has a characteristic salmon color and reduces light coming through the lens by two-thirds of a stop (filter factor of 1.6; see below).

Some color negative stocks have sufficient latitude to allow filming in daylight without an 85 filter (which can be helpful in low light or when there isn't time to put on a filter). Though the color can be corrected in telecine or printing, shooting without the 85 decreases the film's latitude. Color reversal always needs the conversion filter, since the lab cannot adequately compensate.

DAYLIGHT BALANCE. Film stocks balanced for color temperatures around 5500°K are considered daylight-balanced. In fact, actual daytime color temperature varies from 2000°K to well over 10,000°K depending on the relative amounts of sun and sky light and any cloud cover. During a red sunrise or sunset, the color temperature is far below tungsten.

Daylight-balanced film shot under tungsten illumination will appear red-brown, so add blue. The 80A conversion filter is blue and converts most daylight films for use under 3200°K illumination. The 80A has a filter factor of 4 (a loss of two stops).

Color conversion filters are used so frequently that cinematographers tend to think of film speeds in terms of the ISO that compensates for the filter factor. Manufacturers will list a color negative balanced for tungsten as ISO 100 for tungsten light and ISO 64 for daylight with an 85 filter (100 divided by filter factor 1.6 is approximately 64). See p. 280 for further discussion of tungsten- versus daylight-balanced films.

BLACK-AND-WHITE FILM. Black-and-white film doesn't require color conversion filters, but there is a set of filters that can be used to darken a sky or to change the relative exposure of different-colored objects.

Red and green objects that are equally bright may photograph in black-and-white as the same gray tone. Photographing the red and green objects with a red filter makes the green object darker than the red (since the red filter absorbs much of the green light).

The sky can be darkened using graduated neutral density filters and polarizers (see below). Black-and-white film allows the use of colored filters to darken a blue sky but not a white, overcast sky. Red and yellow filters will darken a blue sky. Unlike the effect with a polarizer, the darkening doesn't change as you move the camera, so the camera may be panned without worry.

Commonly used black-and-white filters include: Wratten #8 (K2; yellow or light orange) for haze penetration, moderate darkening of blue sky, and lightening of faces; and Wratten #15 (G; deep yellow) for heavy haze penetration, greater sky darkening, and, especially, aerial work and telephoto landscapes. The red filters (for example, #23A, #25, #29) have increasing haze penetration and increasing power to darken skies.

Measuring Color Temperature

The color temperature of a source of illumination can be read with a *color temperature meter*. A *two-color meter* measures the relative blue and red components of the light, while a *three-color meter* also measures the green component. A two-color meter is adequate for measuring light sources of continuous spectral emission, including tungsten, firelight, and daylight. For light sources such as fluorescents and

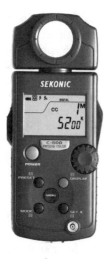

Fig. 8-5. Color temperature meter. Sekonic C-500 is a three-color meter that can be used with digital cameras and film. Can display color temperature in degrees kelvin or as a color-compensating (CC) index for selecting appropriate filters. (Sekonic)

mercury arc lamps, you should also measure the green component with a three-color meter.

Color temperature meters are more often used when shooting film than video, since in video you can see the color on the monitor. Most lighting situations don't require a color temperature meter, as it is enough to know the approximate color temperature of a light source. Large differences can be corrected by a filter and smaller differences can be corrected in postproduction. Color meters prove most handy when balancing the color temperature of different light sources. For example, the meter can measure if adequate compensation has been made by putting gels on windows to match the color temperature of tungsten light fixtures (see Chapter 12).

FILTERS

Lens filters are used in shooting for a variety of reasons. Some are used to make a scene look "normal" on video or film (that is, close to the way the scene appears to the naked eye). Others are used to create special effects. In some cases, filtration must be done in the camera to achieve the look you want. However, many filter effects that were traditionally done on the shoot are now done digitally in postproduction. Leaving some of the adjustments to post can help you shoot faster without worrying about getting everything just right on the shoot.

Filter Factors

All filters absorb some light, and compensation must be made for the loss of light to avoid underexposing the film or digital image. The *filter factor* is the number of times exposure must be increased to compensate for the light loss. Each time the filter factor doubles, increase the exposure by one stop. Manufacturers supply filter factors for each of their filters.

If you know that a filter decreases exposure by one stop (a filter factor of 2), compensate by opening the lens one stop. When two or more filters are used simultaneously, the filter factor of the combination is the product of their individual factors. If one filter has a factor of 4 and the other a factor of 2, the combination will have a filter factor of 8 (4 × 2). To compensate, open the iris three stops.

When shooting digital, any light loss from a filter will become apparent as you look through the viewfinder. Be sure to set the exposure with the filter in place on the lens.

When shooting film, you can divide the filter factor into the ISO number to calculate exposure directly from the exposure meter. If you were using a filter with a filter factor of 4 with a film rated ISO 100, the meter could be set at ISO 25 (100 divided by 4) and the exposure calculated directly. In this case, don't open the iris beyond what the meter indicates. Film stock data sheets list filter requirements and factors for various light sources.

Neutral Density Filters

Neutral density (ND) *filters* are gray in color and are used to reduce the amount of light passing through the lens without affecting the color. They allow you to open the lens to a wider aperture to reduce depth of field, to shoot at an aperture that yields a sharper image, or to shoot at all if the light level exceeds the ability of the video camera or film stock to handle it.

With video cameras, ND filters are often marked as a fraction, such as ¼, ¹⁄₁₆, or ¹⁄₆₄ (two, four, and six stops respectively). You can also get *variable ND filters* (also called *fader filters*) that are adjustable for different amounts of darkening, using two pieces of polarized glass mounted together. Some NDs have inferior optics, so test yours carefully for softening of the image, or darkening around the edges of the frame, especially with thick filters and wide-angle lenses. For more on NDs with digital cameras, see p. 134.

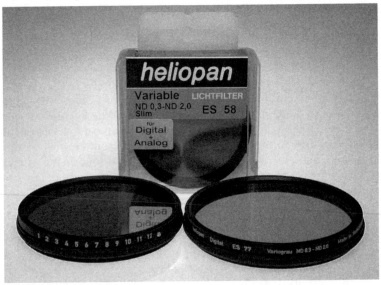

Fig. 8-6. Variable neutral density filters. Also called faders, variable NDs allow you to dial in different amounts with one filter. The Heliopan model shown ranges from 0.3 ND (one stop) to 2.0 ND (six and two-thirds stops). (HP Marketing Corp.)

In the film world, ND filters are generally marked in increments of 0.1 ND, which is equivalent to one-third of a stop; 0.3 ND cuts down the light by one stop, 0.6 ND by two stops, and 1.2 ND by four stops. When you combine ND filters, these numbers should be added, and not multiplied, as is done with the filter factor. Sometimes ND filters are marked 2X or 4X, in which case you are given the filter factors (one and two stops, respectively). With film, ND filters are often combined with color conversion filters for daylight filming when you want to reduce the amount of light. For example, an 85N3 combines an 85 filter with one stop of neutral density.

Graduated Filters

Graduated filters (also called *grads* or *wedges*) have one section neutral density and one section clear. The transition from dense to clear can be abrupt or gradual (filters with a smooth transition from dense to clear are sometimes called *attenuators*). Grads are primarily used to darken a sky that would otherwise bleach out and show no detail. Grads can be used to make day-for-night scenes more realistic by darkening the sky. Some grads have a color, such as orange to heighten a sunset effect.

Grads should be used with a matte box (see p. 317). The larger the filter you use, the more freedom you will have to position it correctly. Position the neutral density portion to cover the sky, aligning the graduated region with the horizon line or higher. If you're working with great depth of field (say with a wide-angle lens at small aperture), the grad itself may be too sharply in focus to achieve the effect you want. Keep it as close to the lens as possible and use a soft-edged grad if stopped down.

Selectively darkening the sky or any portion of the frame can also be done in postproduction. One advantage of using a grad on the camera is that it may prevent the sky from being grossly overexposed (burning out cloud details, for example), which might not be correctable in post.

Fig. 8-7. Graduated filter. A grad can be used to selectively darken or color the sky. Grads vary in the sharpness of their transition from dark to light. (Stephen McCarthy)

Polarizing Filters

Aside from graduated filters and special effects, the *polarizer* is the only way to darken a sky when shooting in color. A polarizer is somewhat like a neutral density filter in that it affects all colors equally. The difference is that it selectively cuts down light oriented in a single plane—that is, polarized light. On a clear day, some of the light from the sky is polarized, as is light reflected from glass and water, but not metal. Polarized light can be progressively eliminated by rotating the polarizer. Reflections from glass and water can sometimes be totally eliminated, but be careful not to overdo the effect; otherwise, a car may look as though it has no windshield or a pond as though it is dry.

As you move the camera, the orientation of the polarizer to the light source may change, altering the amount of light that is filtered out. The exposure of an object may thus change during the shot. When the polarizer is used to darken the sky, this change is particularly noticeable when the camera pans. Maximum darkening of the sky occurs with the filter oriented at a right angle to the sun. When it is pointed toward the sun or 180 degrees away (the sun directly behind), the polarizer has no effect. Similarly, polarized shots taken at different angles to the sun may not edit together well, since the sky will appear different from one shot to the next. Clear blue skies can most easily be darkened with the polarizer. The hazier the sky, the less noticeable the effect will be. An overcast sky, whether in color or in black-and-white, can be darkened only by a graduated filter.

The polarizer has a filter factor varying from 2 to 4 (one to two stops), depending on its orientation and the nature of the light in the scene. Side lighting and top lighting, when the sun is at right angles to the polarizer, may require a compensation of two or more stops.

When shooting video, set the exposure with the polarizer in place and oriented as it will be for the shot. When shooting film, calculate exposure compensation by taking a reflected light reading through the polarizer, with the polarizer oriented as it will be on the lens.

Fig. 8-8. (left) Without polarizer. (right) With polarizer filter. The polarizer minimizes the reflections from the windshield. (Schneider Optics)

Ultraviolet and Infrared

Unlike the human eye, digital and film cameras are sensitive to *ultraviolet light*. Atmospheric haze scatters large amounts of ultraviolet light, making the haze appear heavier when shooting distant landscapes. To minimize this effect, use a *UV* or

1A (skylight) filter. The UV is clear to slightly yellow in color, while the 1A is slightly pink. The filter factor is negligible, and no exposure compensation need be made. Haze filters have no effect on fog and mist because these atmospheric effects are due to water droplets and not the scattering of ultraviolet rays.

The 1A filter is useful to warm up the blue cast caused by ultraviolet light present in outdoor shade, which is especially noticeable when snow scenes are filmed. Since the 1A and haze filters don't significantly affect exposure, they're useful in protecting the front element of the lens in difficult environmental conditions—for example, in salt spray or sand. Some filmmakers leave this filter in place at all times.

Some HD digital cameras can be sensitive to *infrared (IR) contamination* when filming in bright sun. Infrared energy (essentially heat) isn't visible to the naked eye, but it may cause the image as seen by the sensor to have lower contrast and it can make black areas appear brown. Filters such as Schneider Optics' True-Cut 750 IR can help.

Diffusion Filters

Diffusion filters soften hard lines and are often used to minimize facial lines and blemishes. They are sometimes used to indicate a dream sequence or a historical sequence or just make the image a little mellower or less harsh. As diffusion increases, flare from bright areas creeps into adjacent areas. A diffusion effect can be achieved by stretching silk or nylon stocking material in front of the lens or over the rear element (see below for discussion of mounting filters behind the lens).

Tiffen's Softnet filters have netting material laminated within a glass filter. Black net or dot pattern diffusion filters don't affect contrast; white net filters do soften contrast. Diffusion filters generally require no exposure compensation, though net material may cut out some light. Wherever a net is mounted, keep it as close to the lens as possible and check that the net pattern is blurred and not in focus on the image. Use a good lens shade or matte box to keep stray light from striking a diffusion filter directly.

In HD video and 35mm film, a softened image is often desirable. In 16mm, and most SD video formats, the image is softer to begin with, and diffusion should be used sparingly unless an exaggerated effect is desired. Sometimes diffusion or nets are used in video to soften the image slightly and give it more of a "film" look. You can evaluate the effect in a good monitor (though it may look different on a larger screen).

The same diffusion will seem more pronounced through a long focal length lens than with a short focal length lens, so you may want to use less diffusion when zoomed in for a close-up if you're trying to match the look of a wide shot.

Various methods can be used to soften or diffuse an image in digital post.

LOW-CONTRAST FILTERS. *Low-contrast (low-con) filters,* available in several grades, reduce contrast without softening lines or reducing definition as much as diffusion filters. Low-cons affect the shadow areas particularly by smearing the highlight areas into the shadows. Colors are less saturated and the overall look is softer. There are a few variants of low-contrast filters, including Tiffen's Pro-Mist and Ultra Contrast filters. No exposure compensation is required when using low-con filters.

Fig. 8-9. Various Tiffen filter effects. (1) No filtration. (2) A Pro-Mist filter softens the sharpness and contrast and creates a halo around highlights and light sources. (3) A Soft/FX filter softens facial details. (4) A low-contrast filter spreads highlights into darker areas and lowers contrast. Filtration in these images was done with the Tiffen Dfx digital filter suite after the image was shot. Very heavy filtration is used in this illustration so that the effects are visible, but in production subtler levels would be used. These digital effects emulate actual glass Tiffen filters for mounting on lenses, which produce somewhat different looks.

Fog Filters

Fog filters are available in various grades to simulate everything from light to heavy fog. In general, the more contrasty the scene, the stronger the fog filter needed. With too strong a filter, objects may lose so much contrast that they become invisible. Fog filters are sometimes used for heightened mystery or romanticized flashbacks.

In natural foggy conditions, objects tend to become less visible the farther away they are. Most fog filters do not simulate this effect, so try not to photograph objects too close to the camera or let a subject move toward or away from the camera during a shot. Double fog filters lower image definition less than standard fog filters do. There's no exposure compensation for fog filters, though slight overexposure can increase the fog effect.

Color-Compensating Filters

Generally, major color corrections are made during shooting, and fine-tuning of the color is left for postproduction. There are times, however, when specific color adjustments may be made via filtration on the lens: for example, when shooting with certain discharge-type light sources such as fluorescent, mercury vapor, or sodium vapor lights (see Chapter 12); when video will be broadcast or shown directly without further color correction; or when you want to create a specific color effect, such as a sepia look for scenes intended to look old.

Sometimes a little warming is done with a camera filter to provide a more appealing look. The Tiffen 812 filter has the nice effect of improving skin tones without making the whole scene look too red; it can also be used to make a cloudy day seem less cold. When using an 812 with a video camera, be sure to white-balance *without* the filter in place, or the camera will undo the filter's effect.

For film shoots, precise color adjustments are sometimes made with a set of *color-compensating (CC)* or *light-balancing* filters. The most advantageous system assigns a *mired value* to every color temperature. To convert from one color temperature to another, subtract the mired value of the color you're starting with from the value of the color you want. If the result is a positive number, use yellow filtration to warm the scene, as yellow increases mired value and decreases the color temperature. A negative number calls for blue filtration to decrease mired value and raise the color temperature. Unlike the Kelvin scale, where a difference of 100°K is more significant at 3200°K than at 5500°K, mired values indicate a constant shift across the scale. (Consult *American Cinematographer Manual* for mired values of typical light sources and filters and for the Kodak color-compensating filter system.)

MATTE BOXES AND LENS SHADES

Use a lens shade (see Figs. 4-16 and 3-15) or matte box (see Figs. 1-3 and 8-10) to prevent stray light from hitting the front element and causing flare. If you look at the front of the lens and see the reflection of any light source, there is the potential for flare. A deeper matte box or shade gives better protection. Matte boxes are often adjustable and should be adjusted as deep as possible without vignetting the image. Similarly, use a lens shade as deep and narrow as possible. Long focal lengths allow for a narrow shade. The shades for extreme wide angle are often so wide that they offer little protection from stray light. A *French flag* or *eyebrow* (see Fig. 8-10) can be set to cut light sources that the lens shade or matte box misses. When light sources are in the scene you're filming, sometimes you can shade the source itself to minimize flare (see Chapter 12).

Matte Boxes

Matte boxes have slots that accommodate one or more filters. Often one of the slots rotates for filters such as polarizers or special effects filters. Glass filters are

Fig. 8-10. The French flag attached to the top of the matte box (also called an eyebrow) helps block light sources from above. (Bob Corkey)

expensive; with a matte box, one set of filters can be used for different lenses. Gelatin filters can be mounted in frames that fit into the slots.

Matte boxes often mount on *rods*, which extend from the camera to support the lens, the matte box, and/or other accessories. If the front element of the lens does not rotate during focusing, a lightweight matte box can sometimes be attached to the lens itself. A *lens doughnut* is sometimes needed as a seal between the lens and the back of the matte box, to keep light from entering from behind.

CHECKING FOR VIGNETTING. To check for vignetting, point the camera at a white or gray card that is uniformly lit (sunlight can work well). Make sure you can see all the way into each corner of the frame, with no darkening at the edges, and without seeing the matte box or lens shade. Try this test at close focusing distances and, with a zoom lens, at its widest angle. If you see darkening, you may need to reposition matte boxes or filters. Vignetting is inherent in some lens designs and you may not be able to get rid of it all. Some DSLRs have a menu setting to compensate.

Lens Shades

A glass filter can usually be mounted between the lens and the lens shade. On some shades a filter can be dropped in place. Some shades have provisions for rotating a filter. Lens shades are available in metal, hard plastic, and soft rubber. Rectan-

Fig. 8-11. Sony FS100 camera shown with Zacuto base plate, riser, rods, and lens support. (Zacuto USA)

gular lens shades work more efficiently for their size but can be used only on lenses with nonrotating focusing mounts.

Mounting Glass Filters

It doesn't make sense to use an expensive lens with a poor-quality glass filter that may impair the image, so use high-quality filters. Gels sandwiched between glass are generally of lower quality. Dyed glass filters should have an antireflective coating (*coated filters*). To avoid an unwanted optical phenomenon known as *Newton's rings*, don't mount two or more glass filters so that their surfaces touch.

Some cinematographers like to keep a glass filter over the front element of the lens to protect it from scratches or from poor environmental conditions, such as sand or salt spray. Use a high-quality coated filter. Clear, skylight 1A, or haze filters will not alter image color or tonal rendition to any serious extent, though any filter may cause reflections and lowered contrast.

Glass filters may be square shaped for matte boxes or round for mounting on lenses. They come in a variety of sizes, sometimes designated in millimeters and sometimes by *series size* in Roman or Arabic numerals.

ADAPTER RINGS. Most lenses accept an *adapter ring* that screws into the area around the front element or slips over the barrel for mounting glass filters in front of the lens. The filter of appropriate size is then secured with the lens shade or another adapter ring. A *retainer ring* lets you mount two filters. Use *step-up rings* to mount a large filter on a smaller lens.

Behind-the-Lens Filters

Some cameras have a behind-the-lens slot for gels, and there are adapters for mounting gels on the rear of some lenses (inside the camera). When a gel is mounted behind the lens, it refracts light and moves the focal plane back about one-third the thickness of the gel. If you plan to use behind-the-lens filters, have the flange focal distance adjusted by a technician to compensate for the change. You must then always use a clear gel (UV 1A or 2A) when not using another filter.

Handle gels in paper or only by their edges, preferably with tweezers; avoid scratches and crimping. The closer the gel is to the film or video sensor, the longer the focal length of the lens, or the more a lens is stopped down, the more likely it is that physical imperfections and dust will show up in the image.

As discussed above, sometimes nets or stocking material is mounted behind the lens for a diffusion effect. These don't affect the collimation the way gels do, but they must be used with care to be sure they don't come off or damage the lens or camera. Rubber bands or special *transfer tape* (also known affectionately as *snot tape*), which has a rubber cement–like adhesive, can be used to attach the net to the lens.

CHAPTER 9

Shooting the Movie

This chapter is about the production phase of making a movie: planning and organizing the shoot, directing the film, and camerawork. Given the range of possible types of productions—dramas and documentaries, student projects, and professional films—you may find parts of the chapter more or less relevant to your work. But the concepts and methods of one kind of production often apply to others, even if somewhat different in scale or execution.

Because shooting a movie draws on all the skills and techniques of filmmaking, in some sense all the other chapters in the book are relevant to this one. More specifically regarding the choices made by the director or camera operator, it's important to have an understanding of cameras (Chapters 3 and 6), lenses (Chapter 4), and editing (Chapter 13). The financial and legal aspects of the topics in this chapter are discussed in Chapter 17.

THE GOALS OF PRODUCTION

At the most basic level, production is the time to capture images and sounds that you'll use to tell a story. For a drama, production represents a tremendous collaboration between all those behind the camera (producers, writers, director, art director, cinematographer, etc.) and the actors who perform in front of it. In a documentary, there's another kind of collaboration between the film crew and the film's subjects.

It's important to keep in mind that production is not an end in itself, but a means to an end: everything you do in production is to ensure that when you get to the editing room you'll have the elements you need to tell the story. The director must constantly think about not just what the camera is capturing, but how that footage can be edited together. Part of the director's skill is being able to visualize how scenes being filmed will translate to the screen and how they'll integrate with scenes that have already been filmed and ones not yet shot. Having some editing experience is extremely useful for directors and cinematographers.

This is not to say that going into production the director needs to pre-edit the movie (though more on that below). In fact, hopefully the director will provide the editor with material that can go together in multiple ways. Even tightly scripted films are often transformed in terms of pace, point of view, and storytelling in the editing room, and the director should anticipate the editor's needs.

Thinking about shooting and editing at the same time can be even trickier with documentaries, where you may have limited or no control over what happens in front of the camera. You're capturing events or moments, but you may not know their meaning and place in the film yet. This calls for even more flexibility on the part of the director and cinematographer.

This chapter is in part about the language of cinema, the grammar of how shots flow from one to the next. The kinds of shots you get and how they're ultimately edited constitute a key part of the film's style. People sometimes think of style and content as separate things, but each reflects on the other and affects how audiences understand the film. There's meaning in every shot.

Though parts of this chapter address narrative filmmaking in particular, documentary work often involves similar concerns in terms of filming, editing, and production. Documentary and fiction filmmakers should be versed in each other's methods.

Fig. 9-1. In these shots from Alfred Hitchcock's *Psycho*, composition, lighting, and selective focus work together to draw us into the scene and make us want to see what Norman Bates (Anthony Perkins) is seeing through that hole. (Universal)

Scenes, Takes, and Sequences

Some terms that define how the camera captures action:

A *scene* is an event that takes place in one setting in a continuous time period. Two actors talking in a kitchen might be indicated in the script as a scene. However, if one of the actors walks into the dining room, and the camera follows or moves to the next room, that is often considered a separate scene in the script.

A *sequence* is generally a scene or a series of scenes that make up a unit. The above-mentioned scene could also be referred to as the "kitchen sequence." However, sequences can be made up of shots that take place in different locales but together form a conceptual whole. For example, you might refer to the "baptism sequence" in *The Godfather*, which includes a scene in a church intercut with a series of scenes of murders being committed around the city.[1]

A scene may be made up of a single *shot* (such as a wide shot of the entire action)

---

1. Nonlinear editing systems employ a different use of "sequence." In an NLE, a sequence is a single timeline or grouping of shots that could range from one shot to the entire movie.

or it may be divided into several shots or *camera angles* (or just *angles*) that will eventually be edited together (such as paired close-ups of two actors talking to each other; see Fig. 9-3).

During production, whenever the camera is moved to a new spot to get a different camera angle or scene, that's considered a new *setup*. Changing setups often means not only changing camera position, but changing lighting and other aspects as well. Simply changing the focal length of the lens to get a new shot from the same position is not a new setup.

Various *takes* are filmed, each trying to capture a particular shot. For example, "Scene 8, Take 14" is the fourteenth attempt to capture scene 8 in the script. Letters can be used to indicate a particular angle called for in the script. "Scene 8A, Take 4" is the fourth attempt to get the second camera angle (A) of scene 8. Another way to notate it would be "Scene 8, Shot 2, Take 4."

"Take" (or *camera take*) refers to each section of footage from the time the camera begins shooting until it is turned off. "Shot" is sometimes used to mean camera take and sometimes to mean the edited take—that is, the portion of the take used in the edited version of the movie. To confuse things further, "scene" sometimes means shot (as in, "scene-to-scene color correction"). Usually the context distinguishes the meaning.

COMPOSITION AND SHOT SELECTION

Types of Shots

Shots are divided into three basic categories—the *long shot* (LS), *medium shot* (MS), and *close-up* (CU). The long shot includes the whole body of the person in relation to the environment, usually taken from fairly far away from the subject. A wide view of a landscape is sometimes called a long shot or a *wide shot*. The *establishing shot* is a long shot that defines the basic space or locale where events will take place. The medium shot is not too detailed, includes part of the subject, and usually includes people from head to knee or from waist up. The close-up shows a detail of the scene; in the case of a person, it is a head-and-shoulder shot. A "two-button close-up" shows everything from the face down to the second button on a person's shirt. In a *big close-up*, just a face fills the screen, or in an *extreme close-up* (ECU) part of a face or a small object fills the screen—for example, a watch or a fly.

Two shots taken from opposite angles are called *reverse-angle shots*. A conversation between two people is often shot with each person alone in the frame in three-quarter profile. When the scene is edited, we see one person looking right, then the other looking left (see Figs. 9-3 and 13-4). This shooting-editing style is called *shot/reverse shot* or *angle/reverse angle*. These shots are typically close-ups, but the back of the other person may be visible (a close-up that has the back of another person's head or another element in the foreground is sometimes called a *dirty close-up*).

Shot/reverse-shot cutting is often contrasted with the *two-shot*, which is a single shot of two actors from the front showing them from the knees up (*knee shot*)

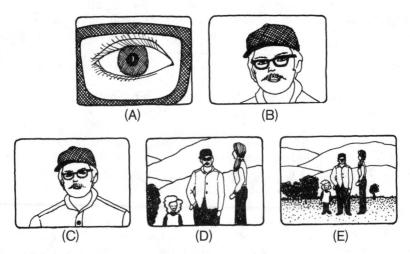

(A)   (B)

(C)   (D)   (E)

Fig. 9-2. Shot division. The categories are not exact. (A) The *extreme close-up* fills the screen with a small detail. (B) The *big close-up* fills the frame with a face. (C) The *close-up* includes the head and shoulders. (D) The *medium shot* includes most of the body. When two people are shown in medium shot, it is a *two-shot*. (E) The *long shot* includes the whole body and the surroundings. (Carol Keller)

or waist up. The *point-of-view* (*POV*) shot is taken from someone's or something's vantage point (such shot 2 in Fig. 9-16). It can be taken from behind an actor over her shoulder or with the camera at the position of her eyes. POV shots also include shots from extreme vantage points, such as from directly overhead (*bird's-eye view*).

Fig. 9-3. This sequence from *Born Yesterday* begins with a two-shot, then cuts to a medium shot of Judy Holliday, followed by a reverse angle of William Holden. (Columbia Pictures)

Composition

Each shot is *composed* or *framed* in the camera viewfinder. When you film from a script, the action and framing for each shot can be *blocked out*, or planned, before the take. In unscripted work, framing and movement are improvised based on both what is seen through the viewfinder and what is seen and heard outside the frame. Framing can be thought of as a way to control viewers' attention: directing them to certain elements in the scene, excluding other elements, and creating an image that's visually satisfying.

The notion of composition comes from painting and in part from still photography, and it refers to the arrangement of objects within the frame—their balance and tensions. Composition in motion pictures is quite different, since objects move within the frame (subject movement) and the frame itself can move (camera movement). Furthermore, one shot is edited next to another, creating an entirely new set of tensions and balances through time.

Perhaps the most commonly cited compositional guide is the *rule of thirds*, which can help you avoid placing important areas of interest dead center in the frame, which tends to be dull. Instead, position important areas one-third of the screen width from one side or the other (see the upper-left image in Fig. 9-20). In a close-up or medium close-up shot, you can place the subject's eyes about a third of the screen height from the top (the nose will then be roughly centered in the frame; see Fig. 12-33). It should be noted that a great many well-balanced compositions do not conform to this "rule."

Try to place objects and people naturally in the static frame—either comfortably within the frame or using the edge to cut them off decisively; don't place them so close to the edge of the frame that they seem to fight with it. Avoid large dead spaces or losing the subject in a mass of irrelevant details. Be particularly attentive to what's directly behind the subject, such as plants that may seem to be growing out of a person's head, or activity that distracts from what you want the audience to focus on.

A key consideration when framing a medium shot or a close-up of a person is how much *headroom* there is between the top of his or her head and the top of the frame. Individual shots vary tremendously in terms of how much headroom feels comfortable. In Fig. 9-14, the subjects' heads nearly touch the top of the frame, which works well in this scene. In shot 3A in Fig. 9-16, the space above Grace Kelly's head feels natural in the wide shot, but in the close-up (3D), the same amount of headroom seems perhaps unnecessary (the final frame might feel better balanced if the camera tilted down just a bit as it moves in). Many of the shots in Fig. 13-4 are framed so tightly that there's no headroom at all. Headroom—and composition in general—is subjective, and cinematographers and directors must go by their instincts in each setup.

Although there are no set rules for composition, compositions create expectations, and that may be used to surprise the audience or to confirm or deny their expectations. For instance, camera angles from below can be used to suggest the importance, stature, and height of the subject (or in some cases, it may just be an unflattering angle). In horror films, compositional imbalance often suggests something scary lurking outside the frame.

Because a shot often reveals its meaning through motion, it's possible to have strong film composition without well-composed still frames. Composition that is dynamic usually resolves tension by the use of subject or camera movement or through editing. A frame that seems off balance at first may fluidly become better centered as it develops. Or the off-balance quality itself may be used as an interesting pictorial element. These days, gross imbalances that violate the conventional notions of composition are often used to add flavor.

Leading the Action

When a subject has a definite movement toward the side of the frame, place the subject closer to the edge from which he is moving (see Fig. 9-4). For example, if you track someone walking from right to left, frame him closer to the right side of the frame as if to leave room for walking on the left. If the shot continues for some time, the person can advance in the frame to suggest forward movement, and even exit the frame to the left. Similarly, someone in profile looking off screen to the right should generally be framed closer to the left side of the frame, leaving space on the right.

(A)   (B)   (C)

Fig. 9-4. Leading the action. (A, B) Leave more room on the side of the frame toward which the action points. (C) The void on the left throws the frame off balance and may feel awkward or suggest something will happen (for example, someone may approach from behind). (Steven Ascher)

Other Elements in the Dynamic Frame

The focus may be "pulled" from the background to the foreground to shift audience attention. Some filmmakers consider this technique mannered unless it is used to follow a movement. Selective focus is used to accentuate a portion of the subject. In a close-up, it's usually advisable to focus on the eyes. A *tilt-focus lens* (see Fig. 4-23) allows you to tilt the plane of focus, drawing attention to a narrow area. Lighting may be changed within a shot; for example, car headlights might suddenly illuminate a person.

Shots tilted sideways (tilted horizon line) are called *Dutch angle* or *canted* and are

Fig. 9-5. A shot with a tilted horizon is called a canted or Dutch angle shot. (Stephen McCarthy)

sometimes used, often in medium close-up, to add tension to a static frame (see Fig. 9-5). Sometimes one tripod head is mounted perpendicularly on another; the lower head sets the basic angle of the shot, while the upper head controls the amount of sideways tilt and even allows the camera to be smoothly tilted from side to side during the take (see Fig. 9-6).

Cinematographers often shoot at an angle that reveals as many sides of the object as possible in order to enhance the feeling of depth. For example, a building filmed head-on reveals one side; shot from an angle it reveals two sides; and shot down and at an angle it reveals three sides. Use familiar references to establish scale. An enormous boulder will seem larger if there is a person in the frame.

Fig. 9-6. The Cartoni Dutch head enables you to mount a second fluid head perpendicular to the first, allowing side-to-side as well as front-to-back tilts. (Cartoni)

Hollywood directors frequently use camera angle, movement, and lighting to create a feeling of deep space in an image. This allows them to clearly distinguish foreground from background and exclude large areas of unmodulated black or white. European directors in the 1960s and 1970s often emphasized the flatness of the screen through their use of lighting and camera angle, sometimes shooting perpendicularly to a wall or allowing large areas of the frame to be overexposed or underexposed.

Composition in the Monitor or Viewfinder

There's a computer expression, "what you see is what you get." Unfortunately, when framing up a shot in a video or film camera, what you see is often *not* what you get. That is, the image that's ultimately delivered to the audience may look a lot different from the one you're seeing, not just in color or exposure, but also in the shape of the frame and where the edges of the picture are. It can be tricky in shooting to try to compose for the frame you're seeing while keeping in mind the different ways it may get transformed.

TV CUTOFF. Traditional CRT television sets were designed to enlarge the picture slightly inside the bezel on the front of the TV, which crops off the edges of the frame (called *TV cutoff* or *overscan*). Web videos, on the other hand, usually show the entire frame, edge to edge. Between these two are flat-panel LCDs and plasma TVs, which are not supposed to cut off the edges, but sometimes do.

Because the audience may not see the edges of the frame, remember when shooting to avoid positioning anything crucial too close to the edges of the viewfinder frame (top, bottom, or sides). TV cutoff is inconsistent from one TV to another—you can't *count* on how much the edges will get cut. Something undesired—like a microphone in the corner of the shot—may or may not show up.

Fig. 9-7. Safe action and safe title areas. The outer boxes show TV safe action and safe title areas when working in 16:9; the inner boxes show the same when doing a 4:3 center-cut crop for SD television. The safe areas here are conservative and based on older CRT standards. Most modern flat-panel displays have less cutoff, and you can usually get away with positioning things closer to the edges of the frame, especially with regard to safe title. (Steven Ascher)

The camera viewfinder should be able to display a *TV safe action* frame as a guide to show which parts may be cropped. The *TV safe title* area is even closer to the center of the picture to protect text and titles that have to be readable (see Fig. 9-7). Some monitors are switchable between *underscan*, which shows you the entire image, and *overscan*, which shows you typical CRT cutoff. Underscan will show you when unwanted things are definitely out, and also what the image will look like when shown on the Web.

ASPECT RATIO ISSUES. If you shoot in a widescreen format, be aware that your movie may be shown in a nonwidescreen format, particularly if broadcast. Similarly, if you shoot nonwidescreen, the footage will quite likely be converted to widescreen at some point. Please read the discussion of aspect ratio starting on p. 74 and particularly How Aspect Ratio Affects Your Shooting on p. 80. Fig. 9-7 shows the safe action and safe title areas of a center-cut 4:3 image extracted from a 16:9 frame.

Some cameras have interchangeable viewing screens or can display different aspect ratios, such as 1.66, 1.85, and 2.39. Sometimes a widescreen look is achieved by shooting in a relatively less wide format and cropping or masking the image in postproduction or projection. For example, you might shoot digital in 16:9 and then crop the top and/or bottom of the image to create 1.85 during post (see Fig. 9-8). If this is the case, be sure to shoot a framing chart at the beginning of the production so that the cinematographer's intentions in terms of framing are clearly indicated (see p. 269).

THE MOVING CAMERA

Static or *locked-off shots* (that is, shots that have no camera movement) can be contrasted with moving camera shots. A camera pivoting from a single point can *pan*

Fig. 9-8. This production is being shot in 16:9 and will be cropped in post to 2.35. The monitor is taped to show the eventual framing. Some monitors can display frame lines in a variety of aspect ratios. Waveform monitor overlay is in lower right. (David Kruta)

(move in a horizontal axis left or right) or *tilt* (pivot in a vertical axis up or down). If the support that's holding the camera can be raised, this may be *boom* up or *pedestal* up or *crane* up. If the support is on wheels, you can make a *dolly* or *tracking shot*.

Pans and Tilts

Pans work best when motivated by a subject moving through space. Panning with a moving subject makes the rate and movement of panning natural. Panning to follow a subject is sometimes called tracking, but this should not be confused with the tracking shot, where the camera itself moves through space (see below). However, panning with a long focal length lens can be used to simulate a moving camera shot (more on this below).

The most difficult pans are across landscapes or still objects, as any unevenness in the movement is evident. These pans must be fairly slow to avoid judder or strobing (see p. 393). The *swish pan*, a fast pan that blurs everything between the beginning and end of the movement, also avoids the strobing problem.

Panning is sometimes thought to be the shot most akin to moving your eye across a scene. If you look from one part of the room to another, however, you will see that, unlike the pan, equal weight is not given to all the intermediate points in the visual field. Viewers often read images from left to right, and scene compositions can take this into account. Pans often cross still landscapes from left to right, as though the world unfolds in this way.[2]

2. It would be interesting to compare films from countries where the language is written right to left (like Arabic and Hebrew) to see if there's any difference in how pans are typically done.

Cinematographers sometimes say that shots with camera movements like pans, tilts, zooms, and dolly shots are supposed to start from a static position, gradually gain and maintain speed, and then ease down to a full stop. This rule is often honored in the breach, and shots often appear in films with constant speed movement.

Keep in mind that the larger the movie is projected, the more exaggerated any camera movement will be. A quick pan or shaky camera may be far more disorienting or objectionable on a large screen than on a small one.

Dolly Shots Versus Zooms

When the camera moves through space, the viewer experiences the most distinctly cinematic of the motion picture shots. The moving camera is perhaps the most difficult and often the most expensive shot in the cinematographer's vocabulary. A wheeled vehicle with a camera support is called a *dolly*. Moving camera shots are called *dolly*, *tracking*, or *trucking* shots: When the camera moves in, it is called *dolly in* or *track in*; when the dolly moves out, *dolly out* or *track out*. If the camera moves laterally, it is called *crabbing* or *trucking* (for example, *crab left* or *truck right*). A dolly with an integral *boom* provides up-and-down (vertical) movement, which adds enormously to the lexicon of possible shots. Of course you can also do tracking shots without a dolly, either by shooting handheld or by using devices such as a Steadicam or a slider to move the camera (see below).

Zooming, unlike the shots just described, does not involve camera movement. A zoom lens allows you to increase or decrease the focal length during a shot (for more on zoom lenses, see p. 163). Some people object to the zoom effect because

Fig. 9-9. The DSLR on the slider on the floor can make lateral movements; the camera on the jib arm can get high-angle shots and vertical movements (boom up or down). The operator watches a monitor mounted on the jib. (Amanda Kwok/SmallHD)

the viewer is brought closer to (or farther from) the filmed subject without changing perspective. In Fig. 4-3, you can see that with zooming, the entire image is magnified equally, similar to when you approach a still photograph. In a dolly shot, however, the camera moves in toward the subject and the perspective changes; objects also pass by the side of the frame, giving the viewer the sense of physically moving into the space.

The moving camera creates a feeling of depth in the space. The zoom tends to flatten space and can call attention to the act of filming itself. Some filmmakers like this feature and will use the zoom to pick out a significant detail in the subject.

Zooming in the opposite direction of subject or camera movement results in a treadmill effect. If an actor runs toward the camera but the lens zooms back, the viewer feels as though the actor has made no progress. Similarly, if you shoot out of a car's front window and zoom wider, the viewer will feel as though the forward movement is disrupted. In *Vertigo*, Alfred Hitchcock combined zooming in one direction and moving in reverse to simulate the feeling of vertigo. The camera appears to move down a staircase and the lens simultaneously zooms back to keep the size of the field constant. Although the viewer sees the same subject matter, the perspective is exaggerated (since the camera moves closer), evoking the sensation of dizziness due to height. Similar moves were used by Steven Spielberg in *Jaws* and Martin Scorsese in *GoodFellas*—dollying in one direction while zooming in the other to create a disorienting effect.

The Zoom Effect

Zooming changes the image significantly and, unless it is handled well, can be quite disruptive. The classic, graceful zoom starts up slowly, reaches the desired speed, and gradually slows to a stop. There are also times when a "pop" zoom that jumps suddenly from one focal length to another can be effective. As discussed earlier, some people feel that all zooms should come to a stop before a camera cut. However, there are many instances of cuts while the camera is still zooming, especially if the zoom is slow, that work fine.

If you don't like the zoom effect, but want to zoom within the shot to change focal length, you can hide it with another camera movement—for example, a pan. "Burying" a zoom in a pan can make the zoom almost invisible. Novices tend to zoom too often ("zoom happy"), which can be annoying. Zooms are most effective when they are motivated and deliberate, not random.

For a slow, smooth zoom, use a motorized zoom. Almost all video lenses have built-in zoom motors. External zoom drives are available for cine-style lenses used with 16mm and 35mm film cameras, digital cinema cameras, and some HD cameras. Zoom motors usually have a range of speeds. It's helpful to have a very fast speed to reset the lens even if you don't plan to use that speed in the shot.

It's *very* important that the zoom control be able to accelerate smoothly from a stop and feather smoothly back to a stop. Sometimes an external zoom control has a more delicate rocker switch than a camera's built-in switch. When shooting on a dolly or tripod, you'll want an external control mounted on the handle of the tripod head so you don't have to reach around to the lens. Some video cameras can be preprogrammed to execute a smooth move from one focal length to another.

Some filmmakers prefer a manual (nonmotorized) zoom, which puts you in direct contact with the "feel" of the zoom. Many powered zoom lenses can be switched to manual mode. Manual zooming allows you to respond more quickly to fast-changing action. It can also be used for a deliberately "rougher" shooting style.

Some lenses can accommodate a zoom lever for manual zooming that extends perpendicularly from the zoom ring; the longer the lever, the smoother the zoom can be. Detachable drag mechanisms are available that adjust the resistance of the zoom.

STYLE AND DIRECTION

Style in movies, as all art forms, is continually evolving. At any given time, different types of movies make use of various conventions in shooting and editing. The conventions shift over time for a variety of reasons: a stylistically new film will spawn imitators; changes in technology make new techniques possible; ideas are borrowed from one type of moviemaking and applied to others. What follows is a deliberately sketchy history of some styles used in moviemaking, and some thoughts on directing, as a stimulus to thinking about the relationship of style and shooting possibilities. Also see the sections Some Film Theory and Approaches to Editing in Chapter 13.

DRAMATIC FILMS

Narrative Styles

In fiction and other scripted filming, the director must plan how individual shots relate to the action of the scene and to the juxtaposition of other shots through editing. At the most basic level, the director and cinematographer must decide where to place the camera and what to shoot in each shot.

In the deep-focus shot (see Fig. 9-10), the whole frame is in focus. The meaning of the scene thus develops in the deep space of the frame. The camera movement, subject movement, dialogue, lighting, costumes, and so forth all contribute to the forward movement of the film. The long take—that is, a shot of long duration—allows the action to unfold in real space and underlines the fact that the shot's meaning comes from filming, not from editing.

This staging of the shot, or *mise-en-scène*, is contrasted with *montage*, in which meaning and forward movement are conveyed through editing—through the juxtaposition of various shots that by themselves may contain less information or content. When the action of a scene is captured in many shorter shots, the filmmaker has an opportunity to control pacing and to direct the audience's attention in ways that may not be possible with longer takes. Montage also opens up the possibility of constructing entirely new meanings by suggesting connections between shots that otherwise might seem unrelated (for more on montage, see Chapter 13).

André Bazin, the French film critic often credited as the decisive influence on the French New Wave, thought it characteristic of advanced film directors of sound pictures to be concerned with mise-en-scène, with the integrity of the photo-

Fig. 9-10. Deep-focus shot from *Citizen Kane*. A wide-angle shot with both foreground and background in focus allows the action to develop within the frame. (RKO General)

graphed space. If you think of dangerous stunts, it is easy to grasp the visceral effect of seeing the events photographed rather than constructed. Among all the silent filmmakers, Buster Keaton seemed to understand best the power of unmanipulated space. His stunts, often performed in long shot, were clearly incredible feats. Much of the attraction of unmanipulated documentary is its ability to convince the viewer that what is seen on the screen actually occurred.

On the other hand, when audiences "suspend disbelief" and enter into the world of the movie, a carefully constructed edited sequence can deliver enormous emotional impact or bring out otherwise buried meaning. Staging and editing should not be thought of as opposites but as two stylistic tools at the filmmaker's disposal.

The first dramatic filmmakers approached motion pictures as an extension of theater. A story would be acted out in front of a fixed camera. Though the early silent films of the 1900s were not actually shot on a proscenium stage, the camera's relationship to the action was much like a theatergoer's view of a stage play. D. W. Griffith is credited with first exploiting the power of the close-up. The camera comes in close to reveal nuances of an actor's expression, creating a new relationship between audience and actor, necessitating a new, more subtle style of acting. The silent cinema defined the basic vocabulary of the film image. Today, shots taken without sound are referred to as *MOS*. The story goes that when the German directors came to Hollywood in the early 1930s, they referred to silent footage as "mit-out-sprache" (a kind of fractured German for "without speech"), hence MOS.

Hollywood sound films until the 1950s generally were shot in studios using a classic shooting/editing style: Scenes are first filmed all the way through in *master shots* (relatively wide-angle, continuous takes). Then close-ups are filmed, if needed. The edited scene begins with the wide establishing shot to ensure that the audience is well oriented and comfortable in the setting before cutting to the closer shots. From this classic approach evolved a "traditional" style of filming a two-person scene using four camera angles: a master shot, a two-shot, a close-up of one character, and a reverse of the other. A radical exception to this style is found in Robert Montgomery's *Lady in the Lake*, filmed with a subjective, point-of-view camera meant to reveal what the audience would see if they were inside the protagonist's head.

In the 1960s and 1970s, as the general culture loosened up, so did narrative style in many films. The old dictates of master shot/close-up coverage gave way to a freer-form shooting that assumes audiences have the visual sophistication to understand a scene that might be played in, say, only an extreme close-up. John Cassavetes experimented with a style that seems to merge documentary and narrative sensibilities. To the audience, both the acting and the camerawork may appear spontaneous and improvised, with scenes that flow organically from one moment to the next. It has become increasingly popular to shoot dramas in a handheld, documentary style. This may be done to add a sense of "realism" to a fictional or semifictional story or as a parody of documentaries ("mockumentaries," such as *This Is Spinal Tap*).

The 1980s brought the music video. Made by and for a generation that was raised watching TV, music videos introduced a new lexicon of quick cutting and the juxtaposition of wildly differing types of imagery. Stylistic touches exploited in music videos and TV commercials have found their way into many other types of movies; these techniques include deliberately shaky camerawork, distorted images, fast cutting, and intentional jump cuts (see below).

Today narrative films combine elements of all these styles. Many mainstream Hollywood or TV dramas are very straightforward stylistically, employing a style that will not "intrude" on the storytelling. Independent dramas tend to take more risks, but more often what sets them apart is the kind of stories they tell, rather than the fundamental visual language of shot selection and editing. As the Internet becomes increasingly important for distribution, it's interesting to see how narrative styles adapt to the small size and generally short duration of online videos.

Perhaps the best way to think about shooting and editing style is to watch movies and note which scenes work especially well or badly. To understand the relationship of camerawork to editing, it can be particularly instructive to watch films with the sound off.

Coverage

As discussed above, one approach to capturing a scene is to shoot the entire action in a single, continuous master shot. Woody Allen often films scenes in an uninterrupted master, such as many dialogue scenes in *Manhattan* and *Annie Hall* (see Fig. 9-11). In some scenes there may be little or no camera movement. This puts a special emphasis on the performances and writing and at times may de-emphasize the filmic aspects of the scene.

Fig. 9-11. This scene from *Annie Hall* runs about three minutes as an uninterrupted master shot. It ends with Woody Allen directly addressing the camera, breaking the "fourth wall" and transforming an observational scene into one that calls attention to the act of filming. (United Artists)

On the other hand, the opening scene of Orson Welles's *Touch of Evil* is an intricately choreographed continuous take that covers about three and a half minutes of action in close-ups and wide shots from high and low angles (accomplished with a mobile crane) in a tour de force of cinematic technique (see Fig. 9-12). At times, long master shots can give an audience a satisfying sense of being able to observe and discover things about a scene on their own.

For both aesthetic and practical reasons, filmmakers much more commonly parse or divide the action into various shots instead of simply shooting a single master. This helps both in shooting the scene and editing it. *Coverage* refers to the options (that is, different camera angles) that have been filmed in addition to the master. Having multiple camera angles available in the editing room allows you to change the pace of the scene, direct audience attention to different aspects, make use of the best performances, and edit around camera or acting errors. If a scene is covered with only one or two angles or takes, options are limited. Many an editor has lamented a director's lack of coverage.

One logical and traditional way to break down a scene is to move from a long shot to a medium shot to a close-up. This orients the audience to the physical space and the progression of increasingly tight shots suggests forward movement into the scene, as though the camera is delving deeper into the action (see Fig. 13-2). When a scene goes wider, from a medium shot to a long shot, we expect action on a larger scale (for example, a new arrival in the scene) or a leave-taking from the action (as might happen at the end of a movie). Nevertheless, contemporary audiences are comfortable with a wide variety of cutting styles and the traditional rules about the relationship of shots don't always apply.

Point of View

Among the arts, cinema has a unique ability to influence our thoughts and emotions and to allow us to see the world through the experiences of real and fictional characters. In a sense, the camera becomes the audience's eye, and the filmmaker, through shooting and editing, has an enormous power over what the audience feels and understands.

What audiences know about the characters and which ones they identify with depends in part on how individual scenes are constructed and how the story unfolds

Fig. 9-12. The opening sequence from *Touch of Evil* is an uninterrupted master shot that reveals the planting of a bomb, introduces central characters, and explores the urban landscape in continuously unfolding action. When Charlton Heston and Janet Leigh react to the sound of an off-screen explosion, the opening shot ends (1K) with a cut to a cutaway of the burning car (2). (Universal Pictures)

overall. How point of view is expressed in scene and story structure results from the way the script is written, how the director chooses to film it, and how the movie is edited. These aspects must be considered carefully before you go into production.

Let's take the example of a series of scenes in which a man goes to his doctor, the doctor reveals that some test results are bad, then the man goes home (see Fig. 9-13). The following are a few possible ways to shoot and edit this sequence of events.

The camera could witness the day along with the man. We see him saying good-bye to his wife as she drops him off at the doctor's office. He goes into the building alone. We see the doctor tell him about the test results and the man asks some questions. We cut to him at home, telling his wife the news.

In another way of portraying these events, we might start with the same shot of his wife dropping him at the doctor's, but have the camera stay with her as he enters the building and she drives off. We cut to her later, thinking about the possibilities. Then we cut to her serving dinner as she asks how the checkup went.

In a third scenario, we begin with the doctor alone in his office, reading and reacting to the test results. Then the man enters. The audience already knows the news is bad. There might be no dialogue at all, just a silent shot of the doctor's face. We then cut to the man silently at the table, not ready to tell his wife what happened.

Scenario 1 Scenario 2 Scenario 3

Fig. 9-13. Three ways of covering the same events. See text. (Greg High)

Each of these approaches stresses different aspects of the story. In the first option, the camera is closely identified with the man and his experience. The second version is obviously more from his wife's point of view—how *she* experiences these events. Depending on the story you're telling, you might want to restrict what the audience knows and sees to what a particular character experiences. In *Chinatown*, like many noir and mystery stories, the camera stays with the detective (Jake Gittes, played by Jack Nicholson) and the audience gathers clues along with him. We have no access to events that Gittes doesn't witness.

The third version of the doctor scenario differs from the first two in part because it may involve little or no dialogue. The audience understands the outlines of the story and gathers emotional clues through expression and gesture. Another difference is that in this scenario the audience gets information independently of the main characters (since we learn of the test results before the man does). This approach affects the narrative in direct and indirect ways. When the audience has knowledge that a character doesn't possess, a scene can at times be invested with irony, tension, or foreboding.

In interviews with François Truffaut, Alfred Hitchcock talked about the difference between surprise and suspense. He imagined a mundane dialogue scene in which there is a bomb under the table, which suddenly goes off, surprising the audience. He contrasted that with a different scene structure: in the second version, we see an anarchist plant the bomb, which is set to go off in a few minutes. Now, the same "innocuous conversation becomes fascinating because the public is participating in the scene. . . . In the first case we have given the public fifteen seconds of surprise at the moment of the explosion. In the second case we have provided them with fifteen minutes of suspense." As shown in Fig. 9-12, Welles used this second technique in *Touch of Evil*.

CAMERA ANGLES AND MOVES. The different approaches to the doctor scene or Hitchcock's bomb example represent choices that need to be made in the script and direction. Another set of choices apply to cinematography, since the camera's point of view is expressed most directly through individual camera angles and moves. The *eye line* or *sight line* is the direction a person is looking relative to the scene and relative to the lens. A character's eye line can indicate who or what she is looking at, and the angle of the eye line relative to the camera position can affect the way the audience experiences the scene.

The sequence from *Born Yesterday* in Fig. 9-3 is shot in a straightforward, observational style. The profile two-shot establishes the setting; the over-the-shoulder medium shots of Judy Holliday and William Holden cover the dialogue in a relatively objective way.

By comparison, in the scene from *The Last Picture Show* shown in Fig. 9-14, the camera is physically closer to the characters, and their eye lines are closer to the lens. Cybill Shepherd is filmed from above, representing Clu Gulager's point of view. Similarly, he is filmed from below, at about the height of her position on the

Fig. 9-14. In this scene from *The Last Picture Show*, the camera is positioned close to the actors' eye lines. High-contrast, hard light adds a moody feel (the shot of Cybill Shepherd evokes Hollywood black-and-white glamour photography from the 1930s and '40s). Clu Gulager's reflection in the mirror adds another dynamic element. (Columbia Pictures)

couch. These shots are not over-the-shoulder, but are clean medium shots, which can sometimes heighten the audience's sense of sharing the characters' point of view.

In some films and some scenes, the camera will more closely take on a character's point of view. For example, the shots from *Rashomon* in Fig. 9-15 represent the subjective point of view of each character looking at the other. The eye line of each man is very close to the lens, but not directly into it. In some films, actors will look directly into the lens and talk to it as if the camera were inside the head of the other character (perhaps for an intimate kissing scene). This type of shot can easily seem awkward.

Fig. 9-15. POV shots. In this dueling scene from *Rashomon*, the shot of Toshiro Mifune on the left represents Masayuki Mori's point of view; the shot on the right represents Mifune's POV. The eye line of each actor is toward the lens, but not directly into it. (The Criterion Collection)

Handheld camera moves are often used to represent a character's point of view and sometimes a character's emotional state. Panic or frenzy can be reinforced by a shaky or nervous handheld camera style. In real life, our remarkable human skeleton, gait, and sense of balance keep our head upright and steady and our field of view level in most circumstances, but the convention that wobbly handheld camerawork equals interiority or a subjective viewpoint is universally accepted. Horror films notoriously exploit tremulous handheld shots to telegraph the presence of an unseen onlooker.

Camera moves are often used to represent a character's experience. A character enters a room and the camera dollies forward, representing what the character is seeing. Audiences quickly make an association between a shot of a character looking off screen and a shot of what that character is supposed to be seeing. For example, in the scene from Hitchcock's *Rear Window* in Fig. 9-16, we start with a shot of Grace Kelly and James Stewart looking out the window, then cut away to their point of view of Raymond Burr across the courtyard (for more on this cutting pattern, see Chapter 13). When we cut back to Kelly (shot 3 in Fig. 9-16) the camera dollies in on her as the realization dawns on her that Burr's character may be a murderer. This kind of push-in to a close-up is commonly used in films to underscore a character's thoughts or to emphasize the seriousness of a situation.

Fig. 9-16. This scene from *Rear Window* begins with three shots: (1) Grace Kelly and James Stewart looking off screen; (2) a POV shot of Raymond Burr; (3) their reaction shot. Shot 3 dollies in on Kelly to emphasize her shock. (Universal; Steven Ascher)

In many films, fluid movement by means of Steadicam, slider, dolly, crane, and boom (sometimes in combination) is used to add flow and lyricism to a scene, but not to represent any particular character's POV. In *Psycho*, Alfred Hitchcock at times uses camera moves in which the camera itself almost becomes a character, prowling around a room, manipulating the audience in a carefully calibrated way.

When determining camera position and moves, think about how you want the audience to experience the scene. Should any of the characters be favored in terms of point of view? When do you want the camera positioned at a distance, observing the action? When do you want it in close? Should the camera be a voyeur or a participant? Do you want it to lurch impulsively, creep stealthily, or weave with uncertainty?

Whether shooting dramas or documentaries, try to put yourself in the minds of the audience. What do you want them to see? How do you want the scene to unfold? Use blocking to *reveal* things rather than to merely show everything up front. Use mystery to your advantage. Some shots are most interesting for what they *don't* show.

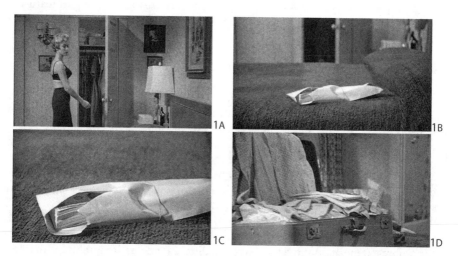

Fig. 9-17. In this continuous tracking shot from *Psycho*, the camera reveals the stolen money and a suitcase that tells us Marion Crane (Janet Leigh) is packing to leave town. There is a tension in the way these things are revealed in a continuous shot that feels very different than if they were shown in separate shots with cuts between them. (Universal)

The Illusion of Continuous Time

Live television shows are typically shot with several cameras. A talk show, for instance, might have one camera shooting a close-up of the host, another shooting a close-up of the guest, a third getting a two-shot of both, a fourth shooting the audience, and so on. By cutting back and forth between the various camera angles, we are shown many aspects of the scene, all in continuous time.

Dramatic films, on the other hand, are often shot with a single camera. The action is filmed from one camera angle. Then the camera is moved to a new angle, and the action is repeated or a new part of the action is staged. Depending on the action, it may be filmed from many different angles that may be shot on different days and/or at different locations.

Continuity style is the technique of shooting and editing shots filmed at different times so that the action on screen seems to flow continuously in time from one moment to the next. Continuity style is a grammar that audiences are familiar with from years of watching movies, and it is sometimes thought of as "invisible cutting" since the technique is so common as to be at times unnoticeable. Some scenes and films demand continuity style; others don't (more on that below).

The rules of continuity style (they're more guidelines, really) depend on the scene. Take the example of two people talking across a table (see Fig. 13-4). As noted above, this is commonly shot with a shot/reverse-shot approach. One camera angle features character A; another features character B. As long as the 180-degree rule is observed (see below), we can cut back and forth between them with a sense that the conversation is continuous. Sometimes the angles on the two characters are balanced to match each other as closely as possible (see Fig. 9-3). However, in some scenes, the angles can be quite different.

We've been discussing a scene in which there are two camera angles featuring different people. What about a situation that involves two shots of the same person? Say you have a close-up of character A and you cut to another take of the same close-up (without changing focal length or camera position). In this case, the jump or discontinuity between one take and the next will be very noticeable (see Fig. 13-3). This is called a *jump cut*. To avoid jump cuts, there needs to be a significant difference between the first and second shot, both in terms of the size of the shot and usually the angle from which it's filmed. Thus, a wide shot will usually cut easily with a medium shot or a close-up, but a cut between two medium shots will often feel unsmooth. The change in size between the first shot in the sequence and the next might be accomplished by changing the focal length of the lens or by moving the camera forward or back. The camera should also be moved laterally (left or right) between the two shots to avoid the feeling of a jump cut (some say that the angle should change by at least 30 degrees to provide enough difference between the two shots). Whether a cut feels smooth or jumpy is also affected by the action, the background, and especially continuity in sound (see below for more on jump cuts).

When restaging action to be filmed from different angles, it's important that the action be consistent from take to take. So if the actor picks up his coffee cup on a certain line in one shot, he should do it at the same point when filmed from other angles. The script supervisor (sometimes called continuity supervisor) is responsible for noting a wide range of continuity issues, from gestures to wardrobe to line readings, to ensure that shots will match when edited together. If you're shooting digital, when a continuity question arises it may be relatively easy to check a previous take. Even so, when there's an unintentional mismatch it's often the case that you can shoot or cut around it because the audience's attention is focused elsewhere (of course, there will always be people on the Internet with nothing better to do than troll for continuity errors).

A *cutaway* is a shot away from the main action that can be used to cover discontinuities or to condense the action. For example, when filming a politician giving a speech at a rally, a shot of a woman in the audience could be considered a cutaway or a *reaction shot*. In editing, the cutaway can be used to smoothly join one part of the speech with another. You cut from the politician (in sync sound) to the woman and back to the politician at a later part of the speech. Without the cutaway, the condensed speech would be more obviously discontinuous.

Even if you plan to shoot each part of the action from only one angle, allow for an overlap of action from one shot to the next in the scene to be sure there won't be temporal discontinuities in the editing. For example, say the script calls for a wide shot of a man getting in a car and slamming the car door, followed by a close-up of his face as he starts the engine. Shoot the wide shot all the way through the slamming of the door. When you start the close-up, shoot the action from a point *before* the first take ended, including the slamming of the door. This gives the editor options to cut the two shots together at several different points without discontinuity. As noted above, the camera should also be moved laterally between the wide shot and the close-up to make a smoother cut and to minimize any slight discontinuities in action.

When a character walks off camera, the viewer generally accepts a time jump when the next shot begins with him later on. For instance, if someone walks off frame toward the door, a cut to the same person walking down the street or sitting at a restaurant doesn't seem discontinuous. When panning or tracking with a moving subject, it's usually a good idea to let him walk out of frame at the end of the shot to provide more options in editing.

When shooting uncontrolled documentary scenes, you can't restage the action to get new camera angles. However, continuity issues still come into play. Always try to have in mind what shot you can cut the present one with. Whenever you feel there will have to be a cut made to another shot, change camera angle and focal length to make continuity editing easier. When shooting a scene with repeated action (for example, someone cooking or chopping wood) you can cover it from different angles, and be sure to include an overlap of action. In documentary, cutaways are often essential to making a scene work (see below).

Compressing and Expanding Time

Much like the issues of point of view discussed above, the flow of time in a movie depends in part on structural decisions made in writing, directing, and editing and in part on how individual shots are filmed. Storytelling always involves balancing moments that are described in detail with scenes in which the action is highly compressed (or omitted altogether). You want the audience to focus on those moments that have the most interest, meaning, and emotion while moving as quickly as possible through story points that may be necessary but are not in themselves worthy of much screen time.

Let's go back to the doctor's office scenarios described on p. 337. In the first version, the entire trip to the doctor is shown in a fair amount of detail. The man and the doctor engage in dialogue about the tests, and when the man returns home he tells his wife about it. In the second version, we know that he went to the doctor but we go directly to the conversation with his wife, essentially skipping the office visit. One approach is not better than another, but they use screen time and place emphasis in very different ways. The third version is almost like a silent film; it could be done in a few short or long shots, with no dialogue. It might convey ample emotional weight in relatively little time.

The script should be written (and rewritten) with a close eye to which scenes, dialogue, and details are truly important and which could be condensed or dispensed with altogether. Similarly, when planning coverage of a scene, the director should consider which action is worthy of being filmed in detail. In the third version of the doctor's office scene, you might decide that showing the man sitting in the waiting room is suspenseful, since we know he's about to get bad news. Conversely, in the first version, the same shot in the waiting room may just be dull. These kinds of judgments need to be evaluated before the shoot, but will ultimately be decided in the editing room (more on this in Chapter 13).

There are many techniques for shortening action when a film is shot and edited in continuity style. Say you're shooting a character painting a picture and you want to show her starting with a blank canvas and in the next shot show her putting the last touch on the finished work. To simply cut from one wide shot to another would probably seem too severe. The routine solution is to dissolve from one shot to the other. Another possibility is to do a *reveal*. The first shot ends as a wide shot. The second shot might begin with a close-up of her face and pull back (either by zoom or by moving camera) to reveal the finished painting. Alternatively, as described above, you can use cutaways to bridge from one moment to another later on. So you might cut to the painter's cat watching her work, and then cut back to the canvas almost completed.

At one time, jump cuts were seen as a radical new grammar that called attention to the discontinuity in time and to the medium of film itself (in contrast to "invisible cutting"). Today, they are far more commonplace, and audiences have come to accept them as routine. There are many situations in which jump cuts don't work, but increasingly filmmakers use them not only for scenes in which they want to highlight the jump in time, but simply because they want to shorten a scene and jump cuts will do the job.

When filmmakers want to expand time and make a moment or scene linger on screen, there are a number of possibilities. The first, as just discussed, is to block the action and cover it in a way that gives it lots of screen time. Some scenes or moments can benefit from slow motion (see p. 389). Martin Scorsese famously filmed boxing scenes in *Raging Bull* with a variety of slow-motion shots, sped-up shots, shots that linger, and very short shots in a fast-cut montage; these techniques together extend and compress time in a way that tries to capture the sensation of being assaulted in the ring.

The 180-Degree Rule

Screen direction refers to the right or left direction on screen as seen by the audience. If a subject facing the camera moves to his left, it is screen right. The *180-degree rule* (also called the *director's line* or the *line*) tells how to maintain screen direction when different shots are edited together. If a subject is moving or looking in one direction, in general it's best not to let screen direction change when cutting to the next shot. For example, when you're watching football on television, you see the blue team moving from screen left to screen right. If the camera were now to shift to the opposite side of the field, the blue team would appear to be moving in the opposite direction (that is, their screen direction will have changed from right to left). It's likely that you would be confused. To avoid this confusion, TV crews generally keep their main cameras on one side of the field, and when they use a camera position from the opposite side of the field, a subtitle may be flashed on the screen saying "reverse angle."

To help plan your shots, imagine a line drawn through the main line of action—be it a moving car, a football field, or the eye line of a conversation. If all camera setups are on one side of the line, screen direction will be preserved from shot to shot. Shots *on* the line (for example, someone looking directly into the camera or a shot from the end zone in the football example) are considered neutral and can go with shots on either side of the line.

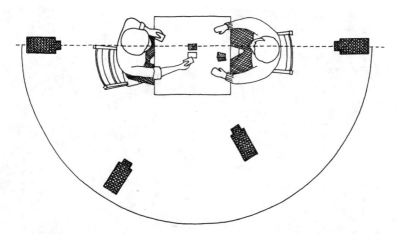

Fig. 9-18. The 180-degree rule. If all the camera positions are kept on one side of the sight line, screen direction will be preserved in editing. (Carol Keller)

During a take, the camera can move across the line with minimal disorientation. But if later in the editing room you don't use the shot where the camera crosses the line, you may have to violate the 180-degree rule. Rule violations may disorient the audience, but rarely are they disastrous. Sometimes inserting a neutral shot minimizes disorientation. The problem is most serious when screen direction itself has been used to construct the space of the scene. For example, in a shot/reverse-shot scene of two people talking, they must be looking in opposite screen directions when there is a cut from one to the other; otherwise they will not appear to be talking to each other. Similarly, chase sequences depend on screen direction to establish whether one car is chasing another or if the two are headed toward each other.

Screen direction issues can sometimes apply to shots that aren't even in the same scene. For example, documentary interviews are often filmed so that one subject is facing camera left and a subject with a contrary opinion (often filmed in a completely different setting) is facing right. Cut together, there's a sense of opposition or contrast in the framing as opposed to the uniformity that would result if each were looking to the same side of the lens.

Sometimes there are two different lines of action and there is no way to avoid breaking the rule. For example, a couple is talking in the front seat of a moving car in a scene that is shot angle/reverse angle. When the driver is shot, the background is moving left; but when the passenger is shot, the background is moving right. Since the relation of the couple is most likely the key element of the scene, draw the line of action along their eye line to preserve their screen direction in the editing.

For more on directing and working with actors, see below.

Fig. 9-19. This sequence from *The Last Picture Show* begins with a POV shot of Ben Johnson through a windshield. The cut to Timothy Bottoms and Jeff Bridges makes it clear that shot 1 was their point of view. Their conversation is then covered shot/reverse shot, moving tighter on the boys as the scene progresses. The 180-degree rule is preserved since they look screen right and Johnson looks screen left. (Columbia Pictures)

DOCUMENTARIES

Documentary Styles

People who are unfamiliar with how films are made sometimes think of documentaries as "documents" of reality—as though a film is simply a collection of footage of "real" people doing things or being interviewed. In fact, documentary filmmakers can have very different goals and strategies, and their films can vary widely in terms of style and genre. Some of the key stylistic questions relate to how much the filmmaker attempts to control or interact with the subjects, and to the way information is conveyed in the movie.

Some of the first motion pictures were made by Thomas Edison in the 1890s. These were "documentaries" in the sense that a camera was set up to record actual events, such as the electrocution of an elephant. The Lumière brothers' *Train Coming into a Station* (1896) is a single, continuous shot of a train arriving. It was an amazing novelty to see the world on film.

The style adopted by UK documentarians such as John Grierson in the 1930s and 1940s is a kind of hybrid that can involve staged events and real people (nonactors). It started in the days when cameras and sound recording equipment were heavy and hard to move around, so action would often be produced and orchestrated for the camera. In this approach, scenes may be scripted and shot much like a narrative film. Many of these films use a "voice of God" narration—the authoritative male voice that provides factual information and often spells out the message intended for the viewer to take from the film.

In the 1960s, lightweight 16mm cameras were introduced that could record sync sound with portable tape recorders. The advent of handheld cameras meant new access to locations and people's lives. Jean Renoir spoke of the heavy studio camera as an altar to which actors had to be brought. The handheld camera could now go out into the world instead of the filmmaker bringing the world to the camera. *Cinema verité* (also called just *verité* or *direct cinema*) films attempt to spontaneously react to events and capture life as it is lived. With a small crew and enough time for subjects to get comfortable, the filmmaker can become very unobtrusive. Subjects who are not self-conscious will reveal to the camera how they really live and self-conscious subjects will reveal themselves in how they choose to perform. Many of these films use no narration or interviews, and viewers may have the impression they're seeing a form of unmediated reality that hasn't been influenced or interpreted by the filmmaker (which was the goal of many early verité filmmakers). However, all filming and editing involves selection and point of view, so documentary film should never be confused with unmediated reality.

In the 1970s, a "personal documentary" movement emerged. In these movies, filmmakers explore their own lives, or shoot others with the explicit acknowledgment of the camera's presence and the filmmaker's role in interpreting events for the audience. Rather than creating an illusion of objectivity, these films embrace a subjective and personal view and are often narrated by the filmmakers themselves.

In the 1980s and 1990s, nonfiction programming grew in popularity on network television. Magazine-style shows such as *60 Minutes* are structured around short segments in which a correspondent is the guide and narrator of a particular story. These productions have their roots in journalism. The correspondent is seen interviewing subjects and doing *stand-ups*—telling the story directly to the camera. These shows usually contain some amount of "verité-style" footage in which people are seen living their lives or doing their jobs. This footage is often referred to with the antiseptic term *B-roll*. B-roll is noninterview material that is often only allowed to play for a few seconds in sync sound. Then the location audio is dipped down and the picture becomes a bed over which to lay narration.

Today nonfiction films are made using all of these styles, or combinations of them. When you embark on a documentary project, you need to determine the stylistic framework for the movie. In what ways will the audience learn about the subject? By watching events unfold in a verité-style approach? By seeing interviews with the subjects or hearing them over other footage? By seeing interviews with "experts" commenting on the subjects? Will there be narration (also called *voiceover*)? If so, is the narrator a disembodied voice or someone also seen on screen (either a subject, the filmmaker, or a correspondent)?

Often the film's topic will dictate style. Documentaries about past events generally use a combination of interviews (*talking heads*) and archival material (*stock footage*). Often this is combined with present-day footage of locations where events took place. Sometimes *reenactments* of past events are shot using actors. This footage may be shot in a stylized way to avoid being too literal; for example, actors might be filmed without any dialogue or without showing their faces. Of course, the more screen time devoted to reenactments (and the more dialogue they contain), the closer you get to the hybrid genre *docudrama*, which exists somewhere between documentary and fiction.

Fig. 9-20. The documentary *Inside Job* develops a story of financial collapse using interviews, exterior shots, graphics, archival footage, and narration. The choice to shoot in widescreen 2.35 aspect ratio results in talking-head shots in which the background plays a prominent role. (Sony Pictures Classics)

SCRIPT OR NO SCRIPT. Historical and issue-based films often begin with research, followed by a script or detailed treatment. Sometimes "preinterviews" are done to determine what someone will say (more or less) before they're filmed. The film is structured as much as possible in the writing, and the footage shot in the field or acquired from other sources is intended to illustrate a set of ideas that have already been laid out.

One of the reasons television tends to favor correspondent- and interview-based productions is that they can be produced on a short schedule. Interviews can be done and stand-ups scripted fairly quickly. The interview *bites* (responses) are edited together with B-roll. It's not unlike writing a newspaper piece.

This is in contrast to documentaries in which the shooting *is* the research. Contemporary stories that are still unfolding often call for a much more spontaneous approach. You should have an idea of what you're looking for, and focus on particular story threads and characters, but often it's in the shooting that you find what the arc of the story is. Some stories have an obvious arc—a film about an election, for example.

Reality TV is a loose genre of programming about the lifestyles of minor celebrities or in which people engage in competitions or are thrown into preplanned situations. While the dialogue may not be scripted, the idea is usually to shoot a situation, event, or setup that can be edited into an hour or half-hour episode.

When you make documentaries about real people living their lives—without trying to "direct" them or structure what they do—you're never sure what's going to happen or when. Many a filmmaker has completed weeks, months, or years of shooting with no idea if enough of a story has emerged to make a film. Then it may take an extended period in the editing room to weave together a coherent piece. But the payoff to this risky approach is in the power of stories that develop over a long period of time, in which characters change and grow, are born or die. The result can be a complexity and depth that can't be achieved any other way.

Filming Real Life

Documentary film provides a uniquely rich opportunity to experience how other people live their lives. There's a particular thrill about seeing dramatic moments unfold, knowing that they're spontaneous and unscripted. Creating the environment in which people will reveal themselves with a camera present is part of the documentarian's art.

The more the people you're filming trust you, the more comfortable they'll be in front of the camera. Filmmakers use different approaches to building trust.

Some like to spend a long time with their subjects before filming begins, to give everyone a chance to get to know one another. If you do so, you can expect many moments when you'll wish you had your camera. Regardless of when you start filming, spending some personal time together when the camera's not rolling (sharing a meal or a cup of coffee) can be an important part of learning about and getting comfortable with your subjects and their learning about you.

You should discuss with your subjects what kind of film you're making and where you plan to show it. You may want to talk with them about what's okay to shoot and what's not. Some filmmakers have the subjects sign a release at the outset, granting permission to use whatever is filmed (see Talent and Appearance Releases, p. 739). Others wait until later. From a journalistic standpoint, it's not a good idea to give subjects a formal right of approval over what gets used in the film and how it's edited (you're making the movie, not them).[3] However, you may or may not want to offer to show them the film before it's done to get their response. Public exhibition of a film can have an enormous impact (both positive and negative) on the subjects' lives, which you need to consider seriously as you shoot and edit. In some situations, people will let you film them only if they have some input in the process.

Once production begins, keep the crew small and use as few lights as possible, so the shooting is relaxed and low-key. When you start shooting, don't make a lot of commotion. Some camerapeople like to keep the camera on their shoulder or in position much of the time so there's not a big distinction between the times they're shooting and when they're just waiting. On a video camera, turn off the tally light that announces when you've pulled the trigger. When shooting double system, keep slates quiet, do tail slates, or avoid them altogether if you're also recording audio in the camera (see Chapter 11). The point is not to be sneaky, but to make filming as subtle as possible, with a fluid transition between shooting and not shooting.

Using wireless mics can be particularly useful in documentary. When subjects wear a mic, they're free to roam where they want without a soundperson sticking a mic boom in their faces. Be sure to show them where the mute button is so they can have privacy when they want it.

---

3. Some broadcasters may consider the film compromised if the subjects have control or if it feels like a puff piece promoting a group or individual.

Though people may be self-conscious at first, the fact of the matter is that being filmed over a period of time can be quite boring—the novelty wears off quickly. This is what you want—for your subjects to go about their lives without worrying about what you're shooting. Some filmmakers try to become a fly on the wall and interact very little with their subjects. Others are friendly and conversational when they're *not* shooting, but silent when the camera's rolling. In some filmmaking styles, the conversation between filmmaker and subject continues the whole time. It's up to you.

Fig. 9-21. Like most of Frederick Wiseman's documentaries, *Boxing Gym* explores an institution using only sync-sound scenes of contemporary life, with no narration, interviews, added music, text, or other framing devices. (Zipporah Films)

Shooting Uncontrolled Scenes

For the cameraperson, filming people without controlling what they do takes a special combination of sensitivity, luck, and quick thinking. Perhaps more than any other kind of shooting, cinema verité filming requires that the camera operator *think like a director and an editor*, all while spontaneously reacting to changing events. The tendency while shooting is to concentrate on the central action or person talking; remind yourself that the audience may also need to see the context (wide shot) and reactions from others in the scene. Think about the sequence as a whole. Ask yourself if you've gotten enough coverage. Though you don't yet know how the sequence will be edited, try to provide multiple options for editing and shots you think might make interesting beginnings or endings. The audience will see the scene through *your* eyes, so always have them in mind while you shoot.

It's especially important to think of individual shots and camera movements as having a shape, with a beginning and end. Novices, especially when shooting video, tend to move the camera constantly, which makes the footage very hard to cut. When doing a camera movement (whether it be a zoom, pan, dolly, or walking shot), it's often a good idea to begin with a static frame and hold it for a few seconds, then transition into the movement, and glide to a stop on another frame and hold that a few seconds. The editor may cut out the static beginning and end, but at least he or she will have them if needed.

A few documentary filmmakers, notably Frederick Wiseman, have a style in which scenes often play out in nearly real time with relatively little cutting within the scene. This can allow human interactions to unfold in a natural way. Far more commonly, scenes as edited on screen must play much faster than the actual events take in real time. The filmmaker must shoot so that time can be condensed. This means judiciously shooting the action so that the editor can cut out the uninteresting parts and weave together the essential parts. Take the example of shooting two people talking over dinner. The meal might take two hours in real time and run two minutes in the edited movie. If the camera remained locked in a two-shot the entire time, the sequence would be almost impossible to cut. Instead, get a variety of angles, some two-shots, some close-ups. Be sure to shoot ample footage of the person *listening* as well as the person talking. An over-the-shoulder shot taken from behind the person talking shows the relationship of the two subjects without showing moving lips; this can be very useful in the editing room. Similarly, when shooting someone on the phone, try to get some angles from behind or where the phone blocks the camera's view of the person's lips. When shooting someone playing an instrument, be sure to get neutral shots in which no finger or hand positions are visible. See Dramatic Films, p. 332, for more on shooting and editing conventions that apply to both narrative films and documentaries.

Shooting Interviews

Filmmakers incorporate interviews in various ways. In a typical news or journalistic piece, they may be the primary source of content and take up much of the screen time. In some films, interviews are woven in with other types of footage and feel more like an opportunity for conversation or storytelling than for information delivery. In some films, the audience never sees the interview; instead, the filmmaker edits the audio and uses it as voice-over, to give the sense that the character is narrating the movie.[4]

A key issue when doing interviews is whether the interviewer's voice will be heard in the edited interview. That is, will the audience hear the questions and follow-ups (as is common when a correspondent does a magazine piece) or will they just see the subjects' responses edited together (which is typical when there's no host or filmmaker shown or heard on screen)? Doing interviews when the questions *won't* be heard creates a unique, somewhat bizarre dynamic that takes some practice to pull off smoothly. You need to get the person talking, but not exactly *to* you (since you don't exist in the conversation). You may have the urge to respond, to reassure the person that what she's saying is interesting, but you can't make a sound—at least not while she's talking. Some things that may help:

- Set a relaxed tone at the outset. Have the subject talk to you and try to ignore the camera. Tell him it's okay if he needs to stop to think, or to redo a question. (Though, for some types of interviews, such as challenging a poli-

---

4. If you know *for sure* that you want only the audio from an interview, recording with only an audio recorder can sometimes put people more at ease. Or use a video camera but point it away.

tician about questionable policies, you might *want* to put your subject on the spot.)

- Explain that your voice won't be in the piece, which is why you may be nodding but not responding when he talks.

- Answering questions the audience doesn't hear can produce awkward results. If you ask, "Where were you born?" and all your subject says is, "London," you'll have a problem in the editing room. Instead, ask her to incorporate your question into her answer ("I was born in London") or at least ask her to respond in full sentences.

- Don't let subjects say, "As I said before" or refer to earlier conversation. There's no way to know what order the material will be used, or if you'll use both bites. Every statement should stand on its own. If you're not part of the piece, don't let them refer to "you" either.

- Filmmakers differ in how much to let people talk during an interview and how much to try to influence how they phrase things (it also depends on the project). Long, run-on sentences may be unusable. Always be listening for how you can edit what's being said, to shorten it while retaining the meaning. Some people have a knack for speaking in long strings of dependent clauses that are simply not editable. You may want to stop and ask them to say the same idea more succinctly, or to address the content in separate short bits instead of one long chunk. Often, the first time someone answers a question is the freshest. If you need to do a "re-ask," change the focal length of the lens so you can edit the first part of one answer with the second part of the other, if you want.

Sometimes interviews feel more natural if the subject has a physical activity to do, is walking or driving, or is in a familiar setting, like a kitchen. The background and setting can be used to tell the audience something about the person. Another approach is to use a neutral backdrop to provide consistency from one subject to the next. A textured cloth or black (*limbo*) backdrop can be brought from location to location, but if there are many talking heads, a uniform backdrop can become dull. Sometimes interviews are filmed in front of a green screen, with the background added in postproduction (see Green Screen and Chroma Keys, p. 211). This opens the door to all sorts of imagery in the background, including motion shots. Keyed backgrounds sometimes feel artificial, but when appropriate, they can be very interesting.

CAMERA ANGLES AND MOVES. For sit-down interviews, usually the interviewer sits close to the camera so the eye line of the subject is toward the lens but not directly into it (which can sometimes feel awkward). When positioning the subject, be attentive to screen direction—try to alternate setups with subjects facing screen left with those facing screen right (see Fig. 9-20). Opposing screen direction is classically used for people with opposing opinions. When the interviewer is to be shown on camera, or if there is more than one camera, sometimes one camera angle is from the side, to get more of a profile shot. Filmmaker Errol Morris uses what he calls the "interrotron," which is basically a teleprompter (see Fig. 9-33) that projects his face on a screen in front of the lens, so the interviewee can look directly *into* the lens while talking to him. On-camera hosts or correspondents generally look directly *to camera* when addressing the audience.

Some filmmakers shoot interviews with no camera movement during shots, but zoom in or out to vary the focal length between shots. This allows cutting in or out of the material without ever having to cut during a zoom, which some people find objectionable. However, a well-timed zoom can enhance an interview by bringing the viewer closer for important or emotional material, or pulling back to capture, say, interesting hand gestures. If the zoom is gradual and properly timed to the phrases of speech, cutting opportunities should not be too limited.

Sometimes interviews are filmed with a dolly-mounted camera to keep some sense of movement throughout. Curved track can help you maintain the same distance from the subject while moving around. Timing is everything, since even a slow dolly move will reach the end of the track before long. It may just be luck if you're moving in the right direction at the right place at the right time.

When more than one camera is used, as is typical with news and magazine shows, one camera can hold a more conservative, wider shot while another is more active. DSLRs are sometimes used to add an additional fixed camera angle without an operator. Shooting interviews with multiple cameras provides flexibility for editing and makes it much easier to condense time without jump cuts. It also avoids the fake reaction shot problem that happens when there's only one camera and the interviewer's questions and reaction shots are filmed after the interview is over. (For a wonderful example of this, see James Brooks's comedy *Broadcast News*, in which a correspondent is seen tearing up on camera during a moving interview, even though the shot of him crying had to be filmed as a retake after the actual interview was done.)

If lower-thirds will be used to identify subjects (see p. 543), be sure to leave room at the bottom of the frame.

See Lighting Interviews, p. 508, for more on interview setups.

PREPARING FOR PRODUCTION

Preparing well for your shoot can mean the difference between an organized, productive filming experience and a chaotic, haphazard one. Actually, shooting movies is almost always chaotic—there are an enormous number of things going on at once, decisions being made, events out of your control—but if you're prepared, and lucky, it will be a kind of controlled chaos that results in getting the footage you need while staying close to your schedule and budget and keeping everyone relatively happy.

Preparation can take many different forms. For a director, it may mean previsualizing the action and camerawork. Alfred Hitchcock prepared so meticulously—working out the entire film beforehand—that he claimed that shooting was an uneventful execution of the movie he'd already seen in his mind.

For a producer, preparation means hiring a good team and making sure the resources needed are available on time. No matter what budget you're working with, there are always financial pressures, and you may not be able to deliver what's on everyone's wish list. Knowing which things you can do without—and which you can't—is part of the producer's skill.

For the director of photography, preparation means having the equipment you need, knowing how to use it, and being confident that it's working. Together with the director you'll have worked out a visual style and, depending on the shoot, planned individual shots, angles, and lighting.

Some shoots can be planned to the nubs; others have to be highly improvised in the moment. As a Roman philosopher said, "Luck is what happens when preparation meets opportunity." Two thousand years later, it's a tired cliché, but still useful for film shoots.

Fig. 9-22. Shooting a scene. Video can be monitored, logged, and recorded directly on a laptop. (Adobe Systems, Inc.)

PREPARING THE SCRIPT AND APPROACH

Script Preparation

Narrative films often begin with a story or treatment. Then a more detailed screenplay (script) is written. It's important to put the script in standard page format since that's what actors and executives expect and, particularly if you're a novice, you want to show that you understand industry practice. You can use a scriptwriting program like Final Draft, a free app like Celtx, or just use a word processor (formatting guidelines can be found in scriptwriting books—see the Bibliography—or on the Web). When writing a script to be read by potential funders or actors, it's a good idea to keep camera direction and *blocking* (the actors' movements) to a minimum.

The reader should experience the movie as it will play on screen and not be burdened by the mechanics of how it's put together.

When you read the screenplay of a movie you admire, or recall the dialogue in a memorable scene, you may be surprised at how few words are used. Powerful moments in films are often made up of looks, actions, and relatively terse exchanges rather than long stretches of expository dialogue. Novice (and experienced) filmmakers often find in the editing room that scenes play better with much less dialogue than was written (see Chapter 13). This is in part because of pacing, and in part because some things you might think need to be explained actually play better when the audience makes the connections themselves. Be sure to read through every line of dialogue *aloud* before going into production. This is often best done with the actors (see below). There's no better time to trim dialogue and entire scenes than before you shoot!

Another consideration is estimating how long the finished film will run. You may want to hit a standard length, such as ninety minutes or two hours, and you may be required to if a contract calls for it. There's a general assumption that scripts in standard layout run about a page a minute. Dialogue scenes are more predictable than action scenes in terms of the relationship of page length to running time. Even so, some dialogue is delivered as rapid-fire repartee and some is slow-paced. You can estimate running time by speaking the lines with a stopwatch.

Before you go into production, every scene and description in the script should be considered for its financial and technical implications (see Working Backward from the Budget, p. 58). Also, be sure the total number of scenes and locations is within your budget (more on this below).

You may want to have a lawyer or script service vet the screenplay for any potential legal issues. For example, if you have a character named Roy Cornelius who lives on Houston Street in New York, you'll want to check that there isn't a real person with that name on that street. If the script calls for a specific piece of music to be performed or used, that will also need to be cleared. For more on legal and clearance issues, see Chapter 17.

THE SHOOTING SCRIPT. As you approach production, a *shooting script* is prepared that includes specific camera angles and may have more details on action. Every scene is numbered and all scene and page numbers are locked. That way, if changes are made to a page, any replacement pages can be inserted without reprinting the whole script. If page 18 is rewritten and becomes longer than a page, the extra page would be 18A. Similarly, if a new scene is added after scene 20, it becomes scene 20A. Revision pages are dated and typically printed on different-colored paper: the first revision on blue, the second on pink, then yellow, and so on.

Previsualization and Rehearsal

If you were setting out to design an environment that fosters creativity and relaxed, fresh thinking, a film shoot would *not* be it. On a typical day, if you're not already behind schedule, you will be if you stop too long to ponder. Not to mention the fact that there may be hordes of people busily executing the ideas as planned who won't be happy when you decide to change *everything* at the last moment.

There are many ways to explore, experiment, rehearse, and previsualize before you actually go into production.

Having a group of actors read through the script gives you a chance to hear the dialogue and get ideas for direction. This can be done as a *table read*, where everyone sits together, or you may want actors to move around to get the physical sense of a scene. If you can afford it, reading with the actual actors who will play the parts can be a productive time to work out ideas and to form relationships. Some directors insist on rehearsal time. Director Mike Leigh uses rehearsal as a time when the actors can actually shape the story and dialogue. Other directors prefer that actors do the material fresh on the shoot with little prep. There are benefits to rehearsing in a separate space prior to the pressures of production, but sometimes you just have to rehearse in the moment on the set.

The physical aspects of the set or location are an integral part of how scenes are blocked and shot. Sometimes the physical space is designed or modified according to how you want to play a scene, and sometimes you're on location and just have to use what you've got.

The director, director of photography, and other members of the production team need ways to plan and collaborate how the film will be shot. Perhaps the simplest tool is to draw basic sketches of camera angles and blocking. These can be floor plans and/or drawings of what would be seen through the lens (see Fig. 9-23). The DP may also want to make charts of lighting setups.

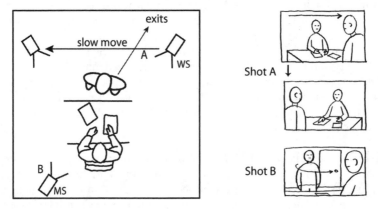

Fig. 9-23. Basic sketches for planning scene coverage. (left) An overhead diagram of camera angles and blocking. (right) Simple sketches of individual shots from the same sequence. (Steven Ascher; Greg High)

Storyboards are shot-by-shot drawings of how the action and camerawork are supposed to play on screen. These can be particularly useful for effects shots and complex setups where many people may be needed to make the shot work. A storyboard artist may draw them or you might make sketches yourself. Some directors use detailed storyboards as a way to previsualize a scene; others find them limiting. Often there are many changes between the storyboard and what is actually shot and edited into the movie.

Computer storyboarding programs, such as StoryBoard Quick and StoryBoard

Fig. 9-24. Storyboards can be created with apps like StoryBoard Artist. (PowerProduction Software)

Artist, may save time and can be helpful if you lack drawing skills (see Fig. 9-24). You can also use apps such as Poser, FrameForge, and After Effects to create video sequences to which audio can be added; some applications can simulate what a camera would see if moving through a physical space—useful for planning set construction or a CGI shot.

Some filmmakers like to rehearse not just the actors but the entire movie, including shooting and editing. Francis Coppola and others have used video as a tool to shoot essentially a rough draft of a movie (or scenes) and edit prior to production. You might go out with a small digital camera and experiment with camera angles, moves, dialogue, or blocking. Cut it together and see how it flows. Even if you can't shoot the real locations or real actors, you'll get ideas, and you'll either use them for the movie or you'll realize—with plenty of time to make a new plan—that you want to do something completely different.

SCHEDULING AND PLANNING

Script Breakdown and Scheduling

As you prepare for shooting, every scene in the script is broken down for the production elements required. A *script breakdown sheet* lists the people and resources needed for each scene, including cast (both principal players and extras), crew, stunts, props, wardrobe, makeup/hair, vehicles, special effects and equipment, music, and so on. The length of each scene is indicated in one-eighth-page increments (a half-page scene is four-eighths).

Once the script is broken down, a shooting schedule is created. This may be done by the first assistant director, the production manager, or sometimes the producer. The *production board* (also called *production stripboard*) is a chart with strips of paper for each scene, color coded according to whether the scene is interior or exterior, day or night. Strips can be moved around to form the schedule and modify it as necessary. This organizational system can also be done on a computer with software like Celtx or Movie Magic Scheduling (see Fig. 9-25).

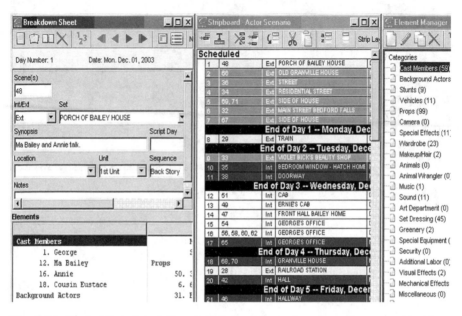

Fig. 9-25. Movie Magic Scheduling. (left) A breakdown sheet for each scene, with talent, props, and equipment needs. (middle) Stripboard for planning the shooting schedule. (Entertainment Partners)

Production scheduling is a complex task that takes experience to do well. The goal is to maximize efficiency and remain flexible for contingencies. On a low-budget film, it's common to shoot about three or four pages in a twelve-hour day. Dialogue scenes may go faster than action scenes that require many camera setups (lots of short scenes often take longer than a few long ones). The pace of shooting is usually dictated by the budget. If you can afford only two days at a location, you'll have to get the scenes there done in that time even if it means compromising the original plan. It's not unusual to go into a shoot with a full list of camera setups on the schedule, then pare down the list to bare essentials as the time—and, often, the light—run out.

Generally, filming in the order the scenes appear in the script is not optimal. You usually need to film all the scenes that occur in one location together because it's too inefficient to return to the same place to set up multiple times. Similarly, you may need to *shoot out* an actor (group together all his or her scenes) if that person's availability is limited. If you use scheduling software, it's easy to print out a *day-out-of-days schedule* that allows you to see all the days when individual actors or other elements are scheduled so you can see if rearranging things might allow you to film an actor's scenes back-to-back.

Planning *within* each day's shoot should also take into account when cast members and resources are needed. For example, shoot the wide shots of a crowd scene first, then shoot close-ups after most of the crowd has been dismissed.

The production team will work faster and get more comfortable with one another after working together for a while, which argues for shooting relatively easy scenes first, then doing more complex scenes later on. Actually, crews often go through an arc: things are bumpy at first, after a while they get into a groove, and then, as exhaustion sets in, they get more ragged. Don't shoot key scenes on the first day.

Also consider emotional content when scheduling scenes. For example, a film about two people meeting and developing a relationship may be performed more naturally by actors who are just getting to know each other in the early scenes and have the experience of the shoot behind them for later, perhaps more intense scenes.

It makes sense to shoot exterior scenes relatively early in the production in case bad weather sets in later. Always have an interior *cover set* available that you can move to if an exterior becomes suddenly unfilmable due to weather. Duplicate wardrobes and props allow the production to continue even when a prop has been misplaced or a shirt has gotten dirty.

When you move from one location to the next (a *company move*) you invariably lose a lot of time. Avoid moves during a day when possible. Schedule meal breaks every six hours (or more often) and have plenty of drinks and snacks (called *craft service*) available at all times. The time between the end of one workday and the start of the next is *turnaround time*, and it should normally not be less than twelve hours. Turnaround can be a particular issue with night shoots if filming is scheduled for the next day; you can't stop shooting at 3:00 AM and ask the crew to start again at 8:00 AM. Exhaustion has caused serious accidents.

On some productions, everything is shot during the period of principal photog-

Fig. 9-26. When shooting exteriors, the time of day and weather can be as important as the location. For example, light at midday tends to be flat and may be harsh. Light earlier or later in the day may cast interesting shadows. The magic hour just before sunrise or after sunset may show lights as well as the landscape. Thin cloud cover can enhance colors and soften shadows, which is often helpful in close-ups. Haze buildup may obscure distant shots.

raphy. On others, time is left in the schedule for *reshoots* (often after editing has begun) or for the occasional *pickup shot* needed to fill in a gap or transition (pickup shoots are generally done with a reduced crew). ADR may be needed to replace dialogue before the mix (see p. 532). It's smart to anticipate these things by building them into the schedule and the actors' contracts.

See Chapter 17 for more on scheduling and business arrangements.

The Shooting Ratio

Drawing up a budget and a plan helps you address a key question: how much material should you shoot? The total amount of footage shot is invariably greater than the length of the final edited movie. The ratio of total footage filmed to final running time (*the shooting ratio*) varies widely by type of movie, budget, and the director's style. A carefully planned drama might be on the order of 5:1 or 15:1. A reality television show with multiple cameras could have up to 450 hours of footage for a one-hour program.

On a drama, the footage shot will depend on several factors: the length of the script; how many scenes there are; the number of different camera angles (setups) required; how many takes of each need to be shot. Sometimes directors shoot a whole scene in wide shot, then reshoot the whole scene again in close-up to give the most flexibility in editing. This results in a higher shooting ratio than if you decide in advance that you'll film, say, only the opening and closing of the scene in wide shot and do the bulk of the dialogue in close-up. By "pre-editing" in this way you'll save time in the shoot and reduce the amount of footage (you'll also reduce your options in the editing room somewhat). Hitchcock was so precise in filming just what was needed that editor George Tomasini joked that sometimes editing a scene meant simply trimming off the slates and stringing the shots together.

No matter how predictable you assume the action will be, the unexpected always seems to happen: changes in the weather, flubbed lines, or technical difficulties with picture or sound. Additional takes are invariably needed in acted work, and documentary is always unpredictable.

One big factor in the shooting ratio is whether you're shooting digital or film. Film is obviously expensive, so there's always pressure not to shoot too much. Digital is cheaper on a per-minute basis, so people tend to shoot it at a much higher ratio than film. When you shoot film, you have to edit in your head and make every foot of film count. With a digital camera, it's almost harder to turn it off than to just keep shooting.

The benefit of shooting at a high ratio can be a more relaxed feeling on the shoot. You can take bigger risks in terms of trying things out, letting actors play with a scene, or not stopping between takes. With unpredictable documentary scenes, shooting liberally may allow you to capture things you'd otherwise miss. However, there can be real problems with shooting too much. Aesthetically, shots can become too relaxed and rambling, with no particular beginning or end, and may be impossible to cut. It's interesting to note that students who first learn how to shoot on film tend to shoot more carefully and thoughtfully than those who start with digital.

Then, of course, high shooting ratios mean extra costs for added production time, film or tape stock, and processing (even digital will have costs due to transcoding, debayering, or hard drive storage). Managing a project that has hours and hours of material can be a headache in the editing room and may require many days simply to view and log the footage.

With experience, you will find the ratio that's right for your style of working.

ORGANIZING THE PRODUCTION

The Crew and Production Tasks

The following is a brief description of the roles of key members of a large Hollywood-type film production unit, which gives an idea of the range of tasks involved in a movie shoot. The use of terms like "cameraman" is not meant to imply that the job is performed by a male.

The *executive producer* may arrange for financing or contribute in other ways to developing the production. The *producer* raises money and often creates the "package," which may include the script (*literary property*), the director, and the actors. The producer is responsible for the budget and the overall production and can hire and fire personnel. The *director* is responsible for the production unit, translating the script into visual terms, and directing the actors. In some television productions, the producer's functions overlap with those of a film director.

The *first assistant director* (*1st AD*) is responsible for keeping the shoot on schedule and maintains order on the set. The *second AD* manages call sheets (see below) and makes sure that needed actors are present. The *script supervisor* is responsible for continuity and making sure shots match in everything from weather to hairdo and that everything has been shot from the angles called for in the script.

Fig. 9-27. Crew on location. (Chris Freilich)

The *unit production manager* (*UPM*) is responsible for the relations between the production and outside labor and suppliers. He or she works with the first AD to keep the production on schedule. A *line producer* performs similar tasks in a supervisory role. A *production coordinator* handles details such as shipping, transport, and lodging. A *location manager* or *scout* finds locations as needed and helps arrange logistics.

The *director of photography* (*DP* or *DoP*), also called the *cinematographer*, *first cameraman*, or *lighting cameraman*, composes the shots, plans camera movements, and decides how to light scenes, usually in consultation with the director. On small units, the DP may operate the camera, but on large units, the *camera operator* or *second cameraman* sets the controls and operates the camera during a take. The *first assistant cameraman* (*1st AC*) operates the follow focus, checks the film camera gate for dirt, and manages the camera equipment. The *second assistant* or *clapper loader* operates the slate, loads film in a film camera, and keeps the camera report sheet.

On a digital cinematography or video shoot, job descriptions are somewhat different, as there's no film to load or gates to check, but include other responsibilities, such as managing tapes or data files, setting up monitors, and so forth. A *DIT* (*digital imaging technician*) may be on the crew to adjust camera parameters, supervise recording, create a visual look, and offload and back up camera files.

The *gaffer* and a crew of *electricians* place the lights as directed by the DP. The *best boy* or *second electric* assists the gaffer in setting up lights and cables. The *grips* move things around, place props, and build scaffolds and other rigging for cameras or lights. The *dolly grip* pushes the dolly. The sound department is run by the *sound recordist* (also called *production sound mixer* or *location sound engineer*), who records the sound and directs the *boom operator*, who maneuvers the microphone, sometimes assisted by a *cableman*.

The *second unit* is usually responsible for stunts, crowd scenes, battle scenes, and special effects—essentially those scenes that are shot without sound. These scenes have their own director and camera crew.

The crew is divided into departments (camera, sound, art, wardrobe, etc.), each with a department head. Production design, art direction, set construction, props, makeup, hairdressing, costume design, wardrobe on the set, and countless other jobs are specialized tasks, each requiring one or many people to perform them. Job responsibilities vary by country and by type of production. On union productions there are strict rules about what duties fall within or outside a given job's jurisdiction. For example, the camera crew usually shouldn't touch a lighting fixture. On nonunion or smaller productions, there may be significant overlap in responsibilities, and one person may be called on to perform a variety of tasks. *Production assistants* (*PAs*) are low-paid "gofers" (go for this, go for that) who do all sorts of underappreciated tasks. Don't confuse PAs with APs (*associate producers*).

Crew Size

Finding the right crew size is a balancing act. If the crew is too small for the complexity of the production, crew members get overburdened and the work becomes inefficient and slow. However, as crew size grows, there is a kind of instant multiplying effect: more people require more support (cars, meals, accommodations), which requires more people.

The size of the crew can affect not just the process, but the nature of what gets filmed. The larger the crew, the more expensive each hour of work becomes, which adds pressure to the shoot and makes it that much harder to experiment and try out ideas. Particularly on documentaries, a small crew will have better access to the subjects being filmed and create less disruption in their lives. A small documentary crew might consist of a cameraperson and a sound recordist, with either or both functioning as director. A third person may be needed to drive the car, help with equipment, and run errands. Some documentary filmmakers like to shoot alone, working unobtrusively with a small camera. See p. 731 for the business aspects of hiring crew.

Casting

For any production that involves actors, casting is vital. Finding actors who are not just right for their roles but who also work well as an ensemble can make all the difference. If the casting is good, the director's job is enormously easier. If the casting is bad, a great script and director may not be able to save the project. For a dramatic feature, having some known stars may enable you to get financing and is a boon for marketing. Many stars have been known to appear in low-budget films if the script is good and the number of days required is small.

Depending on the production, you may have a choice whether to work with union or nonunion actors. Union actors are generally more experienced and expensive, though they may reduce or defer their salaries for low-budget productions.

At the start of the casting process, prepare a *casting breakdown*, which is a list of all the roles in the film with a short description. Professionals usually work with a casting director or a casting agency that has files on hundreds of actors and conducts regular auditions for new talent. A casting director can point you to actors who would be good for a role and may help when negotiating with them. For a Hollywood picture, a talent agency might assemble a "package" of lead actors for a project. Breakdown Services, Ltd., is a company that posts breakdowns for agents and actors to view. In many cities there are agencies and casting websites that can give you quick access to a local pool of actors. Some producers hold open auditions, advertised to the general public; if you do this, be prepared to find a few undiscovered gems and a lot of people who have little experience and ability. Beware of actors' *headshots* (posed portraits)—they can be misleading. However, when casting *extras* (nonspeaking background players) headshots are typically all you have to go on.

When holding auditions, prepare *sides* (portions of the script excerpted for each character) and get them to the actors prior to the audition. Sometimes casting directors do the first auditions themselves, which the producer and director review online. Then *callbacks* are scheduled to read the promising actors again, often in different combinations. With some casting decisions you know instantly if an actor is right or wrong for a part; other times it takes a lot of thought. Be sure to record everything on video so you can review. It's important to see how actors take direction, so ask them to try their lines a few different ways. Pay attention not just to line readings, but to how actors handle themselves when they're listening and performing action without dialogue. A major part of acting is nonverbal.

For more on hiring actors, see p. 732.

Locations

The producer can seek out locations for film shoots or hire a location scout who may already keep a database of likely places. Many states have film commissions that can assist in finding locations and securing public areas like parks and government buildings. Potential sites should be photographed from multiple angles or shot on video to give a sense of the space.

Location scouting—the British call it *doing a recce* (from "reconnaissance," it's pronounced "rekky")—is important to assess how suitable a space will be for shooting. For a drama, ideally the producer, director, DP, AD, production designer, soundperson, location manager, and other members of the team will scout each location. For a documentary, sometimes just the director and DP go along. A *technical survey* is done to determine:

1. *Direction and art direction.* Is the space adequate for shooting? Are the rooms cramped or is there enough space to get the camera back away from the action? If a dolly will be used, is there room for the tracks? Are the walls, furniture, and artwork usable for your movie or will they need to be changed? Any problems with views out the windows? For an exterior location, will there be a problem with crowd control? A digital camera or *director's finder* (a small handheld finder for viewing a scene at different focal lengths) is useful to block out shots.

2. *Lighting.* What is the natural light and how is it expected to change over the shoot? (Apps for mobile devices like Helios Sun Position Calculator can show which way the sun will be shining at different times of day on a given date.) How much artificial light will you need? Are the ceilings high enough to hide lights out of frame? How much electric power is available; will generators or other sources be necessary? Try to meet with maintenance personnel to check out the power and other issues (see Chapter 12).

3. *Camera.* Will any special lenses be needed (for example, a wide-angle lens for small spaces)? Can the usual camera supports be used or will you work handheld or with a Steadicam? Will you need to adjust camera, filters, or film stocks due to high or low light levels?

4. *Sound.* Is the location quiet enough to shoot? Is it under an airport flight path or near a highway? Do the floors squeak when you walk on them? Is the space too reverberant (see Chapter 11)? Ask if the noise level changes a lot at certain times of day.

5. *Production and support.* What are the restrictions in terms of when filming can take place? Will it be difficult or costly to secure permission? Is there adequate parking or can permits be obtained to reserve more? Are there enough bathrooms? Are there staging areas where equipment, wardrobe, and makeup can be set up separate from the shooting area? Will you need fans or air conditioners to keep the space from getting too hot? Is the location difficult to find? Is there Internet access?

You will usually need a location release and in some locations a permit and/or an insurance bond (see Chapter 17).

Fig. 9-28. A director's viewfinder allows you to view a scene with different focal length lenses, to get a feel for what focal length you want to use on the camera. This iPhone version combines a Zacuto handgrip with the Artemis director's viewfinder app. Director's finders are helpful for scouting locations and planning shots. (Zacuto USA/Chemical Wedding)

Finding a good location that suits all your needs is difficult. Often filmmakers will shoot exteriors in one place and the interior that is meant to represent the inside of that building in an entirely different place. If the production budget will support it, shooting in a studio can solve many of the typical problems of locations. Even on a low-budget production, a quiet space, a few *flats* (movable walls), and some props can take you a long way if you have good lighting and clever art direction.

Backtiming from Production

Shooting a film is a bit like a rocket launch: there are countless things that require lots of preparation so that all systems are "go" when the ship blasts off. As a producer, you should begin preproduction at least three or four months ahead of the first day of shooting. Among the tasks to be accomplished: scheduling, casting, hiring department heads, hiring other crew, arranging for equipment, props, costumes, vehicles, catering, and determining the postproduction workflow. It can take months to get music licenses if you need them for songs performed during the shoot, and other forms of paperwork, including location permits, insurance, and contracts, also take time. For an excellent preproduction checklist, see Maureen Ryan's *Producer to Producer* (see the Bibliography).

THE EQUIPMENT PACKAGE

Equipment Prep

Equipment for a shoot may belong to you, people you hire, a rental house, or a school or other institution (see Equipment, p. 733). Prior to the shoot, the *equipment package* needs to be assembled and tested to be sure everything's working. For camera tests, see Chapters 3, 6, and 7. For audio equipment, see Chapter 11. The night before the shoot, make sure that replaceable batteries are fresh and rechargeable batteries are charged (see Chapter 3).

If you're traveling to the location, use solid shipping cases to protect the gear in vehicles or planes. Many people prefer to hand-carry the camera itself and delicate lenses or audio gear on planes (see p. 270). Bring batteries when hand-carrying; inspectors may demand that you operate the equipment to show it's legit (but see p. 132 for limitations). See p. 285 for shipping film.

Having your equipment and supplies well organized and easily accessible is extremely important. In the pressure of a shoot, you want to be able to quickly put your hands on whatever you need. When shooting with a large crew and plenty of support vehicles, things can be divided into many cases or storage containers. However, when you need to pack light for portability—and especially when working alone—having the right amount of gear in the right cases makes a huge difference. Particularly for documentary work, you'll want a soft shoulder bag or belt bag for batteries and supplies that you can wear while shooting.

Fig. 9-29. The RED Scarlet can capture 5K REDCODE RAW stills and 4K motion. Available with PL mount or Canon EF mount (shown). Also shown: touch-screen LCD monitor, batteries, REDMAG SSD recording media, and module to accept the SSDs. (RED)

A Field Package

The following is a basic list of equipment for a professional field shoot in video or film. Depending on your camera and production style, you may need more or less stuff. Typically, many items are rented; others may be owned by the production group. *Expendables* (supplies like gaffer's tape or gels that will be consumed on the shoot) are purchased before the shoot or supplied as needed during the production. All items are discussed elsewhere in the book.

DIGITAL CAMERA

Camera with zoom lens and/or set
  of primes
Two to four batteries, with charger/
  AC power
Field monitor
Cables for camera-to-monitor
  connection
Soft camera case
Media: flash memory cards, tape,
  solid-state drives; possibly an
  external recorder
Laptop and/or external device for
  downloading; additional external
  drives
ND (neutral density) filters if not
  built in; close-up diopters;
  circular polarizer

FILM CAMERA

Camera body
Lens package: zoom lens and/or set
  of primes
Two or three magazines
Three batteries and charger
85 and ND filters; close-up
  diopters; polarizer
Sound barney if needed
Zoom motor and controller
Light meters; changing bag
Spare film cans; camera tape

CAMERA SUPPORT AND ACCESSORIES

Tripod with fluid head and spreader
Shoulder brace for small cameras (if
  desired)
Matte box, French flag, and/or lens
  shade
Mounting plate with rods
Follow-focus control
Hi hat and/or table stand
Dolly; curved and straight track and
  wedges (if applicable)
Slider (if applicable)
Expendables
See p. 270 for other items

AUDIO GEAR

Cardioid (directional) or
  hypercardioid ("shotgun") mic
Lavalier mic; assorted clips
Wireless transmitter(s) and
  receiver(s)
Fishpole mic boom with shock
  mount
Softie or Zeppelin windscreen
Field mixer
Headphones
Cables for mic-to-mixer and
  camera-to-mixer connections
  (often XLR-to-XLR)
Extra batteries

DOUBLE-SYSTEM RECORDING

(If applicable)
Digital audio recorder
Slate; timecode generator

LIGHTING AND GRIP

Lighting units with stands, spare
   lamps
Small onboard or "Obie" eye light
AC power cables; cube taps or
   power strips
Gels: CTB and CTO (small sheets
   for lights, large rolls for windows)
Spun and/or other diffusion
Collapsible reflector
C-clamps, Mafer clamps, spring
   clamps
Wooden clothespins, sash cord, etc.
Gaffer's tape; black wrap
Dimmers

OTHER LIGHTING AND GRIP

C-stands with arms
Sand or water bags
Flags, silks, nets (various sizes)
Foam-core or white bounce cards
Apple boxes
Duvetyn (black cloth)
Sound blankets
Overhead with silk, net and solid
Tie-in cables and boxes

IN PRODUCTION

After all the preparation, it's time to shoot.

Staying Organized

Create a *production book* that has all the key information needed for the shoot: all cast and crew contacts, directions, names of vendors, budget and financial information, etc. Be able to answer any question that comes up quickly.

Every day during production, an AD prepares *call sheets* that inform every member of the cast and crew when they should report for shooting and what will be filmed that day. The call sheet includes contact numbers, directions, and any other useful logistical information. Mobile apps like *doddle, Pocket Call Sheet,* and *Shot Lister* can also be used to coordinate the production team.

The director should have a shot list for each day. The planned setups and schedule should have been discussed in advance with the production team.

Don't assume that people know the plan unless you confirm that they do. Have backups in case equipment goes down, weather turns bad, or someone doesn't show up.

Preparing the Slate

The *slate* (also called *marker, clapper board, clap sticks,* or simply *sticks*) originated in traditional film production as a way to help synchronize sound and picture during editing. The classic slating device is literally a piece of slate on which information can be chalked, with a hinged piece of wood on top that makes a sharp noise when it makes contact with the board. Modern slates are usually plastic or electronic and often include a timecode display that freezes when the hinged board is slapped down (see Fig. 11-19). There are also slate apps for tablets and mobile phones (see Fig. 9-30).

Slates are used today for digital or film productions shot double system (with a separate audio recorder; see p. 36). When shooting video without a separate audio

SLATE	108	ROLL	24	SCENE	8	TAKE	15

16:23:42.00

PROD	My TV Series	CDL	4	FPS	30
DIR	A. Director	DATE	8/11/11		
DP	D.P. Cameraman	CAM	A	INT NITE	EXT MOS

Fig. 9-30. MovieSlate app for iPhone or iPad. Displays time-of-day (TOD) timecode or you can jam timecode from an external source. A shot log—including scene and take info, notes, and other data such as GPS location—can be exported easily via the Web. A plug-in is available for generating detailed sound reports. (PureBlend Software)

recorder, slating is not needed for syncing purposes; however, it's a good idea to use a slate on all dramas—in film or digital—to visually ID the scene and take number at the head of the take. Even MOS scenes with no sound should be slated for identification ("MOS" is written on the slate). When a slate is used to ID a take, but not for syncing, the hinged bar should not be raised.

Information written on the slate includes the production company, name of project, director, DP, scene and take numbers, and date. If more than one camera is being used, that is usually indicated by letter (A, B, C, . . .). The camera roll number is indicated (which may be a film roll, videotape, or memory card number).[5] The sound take number (if used) and sound roll may also be indicated. A small gray card (see Fig. 8-4) or chip chart will assist in color correction.

As noted on p. 323, there are different ways of notating scene and take numbers. In one common system in the U.S., the scene number alone is used for the first setup of a scene ("Scene 8"), with letters added for each additional camera angle or setup ("Scene 8A" would be the second angle).[6] Filmmakers sometimes use a sys-

---

5. Although memory cards and drives are recycled, i.e., copied and erased for further use, it's a good idea to number them and keep track of their use in case of technical problems with a particular card or drive, which can be traced only if you maintain a clear record of their use.

6. The letters *O* and *I* are often skipped since they look like numbers.

tem that tracks *slate numbers*. The first setup of the first day of shooting is slate number 1 and the slate number increases with each new camera angle until the end of the production (the slate in Fig. 9-30 indicates slate 108, take 15). Numbers are often written on pieces of tape that can be stored on the back of the slate and quickly stuck on the front as needed (obviously not necessary with tablet or smartphone slates). The assistant should increment the numbers immediately after slating to be ready for the next take.

Today, much of the information on the slate can be logged electronically and included as metadata with the picture or sound files (see p. 242). For more on slates and slateless timecode systems, see Syncing Audio and Picture, p. 465.

Shooting a Take

For staged work, there's a basic protocol for beginning each take. The following assumes that double-system audio and slates are being used.

The assistant director announces the upcoming take and calls "last looks" so everyone finishes their prep. The AD then calls for quiet and says "sound." The audio recorder is started, and the recordist says "speed" when ready to record. The AD then says "camera," and the camera operator calls "speed" or "rolling" when the camera is ready to record. The AC reads aloud the scene and take numbers from the slate, says "mark" or "marker" (to help the editor find the sound) and closes the clap sticks.[7] When ready, the director calls "action." Normally, the camera and recorder are not turned off until the director says "cut."

After the take is over, the director should indicate to the script supervisor or person logging if the take is good (*circle take*) and any notes. With digital postproduction, often all the takes are available in the editing room (unlike traditional film, in which only the best takes are printed), but there should be a record of which takes the director liked best.

When shooting the slate, be sure it's large in the frame and in focus so the numbers are readable. If the slate is in place for the very first frame of the take, it will appear in the clip's thumbnail in editing, which can save time. Even when using a slateless timecode system, a clap stick with manual slates may still be done as a backup in case of timecode problems and for scene/take information.

When possible, do *head slates*, which are done at the beginning of the shot. Head slates speed the process of putting the sound and picture in sync in the editing room. *Tail slates*, done at the end of the shot, are sometimes preferable for unstaged documentary filming since they don't loudly announce to everyone that filming is about to begin; they may also be less disruptive for acted scenes where the mood is delicate. However, tail slates can slow down syncing, since you have to locate the end of the take and work backward. The clapper board is held upside down to indicate a tail slate; the person slating should call out "tail slate" or "end sticks."

If either the camera or the audio recorder misses a slate and you have to do it a second time, announce "second sticks" or "second marker" to alert the editor. In any

---

7. If the sound files are labeled with the scene and take numbers, reading them aloud may not be necessary. Different productions use variations on the above protocol.

situation, a gentle slate helps put actors or film subjects at ease. Generally actors should not be rushed to begin the action immediately after the slate.

Fig. 9-31. Slating on a DSLR shoot. (Sean Ellis/SmallHD)

Covering the Scene

Be sure to first read Style and Direction starting on p. 332.

When shooting, ask yourself how the shot you're taking might work with the other shots you've gotten or need to get. Do you have enough coverage—that is, have you provided enough options for editing? Do you have an establishing shot? Cutaways? Have you got interesting close-ups?

Both the order of scenes in the original script and the overall length of the movie are often changed substantially in the editing room. Keep this in the back of your mind as you plan your coverage. Don't paint yourself into a corner so that shots and scenes can only be put together *one* way. Filming a continuous master shot of an entire scene can be time-consuming on set to get everything right. Even if you plan to do the scene in a single shot, surprise errors often show up in the editing room and you'll want to cut around them. Shooting a reaction shot or a cutaway as editing insurance can be valuable even if you don't intend to use it. Sometimes a long take is good, but you need to cut the sequence shorter and your beautiful three-minute shot now becomes a burden.

Directors often concentrate on the characters who are talking. Keep in mind that some scenes are more interesting for the reactions of other characters. When filming a close-up of one actor talking to an off-screen actor, it's a good idea to set a microphone for the off-camera actor as well—the performances from these takes can sometimes be better than the on-camera takes. Higher-budget films often shoot with two cameras simultaneously in this situation.

For very wide shots in which a boom mic can't get close to the actors (and you're not using lavaliers) consider recording the dialogue a few times *wild* (sound but no picture) with the mic in close. This may help you in the edit and is a lot cheaper than doing ADR.

Blocking the camera and actors is a kind of choreography. Keep the image as dynamic as possible. Be attentive to the depth of the space you're shooting in, either to show it or to let actors move through it.

How Many Takes?

Directors differ in terms of how many takes they typically shoot. Sidney Lumet, whose background was early television, liked to rehearse actors prior to the shoot and only film a few takes because the first ones have the freshest performances. Stanley Kubrick, with a background in photography, would often shoot numerous takes in order to groom each shot to perfection. One saying has it that the best takes are the first and the tenth (the advantages of spontaneity versus practice), but the budget may not permit ten takes.

Inexperienced directors tend to shoot more takes and choose more of them as preferred (circle takes). At minimum, always shoot at least two keepers of any shot to have a *safety* in case one gets damaged or has unnoticed technical problems. Even if a take is good, it can be productive to try it again faster or slower or to vary something in the reading or action. Often in the editing room, you wish you had more options to choose from, not just more versions of the same reading and blocking.

When something goes wrong in the middle of a take (*busted take*) try to reset quickly ("back to one") without a lot of chatter and keep the momentum and concentration going. Some directors like to go immediately into a second or third take without stopping to reslate. This can be helpful to actors but may create some confusion in the editing room.

For more, see The Shooting Ratio, p. 360.

Reviewing the Footage

Some directors like to play back each good take on video after shooting it; this can slow production down a lot. However, it's generally a good idea to check the best takes before breaking down a camera- or lighting setup and moving on to the next one.

Looking at dailies is a good way for the director, cinematographer, and others to evaluate the footage as it gets shot, preferably on a relatively large screen. Some directors invite actors to attend dailies screenings; others prefer that actors not see themselves and get self-conscious. Uncut dailies don't look like polished movies—they're repetitive, rough, and often messy. It takes experience to see the potential in the raw footage. On larger productions, dailies are often uploaded to the cloud so that executives and members of the production team can monitor progress wherever they are on a tablet or computer (see p. 94).

On some productions, the editor cuts scenes as they're shot, which can be a good feedback mechanism for the director. You'll either know things are working or you'll see where adjustments need to be made (or even when scenes need to be reshot).

Errors discovered while viewing rushes or during editing often necessitate pickup shooting, which entails going back to get additional shots to fill in a sequence. A documentary crew might return to get a cutaway from a car window, or, in a fiction film, there might be a need for a reaction shot of an actor. Take stills of sets, lighting setups, makeup, and costumes to help match shots that may need to be redone. Many DPs (or their assistants) keep detailed notes about lenses, camera angles, and lighting to facilitate reshoots, some of which may be recorded as metadata in camera files or with an app such as MovieSlate (see Fig. 9-30).

Working with Actors

As much as films vary stylistically, directors vary in their style of working with actors and in the tone they set for the talent and the crew. Some like to plan and control every line and gesture. Others, such as Robert Altman, like to create an environment in which actors are encouraged to experiment with their roles. Some like to discuss deep psychological motivation and others are more interested in basic blocking and line readings. Michael Caine once complained to director John Huston that he didn't give him any instructions. Huston replied, "The art of direction, Michael, is casting. If you've casted right, you don't have to say anything."[8]

As noted above, some directors see rehearsal as a chance to work out ideas with the actors; others prefer to go into the shoot with as much spontaneity as possible.

Whatever your style, do what's necessary so actors can deliver their best performance. Actors are often extremely vulnerable to disruptions of mood and should be treated with respect and deference. Only the director should give performance instructions to actors; anyone else wishing to communicate should tell the director. Particularly in intimate or difficult scenes, some actors prefer that crew members not even make eye contact with them while the camera is rolling (in some scenes it may be best to clear the set of unneeded crew). Use your tone of voice even in calling "action" as a way to set the mood for the take.

Rehearsal is done both for the actors and for the crew. The actors' blocking will affect the lighting and the camerawork (and vice versa). You may want the actors to take part in working out the blocking but don't make them stand around while the lighting crew does its work (that's what *stand-ins* are for). Marks for the camera or the actors to hit are "spiked" with a piece of tape on the floor. Keep in mind that once lighting, props, and dolly tracks are set, your flexibility to change things is limited.

Avoid shouting and arguments in front of the actors (or anyone else, for that matter) and don't involve them unnecessarily in your technical business. Make sure they have a comfortable space to go to off the set to relax.

It's very helpful for the director to get a wireless headphone feed from the sound recordist to hear how dialogue sounds as it's actually being recorded. When a dramatic shoot is done with a live video monitor, there's a tendency for some directors to bury themselves in *video village* (the place where monitors and playback equipment are located, sometimes under cover when shooting outside). This can leave actors feeling isolated. When video village is filled with a lot of people kibitzing over the video monitor, you can easily end up with a "too many cooks" problem.

8. From Michael Caine interview on NPR's *Fresh Air*.

Fig. 9-32. Kibitzing in video village. (Steven Ascher)

Wardrobe, Makeup, and Set

An actor's wardrobe, makeup, and hair can have a huge impact on the look of the movie and on the character's presence on screen. Don't overlook the importance of good makeup and wardrobe as well as art direction. With documentaries, it's often not appropriate to deal with these issues, but in some situations—such as shooting interviews—you can choose the setting, make suggestions for wardrobe, and apply some minimal makeup.

Guidelines for clothing also apply to wall treatments, furniture, and other items on the set.

In general it's a good idea to avoid very bright or very dark clothing. White shirts often burn out (overexpose) when the camera is exposed for proper skin tones, especially in daylight. Pastel or off-white shades work better. Video cameras and particularly DSLRs can react badly to fine patterns like checks and stripes, which can cause moiré patterns (see Fig. 5-18).

Avoid shiny surfaces or jewelry. Washable *dulling spray* or even a little dry soap can be applied to bright items, or lights can be flagged (see Chapter 12) to minimize reflections. When shooting people with glasses, light them from high above or to the side to avoid kicks in the glasses.

Applying makeup is an art and needs to be tailored to individual faces. Facial shine, caused by sweating under hot lights, is a common problem that is easily remedied with a little translucent face powder, which can be brushed on actors or interview subjects and will be totally invisible. Apply the powder first to the brush, not directly to the skin, and touch up faces whenever you see shine. Many cinematographers carry powder in their ditty bag.

Prompters and Cue Cards

Actors may forget their lines. Correspondents or on-camera narrators may be asked to speak long passages directly to the camera. Lines can be written on *cue cards*. When a host or correspondent reads to camera, her eye line must be directed as close to the lens as possible so she won't appear to be reading. A low-budget technique is to cut a hole in the center of the cue card for the lens. A better solution is to use a *teleprompter*, which mounts in front of the lens and displays written copy from a computer (see Fig. 9-33). Larger teleprompters may limit camera mobility and usually require a solid camera support. Smaller teleprompters based on tablet computers and smartphones are lighter and can sometimes attach directly to the lens, permitting use of a handheld camera. Some actors are adept at using an *ear prompter* (also called an *earwig*), which is a miniature receiver that fits in the actor's ear and can be fed wirelessly from a pocket-sized recorder. The actor reads his lines into the prompter prior to the take; then during the take he hears the words played back while he speaks to the camera (this only works for scenes in which no one else talks). It takes practice to talk while listening, so don't let the talent try this for the first time on the shoot.

Fig. 9-33. Teleprompter. (left) In this lightweight ProPrompter model, the person being filmed can look directly into the lens and read, via the partially reflecting mirror, text displayed on an iPad. (right) This bracket holds an iPad displaying text that can be positioned near the camera and controlled from an iPhone. (Bodelin Technologies)

LOGGING

As you move from production to postproduction, it's essential to organize the material that was shot and keep good records of what went on during the shoot. Once you're in the editing room, you'll want to be able to quickly find every bit of picture and sound that was recorded. Several different kinds of logs or reports are used in production.

Basic Log

The simplest kind of log is a record of each take. It's easy enough to create your own log form by making a table with a word processing program. There are also several apps for mobile devices. The log includes information on:

- Date and location.
- Tape number, card number, optical disc, or hard drive. Never have two tapes, optical discs, or film rolls with the same number. Use letters if necessary.
- Scene number and/or description.
- Take number (if any).
- Timecode start for each take. (Usually the starting timecode of the next take tells you the ending timecode of the previous take, but some people note both start and stop codes.)
- Indicate if the take was good; any performance or content notes.

Devices such as ScriptBoy can provide a wireless remote readout of the camera's timecode to aid the person logging (so he or she doesn't have to keep bugging the cameraperson for timecode numbers). When practical, timecode can also be superimposed on a video monitor for the logger. There are various logging apps for mobile phones and tablets that allow you to email the logging file to the rest of the production team. NLEs often provide a way to import logging data as XML text files, which they then map into their own metadata fields.

Fig. 9-34. For logging in the field, the ScriptBoy provides a writing surface with built-in timecode display. The transmitter sends timecode wirelessly from the camera. (Vortex Communications, Ltd.)

In unscripted documentary work there tends to be little time for detailed logging. It's important to write down notes whenever you can, at least at the end of every day, indicating what has been shot and which files/tapes/film rolls cover what.

Continuity Script

For feature films and other scripted work, the script supervisor creates a marked script to show what camera angles were used to cover each page. This *continuity script* serves as a reminder of what coverage has been shot and needs to be gotten, and it tells the editor what shots were filmed during production (see Fig. 9-35). Script supervisors will also create an *editor's daily log* (or similar name), which lists all picture and sound takes in the order they were shot, or at least all the selected takes. The script supervisor will also prepare *script notes*, which include descriptions and comments on each take and may include items about lenses used and continuity issues. Sometimes camera reports include lens settings.

Some systems can upload script information to the telecine shot log to help organize video clips by their content (see Shot Logs, p. 693).

On a feature, a *daily production report* is done every night to track what was filmed that day.

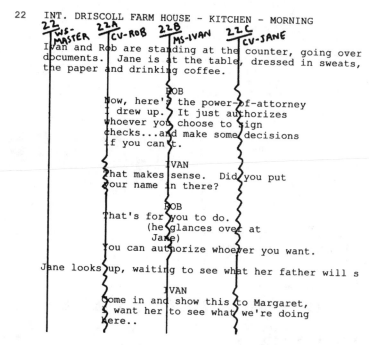

Fig. 9-35. Lined script. Each vertical line indicates a different camera angle or shot that was filmed. Zigzag portions indicate off-camera dialogue or action. The script is normally marked by the script supervisor during the shoot.

Camera and Sound Reports

When shooting film, the camera assistant fills out a *camera report* that indicates every take on a given roll of film, including the length of the shot and any remarks (see Fig. 9-36). Good takes are normally circled when shooting 35mm. This tells the lab which 35mm takes to print and/or transfer to digital. The camera report should also include scene and color information that will help the lab or transfer facility with picture adjustments, such as exterior ("Ext") or interior ("Int"); special instructions ("print slightly red"). Without instructions, the lab may attempt to bring intentionally underexposed scenes (for example, day-for-night shots) or scenes with colored gels (say, at a nightclub) back to normal.

When double-system sound is recorded for film or video shoots, the sound recordist may fill out a *sound report* (see p. 442).

DuArt FILM AND VIDEO
245 West 55th Street   New York, NY 10019
Phone 212-757-4580   Fax 212-333-7647 or 212-977-7448

CAMERA REPORT

Roll # 15   Sheet # 1

Production ON A ROLL   Director H. TESSMAN   Date 6/7/99
                                                           Job #
Camera Person J. BRACK   Assistant A. JULIA
Recordist   Loader   Camera # 610   Mag # 236

Scene#	TK#	SD.	Dial	Ftg	Remarks	Scene#	TK#	SD.	Dial	Ftg	Remarks
22	1		100	110	INT. KITCHEN -WS						
	2		210	100							
	③		310	90	BEST						
	④		400	50							
	5		450	100							
22A	1		550	120	CU - ROB						
	②		670	110							
	③		780	120	tail slate						
22B	①		900	90	CU - IVAN						

OUT AT 990   NEG. TYPE 5279
PRINT 450
NO PRINT 440   EMUL. NOS. 184-1704
WASTE/END 110   EXP INDEX NORMAL

FILM-TO-TAPE TRANSFER SPEED ☑ 24 F.P.S.   INSTRUCTIONS TO LAB TIMER
                            ☐ 30 F.P.S.   Print warm for early morning
                            ☐   PRINT CIRCLED TAKES ONLY
SUBJECT TO CONDITIONS ON REVERSE SIDE.

Fig. 9-36. The camera report accounts for every take on each camera roll. The best takes are circled. In 35mm, usually only circled takes are printed.

SUPPORTING THE CAMERA

The Tripod

The *tripod* is a three-legged camera support. The camera mounts on the *tripod head*, which sits on the tripod's *legs*. Heads designed for motion picture work are able to *pan* (short for *panorama*), which means to rotate the camera horizontally, or to *tilt*, which is a vertical rotation. *Friction heads* for tripods are the cheapest, but they make it hard to pan smoothly. *Fluid heads* have a built-in hydraulic dampening device to make panning much easier (see Fig. 9-37). Their light weight and ease of operation make them the best for most situations. Large cameras are sometimes used with *geared heads* that use two gear wheels to control movement (see Fig. 9-38). These are heavy and take experience to operate but can produce smooth, repeatable movements.

Heads have an adjustment for the amount of drag or dampening for panning (it's easier to pan smoothly when the head "sticks" a little). Most heads made for video cameras have a balancing mechanism, either a spring affair or a forward/back adjustment. When the camera is properly positioned and balanced, it should not move

Fig. 9-37. Fluid heads are the most versatile and easiest to operate. This Sachtler head has seven-step pan and tilt drag controls and a quick-release plate that attaches to the camera and can be snapped on and off the head. The top surface slides forward and back for balance. (Fletcher Chicago/Sachtler Corp. of America)

legs but don't tighten them yet; hold the tripod in a vertical position and press down on it until the legs are even, and then tighten all of them. Point the legs so you can stand comfortably next to the camera. With a ball-in-socket head, loosen the ball and move the head until the bubble on the attached spirit level is centered. If the tripod has no level, align a true vertical (like the edge of a building) with the vertical edge of the frame; or align a true horizontal, viewed head-on, with the top or bottom of the frame.

Quick-release mechanisms save an enormous amount of time mounting and releasing the camera from the tripod head without having to screw and unscrew the connection each time. Avoid tripods that lack a quick-release plate. Tripod legs often have a point or spike at each toe that can be secured in dirt or sand. A *spreader* (also called a *spider* or *triangle*) is a three-armed device that spreads from a cen-

when the head is unlocked. Use the lock on the tripod heads to prevent an unintended tilt, since camera and tripod can fall over.

Tripods have aluminum or carbon fiber legs (which are lighter and more expensive). Standard legs will telescope out to around six feet, and *baby legs* raise to around three feet. Dual-stage legs have three sections, allowing them to go lower than single-stage legs while reaching the same height or higher (see Fig. 9-39). The *hi hat*, used for low-angle shots, does not telescope and is often attached to a board. A *table stand* can be useful for small cameras. Tripod legs and heads are rated by the weight they support; don't use a camera heavier than the rating.

Level a tripod so that the horizon line is parallel to the top or bottom of the frame. Unleveled tripods result in canted shots and tilted pans. To level a tripod, extend one of the legs (loosen the leg lock and tighten at the proper length); extend the other two

Fig. 9-38. Geared head. Arrihead 2 shown with Arriflex 535B 35mm camera. (ARRI, Inc.)

Fig. 9-39. (left) Tripod legs with the spreader mounted midleg can have an advantage when shooting on uneven surfaces. (right) Dual-stage legs (note three sections on each leg) can often go both lower and higher than comparable single-stage legs. This spreader is at ground level and attaches to the tripod feet. (Miller Camera Support)

Fig. 9-40. A tripod that allows the legs to be spread wide permits low-angle shots. An external monitor makes viewing easier when the camera is low or high. (Toby Ralph/SmallHD)

tral point and clamps to each tripod leg; this prevents the legs from sliding out from under the tripod head. A spreader that remains attached to the tripod even when stored for travel saves a lot of setup time. A spreader that attaches midway up the legs instead of at ground level can be helpful when shooting outdoors or on uneven surfaces.

When shipping or transporting a tripod, loosen all locks and drag mechanisms on the fluid head so the head is free to move in its case and is less likely to be damaged by rough handling.

A *rolling spider* or *tripod dolly* (a spreader with wheels) facilitates moving the camera between shots. Don't use it for dolly shots except on the smoothest of surfaces. When no spreader is available, a four-by-four-foot piece of rug can be used. You can tie rope or gaffer's tape around the perimeter of the legs for an improvised spreader.

Some tripods (usually made for still photography) have devices for elevating the center of the tripod. On some tripods this extension may contribute to the unsteadiness of the image; it's usually better to extend the legs. If additional height is needed, mount the tripod on a platform. On larger productions *apple boxes*—strong, shallow boxes of standard sizes—are put together to make low platforms. Apple boxes are available in full, half, and quarter size.

If you'll be shooting with a digital camera for extended periods on a tripod or dolly it's very helpful to have an external monitor or, for a film camera, a viewfinder extension. Remote controls for the lens and camera are available for both video and film cameras. Some mount on the tripod handle; some extend from the lens or camera directly or on cables. When shooting from a tripod or dolly, it can often be difficult to reach the lens or camera switch without them.

Dollies

The *doorway* or *door dolly* is basically a board on rubber wheels with a simple steering mechanism; this is a lightweight, portable, and inexpensive dolly. You can place a tripod on it and anchor it with sandbags. The *western dolly* is a larger version. Though these dollies are steerable, they can't move laterally, as a *crab dolly* can.

A dolly with an integral *boom* provides up-and-down (vertical) movement, which adds enormously to the lexicon of possible shots. A *jib arm* can be used with a tripod and/or a dolly for up-and-down or side-to-side movement. Jib arms are harder to control than built-in booms, but they can provide extended reach for high-angle shots. If the support can reach great heights, it is called a *camera crane*. Industrial "cherry pickers" (like a telephone repair truck) may be used to raise the camera up high for a static

Fig. 9-41. Doorway dolly. Lightweight, affordable, basic dolly. (Matthews Studio Equipment, Inc.)

Fig. 9-42. Dolly with boom permits vertical as well as horizontal movements. (J. L. Fisher, Inc.)

shot, but they don't have the proper dampening for a moving shot that ends with the camera motionless.

Most dollies can be run on plywood sheets or smooth floors. Use air-filled tires when running on pavement. Large tires, especially when underinflated, give smoother motion on rougher surfaces. For the smoothest, most repeatable movements, use a dolly that runs on tracks. Track comes in straight and curved sections of various lengths that can be combined as needed. Track can be used indoors or out, but it needs to be carefully positioned and leveled with *wedges* to produce bump-free, quiet movements. A little lubricant helps stop squeaks. Some dollies with flat wheels can be switched to or mounted on *bogey wheels* or skateboard wheels for track.

There are substitutes for professional dollies—wheelchairs, shopping carts, a pushed automobile, a blanket pulled along the floor or a table. Don't secure the camera rigidly to most of these improvised dollies. Hand-holding or using a Steadicam insulates the camera from vibrations.

The person pushing the dolly (the *dolly grip*) becomes an extension of the camera operator and needs just as much practice and finesse to get the shot right. Keep this in mind when hiring your dolly grip. Even if you don't plan to do moving shots, having the camera on a dolly with a boom can save a great deal of time on the set, allowing you to quickly put the camera in positions that would be slower or impossible to do with a tripod.

Fig. 9-43. Compact jib arms can be used for location and studio work, and can be mounted on a tripod or a dolly. (Miller Camera Support)

Fig. 9-44. Briefcase dolly. Can be used with straight or curved track or on bare floor. The dolly platform folds up, becoming a thin carrying case for travel. (Fletcher Chicago/Egripment USA)

Fig. 9-45. The dolly grip (left) plays a crucial role in executing a well-timed dolly shot.

Fig. 9-46. Cinevate slider permits lateral or vertical moves. Can be mounted on a tripod or on the ground. When doing any kind of camera move, placing the subject or objects in the near foreground helps accentuate the sense of movement. See also Fig. 1-19. (Cinevate)

Short camera moves can be done with *sliders*, which are compact rail systems often small enough to fit on a single tripod. Different lengths are popular, from a mere two feet to six feet and longer. Some are ultralight, designed for the DSLR weight class; others are sturdy enough for the largest 35mm film cameras (and require more support than a single tripod). With even a two-foot slider, the use of a wide-angle lens to emphasize movement through space and a slow, deliberate forward glide or lateral move of six seconds or more can add welcome production value to documentary and dramatic sequences alike. The movement will be most visible on screen if the camera moves past objects in the foreground.

Shooting in a Moving Vehicle

When you need a tracking shot that's faster than what you can get from a dolly, use a motorized vehicle. A vehicle, especially if it is equipped with a shooting platform, is extremely versatile. In general, the larger the car, the smoother the ride. Automatic transmission is preferable, since manual shifting may create a jerky movement. Keep tire pressure low to smooth out the ride. If you're not using a professional camera vehicle, it's usually best to hand-hold the camera to absorb automobile vibrations. It's easiest to achieve smooth camera movement if the car's speed remains constant, and most difficult if the vehicle goes from a stop into motion.

Shooting in the same direction as the moving vehicle results in the motion appearing normal on the screen. Shooting at right angles to the direction of the vehicle makes the car appear to be going roughly twice as fast as it is. At intermediate angles, the speed is between these extremes. Wide-angle lenses increase apparent speed and long focal length lenses can decrease apparent speed (see Perspective Effects, p. 385). By shooting at a higher frame rate you can smooth out unevenness in the ride (similarly, you can slow down normally shot footage, but this won't look as natural).

When shooting action that takes place in a car, you may be able to get the shots you need by shooting from inside the car, which might involve shooting handheld

Fig. 9-47. Suction mounts can be attached to cars, windows, and nonporous surfaces. Car mounts should be set up by experienced persons using safety lines when possible. (Filmtools)

from a passenger seat or mounting a camera inside the car or out. Heavy-duty suction mounts and clamps allow you to attach cameras to the hood or side of the car. The surface must be smooth, clean, and dry to use suction mounts. If the camera is mounted on a moving vehicle or in a precarious spot, be sure to tie it down with safety lines.

For better control and lighting, as well as a wider range of camera angles and moves, larger productions use a camera vehicle to tow the car that the actors are in (which is called the *picture car* or *picture vehicle*) either on a hitch or on a trailer. A trailer facilitates doing shots through the side windows, including dolly moves. Towing the picture car frees actors from having to concentrate on driving while doing their scenes and is safer.

The Handheld Camera

The handheld camera was first experimented with during the silent era, especially in the films of Dreyer, Clair, Vigo, and Vertov. Cameras then were hand-cranked or spring-wound, or they used heavy motors, and sound, if possible, was nonsynchronous. Not until the early 1960s, when lightweight 35mm and sync-sound 16mm cameras arrived—launching New Wave fiction filmmaking and cinema verité documentary filmmaking—was the potential of the handheld camera realized. Not only could the camera now capture new subject matter in new locations, but handheld shooting, at its best, imparted a new electricity to the image. The extreme mobility of a handheld camera permits following every action, achieving a feeling of intimacy and spontaneity impossible when using a tripod- or dolly-mounted camera, which is why handheld shooting is often best in unscripted situations—whether a documentary or with improvised acting.

Sometimes a handheld camera is used specifically to bring a "documentary" feel to the footage, in which case a little bit of shakiness may be desired. On the other hand, a skilled cameraperson can hand-hold with real steadiness, maintaining mobility but keeping the image very stable. Cameras that ergonomically lend themselves to comfortable, balanced hand-holding are often used to squeeze off shots that would take too long to set up otherwise. It is not uncommon these days to see an occasional handheld shot mixed in with mostly tripod and dolly shots. Audiences, whether they know it or not, have grown used to seeing this mix of mounted and handheld shots in both movies and particularly television dramas that are limited to tighter budgets.

TIPS FOR HANDHELD SHOOTING. Shoulder-mounted cameras are the steadiest, because the operator's body braces the camera and dampens vibrations (see Fig. 2-16). Cameras that are held in front of the eye, like small digital camcorders, are harder to hold steady and can feel heavy after a few hours of shooting, especially when you add items like a matte box, focus control, onboard monitor, wireless receiver, portable recorder, and/or light. A single lightweight item can often be mounted to the camera's shoe; others can be attached to rods or a "cage" (see Fig. 10-15). Heavier items, like a wireless receiver, can be mounted on your belt or put in a small shoulder bag with wires to the camera (see Fig. 11-1).

Most small camcorders feature some type of internal image stabilization, which can be very effective. Cameras that don't balance on the shoulder can be used with a brace. Some braces increase stability but still require you to support the front of the camera (see Fig. 3-15). A larger body brace can take more weight off your arms and allow steadier shots, but some cinematographers feel it imparts a mechanical feel to the shooting and makes it harder to respond to unpredictable events or to shoot in small spaces, like a car.

With each different make or model of camera or camcorder you must memorize which way to turn the lens controls for focus, aperture, and zoom. Make up your own memory aid, such as "pull to bring infinity close and bright," which means (assuming the lens is operated with the left hand) pull counterclockwise for farther distances (infinity), to open up the aperture (bright), and to zoom in closer. The controls on your lens or camera may be completely different, so you may need to make up another memory aid for your rig.

To shoot a handheld camera over extended periods of time, it helps if you're in good physical shape. Find a comfortable position for shooting by practicing before you begin. Some people shoot with one foot in front of the other, others with their feet shoulder-width apart. Don't lock your knees; keep them slightly bent. Stand so you can smoothly pan in either direction and move forward or backward. For filming while walking, walk Groucho Marx–style, with your knees bent and shuffling so that the camera doesn't bob up and down.

When you film without a script, avoid excessive zooming and panning, which could produce results that are unwatchable and uncuttable. To get in the rhythm, students should try counting slowly to six without making any camera movements.

When you shoot while walking backward, have someone (say, the sound recordist on a small crew) put his hand on your shoulder and direct you. Try cradling the camera in your arms while walking and shooting; use a fairly wide-angle lens, positioned close to the subject, and keep in stride. Put the camera on your knee when shooting the driver in the front seat of a cramped car.

To steady a static shot, lean against a person or a support, such as a car or building. When shooting landscapes or scenes with strong architectural elements, any jiggles become obvious due to the stillness of the subject. Consider using a tripod or putting the camera on a surface for these shots. The *Steadybag* is like a small beanbag and allows you to perch a camera quickly on a flat or uneven surface for a steady shot.

Documentary filmmaking creates some of the most difficult follow-focus situations, as the camera-to-subject distance constantly changes in unpredictable ways. This is especially problematic with large-sensor cameras that have shallow depth of field. When careful focusing is not possible, zoom to a wider angle to increase depth of field and move the distance ring to the approximate position. As your skill increases, it will become easier to pull something directly into focus by looking through the viewfinder. As previously said, remember that the wider the angle of the lens, the less annoying any camera jiggle will be in the image (see Chapter 4).

Image Stabilization Devices

Image stabilization methods can be used to lessen unwanted camera vibrations and jiggles. These range from common *optical image stabilization* (*OIS*) systems built into small camcorders and DSLR lenses to built-in systems for B4- and PL-mount lenses (by Canon) to lens peripherals (also Canon) to handheld or body-mounted devices, including helicopter and other vehicle mounts. In post, there are numerous software applications to remove unwanted camera shake, notably Adobe After Effects. Most professional editing systems now offer this function; Apple Final Cut Pro X, for example, can automatically stabilize when you import the footage (see p. 593).

INTERNAL IMAGE STABILIZERS. *Electronic image stabilization (EIS)* requires a sensor larger than the actual image itself (or first must slightly enlarge the image) to digitally reposition the image while you're shooting to reduce image shake, which may noticeably affect image quality. For this reason it is found mostly in cheaper consumer camcorders. As mentioned above, internal optical image stabilization is used in DSLR lenses and camcorders favored by professionals to dampen vibration and shake. Experiment to see whether you like the effect of optical image stabilization. Some OIS systems add a slight lag to certain camera movements, giving an unwanted floating effect. Some newer camcorders offer a choice of different levels and types of OIS.

THE STEADICAM. The Steadicam, Glidecam, and similar devices allow the camera to be mounted on a gimbaled arm attached to a harness worn by the camera operator that isolates the camera from body shake, enabling smooth movements (see Fig. 9-48). This enables camera movements similar to those from a dolly, but with much faster setups, shooting in tighter quarters, and significantly increased mobility. Any vehicle—automobile, boat, helicopter—can serve as a platform for dolly-smooth movements. Pans, tilts, running shots, and shots going up stairs can be made with the subtlety of the moves of the human body without any handheld jiggles.

Since the mid-1970s, camera stabilizing systems—first and famously Steadicam—have enabled new camera moves that blend the freedom of hand-holding with the controllability of a dolly or crane. In fact, the very first Steadicam shot ever seen in a movie, from *Bound for Glory* (1976), was produced by Steadicam inventor Garrett Brown riding a tall crane shot all the way to the ground, then hopping off and floating the camera through the movie's set. Prior to Steadicam, this would have been an impossible shot. Alexander Sokurov's *Russian Ark* (2002), a costume-drama romp through the history and galleries of the State Hermitage Museum in Saint Petersburg, is nothing but a single ninety-six-minute Steadicam take—and a virtual encyclopedia of Steadicam timing, technique, and moves.

The impact of a device like this on the language of film shot-flow has been monumental. Not only does it expand the basic repertoire of dollylike shots, but, more important, it creates new relationships between filmmaker and location and between filmmaker and actors. Quick, inexpensive setups relieve the pressure on actors and crew. In documentary, the use of image stabilization devices can be effective for tracking or establishing shots. For filming people in more intimate settings, however, the equipment may be too intrusive.

Although you can respond to unplanned subject movement (unlike a dolly, for which each shot must be blocked), response is slower than that of a shoulder-mounted camera. Steadicam or Glidecam shots have a floating quality that some people find less exciting than well-done handheld shots. And at the end of a move, it is sometimes a challenge to maintain a perfectly stable horizon line without some bobbing.

A Steadicam-type system must be set up specifically for each size, weight, and balance of camera and requires that film cameras be equipped with a video tap for monitoring. Film cameras with vertically mounted magazines or coaxial magazines (see p. 262) work best, since the camera's center of balance remains more stable during a take. The operator needs special training and plenty of practice. Often wide-angle lenses work best when tracking action.

There are various smaller devices designed to smooth out camera movement for small digital cameras exemplified by the Steadicam Merlin (see Fig. 1-15). These are handheld, with no body brace or monitor. With practice, these can provide smooth moves in some shooting situations.

CAMERA MOUNTS. To stabilize large movements (for example, when shooting from a boat) a *gyroscopic stabilizer* can be mounted on a tripod to compensate for motion in the camera platform. When shooting from a helicopter, a Tyler mount or Wescam system can be used to stabilize the camera.

SOFTWARE STABILIZATION. Many software applications allow you to stabilize a shot in postproduction. Some are astonishingly sophisticated and can make a bouncy, handheld shot look dolly smooth. For more, see p. 593.

Fig. 9-48. Steadicam. The camera floats smoothly, isolated from shocks or jarring with springs in the support arm. The operator wears a harness and watches a small monitor mounted on the Steadicam. Steadicam and Glidecam also make smaller, handheld systems for small cameras (see Fig. 1-15). (The Tiffen Company)

SLOW MOTION, FAST MOTION, AND JUDDER

SLOW MOTION

Slow motion can be used to analyze motion or to call attention to motion itself. In Leni Riefenstahl's *Olympia*, a film of the 1936 Olympics in Berlin, the movements of the athletes are broken down and extended in time with slow motion, letting the viewer see things unobservable in real time. Televised sports events often show replays in slow motion ("slo-mo") to analyze the action. Slow motion extends real time, sometimes giving an event more psychological weight. A character's death may occur in an instant, yet be the most important moment in a film. Starting with *Bonnie and Clyde*, countless films have shown the protagonist's death in slow motion, extending the time of death to give it greater emotional emphasis. Today filmmakers often use slow motion to add feeling to otherwise mundane shots.

Slow-motion effects can be achieved in two ways: by running the camera at higher than regular frame rate; and by shooting at normal speed and then slowing the footage down later during postproduction. There can be a noticeable difference between the two methods.

When the camera runs fast, you are capturing many continuous frames in a given period of time (say, 80 frames in a second). This makes the slowed action seem smooth and continuous on playback or projection. This technique is also called *overcranking*.

However, when a film or video camera is shooting at normal speed (say, 24 or 30 frames a second), and you then slow the footage down in post, motion may appear discontinuous and jerky. The slow-motion effect is achieved in post by repeating each frame two or more times, then moving to the next frame. There will be a slight jump when you move to each new frame. Also, the normal motion blur that takes place with any camera and/or subject movement—which is invisible at normal playback speeds—will be more pronounced when normal footage is slowed down (see Figs. 2-14 and 2-15). This effect may be desired, or at times it may just look inferior to true slow-motion shot with a camera running at a higher frame rate.

Software apps like Twixtor and the time warp effect in After Effects can create better slow motion during postproduction by interpolating (essentially creating a new frame that bridges the gap from one frame to the next). If you plan for this, shoot with a fast shutter speed (less than $\frac{1}{2000}$ second) to reduce motion blur.

The effect of overcranking depends in part on the base frame rate of your project. For example, if the rest of the movie is being shot at 30 fps, then shooting at 60

Fig. 9-49. Phantom Flex high-speed digital camera can shoot 5 to 2,570 fps at 1920 x 1080 HD resolution. (Vision Research)

fps will slow motion by half. High frame rates also result in shorter exposure times, which require more light.

High speeds can help minimize the effect of unwanted camera jiggle and vibration. When the camera is handheld or on a moving vehicle, faster camera speeds lengthen the distance between jerky or uneven movements and make the image seem steadier. Of course, any subject movement will also be in slow motion.

High-Speed Cameras

Sometimes very high frame rates are needed for an effect or to capture or analyze fleeting events. If you want to see individual water droplets slowly crashing on the ground or a bullet shattering glass, use a high-speed camera (and sometimes strobe lighting, which is like using a very short shutter speed). High-speed digital cameras, like the Phantom Flex, can shoot 720p HD video at over 6,000 frames per second, and even higher frame rates are possible at lower resolution. As a point of comparison, a camera speed of 250 fps stretches one second of real time into more than ten seconds of 24p film time.

High-speed recording implies very short exposure times, which usually requires a lot of light (and a sensitive chip for a video camera or a fast stock for a film camera). Some cameras can be operated at normal speed and then ramped up to high speed when the key action begins and they'll automatically adjust the exposure.

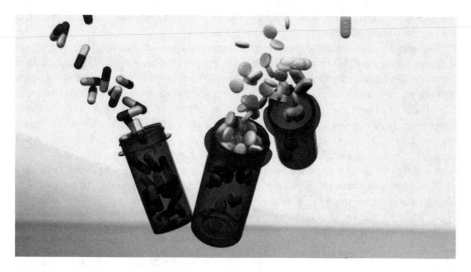

Fig. 9-50. To achieve shots like this, in which rapidly moving objects appear to move slowly but smoothly and are clear and distinct with no motion blur, you need to shoot at a high frame rate and not merely slow down normally shot footage in post.

FAST MOTION

Most film cameras and many digital cameras can be operated at slower-than-normal frame rate (called *undercranking*). This results in each frame being exposed for a greater length of time. For example, shooting at 12 fps gives one stop more exposure than filming at 24 fps. This can be used to advantage in scenes where the light level is too low for exposure at normal speed and there is no movement in the scene—for example, when filming exteriors at night. Keep in mind that any motion, like car headlights, will seem sped up. If shooting in a dark church interior at 12 fps, you might have actors walk at half speed, or move the camera half as fast as usual so the movement will appear normal in playback. If you take undercranked footage and slow it down in postproduction, you can get an interesting ghostlike effect.

Undercranking produces a slower shutter speed. However, it creates a very different effect than shooting at normal frame rate with an adjustable shutter set to a slower shutter speed (see p. 135 and p. 256).

Chase sequences can be undercranked to make motion appear faster and more dangerous. The sped-up motion of silent film comedy was, supposedly, the result of an unintentionally undercranked camera on a Mack Sennett set. You can get this effect by shooting at about 16 to 20 fps and then playing back or projecting at 24 fps.

Time-Lapse

With significantly slower speeds, time is proportionally sped up. In *time-lapse*, the sun can set, a flower can blossom, or a building can be demolished and another constructed in a few seconds (sometimes called *pixilation*). Nonlinear editing systems can speed up shots to create time-lapse sequences from footage shot at normal speed, but for action that takes place over hours or days, you won't want (or be able to) record that much footage to speed it up later.

For very condensed time, you need a camera that can make single-frame exposures. Some digital and film cameras have this option, which may be called *interval recording*. DSLRs are very effective for shooting time-lapse footage and stop-motion animation. Animated films, such as Tim Burton's *Corpse Bride*, have been shot with DSLRs. Filmmakers can put DSLRs on small, motorized tracks to get very exciting moving-camera time-lapse shots. Some film cameras can be used with an *intervalometer* to control time-lapse exposures. GBTimelapse is an app that can provide versatile control of a DSLR and capture images directly to a computer.

Finding the right frame rate for a time-lapse sequence takes some experimentation. Start by estimating how long you want the finished sequence to run on screen. From this you can figure the total number of frames to expose. Say you want to shoot a sunset that takes two hours (120 minutes) and have the shot run ten seconds in the movie. For this example, let's assume this is a 24p digital or film project. Hence, 10 seconds × 24 fps = 240 frames. This means you need to expose an average of 2 frames per minute during the sunset. It's a good idea to start shooting sometime before and continue after the main action to provide flexibility in editing. Unless you're shooting film, it's often safest to record more frames than you think you need in a period of time, and speed the footage up a bit in post if necessary.

Exposures may be programmed for one or several frames at a given time interval or at varying intervals. The fewer exposures at a time and the farther apart, the more jumpy or staccato the motion will look. Single-frame exposures are often slower than the normal camera shutter speed, which can also help reduce flicker when shooting under fluorescents or other pulsed lights. (Avoid fluorescents when possible; if you can't, software plug-ins may be able to reduce flicker in post.) Very slow shutter speeds for each exposure will increase motion blur. You can use this effect to turn car lights at night into colored streaks.

Some time-lapse sequences look best without changing the lens iris or exposure time over the sequence. In this case, base the exposure setting on the light reading at the most important part of the sequence. You could also "ride" the exposure, changing it manually or by using programmed features in the camera or interval-ometer.

In some situations an auto-iris can extend the usable length of the sequence if the light is changing. In others, it might fight with the effect you're looking for: a sunset might look too silhouetted, for example.

Often, a wide-angle lens produces the best time-lapse effect. A wide shot of traffic at a certain frame rate might produce a shot that looks like a fast-moving river of cars; any single car might be seen moving from one side of the frame to the other. However, if you used a telephoto lens to get a long shot of the same scene at the same frame rate, you might end up with a shot that showed individual cars popping into one frame and disappearing in the next. An interesting effect can be had by walking or dollying the camera, shooting a frame or two every step.

Animation

Animation can be seen as a variant of time-lapse photography. A series of paper drawings or paintings on acetate (*cel animation*) is done, with slight changes between the images. A few frames of one drawing are exposed, then the next one is filmed. On projection, the art seems to "move." This technique can also be used for Claymation and other pixilated shots of real objects that seem to move by themselves.

Today, animation is usually generated digitally, but traditional animation can be done with an animation stand and a DSLR or film camera capable of single exposures. In the past, motion-control animation stands such as the Oxberry were used to program moves across an animated or still image. Today it's more common to scan artwork and do the moves in an editing system (see Animating Stills, p. 596).

JUDDER OR STROBING

All motion pictures are based on the illusion that a series of still images, when shown one after another, will appear to have movement. For the illusion to work and for motion to appear smooth, the changes from one image to the next can't be too great. When you shoot video at 60 frames per second (either progressive or interlace) motion tends to look fairly smooth on screen. However, when you shoot video or film at 24 fps, there are fewer images every second, and the changes between frames when either the camera or the subject moves can be greater (see Fig. 2-15). If something moves too quickly, to the audience it can look as though the object is jumping or skipping from one position to the next rather than moving smoothly and continuously. This irregular movement is sometimes called *judder*, *strobing*, or *skipping*.[9] It can give the viewer eyestrain or a headache. Judder is some-

9. The term "judder" is also used to refer to the irregular, sometimes stuttering motion that can result when 2:3 pulldown is used to convert 24 fps material to 30 fps (see Fig. 14-31).

thing to pay attention to when shooting at slower frame rates (like 24 fps) and sometimes even when shooting at higher frame rates when an adjustable shutter is set to a very fast shutter speed.

Judder is most visible in pans, especially fast moves across strong vertical lines. The higher the image contrast or greater the sharpness, the more likely that judder will occur. To minimize strobing when shooting, there are various guidelines or tricks. A rule of thumb is to allow at least five to seven seconds for an object to move from one side of the screen to the other. This applies both when the camera pans or when the subject moves through a stationary frame. If the camera moves or pans *with* a moving subject, the viewer concentrates on the person and is less likely to notice judder in the background. In this situation, use shallow depth of field if possible and focus on the subject, letting the background go soft. Avoid panning across high-contrast scenes that have strong vertical lines. Fast swish pans are usually not a problem. You can get charts of safe panning speeds for different camera and lens settings.

Footage shot with cameras that have relatively small sensors (including SD video cameras, some HD cameras, and 16mm film cameras) may appear to judder more than footage shot with 35mm film cameras or large-sensor HD cameras, in part because shots with large-sensor cameras typically have shallower depth of field, making it easier to throw the background out of focus. Using a slow shutter on a video camera (for example, ¹⁄₂₄ second) may reduce judder. Judder and flicker often look worse in the camera viewfinder than when the image is seen on a normal monitor or projected on screen (see p. 86). However, when it comes to projection on a big monitor or in a theater, bigger screens can make judder seem more severe than on smaller monitors (the jumps in the image are across a greater physical distance). Video projection, because it's brighter, may look jumpier than film.

A phenomenon related to strobing, and frequently referred to by the same term, is often noticed when the wheels of a moving vehicle on the screen seem to be stopped or to be traveling in reverse. This occurs when exposures happen to catch spokes at the same position in consecutive frames (thus, the wheels seem stopped) or catch them in a position slightly behind so the wheels appear to be spinning in reverse.

SHOOTING TVs AND VIDEO MONITORS

There are many situations in which you may want to shoot a video or computer display with either a video camera or a film camera. You may be shooting a scene in which a character is watching TV or you might be getting shots of a website on a laptop.

In some cases shooting video displays is very straightforward. For example, shooting any flat-panel LCD, plasma, or OLED screen with either a video or a film camera usually produces excellent results regardless of the frame rate or shutter speed, at least in most cases.

Sometimes when the frame rate or scanning rate of a display does not exactly match the frame rate or shutter speed of the camera, the screen image will seem to flicker. Many professional and prosumer video cameras have variable electronic shutters. Some have a specific feature to exactly match the shutter speed of the camera to the display's scanning frequency. Sony's system is called Clear Scan; Panasonic calls its Synchro Scan. These provide for a wide range of scanning frequencies that can be dialed in very precisely. Changing the shutter speed of a video camera affects the exposure time, but the basic frame rate is not affected (see p. 135). Don't forget to go back to your normal shutter speed after shooting the screen.

Another approach when shooting a computer display is to change the scanning (refresh) rate of the monitor, using the computer's control panel (Windows) or settings (Mac).

When shooting any display, be sure to white-balance the camera on the display and set exposure carefully. If you want the display's image to look flat and rectangular, shoot with a long lens from a good distance away. Or you might try getting very close and letting some parts of the screen be sharp in the foreground with other parts softer in the background. Sometimes when you focus on the screen you see the pixels too clearly or get a moiré pattern. Try throwing the lens *slightly* out of focus to reduce or eliminate this moiré.

Sometimes people mount a piece of green-screen material over the monitor so that video or computer images can be added later with a chroma key. You might do this if the monitor image isn't available when you're shooting. This is much easier to do convincingly if the camera you're shooting with doesn't move.

When shooting a monitor with a film camera, take a reflected light meter reading, not an incident reading. The color temperature of many monitors is close to daylight (6500°K). Use an 85 filter for tungsten film if you have enough exposure. Some monitors offer a choice of color temperatures. You may need a fairly fast film to get enough exposure.

SHOOTING CRTs. Shooting old-fashioned CRT televisions or video monitors—especially with a film camera—is more complicated since you often get a horizontal *shutter bar* or *hum bar* in the image. Filmmakers working in PAL countries can get a clean image simply by shooting a 25 fps PAL video monitor with a video camera or standard crystal-sync film camera with a 180-degree shutter running at 25 fps. Sometimes filmmakers in NTSC countries will adopt a similar strategy and shoot film at 29.97 fps. When film is transferred to video at 29.97 fps, motion will look normal, but if transferred at a standard 24 fps, motion will appear slightly slowed. Therefore, use of this technique hinges on considerations of frame rate and scene content. Be sure to consult with the transfer house in advance about proper speed for the sound recorder to maintain audio sync.

Another approach to filming a CRT in NTSC countries is to use a film camera with a variable shutter. When filming at 24 fps, a shutter opening of 144 degrees can be used (equals 1/60-second shutter speed), at least for short shots. Some cameras provide a precise 23.976 fps frame rate to perfectly match NTSC's 0.1 percent slowdown (from 30 fps to 29.97), which creates a true frame-rate lock. Motion shot at 23.976 will appear normal when projected at 24 fps and the footage can be transferred to video at real time.

SHOOTING IN 3D

The Basic Idea

Unlike the single camera and lens, we have twin eyes and our visual perception is binocular. The two eyes are required for *depth perception*: How near is that lion? How distant is that lake? How deep is that ravine? Can I reach for that fruit?

When the fourth dimension of time is added, depth perception allows us to perceive velocity. Not only how near that lion is, but also how fast he's traveling toward us.

From cave drawings onward, artists have attempted to represent the three dimensions of space—height, width, and depth—in two-dimensional form. Not until the Italian Renaissance and the development of *scientific perspective* did realism in painting succeed, and it took the invention of cinema in the nineteenth century to incorporate the extra dimension of time in depicting realistic motion. Even so, the outcome was limited to a flat, two-dimensional screen lacking the visual cues needed for genuine depth perception.

Stereoscopy, or 3D imaging, arrived with the birth of photography. By 1840, the English inventor Sir Charles Wheatstone—who was first to explain the role of binocular vision in *stereopsis* or depth perception—had invented a stereoscope for displaying still photos in stereo pairs. Handheld stereoscopes exploded in popularity in the second half of the nineteenth century, as evidenced by their easy availability at flea markets today.

Just as depth perception requires two eyes, stereoscopy requires two images, one for each eye. This means two cameras. Creating dual simultaneous images was feasible using the earliest still cameras but impossible with hand-cranked silent motion picture cameras.

By the early 1950s, theatrical movies dubbed "3D"—three-dimensional—became technically possible and enjoyed a brief heyday, with more than sixty 3D films released in 1953 alone. Notable examples are *Creature from the Black Lagoon* (1954) and Alfred Hitchcock's *Dial M for Murder* (1954). But the technical challenges of manipulating enormous twin blimped cameras (for sound films) persisted, as did the challenges of simultaneous projection of two giant reels each containing a 35mm print, one for each eye. As a result, 3D films died out until the early 1980s,

Fig. 9-51. 3D camcorder. The Panasonic AG-3DA1 has dual lenses and two 1920 x 1080 HD sensors. This kind of one-piece camcorder is easier to operate than 3D rigs that use two separate cameras. (Panasonic Broadcast)

when a second spike in popularity occurred, including *Friday the 13th Part 3* (1982) and *Jaws 3-D* (1983).

This type of 3D filmmaking, using motion picture film, never achieved mainstream status with production crews, audiences, distributors, or exhibitors. Loading and identically exposing two strands of 35mm motion picture film—also developing and printing them identically, with all the costs doubled—was never a picnic; and those funny glasses, whether Polaroid or anaglyphic (red/cyan), which often induced headaches, failed to endear the complex format to the paying public.

Digital 3D

The popularity and commercial success of today's motion 3D (sometimes called *S3D* for stereoscopic 3D, to distinguish it from 3D computer graphics) is driven by the countless advantages of digital video. Compact, silent HD cameras are easily mounted side by side. Since there's no film to load or process, it's possible to view 3D results in real time or upon playback—perfect for realigning the optics, if necessary, for a better stereo experience free of eyestrain.

Even so, 3D doubles the amount and complexity of camera systems: lenses, optical paths, sensors, DSP, frame rate, even storage. All must be perfectly matched and synchronized. Choosing to produce a project in 3D is not a choice to be taken lightly.

The production, postproduction, distribution, and exhibition of digital motion pictures in 3D is an extensive topic warranting its own bookshelf. Since a full treatment of 3D technology and techniques, including the psychophysics of stereo vision, is beyond the means of this book, below is a brief outline of basic 3D concepts and practice, meant as a starting point only.

Fundamentals of 3D Images

The spacing between our eyes is called the *interocular distance* and can range from 55 to 75 millimeters (65mm, or 2.5 inches, is average for adults). The spacing between the two matched lenses required of any 3D camera system is called the *interaxial* distance, the space between the central axis of each lens.

The distance between our eyes, which of course is fixed, is what determines our sense of scale, the depth and size of objects we experience as near and far. Because the interaxial distance between two cameras in a stereo rig can be adjusted, the appearance of depth in 3D space can be collapsed by merely reducing interaxial distance. Increasing the interaxial distance imparts a sense of greater depth.

Convergence (sometimes called *vergence*) is the degree to which two lenses or cameras in a 3D system are angled toward each other, similar to the way our eyes rotate inward as we view an object approaching our nose. As babies we learn both to converge our eyes on an object of interest and, at the same time, focus our eyes on that object.

It's been said that making 3D is easy, making *good* 3D is hard. Many of the problems created for viewers of 3D movies can be found in the fact that when we view 3D, we focus our eyes on a two-dimensional screen, which of course exists at a fixed distance. Meanwhile, because of the 3D effect we are experiencing, our eyes are converging elsewhere, either in front of or behind the screen—an unnatural dissociation of convergence and focus as far as our eyes and brain are concerned (see

Fig. 9-52). Minimizing uncomfortable *vergence/accommodation conflicts* ("accommodation" is the technical term for refocusing our eyes) is the key to making 3D movies that don't tire the eyes.

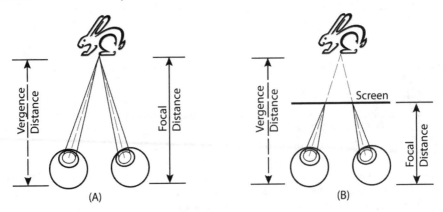

Fig. 9-52. (A) Normally, when we look at an object our eyes converge and focus at the same point. (B) When viewing 3D movies, our eyes focus on the surface of the screen, yet converge at a different point, wherever the object we're looking at is placed.

Angling two 3D cameras to create the illusion of objects behind the screen results in what's called *positive parallax*; placing objects in front of the screen (a spear thrust into the audience, for example) results in *negative parallax*. Consequently, the 3D image area behind the viewing screen is called positive space, while the area in front is called negative space.

The so-called *View-Master effect*, in which objects look like cardboard cutouts, can be avoided by not using long focal length lenses, which flatten object space to begin with.

Production in Digital 3D

Creating a digital 3D movie can be a production process or a postproduction process or a combination of both. A live sporting event on TV is an example of digital 3D that must be captured in production. In contrast, virtually all Hollywood digital 3D movies released before 2010 were shot in 2D, then painstakingly and expensively converted to 3D in post. (The 3D conversion of earlier movies, like *Star Wars*, is sometimes called *dimensionalization*.) However, since 2010, shooting 3D on the set has become the norm due to the arrival of compact digital cinema cameras like RED's Epic and ARRI's Alexa M, which make two-camera 3D rigs more manageable in size and weight. (Think Steadicam.) Additional factors are the growing familiarity of experienced crews with the demands of 3D production and a realization on the part of producers that shooting digital 3D takes about the same time as 2D.

Digital 3D camera rigs take many forms. Countless independent producers have created 3D by placing two identical cameras side by side. Typically, very compact cameras are used for this approach, to get as close to a 2.5-inch interaxial distance as possible. To avoid 3D problems, there must be perfect agreement between the two lenses used for left and right images: identical *f*-stops, no vertical displacement (like our eyes, both lenses must exist on the same horizontal plane), matched geometry for left and right images, and if zooms are used, perfect synchrony in focal length (image magnification), with no center drift in either lens during zooming. It's a tall order, but any deviations will cause eyestrain and entail costly or time-consuming correction in post.

Seen from above

Fig. 9-53. Side-by-side 3D rig. This one uses two GoPro Hero HD cameras (see Fig. 2-8). (Photo by David Leitner)

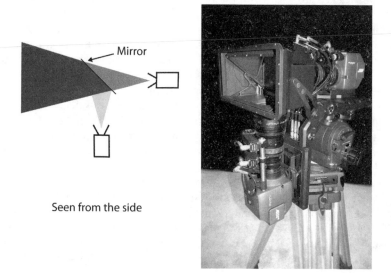

Seen from the side

Fig. 9-54. Mirror 3D rig in which the two cameras (ARRI Alexas) shoot through a partially reflecting mirror. (Photo by David Leitner)

Professional 3D camera rigs come in two basic configurations: side by side and a vertical arrangement featuring a beam-splitting mirror. (See Figs. 9-53 and 9-54.) Achieving a tight interaxial distance is always a problem for a side-by-side rig, limited by the width of the cameras involved. The over/under mirror configuration overcomes this easily, since both cameras can share the same optical axis if they want to. For example, during the production of *The Amazing Spider-Man* (2012), an interaxial distance between 0.25 and 0.75 inch was used throughout. An interaxial distance of 2.5 inches was found to be too wide for shooting objects closer than ten feet without inducing a feel of miniaturization in the scene.

Lastly, a number of consumer and professional all-in-one 3D camcorders have been introduced by Panasonic, Sony, JVC, and others. What they have in common are two side-by-side lenses and two sensor systems bundled into one device. Small CMOS sensors are used, from ¼ inch to ½ inch in size, either arranged as dual single sensors or as dual three-chip blocks. Interaxial distance is fixed by each camcorder's size and design, while adjustment of convergence is achieved by an internal optical element shifted manually by dial or automatically in some cases. Dual image streams are recorded onto file-based flash media in popular compression formats like AVCHD. Onboard viewing is achieved using either 2D viewfinders offering overlays to depict proper convergence or by "glasses-free" *autostereoscopic* LCDs, which flip out from the camcorder in normal fashion. Autostereoscopic displays use *lenticular* screens, which, when held at a close distance from the face, offer each eye a difference image. You're familiar with lenticular screens from postcards that produce animated effects when rotated back and forth. The fine vertical ribs you feel when you touch the front surface of these cards are lenses that magnify different images from different angles, just like an autostereoscopic LCD.

This leads to the issue of how you view or monitor digital 3D during production. Autostereoscopic displays are limited to one viewer at a time. They must be small in size and positioned straight in front of your eyes at a short, fixed distance. Note that this describes the viewing conditions of a cell phone, gaming device, tablet computer held at arm's length, or laptop screen—which is why autostereoscopic displays are beginning to arrive on these devices. Anything larger requires either *passive* glasses, with circular-polarized filters, or *active* glasses, with electronic LCD shutters synchronized to the 3D display (more on this below). For this reason, some choose to monitor 3D shoots in standard 2D, placing emphasis on performance and shot flow, and only later view the results in 3D. Adopting this scenario, peace of mind dictates placing an experienced *stereographer* at the center of the production team.

Editing 3D is an evolving craft. Some edit partway in 2D using either the left- or right-eye recording, then switch to full 3D. Plug-ins to facilitate editing of 3D are available for popular NLEs like Final Cut Pro and EFX programs like Adobe After Effects; there are also plug-ins to detect and correct parallax and alignment errors. Dashwood Cinema Solutions (www.dashwood3d.com) is particularly well regarded for both the information at its website and its plug-ins and software tools for 3D production.

Exhibition and Distribution of Digital 3D

Most commercial theaters exhibiting 3D in the U.S. today use a single-projector system from RealD that alternates left circular-polarized and right circular-polarized images 144 times a second. That equals 72 flashes a second to each eye, or 3 flashes per frame at 24 fps. To preserve polarization, a silver screen is required. (A white matte screen won't work, which is how you can always tell it's RealD.) The viewer wears inexpensive *passive* circular-polarized glasses (thin gray filters), which can be thrown away.

If a theater doesn't wish to replace its perfectly good screen with a costly silver screen, it can use the Dolby system, in which a spinning wheel in front of the digital projector alternates two sets of narrow-band RGB filters. The audience, in turn, wears relatively expensive *passive* dichroic glasses (they reflect colors), which permit one set of narrow-band RGB images to enter the left eye, and the other set, the right eye. These glasses the theater owner does not want you to toss or walk out with.

As an alternative, the theater could install a projection system based on *active-shutter* glasses, in which an alternating LCD filter over each eye is wirelessly synchronized to the projector's output. IMAX has used this technology, but it's the most costly of all.

Flat-screen 3D TVs for home viewing use either circular polarization, which favors cheap glasses, or a system of actively switching left- and right-eye images, which active-shutter glasses are wirelessly synced to. The argument against 3D TVs using circular polarization is that they split odd and even scan lines, so that each eye receives only half of 1080 lines, or 540 lines—half the vertical resolution. This can cause the edges of horizontal action to appear serrated as they did in the days of interlaced CRTs. On the other hand, active-shutter glasses require batteries or charging and are expensive. What parent wants to buy replacements when their kids break, lose, or repeatedly decimate them? And what kid wants to hold his or her head perfectly upright for the proper 3D effect? (You can view a 3D TV with passive glasses lying down or standing on your head, if you wish.) The jury is out on which of these 3D TV technologies will dominate the market, with both types being built and marketed by major TV manufacturers.

Signal standards for 3D TV are in place for cable distribution and several 3D channels are testing the waters. With 3D production costs dropping constantly, with a swelling catalog of 3D box office hits available on Blu-ray, and with growing 3D channels on YouTube and Vimeo, digital 3D appears not to be a passing fad.

CHAPTER 10

Sound Recording Systems

This chapter is about sound and the audio recording equipment used for both video and film. Many of the principles that apply to one type of system are relevant to others. See Chapter 11 for discussion of the sound recordist's role and recording techniques.

SOUND

What we hear as sound is a series of pressure waves produced by vibration. A violin, for example, works by vibrating air rapidly back and forth. When you pluck a string, it makes the body of the violin vibrate—when it moves one way, it compresses the air (pushes it) in that direction; when it moves the other way, that pressure is temporarily reduced. Sound waves travel through the air and cause your eardrum to oscillate (move back and forth) in response to the sound. Like ocean waves breaking on a beach, sound waves alternately press forward and recede back.

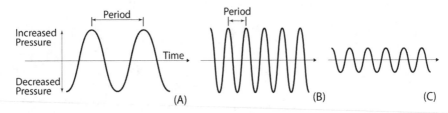

Fig. 10-1. Sound waves. (A) The height of the wave (or *amplitude*) corresponds to loudness. The time from one crest to the next (the *period*) corresponds to the sound's frequency. (B) This is a higher-frequency sound than A—wave cycles occur more frequently in the same amount of time and it sounds higher pitched. (C) This wave has lower amplitude and it sounds quieter.

Loudness

The *loudness* or *volume* of a sound results from the amount of pressure produced by the sound wave (the *sound pressure level*, or *SPL*). Loudness is measured in *decibels* (*dB*), which are used to compare the relative loudness of two sounds. The softest audible sounds occur at the *threshold of hearing*. The volume of normal conversation is about 65 dB above threshold, thus its sound level is said to be 65 dB. The *threshold of pain* is at about 130 dB, equivalent to the noise of a jet passing within one hundred feet.

When we work with recording systems, sound level is expressed in dB units that reflect the electrical voltage (see below). For more details, see Setting the Recording Level, p. 446.

Dynamic Range

For any passage of sound—be it music, speech, or noise—the difference in volume between the quietest point and the loudest is called the *dynamic range*. The human ear has a dynamic range of 130 dB between the thresholds of hearing and pain. The dynamic range of a symphony orchestra is about 80 dB, which represents the difference in volume between the full group playing fortissimo and a single violin playing very softly. Actually, the dynamic range of the orchestra is somewhat lessened by the shuffling and coughing of the audience, which at times may be louder than the quietest solo violin.

Dynamic range is a term used in evaluating audio recording systems, where it is sometimes called the *signal-to-noise (s/n) ratio*. The "signal" is the sound we want to record; the "noise" can be in part system noise from the amplifiers and circuits in the recorder and the microphone. Digital recorders can have a dynamic range up to about 90 to 120 dB or more between the loudest sounds that can be recorded and the *noise floor*, where the sound signal gets lost in the limits of the digital recording format. A bit like the shuffling sounds of the symphony audience, noise determines the lower limit of the dynamic range.

Analog recorders have much more limited dynamic range (up to about 70 dB) due to tape noise or hiss that's always present.

Frequency

Musical notes are pitches; the modern piano can produce pitches from a low A to a high C. The lower notes are the *bass*, the higher ones the *treble*. What is perceived as pitch is determined by the *frequency* of the sound wave. Frequency is a measure of how frequently the waves of sound pressure strike the ear—that is, how many cycles of pressure increase/decrease occur in a given length of time. The higher the frequency, the higher the pitch. Frequency was formerly measured in cycles per second; now the same unit is called a *hertz (Hz)*. Musical notes are standardized according to their frequency. Orchestras usually tune up to concert A, which is 440 Hz. Doubling this or any frequency produces a tone one *octave* higher.

The male speaking voice occupies a range of frequencies from about 100 to 8,000 Hz (8 kilohertz, written kHz). The female speaking voice is slightly higher, ranging from about 180 to 10,000 Hz. The ear can sense low frequencies down to about 20 Hz, but these sounds are very rumbly and are felt throughout the body. At the other extreme, sounds above 20,000 Hz are audible to dogs and bats, but seldom humans. For more on working with voice in postproduction, see Frequency Range and EQ, p. 665.

When sound volume is low, the ear is much more sensitive to midrange frequencies (2,000 to 4,000 Hz) than to low or high frequencies. So if you listen to a music track very quietly, it may seem to lack bass and treble, but if you turn the volume up, the same track will now seem to have a much richer low end and high end. When sound volume is high, the ear responds much more evenly to all frequencies of sound.

Tone Quality and Harmonics

All naturally occurring sounds are made up of a mixture of waves at various frequencies. A violin string vibrates at a basic frequency (called the *fundamental*), as well as at various multiples of this frequency. These other frequencies are called *harmonics* or *overtones*. With tones that sound "musical," the frequencies of the harmonics are simple multiples of the fundamental. Most other sounds, such as a speaking voice or a door slam, have no discernible pitch; their harmonics are more complexly distributed. The relative strengths of the harmonics determine *tone quality* or *timbre*. When a man and a woman both sing the same note, their voices are distinguishable because the man's voice usually emphasizes lower harmonics than the woman's. Pinching your nose while talking changes, among other things, the balance of harmonics and produces a "nasal" tone quality.

Frequency Response

Frequency response is used to describe how an audio system responds to various frequencies of sound. As noted above, at low volume the ear favors middle-frequency sounds, and at high volume its frequency response is more even or flat. A good audio recorder is capable of providing a fairly *flat* frequency response throughout the frequency range of human hearing.

Because all sounds incorporate a spread of frequencies, if you change the frequency response of a recording by increasing or decreasing the low, middle, or high frequencies, you can change the character of the sounds. The bass and treble controls on a radio do this to some extent; most people like to turn the bass up in dance music to make the rhythm, carried by low-frequency instruments such as the bass guitar and bass drum, seem more powerful. *Equalizers* (see Figs. 11-12 and 15-17) are often used to alter the frequencies of sounds during recording or after. With an equalizer, you could boost low frequencies to make, say, a truck engine sound deep, rumbly, or menacing, or you could boost the high frequencies of a piano to make its sound "brighter." If we diminish high frequencies without changing the bass, the effect is like putting cotton in your ears: the sound is muddy and dull.

Telephones have a fairly limited frequency response, which is centered on the middle frequencies needed to understand speech. In movies, the sound of someone talking through a phone can be simulated with an equalizer by cutting the low and high frequencies and boosting the midrange.

HOW AUDIO IS RECORDED

This section is about how analog and digital recording works—the fundamental process of capturing and storing sound. Though most recording is done digitally these days, it's important to understand analog because it's still very much a part of the process.

ANALOG AUDIO RECORDING

In simplest terms, the idea of analog tape recording is to convert sound energy in the air to magnetic energy, which can be stored on tape. When the tape is played back, the process is reversed to reproduce sound (see Fig. 10-2).

The *microphone* responds to sound waves by producing electrical waves that have essentially the same character in terms of frequency and amplitude. Most modern microphones employ an extremely light *diaphragm* that can move with the slightest variations in sound pressure. Mics vary in the way the moving diaphragm generates electricity. The common *dynamic microphone* is also called a *moving-coil* microphone because it has a very light coil of wire attached to the diaphragm. When the diaphragm moves back and forth, the coil moves past a magnet and creates an alternating electric current that flows through the wires in the coil. Thus, sound pressure is translated into electric pressure, or *voltage*.

This voltage travels from the microphone to a *mic preamp* (*preamplifier*), which increases its strength and may supply the mic with power.

In an analog recorder, the sound signal then goes to the magnetic *recording head*. A recording head is an electromagnet, not unlike the ones used in metal scrap yards or that kids sometimes play with. When electricity passes through the head it generates a magnetic field. The head is a C-shaped piece of metal with wire coiled around it. On its front is an extremely narrow opening called the *gap*. The head completes a flow of energy; advancing and receding sound waves become electrical waves, which finally result in a magnetic field that is oriented first in one direction and then in the opposite.

Magnetic tape is made up of a thick support material or *base* and a thin emulsion that stores the information. Tape emulsion is called *oxide* and contains small particles of iron. Each piece of iron is a miniature bar magnet with distinct north and south poles. When a particle of iron passes the gap in the recording head, the magnetic polarity of the particle aligns itself with the magnetic field at the head. When the tape moves on, it maintains that alignment. Since the magnetic field is always alternating back and forth, any given stretch of tape contains groups of particles that alternate in their alignment.

When you play back the tape, it is passed over the same head, or a similar playback head. Now the magnetic field stored in the iron particles creates an electric current in the wires coiled around the head. This signal is amplified and sent to a loudspeaker, which acts like a moving-coil microphone in reverse. Instead of the microphone's diaphragm, the speaker employs a paper cone that is connected to the coil. When current passes through the coil, it moves the cone, which in turn pushes the air to produce sound pressure waves. If you stand in front of a large bass speaker, you can both hear and *feel* the sound waves generated by the paper moving back and forth.

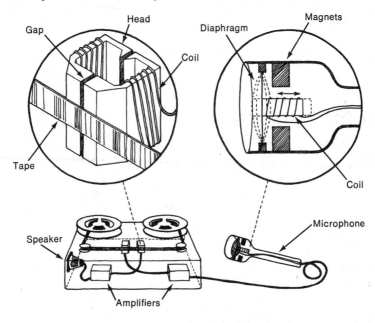

Fig. 10-2. The magnetic recording process. The playback head of the tape recorder is shown in a cutaway view (the width of the gap is exaggerated for clarity). The microphone cutaway shows the components of a dynamic microphone. (Carol Keller)

DIGITAL AUDIO RECORDING

Before reading further, see The Basic Idea, p. 227.

The way digital audio is recorded is similar in many respects to the analog audio process described above. First of all, microphones and speakers are analog, so sound is captured and reproduced using the same equipment regardless of the recording format (the same microphone could feed an analog or digital recorder). The difference is in the way digital recorders process and store the sound.

With analog recording, sound is converted to a voltage; the voltage is converted to a magnetic field, which is then stored on tape. In digital audio recording, we start the same way: sound is converted to a voltage. Then the *analog-to-digital (A/D) converter* processes the sound by repeatedly measuring the voltage level (*sampling* it) and converting those measurements to numbers (*quantizing*). This two-step process is the heart of digital recording. The quality of the recording depends on how *often* we sample the voltage and how *accurately* we measure each sample.

Once we have the sound expressed as digital data we can then store it on flash memory, a hard drive, a CD, tape, or other medium. The basic concepts of sampling and quantizing are quite similar for both video and audio recording. If you understand one, it can help you make sense of the other.

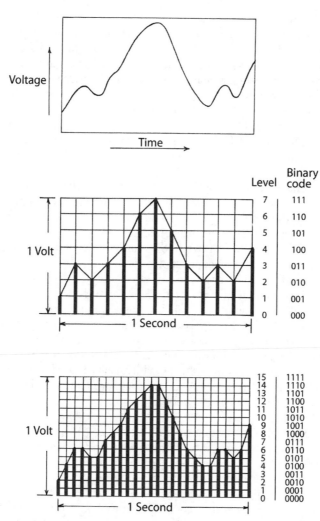

Fig. 10-3. Digital recording. (top) The original analog signal. Note that the voltage level changes continuously over time. (middle) To record the signal digitally, we take *samples* (measurements) at regular time intervals (the vertical lines). The level of the signal at each sample is measured according to a level scale (the horizontal lines). The total number of units in the scale is determined by the *number of bits* in the system; a three-bit system is pictured here. Samples can only be measured in *one-unit increments*. A measurement that falls between, say, level 2 and level 3 must be rounded down to 2 or up to 3. (bottom) This has twice as many samples in the same period of time (higher *sample rate*). And by using more bits (four instead of three), we can measure each sample with greater *precision*. This is a higher-resolution recording that better approximates the shape of the original analog signal. (Robert Brun)

Sample Rate

The first part of the digitizing process is to take a series of samples or measurements of the sound level. Take a look at Fig. 14-24, which shows an audio waveform (a visual representation of a sound). You can see that it's constantly changing (oscillating). High-frequency signals change very fast and low-frequency sounds change more slowly. To accurately measure the level of high-frequency sounds we need to take samples more frequently than for low sounds.

As a simplified example, imagine you're counting the cars of a train going by. When the train is going slowly, you can take your time counting each car (low frequency). But as the train speeds up, you have to count much faster to get an accurate count.

High frequencies are of particular concern because without them, a recording may have poor quality and sound muddy or dull.[1] An engineer named Harry Nyquist proved that the sampling rate has to be at least *twice* the maximum frequency we hope to capture. Because humans can perceive sounds up to about 20,000 Hz (20 kHz), a digital audio recorder needs to sample at least 40,000 times a second (40 kHz) to capture that range of frequencies.

Different digital audio recorders use different *sample rates* (also called *sampling frequency*). Too low a sample rate results in *aliasing*, with poor high-frequency reproduction. The higher the sample rate, the better the frequency response and quality. Increasing the sample rate also increases the amount of data that needs to be stored.

CDs have a sample rate of 44.1 kHz (this rate is sometimes referred to as "CD quality" and is often used for music). Audio on the Web is typically 44.1 kHz. Most video cameras and recorders use 48 kHz, which is a standard professional sample rate. Very high quality recorders used for high-end production and music recording may operate at 96 kHz or even 192 kHz.

Bit Depth or Precision

Sample rate is an expression of how often we measure the audio signal. *Bit depth* or *precision* refers to how accurately we measure each sample.[2]

To get the idea of bit depth, consider this simple example. Say you had to measure people's height with a stick (think of a ruler with no markings on it). The stick is one foot long and you can only record the height in one-stick increments. So you could measure a six-foot-tall man very accurately (six sticks). But when you measure a woman who's five feet, six inches tall, you have to record her height as either five sticks or six sticks—either way, you're off by half a foot.

Now, imagine that we do the same thing with a shorter stick that's only six inches long. We can still measure the man's height precisely (twelve sticks). And when we measure the woman, now we can be just as accurate (eleven sticks).

Digital systems use a measurement scale to record the voltage of each audio sample. The scale has a number of levels. In an 8-bit system there are 256 levels.[3] Each level is the equivalent to one of our "sticks." The quietest sound could be given the level 1 and the loudest would be given level 255. But there's no such thing as a

---

1. If a video recording lacks high frequencies, fine detail in the picture may be lost, making it appear unsharp.

2. Bit depth is also called *bit length* and *word length*.

3. Digital systems use binary (base 2) numbers, and each digit is a *bit*. Eight bits is 2^8, which is 256.

fraction of a level. If the signal level fell midway between 125 and 126, it would be rounded down to 125 or up to 126. Either way, that would introduce an error that could degrade the sound. In the digital audio world, that's called a *quantizing error*; it's a form of noise.

For greater precision we could use more bits. In a 16-bit system (which is fairly typical in professional video cameras) there are 65,536 levels. Now we can measure different voltage levels much more accurately and reproduce sounds more precisely. The more bits used for each sample, the higher the quality and the lower the noise. However, increasing bit depth, like raising the sample rate, increases the amount of audio data to be processed and stored.

Some high-quality recording systems use 20 bits or 24 bits or more. Even though you might not be able to hear the difference between 16 bits and 24 bits, when digital audio gets processed during postproduction, errors get multiplied, so more precision keeps the sound cleaner in the end.[4] Sometimes 16-bit recordings are converted to 24 bits for mixing.

Keep in mind that using more bits doesn't mean recording *louder* sounds. As you can see in Fig. 10-3, the 1-volt maximum signal is divided into eight levels in the middle graph and sixteen levels in the lower graph. The maximum level is the same in both. However, an interesting thing happens at the *bottom* of the scale where the very quietest sounds are recorded. Sounds that are lower than the first level will disappear entirely from the recording (they will be recorded as 0). This is the *noise floor*. But if we use more bits, the first level is now lower, and we may be able to catch quiet sounds that would have been too low to register before. This reduces noise and increases dynamic range.[5]

Resolution and Sound Quality

Together, the sample rate and bit depth contribute to the *resolution* of a digital audio recording. Low-resolution recordings may sound "gritty" or overly crisp ("cold"). When the recording can't capture the subtleties of the original sound, artifacts result, which may be disturbing to the ear. High-resolution recordings sound more faithful to the original sound source in terms of frequency response, dynamic range, and lack of noise.

TYPES OF AUDIO RECORDERS

Today, whether you're working in video or film, you have a wide range of options for recording audio. When shooting film, audio is always recorded with a separate recorder since modern film cameras can't record sound. When shooting video, sound is usually recorded right in the camcorder. However, many digital cameras—particularly DSLRs—lack high-quality audio capability, so external audio recorders may be used for better sound.

---

4. When the sound level is very low—near the noise floor—there is a noticeable difference between 16-bit and 24-bit recording.

5. Systems that use *dither* actually allow you to hear sounds *below* the lowest level. Dither is a special form of low-level random noise. Generally, dither should be used when converting from a high bit depth to a lower one (such as converting 24 bits to 16 bits).

The quality of an audio recording depends in part on the recording format and the settings used, and in part on the quality of the particular recorder. Even a good digital format may sound noisy if the recorder has poor microphone preamps. Before choosing a system, talk to recordists and read reviews.

DIGITAL AUDIO RECORDERS

Types of Digital Recorders

Audio recording technology has come a long way. For years, most professional sound recordists on film shoots used analog recorders with ¼-inch-wide tape (the Nagra recorder was the industry standard). Later, *DAT* (*digital audiotape*) became popular. Today most recordists use digital machines that create audio files that are stored on different types of media—there's no tape involved. This change parallels the evolution of digital cameras that also create digital files instead of recording in a linear fashion onto videotape. File-based recording is "nonlinear": a new file is created whenever you press start on the recorder and each file can be moved, copied, deleted, or played back independently of any other file. This saves time and

Fig. 10-4. The Sound Devices 744T is a file-based digital recorder that can record up to four audio tracks to an internal hard drive, CompactFlash cards, or external FireWire drives. This and similar Sound Devices models are used by many pros. (Sound Devices, LLC)

Fig. 10-5. Tascam DR-680 records up to eight tracks to SD cards. (TASCAM)

offers a lot of flexibility in postproduction.

Digital audio recorders can store
files on flash memory cards, hard
drives, and/or optical discs like CDs
or DVDs. Many digital recorders can
store files on several types of media so
the differences between machines
tend to have more to do with size,
quality, and features than the particular storage system. File-based recording to solid-state media including
CompactFlash, PCMCIA cards (like
ATA flash), and Memory Stick means
no moving parts, so the recorder is
very quiet, needs fewer repairs, and
may be useful for harsh physical environments with a lot of jostling (hard
drives and tape machines don't like to
be treated roughly).

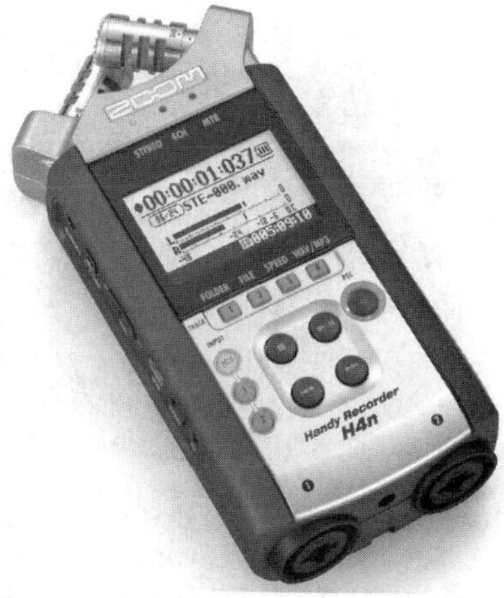

Fig. 10-6. The Zoom H4n Handy Recorder is
a small, affordable device that records up to four
tracks to SD and SDHC cards using built-in
stereo mics or external mics input via either
XLR or phone connectors.

You can also get systems designed
for recording to a laptop or desktop computer; they include a physical box that
contains microphone preamps with professional mic jacks, and a software app for
capturing audio to the computer.

Several digital systems are obsolete or on the way out. DAT machines that use
a small tape cassette are no longer made by Sony. *ADAT* is a system for recording
eight tracks of digital audio to an S-VHS cassette that has been used in the music

Fig. 10-7. The Pro Audio To Go app allows you to record 48 kHz AIFF audio files to an
iPhone using an external mic. See also Fig. 11-12. (Weynand Training International)

Fig. 10-8. A mic preamp like the Tascam US-200 allows you to input mics that have professional XLR connectors to a computer. Digitizes audio at up to 96 kHz/24-bit resolution. Can supply phantom power to mics that require it. (TASCAM)

Fig. 10-9. Apps like Sound Forge allow you to record audio directly to a laptop or desktop computer. Includes editing and mixing capability. (Madison Media Software, Inc.)

industry.[6] *DA-88* machines record to Hi8 cassettes and have been used to deliver final mix stems in the TV industry. *Magneto-optical (MO) discs,* such as Sony's *MiniDisc,* are small and capable of very good sound quality but have fallen into the dustbin of techno-history.

Audio File Formats and Compression

We've seen that the quality of a digital audio recording depends in part on the bit depth and sample rate used. Whatever settings you choose, a good-quality digital

---

6. ADAT is also a protocol for eight-track digital recording that can be used with other recording media.

recorder for video or film work should be able to record the audio file without compressing the data.[7] Uncompressed digital audio is sometimes called *linear PCM*. As long as you have enough storage space, it makes sense to record uncompressed.

Many digital recorders can record audio in a variety of file formats. A standard file format for professional video and film field production is *BWF* (*Broadcast Wave Format*). BWF includes support for uncompressed PCM audio as well as MPEG compressed audio. Broadcast Wave is based on the common Microsoft WAVE (.wav) audio file format but includes an extra "chunk" of information about such things as timecode, date and time, bit depth, sample rate, and so on.[8] This added information is called *metadata* (see p. 242); compared to formats that don't carry metadata, BWF files offer big advantages for managing postproduction workflow. BWF files work equally well on PCs and Macs.

There are two flavors or modes of BWF and they handle multitrack recording differently. *BWFm* (*monophonic*) creates a separate mono file for each channel of audio. So if your recorder can record to four channels simultaneously, when using BWFm you'll get four separate files (they can still be grouped by file name and metadata). Depending on the system and the recording, the files can be put in sync in the editing system either manually or automatically.

BWFp (*polyphonic*) is the other version. Using BWFp, the four channels would be recorded as a single file, with all the tracks interleaved. This is similar to how standard stereo .wav files for music combine the left and right channels in one file. BWFp simplifies editing, but not all editing systems can handle it.

Some recording systems will record to other file formats, including AIFF (.aif), MARF (Mobile Audio Recording Format II), and SDII (Sound Designer 2).

With uncompressed recording, the amount of audio data produced each second (the *data rate*) can be calculated by multiplying the bit depth by the sample rate.

To save storage space, many recorders offer the option to reduce the data using compression such as *WMA* (*Windows Media Audio*), *MP3 audio* (officially named *MPEG2-Layer 3*), or *AAC* (also called *MPEG-4 audio*). Depending on the amount of compression used and what you're doing, compressed audio may be perfectly acceptable for your work or not. Some inexpensive digital recorders are marketed as "voice recorders" because their low-data-rate .mp3 or AAC files are designed for

Fig. 10-10. The Zaxcom Nomad is a versatile mixer and recorder designed for over-the-shoulder use. Can record up to twelve isolated tracks. Able to transmit timecode wirelessly and includes a timecode display that can be used instead of a digislate when needed. (Zaxcom, Inc.)

7. As noted elsewhere, don't confuse data compression used to make smaller files with audio compression used to limit loudness.

8. Standard WAVE files have the extension .wav. Broadcast Wave files can have either .wav or .bwf. Some software can't read the metadata in the BWF file header and will play only the audio using the extension .wav. BWF files may have additional metadata included in iXML format.

longest recording times, not highest audio quality. At the high end of the quality spectrum, FLAC (Free Lossless Audio Codec) compression—file extension .flac—can reduce the data rate without degrading the audio.

Before choosing a file format, be sure to discuss it with the postproduction team!

Recorder Setup

Given the wide variety of technologies and recording systems, it's beyond the scope of this book to go into detail on each. Some general considerations:

SETTING SAMPLE RATE AND BIT DEPTH. Most digital recorders offer a choice of sample rate and bit depth (see above). Most video camcorders record audio at 48 kHz at 16 or 20 bits. A setting of 48 kHz/16 bits is, as of this writing, standard for TV and film delivery and may be the best choice if you're using camcorder audio along with sound recorded separately. However, if you're working with a separate recorder that supports it, you may choose to record at higher resolution. Recording at 24 bits is increasingly common for high-end production. As noted above, increasing either setting will increase the amount of data to be stored (and reduce the amount of time you can record on the media you have).

FILE STRUCTURE AND NAMING. Depending on your system, you may need to format or initialize your hard drive or flash memory in preparation for recording. You may create a "session" or folder for the day's work and/or for each scene. Or you may use a different directory structure for organizing the audio files. Files are easy to lose track of, so good organization will help you stay sane.

You may have a choice about the scheme for naming files. Some recorders automatically generate file names using a number that changes or increments each time you press record. Some recorders can insert the date and time as the file name.

Fig. 10-11. The Zaxcom ZFR100 is very small (2 x 3 inches) and records to MiniSD cards. Can receive timecode wirelessly from the camera, allowing automatic start when the camera rolls and matching code for quick syncing with the picture in post. (Zaxcom, Inc.)

Some machines allow you to manually name files with scene and take numbers; a naming system that can be used with mono Broadcast Wave files is: S002T05_2.wav. This would be scene 2, take 5, track 2. If there are multiple tracks, each has the same file name but the number after the underscore (_2) indicates which track it is so you can put them together later.

You can't have two files with the same name in the same folder; some recorders will add a letter so that won't happen. Depending on the system, a very long take may exceed the maximum file size. Some systems will automatically split the recording over multiple files, which can be seamlessly joined in editing.

Broadcast Wave files are stamped with the time of creation, so check that the recorder's clock is set correctly.

TIMECODE. Some digital recorders are equipped for timecode. See Timecode, p. 223, and Timecode Slates, p. 466.

Recording Media and Backup

Use high-quality memory cards and be sure they can handle the sustained read/write data rate of your recorder. Test cards by recording the maximum number of tracks at a higher sample rate than you plan to use for ten minutes to see if the card can handle the data.

Many audio recorders can write files to two different memory cards or other media at the same time (*mirroring*), which provides an instant backup. See p. 117 for more on media management and backing up files.

Recording

Many digital recorders have familiar controls like a typical tape deck's transport controls (record, play, fast-forward, pause) even though there's no tape and nothing is actually moving.

Setting the recording level is discussed on p. 446.

Many digital recorders have a *prerecord* function (also called a *record buffer*), which captures sound from *before* you press record. Here's how it works: When the machine is on, even if it's in "pause," it's *always* recording, and saving the latest several seconds in a buffer.[9] When you press record, it begins the recording with what's already stored in the buffer. This can be useful for documentary recording, where you may not start recording until you hear something interesting but by then you've missed the beginning of the sentence. When recording for film shoots, some telecines need five to ten seconds of preroll time before the take begins (see Chapter 16); by using prerecord you can capture the preroll automatically. Or, as one recordist put it, even if you're busy eating a doughnut when you hear the director call "action!" you can still get the first part of the take.

Some recorders have buttons that permit you to mark preferred takes (circle takes) for later reference as well as blown takes (false starts to be deleted).

Monitoring

All recorders have headphone jacks. Many will allow you to choose different modes such as mono (all tracks in both ears) or L/R (left channel in left ear only, right channel in right ear only). On a multitrack recorder there may be an option to *solo* one track alone.

On all recorders, you hear the sound as it is processed in the recorder, just prior to being recorded. Some recorders also offer *confidence monitoring*, which means listening to the actual *recorded* sound from file or tape. On a tape recorder, the headphone switch might have two positions: "direct" (or "source") and "tape." The benefit of listening to the recorded sound is that you can be sure everything is recorded satisfactorily and there aren't problems with the tape or file. The disadvantage is that the recorded sound may be delayed by up to several seconds, which can be a bit disorienting for the recordist.

Digital and Analog Connections

Digital field recorders have analog mic inputs for attaching microphones and analog line inputs for recording from other analog sources (see Mic and Line Level, p. 431).

---

9. The size of the buffer varies between machines and may depend on sample rate.

They also have analog outputs for sending the audio to headphones and to various types of analog equipment, such as an amplifier, analog mixer, or speaker system.

However, when sending the audio to another *digital* system (such as a digital mixer or another recorder), it's almost always preferable *not* to use the analog outputs, because that means converting the digital audio to analog and then back to digital again (which can degrade the quality).

For editing purposes, the simplest and best solution with file-based recorders is to do a file transfer to the editing system from the recorder's hard drive or flash memory or to burn a data CD or DVD. Even so, there are many situations where you want to connect equipment digitally before or after recording when a file transfer isn't appropriate.

To pass digital audio data back and forth, professional audio recorders often have digital inputs or outputs that use the *AES* format (also called *AES3* or *AES/EBU*). AES cables use XLR connectors (see Fig. 10-32) or, for the *AES3id* version, BNC connectors (see Fig. 3-14).

The consumer version is called *S/P DIF*. S/P DIF cables are either *coaxial* (electrical) and use RCA jacks, or *optical* and use a *TOSLINK* connector (see Fig. 10-13). Many types of consumer equipment such as DVD players use S/P DIF.

When using any of these systems, be sure to use high-quality cables designed for this purpose, not conventional analog audio or video cables. You can go from a

Fig. 10-12. The MOTU Traveler provides four mic inputs and a total of twenty channels of analog and digital inputs and outputs. A full-featured interface for recording to a laptop in the field. (MOTU, Inc.)

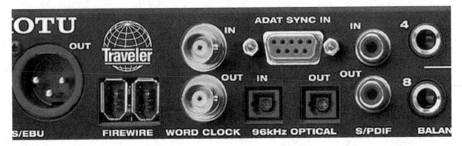

Fig. 10-13. The rear panel of the Traveler provides a good view of various connectors used for digital audio. From the left: XLR (used here for AES/EBU); FireWire; BNC (used here for word clock); nine-pin (used here for ADAT), TOSLINK (for S/P DIF optical); RCA (used here for S/P DIF coaxial); ¼-inch phone jack for balanced analog input. (MOTU, Inc.)

machine with an AES output to one with a S/P DIF input (or vice versa) with the proper adapter.

Digital recorders use a precise timing signal called *word clock*. When two digital machines are connected via AES or S/P DIF, there shouldn't be any variation between the two word clocks. In this situation, one machine may be designated the master and the other the slave to synchronize word clocks.

Another way to transfer audio digitally between video cameras and decks is to use an HDMI, HD-SDI, or SDI link (see p. 237).

AUDIO IN THE VIDEO CAMERA

See Sound Recording for Video, p. 35, before reading this section.

On many video shoots, the camcorder itself is the audio recorder. The audio recording capabilities depend on the particular camera and on the video format. For the basics of operating a camcorder, see Chapter 3. For instructions on setting the audio level, see p. 446.

Mics and Inputs

Consumer and prosumer camcorders usually have a built-in microphone, and professional camcorders typically provide a mount for attaching an external mic. On-camera mics can be very handy when working alone or for quick setups, but they are often too far from the subject to record good sound, they often pick up noise from the camera, and they can have other disadvantages (see The Microphone, p. 420).

The built-in mics on consumer cameras often record in stereo (splitting the sound into left and right channels; see Stereo Recording, p. 461). Some can even record multichannel surround sound. This can be fine for informal recording and for gathering ambient sound or effects. You may also like the feel of stereo or surround sound. However, keep in mind that on professional productions, dialogue is typically recorded in mono, even if the movie is ultimately released in stereo or multichannel sound (see Chapter 15). When using an on-camera mic with a prosumer or professional camcorder you might use a mono mic and record to *one* of the channels.

Another concern with DSLRs and consumer video cameras is that the mic inputs may have only miniphone jacks (see Fig. 10-32) and have no provision for higher-quality mics that use professional XLR cables or that need phantom power (see below). You can get an external preamp unit that has professional connectors (and phantom power if needed) and mounts on the bottom of the camera (see Fig. 10-14).

Sometimes even on a good-quality camera, the mic preamps and audio circuits are noisy or have other defects. Recordists usually prefer to use a separate field mixer (see p. 430) to power the mics and control the volume, using a line-level connection into the camera (see below). Wireless microphones can be connected directly to the camera or through a mixer (see p. 428).

DSLRs often suffer from the trifecta of bad microphones, poor-quality mic preamps, and lots of handling noise whenever you touch the camera. It's worth using an external mic and, for critical recordings, a separate audio recorder as well.

Fig. 10-14. The juicedLink DT454 preamp offers many enhancements for recording audio with a DSLR. Has four mic inputs (XLR and 3.5 miniphone stereo), phantom powering for mics, audio meters, and headphone jack. Provides manual gain control and can disable the camera's AGC. (juicedLink)

Number of Audio Channels

Every video format can record at least two channels of audio, which can be used for recording two separate mono tracks or one pair of stereo tracks. For typical field production, you might put a boom mic on one channel and a wireless mic on the other.

Some formats offer more channels. HDCAM SR can handle twelve. Recording on multiple channels provides more flexibility later, by keeping separate mics separate and not mixed together. However, managing multiple channels can add complexity to the process. If you want to record many tracks (perhaps for a five-channel surround-sound recording) you may have an easier time using a separate audio recorder and recording directly to file.

Audio Quality

Most digital video formats use 48 kHz sampling. Bit depth varies by format: DV, DVCAM, DVCPRO HD, and HDV use 16 bits, which is the most common bit depth for audio recording as of this writing. At a higher quality level, Digital Betacam and HDCAM use 20 bits; HDCAM SR uses 24 bits. DV typically records two channels of audio using a 48 kHz sample rate at 16 bits. Some DV cameras will also record four channels of audio at 32 kHz at 12 bits, which provides much lower quality and should be avoided.

Many prosumer and most professional cameras can record uncompressed audio. This is usually indicated as *PCM* or *linear PCM* and is preferred as the highest quality. Some HDV cameras record compressed audio using MPEG-1 Audio Layer 2 compression at 384 Kbps. This lowered quality may work fine for you, although with some projects it may be better to record uncompressed.

THE ANALOG TAPE RECORDER

The benefits of digital are such that almost no analog recorders are still made. Reel-to-reel Nagra analog recorders have played a venerable role in the industry and some may still be in use.

For an audio recorder to be used for sync-sound work, the speed must be precisely controlled. Digital recorders are generally accurate enough, but with analog, any recorder not specially adapted for sync work will have speed variations that cause the picture and sound to go out of sync. On a Nagra, the *neopilot* (or just *pilot*) tone is a signal that's recorded on tape with the audio. On playback, the pilot is used to control the tape speed (called *resolving*) so the audio plays at exactly the speed it was recorded.

The recording heads on an analog recorder must be kept clean and free from magnetic charge. The first sign of a dirty, worn, magnetized, or improperly adjusted head is the loss of high-frequency sounds—recorded material sounds muddy or dull. Heads should be cleaned with head cleaner or isopropyl (rubbing) alcohol. Buy some head-cleaning swabs or use a Q-tip and clean heads at least every few tapes to remove accumulated oxide.

Fig. 10-15. Everything but the kitchen sink? Mounted on this Zacuto Z-Cage are: a light, an audio recorder, a monitor, and a wireless receiver. (Zacuto USA)

THE MICROPHONE

Microphone Types

A few basic types of microphones are used in film and video production.

Condenser microphones are used extensively. They are often quite sensitive and tend to be more expensive. Condenser mics use a capacitor circuit to generate electricity from sound, and they need power supplied to them to work. Power may come from batteries in the microphone case, on the mic cable, or in the recorder itself. *Electret condenser* mics employ a permanently charged electret capacitor, can be made very cheaply, and may require no power supply.

Dynamic or *moving-coil microphones* are typically used by musical performers, amateur recordists, and many professionals. They are simpler and less sensitive than condensers, but are usually quite rugged and resistant to handling noise and they require no batteries or special power supply.

Fig. 10-16. Electro-Voice 635 omnidirectional dynamic microphone. Simple and durable. (Electro-Voice)

Directionality

Every mic has a particular *pickup pattern*—that is, the configuration of directions in space in which it is sensitive to sound.

Omnidirectional or *omni* microphones respond equally to sounds coming from any direction.

Cardioid mics are most sensitive to sounds coming from the front, less sensitive to sounds coming from the side, and least sensitive to those coming from behind. The name derives from the pickup pattern, which is heart shaped when viewed from above. *Supercardioid* microphones (sometimes called *short shotgun, minishotgun,* or *short gun*) are even less sensitive to sounds coming from the side and behind. *Hypercardioid* microphones (*long shotgun, shotgun,* or *lobar*) are extremely insensitive to any sounds not coming from directly ahead. However, hypercardioid mics (and to a lesser extent supercardioids) have a certain amount of sensitivity to sound emanating from directly behind the mic as well. Because the names for these microphone types are not entirely standardized (one company's "hypercardioid" is another's "supercardioid"), be careful when you select a microphone.

Bidirectional mics have a figure-eight pickup pattern with equal sensitivity on either side; these mics may be used in a studio placed between two people talking to each other.

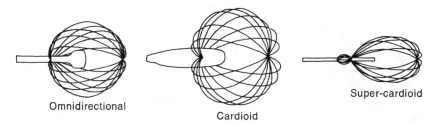

Omnidirectional

Cardioid

Super-cardioid

Fig. 10-17. Representations of the directional sensitivity of omni, cardioid, and supercardioid microphones (not drawn to the same scale). These indicate each mic's response to sound coming from different directions. Imagine the omni mic at the center of a spherical area of sensitivity; the diaphragm of the cardioid mic is at about the position of the stem in a pattern that is roughly tomato shaped. Though the lobes of sensitivity are pictured with a definite border, in fact sensitivity diminishes gradually with distance. See Fig. 10-20. (Carol Keller)

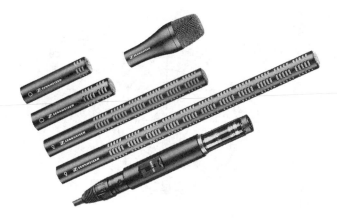

Fig. 10-18. Sennheiser K6 modular condenser microphone system. The powering module is at bottom (works with internal batteries or phantom power). Interchangeable mic heads range in directionality from supercardioid to omni. (Sennheiser Electronic Corp.)

Boundary microphones (sometimes called *PZMs*, or *pressure zone microphones*) are mounted very close to a flat plate or other flat surface and have a hemispherical pickup pattern. These are sometimes used for recording a group of people when the mic can't be close to each speaker, or when recording music (mounted on a piano, for instance).

Manufacturers print *polar diagrams*—graphs that indicate exactly where a microphone is sensitive and in which directions it favors certain frequencies. It's important to know the pickup pattern of the mic you are using. For example, many people are unaware of the rear lobe of sensitivity in some hyper- and supercardioid mics, which results in unnecessarily noisy recordings.

Hyper- and supercardioid microphones achieve their directionality by means of

Fig. 10-19. Mounted on a flat surface, a boundary mic uses the surface to boost its audio response. (Audio-Technica U.S., Inc.)

an interference tube. The tube works by making sound waves coming from the sides or back of the mic strike the front and back of the diaphragm simultaneously so that they cancel themselves out. In general, the longer the tube is, the more directional the mic will be. For proper operation, don't cover the holes in the tube with your hand or tape. Usually, the more directional a microphone is, the more sensitive it will be to wind noise (see Windscreens and Microphone Mounts, p. 424).

Contrary to popular belief, most super- and hypercardioid mics are not more sensitive than cardioid mics to sounds coming

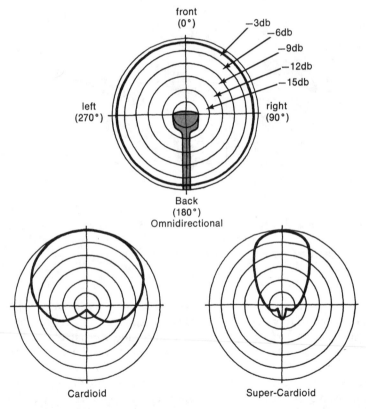

Fig. 10-20. Polar diagrams indicating the sensitivity of omnidirectional, cardioid, and super-cardioid microphones. Imagine each diagram as a cross section of the mic's sensitivity, with the microphone lying along the vertical axis (as the omni mic is here). The microphone's diaphragm would be positioned at the center of the graph. (Carol Keller)

from directly ahead; they are *not* like zoom lenses; they don't "magnify" sound.[10] However, directional mics do exclude more of the competing background sound, so that they can produce a good recording at a greater distance from the sound source—as recordists say, the "working distance" is greater.

One disadvantage of highly directional mics is that you may encounter situations in which it's hard to capture important sounds within the narrow lobe of sensitivity. A classic case is trying to record a two-person conversation with a long shotgun mic: When the mic is pointed at one person, who is then *on axis*, the other person will be *off axis*, his voice sounding muffled and distant. Panning a long microphone back and forth is an imperfect solution if the conversation is unpredictable. In such cases, it may be better to move far enough away so that both speakers are approximately on axis. Unfortunately, the best recordings are made when the microphone is close to the sound source. A less directional mic, or two mics, would be better.

Microphone Sound Quality

Microphones vary in their frequency response. Some mics emphasize the bass or low frequencies, others the treble or high frequencies.

The frequency response of a microphone or recorder is shown on a *frequency response graph* that indicates which frequencies are favored by the equipment. Favored frequencies are those that are reproduced louder than others. An "ideal" frequency response curve for a recorder is flat, indicating that all frequencies are treated equally. Many mics emphasize high-frequency sounds more than midrange or bass frequencies. Recordists may choose mics that favor middle to high frequencies to add clarity and *presence* (the sensation of being close to the sound source) to speech. Some mics have a "speech" switch that increases the midrange ("speech bump"). In some situations, a mic that emphasizes lower frequencies may be preferred. For example, a male vocalist or narrator might like the sound coloration of a bassy mic to bring out a fuller sound. A large-diaphragm mic, like the Neumann U 89, can be used for a "warm" sound.

Sometimes recordists deliberately *roll off* (suppress) low frequencies, especially in windy situations (see Chapter 11).

When you purchase a mic, check the frequency response graph published by the manufacturer. An extremely uneven or limited response (high frequencies should not drop off significantly before about 10,000 Hz or more) is some cause for concern.

One of the things that distinguishes high-quality mics is low "self-noise"—the mic itself is quiet and doesn't add hiss to the recording.

The microphones that come with recorders and cameras are often not great and may need to be replaced. Set up an *A/B test* where you can switch from one mic to another while recording. However, you may find that you prefer the sound of the less expensive of two mics. An A/B test is especially important if you need two matched microphones for multiple-mic recording (see Chapter 11).

---

10. *Parabolic mics,* which look like small satellite dishes (sometimes used at sporting events), actually *do* have a magnifying (amplifying) effect.

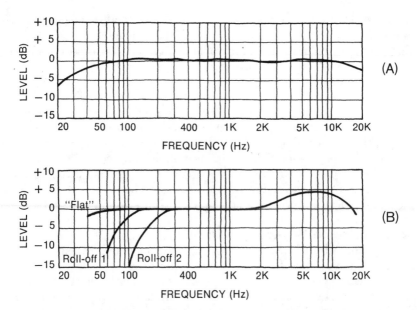

Fig. 10-21. (A) The relatively flat frequency response of a good-quality audio recorder. Where the graph drops below the 0 dB line indicates diminished response. (B) A microphone frequency response curve. This mic is more sensitive to high frequencies. The three parts of the curve at left represent increasing amounts of bass roll-off controlled by a built-in, three-position switch (see p. 459). (Carol Keller)

Windscreens and Microphone Mounts

The sound of the wind blowing across a microphone does not in the least resemble the gentle rustle of wind through trees or the moan of wind blowing by a house. What you hear instead are pops, rumble, and crackle. When recording, don't let wind strike a microphone (particularly highly directional mics) without a *windscreen*. A windscreen blocks air from moving across the mic.

Fig. 10-22. (left) Rycote rubber shock mount and pistol grip. (right) The Rycote Softie windscreen works well in windy conditions. (Rycote Microphone Windshields, Ltd.)

A minimal windscreen is a hollowed-out ball or tube of *Acoustifoam*—a foam rubber–like material that does not muffle sound (see Fig. 8-10). This kind of windscreen is the least obtrusive and is used indoors and sometimes in very light winds outside. Its main use is to block the wind produced when the mic is in motion and to minimize the popping sound caused by someone's breathing into the mic when speaking.

For breezier conditions, a more substantial windscreen is needed. Many recordists carry a soft, fuzzy windscreen with built-in microphone mount, such as the Rycote Softie (see Fig. 10-22). A Softie can also be used to cover a camera mic. For heavier wind, a windscreen called a *zeppelin* can be used.[11] Like its namesake, this is large and tubular; it completely encases the mic. In strong winds, an additional socklike, fuzzy covering can be fitted around the zeppelin. A good windscreen should have no noticeable effect on the sound quality in still air.

When you are caught outside without an adequate windscreen, you can often use your body, the flap of your coat, or a building to shelter the mic from the wind. Hide a lavalier under clothing or put the tip of a wool glove over it (see below). Often, a bass roll-off filter helps minimize the rumble of wind noise (see Chapter 11). Omni mics may be the least susceptible to wind noise.

Besides wind noise, microphones are extremely sensitive to the sound of any moving object, such as hands or clothing, that touches or vibrates the microphone case. *Hand*

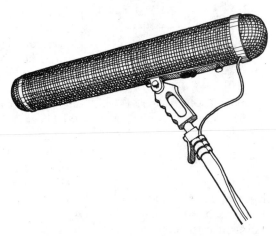

Fig. 10-23. A zeppelin windscreen for a shotgun mic, shown with a pistol grip and mounted on a microphone boom pole. (Carol Keller)

noise, or *case noise*, becomes highly amplified and can easily ruin a recording with its rumbly sound. The recordist should grip the microphone firmly and motionlessly, grasping the looped microphone cable in the same hand to prevent any movement of the cable where it plugs into the mic. Even better, use a pistol grip that has a shock mount (usually some form of elastic or flexible mounting) to isolate the mic from hand noise (see Fig. 10-22).

In many recording situations, a *fishpole* (collapsible) boom should be used to enable the recordist to stand away from the action (see Figs. 1-1 and 1-28). A shock mount will isolate the mic from hand or cable noise on the boom.

11. In the UK, windscreens are called "windshields," and zeppelins may be called "blimps."

Lavalier or Lapel Microphones

Lavalier microphones (lavs) are very small mics generally intended to be clipped on the subject's clothing. Also called *lapel mics*, these are often used with a wireless transmitter (see below) or may be connected by cable to the recorder. Most TV news anchors wear one or two lavs clipped on a tie or blouse. Lavaliers are quite unobtrusive and are easy to use when there isn't a sound recordist. Lavs are often

used for interviews because they can result in clear, loud voice tracks. They're useful for recording in noisy environments because they're usually positioned so close to the person speaking that they tend to exclude background sound and the reverberation of the room. However, this also results in a "close" sound, which sometimes sounds unnatural. Many professional recordists don't like using lavs and prefer the sound from a good cardioid or hypercardioid mic on a boom because it's more natural, more "open," and it doesn't risk clothing or body noises. In some situations like interviews, recordists will mic with a lavalier on one track and a boom mic on another. The lav should get a clear voice track; the boom, if it's a good mic, may actually get a better voice track but will also get more of the room sound. Avoid mixing both mics on the same channels in the field, and even if you record to separate

Fig. 10-24. Lavalier mic. The Tram TR-50 is widely used by ENG video crews. Shown here with a vampire clip for attaching to the outside or inside of clothing.

channels, be careful in post because you can get phase cancellation if both mics are up (see p. 460). Some good lavaliers, like the Sanken COS-11D, sound surprisingly similar to boom mics and the audio from the two can intercut well (see Fig. 10-26).

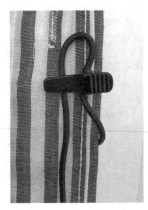

Fig. 10-25. When clipping a lav on clothing, make a loop with the cable under the clip in back to keep the cable neatly tucked in and to provide strain relief so any tugs on the cable won't pull directly on the mic.

Most lavaliers are omnidirectional, although cardioid lavs are available. Many have a flat frequency response. However, when you clip a mic on someone's shirt you may get too much bass (from being right over the chest cavity) and not enough treble (since the mic is out of line with the speaker's mouth). Some lavs have a mid-range speech bump (see Microphone Sound Quality, p. 423), which can compensate for an overly bassy source.

A good position for a lavalier is in the middle of the chest at the sternum (breast-bone). For subjects wearing a T-shirt or sweater, sometimes the mic is clipped on at the collar. The problem with collar placement is it may be too close to the subject's voice box and and/or cause sound variations if the subject turns her head away from the mic. If the subject is looking generally in one direction (perhaps for an inter-view), put the lav on that side of her collar.

There are various types of clips and mounting systems (not all are available for all mics). Most have standard clothing clips. A *vampire clip* has two pins and mounts flat against clothing (see Fig. 10-24). Some mics have rubber enclosures for mount-ing under clothing.

Often it is preferable to hide the mic; for shooting dramatic material, it's essen-tial. Clip or tape the mic under clothing, but listen carefully for case noise caused by the cloth rubbing on the mic. Silk and synthetic fabrics are the worst for noise; cotton and wool are often fine. Small frames or cages are available to provide sepa-ration between the cloth and the mic. You can improvise with some rolled-up tape to prevent rubbing. Some recordists prefer to tape the clothing to both sides of the mic to keep it from moving on the mic case.

Leave enough slack in the cable so that the body movements don't pull on the mic; make a small loop in the cable for strain relief and tape or clip it in place (see Fig. 10-25). Sometimes you can get better sound by hiding a lav in the subject's hair or a hat. Carry some moleskin or surgical tape for taping mics to skin. For more on using lavaliers, see Chapter 11.

Fig. 10-26. The Sanken COS-11D lavalier has a very small capsule that can be hidden in clothing or hair. The mic would normally be tucked under the tie's knot to hide it. Also comes with a rubber sleeve that can be taped inside clothing. (Steven Ascher)

Wireless (Radio) Microphones

Both camera and subject gain greater freedom of movement with a *wireless*, or *radio*, *microphone*. A wireless isn't really a mic at all, just a radio transmitter and receiver. In a typical film or video shoot, a lavalier mic is clipped on the subject and plugged into the concealed transmitter, which is about the size of a pack of cards. A receiver mounted on the recorder or camera picks up the signal with a short antenna. Wireless sound quality is sometimes not as high as with *hard-wired mics* (mics connected by cables), but wireless systems can work beautifully and are used regularly in professional productions. High-end systems can cost thousands, although much more affordable wireless systems costing a few hundred dollars are surprisingly good. Some systems are digital, others analog, and some combine both technologies.

Fig. 10-27. Wireless mic. Sennheiser evolution wireless system with bodypack transmitter, receiver, lavalier mic, XLR cable, and plug-on transmitter for handheld mics. This affordable UHF wireless system offers a wide choice of frequency bands so you can avoid radio interference. (Sennheiser Electronic Corp.)

Using a wireless opens up many possibilities for both fiction and documentary shooting. You never need to compromise camera angles for good mic placement, since the mic is always close to the subject but out of view. In unscripted documentaries, there are great advantages to letting the subject move independently, without being constantly followed by a recordist wielding a microphone boom. Some people feel uncomfortable wearing a wireless, knowing that whatever they say, even in another room, can be heard. As a courtesy, show the person wearing the mic where the off or mute switch is. Some recordists object to the way radio mics affect sound perspective: unlike in typical sound recording, when the subject turns or walks away from the camera wearing a wireless, the sound does not change.

A wireless transmitter and receiver can be used for many purposes: to connect a handheld mic, a standard boom mic, or a mic mixer to the camera or recorder; or to transmit timecode or a headphone feed on the set.

Wireless transmission is not completely reliable. Depending on any physical obstructions and competing radio transmissions in the area, wireless signals may carry up to several hundred feet or they may be blocked altogether. Newer wireless systems offer a choice of radio frequencies, usually within a particular range or "block" (systems that offer multiple frequencies are called "frequency agile"). There have been big changes and restrictions in the frequencies that are legally available for wireless audio. Talk to a recordist or dealer to find the frequencies that are legal and likely to be interference-free in the area where you're shooting; lists of open frequencies should also be available on the websites of wireless manufacturers such as Sennheiser and Lectrosonics.

Always position the receiving antenna as close to the transmitter as possible. If the signal breaks up (either gets noisy or is lost altogether), experiment with different antenna positions. Try tuning to a different channel and make sure the transmitter and receiver are on the exact same frequency. Some systems broadcast on more than one frequency simultaneously to avoid breakup. "Diversity" radio mics use multiple antennas for the same reason. Inexpensive consumer wireless systems can get interference from many household sources. Avoid electric motors, computer monitors, and other electronic interference. Make sure the *squelch* control is properly adjusted to prevent noise when the radio signal is lost.

Check and/or replace transmitter and receiver batteries every few hours.

Many lavalier mics are available with connectors designed for a particular wireless transmitter, allowing them to get any needed power from the transmitter and keeping the cabling compact. Try to get a mic matched to your wireless.

Most professional wireless transmitters use a limiter (see p. 454) to prevent excess volume levels. Many models have a level adjustment and some have a light to indicate excess volume. With the subject speaking normally, turn the level up on the transmitter

Fig. 10-28. Lectrosonics wireless receiver with superminiature transmitter. Lectro makes some relatively affordable units, but many are very high-quality, expensive systems for pros. (Lectrosonics, Inc.)

until the light flashes often, then turn it down a bit. For more on level adjustments, see Chapter 11.

Wireless receivers can be mounted directly on a camera with various brackets or plates. For handheld work with a small camera, this may increase the camera's weight noticeably, especially when more than one receiver is used.[12] You can also put receivers on your belt or in a shoulder bag with a wire to the camera (see Fig. 11-1). It's important to match the output level of the receiver to the audio input on the camera or recorder. Some receivers work at line level, others at mic level, and some are switchable. For more on this, see Mic and Line Level, p. 431, and Gain Structure, p. 455.

12. Zaxcom makes a wireless system that can transmit two audio channels to one receiver, lightening the load a bit.

An Alternative to Wireless

There are some very small recorders that can be placed on the subject to record independently of the camera. These include small flash memory recorders, such as the Zoom H4N (see Fig. 10-6) or the higher-end Zaxcom ZFR100 (see Fig. 10-11). These could be used instead of wireless or if you don't have enough transmitters or if radio reception is poor. You need to sync the audio in editing (see Recording Double System for Film and Video, p. 464). The ZFR100 can be controlled wirelessly with the camera's timecode signal, allowing remote start and stop from the camera and autosyncing in the editing room.

Fig. 10-29. Portable microphone mixer. The Shure FP33 is an affordable analog mixer, used by many crews over the years.

Field Mixers

A *field mixer* or *microphone mixer* allows you to take inputs from various audio sources, combine and control them, and then output the signal to a camera or recorder. A mic mixer could be used to control a single boom mic (see Fig. 1-28) or to balance multiple mics (such as combining a wireless with a boom mic). Sometimes when recording a person giving a speech in a lecture hall, instead of using your own mics you get a house feed from the facility's public address (PA) system. A field mixer can be used to control that signal before recording it.

Most mixers have two or more input channels to control the level of different inputs and one or more master faders to control the level of the combined output. A new generation of mixers combine mixing and recording capability in one unit (see Figs. 10-10 and 10-30). For more on mixer controls, see p. 640.

Microphone Power

The electric power needed to run a condenser microphone may come from a battery in the mic or on the cable. Power may also come from the mic preamp (sometimes called just a "mic pre") in the camera, recorder, or mixer; the most com-

Fig. 10-30. Sound Devices 788T twelve-track, high-end audio recorder, shown with 552 mixer. The 552 mixer can also record digital audio internally to SD or SDHC media. (Sound Devices, LLC)

mon version of this method is 48-volt *phantom power* (the mic input is often labeled "+48V"; see Fig. 10-31).[13] Phantom power frees you from carrying an extra set of batteries for the mic. Always check that your mic is compatible with the power supply before plugging it in or you could damage the mic (dynamic mics and some condensers—especially those that have their own batteries—should not be used with the +48V setting).

On some recorders, if the microphone input is set up for phantom powering, it will not accept dynamic mics or condensers that have their own power; but on many machines it can be switched either way. Phantom powering sometimes involves rewiring microphone cables to reverse, or "flip," the phase, making them not interchangeable with normally wired cables.

AUDIO CONNECTIONS

Microphones, mixers, and recorders can be connected in various ways. Not all are compatible and they may need an adapter or device to make the connection work. It's worth learning the names of connectors used for audio cables. All connectors have male and female forms; the male is sometimes called the *plug*, the female, the *jack* (see Figs. 10-13 and 10-32).

Mic and Line Level

The audio inputs on many cameras and recorders can be switched between *mic level* for taking signals directly from microphones and *line level* for connecting other types of audio equipment. Professional gear may have a three-way switch: "line," "mic," and "mic +48V" (see above). On some machines, there are separate sets of inputs and outputs at mic and line level. Some systems have a *trim control* to tweak the level of an input up or down to better match the source to the recorder.

If you have a choice, it's generally advantageous to use line inputs and outputs

13. Another flavor of phantom power is 12V *T-power*.

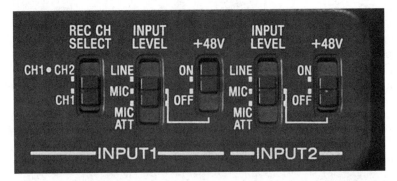

Fig. 10-31. Audio input selector on a Sony camcorder. Note choice of input level including Line, Mic, and Mic ATT (short for "attenuator," this reduces the level by 20 dB for loud situations). When mic input is selected, you can choose "+48 volt" for condenser mics that require phantom power or select Off for self-powered condensers and dynamic mics. (Sony Electronics, Inc.)

to connect mixers, recorders, and wireless receivers. The line level is much stronger than mic level and less susceptible to interference. Never plug a line-level signal into a mic-level input or damage could result. If you plug a mic-level signal into a line-level input, the signal will be weak, but you may be able to boost it enough to be usable.

Another thing to keep in mind is that line level comes in a professional version (+4 dBu) and a lower-powered consumer version (which may be indicated as –10 dBV).[14] This means that if you plug the line output of a consumer camera into the line input of a professional deck, the signal may be too quiet and possibly noisy. Going the other way (from the line output of a professional machine to the line input of a consumer machine), the signal may be too loud and possibly distorted. A *line pad* or *attenuator* can be used to reduce signal level. Also, professional line outputs are usually balanced, while consumer line outputs are usually unbalanced (see below).

Balanced Cables

Interference and hum from nearby power lines, automobile engines, fluorescent lights, and radio stations can be a problem. The best solution is to use a microphone and recorder that are connected by a *balanced cable*. In a balanced mic cable, the two wires of a standard cable are enclosed in a sheathlike third wire that insulates them from electric interference (see Fig. 10-32). Balanced cables can usually be recognized by the three contacts, instead of two, in the connectors at either end. Most professional audio gear that has balanced inputs or outputs uses either XLR cables or cables with three-contact ¼-inch plugs (also known as *TRS* for *tip, ring, sleeve*). If a piece of equipment has only RCA or ⅛-inch mini connectors, these are not bal-

14. The consumer version is actually about 12 dB lower than pro level. The dBu scale measures voltage relative to a 0.7746 volt reference, whereas the dBV scale uses 1.000 volt as a reference. So consumer level is the equivalent of -7.78 dBu.

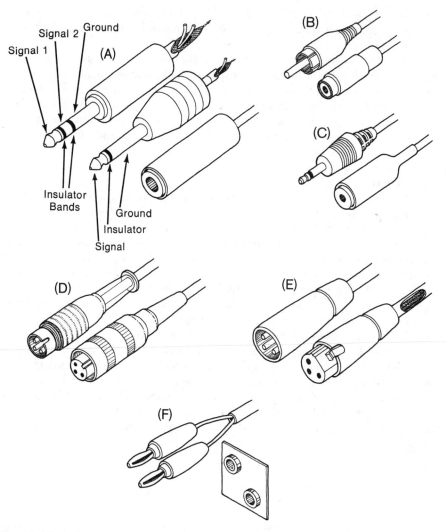

Fig. 10-32. Audio connectors. (A) ¼-inch males and female. A three-contact (also called TRS) stereo plug is at left, a two-contact (TS) mono plug is in the center. The three-contact version can be used for balanced cables. (B) *RCA* or *phono* male and female. (C) *Mini phone* or simply mini male and female. This is a miniaturized version of the ¼-inch connector (diameter is ⅛ inch—3.5mm—instead of ¼ inch). There is a stereo version of this plug, recognizable by the two black insulator bands (see A). There is also a *sub-mini* plug that's even smaller—2.5mm. (D) Three-pin *Tuchel* male and female. The sleeve on the female engages the threads on the male. This Tuchel is a variant of a *DIN* connector. (E) Three-pin *XLR* or *Cannon* connectors. The male and female snap together. Both XLR and Tuchel connectors may have more than three pins. The female XLR is pictured with the insulation cut away to show the balanced or stereo cable with the two signal wires encased in the sheathlike ground. (F) *Banana* plugs and jacks. For more audio and video connectors, see Figs. 3-14, 5-14, and 10-13. (Carol Keller)

anced inputs so mic cables will be susceptible to interference. If you connect a balanced mic cable to an unbalanced cable or unbalanced input using an adapter, the signal will not be balanced.

Whenever you get electrical interference, try moving the recorder or the cable to another position. In the field, it can help to wrap the microphone cable, especially the connectors, or even the recorder, in aluminum foil. Sometimes when you connect two pieces of equipment, a low (50 Hz or 60 Hz) humming sound results if either piece is plugged into the AC wall current. If this happens, connect a ground wire between the case of one machine and the case of the other or ground them both to a common point.

Impedance

Impedance is a measure of the resistance of any audio device to the flow of electric current. Impedance, sometimes represented by Z, is measured in *ohms*. The impedance of a microphone may be low or high; the same is true for the microphone input on the mixer or recorder. Usually, professional microphones with XLR connectors have low impedance. It is important to use a low-impedance mic with a low-impedance mic input, or a high with a high. Exact matching is not necessary.

Historically, low impedance was 600 ohms (often written 600 Ω) or less, while high-impedance devices were around 10,000 (10k) ohms or more. Today many mics and camera inputs have impedances in the range of 100 to 2,000 Ω and most modern mics, cameras, and recorders should work fine together.

Low-impedance equipment is preferable because it allows you to use up to several hundred feet of microphone cable without picking up hum and interference from AC wall current and radio stations. With *high-Z* (high-impedance) equipment, lengths over six to ten feet may result in various types of noise. If you're using an old mic or recorder and impedances are mismatched, use a *matching transformer* on the mic cable. Try to put it closest to the piece of equipment with the higher impedance.

CHAPTER 11

Sound Recording Techniques

This chapter is about methods of recording audio for video and film. See Chapter 10 for discussion of audio recording equipment.

PREPARING FOR A SHOOT

GATHERING GEAR

Lists of useful audio equipment for a video or film shoot appear on p. 367. Here are some considerations in choosing audio equipment.

Recorders and Formats

When shooting video, the choice of camera is usually driven by picture needs, but it clearly has an impact on sound as well. In selecting a system, you must consider: How many audio channels do you need? Does the camcorder allow manual adjustment of audio levels? Can you use external mics? Are there professional mic connectors (such as XLR) or will you need adapters? If you're working with a sound recordist, will you need a mic mixer so he or she can control levels? Does the camera record audio in a highly compressed format or with a low sample rate that might compromise quality?

For film or double-system video shoots, the recordist has more freedom in choosing a recorder. This decision should be made on the basis of what features are needed, the cost, and how postproduction will be done. Many of the questions mentioned above apply here as well. How many channels do you need? Can you easily input professional-type mics? Do you need timecode? What digital format will you use? How will files be exported from the recorder for archive and postproduction? Do you have enough storage media? How will the deck be powered in the field? Do you need a shoulder case? Are the controls easily readable in daylight? Sometimes when a recorder is too small, or has badly arranged controls, it may be hard to use in high-pressure situations.

Spare batteries and an AC power connection for the recorder should be kept on hand.

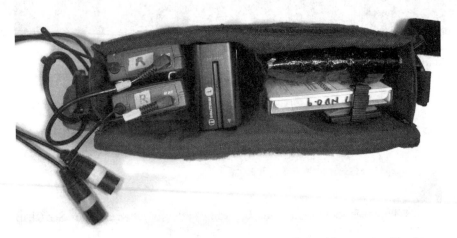

Fig. 11-1. For documentary and handheld shooting, a small shoulder pouch—like this one by Portabrace—can be used to carry spare batteries, filters, memory cards, and accessories. Shown here, two wireless receivers are connected by cables to the camera, but sit in the pouch to keep the weight off the camera.

Microphones

Unless you can carry several mics, your choice of a primary microphone is crucial. Many recordists prefer a short shotgun, which is directional enough to exclude some background sound but has a wide enough pickup pattern for general uses. This type of mic is good for unpredictable documentary or dramatic scenes. The Sennheiser ME 66 and the Røde NTG2 are lower-cost versions; the Sennheiser MKH 60 is more expensive. When shooting alone, these can also be mounted on a camera.

Having a cardioid mic, which is less directional, can be useful for dramatic scenes with more than one character speaking, and for documentary interviews or scenes in relatively quiet locations. For noisy locations, a long shotgun mic, like the Sennheiser MKH 8070, can be useful to help isolate voices when you can't get close to the subject (a sporting event, a news conference). Long shotgun mics tend to be big and awkward, and the narrow pickup pattern is often too directional for recording in tight quarters. In documentary work, subjects can find them intimidating.

Modular microphone systems allow you to use one power supply with several heads of varying directionality (omni, cardioid, and supercardioid; see Fig. 10-18). This provides a great deal of flexibility. There are modular systems at both ends of the price range.

Always try to have at least one backup microphone and cable as insurance. If the second microphone is more directional or less directional than your primary mic, you'll have more flexibility. Lavalier mics (see p. 426) are very small, pack easily, and can be used for general recording in some situations.

For dramatic work and any kind of controlled shooting, a microphone boom is essential to allow the mic to be positioned close to the sound source while keeping the person holding the mic out of the shot (see Figs. 1-28 and 9-27). Typically, re-cordists carry extendable booms that can be adjusted for each shot. Studio mic booms are mounted on a pedestal to relieve the boom person of the considerable fatigue that results from holding a boom all day. For smaller, mobile crews, borrow a stand from a lighting kit and get a bracket so you can mount the boom on it; this is particularly useful for situations such as sit-down interviews or scenes in a drama in which actors aren't moving.

In some documentary scenes, the boom may be too big or intrusive. The mic can be handheld (with or without a pistol grip shock mount) for more intimate situations. A short table stand for the mic can be handy at times.

Headphones

The choice of headphones is also important. For controlled shooting situations, it makes sense to get headphones that have good fidelity and closed ear pads that fit around the ear. These block any sounds coming directly to the recordist without having gone through the microphone first, so you can be sure of the recording without being misled by other sounds around you. Open headphones are light-weight and more comfortable. They usually rest on top of the ear (*supra-aural*). With these, you may not hear some defects that will be apparent on a better sound system. Sometimes sound leaking out of these headphones may be picked up by the mic.

Fig. 11-2. (upper left) Headphones with closed ear pads. (upper right) Headphones with open ear pads. (bottom) Mono earpiece shown with mono connector; stereo-to-mono adapter (so you can hear both channels from the camcorder); and right-angle adapter (so the plug doesn't stick out from the camcorder).

One problem with headphones that fit around the ear for unstaged documentary filming, especially when a directional microphone is used, is that the recordist can hear only sounds he or she expects to hear; if someone speaks outside the mic's range of sensitivity, the recordist will not hear or react to it. Some documentary recordists just put the headphone over one ear so they can better relate to people and react to events.

If a boom person is handling the microphone separately from the recordist, that person should have his or her own headphone feed.

Some camcorders have a small speaker at the operator's ear. All cameras can be used with a wired earpiece that goes in one ear. These are not intrusive and they allow you to respond to what's going on around you. They aren't great for close monitoring of the sound (it's easy to be fooled by what you hear in the *other* ear that's hearing the scene without the earpiece), but you'll hear major problems like breakup or loss of audio.

Stereo headphones should be used with a mono adapter when you are recording only one channel of audio so that you can hear it in both ears. Some headphone outputs can be switched to mono for that purpose. A mono earpiece may need a stereo adapter if you're recording stereo so you can hear both channels.

Other Equipment

A typical professional video package includes a field mixer (see p. 430). Get a *breakaway cable* with a *headphone return* line in it (see Fig. 11-3). This allows the recordist to monitor the sound coming from the camcorder (as a check that the signal is really there), and it breaks apart easily so the camera and sound recordist can separate quickly.

One or more wireless microphone systems (see p. 428) will greatly increase your mobility and flexibility for both film and video shoots.

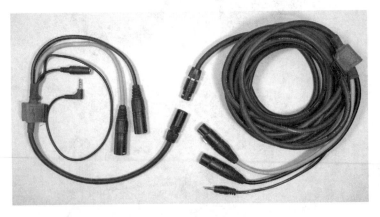

Fig. 11-3. Breakaway cable. The part of the cable on the right plugs into the mic mixer's output. The part on the left is the *pigtail* that plugs into the camera's input. In the middle is a breakaway link for quickly disconnecting the camera from the mixer when needed. Also included is a headphone feed from the camera to the mixer.

Recordist's Tools and Supplies

Having a few tools at hand can mean the difference between easily finishing a shoot and canceling it. After looking online or consulting a technician, even inexperienced persons can often make adjustments or isolate what needs to be repaired.

Permanent felt-tip marker (e.g., Sharpie)
Spare batteries for recorder and mic
Sound report sheets or log
Flash memory cards
CDs or DVDs for backup
External hard drive
Small roll of gaffer's tape

For maintenance and repairs:
Head-cleaning cassette (for videotape or DAT)
Swiss Army knife with scissors
Screwdriver handle and detachable blades: two sets, medium and jeweler's size
Small needle-nose pliers with wire-cutting edge
Small volt/ohm meter ("multitester")
Battery-operated soldering iron, rosin-core solder
Short length of light wire

Preparing the Recorder

Equipment should be checked thoroughly before using. This is especially important if it has been transported, was used by someone else, or came from the rental house. School equipment is often more likely to be malfunctioning than working properly. Many recordists check their equipment whenever they arrive at a new location for shooting. The preparation you do depends a lot on the particular technology you're using. If anything in this list is unfamiliar, look elsewhere in this chapter and in Chapter 10.

1. *Check the batteries.* If possible this should be done with the machine running in "record" position to see how the batteries read under load. Many rechargeable batteries will read fairly high on the meter until they are ready to give out, then the voltage drops sharply, so be prepared if the reading seems at all low. See Batteries and Power Supplies, p. 127, for more on managing batteries.

2. *Check the settings.* There are numerous settings; here are a few to check: Is the limiter or AGC on or off? If recording digitally, what about sample rate, bit depth, file formats? Scan through physical switches and menu selections. Check the manual if you're unsure about any settings.

3. *Timecode and/or pilot.* For a timecode-capable recorder, make sure the timecode can be properly recorded and played back. On analog sync recorders, check that the pilot signal is actually being recorded on tape.

4. *Microphones.* Do you have cables? Windscreen? Various clips for lavs? Are the recorder inputs set correctly for mic level (and phantom power if needed)? Wireless mics should be checked for clear radio channels (without interference) and fresh batteries.

5. ***Clean the heads.*** This should be done as a matter of course for analog recorders (see p. 419). For video cameras that record to tape, or DAT machines, it may not be necessary unless there's evidence of a problem. For most digital recorders, this does not apply.

6. ***Test the audio.*** Do a test recording and listen to it carefully for defects. Check the meter. Make sure you can move the level control without causing static. If there is static, moving the control rapidly back and forth a few times can help. Set the headphone level adjustment, if there is one. Gently move the recorder, cable, and microphone while listening through headphones to be sure there are no loose connections. This should not produce noise or static.

If you can't get the recorder to work properly, systematically isolate various components. Try a different mic or mic cable; plug the mic into a different input; make sure the recorder is not in "pause"; check the AC/battery power switch (if there is one); try running the recorder on AC power; try cleaning the battery contacts with an eraser or grit-free abrasive; and so on.

Before going out to shoot, coil up excess cabling and fasten with Velcro cable ties (see Fig. 11-4). Make the recorder and/or mixer package as neat and compact as possible. It's much easier to concentrate on recording if you can move without getting tangled up. For handheld work, carry the recorder on the side of you that allows easiest access to the controls and the meter, and put some padding under the strap to spread the load. Wear soft-soled shoes and clothing that doesn't rustle.

Recordists on feature films often use a *sound cart* as a platform for mounting the recorder, mixer, and accessories that can be wheeled between setups (see Fig. 1-41).

Fig. 11-4. Cable tie. This Velcro fastener can be used to keep coiled cables under control. (Fletcher Chicago/The Rip Tie Company)

THE SOUND RECORDIST'S ROLE

The sound recordist is responsible for placing the microphones (although someone else may hold them), operating the recorder or mixer, and making sure that the quality of the recording is good. For staged (controlled) work, the recordist, also known as the *production sound mixer*, can usually experiment with various mic positions and monitor the level of a rehearsal before shooting begins.

On video shoots, the recordist usually does not control the camcorder, but he or she must ensure that the sound actually recorded in the camera is acceptable. When possible, this means monitoring from the camera with headphones and/or doing periodic playback to check the recording.

For staged work, there is a standard protocol for starting each take; see Shooting a Take, p. 370.

For unstaged documentary shooting, the recordist should be alert and attentive to the action and not be glued to the meters. With time, your judgment will make you less dependent on the meter. Recordists should be respectful of actors or subjects when placing body mics. Some recordists bring a newspaper to the set and pretty much tune out when they're not recording. Try not to "disappear" on set. Staying alert will help you and others do their jobs. On some sets, people in the sound department are treated like second-class citizens. The recordist may be forced to find mic positions only after all the lighting and blocking is done, making his job harder. He may also be blamed for airplanes flying over and the dog barking next door.

Communication

On all productions, crew members must communicate with each other. The camera operator must be able to signal to the recordist (or boom person) that he is in the frame, and the recordist must be able to indicate his need to change position. Sometimes in documentary work, only the recordist can hear whether a scene is worthy of being filmed. For all of these reasons, the filmmakers should have a set of signals with which to communicate silently. If these are hand signals, they should be sent with minimal commotion, so as not to disturb actors or documentary subjects. This requires that crew members watch each other as well as the action. The recordist, or whoever is operating the microphone, should try not to position himself on the camera operator's blind side (which is usually the right), and the camera operator should frequently open her other eye so that she can see the recordist while shooting. This is most important when filming improvised or unstaged action. After a crew works together for a while they begin to predict each other's needs, and eye contact precludes the need for hand signals.

If circumstances are such that a good-quality recording can't be made, the recordist should say so. If an airplane makes a take unusable, tell the director when the take is over (some directors want you to signal the problem during the take; smart directors will be looking at you as soon as they hear the plane). The director must decide whether to try to salvage a take with ADR or other postproduction cures (hence the solution for every conceivable production problem: "We'll fix it in the mix!").

Labeling and Managing Media

When recording to videotape, the tape box should be clearly labeled with the production title, production company, tape number, date, frame rate, timecode type (drop or nondrop), reference tone level, and any special track assignments (such as "Lavalier Ch. 1, Boom Mic Ch. 2").

When recording to file, either in the camera or using a separate audio recorder, this information can be noted in the log (see below), spoken into the microphone and recorded, or sometimes included in metadata in the file. Additional information may include sample rate and bit depth (which is often 48 kHz at 16 bits).

When recording audio to file with a flash memory or hard drive system, take care in organizing file names; keeping track of drives, memory cards, or optical discs; making backups; and all the other details that will prevent the disaster of losing irreplaceable recordings due to carelessness or a corrupted file. See Managing Data on the Shoot, p. 117.

If recording to tape, develop a system to keep track of which tapes have been recorded and which are fresh (if you reuse tape, it is especially easy to get confused). Cassettes have little record-inhibit tabs that should be pushed in after recording to prevent accidental rerecording.

A reference tone is traditionally recorded at the head of every videotape, audiotape, or other recording, though with digital it is not as useful. This is discussed on p. 452.

Logging

For a video shoot, someone may be assigned to keep logs of all the takes (see p. 376). On a double-system digital or film shoot, the sound recordist often keeps a *sound report*, which is a paper or digital log of each take, noting the length, any problems, and whether the director considers the take good or bad (similar to the camera report in Fig. 9-36). On some productions, a *sound take number* is given each time you record audio (and is included on the slate). This identifies each piece of sync and wild sound. Since sound take numbers advance chronologically throughout the production (unlike scene numbers), in conjunction with the log, they aid in locating pieces of sound and picture. When you're recording to file using a hard drive or flash memory recorder, the system may automatically assign a take or event number to the file name or user bits.

Some NLEs can read the metadata information in a Broadcast Wave file, including scene/take, time of recording, and other info. There are also apps that can automatically generate a sound report from BWF files.

In unstaged documentary work, there's no time for meticulous log keeping. Instead, if using a separate audio recorder, the soundperson can record a quick message after every shot or two, describing what was filmed, if there were problems with the slate, and so on; this can save a great deal of time in the editing room. It's a good idea to keep an informal log, listing the contents of each sound roll or group of files.

Before recording *wild sound* (sound recorded without picture) identify it as such by speaking into the microphone. In some cases you may want to record wild sound to a separate tape or media, especially if a telecine transfer will be done.

RECORDING TECHNIQUE

The general objective in sound recording is to place the microphone close enough to the sound source to produce a loud and clear sound track. A good track should be easily intelligible; lack strongly competing background sounds, unpleasant echo, or distortion; and be reasonably faithful to the tone quality of the original sound. Once a good recording is in hand, you have a great deal of freedom to alter the character of the sound later as you choose.

Placing the Microphone

The ideal placement for many mics is between one and three feet in front of the person speaking, slightly above or below the level of the mouth. If the microphone is directly in line with the mouth, it may pick up popping sounds from the person breathing into it. A windscreen helps. If a directional mic is too close, it will bring out an unnatural bass tone quality. This is the *proximity effect*, which results from the particular way low frequencies interact with directional microphones. If a microphone is too far from the subject, background sound (*ambient sound*) often competes with or drowns out the speaker's voice. Also, undesirable acoustic qualities of the recording space, such as *echo* and *boominess*, become more noticeable (see below).

The microphone's position is almost always compromised by the camera's needs. It's important, however, that the sound source be solidly within the pickup pattern of the mic. Generally a boom mic will be brought in from just above the camera's frame, as close as possible without getting in the shot (see Fig. 8-10). The boom operator should practice during rehearsals. Be attentive to mic shadows—you may need to move away from a light to avoid them. Ask the camera operator for a frame line before the shot begins so you know how far in you can go.

Keep in mind that sound diminishes with distance from the sound source. Sound pressure is inversely proportional to the distance; thus, moving *twice* as far from the sound source diminishes the sound to *half* of its previous level. If the recording level of the sound seems low, especially with respect to louder background sounds, you must get closer to the sound source and not attempt to correct the problem by turning the level way up on the recorder.

Many beginners think the recordist should try to capture all sounds in a general fashion, standing back from, say, a party, a conversation, or a street scene to record all the sounds together. The result of such recordings is often an indistinct blur (which indeed can be useful in some scenes). However, usually the recordist should instead select individual sounds and get close enough to record them clearly. If an overall mix of sounds is desired, it may be necessary to put together several distinct tracks later.

For documentary filming in noisy conditions, you may need to get closer to the subject than you feel comfortable doing. A few experiences with scenes ruined by bad sound will help overcome shyness. Another approach to a noisy situation is to use a lavalier mic on the subject with a wireless transmitter to get the mic in close while allowing the recordist to stand back.

Shooting a group of people at a dinner table or conference table can be difficult. A boom mic is hard to manage if the conversation is unpredictable (and can be really distracting if it swings around wildly trying to catch everyone who talks; using two booms can help). Sometimes you can place a couple of omni mics or lavs in the center of the table and go wireless to the camera or recorder. Or try using a boundary (PZM) mic (see Fig. 10-19). Some lavs have a bracket so they can be taped facedown on a surface as a kind of boundary mic. Be careful about the sound of objects being put down on the table. You may need to keep the mic off the table surface or give people a cushion—say, a placemat for cups and glasses—to soften the noise of putting things on the table.

For placing multiple microphones, see p. 459.

SOUND PERSPECTIVE. Whenever you put a mic very close to the sound source it minimizes both background sounds and the natural reverberation of sound reflecting in the recording space. In some situations a close mic sounds artificial. For example, if the camera is filming a distant long shot and the mic is very close, the recording will lack the proper *sound perspective*. Although distorted sound perspective is found regularly in movies, you may not like it. To correct this, the recordist could move farther back, but at the risk of sacrificing clarity. Alternatively, during the sound mix you could lower the level and maybe use equalization and a little reverb to give a sense of distance to the sound (see Chapter 15). Similarly, any missing ambient sounds can be added later by mixing in additional tracks. These kinds of effects are usually handled better under the controlled conditions of sound editing than they are while making a live recording. You can always *add* background sounds, distance effects, and equalization during sound editing and mixing, but nothing can make a noisy, echoing, or weak recording sound pleasing and clear.

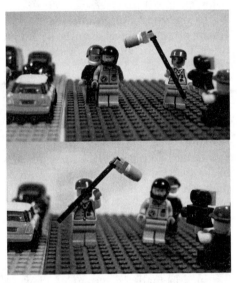

Background Sound

Ambient sounds are the background sounds that surround any recording space. They can come from birds, traffic, waves, refrigerators, fluorescent lights, stereos, and the like. The best way to minimize their effect, when possible, is to eliminate them entirely. Don't shoot the birds, but do turn off refrigerators and air conditioners, and close windows facing out to the street.[1] When possible, locations should be chosen with ambient noise in mind. Try not to set up shoots underneath an airport flight path or by a busy highway. Sometimes you can get a permit to block off a street while you are shooting; otherwise, plan to

Fig. 11-5. Use a directional mic's pickup pattern to your advantage. (top) When filming near a noise source (such as the street) if your mic is pointing at both the subject and the noise, you'll pick them both up on the mic. (bottom) If you reposition so that the mic is pointing away from the noise source, you'll minimize noise and pick up your subject more clearly. In any situation, you want the mic as close to the subject as possible (within a few feet); this is especially important in a noisy setting. (Steven Ascher)

shoot at a quiet time of day. Heavy *sound blankets* (furniture packing pads) can be used to dampen noisy windows or air vents. These can be clipped and hung on grip stands to make a quieter space near the actors or subject.

Ideally, audible background sounds should remain consistent throughout a scene. Consistency is important for editing, since much condensing and rearranging of the movie's chronology is done at that time. An editor needs the freedom to

1. Many a crew has driven off from a location forgetting to turn the fridge back on. Put your car keys in it when you turn it off to remind you.

juxtapose any two shots without worrying that the background tone may not match. The audience will tune out the gentle ambience of an electric fan, but they'll be aware of it if it pops in and out in every other shot. If you begin shooting a scene with the window closed, don't open it during the scene. In situations where you can't control some background sound (a neighbor's auto, for example), try to record some of the offending sound alone in case during editing it's needed to cover sections of the scene that lack it.

Make every effort to turn off or lower any music that is audible at the filming location. Discontinuous music is a glaring sign that the chronology of shots has been changed. Recording music may also create copyright problems (see Chapter 17). If ambient music can't be eliminated, or if it is part of the scene you are filming, plan your editing around it when you shoot.

When shooting in a noisy location, there are a number of things you can do. First, use a directional mic and get the mic as close to the source as possible. Always keep its pickup pattern in mind (see Figs. 10-17 and 10-20). Try not to let the subject come between the mic and a major noise source, like the street. To mic someone on the sidewalk, don't stand with your back to the buildings where you will pick up your subject and the street noise equally (see Fig. 11-5). With a supercardioid microphone, if you can point the mic upward from below (or down from above), you can minimize street-level noise, including sound reflected off buildings.

Lavalier mics are often useful for noisy settings. These are especially effective for a single subject. Sometimes you can even mic two people near each other with one lav (you may want to place the mic a little lower than normal on the person wearing the mic to try to even out the two voices). Lavs can also be hidden, for example, in a piece of furniture.

ROOM TONE. Record 20 seconds of *room tone* at every location. Have everyone be quiet and stop moving while you record. Even if nothing in particular is audible, every site has its distinct room tone, which is very different from the sound of absolute silence. Room tone—an expression that refers to outdoor sound as well—is used in editing to bridge gaps in the sound track, providing a consistent background. When shooting video with a boom mic, if the camera is pointed at the mic while you're recording, it's easier to find the tone when editing.

Acoustics of the Recording Space

The size, shape, and nature of any location affects the way sound travels through it. An empty room with hard, smooth walls is acoustically *live*, reflecting sound and causing some echoing. Bathrooms are often very acoustically live; sound may reverberate in them for a second or more before dying out (try singing in the shower). A room with carpets, furniture, and irregular walls is acoustically *dead*; sound is absorbed or dispersed irregularly by the surfaces. Wide-open outdoor spaces are often extremely dead, because they lack surfaces to reflect the sound. Test the liveness of a recording space by clapping your hands once or giving a short whistle and listening to the way the sound dies out.

The acoustics of a location affect the clarity of the sound track and the loudness of camera noise. It's hard to hear clearly in an overly live room (a *boomy* location), as high frequencies are lost and rumbly low frequencies predominate. If you've ever tried to talk in a tunnel, you know what it does to the intelligibility of voices.

You can improve an overly reverberant location in a number of ways. Use a directional mic and move closer to the sound source. Deaden a room by closing curtains or by hanging sound blankets on stands and spreading them on the floor. Avoid positioning a microphone near a smooth wall, where it will pick up both direct and reflected sound; echo may be increased or sound waves may cancel each other, weakening the microphone's response. This may also occur when a mic is mounted on a short table stand over a smooth, hard surface. Avoid placing the mic in a corner or equidistant from two or more walls, where reflected sound may cancel or echo. Sometimes boominess can be reduced by filtering out low-frequency sounds below about 100 Hz (see Bass Filters, p. 459).

If a space is too live, even a quiet camera's noise will sound loud. When you point the mic away from the camera, you often are aiming at reflected sound bouncing off a wall. When this happens, deaden the space with blankets, move closer to the subject, or use the pickup pattern of the mic to cancel out both direct and reflected camera noise. Put a film camera in a barney if needed.

SETTING THE RECORDING LEVEL

One of the recordist's key jobs is controlling the volume of the recording. The loudness of sound as it passes through a camera or audio recorder is called its *level* or *gain*; this is adjusted with a control labeled "volume," "gain," or "level." This control is sometimes called a *pot* (short for *potentiometer*). All prosumer and professional cameras and audio recorders have a manual control to set the recording level (some consumer cameras only have auto control). In a typical recording situation, you're controlling the level of one or more microphones.

Setting the level isn't hard. In the simplest terms, *you want to record sound as loud as you can without it being too loud.* This provides the best dynamic range and keeps the sound signal as far from the noise floor as possible. In film and video production, sound levels are always readjusted during editing and mixing, so even if you record a sound loudly on the shoot, you can always make it quiet later if that's called for (see Fig. 11-11).

Setting the level too high is sometimes called *overmodulating*, *overrecording*, "going over," or "recording too hot." The opposite is *underrecording* or "recording too low."

To know how to handle levels, you need to know a bit about the nature of sound, what meters do, and the workings of your digital or analog recorder. Please see Sound, p. 402, and How Audio Is Recorded, p. 405, before reading this section.

Understanding Sound Level

Figure 11-6 shows a simplified representation of the level of a sound signal over time. Notice that the level is always changing, with peaks and valleys. The upper black line shows the highest limit of the peaks. Peaks often come and go very quickly, so the ear may not fully perceive their loudness. However, we are very concerned with how high the peaks are because digital recording equipment can't tolerate peaks that are too high.

The lower black line represents the average level. This corresponds most to how our ears perceive the loudness of sound. The relationship of the average level to the peak level varies with the type of sound. With a "normal" male speaking voice, the peaks might be 8 to 10 dB higher than the average. With short, percussive sounds like a hammer, jangling keys, or a chirping bird, the peaks might be up to 50 dB higher than the average—a much bigger ratio.[2]

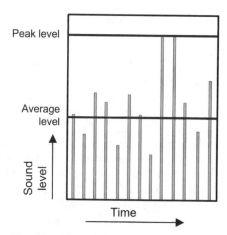

Fig. 11-6. Sound levels over time. Typical sounds contain volume peaks that are higher than the average level (how much higher depends on the sound).

When recording sound, we need some way to measure or meter the sound level.

Most digital systems have *peak-reading meters*. The peak meter responds almost instantaneously to quick surges in volume (called *transients*) and provides a reading of the *maximum* sound level, which helps ensure that you're not recording too loudly.

Peak meters come in various forms, including on-screen displays (see Fig. 11-7) and the *modulometer* found on a Nagra recorder. The *PPM* (*peak program meter*) widely used in Europe responds to transients faster than a VU meter (see below) but slower than a true peak reader. Many audio peaks come and go so

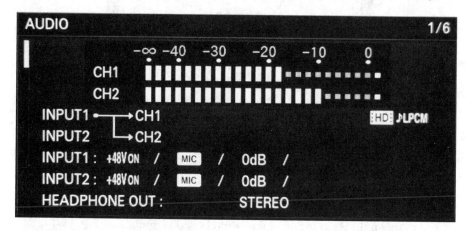

Fig. 11-7. Digital peak-reading meter. You never want the level to reach 0 dB. When the dot to the right of 0 lights up, the sound will be clipped. Indicators below the meter show that Input 1 is going to both recording channels, the mic is being fed +48 volt phantom power, and the camera is recording PCM uncompressed audio.

2. The ratio between peak and average level is called the *crest factor*.

fast that you can't actually see them on a meter. Peak meters may have a *peak hold* function, to let the meter linger a bit at the highest peaks so you can read them.[3]

The drawback of peak meters is that the level shown on the meter may not correspond well to perceived loudness. For example, the clink of two wineglasses in a toast might peak very high on the meter but sound very quiet.

To get a better reading of how loud something sounds, you can use a *VU (volume unit) meter* (see Fig. 11-8). The VU meter is the classic meter for analog equipment and if a meter has a needle and is not identified otherwise, it's probably a VU meter (there are also electronic versions with LED lights). VU meters read the *average* sound level. They give an accurate reading of steady sounds that don't have sharp peaks (like steady reference tones or a violin playing a long, slow note). However, they are designed to respond relatively slowly to changes in sound level (you can think of the needle as being fairly "heavy"), which means that quick transients from sounds like the aforementioned hammer or keys can pass by without deflecting the meter much (see Fig. 11-9). This is the problem with VU meters—they don't give a good reading of how high the peaks are.

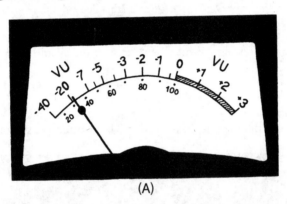

(A)

Fig. 11-8. VU meter. Some VU meters use LED lights or a digital display instead of a needle. (Carol Keller)

Peak and average: keep these two concepts in mind when you record sound. With digital recording in the field, we're primarily concerned with peaks because a signal with overly high peaks causes recording problems (as described below). But when we want to know how loud things sound, peak meters aren't as useful as VU meters and neither is as good as the newer digital loudness meters that are primarily used in postproduction (see p. 662). Meters can help you if used correctly, but in the end, your ears tell you more about loudness than a meter can.

For more on the relationship of levels and how they sound, see Fig. 15-14.

---

3. How quickly a meter responds to a peak, and then releases afterward, is called its "ballistics." PPMs, for example, are defined by very specific ballistics, and there are a few different flavors of PPMs.

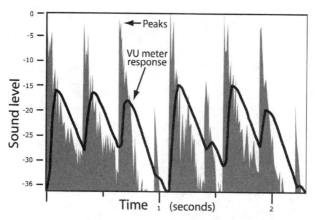

Fig. 11-9. Peak level and the VU meter. The gray area represents the sound level of a drumbeat, with its short, percussive peaks. The black line is the response of a VU meter. Note that the VU meter lags behind the actual spikes in level, and it doesn't rise as high or drop as low as the quick peaks and valleys. The VU meter indicates an average level that gives a good sense of how loud something sounds but is often significantly lower than the actual peaks. (From http://en.wikipedia.org/wiki/VU_Meter)

Digital Level

The peak meters found on digital cameras or recorders typically start at 0 dB at the top of the scale and range down to a negative number like –60 or less at the bottom (see Figs. 11-7 and 11-10). In digital recording, 0 dB represents *all* the digital bits being used; there is nothing higher. This is *full scale*. The units on the meter are marked as "dB" and represent *dBFS* or *decibels full scale*. You could think of them as decibels *below* full scale—the number tells you how close you are to the top. You never want the signal to actually reach 0 dB because anything above this level will be clipped and distorted.

As a general rule, you want to record the signal as high (loud) as you can without letting the signal reach 0 dB. How best to do that depends on your equipment, the sound, and your preferences.

With professional recording, the level is often set so that the average level of voices or music on the peak meter reads around –20 dBFS or a bit higher and the loudest peaks reach about –10 dBFS. This leaves a safety margin of 10 dB before reaching the top, in case of any sudden, hotter (louder) peaks (see Fig. 11-10). If you're looking for a simple rule to follow, this should work fine in most situations.

Some recordists like to record at a higher level, to stay farther away from the noise floor and use the full dynamic range of the system. This is often done with consumer and prosumer machines that have more noise. The average level may be set to around –12 dBFS, with peaks up to about –2. This of course leaves little *headroom* or safety margin in case of a loud peak.[4]

---

4. The idea of "safety margin" as used above is the difference between the highest peaks and the maximum level the system can record without distortion. "Headroom," however, is usually defined as the difference between the *average* signal level and the system maximum. If you're recording the average program level at –20 dBFS with peaks up to –10 dBFS, you have 20 dB of headroom, but only 10 dB of "safety margin."

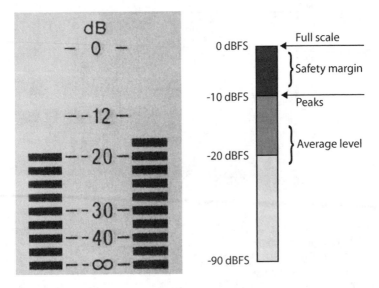

Fig. 11-10. (left) Peak-reading meter. The left channel reads –20 dBFS. (right) Rough guidelines for setting the level during field recording. Average level is around –20 dBFS or so with typical peaks reaching up to –10 dBFS. This leaves a safety margin of 10 dB for unexpectedly loud peaks. Different situations call for different levels.

Many recordists use a limiter as a matter of course with digital recordings to protect against high peaks (see p. 454).

Digital meters often have a clipping indicator, or "over" light, to show when peaks hit 0 dB; sometimes these light up just *before* you hit 0. Some systems *only* have a peaking indicator. In this case, turn the level up until the light comes on frequently, then reduce the level until the light stops flashing on.

With any recorder, be attentive to the type of sound and how high the peaks are. If you're filming a scene of two characters having a fight, the dialogue might go from low mumbles to loud shouts (with a few smashed dishes along the way). In situations like this in which dynamic range is high, you might want to keep the level lower than normal to protect against unexpected peaks. This is a situation in which a good limiter can help.

On the other hand, when you're recording something very even and predictable, you can nudge the level higher without risking overrecording.

If your recorder has an adjustment for headphone volume, set it at a comfortable level and leave it there. This will help you record consistent levels, and when you're in a situation in which it's difficult to watch the meter, it will help you to estimate proper recording level by the way things sound in the headphones.

If you do accidentally record something too hot, there are software solutions, such as iZotope RX 2, that may be able to recover some clipped peaks (see p. 667).

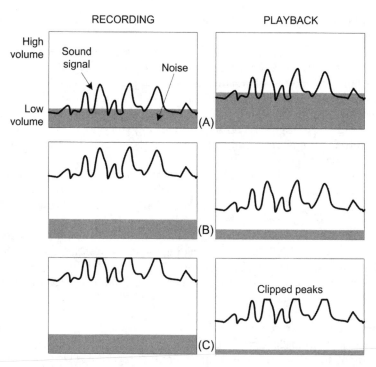

RECORDING   PLAYBACK

High volume

Sound signal

Noise

Low volume

(A)

(B)

Clipped peaks

(C)

Fig. 11-11. Setting the recording level. The sound signal is what we want; the interfering noise could come from the recording system, the recording environment, or, with analog recorders, tape noise. (A) If the sound signal is recorded at a low level—near the level of the noise—when the volume is increased to a medium level in playback, the competing noise gets louder too. (B) If the signal is recorded as loudly as possible without overrecording, you can lower the volume in playback and the noise level will diminish as well. (C) If the level is set so high in recording that the signal is distorted, it will still be distorted in playback even if the level is reduced later (note the clipped peaks). (Steven Ascher)

Analog Levels and VU Meters

You may encounter analog equipment in the form of a tape recorder or perhaps in a field mixer that has a VU meter. With analog, the same rule applies as for digital: you want to keep levels as loud as possible without overrecording. However, the rule is interpreted slightly differently.

VU meters have a scale that goes from about –40 VU to +3 or +6 with a bold change in the color or thickness of the markings at the 0 VU point (see Fig. 11-8). For normal recording, the level should be set so that the highest deflections of the meter read up to 0 VU. Though most recordists are careful to avoid letting the needle pass the 0 dB mark, it's usually the case that occasional, loud peaks can go to +3 or even more without causing problems. With analog tape recording, there isn't a fixed top level as in digital, where the sound is *sure* to be distorted. The actual point of overrecording and distortion is really determined by the type of sound, the recorder's amplifier, and the tape being used. Some sounds may read a few decibels above the 0 point without serious distortion, some will distort, and some will not be badly harmed by the crackle and breakup produced (a gunshot, for example).

Another difference between digital and analog is at the lower end of the scale, where quiet sounds are recorded: analog has a lot more noise. All analog magnetic tape has inherent noise, and both digital and analog recordings can have noise from the physical space where the microphone is, and from the circuits in the mic and the recorder. Ideally the sound you're recording should be a lot louder than the noise. Compared to digital recording, with analog you can be a little less worried about overrecording, but you should be a little more careful about not recording things too quietly.

If you're using a VU meter, keep in mind that the actual peaks will be higher than the meter indicates (see Fig. 11-9). So if you're recording percussive sounds like hammering, a chirping bird, or jangling keys, don't turn the level control way up to try to get them to read high on the scale. Many types of sounds will record just fine even though the VU meter is only in the middle or even the lower part of its range.

Some analog machines have peak-reading meters. With Nagra's modulometer, a typical recording might be in the –8 to –1 dB range; this is easy to remember because the needle will be roughly in a vertical position. If the level goes above 0 dB, lower it somewhat.

Reference Tone

In analog recording, a *reference tone* (also called a *line-up tone*) was recorded at the beginning of a tape or session to help ensure that recordings were played back at the proper level. This would help you or others calibrate the playback level to match the level of the original recording. Much like color bars, tone is much less useful in the digital era since digital levels are fixed when a file is made, and they don't change when you copy the file. However, there are still situations when reference tone can be useful, and it is expected, for example, when making a videotape for broadcast.

Many pro or prosumer recorders, mixers, and cameras have a *tone generator* or *oscillator* that can make a steady tone, typically at 1 kHz. You may have a choice of tone level, often between –12 dBFS and –20 dBFS. The idea is to use a tone level that corresponds to the average level at which you recorded (the *program level*). Though the idea is simple enough, there are variations depending on the type of equipment and style of recording.

- A standard approach for professional digital video recording in the United States is to record the average program level around –20 dBFS. In this case, set the reference tone to –20 dBFS. This is a level that postproduction houses and broadcasters are used to and should result in fairly consistent levels. The –20 tone equates to 0 VU on a VU meter. In Europe and the UK, –18 dBFS is often used instead as the reference level.
- When using a VU meter, tone is typically set at 0 VU. Peaks are not allowed to exceed +3 or sometimes +6 dB.
- When using a Nagra recorder, tone is typically set at –8 dB on the modulometer.
- As noted above, sometimes people record at –12 dBFS average level. In this case, use a line-up tone at –12 dBFS.

It's important when recording a reference tone that you indicate in writing (and sometimes as a recorded, spoken message) what level the tone is recorded at. If you use a nonstandard tone, be sure to discuss it with anyone involved in postproduction sound or dub work.

Reference tones are just that—a reference. Just because a tone is recorded at the start of a tape or program doesn't mean the levels are correct throughout.

Making Level Adjustments

In general, recordings sound better if the level is not changed in a noticeable way during the recording. This may mean, for example, setting the level at a compromise position between the loud and soft voices of two people talking. (Another solution might be to move the microphone closer to the soft-spoken person.) Try to anticipate surges in volume, choosing perhaps to underrecord slightly an orator whose every sentence is greeted with loud cheers from the audience. This is another situation where a good limiter could be helpful (see below).

When possible, set levels during rehearsals, or have an interview subject talk for a bit so you can get a level. Often a certain amount of level adjustment (called "riding the gain" or "riding the pot") is called for during a shot. Try to make level changes between lines of dialogue, not during them; if you have to reset during a line, adjust the level gently and not too suddenly.

Try to maintain consistency in your tracks. If you're recording a scene in a drama, try to keep the characters at roughly the same level so they can be edited together without a lot of level changes.

When recording a single mic with a two-channel (or more) recorder or camera, some recordists use the second channel as insurance against overrecording. Record the mic on one channel at full, normal level. Also route the mic to the second channel, but set the level on this track 6 dB lower than the first channel (some set it even lower than that). This second track is used only if the first one is too hot.

When quiet sounds seem underrecorded, don't turn the level control beyond three-fourths of its full range, as this will usually add system noise. Instead, get closer to the sound source. If extremely loud sounds (like live rock music) require that the level control be set at less than one-fourth of its range, this too may degrade the sound signal. If this is the case, get an *attenuator*, or *line pad*, to place on the cable between the microphone and the recorder (some mics and recorders have built-in attenuators; see Fig. 10-31). The attenuator cuts down the strength of the signal.

Automatic Level Control

Many audio and video recorders are equipped with some form of automatic control of recording level. The names for the various types of automatic systems are not entirely standardized. Some types work better than others, but often the effectiveness depends more on the sophistication of the particular camera or recorder than on the type used.

AUTOMATIC GAIN CONTROL. *Automatic gain control* (*AGC*) or *automatic level control* (*ALC*) works by automatically choosing a predetermined recording level. If the sound signal coming in is too quiet, it will be boosted; and if it is too loud, the gain will be reduced. AGC requires no attention on the part of the operator, and it can be quite effective for straightforward recording in which the sound level doesn't vary too much. However, some AGC devices don't handle sudden volume changes well. Say you're recording someone in a kitchen. While he speaks, the level is fine, but when he stops, the AGC responds to the quiet by boosting the gain, bringing the sound of the refrigerator to full prominence. AGCs sometimes have a slow *release time*, and if a sudden, loud sound occurs while someone is speaking, the recording level will drop, reducing the level of the dialogue, and return to normal some moments later.

For all these reasons, AGC gets a bad rap. Indeed, some AGCs are not very good and in most situations a competent recordist setting the level manually can do much better. However, some AGCs work well and can be a real lifesaver if you're shooting alone or in a challenging situation. Test your own system and judge for yourself.

LIMITERS AND COMPRESSORS. A *limiter* is another form of automatic control that allows you to set the basic recording level; the limiter only kicks in to reduce the level if you're in danger of overrecording. Limiters often cut in fairly sharply when the sound level gets too high, protecting against sudden volume peaks (see Fig. 15-14).[5] Some limiters work so well that they're virtually "transparent" (unnoticeable); others can produce an unnatural, flattened effect in the sound.

Some wireless mics and other systems have limiters with a flashing LED indicator instead of a meter. Turn up the gain until the indicator lights up, showing that the limiter is cutting in; then decrease the level a bit until the limiter operates only on the loudest peaks.

Limiters can be very helpful for scenes in which sound levels change suddenly. They're especially useful for digital recording, where too much level is a particular problem. Limiters can be a kind of insurance policy against hot peaks, but if they're relied upon too heavily (that is, if the recording level is set so high that the limiter is constantly working), the sound may lose much of its dynamic range and seem flat and without texture. Some pros use them regularly; others avoid them.

A *compressor* is another method used in various audio systems (including some wireless mics) for dealing with excess level. Compressors reduce the level by a certain ratio (say, 2:1 or 3:1), which compresses (reduces) the dynamic range of the sound. Compressors and limiters are in the same family. Limiters reduce the level more sharply than compressors usually do, but unlike compressors, they are generally set to act only on the very loudest sounds.

A *compressor/expander* (sometimes called a *compander*) compresses the dynamic range during recording—to lower loud volume peaks so they won't overrecord and boost very quiet sounds so they won't be lost—and then expands the dynamic range during playback by safely raising louder sounds and reducing quieter ones.

Different systems use different methods or different names. Some recorders use the term "compressor" to describe something more like an AGC. Some flash re-

---

5. The threshold point where a limiter cuts in and how much it limits the sound level varies among systems and is sometimes adjustable.

corders can store a backup recording at a lower level and automatically switch to it if the main recording gets too hot.

For more on compressors and limiters, see Level and Dynamic Range, p. 659.

Gain Structure

There are many situations in which you want to use two pieces of audio gear together; for example, using a wireless mic with a camcorder. It's important to co-ordinate how the level is set in each, especially with analog connections. *Gain structure* or *gain-staging* refers to the process of setting the level correctly through the whole audio chain.

As a rule, you want the upstream item (say, the wireless receiver) set to output at normal full level (*unity gain*) but not so high that the sound is distorted. If you feed too low a level from the wireless to the camera, the camera will need to boost the signal, raising the noise level. If you feed a signal that's too hot, the signal will be distorted from that point forward.

In shooting, it's common to use a microphone mixer (field mixer) with a camera or audio recorder (see p. 430). Most mixers have level controls for individual chan-nels and a master fader that controls all the tracks together. Especially when using only one channel, you generally want to avoid situations in which the channel is set low but the master is set high, which may add noise. Set the channel at a healthy level, then use the master to fine-tune the level.

When using a field mixer, typically the recordist wants to set things up so he or she can control the level from the mixer, knowing that the camera will record cor-rectly. Ideally, the field mixer should output to the camera using line level (see p. 431). Make sure any AGC is turned off in the camera. Turn on the mixer's tone generator and set it to 0 VU on the mixer's VU meter or –20 dBFS on a peak meter.[6] Then adjust the gain on the camera so the tone reads –20 dBFS on the camera's digital meter (but see p. 432 for more on reference tones). Now the recordist can adjust the level during the shoot using the mixer's meter and level control. You should still try to monitor the audio output from the camera with headphones, and check the camera's meter from time to time. The same concepts apply when using a mixer with a separate audio recorder.

MUSIC, NARRATION, AND EFFECTS

Recording Music

Some suggestions for music recordings:

1. It's often best to record music in stereo (if not with more than two channels). See p. 461 for more on stereo mics.
2. When you record an acoustic band or orchestra, try to find a mic placement that balances the instruments nicely. Often a stereo mic slightly behind and above the conductor's position on a high stand is used as the master mic.

6. On some mixers the tone is not adjustable.

With many instruments, the sound will radiate out and up, so getting the mic high helps. Hanging mics is another solution. Sometimes a second mic is added to capture a vocalist or soloist. You may also want to put mics elsewhere in the space to record on separate tracks or to mix with the master. When you use more than one mic, be careful to avoid phase cancellation (see p. 459).

3. When you record an individual instrument, place the mic near the point where the sound is emanating (for example, the sound hole of a guitar or the bell of a saxophone).

4. When recording amplified vocalists or instrumentalists, you often want to put your mic by the loudspeaker, not the person. When you record a person at a podium, you may get better sound by miking the person directly, but you must get the mic very close. Often with amplified speeches or musical performances you can get a line feed directly from the public address system (or a band's mixing board) to your recorder. By doing this, you avoid having to place a microphone and you usually get good-quality sound (in the case of the band's mixer, you get premixed sound from multiple microphones).

5. Generally, you want to let the musicians control the volume. Avoid using automatic level control or making sudden manual adjustments to the recording level. Find the highest level that can accommodate loud passages in the music and then try to leave the level alone. For live performances, professional recordists sometimes attend rehearsals, follow the musical score, and make slight adjustments during rests or pauses between soft and loud passages. When recording music, consider using a higher bit depth and/or sample rate.

6. When shooting a musical performance, plan to record fairly long takes. Unlike a lecture that can be cut into short segments and spliced together, musical performance sound must be relatively continuous. The camera should get a number of cutaways that can be used to bridge various sections or tie together takes from different performances. Shooting with more than one camera helps ensure that you will have sufficient coverage. For cutaways, get some neutral shots (such as faces and audience shots) that don't show fingering or specific hand positions, which can be used anywhere.

7. If you want to use an existing recording, transfer the digital source file directly to your editing system. You may need to convert to a different file format. Use uncompressed sources whenever possible.

8. If you plan to use music in your movie, you should be familiar with music copyright laws (see Chapter 17).

Music Videos and Music Playback Scenes

Music videos and scenes in movies that include performers lip-syncing to prerecorded music present some challenges to the sound recordist. Generally, the band will have already recorded the song, and the performers will sing along with it for the video. The recordist is usually responsible for having equipment to play back the song. It's a good idea to also record a *scratch track*—an audio recording that isn't usually intended for use in the final version of the movie—of the performers on the set. In this case, the scratch track will help in syncing the footage to the song and will capture any on-set banter or other sound that may be wanted by the director.

VIDEO CAMERAS. Shooting to music playback with video cameras is fairly straightforward. The music should be played back on a stable, speed-controlled format such as hard drive, flash memory, or good-quality CD player. Use a camera frame rate that won't require speed changes in postproduction. In NTSC countries, 23.976 fps and 29.97 fps should work fine. In PAL countries, you can use 25 fps. The singers' mouth movements captured on video should then match up to the song in postproduction. Some video cameras may drift slightly in speed relative to the audio. A sync generator may be used to keep the audio playback and the camera locked together. Even without it, if shots are kept relatively short, sync drift won't be apparent in the shot.

FILM CAMERAS. Shooting with a film camera for video release in NTSC countries can be somewhat trickier. If the camera is run at 24 fps, the film will be slowed down by 0.1 percent during the telecine transfer (see Chapter 16). Compared to the master recording of the song, the singers on video will then be moving their lips 0.1 percent too slow. One way to solve this is to run the camera at 23.976 fps.

Another solution is to shoot at 24 fps and *pull up* (speed up) the music playback by 0.1 percent on the set. There are several recorders that can be made to play exactly 0.1 percent fast. Or you can create a file in a DAW that's sped up by this amount and play that on the set. The lip-sync singing is then done to the sped-up song, but when the picture is transferred to video, it will drop down to the speed of the original song. Always consult with the transfer house or other professionals before shooting.

When vocalists are to be recorded actually singing on camera but need to stay in sync with prerecorded music, an earwig (see p. 375) can be used to play the music back in their ear without being picked up by the mic. Also, a low-frequency "thumper" subwoofer speaker can be used to supply the beat at a tone that won't interfere with the vocal track. Thumpers are sometimes used for dance scenes where actors need to keep the beat but the actual music can't be played on set (for example, because it would interfere with dialogue).

Recording Narration

Narration (*voice-over*) should generally be recorded in a soundproof booth in a studio, as any background sound in the narration may cause serious problems. Any noise in the recording will be especially noticeable in the movie as the narration cuts in and out. For a low-budget production, or if you have to record on location, you can build an enclosure with sound blankets and grip stands to try to isolate the narrator. Set it up as far from windows and outside noise (such as airplanes) as possible—basements sometimes work best. You might even try a big coat closet.

Be attentive to echoes from reflected sound, especially in the small space of a recording booth. Even the stand used to hold the narration can create unwanted acoustic effects. Use a clip or small stand to hold the script. Narrators often like to use their hands when speaking, so it's better if they don't have to hold the script.

Often the mic is placed quite close to the narrator for a feeling of presence. Position the mic a few inches to the side and use a good windscreen to avoid breath popping. Listen closely for breath sounds while recording; redo takes if necessary. Many people like the warm, full sound of a large-diaphragm studio mic like a Neumann U 87 or U 89. For more on writing and delivering narration, see p. 533.

Recording Sound Effects

Sound effects (*SFX*) are nonmusical, nonspeech sounds from the environment. The sounds of cars, planes, crowds, and dripping water are all considered effects. Effects usually have to be recorded individually. Don't expect to get a good recording of effects during scenes that involve dialogue. An effect may be difficult to record well either because of practicalities (positioning yourself near a jet in flight, for example) or because it doesn't sound the way audiences have come to expect it to (for example, your recording of a running brook may sound more like a running shower). It can be better to purchase prerecorded effects from an online sound library; mix studios often stock a wide range of effects (see Chapter 15). You can also

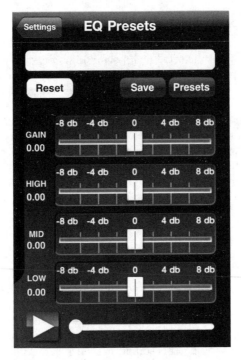

Fig. 11-12. Equalizer screen on Pro Audio To Go mobile app. Equalization can be done, for example, to reduce the level of low frequencies (bass) during recording. See also Fig. 15-17. (Weynand Training International)

try simulating an effect—crinkling cellophane to simulate the sound of "fire," for instance. There are many postproduction processes (reverb, speed changes, filtering) that can be used to create and enhance effects.

OTHER RECORDING ISSUES

Bass Filters

Many recorders, mixers, and microphones are equipped with filters that reduce the level of low-frequency sounds. These filters are variously called *bass cut, bass roll-off, high pass*, and *low-frequency attenuation (LFA)*. Some filters cut off bass fairly sharply at some frequency, say 100 Hz. Others roll off low frequencies more gradually, often diminishing them 12 dB per octave; thus, the filter might reduce 150 Hz somewhat, 75 Hz quite a bit, and 37 Hz almost entirely.

Filtering, also called *equalization*, is done to minimize the low-frequency rumble caused by such things as wind, traffic, machinery, and microphone-handling noise. The low-frequency component of these sounds is disturbing to the listener and can distort higher-frequency sounds. If low-frequency sounds are very loud, the recording level must be kept low to avoid overrecording, and this impairs the sounds that you really care about (like voices).

Microphones and recorders may have a two- or three-position bass roll-off switch. The first position (sometimes labeled "music" or "M") provides a relatively flat frequency response with no bass filtering. The next position ("voice" or "V") provides filtering below a certain frequency. If there is a third position, it rolls off bass starting at an even higher frequency (see Fig. 10-21). Do test recordings with the filter to judge its effect. On some mics, the "M" position is optimal for most recording, and the "V" position should be used only for excessive rumble or when the mic is very close to someone speaking. Sometimes the third position removes so much of the low end that recordings sound very thin and hollow. For the same reason, it's usually best to avoid using a camcorder's "wind" menu setting.

There are two schools of thought on filtering bass: one is to filter as needed in the original recording; the other is to hold off as much as possible until postproduction. The first school argues that the low frequencies will be filtered out eventually, and a better recording can be made if this is done sooner rather than later. This must be weighed against the fact that frequencies rolled off in the original recording are not replaceable later. The sound studio has better tools and is a better environment in which to judge how much bass needs to be removed.

A prudent approach is to filter bass only when excessive rumble or wind noise requires it or when trying to compensate for a microphone that is overly sensitive to low frequencies. Then filter only the minimum amount to improve the sound. If filtering is done, keep it consistent in the scene.

Multiple Microphones and Multitrack Recorders

There are many situations in which you may want to use more than one microphone. Typical examples are when recording two people who are not near each other, recording a musical group, or recording a panel discussion. Many recorders have provisions for two microphone inputs, and some machines can record from microphone and line inputs simultaneously (mics can usually be fed into the line input with the proper preamp). A mic mixer allows several mics to be fed into the recorder. Try to get microphones that are well matched in terms of tone quality. Sometimes a filter can be used on one mic to make it sound more like another.

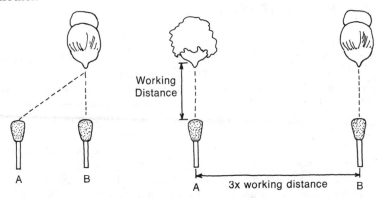

Fig. 11-13. Multiple microphones. (left) Distance from the woman to microphone A is only slightly longer than distance to microphone B, leading to possible phase cancellation. (right) Separation between microphones is three times the distance from each mic to its sound source. Now the distance between microphone A and the woman at right is sufficient to minimize the chance of phase cancellation. (Carol Keller)

When recording with multiple mics, be careful to avoid *phase cancellation*. This occurs when two mics are slightly different distances from the sound source, so the peak of a sound wave reaches one mic slightly before or after it reaches another mic. This diminishes the strength and quality of the sound signal because the diaphragm of one mic is being pushed by the sound pressure while the other mic is being pulled and the two signals cancel each other out. The rule of thumb for avoiding this is that the microphones should be at least three times farther from each other than the distance from each mic to its sound source (see Fig. 11-13). Directional microphones that are angled away from each other can often be placed closer together.

Start with one mic and watch the level on the audio meter when you plug in the second mic—the strength of the sound signal should be increased, not decreased. Sometimes two microphones are wired differently, so that even if the mics are placed correctly, they cancel each other anyway. When recording in stereo, phase cancellation is not always noticeable but becomes apparent when the two mics are combined (*summed*) to one mono channel.

When using multiple mics, when someone is *not* speaking, keep his mic level down to avoid unwanted noise; this is often difficult when recording unpredictable dialogue.

If the recorder has multiple recording channels, this opens up various possibilities for multiple microphones. You can record both a boom mic and a lavalier separately. You can place two mics in different positions and choose whichever sounds best later. If different subjects have their own mics and recording channels, their lines of dialogue can be separated more easily for editing and mixing purposes. Director Robert Altman used recording systems with up to forty-eight tracks with wireless mics on individual actors, each feeding a different channel. With this system, the actors can freely improvise, and everyone's lines will be recorded well, something that is almost impossible to do with only one mic and recording channel. Phase cancellation can often be avoided with multiple recording tracks if the editor can choose the sound from one mic or another without trying to mix them together.

Having many tracks can be cumbersome for dailies screenings or for the picture editor. If you record to multiple tracks, you may need to create one or two *mixdown tracks* that combine the key dialogue tracks. Some multitrack recorders allow you to record a mixdown along with the individual source tracks.

Stereo Recording

Most video and audio recorders have at least two channels and are capable of recording in stereo. Some digital cameras are equipped with dual built-in mics that give some stereo separation between the left and right sides.

When movies are distributed to the public, in theaters, on TV, or as DVDs, they are in stereo (at least two channels) or another multichannel format such as 5.1-channel sound (see Mix Formats, p. 669). However, it's important to make the distinction between *recording* in stereo on location and *releasing* the finished movie in stereo. For very many projects, dialogue scenes and the like are recorded in mono, even if those scenes will ultimately appear in a stereo sound track in the finished movie. A mono recording is made with one microphone (or more) on one audio channel. It's very easy during the sound mix to place a "mono" sound on either the left or the right side of the screen to create a stereo effect if needed.

Nevertheless, there are times when stereo recording is desired either for the entire production or for specific types of sound such as music, effects, or wide shots (perhaps to capture the sound of a horse moving from one side of the screen to the other).

There are various techniques for recording stereo. Stereo mics built into camcorders usually employ the *X-Y* method (see Fig. 11-14). This uses two cardioid mics each pointed 45 degrees to the side (the two mic capsules may be in the same housing). The X-Y method is straightforward and simple, though when the two mics are separate—that is, not in the same case—mounting and controlling them must be done with care. It can sometimes be difficult to get the proper balance between the left and right side.

Some people prefer the *M-S* (*mid-side*) method, which is a bit more complicated. This also employs two mics: one with a cardioid pickup pattern and one with a figure-eight pattern (see Fig. 11-15). Mics like the Shure VP88 have both mics built into a single housing. The cardioid mic picks up sound from the front and the figure-eight mic gets the left- and right-side image; each mic is sent to a separate channel on the audio or video recorder. Later, the two tracks are "matrixed" through an M-S decoder or by tweaking the phase of the tracks in a DAW. The advantage of the M-S method is that it offers a lot of flexibility. In postproduction, you can create the standard two-channel, left-right stereo effect,

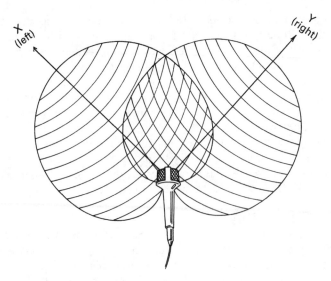

Fig. 11-14. Pickup pattern of a stereo mic in the X-Y configuration. Shown here, the two mic capsules are in one body. (Robert Brun)

and tweak the "width" of the stereo image. You can also easily isolate the mono signal from directly in front, if needed, which is more difficult if you originally recorded with X-Y stereo. Some M-S mics (such as the VP88) allow you to output an X-Y (left-right) signal if you prefer; on some you can even select how wide the stereo pattern is.

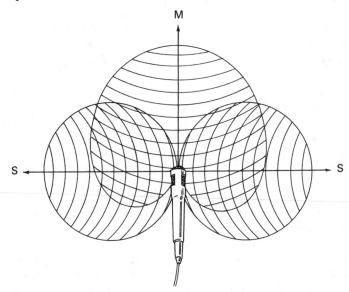

Fig. 11-15. Pickup pattern of a stereo mic in the M-S configuration. Shown here, the two mic capsules are in one body. (Robert Brun)

Fig. 11-16. Shure VP88 microphone. Versatile mic that can output an M-S signal or can be switched internally to provide a stereo (X-Y) output with a choice between low, medium, or high stereo effect. Comes with a splitter cable for outputting the two channels. Use both output connectors for M-S or stereo output, or use just one in the M-S mode to record a mono signal from the cardioid capsule or the figure-eight capsule. (Shure Brothers, Inc.)

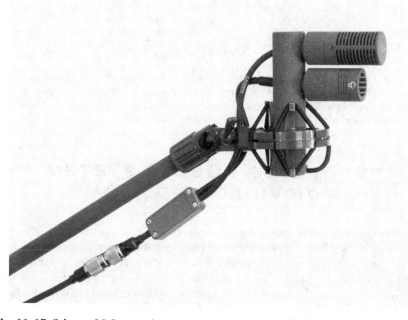

Fig. 11-17. Schoeps M-S setup showing separate cardioid and figure-eight mics that can be combined (matrixed) to create stereo. Schoeps makes very high-quality professional mics. (Posthorn Recordings, NY)

Surround Sound Recording

Some cameras and microphones offer the possibility of recording 5.1-channel surround sound, which provides a feeling of dimensionality and sense of space for productions that will be shown in a 5.1-channel format. Some consumer camcorders have built-in mics that can record the 5.1 channels to two channels (a stereo pair) using Dolby Digital encoding. There are also stand-alone mics, such as those made by Holophone, that simulate the directionality of human hearing and feed five or more separate cables to an external mixer or recorder for a 5.1 or 7.1 surround format (see Fig. 11-18). For more on surround formats, see p. 669.

Fig. 11-18. Holophone's H2-Pro 5.1 can capture up to five channels (left, center, right, left surround, right surround, and low frequency) in one mic body. Outputs each channel via a separate XLR cable to a mixer or recorder. Other models can encode the 5.1 channels to two-channel stereo for recording in a typical camera. (Holophone)

RECORDING DOUBLE SYSTEM FOR VIDEO AND FILM

Double-system (or *dual-system*) recording means using a separate audio recorder from the camera. All film shoots are done double system since film cameras don't record sound. Video shoots are sometimes done with a separate audio recorder in order to record higher-quality sound or more audio tracks or to provide more mobility for the recordist than might be possible by recording sound in the camera. In this situation, it's still recommended to record audio in the video camcorder as well, to serve as a scratch track for reference.[7]

---

7. This could be done as a feed from the audio recorder or just by leaving the camera mic on.

When sound and picture are recorded in separate machines, there are two basic concerns:

- Ensure that both sound and picture can be played back at the same speed or frame rate, so they don't drift relative to each other during a shot.
- Make it as easy as possible to sync the sound to the picture in postproduction—that is, to line up the sound recording with the picture so that when we see something happen on screen we hear it at the same time. Syncing up is discussed on p. 589.

Speed Control

To record double-system sync sound, it's essential that the speed of the camera and recorder be precisely controlled. Today, digital video cameras have precise speed control and film cameras with crystal-controlled motors are used for sync work (see Camera Motors, p. 258).

As for audio recorders, digital machines should have speed control that's accurate enough for sync recording. Small amounts of sync drift with some systems can be corrected in editing. Speed control with analog recorders is discussed on p. 419.

PULLDOWN. When shooting film in former NTSC countries the speed of the audio may need to be adjusted after recording. Film shot at 24 fps will typically be slowed to 23.976 fps when transferred to video (see p. 690). This means that audio recorded in the field may also need to be pulled down (slowed down) by the same 0.1 percent. The transfer facility can do it in the telecine session. Audio playback speed can be also be adjusted in the editing room, by modifying the speed of the audio track in the NLE. Pulldown may not be needed if the project is edited at true 24 fps (see p. 690). Another approach is to build in a speed adjustment during recording by manipulating the sample rate. On some recorders, instead of recording at the standard 48 kHz sample rate, the recorder can be set for 48.048 kHz. This creates 480 extra samples per second when recording. However, the recording is "stamped" as having the normal 48 kHz rate, so the playback machine plays back the usual 48,000 samples per second, making the sound 0.1 percent slower. This has the advantage of avoiding sample rate conversion, which could degrade the quality. With some recorders, to make sure the 48.048 kHz is stamped as 48 kHz, the setting is indicated as 48.048F ("F" for fake or Fostex).

Always discuss settings with the post team before recording!

SYNCING AUDIO AND PICTURE

Many different techniques and technologies are used for making the syncing process easier. Some of them involve timecode (be sure to read Timecode, p. 223, before reading this section). Because there are a lot of options, this topic can get confusing; remember, in the end you'll probably only be using *one* of them on your shoot. As noted on p. 369, slates (see Fig. 9-30) are used both to visually identify what's being filmed as well as to aid in syncing the picture and sound. The following discussion is only about syncing.

Traditional Slates

Syncing involves lining up the sound and the picture. It's much easier to do if there's a distinct event that can be seen clearly in the picture and heard on the sound track. For example, the closing of a car door might suffice. A *slate* is an event in sound and picture that can be used to facilitate syncing.

The traditional slating device is the clapper board, discussed on p. 368. Even if a slate is electronic (such as an iPad app) it may still be based on the same principle of matching the picture of the slate closing to its sound. The advantage of traditional slates is that they're low-tech and fairly foolproof. The disadvantage is that it can take a long time in the telecine or editing system to find the right audio and sync it up to the picture.

Slating can also be done by gently tapping the microphone once or twice or even by snapping your fingers within range of the recorder.

When you make any slate, it's imperative not to turn off the camera or recorder between the slate and the shot itself, as novices sometimes do.

Fig. 11-19. Timecode slate. A "dumb slate" can display timecode sent from the audio recorder or other source. A "smart slate" incorporates its own timecode generator (see Fig. 11-20). (Denecke, Inc.)

Timecode Slates

A *timecode slate* (also called a *digislate*) looks like a standard clapper board with a timecode display on its face (see Fig. 11-19). In one of the simplest ways of using a timecode slate, timecode (often indicated as *TC*) is fed from the audio recorder to the slate. Any video camera or sync-sound film camera can be used (the camera may have no timecode capability or may be running a different timecode from the audio recorder).

Slates are done in the usual way, preferably at the head of the shot. When the top clap stick is lowered on the slate, the timecode at that instant is held on the display. In postproduction, the frame where the clap sticks closed is paused on screen so the audio timecode at that moment can be read on the slate. That number is entered into the editing or telecine system, which locates that same timecode in the audio and, presto, the shot is in sync.

In this method, timecode is sent to the slate from the audio recorder via a cable or a wireless link. With a *smart slate*, the slate has its own timecode generator. *Jam-syncing* means that one timecode source sets the other machine to its timecode. You can jam-sync the slate with timecode from the audio recorder or from another timecode source, and the slate and recorder should maintain the same free run/time-of-day code.

A timecode generator, such as Ambient's Lockit box, Denecke's SB-T, or Horita's PG-2100 Portable Mini Time Code Generator, can be used to jam-sync the slate and/or audio recorder.

When using a slate app for an iPad or other tablet (see Fig. 9-30), keep in mind that even if it has a timecode display, if it doesn't allow for jam-syncing or displaying timecode from the audio recorder, it won't support this kind of precise numerical syncing method.

TIMECODE SLATE ISSUES. Some people prefer smart slates because they require no connection between the slate and the audio recorder. On the other hand, this provides one more opportunity for timecode to go out of whack. A wireless transmitter can be used to send code from the recorder to a dumb slate (timecode reader only), which simplifies things somewhat but requires a good wireless link.

As a safety precaution when using a timecode slate, be sure to record the sound of the clap sticks closing (the old-fashioned slate system) in case there's a problem with the code. Also be sure to frame the slate in the camera viewfinder *clearly* so the timecode numbers are big and easy to read.

Timecode generators tend to drift slightly over time. This can lead to sync errors if the timecode in a slate or camera differs from the timecode in the audio recorder. When using more than one timecode device, pick one of them to serve as the master clock and use it to jam-sync the other machines. Rejam whenever devices are powered down or, in any case, no more than every few hours. The Zaxcom Nomad mixer/recorder can wirelessly and continuously jam timecode to multiple cameras, and it includes a visual timecode display that could be used instead of a digislate in some situations (see Fig. 10-10).

Audio Timecode Frame Rates

Most timecode-capable recorders offer a variety of timecode frame rates. The goal is to pick a frame rate for the audio timecode that will match or be compatible with the video or film timecode rate. Keep in mind that *the audio timecode frame rate does not control the speed of the audio*, it only affects how the timecode is recorded. Not all audio recorders can handle all timecode rates.

- *23.976 fps.* Digital cameras that record "24p" in NTSC countries are usually operated at 23.976 fps (also known as 23.98). This timecode is always non-drop (ND).

- **24 fps.** If a film camera is run at 24 fps, this timecode is sometimes used when the film-to-digital transfer and recording is at 24p.
- **25 fps.** This rate is used for film and video shot at 25 fps or true 24 when editing is to be done in a PAL video environment.
- **29.97 fps.** This is the standard timecode for video shot at 23.976 or 29.97 fps in NTSC countries.
- **30 fps, ND.** This is a *true* 30 fps rate, *not* the same as 29.97, and is often used in NTSC countries for film shot at 24 fps. After the 30 fps audio TC has been slowed down by 0.1 percent, it will match the 29.97 fps rate on the video transfer (and it can still work when the video transfer is recorded at 23.976 fps). This is a standard audio timecode rate used for film production in the United States.

Unless instructed otherwise, it's always safest to record nondrop (ND or NDF) timecode. Be sure to discuss any audio timecode choices with the lab, post house, and postproduction team before recording! Label all boxes, logs, and slate clearly with sound TC speed, drop or nondrop (as well as the usual items listed earlier). Do a workflow test before beginning a production to make sure all systems are set correctly.

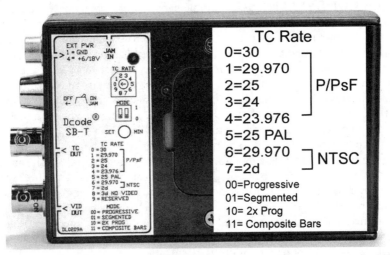

Fig. 11-20. Timecode generator. The Denecke SB-T reads, generates, and jams to all standard frame rates. Outputs timecode and video sync in PAL and NTSC, as well as trilevel sync for HD. Enlargement shows available frame rates. (Denecke, Inc.)

No Slates

When you're shooting with DSLRs or other video cameras and using a separate audio recorder, there are software solutions that can automatically sync audio from the recorder with audio recorded by the camera. The recorder captures high-quality audio. The camera mic picks up lower-quality audio, but it's recorded in sync with the picture, like typical video. In editing, the camera's audio is on one track of the NLE and you import the recorder's audio onto another track. Several NLEs, and software like PluralEyes, can match the audio waveforms of the two tracks and put them in sync (see p. 589).

This saves time on the set, as no slates are necessary, and saves time when syncing is done. The camera can start and stop at will, and as long as the recorder is running, you'll be able to sync up the material. This can be particularly handy when several cameras are used to shoot, say, a concert—you could have several roaming cameras and never need an audio or visual slate to find sync. This can also be useful for interviews in which you want to start and stop the camera while always rolling sound.

Even without software, it's usually not hard to put shots in sync that don't have a slate; it just takes longer.

Another technique that doesn't require slates and doesn't require any audio recorded in the camera (no modern film cameras record audio on film) involves timecode. If you use a digital or film camera that can internally record the same timecode as the audio recorder, then you don't need slates at all. In postproduction, the editing or transfer system simply locates the identical timecode numbers in video and audio; syncing can be totally automated. This can save a lot of time in a telecine session.

There are various ways to record the same code in picture and sound; which one you choose depends on the capabilities of your equipment.

FILM CAMERAS. Some film cameras can expose a running timecode display along the edge of the film (*in-camera timecode*). The *AatonCode* system (also used in Panavision cameras) exposes on the film a combination of human-readable numbers and a machine-readable matrix of dots (see Fig. 6-14). The ARRI system uses a bar code. The camera's timecode is jam-synced to the audio recorder. In postproduction, properly equipped telecines can read the film timecode and automatically sync it to the audio code (see Chapter 16).

VIDEO CAMERAS. In one method, the timecode output from the video camera is connected by cable or wireless link to the timecode input of the audio recorder. This may allow use of record run timecode, which is often preferable. Some audio recorders can be slaved to the camera's timecode so they start and stop automatically when the camera does.

Another method is to use free run/time-of-day timecode and jam-sync the camera and audio recorder with the same TC source. This could be done by cable or with a timecode generator such as the Ambient or Denecke products mentioned above. This may be preferable when more than one camera is being used. For precise sync with more than one HD camera, you need to feed each camera the same timecode via the timecode input and feed trilevel sync via the genlock input.

If your camera won't accept timecode input (many cameras won't), you can put external timecode on one of the camera's audio channels. First, using a TC generator (see above), jam-sync the audio recorder. Then remove the TC source and plug it into one of the audio inputs on the camera (it will need to stay attached while you shoot). Record the TC at an audible level, but don't let it get too hot. Be sure to inform the post team that you've done this.

WHEN TIMECODES DON'T MATCH. Depending on your equipment and what you're trying to do, there may be situations where you *can't* have identical code in the camera and audio recorder. For example, when shooting HD at 23.976

fps, you may find that your audio recorder can't handle that rate. However, if you use 29.97 fps timecode in the audio recorder, you can jam the camera's 23.976 timecode to the recorder and the two will have identical code at the first frame of every second, even though the frames *within* each second are different.[8] Matching up different timecodes with different frame rates is called *cross jamming*.

OPERATING A DOUBLE-SYSTEM RECORDER

Operating an audio recorder on a double-system shoot draws on all techniques described earlier in the chapter and in Chapter 10. However, there are a few additional things to keep in mind.

If your recorder is equipped with confidence monitoring, it's a good idea to monitor it and not the microphone directly (see Monitoring, p. 415). This allows you to check the recording quality. Running out of storage space on a flash card or other storage medium during a take is unnecessary and embarrassing. Some record-ists routinely change cards when they start to fill even if some recording time is remaining, which ensures adequate supply and means the camera crew won't have to wait for you to make a change later. If you don't have enough storage space to complete a shoot, in emergencies you may be able to switch to a lower sample rate, but don't forget to log this and to inform the postproduction team.

In unstaged documentary work, it's important that the soundperson be ready to record at a moment's notice. If shooting appears imminent, the recorder should be put in the standby position (on some recorders this is done by pressing the record button, but not the forward button) and the recording level should be set. If the scene looks interesting, the recordist should not hesitate to record. If the scene doesn't pan out, simply say "no shot" into the mic and stop recording. If the scene is good, the camera should roll. The first part of the scene that has no picture can usually be covered with another shot or a cutaway. There is no advantage to rolling vast amounts of sound, but often if you wait too long to start the recorder, the take will be useless (this is another situation where prerecord can help).

When shooting film, some telecines require five to seven seconds of preroll before the slate or first usable audio. Consult the transfer house before you shoot to find out how much preroll, if any, they need. Make sure you let the recorder run the allotted time before the slate is done or the camera starts (and/or use prerecord to build in the preroll time; see p. 415).

When a film roll runs out during a shot, it's helpful to announce "run out" into the mic when it happens. It's especially useful when using tail slates.

If shooting film, it's generally a good idea to record or store all wild sound (sound without picture) separately so that no one has to wade through it during the telecine session or when syncing up.

---

8. The same thing happens when you transfer film to 24p video but have audio timecode at 30 fps.

CHAPTER 12

Lighting

The Function of Lighting

Everything we do with cameras and lenses is about capturing light. Light is needed to register an image on a video camera's sensor or on film, but the lighting in a movie plays a much more complex role than just that. A scene may be lit by nature (the sun), with *available light* (using whatever natural or man-made light is already at the location), or with lighting fixtures that the filmmaker controls. The way a scene is lit influences both how we understand the scene—what we can see in it—and how we experience the scene emotionally.

Lighting directs the viewer's attention, since the eye is naturally drawn to bright areas of the frame. Lighting gives the audience cues about the time of day and season in which a scene takes place. The angle from which light strikes an object or a face affects how we see shapes and textures. Side lighting casts shadows that emphasize depth, dimension, and surface texture, while frontal lighting tends to flatten, compress, and smooth over features.

Qualities of light have a powerful effect on the mood of a scene. Painters are often celebrated for the way they manipulate light and create particular moods. Andrew Wyeth, for example, evokes the gray, quiet feeling of the Maine landscape with extremely flat and even illumination. Rembrandt creates a much more dramatic effect by using a chiaroscuro style, in which pools of light and shadow are used to obscure as much as they reveal of a subject. Think of the qualities of light over the course of a day. A bright morning sun can feel cheery and safe, while a moonless night evokes mystery or tension.

On feature films, lighting is usually a top priority. The actors and sets must look their best and the mood of the scene must be right. Lights are positioned carefully, consuming much time and expense. The director of photography is usually responsible for the lighting design, which is as important as his or her mastery of cameras and lenses.

In documentary production, light is sometimes a low priority, thought of less for its mood than for its exposure value. In some cases there's just no time for careful lighting. But sometimes good lighting takes no more time than bad. It may be as simple as using available light smartly.

In all productions, one of the key concerns is controlling contrast. Most natural and available light situations have a range of brightness that exceeds the camera's ability to capture it. Often lighting equipment is needed to make shadows less dark or highlights less bright.

People get into fierce debates about the virtues of one camera over another, video versus film, one type of setting or another, but the fact of the matter is that lighting often plays a huge and unacknowledged role. Good lighting can make even a "bad" camera look good, and bad lighting looks bad regardless.

This chapter is written for people working in video or film, who may have a large crew or be shooting alone. For simplicity's sake, the person doing the lighting will be referred to as the DP (director of photography).

LIGHT

Look at a painting, a photograph, or a scene in a movie that you think has interesting light. How is the painter or photographer achieving that effect? Start by identifying the light sources (you may not be able to see the source itself, just the light it produces). Examine each source for these factors that contribute to its effect in the scene:

- What kind of shadow does it cast (crisp or diffuse)?
- What angle is it coming from?
- How bright is it (its intensity)?
- How bright is it relative to other lights (the lighting contrast)?
- What color is it?

When you're ready to shoot a scene, ask the same questions about the light sources. At times you may specifically check, say, the angle or intensity of a given light. But at other times you will look at things more instinctively, evaluating the overall "feel" of the lighting but keeping these factors in the back of your mind.

Qualities of Light

The *hardness* of light is a way to describe the type of shadow it casts. *Hard light*, also called *specular light*, like direct sunlight on a clear day, is made up of parallel rays that produce clean, hard shadows that neatly outline the shapes of objects (see Fig. 12-1). Hard light is crisp and can sometimes feel harsh.

Soft, or *diffuse*, light is less directional. It's made up of rays going in many different directions and produces much softer, gentler shadows. The light on a hazy or overcast day is soft. It emanates from all parts of the sky at once. If it casts shadows at all, they are dull and indistinct.

Hard light can be produced artificially with *lensed* or focused lamps that emit a clearly directed beam. The spotlights used to single out a performer on stage are extremely hard. The light from a car headlight is quite hard. Hard light can be created with a fairly compact lighting fixture.

Because hard light casts very distinct shadows, it is used to delineate shapes. It brings out surface textures and can cast dramatic, sculpted shadows. The classic Hollywood look of the 1940s is based on fairly hard light sources (see Fig. 9-14). In

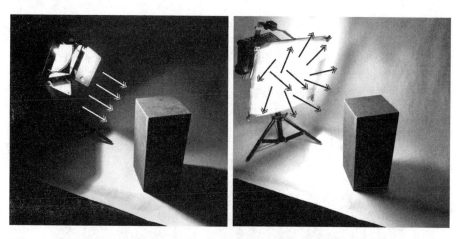

Fig. 12-1. (left) The relatively parallel rays of hard light cast a sharp shadow. (right) The scattered, more random rays of soft light cast a diffuse shadow.

a less flattering use of hard light, news photographers often use a simple, hard light that creates sharp shadows across the face.

Soft light sources produce a broad and even glow, not a beam of light. Soft sources are usually indirect; that is, the light from the bulb is first bounced off a white or silvery surface before striking the subject. In a classic umbrella light (see Fig. 12-28), the bulb shines into the umbrella, which reflects back a wide, diffuse pattern of light. To soften the light from any bulb, we need to spread the light out and disrupt the parallel rays. Another way to soften light is to put some type of

Fig. 12-2. Hard light. This scene from *Dr. Strangelove* is lit with a hard source that casts crisp shadows and provides a glint in Sterling Hayden's eyes. Harsh lighting is used throughout the film to accentuate the craziness of Hayden's character, Jack D. Ripper. (Columbia Pictures)

translucent material between the source and the subject, which is not unlike what a typical cloth lampshade does on a household fixture.

Soft light is relatively gentle and tends to smooth out features and textures. Traditionally, female actors are lit with soft light to disguise any facial wrinkles or imperfections. A single soft light off to the side can provide delicate modeling of curved surfaces such as the face, because of the way it "wraps around" the curve with gradual shading (hard lights produce shadows that are more sharp edged). Some people feel that soft lighting is more "natural." This is true in some situations; for example, window light is often fairly soft and may cast gentle, soft shadows. On the other hand, direct sunlight streaming through a window is usually quite hard and casts hard, crisp shadows.

Fig. 12-3. Soft light. The diffuse light in this shot wraps around the woman's arm and face and produces very gentle shadowing.

Directionality

As noted above, the direction or angle from which light strikes the subject influences how the subject appears on screen. Light coming from the general direction of the camera is called *front light*. *Front axial light* comes from very near the camera's lens; its shadows are mostly not visible from the camera position. Camera-mounted fixtures, such as flash units used on still cameras, provide front light, which illuminates all the visible surfaces of the subject. Full frontal lighting can be quite harsh and usually uninteresting, since dimensionality and surface texture are minimized. However, the flattening effect may be desired. Models are often photographed with very frontal light (see Fig. 4-5). In fashion shoots, sometimes a *ring light* is used that encircles the lens and can makes faces seem flawless and without dimension (of course, a little retouching in Photoshop makes them even more flawless).

You can think of full frontal lighting as projecting from the number 6 on a clock face whose center is the subject. (Think of the camera as also positioned at the number 6.) *Offset* (the light at number 5 or 7) and *three-quarter front light* (around 4:30 or 7:30) can be used for portraiture when more shadowing is desired.

Full side light (around 3 or 9) provides good modeling and indication of texture (since texture is revealed by the pattern of tiny individual shadows visible from the camera position). Side light can be quite dramatic. It produces shadows that fall clearly across the frame and distinctly reveal the depth of various objects in space.

Backlight originates from behind (and usually above) the subject. It tends to outline the subject's shape and to differentiate it from the background. Backlight can produce a bright edge or halo on a subject's hair and shoulders. When backlight predominates, sometimes called *contre-jour*, it can create a moody and romantic ef-

Fig. 12-4. Directionality of light. The subject is lit by one light. (A) Backlight or kicker. (B) Side light. (C) Three-quarter front light. (D) Full frontal light. Also see Fig. 12-40. (Ned Johnston)

fect. If the background is bright and no light falls on the camera side of the subject, the subject will be in silhouette.

We are also concerned with the *vertical* angle of light—that is, the height from which it strikes the subject. *Top light*, which shines down from directly above the subject, can make deep shadows in eye sockets. Cinematographer Gordon Willis used top light in *The Godfather* to cast menacing shadows in Marlon Brando's eyes. Top light can also make landscapes seem more two-dimensional, because few shadows are visible (think of sunlight at noon on a bright day). Most movie lighting is done with the key lights angled about 40 degrees from the floor or slightly higher for the best modeling without casting excessive shadows. *Underlighting*, in which the light comes up from below the subject and casts shadows upward, occurs rarely in nature and is used in horror films to lend a ghoulish look to faces.

Fig. 12-5. Lighting depends on the camera angle. From this side, the performer is backlit by the spotlight, with a very high-contrast, edge-lit look. If you shot from the other side, she would be front lit with a much flatter look. The camera on the crane directly above is seeing a side-lit shot of the keyboard. (Sony Electronics, Inc.)

Lighting Contrast

Much of the mood or atmosphere of a lighting scheme is determined by the *lighting contrast*—that is, the relationship in light intensity between the brightly lit areas and the shadow areas. With great lighting contrast, there is a great difference in intensity between the bright areas and the deep shadows. With low lighting contrast (often achieved by using secondary lights to fill in the shadows), the lighting appears fairly flat and uniform throughout the frame. The degree of lighting contrast is often expressed numerically in terms of the *lighting contrast ratio* (see

p. 512). Lighting contrast results from the relationship of the *key light* (which casts the primary shadows) and the *fill light* (which fills in the key's shadows). See below for more on these terms.

A *low-key* lighting design has high lighting contrast and a Rembrandt-like look, with dark shadow areas predominating over light areas. Low-key lighting is associated with night, emotion, tension, tragedy, and mystery. Film-noir movies, as well as *Citizen Kane*, are lit in moody, low-key lighting; the dramatic feel of the lighting is well suited to the black-and-white image.

With *high-key* lighting, the lighting contrast is low and bright tones predominate, making everything appear bright and cheery. High-key lighting is often used for daytime scenes and comedy. Most studio-shot television shows use this kind of low-contrast lighting scheme because the light is evenly distributed around the set, which is convenient in situations in which several cameras are shooting simultaneously from different angles or when an actor must be able to move freely around the set without walking into deep shadows.

Fig. 12-6. The single candle produces hard light (note the crisp shadows) and a very high-contrast lighting scheme with no fill lighting and deep shadows. (*The Penitent Magdalen* by Georges de La Tour, The Metropolitan Museum of Art, Gift of Mr. & Mrs. Charles Wrightsman, 1978)

Fig. 12-7. In this scene from *Get Low*, smoke is used to reveal the rays of light streaming through the window. Lighting contrast on the face is high, with little fill lighting for a stark look. The frame has a great feeling of depth that ranges from the foreground subject to the middle ground window, and then to the back wall of the church. (Sony Pictures Classics)

Fig. 12-8. The window light here is quite soft (note the gentle shadow angled downward from the windowsill). Compared to Fig. 12-7, this lighting is lower contrast, since the light source is bigger and softer, and reflected light in the room helps fill in shadows. See other works by Vermeer for his masterly rendering of natural light. (*Young Woman with a Water Jug* by Johannes Vermeer, The Metropolitan Museum of Art, Gift of Henry G. Marquand, 1889)

Fig. 12-9. This scene from *Born Yesterday* is lit in a classic high-key, low-contrast style of Hollywood comedies of the 1940s and 50s. Lighting units are fairly hard, and no part of the set is allowed to go very dark. (Columbia Pictures)

LIGHTING EQUIPMENT

Lighting equipment may be owned by the filmmaker, a production company, or a school, or it may be rented for individual shoots. Often the DP and/or gaffer (see p. 362) assembles a lighting package from a rental house according to the needs of each production or day's work.

Lighting Fixtures and Light Intensity

In the world of movie lighting, a lighting fixture may be called a *lighting unit, instrument, head,* or *luminaire.* The bulb is referred to as a *lamp* or *globe*; changing a bulb is *relamping.* Lighting units are identified by type and power consumption. A 5K spot is a 5,000-watt (5-kilowatt) spotlight. Lights are balanced for tungsten (3200°K) unless stated otherwise. Don't confuse degrees kelvin with use of *K* that indicates wattage.

On the set you'll find many names used for various pieces of equipment; some are based on manufacturers' names, and others are nicknames used in different regions or countries.

The brightness of a lightbulb is usually discussed in terms of wattage. *Wattage* is actually a measure of how much electric power is used (see Location Lighting, p. 518); some bulbs and fixtures put out more light than others for the same power consumption (that is, they are more efficient). In the case of two lights that employ the same type of bulb in the same fixture, a doubling of wattage implies a doubling of light output.

With the exception of certain focusing lighting fixtures, the intensity of illumination decreases the farther the subject is from a light. This is known as light *falloff.* The rule for typical open bulbs is that the falloff in intensity is inversely proportional to the *square* of the distance (see Fig. 12-10). Thus, moving an object *twice* as

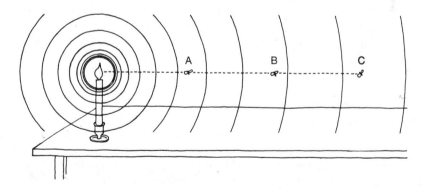

Fig. 12-10. The inverse square law. (1) Light falls off rapidly as you move away from the source: moth B is twice as far from the candle as moth A but receives one-quarter the amount of light. Moth C is three times farther from the candle than moth A and receives one-ninth the amount of light. (2) Light falloff is less severe when you are farther from the source: moving from B to C is the same distance as moving from A to B, but the light falloff is much less (it falls off to about half the previous level instead of to one-quarter). (Carol Keller)

far from a lamp results in it being lit by *one-quarter* the amount of light. Because of this, falloff is especially sharp when you are *near* the light source. Imagine a couch lit by a floor lamp at one end of the couch. A person sitting near the lamp could be lit four times as brightly as the person sitting next to him (an exposure difference of two stops). This difference will look even more extreme when captured on video or film. For even illumination, lights should be kept far away from the subjects so that slight changes in distance do not cause large changes in exposure. Soft light sources fall off more sharply than focused, hard light sources.

BULBS

Bulbs differ in the type and color of light they emit. If you're unfamiliar with color temperature and its use in video and film, see Chapter 8. Further discussion of white balance and video cameras is on p. 109.

Household Bulbs and Photo Bulbs

It used to be that most home interiors were lit with tungsten incandescent bulbs. These are rapidly being replaced with compact fluorescents (see below). Nevertheless, there are still tungsten bulbs in use. Common household incandescent bulbs can be used with video cameras as long as the camera can get a good white balance. They can also be used for black-and-white film shoots. Their color temperature, however, is about 2900°K, so the light they produce looks yellow-orange instead of white on tungsten-balanced color film. Sometimes professional 3200°K lighting units are used for the primary illumination for a shoot, and household incandescents are used in a table lamp or other practical fixture (see Lighting Styles, p. 498). In this case, though the household bulb may look yellow relative to the movie lights, it may seem natural in the scene. See Practicals, p. 491.

Photo bulbs are available that use tungsten filaments similar to those in household bulbs, but the light emitted is designed to match tungsten-balanced film. Both 3200°K and 3400°K versions are available. A bluer, "daylight-balanced" version (rated at 4800°K) can also be purchased. Photo bulbs may be either *photofloods* or *reflector floods*. Reflector floods, such as the R-40, are mushroom shaped with a built-in reflecting surface that projects a more directed beam of light.

Tungsten-Halogen Bulbs

Also called just *tungsten* or *quartz*, these bulbs employ a tungsten filament surrounded by halogen gas encased in a quartz glass bulb (see Fig. 12-17). Tungsten-halogen bulbs have been the most commonly used bulbs for professional lighting instruments. The standard "tungsten" lighting unit is assumed to have a tungsten-halogen bulb rated at 3200°K. The bulbs are small and the brightest ones are rated at about 20,000 watts. They burn for hundreds of hours, do not diminish in brightness or color temperature over their life span, and are relatively resistant to breakage during transport. Tungsten bulbs become very hot and are used mostly in heavy-duty fixtures for maximum safety and control. Finger oils damage quartz glass, so use gloves or paper when handling the bulb. If the glass is touched, wipe it with alcohol. Carry a metal clamp for removing hot bulbs. Since quartz bulbs can explode, never turn one on when you or anyone else is directly in front of the fixture.

As noted above, tungsten bulbs are rated at 3200°K and can be used with tungsten-balanced film without a filter. These bulbs, and any other tungsten-balanced source, can be raised in color temperature to better match daylight illumination with a blue *dichroic* filter or with blue gel material (see p. 497). This normally cuts the light's output by about half.

Fig. 12-11. HMI lights being used outdoors. Note the ballast unit (circled). HMIs are an efficient source of daylight-balanced illumination.

HMI Bulbs

Hydrargyrum medium-arc iodide (*HMI*, also called *metal halide*) bulbs are an efficient lighting source that produces daylight-balanced illumination (5600°K or 6000°K). HMIs put out three to four times as much light as tungsten bulbs for the same amount of electric power used. This improved efficiency means that bright lights can be run off a smaller power supply, possibly avoiding the need for special power lines or generators. Trying to match daylight with a tungsten source requires filters that cut out half the light; HMIs require no filters for daylight and are far more efficient for daylight applications. HMIs also give off less heat than tungsten lights, making them popular with actors and crews. HMIs are generally operated using AC power (wall current) and require a ballast unit to control the electricity going to the lamp. Most HMIs produce a pulsed light that seems continuous to the eye but may result in flicker in the video or film image if used improperly.[1] To avoid flicker, the light pulses must be evenly distributed on each video or film frame. These are the guidelines:

1. Use a crystal-controlled camera. All video cameras and most sync-sound film cameras are crystal controlled.
2. Use a very stable power supply. In most technically advanced countries, the frequency of AC current is very stable. Care must be taken when using generators (use a crystal-controlled generator) or when shooting in the developing world.
3. Use a frame rate that is divisible into twice the AC frequency. Thus, in the United States and other countries where the AC power is at 60 Hz, a frame rate of 12, 15, 20, 24, 30, 40, or 60 can be used. At 24 fps, camera shutter angles from 60 to 200 degrees will work fine, but a shutter angle of 144 degrees allows for the maximum variation if camera or power is slightly off speed. In countries with 50 Hz power, you can shoot at 10, 12.5, 16.666, 20, 25, 33.3, or 50 fps without danger of flicker. In these countries, a camera run at 25 fps can use any shutter angle. A camera run at 24 fps can avoid flicker by using a 172.8-degree shutter.
4. When shooting in former NTSC countries that use typical 60 Hz power, standard video frame rates of 30p or 60i can be used without flicker (and use a shutter speed of $\frac{1}{65}$ or $\frac{1}{120}$ second). In former PAL countries with 50 Hz power, video cameras run at 25p or 50i should be flicker-free (use a shutter speed of $\frac{1}{50}$ or $\frac{1}{100}$).

These principles apply to all AC discharge lamps, including some fluorescent tubes (see below), HMI, CSI, sodium vapor, and mercury vapor lamps (the latter two are often found in sports stadiums and parking lots; they may require special filtering for color balance).

There are *flicker-free* ballasts available that allow filming at any frame rate without risk of HMI flicker and may output more light; however, they can produce a high whistling sound in some settings.

Fig. 12-12. Bron's Kobold 200-watt HMI with ballast unit. (Bron-Kobold, USA)

---

1. Flicker means that some frames seem more brightly lit than others.

Some HMIs can be battery powered. A 200-watt HMI puts out nearly as much light as a 1K tungsten unit (see Fig. 12-12).

Fluorescent Bulbs

Fluorescent lighting falls into three categories: compact fluorescents often found in the home, conventional fluorescent fixtures typically found in office and institutional settings, and specially designed fluorescent lighting units for film and video work.

COMPACT FLUORESCENTS. Many homes are lit with compact fluorescent lamps (CFLs), which typically have a spiral-shaped or short, folded tubular bulb, most of which screw into the same household receptacles used for incandescents. CFLs are available in various color temperatures ranging from a warm white that is close to tungsten up to daylight (for more on CFL color, see p. 308). CFLs can be used for video assuming the camera can get a good white balance and for film as long the color works with your stock and any other lighting units. Some CFLs are dimmable. CFLs can be used in some professional lighting units (see Fig. 12-13). CFLs and LEDs (see below) produce the smallest carbon footprint.

Fig. 12-13. This Lowel Rifa light (see Fig. 12-19) has a receptacle for professional tungsten-halogen lamps, or you can quickly replace it with a screw-in (Edison) fitting that accepts standard household bulbs and compact fluorescents (shown here). CFLs are cheap and use very little power. You can get daylight-balanced, professional CFLs (5500°K) or use conventional household bulbs of various color temperatures.

CONVENTIONAL FLUORESCENTS. Standard fluorescent lighting fixtures have long, straight tubular bulbs and are usually undesirable for shooting—but they may be unavoidable. The spectrum of light from standard fluorescent tubes is discontinuous and matches neither tungsten nor daylight illumination. There are several types of fluorescent tubes available (daylight, cool white, warm white) that vary in color. Daylight and cool white tubes may produce an unpleasant blue-green color cast. Some warm white bulbs, however, are fairly close to tungsten.

As long as all fluorescent tubes in a scene are the same type, most video cameras can achieve an acceptable white balance (you may want to experiment with the "daylight" position on the white balance control). Film cameras can be used with filters on the lights or the camera to improve color rendition, such as using either an 85 or an FL-B filter for tungsten films or an FL-D filter for daylight-balanced films. However, with many color film stocks, acceptable color balance can be achieved in the lab even if no filters were used. It's better to get a good exposure with no filter than to be forced to underexpose with a filter.

Fluorescent lighting causes similar but less severe flicker problems than HMIs (see above). Standard frame rates of 24, 25, and 30 fps are fine. (In North America and other places where 60 Hz power is used, the rule of thumb is simply not to use shutter speeds faster than 1/60 second; in other parts of the world where power is delivered at 50 Hz, 1/50 second should work.)

Mixing fluorescents with other sources of light can cause problems (see Mixed

Fig. 12-14. (left) Kino Flo high-output, flicker-free fluorescent bulbs are available in true tungsten (3200°K) or daylight balance (5500°K). (top) Kino Flo Diva-Lites are useful as a soft source and for large areas. (right) The BarFly is handy for tight spots and accents. (LocLum.com/Kino Flo, Inc.)

Lighting, p. 514). Fluorescent fixtures at workplaces often shine straight down, resulting in overexposed hair and deep eye and nose shadows. Many DPs choose, whenever possible, to replace standard fluorescents with color-balanced tubes (see below) or to turn off the fluorescents altogether and relight with some other source. When shooting in supermarkets and other settings in which it's impractical to either turn off or replace existing tubes, a DP will sometimes use a professional fluorescent fill light fixture that uses the same tubes, to at least maintain consistency.

FLUORESCENTS FOR VIDEO AND FILM. Fluorescent lighting units are available that overcome the problems mentioned above. A wide range of fixtures are made by Kino Flo using high-frequency ballasts that are flicker-free and avoid the humming noise of standard ballasts. The KF55 tube is daylight balanced at 5500°K and the KF32 is tungsten balanced. Other manufacturers make fluorescent units as well. Banks of fluorescents can be used as key or fill lights. The light output is bright, soft, and very even. Individual tubes—sometimes very small ones—can be used for out-of-the-way spots or built into a set.

There are also fluorescent tubes available that can be used with conventional fixtures but produce a true color that reads correctly with either video or film. The Optima 32 bulb is tungsten balanced and the Vita-Lite and Chroma 50 tubes are daylight balanced. When shooting in an office or other institutional setting, a movie crew will often replace the existing tubes with these bulbs.

LEDs

A newer type of lighting unit uses *LEDs* (*light-emitting diodes*) and offers lots of advantages for shooting. These compact units produce heat-free, flickerless, silent light and some units can be dimmed from 100 percent to full off with no color shift (unlike many other types of light). Some LED instruments combine different-

Fig. 12-15. Litepanels MiniPlus LED lights mounted on a car mirror and camera. LEDs are efficient lighting, available in daylight and/or tungsten balance, and fully dimmable with virtually no shift in color. LEDs are available in large and small panels. (Litepanels, Inc.)

colored diodes, so they can be switched between 5600°K daylight and 3200°K tungsten balance (and some offer color balances in between). Other units are designed for daylight *or* tungsten color temperature and need a filter to convert to a different color. LEDs are highly energy efficient and have an extremely long life span. LEDs are available as flat panels, as focusable lensed lights, and as individual "bulbs" (such as those used in the home, which are bulb-shaped to emulate tungsten lights). As costs come down, LEDs are starting to replace other types of bulbs both in the home and on movie shoots because they are versatile and eco-friendly. See Figs. 12-15 and 10-15.

Plasma

Plasma is a type of lighting technology just coming into use for video and film. Plasma units produce daylight-balanced, flickerless light and are twice as efficient as HMI—a 275-watt plasma is equivalent to a 575-watt HMI. They can be used with high-speed cameras and run on AC or batteries.

TYPES OF LIGHTING INSTRUMENTS

Lensed Spotlights

The most controllable kind of lighting unit is a focusing spotlight. Some spots have a *Fresnel lens* (silent *s*, pronounced "fray-NEL") in front of the bulb (see Fig. 12-16). These lights emit focused, parallel rays of light that don't spread out much or diffuse over distance. Most spotlights are focusable, which means the bulb can be moved back and forth relative to the reflector or lens to produce either a hard, narrowly directed beam of light (*spot* position) or a wider, more diffuse, less intense beam (*flood* position). These, like most other movie lights, have a set of adjustable baffles called *barndoors*, which are used to block the beam from going where you don't want it (see Fig. 12-18).

Mole-Richardson makes a widely used line of studio equipment and you should learn Mole's names: a 5K lensed spotlight is a *senior*, while the 2K is a *junior*, and the 1K is a *baby* spot. A *baby junior* is a 2K in a small housing. A *tweenie* has a 650-watt bulb and a *mini* or *tiny* (also called an *inkie*) is 250 watts or less.

Focusing, lensed spotlights are versatile and very controllable and used extensively on typical movie sets. They may also be used on location shoots, particu-

Fig. 12-16. LTM Pepper Fresnel. Compact, focusing lensed spotlight. Note Fresnel lens. (Fletcher Chicago/LTM)

larly when the production is supported by a truck and a larger crew. However, lensed units are sometimes too heavy for a documentary being done with a small crew or involving a lot of travel. Some documentary DPs carry one or two lensed units and use mostly open-faced lights (see below).

Open-Faced Spotlights

Open-faced spotlights have no lens in front of the bulb. These are lighter and cheaper than Fresnel units and are often used on location and in small-scale filming. While these nonlensed instruments can be focused by moving the bulb from spot to flood positions, they are less controllable or "cuttable" than lensed units (because the beam is not as sharp-edged), and the quality of light is not as hard.

Open-faced lights have various names. Mole's 1K is a *Mickey*, Ianiro's is a *Redhead*. A 2K may be a *mighty* or a *blonde*. Lowel's open-faced spots include the *Omnilight* (maximum 650W) and the *DP light* (maximum 1K).

Fig. 12-17. Lowel DP open-faced spot. The quartz bulb is clearly visible. (Lowel Light Mfg., Inc.)

Nonfocusing Lights

Lights that are not focusable come in many configurations. Some have lenses, some don't. *PAR lamps* (for *parabolic aluminized reflector*) are sealed beam lights that look like automobile headlights. PAR lights are available with different fixed lenses; some project a very narrow beam over great distances, while others have a wider pattern. PARs may be used singly or in groups—typically, a grid of 2 x 3 or 3 x 3 lights on a frame (called *six lights* and *nine lights*, respectively). PARs put out a lot of light, and they can be used to simulate or augment sunlight, but they can be hard to control. *FAY* bulbs are PARs that incorporate a dichroic filter to produce daylight-balanced illumination. You can also get HMIs in sealed-beam configuration.

There are several types of nonfocusing, open-faced floodlights. *Scoops* are dish-shaped floodlights. *Broads* are rectangular and have a long, tube-shaped bulb (see Fig. 12-18). Floodlights are sometimes used on the set as fill lights or to provide even illumination over a broad area. They can be hard to work with because the light tends to spill where you don't want it.

Fig. 12-18. Broad. Bardwell & McAlister 1,000-watt Mini-Mac with four-leaf barndoor. Note the tubular bulb. (Bardwell & McAlister, Inc.)

Soft Lights and Reflectors

The relatively hard light produced by a spot or a flood unit can be softened by placing some *diffusion* material in front of the unit. Diffusion spreads the light, disrupts the hard parallel rays, and cuts down the light's intensity. One of the most common types of diffusion is light fiberglass matting called *tough spun* or *spun* (for spun glass), which will not burn under the high heat of movie lights. There are many other types of professional diffusion, including translucent plastic sheets such as Lee 216 White Diffusion and the slightly milder Opal Tough Frost made by Rosco (see Fig. 12-1). Rosco's Soft Frost looks a bit like shower curtain material; because it's flexible, it won't rattle in the wind like some other diffusion material. Most types of diffusion are available in various grades, including full, ½ (medium), and ¼ (light). If placed far enough from the heat of the fixture, any number of materials can be used for diffusion, including thin cloth, silk, or rolls of tracing paper.

To obtain softer lighting, the light from the bulb can be bounced off a white or silvery surface; the larger the surface and the farther it is from the bulb, the softer the light. A *soft light* is a large, scoop-shaped fixture that blocks all direct light from the bulb so that only bounced light escapes. Studio soft lights are bulky, but there are collapsible models available that pack easily for travel.

A *soft box* encloses the bulb in a collapsible reflector with a soft diffuser over the opening. These can provide very nice, soft light and are quick to set up and easy to

Fig. 12-19. Collapsible soft boxes produce very soft, very even illumination and fold up for travel. Shown here, Lowel Rifa lights of various sizes. See also Fig. 12-13. (Lowel Light Mfg., Inc.)

use. Chimera makes popular soft boxes (called *lightbanks*) that can be mounted over a conventional spotlight with a *speed ring* adapter (see Figs. 12-20 and 12-26). Lowel's Rifa light is a self-contained soft box (see Figs. 12-19 and 12-13) that sets up quickly. Compared to simply bouncing light against a card to produce soft light (see below), a soft box is more controllable—you can direct it at the subject without light spilling all over the room. Many soft boxes are available with an *eggcrate* (a fabric baffle that mounts on the front surface) that helps keep light from spreading (see Fig. 12-26).

Chimera also makes *lanterns*, which have rounded or pancake shapes that can be used to provide a gentle glow by a subject or for even illumination over a dinner table. You can make your own low-cost lantern using a household paper Japanese lantern.

Soft lighting can also be created with a spot- or floodlight by bouncing the light off walls, ceilings, or reflecting cards. Bounced light is good for lighting a large space. *Foam-core sheets* are lightweight and rigid and make a versatile bounce board that can be easily cut and taped to walls or mounted on stands. White cardboard *show cards* are cheaper but sometimes not rigid enough. Using foam core or cards for fill lighting can be a good way to fill shadows from lights without creating new ones (see Fig. 12-34).

An extremely lightweight *space blanket* or foil sheet can be taped shiny side out to make an excellent reflecting surface on a dark or colored wall, and it will protect

Fig. 12-20. Chimera lightbanks being used for soft key lighting. A reflector provides fill. See the results in Fig. 12-29D. (Chimera)

Fig. 12-21. A light source can be softened by bouncing it and/or by projecting it through diffusion material. The xenon light source here produces a very circular, focused, narrow beam of light. Shown with Xeno mirror reflector. (Matthews Studio Equipment, Inc.)

the wall from burning. Another way to create soft light is to use a photographer's umbrella, which is silver or white on the inside. The lighting unit is mounted on the stem and directed toward the inside of the umbrella. Umbrella reflectors fold to a compact size for traveling.

Generally the reflecting surface should not have a color cast. However, sometimes a colored surface is used deliberately to create an effect. A reflector with a gold surface may be used to provide a warm fill light. Space blankets usually have a blue side that can be used to approximate daylight when bouncing tungsten lighting units.

Reflectors of various kinds are also used outdoors to redirect sunlight. This is commonly done to fill shadows on a sunny day (see Figs. 12-22 and 12-40). Usually you can get much more punch from a reflector than you can from a powered lighting instrument and it requires no electricity. Smooth, silvered reflectors provide relatively hard light, while textured silver or white surfaces are softer. Collapsible, cloth reflectors such as the Flexfill are popular for location shoots. They fold into a small disc for travel, and open to a larger circle with one side white and the other silver or gold. On windy days, all reflectors must be carefully steadied or the intensity of light on the subject will fluctuate.

Fig. 12-22. Flexfill reflectors. Useful for filling shadows and reducing lighting contrast. Available in different surfaces: white maintains the character of the light; silver for more punch over longer distances; gold for adding warmth (shadows lit by skylight can sometimes look blue); translucent softens the light (when placed between light source and subject). Flexfills collapse to roughly one-third size when not in use. (Allen Green)

Practicals

When a typical household table lamp is used on a movie set, it is called a *practical*. Practicals are often part of the set design (see Fig. 12-31). They may also be present in documentary shoots. Often a dimmer or diffusion material is used with a practical to cut down the intensity or at least minimize the light falling below or above a lampshade. You can get inexpensive dimmers at a hardware store that screw into the socket or plug between the power cable and the wall. If you're looking for more intensity from a practical, and you use a photoflood or screw-in halogen light, be sure the fixture is rated for the wattage of the bulb and that there's adequate upward ventilation to prevent burning or melting. For more on working with practicals, see Lighting Wide Shots, p. 506.

Camera Lights and Handheld Lights

Camera-mounted lights are commonly used for newsgathering or documentary (where they are sometimes called *sun guns*) and feature films (where they may be called *Obie lights, eye lights,* or *bash lights*). A camera-mounted light is useful when the camera is moving because the unit moves with the camera and provides shadowless light on the subject. This shadowless light can be a blessing if it is filling the shadows cast by other, stronger lights. However, if it is the only light on the subject, it can be a curse, as full frontal lighting tends to be flat and harsh. On the other hand, ring lights, which circle the lens, provide totally flat, frontal light and that shadowless look is often seen as glamorous.

Fig. 12-23. Cool-Lux on-camera light with battery belt and diffuser. (Cool-Lux)

Sun guns (originally a trade name that gained wide use) are often handheld and powered by battery. Even a standard tungsten spotlight can sometimes be fitted with a 30-volt bulb and powered with a 30-volt battery pack or belt. Lights and power packs vary in capacity, and most require several hours to recharge (see Battery Power, p. 128). With tungsten bulbs, when the batteries run down, light intensity and color temperature drop. LEDs are more efficient, will run longer on a battery, and should maintain constant color temperature (see Figs. 12-15 and 10-15). Battery-powered lights are useful for scenes in cars; some can be run off the car battery by using an adapter.

When a scene is lit with only one small light, it's not easy to make the lighting pleasant. With a handheld light, it's probably best to position the light a few feet to the side of the camera. The harsh shadows can be softened with diffusion on the light, although this sacrifices brightness. Some DPs bounce handheld lights off the ceiling or a wall, producing a very diffuse light. To maintain constant illumination, hold the unit steady. It's often best to have an assistant hold the light.

Lighting Accessories

The art of lighting begins with the lights themselves, but the tools for controlling light are just as important. The lighting package includes many accessory items for working with light.

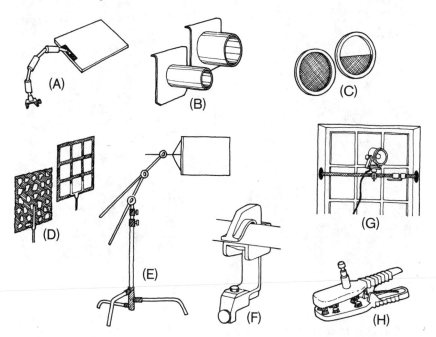

Fig. 12-24. Lighting accessories. (A) French flag. (B) Snoots. (C) Full scrim and half scrim. (D) Cookies. (E) Century stand with three gobo heads and flag. (F) Hanger for mounting on pipes or small beams. (G) Polecat mounted in window well. (H) Gator grip. (Representations are not drawn to same scale.) (Carol Keller)

Spilled light, or just *spill*, is light (usually from the edge of the beam) that illuminates an area where you don't want it. Spill is primarily controlled with *barndoors*, which are adjustable flaps that mount on the front of the lighting instrument (see Fig. 12-18). Barndoors come in two- and four-leaf versions, the latter providing more control. They can be opened wide or closed down to produce a relatively narrow beam of light. An even narrower beam can be made with a *snoot*, which is a cylindrical baffle that fits over a spotlight.

Flags, which are also called *cutters* or *gobos*, are either rectangular metal cards, dark cloth on wire frames, or pieces of cardboard. They are usually mounted on stands to cut off unwanted spill. The farther the flag is from the light, the sharper its shadow will be.

A *French flag* is a small card mounted on the camera as an effective lens shade to block light spilling into the front of the lens. These are sometimes attached to small flexible arms, and sometimes to the top of a matte box (see Fig. 8-10).

At times you need to flag off a light softly, creating a gradual transition from light to dark rather than having a hard shadow line. This may be done with a *scrim* or *net*—a piece of very thin, dark netting often mounted on a three-sided frame (see

Fig. 12-25). Nets come in single and double thicknesses and can be used in multiple layers for increased shadowing.

Fig. 12-25. Adjusting a double scrim on a grip stand. Useful for shading off the light on part of a scene.

Spill leaking from the back of a lighting unit can cause flare in the lens, or, if gels are being used, it can disrupt the lighting scheme with light of the wrong color. This spill can usually be blocked off with cards or flags. *Black wrap* is black aluminum foil that is very handy for controlling spill.

A *cucoloris* (usually called a *cookie* or *kook*) is a cutout piece of material placed in front of a light to cast a patterned shadow. Cookies are typically used to project the shadow of a window frame or venetian blinds. By adjusting the color and angle of a light projecting through a window cookie you can suggest a mood or indicate a time of day. Sometimes an abstract, dappled pattern is used to break up a uniform expanse of wall or floor or to create a transition zone between sunlit and shaded areas. The shadow cast by any cookie or flag will be sharpest if it is placed closer to the subject than to the light and if the light source is hard.

There are many ways to reduce the intensity of a light. The simplest is perhaps just to move it farther from the subject. Nets can be used to shade or "feather" a light. *Silks* are white silk material mounted on frames like nets; they cut down the light while diffusing it somewhat (see Fig. 12-27).

Scrims (not to be confused with the fabric scrim mentioned above) are circular wire mesh screens that are placed in front of a lighting unit, usually inside the barndoors, to reduce the intensity without changing the color temperature or the quality (hardness) of light. Inserting a scrim is the best way to reduce light intensity without changing anything else. A single scrim (usually indicated by a green frame) reduces the intensity about a half stop; a double scrim (red frame) cuts out a full

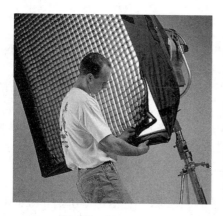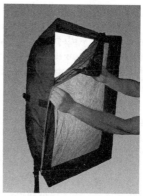

Fig. 12-26. (left) Cloth grid eggcrate being mounted on a large Chimera lightbank to reduce spill and direct light mostly toward the subject. (right) Using a scrim to reduce the output of a soft box. (Chimera)

stop. On a half scrim, half of the circle is left open. A half scrim can be used to solve the common problem that occurs when someone walks toward a light. Normally, as he approaches the light he'll become brighter. To even out the illumination, raise the lighting unit fairly high above the subject and point it down at an angle. Use a half scrim to reduce the intensity of the bottom of the light beam (which falls near the unit) without diminishing the top of the beam (which reaches into the distance). You could use a net or a silk to do the same thing (see Fig. 12-27). Roscoe makes a black plastic scrim material in wide rolls (Cinegel 3421) that you can place over windows to reduce the light coming through by two stops; if not in sharp focus you can shoot through it without seeing the scrim (see Fig. 12-39).

Studio lighting is sometimes dimmed with *shutters*, which act like venetian

Fig. 12-27. A silk being used to cut the bottom half of the light beam; this evens out the illumination close to and far from the light. This light is attached to the telephone pole using a poultry bracket. (Matthews Studio Equipment, Inc.)

blinds. *Dimmers* are used in theatrical lighting, as in the home, to regulate light intensity. Dimmers lower the voltage going to the light, which not only makes the light dimmer, but with tungsten lights results in the color temperature dropping as well (making tungsten lights more orange). There are some situations in which the lowered color temperature may seem natural (see Mixed Lighting, p. 514). LEDs and some fluorescents can be dimmed without changing the color.

There are hundreds of devices for supporting lights and mounting them on various surfaces. Lights are usually supported by stands, which are collapsible for transport. *Century stands* (*C-stands*) have low-slung legs at different heights that allow several stands to be positioned close together. *Gobo heads* with multiple locking arms can be positioned in endless ways. *Roller stands* have wheels that make it easier to reposition heavy lights.

A *gator grip* is a spring-loaded clip for attaching lights to doors, pipes, and moldings. A *C-clamp* with a *spud* to mount a light is more stable. A *polecat* is like an expandable closet bar. A heavier-duty version is the *wall spreader*, which allows you to run a piece of lumber, such as a two-by-four, between two walls. A polecat or a wall spreader can be used to hang lights near the ceiling without stands that might show in the scene. When shooting in offices or other rooms that have hung ceilings, a *scissors clip* allows you to mount lights right on the ceiling. A *wall plate* for mounting fixtures can be screwed or taped to vertical or horizontal surfaces.

Several feet of opaque black fabric such as *duvetyn* ("doova-teen") can be extremely useful to have on hand for creating limbo backgrounds, darkening a window, or placing on a table for filming objects.

Other items for a lighting package include apple boxes (see p. 381), *sandbags* for stabilizing lights and stands, *stingers* (extension cords), gloves for handling hot lamps, and plenty of *gaffer's tape* (a gray fabric tape sold in equipment houses—*not* duct tape). See p. 368 for a typical lighting and grip package.

Colored Filters and Gels

A common way to change the color of light is to use *gels* (gelatine), which are made of flexible, transparent plastic that comes in small sheets and large rolls. Gels can be mounted on lights in gel frames or just attached to barndoors with clothespins.

CTO (*color temperature orange*) gels are used to lower color temperature for converting daylight to tungsten-balanced light or otherwise warming a light source. *Sun 85* or ¾ *CTO* gels are roughly equivalent to an 85 camera filter (see Chapter 8) and are used to convert standard 5500°K daylight and HMI sources to tungsten. These filters cut out about two-thirds of a stop of light. Lee 204 and Rosco 3407— full CTO gels that are slightly more orange—are used to convert skylight (6500°K) to tungsten.

CTB (*color temperature blue*) gels are used to raise color temperature and make any source bluer. Some blue gels are referred to as *booster gels*, since they boost the color temperature. Rosco 3202 and Lee 201 are full CTB gels, used to bring a 3200°K tungsten source up to 5700°K daylight. These cut out a little less than two stops of light (one and two-thirds).

Gels can be purchased in full, ¾, ½, ¼, and ⅛ intensity versions, from deep color to pale, to make large or slight changes in color for precise matching of light sources. The deeper the color of the gel, the more it cuts down the light intensity. Often the full CTB cuts out too much light, and a ¾ or ½ CTB is used instead, allowing a tungsten source to appear slightly yellow compared to daylight.

Gels are available in many other colors besides orange and blue. Sometimes the light from an HMI lamp seems *slightly* too blue; a ⅛ Straw gel or a pale yellow may be used to "take the curse off" and warm the light a bit. There is a wide range of other colors for creating more theatrical effects.

Gels are also available in combination with neutral density (ND; see p. 312) or diffusion material. Blue Frost converts tungsten to daylight while adding diffusion—having both effects in one gel may prevent unneeded loss of light.

Gels should be replaced when heat from the lamp causes the center of the gel to become paler. Gels and the more rigid *acrylic filters* may be attached to windows to filter daylight (see Mixed Lighting, p. 514).

Another way to raise color temperature is to use a *dichroic* filter, sometimes called a *dike*, which is a special blue glass filter used to convert 3200°K tungsten sources

Fig. 12-28. Lowel Super Ambi Kit. Location package includes two Omni-lights (650-watt-maximum open-faced spots); two Tota-lights (1,000-watt-maximum broads) with umbrellas; one Rifa eX 55 soft box; one Pro-light spot. Accessories include stands, flags with flexible stems, scrims, door/wall brackets, clamps, gel frames, etc. Everything fits into the carrying case. (Lowel Light Mfg., Inc.)

to about 5500°K to match the color of daylight. These cut out about 50 percent of the light, reducing intensity by one stop. Dichroics are expensive and fragile and must be fitted to a particular light.

Mounting Lights Safely

In close quarters a hot, falling light can do serious damage. Spread legs of a light stand wide for maximum stability. Weigh down light stands with sand or water bags or tape them down with gaffer's tape. When raising a light, use the lower, thicker extensions of a light stand before the thin, upper ones.

Tape all power cables neatly to the floor or put mats over them in high-traffic areas so no one trips on them. Use plenty of good-quality gaffer's tape when you attach lights to a wall, and if you can, place lights where they won't strike anyone if they fall. Remember that tape loses its stickiness when hot. When possible, "safety" a hanging light by attaching a piece of sash cord or chain to a fixed point to catch the light if it drops off its mount. Gaffer's tape will often remove paint and wallpaper, so peel the tape back slowly as soon as possible after shooting to minimize damage.

LIGHTING TECHNIQUE

LIGHTING STYLES

Before beginning any movie that involves controlled lighting, decide on the lighting style you hope to achieve. The DP and director can look at movies, photographs, and paintings for ideas.

Like everything else, lighting styles have evolved over the years. Black-and-white feature films of the 1930s and 1940s were usually lit in a highly stylized way. The goal was not "realistic" lighting but something that would heighten the drama and the glamour. These films were shot on studio sets that often had no ceiling and only two or three walls. Lights mounted outside the set on overhead grids and elsewhere struck the actors from directions that would be impossible in a normal building interior. Strong edge lighting was needed with black-and-white to separate actors from the background.

In many feature films today, lighting is intended to be more "naturalistic"—that is, like the kind of light one would find in the real world. Many lights may be used, but the intent is to simulate the light that might normally occur in the filming space, whether it be from sunlight or man-made fixtures. One way to help give lighting a natural feel is to make sure that the chief light sources seem "motivated." Motivated lights are ones that appear to come from a logical source. For example, actual window light may be used for illumination, or lighting instruments may be set up near the windows to give the illusion that the light comes from the windows. Even if the goal is naturalistic lighting, usually liberties can be taken to improve the lighting of faces or achieve particular effects.

Often a few household fixtures are placed in a scene as practicals. These may actually light the subject or merely act as motivation for light from professional lighting instruments.

Of course, many movies don't seek realism at all, and instead use lighting to create a dramatic, expressive ambience. Horror films, action films, and many dramas use a more theatrical approach to lighting that creates a unique world that doesn't particularly look like the one you live in.

The sensitivity of digital cameras and film stocks has improved, and it's increasingly possible to shoot indoors entirely with available light without introducing any special lighting equipment. This can be a real boon for documentaries (see below). For fiction films, ironically, it sometimes takes a lot of light to make a scene look really *unlit*, the way it does to the naked eye. For example, you may be able to shoot an interior scene with just window light, but this may result in the windows being overexposed and the people appearing somewhat underexposed (see Fig. 7-17). To get a natural balance between the interior and exterior may require gels on the windows and/or a significant amount of light from inside (see Mixed Lighting, p. 514).

Documentary Lighting

Lighting a documentary can be tricky. You have to balance your desire for a certain style or look with the typical constraints of a small crew, small lighting package, and short shooting schedule. Interviews can be lit fairly fast, but providing good lighting for an uncontrolled scene in which people move around a large space, either at work or at home, often takes more time and equipment. Sometimes large spaces are lit with a few lights bounced off the ceiling. This may give you enough light for exposure and is fairly even. However, this kind of light is flat and tends to be "toppy"—that is, coming from above and causing dark shadows in the eye sockets.

When shooting unscripted scenes of people living their lives, consider the effect the lights have on your subjects. If you're filming intimate scenes of family life and other potentially delicate moments, you want to do everything you can to minimize the disruption caused by the film crew. Bright lights can create an "on-the-set" feeling, and people under the lights may feel like they should "perform" when the lights go on. Also, because it's hard to light an entire house or location, the use of lights transforms some areas into filming spaces while others remain living space. All of this may disrupt the natural flow of life that you hope to capture. Sometimes you can mount a few lights on the wall or ceiling and basically leave them in place for the duration of a shoot, turning them on when needed. The less light you use, the more mobile and unobtrusive you can be. But this may come at some sacrifice to the image quality. For every scene, you have to balance these concerns.

POSITIONING LIGHTS

A Basic Lighting Setup

A classic lighting technique is sometimes called *three-point lighting* because three basic lights are used to illuminate the subject: the key, fill, and backlight. Each light has a particular function. Even if many lights are used to cover a large set, each light plays one of these three roles.

KEY LIGHT. The key is the brightest light and casts the primary shadows, giving a sense of directionality to the lighting. The key may be hard or soft; the harder the light, the bolder or harsher its shadows will be. The key's shadows must be watched carefully for the way they interact with the subject. The key light is usually placed somewhat off the camera-to-subject axis, high enough up so that the shadow of the subject's nose does not fall across the cheek but downward instead. This height helps ensure that body shadows fall on the floor and not on nearby walls, where they may be distracting.

Fig. 12-29. Three-point lighting. (A) Key light only. In this shot, the key is quite far to the side. (B) Key plus backlight. The backlight separates the man from the dark background and brings out texture in his coat and hair. (C) Adding fill light from near the camera on the opposite side from the key brings up the light level primarily on the dark side of his face, making the shadows less severe. See Fig. 12-30 for this lighting setup. (D) Another example of three-point lighting, with a softer, more frontal key coming from the other side of the camera, and a lower-contrast look. Additional lights highlight the background. See Fig. 12-20 for this lighting setup. (Stephen McCarthy; Chimera)

FILL LIGHT. The main function of the fill light is to fill in the shadows produced by the key without casting distinct shadows of its own. Fill lighting is almost always softer than the key; it's usually created with a soft light fixture or a bounced spotlight. If the fill light emanates from a point close to the camera's lens and at the same level, its shadows will not be visible to the camera. The fill is generally placed on the opposite side of the camera from the key. Sometimes light is bounced off the wall or ceiling to provide flat, even fill over a broad area.

BACKLIGHT. Backlights (variants are called *hair*, *rim*, or *edge lights*) are placed on the opposite side of the subject from the camera, high enough to be out of view. Backlight should generally be fairly hard, to produce highlights on the subject's hair. If a backlight is at about the same level as the subject and somewhat off to the side, it is called a *kicker*. Kickers illuminate the shoulders and the side of the face more than hair lights do. All backlights are used to give a bright outline to the subject, helping to separate the subject from the background and define shape.

SET LIGHTS AND SPECIALS. In some situations, the key and fill lights adequately light the background. In others, a fourth basic type of light, the *set light*, is used to illuminate the background and selected objects. Sometimes parts of the

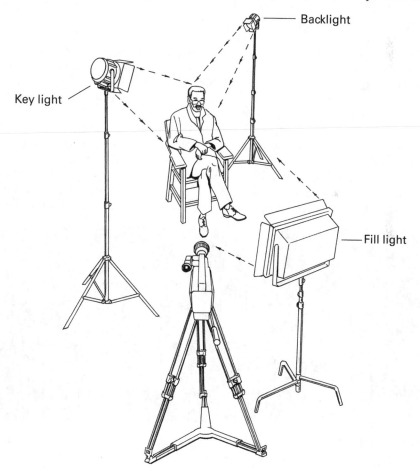

Fig. 12-30. A three-point lighting setup, similar to the one used for Fig. 12-29. (Robert Brun)

set need to be given their own key, fill, and/or backlights. A *special* is a light used to solve a particular problem, such as a light to bring out an especially dark object in the background.

Lighting Faces

In medium and close shots that include people, the lighting on faces is extremely important. When lighting a set or location, if you know there will be significant close shots of people, the overall lighting should be designed to provide good facial lighting (even so, the lighting for wide shots will generally be tweaked or cheated somewhat when it comes time for close-ups). For the purposes of this discussion, let's assume you're lighting a single subject in a chair. Start by positioning the key light alone, paying close attention to the shadows of the subject's nose and eye sockets. Every face is different; people with deep-set eyes and prominent noses will have more shadowing than those with flatter faces. The closer the key light is to the camera, the less shadowing there will be. Television news programs tend to be done with very frontal, flat lighting (see Fig. 12-9). This is a functional lighting approach, and minimizes possibly objectionable shadows, but it may be dull. If the key is brought around somewhat to the side (three-quarter light), the face takes on more dimensionality (see Fig. 12-29D). About 45 degrees from the camera is considered fairly standard for the key position. In Fig. 12-29C, the key is positioned quite far to the side (almost 90 degrees) for a dramatic look. In this case, it is also fairly high to avoid reflections in the man's glasses.

Pay close attention to the way the eyes are lit. As the poet tells us, eyes are the windows to the soul. When you can't see the eyes, sometimes you feel like you can't see into the *person*. Generally subjects face one side of the camera or the other. Often the lighting looks best if the subject is looking *toward* the key light (thus, if the subject is facing camera left, put the key light on the left side of the camera; see Fig. 12-38). This puts both eyes in the key light. If one eye is in shadow, the fill light

Fig. 12-31. In this scene from *Capote*, the key light comes from the left, on the far side of the subject, leaving most of his face in shadow. The practical in the background helps motivate the light on the table and subject. When the camera shoots from the shadowed side of the face, the light often brings out interesting modeling (shooting from the other side would look much flatter). (Sony Pictures Classics)

can be used to bring up the illumination on that side (see below). Of course, you might choose to put one or both eyes in shadow, perhaps to create a mysterious or spooky feel.

The key should generally be high enough so that the nose shadow falls down, not across the face (some DPs try to place the nose shadow on the "smile line," which extends from the nose to the corner of the mouth; see Fig. 12-2). The "standard" key is 45 degrees above the subject.

Though it may seem counterintuitive, lighting is sometimes more interesting when the key light is illuminating the side of the face *away* from the camera. In Fig. 12-31, the key is positioned in front of the man, to the left, and the majority of his face is *not* lit by the key. Other examples can be seen in Fig. 13-4. For a more dramatic look, using less fill light (or none) makes the shadowed side of the face go darker. In Fig. 12-32, the subject looks off screen into a light that might suggest a distant window or lamp. His nose is rim-lit with strong shadows falling across his face and the camera side of his face is left quite dark. This kind of look is well suited to a very low-key nighttime scene (see Special Lighting Effects, p. 516).

Should the key light be hard or soft? It depends on how you want the audience to interpret the lighting. Direct sunlight is quite hard; indirect window light or the

Fig. 12-32. Far-side key. Key light positioned on the far side of the subject produces a rim of light on the nose and brings out skin texture. Having virtually no fill light creates a low-key dramatic look, which could be used for a nighttime scene. (*Portrait of Martin Baer* by Johan Hagemeyer, The Metropolitan Museum of Art, Gift of the Estate of Johan Hagemeyer, 1962)

light of an overcast day is soft. You may like dramatic, crisp shadows or you may prefer a gentler look. Generally, some diffusion material (see Soft Lights and Reflectors, p. 488) should be used to help make the key less harsh. Hard light will accentuate skin defects, makeup, and lighting errors more than soft light. Soft light is more forgiving. One look that can be appealing is to use a quite soft key. The light will wrap around the face and you may need little or no fill light (see Figs. 12-3 and 12-29D). Diffused lights do not "throw" as far as hard ones, so soft light sources need to be placed closer to the subject. For soft lights, as a rule, the larger the surface of the light source and/or the closer it is to the subject, the softer the light will be.

Fig. 12-33. Window-lit scene. Nearby window provides key light. Light reflected from the wall on the right provides fill on the dark side of the man's face. A splash of light on the back wall reinforces the sense of sunlight. (Stephen McCarthy)

After the key has been placed, some DPs "rough in" the fill light; others go next to the backlight. Backlight should be used when needed, but it can sometimes seem artificial or stagy if overused. Backlight can be very important to provide separation between the subject and the background (see Fig. 12-29B). Some scenes just look *dull* without some backlight to add luster to the hair and put some bright "kicks" in the scene. On the other hand, sometimes the subject and the background have adequate separation simply because one is significantly darker or lighter than the other, and you don't really need a backlight on the subject (see Fig. 12-7). Some scenes are meant to appear lit only by one source, and backlight might spoil the effect (see Fig. 12-33). However, if a backlight isn't overdone, it can often add a helpful shine without calling too much attention to itself (see Figs. 12-29D and 13-4).

Fig. 12-34. "Window-lit" scene. A lighting setup that might be used to simulate the light in Fig. 12-33. Key light is bounced for a soft look. Fill lighting is provided by a white card just out of frame to the right. A set light provides the sun effect on the back wall. Flags and/or a cookie might be needed to create the desired effects on the walls. Compare with Fig. 12-37. (Robert Brun)

Backlights should be placed high enough to avoid lens flare in the camera and angled down so that they don't strike the tip of the subject's nose. If a backlight causes flare or casts a noticeable shadow in front of the subject, flag it off with the barndoors or a gobo.

The fill light is used to bring up the light level in the shadows cast by the key or the backlight. Put the fill light close enough to the camera so that it doesn't create a second set of shadows of its own. The difference in brightness between the shadows and the highlights is the lighting contrast. The contrast plays a big part both in how details will be reproduced in the video or film image and in the mood of the lighting. (See Lighting Contrast, p. 476.)

Sometimes fill lighting is provided not by a separate lighting unit but by a reflecting surface (this has the advantage of not casting another set of shadows). In Fig. 12-33, the wall on the right side of the room reflects back the sunlight, filling the shadows on the dark side of the man's face. In Fig. 12-34, a piece of white foam core is used to simulate the same effect. A Flexfill or other reflector (see Fig. 12-22) may be used indoors or out to do the same thing. Often a white reflector needs to be quite close to the subject to provide significant fill.

Various other techniques and tricks will improve facial lighting. A low-powered eye light is sometimes used to add a little sparkle to the eyes, giving the subject an alert or alluring look. An eye light should not be so bright that it washes the face out with flat fill. Sometimes nets are used to delicately shade the top and bottom of the face, focusing attention on the eyes and mouth. A special (see p. 502) may be used to bring up the illumination on particularly dark or absorptive clothing.

Facial shine can be very distracting and can be avoided with a basic application of powder (see p. 374).

It should be noted that a certain amount of "relighting" can be done digitally in post. Particularly for a locked-off shot, it's easy to shade off the background or selectively darken parts of the frame to create a more interesting look (see Fig. 14-39).

Lighting Wide Shots

Wide shots or long shots that show a large part of a set or location can be harder to light than close-ups because of the greater area to be covered and the problem of hiding lights and light stands. Wide shots often involve people moving from one place to another, which adds the challenge of providing good light in several different parts of the set.

Generally, wide shots should be lit to establish mood and to cover the actors' blocking (movements). Proper facial lighting is a lower priority. Keep in mind that the eye is naturally drawn to light areas of the frame. Thus, the area in which the actors move is normally lit slightly brighter than the background or extreme foreground. Flags or nets can be used to diminish the light falling on unimportant areas such as broad expanses of wall. Much of the mood of the shot is established by the relation between the brighter action area and the darker background. Try to maintain this balance when you change camera position or lighting.

When you light any scene, it's usually more interesting to have pools of light and areas that are relatively dark than to have flat, even illumination throughout the frame. Pools of light also create a greater feeling of depth; a corridor, for example, seems longer if bright and dark areas alternate. Use fill light to provide illumination between the brighter areas.

When subjects move closer and farther from a light, the illumination falling on them can change significantly (see Fig. 12-10). Sometimes a half scrim or other material can be used to even out the light (see Fig. 12-27). In general, using a brighter, harder light from a greater distance away from the action will result in more even illumination than a softer unit closer to the subject. Sometimes a very bright light positioned outside a window or on the far side of the room is the best way to keep interior action evenly lit.

If you're going for a naturalistic look, examine the location for appropriate "motivating" sources for the lighting. Most daytime scenes include light coming through a window. Actual window light may be used, but often it must be simulated because the sunlight would change during the course of filming. If the window itself is not visible, you can position the light source wherever seems plausible. You can bounce light off a large white card for an overcast or "north light" look or use a large, focused spotlight or PAR light to simulate sunlight streaming in. When simulating sunlight, a warming gel (CTO; see Colored Filters and Gels, p. 496) is sometimes used over the light. If tungsten light is mixed with actual window light, some filtering must be done (see Mixed Lighting, p. 514).

If household fixtures are being used as practicals in a scene, sometimes they can provide significant illumination. You can replace the bulb with a photoflood or a screw-in halogen bulb. Or you may be able to use just a brighter household bulb; if it's a tungsten bulb or warm CFL, the color may read too red/yellow on camera depending on what other sources are used and how the camera or film is color balanced. Many practicals can't handle much heat or electricity, and often a bright bulb makes the practical appear too bright on camera. The shade may overexpose, looking burned out. To seem natural, the lampshade of the practical should read about two to three stops brighter than the faces of nearby actors. This varies, of course, with the type of shade and fixture.

Often the opposite approach is taken with practicals. Instead of trying to light the subject with them, the DP treats them simply as set dressing. Sometimes a low-intensity bulb or a screw-in dimmer is used to keep the light subtle. Neutral density gels or diffusion material can be hidden in the lampshade to dim down the shade or the spill coming out of the light. Then a professional lighting instrument is aimed in from off camera to simulate the light that would come from the practical (see Fig. 12-31). Be sure the instrument is flagged so it doesn't shine *on* the practical and cast a shadow—a dead giveaway.

Frequently one light can be used to accomplish several functions. If two people are talking across a table, a light can key one person while it backlights the other. This is called *cross lighting* (see Fig. 12-35). When an actor moves through his blocking, a given light may change from a key light to a backlight.

Cinematographer Néstor Almendros (*Days of Heaven*) prided himself on being able to light a scene with as little as one or two lights. Many scenes require more lighting fixtures, but often, the fewer the sources, the cleaner the image looks. When there are many lights, you run the risk of many distracting shadows falling in different directions. To minimize this, keep actors away from walls, place them against dark rather than light walls, position furniture or props to break up the shadows, and use diffusion to soften secondary lights. Moving a light closer to a person will diffuse the shadow she casts.

Bright, shiny surfaces in the frame attract the eye and are usually undesirable. Glints or kicks can be diminished by repositioning a shiny object or by applying washable *dulling spray* or even soap. Sometimes you can get rid of the reflection of a light in a surface by raising or lowering the camera a few inches or wedging a little tape behind a picture frame to angle it away from the camera. Reflections from smooth, nonmetal surfaces such as plastic, glass, and water can be reduced by putting a polarizer filter on the camera. Avoid shooting glass or mirrors that will pick up the lights or the camera. If you have to film against white walls, take care not to overlight them. Usually broad expanses of wall are broken up with pictures or furniture.

When a scene is to be filmed with both long shots and medium or close-up shots, it's common to determine the blocking, set the lighting, and shoot the long shots first. Then, as the camera is positioned closer to the subject, the lights can be cheated

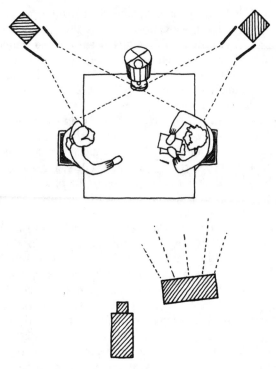

Fig. 12-35. Cross lighting. Each spotlight keys one subject and backlights the other. Lights are used in part to simulate practical illumination from the table lamp and are thus flagged off of it. Fill light is placed near the camera. (Carol Keller)

(moved) to maintain the general sense of the long shot while providing more desirable facial lighting. Close-ups are usually lit with slightly lower contrast lighting than long shots are so that facial detail will be clear. When the camera angle changes significantly, you can make many changes in the light without the audience noticing.

When shooting video, or when using a film camera with a video tap, watching the image in a monitor can help you light, but beware of small and poor-quality monitors. Make sure the monitor is set up properly (see Appendix A) and that there isn't light falling on the monitor screen. Shooting stills can be very helpful for continuity purposes to record how props were arranged, how actors were dressed, and if lighting setups need to be re-created.

Before you shoot, scrutinize the frame to make sure no light stands or cables are visible. Be sure no lights are producing flare in the lens (stand next to the camera and look at the front of the lens; if you see any light sources in the glass, try to flag them off). Rehearse the shot to check that movements of the crew and especially the microphone boom don't produce visible shadows.

Lighting Interviews

With the widening range of news, documentaries, and reality television, interviews have almost become a filmmaking form unto themselves. Considerations of shooting interviews are discussed in Chapter 9. Decisions about lighting should start with the setting: how do you want to place your subject and what do you want to see in the background? Some interviews are done in wide shot (see Fig. 9-20), but more typically, medium shots and close-ups are featured. Adjusting objects in the background by a few inches can often make all the difference in what the audience sees and in compositional balance at different focal lengths.

The lighting scheme may use available light (or simulate what the light might normally look like). Or you may decide to turn off or block any existing light and create a very different mood. The lighting style can convey a lot in terms of how the audience understands the interviews, so at the start of production consider the look you want, and whether there should be a consistent look throughout or if different interview subjects call for different styles. Lighting contrast is a central concern. Some projects seem to demand a flatter, brighter look (such as Fig. 12-29D); others benefit from darker backgrounds and darker facial shadows with more modeling.

The following four illustrations are offered not as recommendations, but to discuss some different approaches. All were done with very few lighting instruments. The sensitivity of your particular camera will play a large part in how much light you need.

The lighting setup in Figure 12-36 began with turning off the office's overhead fluorescents, since the light was flat and the bulbs were of mixed color temperature. The windows were covered to block out daylight (to create a darker feel and prevent any changes during the interview). The key light was a small Lowel Rifa soft box (see Fig. 12-19) on the left side, with no additional fill. A low-wattage bulb was used in the soft box so that the lens iris could be wide open for shallower depth of field (throwing the background out of focus). The fluorescent fixture built into the cabinet provides light on the background and adds a little edge on the dark side of the face. A small backlight on the left side creates highlights on the shoulders and lights the front of the desk.

Fig. 12-36. Lighting interviews. Key and backlight. See text. (Steven Ascher)

The lighting in Figure 12-37 also began with turning off the overhead fluorescents and was done with no added lights. The subject is lit with window light coming through a fairly small opening in the vertical venetian blind off screen on the right. The rest of the window was kept shaded to make the background relatively dark, so the details on the shelves wouldn't compete with the subject. No back or fill light was used. Black duvetyn fabric was hung on the left side of the frame as *negative fill* to prevent reflected light in the room from striking the shaded side of his face, which would have flattened contrast. (More typically, white cards or reflectors are used on the dark side in a situation like this because contrast is often too great; see Fig. 12-34.) A low-intensity bulb in the practical on the right provides a little accent on the table.

Fig. 12-37. Lighting interviews. Window light. See text. (Steven Ascher)

The lighting in Figure 12-38 was done with a single soft light on the left. Flags and an eggcrate were used to keep the light from spilling on the background. Unlike in Figures 12-36 and 12-37, here the subject is looking toward the key light, which creates shadowing on the camera side of the face and sparkles in the eyes. This scene has high lighting contrast with deep shadows, but both eyes are fully lit, so it doesn't feel harsh. The practical on the table provides some light in the background. Lamps, plants, and flowers turn up routinely behind interview subjects as set dressing—for obvious reasons—but don't neglect to look for alternatives too.

The shot in Figure 12-39 is directly into a bright window, which calls for relatively bright light on the subject. In this shot, the light on the face (from a soft box with a daylight-balanced compact fluorescent bulb) is quite flat, but because the background is busy and bright, the light doesn't seem dull. Rosco Cinegel black scrim was taped to the window behind the subject to cut two stops of light from outside. A neutral density filter on the camera allowed for a wider iris and shallower depth of field. Diagonals in the background provide a sense of dimensionality. The time of shooting was chosen so that there wouldn't be too much direct sunlight on the buildings.

Fig. 12-38. Lighting interviews. Key light only. See text. (Steven Ascher)

Fig. 12-39. Lighting interviews. Bright background. See text. (Steven Ascher)

Lighting and Exposure

When setting lights, the question arises: how brightly should a scene be lit? For starters, you need enough to get an acceptable exposure with your camera/lens combination (plus film stock if you're shooting film). You might use more light if you want to shoot at a higher *f*-stop to increase depth of field. Lens sharpness for many lenses can be maximized by shooting at apertures about two stops closed down from wide open (on an *f*/2 lens, shoot around *f*/4; see p. 173). On a feature film, many DPs try to work at a given *f*-stop consistently throughout the movie, which helps them judge lighting setups by eye. As a rule, the discomfort of both crew and actors, or documentary subjects, rises with the amount of light.

CONTROLLING LIGHTING CONTRAST

As discussed in Chapters 5 and 7, both digital and film systems have a limited ability to capture the range of brightness that the eye can see. When lighting a scene, you must pay close attention to the *lighting contrast* (see Lighting Contrast, p. 476). To the eye, scenes always have less contrast than they do as rendered on video or film. Shadows that look natural to the eye may be rendered as black and without detail. Bright highlights can easily overexpose and appear as areas of featureless white.

A good monitor can help you judge how the contrast looks on video, but be sure it's properly set up (see Appendix A). Low-quality monitors often have too much contrast, making it hard to tell where you really are losing detail. Of course, if you're using cine gammas or log or RAW capture, you may be capturing far more in the shadows and highlights than the monitor shows (see Chapter 5).

If you're shooting film you'll have a light meter, but one can be useful on video shoots as well to measure the *lighting contrast ratio*. This is the ratio of key plus fill lights to fill light alone (K+F:F). For a typical close-up, the lighting contrast is measured by reading the light on the bright side of the face (which comes from both the key and fill lights) and comparing it to the light in the facial shadows (which comes from the fill light alone). The measurements are most easily taken with an incident light meter, blocking or turning off the key light(s) to take the second reading. Some DPs prefer to use the incident meter's flat-disc diffuser when doing this to make it easier to isolate the light coming from individual sources.

If the bright side of the face is one stop lighter than the facial shadow, the ratio is 2:1. Two stops would be 4:1; three stops, 8:1. To the eye, 2:1 and 3:1 look quite flat, but this lighting contrast is considered "normal" by Kodak. This is a conservative standard. Low-key scenes, nighttime effects, and many outdoor sunlit scenes are shot at ratios much higher than 4:1.

For either digital or film, you should use lighting contrast to create the mood and look you want. If you choose a high lighting contrast, bear in mind that you may lose detail in shadow or highlight areas. How much you lose depends on several factors: the exposure; the camera and internal settings (for digital); the film stock (film cameras); and how the project is handled during post.

As a rule of thumb, the image will generally *pick up* contrast through the various stages of postproduction and distribution (such as when people watch on their TVs or computer screens). So if you start with a somewhat lower contrast, you may find the image gets "snappier" without your doing anything. You can always *increase* contrast later in post if you find the image too flat, but if footage is originally shot with too much contrast, it may be difficult or impossible to recapture the lost shadow or highlight detail afterward.

If the contrast seems too high, move the fill light closer to the subject or use a brighter fill light. Alternatively, dim the key light with a scrim or move it back.

Lighting contrast should be evaluated with respect to all parts of the frame, not just the light and shadow on faces. Walk around the set or location with an incident or reflected meter, or point a digital camera at various parts of the set, to get a sense of the range of exposure in the scene. If the background is in deep shadow, it may need additional light to keep the overall contrast down. If a window is too bright, it may need a neutral density gel to darken it up a bit. A bright wall can be made darker by flagging the light off it, or you can use a net to gradually shade the light (often you want keep the light on the actors and darken the upper part of the wall above them). Further measures include making sure actors or subjects don't wear very bright or very dark clothing, replacing high-contrast props, and repainting set walls in medium shades. In general, it's less disturbing if some areas of the frame are underexposed than if large or important areas are significantly overexposed.

Lighting Contrast in Daylight

On a sunny day outside, the direct sunlight usually acts as the "key light." The "fill" is provided by skylight and, to a lesser extent, reflections from buildings, objects, and clothing. On a bright day, the lighting contrast is often too great. If you expose properly for the bright areas, the shadows end up looking very deep and harsh. A classic problem is shooting people at midday under a bright sun; the eye shadows may make it almost impossible to see their eyes. That's why hazy or lightly overcast days, with their lower lighting contrast, are often ideal for shooting people outdoors.

There are a number of solutions to the problem of shooting in sun. For an interview or close shot, you can use a white card or a small reflector such as a Flexfill to help fill the shadows. For a larger scene, you can use a bigger reflector such as a shiny board with a silver or gold surface. You can use daylight-balanced lighting instruments, but it may take a lot of intensity to match the sun on a bright day.

Another approach is to try to diminish or soften the direct sunlight. An *overhead set* (also called a *butterfly*) is a pipe frame (often six by six feet or twelve by twelve feet) that can be placed over the action to hold either a *silk* to diffuse the light, a *scrim* to cut down the light without diffusing it, or a *solid* to block the light altogether. Overheads must be used carefully so that the shadow of the frame doesn't show in the shot, and the brightly (and more harshly) lit background doesn't either. The overhead must be held down securely when the wind blows. If sunlight is diffused in this way, it's easier to maintain consistency in the light over a day's shooting, since the material can be removed if a light cloud passes.

Whenever possible, use the angle of the sun to your advantage. You may want to put your subject in gentle shade near a building or by a tree. Don't shoot against a hot (bright) background like a bright sky or a white wall. Sometimes it's best to avoid shooting at all in the middle of the day, when sunlight is the harshest.

When shooting in direct sun, if the sun is not directly overhead, changing the position of the camera and/or the subject will have a big effect on the contrast (see Fig. 12-40).

When you shoot in cars or near windows, lighting contrast can be extremely high between the darker foreground interior and the brightly lit exterior (see Fig.

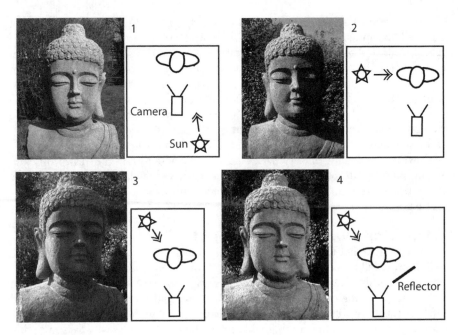

Fig. 12-40. Using the sun to your advantage. (1) Shooting a person front lit (with the sun behind the camera) fully illuminates the subject, but the lighting is flat and it can be uncomfortable with the sun directly in the person's eyes. (2) Positioning the subject so the sun comes from the side provides more dimensionality, but dark shadows on the face can be harsh. (3) Backlighting (or three-quarter backlight) with the sun behind the subject provides nice highlights on the shoulders and hair, and is comfortable for the subject, but since the face is mostly unlit, contrast can be severe. (4) By placing a small reflector (a Flexfill or a white card) so that it reflects sun back toward the dark side of the face, you can adjust the fill light as needed and create a flattering effect on the subject. (Steven Ascher)

7-17). You might choose to add light to the interior or put neutral density gel on the windows. Without these steps, a compromise exposure is normally used.

LIGHTING AND COLOR

Mixed Lighting

Before reading this section, see the discussion of color temperature and filters in Chapter 8 and the discussion of video white balance on p. 109.

A video camera can render colors naturally in daylight or in tungsten light if it is properly white-balanced. Similarly, color film stocks can be used in *either* daylight or tungsten light and produce a pleasing color rendition with the proper filters. However, no video or film camera can shoot a scene that contains *both* daylight and tungsten light without rendering the former blue or the latter yellow/red relative to the other.

To take a typical example: You're trying to shoot an interior scene using window light, but there's not enough light for exposure, so you set up some tungsten movie lights to boost the light on your subject. If you balance the video camera for the tungsten light (or shoot tungsten film without a filter), the daylight from the windows will look very blue by comparison. If you balance the video camera for daylight (or use an 85 filter with tungsten film), the tungsten light will look much too warm (orange).

There are a few ways to deal with this problem. One is to make the tungsten light bluer, to better match daylight. This can be done with dichroic filters or full CTB (blue) gels on the lights (see Colored Filters and Gels, p. 496). However, this will reduce the lights' output by half or more. Also, when shooting tungsten-balanced film—and with some video cameras that have internal filter wheels—an 85 camera filter is generally used for daylight, which cuts down the light intensity almost in half again.[2] This may not leave enough light to shoot.

In this situation, sometimes instead of using a full CTB gel on the lights, only a ¾ or ½ CTB is used. This lets more light through and results in the tungsten light appearing *slightly* yellow compared to the daylight, which can look very nice. Also, if you're shooting film, you could use a daylight-balanced stock that requires no 85 filter.

Another approach is to balance the video camera for the tungsten light (or use no filter with tungsten-balanced film), and filter the *window* light with orange gel or acrylic sheets. Gel comes in large rolls and is easy to transport. Tape it carefully to the windows or it will show in shots that include the windows. Gels crease easily, will reflect the lights if mounted sloppily, and are noisy in windy locations. Acrylic sheets, on the other hand, are inconvenient to carry, but they are good for mounting outside the window where they won't show. They are also optically sharper for shots that involve shooting *through* the window.

A sun 85 or ¾ CTO (orange) gel can be used to warm up 5500°K daylight to 3200°K tungsten balance. For dimming overly bright windows it can be very helpful to have some combination CTO–neutral density gels (for example, 85 N6, which brings down the color temperature and cuts an additional two stops of light; see p. 312). While a ¾ CTO gel will make daylight match the color of tungsten, sometimes you want the window to look a little blue by comparison, to maintain some of the natural difference between the interior and exterior light. In this case, use a paler gel, such as a ½ or ¼ CTO, on the windows.

If a location has large windows and is illuminated primarily with daylight, or when you're shooting outside, often the best solution is to use an HMI, or daylight-balanced fluorescent or LED lights, which require no filter to match daylight (though a little warming gel often improves the look). However, if window light is insignificant in a scene, it is often easiest to block the daylight out altogether (using curtains, sound blankets, or show cards) and then light completely with tungsten.

MIXED FLUORESCENTS. See p. 483 for discussion of fluorescent lighting. Ideally, anytime you are shooting with fluorescent light you should use Kino Flo or

---

2. With many color negative stocks and digital cameras you can get away with shooting in daylight without a filter, and this is one instance where you may need to.

other true tungsten- or daylight-balanced tubes. However, if you are forced to shoot with conventional fluorescent tubes and plan to mix in daylight or tungsten sources, filtration is usually called for. Unfortunately, conventional fluorescents come in a variety of colors, so different gels may be needed. Some fluorescents can be thought of as daylight with a green spectral element. Thus, window light can be filtered with Rosco's Windowgreen to match "cool white" or "daylight" fluorescents better; HMIs can be filtered with Tough Plusgreen; and tungsten sources can be filtered with Tough Plusgreen 50.

Alternatively, the fluorescent tubes themselves can be filtered. For example, you can use Rosco Minusgreen to match cool white fluorescents to daylight. Various gels come in sleeves that can be fitted over the fluorescent tubes; these can reduce the green halo effect that sometimes occurs when fluorescent units are visible in a shot. If filtration is not possible, fluorescent lighting fixtures, such as the Molescent unit by Mole, can be brought in for additional light using the same type of tubes that are already in the room. Mixing conventional fluorescent light with other sources and mixing various types of fluorescent tubes can be very tricky. A three-color color temperature meter helps (see Fig. 8-5).

Color Contrast

Differences in color between two objects (their *color contrast*) help us to tell them apart and determine their position relative to each other. In black-and-white, however, a red bug and a green leaf may be indistinguishable because their tonal values are the same (they reflect the same amount of light). Thus, when shooting in black-and-white it is usually necessary to use slightly higher lighting contrast than you would in color and to make sure that there is adequate shading and/or backlighting to differentiate various objects from each other. It is also possible to use color contrast filters on the camera to separate tonally similar areas (see Chapter 8). If you are shooting video and converting to black-and-white in post, you can do color balancing in post to heighten the difference between areas that might otherwise blend together.

Color contrast is also important when shooting in color because the shades and intensities of colors play a large part in setting the mood of a scene. The color scheme in a movie can be controlled in wardrobe planning, set design, the setup of a video camera, or the choice of film stocks. To make colors appear more pastel or desaturated, you can use camera filters such as a diffusion or low-contrast filter (see Fig. 8-9). Underexposure and overexposure also affect color saturation. During postproduction you can make many adjustments to both color saturation and the reproduction of individual tones.

SPECIAL LIGHTING EFFECTS

Night-for-Night

Sometimes you can shoot at night without supplementary lighting, particularly on city streets. However, often you need to augment whatever existing light there is. When using lights to simulate a nighttime effect (such as moonlight or streetlight), use hard lighting fixtures in an extremely high-contrast, low-key lighting scheme. Lights should be used to produce sharp highlights or rim lighting with very little fill. Shadows should be crisp and not diffused. Create pools of light—not flat, even illumination (see Fig. 5-10).

When the light level is low, the eye is less sensitive to color. If you go out on a moonlit night, the landscape seems desaturated and slightly bluish. Lighting fixtures on movies are often gelled blue to simulate moonlight. A pale grayish blue often looks more natural; avoid an intense, saturated blue. Some DPs like to wet down streets and surfaces at night so they reflect highlights.

Because night scenes can require many lights, especially for a wide shot, it is often better to shoot at the *magic hour* just before sunrise or just after sunset when there's enough light to get exposure on buildings and the landscape but it is sufficiently dark that car headlights and interior lights show up clearly (see the upper-right image in Fig. 9-26). Although beautiful, the magic hour is fleeting, often lasting only about twenty minutes, depending on the time of year and your location. Rehearse and be ready to go as soon as the light fades. It helps to have some supplementary light on hand for additional fill in the waning moments and for shooting close-ups when it gets darker. When you shoot magic-hour scenes with tungsten-balanced color film, you don't need an 85 filter. In general, avoid shooting the sky during the magic hour, because it will look too bright, or use a graduated filter (see Fig. 8-7).

Day-for-Night

Hollywood invented the technique of shooting night scenes during the day, using filters and underexposure to simulate a night effect (the French call this *la nuit Américaine*—"American night"). *Day-for-night* often looks fake. It's easier in black-and-white, where a red or yellow filter can be used to darken a blue sky (see Chapter 8). For color work, a graduated filter can be used. Ironically, day-for-night works best on bright, sunny days. Shoot early or late in the day when distinct side light or backlight casts long shadows that will seem like moonlight. Avoid shooting the sky and use intense lights in windows to make interior lights look bright relative to the exterior. Underexpose by two or three stops while shooting (after making the normal compensations for any filters). When shooting film, do not rely on trying to print down a normally exposed negative.

Rain, Smoke, and Fire

In order to be visible on film or video, rain, smoke, and fog should be lit from behind (see Figs. 12-7 and 5-10). Aim the lighting instruments as close to the camera as possible but flag them off so that no light shines directly in the lens and causes flare.

Sometimes firelight is simulated by placing an amber gel over the light and jiggling strips of paper or cloth suspended from a horizontal bar in front of the light. Even better, get a *flicker box*, which is an electronic device that allows you to dial up different rates of flicker. Sometimes DPs make fire effects (or simulate the light from a television) with very intense flickering and virtually no fill light, making the scene seesaw between very bright and very dark. In real life, that kind of flicker generally happens only if there's *no* other light in the room. In a typical room with

THE FILMMAKER'S HANDBOOK

a fireplace, or in a TV-watching environment, usually people have at least *some* other light on, and the flicker on people's faces from a fire or TV is usually subtle. Sometimes the most convincing effects are done with two or more lights that can be flickered alternately.

LOCATION LIGHTING

The Location

Whenever possible, scout locations prior to filming to assess lighting needs, check the availability of electric power, and formulate a shooting plan (see p. 364). When scouting an interior location, bring a camera and/or a light meter and try to estimate the natural light at various times of day (there are apps for mobile phones that can tell you when and where you'll have sunlight). With a camera or a director's finder (see Fig. 9-28) you can block out actors' movements and camera angles. Determine what lighting package you need. If any windows need to be gelled, will you need a tall ladder to reach them? A day at a cramped location helps you appreciate why many movies are made in studios with high ceilings, overhead lighting grids, movable walls, air-conditioning, and plenty of work space. Movie crews on location often break furniture and mar walls with lighting gear. You can save a lot of time by coming prepared with paint and repair supplies.

Electric Power

Lights for moviemaking can consume a great deal of electric current. Before you shoot, try to determine if the location has enough power for your needs; otherwise, circuit breakers (or fuses in older homes) may blow, the production could be shut down, or a fire could erupt.

To estimate your power needs, use this formula: volts × amps = watts. You want to find the number of amps your lights will use, as this is what overloads circuits and causes breakers to blow when too many lights are put on one circuit. Standard household current in North America is delivered at about 110 volts, which can be rounded off here to 100. Every lamp is rated by the number of watts it consumes. In the home, a 60-watt bulb is typical, while, for filming, 1,000 watts (1K) is common. If you simply read the bulb's wattage and divide by 100, you get the number of amps the lamp requires (this formula includes a safety margin). A typical home circuit can handle 15 (or 20) amps, which is thus enough to run three (or four) 500-watt bulbs. Using any more lights will trip the circuit breaker or blow the fuse. Newer lighting units are more efficient, using less power for the same light output. Using LED lights, for example, allows you to get much more light from the same circuit compared to tungsten.

In Europe and most of Asia, the wall current is delivered at 220 to 240 volts. The same calculation can be done by dividing the wattage by 220 (or to make the math easier, and the safety margin greater, just divide by 200).

To determine how much power is available at the location, examine the circuit breakers or fuse box (often found in the basement). Count how many circuits there are and the maximum amperage of each one (amps are indicated with a number followed by "A"). Circuit breakers, which can be reset by flipping a switch when they are tripped, are found in most houses with newer wiring.

Often, circuits are labeled to indicate which rooms they are connected to. If not, plug lights into various wall outlets and turn the breakers off one at a time and see which lights go out.[3] Extension cables can be run to other rooms to distribute the load if necessary. Don't use thin, home extension cords, as they increase the load and may melt.

When too many lights or overly long cables are used, the voltage may drop (the equivalent to summertime brownouts), which lowers the color temperature of tungsten lights. A 10-volt drop in supply lowers tungsten lights about 100°K. If there is no window light and all light sources are on the same supply, this color change is usually correctable.

To get around this and other typical problems of location power supplies, professionals often *tie in* to the electric supply as it enters the house and use their own set of circuit breakers and electrical distribution cabling. This should be done only by a trained electrician; in some places, a permit must be obtained and the electrician must also be licensed.

In outdoor locations, a generator ("genny") or a set of car batteries can be used for power. You can buy or rent portable, low-cost, but relatively noisy generators (often ranging from 1,600 to 6,500 watts). Large truck-mounted generators are also made for movie work that are much more powerful and quiet. Ten 12-volt car batteries ("wet-cells") wired in a series can run regular tungsten lights at normal color temperature. As the batteries weaken, the color temperature and light output drop.

WORLDWIDE POWER SYSTEMS. Household power in North America is supplied at 110 to 120 volts. It is *alternating current* (*AC*)—that is, it pulsates back and forth; it does so sixty times a second (60 Hz). As noted above, in most parts of the world power is supplied at 220 to 240 volts, alternating at a frequency of 50 Hz.[4]

Most AC equipment works equally well at frequencies of 50 or 60 Hz. However, clocks, some battery chargers, and other equipment will not run properly if the frequency of the current is incorrect. Tungsten lights work fine with either system, but AC discharge lamps, including HMIs and fluorescents, may be incompatible with the camera speed or shutter.

Virtually all equipment should be used only with the voltage it was designed for. Some equipment may have a switch to select 110- or 220-volt use. Tungsten fixtures can be converted from one voltage to another simply by using a different set of bulbs. Other equipment requires a voltage-changing device, of which there are two types. The *transformer* is relatively heavy for the amount of power (wattage) it can handle. It can be used with any equipment but should not be overloaded. Transformers don't affect the frequency of the current. *Diode-type voltage changers* are extremely light (usually a few ounces) and, for their size, can handle much more power than transformers. They should be used only for lights. Since these work by converting AC current to DC, they should not be used with anything that is fre-

---

3. You can also get an inexpensive device that you plug into an outlet, then you wave a sensor over the circuit breaker to see which circuit the outlet is on.

4. Some countries, particularly in Central America, may supply power at 220 volts but at 60 Hz.

quency dependent. Check with a technician on the requirements of your equipment.

While typical electric plugs in North America and most of Central America use two flat blades and sometimes a round grounding pin, outlets found in much of the rest of the world have a different configuration. Other systems use plugs with two or three round pins or angled blades. Adapters are available to convert from one type to the other or you can replace the plugs on your equipment if needed. Search the Web for electric power and plug configurations wherever you're planning to shoot.

CHAPTER 13

Picture and Dialogue Editing

My movie is first born in my head, dies on paper; is resuscitated by the living persons and real objects I use, which are killed on film but, placed in a certain order and projected onto a screen, come to life again like flowers in water. —ROBERT BRESSON

E diting is the selection and arrangement of shots into sequences and the sequences into a movie. It's sometimes thought to be the most important element in filmmaking. On many films, the storyline is substantially formed or re-formed in the editing room, sometimes "saving" the film.

The earliest filmmakers made films from one unedited camera take or shot. A few years later, it became obvious that shots could be trimmed and placed one after another, with the audience accepting that the action occurs in the same setting. The joining of two shots, with the abrupt ending of one shot and the immediate beginning of the next, is called a *cut*. In traditional film editing, the word "cut" applies not only to the transition from one shot to another on screen, but also to the physical cutting and joining (splicing) of pieces of film (hence editing referred to as cutting). In video, the term *edit point* is often used to indicate the point where a cut takes place. When editing on a digital system, the *head* (beginning) of a shot may be referred to as the *In Point* and the *tail* (end) as the *Out Point*.

SOME FILM THEORY

Montage

Perhaps the most developed theory of film comes from the silent era; it's called Russian *montage theory*. The word "montage" is derived from the French and means to "put together" or "edit." The Soviet filmmakers held that the ability to change images instantaneously was unique to film and in fact constituted its potential as an art form. In editing, the image can shift from one person's point of view to another's; it can change locales around the world; it can move through time. The Soviets, for the most part, looked at the shots themselves as meaningless atoms or building blocks and asserted that meaning first emerges from the images through the juxtaposition of the shots.

In the early 1920s Lev Kuleshov, a Soviet film teacher, created experiments to show how the meaning of a shot could be totally altered by its context. He took a series of shots of Ivan Mosjoukine, a famous contemporary actor, looking at something off screen with a neutral expression on his face. He then constructed a few

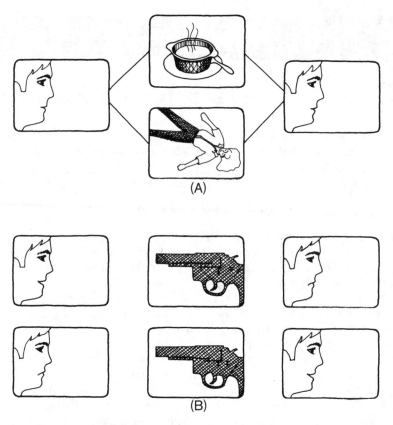

Fig. 13-1. Three-shot sequence. (A) The meaning of the actor's expression depends on the insert shot. (B) The meaning of the actor's expression depends on the ordering of the shots. (Carol Keller)

different sequences. In one sequence, he cut from a medium shot of Mosjoukine to a close-up of a bowl of soup and then back to a close-up of Mosjoukine. In the next sequence, the middle shot, called an *insert shot*, was replaced with a shot of an injured girl. Kuleshov's students commented that the last shot in each of the sequences, called the *reaction shot*, showed the actor's great acting ability to convey with subtlety hunger in the first sequence and pity in the next.

In another of the Kuleshov experiments, a sequence was constructed as follows: an initial shot of Mosjoukine smiling, an insert shot of a gun, and a reaction shot of Mosjoukine frowning. Kuleshov then rearranged the order: first the frowning shot, then the gun, and finally the smiling shot. In the first sequence, the actor's reaction seems to be one of fear; in the second, one of bravery. The important point of these experiments is that the actor's expression is constant, but the viewer attributes changes in emotional states to him on the basis of the editing. A woman looks off screen; there is a cut to a bomb blast and then a reaction shot of the woman. The audience assumes the woman is looking directly at the blast, even though the blast could have, in fact, occurred in another part of the world at another time (see Fig.

9-12). Sergei Eisenstein, the most renowned of the early Soviet filmmakers, felt that film space is the constructed space of montage, not the space photographed in the shot. Film space is more than the simulation of real space; it can also be abstract. It is possible to cut from a shot of Kerensky, who was head of the provisional government, and whom Eisenstein portrays as a villain in his film *October*, to shots of a glass peacock to suggest that Kerensky suffers from the sin of pride. There is no suggestion, however, that the peacock and Kerensky share the same physical space. Two shots, edited together, produce a new meaning, and film space allows for these kinds of metaphorical relationships between images. In addition to narrative content and metaphor, shots can be held together by abstract elements such as movement, tone, compositional weight, and image size.

Similarly, Eisenstein saw film time not as the duration of real movement but as the time set up by the rhythms and juxtaposition of montage. An event may take only a split second in real time, but, as its importance may be great, its duration should be lengthened in film. In *Potemkin*, Eisenstein extends time by showing a crying baby in a carriage teetering on the edge of a steep flight of stairs and then cutting to other shots before returning to the baby. Suspense is heightened by prolonging the event. Real time can also be condensed. Cutting from a horse race to a reaction shot of the crowd (a shot away from the main action is called a cutaway) and then back to the race allows a large portion of the race to be deleted. Similarly, a character's walk will seem continuous if you cut from him walking off screen to a point much further along in the action. Like film space, film time is also a construction created in editing.

Eisenstein also experimented with the montage of very short shots. In *Potemkin*, a sequence of brief shots of statues of lions in different positions cut quickly gives the illusion of their movement. A few frames of an attacking Cossack convey horror. There is no absolute rule for the minimum length of a shot; the minimum depends on the nature of the shot and the context. During World War II, it was found that plane spotters could recognize a female nude in just one frame, but it took them much longer to recognize a Messerschmitt.

The directors in Hollywood never adopted the Soviet concept of montage in its broadest sense. In Hollywood, a "montage sequence" is a sequence of short shots that condenses a period of time. For example, the hero might be shown growing up through a sequence of five or six shots that show him at different ages. The aspect of montage that was accepted by Hollywood (indeed, the Soviets had discovered it in early American films) was the *three-shot sequence*—that is, actor looks off screen, cut to a shot from his point of view, and then cut back to the reaction shot. Alfred Hitchcock constructed *Rear Window* almost entirely using this cutting technique (see Fig. 9-16).

Montage theory underlies much advertising and some experimental films. The juxtaposition of women, happy teenagers, and upbeat music with automobiles, soft drinks, and other products is used to manipulate consumers. In experimental films, the tradition of montage seems to find new life. In *A Movie*, Bruce Conner cut together *stock footage*—that is, footage purchased from a service (also called *library* or *archival footage*)—from widely disparate sources, ranging from pornography to newsreels, to form a unified whole. Music videos popularized a shooting and editing style with seemingly no rules about how images can be combined. Although the shots come from different times and places and are shot in vastly different styles, the viewer integrates them into a flow.

In *What's Up, Tiger Lily?* Woody Allen dubbed new dialogue into a Japanese action film to change the storyline completely. It is not that the original film loses its meaning. The joke is the ease with which meaning is changed by editing, in this case, by altering the relationship of sound and image.

APPROACHES TO EDITING

While the general public tends to focus on the role of the director and the creative decisions made on the set or during production, the decisions made in the editing room by the editor and director are just as important to the success of a film. As noted earlier, production is a time to gather footage that can be put together in any number of ways. It's in editing that the movie truly takes shape. Editing can have an enormous impact on pace and mood, on content and meaning, and, for dramas, the effectiveness of actors' performances. With a scripted film, the script is a starting point; but as the edited movie comes together, it is the footage and the edited sequences that determine the best way to tell the story, which may or may not follow the script. With documentaries there may be no script at all, and the editor plays a key role in the storytelling.

As the editor shapes the film, he or she must anticipate how audiences will experience the movie, and use structure and pacing to guide them through the story. But when an editor has been really successful, the craft that goes into the film may go completely unnoticed by the viewers. Editor Walter Murch (*Apocalypse Now*) likes to quote director Victor Fleming (*Gone with the Wind*), who said in 1939, "Good editing makes the film look well-directed. Great editing makes the film look like it wasn't directed at all."

Before reading further, be sure to read Style and Direction, starting on p. 332.

Story Structure

Think of someone you know who's a good storyteller—a person who can tell an anecdote, perhaps an event from his or her life, in a way that's engaging, well-paced, clear, funny, or sharp. Good storytellers know what facts you need to understand the story, in what order you need to know them, where to stretch out the tale with specific details, and where to gloss over events to get to the good parts. We all know bad storytellers as well—people who overload their audience with information or leave them confused or focus on irrelevant details—whose stories seem to go nowhere. Good stories have a discernible shape, with distinct *story beats*—moments in which something important happens, a key piece of information is revealed, or emotion is expressed.[1] The audience may not be consciously aware of the story's overall shape or of individual beats, but they feel them nonetheless. In a similar way, after years of watching different kinds of movies, audiences have instinctive expec-

---

1. The term "beat" can also mean simply a short amount of time in a scene, as in "wait a beat after she turns before cutting to the man."

tations about length and, for feature films, how far the story should have progressed by the ninety-minute or two-hour mark (more on this below).

It's commonly said that every story needs a beginning, middle, and end, but engaging stories can start in completely different ways. Some start broadly, helping the audience get oriented to the time and place, the physical environment, and the characters. Once those things are established, the plot or storyline is initiated. Other stories start much more narrowly, perhaps with a specific action, like a robbery. In this structure, unfolding events pull us along, and as they move forward we learn more about the characters, the environment, and so on.

Filmmakers can sometimes feel pressure to crowd as much information as possible toward the front of the film. This is particularly true in documentary. They want to set everything up, revealing all the *backstory* (history and events that took place before the contemporary action of the film) so the audience can be fully informed and prepared for the film's story. *Expository scenes* are sequences that are primarily concerned with bringing out information. Exposition, while necessary, can bog down the forward movement of a film. One of the chief tasks of the editor is to parcel out information, and good editors understand when to *hold back* details because exposition at a certain point might slow the film down and/or because audiences can find it intriguing to put pieces of the puzzle together themselves.

Stories, whether scripted dramas or unscripted documentaries, are divisible into *acts*. Acts can be defined in various ways, but in general terms, an act is a unit of storytelling made up of a series of scenes that may share a tone and build to a particular dramatic point or climax. In dramas, at the cusp between one act and the next there is often a reversal that sends the story in a new or unexpected direction and builds to a higher level of tension.

In a traditional three-act structure, the first act introduces the protagonist(s) and the *inciting incident*, which sets the story in motion. The second act brings conflicts or obstacles that prevent the protagonists from reaching their goals. The third act builds to a major climax, then resolves in a denouement.

People debate about how many acts a dramatic film should have, and even whether asking that question implies a formulaic approach. Nevertheless, it's helpful to look at where the acts fall in your story and how you can sharpen the flow and intent of each one. Each act should have a set of ideas and objectives, and scenes that don't contribute to that intent may need to be cut. In television dramas, acts are defined by commercial breaks, with the goal of locating a key plot point or cliffhanger at the end of each act, to keep viewers from changing channels.

With both dramas and documentaries, it's very helpful to chart out the scenes in the movie and look at their structure in terms of acts. Some editors like to make a three-by-five-inch card for each scene and put the cards on a bulletin board so they can quickly see the overall structure and easily rearrange individual cards. Some use software like Final Draft to display and arrange scenes. You can also create a *continuity*, a list of all the scenes, with any word processor.

For more on story structure, see the screenwriting books in the Bibliography.

Joining Sequences

One traditional method of editing connects shots into a sequence with straight cuts and then brackets the sequences themselves with *fades* and *dissolves*. Fades work like theater curtains opening and closing on an act or like a sunset followed by a sunrise. Dissolves, on the other hand, suggest a closer connection between one sequence and the next. Like fades, dissolves convey the passage of time—sometimes short time gaps within a sequence and sometimes long periods, as when a close-up of a person dissolves into another close-up of the same person shown at a much older age. When dissolves are used within sequences to signal short time gaps, their only function often seems to be to avoid jump cuts. Sequences can also be joined by wipes and many other visual effects (see Chapter 14).

In contemporary filmmaking, two sequences are typically joined with a straight cut (that is, one follows directly after the other with no dissolve or other effects). This sometimes creates the problem of distinguishing cuts *within* sequences—those that signal no significant time change—from cuts *between* sequences where there is a significant change of location or time. Filmmakers like Luis Buñuel and Alain Resnais like to explore this ambiguity. On the other hand, even with straight cuts there are many cues to signal the audience that the sequence has changed, including differences in sound level, lighting, dress, locale, or color. Even dream and fantasy sequences may be introduced with a straight cut, unlike in the American films of the 1930s and 1940s in which they would be signaled by eerie music and a *ripple* or *oil dissolve*. It's not unusual to see a contemporary movie with no effects other than a fade-in at the opening of the film and a fade-out at the end.

Another way to join two sequences is to *intercut* them (also called *parallel editing*). For example, the perils of the heroine heading toward a waterfall in a canoe are intercut with the hero's race to arrive in time to save her (always just in the nick of time). We cut back and forth to develop two threads of action simultaneously. More on this below.

Beginners tend to think of scenes as separate units to be shaped and polished individually. Always keep in mind the story as a whole and how one scene can best draw the audience forward to the next one. As discussed above, cuts between sequences can be used to make associations between them or suggest metaphors. In *The Graduate*, Dustin Hoffman pulls himself up on an air mattress in the pool and lands in one motion—across a brilliant cut—on Anne Bancroft in bed. Be attentive to any kind of similarities between the last frames of one scene and the first frames of the next in terms of where characters are in the frame, color, sounds, movement. You can create momentum and deliver meaning by drawing connections between scenes that might otherwise seem unrelated.

Continuity Editing

As discussed in Chapter 9, *invisible* or *match cutting* usually refers to the construction of sequences (or scenes) in which space and time appear to be continuous. Typically, both fiction and documentary sequences are match cut to appear continuous. On a film set, however, shots are rarely done in the order that they will appear in the final movie and it is the director's responsibility to shoot scenes with adequate coverage so that the editor can construct continuous sequences. On a documentary shot with one camera, every cut alters continuous time, which may be disguised in editing or not, depending on the context.

There are various ways to make action seem continuous. If the eye is distracted, a cut becomes less noticeable; therefore, editors "cut on the action" (a door slam, punch, or coin flip) to hide a cut. The action draws the viewer's attention away from the cut and from any slight mismatch from one shot to the next. Overlaps of action allow the editor to cut just before or just after the action or on the action itself. Cuts tend to propel time forward and to pick up the pace. Sometimes the action looks

Fig. 13-2. In the opening sequence of *Rashomon*, the camera moves from an establishing shot to close-ups, orienting the audience to the locale and environment before delving into details. At each cut, there is a significant change of camera position, focal length, and/or angle, which helps maintain the sense of continuity in time and space within the scene. Compare to Fig. 13-3. (The Criterion Collection)

too fast due to cutting, and the editor must include a few frames of action overlap between two shots.

Changing camera angle and focal length between consecutive shots disguises discontinuities and may make the cut "work"—that is, look as though it matches and is not jarring. Cutaways and reaction shots are tools that maintain continuity between shots that do not match. Cutting away from the main action to a reaction shot allows you to delete uninteresting dialogue or mistakes in the main action. Cutaways and reaction shots also allow you to control the tempo of the film through editing, which would be impossible with a continuous take.

THE JUMP CUT. The sequence of cuts that moves from long shot to medium shot to close-up is generally made up of match cuts. In other words, each of the cuts appears to occur in the same space and time period. However, when there is a noticeable discontinuity between two similar shots, that may be considered a *jump cut*. For example, to cut from a shot of a person sitting to a shot of the same person standing in the same spot creates a noticeable jump in time. If the image size and angle don't change very much from one shot to the next (for example, two medium shots of the same person cut next to each other), that may also be considered a jump cut. There is no fixed rule about when joining two shots will result in a jump cut, but generally speaking the smaller the change in image size or angle, the more likely it is the cut will seem discontinuous. Also, whether or not sound (including background sound) seems continuous from one shot to the next makes an enormous difference in whether a cut seems to jump or not.

The director Jean-Luc Godard, in the early 1960s, began to use the jump cut as a creative element in his filmmaking. He cut out what he felt were boring middle parts of shots or spliced together two close-ups of the same character with a definite jump in time. Not only did these jump cuts comment on the nature of film space, but they also created exciting rhythms that seemed to express the feeling of modern life.

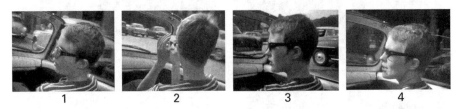

| 1 | 2 | 3 | 4 |

Fig. 13-3. In this sequence from *Breathless*, there is no change in focal length or angle from one shot to the next, creating a jump cut that results in an obvious discontinuity in time. (The Criterion Collection)

Today jump cuts are used widely in sequences where match cuts were traditionally used, and audiences have come to accept them as a routine part of the visual language of editing. Some films establish a visual language in which jump cuts are part of the editing grammar throughout the film. In some sense, the meaning of jump cuts is disappearing since they no longer really command attention. On the other hand, many movies are constructed using continuity editing from the outset, and the sudden use of a jump cut would seem jarring or even an error. While shooting, it makes sense to cover yourself with alternate shots, cutaways, and the like, rather than be forced to resort to jump cuts to salvage a sequence. Sometimes a quick dissolve or a fade-out/fade-in is used to cover what otherwise would be a jump cut.

Screen Direction

A basic rule of film editing is to try to preserve screen direction at cuts (see The 180-Degree Rule, p. 344). If you cut from person A looking off screen to the right to a shot of person B also looking to the right, it will appear that they are both looking in the same direction rather than at one another. Much of the directional information in a chase sequence comes from screen direction.

When two shots violate the 180-degree rule and there is no shot available where the camera crosses the line, you can separate the shots with a neutral shot (for example, a shot taken on the line).

In editing, if a character walks off screen right, he should generally come in from screen left to appear that he is continuing on his walk (if he comes in screen right, the audience may think he's returning to his previous spot, though in many cases this is not an issue). Screen direction to the right is usually accepted by audiences as meaning travel from west to east; to the left is travel from east to west. A plane flying from New York to Paris is typically shown flying left to right.

Intercutting

The idea of intercutting is to advance two or more scenes at the same time by cutting back and forth between them, which at times may involve placing sound from one scene with the picture from another. Done right, intercutting can be a powerful tool to develop several ideas or plotlines at once, helping the audience draw connections between the different ideas, using one scene to provide a kind of commentary on another. Done wrong, intercutting can be confusing or irritating.

Figure 13-4 is a sequence from *Out of Sight* (directed by Steven Soderbergh, edited by Anne V. Coates) that shows an interesting use of intercutting, screen direction, and other shooting and editing concepts.[2] The sequence begins as George Clooney sits down with Jennifer Lopez in a bar—we see a two-shot followed by angle-reverse shots of each actor. As the sequence progresses, the framing of their shots becomes tighter, something that is commonly done as scenes develop and become more intense or intimate. In frame 6 we cut to Lopez putting her hand on her glass. In frame 7 Clooney puts his hand on her knee, which might appear to be taking place under the table. In frame 8 we see Lopez with reversed screen direction (and also a warmer color balance), the implications of which—and location of the shot—are unclear at first. The conversation continues in the sound track and frame 9 is clearly still in the bar. However, as the sequence goes on we realize that their seductive talk at the table is being intercut with the next scene in her hotel room in which they go to bed together. The use of very close shots plays with the ambiguity of which space we're in. The intercutting moves the story along by combining the

---

2. Fig. 13-4 does not include every shot in the sequence.

Fig. 13-4. Intercutting. Selected shots from *Out of Sight*. See text. (Universal Pictures)

seduction with the results—it's economical (relatively little of the hotel room scene is shown) and a deft way to hint at what they're thinking about while they talk. Also used in this sequence and elsewhere in the film are very short freeze frames that call attention to little moments, as though remembered by the characters or singled out by the filmmaker for our notice. Frames 17 and 18, though not contiguous in the sequence, make a lovely parallel by pairing profile shots, first at the table, then in bed.

DIALOGUE EDITING

Dialogue and Scene Structure

In both fiction and documentary, dialogue editing is part of shaping the basic storyline. What gets said, and when, is a fundamental part of moving the story ahead. Careful editing of dialogue can have a big impact on individual sequences, even if the scene has been carefully scripted.

Unlike stage plays, which may include long speeches that work well when delivered to a live audience, film dialogue tends to work best when it's quite simple and spare. Images, facial expressions, and juxtapositions of editing should tell the story as much as dialogue, when possible. In documentary, even expository material usually plays best when pared down to essentials. For more on this, see Script Preparation, p. 354.

When editing a scene, look for places where you can remove unnecessary dialogue. Sometimes you can begin the sequence after most of the setup has already taken place, doing away with unneeded exposition. Sometimes a pivotal line can be moved to the beginning of a sequence, allowing the rest to be made more succinct. Real people often speak with false starts, digressions, repetition, long pauses, or uninteresting detail; people on screen (whether they're in documentaries or dramas) generally need to be a lot terser to hold audience interest. Find places where a look from one character to another might replace dialogue. Let the audience fill in the details.

The use of simple cutaways is the most common method of condensing or rearranging speech. A three-shot pattern is used. While one person is speaking, we cut to a person listening or to another relevant shot. During the cutaway, the speaker completes one thought and the sound cuts to another sentence (to the audience this sounds like the normal flow of speech). Before the picture cuts back to the speaker's face, pauses, words, and whole sections of dialogue can be removed or added. The editor can construct any number of possible sentences from the collection of recorded words. Sometimes cutaways are not needed to condense dialogue: a match cut or jump cut may work just as well.

Cutting away from sync-sound dialogue can be a useful tool for providing a sense of dynamic flow in a conversation. Say you cut from one person asking a question to a shot of someone else responding. If the picture cuts from the first person to the second before the question is finished, the editing may take on a more natural, less mechanical feeling (see Fig. 14-25). Showing the person being spoken to, and not just the person speaking, can give the audience insights into the characters as well as clues on how to interpret what is being said. Hitchcock insisted that what is said on the sound track should contrast with what is seen. Cutaways may be chosen to provide an interesting counterpoint to the spoken dialogue.

When the sound cuts before or after a picture cut (instead of in sync with it) this is called a *sound overlap*, *split edit*, or *L-cut* (see Basic Sound Editing, p. 584). Sound overlaps play a big part in creating the illusion of continuity across cuts (see Sound and Continuity, p. 642).

Replacing Dialogue

It's essential that the audience be able to understand spoken dialogue. Bad sound and unintelligible dialogue can quickly alienate viewers and make them lose interest in the movie. Listen critically to your dialogue tracks and avoid using takes that are hard to hear (for more, see Evaluating the Sound Track, p. 642).

In fiction films, where the pacing of dialogue may be quite consistent from one take to the next, it's often possible to substitute the sound from one take with that of another (while keeping the picture from the original take). This can be used not only to improve sound quality, but to find better performances as well. Pauses between words usually need to be trimmed or expanded slightly to maintain sync.

When location audio on feature films is unacceptable, dialogue tracks may be replaced using *ADR* (*automatic dialogue replacement*), also called *looping*. Actors are brought into a sound studio to redo their lines while watching repeating loops of picture. An *ADR cue sheet* is prepared that lists every bit of dialogue by timecode with space to indicate best takes when they're recorded. In the session, ADR software plays three beeps before each bit of dialogue and a visible streamer goes across the screen, which cues the actor to start speaking. It's easier to do short sections, but actors may get into character better with longer passages.

ADR can be slow and expensive. Often the timing is wrong or the voices sound "canned" and unnatural. The dialogue must be mixed properly with Foleys or other sound effects to make the takes believable and to try to match them with the ones recorded on location. Software such as Synchro Arts' VocAlign and Adobe Audition can automatically adjust the timing of a redone take to match the pacing of the original take. During sound editing, the ADR lines are put on their own tracks and the original audio is moved to the *X and Y production dialogue tracks* in case the director wants to hear them.

When dialogue contains swear words that are unacceptable to a TV network, there are various solutions to creating a *soft version* of the film. In a drama, the actors may record similar but inoffensive words during production that can be edited in when needed; or this may be done in ADR. For a documentary, you might choose to edit in a beep sound over the offending word (which makes it very clear what you're doing) or you might simply drop the audio for an instant (but be sure to have some tone underneath). Some networks require that people's lips be blurred if you can see what they're saying without the sound.

Cutting Dialogue Tracks

When editing dialogue, it's often necessary to separate words that are spaced closely together on the track. This is a skill that improves with practice. Use the NLE's audio waveform display to help locate the beginning and end of a word (see Fig. 14-24). Sometimes you can't avoid clipping a word—perhaps because someone else starts talking—which sounds jarring (chopped-off words are sometimes called *upcut dialogue*). Often a two-frame crossfade can make an otherwise awkward cut sound natural. Some NLEs can cut within a frame (subframe editing), which may make a cleaner cut. If a word is cut off, sometimes you can find a different take where the same word appears and substitute the word or even just the end of the word. Be attentive to breaths between words—avoid cutting in the middle of a breath. It's often better to leave the whole breath in place and fade it down quickly.

Narration

Narration, or *voice-over* (*VO*), is used in both documentary and fiction. It may be used to deliver information, provide the point of view of an unseen character, or allow an on-screen character to comment on the action.

Narration should be kept simple and clear—it shouldn't sound "written." When writing narration, practice speaking it aloud to be sure it sounds like natural speech. Avoid complex phrasing or vocabulary that taxes the audience's ability to understand.

Narration sometimes works best when woven in with sync sound from the scene. Look for places where you can float a line of narration, then bring up sync sound, then run another line of narration. This needs to be done carefully—if the narrator speaks over a close shot of someone else talking, it can be distracting.

Editors or directors often record their own voices as a "scratch" narration during editing that will be replaced by the actual narrator after the picture is locked. Many NLEs have a voice-over or direct recording tool that allows you to record a scratch narration straight to hard drive, while watching the picture if you want.

Narration recording sessions should be logged to keep track of good and bad takes; often you want to combine parts of several takes. Recording narration with timecode facilitates logging and editing.

Ideally, final narration should be recorded in a sound booth to get high-quality, clean sound with no background noise. Some narration sessions are done while watching the picture, but this can be distracting and is usually not necessary. Instead, prepare your scratch narration to be sure the copy fits properly in each scene, then record the final narration at a similar pace. You can bring a stopwatch to the session to ensure the narrator reads at the same speed. If the recorded VO is too slow, you'll need to edit out pauses between words or perhaps extend the picture to make it fit. See p. 457 for narration recording suggestions.

See Chapter 15 for editing music and other sound editing concerns.

THE EDITING PROCESS

The editing process varies by type of production, type of editing equipment, and individual editors' preferences. In the sections below, procedures from different types of productions are discussed together.

The Editing Team

Today many independent filmmakers, journalists, and corporate videomakers edit by themselves on a laptop or desktop system. A Hollywood feature, on the other hand, will have a large hierarchy of editors doing specialized tasks in several locations. It's instructive to see how that system is organized, even if you're working on a much smaller team.

In the studio system, the *supervising film editor* oversees the entire organization. Under that person are one or more *film editors*, a *supervising sound editor*, a *music editor*, and a *supervising VFX (visual effects) editor*. Under each of those people may be several other editors. For example, sound editing may be done by a *dialogue editor*, an *FX (effects) editor*, and a *Foley editor* (see Chapter 15). Under those editors may be several assistants, apprentices, and production assistants.

On a small team, the editor may be responsible for a number of those tasks, and assistants do things like manage data and hard drives, synchronize rushes, keep logs, and output files and DVDs when needed for screenings.

When the picture and sound for a project are stored on shared drives that can be accessed by several editing systems, picture editors, dialogue editors, effects editors, and assistants can all work on the project at the same time and easily pass updated files back and forth.

The Editing Schedule

On feature films, it's typical for the editor to begin cutting during production, both to provide feedback for the director on the shoot and to shorten the overall schedule. The editor will produce an *editor's cut*, which becomes the *director's cut* after the director has had a chance to view and make changes. On some productions, editing begins after the shoot has wrapped. Projects vary widely in terms of how long editing takes. For a feature film, the DGA (Directors Guild of America) contract allows ten weeks, or a day of editing for each two days of shooting, to prepare the director's cut. Many films are edited much faster, and some slower.

Unscripted documentaries may begin editing during production, but it's often only after most of the material is shot that the film can really be shaped. Many documentaries are essentially "written" in the editing room (whether or not there is literally writing involved for, say, narration). Independent documentaries often take months and sometimes years to edit; a span of time that is not uncommonly punctuated by downtime for fundraising.

The Editing Room

Editing equipment is discussed in Chapter 15. The editing room should have a comfortable workstation for the editor and ideally a large monitor and viewing area for other members of the production team.

Make certain all the material for the project is clearly labeled with the (working) title of the production, the name of the production company, and any reel, roll, or drive numbers. The backup files of all camera footage and any camera original master tapes and/or camera original film footage should clearly labeled as such and stored in a safe place—preferably offsite, in a storage facility, a lab vault, or postproduction house.

Organizing Material

Editing involves juggling many elements including picture, production audio, music, effects, and so on. As editing goes on there may be several versions of the movie in different forms. It's essential that the editor be able to quickly locate anything that's needed. Many editors create their own log that accounts for all the material in the editing room along with their own notes about takes and performances. Many other tools and techniques are available for organizing and identifying editing assets:

- On a dramatic film, the script supervisor will prepare a continuity script that shows the editor how each scene was covered in terms of camera angles and takes. There will also be an editor's log and the script notes (see p. 377). Camera and sound reports also indicate what was filmed and recorded, along with notes (see p. 377).
- On a documentary, there may be a log of what was shot or topics discussed in interviews. Verbatim transcripts are usually made of any interview material.
- Various applications let you review footage prior to editing. Some, such as Digital Heaven's MovieLogger and Adobe Prelude, can capture timecode and mark In and Out Points that can be exported to the NLE. Sometimes directors use logging programs or NLEs to assemble their preferred takes into a sequence, then pass that to the editor. Intelligent Assistance's prEdit allows a director to make selections from a transcript, rearrange them, see the associated video clips, and export the sequence to an NLE. On a documentary or reality program with lots of footage, assistants may log the material for the editor.
- Several programs can phonetically index your media so that you can type in a phrase and the software will find every shot or section of audio media that contains the phrase. Avid's PhraseFind and AV3's Get are two examples. Avid's ScriptSync goes a step further in synchronizing the text version of a feature script with every take of audio or video media that was recorded for that part of the script. You can quickly find all the takes recorded for any section of dialogue. On a documentary, you can use these apps to go quickly from the transcript to the relevant sections of media. Adobe Premiere Pro can automatically generate a written transcript from your media, but in the current version it's far less accurate than a human transcriber (albeit, far cheaper too) so the document will need some touching up by hand.
- Smart use of metadata (see p. 242) is essential for wrangling large amounts of media. NLEs have increasingly sophisticated tools for identifying and searching for media based on different labels and criteria. For example, starting with version X, Final Cut Pro allows you to assign keywords to clips or sections of clips, such as "interviews," "exteriors," or "shots of Zoe." You can then easily find any material that has that particular keyword, regardless of when it was shot or where it is on your system. Some NLEs have face-detection capability; after the system analyzes the footage, it can indicate which shots have one or more people in them.
- For projects shot on film and edited digitally, a shot log will usually be generated in the telecine for every camera roll, correlating key numbers and timecode numbers (see p. 693). This log should be checked for accuracy when loading material into the NLE (see p. 698).

See Chapter 14 for more on organizational systems.

Selecting Shots

As useful as they are for organizational purposes, production logs and continuity scripts can sometimes get in the way of editing judgments. On the set, directors indicate the takes they like, often having seen them only once. Sometimes the director may be attached to a shot because it was hard to get. The editor, on the other hand, can bring to the project a fresh set of eyes, unbiased by what took place during production. Some editors prefer *not* to view dailies with directors so they can form their own opinions about what works and what doesn't. In this case, the editor may put together a first cut from the script and then discuss it with the director. Similarly, though it may save some money not to include or transfer takes considered "bad" on the shoot, these takes can be a gold mine to the editor who may be looking for something very specific to solve an editing problem. A take with a bad line reading may make a perfect cutaway. The dead air before a slate may supply just enough room tone to fill a hole.

In his book *In the Blink of an Eye*, Walter Murch talks about an interesting, unexpected drawback caused by the ability of nonlinear editing systems to instantly locate any shot. In film and linear videotape editing, you're forced to wait and watch while fast-forwarding to find a shot. NLEs save this "wasted" time, but that may deprive you of some serendipitous discoveries—shots you weren't looking for that trigger new ideas for the cut. You can do something similar with an NLE by making a sequence of all the unedited takes together, forming a string of rushes that can be easily viewed from beginning to end.

On documentaries, sometimes producers or directors go through a transcript marking up the bites they want, creating a script before editing begins. If done without actually watching the footage, this can be tremendously misleading, since something that reads well on the page may actually sound terrible, or can't be cut where you want because of the way the words were spoken. Also, working straight from a transcript can lead to visually dull editing.

All of these are reasons to avoid too much "preselecting" of material prior to real editing.

That said, it must be pointed out that on some projects, particularly in news and documentary work, the edit is highly determined by preselection. The director may view the footage and create a *paper cut* or *paper edit*—a list of the selected shots or interview bites in their proper order, identified by timecode; or, as noted above, an NLE or other app can be used to actually assemble shots. Starting with this selection, the editor then puts together the sequence, tunes the transitions, and makes other adjustments. If your budget is limited, this technique can save a lot of time and money in the editing room.

PICTURE AND SOUND QUALITY. You must always try to translate what you see and hear on the editing system to what the audience will see and hear in the finished movie. Sometimes the editing system is not a reliable indicator of what the footage will look like.[3] When using a small monitor or editing with a low-resolution codec, fine details may be harder to see and landscapes and detailed shots may be harder to read. Wide vistas or even medium shots that may ultimately look great

---

3. For projects that originate on film and are edited digitally, the telecine transfer may not capture details in the highlights or shadows that may be visible later when a more careful transfer is done. You may or may not be happy when you later see the hidden details. Be sure to check carefully for flash frames and overexposed frames nearby.

when the project is shown at high resolution on a bigger screen can seem paltry during editing. The need for good sound quality is noted above. Bear in mind that small speakers and fan noise of an editing system can mask a lot of detail in the original audio recording. You may not be able to hear problems or even desirable-but-quiet sounds (see Chapter 15).

From Rough Cut to Picture Lock

Different editors have their own process for sculpting a movie from the footage that comes out of the camera (the dailies or rushes), and different projects may call for different approaches. Start by organizing the bins or folders in the NLE's browser. You might create a bin for every scene as well as separate bins for music, stills, visual effects, sound effects, and the various cuts (sequences). In Final Cut Pro X, there are no bins, but you can use keywords or events to organize the different elements.

The next step is to view the dailies, log them if necessary, and then divide the material into the shots you want to use (the *selects*, *in-takes*, or *ins*) and the shots you put aside (the *outtakes* or *outs*). Some editors like to mark and rearrange clips in the NLE's browser; others immediately start adding the in-takes to a timeline and begin building the cut.

An *assembly* (sometimes called a *string-out*) puts the shots in the order called for by the script. For unscripted material, an assembly may simply be all the sequences in chronological order. The *rough cut* is the first attempt at shaping the film. For scripted films, the assembly and first rough cut may be essentially the same thing. In a documentary, the rough cut may be made by shortening and reordering the sequences from the assembly. The editor usually attempts to put together the rough cut fairly quickly, worrying less about the pace of scenes and getting everything to work well, and concentrating more on establishing the overall direction of the work. Most editors prefer to edit rough cuts on the long side, in order to try out shots and scenes, even if they're questionable and likely to be dropped later. Rough cuts are usually a great deal longer than the final film will be. This is nothing to worry about. Starting loose and then refining is often the best way to proceed.

As the movie continues to be edited and refined, you may have several rough cuts. You may want to save old versions for comparison—be sure to name each version in a clear way so you can tell when it was made and what type of cut it is (such as editor's cut, director's cut, etc.).

When the basic scene order is in place and you start polishing individual sequences and transitions, this is called *fine-cutting*. It's usually easier to fine-cut and pace individual sequences after you've seen the overall flow of the rough cut. As you continue to work, the rough cut becomes a *fine cut*.

Some people prefer to fine-cut from the start of editing instead of making a rough cut. Even though this approach requires more time to complete the first cut, you may be better able to judge the editing and whether scenes are working if you get them relatively tight as you move forward. The two approaches have been compared to carving a work out of a mass of material versus building up a structure piece by piece. With experience, you'll find what works best for you.

As you progress, a continuity (also called a *reel continuity*) should be prepared, which is a list of all the scenes in the movie, the running time, and, for a theatrical film, where the reel breaks fall (see p. 705). The continuity is useful to help structure the film, compare different versions, and aid in feedback screenings. As noted above, some editors like to make file cards with individual scenes and move them around get a feel for structure.

Picture editors differ in how much they like to fine-tune sound, color, and music during the rough-cut/fine-cut stages. Some want to concentrate mostly on the story and flow of the film; others feel that until details like the sound balance and color consistency within scenes are done carefully, it will be harder to judge if the picture is really working. This becomes even more of an issue when outside audiences view the work in progress (see below). Sometimes other editors or assistants will work on audio and color in preparation for a screening.

For larger projects, as editing continues you will often need to export a cut of the film for such things as publicity, trailers, special effects, or music. Since the movie is still changing, you may need to send out updated cuts, or *change lists*, generated by the NLE, that indicate with frame-accurate precision which shots have been lengthened, shortened, or *lifted* (dropped altogether). A sound editor, for example, might use a change list to update her DAW to the new version of the film.

When you're done making changes to the picture, this is *picture lock* or *picture freeze*.

Test Screenings and Feedback

Editing requires an intense, focused kind of thinking. You sit close to the screen and get deeply involved in large problems and tiny details. This is not a good environment to judge whether the movie is really working. You need to step back occasionally and see it from a different perspective.

For projects that will ultimately be shown on a big screen—either in large-screen digital projection or on film—it's imperative that you view the movie on a big screen during the editing process. The transition from small screen to large can be startling. Sometimes the pace of the movie seems to speed up and sometimes to slow down. Wide shots that may seem boring on the small screen suddenly reveal fascinating detail. Close-ups may seem overpowering when ten feet tall. Cuts in which the eye's attention shifts from one side of the screen to the opposite side may seem a little jumpy on the small screen and very jarring on the big one. If you can't get access to a big screen, at least make a DVD or Blu-ray that you can take out of the editing room and view in a different setting.

Watching the movie with outside viewers—a few at a time, or many—is another important part of getting a fresh perspective. Screenings can be invaluable to determine whether something in the movie is confusing or boring or really doesn't work. Even watching the movie with one person who is not part of the editing team will cause *you* to see it in a different way, with a different sense of the timing and content. Try to leave a few days off between when you last work on a cut and when you view it, so you can see it with freshest eyes.

Filmmakers vary on the value of test screenings with large audiences. Some love to get feedback (or may be forced to get it by backers or studios). Some resent the idea of putting important, personal decisions to something that seems like a popular vote. Since a few vocal audience members can sway or overwhelm those who are uncertain, it can help to have people fill out paper questionnaires prior to any discussion, then have a moderator (not the filmmakers) lead a directed conversation with specific questions about what's working and what's not. Often test audiences disagree with each other on which scenes should stay or be cut. One group may laugh where another is silent. The differences in "temperature" between different screenings can be stunning (which you'll continue to find as you screen the finished film).

Another factor in test screenings is the problem of showing unfinished work. You can explain all you want about what a rough cut or a rough mix or uncorrected picture means, but even experienced professionals often lack the ability to imagine what the movie will be like when finished. For more on showing unfinished work to backers or distributors, see Chapter 17.

Whether you show the work in progress to one or many people, it's important to learn how to receive *notes*, and to listen to feedback and criticism. Don't argue or try to talk them out of their position. You've asked for their thoughts, so take in what they say. Don't react too quickly, even within yourself. After some time goes by, and you've had a chance to talk it over with your collaborators, you may find new solutions that hadn't occurred to you before. It sometimes takes days (or more) to sort out which bits of feedback constitute valuable new perspectives and which are just unhelpful and to be ignored. Then of course there are the truly off-the-wall comments that always seem to pop up at screenings, which you have to train yourself not to respond to or mull over on sleepless nights.

Something to keep in mind when you're *giving* notes: calibrate your comments to what the filmmakers can actually use. If you're looking at an early rough cut—and there's time to change things—then let them know what works, what doesn't, or what might improve things. If the film is nearly complete, then limit your suggested changes to what's still fixable, not aspects for which there is no turning back.

Finding the Right Length

If your movie miraculously lucks out in the combination of writing, direction, and editing, it occasionally happens that the rough cut plays just fine at the length it was intended to. If so, congratulations, and enjoy the easy finishing process ahead.

For most projects, however, you may face some tough decisions. The rough cut may be many hours long. Or the fine cut may seem too *short*. How do you find the right length for the project? Do you let the material dictate length, or do you try to cut it to a standard length?

Start by asking yourself what would make the best, tightest movie. If a movie is too long, audiences can turn on it, even if they liked it at first. Well-edited, taut movies keep audience energy high and allow the ideas and emotions in the film to emerge clearly. Be hard on yourself—don't hold on to a sequence just because you're in love with it; only keep it if it really works in the context of the whole film. The advice to "murder your darlings" applies when paring down a rough cut. If two sequences repeat the same idea or emotion, consider dropping one of them. If you can get away with starting a shot ten seconds later, trim off the head. Sometimes ideas or plot points you cut out have a way of emerging subtly in other scenes, and don't need to be explicated.

It's easy for filmmakers who have nurtured material from script through production to feel attached to things the audience won't be attached to in the least. The editor must always try to see the film through the eyes of the audience, and to understand which shots and scenes are essential and which aren't. One of the qualities of good editors is their ability to take an unsentimental and coldhearted view of each sequence and make the required cuts. A strong scene, idea, or joke can lose a lot of power if later scenes seem to be repeating it.

Many filmmakers have had this experience: They finish a fine cut, declaring the movie finished and tight and done. Then, perhaps to fit a broadcast slot (see below), they begrudgingly have to cut some time out. They comb the film for every slack or wasted moment. In the end, they like the shortened version better. Barry Sonnenfeld (*Men in Black*) has remarked that he's one of the few directors whose director's cuts are sometimes *shorter* than the released version of the movie.

Be especially attentive to the first few minutes of the movie. Outside of a theater (where the audience is captive) some people will choose to watch a movie only if they're hooked in the first several scenes. On the other hand, if you start things out too quickly (in the first minute or so) you may lose people who haven't settled into their seats. If the movie begins with head titles and credits (see below), consider developing the story visually under or between the titles—this keeps things moving even while people settle in.

LENGTH AND DISTRIBUTION OPPORTUNITIES. In determining length, you must also consider potential distribution. If you're making a feature film, typically these run about ninety minutes to two hours, give or take. If a film is only slightly over an hour, it may not be considered a "feature" for theatrical, festival, or broadcast slots. If a feature runs substantially over two hours, exhibitors (theater owners) get nervous because it means they can have fewer shows per day and broadcasters may want to cut the film shorter to fit a two-hour (or even ninety-minute) program slot. Documentaries may be feature length, or they may be shorter. A one-hour documentary is much easier to sell to cable or broadcast television than a ninety-minute doc (even a series may sell to more markets if each show is an hour or a half hour). For any broadcast slot, you need to deduct time for station IDs and advertising or promotions. A "one-hour" program may run fifty-seven minutes or a whole lot less, depending on the broadcaster's needs. Feature-length docs are often trimmed to fifty-seven or fifty-two minutes in order to get a TV sale.

When producing something for an educational market, keep in mind the typical length of a class in whatever age bracket you're targeting. Sometimes a one-hour film is cut down to twenty to forty minutes for educational distribution, and any particular content that might be inappropriate for a school environment is removed. Movies for young children are often ten minutes or less to accommodate short attention spans.

For corporate and industrial projects, about ten to fifteen minutes is sometimes the longest that busy executives or workers want to spend watching a movie. For training pieces you must weigh how much information people can absorb and how much "seat time" they want to put in. Short and punchy is better than too detailed and long. Training is often done with short chapters and/or with interactive tools on the Web, allowing users to answer questions and digest material before moving on.

Fig. 13-5. Supered title. Text should stay inside the title safe area (the inner box; see also Fig. 9-7). Drop shadows help separate the text from the background and add dimensionality. Shown here is one of the title tools in Avid Media Composer. (Avid Technology, Inc.)

TITLES

Planning the titles and credits and placing them in the movie is part of the editing process (though the actual title design and production may be done after editing is finished). You can hire a professional designer or a postproduction facility to create titles and credits, or you can work them out on your editing system. Sometimes people shoot titles with physical objects or artwork—like shooting a wall with graffiti titles spray-painted on.

Some titles and credits appear as lettering over a plain background or other nonmoving graphic. Titles that appear over action (a moving film or video image) are called *supers* (for superimposition, see Fig. 13-5).

When a name appears as static (nonmoving) lettering, this is considered a *title card*. If there are *head credits* at the beginning of the film, these are usually individual cards that fade in or cut in. Title cards may be supered or nonsupered, though some people use the term "title card" to mean a nonsupered title. End or tail credits may be done as cards, but more often they are done as a *credit roll*, in which a long list of names moves up from the bottom of the screen. Vertically moving titles are also called *scrolls* or *crawls* (though in video, "crawl" is often used to mean a line of horizontally moving type). The advantage of a credit roll is that the various credits can be given equal screen time (whereas cards tend to favor the names at the top of the card) and the whole list can be read comfortably in less time. With cards, on the other hand, it may be easier to make changes or correct errors. Cards also have the advantage of no motion artifacts, which credit scrolls often exhibit, especially when there's any difference between the frame rate the titles were produced in and the frame rate of the broadcast or distribution format or the display.

Extensive head credits are common in Hollywood films (with the biggest star credits coming before the title), but lengthy head credits on a student film can seem pretentious. Some films start better without head credits, to plunge the audience straight into the story, without reminding them that it is just a story, which was written, directed, produced . . . you get the idea.

There is a generally accepted order for various credits, which is often stipulated in contracts or union rules. Be aware that some broadcasters have restrictions on how credits are done in terms of placement, length, and who can be thanked or credited. They may also impose restrictions on including Web addresses.

Double- and triple-check for correct spellings and proper job titles, and make sure you don't omit important credits! Start collecting your list of personnel and thank-yous during production so you don't forget anyone.

Timing

Different movies use different timing for titles. One rule of thumb is to keep titles on screen long enough to read them twice (or read them aloud once). Experiment with pacing. Titles that linger too long may slow down the film and bore the audience. Too quick titles may leave them frustrated. Another rule of thumb for credit rolls is that it should take about seven to twelve seconds for a line of text to travel from the bottom of the screen to the top; however, rolls may go slower on feature films and often go a great deal faster on TV programs (where broadcasters, who couldn't care less about your credits, are racing to get to the next show).

Typeface and Placement

When choosing a typeface for the lettering, avoid fonts that have very narrow lines or serifs (the angled lines that extend from and ornament some type styles). The smaller the font size, the more likely it is that thin lines or elements will flicker, look noisy, or disappear altogether. Small titles, especially if they move, look worse on interlaced video formats than progressive.

Usually lettering should be no smaller than about 1/25 of total image height (that is, no more than 25 lines on screen at once). The maximum characters per line seems to work well at around 40 for many formats; in theatrical films, up to about 55 characters may work. The longer the line, the harder it is to read quickly. When doing subtitles for dialogue, consider breaking the titles into two shorter lines rather than one long one.

Today almost every project for TV or theaters is produced in a widescreen format (16:9 or wider). Sometimes titles extend across the wide-screen image. However, because movies are often shown at some point on nonwidescreen TV, it may be safer to prepare titles that fit within the 4:3 rectangle (see Aspect Ratio Choices, p. 74).[4] Regardless of whether you're laying out titles in 4:3 or 16:9 aspect ratio, all

---

4. Of course, widescreen films are often letterboxed when shown on nonwidescreen TV, in which case the whole frame is visible, but the titles will look smaller (see Fig. 2-12E).

lettering should fit within the *TV safe title area*, which is smaller than the *TV safe action frame* (see Figs. 13-5 and 9-7). Credit rolls often look best if centered on a central *gutter* with the job title extending to the left of the gutter and the name extending to the right. Look at movies for layout ideas.

Try to put superimposed titles over shots without excessive movement or complexity that might fight with the titles. Titles will make any camera jiggle especially noticeable. Supers should almost always be done with *drop shadows*, which rim the letters with a dark edge to separate them from the background. When a movie is subtitled in a foreign language, it's common to use an *outline font* that has a dark edge all the way around each letter to improve readability against bright backgrounds.

Supers used in documentaries to identify film subjects are sometimes called *lower thirds*, since they fall in the lower third of the frame. Lower thirds are frequently set against a darker *pad* to help separate them from the background (which can be opaque or semitransparent). If lower thirds are anticipated, be sure to shoot your subjects with enough room at the bottom of the frame to accommodate titles. If the project is distributed in foreign markets, broadcasters will ask for a textless version of the movie so they can do foreign language titles. If you plan for this during post, you can create textless background elements on which titles can be added later.

In digital, it's easy to do either supered or nonsupered titles. When finishing a film project the traditional way on film, supered titles may cost more than non-supered titles, depending on the printing method used. For more on generating digital titles, see p. 594.

CHAPTER 14

Editing Digital Video

This chapter is about digital video editing using nonlinear editing systems, or NLEs (the term is used to refer both to the entire editing system and to the particular editing app—the software—it uses). Information is also included about tape editing, which is less common today but continues to play a role.

See Chapter 1 for an overview of video editing concepts, Chapter 13 for a discussion of editing choices and styles, and Chapter 5 for more technical aspects of video.

See Chapter 16 for specific issues for projects that are shot on motion picture film, including film-to-digital transfers and editing considerations when working with a film original. You'll also find information on digital-to-film transfers when making film prints. However, if you are editing film workprint in the traditional way using flatbed editing machines, please see excerpts from the third edition of this book posted at www.filmmakershandbook.com.

The State of Digital Editing

Video editing lives in two worlds. On the consumer side, some NLEs are amazingly easy to use and intuitive. Even young kids can shoot some video, load it into a basic editing program like iMovie, and put a movie together.

On the professional side, the profusion of formats, choices, and technologies has resulted in NLEs that are amazingly sophisticated and powerful. You can do so much with an NLE that many editors find their role now routinely includes whole areas that used to be *someone else's* job (sound mixing, color correction, graphic design, computer repair, etc.). When you first encounter a professional NLE, it can be frightening for all the menus, icons, and ways of working. Remember that the same basic editing functions exist somewhere in each popular NLE, so your knowledge of one—even a consumer version—will help you figure out the next.

Filmmakers vary in their interest in or ability to deal with technical stuff. Some editors with great filmmaking skills know very little about the systems they work on. Others are techno-geeks and proud of it. They want to know everything about the software and hardware and how to do the most complex tasks.

Whatever your level of interest or ability, try to find people who can advise you. Other filmmakers working with the same NLE can be a great resource. Online user groups like the ones at www.creativeCOW.net are great places to post technical questions and find problems being discussed (see the Bibliography for more). You can find free video tutorials on YouTube, and sites like Lynda.com and macProVideo.com offer entire courses in different NLEs with video demonstrations. And when you're stuck, you'll often find that just doing an online search with some keywords turns up helpful solutions.

This chapter covers both basic concepts as well as some more specialized details (particularly later in the chapter). If a section gets too technical for you, skip ahead to the next one. Also, a disclaimer: there are far too many editing systems, techniques, and different names for the same thing to cover them all. When it comes to working with *your* particular system, be sure to read the manual and consult the help section in the software.

Before reading further, be sure to see Video Editing, p. 36, where key ideas are introduced.

COMPONENTS OF A NONLINEAR EDITING SYSTEM

Think of your NLE as a kind of factory. You put into it the raw materials: images and sounds from the camera, maybe graphics and music. You use the NLE to process all that material—to cut it, rearrange it, add titles and effects, and balance the audio. When you're done, you ship the finished movie out of the factory in various forms: you might create a file to post on the Web, make a DVD, or record the movie

Fig. 14-1. Nonlinear editing system. Grass Valley Edius software running on a desktop computer. (Grass Valley)

on videotape. A nonlinear editing system is basically a computer running specialized software. Various devices are attached or installed internally to get material in and out of the computer. Hard drives store the video and audio. And picture and sound monitors allow you to see and hear what you're working on. Depending on your situation, you may be working on a system assembled by someone else, or you may be putting one together yourself. If you're getting your own, you can buy or rent the elements separately, or you may have a vendor sell you a *turnkey system* (a preassembled package). If you intend to buy, read about your options and get recommendations from vendors and people working with the gear. What you need depends in large part on the kind of work you're doing and where your movies will be shown.

Fig. 14-2. Laptops are portable for editing in the field and can be connected to external monitors and other devices in the editing room. (David Leitner)

Software

While the hardware and other equipment that go with an editing system are important, the software application—the NLE program itself—may have the biggest impact on your editing experience. There are numerous NLEs on the market, and they span a wide range of price and power. Since the early 1990s, Avid's suite of NLEs has played a leading role in the mainstream feature film and television industries. Then Apple Final Cut Pro became popular with independent filmmakers and mainstream facilities as well. The introduction of Final Cut Pro X caused a lot of controversy in these markets (more on this below). Adobe's Premiere Pro is also a key player with over 2 million users worldwide. Home users have various low-cost, stripped-down programs to choose from, including ones from Ulead and Apple. Professional NLEs are also made by Sony, Grass Valley, Discreet, Lightworks, and others.

How should you select an NLE? Start by talking with others who do the kind of work you're doing or want to do. Brand names are only part of the story because the same company may offer a range of products. Some companies offer their NLEs along with a suite of applications that integrate with the NLE to do specialized tasks such as visual effects, audio mixing, and DVD/Blu-ray authoring. This makes it easier to move back and forth from one application to another. Today there's better integration between different brands, and it's common for filmmakers to use one brand for part of the process, then work with an app by another company for a different part. Almost all NLEs are available for free trials, so you can see how they feel.

One consideration in choosing an NLE is your computer and/or operating system (OS). Some applications, like Final Cut Pro, run only on Mac OS, some run only on Windows, and some run on both. The latest NLEs work fastest with a 64-bit operating system; if your OS or computer is only 32 bit, consider upgrading. High-end professional systems may include hardware and software as an integrated package.

If you're working alone, or on in-house projects, choose an NLE based on features and price. If you need to interact with outside production facilities and workers, use something standard in the industry or at least compatible. For example, you may want to bring a project to a post house for finishing and if you're both using compatible software it's a lot easier to move the project over.

Another consideration is employment. If you hope to work in the industry it makes sense to get trained on the tools being used by professionals. To date, that has usually meant Avid, Final Cut Pro, Premiere Pro, and Sony Vegas. Fortunately, if you know one you can learn another without too much pain (well, a fair amount of pain). Many apps offer guides for those switching from one NLE to another. Some, like Premiere Pro, allow you to continue using keyboard shortcuts you've memorized from other NLEs.

Starting with Final Cut Pro X, Apple radically reconfigured not just the editing interface of Final Cut but fundamental workflows and terminology. As of this writing, it's not clear whether Final Cut Pro X will achieve an important role in the broadcast and feature film world, or if its chief market will be filmmakers outside of these industries. At times in this chapter you'll find a general discussion of NLEs that includes earlier versions of Final Cut Pro followed by a separate discussion for Final Cut Pro X.

The Computer

When it comes to video editing, you can't have too much computing power. A high-performance machine can mean the difference between being able to concentrate on creative tasks and having to wait repeatedly while the computer renders (computes) effects, prepares your material for output, or simply chokes because the processors or drives can't keep up with the data. The need for power is especially acute if you're working in HD or today's highly compressed acquisition formats utilizing codecs like H.264.

When computer shopping look for several things. First is the speed of the central processing unit (CPU), expressed in gigahertz. The faster the better, but speed costs money. Often a smart strategy is to get a computer near, but not at, the top of a manufacturer's line—it will still be fast but you won't pay extra for the absolute best. Many NLEs are designed to make use of multiple processors, and your work will go faster with dual-, quad-, or multicore chips. If you're editing on a laptop, bear in mind that faster multiprocessors (if available) drain batteries faster. CPU speed (also known as clock speed) isn't the only thing that determines overall performance; also look at the on-chip memory caches and attached buses.

Another key item is random-access memory (RAM). Many tasks need lots of it and each NLE maker will have a minimum recommended amount. Adding more RAM will substantially improve the performance of a relatively slow computer. You can often find better RAM prices from aftermarket manufacturers (that is, *not* the computer maker). RAM comes in different sizes, types, and speeds, so make sure the RAM you get is right for your computer and comes from a reputable company.

The video or graphics card drives the computer monitor(s). Video cards contain the graphics processing unit (GPU) and have their own RAM. Many newer applications use the GPU not just for viewing video but to take computing load off the CPU for tasks like effects and compression. Seek advice on getting a card, because certain applications work significantly better with particular cards, especially when working with HD or larger frame sizes. As one example, Premiere Pro's Mercury Playback Engine leverages GPU acceleration to enable playback of several streams of HD simultaneously and make the entire NLE faster. Video cards also differ in the types of monitor connections, whether they'll drive more than one monitor, and the resolutions they can handle.

The computer is the heart of the NLE, but it only works when connected to other gear. You want a machine with lots of flexibility in terms of available ports for connections, such as USB, FireWire 800, Gigabit Ethernet, Thunderbolt, DVI, or HDMI (see Digital Connections, p. 237). With desktop systems, also look for the number of open expansion slots (especially PCI Express slots) into which you can put cards for various other connections, such as eSATA, which is commonly used for external drives.

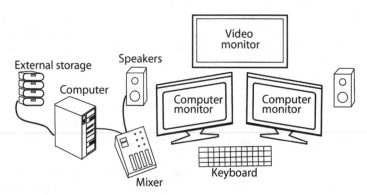

Fig. 14-3. Professional editing setups often have two computer monitors to provide plenty of room for the NLE interface. A broadcast video monitor displays the picture with proper color values for television. A mixer controls the speaker level. External hard drives may be configured in a RAID for speed and data integrity. Compare with the online suite in Fig. 1-30 (which has yet more gear). (Steven Ascher)

You'll need a DVD burner for creating DVDs and importing and exporting all manner of other data (you may also want a Blu-ray burner). Consider an *uninterruptable power supply* (*UPS*) that allows you to shut down in an orderly way in the event of a power outage.

It's essential to have a high-speed Internet connection, or at least be able to connect when needed. You'll use the Internet for accessing help files, getting software updates, sharing files with others, and downloading sound effects or stock footage, among many other uses. And of course hard drives or SSDs are essential for storing your media and need to be managed carefully. Be sure to read Hard Drive Storage, starting on p. 238.

Input and Output

There are many different ways to get video and audio into and out of an NLE. Which methods you use depends on how the video was recorded and what your final product(s) will be.

Today most cameras and audio recorders are file based, which means they create digital files that, by the time they get to the editing room, may be saved on flash memory cards, hard drives, SSDs, or optical discs like DVDs or Blu-rays. Importing files from a memory card into the NLE requires a computer with a built-in card slot of the appropriate size, or you can get an inexpensive external card reader with many different-sized slots that connects via USB.

For transferring files from a hard drive or SSD, you'll want a fast input connec-

Fig. 14-4. (left) AJA Io Express supporting a broadcast video monitor. (right) AJA Io XT with Thunderbolt connectivity between a laptop and a RAID. Both products offer a wide range of input/output and monitoring options, as well as conversions between SD and HD formats. Can capture to ProRes, DNxHD, and CineForm codecs. (AJA Video Systems)

tor. FireWire ports have been widely used for many years for connecting drives, video decks, and cameras. If your desktop computer doesn't have FireWire, it can be easily added. Today there are a number of faster options, including Thunderbolt, eSATA, and USB 3.0, which may be preferable if your drives and computer support them. For more on all of these connections, see p. 237.

If you need to capture material into the NLE that was recorded on videotape, you'll typically need a video deck (VTR) to play the tapes. If you don't have one, you can rent one for the time needed to capture the material or you can have a post facility create files from your tapes. Many digital formats can be captured from a tape deck or camera via a FireWire connection directly to the computer, including high definition codecs like HDV and DVCPRO HD and standard definition formats like DV, DVCAM, and DVCPRO. The FireWire cable controls the deck and transfers video, audio, and timecode.

Tape formats with higher data rates, such as HDCAM, usually require a capture card (see below) and instead of FireWire may use HD-SDI connections. Professional VTRs often use *RS-422 serial device control*, which provides precise control and allows insert editing (the RS-422 cable has a nine-pin connector; see Fig. 14-5).

If you're using footage from an analog tape source like Beta SP or VHS, you'll usually need a capture card to digitize the material at best quality. Or you may be able to route the signal from an analog camera or deck through a digital deck that can make the digital-to-analog conversion.

Fig. 14-5. The back of the AJA Io XT shows various connectors. (lower row, left to right): XLR for power; two Thunderbolt ports (one connects to the Mac, the other can daisy-chain to storage or other peripherals); BNC jacks for SD or HD component video out (composite video is on the Y connector); HDMI out (carries video, audio, and timecode); 3G/HD/SD-SDI out; and LTC (timecode) out. (AJA Video Systems)

CAPTURE CARDS AND INPUT/OUTPUT DEVICES. A number of products serve as an interface so you can bring various formats of video and audio in and out of the computer. Depending on your workflow, these may or may not be needed or useful. Input/Output (I/O) devices such as AJA's Io XT connect to an Apple computer via a Thunderbolt connection (see Fig. 14-5). PCI card systems (also called *capture cards*) plug directly into a desktop computer's PCI Express (PCIe) card slot and often include a *breakout* cable with various video and audio connections (see Fig. 14-6). I/O cards and boxes are made by Blackmagic Design, AJA, and Matrox, among others. These devices vary enormously in their capabilities and ·rice. Some of their functions you can also do with software—without needing the vice—though in some cases the hardware can do it faster or with better quality. ·lable functions may include:

- *Transcoding between digital formats.* Some devices may convert your video to different codecs at different data rates. Useful if you want to transcode for editing or output (see p. 558).
- *Up- and downconversion between SD and HD.* Some can take in HD or SD and output the other. They can also cross convert between HD formats (such as between 1080i and 720p).
- *HD-SDI and/or HDMI connections.* Some allow you to input high definition via HD-SDI or HDMI from a video deck or camera. Or input uncompressed standard definition via an SDI link (see p. 237). They may also provide HDMI, HD-SDI, or SDI output to feed a video monitor.
- *Digital audio input and output.* Some may have connectors for digital audio formats such as AES/EBU (see p. 416).
- *Hardware acceleration.* Some are designed to take some of the processing load off the computer's CPU. This can provide more real-time effects (see p. 553) and make for a more streamlined editing experience. Some can output edited HDV with no rendering.
- *3D workflows.* Some can output separate or combined stereoscopic signals for monitoring.
- *2K or 4K workflows.* Some can ingest or display 2K and/or 4K material.
- *Conversion between analog and digital.* If you have an analog source (composite, component, or S-video) the device may convert to digital files for editing.

Fig. 14-6. Blackmagic Design's Intensity Pro is an affordable input/output card that allows you to connect an HDMI video monitor to a desktop computer via its PCI Express slot. Can also be used to capture HDMI directly from a camera, bypassing the camera's internal compression. Breakout cable on left provides connections to analog video and audio gear. The Intensity Extreme can be used with a laptop. (Blackmagic Design)

Picture Monitors

It's easiest to use an NLE when your computer monitor is big and there's plenty of room for the many parts of the application. Even better, use two monitors for more screen real estate so you can make parts of the interface bigger and easier to work with.

Unless you're creating video *exclusively* for the Web or to be seen only on computer or mobile devices, keep in mind that most computer monitors will not display the picture correctly for television or other types of video distribution. The differences between RGB computer monitors and true component ($Y'C_BC_R$, also called YUV) video monitors in terms of brightness and color values are explained on p. 218.

Whenever possible, you should have a true HD video monitor (or NTSC/ PAL monitor, if working in SD) as part of your NLE setup. A good-quality plasma, OLED, or LCD display is a starting point, and for really accurate color (a necessity if you'll be doing color correction on your projects), get a professional broadcast video monitor with adequate controls (see Appendix A). If you can't afford or can't use an HD broadcast monitor, workarounds for using a computer monitor to display component video are discussed starting on p. 218.

Fig. 14-7. A small mixer is a helpful addition to the editing system for connecting audio equipment (like mics and tape decks) and controlling speaker volume. (Behringer)

Audio Monitoring and Input

Audio monitor is a fancy term for a set of speakers. Often people use a pair of self-powered desktop speakers for editing. Get good speakers whenever possible. For more on speaker selection and the audio environment of the editing room, see p. 639.

It's very helpful to have a small *mixer* (see Figs. 14-7 and 15-4) as part of your editing setup. You can use it to record from a microphone or from other analog sources.[1] Often the speakers are patched through the mixer, which allows you to easily adjust the level and choose which channels you want to monitor.

HOW THE NLE PLAYS
AND EDITS MEDIA

Media Files and Clips

To start work on an NLE, you load the video you want to edit into the system. If you're working with material that was originally recorded to a file, bringing it into

---

1. If your computer lacks analog inputs, you can also record analog audio sources with an ~pensive A/D converter that plugs into a USB port, such as the Griffin iMic or the Tascam US-200 ~ig. 10-8).

the NLE is usually called *importing, ingesting,* or *transferring.* If the camera recorded files to a hard drive or memory card, ingest basically involves copying the files to the NLE's drives.

If the material was recorded on videotape, bringing the material into the NLE may be called *capturing, importing,* or, for analog tape, *digitizing.* You use the NLE's capture tool to capture the video and audio from a VTR or camera.

Either way you bring the material in, the video and audio files will be written to the NLE's hard drives. These imported chunks of video and audio are the *media files* (also called *source media files*).

Media files are contained in a wrapper file format such as MPEG-4 (.mp4 file extension), QuickTime (.mov), MXF, Windows Media (.wmv), or another format (for more on wrappers, see p. 242). Sometimes camera files need to be rewrapped by the NLE to a format that's more compatible. On many systems, the video and each channel of audio are wrapped together in one file; on others, they are stored as separate media files.

When each media file is imported, the NLE creates a *master clip* to go with it. A clip is like a pointer that tells the NLE to go to that media and play it. The clip doesn't contain any audio or video data, but it links to the media file that does.

The idea of "editing" using a nonlinear system is really just repositioning clips that tell the computer which media file to play next. Let's say we've imported three shots: A, B, and C. When we edit these three clips together in order, we're simply telling the computer to find the media for shot A, play it, instantly jump to shot B, play it, and so on.

If we decide to shorten shot B and insert shot N before it, all we do is alter the "playlist." Now the computer is told to play shot A, then jump to N, then jump to B, but this time play less of the shot than it did last time. Even though we have re-ordered and changed the length of the shots, the actual media files are not moved or changed. All we've done is altered the length and order of the clips that point to them. We can have many different versions of the movie with different clips pointing to the same media or different parts of it. Clips can "reuse" the same source media as often as needed (unless this is a project that was shot and will be finished on film; see p. 700).

Real Time and Rendering

When an NLE can play clips in a sequence and jump instantly from one to another, we say that it is processing in *real time.* Depending on your system and what you're trying to do, there are occasions when the NLE may not be able to play or perform various effects in real time. Say, for example, instead of a hard cut between shots A and B, you decide to dissolve between them. The computer will play the end of shot A and meld it with the first few frames of shot B. If the computer can do this on the fly, that's a *real-time effect.* But with some effects, the computer can't do all the calculations fast enough. In this case, the effect must first be *rendered,* which means creating a new file (a *render* or *precompute file*) that contains the effect. If we render the dissolve between shots A and B, the frames that contain the A/B overlap become a render file that the NLE inserts between A and B in playback.

Generally speaking, the faster your computer and/or the lower the resolution of your video the more you can do in real time. When dealing with material that requires a lot of processing, many NLEs will reduce the picture quality or frame rate on playback. You always have the choice to render when you want to maintain normal quality. With some NLEs, rendering means stopping work while the system processes; with others, rendering can take place in the background while you work.

POSTPRODUCTION WORKFLOW

Projects vary a lot in terms of the raw materials and the end products. You may have shot the movie with a smartphone or a top-of-the-line professional HD rig. Your ultimate goal may be a little movie to share with friends on YouTube, or a 7.1-channel surround-sound digital cinema production for screening in a two-thousand-seat theater.

NLEs vary a lot too, in software and hardware. You might be running an old version of a consumer program on a slow laptop, or you might be working at a post house with the latest HD system with the fastest processor and terabytes of storage.

With each project, you need to chart out a workflow—a plan for how you're going to work with your materials and tools. As a rule, most filmmakers have three overarching needs: maintain the highest quality; find the fastest, most efficient route; save the most money. You can't necessarily achieve all three. (The old saying has it that among good, fast, and cheap you can have any two.)

A smart strategy in postproduction, like many other aspects of making a movie, is to think backward from the distribution you're aiming for, to make sure your postproduction workflow will deliver what you'll need creatively and technically. With so many formats, editing systems, and ways of working, it's impossible to cover them all in a book like this. However, there are some standard ways of working based on what you're starting with, the capabilities of the editing system, and the end product you hope to achieve.

The Idea of Offline and Online

The terms *offline* and *online editing* come from the days when video was edited exclusively on videotape, rerecording from one tape machine to another. In this traditional method, the camera tapes are dubbed to a lower-quality format and offline editing is done with more affordable offline editing decks (the original systems were called "offline" because the system was not computerized). In the offline edit you shape and structure the movie—every shot is cut to its proper length and is in its proper order. But at the end of offline editing you don't have a finished, high-quality product—offline cuts often have poor image quality and rough sound. The goal of offline editing is to produce essentially a list of shots used in the movie, a sort of construction blueprint; this is called an *edit decision list* (*EDL*). The list indicates the timecode for the first and last frame of every shot used in the movie (see Fig. 14-41). You then take the EDL to an online editing suite, where the original, high-quality tapes are conformed by timecode to the sequence you created in the offline, using expensive online video decks. The end product of the online is the high-quality, finished *master*.

The terms "offline" and "online" continue to be used today, in the era of digital nonlinear editing. What do they mean now? We can see from the above description that, in one sense, "offline editing" means working on something that is not a finished product; the finished piece will be created later in the online stage. Offline and online are thus stages in the editing process. But in another sense, the idea of offline editing equipment suggests something that works at a lower or "draft" quality while online equipment is capable of "finished" or high quality. Today these distinctions can become blurred. You might be able to use the same NLE to turn out an offline or an online product, simply by using different files or settings. Or your editing system might be capable of onlining a nonbroadcast or Web project, but not an HD movie for television.

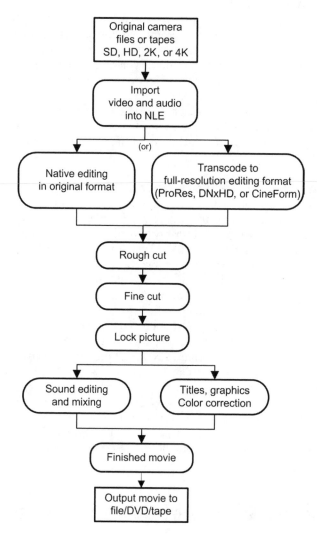

Fig. 14-8. An online workflow. In this scenario, all the work is done on one NLE. (Steven Ascher)

Many workflows used with NLEs involve offline and online stages; how those stages are accomplished varies widely. Though many nonlinear editing systems can generate an EDL, there are now far better, more powerful methods for making the transition from offline to online (for more on this, see Managing Media, p. 609).

A note about language: as you've probably already noticed, "offline" and "online" can be used as verbs ("We're offlining Tuesday"), nouns ("The offline is in my car"), and adjectives ("This is an offline deck"). In a completely different context, the terms can also be used to indicate whether or not media files are connected to the system and available for editing ("These clips are offline").

An Online Workflow

Perhaps the simplest, most straightforward workflow is to import the video footage into the NLE and edit it at full resolution either by using the native camera format or by transcoding to an edit-friendly format like Apple ProRes, Avid DNxHD, or CineForm. When you're done, you output the final product(s) from the same machine (see Fig. 14-8). This can be thought of as an online workflow (there is no offline), and it is used for everything from simple student projects to professional projects of many kinds. This workflow is very convenient in the sense that you are working in one location on one machine with one set of tools, but it also means you're limited to the capabilities of the software and hardware that are on your system.

An Offline/Online Workflow

For several reasons you may choose an offline/online workflow. You may want to do an offline at "draft" quality because your NLE doesn't have enough hard drive storage or processing power for full quality (which may happen when working with data-intensive, high-resolution formats). Or you may do the offline at full quality, but prefer to do the online on a more powerful NLE with better equipment for color correction and mastering. Figure 14-9 outlines a possible workflow that involves shooting either SD, HD, 2K, or 4K format, capturing to one NLE system for offline editing, then moving to an online NLE for finishing. As this flowchart shows, regardless of what format you shoot in, you can reduce offline storage needs by transcoding to a lower-data-rate codec for editing. Some cameras and editing systems create *proxy files* (low-resolution copies of the original camera files), which are useful for offline editing, particularly on a laptop with limited storage space. To do the online edit, the edited sequence is separated from the proxy or low-res files used for the offline and relinked to the original high-resolution camera files. (Sometimes this requires reimporting files or recapturing tapes prior to the online.) In this workflow example, audio is exported to a digital audio workstation (DAW) for sound work and mixing at a sound studio. It's also possible to do both the offline and the online on your own NLE.

WHAT FORMAT OR RESOLUTION TO EDIT IN?

A key decision in postproduction workflow is to determine whether you're going to edit in the same video format that the camera produced or if you're going to

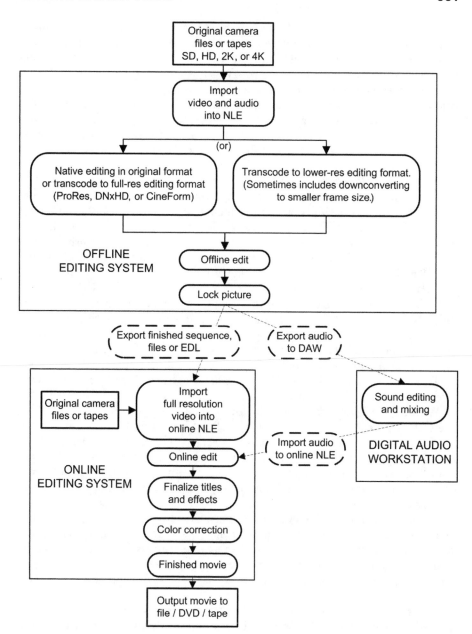

Fig. 14-9. An offline/online workflow using two nonlinear editing systems and a digital audio workstation. (Steven Ascher)

convert the video to a different format or resolution for editing. Virtually all digital video cameras use a codec to compress the video signal before recording (see p. 19 and p. 245). Which codec is used (and at what data rate) depends on the format you're shooting and the particular camera. When you're ready to edit, and you want to import what you've shot into the NLE, you may have a choice about whether to edit with that same codec (called *native editing*) or convert to a different codec (called *transcoding*), or you may even decide to edit with uncompressed video. After you're done editing, you could export in the same codec you used for the edit or, more often, you'll transcode to a number of different formats for distribution.

Native Editing

When an NLE can work in the same codec that you shot with (and therefore allow you to import the video without changing it) it is said to handle that format "natively." With native editing it's a very simple path to import files from a drive or memory card (or capture from digital tape), edit, then export the finished movie back out of the NLE in the same format with no quality loss. The simplicity and ease of native editing are part of how digital video created such a revolution for consumers and pros alike.

Today professional NLEs can work with most camera codecs natively, and consumer NLEs can handle at least the common consumer formats. Native editing can be done in an online-only workflow (you start at native quality and finish at native quality on the same editing system). Native editing can be fast because no time is spent converting to another codec. If you're using a fairly compressed codec, such as DV, DVCPRO HD, HDV, or XDCAM EX, it can be cheap too, because no capture card or fast RAID hard drive array is needed.

With RAW digital cinematography formats, the files can be very large and native editing usually requires a RAID. Not all NLEs can handle these files at full resolution, but one advantage of working natively with REDCODE R3D files from RED cameras, for example, is that you can make the full range of adjustments to color balance, ISO, and other parameters nondestructively (so you can change them later) without having to "bake in" any corrections by transcoding prior to editing (see Fig. 2-21).

While native editing offers various benefits, including being able to get right to work without first converting to another codec, it should be noted that all the codecs mentioned above are *acquisition* codecs used in cameras; they are not typically used to *distribute* a finished movie. So even if you choose to edit natively, you'll generally convert the project to other codecs at the end of the process.

Transcoding for Editing and/or Finishing

If editing natively is so easy, why not edit everything that way? In fact, depending on your situation, you may never need to transcode. However, for various reasons you might want to. In some cases, an NLE can indeed work natively with a format, but the system slows down or works at less than full resolution. Or the format requires more hard drives or faster storage than you have. With some formats you may save time and maintain higher quality by transcoding.

Apple, Avid, and CineForm each offers a suite of codecs to which you can convert any format for editing and finishing. They can deliver very high picture quality at data rates much lower than uncompressed video. Apple's codec is ProRes and Avid's is DNxHD (be sure to read about them in A Few Common Codecs, p. 250). Many other NLEs and camera systems can work with these codecs as well. ProRes and DNxHD are each really a family of codecs: there are high-data-rate versions with alpha channels for effects-heavy productions (see p. 590); there are midlevel versions that have reduced file sizes but ample quality for editing and finishing; and there are low-data-rate versions that are generally intended for offline editing only.

If you decide to transcode to ProRes, DNxHD, CineForm, or another codec for editing and/or finishing, you may have options about *when* to do it. In some cases you may transcode during import or capture from camera files or tapes.[2] Or you could import files natively, then transcode all your footage for editing. Since transcoding takes time and creates a second set of files to store (the originals plus the transcodes), in some cases people edit natively with the original camera files, then transcode just the final edited movie before exporting from the NLE (more on this below).

Transcoding can usually be done within the NLE, or you may prefer to *batch process* a number of files at once before importing to the NLE using a separate application like Apple Compressor, Adobe Media Encoder, Adobe Prelude, or a free program like MPEG Streamclip or HandBrake.

Sometimes when a project has a wide variety of material created in different codecs or frame rates, filmmakers will choose to convert everything to ProRes or DNxHD, perhaps doing frame rate conversions at the same time, as a way to standardize and simplify the post process.

EDITING AT A LOWER DATA RATE. Appendix B shows the data rate and storage requirements of various formats and codecs. As you can see, there are big differences between some of them. For example, you'd need only 217 MB to store a minute of standard definition DV but it takes more than 17 GB to store a minute of uncompressed 2K footage—that's over eighty times more space on a hard drive. High-data-rate formats not only use up a lot of storage, but they can require much faster processing in the storage system and the NLE. For some forms of HD, for example, you need a RAID and can't edit with single drives (see p. 240). If the video is stored on a network with shared storage, high data rates can cause bottlenecks.

Transcoding to a format with a lower data rate can be done in an offline/online workflow. The video is converted to a more compressed codec or format for offline editing. When you're done, you configure a high-quality version of the movie using the original files at the full resolution.

This is a situation in which DNxHD and ProRes can be very useful. DNxHD 36 and ProRes Proxy are designed for offline editing and produce full-raster HD at 36 Mbps, hardly more than standard definition DV's 25 Mbps. Alternatively, you could transcode to a less-compressed flavor of ProRes or DNxHD that maintains higher picture quality but still has a manageable data rate; in which case you could simply finish at this resolution without any further conforming.

---

2. With Final Cut Pro X, if you choose to transcode on import, the system stores both your original media and the transcoded media in your Final Cut Events folder. Transcoding can take place in the background while you work.

Working with low-res proxy files (which may be generated by the camera or in the editing system) makes it easy to edit on a laptop and send files over the Internet. When you're ready, you link the offline edit to the full-resolution original media for the online edit and finishing.

There are various other methods of reducing data rate for offline editing. Some systems offer other codecs such as M-JPEG that can be used at various resolution levels. Resolution may be indicated as a compression ratio, such as 2:1 or 15:1. Higher compression (in this case, 15:1) means lower data rate. Some systems allow you to capture only one field of an interlaced format, instantly cutting the data rate in half. Avid indicates single-field resolutions with an "s" after the compression ratio (such as 15:1s).

When working with RED files, you can use the REDCINE-X application to transcode the original R3D files into lower-resolution, self-contained QuickTime, MXF, or DPX files for editing (and finishing if you choose). Any particular looks you create in terms of color, contrast, and exposure are stored in RMD files, allowing you to reference back to the original R3D files if needed to re-create the same look at full resolution.

EDITING IN A SMALLER FRAME SIZE. In various situations you may decide to downconvert material from a large frame size to a smaller one for editing. For example, you may downscale 4K or 2K material to 1920 x 1080 HD because the NLE can't handle all the data and/or because you plan to finish the project in HD.

Or you may be creating a Web video and decide you don't need Full HD files. When working in iMovie, for example, you have the option to convert 1920 x 1080 HD footage to half size (960 x 540) either on import or export. The smaller size saves storage space and may still be large enough for the website where the video will reside.

In an older methodology, some people choose to offline HD projects in SD. The downconversion can be done by a card, deck, or camcorder during capture (some HDV cameras, for instance, can downconvert to DV in playback). Another approach is to make a set of SD tapes or files from your HD material, then capture those into the NLE. While this may make it easier to work with a low-powered editing system, and can speed up tasks like making a DVD of a rough cut when you need one, there are disadvantages to editing an HD project in SD, which has a different frame size, pixel shape, and color space. Editing in HD but using a more compressed codec (like ProRes Proxy or DNxHD 36) can provide a better editing experience and an easier translation between offline and online.

EDITING AT A HIGHER DATA RATE. We've seen that using compression to reduce the data rate can be helpful for offline editing. Are there times when it helps to go the other way, to a *less* compressed codec or all the way to uncompressed for editing? As you've probably guessed, the answer is yes. People sometimes convert highly compressed material to a less compressed codec for editing or finishing. There are a variety of reasons.

First, highly compressed codecs like the H.264 used in many DSLRs and other MPEG-2 and MPEG-4 codecs require a lot of computer processing to decode and

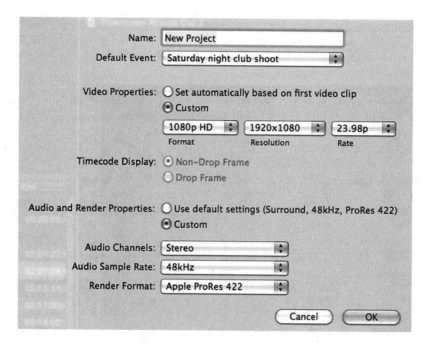

Fig. 14-10. When setting up a new project or sequence, the NLE needs to know the format, resolution (frame size), and frame rate of the movie you're editing. These can be set manually, or some systems can set them automatically based on the first video clip. Audio may be stereo (two channels) or surround (usually 5.1 channels). The selection at the bottom of this screen from Final Cut Pro X shows that even if you're editing natively, any material that needs rendering will be rendered in ProRes 422. (Apple, Inc.)

edit (since they use long-GOP interframe compression; see p. 246). While your NLE may be able to play them natively, performance may be compromised. Also, when you're ready to output the project from the NLE, the system will need to "conform" or render the movie first, which can take a lot of time at a point when you may be under deadline pressure.

Another issue is that when editing with a compressed format, whenever you manipulate a shot by changing its speed, color correction, or other effects, the system needs to recompress the footage to store it. The same is true when you composite one shot with another, do a dissolve, or add a title over picture. The more compressed a format is to begin with, the worse it will look on recompression.

You can minimize these problems in a few ways. One method is to transcode all your camera footage to ProRes, DNxHD, or CineForm and use the transcoded files for editing and finishing. Being I-frame codecs, they put less demand on the computer's CPU and require no conforming (other methods of speeding up the conforming process are discussed on p. 248). Working with these codecs will give you faster renders and better compositing.

If you don't want to transcode *all* your footage, some NLEs, like Final Cut Pro, can be set to edit natively with the compressed codec, but will create ProRes 422 render files *only* for effects. This helps minimize recompression artifacts and saves time and drive space compared to transcoding everything. In general, if your NLE has an option to render to ProRes or another intermediate codec, it's a good idea to do so.

Another consideration comes when it's time to finish the project. Highly compressed formats are usually 8 bit and use 4:1:1 or 4:2:0 color subsampling, which can compromise graphics and chroma keys and make titles less sharp and distinct (see p. 212 for more on this). Titles, composites, and effects will look better if created in a less compressed, 4:2:2 format. Color correction and chroma keys work better in a 10-bit than an 8-bit environment.

For all these reasons, it's common to bump up from a compressed codec to something less compressed for finishing (often using one of the higher-data-rate ProRes or DNxHD codecs). You might do this for offline editing, or you might wait until the online to transcode to a less compressed codec.

While there are potential quality advantages to higher-data-rate formats, when transcoding files you should pick a codec that's appropriate to your workflow without increasing file size too much. For example, if you shoot with AVCHD and decide to transcode to ProRes, you may be fine with ProRes 422 (LT), which is only 102 Mbps, or even ProRes 422 (147 Mbps), while you would gain little or nothing by going up to ProRes 422 (HQ), which is 220 Mbps. On the other hand, if you're sending a shot out to an animator for compositing, for example, you might save it as an uncompressed file to maintain the best possible quality during the later stages of work.

IMPORTING AND ORGANIZING YOUR MATERIAL

When the editor receives material from the production crew, the footage may be well organized and carefully logged as to which drives or tapes contain which scenes. Or the material may be a chaotic mess of undocumented footage. It's essential that the editor organize the material thoroughly so that anything can be found easily when needed.

Organization takes place on several levels. The first is prepping files and folders before ingesting anything into the NLE. Amateurs (and sometimes professionals in a hurry) may be used to simply grabbing camera files and throwing them into an NLE to start editing. But on a serious production, especially one involving a lot of elements, it's crucial that what you do at every step ensures that original files are safe and that you be able to work backward from the edited project to find any original media (video, audio, graphics, etc.) when needed. Drives may fail, or you may be working in more than one resolution, and you'll want the NLE to be able to quickly link back to original files or tapes. This can only happen if you're careful in structuring and identifying your material.

Another kind of organizing is done in the NLE during or after import or capture, when you'll have an opportunity to name clips, set parameters, and add comments and/or keywords to help you find things later. The goal is to organize all your clips and files in a logical way that allows you to see what you have and find every-thing easily.

Setting Up a Project

With most NLEs, the first step to begin editing your movie is to create a new *project* in the NLE. The project is command central for the editing process, giving you access to all your material. With some NLEs, the project also stores various settings for the movie and organizes the editing interface. The project is saved on your hard drive as a relatively small *project file* that can be easily moved from one computer to another.

As discussed earlier in the chapter, when you capture video from tapes or import from camera files, the NLE will typically create new media files for the video (and/or audio) as well as master clips that point to those media files and allow you to edit with them. The project is where the clips are kept. The media files are stored separately—exactly where depends on the NLE and how you're working. In general, you'll get better performance if media files are not on the same physical hard drive on which the NLE app and the operating system are running.[3] Usually external drives are best.

So when you start a new project, one of the first settings is to specify where to store captured media, transcoded media, and render files. This is called setting the *scratch disk* or *target drive*. Actually, the media files will go in a particular folder on the scratch disk. In Final Cut Pro versions prior to X, this is called the *capture scratch folder*, and it's found within the "Final Cut Pro Documents" folder that Final Cut automatically creates. The Avid equivalent is the "Avid MediaFiles" folder, which should be placed at the root level on the drive.

Depending on your NLE, the next step may be to specify the base format, frame size, frame rate, codec, and other parameters of the sequence (movie) you want to create, which is typically—though not always—the same as whatever you've been shooting. Most NLEs have presets for common camera formats—pick the one that corresponds to the footage you're working with. If you're working with mixed formats, the frame size or frame rate of particular video or audio material you're bringing into the system may be different from the movie you're making.

The Project Window or Browser

Once you open the new project, you'll find the *browser* or *project panel* in which clips are stored and organized (see Fig. 14-15). This is your main tool for organizing all your video, audio, graphics, and titles. In the browser you can create *folders* or *bins* into which you put clips and sequences. You might put all the clips from a certain scene in one bin, original music in another, edited sequences in a third, and so on (see Fig. 14-11).

The project window has columns for many types of information, including clip name, media starting and ending timecode, reel (tape) number, codec, etc. You can customize it with more categories, such as notes, shoot date, location, or anything you like. By clicking on column headers you can quickly sort the clips in a bin to find, say, all clips from a certain reel or scene.

---

3. With fast SSDs, this may not be necessary.

With most NLEs you can have the browser display the clips as text, or you can switch to a *frame view* that shows *thumbnails* (still frames) from each clip and may be able to play the clips in motion. You can rearrange clips to experiment with the order before editing them together—a bit like storyboarding.

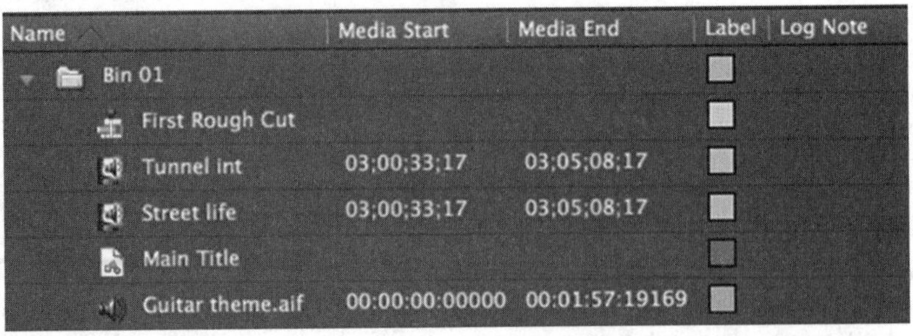

Name	Media Start	Media End	Label	Log Note
▼ 📁 Bin 01			☐	
⚏ First Rough Cut			☐	
🎞 Tunnel int	03;00;33;17	03;05;08;17	☐	
🎞 Street life	03;00;33;17	03;05;08;17	☐	
🖺 Main Title			☐	
🔊 Guitar theme.aif	00:00:00:00000	00:01:57:19169	☐	

Fig. 14-11. Bin. This Adobe Premiere Pro bin contains (top to bottom) one sequence, two video clips with audio, one title graphic, and one audio-only music clip. These different types of elements are often placed in separate bins for better organization. Compare with Fig. 14-16. (Adobe Systems, Inc./Steven Ascher)

Sometimes one clip contains different sections you want to identify to make it easier to find them later. With some NLEs, you can break a master clip into *subclips*, which are sections that act like new, separate clips. For example, with a long interview you might create different subclips for each new question. Some NLEs also allow you to use keywords for this purpose (more on this in the next section).

Some NLEs can import the script or a documentary transcript and associate individual clips with lines from the written document (called *script-based editing*). If you find what you want in the script, you can quickly locate all the video clips that contain that bit of dialogue (see p. 535).

Newer NLEs offer various automated methods of identifying shots that have people in them, or wide shots, or other attributes.

For a project that originated on film, you may need to track keycode numbers, in-camera or audio timecode, as well as camera roll, sound roll, and telecine reel numbers. Though you could enter this data by hand, it's far better to automatically import it from a shot log generated at the telecine session (see Chapter 16).

For more, see Organizing Material, p. 534.

Getting Started with Final Cut Pro X

When Final Cut was redesigned for version X, Apple changed the existing interface, invented new terminology, and repurposed existing terms in ways that can put people familiar with other NLEs through mental gymnastics.[4]

When you import media files, they are stored as part of an *event*. You can create a new event for each set of files you're importing or you can bring new files into an existing event (so, for example, an event might include everything that was shot on a given day, or everything that was shot for an entire film). Each event has its own

---

4. If you've used iMovie, you'll find more things in common.

event folder inside the "Final Cut Events" folder at the root level of the hard drive you choose. The event folder contains unedited clips, any transcoded media files, and sometimes a copy of your original media files.

In the *event library* you can select and view clips (see Fig. 14-17). With most NLEs, unedited clips are typically stored in a bin within a particular project and you can only view them if that project and bin are open. With Final Cut Pro X, you can always see all the clips from all the events on your system (unless you choose to hide them). So if you want to use something you shot last year as part of a biking movie, you can easily grab it for the music video you're making this year. Obviously you don't want hundreds of clips in an unorganized mass. Instead of bins, Final Cut Pro X (FCP X) uses *keywords* (metadata) to help you locate and organize what you need.

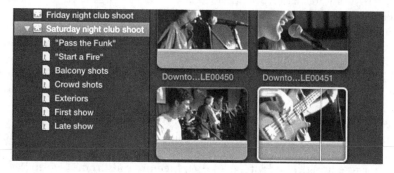

Fig. 14-12. Organizing with keywords. In Final Cut Pro X, you can assign one or more keywords to each clip. By clicking on a keyword collection (the items shown in the event library on the left), the browser will display all the clips with that keyword. Clips are not in bins, but are simply displayed when you click a keyword collection. Different groupings of clips can be viewed depending on what keywords you give them. (Apple, Inc./Steven Ascher)

When you import footage into the system (or afterward) you can assign one or more keywords to each clip or part of a clip. Say you're doing a video for a band, and you create separate events for their Friday show and their Saturday show (see Fig. 14-12). You could assign a keyword with the name of a particular song to every shot you filmed of that song. By clicking on the *keyword collection* of that song in the event library, you can quickly find all the shots of that song regardless of which night or show they were filmed. You could assign additional keywords to any shots that show the crowd, or that were taken from the balcony. By tagging clips with keywords and other identifiers, you create a kind of "virtual bin" that identifies shots and can gather them in different combinations (it's "virtual" because you're not moving clips around, just linking to them). You can refine the groupings using *smart collections*, such as "crowd shots on Saturday night," or "crowd shots from the balcony." The same clip can be part of many different collections. Using metadata to organize and locate your clips can be a powerful tool, and many other NLEs have their own organizational systems that employ metadata.

In Final Cut Pro X, the word "project" refers to what in other NLEs would be considered an individual sequence on the timeline (more on this below). The project file in FCP X contains the clips used in that sequence but not the media files they reference (which are stored with the event).

IMPORTING FILES

When working with file-based video or audio stored on memory cards and hard drives, importing, ingesting, or transferring means bringing the media into the NLE so you can work with it.

Prepping Files Before Importing

If you're really in a rush on location, you can edit directly from flash memory cards, but you'll get better performance and be better organized if you copy the contents of the card to a hard drive or SSD drive before editing. As noted above, keeping your files organized and backed up is paramount. Different people use different systems, but the main idea is to keep all the original media from the project together, grouped into folders in a logical way so you can identify everything you need. It can help with organization to group folders by the type of content. For example, you might have separate master folders for camera files, stills, graphics, audio, stock footage, and so on.

See Folder Management, p. 119, for suggestions of possible ways to organize downloads from camera memory cards. If folders weren't well organized when the cards were originally downloaded at the shoot, the editor can set up a folder structure prior to editing. The contents of each memory card from the camera should be copied to its own folder on the hard drive that includes *all* the files and folders from the card (and be sure to keep the structure of the subfolders on the card unchanged). Give this folder a unique name such as BIKES003, or include the date, such as BIKES-003-120814. Use a consistent naming system for all the cards. This doesn't have to be the same name used on the original camera card. When you import the files from this folder into the NLE, the folder name should be used as the *reel name* for each clip (equivalent to the reel or tape number when shooting videotape). Having this association between a clip's reel name and the folder it came from helps you and the NLE locate files. Don't rename these folders after you import material into the NLE.

If for some reason the original media hasn't been backed up yet, stop what you're doing and make one or more backups and store them in different locations (for more on this, see p. 118).

With some NLEs, when you import files you have the option to duplicate the media files and place a copy within the NLE's folder structure (for example, with Final Cut Pro X you can choose to copy files to the Final Cut events folder). This is an alternative way to organize and back up media files. On advantage is that you'll have all your media consolidated in a central location as part of the NLE's folder system. If you select this option when importing directly from a camera flash media card that will be erased later, don't forget to make a separate backup on another hard drive.

As noted above, some people choose to transcode camera files with a separate application before importing into the NLE. For example, Red Giant's Magic Bullet

Grinder can be used to convert DSLR files into both a full-resolution ProRes or Photo-JPEG file and a low-res proxy for logging and offline editing. It will generate timecode (continuous or reset with each clip) and allows you to burn in the time-code on the proxies (see Fig. 5-24). VideoToolShed's Offloader can automate back-ups and generate Avid DNxHD files with QuickTime or MXF wrappers.

If media files are transcoded to a different codec on import or before, some people back up the transcoded files to save transcoding time in case the files are lost or damaged; however, even if you don't back up the transcodes you should be able to re-create them if needed.

Importing

As discussed earlier, when you import files, the NLE will create master clips (which you'll edit with on the timeline) and you need to tell the NLE where to store them. With many NLEs, you simply create a new bin in the browser or project window and select it as the *target bin* or *logging bin*. In Final Cut Pro X, instead of a bin you select an *event* in which new clips are stored.

With some NLEs you can import files by dragging and dropping them into the NLE's browser from the Finder (Macs) or Windows Explorer. However, with some NLEs importing files from the camera should (or must) be done using commands or tools within the NLE, so the system can process files correctly. With Premiere Pro, you can use the media browser for importing file-based formats (Adobe Bridge, a companion application, can be very useful and provides some functions beyond the browser). In legacy versions of Final Cut Pro prior to X, you use the log and transfer tool to import camera files.

If you're transcoding files, you'll need to choose the resolution (and sometimes codec) that you want to transcode to. Depending on the system you're using, you may have an opportunity to preview the clips before importing, choose which clips (or which portions of a clip) you want to import, and enter metadata like clip names, scene numbers, and notes. As mentioned above, the reel name can be an important organizing tool. Some systems will automatically insert the name of the source folder that the media files came from in the "reel" field; if not, you can do it manu-ally. With Final Cut Pro X, you can associate clips with their source folder by choos-ing to "import folders as keyword collections," which creates a keyword for the source folder name and applies it to all the files from that folder.

Cameras automatically give each clip a name (often a string of numbers and let-ters), which aren't very friendly for editing. It's more useful to give clips names like "Sc. 4, Tk 5" or "Sal on the train," or even "Clip #1." One issue with renaming clips is that, since they occasionally become corrupted or mysteriously go offline, you may need to reimport them later—at which point you'll want to know a clip's orig-inal file name so you can find it in the backups. Many NLEs use hidden metadata to store the original file name even if you change it in the browser, in which case you'll probably be able to find the file. However, some people prefer to leave the original names as they are and use the "notes" column or make a new field in the browser to give each clip a friendlier description. Some systems allow you to re-name clips with a combination of the original name and a description you assign, so you're covered both ways.

On import, you may also have options for various types of automated analysis or processing, such as image stabilization, color adjustment, and content analysis. Any adjustments are usually nondestructive and can be undone later.

Because of file size limitations, sometimes when cameras record a very long take, they store the recording in more than one media file, "spanning" from one file to the next to form one long, continuous clip (the clip is called a *spanned clip*). Sometimes you get a spanned clip when a flash media card fills up and the recording switches to the next card. Different cameras and NLEs handle spanned clips in different ways. For example, with P2 or SxS media, spanned clips get combined into a single clip with continuous timecode on ingest into the NLE. With RED cameras, the individual R3D files that make up a long take are linked to a single QuickTime reference file to form a continuous clip.

NATIVE OR NOT. As NLEs become more flexible and can handle more video formats natively, you may be able to work with files without technically "importing" them. For example, when using Avid Media Composer with Avid Media Access (AMA), the system can *link* to many types of video files that reside on memory cards or external or networked drives without processing or moving them to the NLE's storage.[5] This is handy for getting right to work and avoids unnecessarily duplicating or transcoding files. Even so, performance is generally better if files are on hard drives instead of cards, and some codecs are harder than others to handle natively.

Sometimes even when an NLE can work natively with a given video format or codec, it still needs to process, index, or rewrap the files (for example, converting the wrapper from MXF to QuickTime). Or, you may decide it's preferable to transcode to ProRes, DNxHD, or another codec for better editing performance. Apple refers to rewrapping or transcoding to ProRes as creating *optimized media*. In these cases, when you import or transfer material, the system creates new files that may take some time to process and store on your scratch disk.

AUDIO. When ingesting media, you may have the option of which audio channels from the original recording you want to import (A1, A2, etc.). These may be separate mono channels (1 + 2), which is typical when different mics are used on different channels. Or two channels may form a *stereo pair*, which is common when the recording was done with a stereo mic or when you're importing stereo music. In some cases you'll have audio recorded in 5.1- or 7.1-channel surround sound. In general, you should only import audio channels that were actually recorded by the camera, not any additional, silent ones. Some NLEs offer the option to remove silent channels on import, which is a good idea.

There is usually a setting for audio sample rate (or to allow you to convert to a different sample rate during import). The current standard for professional broadcast video postproduction is typically 48 kHz at 16 bits per sample.

You have no control over audio level when importing digital files or capturing videotape formats over FireWire. When you're editing material that was shot on film, you may need to speed-adjust the audio before capture; see p. 690.

---

5. Depending on the NLE, the ability to handle files natively may depend on having the proper plug-ins or codecs on the system.

FRAME RATE AND PULLDOWN REMOVAL. You may need to select the proper frame rate for your video. Footage shot in 24p may need to have pulldown removed; see p. 601.

CAPTURING FROM TAPE

If your camera records to videotape, you'll need to capture the footage into the NLE for editing.

Start by inserting the tape into the VTR or camera, connecting it to the computer, and opening the capture tool in the NLE (see Fig. 14-14). The capture tool should be able to control the deck or camera, allowing you to play and rewind the tape.

As with importing files, there are some basic settings to attend to. You'll need to indicate which scratch disk you want to store the media files on and which bin in the browser to put the master clips (the logging bin).[6] You may also have a choice of resolution and/or codec. For formats like DV and HDV it's common to edit natively. Unless you're using a higher-end format with a professional deck, you're probably using FireWire (1394) device control.

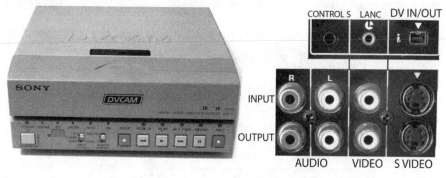

Fig. 14-13. (left) The Sony DSR-11 is a standard definition deck that can play and record DV and DVCAM in NTSC or PAL. (right) The rear panel on the DSR-11 has analog inputs and outputs for stereo audio, composite video and S-video. The FireWire (iLink) connection ("DV IN/OUT") provides input and output for digital component video and audio.

LOGGING. There are several approaches to capturing and logging tapes, depending upon the tape format and playback device you use.

For instance, when capturing DV, DVCAM, or DVCPRO from MiniDV tapes using a camcorder connected with a FireWire cable, one method is to capture the entire tape at once, which can create a giant one-hour clip. Some NLEs allow you to set a maximum clip duration, say thirty minutes, which would result in two half-hour clips. Logging of clips is done after capture, by creating and organizing subclips in the NLE.

With these tape formats, it is also possible to go through each tape before cap-

---

6. In Final Cut Pro X, you select which event to capture to.

ture and *log* it first, which means marking which sections you want to capture, marking an In Point (beginning) and Out Point (end) for each individual clip, giving the clip a name, indicating scene numbers, and adding any comments. After you've logged everything, you do a *batch capture*, in which the NLE automatically captures the media for the clips that you logged (all you have to do is put in the right tape when requested).[7] Using this approach, the material is already tagged and organized when you ingest it into the NLE.

When logging and capturing DV, DVCAM, or DVCPRO tapes in this fashion, use a tape deck (VTR) to save wear and tear on your camcorder. Small camcorders are not designed for heavy shuttling of tape back and forth like professional tape decks, which is why some people prefer to capture an entire MiniDV tape at once and log afterward.

In the case of capturing HDV from MiniDV tapes using an HDV camcorder with FireWire for playback, it's not possible to log the tape before capture. This is because HDV is a long-GOP format that does not offer frame-accurate machine control through FireWire.

Fortunately most NLEs today can do *auto scene detection* (also known as *scene extraction*), which allows you to capture an entire tape in one pass while the NLE uses timecode or picture changes to automatically create a new clip at every camera stop. You can name and comment on clips as they're being captured, or after they're captured.

Fig. 14-14. The tape capture tool in Avid Media Composer controls the video deck and allows you to name and define clips to be captured. (Avid Technology, Inc.)

7. Some people instead mark individual clips and capture them one at a time—sometimes called "capture in to out," which results in a lot of unnecessary rewinding and wear on the tape and machine. Final Cut Pro X *only* works this way and will not do batch capturing.

When logging a tape before capture, keep in mind that every clip needs continuous timecode, so when marking clips be sure that they don't include spots on the tape where there's a break in timecode or control track (if you do, the system will usually create a new clip at the break).[8] If there are no timecode breaks, you can make clips as long or short as you want; however, the longer they are, the more you have to redo if there are problems or a file gets corrupted.

REEL NAME. Every tape needs a unique *reel name* (also called *tape number* or *tape name*). You can name tapes however you like, but if there's any chance you will be making an EDL to move the project to another system, it's traditional to use tape names that are less than six characters with no spaces or punctuation (the name can have numbers and letters but it should start with numbers). A numbering scheme like 001, 002, etc., is always safe. In any case, be sure every tape has a unique name and that you've indicated it correctly on the tape itself, on the tape box, and in the NLE when capturing. If you have a tape with timecode restarts (places where the timecode resets to 00:00:00 in the middle of a tape because the tape was removed and restarted; see Avoiding Timecode Problems, p. 226), give each section its own tape number, such as 003A, 003B, etc.

CREATING AND EDITING SEQUENCES

Now that you've got your material stored on the hard drives, you're ready to start editing. The moment has arrived.

The Editing Interface and Timeline

All NLEs have certain things in common, even if they differ in their particulars and the names for various parts and actions. The *editing interface* is the main display used to control the system. This is divided into several areas or windows, which may be spread over one or two computer monitors, depending on your setup.

Most NLEs use two windows to display video (see Fig. 14-15). One is for viewing and marking clips you want to use. This may be called the *viewer* or *source monitor*. The second window is for viewing the edited movie or sequence you are creating. This may be called the *record monitor*, *program monitor*, or *canvas*. Some NLEs have only a single monitor window in which you can view individual clips or the edited sequence.

The *timeline*, where you actually build the movie, shows how the clips are edited together (see Fig. 14-16). In nonlinear editing, a group of clips on the timeline is a *sequence*. With NLEs, the word "sequence" refers to everything on a given timeline, which might mean an entire movie or just a few shots. Don't confuse this use of "sequence" with the general film usage of "sequence" to mean an individual scene (see p. 322).

---

8. You should set the NLE to make a new clip at each timecode break and to abort capture on dropped frames. If there are many timecode breaks, sometimes it's best to dub the material to another tape with continuous timecode, and use that tape as the master for capturing and online editing.

Project Panel   Source Monitor   Program Monitor

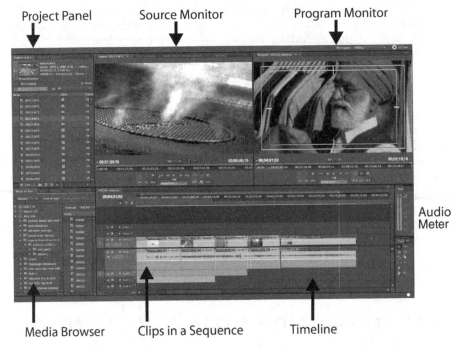

Audio
Meter

Media Browser   Clips in a Sequence   Timeline

Fig. 14-15. Adobe Premiere Pro main editing interface. (Apple, Inc./Steven Ascher)

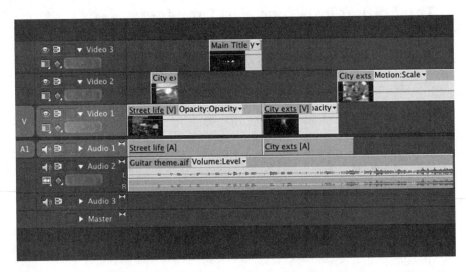

Fig. 14-16. Timeline in Adobe Premiere Pro. Video clips with their associated audio clips are on the Video 1 track and Audio 1 track. A title graphic is on the Video 3 track. Audio 2 contains a stereo music clip with left and right channels paired together. These items are in the bin in Fig. 14-11. (Adobe Systems, Inc./Steven Ascher)

NLEs use colored rectangles along the timeline to represent video and audio clips, often with a *thumbnail* (still frame) showing what the clip contains. Clips are arranged on one or more *tracks*, allowing you to move clips in relation to each other. Transitions between clips, such as fades and dissolves, are shown graphically.

Audio clips are represented in another set of tracks. These tracks can be edited independently of the picture or locked together with it. Many systems will display *audio waveforms*, which are a visual representation of the sound signal that's helpful for finding sounds on the timeline (see Fig. 14-24).

A thin vertical bar moving over the timeline indicates where the system is playing in "play" mode, or the point at which an edit may take place when you are in "edit" mode. This bar is variously referred to as the *cursor*, *play head*, *position indicator*, or *current time indicator* (*CTI*). The cursor usually moves across the timeline from left to right when you are playing a sequence.

You can *zoom in* on the timeline to see in detail how audio and video fit together at a particular cut or transition, or *zoom out* to see a sequence or the entire movie as a whole, to get a sense of the pacing and overall balance. Once you work with this graphical representation of the movie, you'll find it becomes an important tool in how you think about the structure and layout of the movie you're making.

Clips and sequences can be played using keyboard commands or by clicking on-screen buttons using the mouse. Professional editors usually rely on *JKL editing*, which is supported by most NLEs. The J key is "play reverse," the K key is "stop," and L is "play forward." Hitting either J or L twice doubles the speed. Often the space bar on the keyboard is both "play" and "stop."

Most NLEs allow you to customize the keyboard as you like. Some editors like to work with a multibutton mouse, trackball, or graphics tablet to control the NLE. NLEs usually give you several different ways of doing the same task, so you can find the style of working that suits you best. You can use the keyboard, mouse, trackpad, or a combination. Many pros find that once they know (and have customized) the keyboard, they use the mouse or trackpad relatively little for basic editing tasks.

THE FINAL CUT PRO X INTERFACE. Instead of the two-window layout most professional NLEs use, FCP X has a single viewer, which shows source clips or edited sequences depending on what you point at with the mouse.[9]

With other NLEs, as you edit you are building a sequence of clips on the timeline. With FCP X, that sequence is called a *project*. With other NLEs, a project can contain many sequences; with FCP X, each project is just one sequence. The project defines certain aspects of the movie you're building (such as the frame rate and format) and contains information about the clips, titles, and effects in it.

In most other NLEs, such as Premiere Pro, you might have video clips on video tracks 1, 2, and 3 and audio clips in a parallel set of audio tracks (see Fig. 14-16). In FCP X, there aren't tracks. Instead, the *primary storyline* contains the main clips used in the project (see Fig. 14-18). Unlike other NLEs in which each clip on the timeline is *either* video or audio, FCP X clips can contain *both* video and audio (though you can detach the audio from the video as needed).

9. Later versions will have an option for a two-window layout.

Event Library
        Event Browser   Viewer   Inspector

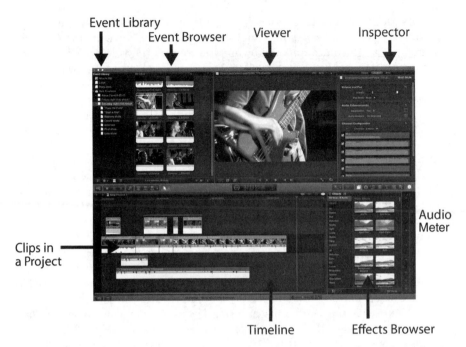

                                                                        Audio
                                                                        Meter
Clips in
a Project

                              Timeline   Effects Browser

Fig. 14-17. Apple Final Cut Pro X main interface. Areas of the screen change depending on what's selected. The single viewer displays both source clips in the browser and the edited movie in the timeline. (Apple, Inc./Steven Ascher)

                              Secondary storyline

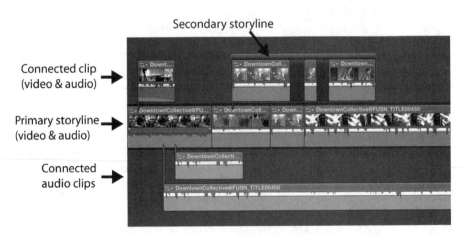

Connected clip
(video & audio)

Primary storyline
(video & audio)

Connected
audio clips

Fig. 14-18. Final Cut Pro X timeline. The primary storyline contains clips with both video and associated audio. Shown here, the first clip in the storyline has a connected video/audio clip (above) and two audio-only clips (below). The secondary storyline groups another set of clips, which are attached to the primary storyline. (Apple, Inc./Steven Ascher)

Above and below the storyline you can attach *connected clips* (essentially like additional tracks, but the clips stay glued to the storyline). You can also have *secondary storylines* (which can contain a few or many clips) that float above the primary storyline and function like big connected clips, and can be edited and moved around as a group. So, for example, in a documentary you might use the primary storyline for interview clips and use a secondary storyline for cutaways or additional audio.

Secondary storylines and attached clips in FCP X are not locked into conventional vertical tracks and, as you edit, they automatically reposition themselves up or down, either in the video area above the primary storyline or in the audio area below it. By doing so, they preserve their exact sync relationships to the primary storyline as you move clips around. One of the main achievements of FCP X is its rock-solid preservation of sync relationships among all the clips in edited sequences, including video, audio, and effects. Unlike most other NLEs, FCP X makes it almost impossible to knock the timeline out of sync.

In this book, it's not possible to go into full detail about all the terms and methods used in different NLEs. The following discussion, covering important principles, uses the most common terms that apply to timeline sequences in all NLEs, including FCP X.

You Won't Hurt Anything

As you get started, remember that clips arranged on the timeline are nothing more than pointers to media files stored on the hard drives (see Media Files and Clips, p. 552). You can delete, change, move, or copy clips without in any way affecting or damaging the original media that they point to. Nonlinear editing is thus completely *nondestructive*. You can totally mess up a sequence and then return to a previously saved version with no harm done.

To further relax you about the editing process, keep in mind that all systems have undo commands (*Ctrl-Z* on Windows or *Command-Z* on Macs), which allow you to easily undo editing mistakes. Some NLEs allow you to select how many "levels" of undo are stored (that is, how many actions in a row can be undone). It's a good idea to set this to twenty or more steps so you can fix things that go wrong.

When experienced editors have a sequence they like, but want to experiment with changes, they will *duplicate the sequence*—make a copy of it and park it in a bin. In doing this, you know you can always get back to where you were before. Sequences by themselves take up very little storage space. FCP X has an *audition* function that permits you to store alternative versions of sequences and switch between them.

Even so, anytime you're using a computer, all sorts of things can go wrong (power outages, crashes, corrupted files) to make you miserable. Be sure to save your work regularly, especially before and after doing anything complex. Many NLEs have an *autosave* function that stores a backup copy of your project file in a location you indicate (on Avid systems, this place is called the *attic*). If you set autosave for every fifteen minutes, that's the most work you'll lose in a crash. Opening a backup file can be helpful if you need an earlier version of a sequence made prior to recent changes. With some newer systems, especially Mac apps under OS X Lion 10.7, the system saves automatically and you can't do it manually. In Lion, for instance, FCP X autosaves continuously. If you experience any sort of crash, FCP X starts up instantly, with no loss of data or editing. Furthermore, if the Final Cut Projects folder is located on your boot drive, Apple's Time Machine can create an automatic hourly backup.

At the end of each day, be sure to back up (or duplicate) your project file to a separate hard drive, a thumb drive, or the Web (FCP X being a possible exception). This is to protect your sequences and editing work. Normally, you don't back up the media files each day. They're too big and it shouldn't be necessary if they were backed up properly before or during the importing process. In the event of a disaster, you can recover your work the way you left it as long as you have a clean copy of the project file, and of the original media files or tapes, and you've been careful when importing and labeling your clips, files, and folders.

Marking Clips and Putting Them on the Timeline

To begin editing, start by identifying the clips you want to use in the bin or browser. On most systems, you can double-click a clip in the browser to view it. You can also drag it to the viewer/source monitor.

The entire, uncut clip is the *master clip*. To use only a portion of it, mark an In Point (start mark) and Out Point (end mark) in the source window. On many systems, the I key marks In and the O key marks Out (these are conveniently located above J, K, and L on the keyboard for one-handed operation). You have just *marked* the clip. It's ready to be put into the movie.[10]

You then mark an In Point on the timeline, indicating where you want the new clip to go (if you don't mark an In Point on the timeline, the NLE will make the edit wherever the play head is positioned, which can be a timesaver).

To edit the clip to the timeline, your options may include: clicking on it in the source monitor or bin and dragging it to the timeline (*drag and drop*) or using on-screen buttons or keyboard commands to select the edit type.

You also need to select which video and audio tracks to add the new clip to. Typically, you'll start by putting the picture on video track 1 and the sound on audio track 1 (and often 2 as well). In FCP X, you'll start by adding clips to the primary storyline.

If you haven't done so already, you may need to choose the base format, frame size, and frame rate for the new sequence in the timeline. Some NLEs will automatically set it to be the same as the first clip you add to the timeline, which is a nice shortcut (but it's a good idea to check that the settings are correct). If your project includes material in more than one format, or you're setting up the sequence manually, see Mixing and Converting Formats, p. 598, for options.

Adding Clips to a Sequence

As you edit, you build up a string of clips on the timeline. When you want to add a new clip to an existing sequence, you have two main options about how the new clip will affect the clips already on the timeline. Different NLEs use different terms for these two styles of edits.

Say you've already built a three-shot sequence using clips A, B, and C. Now you want to insert a new shot after clip A. There are a couple of ways to do this.

10. In Final Cut Pro X, the same thing is done by selecting a range on the source clip, which can be done by dragging across the clip or by marking with keyboard commands.

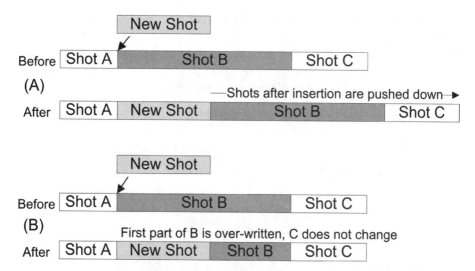

Fig. 14-19. Adding a shot. (A) With an *insert* or *splice* edit, adding a new shot causes existing shots after the insertion point to be pushed later in the sequence. (B) With an *overwrite* edit, the new shot replaces existing material without changing the position of other shots. (Steven Ascher)

INSERT OR SPLICE EDIT. In this type of edit, you *insert* (*splice*) the new clip, and material moves to the right to make room for it. In Figure 14-19A, the new clip goes in at the end of shot A. Shot B remains intact but is pushed back later in the sequence. Note that the sequence gets longer when we add the new clip. If shot B began in the edited sequence at, say, one minute timecode prior to making the edit, it will begin at one minute plus the length of the new clip after we make the edit. Any clips following B will also be pushed back the same amount.

In Premiere Pro and Final Cut Pro this type of edit is called an *insert*. Avid calls it a *splice edit*. It's sometimes called a *ripple edit* because in video terms, this edit has *rippled* all the clips after the edit point; that is, it has changed where they occur on the timeline.

OVERWRITE OR OVERLAY EDIT. In an *overwrite edit*, when we add the new clip we overwrite (cover over) the existing sequence starting at the edit point and continuing until the end of the new clip. In Figure 14-19B, the new clip replaces the beginning of shot B. The end of shot B and the rest of the sequence are unaffected. Note that the total length of the sequence does not change. Clips following the edit (later in the sequence) do not ripple; they remain in their original positions.

Insert edits on an NLE are a basic way of adding new material as you construct a sequence. Overwrite edits are useful for changing a sequence you've built without changing its length or the sync relationship between picture and sound. Say you'd constructed a sequence of images edited to a music track, so that cuts in the picture match up to musical beats and the overall sequence is exactly the length of the song. Using overwrite edits, you could add or change shots in the picture without changing the length of the sequence or the basic sync between picture and sound.

Removing Clips from a Sequence

Now, instead of adding a clip to the sequence A, B, C, we want to remove shot B. Again we have two options for doing so.

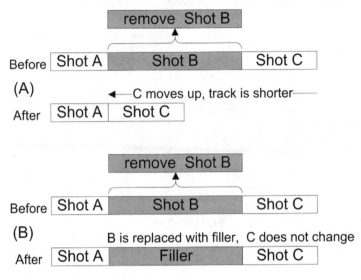

Fig. 14-20. Removing a shot. (A) With a *delete* or *extract* edit, removing a shot causes all the following shots to be pulled earlier in the sequence. (B) With a *lift* edit, any material that's removed is replaced with *filler* (on some systems, the space is maintained without filler). The rest of the sequence remains unchanged. (Steven Ascher)

DELETE OR EXTRACT EDIT. If we simply want to remove shot B, we can *delete* it. This is essentially cutting out shot B and attaching the beginning of shot C to the end of shot A (see Fig. 14-20A). The total length of the sequence is reduced—it becomes shorter by the length of shot B. Some people just call this *delete*; other names include *extract edit* or *ripple delete*. With Final Cut Pro X's "magnetic timeline," the system will perform a delete edit by default unless you instruct it otherwise.

On some NLEs, when a clip is deleted, it is sent to the clipboard (a temporary storage area) and can be easily reinserted elsewhere in the sequence. Even without the clipboard, you can always go back to the original clip in the browser to insert the shot elsewhere.

LIFT EDIT. In a lift edit, when we mark and remove shot B, it is replaced with black filler (see Fig. 14-20B). The filler (also called *slug* or *gap*) is just a placeholder that keeps clips A and C in their original positions, leaving a gap the exact size of shot B between them. The sequence maintains its original length, shot B is gone, and the gap can easily be filled with another shot later. Sync relationships and the total length of the sequence do not change. On some systems, the same thing is done with the *replace with gap* command. With some NLEs, the space left behind after a lift edit is maintained without filler or slug.

Many editing systems offer several other variations on the above-mentioned edits. However, you can perform most editing tasks with these four basic edits. To review: You can bring a clip to the timeline by inserting or by overwriting. You can remove a clip by extracting or by lifting.

Three-Point Editing

When we add a clip to the timeline using an overwrite edit, four edit points play a part in the process. First we decide which part of each source clip we want to use by marking an In Point and Out Point on the clip in the browser or viewer. Then we decide where on the timeline to put it, which involves an In Point and Out Point on the timeline. In Fig. 14-40, you can see the equivalent four points when editing on tape.

To perform an insert or overwrite edit, you need to give the editing system only *three* of those points; it will calculate the fourth itself.

Say, for example, on our timeline we have a shot of an airport runway that shows a red plane taking off, followed a little while later by a green plane taking off. Between them, we want to add a close-up of a blue plane taking off. We could mark the clip of the blue plane with an In Point just before it starts moving and an Out Point just after it lifts off. We then mark an In Point on the timeline, telling the NLE to place the clip after the red plane takes off. That's three points.

Alternatively, we might mark an In Point on the timeline just after the red plane takes off, and an Out Point just before the green plane starts down the runway. Then we mark an In Point on the close-up of the blue plane. Again, only three points.

Or we might choose to mark the timeline the same way, but rather than marking an In Point just before the blue plane starts moving in the close-up, we mark instead an Out Point just as it lifts off the tarmac. It's still three points. By the way, using the Out Point as the mark instead of the In Point is called a *backtimed edit*.

This concept is called *three-point editing*. If you happen to mark all four points, the NLE will normally use only three of your marks: the In and Out Points on the timeline and the In Point on the source clip.

Trimming Clips

After clips have been added to the timeline, you need to be able to adjust their length. This is a fundamental part of editing—fine-tuning how one shot moves into the next. In video terms, *trimming* means to adjust an edit point, either to extend or shorten a shot.

There are several ways to trim shots. Most NLEs have a special *trim mode* that helps you to adjust the cut between two shots. Trim mode often has two or more windows: one displays the last frame of the outgoing shot; another shows the first frame of the incoming shot (see Fig. 14-21). Once in trim mode, you can extend or shorten the *tail* (end) of the first shot, the *head* (beginning) of the second shot, or both. The trim editor allows you to preview the edit with a looping feature, which can play the transition repeatedly while you adjust it.

You can also trim shots right on the timeline by using keyboard commands or by clicking on the end of a clip and dragging one way or the other with the mouse. With most editing systems you have a choice: you can adjust trims by eye, you can click or use a keyboard command to move the edit point by a preset number of frames, or you can type in any number of frames you want.

Fig. 14-21. Trim mode. This Avid trim tool displays the last frame of the outgoing clip and the first frame of the incoming clip. You can select to trim the ends of either or both clips. (Avid Technology, Inc./Steven Ascher)

Types of Trims

Like other types of edits, trims also come in different flavors.

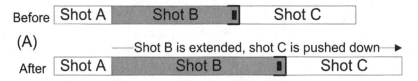

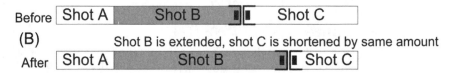

Fig. 14-22. Types of trims. (A) With a *ripple trim* (*single-roller trim* or *trim tail*), the tail of shot B is extended and shot C is pushed later in the sequence by the same amount. (B) With a *roll trim* (*dual-roller trim* or *trim joint*), the tail of shot B is extended and the head of C is overwritten by the same amount. Shot C becomes shorter, but its position in the sequence doesn't change. (Steven Ascher)

RIPPLE EDITS. Let's go back to our sequence of clips A, B, and C. If we perform a *ripple edit* to the tail of clip B, we can extend the shot—that is, move the tail of the clip to the right, which adds frames (see Fig. 14-22A). This will push clip C further down, lengthening the overall sequence and rippling all the subsequent clips. If we wanted to shorten the tail of B, we could just as easily delete frames, moving the tail of clip B to the left. This will shorten the entire sequence and bring up all clips following the edit. Avid calls this a *single-roller trim*; it can also be called a *ripple trim*.

ROLL EDITS. Let's start again with the original A, B, C sequence and apply a *roll edit* (or *roll trim*) to the cut between clips B and C (see Fig, 14-22B). In this trim, we add frames to the tail of B and delete the same number of frames from the head of C. Clip B is extended and clip C is shortened. Clip C now starts later, but because the clip has also gotten shorter by the same amount, the clip does not move relative to the timeline. The tail of C remains in the same place and the overall sequence does not change length. Avid calls this a *dual-roller trim*; in Premiere Pro it's called a *rolling edit*.

Trimming Entire Clips

Two more specialized trims can be used to trim both ends of a clip at once.

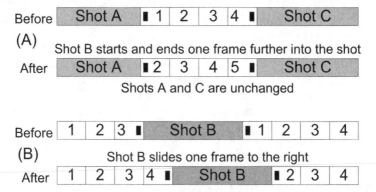

Fig. 14-23. Slip and slide trims. (A) After doing a *slip trim*, all shots remain unchanged in length and relative position, but we now view a different portion of shot B. (B) With a *slide trim*, shot B is itself fixed, but its position in the sequence can be changed. As shown here, shot B is slid to the right, which causes the tail of A to be extended and the head of C to be overwritten. (Steven Ascher)

SLIP EDITS. A *slip edit* (or *slip trim*) allows you to use a different portion of a clip without changing its length or position relative to other clips (see Fig. 14-23A). If you slip a clip to the right, you effectively trim back the head of the clip while extending the tail the same amount. This has the effect of allowing you to view a later portion of the shot without changing anything else. Slip edits are very handy when you want to fine-tune a cutaway or adjust audio sync without changing clip positions.

SLIDE EDITS. A *slide edit* (or *slide trim*) allows you to grab a clip and slide it over adjoining clips (see Fig. 14-23B). For example, in the A, B, C sequence, you could grab shot B and slide it to the right on the timeline. The NLE does this by extending the tail of A and trimming back the head of C. Clip B is itself unchanged but is in a new position. The length of the sequence is unchanged.

Handles and the Limits on Trims

NLEs make it easy to execute your creative ideas. If you want to shorten or lengthen a shot, you just click on it and perform the trim—within limits. Say you have a two-minute master clip in the bin and you put the entire clip on the timeline.

If you later try to extend the head or tail of the shot, you'll get an error message about having "insufficient media" to do the edit. You've used the whole clip (which represents the entire media file)—there is no more. This is pretty straightforward, but some people are puzzled by the error message.

One issue with putting an entire master clip in a sequence is that if you later decide to dissolve in or out of the shot, you won't have the needed extra frames at the head or tail. For example, if you want a 30-frame dissolve at the start of a clip, you'll typically need 15 extra frames at the head of the clip to use for the overlap with the previous clip. To solve this problem, you can simply trim the head of the clip back by at least 15 frames.

When extra media at the head or the tail of a clip is available for use but is not currently visible (or audible) in the sequence, it's called a *handle*. Having handles on your clips gives you the flexibility to extend them or apply transitions later if you want (see Fig. 15-10).

Some NLEs show you available handles when making trims, such as the Inline Precision Editor in newer versions of Final Cut Pro. Another way to check whether you have handles on a clip is by using the *match frame* command. Put the cursor on the first frame of a clip in the timeline and hit "match frame." The master clip will appear in the viewer/source monitor and you can see how much longer it is than the portion you're currently using in the sequence. You'll find many other uses for the match frame command—such as hunting for other shots near the one you're matching.

Transitions Between Clips

A *straight cut* (also called *hard cut* or simply *cut*) is when one shot ends and the other begins cleanly. In NLE terms, all the other ways of bridging from one shot to another (including a dissolve or fade-out/fade-in) are called *transitions*. See Joining Sequences, p. 525, for more on the use of transitions in storytelling.

Transitions are easy to do. You can select the type of transition, its duration in frames, and its position relative to the cut (centered on the cut, beginning on the cut, or ending on the cut). Some systems let you fine-tune the center of the transition at any point near the cut. As noted above, if you want to do a dissolve you'll need handles of half the dissolve length from each shot. When doing dissolves, keep in mind that a bright shot will tend to overpower a dark shot, so a brighter shot will seem to dissolve in faster on a dark shot than vice versa.

Moving Clips on the Timeline

There are several ways to move a clip that's already on the timeline. One way is to click on it and drag it with the mouse. Most NLEs have a *snapping* function that makes clips attach "magnetically" to nearby items (including other clips, the play head, or marks you've set). Turn snapping on to avoid accidentally leaving a small gap between two clips you want to join. Sometimes you want to position two clips very close to each other but not touching—in that case you'll have more control if you turn snapping off.

Snapping is very handy when you want to mark a clip or area for removal. The cursor will snap to the head of the clip, where you can mark an In Point. It will also snap to the tail of the clip (but on some systems you then have to move *one frame to the left* before marking the Out Point to avoid unintentionally cutting a frame from the following clip). In some systems you can click on a clip to select it or you can *lasso* a clip or a group of clips by dragging around them with the mouse.

The NLE has options for how clips behave when moved over each other. In one mode, pushing one clip into another will overwrite the second clip. In another mode you can drag one clip ahead of another and make them swap positions. Clips can also be moved numerically by typing in a frame count plus or minus. Consult your NLE's manual for the various options and how to execute them.

As discussed above, Final Cut Pro X uses a different methodology than most NLEs in terms of arranging and moving clips. Instead of fixed, separate tracks for video and audio, you have a primary storyline, which is a central track containing video and/or audio, to which you can add connected clips and other storylines. You can also collapse a group of clips into a *compound clip*, which makes it easy to move them around together (you can expand a compound clip as needed and fully edit the contents inside). When you move one group of connected video and audio clips toward another, in a situation where they would simply collide with other NLEs, clips automatically jump up or down on the timeline to make way for any overlap, which may be helpful for certain kinds of edits.

All NLEs have *copy* and *paste* functions that can be used to move single clips or many clips on several tracks in a large portion of the timeline. This is a good way to move clips from one sequence to another.

Using Multiple Video Tracks

All NLEs allow you to create more than one layer of video, which is done by stacking two or more clips on different video tracks. A simple example is a title *superimposed* over picture. Normally the top track is the one that is seen "first," so the title goes on the upper track and the picture appears under the letters (see Figs. 14-16 and 13-5). By adjusting a clip's *opacity*, you can change how visible it is (lowering opacity makes it more transparent). For more on layers and compositing, see below.

Even if you're not doing layered effects, using two video tracks can simplify some basic cutting decisions. For example, if you have a continuous shot of a woman talking on the lowest video track and a short cutaway of a man listening on the track above, you can just push the cutaway forward and back, experimenting with placement without having to do a new overwrite edit every time you move it, as you would if the two shots were on the same track.

Often, you want to move a clip vertically to another track while maintaining its original horizontal (time) position. In Premiere Pro, clips will stay in their horizontal position if snapping is turned on. With some NLEs, you need to hold down the command or shift key while dragging to keep clips from sliding forward or back.

NESTED CLIPS. Complex video or audio effects may require many layers of clips. Sometimes when you need several clips in several layers to accomplish an effect, you'll want to *nest* those clips into a single clip, which is easier to move around and work with. Different NLEs use different terms and methods for nesting. With some, you select one or more clips and use the "nest" command. Some allow nesting by creating a separate sequence that contains the various clips on different tracks;

you then insert that sequence into the master sequence as a single clip on the time-line. The nested clip is like a box that keeps things neatly packaged and allows you to do things like add a color effect or audio filter to all the clips in the nest at one time. You can "step into" the nested clip (often by double-clicking on it) whenever you want to work with the clips within.

In Final Cut Pro X, the rough equivalent is a compound clip. Final Cut Pro X also offers *auditions*, which is a method of nesting an alternative clip or group of clips in the same place, so you can easily try different versions to see which you like best.

Other Types of Edits

In addition to the standard insert and overwrite edits discussed above, there are some more specialized ways of bringing clips to the timeline.

If you have a gap you want to fill on the timeline, but the clip you want to fill it with is either too long or too short, you can use *fit-to-fill*. To do this edit you mark In and Out Points on both the new clip and the gap. Fit-to-fill will either speed up or slow down the clip to make it fit the gap exactly.

If you have a clip on the timeline that's the right length and in the right position but you don't like the picture, you can do a *replace edit*. With some NLEs, you park the play head at the start of the clip you want to replace on the timeline; go to the viewer and put that cursor at the head of the replacement shot; then hit "replace." This saves you having to set any In or Out marks.

Avid offers a variation called *sync point editing*, which lets you overwrite a clip so that a particular point in the source clip is in sync with a particular point in the sequence. So you might mark a musical beat in the audio track and a hand clap in a new video clip, then do an overwrite edit so those two things line up. Very handy for syncing up (see below).

BASIC SOUND EDITING

NLEs are powerful tools for editing and mixing sounds. On some projects, all the sound work is done with the NLE. On others, audio is exported to a DAW for final mixing. For more on sound editing, see Chapter 15.

Working with Audio Tracks

Footage from a video camera typically has one or two channels of audio (and sometimes more). When you capture or import that footage, the NLE may create separate clips for the video and each audio channel, but all those clips are *linked* together to make editing easier (you can unlink them when needed).

With most NLEs, when you edit a clip from the source viewer to the timeline, the video clip goes to a video track on the timeline and the associated audio clips go to one or more audio tracks (see Fig. 14-16). The NLE has a *track selector* where you can choose which tracks to place the clips on. You can select *not* to include any combination of the clips in the edit.

With Final Cut Pro X, audio and video appear in the same clip on the same storyline (track) on the timeline (see Fig. 14-18). The audio and video clips can be manually separated and unlinked if desired.

Audio recorded and captured in stereo (for example, most music) normally has two paired channels, left and right. When you edit a stereo clip to the timeline the audio will appear as a *stereo pair*. With some NLEs, both channels occupy the same track; on others, a clip containing the left channel will be on one track, and a paired clip containing the right channel will be on the next track. Any level changes or other adjustments will affect both tracks, unless you choose to unpair them.

Often, a sound recordist will record one mic on channel 1 and a separate mic on channel 2. These should not be edited as stereo pairs, but instead should be treated as the separate *dual mono* channels that they are. If you imported the footage in stereo, you should generally unpair these tracks before editing. For more on working with stereo pairs, see p. 649.

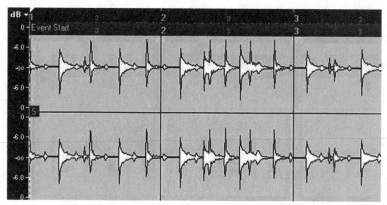

Fig. 14-24. Audio waveforms. A visual representation of a clip's sound, waveforms make some editing tasks easier. Shown here, stereo tracks of a percussive drum sound. The height of each waveform above the centerline corresponds to loudness. (Steinberg Media Technologies GmbH)

Audio Levels

You often need to adjust the sound level (volume) of clips in a sequence, either to correct audio that was recorded too loudly or too quietly in the field, or to balance sounds you're editing together. Changing the audio level is called adjusting the *gain*.

Audio levels can be adjusted in several ways. Most NLEs can display the audio gain as a line on the clip itself. Pushing the line up with the mouse increases the sound level for the entire clip. To set different levels in different sections of a clip, you can add *keyframes* on the line in any area where you want to raise or lower the level (this is also called *rubberbanding* or *audio gain automation*).

With some NLEs, the audio waveform display in each clip shows you its audio levels, so you can make quick adjustments visually.

Sometimes it's easier to use keyboard commands when you want to change the level of a clip, a group of clips, or the level of a keyframe. Keyboard commands can be very precise when you want to nudge the level up or down a few decibels. The gain is normally 0 dB if nothing has been done to the clip. Raising gain by 6 dB will make the clip sound about twice as loud.[11]

When you're editing, what level should the sound be? Most NLEs have a peak-reading audio meter in which 0 dBFS represents the maximum level (see Fig. 11-10). In no case should the audio level reach 0 dB. If the peaks (the loudest parts) are reaching 0 dB, bring the level down. When using a peak meter, keeping the dialogue peaks around –10 dBFS is a reasonable average for typical broadcast audio levels. For more precise instructions on using meters and setting levels, see The Sound Mix, p. 658.

After you've got a few clips playing normally and showing a good level on the meter, adjust the volume of the speakers (or headphones) to a comfortable level. Then *don't change the speaker level* while you edit. You'll be able to tell a lot about the level just from listening. However, if you constantly raise and lower the speaker level, you won't know if something is really too loud or too quiet.

Working with Dialogue

Before reading this, see Dialogue Editing, p. 531.

NLEs are wonderful tools for editing dialogue. You can quickly balance levels if one character is louder than another. You can do precision surgery when you need to make a cut in midsentence or remove a breath. You can create multiple tracks for overlapping dialogue.

One very common dialogue edit is when you want the sound to cut before or after the picture cut. Various terms for this effect include *split edit*, *overlap edit*, and *sound overlap*. Some people use the terms *L-cut*—where the picture cut precedes the audio cut—and *J-cut*, in which the audio cut leads the picture cut (see Fig. 14-25). Say you have a clip of a man talking, followed by a clip of a woman responding, and you want the picture to cut to her before she starts talking (which may make a more natural transition). Make sure the audio tracks are locked or disabled (so they won't move). Then, on the video track *only*, select the picture cut between the man and

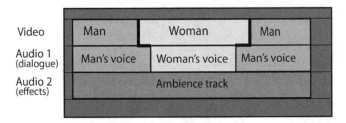

Fig. 14-25. Dialogue often feels more natural when the audio cut between two shots follows or leads the picture cut (sometimes called a *split edit*). Shown here, an *L-cut* from the man to the woman and a *J-cut* from the woman back to the man (the names are suggested by the shapes of the cuts on the timeline). An ambience track may be added to reinforce continuity by remaining consistent across the three shots. (Steven Ascher)

---

11. Note that the dBs on a clip in the timeline refer to level *adjustments* on that particular clip; only the audio meter can tell you the *resulting audio level* of that clip and any other clips playing together with it. Also see the discussion of sound level starting on p. 659.

the woman and do a rolling edit to the left, into the tail of his shot. You might want to have continuous *ambience* (background sound of the location or setting) on another track to help smooth the cut if there's a noticeable change in the background sounds or dialogue sound quality between his take and hers.

Sometimes it can be very effective to do a split edit from one scene to another, letting the audio from the incoming scene start during the end of the outgoing scene, pulling us forward into the next scene.

Many NLEs can perform an *extend edit*, which is handy for making split edits. You simply click on the picture cut, put the play head where you'd like that cut to be, then hit "extend" or "enter."

Audio Transitions and Filters

The audio equivalent of a dissolve is called a *crossfade*. The outgoing clip fades out while the incoming clip fades in. Like picture dissolves, you can set the length and position of the crossfade relative to the cut (assuming you have sufficient handles). Crossfades come in different styles; often you want to use an "equal-power" version, which maintains a constant volume level through the transition. This type of crossfade is sometimes indicated as "Crossfade (3 dB)."

At a cut between two clips you'll sometimes hear a slight click, even though neither clip has a clicking sound in it. If you put a short crossfade (as short as two frames) between them, the click will usually go away.

Various filters can help you to reduce noise, equalize the sound, or add special effects. You can apply these to individual clips, to a nested group of clips, or—on some NLEs—to entire tracks. For more, see Chapter 15.

Maintaining Sync

When you import a typical clip from a video camera, the sound will be in sync with the picture (that is, when you see someone's lips moving, the sound comes out at the exact same time). However, if you're not careful as you edit, the sync relationship between picture and sound tracks can go out of whack, making the sound early or late relative to the picture.

When you make an insert (splice) edit, as long as you insert the same amount to every track on the timeline, all the clips that are already on the timeline will stay in sync. For example, if you insert a 15-frame clip into the middle of a sequence, as long you add 15 frames to all the tracks, they will all stay in sync. However, if you were to add 15 frames to the picture but *not* to the audio tracks, the sound following the insertion would be 15 frames out of sync (that is, sound would be 15 frames early; see Fig. 14-26).

Most NLEs can automatically add the same amount to all tracks when you make an insertion, keeping the tracks in sync. For this to happen, all the tracks need to be unlocked or enabled so they can expand with the insertion (see your NLE's manual for how to accomplish this with your system). The same idea about sync applies when removing clips via delete (extract) edits. If you delete the same number of frames from all tracks, they'll stay in sync.

Unlike insert and delete edits, when you use overwrite edits to add clips to the timeline, or use lift edits to remove them, you don't have to worry about messing up sync relationships. When you use a lift edit to get rid of a clip, the space where

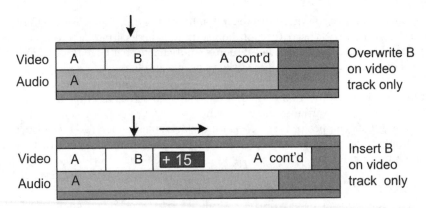

Fig. 14-26. A sync break. (top) If clip B is added *to the video track only* using an overwrite edit, the rest of clip A stays in sync with its audio. (bottom) If clip B is instead added to the video track using an insert edit—and the audio track is locked—the rest of shot A and any clips that follow go out of sync. The +15 indicator tells you that the picture is 15 frames late relative to its audio. Different NLEs use different methods to indicate a sync break.

the clip was located remains as a gap, maintaining the original spacing between the other clips on the timeline.

Sometimes you want to put audio and video out of sync with each other for creative reasons, and sometimes it happens by accident. With some NLEs, if you do anything that causes a video clip and its associated audio to go out of sync (called a *sync break*), you'll see a numerical display on the clips showing how many frames you need to move one relative to the other to put them back in sync (see Fig. 14-26). For example, on some systems, if you see a +7 appear on an audio clip, that tells you that the sound is 7 frames late compared to the picture. One way to fix that is to move the audio clip 7 frames earlier (to the left on the timeline) to put it back in sync. If you see that *all* the audio clips to the right of a certain point are out of sync, that's the point where you need to add or remove some frames on either the audio or video track(s).

Sometimes you create a group of clips (such as music and sound effects) that have a specific sync relationship to the picture but since they're not linked to the video clip, they don't display any sync break numbers if they get out of position. One solution is to add markers (locators) on picture and sound clips so you can see how they line up. Some editors like to put a tail leader and/or set of clips on every video and audio track at the end of the sequence so they can quickly see if one or more tracks have gone out of sync, and by how much.

In Final Cut Pro X, you can connect a group of audio and video clips to maintain sync even when you move the group, or you can create a compound clip or secondary storyline to keep them together. Also, when you add a sync clip to a project, the primary video and audio tracks form one joined clip, so it's much less likely you'll throw them out of sync accidentally.

WORKING WITH DOUBLE-SYSTEM SOUND

Double-system or dual-system sound means using an audio recorder that's separate from the camera (see p. 464). Film is always shot double system, and some video projects are too, particularly when shooting with DSLRs. When the sound and picture are recorded separately, they have to be put in sync before you can edit. This process is called *synchronizing the dailies, syncing the rushes,* or, more commonly, just *syncing up* (pronounced "sinking"). When syncing is complete, every sync-sound shot on the picture has its audio properly lined up.

On some projects shot on film, syncing takes place in the telecine or on another system before the footage gets to the editing room. On other film projects syncing is done in the NLE. Audio speed adjustments needed for projects shot on film are discussed on p. 690.

The first step for both film and video projects is to import the picture and sound into the NLE. Lining up the video and audio clips can happen several ways:

- If manual slates (clap sticks) were used, you find the first frame in which the hinged bar of the slate closes and place a marker or In Point on the video clip. Then find the first moment where the sound of the slate is audible (which is also visible in the audio waveform) and place a mark on the audio clip. This method also works with slate apps like MovieSlate (see Fig. 9-30) if there's no timecode in the audio.
- If a timecode slate was used, you can read the visual timecode display and enter that number to locate the matching code in the audio. Or, if both picture and sound have the same embedded timecode, this can be done automatically and doesn't require slates.
- If you shot with a digital camera that recorded a scratch audio track along with the picture, some NLEs can automatically line up the low-quality audio from the camera with the high-quality clips from the external sound recorder by matching their audio waveforms. Singular Software's PluralEyes plug-in can also do this. This method is very useful for a multicamera shoot without slates, allowing all the video clips from different cameras to align with a master sound track.

Once the video and audio clips are in sync, different NLEs and software use different methods to link them so they stay together and display sync breaks if they should get out of sync later. Avid has an *AutoSync* function that allows you to simply mark In Points on the sound and picture where the clap sticks hit, then use Auto-Sync to create a new, merged clip. In Premiere Pro, choose *synchronize* from the clip menu. If you've created a synchronized, merged clip that contains high-quality audio from a recorder and low-quality audio from a camera like a DSLR, don't forget to mute or delete the camera audio track(s).

Accuracy and Lip Sync

When manually syncing up a slated shot, be sure to line up the *first* point in the picture where the slate makes contact and the first point where it is audible in the sound. Sometimes the picture slate occurs between frames. Simply line up the exact point where you think the slate occurred in the picture with the first point where you can hear it on the sound track. On some NLEs you can slip an audio clip with subframe accuracy, allowing you to nudge the clip in tiny increments to get the precise beginning of the slate's sound.

At some point you will probably need to sync up a shot that has not been slated. To do this, find a surrogate slate in the scene—the closing of a door or an object being placed on a table. Learn to sync up the movements of people's lips with the sound of their words. Look for words that contain hard labial sounds like *b* and *p* for which the sound becomes audible just as the lips part. The *m* sound can be used, but it's not as precise.

After you have determined approximate sync, experiment by sliding the picture two frames ahead or two back to see if you can improve it. Then try moving it one frame each way. A sync error of one or two frames is usually noticeable to attentive audiences. Sound that is slightly late is less objectionable than sound that is early (the former happens often in nature; the latter never does). Sync should be checked carefully, preferably on a big screen. Sync errors detected after a project is done are very upsetting!

BASIC VIDEO EFFECTS

NLEs are capable of a wide range of digital effects, and hundreds of *plug-ins* (standardized, add-on tools that work inside another program) can be purchased for specialized tasks. *Compositing* is the art of building shots from layers of disparate elements that may include live action, *computer-generated imagery* (*CGI*), text, graphics, and effects.

While all NLEs will do compositing, for more complete control consider applications like Adobe After Effects, Apple Motion, Autodesk Smoke or Flame, eyeon's Fusion, and the Foundry's NukeX. These apps offer a wider set of tools for compositing, editing, and finishing in 2D or 3D. While many of these are expensive, some can be rented for a project or used free on a trial basis (for example, After Effects and Smoke offer free thirty-day trials and students can use Smoke free for three years).

The complexity of video effects and compositing is beyond the scope of this book. What follows are some basic NLE effects you might typically use.

Layers, Alpha Channels, and Keys

As noted above, when you have two or more tracks (layers) of video, the resulting video image is as if seen from above the timeline; that is, the top track is seen first. If the clip on top is totally *opaque*, that's all you'll see. If it has areas of transparency, layers below will be visible through it.

Typically, when you have a superimposed title over a video image, you want the title to be opaque where the lettering is and transparent everywhere else so the picture underneath shows through (see Fig. 13-5). Titles and graphics may be created with an *alpha channel*, which is a fourth information channel in addition to the red, green, and blue channels. An alpha channel is a gray-scale image (black-and-white) that defines which parts of a clip are transparent. In many systems, white areas in the alpha channel are opaque, black areas are transparent, and gray areas are *partially* transparent.[12] Graphics with transparency have an extra layer for the alpha channel. An example of a video format with an alpha channel is ProRes 4:4:4:4 (the extra 4 in addition to the typical 4:4:4 indicates that it has an alpha channel).

A video layer can include a moving alpha channel, sometimes called a *traveling matte*. A traveling matte allows you to superimpose a moving foreground layer (whether it be an actor or a graphic) on a different background. A *garbage matte* is a rough matte used to exclude parts of the frame that don't belong in the shot (like light stands or areas outside a green screen) so that other effects can be applied to just the areas you're interested in.

One way to modify the alpha channel and create transparency in portions of the image is to use a *key*. When keying, a portion of the image is selected, based on color or brightness, to be made invisible or transparent. In the example of white titles over a video background, a *luma* (luminance) *key* could be applied to the titles. The luma key would identify the brightest part of the frame only (the white letters), make them opaque, and make everything else on the clip transparent. Chroma keys are used with blue- or green-screen shooting to make colored areas transparent (for more, see p. 211).

When you stack up layers of images and effects, NLE playback can become rough or choppy due to all the processing involved. In some cases you may need or want to render the effects to see them at full quality and full speed. With some NLEs, it's fastest to simply render the top video track, which will include the layers below.

Fig. 14-27. Compositing. The subject is shot in front of a green screen, which is then keyed out. The subject can then be composited on a new background. Autodesk Smoke is a sophisticated compositing application. (Autodesk)

12. In some cases, you may need to "invert" an alpha channel (reversing the tonal values) to make it compatible with your system.

Wipes

In a wipe, image A replaces image B at a boundary edge moving across the frame. Think of scene transitions in *Star Wars*, which are patterned after old wipe styles that were once popular in Hollywood. There are hundreds of wipe patterns. In some wipes, image A pushes image B off the screen vertically, horizontally, or in a particular pattern (stars, a cross, etc.). The edge of the wipe can be soft or hard or have a colored line. These days, flashy wipes can seem pretty tacky and should be avoided unless that's the look you're going for.

Speed Effects

Changing the speed of a shot is often used to add an energetic or frantic feel (high speed) or dreamy quality (slow motion). It's very easy to apply speed effects to clips in a timeline. When you double a clip's speed, the system simply skips every other frame; when you slow a clip to 50 percent speed, it plays each frame twice. When slowing down footage shot at normal speed, most NLEs can do *frame blending*, an option that may produce a smoother look by creating dissolves between frames. Even better, systems or plug-ins with *optical flow* processing can analyze the motion of objects in the frame (*motion estimation*) and construct intermediate frames (*interpolated frames*) between the existing frames to make the slow motion seem more continuous (this is sometimes called "inbetweening"). Optical flow is especially helpful when you want to play a shot much slower than its original speed. The best slow motion is produced by shooting at high frame rates (see Slow Motion, p. 389).

If you double the speed of a clip it gets shortened by half, causing the sequence to be shorter as well. Often you'd rather maintain the length of the clip and sequence, but have the motion in the shot be faster. Some NLEs have an option to change speed without rippling the sequence. In others, the workaround is to move the clip to its own video track, change its speed, then move it back to the main sequence or storyline.

A constant speed effect is one that's applied uniformly to the entire clip. However, some NLEs permit *variable speed effects* (different speeds in different parts of the clip, which is sometimes called *time remapping*).

Sometimes you want to fill a hole in the timeline with a clip that's too long or too short. With fit-to-fill edits, the NLE will adjust the speed of the clip as needed (see p. 584).

Changing the playback speed of audio will affect the pitch of the sound. The faster you make the clip, the higher the pitch (think of the chipmunk sound when voices are made really fast). Many NLEs or audio editing programs have a *pitch shifter* that can restore the pitch (see Fig. 15-19). Voices and short sounds respond better to this process than long, continuous musical notes, which may hiccup after being pitch shifted, especially when going down in pitch.

Scale, Orientation, and Distortion

You can always make the picture smaller, so it becomes a frame within the frame (*picture-in-picture*, or *PIP*). With HD and larger formats like 2K and 4K, you can scale up (enlarge) the frame quite a bit—25 percent or more—with acceptable quality. This allows you to reframe the shot or do a zoom-in. With SD, enlarging the image results in noticeable softening and may not hold up. Upscaling is often necessary when you're introducing nonwidescreen SD footage into a widescreen SD or HD movie (see p. 599).

For techniques for zooming in on stills, see p. 596.

An image can be reversed horizontally (mirror image), which is useful when a shot has the wrong screen direction. An image can also be reversed top to bottom. Some people call the former *flipping* and the latter *flopping*, while others call them both *flopping*. A discussion topic for long winter evenings?

There are numerous ways to *distort* the image, squeezing it or changing perspective or wrapping it around a shape like a sphere or a box.

Keyframes and Effect Curves

Many effects are designed to change image size, position, rotation, or speed as the shot progresses. You can start at the beginning of a clip, get the various settings (parameters) the way you want them, and set a *keyframe* (actually you can set a keyframe for each parameter). You then go to a later part of the clip, change the parameters as you please, and set another keyframe. Each keyframe is a waypoint, and the computer will interpolate between them, making a transition from one to the next. How that transition is made may be adjustable. A *linear* transition is just that—a straight line from one keyframe to the next. Often you want more of an *S-curve*, allowing an effect or movement to *ease in* (picking up speed or intensity gradually) then *ease out* by decelerating gracefully at the end. Many systems offer tools like *Bezier handles*, which you use to adjust the shape of the curve between keyframes, or an option to apply "smoothing" to keyframes.

Other Image Effects and Controls

Filter effects number in the hundreds. These allow you to process the texture or appearance of the image, such as adding blur or distorting colors.

Image stabilization can smooth out a shot that was filmed shakily or from a bumpy vehicle. Most NLEs have a stabilization feature or you can get a plug-in like CoreMelt's Lock & Load or use separate applications like Adobe After Effects. Stabilizers attempt to keep objects in the frame relatively steady while the frame itself moves around them (for example, if the objects go left, the frame goes left too, keeping the objects in the same place on screen). This will result in a constantly moving black border around the frame if you don't enlarge the image to push the border off screen (which lowers resolution a bit). Nevertheless, some image stabilizers are amazingly effective and can make a bumpy walking shot look like it was shot with a Steadicam. Sometimes a stabilizer can even smooth out a jerky zoom.

In FCP X, image stabilization is built in, available as an option in the video inspector window of every video clip, with controls for smoothness of scale and rotation. Clips can be also be automatically stabilized when you import them if "analyze for stabilization and rolling shutter" is clicked in Preferences.

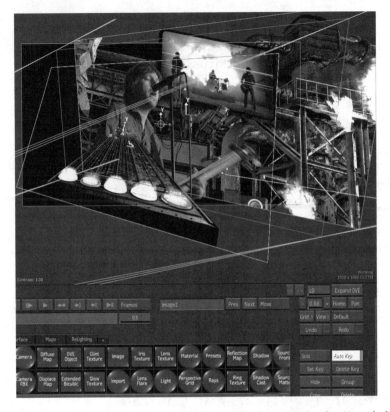

Fig. 14-28. Compositing in 3D, with multiple layers of video using Smoke. (Autodesk)

TITLES, GRAPHICS, AND STILLS

Virtually every movie makes use of titles, text, and graphics of various kinds. NLEs can create text elements as well as shapes, gradients, and other patterns for graphics. For more sophisticated control over text and graphics, you can use programs such as After Effects, Photoshop, and Motion, and plug-ins like Boris Red, together with your NLE.

Titles

See Titles, p. 541, before reading this section.

On-screen text in video is sometimes called *CG* (produced by a *character generator*) or *chyron* (after an early maker of video text devices). NLEs include basic text generators and often have complex tools for animating titles within the NLE or as part of the NLE suite.

The NLE's title tool should give you simple controls over font choice, font size, color, position, justification, kerning (the space between characters), and leading (rhymes with "sledding"—it's the space between lines). This is all you need to make basic titles. "Supered" video titles (those that appear over picture) generally need drop shadows or some kind of graphic pad under them so the letters don't blend into the background. Another technique is to slightly blur the background under a title to make it stand out more. Usually titles in video shouldn't be overly bright or they'll get noisy.

Bitmapped (also called *raster*) *graphics* and titles are made up of individual pixels and look best when made at high resolution and with low compression. If you try to enlarge a bitmapped title it may look soft. Many NLEs and design apps can create *vector graphics*, which are defined by geometrical formulas instead of pixels. Vector-based titles or other shapes can be scaled to any size with smooth results (you could build them for an offline edit at one resolution, then import them into an online sequence and rerender them at full resolution).

As noted in Chapter 13, avoid fonts that have serifs or any graphics with fine horizontal lines, especially for interlaced video formats where they might cause flicker.

Graphics

For optimum control over graphic elements, the NLE is usually not the best tool for the job. Graphic artists often use programs like Photoshop or Illustrator to create graphics, then import them to the NLE using a variety of file formats. Generally you want to use uncompressed or lossless formats. Depending on your system you might use TIFF (.tif), PNG (.png), Photoshop (.psd), or highest-quality JPEG (.jpg). Often, graphics involve a number of layers and some NLEs can import a Photoshop file with the layers on different video tracks, giving you easy access to create effects or alternate versions of the image (for example, different layers might have the same text in different languages).

Over time, the process of moving graphics from outside programs to the NLE has gotten simpler. However, keep two issues in mind when you're creating graphics on other applications.

First, remember that most graphics programs work in RGB color space while most NLEs work in component ($Y'C_BC_R$, also called YUV) color space. See Video Color Systems, p. 207, for more on this. Be aware that colors that may seem dull in RGB on the computer monitor can look very bright on a component video monitor. Avoid choosing rich, saturated colors in the graphics program; they may end up looking garish and noisy in video and exceed the legal range in component 709 or 601 color space (see Fig. 5-12). Choose "broadcast safe" colors in the graphics app or NLE.

Another concern is pixel aspect ratio (see Pixel Shape, p. 232). Graphics programs (and all computers) use square pixels, as do true HD formats. However, SD formats (NTSC and PAL) and some HD formats (like DVCPRO HD and certain versions of HDV) use nonsquare pixels. This means that graphics may look distorted if you're not careful (see Fig. 5-27). In some cases you may need to build the graphics at a larger frame size so they'll look correct when shown in nonsquare pixels.[13] Consult the documentation with your NLE for suggested frame sizes.

Fortunately, newer versions of many NLEs and graphics programs can auto-

---

13. For example, Apple recommends building a graphic at 720 x 540 in a graphics program so it will look normal when shown in nonwidescreen NTSC 720 x 480 DV.

matically adjust for frame size, pixel shape, and color space if you tell them what formats the video and graphics are in.

Animating Stills

You may want to incorporate digital stills or scanned photographs into a movie. Further, you may want to animate them with moves: panning across the image, zooming out from a detail to the whole picture, or moving closer on someone's face. At one time, moves on still images were done by shooting photographic prints on an *animation stand* (also called a *rostrum camera*). Today, they're done in the NLE or in applications like After Effects or Motion, which may provide more precise control and more fluid moves (in which case you might export the animation still as a movie file to be imported into the NLE).

Before reading further, be sure to see Still Images and Video, p. 235.

Start with a still or graphic that has at least the same dimensions in pixels as the video format you're working in, because if you scale up a smaller image in the NLE it can cause a loss of sharpness. If you plan to move in on a portion of the image, prepare the image at a larger frame size than the project. For example, if you want to scale up an image to 200 percent in the NLE, prepare the image at twice the project frame size before you import it. For a tighter zoom, say 3x to 4x, multiply by that amount. With 720p HD formats, a still that's about 4,000 pixels wide will give you room to do a moderately tight zoom-in. When working in SD formats, aim for an image at least 2,000 pixels across.

If you're starting with a digital still, you can use Photoshop or another app to scale the image up. If you're scanning a photograph printed on paper, make sure the scanner is set to a high enough resolution to produce the digital image size you need. For example, if you scan an eight-by-ten-inch photo at 150 dpi, this will produce an image size of 1200 x 1500 pixels. The smaller the photo, the higher-res scanner setting you'll need to create an adequately sized digital image.

While applications like After Effects and Motion can accept very large stills, not all NLEs can (while legacy versions of Final Cut Pro were limited to 4000 x 4000 pixels, FCP X appears to have no limit). With many applications, performance is slower with large images. When importing a still to an NLE, check the import settings because some may scale the still to the project size, which you want to avoid if you made it bigger to accommodate moves.

When adjusting the moves across the image, experiment with speed and motion settings. Generally you want to "ease" into a move (ramping up in speed) and then ramp down as the move finishes in a different place, to create a graceful, nonmechanical feel.[14] With some systems, you can set keyframes along a path as waypoints for *X-Y moves* (horizontal-vertical) and *Z moves* (in-out). With others, you simply indicate a starting frame and an ending frame, and the system moves from one to the other. Bezier handles (see p. 593) can smooth transitions.

When scanning and editing stills into your movie, bear in mind the aspect ratio of the format you're working in. Vertically oriented stills won't fill the frame if you try to show the whole photo, which could look awkward, especially with widescreen video formats. This is why filmmakers often start tight enough on vertical pictures

---

14. Motion and After Effects both offer preset moves to provide smooth ramping.

so the photo fills the frame; then they do a move up or down (such as a move from feet to face on a portrait). Another approach is to put some kind of background behind the picture so the sides aren't completely empty.

Some people like to animate stills with a kind of pseudo-3D technique. Say you have a shot of a man standing by lake. Using Photoshop, create a layer that isolates the man on a transparent background. Then create a separate layer with *only* the lake, filling in the hole where the man was by cloning nearby areas. Load the layers into the NLE and, as you pan across the image, move the man's layer at a slightly different rate than the background to create the illusion of dimensionality.

FREEZE FRAMES. Sometimes you want to use a still that comes from your video footage—otherwise known as a *freeze frame* or *frame grab*. NLEs can easily generate a freeze frame from any shot on the timeline, which you can then edit back into your sequence as a still. However, if you try to enlarge part of the freeze frame, it will look softer, as described above.

When working with interlaced formats, freeze frames may look ragged or show edge tear (see Figs. 1-11 and 5-17) if there's any movement between the two fields that make up the frame. In this case, you'll want to *deinterlace* the still (this command may be among the video effects). The NLE will discard one of the fields and, if you select the *interpolation* option, will fill in the missing lines with an approximation of what would be there if you had shot with a progressive camera. You'll usually want to deinterlace when making frame grabs (still photos) from your movie, say for publicity purposes. For more on deinterlacing moving footage, see p. 213 and p. 600.

Fig. 14-29. Multicam editing. For shoots in which multiple cameras cover the same action (like a concert shoot), some NLEs allow you to load the different camera angles in the same timeline and easily switch between them to create the edited sequence. Shown here, Edius NLE (with lines added for clarity). (Grass Valley)

MIXING AND CONVERTING FORMATS

Today it's common to work on projects that use footage shot in different formats or codecs. For example, you might be working on a documentary in HD that uses archival footage shot in SD. Or you might be working on a dramatic feature shot with a high-end HD camera that has some *B camera* (second camera) footage shot with a DSLR.

Sometimes filmmakers choose to work with mixed formats as a stylistic device, and sometimes they're forced to do so by circumstances of available equipment or preexisting footage. When you put different types of source material in a movie, the differences between them in look and feel will be accentuated anyplace there's a hard cut from one to another. This may serve the effect you're trying to achieve, or it may have the unintended result of making some of the footage look worse by comparison.

Most newer NLEs can play different formats or codecs in the same sequence, allowing you to mix and match. You choose one format (with a given frame size, frame rate, and codec) as the base for the sequence, and any footage that's in another format or codec is adjusted to play within the sequence. Though makers of NLEs like to claim this is a seamless process, you still may need to address various issues. First, while the NLE may indeed be able to play footage that was shot in different formats in one sequence, it may sacrifice some processing speed or stability. Some effects may not play in real time, but need to be rendered first. If mixing codecs is slowing things down, you might consider transcoding some or all of the footage to ProRes, DNxHD, or CineForm (see p. 558).

Even if the NLE can play different formats, you may still be dealing with differences in frame rate, frame size, aspect ratio, and other factors. In some cases the NLE may make automatic adjustments; in others, you may need or want to control things manually.

Frame Rate

Depending on your NLE, you'll need to set either the project as a whole or an individual sequence on the timeline to a particular frame rate or *timebase*. This is the basic frame rate for the movie, and any footage you're using that has a different frame rate will need to be converted to it. Sometimes material is converted from one frame rate to another when you import it into the NLE. Sometimes the footage itself is not really "converted"; you simply have clips with different frame rates on the timeline, and the NLE displays them at the project timebase (or attempts to) when you view the sequence.

As discussed in the next section, material shot in 24p can have pulldown applied to create 60i or other frame rates. Often, footage shot at 24p has pulldown added during recording (or, if shot on film, during video transfer), then the pulldown is removed in the NLE so you can edit at 24p. PAL material shot at 25 fps can be slowed down by 4 percent to match a 24 fps timeline.

Conversions between 24, 30, 50, and 60 fps are discussed below and in Chapters 2 and 16. Frame rate conversions are needed when going between NTSC and PAL, or between various HD formats. Not all frame rate conversions can be done successfully without motion artifacts. Interpolation can help, particularly when going from, say, 60i to 24p. Rather than simply throwing away some fields—which can cause judder—some fields are blended (combined), which can create smoother motion. Many NLEs and plug-ins offer frame blending or optical flow analysis (see p. 592) when slowing down a clip.

For some frame rate conversions, NLEs produce inferior results compared to more sophisticated software plug-ins or apps, or hardware devices like Snell's Alchemist or Blackmagic Design's Teranex system. Filmmakers sometimes have footage converted with specialized software or a hardware transcoder prior to editing, or they send selected material out to a post house for transcoding after the offline edit. Do some tests to see how the footage responds. In some cases you can download a free trial version of conversion software to check it out.

Frame Size and Aspect Ratio

When working in a format with a relatively large frame size (such as 4K, 2K, or HD), there may be times when you want to include footage shot in a smaller frame size. A classic case is when you want to use SD material—perhaps from archival stock footage—in an HD project. This can create two problems.

First, the SD frame has fewer pixels, so it will need to be scaled up to fill the HD frame. This will make it look less sharp and possibly noisy in comparison to the HD. This may be unavoidable.

Conversions can often be done with software or hardware devices. For example, you might be able to up-res from SD to HD using your NLE's scaler, a dedicated plug-in, or a separate application like After Effects, or you might send the footage out to a post house to be processed by a high-end hardware conversion system. Both software and hardware solutions vary in their sophistication and in the quality of the output.

Another potential problem is cutting together widescreen 16:9 material with nonwidescreen 4:3 material. This can happen with SD or HD movies. Several options are available for accommodating one aspect ratio within the other; these are discussed in Aspect Ratio Choices, p. 74. If you try to blow up the 4:3 footage so it fills the widescreen frame, that clip will have lower resolution and you'll lose the top and/or bottom of the image, which may be objectionable. Sometimes people display the SD as a smaller box centered in the HD frame to avoid scaling it up (see Fig. 2-12A). Some broadcasters won't allow this technique. You can also place the SD material over an HD background (such as a blurred, full-screen version of the SD shot) to avoid black side bars.

Generally speaking, downconverting from a high definition format (many pixels) to a lower definition format (smaller frame size) works much better than going the other way. When done right, the image often looks superior to native images in the lower def format. However, downconversion must be done carefully and the NLE may not be the best tool for the job. People making their own standard definition DVDs from HD masters are often disappointed by the results. Seek advice on the best settings for your software. Going up or down in resolution, if you just repeat or delete pixels you can get artifacts (one common up-resing technique is *line doubling*, which repeats existing lines of pixels, and a common but low-quality method of downconversion is *line skipping*, where entire rows of pixels are deleted).

Better systems use *interpolation* to calculate either a larger or a smaller set of pixels based on averaging adjacent pixels.

Interlace and Field Order

When editing interlaced footage, particularly when mixing different interlaced formats in the same sequence, you may need to check that the *field order* (also called *field dominance*) is set correctly. There are two types of fields in an interlaced frame. The *upper field* (also called *field two* or *F2*) contains the odd-numbered scan lines. The *lower* field (also *field one* or *F1*) is made up of the even-numbered lines. Field order refers to which field occurs first in each frame. Digital video formats derived from NTSC and all DV formats are "lower field first" or "lower field dominant." "Upper field first" is found in 1080i HD, video generated by computer graphics systems, and standard definition PAL. See Fig. 5-17 to get an idea of the two fields.

When creating a sequence in the NLE or when doing a reverse pulldown process on capture, it's also important to make sure the setting for field order matches the footage you're working with. If there's a mismatch between your sequence and footage you want to use, you may need to change the field order of some of your material. Sometimes if the field order is set incorrectly on a clip, it will stutter or the image will tear.

There is no field dominance or field order with progressive formats because there are no fields. Mixing interlaced and progressive formats in the same sequence doesn't seem to present any issues. All modern displays are progressive (including LCDs, plasma screens, and OLEDs) and have no problems showing interlaced video, which they convert on the fly to progressive. If you're preparing video for display on the Web, you should generally deinterlace any interlaced footage. Most NLEs have deinterlacing filters, you can get specialized plug-ins, and applications like Compressor and Adobe Media Encoder can also deinterlace.

Traditional CRT TVs are still in use in the world, and these will reveal some field-order problems in your movie that you won't see if you only watch on a progressive display. However, few editing rooms have a CRT around to check for errors. For more on deinterlacing, see p. 213.

Pixel Type

HD uses square pixels; SD uses nonsquare pixels. When mixing formats with different pixel shapes, to avoid distortions in the image you may need to convert some of the footage when importing it to the sequence. See Pixel Shape, p. 232.

Bit Rate

Many cameras record with 8-bit codecs. Some higher-end cameras and recorders operate at 10 or 12 bits. Editing in HD at 10 bits may mean converting to ProRes 4:2:2 or DNxHD 220, or working with uncompressed video. To avoid artifacts when downconverting from a high bit rate to a lower bit rate format, use *dither* (which may be an option with your software).

WORKING WITH 24P AND PULLDOWN

Be sure to read 24 fps Film and Digital, p. 82, before starting this section.

Since the introduction of sound in 1927, virtually all movies have been shot at 24 frames per second, and that continues to be the standard frame rate for theatrical movies and many other types of films. When NTSC television came along, the TV industry (at least in North and South America and Japan) adopted a different frame rate—essentially 30 frames per second (60 fields per second taking into account interlace). To convert movies shot on film so they can be broadcast on TV, the film is run though a *telecine*, which is a machine that scans the film frames and records them to video (see p. 676). But you can't simply speed up a 24 fps film to 30 fps for TV; if you did, motion would be unnaturally sped up, people's voices and music would rise in pitch, and a ninety-minute film would run for only seventy-two minutes.

Instead, using a process called *2:3 pulldown* (also called *3:2 pulldown*), every four film frames are recorded to five video frames (see Fig. 14-31). By distributing each group of four film frames in this way, the overall speed of the movie doesn't change, motion looks normal, and the resulting video can be edited like any other 60i video.[15] If you prefer to edit a film-to-tape transfer at 24 fps, you can do a *reverse telecine* process (also called *reverse pulldown*) to extract the 2:3 pulldown and restore the original film 24 fps in the NLE.

But pulldown is not used just for projects shot on film. Many digital cameras use an internal pulldown process to record 24p to 60i video. In part this is because 60i has been a standard for over sixty years in NTSC countries (originally as SD), and manufacturers want to ensure that their 24p format can be used with existing 60i-compatible decks and monitors. Broadcast and cable HD signals, for instance, are mostly 60i (720p broadcasting, which is rarer, being the exception).

Different types of pulldown can be used to convert between different frame rates. What they all have in common is the idea of changing the base frame rate without changing the overall speed of the footage, so the material after pulldown plays like the original as much as possible.

Let's look at different types of pulldown, with a particular focus on 24p because it can require special attention in editing.

Before proceeding, there are a couple of things to note that depend on where you live:

- Pulldown is a product of mismatched NTSC and film frame rates. In former PAL countries, the issue of pulldown was nonexistent, since film intended for TV was shot at 25 fps, the same frame rate as PAL. For a discussion of converting 24 fps to 25 fps in PAL territories, see Frame Rate and Scanning, p. 685.
- In former NTSC countries, bear in mind that when we talk about video frame rates in whole numbers, we mean rates that are 0.1 percent slower—so 30 fps really means 29.97 fps and 24 fps in video means 23.976 fps (some-

---

15. Actually, when film is converted to 60i, the speed *is* reduced by 0.1 percent. More on this below.

times written 23.98 fps). This is explained on p. 14. In the discussion below, round numbers are used but mean the lowered fractional rates, unless specified otherwise.

Native 24p

Some digital video cameras can record 24 fps "natively," which in this case means recording 24 progressive frames per second to nonlinear (nontape) media like memory cards, hard drives, optical discs, or SSDs. With Panasonic cameras, this is called "24pn" when recording to P2 memory cards. As an analogy, you could think of shooting film as a kind of native 24 fps format: you're simply capturing entire frames, 24 times a second.

Native 24p is simple and straightforward and allows you to record 20 percent more material on a memory card or hard drive compared to the pulldown methods described below. However, if you need to output the footage to a 60i format, then you need to apply one of the pulldown methods. Most cameras and decks that are capable of shooting native 24p can apply pulldown on output, which is useful for monitoring or rerecording.

Progressive Segmented Frame

Some cameras record 24p using a technique called *progressive segmented frame* (*PsF*), also called *segmented frame* (*sF*). With PsF, the entire frame is captured in one exposure at the camera's sensor and then split into two fields, each with half the horizontal lines, prior to recording. As a result, 24 PsF is recorded as though it were 48i (see Fig. 14-30). But the difference between PsF and interlace is that in PsF, both fields are captured *at the same moment in time* (as halves of a true progressive frame), instead of one field being exposed after the other, as in the case of interlace. In postproduction, you can recombine the two fields to remake the original, single progressive frame with no artifacts like the edge tear or aliasing that may result with interlaced material.

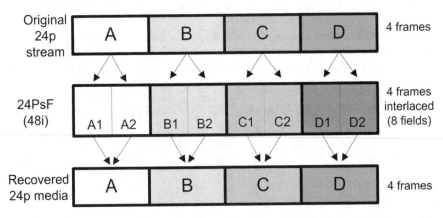

Fig. 14-30. Progressive segmented frame (PsF). The top line represents four frames of the original 24p stream captured by the camera. The middle line shows how each frame is divided into two fields for recording. Later, the 48i fields can be recombined simply to recreate the original 24p stream.

If 60i video is needed from 24 PsF, normal pulldown is done prior to output, with the segmented frames again treated as fields. The segmented frame method can be used with a variety of frame rates, including 25p and 30p.

24p Normal Pulldown (2:3 Pulldown)

As noted above, 2:3 pulldown is the traditional method used when movies shot on film are converted to video in former NTSC countries like the U.S. Many digital video cameras use the same technique to convert 24p to 30 fps (60i). The 24p video signal is processed within the camera so that every group of four frames is translated into five frames of 60i that can be recorded on tape or file. If you're planning to finish your movie on video at 60i, then using *24p normal* is a good pulldown choice; you'll get the look of 24 fps motion and can edit in the normal way you would with 60i. This pulldown is sometimes called *24p over 60i*.

To see how 24p normal works, take a look at Figure 14-31. The original 24p stream is shown at top. Each group of four frames (A, B, C, and D) is converted to five frames (ten fields) of video in the 60i stream shown in the middle row. Frames A and C are transferred to two fields each (which is what we'd expect in an interlaced format—two fields per frame). However, frames B and D are transferred to *three* fields each. This pattern, or *cadence*, is why normal pulldown is also called 2:3 or 2:3:2:3. The point of this whole operation is to create six extra frames every second, bringing us from 24 fps to 30 fps.

Normal pulldown creates smooth motion and is how most 24 fps material (whether from film or digital) is converted to 30 fps. For productions that will be edited and shown in 60i (without ever returning to 24p) you can work with the footage essentially like any other video material that originated in 60i.

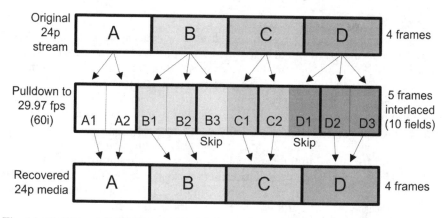

Fig. 14-31. Normal (2:3) pulldown. Again, the top line shows four frames of the original 24 fps material. The middle line shows how extra fields are added to create five frames of 60i. The bottom line shows how reverse pulldown (reverse telecine) works: by deleting two fields and combining others, the 24p stream can be rebuilt.

REVERSE 2:3 PULLDOWN. On some productions, the workflow is to shoot at 24p, use pulldown to convert to 60i (which might happen because the camera uses pulldown internally or because 24p video or film has been transferred to a 60i video format), and then do a reverse pulldown to return to 24p for editing (see below for more on why you might want to do this).

Not all NLEs can do reverse pulldown, also called reverse telecine. In some cases, pulldown and reverse pulldown can be done with software as a render process, but if you are capturing from tape and have a capture card or external hardware, reverse pulldown can be done on the fly in real time.

In Figure 14-31, reverse pulldown is represented by going from the middle row to the bottom row. The bottom row is the "recovered" or restored 24p stream in the NLE. Here's how it works: The first frame of the 60i has only two fields (A1 and A2), which are combined to restore the A frame in the bottom row. The same thing happens with the next frame of the 60i. But then things get a bit messier. There's an extra field—B3—that gets discarded. Then we find that the two fields of the C frame (C1 and C2) are split across two frames in the 60i. Then we have an extra D field to throw away.

For the NLE to do reverse pulldown, it needs to orient itself within the pattern so it knows which fields to save and which to discard. Notice that the A frame is special. It's the only frame of the 24p material that is transferred to exactly one frame of 60i (two fields with no timecode change between the fields). The A frame can be used as a marker to indicate the start of the pattern. Some NLEs can automatically recognize the A frame but in some cases you need to help the system locate the A frames (for more on this, see Managing Pulldown, p. 698).

When working with compressed digital formats that you are importing natively into the NLE (typically done with DV, for example), one disadvantage of 2:3 pulldown is that it requires decompressing frames 3 and 4 to extract the C frame. That is why *24p Advanced pulldown* was created.

24p Advanced Pulldown

Another pulldown pattern, called *24p Advanced* (which may be indicated as *24pA*), is similar to normal pulldown in that some frames of the 24p stream are transferred to two fields of 60i and some to three. However, Advanced uses a slightly different cadence. Instead of 2:3:2:3, the advanced pattern is 2:3:3:2 (see Fig. 14-32).[16]

The 60i footage that results is not quite as smooth as with normal 2:3 pulldown. Advanced pulldown can be thought of as a kind of intermediate format that is not meant to be shown at 60i, directly from the camera tapes or files. It's designed for material that will be edited at 24 fps, and its benefits come when converting back from 60i to 24p. With 24pA, reverse pulldown can be done simply and in real time with no decompression required. The camera sets a flag in the data stream, telling the system to simply discard the third frame in the 60i, leaving us with a tidy package of the original A, B, C, and D frames in compressed form.

Shooting in 24p Advanced can result in a higher-quality capture into the editing system and reduces the amount of data you need to store by 20 percent. It can result in a better end product if you plan to edit in a 24 fps timebase, but not if you're

---

16. If you have a 60i clip that came from a shot with 2:3:3:2 pulldown, you can recognize it because every group of five frames has one interlaced frame, whereas material shot with 2:3 pulldown has two. To tell which frames are interlaced, step through the footage one field at a time and look for unevenness between fields.

editing at 30 fps. There are various workarounds and conversion methods if you shoot in 24pA but would rather have 24p normal footage.

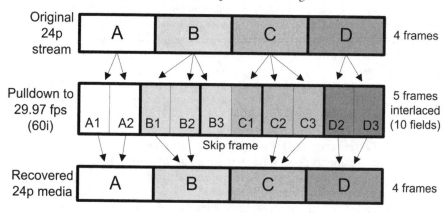

Fig. 14-32. Advanced (2:3:3:2) pulldown. Note the difference between this and Fig. 14-31. Instead of deleting separate fields B3 and D1 to re-create the 24p media, here we delete the entire third frame (B3 and C1), which makes for a cleaner, simpler reverse pulldown process.

24p and 30p over 60p

Cameras that record HD in the 720p format, such as Panasonic cameras using DVCPRO HD, employ another pulldown method to record at a variety of frame rates. In this system, the camera is *always recording* at 60p. To shoot 24p, the camera exposes images at 24 fps, then applies 2:3 pulldown internally to repeat one frame twice, then the next frame three times, and so on as it records the 60p stream (see Fig. 14-33). This method is sometimes called *24p over 60p*. If you want to do reverse

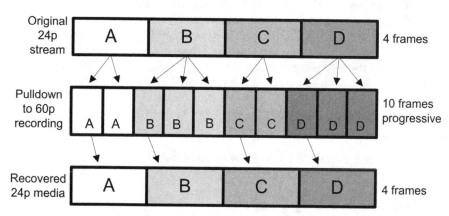

Fig. 14-33. 24p over 60p. The 720p HD format is always recording at 60 fps. When you shoot at 24p (top row), pulldown is used to record each frame either twice or three times in the 60p recording (and each recorded frame is a complete, progressive frame—not divided into fields as shown in Figs. 14-30, 14-31, and 14-32). To re-create the 24p stream, the system simply ignores the extra recorded frames in the middle row.

pulldown, the system knows which frames come from the original 24p stream and which are the repeat frames to be discarded.

A similar method can be used to embed other frame rates in the 60 fps stream. For example, if you shoot 30p, the system records two identical 60p frames at a time and ignores one of them during playback, giving you a 30p stream. In former PAL countries, the 720p format natively records at 50p, and can easily record 25p by repeating frames.

With some cameras, you can shoot at 60 fps with no pulldown. If you're editing at 24p, that footage can be used for 2.5x slow motion, much like shooting film at 60 fps (for more, see Slow Motion, p. 389).

Some Consumer/Prosumer Methods

A number of cameras don't shoot true 24p but offer various "fudged" methods that try to simulate something like it. Manufacturers may claim that these look a lot like 24p, but there are important differences.

Some Sony HDV camcorders offer a *Cineframe 24* mode (sometimes written *24F*). The camera's sensor captures 60i, from which fields are selected to simulate the motion of 24p. The result is that motion is uneven, which any attempt at a reverse pulldown will reveal to the discerning eye. This is a consumer-oriented feature that should not be confused with true, professional 24p and should not normally be used for blowup to 35mm or bump-up to HDCAM for the festival circuit.

Sony's *Cineframe 30* and *Cineframe 25* modes function in 60i and 50i camcorders, respectively, by dropping one field and doubling the other—the same technique found in slow shutter speed effects in Sony camcorders. Some may feel this simulates the motion blur of 30p and 25p but at half the vertical resolution (since you're recording only one of each two fields). The loss of resolution may or may not bother you depending on the application.

Some Canon HDV camcorders offer a 24F mode in which the camera records at 48i, deinterlaces to 24p, then adds 2:3 pulldown to create 60i. While impressive to many, this method doesn't deliver the resolution of true 24p.

Cameras from other manufacturers have various types of frame modes to simulate progressive recording or frame rates in which they don't really operate. Experiment with them to see if you like the look, but ask questions about how they work so you'll know whether they might cause problems for you later.

EDITING 24P FOOTAGE

How you edit 24p material depends on the kind of project you're doing, the workflow you choose, and the equipment you have.

Working in a 24p Project

When working with footage that originated at 24p, be it film, 24p compressed or uncompressed HD, or a RAW format, it's often best to edit at 24 fps on the NLE. This is sometimes referred to as working in a 24p *timebase*. Editing at 24p is well suited to making a 24p end product, like a 24p DVD or Blu-ray or a 24p master for theatrical screenings. This is also a good choice when you're doing an offline edit and want to return to the 24p original material for the online, to make a digital intermediate, or to cut film (for more on these, see Chapter 16). If you make a 24p master, this can be a good source from which many other formats (60i, 50i, 25p) can be created.

SPEED CONSIDERATIONS. As mentioned above, virtually all HD and SD cameras operating at "24p" in former NTSC countries are actually recording at 23.976 fps, which is often rounded to 23.98.[17] If you recorded sound in the video camera or with a separate audio recorder, you should have no problems with sync as long as you edit using a 23.976 timebase.

However, film projects in the United States are traditionally shot at *exactly* 24 fps. Film footage is then generally slowed down to 23.976 in the telecine when transferred to any type of video. Regardless, projects shot on film are sometimes edited at 23.976p and sometimes at true 24p. The choice will affect the way audio speed adjustment is handled. This is discussed on p. 690. Note that slowing the sound to match the picture is often referred to as "pulling down" or "pulldown," but this is different from the pulldown discussed above, which means changing the picture frame rate.

TIMECODE CONSIDERATIONS. In some workflows, 24p HD or film material is transferred to a 60i tape or file format before capturing to the NLE. Keep in mind that the 24p timecode used in the original footage and in the 24p nonlinear editing sequence is not the same as the 30-frame timecode of the tape or files. The count of hours, minutes, and seconds will be the same, but the frame count won't be, since with 24 fps there are 24 frames each second and with 30 fps there are 30. The editing system may be able to make the conversion automatically, but care needs to be taken that pulldown is done correctly and that the timecode of the NLE sequence does indeed match the original 24p source (ultimately, you'll be doing the online with the original material, and it's imperative that timecode of the clips in the sequence is identical). This is especially critical when working with film (see Editing Film Digitally, p. 696).

Working in a 60i Project

When producing a movie that will be shown in 60i (say, a television movie), or if your project uses a lot of 60i footage (for example, existing archival material), you may want to edit at 60i instead of 24p. In this case, any 24p material you're using can have 2:3 pulldown applied and then be treated as 60i footage.

Keep in mind that if you edit 24p material at 60i, and then go back to do an online with the original 24p footage, there may be slight cutting discrepancies between the offline NLE sequence and what you end up with in the online. These errors come from the difference between the 30-frame timecode used in the sequence and the 24-frame timecode of the original source footage. For more on this concept, see Matchback from a 30 fps Project, p. 702. For this reason, you may want to plan your workflow to transfer any 24p footage to 60i for use as a source for the finished edit.

17. Some high-end digital cinematography cameras can be operated at exactly 24 fps.

FINISHING AND OUTPUT

Now you're done editing (you've "locked" the picture) and you're ready to get the movie out of the NLE and into the world.

Final Products and Versions

Different projects can have very different needs when it comes to finishing. You may just be outputting a short video to share on the Web, and with many NLEs the finishing process is highly automated and very simple. On the other hand, you could be delivering your project to a broadcaster or distributor who will have specific technical requirements and request different versions and deliverables (see p. 758). For a typical independent film, you may potentially need:

- High-quality master file of movie.
- HDCAM or other tape format for broadcast or film festival use. Whenever tapes are involved, you'll want a *master tape* to store safely and *clones* to use for actual distribution. You'll want at least one of each for every version of the movie.
- Textless version. If you hope to distribute in a foreign country, you'll want a version of the project that has no on-screen text or titles over picture. Sometimes you do this by building a "clip reel" that contains a second copy of any shot that has text over it, but without the text. (Alternatively, you can remove the text from the movie itself, but include those shots with text at the end so a foreign distributor or broadcaster can see how the text should look.)
- Sometimes nonwidescreen (4:3) versions of a widescreen movie are required. In SD, this might involve both full-height anamorphic and letterboxed versions.
- Audio tracks. Audio deliverables are discussed on p. 673. For more on preparing audio tracks for foreign distribution, see Foreign Release, p. 673.
- For theatrical distribution, you may need a Digital Cinema Package (see p. 625) and/or 35mm film prints (see Chapter 16).
- Compressed files for the Web. You may need versions in different codecs, audio formats, sizes, or bit rates for YouTube, Vimeo, Hulu, and others.
- DVDs and/or Blu-ray Discs. A typical retail disc will have extras including deleted scenes, commentary, and other features.

Planning Your Workflow

As you prepare to finish your project, take some time to plan out your path. You may be doing everything yourself on your own system or you may be preparing to send your project out to sound editors, mix studios, online facilities, and transfer houses. No matter what your route, seek advice about how to accomplish the tasks for finishing. If you're doing the work by yourself, consult manuals, do some research on the Web, and talk to people about the best workflow. There are lots of "gotchas" to be avoided: hidden settings that need to be changed; equipment that's incompatible; technical requirements you're unaware of.

If you're working with outside facilities, it's absolutely essential that you start with them and work backward so you can deliver what they need. Ask them about their preferred workflow, file formats, track layouts, frame rates—anything. Many facilities have instructions posted on their website about how they want materials prepared. There's no "standard operating procedure" when it comes to postproduction; it all depends on the particular project, equipment, software, and techniques being used. See p. 733 for the business aspects of booking an online edit session.

If you've been working with a simple online workflow (with no separate offline edit) on your own NLE, you may be ready to export the movie directly to a finished file, the Web, a DVD, Blu-ray, or even a videotape master.

Or you may be using an offline/online workflow, in which case you're getting ready to do the online edit. This may involve linking to higher-resolution media on your NLE or moving the project to a different system—perhaps at a postproduction facility where you'll do the online edit. For the basics of offline/online workflow, see p. 37 and p. 556.

The next sections are about managing your media and project and the steps involved in preparing for an online edit. Many of these steps also apply to situations in which you want to share your project with another editor, or when you want to archive the project for long-term storage.

If you're not doing a separate online and are ready to output your movie, you may want to skip ahead to p. 614.

Color correction is a central part of finishing a project, and it may be done on the NLE before output, during the online edit, or later. This is discussed on p. 626.

MANAGING MEDIA

Managing your media and other files is a central part of getting ready for an online edit, moving the project to another computer, or archiving a project when you're done with it.

File Types

Let's review the types of files the NLE uses:

- *Source media files.* The video and audio media files imported from the camera tend to be very large and therefore the most difficult to store and move around. Often, some of the media files are excluded when preparing for an online edit or archiving the project (more on this below).
- *Project files.* With most NLEs, the project file contains all the bins, clips, and sequences.[18] Project files tend to be relatively small, since the clips and sequences only point to the media files and don't actually contain them. It's usually a good idea not to delete project files or clips, as they may come in handy later. However, if there are many clips and sequences you rarely use, it can be a good idea to store them in a separate project.

18. In FCP X, each project contains only one sequence.

- *Render or precompute files.* These are created during editing and can easily be deleted and rerendered later if needed. Old, unneeded render files have a habit of piling up on the hard drive if you don't occasionally clear them out. Corrupted render files often cause playback problems. Many NLEs have a tool or command to identify unneeded render files so you can delete them.
- *Other media.* You may have imported graphics, stills, music, sound effects, and other media that have become part of the project.

Many NLEs have a system or tool for working with media. Avid has its *media tool*; Premiere Pro has a media browser and Adobe Bridge. Final Cut Pro X has its event library. These tools can simplify the process of moving or deleting files. When you need to manually move media or render files, often it's best to do it with the media management tools in the NLE rather than accessing them directly via Windows Explorer or the Mac's Finder, though tasks and NLEs vary.

Preparing the Movie for Finishing

Your movie is on the timeline. Editing decisions are done. The final steps of finishing await. Just to remind you one more time, all the clips in the sequence are merely "pointers" that link to the actual media files—the files that contain the video and audio (see Media Files and Clips, p. 552). Sometimes people use the word "clip" to refer to both the pointer and the media file, but it's important to make the distinction.

Before doing anything more, duplicate the sequence, put the copy in a new bin, and use the copy for the next steps. In Final Cut Pro X, you'd duplicate the project and store it outside of the Final Cut Projects folder (so FCP X can't see it). The original is now safely stored away.

Often, when you're finished offline editing, there are still a number of clips in the sequence that serve no function. For example, audio clips that you made silent, or video clips hidden under another clip on the timeline that are never seen in the movie. Delete those so they don't add unnecessary media and work.

If you're making a master file for broadcast use or for sending to another facility, see p. 621 for instructions on adding color bars, slate, and countdown, and resetting the sequence timecode.

For instructions on handling the audio portion of the sequence, see Chapter 15.

PREVENTING ERRORS. Because various things can go wrong during the finishing process (especially if you're moving the project to another system), it's a good idea to make a copy of the movie as you now have it; this can serve as a check against errors later. Typically you might export a self-contained QuickTime file of the sequence, sometimes with burned-in timecode. For the online session, if there is one, the offline movie can be loaded as one video track in the online NLE. This is sometimes called a *guide track*, a *reference track*, or a *reference movie*. A guide track helps prevent errors and shows the online editor your intentions for any effects that don't automatically carry across to the online.

Consolidating Media

If you need to work on your movie on a second NLE (either because you're coediting the project with someone else or because you're going to a postproduction facility for the online edit), typically you'll put a copy of your media files on an external drive and bring it to the other system.[19] If you're coediting, the other editor will normally want *all* the media. If you're doing an online, you'll only want to copy the media *actually used* in the final movie. *Consolidating media* is the process of gathering your media files together into one location (Premiere Pro calls it *collecting* files), often with the option to delete or exclude any unused material. Different NLEs do this in different ways, with somewhat different terminology.

To distinguish what you need from what you don't, remember that when you first imported media from camera files or videotapes, each master clip was at its full length, and all the media files were taking up space on the hard drive. However, now the movie has been edited; many clips didn't make it into the movie, and of the ones that did, you may have only used a small section. In some cases when you consolidate, the NLE can create new, shorter clips of just the portion you used, and it will exclude anything that's not part of the final sequence. Avid's *consolidate* command can do this. Avid also has a *select media relatives* command that can help you identify all types of files being used by a sequence or clip, in case you want to move or delete unused files.

Getting rid of unused media is sometimes called *trimming*. You can trim individual timeline sequences or, depending on your NLE, an entire project (which may contain more than one sequence). You might trim a project prior to archiving to delete unused footage and preserve only the media files you actually ended up working with.

If you trim or shorten sequences as part of the consolidating process, you'll generally want to leave a little wiggle room to adjust things later. This can be done by adding one- or two-second *handles* to the timeline clips, giving you some extra media at the head and tail of each clip (you won't see the handles in the movie, but they're available for future edits if needed). Not all NLEs can add handles, but if yours can, it's usually an option when consolidating.

Moving and deleting media files should always be done with utmost care. However, keep in mind that as long as you have a safe copy of the original, full-length media files or camera tapes, and an intact copy of the project file, you should be able to rebuild your original sequence even if you accidentally delete some media files. This assumes your files are well organized, of course. In the event of a disaster, timecode on the media is invaluable too, although not all of your sources will have the benefit of timecode. Sources without timecode include music clips, sound effects, and stills for animation, and these may or may not have to be painstakingly reinserted into the timeline, depending upon the situation and the capabilities of the NLE.

Linking to Higher-Resolution Media

You may have chosen to do the offline edit with a low-res copy of the footage (see Editing at a Lower Data Rate, p. 559). When it's time for the online, you'll want to link the sequence to the full-resolution original media.

If the high-res media files have already been imported to the NLE, this process

19. Assuming you're not working with a shared storage system, in which case moving the files is not necessary.

may be very simple. You *unlink* or separate the clips in the sequence from their low-res media files. This is sometimes called "making a clip offline" (this use of "offline" doesn't refer to offline editing—it just means that the clip is no longer connected to its media file). You then instruct the NLE to *relink* to the high-res media files.

If the footage came from videotape, the workflow often involves unlinking the clips, then trimming the sequence to create new, shorter master clips of just the footage actually used in the movie (as described in the previous section). Avid's *decompose* command can do this. In Premiere Pro, you can use the Project Manager to "create new trimmed project." You create a new project with shortened master clips, then *batch capture* the original tapes at full resolution. Batch capturing is just an automated process in which the NLE puts the clips in order by reel number and timecode, captures them all, and alerts you along the way when to put the next tape into the deck.

Moving the Project to Another System

You may want to move or copy the entire project (including all the bins, clips, and sequences) to another NLE for editing, or you may be ready for online editing and want to bring only the final sequence to the online NLE, perhaps at a postproduction facility. If the two NLEs are running the same software (or sometimes different applications by the same brand), then the transition from one machine to the other can be very simple. If your system and the one you're moving to use different software, then things may be more complicated.

WHEN BOTH NLEs ARE THE SAME. When you're moving or sharing the project between two machines using the same NLE and OS (operating system), they'll both be able to handle the same media files and the transition between one system and the other should be seamless.

As an example of porting a project from one system to another, look at the Duplicate Project screen from Final Cut Pro X in Figure 14-34. The first option, *duplicate project only*, makes a copy of the project but doesn't include any source media files (you might choose this if the media files were already on the second system). The second option, *duplicate project and referenced events*, would copy the project as well as *all* the media in the event library collected for use in the project. The third option, *duplicate project and used clips only*, copies only the media files *actually used* in the project timeline. You're now ready to work on the second machine running Final Cut Pro X.[20]

WHEN THE TWO SYSTEMS ARE DIFFERENT. Perhaps the most common reason you'd move a project between different systems is that you're doing an online in a post facility that uses a different NLE. Or you might want to do graphics, compositing, or audio work using applications that aren't NLEs. Re-creating an offline project on an online finishing system is called *conforming*.

The key issues in moving between systems are, first, that in order to play back

---

20. Note that this doesn't work between legacy versions of Final Cut and FCP X. Also, as of this writing, the third option will exclude unused media files, but it won't trim or shorten the included files to the length actually used in the project.

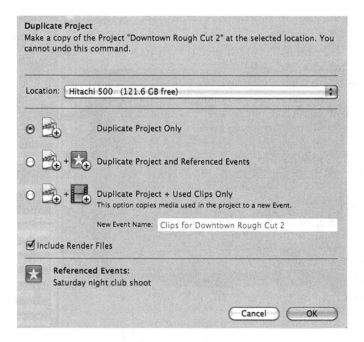

Fig. 14-34. When you duplicate a project in Final Cut Pro X, or move it to another system, you have a choice to duplicate the timeline clips without any media (top button); duplicate the timeline clips and *all* the media files in the event library associated with that project (middle button); or copy the timeline clips and only the media files *actually used* in the timeline. With the last option, FCP X doesn't trim (shorten) media files; it just excludes entire files not used in the project. (Apple, Inc.)

your movie, the NLE needs to be able to read the source media files (the actual pictures and sounds). Different NLEs are designed for different file formats and wrappers (see p. 242). Sometimes they can handle each other's media; sometimes they can't. You may have to rewrap media files to make them compatible, or you may have to import or capture them a second time from the original sources.

The other issue is that the NLE creates a vast array of instructions about the edited sequence: the length and order of the clips, effects, transitions, levels, titles, colors—you name it. All these instructions are metadata (see p. 242). Unfortunately, one brand of NLE can't necessarily read the metadata from another or reproduce the effects, titles, or color correction created on the other system.

There are ways to standardize data so it can be passed from system to system. Formats such as AAF, OMF, and XML are designed to create a common language that applications can use to talk to each other. Programs such as Boris Transfer Suite can move metadata between different applications (for example, when transferring sequences between Adobe After Effects and Avid or Final Cut Pro). An app called 7toX can convert a project from Final Cut Pro 7 to FCP X.

In planning your postproduction workflow, some of your decisions will be based on translation concerns between different systems. These are some of the possible situations you'll encounter:

- You can move the sequence and related metadata from one system to another, along with the media files themselves. This "one-stop shopping" can be a real timesaver. An example is exporting an OMF or AAF of your audio tracks with embedded media.[21]
- You can move the sequence from one system to another but not the media. This means you'll have to reimport the media on the second system. If you were planning to reimport or capture the media anyway for a high resolution online, this may be the best way to go. Sometimes you'll actually prefer to send just the sequence (perhaps over the Internet) without the media embedded, because the media files are so big.[22]
- You can send only an EDL. The edit decision list (see Fig. 14-41) contains the basic information about clip In and Out Points, reel numbers, and a few effects. This is a far more limited information set than what's contained in a sequence, but sometimes it's all one system can take from another. Using the EDL, the finishing system can reimport the media and conform the sequence. For more on EDLs, see p. 632.
- You can send only the media. When there's no communication between systems, all you can do is send the movie or footage itself. For example, you might output your movie from the offline system to a file and import that into the online system.

EXPORTING A FILE

When it's time to export or "share" your movie from the NLE, today that usually means creating a file. Files can be made at different quality levels. You might need a full-quality, full-sized master file for broadcast use. Or you might be making a compressed, lower-quality file for mobile devices or the Web. Many NLEs and other applications have presets or automated workflows that allow you to export with just a few clicks, including uploading to YouTube or other sites. In other situations, you may need to carefully manage the details of the file you're creating.

WHAT'S IN A FILE. When we make a movie file, we're really making three elements: a container file inside of which live a video file and an audio file (see Fig. 5-32).

To create the video file, we typically compress (encode) the video with a particular codec (for more about codecs, see p. 19 and p. 250). As an example, video for the Web is often compressed with the H.264 codec. In some cases, files are created with uncompressed video (requiring no codec).

Similarly, the movie's audio may be exported as an uncompressed file (called linear PCM) or it may be compressed with an audio codec. AAC (Advanced Audio Codec) is commonly used for the audio in Web movies.

Finally, the encoded video and audio files are wrapped together in a container

---

21. In some cases, not *everything* in a project translates correctly. For example, titles may be in the wrong font, or audio levels may be lost.
22. Media without timecode may need to be replaced manually.

(for more on wrappers, see p. 242). MPEG-4, QuickTime, and WebM are all container formats. The wrapper must be compatible with the intended playback system (more on this below).

As a filmmaker, you'll want to be sure the file you're making will work for its intended use. If you're using one of the NLE's presets for exporting a file, that may work fine. However, you'll want to check that the codec(s), wrapper, file size, or other details are compatible with the system or recipient you're sending the file to.

Making a Master File

Outputting a master file could mean making a top-quality file for a broadcaster or distributor, or it could be simply the best copy of your work that you'll use to make other types of files. What constitutes best quality? First of all, if you've been editing in a lower-resolution format than the original camera files or tapes, you should up-res to the full-resolution material before outputting the file (this is an offline/online workflow, described earlier in the chapter). If you've been editing natively in a highly compressed, long-GOP codec like H.264, it's a good idea to output the master in a much less compressed codec such as ProRes 422, ProRes HQ, or DNxHD.[23] You won't gain quality by transcoding, but given that later stages of distribution will involve more cycles of compression and recompression, the image will hold up better in the long run (for more, see p. 558).

You could also output without any compression, making a "full-bandwidth" uncompressed master. The advantage is no compression artifacts, though you will be hard-pressed to see any difference between an uncompressed file and one of the high-quality versions of ProRes or DNxHD. Uncompressed is a "universal format" in the sense that people don't need to have any particular codec on their system to play it. The disadvantage of uncompressed is enormous file sizes and the related need for fast storage to work with the material.

An alternative to exporting video files is to export an *image sequence* (also called a *numbered image sequence*), particularly when large frame sizes (2K, 4K, sometimes HD) are involved. This creates a separate file for each frame using a file format such as DPX, TIFF, or PICT and stores them together in a folder. Each file is numbered so the system knows the proper order. This is sometimes done when preparing a digital intermediate, for example. The vast amount of data created by an uncompressed image sequence is often stored on a tape backup system such as DLT. Audio is exported separately. Later, an NLE or other app can convert the image sequence files back to motion video.

At times you need to export an individual shot rather than the whole movie at top quality. For example, a feature film might have editors, animators, and special effects people all working on the same shot. To pass the footage back and forth, a file of the shot may be created using little or no compression for maximum quality.

PREPPING AN EDIT MASTER. Some master files begin at the first frame of the movie (with nothing preceding it) and end at the last frame. If you're uploading to the Web, this may be all you want. If you're preparing a project for broadcast,

---

23. Other intermediate codecs that can be used for mastering include AIC (Apple Intermediate Codec), Animation, and CineForm.

on the other hand, elements such as color bars and tone, a slate, and a countdown leader may be expected (see Managing the Output to Tape, p. 621, for a format used by many post houses). If you prepare the sequence with these elements, reset the starting timecode of the sequence in the timeline so the program itself (after the countdown) begins at 1:00:00:00 timecode.[24] If you ever need to export just the movie itself without these elements at the head, you can simply select the movie itself with an In Point at the first frame of action before exporting.

Compressed Files for the Web and Devices

You'll likely need to make compressed files for use on the Web, mobile phones, tablets, game boxes, or anywhere else that lower-data-rate, fast-streaming video is required. As a rule, some picture quality is sacrificed to make files smaller and easier to store and transmit.

This topic is tricky to address in a book, since technical standards are evolving as you read this. One major development is HTML 5, which is replacing earlier standards for how Web browsers interact with video. Also, as more people get high-speed ("high-bandwidth") Internet connections, Web videos keep expanding to higher data rates and larger frame sizes. For example, YouTube allows you to upload 4K footage, a vast increase from only a few years ago.

For many filmmakers and consumers, posting video to the Web or creating a file to be shown on an iPhone or iPad couldn't be easier. Simply use one of the preset selections in your NLE or compression software, then save the file to your desktop and upload to the Web. As long as your software is up to date, this can work fine.

However, in some situations manually controlling the compression process will give you better quality, or allow you to create a file that's optimized to a particular website or use. For full control you'll want to use a dedicated compression program like Adobe Media Encoder or Apple Compressor or one of the free programs like HandBrake or MPEG Streamclip. Check the specifications of sites you are uploading to so you can deliver the optimal files for their system.

Whenever you make a compressed file, be sure to test it on your own system to check that it looks and sounds the way you want it to before uploading or sending it off.

The following are some general considerations and guidelines for making compressed files for the Web and various devices. Even as standards evolve, these categories will give you a basis to check out the latest practices.

SOURCE FILE. Start with as high a quality of file as possible. If you've been editing with the camera files natively you might choose to encode directly from your timeline in the NLE. Or, if working from an exported file, avoid heavy compression prior to creating the Web encode.

CONTAINERS AND CODECS. When uploading your movie to a video sharing site, you may have a lot of flexibility in what codec and container formats you use (as an example, look at YouTube's instruction pages for the wide range of formats it accepts). Other sites, like Vimeo, have a more limited set of preferred

---

24. In Europe and the UK, programs often start at 10:00:00:00 timecode.

formats. Investigate the requirements of whatever sites you're using so you can supply each one with optimal files to maintain best quality. They will generally recompress and/or rewrap your files, often to H.264.

Video sharing sites create video that's compatible with most browsers. If you're creating files for your own site, you could choose to embed a video you posted to a sharing site (more on this below) or you could upload a file directly. Use a broadly supported format. As of this writing, perhaps the most flexible combination is to encode video with the H.264 codec, encode audio with AAC, and use an MPEG-4 container (when people talk about compressing to H.264 this is usually what they mean). This is playable on Apple devices, and H.264 is compatible with the video players used on many sites.

As HTML 5 is implemented, in theory things may become more standardized, but as of now it's not clear which browsers will support which formats. Many will support H.264 and most should handle the open-source WebM container format and Vorbis audio codec. A quick search on the Web will turn up recommended codecs and wrapper formats for different browsers in HTML 5.

DATA RATE. When you encode video and audio, you'll usually have a choice about the data rate of the encoded file (see p. 236 for more on data rates). Generally speaking, as the data rate goes up, so does the quality (to a point). However, high data rates can choke the playback system, frustrating viewers who have low-bandwidth connections.

Different video sharing sites have different recommended data rates for submitting material, depending on the size of the video and other factors. For example, as of this writing Vimeo recommends limiting the data rate of SD material to 2,000 kilobits per second (Kbps) and HD material to 5,000 Kbps. When calculating data rates, keep in mind that the total bandwidth equals the video bit rate plus the audio bit rate (each is encoded with separate settings).

Variable bit rate (VBR) encoding can produce better quality with a lower data rate. This requires two passes for the encoder: one to analyze the footage and one to encode.[25]

When using MPEG codecs with interframe compression, you have a choice of how often to set a *keyframe* (this is the I-frame; the distance between one and the next determines the length of the GOP—see p. 247). Normally you can let the compressor set keyframes automatically. Or you can manually increase the distance between keyframes, which decreases the file size but could lead to playback problems.

RESOLUTION (FRAME SIZE). The frame size depends a lot on the website or platform where the file will be viewed. Check for recommended sizes. The larger the image size, the larger the file and the more data that users must download. Large sizes like 1080p may cause systems to choke when displaying the video on a smaller screen.

Use care when downconverting a higher-resolution source to a smaller frame size (for example, when compressing an HD source to SD or smaller frame sizes).

25. Some servers and playback devices require constant bit rate (CBR) encoding.

Artifacts can result if done poorly. Use higher-quality resizing settings in the compressor. For more, see p. 599.

PIXEL TYPE. The Web and most HD platforms use square pixels (pixel aspect ratio 1:1, or 1.00), which works well with most HD camera formats, since they also use square pixels. If you have an SD source or other material that has nonsquare pixels (like 1080 HDV and DVCPRO HD), it will need to be converted to square pixels while encoding (for more, see p. 232). Sometimes this is a factor in choosing the encoded frame size. For example, to display a nonwidescreen 720 x 480 SD image correctly at full size on a computer, it may be encoded as 640 x 480 to compensate for the conversion to square pixels.[26]

ASPECT RATIO. HD is natively 16:9, which should display well on most platforms. If you have any material that's been letterboxed, try to find the original source before the letterbox was applied to use for encoding. If unavailable, crop out the black bars on top and bottom before encoding. Similarly, if you have 4:3 material that's been pillarboxed in a 16:9 frame, crop out the black bars on the sides.

INTERLACE. If your material is interlaced, deinterlace it during encoding to create progressive files. Use better-quality deinterlace settings in your compression software to avoid artifacts and maximize resolution (see p. 213 and p. 600).

FRAME RATE. Encode using the same frame rate as the original footage whenever possible. If you edited at 24 fps, use a 24p source for encoding. If the movie had 3:2 pulldown applied, use reverse telecine to restore to 24p for encoding.

COLOR SPACE AND GAMMA CORRECTION. After compression, the picture may look too dark or the contrast may be off. This can result from the color space conversion from HD or SD video to RGB color space. Also, downconverting to a smaller frame size sometimes makes colors look more intense. Do a test. You may need to adjust gamma settings. Also, if blacks look noisy, *black restore* may create a clean, dark black and improve the overall encode. Unfortunately, different websites may display the same video with very different contrasts.

AUDIO. As of this writing, audio on the Web is typically 44.1 kHz sample rate. See above for information on data rate and codecs.

SELF-CONTAINED AND REFERENCE MOVIES. When you want to export a movie from the NLE to make a compressed file for the Web or a DVD, with some NLEs you can simply send the movie directly from the NLE's timeline to the compression app and go on working with the NLE. With other systems, that process, or compressing using the NLE itself, ties up the NLE until the compression is done. It's often better to export a file from the timeline in its native format, then import that file into the compression or DVD app.

To export the file from the NLE, it's often a good idea to use a QuickTime file

26. Anamorphic widescreen (16:9) SD would be 853 x 480.

(file name extension is .mov). There are two types of QuickTime movies you might use. A *self-contained movie* contains all the video and/or audio in one file and can be sent and played on its own. Self-contained movies are the simplest and safest, because they don't rely on any other files to play. You must use this option whenever you're sending a file from your system to someone else. However, if you're simply passing a file from one app to another on your own system, it's often better to make a *reference movie*. QuickTime reference movies don't contain any media themselves; they simply point to media files stored elsewhere on the system (much like clips on the timeline point to media files). Making a reference movie can save time and requires less storage space on the hard drive.

ADDING METADATA. In some cases when encoding or posting files you can add keywords that help search engines find your files on the Web, as well as information about copyright, licensing, and so on.

Posting on the Web

Once you've made a file for the Web, what's the best way to get it out there? One popular method is to upload to a video sharing site like YouTube, Vimeo, or Myspace—there are dozens of them. People can discover them there, or you can include links on your own website or Facebook page to the posted video. If you want the video to appear in a player on your site or blog, you can copy the *embed code* from the sharing site and paste that into the code on your site (it's not hard). The advantage of this method is that even though the video appears on your site, the video itself is *hosted* by the other site (the files reside there and are played from their server). That gives you less to worry about in terms of compatibility with different browsers, and you can handle high traffic if a lot of people watch your video. Some of these sites allow you to restrict who can see the video (including password protection), which other sites can embed it, what the player looks like, and so on. You may have to pay extra for these features.

Another alternative is to post it directly on your own site in a simple video player. This is also not difficult and may give you more control over how things look. Posting directly on your site usually means your Internet service provider (ISP) is hosting the video on its servers, and may charge extra fees if your videos get a lot of traffic.

OUTPUT TO TAPE

Videotape is now used far less for shooting, but as of this writing it still plays a part in postproduction and distribution, including broadcast and film festivals. Tape remains a convenient and inexpensive way to store and transport movies.

This section is about getting a movie out of the NLE and onto tape, which sometimes requires some editing. However, traditional editing between two videotape machines is discussed at the end of the chapter.

Different filmmakers and projects have different needs when it comes to getting the movie onto tape (sometimes called doing a *layover*). For a school project, you might need to dump the movie from the NLE to tape so you can screen it for your classmates. However, when creating an edit master tape for broadcast or other high-end use, you'll need to position the movie precisely by timecode and be sure there are no flaws in the output, which calls for a high level of care. Since a deck for outputting may only be needed for a day or so, filmmakers who don't have one may rent a deck. In some cases it's simpler, and maybe cheaper, to export a master file from the NLE and bring it to a post house and have its technicians record it to tape, especially when a high-end format like HDCAM SR is involved.

How you actually do the output depends in part on your approach and in part on the tools you have to work with.

Fig. 14-35. HDCAM deck. This high-end Sony VTR records high definition HDCAM SR. (Sony Electronics, Inc.)

Assemble and Insert Recording

All digital video decks and camcorders can do basic *assemble-edit* recording. In assemble mode, the VTR records everything at once: video, audio, timecode, and a control track if there is one. With assemble editing, anything on the tape beginning at the point where you start recording is erased. If you want to record a tape straight through without stopping, assemble mode works fine.

The limitation of assemble-mode recording becomes apparent when you record a shot, stop, then record a second shot. Whenever you stop recording there is a break, which can make the picture go blank or break up. You can begin the next shot cleanly with a digital VTR as long as the editing system rolls back over the outgoing shot (called *preroll*) and gets properly up to speed before editing in the incoming shot. A greater limitation of assemble editing is that you can't edit in *just* audio or *just* video. With every assemble edit, *all* the tracks get replaced (audio, video, and timecode).

True editing decks have a recording mode called *insert-edit* recording.[27] In

27. Note that this use of "insert" is different from insert edits used in NLEs. In fact, insert editing with a tape deck is much more like *overwrite edits* with an NLE.

"insert" mode, you have a choice between recording video, any combination of audio channels, and/or timecode. Insert recording does not automatically erase anything on the tape—you get to choose what is replaced and what remains from any previous recording. Prior to recording you must prepare the tape with continuous control track and timecode. This is variously called *blacking* a tape, *striping* a tape, or *blacking and coding*. With continuous control track, you can insert a shot in the middle of the tape and expect it to edit in and out cleanly. Not all NLEs, decks, and formats support insert recording (particularly in DV). In a typical professional editing setup, insert recording is done with RS-422 device control (see p. 550).

NLE Editing Modes

Depending on your NLE and your video deck, you may have various options for how the NLE and VTR interact.

The simplest way to output to tape is to play back the sequence from the NLE timeline and *crash record* to a deck or camera that isn't controlled by the NLE. You put a tape in the deck, manually press record, then play the sequence on the NLE. Of course, the deck and NLE need to be connected with the proper cables; for DV, for instance, all you need is a simple FireWire.

A better way to output is to have the NLE control the deck and the recording process. Different NLEs use different terms for this, including *print to video*, *export to tape*, *edit to tape*, and *digital cut*. This requires a deck that supports timecode. The NLE will usually allow you to mark In and Out Points on the sequence and/or the tape.

Managing the Output to Tape

If you're using insert editing to record the master tape, you need to prepare it by blacking it first. Many NLEs have a setting to do this. Some decks can black a tape by themselves, or they use a black signal from an external sync generator. If you're using assemble editing, you don't need to black the whole tape in advance, but you should black at least 30 seconds to provide a clean start point for the recording. With crash recording, no tape preparation is necessary.

Depending on your system, you may be able to preset a starting timecode for the tape using settings on the deck or in the NLE.

Professional edit masters have a standard order of color bars, a slate, and a countdown leader at the start of the program. You might build these elements into the sequence on the NLE timeline, or you might edit them separately onto the master tape. Some NLEs can include them automatically on output.

The following are typical elements at the head of a master tape:

1. Begin the tape at 00:58:30:00 timecode ("fifty-eight minutes, thirty seconds") and record 30 seconds of black leader.
2. Then come color bars and tone (see below) for one minute (from 00:58:30:00 to 00:59:30:00), followed by 10 seconds of black.
3. Then put in a 10-second video slate (create a title card that identifies the project name, production company, running time of the movie, date, aspect ratio, audio channel assignments, etc.).

4. At 00:59:50:00 place a clip of a ten-second countdown leader (your NLE should have leader or you can find one on the Web). The countdown displays numbers every second from 10 to 2, with a single-frame beep (tone) in the audio at each second—or at least on the number 2—so you know the picture and sound are in sync. Since video and audio may get separated and remarried during postproduction, it helps to have this visual check. Following the 2 (which is a single frame) is black and silence. If you don't have a countdown leader, just put black in its place.

5. The program begins exactly at 01:00:00:00 ("one hour," also called "one hour, straight up"). If you are editing a project that will be finished on film, see Preparing and Delivering Tracks, p. 655, for guidelines on leaders.

Your NLE should be able to generate color bars. Use HD bars or, for standard definition, SMPTE (NTSC) bars or EBU (PAL) bars, as appropriate. The audio reference tone as indicated on a digital/peak-reading meter is typically set to –20 dBFS for professional projects in the U.S., –18 dBFS in the UK. The equivalent as read on an analog/VU meter is 0 dB. Whatever the level of your reference tone, it's a good idea to note it on the slate and/or elsewhere in the packaging. For more on reference tones, see p. 452.

At the end of the movie, you should include 30 seconds of black so the program ends cleanly and has padding at the end. You may want to include a few frames of color bars several seconds after the film ends as a signal that it's over and as a tail sync mark.

Consult your NLE manual for instructions on output settings, including audio channel assignment, deck control, timecode settings, and others. It's imperative that the sequence play out of the NLE cleanly with no *dropped frames*, which appear as a stutter or instantaneous black. There may be a setting to *abort output on dropped frames*, which is a good way to avoid dropped frames you might not see. To minimize dropped frames, do an *audio mixdown*, which essentially creates a single, easy-to-play render file of all the audio. Most NLEs will automatically render all video effects prior to output; if not, you can do so manually. Close all sequences but the one you're playing. Consider breaking a long movie into shorter sequences or reels. Interframe codecs like HDV and H.264 may require a long rendering process (sometimes called conforming) before output. See p. 249 for possible workarounds.

When outputting to tape, it's very important that you watch the movie as you do so for technical problems. After recording a tape, be sure to set the *record-inhibit* device on the tape cassette to prevent accidental rerecording or erasure.

CREATING A DVD OR BLU-RAY

See DVDs and Blu-ray Discs, p. 34, before reading this section.

We're all familiar with DVDs, which play standard definition video.[28] In 2006,

---

28. It is also possible to store an HD file on a DVD; it won't play in a DVD player but can be played on some computers.

Blu-ray Discs (BDs) were introduced, which can handle both HD and SD content and have much larger storage capacity. Blu-ray players can play both BDs and DVDs, but DVD players can only play DVDs.

DVDs and BDs are useful at many different points in the filmmaking process. You might burn a DVD from your NLE to output a rough cut. You might burn a BD for festival screenings. You might make twenty copies of a trailer for fundraising purposes. Or you might have a replicator manufacture twenty thousand units of the finished movie for retail distribution. Each of these uses calls for a different approach to making the disc.

The simplest DVDs can be created with a stand-alone disc recorder. You feed it video and it records in real time. Very straightforward, but limited in menus and controls.

Burning a DVD or BD directly from your computer gives you much more control over the product. You need a DVD or BD burner in the computer or as an external unit. There are many easy-to-use programs (like iDVD for DVDs) that are highly automated and have simple drag-and-drop tools for making menus.

Authoring a DVD or BD, as it is understood in the industry, means building menus, setting chapter markers, and dealing with various forms of extras, such as sound tracks in different languages, director commentary, deleted scenes, and all the other features that add value to the disc. Prosumer and professional apps provide much more control over authoring and offer better compression, which affects picture and sound quality. If you send your project to a professional DVD facility, a *compressionist* may go through the movie, determining the proper compression level for different shots and scenes.

When you need a limited number of discs (up to about one thousand), generally the process is to compress the video, then burn that file onto a recordable disc type, such as DVD-R or BD-R. This is known as *duplication*. This is what you do when you burn your own discs; you can also have duplication done quickly by an outside supplier. With duplication, it's not hard to make changes and burn a new version when needed. The disadvantages of duplication include higher per-unit costs for discs (though it's still cheaper for small runs) and the fact that recordable discs may not play well in all disc players. When making BD-R/RE discs, for example, playback reliability can depend on the particular software, burner, or player being used.

When you're making a larger number of discs, rather than copying ("burning") files directly to writable media, a *glass master* is made first, which is then pressed (stamped) onto commercial-grade discs. This is called *replication*. This process takes longer and the glass master is an additional charge, but the manufacturing savings per unit make up for it when dealing with mass quantities. Replication is how standard retail discs are made and ensures reliable playback across all players for DVDs and BDs.

Discs can be packaged in a number of ways. The classic, folding *Amaray case* has a clear plastic sleeve. In it you can insert a cover, which you can print yourself, or you can have a supplier offset print one for large runs.

With BDs, you need to pay a licensing fee to sell discs recorded with the format, in addition to replication fees. A replication house can help you navigate the fees and get the most flexible deal. See Chapter 17 for more on distributing DVDs and BDs.

Encoding a Disc

Whether you burn your own discs or send your movie out to have DVDs made by a supplier, it helps to understand some of the technical issues involved.

The user's experience of the disc comes in part from the packaging, menus, extras, and such, but perhaps the most important aspect is the picture and sound quality. In compressing the movie for a DVD or BD, some of the same issues discussed in Compressed Files for the Web and Devices, p. 616, apply here as well. Compression can be done with some NLEs, with separate compression applications, or with DVD creation software. Applications vary in quality and in their ability to control aspects of the encoding. With DVDs, there is only the MPEG-2 codec, but with BDs you have a choice of codecs (see p. 34).

As a rule, you want to use the least amount of compression that will allow the movie to fit on the disc. Your software will normally have presets based on how long the movie is; shorter projects get encoded at higher quality. If you're setting data rates yourself, look into proper settings for maximum and average data rates; these will affect picture quality and how smoothly the disc plays. Don't push the limits of the format; use somewhat lower settings. If you're having discs replicated instead of burning your own, you may have more flexibility; talk with the replicators.

Encoding with multipass, variable bit rate (VBR) compression takes longer, but it can deliver better quality at lower bit rates. As for audio, Dolby Digital provides excellent quality with much smaller files than uncompressed PCM.

Recordable discs include DVD-R, which can be recorded once, and DVD-RW, which can be erased and rerecorded many times (the equivalents with Blu-ray are BD-R and BD-RE). Since BDs are more expensive, you might experiment with a BD-RE to be sure everything's okay, then burn BD-Rs. Inevitably, lots of plastic gets wasted in the process of making a working disc. Buying discs in bulk is cheaper per disc.

If you're making a number of identical discs, rather than encoding, formatting, and burning them one at a time, there are better approaches. With some DVD programs, instead of burning a disc directly, you can export a *disc image*, which is a file that appears on the desktop as a virtual hard drive (volume). If you make a disc image, you only have to format the project once. You can play the disc image with your computer's DVD player application to make sure everything works. Then simply burn the image to as many DVDs or BDs as you need (on a Mac, this is done using Disk Utility).

A replicator will print labeling info and graphics right onto the disc. If you're making your own, you can get a professional look by buying printable discs (they usually have a white surface) that you can use with certain inkjet printers. Don't use stick-on paper labels as they can unbalance the disc and interfere with playback.

Not all recordable Blu-ray Discs will play on all players, and DVD-Rs can have playback issues even if they're supposedly compatible with the player. Whenever you burn your own discs, test each one to be sure it plays properly without glitches and has no *navigation* problems (when the menus don't get you where they should). Try your discs in a different machine than the one you recorded on.

Another compatibility issue comes from the Hollywood studios that divided the world into different "regions" to limit piracy and control markets. DVD players in different parts of the world scan for region codes on the disc and, unless they are multiregion players, may not play another region's DVDs. Region 1 DVDs are made for North America; Region 2 discs play on European machines; and Region 3 is for parts of Asia. Region 0 discs are—in theory—playable everywhere. Note that this coding has nothing to do with differences between actual video standards like NTSC and PAL (which create other incompatibilities when you want to send discs to foreign countries).

Ripping a DVD

Sometimes you may want to extract video from a DVD to use in a project. If this isn't one of your own discs, or one that you have permission to use, this may be a violation of copyright. However, there are circumstances when using content from a commercial DVD is legal; for example, there are fair use exemptions that permit breaking the encryption on commercial DVDs (see Fair Use, p. 742, for more).

Extracting the files from a DVD is called *ripping*, and various free programs such as HandBrake can rip a DVD and transcode the MPEG-2 TS (transport stream) video, which is not playable in a typical NLE, to other formats. Don't expect the quality of these files to be as high as other video that hasn't been so compressed. You may need to try a few programs (do a search online) to find one that can break the copy protection of an encrypted disc (called *decrypting*).

CREATING A DIGITAL CINEMA PACKAGE

A *Digital Cinema Package* (DCP) is a standardized set of files for showing movies digitally in commercial theaters equipped with a server (hard drive) for digital cinema projection. The DCP specifications, which include picture, sound, and file formats, are determined by Digital Cinema Initiatives (DCI), a group created by Hollywood studios to transition theaters to digital, which will eventually make distribution via 35mm film prints obsolete. These standards are intended for global use, and already over half of American theaters can screen a DCP. If you're planning theatrical distribution in larger theaters—and if you hope to qualify for Academy Awards consideration in the U.S. using a digital source instead of a film print—you'll need to create a DCP from your movie. For projects that have been shot on film, a DCP is typically made from a digital intermediate (D.I.; see Chapter 16). For projects shot digitally, the DCP can be made from your master file of the movie; often the color is adjusted with a LUT tailored to digital cinema projection.

A DCP can be made from standard digital cinema formats including Full HD (1920 x 1080), 2K, and 4K (see Fig. 1-7). Some are flat (1.85:1 aspect ratio); others are Scope (anamorphic 2.39:1), in either 2D or 3D. Lesser-resolution formats like SD and 1280 x 720 must first be upscaled to be included in a DCP.

A Digital Cinema Package can support common frame rates of 24, 25, 30, 48, 50, and 60. Note these are true integer frame rates only (23.976 is no longer directly supported). As of this writing, most films distributed as DCP are shot at 24 fps, but if you shoot 23.976 fps, no problem. Conversion to true 24p is readily available at most post houses.

DCP compression is 12 bits per pixel using the JPEG 2000 codec (intraframe, wavelet based) along with an MXF wrapper. Color space is wide-gamut XYZ. The DCP audio format is uncompressed 24-bit PCM at either 48 kHz or 98 kHz. Sound is typically in a 5.1- or 7.1-channel configuration (see Mix Formats, p. 669).[29] DCI standards also include subtitling as well as encryption to protect against piracy.

Typically you'll have a professional mastering facility create your DCP and help you meet the quality and technical requirements, but if you search the Web you can find commercial tools as well as some open-source, home-brew solutions to creating DCP files. A DCP is typically delivered on a hard drive. For more on DCPs and Academy Awards regulations, see the Bibliography.

COLOR CORRECTION

Some people think of color correction (also called *color grading*) as just another video effect, but its importance in the production process warrants special consideration. Adjusting the overall color and brightness values in your movie, and fine-tuning individual clips, can be critical to both how the movie plays for the audience and where it can be shown. Color correction fills many purposes:

- *Establishing an overall look for the movie.* Do you want bright saturated colors, or are more muted, pastel shades better suited to the story? How much contrast do you like? Is there an overall color cast you want for the film or certain sections of it?
- *Maintaining consistency from shot to shot.* Most scenes are made up of several shots. It's important that these shots feel like they belong together and flow from one to the next (this is especially crucial for dramas). A wide shot of a character might cut to a close-up filmed on a different day, but both are supposed to represent one moment in time. It's essential that the two shots match in color and feel.
- *Correcting errors.* A shot may be over- or underexposed, or be too blue or red because improper white balance was used in shooting.
- *Ensuring that the movie is broadcast legal.* Broadcasters have very particular requirements about luma (brightness) and chroma (color) levels. If you're making a video for nonbroadcast use, these levels are useful guidelines.[30] If you're intending to get your movie on TV, video levels must be within specified limits. Similarly, if you're planning a film-out or DCP for theaters, there will also be target levels.

Color correction is both an art and a science, and a good *colorist* is essential to supporting and enhancing the work of the director of photography, the editor, the art director, and, of course, the director. Many filmmakers know the importance of a sound mix not just in polishing the film, but telling the story. Color correction can be equally critical.

Color correction is a delicate thing. You're trying to create a look that reveals

---

29. For Academy Awards qualification you need *at least* three audio channels (left, center, right) and not merely two-channel (left, right) stereo.

30. If your project will be shown *only* on computer monitors and never on video, you have more leeway in setting levels.

the content and expresses the emotion of the movie, while working within technical limitations that can be quite restrictive at times. A shot that looks great to you often exceeds legal levels. Talented colorists find a way to capture the feel you're looking for while keeping the signal "safe." Aesthetically, there's no one "right" color balance—it's up to the filmmakers to decide what serves the story best. Technically, however, there definitely are "wrong" choices that will cause broadcasters or other gatekeepers to reject the project.

How color correction is done depends on the project. For a small video project, you might just go through the sequence on your NLE, tuning things up before exporting to file or tape. For a larger project, rough corrections might be done during the offline edit, with final color correction done in the online edit, where high-end tools, monitors, and external scopes are available. Sometimes color work is done after the online, in a room dedicated to the task, using an image processor such as a DaVinci system (see Figs. 14-36 and 16-7).

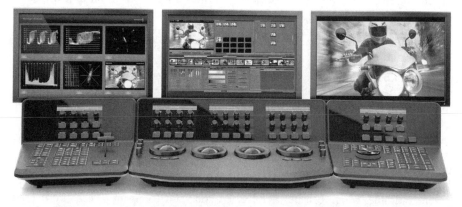

Fig. 14-36. DaVinci Resolve color correction system. (Blackmagic Design)

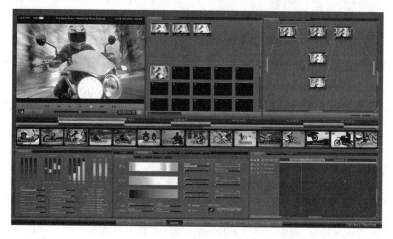

Fig. 14-37. Color grading screen in DaVinci Resolve. Resolve is available as a free, Lite version; as a software app; and as part of a full system with control surface. (Blackmagic Design)

You can also purchase tools, such as Red Giant's Magic Bullet Suite, that offer a universe of different looks and feels with a few clicks.

Whether you do color correction yourself or have an editor or colorist do it, it helps to understand what's involved. For an overview of terms, see Chapter 8 and the discussion of exposure and contrast in Chapter 5.

Color Correction Tools

MONITORS. The most important tools for color grading are your eyes and a monitor you can trust. If you're working on a project that will be shown on TV or via DVD, Blu-ray, or any video format, you must use a monitor properly set up to display component ($Y'C_BC_R$, also called YUV) color space (for more on this, see Video Monitors and Projectors, p. 216). A professional facility will usually have a high-end reference or broadcast monitor. At minimum, you need a decent monitor that has been calibrated correctly (see Appendix A). Having a blue-only setting for calibrating to color bars helps enormously. If the color in your monitor is off, decisions you make about color correction will be too.

You should also have consistent illumination in the room (usually a dim but not dark room) without window light that changes during the day.

SCOPES. Various devices for monitoring the video signal may be built into your NLE or attached separately. The *waveform monitor* (see Fig. 5-3) is used to measure luma (luminance) levels, which correspond to brightness. A *vectorscope* gives a visual display of color (see Fig. 8-3). You can use it to read the hue (sometimes called phase), which is a measure of the particular color—for example, to determine whether it is more blue or red. Both vectorscope and waveform monitors can be used to display the chroma level (also called saturation), which is a measure of the intensity of a color. An *RGB parade monitor* can show you relative levels of red, green, and blue, which can be useful when you want to ensure there's no overall color cast.

Many NLEs have a feature that will indicate clips in the timeline that exceed legal video limits for brightness and color so you know what needs fixing.

CONTROLS. NLEs and image processing systems vary widely in their color correction toolset. You may have a choice between using a very simplified (or automated) set of controls and using a more powerful control panel. Color correction in an NLE is almost always nondestructive (you can change anything later).

Sometimes there's a set of three controls for blacks, midtones, and whites (highlights). Each might have a color control to adjust hue and saturation and a slider to increase or decrease the brightness of that tonal area (see Fig. 14-38).

If there's a color wheel, move the color balance toward the color you want or move it directly away from one you don't want. For example, to fix a shot with a green color cast, move the control toward magenta. Experiment with changing saturation and hue separately. Sometimes a color looks off, but the problem isn't the color itself (the hue), only that there's too much of it (excess saturation).

Some NLEs include gamma controls, which primarily affect the contrast of the midtones. Some NLEs let you manipulate gamma curves in individual color channels. These take some experience to work with.

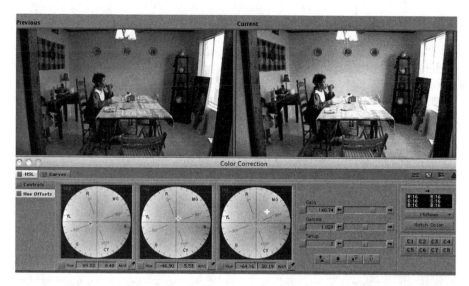

Fig. 14-38. This color correction tool in Avid Media Composer allows you to adjust color and level of the shadow areas, the midtones, and the highlights individually. Other controls affect the image globally. (Avid Technology, Inc./Steven Ascher)

Often you'll have several shots that need the same color correction. You should be able to save the setting from one shot and apply it to others. This may involve dragging a color correction of the first clip to a bin, where you can save it to use later. It's also helpful to compare previously corrected shots with the one you're working on; some systems allow you to display frames from a few different shots at a time. Some newer NLEs can automatically match color balance from one clip and apply it to another; this works better with some shots than others.

Staying Legal

If you're working on a project that will be seen exclusively on the Web, mobile devices, and nonbroadcast outlets, then you have the freedom to adjust color and brightness pretty much as you like. If you'll be showing your work in any component video form—DVD, Blu-ray, tape, video projection, or broadcast TV (including cable)—keep in mind that any elements such as graphics or titles created with a graphics program in RGB color space may appear too bright or with oversaturated colors in video and may need to be adjusted accordingly (see Fig. 5-12).

If you're preparing a movie for broadcast, contact the broadcaster for its technical requirements. In the United States, PBS guidelines are often considered a standard (see the PBS Red Book at www.pbs.org). Technical requirements include a wide range of items including video levels, aspect ratio, audio levels, and channel assignments—be sure to discuss them in advance.

As a rule, for digital HD the luma level should stay below 100 percent on the waveform monitor. Black level on a digital system can be no lower than 0 percent. On some NLEs, the waveform monitor is marked in digital bits instead of percentages. For an 8-bit picture, the video level should be between code 16 (0 percent) and

235 (100 percent). Chroma level on the waveform monitor should stay below 110 percent.

Many NLEs have a filter or effect that ensures that luma and chroma levels stay within legal limits. Avid has a *safe color limiter* (as well as other methods to keep colors safe). Premiere Pro's *broadcast colors* effect is similar.[31] These types of effects are an easy and simple way to guarantee levels are legal. One potential drawback is that the filter may clip highlights (resulting in lost detail) in some situations where it would be better to lower the video level manually. Some people adjust levels manually but throw the broadcast filter on the entire sequence at the very end just to be sure everything's safe (which may be done by nesting the entire sequence or creating a compound clip and applying the filter to the whole thing).

Color Correction Techniques

As long as luma and chroma levels are within any applicable legal limits, it's up to you to set the color and contrast. See p. 191 for a discussion of video levels and contrast.

Generally speaking, you want to be able to see detail in important parts of the scene, without clipping the highlights or crushing the blacks. Sometimes you have to sacrifice the shadow areas to bring highlights within safe limits. Conversely, you may decide to bring out shadow detail and let some highlights be clipped.

A pleasing image usually contains a full tonal range from dark to light. If an image has muddy blacks or flat whites, start by setting your black levels with the "black" or "shadow" part of the color control. Make sure they are really dark, but not so much that a lot of detail is lost. Then adjust the white levels so they max out around 100 percent. Many NLEs have an auto-contrast button that will do essentially that (or separate controls for auto-black and auto-white). You might start with the automatic adjustment, then tweak from there. Then adjust the mid-tones to look pleasing, using the midtones slider or, in some cases, with a gamma adjustment. With some NLEs, you can display the full gamma curve and tweak it manually.

As for color, usually the most important thing is to get the flesh tones right. Warmer flesh tones are often the most flattering, but if Caucasian skin gets too red, cheeks can look flushed or ruddy. Cool tones might be used for a darker or more sinister look. Some vectorscopes have a *flesh tone line* (*I-bar*), which helps in setting Caucasian skin tones.

To establish the overall look, you may choose to increase saturation for more vivid color, or desaturate for more pastel shades (extreme desaturation takes you all the way to monochrome, otherwise known as black-and-white).[32] Actually, black-and-white is often deliberately given a slight color cast for a warmer (think sepia) or cooler look.

Some systems have an *eyedropper tool* that lets you click on a color that should be

---

31. Premiere's filter will also remove unsafe RGB colors that fall outside the NTSC or PAL gamut.

32. Some applications, like Photoshop, have a black-and-white filter that allows you to adjust how color converts to monochrome, which can be very useful for separating, say, a red area from a blue area that would otherwise have the same tone in black-and-white.

white and reset it. This can be handy for correcting a shot that has an overall color cast or poor white balance. An eyedropper can be used to match any tone from one shot to another.

In some scenes, you'll make an overall correction to get flesh tones right but find that something else (say, clothing or the landscape) no longer looks good. Many systems can do *secondary color correction*, which targets a particular area or color without affecting the scene as a whole (you can repaint the walls without affecting the couch).

Many NLEs have a *sharpening* filter, which isn't technically a color correction, but used sparingly can save a slightly out-of-focus shot.

Though individual scenes or sections may call for different looks, generally speaking you want to create a consistent look throughout the movie. If you later find that the project looks different on another monitor (perhaps because yours was off), you can make a global adjustment to tweak the whole movie at once.

Fig. 14-39. Vignette effect. By selectively shading the edges of the frame you can add dimensionality to a scene that has flat lighting. The look is exaggerated here so you can see it, but a subtle vignette can be effective even if not consciously noticed by audiences. During color grading, scenes can be essentially relit in post. (Steven Ascher)

COLOR SPACE. Different types of color space are discussed above and in Chapter 5. Some systems can automatically compensate when converting from, say, 709 HD video to RGB. High-end systems may offer custom *lookup tables* (*LUTs*) that map how the color or brightness of the pixels in one format or version will be rendered in another, allowing precise control over tonal values. Starting with the same master, you might use one LUT when doing a film-out, another when creating a Digital Cinema Package, a third for HD television, and so on.

TAPE EDITING

Traditional video*tape* editing—from one tape deck to another—is pretty rare at this point. However, aspects of tape editing continue to play a role in postproduction. See Editing on Tape, p. 38, before reading this section.

Tape Editing Systems

Tape editing systems are based on the idea of using two or more VTRs and a controller that operates them. The *source* or *playback VTR* plays the raw video footage while selected portions are rerecorded on the *record* or *edit VTR*. Usually there are two monitors to view the material: the *source monitor*, which shows what's playing on the source VTR, and the *record/edit monitor* (also called *program monitor*), which shows the edited program.

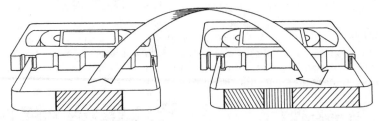

Fig. 14-40. A basic video edit. When editing from the source tape to the edit master, each edit can be described by four points: Source In and Source Out specify which part of the source tape to use, and Record In and Record Out indicate where the shot is to be placed on the edit master. (Robert Brun)

Making an Edit

Tape editing systems, like NLEs, work by three-point editing (see p. 579). Using the edit controller, you select the In Point (sometimes called *Mark In*, *Video In*, or just *In*) of the shot you want to use on the source tape. You then go to the end of the shot and mark the Out Point (also called *Mark Out*, etc.). See Figure 14-40. You have just marked In and Out on the source side (*Source In* and *Source Out*), and since you will be rerecording this shot onto the edit master tape, you need to tell the record deck where to put it. You now roll the record deck to the point where you want the shot to begin and mark this In Point (*Record In*).

Normally you'll be recording using insert edit mode (see p. 620). You can now select "preview," and the controller will rehearse the edit for you, allowing you to see how it looks. If you're happy with the preview, you then select "edit" and the controller will perform (execute) the edit. It's always a good idea to review an edit after you make it to ensure that everything worked mechanically and in terms of the picture or audio transition you were hoping for.

THE EDL AND ONLINE EDITING

Today, even if VTRs are used as sources to play tapes in the online, the edit master will usually be assembled on an NLE. When you do both the offline and the online edit with an NLE, it maintains a lot of information from the offline about effects, titles, color correction, and so on that can be carried forward digitally to the online (see Managing Media, p. 609).

However, if you do offline editing with two tape machines, the information transfer to the online is much more limited. When you're done with a tape offline, you can have the system generate an edit decision list (EDL). The EDL is like a road map you use in the online to reconstruct what you did in the offline. It indicates the In and Out Points by timecode of every bit of video and audio that came from the camera source tapes and shows exactly where each piece is to be recorded on the online edit master.

If the EDL is done properly, you can go into the online session with the source tapes and, by following your list of numbers, rebuild the edited movie from scratch. The machines should be able to use the EDL to *auto-assemble* (also called *auto-conform*) the show. EDLs are sometimes used when conforming high-resolution files or tapes when making a D.I.

Keep in mind that an EDL works only with sources that have timecode. If there's anything in the movie that comes directly from a nontimecoded source (such as music from a CD, scratch narration, or computer-generated graphics), you'll have to reedit these manually in the online session. Whenever possible, rerecord every element that lacks timecode onto a timecoded format before you edit it into the offline program.

An EDL is basically a list of numbers arranged in a particular column format. Standard EDL formats include CMX 3600, which is common, and GVG and Sony. All EDLs include the following data about each edit (see Fig. 14-41):

- *Edit number.* A sequential number to help locate edits. Sometimes called event number.
- *Source reel.* Tells you on which tape to find the source material. This is generally the camera tape number (reel number) if the movie was shot in video. If shot on film, the source reel is the telecine transfer reel (which may have more than one film camera roll on it). Use numbers, not names, for reels (see p. 571).
- *Edit mode.* Indicates if the source for the edit is *V*ideo, *A*udio, or *B*oth. A1, A2, etc., indicate which audio channel to use.
- *Edit type or transition.* May be a *C*ut, *D*issolve, *W*ipe, or *K*ey.
- *Duration.* The length of the transition, in frames. Cuts, being instantaneous, have no duration.
- *Playback In and Out.* Also called *Source In* and *Out.* These tell you the beginning and end points of the source material to use.
- *Record In and Out.* These give you the timecode address on the master tape or sequence where the source material is to be recorded.

Edit Number	Source Reel	Edit Mode	Edit Type	Dura-tion	Playback In	Playback Out	Record In	Record Out
001	004	B	C		04:22:14:02	04:22:31:15	01:00:00:00	01:00:17:13
002	005	A1	C		05:06:30:11	05:06:31:09	01:00:16:11	01:00:17:13
003	005	B	C		05:06:31:09	05:06:42:02	01:00:17:13	01:00:28:06

Fig. 14-41. Information typically contained in an edit decision list (EDL). The column headings and lines have been added here for clarity. The events in the EDL may be listed in the order they appear in the program (A-mode) or be grouped by source tape (B-mode).

There are different ways to structure an EDL, which can affect how the online is done. The events in the EDL can be listed in the order they appear in the program (*A-mode*) or grouped by source tape (*B-mode*).[33] In an A-mode assembly, you start at the beginning of the show and work your way down. This is the least efficient because the same source tape must be inserted in the VTR multiple times, with time wasted for threading and unthreading. Doing a B-mode assembly means recording all the shots from a given source reel at a time, then moving on to the next source reel and capturing all the shots from it. *C-mode* is a variant of B-mode that pulls shots from individual source reels but takes them in ascending order on each source reel instead of the order in which they appear in the movie.

33. This use of "mode" is different from the edit mode discussed on p. 633.

CHAPTER 15

Sound Editing and Mixing

This chapter is about sound work in postproduction. Be sure to read Chapter 13, for issues of dialogue editing. Recording and processing sound is discussed in Chapters 10 and 11.

The Idea of Sound Editing and Mixing

Sound editing refers to the process of creating and refining the sound for a movie in postproduction. *Mixing* is the process of enhancing and balancing the sound. On a large production, sound editing is generally done by specialized *sound editors* who are not involved in the picture editing. The team may include different editors working specifically on music, ADR (see p. 532), sound effects, or Foleys (see below). A *sound designer* may create unique textures or effects. On a small production, the same people may do both picture and sound editing.

Sound is often treated as an afterthought, something to be "tidied up" before a project can be finished. But sound is tremendously important to the experience of watching a movie. An image can be invested with a vastly different sense of mood, location, and context, depending on the sound that accompanies it. Some of these impressions come from direct cues (the sound of birds, a nearby crowd, or a clock), while others work indirectly through the volume, rhythm, and density of the sound track. The emotional content of a scene—and the emotions purportedly felt by characters on screen—is often conveyed as much or more by music and sound design as by any dialogue or picture. Even on a straightforward documentary or corporate video, the way the sound is handled in terms of minimizing noise and maximizing the intelligibility of voices plays a big part in the success of the project.

It is said that humans place priority on visual over aural information. Perhaps so, but it's often the case that film or video footage that is poorly shot but has a clear and easily understood sound track seems okay, while a movie with nicely lit, nicely framed images, but a muddy, harsh, and hard-to-understand track is really irritating to audiences. Unfortunately for the sound recordists, editors, and mixers who do the work, audiences often don't realize when the sound track is great, but they're *very* aware when there are sound problems.

The editing of dialogue, sound effects, and music often evolves organically during the picture editing phase. While the dialogue and picture are being edited, you might try out music or effects in some scenes. You might experiment with audio filters or equalization and often need to do temporary mixes for test screenings. Nonlinear editing is *nondestructive*, which means you can do many things to the sound and undo them later if you don't like the effect.[1] For some projects, the picture editor does very detailed mixing in the NLE, which may be used as the basis for the final mix.

Fig. 15-1. Mix studio. (Avid Technology, Inc.)

Even so, sound work doesn't usually begin in earnest until the picture is locked (or nearly so) and the movie's structural decisions are all made. The job of sound editing begins with the sound editor screening the movie with the director and the picture editor. If you're doing all these jobs yourself, then watch the movie with a notepad (and try not to feel too lonely). In this process, called *spotting*, every scene is examined for problems, and to determine where effects are needed and where a certain feeling or quality of sound is desired. A spotting session is also done for music, with the *music editor*, the *composer* (who will create music), and the *music supervisor* (who finds existing music that can be used, and may play a larger role in hiring or working with the composer). If the music spotting session is done prior to effects spotting, you'll have a better sense of which scenes need detailed effects. Spotting information can also be noted with markers directly in the sequence in the editing system (the markers can later be exported as a text list if desired).

The sound editor or editors then begin the process of sorting out the sound. The audio is divided into several different strands or tracks. One set of tracks is used for dialogue, another for effects, another for music, and so on. Portioning out different

---

1. A few effects do in fact alter the captured audio files—avoid those until the final mix and/or be sure to save a copy of the original clip (prior to applying the effect) on the timeline.

types of sounds to separate tracks makes it easier for the mixer to adjust and balance them. This process is called *splitting tracks*. Effects are obtained and other sounds are added, building up the layers of sound; this is *track building*.

When all the tracks have been built, a sound mix is done to blend them all back together. Enhancing the way the tracks sound in the mix is sometimes called *sweetening*. The mix may be done in a studio by a professional mixer, or it may be performed by the filmmaker using a nonlinear editing system (NLE) or a digital audio workstation (DAW). A professional mix studio (also called a *dub stage* or *mix stage*) is designed with optimal acoustics for evaluating the audio as it will be heard by audiences. Though more costly, studio mixes are preferable to mixes done in the editing room or other multiuse spaces that may have machine noise, poor speakers, or bad acoustics. For theatrical and broadcast projects, it's essential to mix in a good listening environment. Also, professional mixers bring a wealth of experience about creating a good sound track that most filmmakers lack. Nevertheless, with diminishing budgets and the increasing audio processing power of NLEs and DAWs, many types of projects are successfully mixed by filmmakers themselves on their own systems.

After the mix, the sound track is recombined with the picture for distribution. Different types of distribution may call for different types of mixes.

THE SOUND EDITING PROCESS

How sound is handled in postproduction depends on the project, how it was shot, your budget, the equipment being used, and how you plan to distribute the finished movie.

As for the tools of sound work, the distinctions between the capabilities of an NLE, a DAW, and a mix studio have broken down somewhat. For example, some NLEs have powerful sound editing capabilities. A DAW, which is a specialized system for sound editing and mixing, might be just another application running on the same computer as the NLE. And a mix studio might be using the same DAW, but with better controls, better speakers, in a better listening environment.

For most video projects, the *production audio* (the sound recorded in the field) is recorded in the video camcorder along with the picture. For some digital shoots and all film shoots, the audio is recorded double system with a separate audio recorder. For workflows involving double-system sound, see Working with Double-System Sound, p. 589, and, for projects shot in film, Chapter 16.

The simplest, cheapest way to do sound work is just to do it on the NLE being used for the picture edit. For many projects this is where *all* the sound editing and mixing is done. Audio is exported as a finished sound track, either with the video or separately (to be remarried to the picture if a separate online edit is done). This method is best for simple and/or low-budget projects but is often not a good idea for complex mixes.

Even when following this workflow, you might also make use of a specialized audio application, like a version of Avid's Pro Tools, that works easily with your NLE.

Fig. 15-2. Digital audio workstation (DAW). Most DAWs, including the Pro Tools system shown here, can be used for movie track work and mixing, as well as creating music. (Avid Technology, Inc.)

For the most control, audio is exported from the NLE and imported to a full-featured DAW for track work and mixing. Depending on the project, this may mean handing over the project from the picture editor to the sound department. Or, on a smaller project, you might do the sound work yourself, then hand over the tracks to a professional mixer just for the final mix. A professional mix studio will have good speakers and an optimal environment for judging the mix. Professional sound

Fig. 15-3. DAWs, like the Nuendo system shown here, display audio clips on a timeline, much like NLEs do. (Steinberg Media Technologies GmbH)

editors and mixers use DAWs with apps such as Pro Tools, Nuendo, and Apple Logic. Among the advantages of DAWs are more sophisticated audio processing, better control over audio levels and channels, and better tools for noise reduction, sample rate conversions, and the like.

In the past, sound for projects shot on film would be transferred to 16mm or 35mm magnetic film for editing, and the mix would be done from these mag film elements (see Fig. 15-11). Today, even if the film is edited on a flatbed with mag tracks, the sound is usually transferred to digital for mixing.

Planning Ahead

Many of the decisions made during picture and sound editing are affected by how the movie will be finished. Some questions that you'll face later on, which are worth considering early in the process, include:

- Will sound work and mixing be on the same system you're using for picture editing or will you transfer the sound to a DAW? If so, how will you export the sound from one system to the other? How will you get the mixed audio from the DAW to the master file or tape of the finished movie (see p. 655)?
- How many audio channels will you have in the final mix? There are several audio formats with different numbers of channels (ranging from single-channel mono to 7.1-channel formats). Format choice affects every stage of sound editing (see p. 669).
- What about bit rates? As of this writing, most digital projects are edited and finished with 48 kHz/16-bit audio. Sometimes projects are mixed and exported at higher bit rates, such as 24 bits for a Digital Cinema Package.
- How will distribution affect mix style? Different types of distribution (including theatrical, television, and Internet streaming) may benefit from different approaches to sound prep and balancing (see p. 659).
- Will you distribute the project in other languages? This affects track layout and mix (see p. 673).

Some topics in this chapter, such as the sections on sound processing and setting levels, are discussed in terms of the final mix but apply equally to working with sound throughout the picture and sound editing process. It will help to read through the whole chapter before beginning sound work.

SOUND EDITING TOOLS

The Working Environment

Sound work is first and foremost about *listening*, so it's essential you have a good environment in which to hear your tracks. If you're working with computers, drives, or decks that have noisy fans, make every effort to isolate them in another room or at least minimize the noise where you're sitting. Sometimes you can get extension cables to move the keyboard and monitors farther from the CPU, or use sound-dampening enclosures.

The editing room itself will affect the sound because of its acoustics (how sound reflects within it), noise, and other factors. Make sure there's enough furniture, carpeting, and/or sound-dampening panels to keep the room from being too reverberant and boomy.

Speakers are very important. A good set of "near field" speakers, designed for close listening, are often best. They should be aimed properly for your sitting position—usually in a rough equilateral-triangle arrangement (with the same distance between the two speakers as between you and each speaker, and each turned in slightly toward you). Avoid cheap computer speakers. Some people use "multimedia" speakers that have tiny little tweeters on the desktop with a subwoofer on the floor for bass. The problem with these is that they reproduce the high frequencies and the lows, but may be deficient in the midrange, where most dialogue lies.

One philosophy is that you should listen on the best speakers possible, turned up loud, to hear every nuance of the sound. Another suggests that you use lower-quality speakers at a lower volume level, more like the ones many people watching the movie will have. Ideally, you should have a chance to hear the sound on both. The great speakers will have detail in the highs and lows that *some* people, especially theater audiences, will hear. The smaller speakers will create some problems and mask others that you need to know about. Some people use headphones for sound work, which are great for hearing details and blocking out editing room noise, but can seriously misrepresent how people will hear the movie through speakers in the real world. To learn what your movie sounds like, get it out of the editing room and screen it in different environments—such as in a theater with big speakers turned up loud and in a living room on a TV that has typical small speakers.

It's helpful to have a small mixer (see next section) to control the level and balance of editing room speakers.

Fig. 15-4. Mackie 802-VLZ3 mixer. Mackie makes a series of popular, versatile mixers. (Mackie Designs, Inc.)

The Mixing Console

The *mixing console* (also called *recording console*, *mixer*, or *board*) is used to control and balance a number of sound sources and blend them into a combined sound track. The most sophisticated consoles are massive, computer-controlled systems used on a dub stage (see Fig. 15-1). At the other end of the range are simple, manually operated boards often used with an editing system for monitoring sound and inputting different gear into the NLE (see Figs. 14-7 and 15-4).

Today virtually all mixing is done with computer control. Software apps and DAWs often have on-screen displays that look a lot like a mix board. Sometimes apps are used with an attached physical console that has sliders you can move by hand (a "control surface"; see Fig. 15-12), which is a lot easier than trying to adjust levels with a mouse.

Because many NLE setups use a virtual or physical mixer to control various audio inputs, a short discussion may be helpful. The mix board accepts a number of *input channels*, or just *channels*. Each channel is controlled with its own *channel strip* on the surface of the board that has a *fader* (level control) and other adjustments. You might use one channel to input a microphone, and another pair of channels to bring in sound from a video deck. The channels can be assigned to various *buses*; a bus is a network for combining the output of two or more channels and sending it somewhere (a bit like a city bus collecting passengers from different neighborhoods and taking them downtown). The *mix bus* is the main output of the board, the *monitor bus* is the signal sent to the monitor speakers, and so on. You can send any channel you want to the *main mix*, where a *master fader* controls the level of all the channels together. You might choose to assign some channel strips to a separate output channel. This is sometimes done to create alternate versions of a mix, or when two people are using the board for different equipment at the same time.

- Jacks for a *microphone input* and a balanced or un-balanced *line level input* (see Audio Connections, p. 431).
- *Low-cut filter*, which rolls off low frequencies below 75 Hz (often a good idea, especially for monitoring during picture editing; see Bass Filters, p. 459).
- *Gain control* (also called *trim*), which adjusts the level of the mic or line as it comes into the mixer (see below for setting this).
- *Aux* (*auxiliary*) *pots* for sending the signal out for various uses.
- *EQ* (*equalization*) controls, for high, mid, and low frequencies. Turning each knob to the right boosts that frequency band; turning to the left cuts it. Some mix consoles have "fully parametric EQ," which allows you to fine-tune both the width of the band and where it is centered.
- *Pan pot.* Turning the pan control to the left sends the signal to the left channel/speaker; the other way sends it to the right. When using a mixer to play audio from the NLE, generally you should have the left channel out of the NLE panned fully left, and the right channel panned fully right. If you leave both channels panned in the middle, both will go to both speakers with no stereo separation.
- *Mute button.* Kills the sound from this channel (so you can hear the other channels without it).
- *Pre-fader solo.* Allows you to hear *only* this channel, at its original level (before going to any fader).
- *Level control.* Also called *gain*, it adjusts the volume level for the channel. Twelve o'clock on the dial is marked "U" for *unity gain* (on some mixers this is marked "0 dB"). Setting the level higher than U may add noise.

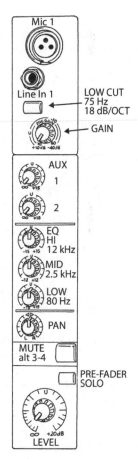

Fig. 15-5. Channel strip from Mackie 1202-VLZ3 mixer. See text. (Robert Brun)

To set up a channel on a mixer, plug the sound source (say, a video deck or microphone) into the channel input. Turn the gain control all the way down, and set the channel's level, the master fader, and the EQ controls to U or 0 dB. Now play the sound source (with nothing else playing) and adjust the gain (trim) control until the level looks good on the mixer's level meter. See Chapter 11 for more on setting levels. Now you can set the EQ where you like it, and use the channel strip and master fader to control the level as you choose. Generally you want to avoid a situation where a channel's gain is set low and the master fader is set very high to compensate. If you're just using one channel, often it's a good idea to leave the channel's gain at U and use the master fader to ride the level (see Gain Structure, p. 455).

SOUND EDITING TECHNIQUE

Editing dialogue and narration is discussed in Chapter 13. Basic sound editing methods are discussed in Chapter 14.

Evaluating the Sound Track

All the audio in the movie should be evaluated carefully at the start of sound editing. Is the dialogue clear and easy to understand? Is there objectionable wind or other noise that interferes with dialogue? Go through the tracks and cut out any noise, pops, or clicks that you can, and usually any breaths before or after words (that aren't part of an actor's performance). You can fill the holes later with room tone (see below for more on this). Pops that occur at cuts can often be fixed with a two-frame *crossfade* (sound dissolve).

If you have doubts about the quality of any section of audio, try equalizing or using noise reduction or other processing to improve it. Be critical—if you think you're unhappy with some bad sound now, just wait till you see the movie with an audience. For nondialogue scenes, the remedy may be to throw out the production sound and rebuild the audio with effects (see below). For dialogue scenes in a drama, you may need to use other takes, or consider automatic dialogue replacement (ADR; see p. 532). Consult a mixer or other professional for possible remedies. If it's unfixable, you may need to lose the whole scene.

Sound and Continuity

Sound plays an important role in establishing a sense of time or place. In both fiction and documentary, very often shots that were filmed at different times must be cut together to create the illusion that they actually occurred in continuous time. In one shot the waiter says, "Can I take your order?" and in the next the woman says, "I'll start with the soup." These two shots may have been taken hours or even days apart, but they must maintain the illusion of being connected. The way the sound is handled can either make or break the scene.

When you're editing, be attentive to changes in the quality, content, and level of sound and use them to your advantage. If your goal is to blend a series of shots into a continuous flow, avoid making hard sound cuts that butt up two sections of audio that differ greatly in quality or tone, especially right at a picture cut. A crossfade can smooth out a hard cut. Certain differences in quality and level can be smoothed over by adjusting levels and doing some EQ. Sometimes just moving the audio cut a few frames before or after the picture cut helps (see Fig. 14-25).

Audiences will accept most changes in sound if they're gradual. One technique is to add in a background track that remains constant and masks other discontinuities in a scene. Say you have a shot with the sound of an airplane overhead, preceded and followed by shots without the plane. You could add airplane sound to another track (which you can get from a sound effects library); fade it in before the noisy shot, then gradually fade it out after it (see Fig. 15-6). This progression gives the sense that the plane passes overhead during the three shots. As long as the sound doesn't cut in or out sharply, many discontinuities can be covered in a similar way.

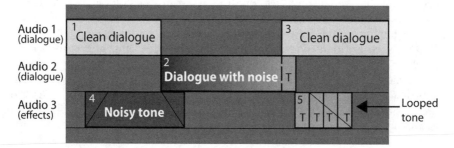

Fig. 15-6. Smoothing out a noisy shot. On audio track 1 are two clean dialogue clips (1 and 3) that have no background noise. On track 2, the dialogue clip (2) has noise from an air conditioner that was running when that part of the scene was shot. Room tone with air conditioner noise was found earlier in the shot and a copy (4) was pasted on track 3. It is crossfaded with clip 2, so the noise level comes in gradually, not abruptly. Normally, a second copy of clip 4 could be placed at the end of clip 2 and faded out, to smooth the transition out of the noisy section. However, the noise at the end of clip 2 is different and doesn't match. So room tone (T), which was found in a short pause at the end of clip 2, is copied, then pasted repeatedly as a loop on track 3. Crossfades from one section of the loop to the next can help blend them together. Then the looped clips as a group can be faded out (on some systems this requires making a nest or a compound clip).

If you're cutting a scene in which there was audible music on location, there will be jumps in the music every time you make a cut in the audio track. Try to position cuts in background sound under dialogue or other sounds that can distract the audience from the discontinuous background.

While gradual crossfades ease viewers from sequence to sequence, it's often desirable to have hard, clear changes in sound to produce a shock effect. Opening a scene with sound that is radically different from the previous sequence is a way to make a clean break, start a new chapter. When cutting from a loud scene to a quiet scene, it often works best to allow the loud sound to continue slightly beyond the picture cut, decaying (fading out) naturally. When a loud scene follows a quiet scene, a straight cut often works best.

When building tracks, don't forget the power of *silence*. A sense of hush can help build tension. A moment of quiet after a loud or intense scene can have tremendous impact. Sounds can be used as punctuation to control the phrasing of a scene. Often, the rhythm of sounds should be used to determine the timing of picture cuts as much as or more than anything going on in the picture.

Sound Effects

For feature films, it's common during shooting to record only the sound of the actors' voices, with the assumption that *all* other sounds (such as footsteps, rain, cars pulling up, or pencils on paper) will be added later. Shooting often takes place on an acoustically isolated soundstage. Without added sound effects to bring a sense of realism, the footage will seem very flat. Documentaries often need effects as well, to augment or replace sounds recorded on location.

Sound effects (*SFX*) are available from a number of sources. You can download effects from the Web or buy them on discs. Most mix facilities keep an effects library. A good library has an astounding range of effects: you might find, for example, five hundred different crowd sounds, from low murmurs to wild applause. Libraries such as Sound Ideas or the Hollywood Edge offer effects for specific models of cars, species of birds, types of shoes, guns, or screams.

The most compelling effects may not be the obvious library choice. A car zooming by in a dramatic scene could have engine and tire sounds, plus rocket sounds or even musical tones. To create unusual effects, the sound designer will collect, sample, and process all sorts of sounds and textures.

Fig. 15-7. Foley room. The various floor surfaces are used to make different types of footsteps. Items in the background are for generating other sound effects. (Sync Sound, Inc.)

A *Foley stage* is a special studio for creating effects while watching the picture (named for Jack Foley, who invented the technique in the early days of sound films).

The floor may have different sections with gravel, wood, or other surfaces to simulate different kinds of footfalls. A good Foley artist can pour water, make drinking sounds, and do other effects that work perfectly with picture. When doing foreign language versions of a film, Foleys are often needed because the original effects that were recorded with the dialogue have to be cut out.

Effects can also be used to help define a place or a character and can be used as a narrative element. Some effects are clichéd (the creaking floors and squeaking doors of a spooky old house), but imaginative use of sounds can add a vivid flavor to an otherwise bland location.

Effects are sometimes used to create moods or impressionistic backgrounds that don't relate literally to anything in the image. Creative sound editing may involve burying abstract or unrelated sounds under the more obvious sounds created by people or objects on screen. Sometimes these effects are very subtle. A quiet, very low-frequency sound may be barely audible but can create a subliminal sense of tension. As editor Victoria Garvin Davis points out, often the mark of a good effect is that you never even notice it.

Room Tone and Ambience

The sound track should never be allowed to go completely *dead*. With the exception of an anechoic chamber, no place on earth is totally silent. Every space has a characteristic room tone (see p. 445). For technical reasons as well as aesthetic ones the track should always have some sound, even if very quiet. Whenever dialogue has been edited and there are gaps between one bit of dialogue and the next, room tone is particularly important to maintain a sense of continuity. Filling in room tone is sometimes called *toning out* the track.

If the recordist has provided room tone at each location, you can lay it under the scene to fill small dropouts or larger holes or to provide a sense of "air," which is quite different from no sound. If no room tone has been specifically recorded, you may be able to steal short sections from pauses on the set (such as the time just before the director says "action") or long spaces between words. You may need to go back to the original field recordings to find these moments.

Short lengths of tone can sometimes be looped to generate more tone. On an NLE, this can be easily done by copying and pasting the same piece more than once. Listen closely to make sure there's nothing distinct that will be heard repeating (one trick is to insert a clip of tone, then copy and paste a "reverse motion" version of the same clip right after it so the cut is seamless).

Often, you want to create a sonic *atmosphere* or *ambience* that goes beyond simple room tone. For example, vehicle and pedestrian sounds for a street scene. *Background* (*BG*) or *natural* ("nat") sound is often constructed during sound editing or the mix from several different ambience tracks together. A background of natural sound or music under dialogue is sometimes called a *bed*.

You could try recording your own backgrounds, but many atmospheres, such as the sound of wind in the trees, are simpler to get from an effects library than to try to record. Another background is *walla*, which is a track of people speaking in which no words can be made out, which is useful for scenes in restaurants, or with groups or crowds.

MUSIC

The Score

Music may be *scored* (composed) specifically for a movie or preexisting music may be licensed for use. An *underscore* (or just *score*) is music that audiences understand as being added by the filmmakers to augment a scene; *source music* seems to come from some source in a scene (for example, a car radio or a pianist next door).[2] Songs may be used over action, either as a form of score or as source music. To preserve continuity, music is almost always added to a movie during editing and is rarely recorded simultaneously with the dialogue. (Of course, in a documentary, recording ambient music may at times be unavoidable.)

Music is a powerful tool for the filmmaker. Used right, it can enhance a scene tremendously. Most fiction films would be emotionally flat without music. But if the wrong music is used, or at the wrong time, it can ruin a scene. Though there are many movies with catchy themes, or where well-known songs are used to great effect, it's interesting how many movie scores are actually quite subtle and nondescript. Listen to the score for a movie you've liked. Often the most powerful scenes are supported by very atmospheric music that doesn't in itself make a big statement. A case can also be made for times when music should be avoided. In some documentaries and in some moments in dramas, music can have a kind of manipulative effect that may be inappropriate. No matter what music you choose, it unavoidably makes a kind of editorial comment in terms of mood and which parts of the action are highlighted. Sometimes audiences should be allowed to form their own reactions, without help from the filmmaker (or composer).

To get a sense of music's power, take a scene from your project and try placing completely different types of music over it (hard-charging rock, lilting classical) or even try faster or slower tempo examples from the same genre. Then slide the same piece earlier or later over the picture. It can be quite amazing how the same scene takes on completely different meanings, how different parts of the scene stand out as important, and how different cuts seem beautifully in sync with the rhythm and others wildly off.

Typically, during the rough-cut stage, movies are edited with no music or with *temp* (*temporary*) *music*. The editor and/or director bring in music they like and "throw it in" to the movie during editing to try it out. This can be a great way to experiment and find what styles work with the picture. The problem is that after weeks or months of watching the movie with the temp music, filmmakers often fall in love with it and find it very disturbing to take it out. The temp music must come out for many reasons, ranging from its having been used in another movie to the likelihood that you can't afford it to the fact that you've hired a composer to write a score. Often composers have ideas that are very different from the temp music you've picked, and they may not be able or willing to write something like the temp track if you ask them to.

Every composer has his or her own method of working, and the director and

---

2. Source music or other sound from within the story's space is sometimes referred to as *diegetic* sound, as opposed to the nondiegetic sound of the movie's score.

composer must feel their way along in finding the right music for the project. *Spotting sheets* (sometimes called *spot lists*, *cue sheets*, or *timing sheets*) should be prepared, showing every needed music cue and its length. Cues are numbered sequentially on each reel with the letter "M" (2M5 is the fifth cue on reel 2). Music may be used within a scene or as a *segue* (pronounced "seg-way"), which is a transition or bridge from one scene to next. A *stinger* is a very short bit used to highlight a moment or help end or begin a scene.

The director should discuss with the composer what each scene is about, and what aspects of the scene the music should reinforce. Even if you know musical terminology, describing music with words can be tremendously difficult. The conversation often turns to far-flung metaphors about colors, emotions, weather—whatever is useful to describe the effect the music should have on the listener. What makes great composers great is their ability to understand the ideas and emotions in a scene and express that in music.

When auditioning different cues, try out different moods and feels. You may discover humor where you never saw it before or, with a more emotional cue, poignancy in a commonplace activity. Pay particular attention to tempo. Music that's too slow can drag a scene down; music that's a little fast may infuse energy, but too fast can make a scene feel rushed. The musical key is also important; sometimes the same cue transposed to a different key will suddenly work where it didn't before.

Scoring is often left until the last moment in postproduction, but there is a lot to be gained by starting the process as early as possible.

Licensing Music

If you can't afford or don't want an original score, you can license existing music. Popular songs by well-known musical groups are usually very expensive. Often a music supervisor will have contacts with indie bands, composers, or others who are eager to have their music used in a movie, and that music may be much more affordable. Music libraries sell prerecorded music that can be used for a reasonable fee with minimal hassle. Many of them offer tracks that sound *very much* like famous bands (but just different enough to avoid a lawsuit). See Chapter 17 for discussion of copyright, licensing, and the business aspects of using music.

Music Editing

When delivering a cut of the project to the composer, it's usually a good idea to pan any temp music to the left audio channel only, so the composer can choose to hear the clean track without the music if desired.

The composer will supply each cue to you either with timecode in the track or with starting timecode listed separately so you can place the music where intended. Nevertheless, sometimes music needs to be cut or repositioned to work with the edited scenes. Not infrequently, a cue written for one scene works better with another.

When placing music (and when having it composed) keep in mind that in dialogue scenes, the dialogue needs to be audible. If the music is so loud that it fights with the dialogue, the music will have to be brought down in the mix. A smart composer (or music editor) will place the most active, loudest passages of music before or after lines of dialogue, and have the music lay back a bit when people are talking. If the music and the characters aren't directly competing, they can both be loud and both be heard.

Cutting music is easier if you're familiar with the mechanics of music. Some picture cuts are best made on the upbeat, others on the downbeat. Locating musical beats on an NLE may be easier if you view the audio waveform (see Fig. 14-24). Short (or sometimes long) crossfades help bridge cuts within the music. A musical note or another sound (like some sirens) that holds and then decays slowly can sometimes be shortened by removing frames from the *middle* of the sound rather than from the beginning or end; use a crossfade to smooth the cut.

In the mix, source music that is meant to appear to be coming from, say, a car radio is usually filtered to match the source. In this case, you might roll off both high and low frequencies to simulate a tinny, "lo-fi" speaker.

On some productions, the composer will premix the music herself and deliver it to you as a stereo track. On others, the composer may deliver the music with many separate tracks of individual instruments that the rerecording mixer will premix prior to the main mix (or the composer may supply a set of partially mixed stems with rhythm, melody, and vocal tracks).

Music Creation Software

A number of available apps allow musicians and nonmusicians to construct music tracks by assembling prerecorded loops of instruments that contain snippets of melodies and rhythms. The loops can be combined with other tracks performed with a keyboard or recorded with a mic. You can create an actual score this way, or it's handy for quickly trying out ideas for a scratch track.

There are apps just for music, such as GarageBand, and there are DAWs that can be used for both building music tracks and general mixing; these include Logic, Nuendo, and Pro Tools. The loops may be sampled from real instruments and you can adjust them for tempo and pitch. You can buy additional loops in different musical styles on the Web. These apps may also include a library of stock cues you

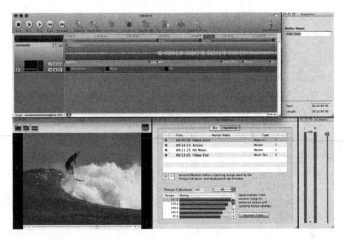

Fig. 15-8. Sonicfire Pro can connect to a royalty-free music library where you can locate appropriate music cues, then adjust them to scenes in your movie. (SmartSound)

can use. Sonicfire Pro is a hybrid app that helps you find appropriate stock music from the SmartSound library, then customize it for individual scenes in your project.

SOME SOUND EDITING ISSUES

POPS AND CLICKS. Often on NLEs, you get a pop or click where two audio clips meet on the same track (even if neither pops by itself). To avoid this, put a two-frame crossfade between them or try trimming one side back by a frame (or less). Some DAWs can routinely add a crossfade of several milliseconds to avoid clicks at cuts.

AUDIO SCRUBBING. Many sound edits can only be made by listening to the track slowly. The term audio *scrubbing* comes from the use of reel-to-reel tape recorders, where you would manually pull the sound back and forth across the playback head in a scrubbing motion to find individual sounds. Some digital systems offer the choice of analog-style scrub (slow and low-pitched) and a digital version that plays a small number of frames at full speed. See which works best for you.

STEREO PAIRS. As noted on p. 585, paired stereo tracks include one track that's panned to the left channel and one that's panned to the right. This is appropriate for music, or other stereo recordings, but sometimes two mono tracks from a camcorder show up on the timeline as a stereo pair—for example, the sound from a boom mic and a lavalier may be inadvertently paired. In this case you should unpair them, then pan them to the center so that both go equally to both speakers. Then, you should probably pick one and lower the level of the other completely (or just disable or delete the other clip if it's clearly inferior).

Summing (combining) two identical tracks on the same channel will cause the level to rise by about 6 dB. You can use summing to your advantage when you can't get enough volume from a very quiet clip by just raising the gain. Try copying the clip and pasting the copy *directly* below the original on the timeline to double the level. While this can work on an NLE, most DAWs have better ways of increasing level. For more on stereo, see Chapter 11 and later in this chapter.

TRIMS AND OUTTAKES. One advantage of doing at least basic track work on the NLE used for picture editing is to get instant access to outtakes. There are many situations in which you need to replace room tone or a line of dialogue. It's very handy to be able to quickly scan through alternate takes, or to use the match frame command to instantly find the extension to a shot. These things take longer on another machine if you don't have all the media easily accessible on hard drive.

Whoever is doing the sound editing may want access to *all* the production audio recorded for the movie. Crucial pieces of room tone or replacement dialogue may be hiding in unexpected places in the tracks. Be prepared to deliver to the sound editor all the audio, including wild sound, and the logs, if requested.

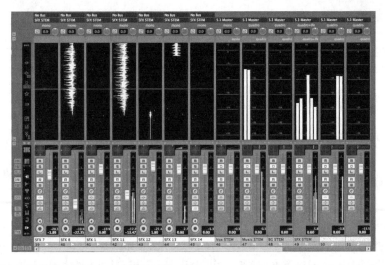

Fig. 15-9. DAW mixing panel. This Nuendo screen shows sound effects tracks in a 5.1-channel mix. (Steinberg Media Technologies GmbH)

PREPARING FOR THE MIX

Everything done in sound editing is geared toward the mix. The better your preparation, the better the movie will sound and the faster the mix will go. Regardless of whether the mix will be done by a professional mixer or by you on your own system, go through the entire sound track and be sure you've provided all the sounds needed. During the mix, changes or new effects may be called for, but try to anticipate as much as you can.

Mixes are done with different types of equipment, but all mixes share the same fundamental process:

1. All of your audio tracks are played back together, in sync with the picture.
2. The relative levels of the tracks are adjusted and various types of EQ and processing are applied as needed.
3. All the sounds are combined and the mixed sound track is rerecorded on other tracks for final output.

The *sound mixer*, also called the *rerecording mixer*, presides at the console. Like an orchestra conductor, the mixer determines how the various tracks will blend into the whole. Some mixes require two or three mixers operating the console(s).

Splitting Tracks

During picture editing, the sound may be bunched on a few or several tracks in the editing system. After the picture has been locked, and it's time to prepare for the mix, the tracks are split in a very specific way to facilitate the mix. Sounds are segregated onto different tracks according to the type of sound; for example, dialogue, music, narration, and effects are usually all put on separate tracks. Actually, each type of sound is usually split into a *group* of tracks (for example, you may need many tracks to accommodate all your dialogue or effects). This layout is used partly so the mixer knows what to expect from various tracks, but also so that he can minimize the number of adjustments made during the mix. Say you have narration in your movie. If all the narration is on one track—and there is nothing else on that track—then the mixer can fine-tune the level and EQ for the narrator's voice and then quite possibly never touch that channel again during the mix. If, on the other hand, the narrator's voice keeps turning up on different tracks, or there are other sounds sharing her track, the mixer will constantly have to make adjustments to compensate.

A simple documentary might be mixed with anywhere from eight to more than twenty tracks; a simple dramatic mix might involve twenty to forty tracks. A complex, effects-filled drama for 5.1-channel surround sound might have well over one hundred tracks. When there are many tracks, often a *premix* is done to consolidate numerous effects tracks into a few that can be more easily balanced with the dialogue and music.

Talk to your mixer for his preferences before splitting tracks. Some mixers prefer tracks to be laid out in a particular order. For example, the first tracks contain dialogue and sync sound, the next narration, then music, and the last effects. If there is no narration or music, the effects tracks would follow immediately after the dialogue. If your movie has very little of one type of sound (say, only a couple of bits of music), you can usually let it share another track (in this case you might put music on the effects track).

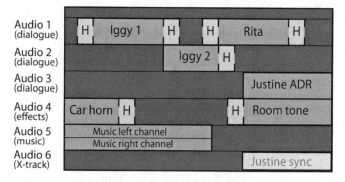

Fig. 15-10. Track work. Prior to the mix, audio is split into separate dialogue, effects, and music tracks. Shown here, a wide shot of Iggy (Iggy 1) and close-up (Iggy 2) are placed on separate tracks because they were miked differently and call for different equalization. Rita's dialogue sounds similar to Iggy 1, so they are on the same track. Justine's dialogue was rerecorded after the scene was shot because of background noise; the replacement lines require room tone. The original sync version of Justine's dialogue is on audio track 6 if needed, but for the time being the clip is inaudible (clips can be made silent by *disabling* or *muting* them). The sections marked "H" are handles available for crossfades, which are often needed to smooth out dialogue cuts (handles are normally invisible on the timeline). The two channels of stereo music shown here share the same track; on some NLEs, stereo sound is displayed as two linked clips on separate tracks.

A common method of labeling tracks uses letters for each track in a group: you might have Dia. A, Dia. B, Dia. C, and SFX A, SFX B, etc. If the movie is divided into reels (see below), each reel is given a number, so a given track might be labeled, say, "Reel 3, Mus. A." Ask the mixer for track labeling preferences.

CHECKERBOARDING. To make mixing go faster, tracks within any group may be split into a checkerboard pattern (see Fig. 15-10). For example, two characters who are miked differently might be split onto separate dialogue tracks. This can make it easier to adjust the EQ and level differently for the two mics.

In general, if one clip follows another on the same track and you can play them both without changing the EQ, hearing a click, or making a large level change, then leave them on the same track. Tracks should be split when two sections of sound are *different* from each other in level or quality and you want them to be *similar*, or if they are *similar* and you want them to be *different*. Thus, if two parts of a sequence are miked very differently and need to be evened out, put them on separate tracks. If you have a shot of actor A followed by a separate shot of actor B and the level or quality of the sound changes at the cut, they should be on separate tracks.

If the difference between two clips is caused by a change of background tone, it usually helps to ease the transition by doing a crossfade between the two shots (assuming there's enough media to do so).

How many tracks do you need for each type of sound? Say you're splitting your dialogue. You put the first clip on one track, then put the next on the second track. If the next split comes in less than eight to ten seconds, you probably should put that piece on a third track rather than going back to the first. But not necessarily. There are different schools of thought about how much to checkerboard tracks. The idea of splitting tracks originated when mixes were done with mag film dubbers (see Fig. 15-11). With a dubber, it's only possible to do a crossfade between two shots if they're on separate tracks; you *have* to checkerboard them to do the effect. With a digital system, however, it's easy to set up a crossfade between one clip and the next on the same track. Mixers differ in how much they want tracks checkerboarded; ask yours for his preferences. On some systems, EQ and other effects may be applied to *individual clips*, so checkerboarding may not be helpful, particularly if you're doing your own mix. However, on some systems effects are applied to an *entire track*, or the mixer may be trying to set levels by hand (the old-fashioned way); splitting tracks can make those tasks easier.

After talking with the mixer, work through the movie shot by shot to determine how many tracks you need. Sometimes you'll want extra tracks for optional effects or alternate dialogue takes to give the mixer more options. You don't want to use more tracks than are necessary; on the other hand, having more tracks could save you time and money in the mix.

Reel Breaks and Reference Movies

To be absolutely sure that there aren't any sync errors, it's best to do the mix with the *final picture* (either from the online video edit or, for a project finished on film, a digital transfer of a print or other film element). That way, any sync discrepancies can be fixed in the mix.

However, it's often the case that you have to mix with the locked picture from the offline edit. Create a *reference file or tape* of the offline edit that includes your rough sound mix as a guide for the mixer.[3] Talk with the mix studio people about what file format, frame rate, frame size, and codec they want. Often, they'll want burned-in sequence timecode.

FOR PROJECTS SHOT ON VIDEO. The mixer will usually want a file or tape of the offline edit with sequence timecode burned in (window burn). Mixers often prefer that you deliver the movie as a file, in QuickTime or another format. Follow the instructions for leaders on p. 621, so that the file begins at 00:58:00:00, has the correct countdown leader, and the *first frame of action* (*FFOA*, also called *first frame of picture* or *FFOP*) starts at 01:00:00:00. The same layout should be used when making a tape. Be sure it has the proper countdown leader, continuous timecode, and no dropped frames.

Put a *sync pop*[4] (the audible beep in the countdown leader that syncs to the picture exactly two seconds prior to the start of the program) on *all the audio tracks* as a sync check. Also add 30 seconds of black after the last frame of action, followed by a tail leader with visible sync frame and sync pop on all the tracks. This is done on the NLE prior to output.

In some cases, the project will need to be broken into shorter lengths (*reels*) if the entire movie can't be edited, mixed, or finished in one chunk (which may happen, for example, if files get too big). If so, each reel is made into a separate sequence, beginning with a different hour timecode. Accordingly, reel 1 would begin at 01:00:00:00, with reel 2 starting at 02:00:00:00, and so on. The reels can be joined together later.

FOR PROJECTS THAT WILL BE FINISHED AND PRINTED ON FILM. See Reel Length, p. 705, for guidelines on dividing up reels, and the note above for setting the starting timecode on each reel.

When preparing film projects, each reel should begin with a standard *SMPTE leader* (also called an *Academy leader*). This has the familiar eight-second countdown. Your NLE should have a leader included as a file or you can download one. The leader counts down from 8 to 2 with two seconds of black following. The frame *exactly* at 2 should have a sync pop or beep edited into *all sound tracks*. The sync pops aid in keeping the tracks in sync during the mix and are essential for putting the film optical track in sync with the picture; see Optical Tracks, p. 713. A tail leader with a beep should also be added.

With projects that are going to be finished digitally, the SMPTE leader is often edited in before the hour mark, so that the beep at two takes place—for the first reel—at 00:59:58:00 and the first frame of action appears at one hour straight up (01:00:00:00). However, for projects that involve cutting and printing film, the

---

3. "Reference" here means something to refer to in the mix; if you're making a QuickTime file, the term "reference file" has another meaning (it's a file that doesn't contain media; see p. 618). Any QuickTime files you make to give to the mixer should be *self-contained*.

4. In the UK, it's called a sync *pip*. Also note that in Europe and the UK, programs often start at 10:00:00:00 timecode.

lab may want the SMPTE leader to *begin* at the hour mark, so the beep at two would appear at 01:00:06:00 and the FFOA starts at 01:00:08:00.[5] Talk to the mix facility, lab, and/or post house technicians for the way they want the reels broken down.

On some projects, the 35mm film footage count is also included as a burned-in window, with 000+00 beginning at the SMPTE leader start frame.

Fig. 15-11. For decades, film mixes were done with multiple reels of analog magnetic film playing on dubbers. Six playback transports are at left; one master record dubber is at right. Now, most of the dubbers that survive are only used to transfer mag film to digital for mixing. (Rangertone Research)

5. In 16mm, with the "Picture Start" frame of the SMPTE leader used as zero (01:00:00:00 in video), the first frame of action occurs at exactly 4 feet, 32 frames.

Preparing and Delivering Tracks

If you're working with a mixer or a sound studio, ask how they like the tracks prepared and delivered. Following their preferences, split the tracks as discussed above. Clean up the sequence by deleting any disabled or inaudible clips that you don't need for the mix. When the tracks are ready, you need to export them from the NLE and import them into whichever online edit system or DAW the mixer uses. There are a few options. For an overview of this process, see File Formats and Data Exchange, p. 242, and Managing Media, p. 609.

EXPORT THE SEQUENCE AND MEDIA. Usually the best way to move the audio tracks to another system is to export the entire sequence with its media. This is often done by exporting the timeline from the NLE using an OMF or AAF file (see p. 244). OMF/AAF files include a wealth of metadata about where each clip belongs on the timeline, audio levels, media file names, and so on. In addition, when you create the file, you have the choice of whether or not to include (*embed*) the actual audio media in the file.

When you import an OMF/AAF file into the DAW, all the audio clips should appear in the new sequence in their proper timeline position on their own tracks. Ideally, you chose to embed the audio media in the OMF/AAF file, so you can give the sound studio a self-contained file on a DVD or hard drive that has the sequence and all the sound in one neat package—what could be easier?

In some situations this process isn't quite so simple. For example, not all systems can export or import OMF/AAF files. Some systems can exchange sequences using XML files or apps like Boris Transfer. In the past, Automatic Duck programs have also been used for this purpose.

Sometimes you want to send the OMF/AAF sequence (also called the *composition*) separately from the audio media files; for example, when there are ongoing changes to a project during sound editing or if the OMF/AAF file is too large.[6] In this case, the media (either *all* the audio media for the project, or a consolidated set of files with just the audio used in the sequence) is delivered first, and an OMF/AAF of the most recent sequence is delivered separately. The OMF/AAF composition will then *link* to the media.

Depending on the systems involved, not *all* the information in your offline sequence may be translated to the DAW. For example, some or all clip level adjustments may not carry over from one system to the other. You may also want to remove any filter effects or EQ (see below).

Be sure to include ample *handles* on your clips. Handles are extensions of clips that remain hidden (inaudible) but are available in case the mixer wants to use them for crossfades or to lengthen a clip (see Fig. 15-10). Mixers may request handle lengths anywhere from 30 frames to ten seconds or more, which you can select with the OMF/AAF export tool. Whenever possible, confirm that the exported OMF/AAF file actually plays and links to the media before sending it on to the mix studio.

Be sure all audio clips are at the same sample rate (typically, mix sessions are done at 48 kHz/16 bits).

---

6. As of this writing, OMF files are limited to 2GB. Sometimes it's necessary to break the movie into shorter sections or only export a few tracks at a time to keep each OMF file under the limit.

EXPORT AUDIO FILES. If your system doesn't support OMF/AAF, you can export each track as a separate audio file (in a format such as AIFF or WAV). You *must* have head leaders with a sync pop because, depending on the format, there may be no timecode. This method is cumbersome and doesn't allow for handles. (That is, you can include extensions of shots if you want, but they aren't "hidden" and the mixer will have to manually fade or cut any extra audio that's not needed—not very useful.) Also, unlike OMF, the files will appear in the DAW as a single, uninterrupted clip, which makes it harder to see where different sounds are, see how they relate, and slide clips around when needed.

EXPORT AN EDL. An EDL contains the basic data about where each clip begins and ends and where it belongs on the timeline (see Fig. 14-41). An EDL contains no media. It's a bit like using OMF/AAF but with no media and less metadata. An EDL is sometimes used when the sound studio prefers to recapture the original production audio instead of using the media from the NLE. An EDL can also be used with systems that don't support OMF.

PREP AND DELIVERY. No matter what method you're using, as a rule you should remove any filters or EQ you've done in the offline edit so the mixer can create his or her own.[7] This is especially the case when exporting AIFF or WAV audio files, because once the effect is applied to those files, the mixer can't remove them later. (When exporting AIFF or WAV or laying off to tape, you may also want to remove any level adjustments you made to clips.)

Some editors put a lot of work into their rough mix and want to preserve any level adjustments they made as a basis for the final mix. If you're using OMF/AAF and a system that can translate audio clip levels from the NLE to the mixer's DAW, this may indeed save a lot of time in the final mix. However, some mixers prefer to start with a blank slate, and don't want the editor's levels at all, since things change a lot once you start sweetening (and he can always listen to the tracks on the reference file or tape if he wants to hear what the editor had in mind).

Mix Prep and Final Cut Pro X

As discussed in Chapter 14, starting with version X, Apple completely redesigned Final Cut Pro. Unlike virtually every professional NLE, FCP X doesn't use fixed, sequential audio tracks, so you can't checkerboard sound as described above. However, it does offer other techniques to separate different sound clips using metadata. For example, you can give every clip a *role* name that identifies what type of sound it is. The default FCP X role categories are dialogue, music, and effects, although you can create as many more as you like. You can further divide these into *subroles*. Under the dialogue category, for instance, you could add "Jim in Office," "Jim in car" or "Jim, Scene 6." You could create separate subroles for "truck effect" and "boat effect." Whatever makes sense for your production. It's very easy to find and listen to all the clips that share the same role or subrole. You can also select various clips and group them together in a compound clip, then apply a volume adjustment, EQ, or other effect to the entire group. By le-

---

7. Some DAWs, such as Pro Tools, allow the mixer to disregard any plug-in effects on import.

veraging audio processing tools from Logic Studio as well as Final Cut, FCP X offers much improved audio mixing *within* the app. If you want to output mix stems (see p. 673), you can export each type of sound according to its role to an AIFF or WAVE audio file.

However, if you're planning to export audio to a DAW for mixing, things are not as flexible. First, if you have three different effects clips playing together that have the same "effects" role, they'll be folded together on export. The solution is to assign separate roles or subroles to any clips you will want separate control of during the mix. Also, as just described in Export Audio Files, creating an AIFF means no handles, which could be a problem if you decide to add a fade or dissolve during the mix that requires extra frames. Lastly, each track is just one long clip, so you don't have the flexibility you would have with an OMF/AAF to find and reposition clips. As of this writing FCP X is relatively new, and better solutions are emerging for mixing in other systems, such as the X2PRO Audio Convert app by Marquis Broadcast that can convert an FCP X timeline into an AAF file that can be opened in Avid Pro Tools.

Fig. 15-12. A control surface has mechanical faders that can interact with software apps, allowing you to make level adjustments using the sliders, which is faster and more comfortable than using a mouse. The Mackie MCU Pro can be used with many different apps, including Logic, Pro Tools, Nuendo, and Ableton. (Mackie Designs, Inc.)

Cue Sheets

In a traditional mix, the sound editor draws up *mix cue sheets* (also known as *log sheets*). These act like road maps to show the mixer where sounds are located on each of the tracks. The mixer wants to know where each track begins, how it should start (cut in, quick fade, or slow fade), what the sound is, where it should cut or fade out, and how far the track actually extends beyond this point (if at all). These days, few people bother with cue sheets, since the timeline on the DAW shows the mixer where all the clips are.

THE SOUND MIX

This section is in part about doing the mix in a sound studio with a professional mixer. However, most of the content applies if you're doing either a rough or a final mix yourself on your own system.

Arranging for the Mix

Professional sound mixes are expensive (from about $100 to $350 or more per hour); some studios offer discounts to students and for special projects. Get references from other filmmakers before picking a mixer.

Depending on the complexity of the tracks, the equipment, and the mixer's skill, a mix can take two to ten times the length of the movie or more. Some feature films are mixed for months, with significant reediting done during the process. For a documentary or simple drama without a lot of problems, a half hour of material a day is fairly typical if the work is being done carefully. Some studios allow you to book a few hours of "bump" time in case your mix goes over schedule; you pay for this time only if you use it.

The more time you spend in the mix talking, or reviewing sections that have already been mixed, the more it will cost. Sometimes filmmakers will take a file or tape of the day's work home to review before the next day's session (though even this output may be a real-time process, adding time to the mix).

Some mixers work most efficiently by making the first pass by themselves without the filmmaker present. Then you come to the studio, listen, and make adjustments as necessary.

Fig. 15-13. Rerecording mixer at work. (Sync Sound, Inc.)

Working with the Mixer

The sound mix is a constant series of (often unspoken) questions. Is the dialogue clear? Is this actor's voice too loud compared to the others? Is the music too "thin"?

Have we lost that rain effect under the sound of the car? Is the sync sound competing with the narration? Left alone, a good mixer can make basic decisions about the relative volume of sounds, equalization, and the pacing of fades. Nevertheless, for many questions there is no "correct" answer. The mixer, director, and sound editor(s) must work together to realize the director's goals for the movie. Trust the mixer's experience in translating what you're hearing in the studio to what the audience will hear, but don't be afraid to speak up if something doesn't sound right to you.

Mixers and filmmakers sometimes have conflicts. Mixers tell tales of overcaffeinated filmmakers who haven't slept in days giving them badly prepared tracks and expecting miracles. Filmmakers tell of surly mixers who blame them for audio problems and refuse to take suggestions on how things should be mixed. If you can combine a well-prepared sound editor with a mixer who has good ears, quick reflexes, and a pleasant personality, you've hit pay dirt.

Mixing for Your Audience

Before an architect can design a building, he or she needs specific information about where it will be sited, how the structure will be used, and what construction materials can be employed. Before a mixer can start work, he or she will have a similar set of questions: Where will the movie be shown? What technologies will be used to show it? How many different versions do you need? Some projects are designed solely for one distribution route. For example, a video for a museum kiosk might be shown under very controlled conditions in one place only. But for many productions, there are several distribution paths. A feature film might be seen in theaters, in living rooms on TV, and in noisy coffee shops on mobile phones and iPads. A corporate video might be shown on a big screen at a company meeting, then streamed on the company's intranet. Each of these may call for different choices in the mix. On some projects, the mix may be adjusted for different types of output.

LEVEL AND DYNAMIC RANGE

How or where a movie is shown affects the basic approach to sound balancing, in particular the relationship of loud sounds to quiet sounds. See Sound, p. 402, for the basics of dynamic range, and especially Setting the Recording Level, p. 446, before reading this section.

In a movie theater, the space itself is quiet and the speakers are big and loud enough so that quiet sounds and deep bass come across clearly. Loud sounds like explosions and gunshots can be very exciting in theaters because they really sound *big*. This is partly because they are indeed loud (as measured by sound pressure), but it is also due to the great dynamic range between the quieter sounds and the explosions. Our ears get used to dialogue at a quieter level, then the big sounds come and knock us out of our seats. This idea applies to all types of sounds, including the music score, which can include very subtle, quiet passages as well as stunning, full crescendos.

When people watch movies at home, it's a very different story. First, the movie is competing with all sorts of other sounds, including people talking, noises from the street, appliances, air conditioners—whatever. Though some people have "home theaters" equipped with decent speakers, many TVs have small speakers that are pretty weak when it comes to reproducing either the high frequencies or the lows. And the overall volume level for TV viewing is usually lower than in a theater. Subtlety is lost. If you make any sounds too quiet in the mix, they'll be drowned out by the background noise. Everything needs to punch through to be heard. A common problem happens when mixing music. In the quiet of the mix studio, listening on big speakers, you may think a soft passage of music sounds great. But when you hear the same mix on TV at home, you can't even *hear* the music.

When people watch movies streamed over the Internet, it's usually even worse. A computer may have small speakers, a mobile phone has tiny speakers, and the audio may be processed for Web delivery. So it's not just the screening environment that limits dynamic range—it's also the delivery method.

What does this mean for the mix? For a theatrical mix, you have a lot of dynamic range to play with; for a TV or Internet mix you have much less. Here's one way to visualize it: all recording systems have an upper limit on how loud sounds can be. Regardless of the format, you can't go above this level. For a theatrical mix, you can let quiet sounds go much lower than this level. But for a TV mix—or for any format where there's more noise involved—"quiet" sounds should stay much closer to the top.

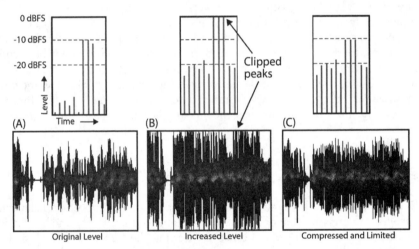

Fig. 15-14. Compression and limiting. (A) This audio has great dynamic range—note the difference in level between the quietest sounds and the peaks. (B) If we raise the level so that the quieter sounds are loud enough to be heard clearly, the peaks are now too high and will be clipped and distorted. (C) Using a compressor, we can reduce the height of the peaks while keeping the average level up. In this case, a limiter is also being used to ensure that no peaks go over –10 dBFS. Note that we've now significantly reduced the sound's dynamic range. Because the average level has been raised, C will sound a lot louder than A, even though the highest peaks are the same in both. (Steven Ascher)

Compression is a useful type of processing for many mixes. An audio compressor reduces the level of the loudest sounds to keep them from overrecording.[8] In some

---

8. Don't confuse audio compression with the digital compression used to make files smaller.

mixes, a compressor and/or peak limiter (see p. 454) might be used just to prevent overrecording of the loudest peaks. But for a TV mix or especially for an Internet mix, compressors are often used like a vise to squeeze the dynamic range of the sound. The overall level of the sound is raised, making the formerly "quiet" sounds pretty loud, and the compressor and limiter keep the loudest sounds from going over the top (see Fig. 15-14). The result is that everything is closer to the same level—the dynamic range is compressed—so the track will better penetrate the noisy home environment. However, too much compression can make the track sound flat and textureless, and that makes for an unpleasant experience if you do show the movie in a quiet room with good speakers. In the past, TV commercials were highly compressed, which is why they seemed to blast out of your TV set, even though their maximum peak level was no higher than the seemingly quieter program before and after. Typical pop music is also highly compressed, with dynamic range sometimes as little as 2 or 3 dB between average level and peaks, so everything sounds loud and punches through in a noisy car.

USING A COMPRESSOR. Compressors and other devices share certain types of adjustments that can seem really intimidating when you first encounter them, but will make more sense when you start using them (see Fig. 15-15). Take the example of using a compressor to reduce dynamic range so you can raise the overall level and make the track sound louder.

The *threshold* control determines how loud a sound must be for the compressor to operate; signals that exceed the threshold will be compressed. If you set the threshold to 0 dB, the compressor will do nothing.

The *attack* control determines how rapidly the compressor responds to peaks that cross the threshold (lower value equals faster attack). The *release* control sets the time it takes for the compressor to stop working after the peak passes. You can start with the defaults for attack and release (depending on the sound, if you set these too fast, you may hear the volume pumping; if you set them too slow, you may hear that too).

The *ratio* control determines how much the level is reduced. A 2:1 ratio is a good starting point, and it will compress signals above the threshold by one-half. The higher the ratio, the more aggressive the compression, and the flatter the dynamics. Limiters, which are like compressors on steroids, may use ratios of 20:1 up to 100:1 or more (along with a very fast attack), to create a brick wall that prevents levels from exceeding the threshold at all. Many people use a compressor with a relatively gentle ratio for the basic effect, and add a limiter just for protection at the very top end. You might set a limiter to prevent peaks from going above around –2 dB (or somewhat lower) to guarantee they won't be clipped.

Compressors and limiters often have a *gain reduction meter* that shows how much they are actively reducing the peaks. The meter stays at 0 when the sound level is below the threshold. As you lower the threshold, you'll see the compressor reducing the peaks more, and the track will probably sound quieter. If you now increase the *gain* control (which affects the overall level), you can increase the loudness. By tweaking the threshold, the ratio, and the gain, you'll find a balance you like that reduces the dynamic range a little or a lot (depending on the effect you're going for) and places the audio at the level that's right for the mix you're doing. Generally you don't want a combination that results in the compressor constantly reducing the

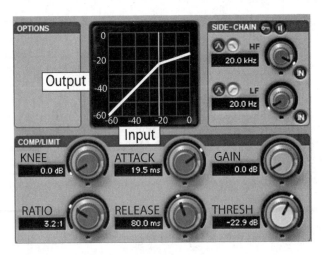

Fig. 15-15. Compressor/limiter. This DigiRack plug-in has a graph that shows the relationship of the sound level going *into* the compressor (the horizontal axis) and the sound level coming *out of* the compressor (the vertical axis). With no compression, output equals input. In this figure, audio levels above the –22 dB threshold will be compressed (reduced in volume). It's interesting to compare this to Fig. 5.1, which shows a graph with a similar slope used to compress video levels. (Avid Technology, Inc.)

level by several dBs (which you'll see on the gain reduction meter) or things may sound squashed and unnatural.

Some apps offer compressor effects that are highly simplified with little user adjustment, such as Final Cut Pro X's loudness effect (discussed below). These may work fine for general purposes and they're obviously easy to use.

After you create any effect, hit the *bypass* button to compare before and after, to see if you really like it.

Loudness Meters and New Standards

There has been a major change in how audio levels for television programs are measured and controlled. As discussed on p. 448, neither peak-reading meters nor VU meters give an accurate representation of how loud something sounds. However, newer *loudness meters* use a sophisticated algorithm to give a reading that much more closely represents how loud the program feels to a listener (*perceived loudness*). Starting around 2010, a new generation of loudness meters arrived that comply with the *ITU-R BS.1770* standard (see Fig. 15-16). Loudness is measured in *LUs* (loudness units); 1 LU is equivalent to 1 dB.

In Europe, loudness meters are marked in *LUFS* (*loudness units*, referenced to *full scale*). In North America, a very similar system uses the *LKFS* scale (*loudness, K weighted, relative to full scale*). A reading in LUFS is essentially the same as one in LKFS.[9]

---

9. EBU meters that read in LUFS use "gating" to ignore moments of silence in determining the average level. For typical television programming the difference between a reading in LUFS and one in LKFS may be less than 1 dB.

Most loudness meters can display the loudness averaged over a few-second period as well as across the entire program (called *program loudness*). They also provide a superaccurate reading of peaks (*true peak level*, which accounts for the highest spikes that can result after digital-to-analog conversion).[10] The key thing to remember about loudness meters is that the reading in LUFS or LKFS is a very good indication of how loud the program will sound.

As loudness metering technology has developed, the rules broadcasters must follow to control the audio level of programming have changed as well. In the United States, Congress passed the CALM Act, which requires that TV commercials be at a similar loudness level as other programming. No longer can ads get away with using extreme compression to sound so much louder than TV shows. In Europe, the EBU is putting in place similar guidelines. Networks are using loudness metering to ensure consistent loudness across all their programming and across different playback devices.[11]

In mixing an individual movie or show, the legal loudness level may be used to set the loudness of an "anchor element" (typically dialogue), with other

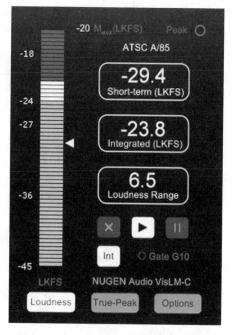

Fig. 15-16. Loudness meter. This plug-in by NuGen displays a variety of information, including the loudness of the audio at any moment, as well as the loudness averaged over the length of the program ("integrated"), which helps you stay legal for broadcast. This meter can display loudness in LKFS units used in North America or LUFS used in Europe. (NuGen Audio)

elements in the mix (music, effects) balanced around it. The various elements do not have to be at the same level. The new standards should permit more dynamic mixing in individual scenes since the measured loudness is an average over the whole program.

Setting the Mix Level

If you're working with a mixer, he'll know what level to record the track at. If your movie will be delivered to a TV network, the broadcaster will give you technical specs for program loudness and true peak levels; be sure to show them to the mixer.

---

10. *True peak* level, which loudness meters can display, can be 2 dB higher than what typical peak meters indicate.

11. With programs encoded in Dolby AC3, a chunk of metadata called *dialnorm* should indicate the loudness at which the program was recorded. Broadcasters and cable operators are required to set it to the average program and commercial loudness. If set appropriately, loudness will be consistent for consumers from channel to channel and from program to program.

In North America, new digital television standards call for the average loudness of dialogue to be –24 LKFS, plus or minus 2 LUs. Short peaks can go very high (up to –2 dBFS) as long as dialogue is correct (which allows for punchy effects or moments of loud music). Loudness does *not* need to read a constant –24, it simply must come out to this average value over the length of a show or a commercial and not vary too much during the program. In Europe, the target for average loudness is –23 LUFS, plus or minus 1 LU.

If you're doing your own mix, ideally you'll work with a loudness meter, which may be available as a plug-in for your NLE or DAW or as a stand-alone application or device.

If you don't have a loudness meter, you're probably using the audio meter on your NLE or DAW, which is typically a peak-reading meter with 0 dBFS at the top of the scale (see Fig. 11-10). NLE peak meters don't give a good reading of perceived loudness, but you can approximate the correct target loudness by keeping the dialogue peaks around –10 dBFS on the NLE's peak meter.[12]

As noted above, occasional peaks can legally go up to –2 dBFS, but don't let the level stay up there. Some mixers use a "brick wall" limiter or compressor to keep peaks safely below.

A reference tone should be recorded in the color bars that precede the program. As discussed on p. 452, a reference tone of –20 dBFS is common in the U.S., while –18 dBFS is used in the UK.

In some cases when mixing for nonbroadcast video or Internet use, people like to mix with a higher average level for dialogue (but as before, highest peaks should not exceed –2 dBFS). If you're mixing for the Web, listen to how your encoded video compares in level to other material on the Web and adjust as necessary. Whether your outlet is the Internet, DVD/Blu-ray, TV, or theaters, the goal is to have an average level that's consistent with the other movies out there, so that your audio sounds fine without people having to set the playback level up or down.

Once you have the recording level set so it looks correct according to the meter, set the monitor speakers to a comfortable level. Then, *don't change the speaker level while you mix*, so you'll have a consistent way to judge volume level by ear. Many mixers work with a quite loud monitor so they can hear everything clearly, but be aware that a monitor set to a high volume level will make bass and treble seem more vivid compared to a quieter monitor. So music, for example, will seem more present when the monitor is loud. When you listen later on a monitor set to a quieter, more normal level, the music will seem less distinct, even though the mix hasn't changed.

In most mix studios, you can switch between full-sized, high-quality speakers and small, not-great speakers, which can be useful in helping you judge how the movie may ultimately sound in different viewing/listening environments.

HITTING THE TARGET. Good sound mixers are able to balance sections of the movie that should be relatively quiet with those that should be loud, all the

12. You can download audio clips at www.atsc.org that are recorded at –24LKFS so you can see how they read on your meters and get a sense for where the peaks should be. Look for documents referring to A/85 calibration.

while keeping the sound track as a whole at the proper level to be consistent with industry standards. As noted above, if the movie will be broadcast, there are slightly different standards for North America, the UK, and Europe. Theatrical mixes often have yet different target levels. A professional mixer can guide you through the process and put you in a good position to pass the (often nitpicky) technical requirements of broadcasters and distributors.

Filmmakers doing their own mixes sometimes use filters or plug-ins to automatically set the level of the entire movie or of individual clips. For example, *normalizing* filters, such as the *normalization gain* filter in Final Cut Pro 7, work by scanning through the audio to find the highest peaks, then they adjust the overall level so those peaks hit a specified level (default is 0 dBFS, but you shouldn't let peaks go this high). Eyeheight makes the KARMAudioAU plug-in, which measures loudness, not just peaks, and can ensure that tracks stay within the different international loudness standards mentioned above.

These kinds of automated features can be useful to ensure that no levels are too hot. However, the risk of using them to push up the level of quieter passages is that you may lose dynamic range, and things that should be quiet will now be louder. If you choose to normalize, be sure to listen and decide if you like the result. Final Cut Pro X offers a "loudness" effect as an "audio enhancement," which is essentially a compressor/limiter as described above. This can automatically increase average level and decrease dynamic range, but it does offer manual override.

FREQUENCY RANGE AND EQ

Another consideration when mixing is the balance of low-, mid-, and high-frequency sounds (from bass to treble).

During the shoot, we make every effort to record sound with good mics and other equipment that has a flat response over a wide range of frequencies (see p. 423 for more on this concept). We want to capture the low frequencies for a full-bodied sound and the high frequencies for brightness and clarity. However, in mixing, we often make adjustments that might include: reducing (rolling off) the bass to minimize rumble from wind or vehicles; increasing the midrange to improve intelligibility; and cutting or rolling off high frequencies to diminish noise or hiss.

Changing the relative balance of frequencies is called *equalization* or *EQ*. EQ is done in part just to make the track sound better. Some people like to massage the sound quite a bit with EQ; others prefer a flatter, more "natural" approach. It's up to you and your ears.

However, as with setting the level, it's not just how things sound in the mix studio that you need to be concerned with. What will the audience's listening environment be? A theater with big speakers or a noisy living room with a small TV? The big bass speakers in a theater can make a low sound feel full and rich. A pulsing bass guitar in the music could sound very cool. The same bass played on a low-end TV might just rattle the speaker and muddy the other sounds you want to hear. Some recording formats (like film optical tracks) can also limit frequency response.

When frequency range is limited, one common problem is that dialogue that sounds clear in the mix room may lose intelligibility later on. Sometimes it's necessary to make voices a little "thinner" (using less bass and accentuated midrange) so they'll sound clearer to the audience.

This is where an experienced mixer can be very helpful in knowing how to adjust EQ for the ultimate viewer.

Setting EQ

You may want to use some EQ during the picture edit to improve your tracks for screenings, or you may be doing your own final mix. *Equalizers* allow you to selectively emphasize (boost) or deemphasize (cut or roll off) various frequencies throughout the audio spectrum. The simplest "equalizer" is the bass/treble control on a car radio. *Graphic equalizers* have a separate slider or control for several different bands of frequencies (see Fig. 11-12). *Parametric equalizers* allow you to select different frequency bands, choose how wide each band is, and boost or cut them to varying degrees (see Fig. 15-17).

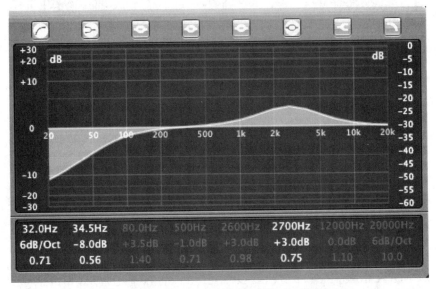

Fig. 15-17. An equalizer can boost different frequency bands (above the 0 dB line) or diminish them (below the line). The controls at the bottom of this Apple Logic equalizer allow you to select the center of each frequency band, how wide the band is, and how much to raise or lower the sound level. The EQ shown here is a basic one for improving the clarity of speech tracks by boosting the midrange and rolling off the bass (compare it with Fig. 10-21B). Equalization should always be done by ear and not by formula. (Apple, Inc.)

To increase the intelligibility of speech, you might boost midrange frequencies that are between around 2 and 4 kHz (2,000 to 4,000 Hz). To increase the "warmth" or fullness of voice or music, experiment with boosting the 200 to 300 Hz region.

Rolling off low frequencies reduces the rumble caused by wind and microphone noise (for more, see Bass Filters, p. 459). Some people reduce frequencies below about 100 Hz, rolling off at a slope of around 24dB per octave. Others use a low-frequency cutoff (high pass filter) set slightly lower (around 75 to 80 Hz or so).

Since bass rumble can force you to record at too low a level, this is one type of EQ that should generally be done.

High-frequency hiss from mic or system noise may be reduced with a noise-reduction plug-in (preferable—see below) or by rolling off frequencies starting above about 5 kHz or so. The upper-end frequencies can be cut off with a *low pass* or *high shelf filter*. The sound of a voice on the telephone can be simulated by boosting frequencies between about 400 and 2,000 Hz and rolling off all others. Many NLEs have EQ presets you can experiment with that may do what you want with one click.

Good equalization is an art, and should always be done by ear, not by numbers.

OTHER SOUND PROCESSING

Many tools are available to manipulate sound, including the compressors and equalizers just discussed, plus pitch shifters, delays, and noise reduction. In the past, separate hardware devices were used for different effects. Today, virtually all types of sound processing can be done with software plug-ins. The following are a few common tools.

Noise Reduction

Ambient noise is perhaps the biggest problem in location sound recording. Other types of noise, including hum or hiss, can be produced by lights, equipment, or analog tape.

Various noise-reduction apps can be very effective in isolating different types of noise and eliminating or reducing them with minimal effect on other sounds. These may be part of an NLE or DAW and/or available as plug-ins, such as those made by iZotope and Bias. With many of these noise-reduction systems, you "train" the software by letting it analyze a section of audio that has *just* the offending noise. It can then reduce that noise in passages that contain dialogue, music, or other sounds.

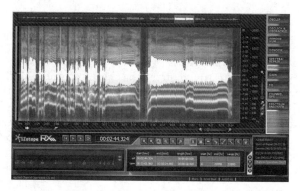

Fig. 15-18. Digital noise reducers, like the iZotope RX 2, can target many types of noise and reduce or remove them, often with little effect on dialogue and music. The RX 2 is available as a plug-in and a stand-alone application. Most NLEs offer some form of noise reduction. (iZotope, Inc.)

If your audio clip has a short section in which the noise is in the clear with nothing else, that's probably enough for the software to analyze. If not, you might include handles or an additional clip with the same noise for the mixer to use.

RX is a suite of audio repair tools by iZotope (www.izotope.com) that includes plug-ins to restore peaks that were clipped due to overrecording and to visually identify noise (such as a siren) so it can be removed from dialogue (see Fig. 15-18).

Another noise reduction method is called a *noise gate*. Noise gates minimize noise by acting like an automatic gain control in reverse: whenever there is no clear sound signal (such as speech) they *reduce* the recording level—because it is during the pauses that noise is the most conspicuous. Noise gates can make a noisy track clearer, but a heavily "gated" track will cause the background level to abruptly rise and fall, making it sound noticeably processed. Noise gates can also be used to make an overly reverberant track drier and to change the character of music.

Notch and Hum Filters

Also called *dipping filters*, these are a bit like very precise equalizers. They allow you to pinpoint one or two frequency bands and *notch* (cut) them or *peak* (boost) them. Notch filters are useful for isolating and removing specific noises, like the 60 Hz hum caused by fluorescent lights (50 Hz in Europe and Asia), with minimal disturbance to the rest of the track. To get rid of a noise, start by peaking it to make it as loud as possible. Once you've located it, then dip at the same frequency.

Many NLEs have *hum filters*, which do a similar thing. There may be frequency setting for the center of the hum and a *Q setting* that controls how far above and below that frequency is affected (the bandwidth). Use the *gain control* to reduce the hum as much as possible without impairing other sounds. Many kinds of interference are audible at both fundamental frequencies and harmonics; notching at two or three frequencies may be necessary for complete removal.

The more sophisticated noise-reducing plug-ins mentioned above may do a better job than either of these filters.

Reverb

The way sound waves reflect off the walls of an enclosed space gives your ear cues about how large the space is. This sound reverberation gives a sense of "liveness" to sound (see Acoustics of the Recording Space, p. 445). A reverb unit can be used to add reverberation to sound after it has been recorded. With more reverb, sounds take longer to decay, making them seem like they were recorded in a larger or more reverberant space. Reverb units can make voices postdubbed in the studio seem more like they were recorded on location. Sound that lacks reverb is sometimes called "dry" or "tight." Many DAWs have sophisticated modules that can simulate any size space from a closet to a concert hall, such as Logic's Space Designer. An *echo filter* repeats the sound as though echoing in a tunnel or canyon.

De-Essers

Compressors used to reduce the sibilance, or whistling, caused by *s* sounds in some people's speech are called *de-essers*. You can hear sibilance distortion sometimes by turning the volume very high on a radio with small speakers. The de-esser

Fig. 15-19. iZotope Radius can be used to change the pitch of an instrument or voice while preserving the timing of the original recording. Or you can change the tempo (speed) of the audio without changing the pitch. Pitch shifters, which may be included in your NLE, can help when you want to change the speed of the movie or an individual clip without the pitch changes that would otherwise occur. (iZotope, Inc.)

compresses high frequencies (where sibilance distortion occurs) without affecting much else.

MIX FORMATS

Sound Formats and Audio Channels

Several different audio formats are used when movies are shown in theaters, on TV, from DVD/Blu-ray, or over the Web. Formats vary in how many channels of audio they can play. In some cases, the producer can choose how many channels to mix for; in others, it's dictated by the distribution method planned for the project. Let's begin with the options in terms of audio channels.

Mono sound means a single channel of audio. For example, 16mm film prints with optical sound tracks reproduce mono sound. The film may be shown on a projector with a single built-in speaker or it may be shown in a theater that has many speakers. Regardless, there is only one channel of sound. Student films are often recorded, edited, and mixed in mono.

Virtually *every other* means of showing a movie today has the possibility of at least two channels of sound. Some have six or more.

In typical music or TV sound in the home, *stereo sound* means two channels (left and right). Stereo (also called 2.0 channels) adds presence to music and allows you to place sounds on one side or the other, giving a sense of dimensionality. A movie can be released in stereo even if all the production sound was recorded in mono. In fact, this is often the case. The sound recorded in the field may be taken with a single mono microphone and recorded on one track in the camcorder or audio recorder. During editing, additional tracks are introduced, such as music and effects. Finally, in the mix, the mixer portions the sounds out to either or both of the two stereo channels. Music tracks may have true stereo separation while dialogue is often positioned identically on the left and right (with the pan control in the center), making it essentially "two-channel mono." Many television programs, corporate videos, and other movies are done this way.

In the film industry, "stereo" is understood to include a surround channel. In a movie theater, surround speakers are placed along the sides and rear of the theater. Sounds that are assigned to the surround channel include ambience (atmospheres) and some special effects, which surround the audience, adding a sense of realism.

Proper theater stereo also has a center channel so that the sound of actors speaking on screen will appear natural, coming directly from the screen instead of seeming off balance for people who are not sitting in the middle of the theater. This format is often referred to as *LCRS* (left, center, right, surround).

Films mixed for analog *Dolby Stereo* can have these four channels, with left, center, and right speakers hidden behind the screen, and surround speakers at the rear and sides of the theater. The four channels are specially encoded so they can be recorded on just two tracks, so a "stereo" (two-channel) recording can carry all the information for the four playback streams. This encoding of four channels in two is also called *LT/RT* (left total, right total).

Moving up the food chain, the *5.1-channel* standard includes the same left, center, and right channels across the front of the room but the surround channel is split into left and right sides. For really deep bass, an additional channel is added to drive a subwoofer—this channel is called *LFE* (*low-frequency effects*). Since this bass channel uses much less bandwidth than the other five channels, this layout is referred to as having "5.1 channels."

The most common 5.1-channel format is *Dolby Digital* (*AC-3*), which is used in a wide variety of applications, including digital broadcasting, DVDs, Blu-rays, and theatrical films. Dolby Digital is digitally compressed and can pack all 5.1 channels into less space than a single channel of uncompressed PCM audio.

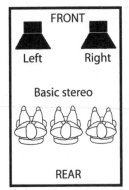 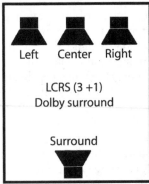 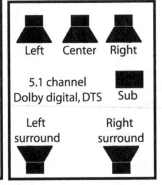

Fig. 15-20. Speaker layouts for different sound formats (as seen from above). The single surround channel in the LCRS format is often sent to more than one speaker. The 5.1-channel format includes a subwoofer for low-frequency effects (deep bass).

A Dolby Pro Logic II encoder can record the 5.1 channels to a two-track recording format (much like Dolby Stereo discussed above). This may be used, for example, in a consumer camcorder equipped for 5.1-channel surround sound recording.

If a movie mixed in Dolby Digital is broadcast on TV or distributed for home video, the system cleverly adjusts for individual playback systems. People who have only one speaker (say, in an older TV set) will receive a mono signal with all the sound. People who have two speakers (in a typical "stereo" TV) receive a two-channel signal (called a *stereo downmix*). And people who have a "home theater" setup with left, right, center, and surround speakers and a Pro Logic decoder in their system can "unfold" the matrix into 5.1 channels for the full effect.

Other formats add more channels. *Dolby E* can store up to eight channels of audio on two compressed channels (it is decoded to Dolby Digital before reaching home viewers). *Dolby Surround EX* adds a center surround speaker for 6.1 channels, *Dolby Digital Plus* has 7.1 channels (the surround speaker array has four parts—left side, left back, right side, right back). *SDDS* offers 7.1 channels by dividing the front speaker array into five parts. The goal of adding more channels is to provide a more dynamic, enveloping sound experience for the audience. Toward that aim, Dolby is developing the *Atmos* format, which includes speakers *over* the audience for a 3D, immersive effect. For more on how these formats are applied to film, see Sound for Film Prints, p. 713.

WORKING WITH AN AUDIO FORMAT. Broadcasters or distributors often require programming in a certain format (increasingly, 5.1 channels is standard for television, DVD, and Blu-ray). In other cases you may have an option.

Mixing for many channels adds time and complexity to the sound edit and mix; it also requires a studio equipped with the necessary speaker layout. While dialogue is almost always placed in the center, you have flexibility about where to place other types of sounds.

Hardware converters, apps, and plug-ins like Soundfield's UPM-1 can take a stereo (two-channel) sound track and "fake" a 5.1-channel mix by putting dialogue in the front speaker channels while placing effects and ambience (as much as possible) in the surround speaker channels. This synthesized upmix can allow stereo programs to be released in 5.1-channel formats for broadcast or other distribution.

As noted above, programming released in 5.1 channels will be viewed by some in mono and by some in two-channel stereo. It's essential that you test your 5.1-channel mix to be sure it "folds down" correctly to stereo and mono without any phasing or other issues. Even a program originally mixed in stereo should be monitored in mono, preferably through headphones.

When a theatrical film is to be mixed in Dolby Digital, arrangements must be made to license the format from Dolby, which is not cheap. (Licensing is also needed for nontheatrical products that bear the Dolby logo.)

Broadcasters now routinely require 5.1-channel sound tracks, but some types of productions may not gain much from a multichannel sound track and aren't required to have one. For example, a corporate video or Web video might be mixed in basic stereo (just two channels) or even mono on the assumption that most viewers will not have a home theater setup and will hear the sound through relatively

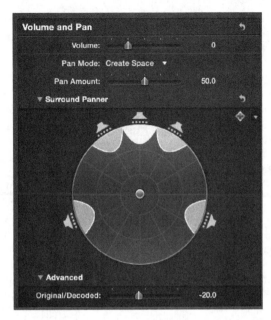

15-21. When doing a 5.1-channel mix, you can use a surround panner to set the direction from which the audience hears different sounds. Shown here, the panner from Final Cut Pro X with left, center, and right front speaker channels, as well as left and right surround channels. (Apple, Inc.)

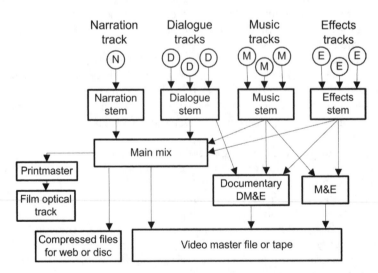

Fig. 15-22. This shows how individual dialogue, music, and effects (and sometimes narration) tracks are combined into stems, and the stems are then output in various combinations for different deliverables. An M&E mix (or a DM&E for a documentary) may be recorded on separate audio channels along with the main mix on the final video master file or tape. (Steven Ascher)

small speakers on a TV or computer. Particularly for nonaction, non-special-effects movies, many audiences never notice the difference.

DELIVERABLES

At the end of the mix, you often need to create several versions of the sound track for different uses.

- *Main mix.* The mixed audio is output from the mixer's DAW so it can be recombined with the edited picture. This often involves importing a BWF or other format audio file into an NLE and then outputting the married picture and sound from there to a file or tape. Sometimes a *layback* is done to record the mixed sound track directly to the edit master tape (or *several* edit master tapes, depending on how many versions there are).
- *Printmaster.* For projects that will be finished on film, an output is done to create the *printmaster*, which is the source from which the film print's sound track will be created. Sometimes the printmaster needs to be speed adjusted (for example to compensate for the 0.1 percent slowdown in telecined film in NTSC countries, or the 4.1 percent speedup in PAL countries; see Chapter 16). There may be one printmaster for 5.1-channel formats and another for LT/RT formats.
- *Mix stems.* *Mix stems* (also called *splits*) are the basic groups or components of the mix, including dialogue, narration, music, and effects.[13] In the main mix, all the stems are combined (see Fig. 15-22). However, having a separate file of each stem alone is extremely useful. You can use or exclude any stem for making trailers or other versions of the movie (for example, you'll often use different music in the trailer, or you may change the music in the movie itself if a music license runs out). Without stems, you'd have to return to the mix studio and try to split out what you need. On features, music stems without any fader moves are often a required deliverable.
- *Compressed files.* You may be making a version of the mix for Internet streaming or other compressed digital formats (which may or may not have the same number of channels as the main mix). Compression is usually done at the same time that the picture is encoded for Web delivery. The AAC codec is typically used for H.264 formats for Web and mobile devices.

Foreign Release

For foreign distribution, when translation to another language is called for, you will need to supply an *M&E* (*music and effects*) track. The M&E mix contains all the nondialogue sound that will be used as a bed on which dubbed, foreign language voices will be added. For a drama, there may be sync scenes in which dialogue and effects (such as footsteps) can't be separated. In this case, Foley work may be needed to create clean effects tracks that have no dialogue—a process that may take several

---

13. Background (BG) sound is sometimes a separate stem from effects, and sometimes they are combined in one stem.

days (see p. 644). A "fully filled M&E" means you are supplying complete and continuous background and effects tracks, along with any music, so that dialogue in another language can later be added without additional track work.

On a documentary, the M&E may just be a mix without narration (sometimes called a *DM&E*), since the dialogue is often inextricable from the "effects" (they're all recorded together on location). When a foreign language version of a documentary is made, interviews and other scenes are often subtitled, but sometimes they are dubbed instead (because broadcasters don't want to make viewers read subtitles). If there is narration, it's usually dubbed even if the dialogue is subtitled. Broadcasters may ask for an "undipped" version of the sound track with no narration (undipped means a track that has not been lowered, or *ducked*, as it normally would be whenever the narrator speaks). You can prepare for this by first mixing the entire film with undipped music and sync sound, then returning to the beginning and making a dipped version with narration exclusively for domestic use.[14] See Chapter 17 for more on preparing a movie for foreign release.

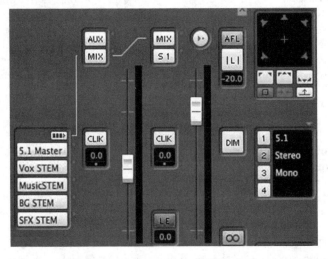

Fig. 15-23. This Nuendo monitor panel has selections for listening to individual stems—vox (voice), music, BG (background), and SFX (effects)—or the combined 5.1-channel master mix. The master can be monitored with all 5.1 channels using a full speaker array in the room, as a stereo (two-channel) downmix on two speakers, or as a mono mix with just one channel of sound. (Steinberg Media Technologies GmbH)

14. DAWs can output undipped tracks simply by removing the added level settings.

CHAPTER 16

Working with Film in Postproduction

This chapter is about working with motion picture film during editing, post-production, and distribution. This concerns projects that are shot on film but edited digitally, as well as projects that are shot digitally but will make film prints for theatrical distribution. You'll also find material on traditional methods of conforming film negative and printing it. Since the vast majority of projects that are shot on film today are edited digitally using NLEs, information on now old-fashioned film editing using workprint and flatbed editing machines has been deleted from this edition of the book. However, if you are cutting workprint in the traditional way, you can find excerpts on editing from the third edition at www.filmmakershandbook.com.

See Chapter 9 for production techniques, Chapter 14 for nonlinear editing, and Chapter 7 for sending film to the lab for processing during production.

OVERVIEW OF FILM-VIDEO TRANSFERS

From Film to Digital and Back Again

In contemporary filmmaking, every movie that isn't shot on digital video gets transferred to digital at some point, usually for editing and certainly as part of distribution.

Though theatrical distribution is increasingly digital, many theaters around the world still show 35mm film prints. So movies intended for theatrical distribution, whether shot digitally or on film, may need to make film prints, which often involves a digital-to-film transfer (film-out).

Your options abound when it comes to taking film original footage and editing it digitally. You've also got options when it comes to taking the digitally edited movie when it's done and translating that to film. Different productions use different strategies, depending on time, budget, and intended distribution. In fact, there are so many strategies and combinations that it can be hard to keep them straight. The good news is that even though there are numerous routes to get from one end of the process to other, eventually you only have to pick *one*.

In overview, there are two chief ways of transferring film to digital: a *telecine*, which can transfer to standard definition and high definition video (and sometimes larger frame sizes) and a *film scanner*, which can create high-resolution files (often 2K or 4K) in formats such as DPX. Telecines tend to be used for material intended for television, for independent films, and for the editing stage of high-budget feature films. Scanners, which are slower and more expensive to transfer on, tend to be used for final transfers of higher-budget features. However, distinctions between telecines and scanners are breaking down; see below for more on both.

Fig. 16-1. Shadow Telecine. CCD imaging. Outputs all common HD and SD video resolutions. (Digital Film Technology)

Some of your options in transferring film to digital include:

- *Recording format.* Film may be transferred to a variety of digital formats (SD, HD, 2K, 4K) and recorded to file or tape.
- *Frame rate conversion.* Film is generally shot at 24 fps (25 fps for TV in PAL countries). The digital transfer may be recorded at frame rates including 24, 25, and 30 fps. Converting from one frame rate to another may involve a pulldown process.
- *Color correction.* In some transfers, a lot of time and care are put into color balancing; other transfers are done quickly without fine-tuning color, or they are done "flat" to maximize color correction options later.
- *Audio speed correction.* When the playback speed of the picture is changed, the audio may need to be sped up or slowed down to stay in sync.

- *Audio syncing.* On a film shoot, sound and picture are recorded separately. It's possible to sync the audio during the telecine session or after.

As for the other side of the process—transferring a digital project to film—regardless of whether the footage originated on film or digital, perhaps the most widely used method is a *laser film recorder*, which can create a film negative from a digital file or tape. Of course, the usefulness of 35mm film prints for distribution is rapidly diminishing as theaters convert to digital.

Choosing your route through production and postproduction should be done in consultation with the lab or postproduction facility, editing team, and audio post facility. Get the cinematographer and sound recordist in on those conversations too. It's hard to overstate the importance of working out your planned workflow with all concerned parties in advance.

A note about terminology: "digital video" includes many different resolutions and frame sizes, including SD and HD. However, when you're talking about high-resolution formats such as RGB or 2K or 4K, while they are digital, many people don't consider them "video" because they can't be recorded or broadcast with typical video equipment. In the discussion below, the term "digital" includes video and nonvideo formats.

SOME FILM-DIGITAL WORKFLOWS

This section examines some possible workflows that can be used for projects that originate on film (or on 24p video). The scenarios are not offered as recommendations, but rather as a way to discuss various options. Elements from one workflow might be combined with another.

Scenario One: Shoot Film, Transfer Once, Finish Digital

This might be used for a project shot on film and destined for the cinema, or geared toward a relatively quick postproduction schedule for television broadcast. If film prints are needed, they are made by doing a film-out from the final digital master. See Figure 16-2.

In this scenario, film may be shot in any format (35mm, 16mm, or Super 8). Production audio is recorded in the field double-system with a file-based (flash memory or hard drive) recorder. Timecode on the audio is highly recommended.

In-camera timecode or timecode slates (see p. 466) during production will greatly facilitate syncing the audio, but timecode on the film is not required. After shooting, the negative is processed and prepared for the film-to-video transfer or scanning (see below). All the footage may be transferred, or the telecine or film scanner can fast-forward through undesired material to record only the selected takes. In this workflow, the film will only be transferred to digital *once*, so the output of the telecine or scanner is recorded to a high-quality digital format such as 1920 x 1080 HD or, in the case of a low-enough shooting ratio or a high-enough budget, 2K or 4K. Some transfers are recorded to a tape format such as HDCAM SR. Others go directly to file on hard drives—bypassing videotape altogether—as

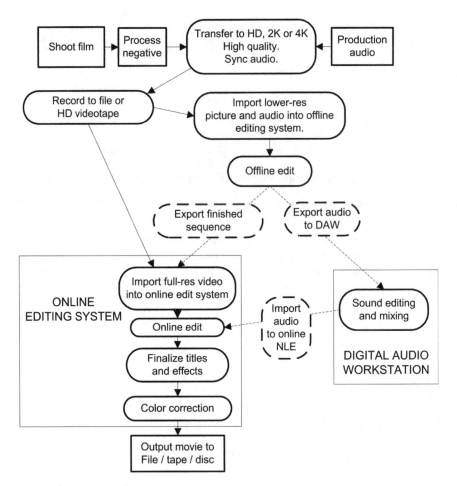

Fig. 16-2. Scenario One. A possible route for shooting film, transferring to digital once, then editing and finishing digitally.

uncompressed DPX files or high-quality Apple ProRes or Avid DNxHD compressed files.

Because this is the only digital transfer that will be done, a degree of care must be taken in color correction—more than for the "digital dailies" used in Scenario Two. Even so, final color correction will be done later in the process.

If possible, it's desirable to sync sound and picture during the telecine session (scanners don't offer this possibility). If the film and audio have proper timecode, there are automated systems that can sync up on the fly during the telecine transfer. However, if picture and sound need to be lined up manually, it can get expensive to do this in the telecine suite. As an alternative, some facilities have a *layback suite*. Here, you could take the picture recorded in the telecine that has no audio and sync it up in this specialized room that bills at a lower hourly rate (see Fig. 16-3).

The reason to sync up at this stage is so that the master recording (tape or file)

Fig. 16-3. The layback suite is an editing room set up for syncing audio to video. Less expensive than syncing in the telecine suite. (DuArt Film and Video)

will have sound on it. This can simplify other postproduction tasks and make it easy to create digital dailies for the production team on location or for whoever needs them. However, on many productions, the sound is synced later, using the nonlinear editing system to do the work. Syncing on the NLE may be the most economical and can result in better sync because of subframe accuracy.[1]

After the telecine or scanning step is completed, the transfer facility uses the HD master tapes or high-resolution files to create compressed HD media that can be directly imported into your editing system. You might choose an even more compressed version tailored to offline editing using a codec such as ProRes Proxy.

After the material has been loaded into the NLE, you're ready to do your offline edit. When you're done with the offline edit and have "locked picture," you're ready to do the online. Often this is done at a postproduction facility. Or you may be doing the online yourself.

If you did the offline edit with high-quality, high-resolution files, you can simply use them for the various stages of finishing. If you used a more compressed codec for offline editing, then you'll need to up-res to the full-resolution files or tapes created in the telecine (this is a typical offline/online workflow; see p. 556). Color correction may be done at this stage or later on a specialized system.

Generally, audio will be exported to a digital audio workstation (DAW) for mixing in a dedicated sound studio (see Chapter 15). The audio is reimported to the online.

At this point, the show is complete and can be duplicated to various formats and

---

1. In the telecine, sync is adjusted in one-frame increments; in the NLE you can slide audio plus or minus one-quarter frame or less.

frame rates as needed. If film prints are required for film distribution, a film-out can be done from the digital master.

Scenario Two: Shoot Film, Transfer Twice, Finish via D.I.

For higher-budget films, instead of using a normal telecine to transfer the camera negative to digital, you can use a high-resolution film scanner to create a 2K or 4K data file. At this resolution, the master edited version of the movie is called a digital intermediate, or D.I. (see below). The D.I. can be used to produce any number of digital file or tape outputs, including a Digital Cinema Package for theatrical use and a film-out to make film prints.

Because film scanners are expensive, create very large files, and may be slow, it's more economical to use them to scan *only* the footage used in the edited movie. In this

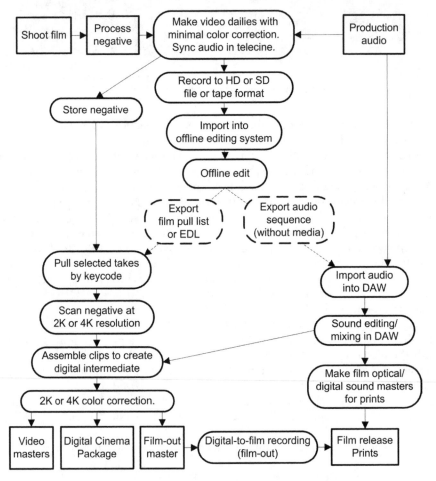

Fig. 16-4. Scenario Two. A possible route for shooting film, transferring to video dailies for the offline edit, then scanning the film to create a digital intermediate.

workflow, the film is transferred to digital twice. The first time captures all or most of the footage that was shot. These are *digital dailies* (also called *video dailies*), made as quickly as possible, often with minimal color correction, to HD using a conventional telecine. These dailies are used for the offline edit. Then, after the movie is edited and you know exactly which shots are needed for the final film, the selected footage is scanned at high resolution (2K or 4K) to create the D.I. (see Fig. 16-4).

In this scenario let's assume the production audio is synced with the picture in the telecine when the digital dailies are made. The telecine also compiles a *shot log*, which is a database that correlates the film keycode numbers and the video timecode generated during the transfer (see p. 693).

To begin the offline edit, you import the dailies (picture and sound) into the NLE. You also import the shot log, which, as you edit, enables the NLE to keep track of which parts of the film negative are being used in the movie.

When the offline is done and picture is locked, the NLE generates a pull list (see p. 701) to locate the selected negative that needs to be scanned. In some cases, selected shots are pulled by a negative cutter from the original camera rolls and strung together on a reel for digital scanning. In other cases, the rolls are left intact, and the scanner simply locates the frames it needs using keycode, fast-forwarding from one shot to the next on the camera roll.

Once the negative has been scanned at high resolution, an assembly (sometimes called a *conform*) is done to rebuild the edited film with high-res media (this is much like an online edit; see p. 611). Visual effects (VFX) are added; dust busting (to remove any dirt) and color correction are done. Actually, several different color corrections may be used for different end products. For example, one LUT (lookup table; see p. 631) is used to translate the image for HD output, and a different LUT is used for film-out (and there are many different LUTs for particular looks).

These days, production audio recorded in the field that has been synced in the telecine or NLE can usually be used for the final audio mix.[2] However, particularly on high-budget films, the sound editors may prefer to use the original production audio files as a source for the final mix. This may be because, on a concert film, for example, the production audio was recorded at a higher sample rate or bit depth or with more channels. In this scenario, rather than export audio from the NLE for the mix, an audio OMF/AAF or composition is sent to a DAW without media, then the production audio files are imported directly into the DAW for mixing. Afterward, the mixed tracks are recombined with the digital master and a printmaster is made for film prints.

Scenario Three: Shoot Film, Transfer Twice, Finish via Film

This workflow is now much less common, but it might be used for a low-budget project that is shot on film and edited without a lot of visual effects. Like Scenario Two, it involves first making digital dailies by transferring the film quickly for of-

---

2. Quality varies among digital formats. Uncompressed PCM audio tracks at 48 kHz, 16 or 20 bits, are common in video formats and will serve fine if the original audio was recorded at a similar resolution.

fline editing. As before, the telecine generates a shot log that allows the NLE to track, via key numbers, what part of the negative you're using for the edit.

In this scenario, since we're trying to save money, the production audio is imported into the NLE and syncing is done in the editing room, which is cheaper than having the transfer house do it.

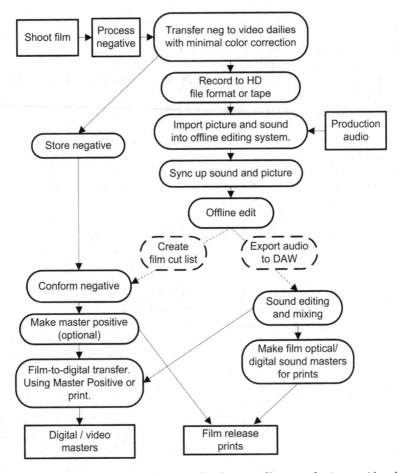

Fig. 16-5. Scenario Three. A possible route for shooting film, transferring to video dailies for the offline edit, then conforming the negative in the traditional way and finishing on film. Final video transfer is done from a film print or master positive.

The big differences between Scenario Two and Three take place after you lock picture in the offline. In Scenario Two, selected negative is then digitally scanned at high res to create a 2K or 4K D.I., from which all digital and film outputs are made. In Scenario Three, the NLE generates a film cut list (or an EDL can be used instead), which a negative cutter uses to conform the camera original negative in essentially the traditional way. This may involve cutting 16mm negative into A&B rolls or, in 35mm, creating a single strand (for more on negative cutting and printing, see p. 706). The lab then makes film prints from that conformed negative.

Since you will also need a digital version of the final, edited movie, this can be made by running a film print or intermediate (see p. 711) through a telecine.

In this scenario, audio is exported from the NLE for mixing on a DAW. The mixed sound track is then used for the video transfer. Analog and digital sound masters are also created for making film prints.

This method has become uncommon for a variety of reasons: there are few traditional negative cutters left, the process is time-consuming, and so on. However, D.I.'s are not cheap, and this method may be more affordable on some projects.

FILM-TO-DIGITAL TRANSFER DEVICES

The Telecine and Lower-End Methods

The *telecine* (pronounced "tel-e-sin-ee") is a device for converting film to video in real time. It has a transport to move film footage continuously across a scanner head that reads each frame and converts it to a digital video signal. High-end telecines are very sophisticated. Many can handle a variety of film formats (35mm, 16mm, Super 16, Super 8, and 8mm), either positive or negative film, at several different speeds with no danger of scratching. Modern telecines can output in HD or SD video and in some cases higher resolutions of 2K or 4K (not in real time).

There are various types of telecines. *Linear array CCD* systems (such as Digi-talFilmTechnology's popular Spirit series) use a bright xenon light to project an image of each frame onto several horizontal rows of CCDs. Some newer systems use LED illumination. The older *flying spot* systems optically superimpose the raster of a CRT onto each frame of film, which is then digitally sampled. Each of the different technologies has its "look," but all can produce superb results.

The *film chain* is a lower-end transfer device made up of a special 16mm film projector that projects the film image directly into a video camera. Film chains, holdovers from the early days of television, are less expensive than telecine transfers, provide much less control, and are not gentle enough to allow transferring negative. Super 8 and 8mm films are commonly transferred on this type of technology.

Sometimes people make a slop transfer by using a video camera to shoot a film image projected on a screen or an image off a flatbed editing system. Quality is low, and speed control is not precise enough for reliable editing.

In general usage, the word "telecine" is often used to mean any film-to-video conversion. It's also used to refer to the pulldown process (see Working with 24p and Pulldown, p. 601).

High-Resolution Film Scanners

Telecine transfers can produce images of very high quality, but which are subject to the limitations of video itself in terms of resolution and tonal reproduction. *Film scanners* are film transfer machines that get around those limitations and can capture all the resolution and tonal range of the original negative. If you're familiar with digital still photography, imagine every frame of 35mm or Super 16 film reproduced as a TIFF or RAW file, and you'll have the right idea. Film scanners typically capture film frames to uncompressed Digital Picture Exchange (DPX) files. DPX is based on a format Kodak devised for its pioneering (now defunct) Cineon film scanning system. DPX files are huge and therefore recorded directly to arrays of hard drives or to digital linear tape (DLT).

Fig. 16-6. The Spirit DataCine series of high-resolution scanners can output HD and SD video formats, and some can output 2K and 4K DPX data files. (DuArt Film and Video)

The two most common types of scans are 2K and 4K, which are typically 2048 x 1556 pixels and 4096 x 3112 pixels, respectively (the vertical pixel dimension of a 2K or 4K scan is determined by aspect ratio). The 4K version most closely approximates the original resolution of 35mm negative. However, when compared to 2K, 4K requires *four* times the data. This means longer scan times per frame and four times the disk storage for the larger 50MB/frame DPX files (2K files are 12MB/frame). This translates into at least double the costs of 2K. As a consequence, 2K scans have been Hollywood's budget choice for most 35mm special effects, digital cinema applications, and digital intermediate work, although this is changing as the price of high-end computing and fast disk arrays drops. For Super 16 scanning, 2K is considered more than adequate.

A 2K or 4K scan can serve as the ultimate "universal master"—a high-resolution 24p source from which to generate a digital intermediate for film release, files for digital cinema projection, as well as downconverts to HD or SD at virtually any frame rate and frame size, including NTSC and PAL. One caveat, however, is that storing and retrieving ninety minutes of huge DPX files is expensive, as is processing them to create downconverts to SD and HD. It is often more economical to simply transfer the negative on a telecine to a 24p HD master, which is then used as the digital intermediate to make HD deliverables.

TYPES OF FILM SCANNERS. Some film scanners have a continuous film transport similar to that of a telecine. They can transfer film to HD video and also create 2K and 4K scans. Examples are the DigitalFilmTechology's Scanity and Spirit DataCine family, and Cintel's C-Reality, DSX, and dataMill. Some can scan film negative to 2K resolution at 24 fps (real time).

Other scanners are based on the slower, intermittent, pin-registered transports of optical printers, and these create high-resolution film scans at less than real time.

Digital Intermediates

Kodak created the term *digital intermediate*, or *D.I.*, to describe the process of scanning film to 2K or 4K digital files, doing color correction, degraining, scratch removal, wire removal, special effects, and so forth, in the digital realm, then outputting the results back to film in a seamless, undetectable manner, with no loss of resolution or tonal scale. However, in the years since the term first appeared, its use has widened to encompass virtually all high-resolution digital postproduction, from HD formats to DPX files. Many people use it to refer to a post workflow that results in no film-out at all—for instance, preparing a feature shot on Super 16 and scanned to HD for digital projection at a film festival.

Perhaps the best use of the term is to refer to workflows that involve shooting with high-quality image capture systems (including 16mm and 35mm film, HD video, RGB 4:4:4, or 2K or 4K files from digital cinematography cameras) with the intent of doing a high-quality theatrical release, either on film or via a DCP.

TELECINE OPTIONS AND CONTROLS

Film gets transferred to digital in various ways and you have many choices.

RECORDING FORMAT AND SCANNING OPTIONS

Frame Size

If a film is only going to be transferred to digital once, an argument can be made for transferring to the highest-resolution format you can afford. For a well-budgeted feature, that means scanning to 2K or 4K DPX files. For an independent film or television production, 1920 x 1080 HD is virtually a match for 2K and it's cheaper.

If you're going to the expense of shooting film, it is counterproductive to transfer to SD, as most broadcasters and screening venues show HD these days.

If you're making digital dailies for the offline edit, choose a lower-data-rate HD file using ProRes or DNxHD codecs. It will not only provide a better offline editing experience, but you'll be able to better inspect which shots are sharp or soft before they make it to the big screen.

Frame Rate and Scanning

Which frame rates you use to record in the digital transfer may depend on the part of the world you're working in (formerly NTSC countries or formerly PAL countries; see p. 7), the equipment available to you, and the end product you want to create.

NTSC COUNTRIES. The universal standard frame rate for shooting film is 24 fps. When editing digitally, there are many advantages to editing at 24 fps as well. Having a direct, one-to-one correspondence between film frames and digital frames simplifies things a great deal, and it ensures greater accuracy when moving back and forth between celluloid film and digital video. If you edit at 24 fps in the NLE, you can still derive other frame rates if needed later (for example, if you're broadcasting at 60i). Since each film frame resembles a progressive scan (each frame captured all at once), it also makes sense to do the digital transfer to a progressive digital format.

There are two main methods of transferring film to digital at 24p. One is to record to a 24-frame format. When recording to file, both ProRes and DNxHD can record at 24p. When recording to tape, formats like HDCAM SR can record at 24 PsF (see p. 602 and Fig. 14-35).

The other method is to record to a 60i format using 2:3 pulldown (see p. 603). If this is done, reverse pulldown can be used to restore the 24p stream in the NLE.

If the movie is being made for television and will be broadcast at 60i (30 fps), some people prefer to transfer the film in the telecine to 60i video using 2:3 pulldown and then just treat it like any other 60i video project. This can work fine, but it may lock you into interlace, which has various disadvantages (see p. 11).

When working with a 24p format, it's important to keep in mind that while the standard speed for film cameras is 24 fps, telecines in countries where NTSC video has been used will usually transfer at video frame rates that are 0.1 percent slower than the integer number (see The Frame Rate, p. 14). So when a video camera or deck indicates it's operating at "24p," that usually means 23.976p.[3]

What does this 0.1 percent slowdown mean to you? Well, first of all, you can't hear it or see it. Footage playing at 24p will look the same as 23.976p. However, if sound is running at one rate and the picture is running 0.1 percent faster or slower, they will go out of sync with each other. It's essential that the 0.1 percent slowdown be taken into account when working with audio (this is discussed below). It's also important to be clear whether you mean 24p or 23.976p as you plan workflows. Many NLEs offer the option of working at true 24p or at 23.976 fps.

PAL COUNTRIES. In countries where PAL was formerly the broadcast standard, frame rates are simpler. Film can be shot for television at 25 fps and telecined to 25p video in a simple frame-to-frame transfer with no speed change or pulldown. HD or SD video at 25p or 50i runs at *exactly* the stated rate.

When film is shot for cinema projection at 24 fps and transferred to 25p video you have options about how to handle it. The most common method is to speed the film up to 25 fps in the telecine (a 4.1 percent increase), which again provides a simple frame-to-frame transfer. This is sometimes called the *24@25* method. It will cause the audio to rise in pitch slightly (about a half tone), which can be digitally processed later if desired to lower the pitch. Depending on your NLE and your preferences, you may then edit at 25p or slow the NLE down to 24p for editing.

---

3. People often round 23.976 to 23.98 or 23.97 for convenience.

When projected in a theater at 24 fps, this will run normally, and when shown on television at 25 fps, it will have a 4.1 percent shorter running time and higher-pitched audio.

You can also use pulldown to transfer with no speed change. With the *24+1* telecine pulldown method, sometimes called *PAL+1*, an extra field is added every 12 frames, adding 1 video frame every second, bringing 24 fps up to 25 fps. With this method, audio remains at normal speed.

Recording Media and Compression

You can record with many video formats in the telecine (though your transfer facility may not have them all).

It is increasingly popular to record directly to file, using codecs like ProRes and DNxHD. The transfer house can transfer the files to your hard drives, which you should then immediately back up.

Some people prefer to record to tape, which can be used for archiving. HDCAM SR offers very high-quality RGB 4:4:4 recording, but it's not cheap. Other HD formats include D-5 HD and standard HDCAM for 4:2:2 $Y'C_BC_R$ recording. You'll still need files for editing, which can be made at the same time as the tapes or later *from* the tapes.

High-resolution 2K and 4K scans may be done to hard drives or media such as digital linear tape (DLT).

IMAGE CONTROL

Transfer and Color Correction Strategy

The telecine works in concert with several other pieces of equipment. The *color corrector* is a dedicated video processing system that allows the telecine operator or *colorist* to program color and other image settings. This is also called *grading* and the colorist may be called a *grader*.

For digital dailies, you have a choice of transferring all the footage so you have easy access to it in the editing room, or you could transfer only circle takes that were indicated in the camera report or log as being good. Generally, digital dailies are made directly from the original camera negative rolls (often two camera rolls are spliced together to form a *lab roll* or *flat* for transfer). You have a few choices in terms of how the footage is color-corrected:

- A *one-light transfer* uses a single color correction for the entire roll. This is the fastest and cheapest and may be done for dailies if the footage is going to be transferred a second time (as in Scenario Two, above).
- In a *best-light transfer*, the colorist may make a few corrections on each roll.
- In a *timed transfer*, the colorist does *scene-to-scene* color correction, making each shot look as good as possible. This is the slowest and most expensive. It's worth noting that no matter how well scene-to-scene grading is done, further color correction will be needed after the movie is edited.
- A *flat transfer* (also called a *flat grade*) is a variant of a one-light and involves

Fig. 16-7. Colorist at work on a DaVinci system. (DuArt Film and Video)

creating an image that has visibly low contrast and preserves as many of the extremes of exposure as possible at one time. This approach is often used when the negative is going to be transferred only once, because it provides the most flexibility for digital color correction at a later stage (otherwise, certain types of color correction in the transfer may lock you into particular looks that can't be undone later). A standard Cineon/DPX 10-bit log transfer characteristic (gamma) is often used to provide consistency in different playback environments. But you (and audiences and clients) won't like the flat image until, at a later stage, a LUT is applied to adjust the color and contrast of the material. The director of photography may choose a given LUT to create a particular look, which can be changed at any point later. Makes for a fast and economical transfer.

Other Telecine Image Controls

Beyond simply reproducing what is on the film, telecines can provide tremendous creative control over the image. Shots can be moved horizontally (*X axis*) or vertically (*Y axis*) or resized (*Z axis*). This allows you to pan and scan a widescreen image for conversion to a narrower aspect ratio. You might want to enlarge the image, in order to remove unwanted objects near the edge of the frame, or to zoom in on something important.

Telecines offer a variety of frame rates. Off speeds can be used for effects on individual shots, or entire films can be time compressed or expanded to fit a certain broadcast length. Speeding up a feature film 3 percent can shave three and a half minutes off the running time without making any cuts. Some movies actually play better if sped up a little for the small screen. With any speed changes, you need to watch carefully for motion artifacts like judder that may be introduced, especially in scenes with fast subject or camera movement.

Film may have a certain amount of weave or unsteadiness in the telecine gate, causing the entire image to float slightly. This may go undetected in a straight transfer but be painfully apparent if nonmoving video titles or effects are later superimposed on the image (titles that are already on the film are not a problem). Some telecines and scanners use pin registration (see Fig. 6-3) or electronic alignment systems to increase steadiness.

Other image processing includes *enhancement* (also called detail; see p. 138), which can make the image appear sharper. This should be used sparingly. Many systems are equipped with *grain reducers*, which can help soften the appearance of film grain.

Cleaning the Negative

Handling of negative should be kept to a minimum and any unnecessary shuttling in the telecine should be avoided. Use extreme care to avoid dirt, scratches, and cinch marks. The transfer facility should clean the negative before making transfers or prints. The safest cleaning method is *ultrasonic cleaning*. As the film passes through a solvent bath, high-frequency vibrations remove all but the most firmly embedded dust particles.

Some telecines and scanners are equipped with *liquid gates* (also called *wet gates*), in which the film is immersed in a liquid with the same refractive index as the film. This can hide base scratches, minimize surface emulsion scratches, and sometimes lessen graininess.

Both ultrasonic cleaning and wet gate printing may weaken or open tape splices. Notify the transfer facility if the footage has any tape splices.

After transfer or scanning there is often some dirt in the image. *Dust busting* is typically done for feature films to clean up visible dirt spots by digitally cloning clean areas from surrounding frames and pasting pixels from those areas over the dirt. This technique can also be used to repair scratches and other artifacts.

AUDIO OPTIONS

Since telecine suites usually charge hundreds of dollars an hour, you want to minimize your time in there. A key cost factor is how audio syncing is handled.

As discussed above, one option is to have the audio synced in the telecine suite. The advantage to the producer is that both picture and sound are taken care of at one time and synced dailies can be delivered quickly to the production team. This workflow is most expensive if traditional clapper sticks are used without timecode. A timecode slate is more efficient: the telecine operator stops at each slate, types in the timecode number, and the audio playback shuttles to the correct piece of sound. The fastest method is to shoot with in-camera film timecode (AatonCode or ARRI Code). In this case the audio can instantly *chase* (find and keep up with) the picture during the transfer and there is no extra time penalty for syncing during the transfer.

A more cost-effective strategy is to transfer the picture first (*silent transfer*), then sync audio to picture later in a layback suite (see Fig. 16-3). Or, even better, you can sync it yourself on your NLE. For more, see Working with Double-System Sound, p. 589.

Speed Control

As discussed in Frame Rate and Scanning, above, the frame rates used for filming, transfer, and editing vary by project and by which part of the world you're working in. The playback speed of the audio often needs to be adjusted to stay in sync with the picture. Speed adjustments may be handled by the transfer facility, or you may be doing them in the editing room.

NTSC COUNTRIES. Film is traditionally shot at *exactly* 24 fps. As noted above, in countries where NTSC video has been standard, video frame rates are not whole numbers, but instead are 0.1 percent slower than what they appear to be. When you transfer film that was shot at exactly 24 fps using a telecine, it will typically be transferred either to 23.976 video or, if pulldown is used, to 29.97. In either case, the digital transfer of the film is playing 0.1 percent slower than real time. We have to take that into account when syncing the audio.

There are various methods to slow the audio down by 0.1 percent in the telecine suite or after. Digital recorders are sometimes set to a sample rate of 48.048 kHz in the field and then played back at 48 kHz to slow the playback 0.1 percent (see p. 465). Or audio can be recorded normally, then slowed down in post.

If you're syncing in the NLE, you can import audio at its normal rate, then modify its speed to 99.9 percent.

Alternatively, if your NLE supports it, you can speed the picture up 0.1 percent to true 24 fps before syncing the audio. This allows you to import audio digitally at standard 48 kHz sample rate with no frame rate or speed conversion that could lower quality.

Confusingly, the term "pulldown" is also used to refer to this slowing down of picture or sound, as in, "Don't forget to pull down the sound 0.1 percent in transfer." Similarly, speeding up may be referred to as "pulling up," as in, "Will this audio recorder pull up from 29.97 to 30?"[4]

When production audio is recorded in the field with timecode, typically a true 30 fps timecode is used. When the audio is slowed down by 0.1 percent, this becomes 29.97 fps timecode, which can stay in sync with either 23.976 or 29.97 fps video.

A film camera can be run at certain speeds that do not require any pulldown in the audio. Modern crystal-sync film cameras can be operated at 29.97 or 23.976 fps. Since these speeds can run on the telecine without being slowed down, real time is maintained, so audio should not be pulled down. Some telecines can be run at precisely 24 fps, so they maintain real time as well.

As long as you keep in mind whether you're working with real-time media or footage that's been slowed 0.1 percent, you can decide if you need to correct for the difference. Some techniques of changing audio speed can degrade the audio quality, so be sure to discuss workflow plans with the post team.

---

4. And the term "pullup" has other meanings as well! See When Reels Are Spliced Together, p. 715.

PAL COUNTRIES. When 24 fps film is transferred to 25 fps video in the typical way, there is a 4.1 percent increase in frame rate. The audio will need to be sped up by 4.1 percent, which results in a noticeable change in pitch, though that may be digitally corrected later. If you slow the video down in the NLE to edit at 24 fps, you can import double-system sound into the NLE with no speed change.

Some people use the 24+1 telecine pulldown method (sometimes called PAL+1), in which an extra field is added every 12 frames to create a 25 fps digital transfer. In this case audio should run at its normal speed.

FILM TRANSFER DATA

Several systems are used to track footage and timecode in the film-to-video transfer, later in editing, and for any retransfers or negative cutting during the finishing process. The following are the main ones in play, though they're not all used on every production.

Film Key Numbers/Keycode

Kodak and Fujifilm expose eye-readable key numbers and machine-readable bar codes along the edge of camera negative that can be read after the negative is processed (see p. 283). Key numbers identify every frame of the original negative and are essential for match cutting after editing. Kodak calls its bar code version *Keykode* and Fujifilm call its *MR code*. Most telecines have keycode readers, allowing them to track the negative as it goes through the machine. Key numbers run in an unbroken sequence from the beginning of each camera roll to the end. Unlike timecode in video, film key numbers are permanent in the film and never change, so they're a solid reference for finding and cutting the sections of negative.

In-Camera Timecode (also called Film Timecode)

All Aaton and some ARRI cameras have the ability to expose timecode along the edge of the negative near the key numbers and keycode (see Fig. 6-14). In-camera film timecode—AatonCode and ARRI Code are 24 fps versions of SMPTE/EBU timecode—is always set to record the time of day (TOD) at the moment each frame of film is exposed. For sync-sound shooting, the audio recorder in the field records identical TOD code, so sound and picture can be matched up by timecode either in a properly equipped telecine or in the NLE.

Audio Timecode

Timecode recorded with the audio in the field is sometimes called *audio timecode*, *production audio timecode*, or *sound timecode*. As noted above, when the film camera records the same timecode as the audio recorder, we can easily sync the sound and picture. However, since many film cameras don't record in-camera timecode, a timecode slate may be used for sync (see Fig. 11-19). A timecode slate displays the same timecode as the audio recorder in big LED numbers so that when the film camera shoots it for a few seconds, we have a convenient way to line up picture and sound for sync.

Video Timecode (also called Telecine Timecode)

Whenever you transfer film to video in a telecine, the video will be given timecode, which is recorded on the videotape or to the metadata of a digital file. Sometimes referred to as *telecine timecode*, this is completely separate from any production timecode that may or may not have been recorded in the film camera or audio recorder. Video timecode allows each videotape reel or file of the transfer to have its own unique, ascending timecode that runs continuously from the beginning of the reel to the end (note that each video reel may contain more than one film camera

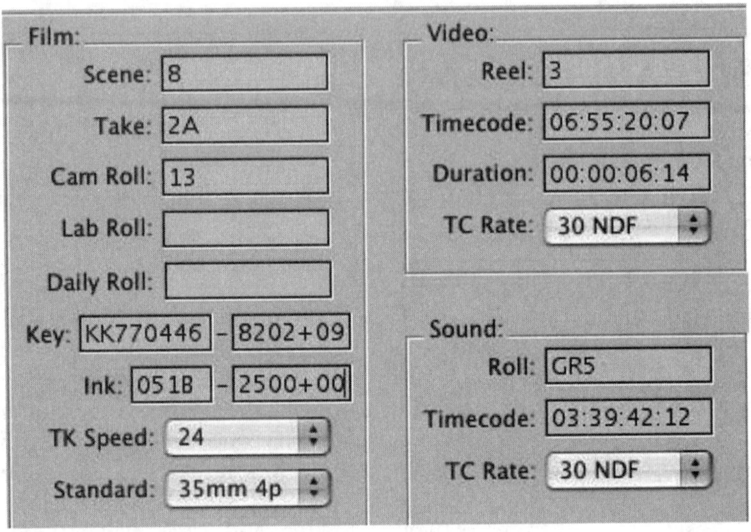

Fig. 16-8. This Cinema Tools screen provides a good opportunity to look at the data associated with a film transfer. (Apple, Inc.)

FILM DATA (from film shot in the field):
SCENE AND TAKE: from slate or log
CAMERA ROLL: original camera negative roll number
LAB ROLL AND DAILY ROLL: each may contain more than one camera roll
KEY: key number read from the keycode exposed in the film when it was manufactured
INK: ink edge code printed on the workprint after it has been synced; used when transferring
   from workprint
TK SPEED: telecine transfer speed in fps
STANDARD: film format; 35mm four-perf shown here

VIDEO DATA (the video being recorded in telecine session):
REEL: reel number of videotape or file, as assigned by production or facility
TIMECODE: timecode of video
DURATION: length of shot/clip
TC RATE: timecode rate of video; 30 fps nondrop shown here

SOUND DATA (from production audio recorded in the field):
ROLL: sound roll number
TIMECODE: audio timecode recorded in the field (and displayed on digislate)
TC RATE: timecode rate of production audio (see p. 467)

roll). When recording to a 1080p/24 format like HDCAM in 24p PsF mode, this will be 24 fps timecode. When recording to 60i it will be standard 30 fps SMPTE timecode. When you capture 60i to a nonlinear editing system, you can either edit at 30 fps or use reverse pulldown to reconstruct the 24 fps frame rate and timecode from the film (see Fig. 14-31). PAL transfers will normally be 25-frame EBU code. Together with the key numbers, it's essential that video timecode be tracked correctly for accurate negative cutting and online editing.

Ink Edge Code

On feature films for which a film workprint has been made, identical *ink edge code* numbers are printed on each roll of workprint and matching roll of mag sound after an editor has put them in sync. Also called *Acmade numbers*, they facilitate traditional film-style editing using a flatbed. Some NLEs can track these numbers to aid in cutting the workprint for, say, test screenings by film projection. Ink edge code numbers must be entered into the NLE manually during logging.

Shot Logs

Without doubt, there's a lot of data to keep track of. You may wonder what you need it for. If you're planning to edit on an NLE and then return to the original camera negative to do additional digital transfers and/or cut the negative for film prints (as outlined in Scenarios Two and Three, above), then you'll want to track the video timecode, key numbers, and production film timecode (if any). However, if you plan to transfer the negative only once, edit digitally, and never return to the negative, you may not need anything more than the video timecode recorded on the master tapes or files.

Rather than you trying to keep track of all these numbers yourself, the telecine facility can give you a computer file called a *shot log* or *telecine log*. A shot log might contain information such as scene, take, camera roll number, lab roll number, dailies roll number, key numbers, telecine frame rate, video reel, video timecode, audio reel, audio timecode, and telecine operator's notes.

Be sure to ask for a shot log and specify which types of data you wish to be included. A good policy is to ask that all timecode and keycode data be included in the log, even if there is an extra charge for this. You never know what information about the picture or synced sound might prove to be a lifesaver at a later date.

There are several logging formats, including FLEx (.flx), ALE, ATN (Aaton), and FTL. The shot log is typically delivered as a file to be imported into your NLE; you may first need to convert it to a format compatible with your NLE. The numbers from the log file should be checked carefully after capturing the clips in the NLE (see below).

BOOKING A TRANSFER

The following are some considerations in planning and ordering a film-to-digital transfer. As noted above, transfers can be loosely thought of in two categories: digital dailies, which are made for offline editing purposes, often with the intent of going back to the original camera negative after editing to do another transfer; and final transfers, which are done for edited films either from the negative before online editing, or from an assembled source such as a master positive or print after the film is done. Many films, ranging from student projects to big-budget television movies, are transferred only once; that transfer is used for the offline edit and for the finished product.

It's essential that you talk with the transfer facility, the video editor, and the negative cutter before making any arrangements for the transfer.

Film-to-tape transfers are generally billed on an hourly or per-project basis. Transfer time will be longer than the running time of the material; how much longer depends on the material and what's being done to it. As a ballpark, digital dailies without scene-to-scene color correction ("one-light" or "best light") may take one and a half to two times the running time of the footage; dailies with sound and color correction may take three to six times the running time; careful color correction of a finished film may take fifteen to twenty times. Footage with many short shots may take more time to transfer than material with long takes.

Digital Dailies

For video dailies, the negative cutter, lab, or transfer facility prepares the footage for transfer. The following items should be specified and/or discussed when you place your order:

1. *Film format.* Specify whether you shot 35mm, Super 16, 16mm, or Super 8. Flat (nonanamorphic) or 'Scope. Color negative or black-and-white. Manufacturer and film type.

2. *Aspect ratio.* Did you shoot 16:9? 1.66? 1.85? 2.39? When shooting 35mm particularly, it's a good idea to film a framing chart at the head of the reel so that the telecine operator can verify your camera's aspect ratio and exact framing.

3. *Video format.* What videotape format are you recording to? Or are you recording direct to hard disk or other data format? What frame rate are you recording to: 24p? 60i? 50i?

4. *Punch head of each camera roll or flat.* A punch mark is made in the negative to serve as a reference point at the zero timecode frame. This is typically done at a key number ending in 00 (such as KJ 23 1234 5677+00). Ask for a list of each roll's corresponding key numbers at punch marks. After you have captured the video into the NLE, you can use the list to check against transfer errors. Many people like to have a punch made at the head of each camera roll or wherever there is a break in key numbers (that is, wherever two pieces of film are spliced together). Sometimes punches are only made at the head of each *film flat* (also called *lab roll* or *lab reel*), which may be made up of a few camera rolls spliced together.

5. *Pulldown.* When transferring from 24 fps to 60i, it's standard practice to do an "A-frame transfer," which should start at the head punch with an even hour of timecode (such as 02:00:00:00). For more, see Managing Pulldown, p. 698.

6. *Timecode.* This is the video timecode that will be recorded on tape or file. For editing purposes, nondrop timecode (ND) is recommended to avoid

errors. Specify the starting timecode for each tape (typically a different hour for each).

7. *Burn-in numbers.* If you're making digital dailies (with the intention of scanning the film again later or cutting negative), there are a set of numbers you may want to have *burned in* so they're visible on screen. These include film key number, in-camera film timecode (if any), audio timecode (if any), and video timecode. You must specifically request from your postproduction facility inclusion of each of these burned-in data windows in your dailies; you can specify where they're placed on the screen. You can also have a "clean picture" (not burned in) with timecode and keycode information on the address track of the videotape and in the telecine shot log. You can also have two sets of tapes or files made, one with and one without burn-ins.

8. *Audio sync.* Do you want audio synced in the telecine session or will you do it later? Is there audio timecode (production timecode)? Timecode slates? Do you want audio code recorded to video?

9. *Color correction.* Do you want the colorist to adjust the image for each scene or just once for the entire roll? See above for more on this.

10. *Shot log.* You will usually want a shot log of the transfer (see above). Ask for a file format compatible with your editing system.

11. *Shipping and storage.* Do you want the negative returned to you or stored by the lab or transfer facility? What type of shipping do you want for the videotape and/or negative?

12. *Contact info.* Be sure to include off-hour phone numbers in case of questions.

Transferring Edited and Finished Films

On some productions, a high-quality transfer or scan is done after the offline edit to create color-corrected, high-res media for the online (see Scenario Two, p. 680). On some productions, the final, high-quality transfer is done from a film print or other motion picture film element (see Scenario Three, p. 681). A good colorist will contribute enormously to the way your film looks, so ask for recommendations and check out the colorist's previous work. In a *supervised transfer* you get to be present. In an *unsupervised transfer*—which usually costs less—you let the colorist work alone. Be sure to let the colorist know in advance of any special looks you're going for. Some transfer facilities will charge you per foot instead of per hour for unsupervised work.

Keep in mind that you may need to make several versions of the movie recorded in different aspect ratios (with or without letterboxing and/or pan and scan), with different edits (full-length and TV cutdown), or in different video standards (HD, SD, and compressed versions for Internet streaming). If you've made a distribution deal, these assorted masters are called "deliverables" and are required by contract. Today it's common to make one master transfer and do your versioning from that. The key to going this route is to make a universal 1080p/24 HD master (or larger frame size). From this single master, all broadcast HD, SD, and Internet submasters can be generated with no loss in quality.

Use a high-quality digital master as the audio source. Even if there's timecode, it helps to have a countdown leader with an audible sync pop at "2" to check against potential errors.

If you've already cut the negative and done film printing in the lab, you may have some choices about what film element to use for the transfer.

1. *Original negative.* Using the original negative for the transfer results in the sharpest picture with the most flexibility for color correction in terms of color and tonal scale. Because color negative reproduces a full tonal scale at about half real contrast, all shadow and highlight details are visible (including perhaps those power cables on the floor you thought were hidden in the dark corner of the set), details that will be unavailable in later prints that have higher projection contrast. However, for transfers done after the movie is edited, going back to the original negative may entail doing an online edit of the show after it is retransferred to video, which adds cost.

2. *Master positive.* For movies that have already been edited, a *color master positive* (sometimes called an *interpositive*, or *IP*) makes a second-best source for the video transfer. A master positive is a single-strand, low-contrast, positive copy of the original negative made from a special intermediate film stock (for more, see Intermediates, p. 711). A master positive preserves the original negative's full latitude yet has finer grain than the original. It is typically struck from a negative that has been scene-to-scene color-corrected, so it will already be fine-tuned for color and density before it gets to the telecine suite (although more correction will be necessary in the te-lecine). No online edit is needed after transfer.

3. *Duplicate ("dupe") negative.* Made from the same intermediate film stock as a master positive, a duplicate negative is also printed from a master posi-tive. A dupe negative is less desirable than a master positive as a video trans-fer element because is it one generation further removed from the original, with consequent loss of sharpness and a buildup of grain and contrast.

4. *Print.* For reasons of cost, a master positive, which costs considerably more than a simple print, may not be feasible. Standard answer or release prints, although more contrasty, are the only alternative. Prints are generally com-plete with all titles and credits, which may or may not be an advantage de-pending on your needs (foreign broadcasters or distributors may want a "textless" version). For transfer to video, a black-and-white print can be developed to lower contrast (gamma) to facilitate a less contrasty transfer, an option not available in developing a color print.

EDITING FILM DIGITALLY

As described earlier, film is mostly used today as an acquisition format for digital postproduction. In other words, projects that shoot film generally transfer or scan the footage to create digital files, and from that point forward they do editing, visual effects, and color correction digitally.

On many productions, film is transferred to digital once, and the camera original negative is never used again. The digital files or tapes created during the telecine or scanning process essentially become the new camera original materials. So you can handle the editing the same way you would for other video projects. See Chapter 14 for digital editing, and in particular the discussion of working with 24 fps media that starts on p. 601. If this is your workflow, the following discussion doesn't apply to you.

However, as outlined in Scenarios Two and Three above (see p. 680), on some productions, the camera original footage is transferred once to digital dailies for the offline edit. Then, after the offline edit is locked, the film footage is rescanned and/or physically cut. If you are using one of these types of workflows, then you need to ensure that you can translate the offline edit back to the film without errors. This includes (1) making sure the NLE is working with accurate metadata about the film transfer and (2) making sure that any edits you do in the offline won't create problems later (the rules are slightly different if you plan to rescan the film versus cutting negative in the traditional way). There are also things to keep in mind if you plan to eventually make film prints.

PREPARING TO EDIT

One of the first considerations is what frame rate you will be editing in (also called the editing *timebase*). For example, editing at 24p can work nicely with film shot at 24 fps and transferred to 24p files. Or you may be delivering the project to a broadcaster at 60i and choose to edit at 29.97 fps. Reasons to choose different editing timebases are found elsewhere in the book and should be discussed with the postproduction team.

Importing audio to the NLE is discussed on p. 690. Syncing is discussed on p. 589.

Managing Data

When an NLE is used to edit material that originated on film, it's essential that for every shot you edit digitally in the NLE, you can later identify the physical piece of film that shot came from. Once you're done editing, you need to be able to precisely locate each piece of film used in the movie, and know with utter precision which frames of film to scan or cut. Working backward from a video edit to the original film footage is sometimes called *doing a matchback* or *matching back*.

In the days before NLEs existed, film projects were sometimes edited on linear videotape. Translating the video edit back to film was done simply using video timecode, a method you could still use today. Every roll of camera original negative has a hole punched in the center of a certain frame at the head of the roll. Once it has been transferred to video, we know the video timecode of that punched frame and every other frame of film on the roll. So, after editing the movie in video, you can use an EDL (see p. 632) to identify every frame of film used in the video edit via timecode.

Today NLEs still keep track of video timecode, but some NLEs also offer a more accurate and automated way to match back using film key numbers (keycode; see p. 283 and p. 691), which are actually printed on the film. After you're done with

Fig. 16-9. Telecine and video data. This Avid display shows the data that the NLE is tracking, which includes: the timecode of the video transfer (09:10:23:03), the pulldown phase (C2), the film keycode (K? 05 7788-8336+02), and the timecode of the production audio (10:29:40:19). Keycode, which is recorded on the film's edge by the manufacturer and references each original film frame *exactly*, is the most reliable common reference when doing multiple video transfers. (Michael Phillips/Avid Technologies, Inc.)

the offline edit, the NLE should be able to produce an accurate list of all the negative using key numbers.

As discussed above, a telecine log (also called a shot log) allows you to import into the NLE information about the transfer, including video timecode, key numbers, and many other kinds of metadata. It's important to verify that those numbers are correct before you start editing. To begin with, make sure that the key numbers and timecode are the same in the telecine log, any burn-in numbers on screen, and in the NLE's bin or browser.

For further verification, you can also make a *confidence list*. (These instructions are for Avid systems, but you can apply a similar method to other systems.) To do this, create columns in each bin with these headings: "start," "camroll," "kn start," "kn mark-in," "clip name." Then load each clip in the source monitor and mark an In Point at the frame where the slate closes. This should bring up the key number for that frame in the kn mark-in column. Do this for every clip and then generate a bin list and send it to the negative cutter or lab. The negative cutter can then check a few takes by running down the slate and examining the actual key number on film. This way, he or she can verify that the key numbers entered into the system are correct.

Managing Pulldown

If you've transferred 24 fps film to 30 fps video (60i) and want to edit at 24 fps in the NLE, you need to do a reverse pulldown to convert back to 24p. To do this accurately, and to track timecode and key numbers correctly, the NLE needs to know the *pulldown type* (also called *pulldown phase* or *pulldown field identifier*) of the first frame of each clip (the pulldown type of the first frame may be called the *pull-in*). Pulldown type is often indicated as A1, A2, B1, B2, B3, etc. (see Fig. 16-10). With standard A-frame transfers, A frames will have timecode ending in :00, :05, or multiples of five frames. Pull-in information should be in the shot log and you may never have to worry about it.

Sometimes there are errors and you need to enter the pull-in manually. The pulldown type for any frame may be visible following the key number burned in on screen (see Fig. 16-9).

UNDERSTANDING PULLDOWN TYPE. How pulldown works can be confusing. To see what's going on, look at Fig. 16-10 (you may also want to look at Fig. 14-31). Figure 16-10 shows a group of four film frames transferred to five frames of 60i video. Notice that film frame A is transferred to two fields of video (A1 and A2). Frame B is transferred to three fields (B1, B2, and B3). Frame C is also transferred to two fields, but they are split between two *different* video frames.

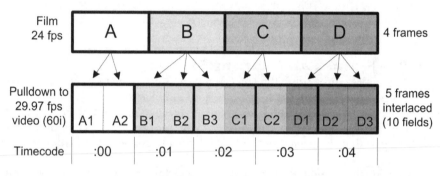

Fig. 16-10. This shows the relationship of pulldown and timecode in an A-frame film transfer using normal pulldown. See also Fig. 14-31.

Here's a way of looking at them:

1. Frame A is transferred to both fields that make up video frame 1 with no timecode change between the two fields.
2. Frame B is transferred to both fields of video frame 2, and to the first field of video frame 3. (Three fields total—B1, B2, B3—timecode change between fields 2 and 3.)
3. Frame C is transferred to the second field of frame 3 and the first field of frame 4. (Two fields total—C1, C2—timecode change between the fields.)
4. Frame D is transferred to the second field of video frame 4 and both fields of video frame 5. (Three fields total—D1, D2, D3—timecode change between fields 1 and 2.)

If the pulldown type is not indicated, you can figure it out by slowly stepping through the video field by field while watching on a monitor. Find a distinct frame, say a hole-punch or the moment where the clap sticks come together. If two fields are identical and there is no timecode change between them, you're looking at an A frame (note that the A frame is special in having this simple one-to-one relationship between film and video frames). If two fields are identical but the timecode changes between them, that's a C frame. If three fields are identical but there is a timecode change between the first and second field, you're looking at a D frame.

When working with PAL or other direct frame-to-frame transfers where no pulldown is used, pulldown type doesn't exist. What a relief!

EDITING CONSIDERATIONS FOR TRADITIONAL FILM FINISH

This section applies *only* to projects like the one described in Scenario Three, in which the workflow involves a digital offline edit followed by traditional film conforming to make film prints—in other words, if you're cutting negative the old-fashioned way. It does *not* apply to anyone making a D.I. or other digital master immediately after the offline edit that will be used to make digital outputs and perhaps a film-out.

Dupe Frames and Cutting Frames

When you're editing digitally you can repeat a shot as many times as you like. For example, you might want to use a certain establishing shot several times in your movie. In film, every shot is based on one piece of negative, which normally can be put in only *one* place in the movie. If you want to use the same shot twice, that footage will usually need to be *duped* (physically duplicated on another piece of film).

Also, at the head and tail of every shot removed from the original camera rolls during negative conforming ("cutting the negative"), the negative cutter needs a fraction of the next frame beyond the first and last frame of the shot for the overlap required by a cement splice. If you take a shot and cut it into two pieces, you need to leave at least one unused frame between the pieces. This is called a *cutting frame* or *cutback frame*. Many nonlinear editing systems have a "dupe detection" feature that warns you if you've reused any part of a shot or left insufficient cutting frames between shots. When editing at 30 fps on an NLE, leave at least *two* video frames unused so you will be sure to have at least *one* film frame.

Fades and Dissolves

When making fades and dissolves, video editors can choose virtually any length effect. Film contact printing machines, on the other hand, offer a standard set of fade and dissolve lengths and you should try to use one of them. Check with your lab for available lengths. Standards usually include 16, 24, 32, 48, 64, or 96 frames, which (at 24 fps) is 0.67, 1, 1.33, 2, 2.67, or 4 seconds. Some nonlinear systems can print out an optical list (see below), which will help you identify any nonstandard effects you may have used.

Reel Divisions

The film needs to be divided into sections that will fit on reels for printing. This is discussed on p. 705.

WHEN YOU'RE DONE WITH THE OFFLINE EDIT

You've edited the movie on your NLE and locked picture. Now it's time to go back to the original camera negative to rescan it for a D.I. or to cut it for traditional film finish.

If you edited at 24 fps (either true 24p or 23.976p), you should be able to generate a frame-accurate list of the negative used in the final sequence. Sometimes you do this from an EDL using timecode. However, it's preferable if your NLE can make the list using film key numbers (keycode) from the original transfer (particularly if you plan to do a D.I. with DPX files). Specialized software is sometimes required. Avid uses FilmScribe.

The lab or negative matcher will use the key numbers and/or the timecode to find the negative that corresponds to the clips you used in the NLE sequence.

Film Cut Lists

Several types of lists are used to translate from the NLE to the film negative or workprint. Remember, when talking about negative cutting and film postproduction, an *individual* shot or clip is called a "scene" (as opposed to the meaning of the word in shooting, where a "scene" can be made up of several shots).

- *Pull list.* Tells the negative matcher which scenes to take (pull) from each camera roll. There are various types of pull lists, including *scene pull lists* and *optical pull lists*.
- *Assemble list.* Shows all the scenes in their proper order. Includes the beginning and ending footage and frame count of each scene; the first and last key number of each shot; the lab roll number; the camera roll number; and the clip name.
- *Dupe list.* Shows which material needs to be duplicated prior to conforming the negative because it's used more than once in the movie. A dupe list can be generated at any time during editing to check that no material has been unintentionally duplicated.
- *Optical list.* Shows what source material is needed to create special effects, including freeze frames, slow motion, fast motion, etc.
- *Change list.* Shows only the changes (additions or deletions) that have been made since an earlier version. This is helpful if a film workprint is being cut along with the edited video for test screenings or if the negative has been transferred and edited already and only certain sections need to be changed.

Retransferring for a D.I.

If you'll be rescanning the negative for a D.I., the NLE can generate a pull list of the shots used in the film. You may want to pull shots with handles (a few extra frames) or take shots from flash frame to flash frame. You might even choose to avoid cutting the negative *at all*, and have the telecine or scanner fast-forward to the sections you need. The benefit is that you minimize handling and don't destroy any footage in case you want to edit another version differently.

After the footage is scanned, you transfer the project to a finishing system capable of working with high-resolution files. The offline sequence is then relinked to the new high-res media, and the D.I. is conformed with any visual effects, graphics, titles, and so on.

Matchback from a 30 fps Project

If you shoot film at 24 fps, transfer to 30 fps video (60i), then edit the offline video at 30 fps, be aware that certain errors may creep in when you translate the video edit back to film. This is because there won't be an exact match between the 30 fps video timecode and the 24 fps film frame count.

Take a look at Figure 16-10. You can visualize the lower row as a shot that's five frames long in video and see that it translates neatly and exactly back to four frames of film (the upper row). The same is true of any shot in video that's a multiple of five frames.

Now imagine a three-frame shot in video (say, the first three frames in Fig. 16-10). This could be thought of as two and a half frames of film. If we use only the A and B frames from the negative, the film shot will be slightly shorter than the offline video. If we include the A, B, and C frames, the film will be slightly longer than the video.

The software that performs the matchback from 30 fps to 24 fps will drop or add a frame when needed to keep the overall running time the same between the video and film. This may cause slight sync drift, but never more than plus or minus one frame. It can result in some bad edits, such as when you thought you cut something out of the movie (like a flash frame) and you find it's back in after the matchback. You should be able to review the cut list and see where the software made changes to check for potential problems. This is also the reason you should leave *two* cutting frames in the video for the negative matcher so she'll be sure to have at least one in the film.

These kinds of problems apply *only* when you go back from a 60i video offline to cut the negative (or to do a rescan at 24 fps). If you're planning to transfer from film to video only once and stay in 60i, it's nothing to worry about.

FROM DIGITAL TO FILM

A digital video-to-film transfer, or a transfer of digital files to 35mm, is called a *film-out* or *scan-out*. These conversions are primarily used by two distinct markets.

At the high end are big-budget feature filmmakers who are working with high-resolution files in a digital intermediate. These may be 4:4:4 RGB or DPX files (or other formats) acquired with high-end HD or digital cinematography cameras at resolutions including HD, 2K, and 4K. Or the movie may have been shot in film and scanned in a high-resolution scanner.

In this workflow, the postproduction and effects are done in the HD, 2K, or 4K realm, and at the last stage the D.I. is recorded to film to make prints for theatrical distribution in cinemas.

The other transfer market is for independent or television movies that have been shot in HD or SD video, but where the filmmakers want to make film prints to show in festivals or for theatrical release. If necessary, the video is up-resed and converted to 24p before doing a film-out.

Digital projection is becoming the norm, so the need for 35mm prints is diminishing rapidly.

Digital-to-Film Recorders

There are various technologies for writing digital video or digital files to film, and they range in quality and cost. At the highest level currently are *film recorders*. These systems use either a laser, a high-res LCD panel, or a cathode ray tube to record high-resolution HD, 2K, or 4K images directly onto 35mm film. Most of these machines work slower than real time, but some newer ones can operate at 24 fps. Generally film recorders are used to create film negatives or intermediates from which quantities of prints can be made. But some, like the Cinevator, can create prints directly; a filmmaker who only needs a film print for a few festivals may prefer this method.

Fig. 16-11. Arrilaser film recorder for making film-outs. (DuArt Film and Video)

The most popular *laser film recorder* is the Arrilaser, which uses three solid-state lasers—red, green, and blue—to write directly to the color negative. *LED recorders* include the Definity from CCG. *CRT film recorders*, including models made by Celco, use a high-resolution black-and-white CRT whose image is projected into a film camera. Each film frame gets three exposures: one each through a red, a green, and a blue filter.

The original video-to-film conversion method is the 16mm *kinescope*, a device mainly consisting of a special film camera shooting a high-quality video monitor in real time. This type of kinescope (the color negative that results is also called a kinescope, or "kine"; rhymes with "skinny") is the most economical transfer method. Since 16mm has all but died as a distribution format, few people make 16mm kinescopes or choose to film-out to 16mm anymore.

PREPARING FOR THE DIGITAL-TO-FILM TRANSFER

Before choosing a transfer facility, talk to filmmakers you know and ask to see samples of the facility's work. Once you choose a facility, work closely with it to prepare your video prior to transfer. Do short tests of footage before investing in the full transfer.

Color and Image Considerations

The process begins with making your digital cinematography look as good as possible. When shooting your movie, use a high-quality digital camera at the highest resolution you can afford. Shoot HD, 2K, or 4K if possible. Shoot at 24p. Using high-quality PL-mount cine lenses when the camera has a Super 35–sized sensor can make a huge difference. If you're shooting with a ⅔-inch HD camcorder, Zeiss DigiPrimes can't be beat. (Remember that primes are faster and sharper than zooms.) Be fastidious about focus. Use a properly set up field monitor (see Appendix A) to avoid unintentional over- and underexposure. If using an HD video camera, turn down the sharpness or enhancement (see p. 138). You may want to use a special gamma or even a log curve instead of standard Rec. 709 gamma to preserve as much shadow or highlight detail as possible (see Chapter 5). Before you begin shooting, consult with a transfer facility about the use of nonstandard gammas.

During editing, project the video on a big screen and look for things like poor focus that may not be noticeable on a small monitor but will be in a theater. Hopefully you didn't shoot interlace (see p. 11), but if you did, watch for interlace artifacts in which straight diagonal lines look like stair steps. These and artifacts like color fringing may lead you to reedit sections or do some video fixes.

Color correction that looks good in video won't necessarily translate directly to film. Video and film possess different color gamuts and tonal scales. Each post facility has its particular film recorder tweaked with custom color lookup tables (LUTs), which means that you can't take the same set of color corrections from one facility to another. But this is also an area where a lot of creative input can be had in terms of the look on film. If you're on a tight budget, you may be going more or less directly from your color-corrected video with a best-light or minimal correction, but the facility will still have to assign overall values for color correction, gamma, and sharpness. Discuss using noise or grain reduction.

Frame Rate

If you shot at 24p, then you're way ahead of the game in terms of the film-out. Since film is also 24p, there should be no problem with motion or interlace artifacts. If you shot at 25p or 50i, the film-out will be made on a frame-for-frame basis, so there won't be motion artifacts, but the projected movie will run 4 percent slower. You may want to give the composer in advance a version that has been slowed down 4 percent in case any music adjustments need to be made prior to the film-out.

When material has been shot at 24p, transferred to 60i video and edited at 60i, then transferred to film, you can get strange motion artifacts. Better to use reverse pulldown and edit at 24p. If you mastered at 60i, the transfer facility will do the reverse pulldown.

If you shot at 60i, the footage needs to be deinterlaced (see p. 213) and pulled down to 24 fps. Poorly done, this may result in some scenes looking soft (unsharp) or having judder (stuttering motion). Various transfer houses have proprietary software for doing the frame rate conversion and some are superior to others.

Resolution

High-quality transfers are done from HD, 2K, and 4K files. If you shot in SD, the facility will up-res your video prior to the film-out. Some facilities favor high definition RGB 4:4:4 instead of 2K for film-out, maintaining that it matches 2K quality while being more economical. Of course, the higher the resolution you start with, the better it will look when recorded to film.

Titles

Credit rolls can create weird motion artifacts. If you have an SD or HD master in 60i, it's best to remake the titles in 24p, and don't use fonts with fine lines. Some people prefer cards for end credits instead of a moving roll to avoid any motion issues.

Subtitles can be done in video but, if so, they can't be removed from the film negative. If you're only making a few prints to distribute in different languages, consider making them without subtitles, then use a laser-burn process to add them to individual prints.

Aspect Ratio

Cinema projection is virtually always widescreen, so you need to consider any potential aspect ratio conversions (see p. 74).

Most theaters will crop or mask the top and bottom of the full 35mm frame to project a 1.85 widescreen image. Since HD video masters are typically 16:9 (the equivalent of 1.78 film aspect ratio), not much adjustment is needed to fit the 1.85 frame. One method is to crop the digital image 2 percent at the top and bottom. Another option is to scale down the digital image just a bit, to bring the top and bottom inside the film frame. This way, you don't crop anything out and the thin black bars on the sides can be masked by the theater curtains.

For some productions, an anamorphic ('Scope) film-out is made for widescreen aspect ratios like 2.40.

Reel Length

Films are divided into manageable lengths, called *reels*, for editing and printing. A typical feature film will be made up of several reels. Before doing a film-out (or making prints the traditional way), if the movie isn't already divided into reels, it needs to be broken into roughly twenty- to twenty-one-minute sections, since 35mm films are generally printed and released on 2,000-foot reels. Talk to the lab and transfer facility for their preferences; they can usually do this *reel balancing* for you.

Choosing the reel breaks involves a bit of care and artfulness. Be attentive to the scenes at which reel breaks take place, particularly the first scene on a new reel. Avoid having reel breaks in midscene or where music is playing or before scenes with important information (in case the projectionist messes up the transition from one reel to the next). The heads and tails of reels tend to get a lot of wear and tear, so try to avoid very light scenes, which show dirt more.

If you're cramped for space on a reel, remember that the head and tail of the reel are reserved for printing leaders so the movie itself can't be more than about 1,900 feet (35mm film runs at 96 feet per minute). The reels should also be balanced so each reel is full (or nearly so), with the last reel shorter if necessary.

If you're doing the reel breakdown on your NLE, see p. 653 for information about leaders and sync pops, which are needed to keep the picture and print sound track in sync.

After a film is printed, the reels are often spliced together for projection or shown alternately on two projectors, using a changeover device. See 35mm Release Prints, p. 713, for inscribing changeover marks on the release prints. See p. 715 for special precautions when preparing sound tracks for multireel films.

Film Stock

Some film recorders are designed to record to particular film stocks, and others offer a range of options. Be sure to discuss this with the transfer facility.

Alpha Cine Labs in Seattle, popular with many independents, uses Kodak Color Intermediate II 5242/2242 (acetate/polyester) or Fuji Eterna-RDI 8511/4511 (acetate/polyester). All are intermediate stocks that produce a negative with sharper resolution than camera original negative, and they are better suited to printing a large number of release prints. The polyester-base stock is more resistant to wear and tear compared to acetate. If using an acetate negative for more than ten prints, Alpha Cine recommends creating an additional master postive and dupe negative.

Filmmakers are often unaware that they have a choice of print stocks on which to print their film-out. Kodak, for instance, offers Kodak Vision color print film 2383 and Vision color print film 2393. The 2383 is Kodak's workhorse print stock, but the more contrasty 2393 has richer blacks and more saturated colors (and costs more). Fuji offers three Eterna print stocks that differ in density, contrast, and color saturation.

As noted above, sometimes a *direct print* is made with no negative if only one print and a few screenings are anticipated.

For more on these topics, see Making Film Prints, p. 709. Sound tracks for film prints are discussed starting on p. 713.

TRADITIONAL FILM
CONFORMING AND BLOWUPS

As described on p. 49, not that many years ago the standard workflow for a movie shot on film involved editing a film workprint, then cutting the camera original negative to match the edited workprint. *Negative cutting*, also called *conforming*, is the process of assembling the camera original in rolls so that prints and intermediates can be made. Conforming must be done with utmost care and precision and cutting errors made during conforming can be disastrous.

As time and technology have moved on, most people now edit digitally. As described in Scenario Three on p. 681, it is still possible to go from a digital offline edit to conform negative in the traditional way. However, this workflow is falling by the wayside. Independents just don't need film prints as much as they used to, and studio filmmakers usually prefer to do a D.I. with a film-out rather than conform and print from the negative in the traditional way.

This section is included as an overview of methods you may want to be familiar with and may still be using. Film restoration and archival work often involves traditional methods.

PREPARING THE ORIGINAL FOR PRINTING

Films are conformed in different ways depending on the film gauge and what kind of printer is being used. A *printer* is essentially a machine that duplicates one piece of film onto another. The camera original and the unexposed printing stock move past an aperture where the intensity and the color of light exposing the stock can be controlled. Prints can be made either by putting the original in contact with the print stock on a *contact printer* or by projecting the original onto the print stock through a lens on an *optical printer* (see Fig. 16-12).

Below are two principal ways of laying out the original for printing (and sometimes digital transfer).

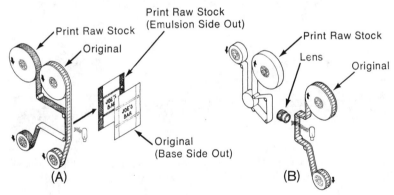

Fig. 16-12. Contact and optical printing. (A) The contact printer: the original is printed in emulsion-to-emulsion contact with the print stock. The inset shows how this changes the wind. Usually the original reads through the base (B-wind), and the contact print reads through the emulsion (A-wind). (B) The optical printer: a lens is used between the original and print stock. The wind can be preserved or changed on an optical printer. (Carol Keller)

Single Strand

Splicing the conformed original into a *single strand* (also called *A-rolling*) is simple and straightforward. This is the standard process in 35mm printing, since the frame line is wide enough to make cement splices that aren't visible on screen.

However, when you're printing from a single strand in 16mm and Super 8, splices—whether made with cement or tape—will show on the screen. Virtually all professionally made 16mm films are printed using a more expensive technique that makes cement splices invisible (see below).

Single-strand printing has some disadvantages. When you use a contact printer, fades on negative stocks and double exposures, superimposed titles, or dissolves on either negative or reversal stocks are normally not possible, since these effects require the overlapping of two shots. You can do these effects from a single strand if the effect is optically printed or done digitally; then a new piece of negative with the effect is spliced into the roll.

A&B Rolls

Printing in multiple strands of original can make splices invisible in 16mm. *A&B rolling* (also called *checkerboard printing*) is the most common way of printing 16mm films. This involves dividing the shots from the original onto two rolls and spacing them with black leader. Thus, the first shot of the movie is on the A-roll, with black leader opposite it on the B-roll. The second shot is spliced onto the B-roll, and leader of the same length fills the space on the A-roll. To print the A&B rolls, first the A-roll is run through the printing machine with the print raw stock. The shots on the roll are exposed onto the print stock, but wherever there is black leader nothing happens. Then the B-roll is threaded up with the print stock. The shots on this roll occur only where black leader was on the A-roll.

This technique leads to invisible splices because the overlap needed to make the cement splice occurs over black leader, through which no light reaches the print stock. A&B rolls allow you to do fades, dissolves, double exposures, and superimposed titles.

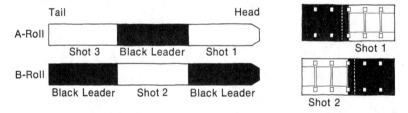

Fig. 16-13. A&B rolling. (left) Three shots laid out on A&B rolls with black leader as spacing. (right) The overlap for the 16mm cement splice occurs over the black leader, not over the picture. (Carol Keller)

BLOWUPS

Enlarging from a smaller gauge to a larger (for example, from 16mm to 35mm) is called a *blowup*. Going from a larger gauge to a smaller is called *reduction printing* or, sometimes, *blowdown*. Today most filmmakers who shoot Super 8, 16mm, or Super 16 and need 35mm film prints do so by running the film through a telecine or scanner and then doing a film-out to 35mm. However, the traditional method is to use an optical printer for blowups.

16mm and Super 16 Blowups

Blowups from 16mm and Super 16 to 35mm (see Fig. 1-39) may be done for low-budget feature films that receive theatrical distribution. The Super 16 format, having a larger frame and wider screen aspect ratio, was basically designed for blowup so if you know at the start of the project that you will need a blowup, shoot Super 16 whenever possible.

When shooting 16mm or Super 16, do everything you can to minimize grain. Use fine-grained film stocks and avoid underexposure of color negative. *Slightly* overexposing color stock up to one stop produces the finest-grain blowup (for more on grain and exposure, see Chapter 7). Avoid flashing and force processing (pushing).

When composing images during the shoot, keep in mind the aspect ratio you intend to distribute the film in. In the United States, most theaters show films at 1.85:1, though some can accommodate 1.66:1, which is a standard used in European theaters. When shooting regular 16mm, be aware that the top and bottom of the frame will be cropped. Some viewfinders are marked for 1.85 aspect ratio (see Fig. 6-6). The lines marked for the top and bottom of the TV safe action area are very close to 1.66 cutoff. Even if the film was not shot with blowup in mind, if the framing is not too tight you'll probably be fine.

MAKING FILM PRINTS

You may have done a film-out to create your film negative from a digital file, or you may have shot film and conformed negative in the traditional way. In either case, you have options when it comes to making film prints. For projects that are shot on film, the terms *camera original* and *original camera negative* (*OCN*) refer to the footage that went through the camera. For the purposes of this section, "camera original" will also refer to the first negative produced in a film-out.

PRINTING BASICS

A print made directly from the camera original is referred to as a *first-generation print*. A print made from a copy of the camera original would be a second-generation print. Sharpness is lost and grain increased every time a duplicate is made. The filmmaker has to decide how many generations are acceptable.

Film must be as clean as possible before you make any prints or intermediates (see p. 689).

Print Exposure and Color Correction

The exposure and color for each scene must be controlled in printing to correct errors in the original and to provide creative adjustments. Contact and optical printers usually have an exposure scale divided into one to fifty steps called *printer lights* or *printer points*. Color balance is controlled by dividing an intense beam of white light into three separate beams of red, green, and blue light by means of a beam-splitter. Each of these colored beams is first modulated in fifty incrementing steps by light gates (little barndoors) and then recombined at the printer aperture (*additive printing*).

Different labs use different machines and standards, but as a rule a normally exposed negative will print near the middle of the range, usually between 25R, 25G, 25B ("25 points across") and 30R, 30G, 30B ("30 points across"). A negative that was overexposed in shooting will appear darker or "heavier" and will need brighter printer lights to compensate when printed. One stop of overexposure will need a correction of +6 points or +7 lights applied to all three colors.

At the lab, the color *timer* (U.S. term) or *grader* (British term) adjusts exposure and color balance, much as a colorist corrects the image during a video transfer and uses his judgment about how corrections will ultimately translate to the film print.

The types of corrections available in film printing machines will seem primitive compared to working in video. In a film printer, an overall color balance must be chosen for each scene. In video, you can change the color of, say, a person's shirt without affecting the skin tone; or you could darken only the sky while leaving the landscape unchanged. This is yet another reason why many film projects are finished digitally, with a film-out to make prints.

Print Stocks

Camera stocks are matched to companion print stocks to produce an image of proper gamma (see Chapter 7). There is no reason, however, that a Fuji print can't be struck from a Kodak negative, or vice versa. (It happens all the time.) If your overall imagery has less contrast than normal, consider a Kodak or Fuji print stock with higher contrast or deeper color. Different negative and print stocks combine to produce a range of looks and palettes. Don't be afraid to test them.

ANSWER PRINTS

The first print from the conformed original is the *answer print*. It is a timed, color-corrected, trial print. The first answer print is rarely perfect. You'll make corrections, then a second (or third) answer print to check them. Generally you should let the timer do the color corrections for the first answer print on his or her own. Then screen and/or discuss it with the timer to make any changes for the next print. Nevertheless, tell the timer in advance of any special timing instructions, such as night scenes or scenes that should have an unusual color cast. Often filmmakers get used to the timing of the dailies and are shocked by the new timings in the answer print.

Evaluating the Answer Print

View the answer print (or any other print being evaluated) on a projector you know or under standard conditions. The lab will often have a projection room that meets industry standards for image brightness and color temperature. Carefully check for conforming errors, invisibility of splices, smooth cuts without image jumping, quality of effects. If the print shows dirt from the original, have the printing rolls cleaned before striking the next print. If there are scratches or cinch marks, you may want to see if wet gate printing will help. If there is a sound track, listen carefully for good sound reproduction without distortion or excess noise.

Write down a list of shots that need correction. It's best to screen the print with the timer at this point or note errors by footage count from the "Picture Start" mark on the head leader of each reel. See p. 626 for some color correction guidelines that apply to both film and video.

INTERMEDIATES

Even if handled carefully, the camera original will start to show wear after several prints. Splices can pull apart after repeated trips through the printer. Some labs do not like to pull (make) more than a few prints from color negative original; however, as noted above, polyester-base stocks sometimes used for film-outs are more rugged. If more than ten prints are to be made from acetate original, standard practice is to duplicate the original onto an *intermediate*, which you then substitute for the original when making *release prints* (that is, the prints for distribution). Intermediates serve several purposes: they protect the original from handling; they serve as an insurance copy; and they allow quantity printing at a lower price. However, if you are making only a few release prints, printing directly from the original saves money and achieves the highest quality. Intermediates are sometimes referred to as *preprint elements*.

Original Color Negative

Intermediates for original color negative are usually made in a two-step process. The original negative is first printed to a *master positive*. (*Master positive* is the correct term for color positive intermediates, but *interpositive*, *IP*, and *interpos*, terms from the earlier days of black-and-white printing, are often used instead.) Master positives are commonly made with Kodak 5242 for 35mm or 7242 for 16mm (both are acetate stocks). Also popular are master positives with an indestructible polyester base made with Kodak 2242/3242 (35mm/16mm). Equivalent Fuji intermediate stocks for making master positives are Eterna-CI 8503/8603 (35mm/16mm, acetate) and 4503 (35mm, polyester).

Master positives have a gamma of 1.0, which reproduces a positive version of the original negative's tonal scale with a 1:1 contrast. After the master positive is made, it is printed to the same intermediate stock it was made with, which reverses the tonalities again, to produce a *duplicate negative* (*dupe neg*). Release prints can then be struck from the dupe negative. This two-step process not only protects the original negative, but the master positive makes an excellent low-contrast, first-generation source for a video transfer (see p. 696).

When the same shot is used twice in a movie, a dupe neg can be made of the original shot and cut in with the original camera negative. In this case, be sure to have the dupe neg printed on acetate stock so it will splice with the OCN (acetate and polyester can't be cement-spliced together).

There are other forms of intermediates for color negative originals. *Color separation negatives* (also called *YCM masters*) are three separate records of the color original made on black-and-white film using red, green, and blue filters, respectively.

Although expensive, YCM masters use no color dyes and create a permanent, non-fading record of the colors for archival storage.

Reversal Original

For films shot with reversal original, an *internegative* (*IN*) can be made from the original. This allows release prints to be made in the standard negative/positive process instead of trying to strike reversal prints from reversal original, a process that may not be available and often results in lower-quality optical sound tracks.

Black-and-White Negative

To control contrast, black-and-white negatives are duplicated by the same two-step process used for duplicating color negatives. First the negative is printed onto Eastman Fine Grain Duplicating Positive Film 5366/7366 (35mm/16mm, acetate), and then the master positive is printed onto a duplicate negative made with the same stock.

Check Prints

A *check print* is like an answer print but made instead from a dupe negative or internegative. After a dupe negative or internegative blowup to 35mm is made, for instance, a check print is struck to verify that all went well.

RELEASE PRINTS

A *release print* is a print intended for distribution—finished and ready to be shown. Minor timing errors on a check print or an answer print can usually be corrected when the release print is made. Today most movies projected on film are distributed in 35mm. A few film festivals still accept 16mm, but 16mm distribution has largely disappeared.

Fig. 16-14. Release prints being prepared for shipping. (Film-Tech.com)

35mm Release Prints

Usually 35mm prints are mounted on plastic or metal reels and shipped in plastic cases or heavy-duty *ICC* or Goldberg metal cases. The reels of film should be taped or otherwise secured to prevent unspooling in shipment. Reels are usually about twenty minutes long. Some theaters will splice all the reels into a single *platter* for projection (see Fig. 16-17). The sound should be prepared with pullups in anticipation of the reels being spliced together (see Analog Optical Tracks, p. 715).

Some theaters will keep the reels separate and use two matched projectors. They change over from one projector to the other at the end of each reel to avoid an interruption for reloading. *Changeover marks* are small circles inscribed in the upper-right-hand corner of a few frames at the end of each reel to cue the projectionist when to start the next projector. The lab can put marks on the print, or on a dupe negative so they appear on all prints. Counting backward from the last frame on a reel, the marks appear on frames 25 to 28 and 196 to 199.

Print Care and Handling

When labeling print containers for shipment, be sure to put your return address inside the case, since many shippers will cover over exterior labels. Indicate whether a case or reel is part of a set (for example, "Reel 2 of 3"). Prints should be kept clean and free from damage. Broken perforations may be repaired with splicing tape or preperforated tape applied to just the edge of the film without obscuring the picture.

Release prints today are generally made on polyester stock. All prints get scratched, but 16mm prints are particularly vulnerable. Always clean the projector gate before use (see below). For distribution, you may want to use a film shipping house (see Chapter 17) that can inspect and repair prints whenever they come back from being shown. For more on prints and projection, see below.

SOUND FOR FILM PRINTS

Before reading this, see Mix Formats, p. 669, for information about sound mixing and release formats for sound. This section is about putting the finished track on a film print. A film print with sound is called a *composite* or *married* print.

ANALOG OPTICAL TRACKS

Optical Tracks

The traditional type of composite print employs an *optical sound track*, which uses a photographic process to record and play the sound. Optical tracks are a worldwide standard in 16mm and 35mm. Conventional optical tracks look like jagged lines along the edge of the film (see Fig. 16-16). In the projector, an *exciter lamp* shines a narrow beam of light through the sound track. As the area (thickness) of the track varies, so does the amount of light that can pass through it. A *photocell* on the opposite side of the film converts the changes in light into a changing electrical signal, which is reproduced as sound.

In 35mm, optical sound may be mono (one channel of sound) or stereo. With *Dolby SR* (*Spectral Response*) tracks, four channels of sound (LCRS; see p. 670) can be encoded in one pair of stereo tracks. Dolby SR increases the dynamic range and reduces the noise of optical tracks; it can produce very good quality. In 16mm, optical tracks are mono and the sound quality is relatively poor.

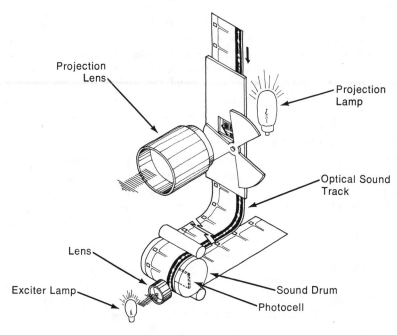

Fig. 16-15. Film projector and optical sound. Light from the exciter lamp shines through the optical sound track. The resulting variations in the light are registered by the photocell (shown in cutaway). In 16mm, the optical sound reader is separated from the film gate where the image is projected by 26 frames. (Carol Keller)

Making Optical Tracks

To make an optical track, you supply the lab or sound facility with the movie's sound track (the printmaster; see p. 673) on disc, hard drive, mag film, or other format. Using an optical recorder, the track will be exposed photographically on a piece of film called an *optical sound negative* or *optical sound master*. After development, the optical sound negative is then contact printed with each release print. At each step in the process, the density of the optical track must be carefully controlled. If a sound house produces the optical master, it's imperative that the house have a close working relationship with the lab.

Newer projector technology uses an LED instead of a tungsten exciter lamp, and prints have a cyan-colored sound track. However, these projectors don't read conventional silver tracks well. A compromise *high-magenta sound track* may produce acceptable results on either type of projector.

KEEPING OPTICAL TRACKS IN SYNC. When you submit a sound track to the lab to make an optical sound master, it should be prepared according to the standard SMPTE leader format with an audible beep at the "2" (see Reel Breaks and Reference Movies, p. 652). On the optical master, the beep will appear as a frame of squiggly lines in an area where the track is otherwise smooth. The lab will position this frame several frames ahead of the "2" when it makes the release print. The separation is 26 frames in 16mm and 20 frames in 35mm. Without the beep, the lab may have no accurate way to put the track in sync with the picture. Be sure to discuss with the lab the frame rate at which the film was edited to ensure proper speed adjustments have been made.

WHEN REELS ARE SPLICED TOGETHER. For projection it is common to splice together the various reels that make up a movie and show it in one continuous strand. An interesting thing happens if you splice together two reels of a release print. Say you have a 35mm print and you splice the first frame of picture of reel 2 to the last frame of reel 1. When the splice runs through the projector, the picture will cut from one reel to the next, but the sound won't change until almost a second later. Actually, you get 20 frames of silence after the cut, at which point the sound from reel 2 starts with the first 20 frames cut off. Not good.

Why does this happen? Look at the 16mm projector in Figure 16-15. The film is moving from top to bottom, so as the cut moves through the projector it first passes the film gate but doesn't reach the sound reader until about a second later. This separation is the reason the optical sound for any frame of picture is located on the print 26 frames ahead of the picture in 16mm (20 frames in 35mm).

To create a smooth, natural cut in which the sound and picture change in sync, we must repeat sound from the *head* of reel 2 to the *tail* of reel 1. This can be done before, during, or after the mix. It simply means duplicating this short section of sound and adding it onto the tail of reel 1's track. Mixers do it as a matter of course at the mix. This is sometimes called a *pullup* (but should not be confused with the use of "pull up" to mean speed up). A pullup should be done to the tail of every reel in the film except the last one. This is *only* needed for film prints and does not apply to editing together reels of video.

DIGITAL SOUND TRACKS

On most modern film releases, digital tracks are used on the film prints to provide better quality and more audio channels.

Dolby Digital

Perhaps the most common digital film print format is *Dolby SR-D*. With this system, a pattern of dots that carry digital data is printed between the sprocket holes of the film print (see Fig. 16-16). Also called *Dolby Digital*, this format can accommodate a 5.1-channel mix (left, center, right; left and right surround; and a subwoofer for low-frequency effects). Dolby Digital prints also include the analog Dolby Stereo optical track described above, for theaters that can't play the digital track. The analog track plays a four-channel mix folded down from the 5.1-channel digital mix. *Dolby Digital Surround EX* can accomodate 6.1 or 7.1 channels. Dolby

Stereo optical
(analog)   SDDS

DTS | Dolby digital |

Fig. 16-16. The edge of a 35mm release print showing four types of analog and digital sound tracks that can be put on the same print. (Frank Angel)

Digital requires a license from Dolby for each production as well as certification from a Dolby technician that proper procedures are followed.

DTS, SDDS, and THX

Digital Theater Systems (*DTS*) uses a CD-ROM to play six channels of uncompressed digital sound on a disc playback system interlocked to the film projector. This can be used for a four-channel or 5.1-channel mix. DTS needs to be licensed for your production and works only in theaters equipped with disc playback equipment. DTS can be used on 16mm and 35mm prints and requires a timecode track on the print.

Sony Dynamic Digital Sound (*SDDS*) is an eight-channel digital system that uses a matrix of dots, similar to SR-D, but positioned along both edges of the film outside the sprocket holes. This can be used for 7.1-channel mixes.

On major releases, analog, Dolby Digital, DTS, and SDDS tracks may all be included on the same print so it's usable with any projection system.

Lucasfilm's *THX system* isn't an audio format, but it sets standards for the playback environment, regardless of the film format. THX-licensed home theater systems are based on Dolby Pro Logic Surround decoding.

FILM PROJECTION

Projectors (often jittery machines with dirty, low-contrast optics) are usually the weak link in the chain of equipment that transfers the image from the world to the screen. Even so, the image quality of projected film may be more consistent than video projection, which varies widely with the type of equipment and how it's adjusted. When projecting 35mm, the theater will have a set of lenses for different types of prints (flat or anamorphic).

If you're handling the projection, keep the film path of the projector clean, especially the area of the film gate behind the lens. Dirt and emulsion dust regularly accumulate in the gate and can easily scratch the film. Use a cotton swab with alcohol or acetone to clean both sides of the pressure plate (acetone should never be used on plastic or sound heads). Hairs that lodge in the gate during a screening can often be blown out with a can of compressed air while the film runs. Try to focus the picture and adjust the sound before the audience arrives. Focusing can be done with the naked eye, with binoculars, or with an assistant at the screen if the distance from the projector to the screen (the *throw*) is great. If you focus on the *grain* and not the image itself, you'll be sure to maximize sharpness even if the scene itself was filmed out of focus.

Whenever possible, do a tech-check before the audience arrives to set audio levels and ensure that the right lens and masking are being used.

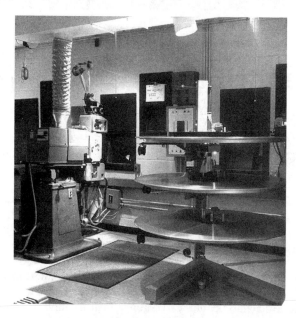

Fig. 16-17. Many theaters use a platter system so that an entire print can be spliced together, fed to the projector in one piece, and spooled up again. The projectionist only has to start the projector at the beginning and turn it off at the end. (Film-Tech.com)

CHAPTER 17

Producing and Distributing the Movie

Cinema is an unhappy art as it depends on money, not only because film is very expensive, but then it is also marketed like cigarettes.

—ANDREI TARKOVSKY

This chapter is about the business and legal aspects of getting a movie made and shown. Many of these concerns apply to any kind of film or video project, from feature film to corporate video to student project. The scope of this book allows for only a general discussion of these topics, to help you frame the questions for which you need answers. A proviso for everything that follows: nothing here should be taken as legal advice or as a substitute for a consultation with an experienced attorney, accountant, or other professional. Also, because laws and customs vary from state to state and country to country, bear in mind that practices may be different where you live. For those who can't afford traditional legal services, organizations such as Volunteer Lawyers for the Arts may be able to assist you.

DEVELOPING THE PROJECT

Be sure to read Getting Your Movie Off the Ground, starting on p. 53, before reading this section.

The development period for an independent film is the movie's first stage of life, when an idea is nurtured and funding is put into place. When development is done, preproduction—the concrete preparations for the actual shoot—can begin (see Chapter 9 for more on that). On some projects, development and preproduction overlap.

What happens during development depends a lot on what kind of project you're doing, how many people are involved, the amount of funding needed, and where the money's coming from. Like everything else in filmmaking, several things are usually happening at the same time in terms of developing the idea, looking for money, and putting together key parts of the team.

Development is in part about getting others interested and involved in your project, but just as crucially, it's a time for you to ripen your vision. If you approach an investor, a commissioning editor for a television series, or a distributor, you will be asked tough questions for which you need clear answers. These days there is virtually no subject about which a previous film (or two or three or four) hasn't already been made. So you'll need compelling arguments about why yours is different, special, and worthy. A half-baked vision can doom you to years of working on a project with a fatal flaw.

To get feedback, talk to friends—does your idea pique their interest, get them excited? Talk to sales agents or distributors. Become part of online communities (like the one for documentaries at www.d-word.com) where you can ask more experienced producers for advice. Of course, some films depend heavily on how they're executed and no one can predict if they'll find an audience or not. But for many projects, the market may simply not be there. Regardless of whether you let that deter you, it's worth knowing the landscape ahead of time and preparing yourself by thinking through your project deeply and thoroughly.

Basic Elements

Different movies sprout from different kinds of seeds. If you're producing a narrative film, you might find a short story or novel, then option the rights to develop a script. Or if a newspaper article sparks an idea for a documentary, you might try to work with the article's author or set off to do your own research. Studios may develop projects based on existing scripts (often rewriting them until they bear no resemblance to the original) or start with as little as a story premise and the name of a star they want to work with.

Once the basic idea is in place, you can look for key people to participate in the project, such as a writer to create a script, an actor for a central role, or a list of potential subjects for a documentary. You're not in preproduction yet, so you're not fully staffing up or necessarily doing all the research, just getting central creative elements together. During development, you want to surround the basic idea with enough elements so that people get excited about the project and feel confident that it can be successfully completed. People are going to ask:

- Is the idea interesting, promising, original?
- Are the people making the film talented and experienced?
- Are any well-known elements involved, in terms of actors, writers, director, etc.?
- Is the production well organized and properly budgeted?
- Is the project likely to be a success in terms of profit, viewership, and/or social value?

Development is in part a time for selling: you're selling yourself and the project to potential funders and to all sorts of people you hope to work with. You have to make the most of what you have and what you think you can get in the future. Often it's a chicken-and-egg situation: with money I could get (Actor X, Director Y, Great Location L); and if I had (Actor X, Director Y, Great Location L) I could get money.

If you don't have much of a track record, it can be extremely valuable to partner with an experienced filmmaker or company. Sometimes an experienced person will sign on as executive producer and help you find funding or support.

The One-Sheet

As a starting point, you'll need a one-page summary of the project you can email around to prospective partners or funders, sometimes called a *one-sheet*.[1] This is an easily read document that distills elements from the proposal (see below) and represents your film to the world. You'll go through many versions of this document and you should edit it until it really sings. Test it out on friends and colleagues in the business.

For a documentary, the one-sheet should convey a distinct, intriguing premise. The reader should quickly glean the dramatic question at the heart of the film, how your project is different from others, who the audience is, and why you're the right person to make this film.

For a drama, the one-sheet is a short treatment that leaps off the page and will serve as an urtext for the construction of a screenplay.

The Proposal

The proposal describes the project more fully than a one-sheet, and it is an important tool for promoting the project. The format and style of the proposal depend on the type of production (such as fiction or documentary) and where you're trying to get funding or support (such as investors, TV networks, foundations, or individual donors). For a low-budget horror film, you may be soliciting investors whose chief concern is whether they'll make a profit. For a documentary about a pressing social concern, you may be asking for support from foundations or donors who aren't looking for financial return but want to know if the project is likely to be widely seen, raise awareness, and bring about change. Your proposal should be tailored to the type of organization or investor you're sending it to and the project should be represented in a way that is consistent with their interests.

When writing a proposal, keep in mind that it will be read by people who are sifting through many competing proposals and applications; they'll need to understand what you want to do as quickly as possible. Simple, direct, and clear prose is important. Some funders will have detailed applications or specified proposal formats; in other cases you'll put together your own document. Be sure to formulate a clear and succinct idea of your project and its goals.

The following are elements that may be included in a proposal (not necessarily in this order).

LOGLINE. As discussed on p. 54, the logline is one or two sentences that describe and pique curiosity about the project. You'll need it for correspondence, conversations, and applications of various types.

OVERVIEW/SUMMARY. Give an overview of the production in one or a few paragraphs. This is a brief summary that outlines what the film is, key participants, what you hope to accomplish, and anything else that makes the project stand out in the mind of the reader (such as major support and endorsements you've already received).

---

1. "One-sheet" is also a term for a movie poster; see p. 763.

SYNOPSIS OR PROJECT NARRATIVE. For a scripted film, the synopsis is a short summary of the characters and plot. Keep it vivid and don't go into too much detail. You'll submit the actual script or story treatment separately.

For a documentary, you might do a synopsis that outlines the movie as you envision it, with the kinds of scenes and stories you hope/plan to capture. In some proposals, instead of a synopsis, a more comprehensive project narrative is done that expands on the ideas in the short overview. One granting organization that funds documentaries asks for a narrative that includes information on the project concept; the film's style and aesthetic treatment (what it will look like); key creative personnel and their unique qualifications; the relevance and timeliness of the project; project schedule; intended audience; and distribution strategies. It may be mostly a question of page layout whether you discuss these items as part of a project narrative (with headings for each subsection) or as separate sections in the overall proposal.

FUNDING AND INVESTMENT. For an investor-funded film, you must detail how money is being raised, how much (if any) has been raised so far, and how income will be distributed to investors and other participants when revenues come in. There are strict investment rules (some of which vary by state) and putting together an investor *prospectus* must be done in consultation with an attorney familiar with both film investment and tax law.

For other types of projects that aren't necessarily expected to turn a profit, you should detail how you plan to obtain the money you need to make the film.

AUDIENCE AND REVENUES. On for-profit films, it helps to list some films that are similar to yours in terms of type of story, talent, target audience, or distribution and indicate how much money they grossed (in the United States, you can usually get box office grosses via IMDb.com or Boxofficemojo.com). A more complete analysis of *return on investment* (*ROI*) includes all forms of revenue (domestic and foreign, theatrical, DVD, etc.) less total costs (including production and marketing).

For a documentary on social issues, you may want to discuss who the intended audience is, and show how comparable productions reached wide audiences. Describe the *outreach campaign* you intend to do to target groups and individuals who will benefit from your project and want to see it.

In the past, many films were made with the assumption that distribution would be funded and handled by distribution companies. Many moviemakers took the attitude that their responsibility ended with making the movie. Increasingly, filmmakers are finding that they are forced to handle distribution themselves or in a hybrid arrangement with a distributor (more on this later in this chapter), or they choose to. Particularly with grants, you can increase your chances of getting funded if you demonstrate a serious commitment to showing the movie when it's done (including budgeting for distribution from the outset). The more specific you are (and the more interest in the project you can demonstrate from broadcasters or potential users), the better your project looks.

SCHEDULE AND BUDGET. Include a project timeline that indicates when each phase of the production should be complete. Readers of a proposal will want to see the budget summary (top sheet; see below), not the detailed line items (though that may be requested separately). Grant organizations often have specific rules about how the budget is laid out and what you can and can't pay for with grant funds.

BIOS. One paragraph on each key member of the creative team, such as producer, director, writer, and main talent, and sometimes cinematographer, editor, or other participants. Grant applications may also ask to have full resumes attached.

SCRIPT, TRAILER, OR SAMPLE. The more you have that's concrete, the easier it is for potential funders to understand and believe in what you're doing. For a fiction film, the script is an important part of the package. For both fiction and documentary, a trailer or sample made from any footage that has been shot can be very useful (see p. 57 for more). In some cases you can only show samples of past work. For grant applications, a tight, well-made ten-minute piece is better than a long, slowly developing feature. In fact, many panels won't watch more than three to five minutes anyway, so be sure there's something strong from the start. Find out the viewing procedures and create an excerpt DVD or file (or give instructions to cue up a DVD to a certain spot). You can "set up" the clip with a short written description. Many filmmakers post clips and samples online (often at a password-protected Web page).

LOOK BOOK. Mainly useful for feature films, the *look book* helps define the look in terms of the cinematography and design that you hope to achieve. It can contain stills from other films or photos as a visual reference and may include casting and location possibilities. Look books are often stylish and graphically appealing. Sometimes a video look book is made using clips from films.

The Production Entity

Because the organization, financing, and responsibilities of making a movie are complex, on many independent feature films a company or other legal entity is created solely for the purpose of producing the movie. If you're seeking investors and need only a few backers, perhaps the simplest arrangement is to form a *limited partnership* (*LP*) or the related *limited liability company* (*LLC*), in which the investors supply capital and the filmmaker may retain control and responsibility for the project.

Even if you're not in a position to form a legal entity for the project, it's essential that key collaborators lay out clearly in writing their respective position in terms of ownership and finances. For example, the producer and director should have a signed agreement that specifies responsibilities and control of the work, payments due, profit sharing, copyright, and an agreement to submit to binding arbitration in case of a dispute. Particularly on smaller projects (in which lawyers aren't involved from the start) it's not uncommon that people collaborate loosely to get a project going, then feel misunderstood or taken advantage of further down the line. Be sure to have a written contract or deal memo with everyone who works on the film and will eventually be in the credits.

Many different versions of these forms, such as an investor agreement, are available on the Internet and can be very useful in saving legal fees. You can amend a boilerplate form and bring it to a lawyer for critical tweaking at the end.

NONPROFIT STATUS. Some grants are available only to nonprofit organizations or indirectly to filmmakers working under the aegis of one. Nonprofit groups in the United States are sometimes referred to by their tax code status, *501(C)3*. Nonprofit status doesn't prevent a funded movie from turning a profit. However, the filmmaker must usually establish that the primary goal of the project is social, educational, or artistic—not just profit. Nonprofit corporations are more difficult to set up than for-profit entities, so it's usually simpler to affiliate yourself with an existing nonprofit group, which can act as your *fiscal agent* or conduit through which to apply for funding. Many organizations, such as film foundations, universities, and church groups, will perform this service. Typically the supporting group will take 5–15 percent of the funds raised as a fee, but this is sometimes waived. Often you can apply for state funds from a state where you don't live, as long as you work with a fiscal agent in that state. Try to find a nonprofit group whose goals and mission are related to the project you're proposing. One advantage of certain types of nonprofit status is that individuals or corporations that support the project may be able to deduct their contribution from their taxes. This can be a powerful incentive for wealthy contributors.

FUNDING SOURCES

Commercial Funding

Feature films intended for theatrical release are usually financed by studios, film distributors, investor groups, or others who invest in exchange for a share of the film's future earnings. *Equity financing* involves investors who provide cash and are given *points*, which are a share of profits. If the film is profitable, the investors get their investment back plus a percentage. Points are also paid to the producer and other profit participants.

Sometimes wealthy investors get involved in films as a way to get in on the "glamour" of filmmaking and to get tax breaks even if the film isn't profitable. Producers may entice investors with a chance be around the set, come to premieres and film festivals, and mingle with the cast. Changes in tax laws have made it harder to get a write-off from a film that loses money.

Many fiction films and documentaries, especially those by filmmakers with established reputations, are funded wholly or in part by the entities that will distribute the finished product—this may include film distribution companies, broadcast or cable TV organizations, Web-based companies, or publishers (for a multimedia project, for example). Bankable projects—like one that features an actor who is popular overseas and can get a *minimum guarantee* (MG) from a foreign sales agent—can be presold to distributors to raise production money. Distribution rights are usually divided so that one distributor buys domestic distribution rights and others buy specific foreign markets.

Often, independent producers are unable to sell a film prior to production, but may be able to raise completion money after the project is under way. Television networks or stations may be persuaded by a proposal or script to fund all or part of a project, or they may wait until the movie is done. Selling a movie prior to production (or completion) is considered a *presale*; when it's bought after it's done, this is considered an *acquisition*. Ironically, television executives generally offer much more money for a movie that hasn't yet begun—and is therefore a greater risk—than for one that's finished. This usually reflects their desire to get credit for, and have some control over, the project.

Completed movies, especially ones without a strong reputation, more than ever face a buyer's market. Single television shows ("one-offs") are often hard to fit into a broadcast schedule and they are much harder to promote than a series. Unless your project fits into the format of a preexisting series, sometimes it's easier to raise a lot of money for a *limited series* than it is to raise much less money for a single show. For more on this, see Distribution and Marketing, p. 747.

Getting Grants

The funding sources discussed above are generally only available to projects that are likely to earn a profit or find a sizable audience on television or through other distribution channels. Many documentary, experimental, educational, and short fiction movies never make a profit (or, in some cases, even recoup their costs) and may be aimed at a relatively small, non-mass-market audience. These projects must usually be subsidized by government, foundations, or private donations. In many countries, there are government-run or private agencies at the national, state/provincial, or local level that give grants for production or distribution. Some grants are given to filmmakers on the basis of their previous work and are not intended to support any particular project. Others are given for specific projects, and the filmmaker's past work is used to determine whether he or she is capable of completing the task. Producers with no track record are always at a disadvantage. If you have no relevant prior work to show, consider teaming up with someone more experienced.

Outright or *direct grants* are cash funds for the project. Sometimes grantors require you to "cost-share" by funding part of the budget with your own or others' cash or with in-kind donations of services, materials, or facilities (see below). *Matching grants* are given with the stipulation that some money be raised first from third-party (outside) sources. A 50 percent match means that the granting agency will give you a dollar for every two dollars you raise from someone else. Often just the fact that the granting agency has endorsed the project by giving you a grant helps you leverage money from other sources.

For most grants, there is a substantial delay between the time you submit your application and when grant funds are released. Six months or even a year is not uncommon. Plan ahead. As one producer said, "It was three years between the time I conceived of the film and when I was fully funded. By then, I wasn't really interested in shooting it." Also keep in mind that many grants will only reimburse expenses that are incurred during the grant period, so you may want to wait until the grant starts to do certain work.

Before submitting an application to a granting organization, do your homework and find out what kinds of projects it has funded in the past and what criteria it uses to select grantees (and see above for more on applications and proposals). If you can, contact the agency's staff, both to learn about the organization and so that they know you and your project before the review panel meets. Prepare a list of questions that will help you target your application toward their concerns. Although the staffers usually do not pass judgment on proposals (generally outside reviewers do), they can help in various ways.

You'll find many sources of information on available grants. Search the Internet, or go to your local library for books on granting organizations. The Foundation Center (www.foundationcenter.org), which has branches in many cities, puts out a directory of granting agencies with a tally of projects funded in the past. State arts councils often have similar lists. See the Bibliography for suggestions of books, periodicals, and websites.

When searching for a grant, don't look at just the obvious choices for media-related funding. Sometimes you can get money from sources that don't specialize in media, but that have an interest in the topic your project addresses. Many private foundations and corporate-giving programs have a particular focus or local interest. A drug company might give a grant for a medical-related project. A bank might give money for a locally produced project as part of its community support. These funders are often looking to maximize the impact of their investment and the amount of publicity they'll get. Be resourceful and prepare yourself for lots of rejection: when they weigh the choice between funding a needed machine at the local hospital and supporting a movie, you can guess what many companies will do.

As noted above, you may need to form, or be associated with, a nonprofit organization in order to apply for some grants.

Crowdfunding

Another form of funding, called *crowdfunding* or *crowdsourcing*, has arisen through sites like Kickstarter (www.kickstarter.com) and Indiegogo (www.indiegogo.com), where you can post your project idea and interested people can donate funds. The sites take a small commission on donations. You can drive people to your project with social networking or email blasts—it's important to reach out widely to anyone you know and anyone your friends know. In the most effective campaigns, people post a video of themselves making a direct appeal to potential donors. You can also post a trailer. Filmmakers offer levels of rewards, such as an executive producer credit for a high contribution or a DVD for a small donation.

Not all filmmakers have the temperament to mount and execute a consistent and well-planned campaign of this nature, which takes hours every day for the duration of the appeal, and when not done right can often feel like begging or harassing your friends.

A listing of other sites can be found at www.crowdsourcing.org.

Noncash Contributions

Resourceful filmmakers (and also desperate filmmakers) are always on the lookout for ways to get goods and/or services donated to a project. Food, air travel, props, and labor may be offered by persons or companies in exchange for a credit in the film, the chance to be part of a film in production, or a tax deduction. A company may support a local film merely to be a good neighbor or, for a larger project, for the advertising. An airline may offer free travel to a project if a shot of one of its planes is included in the film. (Airlines may supply free stock footage of planes in flight, saving you the cost of getting it from a stock footage library.) Or an indie band might let you use their song so they get more exposure.

Sometimes filmmakers barter services. Say you want to shoot a scene in a store, but can't pay a location fee. You might offer to shoot footage the store could use in an ad or on its website.

For high-visibility projects, companies will supply products, locations, or advertising, or they'll even pay a fee to the production if their products are included in scenes. There are product placement specialists whose job it is to create such tie-ins.

Interns will work on productions for experience or sometimes for college credit. Such production assistance can be valuable to both parties but there are also risks for both: unscrupulous producers often ask too much of unpaid assistants; and, on the other side, free labor sometimes proves the dictum that you get what you pay for.

By putting a notice online, you may be able to get extras to act in crowd scenes for free. It's a good idea to offer them something in exchange for their presence (for example, food and/or entertainment).

Tax Incentives

Various government programs provide incentives to support film production; these may include tax credits, rebates, cash subsidies, or low-cost loans. In the United States, such programs are administered by individual states. In some countries, they're handled at the national or provincial level. Many programs are intended to lure big-budget feature films to infuse jobs in a particular region, but some are available to independent and documentary filmmakers as well, and they can cover a significant portion of a film's budget. Indie feature films have been made for a fraction of what they'd otherwise cost through painstaking partnerships between producers from a wide range of countries. Many films have chosen their locations or where they do pre- or postproduction work based on available incentives. Qualifying for a program and providing all the needed paperwork can be complex. Consult the film commission in the area where you're working and consider hiring an accountant or lawyer familiar with the system.

Credit Cards and Debt

While they're arranging funding for a movie, some filmmakers cover temporary cash shortages with loans from banks and other sources of credit (which all involve finance charges). Sometimes they get credit from labs and/or other suppliers to defer particular costs. Some people use credit cards to cover costs of starting or finishing a production. The advantage of a credit card is you don't have to convince anyone to give you the money; the disadvantage is the very high interest rate you'll pay if you carry the debt for more than a month. It's extremely dangerous to use credit cards for anything other than short-term expenses you know you can pay back quickly. At its best, film production is a highly risky business, and even great films often fail financially. Don't use credit cards to finance your project!

Corporate and Sponsored Projects

Many filmmakers earn substantial income (or work full-time) producing projects for corporations. These range from in-house training films to promotional or marketing pieces to projects about various topics that the company funds as part of its image building. Frequently producers will be asked to submit competitive bids to get the job. Be careful of bidding too high or too low—a lowball bid may send the message that you're not very good. Producing a project for a corporate bureaucracy can be fraught with the too-many-cooks problem. Be sure to identify who you are reporting to (and who you actually need to satisfy, which may be an entirely different person or group). Try to structure the deal with payments at clearly defined intervals (completion of script, completion of shooting, and so forth). Have formal *sign-offs* at each stage, to certify that the client finds the work satisfactory; you never want to find out after it's too late that the client didn't like a choice you made several steps earlier.

BUDGETS

The *budget* is an accounting of the cost of every aspect of the movie and managing the budget is one of the producer's key jobs.

Prior to production, the *estimated budget* plays a key role in getting the project financed and under way (see p. 58). For feature films, a producer, production manager, or other personnel reads the script and creates an estimated budget based on the use of locations, size of cast, special effects, and the like. Experienced producers can be hired to budget a script; fees range from about $3,000 to $10,000.

As you enter preproduction, consult each department head (art director, cinematographer, wardrobe, etc.) to discuss what has been budgeted and what each department needs to do its job. If their needs and your budget don't match, you may have to rebalance budget allotments or adjust the scope of work.

During production, you'll use the budget to track expenses to ensure that the movie remains within the estimate (or to painfully detail how much over budget things have gone). Each day, the *daily production report* tracks how long each crew and cast member worked and how much was shot each day. All payments that have been authorized to suppliers (usually with a *purchase order*) must be logged.

As each stage of work is completed, and hard costs are entered into the "actual" column in the spreadsheet, that part of the budget becomes "actualized." When the production is over, an *actualized budget* is done, which details all the actual payments that have been made to produce the film.

BUDGET FORMATS. The total cost is important, but the way the budget is drawn up has an impact too. For professionals, the details of the budget make it clear to funders exactly where the money is going to be spent. For novices, a well-drawn budget helps reassure funders that you understand the production process.

Different types of productions (features, documentaries, corporate projects, multimedia) call for different budget formats. Several software packages (such as Movie Magic Budgeting) will help you lay out a budget and track expenditures. You can make your own using Excel or another spreadsheet program. A widely used system is the *AICP* (*Association of Independent Commercial Producers*) budget format, which uses standard line items that people in the industry are familiar with.

Whatever budget format you use, the first page should be a *budget summary*, or *top page*, which lists only the major budget categories (such as crew labor, equipment, travel, etc.) as well as the total cost. Deeper into the spreadsheet, and linked to the top page, are pages with detailed line items that break out each category into its component parts. For example, the equipment section would detail the camera rental, sound rental, lighting rental, and so forth. In some cases, such as in a typical proposal, funders will *only* want to see the budget summary.

Ask other professionals to share with you the budget format they use. They may be reluctant to share complete budgets with you, but they may give you the layout they use without the actual numbers filled in. See the Bibliography for resources for budgeting.

BUDGET TERMS AND STYLES. One type of budget divides expenses into *above-the-line* and *below-the-line costs*. Above-the-line costs are the fees for the producers, director, and key actors and those costs incurred before production even begins, such as the story rights and/or script (the *property*). Below-the-line costs include all equipment, materials, and other salaries involved in production. *Negative costs* of a film are all items prior to the marketing and distribution costs. *Distribution costs* include making distribution copies of the movie (possibly including release prints, digital files, discs, or tapes), trailers, advertising and promotion, and running the distribution office.

It often helps to divide the budget chronologically, separating the costs of preproduction (research, casting, scouting, and planning), production (equipment rental, digital media or film costs, location costs, crew salaries, travel, and meals), and postproduction (editing and the various finishing costs: music, mixing, online costs or video transfer, titles, and prints or digital outputs).

If materials, equipment, and labor are donated to a production or provided at discount, especially for small or nonprofit projects, it's important to include these contributions in the budget but indicate that they are *in-kind*, not cash, items. One way to indicate in-kind costs is to have a separate column for them in the budget; another is to list all the costs at market value, then indicate in-kind contributions as a part of the total income.

Similarly, crew, actors, or suppliers may agree to *defer* their fees, allowing you to pay them back after the project starts generating money. Both for yourself and to show investors and funding agencies, you'll want the budget to indicate the total *value* of the production (including in-kind and any deferrals) as well as the hard cash *cost* you need to come up with to make the movie.

CONTINGENCY. Near the bottom of many budgets is an item for *contingency*, which is usually 5–15 percent of the entire budget. This figure is intended to cover the unexpected: equipment breakdown and delay, reshooting, or unplanned shooting costs (insurance may cover some of these items). Because movies are often budgeted months or years before they are finished, the contingency allotment may also compensate for script or production changes and inflation; some people figure inflation into each budget line item instead.

INDIRECT COSTS AND PROFIT. In addition to the direct costs of getting the movie made, the production company often adds a fee for overhead and, for commercial projects, profit. Overhead includes the *indirect costs* of running your business independently of the project, such as renting your office space, business insurance, and other related expenses.[2]

---

2. General overhead should not be confused with direct, project-related administrative costs, which could include accounting and legal costs, production insurance, facility rentals, or in-house salaries. These direct expenses of the project are usually specific line items in the budget.

Profit is money over and above any actual expenses. Some producers list overhead/profit as a percentage of the total budget; sometimes this is listed as a "production fee." Sometimes profit, overhead, and/or contingency charges are buried in the budget by marking up all the *other* line items. For a commercial project, for example, the production company will usually mark up outside labor and materials costs as part of their fee for doing business.

Overhead and profit figures vary widely by the type of project, the total budget, and what the market will bear; talk to producers you know for their suggestions. In some cases, such as corporate or sponsored projects, a fee of 15 to 35 percent (or a great deal more) above the direct costs of making the movie is not uncommon. On the other hand, for nonprofit, grant-funded projects, often only direct expenses are reimbursable.

Budget Line Items

Following are some expenses to consider when doing a budget. Not all items apply to all types of productions. Some of the headings are for the purposes of this book and would not be used in a typical budget.

DEVELOPMENT AND PREPRODUCTION

Research
Story/script preparation
Budget preparation
Location scouting
Casting; hiring crew
Setting up the office

ABOVE-THE-LINE COSTS

Producer
Director
Story rights
Writer
Principal cast

PRODUCTION PERSONNEL

Production manager
Assistant directors
DP, assistants, camera operator
Sound recordist, boom operator
Gaffer, electrics; grip
Script supervisor
Makeup/hair
Production designer
Art director; props
Set decorator/stylist
Costume designer; wardrobe
Set construction
Location manager
Production assistants; drivers
Still photographer
Supporting talent, extras
Benefits on salaries

PRODUCTION EXPENSES

Camera package
Sound package
Lighting package
Grip package; dolly
Expendables and supplies
Props and sets; costumes
Studio rental
Film and/or tape and/or storage
    media (audio and video; including backups)
Catering
FX; stunts

TRAVEL AND LOCATION
Airfares
Excess baggage
Vehicles, mileage, parking, tolls
Lodging
Location fees; permits
Crew per diems and/or meals

POSTPRODUCTION
Editor
Editing room rental, supplies
Editing system and peripherals/accessories
Titles and graphics
Foley; ADR
Visual effects
Online edit
Masters and protection masters
Standards/format conversions
Composer; music supervisor
Music rights and recording
Narrator and recording
Transcripts
Stock footage or stills
Sound editing, equipment
Sound mix, recording media

DISTRIBUTION
Digital clones; DCP and/or film prints
Screeners (DVDs, Blu-rays)
Telephone, postage, shipping
Website, poster, press kits, stills, flyers, ad slicks, postcards, trailer
Advertising and promotion
Publicist; press screenings
Mailing lists, study guide
Festival fees; travel

ADMINISTRATION
Office rental and expenses
Telephone, photocopies
Internet and website
Shipping and postage
Insurance (production, negative/tape, E&O)
Repairs
Legal and accounting
Contingency

FILM PRODUCTION
Film processing
Digital dailies: telecine or scanning
Video stock or drives
Audio syncing

FILM FINISH
D.I. or video transfer
Negative cutting or film-out
Film sound tracks
Answer print
IP/dupe negative
Check print
Release prints, reels, and cases

OTHER
DVD/Blu-ray authoring
Replication
Preparing deliverables for a distributor or broadcaster
Digital archiving and storage

BUSINESS ARRANGEMENTS

See Organizing the Production, p. 361, before reading this section.

Hiring Crew

Unless you're a solo filmmaker, you'll need to get people to work with you, either for pay or sometimes not. A well-planned, well-run production creates a good working environment that can lead to you getting good footage, a good reputation, and a good chance of working with people you like in the future. Craft unions were organized in the film industry as a way to standardize how much personnel are to be paid and to limit what they can be asked to do. Productions range from unionized feature or television movies to smaller, nonunion film or video projects to student or independent projects in which no one is paid. Regardless of the type of production, crews work best when they feel they are being treated fairly and the producer is looking out for their needs.

Start by making a workable plan for how large a crew you need (see p. 362). Talk to experienced filmmakers for advice. Even if you have a small production in which everyone is wearing many hats, think through who will perform various tasks. Novice producers often neglect tasks (forgetting, say, that props can't get to the set by themselves or that someone needs to have coffee ready *before* the crew arrives) or they ask too much of the crew (perhaps by failing to schedule enough setup time when the company moves to a new location). To avoid a crisis, discuss with the crew in advance what they will be asked to do, and what resources they need to do it.

STANDARD RATES. Union personnel and other professionals usually have a set *day rate* that they charge; rates may differ depending on the type of production. Union members also get a *pension and health* or *pension and welfare* (*P&W*) payment on top of their base salary.

Outside of union productions (where strict rules guide payment schedules), it's important to be clear about what the day rate entails: some people consider a day eight hours, others ten. On feature films, a day is often twelve hours. After the "day" is over, the overtime period begins. Overtime may start at "time and a half" (one and a half times the hourly rate) for a certain amount of time, then escalate to *double time* or more. Sometimes producers ask for a *flat rate*, which is a fixed day rate with no additional pay for overtime. Many indie films are made on a flat rate—but if you go much longer than ten hours you may get diminishing returns, and an exhausted crew can make expensive and even dangerous mistakes.

On some productions, all the department heads are paid the same rate, then personnel at the next level down in all the departments are paid the same rate. This way no one gets special deals and no one feels cheated when they discover what others are getting.

Don't forget that crew and actors expect to be paid for travel to out-of-town locations. Another issue is *turnaround*, that is, how much time they have between the end of one day and the start of the next; union rules may call for penalties if turnaround is less than twelve hours.

Meals should be offered within six hours from the start of work and from the previous meal (on union productions, there are penalties if you go over). Meal time doesn't count as work time; so an eight-hour day means eight hours of work plus the meal. The meal break officially begins when the last person to be served has gotten his or her food.

Remember that an overworked and underfed crew will not perform well. Keep the craft services table (snacks, drinks, and coffee) well stocked and nearby.

Every member of the crew should sign a *deal memo* (and the producer or someone representing the production cosigns it); this memo specifies their responsibilities and compensation (union members sign a standard deal form).

REDUCED RATES. Producers who are strapped for cash may try to get the crew to work for discounted rates or for free. In one method, crew members are paid a small stipend, with the rest of their salary *deferred*, which means that it's paid after the film is done and is generating income. Another bargaining technique is to offer lower salaries in exchange for *points*—a percentage of the film's eventual profit. Both of these arrangements call for enormous trust on the part of the crew since many films, even very successful ones, never officially recoup their costs and become "profitable" (see Following the Money, p. 750).

Often people will work for less if they feel they're getting a career opportunity: for example, a camera assistant getting a first break to work as director of photography. Or they may have some time free and see your project as a way to boost their resume.

When hiring crew or asking someone to work for free, be up-front and realistic about the schedule. Don't ask someone to work for no money or a low flat rate and neglect to mention that you have fourteen hours of material to cover every day. Be explicit about how overtime will be treated.

PAYROLL SERVICES. To simplify accounting, many productions hire an outside *payroll service* (sometimes called a *paymaster*), which is a company that writes the payroll checks, handles all the paperwork, and certifies that proper union and tax filings are made. A paymaster may be necessary when union talent is hired by a production company that is not a *union signatory* (does not have a contract with the union).

Hiring Actors

See p. 363 for the nonfinancial aspects of casting.

Actors are often referred to in the United States as the "talent." Some actors are unionized; some are not. Professional movie and TV actors in the U.S. generally belong to SAG-AFTRA, the now-merged Screen Actors Guild and American Federation of Television and Radio Artists. The union stipulates a minimum pay rate (*scale*), which varies depending on the type of production and the prominence of the role (more for lead actors with speaking lines, less for silent extras). Many actors charge more than scale but may lower their rates if they like a project.

Depending on where you live, the best actors in your area are usually union members; in smaller markets good actors may stay nonunion because there isn't enough union work. Typically a union actor can't work on a nonunion production. And if you use union talent, you are limited in the use of nonunion actors.

Contact the union or a casting agent to discuss the many regulations associated with using union talent. As noted above, forming an LLC or other production entity solely to make one movie is often recommended for independents when becoming a union signatory, so as not to be restricted on future productions.

At www.sagindie.org you can see several agreements for low-budget productions in the U.S. Depending on the production budget and length, these offer reduced salaries and sometimes deferrals, as well as relaxed rules about using professional and nonprofessional talent.

Established actors can make a big difference to a drama. Some may lend their name to a good script while you develop it, but agents for in-demand talent may require a *pay or play deal*, in which you commit to pay the actor regardless of whether you're able to actually shoot with the actor when scheduled.

As with crew, actors expect to be paid for travel time beyond a certain distance.

Equipment

Large movie productions typically rent equipment because it's expensive and may only be needed for short periods. If you plan to rent, research the rates at a number of rental houses and ask them for bids on your job. It's often cheaper to rent from a big company even if it is farther away and transportation costs are added; some houses charge no rental while the equipment is in transit. Longer-term rentals are discounted. Typically, the weekly rate is four times the daily rate; the monthly rate may be twelve times the daily rate. Some houses allow you to pick up the equipment Thursday afternoon and return it Monday morning for one day's rental charge. Often you can negotiate deals.

See below for information on equipment insurance.

If you're a filmmaker working on your own projects or, say, a camera- or soundperson who hires out to work on other people's productions, it can make sense to buy your own gear. The advantages of owning include certain tax benefits, familiarity with a particular piece of equipment, and the avoidance of rental problems, such as unavailability of equipment, out-of-town rental hassles, and costly short-term insurance policies.

Filmmakers can often raise the money to buy equipment when they've been hired to shoot a project over an extended period of time. They can rent the gear to the production on which they are working, charging rental house rates. Two or three months of use can pay for half the cost of a piece of equipment.

Working with Suppliers

During the making of a movie, many times you may need to obtain services, equipment, or materials from organizations like equipment rental houses, studios, labs, postproduction facilities, and mix houses, as well as from independent contractors like animators or graphic artists. Each type of business has a different set of assumptions about the way things are done, yet certain ground rules seem to apply when working with all different types of suppliers.

To identify suppliers you want to work with, get recommendations from people who have done projects similar to yours. Watch the end credits of movies and read the trade press for ideas. When talking to a supplier, ask for references of projects they've worked on. If you're lucky enough to find a supplier you like where you live, you can avoid the hassles and risks of shipping and travel and you have the advantage of face-to-face contact, which often makes things go more smoothly. Nevertheless, many filmmakers work with suppliers in other cities or countries. Overnight shipping, file exchange over the Web, videoconferencing (like Skype) all help shorten the distance between you and the supplier.

To deal effectively with a postproduction house, lab, or other organization, find out whom to contact if problems arise. Sometimes a salesperson will be assigned to your account. Sometimes it's better to deal directly with a manager or technical personnel.

To minimize the chance of problems, lay out as clearly as you can in advance what you need done and when you need the work performed. Give warnings of impending deadlines and try to get a clear, up-front commitment that the supplier can do the job. If problems do arise, stay cool and try to work through them with the supplier. There are plenty of producers with quick tempers who think that fury and threats are a good way to "get results." If this is your reputation, suppliers may choose not to work with you. Don't be bashful if a supplier has screwed up your order, but maintaining a sense of respect for all involved will increase your chances of getting what you want.

Many companies have a *rate card* of standard prices they charge for goods and services. You can often get a discount, sometimes sizable, from the rate card prices if the supplier likes the project, if you're a student, or if the supplier needs the work. At some facilities, virtually *no one* pays rate card rates. Don't be afraid to negotiate and to ask different suppliers to bid on the job. The worst that can happen is they will refuse to budge on price. You can sometimes get lower rates from a facility by agreeing to work at off-hours (like late night) or with junior, less experienced personnel. Sometimes you can get goods and services donated.

For jobs that are charged on an hourly basis, be clear about when "the clock is running" and when it's not. For example, in some situations, short breaks and lunch are off the clock; in others, it is assumed to be part of a day's work. If a machine goes down or there is a problem caused by the facility, most places will deduct this time from your bill.

Sometimes a supplier will give you a flat bid for an entire job instead of charging you piecemeal for individual items or on an hourly basis. This may be a big cost savings. Flat bids can be problematic, however, if the scope of the job changes as you go along. You might ask for a bid based on, say, three eight-hour days of work. But when the work stretches into long overtime on each of those days because you want things done a particular way, the supplier may want to increase the price. Or the work may be done in the time allotted, just not the way you like it. You have less power to ask for changes when the supplier knows that you're not paying for them. Sometimes suppliers agree to very low bids and later regret them. The work suffers. You may be better off paying a bit more and keeping everyone happy.

Often you have the option to contract with several different suppliers to do different portions of a project. You may get a better deal on one part from Company A and on another part from Company B. These savings have to be weighed against the loss of accountability. If the same company does your titles and online edit, then you won't have to pay for time wasted in the online trying to fix problems with the titles. If two different companies do the work, the title people may fix the problem, but you probably won't get reimbursed for the extra online costs.

PAYING ON CREDIT. Having credit with a supplier simplifies delivery and payments for goods and services. Since filmmakers are notorious for being bad credit risks, you may encounter problems unless you're part of a company with a good credit history or until you establish a clean track record with the supplier. If you don't have credit, the supplier may want you to pay with a credit card and/or pay COD.

Usually credit terms are *net* (the full amount) within thirty days. Suppliers will, at times, defer payment until a movie is completed and may waive an interest charge on unpaid balances. If you don't have credit and have to pay for the work before you see it, you lose an important negotiating position if you feel the facility has made an error and the work should be redone. An outstanding balance increases your leverage in negotiations.

Locations

You should have a signed agreement with the owner of any location you plan to use in the film. Get this nailed down prior to shooting. The agreement should specify when you will use the location and for how long (including a backup date if needed due to weather or other issues), what the rental rate is, and any other particulars of the deal. Part of the agreement (or a separate document) is a release in which the owner affirms that you are permitted to shoot at the location and that you are the sole owner of the footage and can use it without limitations (for similar language, see the appearance release, below). If this is a recognizable business with signs or other visible trademarks, the release should include permission to show the signage. However, if you are making a fiction film, you may be required to replace or not show the signs. The agreement should specify that the producer is responsible for any property or physical personal injury caused by the film team while at the location and that the owner releases you from any claims for invasion of privacy, defamation, and the like. See the Bibliography (or search the Web) for sources of sample location release forms.

For documentary shooting, it often happens that you don't arrange locations in advance or provide any payment, but when possible you should try to get a location release on-site when you film, granting permission to shoot there.

When shooting on public streets, in parks, and in other facilities, you generally need city permits and an insurance bond (not to mention a police detail to supervise). Some producers "steal" locations—by setting up quickly in unapproved spots and leaving before anyone stops them.

Insurance

Many types of insurance are available for film and video production. Some of them are mandatory (because they're required by suppliers, distributors, or others), some are not required but you'd be foolish to work without them, and others provide additional protections that you may buy depending on whether you feel the risk justifies the *premium* (the cost of the policy). Talk with a company that specializes in production insurance. People there can help you put together a policy package with the best coverage.

All productions (including student films) should have *general liability* coverage to insure for bodily injury and suits arising from accidents on the set. You may also need to pay *workers' compensation* insurance to the state, which helps cover people who are injured; the cost is calculated as a percentage of payroll. To insure people driving to and from the job you may need a separate *vehicle policy*. Many locations will insist you have liability and/or damage coverage.

Most equipment suppliers won't rent you gear without *equipment insurance*, which covers loss or damage; they'll supply it for a fee, but you can usually save money by having your own equipment policy with renter's coverage. Your insurance company will issue a *certificate* or *binder*, listing the equipment owner as an "additional insured" on your policy during the time of the rental.

Distributors and broadcasters usually require that you have *errors and omissions* coverage, which is discussed on p. 738.

Additional coverage includes *negative/tape insurance* that pays for damage to the negative or original videotapes or files from fire, theft, or loss in transit. *Faulty camera, stock, and processing insurance* covers loss or damage to film due to defects. *Extra expense coverage* provides reimbursement for delays in shooting due to damaged or late equipment, sets, and the like.

On higher-budget films it's common to need a *completion bond*, which is a policy financial backers take out to protect themselves in case the film is not finished on time or on budget. The bonding company will monitor the production to make sure things are being done according to its requirements, charge a few percent of the budget, and require that a chunk of money be set aside for contingencies.

LEGAL AND COPYRIGHT ISSUES

Movies, books, musical compositions, and other creative works are *copyrighted* so that no one may legally duplicate or use material from the work without permission. When you make a movie, you are granted a copyright to protect your work. If you want to use other people's copyrighted material in your movie (for example, a song or a film clip), you usually need to obtain permission (a *clearance*). Clearing copyrighted material usually involves getting a signed permission or *license*, and paying a fee. There are other types of signed permissions or releases used to establish that you have the right to use someone's appearance or performance, to shoot at a given location, or to tell someone's life story.

Getting required permissions can be a lengthy and expensive process. The permissions themselves may be high priced, and there may be legal fees and administrative costs in tracking down the rights holders and negotiating a license or other deal. Hollywood studios are often extremely careful to clear all needed rights, and even some that may not be needed. Why? They have lawyers on staff and they're looking for maximum protection. If people know you have a lot of money, they may sue you even if they don't have a legitimate claim. Just defending a suit can cost thousands even if you win.

At the other end of the scale, student and independent moviemakers sometimes don't get the permissions they need, hoping that the chance of litigation is low. While the need for some permissions is clear-cut, other types of clearances fall into a gray area: even lawyers may disagree about which ones are needed or from whom the permission should be sought. For example, under the fair use laws, you may be able to use some copyrighted material without permission (see p. 742). However, you can't *always* be sure when fair use covers you. Sometimes lawyers can only offer their opinion. The producer must ultimately make the judgment and take the responsibility.

It's unlikely that anyone will come after you if you put a copyrighted song into a video that you only show privately to friends in your living room. However, as soon as a movie is shown or distributed to the public, especially for a fee, you become vulnerable to a lawsuit if you've used copyrighted material, someone's appearance, or a protected life story without permission. If you lose, you'll pay damages and may also be required to reedit or stop showing your movie. Websites may take down posted videos that contain uncleared copyrighted material. Distributors, TV broadcasters, and film festivals may not accept a movie if the required clearances have not been obtained. But even prior to distribution, you will probably need to deal with E&O insurers (see below), who will want to see your permissions.

The greater exposure your project gets, and the more money it generates (or the more money you have), the greater the chance someone will take legal action—justifiably or not. To protect yourself, consult an entertainment or copyright attorney before finishing your movie. For an excellent review of these issues, read Michael Donaldson's *Clearance and Copyright* (see the Bibliography).

PROTECTING YOUR WORK

Copyright and Other Protections

When you copyright a movie, the copyright coverage includes dialogue, sound track, music, and photography (film/video footage). You can't copyright the ideas or concepts in a film—just the specific expression of them. Broad ideas for plots and settings can't be owned, but verbatim excerpts of dialogue can be.

According to worldwide copyright agreements, copyright applies to a script or movie as soon as you commit it to paper, video, or film. This is automatic and immediate and does not require a formal notice or copyright registration with the government (though there are good reasons to register; see below). Sometimes a script is registered prior to casting, when the project is in preproduction. Generally, the movie as a whole is registered when it is done.

Another form of protection for scripts and written treatments prior to the making of the movie is to register them with the Writers Guild of America (WGA) script registration service. For a fee, the WGA keeps a copy of your script on file for a period of years. If another project comes out that you feel has plagiarized yours, the registered script can help establish that your material predated that one. Be sure that the WGA registration is noted on the cover of your script when you give it to people to read.

When trying to get a project started you're often in a catch-22 situation: if you don't tell anyone about the project, you can't generate interest in it; if you do tell, you're vulnerable to people stealing your ideas. When pitching a feature film idea, your ideas are protected somewhat if you are represented by an established talent agency that can help track whom you told your ideas to in case someone later uses them. Even without an agent, you can back up your claims to having pitched ideas for any project by keeping written records of all your conversations and writing follow-up letters after meetings and calls to establish a "paper trail." Whether it will be worth pursuing a lawsuit if you've been wronged is a whole other question.

TITLES. The title of a movie can't be copyrighted, but it can be restricted on other grounds. A *title search* establishes whether the title you choose is available for your use, and you may be required to have a search done by a broadcaster or distributor. There are various services that do this, including Thomson Reuters (www.thomsonreuters.com).

Registering Your Copyright

As noted above, your work is copyrighted as soon as it exists in tangible form; however, you gain increased protection by registering the copyright. Two steps suffice. First, include a copyright notice in the movie's credits. This is usually something like "Copyright © 2012, [copyright owner's name]. All rights reserved."[3] You can also add "[Your country] is the first country of publication for purposes of the Berne Convention."

Second, to register a copyright in the United States contact the Register of Copyrights, Library of Congress (www.copyright.gov). You'll fill out an application, pay a small fee, and submit a copy of the movie and a written description of it for archiving. It's a good idea to register the copyright as soon as you finish the movie. For maximum protection, the registration should take place within three months of the date of "publication," which is defined as the first time the film is offered for distribution to the general public, whether by sale, rental, or loan. Merely showing the film without offering it for distribution is *not* considered publication. Showing your film to a distributor is not considered publication, but making copies and offering it to the public is. Your copyright extends only to the aspects of your movie that are original to your production; material in the movie licensed from other copyright holders remains part of their copyright.

Errors and Omissions Insurance

Errors and omissions insurance (E&O) is a policy that protects producers, distributors, and broadcasters from suits arising from libel, slander, invasion of privacy, and copyright infringement claims. It covers legal fees and settlements with a specified maximum per claim as well as a maximum for all claims together. Producers of big-budget feature films may get E&O policies before shooting begins or prior to the film's release. Independents often don't think of E&O at all, especially if there's nothing in the movie that is particularly provocative or risky from a libel or copyright standpoint. However, bear in mind that distributors and broadcasters will require you to have E&O coverage, and the price of your policy will be partly determined by how carefully you have covered all your legal bases (that is, made sure

---

3. Often the year is indicated with roman numerals. Since this technique probably didn't begin with ancient Roman filmmakers, it may be intended to make it harder for audiences to read how old a movie is.

you have the permissions, releases, and clearances you need). Your lawyer can help you through the process and may be asked to sign off that all due procedures were followed. The underwriter of the policy will decide if anything seems risky. Many policies are for three years, made under the assumption that if you haven't been sued by then, you're not going to be. Some policies charge additional fees for each different means of distribution (e.g., festival and/or theatrical, broadcast, home video); try to find one that covers all in one blanket policy.

RELEASES FOR REAL PEOPLE, PLACES, AND THINGS

Talent and Appearance Releases

People appearing in movies customarily sign a release in which they give permission for the filmmaker to use and publicly exhibit their picture, sound, and/or likeness. There are many variations of the basic release form that an actor or film subject signs. Some attorneys like long releases that enumerate, and thus hope to protect against, every possible claim against the producer. Others think that a simpler—and for documentary situations, less intimidating—version accomplishes the goal. One version is below.

APPEARANCE RELEASE

I authorize _____ (the "Producer"), the Producer's agents, successors, assigns, and licensees to record my name, likeness, image, voice, sound effects, interview, and performance on film, video, or otherwise (the "Recording"), edit such Recording as the Producer may desire, and use such Recording in connection with the motion picture tentatively titled _____("Picture") and all related materials, including but not limited to literary, promotion, and advertising materials. It is understood and agreed that the Producer shall retain final editorial, artistic, and technical control of the Picture and the Picture content. The Producer may use and authorize others to use the Picture, any portions thereof, and the Recording in all markets, manner and media, whether now known or hereafter developed, throughout the universe in perpetuity. The Producer and/ or the Producer's successors and assigns, shall own all rights, title and interest, including the copyright, in and to the Picture, including the Recording and related materials, to be used and disposed of, without limitation, as the Producer shall determine.

Person Appearing: _____ Date: _____

Signature: _____

Address: _____

Email: _____ Social Security #: _____

Put your name or the production company's name as "Producer." If "motion picture" is inappropriate for what you're working on, you could substitute "project."

For a dramatic, corporate, or other project in which the producer hires or arranges for all persons appearing in the movie, the release may be part of an actor's or participant's contract. In this case, the release may start "For good and valuable consideration, the receipt of which is hereby acknowledged, I authorize . . ." The person's social security number is needed for paid performers so you can file any required tax forms.

Some releases add language in which the subject releases the producer and its successors and assigns from any claims arising from invasion of privacy, defamation, false light, and all other personal and property rights (more on this below).

For some documentaries, it is standard practice to have all subjects sign a release. Usually it's a good idea to get the signing out of the way before shooting. In some documentary situations, however, it's awkward or impossible to get signed releases from everyone. Though a detailed, signed release is preferred by lawyers, it is also possible to record a verbal "release" on video. Explain to the subjects what your movie is about, how you hope to distribute it (that it may be shown on TV, in theaters, on home video, and by other means), and that you're asking for their unrestricted permission to use their appearance. In a group setting, you can explain the project to the group and ask anyone who doesn't consent to let you know so you can avoid filming them. Or they may choose to leave. For concert or crowd situations, sometimes the producer distributes written notices or has an announcement read aloud that states, in effect, that a person's presence constitutes consent to being filmed. In certain circumstances no releases are needed. If you are filming the public goings-on at a newsworthy event, for example, you have the same right as news photographers to shoot without permission (not, however, for product endorsement; see below). If you secretly shoot someone's intimate sidewalk conversation, however, you may go beyond the limit of the public's right to know (though laws vary by country).

E&O underwriters and broadcasters want you to get releases, but experts are divided on the actual value of releases for documentaries. If a subject can establish that he has been defamed by your presentation of him, a signed release may not stand in his way of suing successfully. In a privacy infringement case, on the other hand, the mere presence of a camera crew may be sufficient grounds to establish that the subject was aware that what he said or did would be made public. Court precedents in both libel and privacy law are complex and ever shifting; when in doubt, it's simplest to ask permission before filming or at least to ask those with objections to leave the area.

For all types of productions, you can't use footage of a person to advertise a product or company (or the movie itself) if you haven't got a release and if the release doesn't specifically grant that permission. The release above includes advertising, but some people prefer the legal language that the person appearing waives *right of publicity*. Some people will not agree to this clause without additional payment. Other types of releases and licenses (such as for stock footage) often have special provisions when the footage will be used for promotion or advertising.

People, Places, and Things

Whenever a real person, location, or trademarked/copyrighted item is shown or referred to in a movie, there is a chance that someone may object. If a fiction film incorporates real people or copyrighted things without permission, problems may arise.

On feature films, a *script clearance report* is done by combing the script for references to proper names, addresses, business names, radio stations, etc., and checking to see if these correspond to actual people and places (for example, if there's a character with the same name as a person who actually lives in the city where the script is set). Research services can prepare a report for you or you can do it yourself with a phone directory, the Web, a map, and other sources. Avoid using names of living persons, actual phone numbers, or auto license plates in the area where the story is set. Be particularly careful with negative references: if the criminals in your script run the Acme Corporation in Chicago, and there happens to be an Acme in Chicago, the owners may take action against you. It's safer to make up your own names (and avoid last names when possible). Private individuals may give you a written release allowing you to refer to them, but you do not automatically have that right.[4]

As noted above, you should have a location release signed by the owner of any location where you shoot.

When shooting in the real world (indoors or out), it's common that copyrighted posters, trademarked products, or logos on clothing may be visible in the scene. Since broadcasters and distributors may object to copyrighted items being shown in any form without written permission (they want to avoid being sued by the copyright holders), cautious producers make sure that any protected objects are either out of the shot or are shown only incidentally and are not featured. In some cases, logos are digitally removed or blurred in post.

Nevertheless, as attorney Michael Donaldson points out, you have a right to make a realistic film, and including product names or trademarks in a scene may be fair game. Generally, incidental depiction of or reference to a trademarked product is okay, as long as the reference isn't derogatory. If the item is particularly featured either by the way it is filmed or by how it's commented on, it makes sense to get a written release to do so. For more, see Fair Use, below.

In documentaries, common practice is often somewhat different from the full legal protections described above. Location releases are not always obtained, trademarked objects appear regularly, and people often refer to or comment on other real people. Whenever the movie makes a negative comment that disparages someone, you should be particularly careful. Either make it clear that this is being offered as opinion and not fact or, if it is being presented as fact, try to have at least two independent sources to confirm that it is really true.

USING COPYRIGHTED MATERIAL

Many movies use material previously created by someone else, including stories, music, and film clips. These almost always need to be cleared for use.

---

4. "Public" (famous) persons have more limited rights of privacy. Deceased persons have no right of privacy. Their estate does retain the right of publicity, to control any advertising related to the deceased. The estate may also control use of film clips showing the deceased.

Stories and Scripts

To use an existing work of fiction or nonfiction for your movie, you'll need to *option* it (usually from the author, who can be found through the publisher). The option gives you the right to develop your script for a period of time and try to get the movie funded. Usually an *option-purchase agreement* is done, which provides for a comparatively low fee for the option with a specified higher price paid if the movie actually gets made, the final price depending on the film's budget. Since development usually takes a lot longer than you hope, be sure to include the right to extend the option (with additional fees).

When acquiring story rights, ideally you'll get *exclusive* rights, which prevents others from using the material for a film (*nonexclusive* rights, which are cheaper, make your project much less attractive). If you want to make a film about a living person, by obtaining *life story rights* you are protected from a suit if you use information about the person that's not public.

If you write a screenplay or acquire one written by someone else, a *chain of title* must be established that proves that the work is original or, if based on any other work, that all required underlying rights have been secured. A distributor or insurer will want chain of title for many other elements, including music licenses, talent releases, and anything else for which rights are needed.

Using Uncleared Work

There are a few exceptions when you may not need to obtain clearance to use existing work:

PUBLIC DOMAIN. Works that are in the *public domain* are not protected by copyright. The most common type of public domain material is work that was never copyrighted (e.g., traditional folk songs) or work for which the copyright has lapsed. Works created in the United States more than seventy-five years ago are likely to be in the public domain. But mere age or traditional history is not proof of public domain status; renditions or arrangements of the work may have newer, applicable copyrights. A copyright report can be obtained from a law firm or done at the Library of Congress to determine public domain status.

FAIR USE. Another way copyrighted material may be used without permission is through the *fair use* provisions of copyright law. Fair use is a murky territory, and many people make a lot of assumptions based on a little knowledge. Though some elements in a fictional film may fall under fair use protection, fair use primarily applies to documentary films, news reporting, and scholarship. A group of organizations has pioneered a "statement of best practices" when it comes to fair use and documentary film (see www.centerforsocialmedia.org). These guidelines apply to areas such as: using copyrighted material as part of a social or political critique; using copyrighted works of popular culture to illustrate an argument; capturing copyrighted material in the process of filming something else; using copyrighted material in a historical sequence.

The basis for fair use in the United States comes from a somewhat vague section of copyright law. To determine whether your use of copyrighted material qualifies as fair use, four factors are considered: what you are doing with the material; the nature of the original work (if it is factual or imaginative); how much you are using (and if it is central to the original work); and the impact that your use will have on the market value of the copyrighted work.

As noted in the code of best practices, courts have considered two key questions in interpreting fair use:

- "Did the unlicensed use 'transform' the material taken from the copyrighted work by using it for a different purpose than the original, or did it just repeat the work for the same intent and value as the original?"
- "Was the amount and nature of the material taken appropriate in light of the nature of the copyrighted work and of the use?"

As an example, using a short clip from a Hollywood film to make a point in a documentary about women's rights might be considered transformative, while simply making a compilation movie of long passages from your favorite Hollywood films is not. If the use is transformative, the fact that the film you're making may be commercial and intended to earn a profit does not rule out fair use.

The code of best practices helps filmmakers understand what is permissible, and it can help defend them if someone claims they overstepped the bounds. Even so, there can be gray areas, and you should have an experienced attorney confirm that your use is legitimate (and E&O insurers may insist on it). Happily, insurers, broadcasters, and distributors are supporting the set of practices. Unfortunately, there's a long history of paranoia about copyright infringement, and a distributor or broadcaster may still reject a particular use if it's afraid of a suit, regardless of good arguments for fair use.[5]

In a related development, documentary filmmakers won an exemption from the Digital Millennium Copyright Act, allowing them to break the encryption or other digital locks on commercial DVDs in order to obtain short clips when the use of those clips is permitted under public domain or fair use protections.[6]

For more, also see http://fairuse.stanford.edu and Patricia Aufderheide and Peter Jaszi's *Reclaiming Fair Use* (see the Bibliography).

CREATIVE COMMONS. Some content creators want to share their work widely, and they offer it with a *creative commons* license, which allows for many kinds of uses without permission. For more, see www.creativecommons.org.

Clearing Music

Many filmmakers have had the following experience. They know a song that would be *perfect* for their movie, or their film subject starts singing a famous song. They scurry around, trying to figure out how to get permission to use the song. Weeks or months later, they get a response back from the holders of the copyrights. They discover that the song is not available or, if it is, the fee happens to be tens of thousands of dollars more than they have in the budget. Welcome to the world of music licensing.

---

5. As part of that culture, it is sometimes mistakenly assumed that if you ask for permission to use something and are turned down by the rights holder, that will limit your ability to later claim fair use.
6. The DMCA rules may be revised in the future, preserving or removing this exemption.

Clearing music (and movie clips; see p. 746) is one of the thorniest jobs a producer can do. It usually requires extensive research, long delays, and complex negotiations. If you ever have the experience of trying to clear many songs for a movie, you'll probably never want to do it again. Many filmmakers prefer to hire a music clearing service that can shortcut the process with its network of contacts.

If you want to use a preexisting recording, you'll need to obtain permission to use the musical composition, as well as permission to use the particular recording of it. Often a publishing company controls rights to the composition and a record company controls the recording itself, though sometimes these are owned by the same corporation.

Sometimes filmmakers can't afford the recording if it's by, say, a famous rock star. They may license the rights to the composition and get someone else to perform the song. If you find a song performed by a lesser-known band, the band may give you a good price as a way to get exposure.

To secure rights to a composition, start by contacting the publishing company. Usually the packaging for a recording indicates which *performing rights society* the publisher belongs to; these include ASCAP (www.ascap.com), BMI (www.bmi.com), and SESAC (www.sesac.com). If you don't know which one handles the song you're interested in, you can do a search on these sites. If the song has lyrics, sometimes different publishers control the lyrics and the musical composition.

To include a musical composition in your movie, you need *synchronization* or *sync rights*—so named because the music is synchronized to the picture. To perform the music in public, you need *public performance* rights. In the United States, public performance rights for theatrical films are generally included in the deal you make for sync rights; you don't have to pay for them separately, but make sure they're included. For movies that are broadcast on television, the broadcaster usually obtains the public performance rights.

If you want to use a preexisting recording of the song, contact the owner of the recording—usually the record company (look online or on the sleeve of a CD for the address). You'll need a *master use license* to use the actual recording (performance) in your movie. You should also ask the record company if any *reuse fees* are due the performers on the record. At one time, you would have also needed to arrange to get a copy of the master tape in order to have a high-quality audio dub. Today, you can get the audio recording itself from a consumer CD or other digital format. (Try to get uncompressed or lightly compressed files; see p. 412.)

NEGOTIATING THE RIGHTS PACKAGE. For the classic situation of trying to clear a recording by a musical artist you like, you will be requesting a sync license with public performance rights from the publisher and a master use license from the record company. Both of them will ask you to submit a written or online request that details the nature of your movie, how you plan to distribute it, and the way the music will be used. You'll pay more if the song is used under the movie's titles or otherwise featured; you often pay less if it will only be background music in a scene. The price also depends on how many seconds of music you need.

How the movie will be distributed (by which *media*), where it will be shown (in which *territories*), and for how long (for what *term*) also affect the price of the license fee. Big-budget feature films generally clear music rights for *all media* (theatrical, broadcast TV, free cable TV, pay cable TV, home video DVD and Blu-ray, digital streaming, and "any formats now known or hereafter devised") in *all territories* (domestic and foreign) *in perpetuity* (forever). This *buyout* of all rights is by far the most desirable in terms of simplifying business arrangements. Some rights holders will offer only a limited (say, five-year) term.

If you can't afford a buyout, you can secure only the rights you need right away. For example, students often make a deal to acquire just *film festival rights*. Or you might get *nontheatrical rights*; or theatrical rights to art houses but not first-run movie theaters. It makes sense to negotiate for rights you may need down the road (say, for a TV deal you don't yet have), but build them in as *options* that you can exercise and pay for later. This way, if your film gets picked up for distribution, you'll know exactly what the rights will cost.

Rights for home video usually involve a small royalty payment for every DVD or Blu-ray unit sold (with the first few thousand units paid up front).

As technologies change, uncertain areas of coverage arise, and new digital delivery platforms may not be reflected in the publisher's or record company's contract. For example, some publishers may inclusively define rights for "Web/Internet" while others want separate fees for downloading and streaming (or may allow one but not the other). Seek out professional advice, and be prepared to ask for contract language to be adjusted to meet your needs.

Keep in mind that acquiring rights is a *negotiation*. Rights holders will name a price that may take your breath away; then it's up to you to come back with a lower price. Sometimes they'll consider it; sometimes not. If you're poor and struggling and working on a worthy project, they may make a special exception. If you're too poor (or not part of a reputable organization), sometimes they won't even *talk* to you—it's just not worth their time. If you're negotiating with several rights holders and can find one who offers a lower price, sometimes you can get the others to agree to a lower price too. Often this is done on a *most-favored nations* (*MFN*) basis, which means that for the deal to go through, no one is favored over another, and all parties must agree to the same price. One advantage of using a music supervisor and/or a music clearing service is that these professionals know whom to negotiate with and the standard rates being paid for licenses. You may or may not be able to bargain for a better deal on your own.

Some public broadcasting entities, such as PBS, MTV, and the BBC, have blanket agreements and compulsory licenses that may allow you to use music without clearing it with rights holders. This applies only to the television broadcast. You may still need other rights if the movie is distributed through other media or markets.

Even if the licensing process goes well, it can take months. If a song is integral to the movie (say, if a character sings it), be sure to start as early in preproduction as you can. Many publishers and record companies allow you to request and pay for a license through their website.

After the movie is done, you must prepare a *music cue sheet*, which lists each cue, how it's used, the writer(s), and the publisher(s). This is essential for all parties to collect proper royalties. You can find a sample cue sheet at www.ascap.com.

LIBRARY MUSIC. To avoid many of the rights issues mentioned above, you can use prerecorded music from a production music library (also called *stock music*).

Numerous library collections are available online and on disc with selections in many styles and arrangements. This music is packaged specifically for reuse. A production facility may buy or lease a library of stock music for a period of time, or you can purchase and download individual tracks on a *laser drop* basis (what used to be called *needle drop*, which is a continuous section of a recording used once). The rights for the piece are provided with the fee.

ORIGINAL SCORES. Having an original score written for a movie avoids most of the headaches mentioned above. When producers have an original score composed, often the producer will own the rights to the music, in which case the music is considered a *work for hire*. If, as producer, you own the music, you'll want to set up a publishing entity and register it with one of the performing rights societies (see above) to collect royalties. Sometimes the composer will lower his or her fee in exchange for retaining some or all of the music rights, in which case the producer must have a license from the composer to use the music. If the movie is shown widely on television, or in non-U.S. theaters, sizable royalties can accrue to the holder of the rights. The composer will receive half the royalties regardless of who owns the music.

Whenever music is performed for your film, whether on camera or off, be sure you have both publishing and master recording rights. For example, if an actor sings a song during a scene, or a band or a vocalist records tracks in a studio, that person needs to sign a master recording license. Try to get a buyout agreement.

Clearing Movie Clips

If you want to use a scene from an existing movie in your film (whether it be a full-screen excerpt or something visible on a TV in one of your scenes), you usually need to get written permission. Clearing clips is much like clearing music, and just as much fun. Start by identifying who owns the copyright to the movie you want to use. Sometimes this is the production company; sometimes it is the distributor or television network. Particularly for older films, the film may have been bought and sold several times since it was made. Some companies have a clip licensing department and actively seek deals with licensees like you. Others are extremely protective of their film library, throw up every possible barrier, and may simply refuse you.

As discussed above, you may need to negotiate the fee for the clip. Unfortunately, even after you license the right to use a clip, you may still have to get permission to use various elements in the clip. For example, if there's music in the clip, you generally need to obtain separate licenses for it. The musical composition (even if it is just underscore) may be owned by the studio or by the composer; you need to obtain a sync license (see above), usually for a separate fee. Similarly, the right to use the music recording itself (the master use license) may come with the clip, but sometimes you must license that separately. Some people choose to license the clip without any music and compose their own if necessary.

If there are actors in the clip, SAG and AFTRA (actors' unions; see p. 732) have regulations governing the "reuse" of actors' performances in union productions. Recognizable actors may need to give consent and be paid; stars may waive their fee. The SAG contract governing films made before 1960 is different; it may allow you to use some clips for certain uses without paying actors or getting permissions if you *billboard* the clip by putting the name of the film on screen or having it said verbally each time a clip is shown. You can avoid billboarding by clearing and paying the talent. Contact a SAG office for details. The WGA (Writers Guild of America) and DGA (Directors Guild of America) also have regulations governing the reuse of material. In some cases, you may be able to use uncleared clips based on fair use (see above).

STOCK FOOTAGE LIBRARIES. There are many *stock footage libraries* or *archives* that supply footage to producers specifically for reuse. These services may specialize in particular types of material, such as sports, historical, nature, or news. Usually the fee is determined by the length of the clip and how you plan to distribute your movie (like music rights, you can license rights to many media or only a few). *Royalty-free* footage means you pay once for any type of use. *Rights-managed* clips require negotiations depending on how you plan to use the footage. Still images are licensed in a similar way.

Often, you pay a small fee to get a selection of possible clips; after you edit your movie, you pay a higher rate based on the exact number of seconds you use. Keep in mind that while the library supplies the clip, you sometimes need to separately clear what's *in* the clip, including music, actors, news anchors, and such (see above). Some libraries supply pirated footage for which even the clip *itself* is not cleared and you may risk a lawsuit if you use it without the owner's permission.

Smaller archivists can be your friend—steering you to important footage. Rates, even at big houses, are often negotiable. Many stock libraries are available online, which can be tremendously handy for searching and downloading clips directly to your editing system.

DISTRIBUTION AND MARKETING

Distribution refers to the process of making a movie available to audiences. Distribution channels include theatrical exhibition, nontheatrical screenings, broadcast television, cable TV, video-on-demand (VOD), streaming on the Web, digital download, and home video via DVDs and Blu-ray Discs. Some projects make use of several channels, some only a few.

Marketing includes all the things that are done to increase awareness of and interest in the film, so people will be more likely to find it and watch it. New technologies and changing consumer habits are continually reshaping the landscape of how movies get shown, how they're marketed, and how filmmakers are paid for their work. Because of this constant flux, it's impossible in a book like this to accurately describe all that's happening.

In a traditional model, an independent filmmaker sells his or her film to a *distributor*. That company then handles all distribution itself or brokers every aspect of the movie's distribution through different channels. Many independents have found that this model means giving up too much control for not enough money. Or there may be no distributor offering to handle their film. For these reasons, many filmmakers take a different approach. They may divide up the rights to their film, working with different distributors for different media or markets, and/or they may handle some or all of the distribution or marketing on their own.

Let's start by looking at various distribution possibilities available to independent films, then examine the process of launching a movie into the marketplace.

For the technical concerns of distributing a project, see Chapters 2, 14, 15, and 16.

Theatrical Distribution

Theatrical distribution means showing movies the old-fashioned way: in commercial theaters to paying audiences. Hollywood and independent feature films generally seek theatrical distribution as the first outlet for the movie. However, theatrical distribution can be tremendously risky and for many films it's just not worth the effort or expense. The costs of advertising, promotion, making copies of the movie, and running the distribution campaign are high; the chance of making a profit is relatively low. When a studio releases a slate of several films in a year, usually most of them lose money. The one or two blockbusters that make huge profits are counted on to carry the other movies. However, a theatrical run can play an important part in raising public awareness about a movie, and garnering reviews from major papers and media outlets can affect the value of your film worldwide. A splashy theatrical release will boost the price of the movie when it is later sold to TV or other forms of distribution. So a money-losing theatrical experience is sometimes still a good investment in the long run.

The theatrical equation is changing with the expansion of digital cinema projection in theaters. With digital, DCP files are delivered via satellite or hard drive,

Fig. 17-1. Theatrical exhibition is undergoing big changes. (Film-Tech.com)

instead of the distributor having to manufacture and ship heavy film prints (see p. 712). It's a good-news/bad-news situation for independents. Distributing your film digitally, via a DCP or disc, is cheaper than making film prints, which should make theatrical distribution more affordable. In fact, Hollywood studios save so much with digital that they pass on some of the savings to theaters in the form of a *virtual print fee* (*VPF*), which theater owners use to help cover the cost of purchasing digital projection equipment. The problem is that these deals may come with restrictions about showing nonstudio, independent movies. Smaller theaters that also play indie films may not be able to afford to convert to high-resolution digital cinema projection. This may prevent them from showing digital studio productions, while at the same time they are finding it increasingly difficult to get 35mm prints of new *or* old films. Lots of art house theaters have already gone under.

Many people feel that the days of theatrical exhibition are numbered, and that digital delivery to homes will make traditional theatrical distribution obsolete. The resurgence of 3D has boosted theatrical ticket sales, but 3D in the home is gaining traction. Whether the communal experience of watching movies in a theater will disappear is a question that only time can answer.

NAVIGATING THE THEATRICAL WORLD. If you're an independent producer interested in theatrical distribution for your project, you have two major hurdles to jump. The first is getting a *distributor*, and the second is getting the movie into theaters. Some people choose to *self-distribute*—that is, take on the distributor's duties themselves. Unfortunately many independently produced feature films never get distributed at all.

What does a theatrical distributor do? Typically a distributor will *acquire* a movie after it's completed or nearly so (sometimes distributors develop projects from the script stage or earlier). Independent movies are often picked up for distribution when they're shown at film festivals. If several distributors are vying for a movie, or if strong profits are anticipated, they will offer a sizable *advance* for the film. This is an advance on royalties—whatever the producer is paid as an advance will be deducted from his or her share later. For many low-profile films, the advance is small, or even zero. Even if the advance to the producer is low, the distributor should commit to spending a reasonable amount on *prints and advertising* (*P&A*)—the basic marketing costs for the picture—and to opening the film in a minimum number of cities. The distributor then puts together a marketing campaign for the movie. This includes having a poster (*one-sheet*) created and designing newspaper *ad slicks*. A *trailer* (coming-attractions reel) is produced and sent to theaters and posted online in advance of the movie's opening. TV and Web advertising and other promotions may be worked up.

The distributor then goes about trying to book the movie into various theaters. The theater owners are the *exhibitors*. Exhibitors often need to be convinced to run a particular independent film. Theaters range from large *first-run chains*, which generally show only mainstream Hollywood product, to smaller *independent theaters* and *art houses*, which may also show a variety of other movies, including smaller, older, or foreign films. Independent theaters are currently as endangered as small family farms. Theater chains are programmed from a central office; independent cinemas may hire a *booker* who selects the movies for several theaters.

If you're lucky enough to have interest from more than one distributor, you may have a hard choice to make. The advantage of large distributors is that they may pay good advances and can afford substantial P&A budgets. One disadvantage is that if your movie is not immediately doing well at the box office, they may drop your film and go on to the next one. A distributor with a smaller slate of films will usually have less money, but may work longer at trying to keep your film afloat (by trying it in different markets or playing in small venues).

Fig. 17-2. The cost and logistics of shipping 35mm prints for theatrical distribution is a big reason digital cinema is replacing film. (Film-Tech.com)

FOLLOWING THE MONEY. Novice producers are often shocked by how much of the income generated by their movie does not go to them (more experienced producers aren't shocked, just depressed). The total amount of money paid by audiences buying tickets is the *box office gross.* The exhibitor then takes his share and what's left over goes to the distributor (*gross film rental* or *gross receipts*). There are different types of exhibitor/distributor deals. The 90/10 deal gives 90 percent to the distributor at the start of a film's release, with the exhibitor's share increasing every week the film plays (the exhibitor sometimes deducts his basic expense—the *house nut*—first). This puts exhibitors at a disadvantage since attendance typically drops off after the first week(s), so *aggregate deals* that pay a fixed percentage (often between 50 and 60 percent) over the entire run have become more common. In another arrangement, the exhibitor pays the distributor an agreed-on minimum (*floor*) amount or a fixed percentage of the box office, whichever is larger.

As a ballpark figure for all films, distributors get about half the box office gross. Distributors of independent films may average around 35 to 45 percent of the gross. When you hear that a certain film grossed, say, $10 million and cost $5 million, that movie probably has not broken even when distribution and marketing costs are figured in.

But wait—when do you, the producer, get paid? The exhibitor pays the distributor a film rental and then the distributor deducts *its* fee, often around 25 to 33 percent. Then all the distribution costs, including marketing, the costs of film prints or digital media, and interest charges on any advances are deducted.[7] Note that it's in the distributor's interest to spend as much as possible on promotion to create a big splash and try to maximize grosses, but usually that marketing money comes out of the producer's share, not the distributor's.

Finally, the producer gets what's left over (if anything); this is the *producer's net*. Ouch. A film can gross hundreds of thousands or even millions of dollars with hardly anything coming back to the producer. Of course, if the producer has investors to repay, or cast or crew members who worked on deferrals, they must be paid from this same net amount.[8]

As you can see, the process is stacked against the filmmaker. When you add the fact that film accounting can be notoriously unreliable (How many tickets were *really* sold? How was that marketing budget *really* spent?), it's painfully clear why it's so hard to make a living in this business. In one notorious example, one of the Harry Potter films was reported to have grossed over $938 million worldwide, while the studio accounting statement indicated it was still more than $167 million in the red. This is why it's so important to get the largest advance up front that you can, and not rely on getting your money from the "back end," which may be nonexistent. To avoid all these deductions, powerful stars and directors demand a percentage of the gross. While you probably won't get gross points, you may be able to negotiate payments triggered by the film's reaching certain gross amounts.

Fig. 17-3. Where the money (and candy) is. Exhibitors may make more from concessions than ticket sales, especially when a film first opens. (Film-Tech.com)

DIY THEATRICAL. As we've seen, the economics of theatrical distribution for independent films are dicey at best. Even so, some filmmakers are committed to a theatrical launch and may choose to handle distribution themselves, either be-

7. In some deals, the distribution costs come off the top, before the distributor takes its percentage.

8. Commonly, the investors are repaid what they invested, then deferments are paid, then any remaining funds are distributed according to profit participation points. But there are many different formulas for dividing the pot.

cause they get no good offers from distributors or because they prefer it that way. No one will give your film more TLC than you, but be prepared to put in many months of full-time work. In several ways, you'll be at a disadvantage compared to regular distributors. They know the good theaters in each city and who books them; you will have to figure it out. Distributors can command the best play dates and can sometimes keep a film in a theater even if it's not doing well. Some exhibitors are notorious for not paying up. A distributor can get payment by threatening to pull its next film, which is leverage you don't have.

Nevertheless, self-distribution may be the only way to get your movie out there. You'll have far more say over how the movie is promoted and you'll get to keep more of the profits.

A hybrid approach is a *service deal* with a booker or distributor who handles the booking and/or distribution arrangements for a fee. You get the expertise and connections of the distributor but maintain more control (and all the financial responsibility).

One approach sometimes used by both self-distributors and regular distributors is called *four-walling*. Here a theater is "rented" from the exhibitor for a flat fee. Because the exhibitor has no risk, he may take more of a chance on a small film. The distributor then gets to keep the entire box office (less the rental fee).

Given the glut of "product" (new films), the wariness of exhibitors, and the cost of advertising, many independent filmmakers find that distribution in commercial theaters is not a possibility. Instead they use film festival screenings as their de facto theatrical campaign. Festivals can give you exposure, press coverage, a chance to screen the film with an audience, and sometimes income from screening fees or selling DVDs on-site (more on festivals below).

Another approach is one-off event screenings, often copromoted by nonprofit groups with big memberships. Not exactly theatrical, but satisfying exposure with big audiences.

The Digital Multiverse

While digital technology has transformed the process of making movies, its effect on distribution is perhaps even more radical. There are now so many different platforms for delivering video content (and different economic models that underlie them), it's hard to keep them straight. One popular pay-cable TV network used to be simply that—a service you subscribed to via cable TV to watch whatever it was showing at the time. Now it thinks of itself as a purveyor of "nonstandard TV," which you can watch on its schedule, on your schedule, over cable, over the Internet, or on mobile wireless. A broadcast network that for decades only transmitted the traditional way—over the air to TV sets—recently reported that its programming now goes out via seventeen platforms and only one of them is over the air.

The technologies and economics of content delivery are sometimes inextricably mixed, but let's try to separate some of the methods in use.

MEANS OF DELIVERING VIDEO CONTENT
- *Over-the-air broadcast.* Digital. Received by an antenna on the house or TV.
- *Cable TV.* From cable service provider, through wires to the house.
- *Over-the-top TV.* Streamed video that may come over the same cable as cable

TV, but from a different provider. May play through a Blu-ray player or other device.

- *Satellite*. Like cable but wireless. Requires a satellite dish.
- *Internet streaming*. Viewer watches videos from the Web but doesn't store them on his system.
- *Internet downloading*. Viewer gets files from Web but stores them locally for playback whenever. In some cases streamed video is referred to as a download and vice versa.
- *Mobile devices*. Includes phones and tablets.
- *DVDs and Blu-ray discs*.

REVENUE STREAMS

- *Free*. Viewer pays nothing. Usually advertising supported.
- *Basic cable TV*. Viewer gets many channels with the basic cable subscription.
- *Subscription (pay) TV*. Premium channels; viewer pays extra each month.
- *Video-on-demand (VOD)*. Viewer pays to watch a movie when she wants it. Often allows several viewings in a limited time period.
- *Pay-per-view (PPV)*. Similar to VOD, but often used for live events on a schedule. Some people use this term or *pay-to-view* for various types of online purchases of a movie.
- *Subscription Internet streaming*. Monthly fee to watch anything the service offers.
- *Retail downloading*. Viewer buys and owns a digital movie file.
- *Subscription disc delivery*. Viewer can rent many DVDs and Blu-rays for a monthly fee.
- *Retail disc rentals and sales*. Viewer rents or buys individual DVDs or Blu-rays.

For an independent producer, trying to form a strategy to exploit these options can be daunting. For several of these routes, it can be very hard for a producer to make a deal directly with the distribution entity. Instead you make a deal with an agent or aggregator, who can supply product to, say, a cable system for VOD or to iTunes. With an aggregator, you give up some income, but hopefully open up opportunities. Also, there are numerous technical requirements for the different outlets, and it helps to have someone who knows the ropes.

While there's a lot of excitement about the potential of these systems, the fact of the matter is that there are so many delivery platforms and so many movies getting delivered, it's easy for *your* movie to get lost. No matter what the platform, marketing and advertising still drive the industry. For viewers to be aware of your movie, money must be spent on marketing. In a kind of vicious circle, marketing dollars tend to go mostly to things that are expected to draw lots of viewers (though smart promotion and social networking, such as a highly targeted blog and Twitter campaign, can have an impact here; see below).

The list of revenue streams above indicates how money is derived from the consumer, but how does money flow to the producer? A TV network will buy an independently produced movie for an up-front flat fee, but several of the other revenue models involve charging viewers each time they watch or buy something, with a percentage going back to the producer. In some cases, the producer's royalty is relatively small after the cuts taken by the company that's providing the movie to consumers and by the aggregator that you signed with to get the deal. Then you have to contend with constant downward pressure on prices, since many consumers are accustomed to free content (whether supplied legitimately or by pirates) and balk at paying too much for what they watch. In some cases, revenue doesn't come from consumers but from advertisers. Websites like YouTube offer movies for free, but producers can enter into arrangements to *monetize* their videos (receive money—in this case by sharing in ad revenues) when people watch their movies.

The advent of downloading and file sharing completely reshaped the music industry, at which point many musicians found that sales of their recorded music started providing a smaller and smaller percentage of their income (and they needed to look to live performance and other revenue streams to compensate). The changes in the movie industry are no less dramatic.

Fig. 17-4. Digital delivery has changed our traditions of how we view media.

TELEVISION. In terms of sheer audience size, no means of distribution currently comes close to TV (for the purposes of this discussion, "TV" includes all the traditional broadcast networks as well as cable television services with wide reach). Even an unpopular, low-rated TV program can garner millions of viewers. Many filmmakers complain, justifiably, that the type of programming found on television is limited, but compared with theatrical distribution, TV is a remarkably democratic medium. TV viewers will tune in to many types of programs, including public affairs, documentaries, and even dramas that they wouldn't go see in a theater.

The majority of television programming is either produced by television entities or commissioned by them. If you work for a network or another regular supplier of programming, you're aware of the intricacies of getting a new show on the air. If you're an independent producer hoping to sell your project to television, there are a number of ways to approach it. Start by identifying existing series that might make a good fit with your project (whether you have actually produced it yet or not). Some series, particularly on public television and commercial cable networks, actively solicit proposals and works in progress from independents. As noted above, single programs can be awkward to distribute and market on TV—you're almost always better off being part of a series.

Consider working with a television *sales agent*. Sales agents know who the key decision makers are and how much has been paid in the past for shows like yours. Sales agents can be indispensable for foreign television markets, as they generally attend the international TV markets (see below) and have contacts in countries where it would be nearly impossible for you to make inroads.

In the United States, the chief outlets for independently produced (or coproduced) programs include cable networks such as HBO, Sundance Channel, IFC, and, on the broadcast side, PBS. Actually, PBS is an association of public stations, not a traditional, centrally controlled network. This means that only some PBS programming (including the major series) is broadcast on most of the stations around the country on the same date (*hard feed*). Many shows are distributed to stations on an individual basis: each station chooses when or if to broadcast the show (*soft feed*). The latter makes promotion much more difficult. American Program Service (APS) programming is soft fed, and it may offer more opportunities than national series for independently produced shows. If you're trying to get your project on PBS, you can work with an individual PBS station as a *presenting station* to the network, you can go directly to one of the series, or you can try to work through the PBS national headquarters in Washington, DC.

Unless you've been commissioned to produce a movie by a cable or broadcast organization (in which case it will likely own the movie outright), selling your movie to TV often involves a *licensing deal*, in which you permit the broadcaster to show the movie a certain number of times over a specified period of time. Sometimes other types of exhibition are included in the deal as well, such as VOD, *catch up TV rights* (in which the movie is made available on the Web after each airing), and/or DVD or Blu-ray Discs.

Nontheatrical Distribution

The many types of nontheatrical distribution include *educational* (schools and universities), *institutional* (such as libraries and community groups), and corporate. This is sometimes referred to as *audiovisual (AV) distribution*.

Many projects are made expressly for nontheatrical markets. These include educational pieces designed as curriculum aids, training programs, how-tos, and the like. Nontheatrical distribution can also be a significant aftermarket for movies that have already appeared in theaters or on television. Nontheatrical distribution is typically done with DVDs or Blu-rays or via download. Sometimes schools or universities will license a movie for distribution on their intranet (essentially an internal Web system).

Prices for DVDs sold to schools, libraries, and other institutions for the AV market are generally much higher than for home video (from $50 to $350) and often include public performance rights (which allow the institution to show the movie to groups, though not necessarily to charge admission). Often educational distribution is done with tiered pricing: a low price for community groups, a somewhat higher price for schools and libraries, and the highest price for colleges and universities.

As in theatrical distribution, you may choose to work with a distributor or you may self-distribute. Nontheatrical distribution is a specialized business, and some companies do this exclusively. Some theatrical distributors have a nontheatrical division; others contract with a subdistributor to handle this market. Distributors have a catalog and mailing lists of people who have rented or bought similar movies in the past, and they may have a sales force familiar with key personnel in school systems, libraries, and corporations. For some distributors, however, mailing out the catalog once a year is the extent of their marketing effort. Whereas theatrical distributors generally deduct marketing expenses from the producer's share of the income, many nontheatrical distributors do not deduct expenses. Instead, they pay the producer a flat percentage or royalty for each video sale or rental. The producer might get about 30 to 35 percent of the revenue that comes in to the distributor, depending on the deal.

The term "nontheatrical distribution" is also used to mean essentially theatrical screenings in noncommercial settings; for example, showing feature films in museums, art centers, and such.

Home Video and Nontheatrical Marketing

Home video distribution refers to selling videos either directly to consumers, to wholesale and retail sales outlets, or to video stores or online services that rent videos to consumers. Independent filmmakers may choose to go with a distributor for home video, in hopes that the distributor can expand the visibility of the project and get the movie placed with big retail stores and websites. Depending on the project, you may get a sizable advance, a token advance, or nothing at all up front. The distributor should pay for the manufacturing and authoring of the DVD and/or Blu-ray (see p. 64), but may try to deduct some of these costs from your share.

As of this writing, home videos typically retail initially for around $14 to $25 or so. About half of that goes to the retailer, and half is the wholesale price paid to the distributor. The producer's royalty is a usually a percentage of wholesale, often 10 to 30 percent. Some distributors pay a higher flat rate per disc.

After a title has been around for a while, discount sites will offer it to the public for much less than the initial sales price, driving down the price that other retailers can charge as well.

Because distributors take a lot of the revenue and sometimes don't do much promotion, some filmmakers choose to self-distribute for the nontheatrical or home video markets. Or they may work out a nonexclusive deal with a distributor/wholesaler that allows them to sell and promote the film on their own in addition to what the distributor is doing.

Self-distribution begins with setting up a compelling website where interested buyers can learn about the film and see a trailer or some clips. A *shopping cart* on your site takes orders, collecting the buyer's information and processing credit card payments (this can be done through PayPal if you don't take credit cards directly).

Some people choose to handle the billing and shipping of product themselves, but this can be time-consuming. Alternatively, you can sign up with a *fulfillment house*, which takes the orders and ships DVDs for a fee. Some will manage the whole process (manufacture the DVD, package it, and handle the orders and customer service) for a very reasonable price. It's a simple matter for customer orders placed on your site to be processed by a fulfillment house's.

Self-distributors often do a mass mailing to likely buyers, using mailing lists they purchase. You may send notices via email, but because spam filters may block you from reaching institutional buyers, you may need to print and mail brochures. You can buy lists for almost every category of buyer or field of study. For example, you can get a list of all public libraries across the country or teachers in women's studies programs. Your promotional materials should list awards, reviews, and endorsements by people in the field you are targeting. The response rate to a mailing is often only a few percent, but this may be enough to generate a profit.

For nontheatrical distribution, you should also have a poster made that can be distributed for individual screenings. Many nontheatrical movies are accompanied by study guides or training materials. To self-distribute in the nontheatrical market, plan to invest several thousand dollars. It can be a full-time job, especially in the first few months of the movie's release. The campaign requires an initial outlay for DVDs, a website, publicity, business forms, shipping, and costs such as festival entrance fees. It will require ongoing overhead for telephone and promotional mailings. Those self-distributors who have turned a profit have done so by streamlining the mechanical aspects of scheduling, shipping, and billing. Certain costs, like advertising, don't increase much for two films instead of one, so it can be cheaper to work with someone who is distributing a similar film. Distribution cooperatives, like New Day Films, help keep costs down by pooling resources.

Other Distribution Issues

FOREIGN DISTRIBUTION. Foreign markets can be lucrative for both theatrical and TV distribution. Starting when you first plan, cast, or shoot your movie, try to make it appealing and accessible to a foreign audience. To prepare the movie for foreign distribution, you need to do several things. Make sure the sound is mixed to allow for translation into other languages (see p. 673). You will need a textless ("generic") version of the movie without any titles (see p. 608). You will also need a transcript (*continuity*) of the finished program to facilitate translation. Different parts of the world use different video systems and frame rates, and you will need video masters in different formats (see Chapter 14).

DIVIDING RIGHTS AND REVENUES. Many projects have the potential to make money in several different markets. How the rights to these markets are handled can make a big difference to your bank account.

When you are making a deal with a broadcaster or distributor, the company may ask for many types of rights and territories. For example, a broadcaster may want to share in home video or foreign sales; or a theatrical distributor may want rights to sell the movie to domestic TV. When possible, it's to your advantage to exclude those rights from the deal so you can sell them to another entity for more money.

As noted above, if a broadcaster or other group commissions you to do a project and pays the whole production cost, it will likely expect all rights to foreign, home video, and any subsidiary markets. However, if you initiate a project and the production funds come from several different entities, you're in a better position to retain ownership, control, and the ability to license those often lucrative rights to other buyers. An experienced agent or lawyer can help you negotiate the deal.

If you sell a movie to TV and hope to pursue theatrical distribution, try to get the broadcaster to agree to a theatrical *window* prior to the air date (see below for more on this). On the other hand, if you've already sold to TV before you approach a theatrical distributor, the distributor may be much less interested in your project. Normally the distributor will want to share in the proceeds from a TV sale or home video; this is one of its main hedges against losing money on the theatrical run. Expenses are usually *cross collateralized*, which means that any new income, say from a TV sale, goes first to paying off previously accumulated debt before anything is paid to the producer. Be sure the distributor doesn't try to deduct debt from other films it may be handling.

LENGTH. The running time of a movie can have a big impact on its distribution opportunities. For more on this, see p. 540.

DELIVERABLES. If you sell your film to a distributor or broadcaster, there will be a list of things you need to deliver to satisfy your end of the deal. Many filmmakers forget to factor in the time and (often high) cost to supply the deliverables. Depending on the project and the deal, this could include different kinds of digital masters, film or video elements, multiple sound tracks, and documents including all licenses, contracts, chain of title, releases, and a transcript or spotted dialogue list with all lines listed by timecode for dubbing or subtitling. Even for native 16:9 projects, for instance, some cable operators still require 4:3 alternative masters, which might necessitate the resizing of titles and graphics. See p. 608 for some video deliverables and p. 673 for some audio deliverables.

Fig. 17-5. Obligatory shot of the Hollywood sign.

Launching a Movie

When a Hollywood studio releases a new movie, there's a well-oiled machine ready to distribute and promote it. The studio has an established network of contacts for theatrical, television, and home video distribution. The studio often has an in-house marketing department to create an advertising campaign and work with the press. For independent producers, on the other hand, releasing a movie can be a bewildering experience of trying to get attention for it and ultimately to find it a home with distributors, broadcasters, theaters, or other outlets.

Different movies have different goals or needs when it comes to distribution. If you've just finished an independent feature, you might be looking for a distributor, press coverage, a theatrical opening, and then aftermarkets of television and home video. But many movies are not intended for theatrical distribution (and, increasingly, most just don't get the chance). If you've made a movie intended for TV, you might be looking for a broadcaster (or several in different countries). If your movie has already been bought (or was commissioned) by a TV network, you may only be looking for ways to maximize your press coverage and viewership for the broadcast.

If your movie has the potential to be shown through a variety of distribution channels, it's important to plan the release carefully. When a movie is released to the right markets in the right order and at the right time, exposure and potential profits can be maximized. Traditional distribution models are changing, which affects the sequence of events. The following is an outline for the release of a hypothetical feature film to highlight some of the distribution options.

Often the first step for an independent movie is film festivals and markets (see below). These are used to raise industry awareness about the movie and get some press (but not too much; see below). Distributors attend the major festivals and markets looking for new movies to acquire.

After you sign on with a distributor (or decide to self-distribute), the first commercial release is traditionally theatrical distribution (though, as noted above, theatrical release is becoming less feasible for many independent films). Hollywood films are often released in many cities simultaneously (*wide release*) in order to maximize the effect of advertising and press coverage in national media. Smaller films are often given a *limited release* (also called *platforming*) by playing in a few cities and then expanding to more *play dates* if things go well. Many exhibitors will want to see how a film performs elsewhere before booking the movie themselves. In the United States, opening in major cities such as New York and Los Angeles can be very expensive (advertising costs are astronomical) and very important (everyone's watching the box office).

Because the marketplace is crowded with movies and other entertainment options, you don't want your film to get lost. Independent films tend to be programmed to open in quieter periods, away from the major holiday releases from the big studios. However, with increasing numbers of films on the market, almost *no* time is quiet anymore. Sometimes small films are *counterprogrammed* by deliberately putting them out on holidays, as an alternative to studio fare. The timing of your release should be planned around getting the most press coverage and attention possible. Theaters generally open movies on Thursday night or Friday. Get as many people as you can to go that *first* weekend, because by Monday morning the theater decides whether to pull your film or, if you're lucky, hold it over. Some films open on a Wednesday to increase the chance of press coverage (since so many other films are usually opening—and reviewed—on Fridays). If you have a good per-screen average, you'll get extra visibility in the press.

The next step may be VOD via a cable service, or perhaps pay-to-view via iTunes or Amazon, along with availability via DVD, perhaps on Netflix. That might be followed by a second window in which the movie is streamed on Netflix Watch Instantly and advertising-supported free services like Hulu.

For some films, the next step may be home video or perhaps AV distribution (see above). If a movie has a potential to be used by schools and institutions, you can release it to the nontheatrical market at a higher price than consumers will pay for home video. After several months, you move on to the home video release. Some projects are never released on home video. On the other hand, some movies go directly to home video after a theatrical run to capitalize on any existing public awareness.

Then there is the television release. Some movies are bought or commissioned by free (traditional broadcast) networks, others by pay or premium services (cable or satellite). Some movies play on one and then the other. Some TV executives will commission a film and actively encourage a theatrical run prior to the air date as a way to boost attention and prestige. Others see this as *undermining* their press coverage or prestige and insist on the movie premiering on television, with no prior theatrical or video release. There have been a few notable examples of movies that had a limited TV release on a pay service and then went on to a successful theatrical run, but usually a TV airing means the end of theatrical opportunities. Choosing a good airdate (relative to holidays, elections, major sporting events, ratings "sweeps weeks," and such) can be important. One sequence for release to television submarkets is to start with video-on-demand (right after theatrical), then release on pay cable, basic cable, and finally on free, broadcast TV.

The reason to do VOD or home video prior to TV is the assumption that people are less likely to *pay* to watch a movie if they can see it for free. On the other hand, for movies that don't get released theatrically, an upcoming TV broadcast can help land a home video deal. Some broadcast programs have a *tag* at the end of the show telling viewers how they can buy videos, which can be a good marketing device.

ALTERNATIVE RELEASE SCHEDULES. With so many films competing for consumers' attention, marketing should ideally be done at every stage of release. However, marketing is expensive, so the industry has shortened the time between the initial release of a film (with its biggest marketing splash) and the various aftermarkets. For example, DVDs are often released as soon as possible after the theatrical run or, in some cases, simultaneously. In a *day and date* release, the DVD is sold and/or pay TV or VOD is done at the same time as the theatrical release. HDNet Films released Steven Soderbergh's *Bubble* this way. In this case, a financial connection between the theater chain and the broadcaster provided benefits to both.

Another method involves offering a film on VOD or iTunes *before* theatrical or any other platform, or at a premium price during the theatrical run, for viewers who would rather watch at home. This makes theater owners unhappy, but may be profitable for distributors and producers.

Festivals and Markets

Perhaps the best way to get attention for a new project is to enter it in a film festival. The top festivals worldwide include Berlin, Cannes, New York, Sundance, and Toronto. A large group of distributors, agents, and members of the international press attends these festivals, and a successful screening can be a huge boost to a movie. Generating "buzz" can help in many ways. For films that don't have obviously bankable elements like big stars or hot stories, distributors are usually influenced as much by other people's reactions as by their own. (There's a joke about a studio executive who went to see a movie alone. Afterward, a friend asked him what he thought. He said, "I don't know, I saw it by myself.")

The best festivals are very competitive and often require premieres. (If the film has been shown elsewhere in the same country or sometimes the same continent, you may be disqualified.) You can easily lose the opportunity to play at a "smaller" festival while waiting for a bigger one to decide. There are hundreds of festivals around the world, which can provide a fabulous opportunity for you to travel and see your movie with different audiences. Many festivals specialize in particular topics (nature, gay and lesbian, educational, etc.) and festivals often provide a forum for the most interesting discussions about your movie and others. At one time, there was a clear delineation between film festivals and video/TV festivals. This difference is becoming increasingly blurred. Nevertheless, distinctions remain between festivals geared more toward theatrical films (both fiction and documentary) and those that accept more television-oriented or nontheatrical fare. These days, a festival run may serve as a theatrical release for films that don't get picked up by a distributor. Some filmmakers use this as an opportunity to sell DVDs and some festivals will pay a screening fee to show your film.

Many websites list festivals. One of them, at www.withoutabox.com, has listings of many festivals and allows you to store your application information, making it easy to apply to multiple festivals. See the Bibliography for more sources.

MARKETS. A film or TV market can be thought of as a festival for industry people where the focus is not on watching and enjoying movies but on selling and buying them. Some film festivals, such as Berlin, have a market associated with them. Chief markets in the United States include the Independent Feature Project (IFP), in New York every September, and the American Film Market (AFM), which is geared more toward dramas, in Santa Monica in November. Some markets, such as MIP in France and NATPE in the United States, are primarily for buying and selling television programming. Markets may have selection committees, but are often less selective than festivals. The filmmaker pays a fee and has the opportunity to meet with distributors, broadcasters, and festival programmers to discuss a finished movie, a work in progress, or a script or proposal.

In some markets, a screening is held in a theater, to which you can invite buyers. In many markets, there's a library for buyers who prefer to watch films by themselves, often on fast-forward so they can "see" lots of films in a short time without being pestered by filmmakers.

Many markets have an organized process to bring producers and buyers together. Some use a "speed dating" method, where short meetings are arranged in which you can pitch your project quickly. Some have a pitching forum, in which you get a chance to pitch your project to a large group of assembled buyers. This can be nerve-wracking, but it raises the visibility of the project and gives you a very quick idea if there's interest among buyers. One of the key benefits of any market is the opportunity to find many executives in one place at one time, to meet people who can help you expand your understanding of the industry and meet possible mentors.

Marketing Methods and Materials

A marketing campaign comprises many elements.

- *Website.* Having a website for the film is essential. Your website will be the central online location for information about the film, screening schedules, and press materials. A trailer and/or clips can make a big difference (see below). Before you even go into production, register a *domain name* for the film (such as www.yourmoviename.com). There are many sites where you can do this inexpensively. You will need an Internet service provider (ISP) to *host* your site (i.e., to provide the server where your site resides). Particularly when you have a lot of video assets, or expect a lot of traffic to your site, it can be better to load the video content onto a video sharing site like YouTube or Vimeo and link to them using a video player embedded on your own site. It's not hard to set up. Keep the site fresh with updated news, but don't over-share clips from the film. Leave people wanting more.
- *Networking.* There are many opportunities for networking, blogging, and getting word out via Facebook, Twitter, and so on. Your website should link to a Facebook page and if you're tweeting, you can display Twitter feeds there if you choose.
- *Press kit.* You'll need a *press kit* that can be personally handed to press people and posted on the website. Press notes should include a synopsis, director's statement, lists of awards and festivals, credits, and short biographies of the key participants.[9] Some people put several publicity photos in each press kit or at least links to where people can download them from your site.
- *Stills.* The need for good still images cannot be overemphasized. You should have pictures of the actors in role or, for a documentary, the movie's subjects. You'll also need some shots of the production team, especially the director. Having good still images can mean the difference between a paper running your pictures or not. Offer a few to choose from, as competing media may not want to run the same image. Compelling images are also essential for the poster and ad campaign. On a feature film, stills are usually taken on the set or during production for highest quality. On a documentary or low-budget feature, frame grabs and enlargements made from the movie itself can work, particularly if the movie is shot in progressive HD. Standard definition video often doesn't hold up well for enlargements. You can improve the quality of interlaced frame grabs by deinterlacing and doing other fixes in Photoshop (see p. 213 and p. 600). Your site should have a page for downloading press stills; usually low-res images are displayed, with links to download high-res files for use by festivals and journalists.

---

9. Reviews may be included as well, but generally not for press kits going to other critics.

- *Poster and art.* You'll need a poster (*one-sheet*) and some key art treatments that can be used for ads and other materials. Actually, it's not a bad idea to have a full-sized version of the one-sheet (27 x 39 inches is typical) and some smaller sizes that can be put up on bulletin boards and such.
- *Postcard.* It's extremely useful to have a postcard with basic information about the film that can be handed to people at a festival or market, and left in theater lobbies. You can access many poster and postcard printers online. You send them a digital file and they print out what you need for a few hundred dollars. The larger your print run, the cheaper each copy of the poster or postcard is. You can add individual screening dates and times with a sticker.
- *Trailer.* You should have a *trailer* (coming-attractions promo) for posting on your site and other websites. You must have one for theatrical distribution. In about two to two and a half minutes a compelling trailer gives viewers a sense of the movie and gets them excited about seeing it (watch trailers for ideas and effective length). Trailer making is a unique skill; it often involves throwing together shots totally out of context, which can be hard for the filmmakers who made the film to do. Many producers hire a trailer house or editors who specialize. For film theaters, you'll usually need both flat and 'Scope (anamorphic) versions. There are services that specialize in getting your trailer and other assets posted on movie websites, including iTunes; it can sometimes be hard to get them out there on your own.
- *Clips.* When broadcast critics review your movie, they'll want some short clips from the film to show while they talk about it. They may show the trailer, but you should also prepare a *clips reel.* Post clips on your site for viewing, and make them available as QuickTime files or another format on disc or tape. You'll also need audio clips for radio.
- *Electronic press kit (EPK).* For many movies, an EPK is prepared, which includes clips and video footage of the moviemakers on the set along with interviews of the filmmakers and cast.

PUBLICITY. If you have a lot of money or are backed by a large corporation, you can afford to place ads on the Web, in print, or on TV to increase awareness of your movie. But publicity—in the form of feature articles, interviews, reviews, and Web postings—is a lot cheaper and often more effective. The many types of media available to get the word out include websites, newspapers, magazines, radio, TV, and blogs. For some movies, the goal is to interest the general public. For some projects, such as a corporate or educational video, your publicity may be targeted at a specific market or industry group.

If you can afford it, hire a *publicist*, whose job it is to bring your project to the attention of print, Web, and broadcast entities that might cover your movie. A professional publicist will have a list of editors, writers, and producers to contact. Sometimes publicists are hired for a festival debut, to increase awareness of a film and facilitate its getting a distributor. But be careful about overexposing a movie prior to its actual release in theaters or on television. For example, if a newspaper reviews a movie at a festival, it may decide not to run that review again when the movie is released. For general circulation (as opposed to industry-only) media, insist on short "capsule" reviews at festivals, so the full review can be held off till later. A capsule review, if positive, can be invaluable for preparing posters and marketing materials for the actual release of the project.

Be sure to have plenty of *screeners* (DVDs) to give to writers and critics and/or set up an online screener they can watch on the Web (usually password-protected). When possible, hold press screenings or invite reviewers to public screenings so they can see the movie with an audience. Some critics prefer to watch videos by themselves. To improve the chance of a feature piece being done about your movie, emphasize the "hooks" or angles that make your movie special, timely, or newsworthy. Did you lure a famous actor out of retirement? Is your movie about nuclear war being broadcast on the anniversary of the bombing of Hiroshima? Did the film make use of local talent? Is there an incredible story about how the movie got made?

Keep in mind that substantial lead time may be needed between when a feature piece is done and the date it actually appears in print or on the air. Contact editors far in advance. If you're going to be in a city, perhaps for a festival, you can sometimes do print or radio interviews and have them "banked" until the movie is released.

Selling Your Project and Yourself

A lot of novice filmmakers don't realize how much *selling* they have to do to make movies. It starts at the beginning of the project—getting people interested in your idea—and doesn't stop until long after the film is made and distributed. Some people are drawn to moviemaking precisely for the commercial aspects, but for many, the constant need to sell feels like a painful distraction from what they really want to do—make movies. Nevertheless, being forced to pitch can lead you to distill your vision and arrive at a deeper understanding of the project.

If you've managed to get your movie at least partially under way, you may want to work with a *producer's representative* or a *sales agent* to look for funding and negotiate deals at festivals or markets. The rep or agent has contacts among the potential buyers. Agents and reps have no problem pushing and touting a movie, whereas the people who actually *made* the movie often do. Nevertheless, unless you have a very marketable movie or an established reputation, you may have trouble getting a well-connected producer's rep to handle your project. You may do better to look for offers on your own and use an agent or a lawyer to help negotiate a deal when you actually get some interest from a buyer.

A publicist, as noted above, can do a lot to help a project. Some are very connected to distributors, actors, and other industry types and can function a bit like sales agents to help you make contacts.

Anyone who's tried to sell a movie at a market or festival knows what a demoralizing experience it can be. A few movies get sold with great fanfare while the other filmmakers are left glumly wondering why they've gotten no offers. Be patient— often a market or festival will lay the groundwork for a deal, but the actual offer may take several months or more to materialize. Sometimes one festival gets you noticed, but it isn't until the next one that someone comes forward with real interest. Unfortunately, the brutal fact is that most films never get distributed or even invited to festivals. Given the literally thousands of movies that compete for a few slots each year, excellent films are turned away all the time.

When you go to a market or festival, do your homework and try to determine which distributors or buyers are most appropriate for your project (often you can get the catalog of buyers in advance of a market, or use the previous year's guide). Find a way to invite the buyers or make them aware of your movie. But treat them with respect. There are stories of aggressive filmmakers who stop at nothing until some executive watches their movie or reads their script—and sometimes it works. But this kind of harassment is why many weary buyers and programmers, who see hundreds of movies a year, do whatever they can to avoid being ambushed. Trust that if your movie is good enough, people will talk about it, and things will start to happen.

A LAST WORD

If you've actually read from the beginning of this book to here, you deserve an award for endurance. You now know a vast amount about creating all sorts of motion pictures. There are many ways to put your knowledge to use. You might decide to work in the "industry" (indust*ries* is more like it), which could mean making anything from dramas, documentaries, industrials, TV news, and Web videos to video games or apps for mobile phones and tablets.

Some people go into filmmaking with dreams of making a hit and getting rich and famous. If you go into the business, keep in mind that most careers advance much more slowly than the fantasy of being "discovered" and catapulted to the top. A lot of people labor in the trenches for years, and fame and riches may have nothing to do with it. If you produce your own films, even if you do well, in the midst of success there can be plenty of failure. One audience, critic, or client might love your film; another might be indifferent. Or you might have great success with one project and find no takers for the next. And how do you even define success? Getting into a prestigious film festival? Getting good reviews? Selling the film? Doing well at the box office? Each project has the potential to clear some hurdles and stumble on others.

Sometimes it gets easier as you move forward, and sometimes it doesn't. Learning to live with uncertainty and risk is essential to surviving. Hopefully your drive comes from loving what you do.

Making movies is challenging, but finding a sustaining source of income can be just as hard. Especially when you're starting out, making your own films can help demonstrate your abilities, but what pays your salary is often a completely separate thing. Some people have day jobs in a different line of work. Others use their skills to gets jobs in TV, doing corporate media, or working on a film crew. Many people build their full-time careers around jobs like these.

Finding work can be tricky. Try to stay flexible—you may need to work for little or no money to get your foot in the door or to develop your skills. Most job offers in film don't come out of thin air. More often, you get a job because someone recommends you—thanks to the fact that you're hard-working, upbeat, and reliable. So stay in touch with friends and people you've worked with.

It may be that you decide to do something completely different in terms of your career. These days, no matter what your vocation or avocation, almost everyone has a reason to create media at *some* point in their lives. In the end, all the technology and technique in this book is meant to give you the power to express your ideas and tell stories. Now it's up to you to decide what stories to tell, and how to tell them. Making movies is hard work, an adventure, and painful at times. But if you're lucky, it's also enormously fun and satisfying. Enjoy it!

ADJUSTING A VIDEO MONITOR

The Importance of a Good Video Monitor

We all watch TV and use computers without much thought about how the screens are adjusted for brightness, color, and contrast. When shooting or editing video, however, setting up a picture monitor to professional standards is critical for evaluating and controlling the picture.

During shooting, we use the camera's LCD screen, electronic viewfinder, and/or a separate field monitor to view the camera's input signal. But this is not necessarily identical to the image the camera is *actually* capturing to file or tape. For instance, color, saturation, shadow detail, contrast, or overall brightness shown by the field monitor or viewfinder may or may not match what is later seen on a high-quality "broadcast reference" monitor when the recorded signal is played back in post. Needless to say, when we make lighting and exposure decisions based on what we see in the field, we need to be confident that the display we're viewing is as accurate as possible.

While editing on an NLE, we tend to accept what we see on the computer's display, although RGB computer displays often don't accurately reproduce component video color space ($Y'C_BC_R$, also referred to as YUV). If you use a computer display to color-correct video, things may look quite different when the results are played back on a TV. (For more on this, see Computer and Video Monitors, p. 218.)

And when your movie is finished and it's time to screen it, a properly adjusted digital video projector is equally important. A lot of effort goes into producing your project, and you want it to look its best for your audience.

In other words, there's no substitute for a properly adjusted picture monitor in both production and post. It's a necessity.

Professional video monitors and projectors are *set up* (adjusted) for color hue, color saturation, shadow detail, and contrast using a test signal that contains *color bars*. It's the only method that truly guarantees that what you see is *really* what you get.

The color bar setup described below applies to digital HD video monitors and TVs only. In general, whenever you connect a digital monitor to a video source—be it a camera, an NLE, or a tape deck—use digital connections like HDMI or HD-SDI instead of analog connections like analog component HD (also called $Y'P_BP_R$) or composite SD (often labeled "video in") unless your equipment won't support it. If any terms are unfamiliar, see Chapters 1 and 5.

For anyone who has experience setting up analog NTSC standard definition monitors, there are two major differences in setting up newer digital HD monitors. First, while black level in the analog NTSC signal used in North America was 7.5 IRE units (see p. 205), black level in digital video the world over is 0 percent. The monitor setup instructions below assume you are working with digital video (usually Rec. 709 for HD) with black at 0 percent. Second, NTSC monitors had adjustments for both chroma and phase (more on these terms below). HD monitors connected via digital interfaces (such as HDMI, DisplayPort, DVI, HD-SDI, and SDI) don't offer phase (hue) control. You don't need it, because with a digital connection, the color spectrum will not shift out of alignment. However, digital monitors with analog inputs *can* have hue adjustments that may improperly affect a digital input. (This *shouldn't* be the case, because a digital monitor can sense whether its video input signal is digital or analog, but many monitors are made this way.) If your digital monitor does have a control for hue or phase, you can verify if it affects a digital input signal by adjusting the hue or phase control—if this control does incorrectly alter the appearance of a digital signal, you'll see the result immediately, as colors will go wacky all at once. In this case, use SMPTE HD color bars (described below) to set proper hue.

For instructions on adjusting *computer* monitors to best display video, see the help section in your operating system, video card, or monitor calibration software. Many systems have a simple step-by-step process you can follow to calibrate the display. Products like Matrox's MXO2 series of converters can be used to calibrate a computer monitor for use with $Y'C_BC_R$ component video (and also to set up a consumer TV that lacks professional controls).

If your HD project will only be seen on the Internet and not on broadcast or cable TV, then you don't need a video monitor that displays $Y'C_BC_R$, and a properly calibrated computer monitor will serve fine for color correction.

Color Bars

Most cameras and NLEs generate color bars. You can send a signal directly into the production monitor or NLE video monitor, or you can record the bars for adjustment from playback. There are different types of bars with different features.

Newer professional HD equipment can generate a color bar pattern called ARIB bars (for their original creator, the Japanese Association of Radio Industry and Businesses) or SMPTE RP 219-2002 bars (see Fig. A). These are 16:9 aspect ratio and specifically designed for digital HD. We'll call them SMPTE HD color bars.

Another common type of color bars is an updated HD version of the traditional SMPTE split-field pattern (see Fig. B). Unlike the earlier SD analog version of these bars, which were 4:3 aspect ratio, the HD version is in 16:9. "Split-field" refers to the short rectangular boxes under the main bars, which help adjust both hue (phase) and saturation of analog HD input signals (more on this below). Techniques for setting up a monitor with either type of color bars are similar.

Basic Monitor Controls

Two of the main controls on a professional video monitor are *brightness* (sometimes labeled *black level*) and *contrast* (white level, also called *picture*). These features

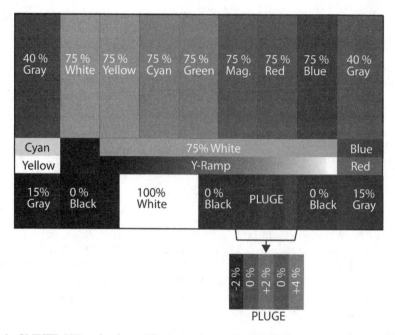

Fig. A. SMPTE HD color bars. The inset shows the PLUGE pattern with raised black levels. When blacks are properly set, only the +2 percent and +4 percent stripes in the PLUGE should be visible, and just barely at that.

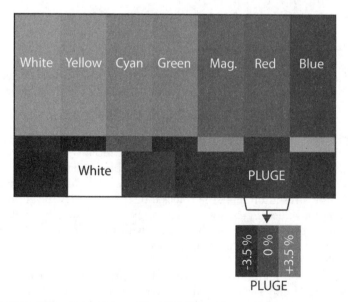

Fig. B. SMPTE HD split-field bars. The PLUGE is shown here with elevated blacks for clarity. Only the +3.5 percent stripe should be visible.

are badly named, as the brightness control mainly raises and lowers the blacks, which your eye perceives largely as a change in contrast.

HD digital monitors have an adjustment for *color* (saturation, properly called *chroma*), which adjusts the intensity of colors but not their hues, which are fixed. However, monitors for older analog signals like NTSC and analog HD also have a *hue* adjustment (also called *tint*, *phase*, or *chroma phase*), which controls the two color-difference, or *chrominance*, signals in the component analog video signal. If these signals aren't precisely aligned, all the colors in the image will appear to shift to something unnatural.

Many consumer TVs have automatic or "smart" settings for color and brightness; turn these off if you are adjusting a TV to color bars. Also turn off any noise-reduction features.

The Viewing Environment

While theatrical projection is usually done in a very dark room, video monitors are by design brighter than projection and usually look better with a *little* light in the room. Make sure light sources don't fall directly *on* the screen (which washes out the blacks, lowering contrast, and can affect color reproduction). For production work outdoors, a hood or shade can be fitted over the monitor to protect contrast.

HOW TO SET UP AN HD VIDEO MONITOR USING SMPTE COLOR BARS

1. **Allow Monitor to Warm Up**

   Run it fifteen minutes to stabilize it.

2. **Check Color Temperature**

   Most monitors have a menu setting for display color temperature (*white point*), which must be set to a world standard of 6500°K (also called D65). If in doubt, check the monitor's menu to confirm the setting. Typically you'll have to make this adjustment only once.

3. **Set Black Level**

   The control labeled "brightness" on many monitors actually controls the black level, which is the value of the darkest black parts of the image. When brightness is set too low, you lose detail in the blacks (crushed blacks). When brightness is set too high, the blacks look milky or gray. Brightness also affects color values, so you want to set this before adjusting color. It can sometimes be easier to evaluate brightness with the color turned down or off altogether (which you can do by reducing the chroma or, on some monitors, switching to monochrome).

   In the bottom right-hand corner of both types of color bars is a patch of thin vertical gray stripes called PLUGE bars (Picture Line-Up Generating Equipment). SMPTE HD bars have five stripes in the PLUGE area. Two stripes are at 0 percent black, two are slightly lighter than that, and one is darker. The idea is to lower the brightness control until the left-hand stripe (–2 percent) and the 0 percent stripe next to it merge together. The +2 percent bar in the middle and +4 percent bar on the right should be just *barely* visible, with the 0 percent bar merged into the darkest black. When you're close, sometimes it helps to tweak the brightness up and down a tiny bit to find the spot where the 0 percent stripe *just* disappears. That's all there is to it.

SMPTE HD split-field bars have only three stripes: one at 0 percent black, one lighter, and one darker. The idea is the same. Lower the brightness until the leftmost stripe and the one in the middle just merge into blackness. The +3.5 percent bar on the right will be just visible.

4. Set Peak White Level

The "contrast" or "picture" control adjusts the level of midtones and bright whites. It also sets the distance or separation between the black level and the brightest whites. The appearance of contrast on your monitor will be affected by local ambient light levels, so setting contrast levels can be a bit of an art form.

In both types of color bars, there's a square in the bottom row that is 100 percent white. Start with the contrast control down, and as you raise it, watch that square turn from gray to white. When it stops responding, you've reached peak white. One technique therefore is to turn it back down and raise it again until you *just* reach the point where it stops responding. The white level is now set. (This doesn't work on OLED monitors, however, in which the 100 percent white square simply gets brighter and brighter. With OLED monitors, perhaps it's best to start with manufacturer's center position for contrast.)

With SMPTE HD bars, as you raise the contrast, on some monitors you'll notice that the Y-ramp, which is only supposed to be white at its far-right side, starts getting whiter toward the middle as contrast becomes excessive. You can also use this to gauge when the white is too bright.

Setting the contrast can affect the brightness and vice versa. Sometimes you have to go back and tweak the brightness after doing the contrast.

5. Set Chroma (and Possibly Hue)

Now it's time to set the chroma (color saturation). This is where SMPTE color bars are so handy. If you have a professional monitor, enable the "blue-only" function (sometimes it's a switch or button on the outside; sometimes it is a menu selection). This will turn off the red and green so that the screen turns deep blue (or sometimes black-and-white). If your monitor doesn't have a blue-only function, you can view the color bars through a Lee 363 blue gel, although this is much less satisfactory. Some I/O and signal-conversion devices like Matrox's MXO2 can supply a signal that allows a similar type of calibration to a monitor that lacks a blue-only mode.

When using SMPTE HD bars with a monitor in blue-only mode, adjust chroma (sometimes labeled "color" or "saturation") until the three vertical bars shown in Figure C achieve the same intensity or brightness, which should make them the same as the horizontal bar below them.

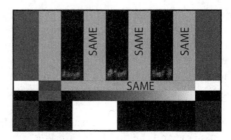

Fig. C. With SMPTE HD bars, when setting chroma (also called saturation or "color") with a monitor in blue-only mode, these four bars should have the same brightness.

When using SMPTE HD split-field bars in blue-only mode, adjust chroma so that the two outer bars have the same intensity as the small color rectangles directly below them. When this is done, the two outer bars should also match each other (see Fig. D).

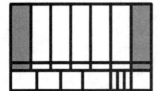   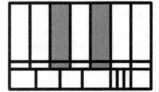

Fig. D. (left) With SMPTE HD split-field bars, when adjusting chroma on a monitor that displays blue only, these two bars and the patches under them should have the same intensity. (right) When adjusting hue (tint) for an analog signal, these bars and the patches under them should look the same. In the case of either a digital or analog input signal, when you finish setting up the monitor, these four bars and the patches under them should all look the same.

If you are adjusting a monitor for an analog HD signal, you can also adjust hue (or phase) in a similar way, so that the near left and right blue bars and the small color rectangles below them are the same. Counting from the left, these would be bars 3 and 5 (see Fig. D). As described above, you may also need to do this with a digital HD signal if the hue adjustment on your monitor affects the picture.

When you are done adjusting the two outer bars—and also, in the case of analog HD, bars 3 and 5—all four bars should now match each other and the small rectangles under them. If this isn't the case, retweak chroma/color—and for analog only, hue/phase—until you achieve this. The two adjustments are interactive, but it isn't very hard to get a good result.

Now turn off the blue-only mode and *voilà!*—perfect color and saturation.

Some cameras only output "full-field" bars without the PLUGE or other bars below (see Fig. E). It's much harder to set up a monitor with these. In former PAL countries, these are known as EBU bars. With a monitor in blue-only mode, match

Fig. E. (left) Full-field bars. (right) When properly adjusted, these appear on a monitor in blue-only mode with three dark bars of equal intensity and four lighter bars that have the same brightness.

the first and seventh bars from the left in blue-only mode by adjusting chroma. If adjusting an analog HD signal, match the third and fifth bars from the left by adjusting hue (phase). Again, all four should then match each other.

If you don't have a way to display blue only, set the chroma by eye so the color level is rich but not oversaturated. If you're adjusting hue for an analog signal, there's only one setting in which both the yellow bar and the magenta bar (second and fifth from the left) will appear correct. The yellow should be a pure lemon yellow, without any hint of green or orange. The magenta bar shouldn't be red or purple.

Getting accurate color without bars is very difficult, since there is no way to know what colors should look like. The best you can do is to go for the most pleasing skin tones. You can adjust chroma and hue (analog only) to make skin appear as natural as possible, bearing in mind that what you are recording will more than likely appear different when viewed later on a properly adjusted monitor.

OTHER SETTINGS

Sharpness
Most video monitors and TVs have a sharpness control (also called aperture or detail) that adds a light line around the edges of things in the scene (see Fig. 3-18). In actuality, this *reduces* fine detail, even though shapes look bolder. Turn this all the way down, then raise it until you just reach the point where added lines appear. Get used to watching pictures without added "sharpness." One exception is that professional camcorders often have a detail adjustment in the viewfinder called "peaking" that can help you focus while shooting. The picture in the finder doesn't look "natural," but you can clearly see what's in and out of focus.

Gamma and Color Space
Computer monitors and some broadcast video monitors have adjustments for gamma. The standard display gamma in Windows, Mac OS, and sRGB (Web

graphics) is 2.2.[1] The standard gamma for HD video monitors, as specified in Rec. 709, is 2.4.

Digital video monitors sometimes offer a choice of "color space" (sometimes called color profile) that includes color gamut and gamma. Typical choices are native display gamma (typically 2.2), SMPTE C (to match phosphor CRTs), EBU (ditto, phosphor CRTs), and Rec. 709. More sophisticated monitors add D-Cine (gamma 2.6) and settings to display log capture, as well as user-defined gammas and extrawide color spaces.

A lower display gamma makes the image appear to have less contrast. Downloadable programs such as QuickGamma can be used for computer monitor calibration. For precise monitor calibration, you can get tools such as Datacolor's Spyder4, which includes automated calibration software and a photometric "spyder" that sits on the monitor surface and measures light output.

As discussed above, gamma differs between computer monitors in RGB color space and component ($Y'C_BC_R$) video. See Chapter 5 for workarounds.

---

1. At one time the Mac (Apple) standard was 1.8, but that no longer applies.

DATA RATES AND STORAGE NEEDS FOR VARIOUS DIGITAL FORMATS*

Frame rate note: "24" = 24 or 23.98; "30" = 29.97; "60" = 59.97

Storage note: GB = 1,000,000,000 bytes (decimal); if media capacity in bytes is binary, media will hold less

Actual storage will vary with size and formatting of media

Video Nominal Data Rate (Mbps)	Com-pression Ratio[2]	Frame Rate	Chroma Sampling	Bits[3]	Estimated STORAGE per minute[4]	Estimated STORAGE per Hour[4]	Notes
			STANDARD DEFINITION[1]				
DVD	3.8[5]	31:1	30, 25, 24	4:2:0	8	37 MB	2.3 GB	MPEG-2, variable bit rate (VBR)
DV	25	5:1	30, 25, 24[6]	4:1:1 NTSC 4:2:0 PAL	8	217 MB	13 GB	
DVCAM	25	5:1	30, 25, 24	4:1:1 NTSC 4:2:0 PAL	8	217 MB	13 GB	
DVCPRO (D-7[7])	25	5:1	30, 25, 24	4:1:1[8]	8	217 MB	13 GB	
DVCPRO 50	50	3:3:1	30, 25, 24	4:2:2	8	423 MB	25 GB	Panasonic DV format
IMX (D-10)	30	6:1	30, 25, 24	4:2:2	8	227 MB	14 GB	Sony MPEG-2 format used in XDCAM
IMX (D-10)	40	4:1	30, 25, 24	4:2:2	8	298 MB	18 GB	
IMX (D-10)	50	3.3:1	30, 25, 24	4:2:2	8	370 MB	22 GB	
ProRes 720 x 486	42	6.1	30	4:2:2	0	320 MB	19.2 GB	Variable Bit Rate (VBR)
ProRes HQ 720 x 486	63	4.31	30	4:2:2	0	470 MB	28.2 GB	
Digital Betacam	90	2.3:1	30, 25, 24	4:2:2	10	675 MB	41 GB	Sony compression
ITU-R 601 (D-1, D-5)	216[9]	uncomp.	30, 25[6]	4:2:2	8	1.6 GB	98 GB	
ITU-R 601 (D-1, D-5)	270[9]	uncomp.	30, 25[6]	4:2:2	10	2 GB	122 GB	

*Table by David Leitner.

	Video Data Rate (Mbps)	Nominal Compression Ratio[2]	Frame Rate	Chroma Sampling	Bits[3]	Estimated STORAGE per minute[4]	Estimated STORAGE per Hour[4]	Notes

HIGH DEFINITION—COMPRESSED

Where multiple frame rates exist, data rates and storage indicated for highest frame rate.

	Video Data Rate (Mbps)	Nominal Compression Ratio[2]	Frame Rate	Chroma Sampling	Bits[3]	Estimated STORAGE per minute[4]	Estimated STORAGE per Hour[4]	Notes
DVD— 1280 x 720	6[5]	various	24	4:2:0	8	45 MB	2.7 GB	MPEG-4 AVC (H.264), VC-1
DVD— 1920 x 1080	8[5]	various	24	4:2:0	8	60 MB	3.6 GB	
Blu-ray	36[10]	various	30, 25, 24	4:2:0	8	270 MB	16.2 GB	MPEG-2, MPEG-4 AVC (H.264), VC-1
HDV 1— 1280 x 720p	19.7	17:1	60, 50, 30, 25, 24	4:2:0	8	142 MB	10 GB	MPEG-2, constant bit rate (CBR)
HDV 2— 1440 x 1080i	25	22:1	30, 25, 24	4:2:0	8	190 MB	13 GB	
AVCHD— 720p	14	16:1	60, 50, 24	4:2:0	8	180 MB	11 GB	MPEG-4 AVC (H.264), variable bit rate (VBR)
AVCHD—1920 x 1080i/p	18	16:1	30, 25, 24	4:2:0	8	180 MB	11 GB	
H.264/MPEG-4 AVC various DSLRs	45	various	30, 25, 24	4:2:0	8	320 MB	20 GB	Variable bit rate. Example here from Canon EOS 7D
XDCAM HD— 1280 x 720	19	n.a.	60, 50, 30, 25, 24	4:2:0	8	140 MB	9 GB	MPEG-2, CBR, subsampled horizontally. Offered by JVC, equivalent to HDV 720p.
XDCAM HD— 1280 x 720	25	n.a.	60, 50, 30, 25, 24	4:2:0	8	190 MB	12 GB	MPEG-2, CBR, subsampled horizontally, equivalent to HDV 1080i.
XDCAM HD— 1280 x 720	35	n.a.	60, 50, 30, 25, 24	4:2:0	8	262 MB	16 GB	MPEG-2, VBR, subsampled horizontally.
XDCAM HD— 1440 x 1080i/p	18	42:1	30, 25, 24	4:2:0	8	140 MB	9 GB	MPEG-2, VBR, subsampled horizontally. HQ Mode.
XDCAM HD— 1440 x 1080i/p	25	30:1	30, 25, 24	4:2:0	8	190 MB	12 GB	MPEG-2, VBR, equivalent to HDV 1080i. SP Mode.
XDCAM HD— 1440 x 1080i/p	35	21:1	30, 25, 24	4:2:0	8	262 MB	16 GB	MPEG-2, VBR. LP Mode.
XDCAM HD 422—1280 x 720p	50	20:1	60, 50, 30, 25, 24	4:2:2	8	375 MB	23 GB	MPEG-2, constant bit rate.
XDCAM HD 422—1920 x 1080i/p	50	20:1	30, 25, 24	4:2:2	8	375 MB	23 GB	

	Video Data Rate (Mbps)	Nominal Compression Ratio[2]	Frame Rate	Chroma Sampling	Bits[3]	Estimated STORAGE per minute[4]	Estimated STORAGE per Hour[4]	Notes
HIGH DEFINITION—COMPRESSED (continued)								
XDCAM EX— 1280 x 720p	35	21:1	60, 50, 30, 25, 24	4:2:0	8	263 MB	16 GB	MPEG-2, VBR. HQ mode recorded to SxS cards. Includes Sony EX1, EX3, F3.
XDCAM EX— 1920 x 1080i/p	35	21:1	30, 25, 24	4:2:0	8	263 MB	16 GB	
MPEG-2 Long GOP—1440 x 1080i/p	25	n.a.	30, 25, 24	4:2:0	8	188 MB	12 GB	
MPEG-2 Long GOP—1280 x 720p	35	n.a.	60, 50, 30, 25, 24	4:2:0	8	263 MB	16 GB	
MPEG-2 Long GOP—1920 x 1080i/p	35	n.a.	30, 25, 24	4:2:0	8	263 MB	16 GB	Constant bit rate. Used in Canon C300.
MPEG-2 Long GOP—1280 x 720p	50	n.a.	60, 50, 30, 25, 24	4:2:2	8	375 MB	24 GB	
MPEG-2 Long GOP—1920 x 1080i/p	50	n.a.	30, 25, 24	4:2:2	8	375 MB	24 GB	
D9 HD—960 x 720p	100	6.7:1	60, 50, 30, 25, 24	4:2:2	8	835 MB	49 GB	
D9 HD—1280 x 1080i/p	100	6.7:1	30, 25, 24	4:2:2	8	835 MB	49 GB	
DVCPRO HD (D-12)—960 x 720p	100	6.7:1	60, 50, 30, 25, 24	4:2:2	8	835 MB	49 GB	
DVCPRO HD (D-12)— 1280 x 1080i/p	100	6.7:1	30, 24	4:2:2	8	835 MB	49 GB	Subsampled horizontally.
DVCPRO HD (D-12)— 1440 x 1080i/p	100	6.7:1	25	4:2:2	8	835 MB	49 GB	
AVC Intra 50—1440 x 1080i/p	50	n.a.	30, 25, 24	4:2:0	10	375 MB	23 GB	Panasonic P2 alternative to DVCPRO HD
AVC Intra 100—1920 x 1080i/p	100	n.a.	30, 25, 24	4:2:2	10	750 MB	45 GB	
AVC-LongG— 1920 x 1080i/p	25	n.a.	30, 25, 24	4:2:2	10	188 MB	12 GB	Panasonic AVC Ultra based on H.264. Long GOP.
AVC Ultra 200—1920 x 1080i/p	226	n.a.	24	4:2:2	10	1.7 GB	102 GB	Panasonic AVC Intra codec based on H.264.
AVC Ultra 444—720p, 1080p, 4K	440	n.a.	24	4:2:2	10/12	3.3 GB	200 GB	

	Video Data Rate (Mbps)	Nominal Compression Ratio[2]	Frame Rate	Chroma Sampling	Bits[3]	Estimated STORAGE per minute[4]	Estimated STORAGE per Hour[4]	Notes
HIGH DEFINITION—COMPRESSED (continued)								
DNxHD 36— 1920 x 1080i/p	36	24:1	24, 25	4:2:2	8	270 MB	16.2 GB	
DNxHD 145— 1280 x 720p	145	7:1	60, 50, 24	4:2:2	8	1 GB	66 GB	
DNxHD 220— 1280 x 720p	220	4:1	60, 50, 24	4:2:2	8	1.6 GB	100 GB	AVID intraframe compression, part of SMPTE 2019-2006 (VC-3) standard.
DNxHD 220— 1280 x 720p	220	6:1	60, 50, 24	4:2:2	10	1.6 GB	100 GB	
DNxHD 145— 1920 x 1080i/p	145	7:1	30, 25, 24	4:2:2	8	1 GB	66 GB	
DNxHD 220— 1920 x 1080i/p	220	4:1	30, 25, 24	4:2:2	8	1.6 GB	100 GB	
DNxHD 220— 1920 x 1080i/p	220	6:1	30, 25, 24	4:2:2	10	1.6 GB	100 GB	
ProRes 422 (Proxy)— 1920 x 1080i/p	45	20:1	30, 25, 24	4:2:2	10	338 GB	21 GB	
ProRes 422 (LT)—1920 x 1080i/p	102	9:1	30, 25, 24	4:2:2	10	765 GB	46 GB	Variable bit rate. Accepts most image file types, from SD to 4K
ProRes 422— 1920 x 1080i/p	147	6:1	30, 25, 24	4:2:2	10	1.1 GB	67 GB	
ProRes 422 (HQ)—1920 x 1080i/p	220	4:1	30, 25, 24	4:2:2	10	1.65 GB	99 GB	
ProRes 4444— 1920 x 1080i/p	330	n.a.	30, 25, 24	4:4:4	12	2.48 GB	150 GB	Includes an alpha channel
CineForm 422—1920 x 1080	115	n.a.	30, 25, 24	4:2:2	10	863 MB	52 GB	Wavelet compression, VBR. Accepts most image file types, from SD to 4K. Compressed file is typically 15% of the original in size.
CineForm 444—1920 x 1080	230	n.a.	30, 25, 24	RGB	12	1.7 GB	104 GB	
D5 HD—1280 x 720p	223	4:1	60	4:2:2	8	2.3 GB	135 GB	
D5 HD—1920 x 1080i	223	4:1	30	4:2:2	8	2.3 GB	135 GB	Advanced M-JPEG, 8 channels audio.
D5 HD—1920 x 1080p	223	4:1	24	4:2:2	8	1.94 GB	116 GB	
D5 HD—1920 x 1080i/p	223	4:1	25	4:2:2	8	2 GB	121 GB	

Video Data Rate (Mbps)	Nominal Compression Ratio[2]	Frame Rate	Chroma Sampling	Bits[3]	Estimated STORAGE per minute[4]	Estimated STORAGE per Hour[4]	Notes
HIGH DEFINITION—COMPRESSED (continued)							
HDCAM (D-11)—1440 x 1080i/p 144	4.4:1[11]	30, 25, 24	3:1:1	8	1.1 GB	65 GB	Sony compression, subsampled horizontally
HDCAM SR (D-16)—1920 x 1080i/p 440	2.78:1	30, 25, 24	4:2:2	10	3.3 GB	198 GB	MPEG-4 Studio Profile
HDCAM SR (D-16)—1920 x 1080i/p 440	4.2:1	30, 25, 24	4:4:4	10	3.3 GB	198 GB	
HIGH DEFINITION—UNCOMPRESSED							
1280 x 720p (8 bits) 353.6		24	4:2:2	8	2.5 GB	149 GB	
1280 x 720p (8 bits) 368.3		25	4:2:2	8	2.6 GB	155 GB	
1280 x 720p (8 bits) 441.9		30	4:2:2	8	3.1 GB	186 GB	
1280 x 720p (8 bits) 737.3		50	4:2:2	8	5.2 GB	310 GB	
1280 x 720p (8 bits) 883.9		60	4:2:2	8	6.2 GB	371 GB	
1280 x 720p (10 bits) 442.4		24	4:2:2	10	3.4 GB	201 GB	
1280 x 720p (10 bits) 460.9		25	4:2:2	10	3.5 GB	209 GB	
1280 x 720p (10 bits) 552.5		30	4:2:2	10	4.2 GB	251 GB	
1280 x 720p (10 bits) 921.8		50	4:2:2	10	7.0 GB	418 GB	
1280 x 720p (10 bits) 1.10 Gbps		60	4:2:2	10	8.4 GB	501 GB	
1920 x 1080i (8 bits) 829		25	4:2:2	8	5.8 GB	348 GB	
1920 x 1080i (8 bits) 994.3		30	4:2:2	8	7.0 GB	417 GB	
1920 x 1080p (8 bits) 795.6		24	4:2:2	8	5.6 GB	334 GB	
1920 x 1080p (8 bits) 829		25	4:2:2	8	5.8 GB	348 GB	
1920 x 1080p (8 bits) 994.3		30	4:2:2	8	7.0 GB	417 GB	
1920 x 1080p (8 bits) 1.66 Gbps		50	4:2:2	8	11.6 GB	696 GB	
1920 x 1080p (8 bits) 1.99 Gbps		60	4:2:2	8	13.9 GB	834 GB	
1920 x 1080i (10 bits) 1.03 Gbps		25	4:2:2	10	7.7 GB	464 GB	
1920 x 1080i (10 bits) 1.24 Gbps		30	4:2:2	10	9.3 GB	559 GB	

	Video Nominal Data Rate (Mbps)	Com-pression Ratio[2]	Frame Rate	Chroma Sampling	Bits[3]	Estimated STORAGE per minute[4]	Estimated STORAGE per Hour[4]	Notes

HIGH DEFINITION—UNCOMPRESSED (continued)

	Video Nominal Data Rate (Mbps)	Com-pression Ratio[2]	Frame Rate	Chroma Sampling	Bits[3]	Estimated STORAGE per minute[4]	Estimated STORAGE per Hour[4]	Notes
1920 x 1080p (10 bits)	993		24	4:2:2	10	7.4 GB	446 GB	
1920 x 1080p (10 bits)	1.03 Gbps		25	4:2:2	10	7.7 GB	464 GB	
1920 x 1080p (10 bits)	1.24 Gbps		30	4:2:2	10	9.3 GB	559 GB	
1920 x 1080p (10 bits)	2.07 Gbps		50	4:2:2	10	15.5 GB	928 GB	
1920 x 1080p (10 bits)	2.48 Gbps		60	4:2:2	10	18.6 GB	1.1 TB	
1280 x 720p	1.69 Gbps		60	RGB 4:4:4	10	12.4 GB	742 GB	
1920 x 1080i/p	1.58 Gbps		25	RGB 4:4:4	10	11.6 GB	695 GB	
1920 x 1080i/p	1.90 Gbps		30	RGB 4:4:4	10	14 GB	834 GB	

DIGITAL CINEMATOGRAPHY

	Video Nominal Data Rate (Mbps)	Com-pression Ratio[2]	Frame Rate	Chroma Sampling	Bits[3]	Estimated STORAGE per minute[4]	Estimated STORAGE per Hour[4]	Notes
CineForm RAW—1920 x 1080	96	5:1	24	RAW	10	720 MB	44 GB	In-camera wavelet
REDCODE (RED One)	267	9:1	24	RAW	12	2 GB	120 GB	Example of REDCODE 36 "R3D" files for 4K capture. REDCODE 28 (12:1 compression) and REDCODE 42 (8:1) also available.
REDCODE (Scarlet)	374	6:1	24	RAW	12	2.8 GB	168 GB	REDCODE "R3D" files for 4K capture
REDCODE (Epic)	1.21 Gbps	3:1 or 18:1	24	RAW	12	9.1 GB	546 GB	Example of REDCODE "R3D" files for full-frame 5k capture.
ARRIRAW— 2880 x 2160, 2880 x 1620	1.25 Gbps	uncomp.	24	RAW	12	9.4 GB	564 GB	ARRI Alexa, Log recording
RAW 4K— 4096 × 2160	19 Gbps	3.1	24	RAW	16	16.7 GB	1 TB	Sony F65, Linear recording. Data rates per Sony.
HDCAM SR— 1920 x 1080p	880	2:1	24	RGB 4:4:4	10	6.6 GB	396 GB	
1920 x 1080p	1.49 Gbps	uncomp.	24	RGB 4:4:4	10	11.1 GB	667 GB	Dual-link HD-SDI
2K (2048 x 1556)[12]	2.29 Gbps	uncomp.	24	RGB	10	17.3 GB	1.04 TB	
4K (4096 x 3112)[12]	9.18 Gbps	uncomp.	24	RGB	10	70.3 GB	4.22 TB	

	Data Rate (Mbps)	Compression	Channels	Bits[3]	Estimated STORAGE per minute[4]	Estimated STORAGE per Hour[4]	Notes
			AUDIO FOR DIGITAL VIDEO				
32 kHz—PCM	0.768	uncomp.	2 channels	12	5.8 MB	0.35 GB	DV only
44.1 kHz—PCM	1.411	uncomp.	2 channels	16	10.5 MB	0.63 GB	
44.1 kHz—PCM	2.117	uncomp.	2 channels	24	15.9 MB	0.95 GB	
48 kHz—PCM	1.536	uncomp.	2 channels	16	11.5 MB	.69 GB	
48 kHz—PCM	2.304	uncomp.	2 channels	24	17.3 MB	1.04 GB	
48 kHz—PCM	3.072	uncomp.	2 channels	32	23 MB	1.38 GB	
48 kHz—MPEG1	0.0384	audio layer II	2 channels	16	2.9 MB	172.8 MB	HDV only
96 kHz—PCM	18.432	uncomp.	8 channels	24	138.2 MB	8.3 GB	

1. Component formats only. Legacy composite digital formats such as D-2 and D-3 not listed.

2. Digital video compression encompasses a variety of competing techniques, from discrete cosine transform to wavelet compression, constant bit rate to variable, intraframe to interframe. Rarely is compression a simple number or constant ratio, even though we refer to it this way. Each set of techniques may yield a different quality even at the same nominal compression ratio. Compression ratios are therefore unreliable indicators of final picture quality.

3. Per color in the case of digital video.

4. Where possible, includes overheads for video stream (header and container format) as well as two to four tracks of 16-bit audio, error detection/correction, timecode, and track information. To avoid fractions, estimates are rounded up to the nearest GB. Actual storage varies depending on size and formatting of hard drives or solid-state media. Always keep 25–30 percent of disk capacity free as headroom to accommodate disk data management and variations in disk speeds.

5. 3.8 Mbps is average video data rate for DVDs. Compression of standard definition video for DVDs ranges from heavy MPEG-2 compression of 2 Mbps to high-quality compression of 6 Mbps. Maximum DVD data rate is about 10 Mbps.

6. 525-line, 29.97 fps digital formats for NTSC countries and 625-line, 25 fps formats for PAL countries share virtually identical data rates. The former has a higher frame rate with fewer lines, while the latter has a lower frame rate with more lines. Listing a format as "25, 30" fps in this chart does not imply that all such camcorders and VTRs record and play both standards. Some can, but most are restricted for use in their respective markets.

7. Formats with "D" names like D-1, D-5, D-9, etc. are SMPTE standards.

8. Where a single chroma sampling ratio is listed, it applies equally to both NTSC-derived and PAL-derived digital formats.

9. These are well-known format rates for Rec. 601 that include audio and timecode. The 10-bit data rate of 270 Mbps is the basis of the SMPTE 259M standard that defines the common Serial Digital Interface (SDI). Rec. 601's video bitrates per se are slightly smaller.

10. Nominal baseline bitrate. Blu-ray can achieve a 54 Mbps (1.5x) transfer rate. Forthcoming application of compression technologies will result in a range of lesser but more practical bitrates to extend programming length.

11. HDCAM MPEG-2 compression is 4.1:1. However, prior to MPEG-2 compression, HDCAM horizontally filters and downsamples an original 1920 x 1080 image to 1440 x 1080. This pre-filtering combined with the 4.1:1 MPEG-2 compression creates a cumulative compression of 7.1:1, which is how HDCAM is often described.

12. Aspect ratio is 4:3 like full-aperture 35mm, not widescreen like 16:9 or 1.85. CMOS can omit top and bottom of sensor to output 16:9, dropping data rate by 25 percent.

APPENDIX C

DEPTH OF FIELD TABLES

See Focusing the Image, p. 153, and Depth of Field Charts, p. 162, before using these tables. For faster reference, you may want to get a depth of field app for a smartphone, such as DOFMaster or pCAM, or get a full set of charts, such as the ones in the American Cinematographer Manual.

This appendix contains two tables to give you an idea of depth of field (one in feet and inches, the other in meters).

To use these tables: (1) Find the lens aperture you are using (expressed as a T-stop) in the Lens Aperture column at upper left. Read across that row to the right until you locate the lens focal length at which you are shooting. (2) Find the point at which the lens is focused in the Point of Focus column on the left side of the chart. Read across that row to the right until you come to the column you located in (1). These figures indicate the near and far limits of the depth of field as measured from the focal plane. For example, at T8, a 100mm fixed focal length lens focused at 10 feet provides a depth of field from 9-0 to 11-4 (that is, 9 feet to 11 feet 4 inches).

This method is used for a ⅟₅₀₀-inch circle of confusion (CoC). For ⅟₁₀₀₀-inch CoC, read depth of field two columns to the right. For ⅟₂₀₀₀-inch, read four columns to the right.

Whether you use charts or an app to calculate depth of field, the starting point is deciding what size circle of confusion you're working with. As discussed in Chapter 4, this is a complex topic involving many factors, including the size and resolution of the recording format and the intended display technology.

The American Cinematographer Manual recommends a 0.025mm (0.001 inch) CoC for 35mm motion picture film and about half of that—0.015mm (0.0006 inch)—for 16mm film.

For DSLRs, based on a 0.030mm (0.0012 inch) CoC for a full-frame DSLR like the Canon 5D Mark II, the CoC for other sensor sizes can be calculated as follows: 0.020mm (0.0008 inch) for a Super 35 sensor, 0.019mm (.0007 inch) for APS-C, and 0.015mm (0.0006 inch) for Four Thirds. You may note that 16mm film and the Four Thirds digital sensor share the same CoC even though the sensor is much bigger (see Fig. 2-7). This is in part because the DSLR CoC is based on viewing still images, where resolution can be precisely detected by the eye, whereas viewing 16mm involves film grain and unsteady projection, which reduce resolution and the eye's ability to discern sharp focus. Similarly, even though a ⅔-inch SD camcorder and a ⅔-inch HD camcorder have the same size sensor, the CoC for the HD image (where fine detail can readily be seen) is considerably smaller than the CoC for the SD image.

So always keep in mind that depth of field is not an absolute, and charts and apps only provide an approximation.

Depth of field is a geometrical calculation, and the *f*-stop, a geometrical measurement, should be used for depth of field estimations. These charts were calculated with *f*-stops but are expressed in terms of T-stops, allowing one-third stop for the difference. If your lens is not marked in T-stops, using the *f*-stop will give a slightly stingy figure for depth of field.

Depth of Field Tables: Feet and Inches
Nearest and Furthest Point of Acceptable Focus

For 1/500 in. circle of confusion use tables as printed.
For 1/1000 in. circle of confusion transpose focal lengths two columns to right.

Lens Aperture (T-stop)	Lens Focal Lengths in Relation to Lens Aperture (mm)										
T2				21	25	30	35	42	50	60	70
2.8			21	25	30	35	42	50	60	70	84
4		21	25	30	35	42	50	60	70	84	100
5.6	21	25	30	35	42	50	60	70	84	100	120
8	25	30	35	42	50	60	70	84	100	120	140
11	30	35	42	50	60	70	84	100	120	140	170
16	35	42	50	60	70	84	100	120	140	170	200
22	42	50	60	70	84	100	120	140	170	200	240

Fixed Focal Length Lenses and Most 16mm Type Zoom Lenses

Point of Focus Measured from Focal Plane (Feet)												
3-0	Near	1-11½	2-2½	2-4¾	2-6½	2-8	2-9	2-9¾	2-10½	2-11	2-11¼	2-11½
	Far	6-7¼	4-8¼	3-11¾	3-7¾	3-5½	3-3½	3-2½	3-1¾	3-1¼	3-0¼	3-0½
3-6	N	2-2½	2-5¼	2-8¼	2-10¾	3-0½	3-2	3-3	3-3¾	3-4½	3-5	3-5¼
	F	9-3¼	6-0¾	5-0¾	4-5¼	4-1¾	3-11	3-9½	3-8½	3-7½	3-7	3-6¾
4-0	N	2-4	2-8½	2-11¾	3-2¾	3-4¾	3-6¾	3-8	3-9¼	3-10	3-10¾	3-11
	F	15-5	7-9¾	6-2½	5-3½	4-10½	4-6¾	4-4¾	4-3¼	4-2¼	4-1¼	4-1
4-6	N	2-6	2-11¼	3-2¼	3-6½	3-9	3-11¼	4-1	4-2½	4-3½	4-4½	4-4¾
	F	25-2	10-1	7-6¼	6-2¾	5-7¾	5-2¾	5-0	4-10	4-8¾	4-7¾	4-7¼
5-0	N	2-7½	3-1½	3-5¾	3-10	4-1	4-4	4-6	4-7¾	4-8¾	4-10	4-10½
	F	75-0	13-1	9-1	7-3	6-5½	5-11¼	5-7½	5-5¼	5-3½	5-2¼	5-1½
6-0	N	2-10½	3-5¾	3-11	4-4½	4-8¾	5-0½	5-3½	5-5¾	5-7½	5-9	5-9¾
	F	Inf	23-10	13-2	9-7¼	8-3	7-5	6-11½	6-7½	6-5¼	6-3½	6-2½
8-0	N	3-3	4-0½	4-8	5-4	5-10½	6-4½	6-9¼	7-1	7-4	7-6½	7-8
	F	Inf	Inf	30-2	16-2	12-8	10-9	9-10	9-2¼	8-9	8-6¼	8-4½
10-0	N	3-6¼	4-5¾	5-3	6-1¾	6-10¼	7-6¾	8-1½	8-7¼	9-0	9-3½	9-5¾
	F	Inf	Inf	Inf	27-6	18-7	14-9	13-0	11-11	11-4	10-10	10-7
15-0	N	3-11¾	5-3	6-4	7-8½	8-10¼	10-1	11-1½	12-0	12-11	13-5	13-10
	F	Inf	Inf	Inf	Inf	50-0	29-6	23-1	19-11	18-2	17-0	16-5
25-0	N	4-5	6-0¾	7-7	9-7¾	11-7	13-9	15-9	17-9	19-3	20-10	21-11
	F	Inf	Inf	Inf	Inf	Inf	Inf	61-0	42-7	36-9	31-4	29-3
50-0	N	4-10	6-10	8-11	11-11	15-0	19-0	23-0	27-4	32-0	35-7	38-9
	F	Inf	Inf	Inf	Inf	Inf	Inf	Inf	Inf	200-0	100-0	70-0
Inf	N	5-4	7-11	10-9	15-7	21-3	30-3	42-3	60-3	80-0	120-0	170-0

35mm Type Zoom Lenses

5-0	N	3-2	3-7	3-10	4-1½	4-3¾	4-6	4-7½	4-8¾	4-9½	4-10¼	4-10¾
	F	19-9	9-9	7-8	6-6¼	6-0¼	5-7¾	5-5½	5-5¾	5-2¾	5-1¾	5-1¼
6-0	N	3-6	4-0	4-4	4-9	5-0	5-3	5-5¼	5-7	5-8¼	5-9½	5-10
	F	177-0	16-2	10-11	8-7	7-8	7-0½	6-8¾	6-5¾	6-4	6-2¾	6-2
8-0	N	3-11	4-7	5-2	5-9	6-2	6-8	7-0	7-3	7-5¼	7-7¼	7-8½
	F	Inf	94-0	23-0	14-1	11-8	10-2	9-10	8-11½	8-8	8-5½	8-4
10-0	N	4-3	5-1	5-9	6-7	7-3	7-11	8-4	8-10	9-1¼	9-4½	9-6¼
	F	Inf	Inf	70-0	23-1	16-11	13-10	12-7	11-8	11-1	10-9	10-6
15-0	N	4-9	5-11	6-11	8-3	9-4	10-7	11-5	12-4	13-0	13-6	13-11
	F	Inf	Inf	Inf	154-0	43-3	26-11	22-2	19-4	17-10	16-10	16-4
20-0	N	5-1	6-5	7-8	9-5	10-11	12-8	14-0	15-5	16-5	17-5	18-0
	F	Inf	Inf	Inf	Inf	195-0	51-0	35-11	28-10	25-8	23-6	22-6
50-0	N	5-8	7-7	9-7	12-6	15-8	19-10	23-6	28-3	31-2	36-0	38-10
	F	Inf	Inf	Inf	Inf	Inf	Inf	Inf	260-0	120-0	82-6	70-3
Inf	N	6-2	8-8	11-5	16-4	22-0	31-9	43-0	61-7	85-6	125-0	170-0

Depth of Field Tables: Metric
Nearest and Furthest Point of Acceptable Focus

Lens Aperture (T-stop)
Lens Focal Lengths in Relation to Lens Aperture (mm)

For 0.05mm circle of confusion use tables as printed.
For 0.025mm circle of confusion transpose focal lengths two columns to right.

T-stop											
T2				21	25	30	35	42	50	60	70
2.8			21	25	30	35	42	50	60	70	84
4		21	25	30	35	42	50	60	70	84	100
5.6	21	25	30	35	42	50	60	70	84	100	120
8	25	30	35	42	50	60	70	84	100	120	140
11	30	35	42	50	60	70	84	100	120	140	170
16	35	42	50	60	70	84	100	120	140	170	200
22	42	50	60	70	84	100	120	140	170	200	241

Point of Focus Measured from Focal Plane (Feet)

Fixed Focal Length Lenses and Most 16mm Type Zoom Lenses

Focus	N/F											
1-0	Near	0-6	0-72	0-78	0-84	0-88	0-91	0-93	0-95	0-96	0-97	0-98
	Far	2-5	1-65	1-40	1-25	1-17	1-11	1-08	1-05	1-04	1-03	1-02
1-2	N	0-72	0-82	0-89	0-97	1-02	1-07	1-10	1-13	1-15	1-17	1-18
	F	4-41	2-30	1-84	1-58	1-45	1-37	1-31	1-28	1-26	1-24	1-23
1-3	N	0-75	0-86	0-95	1-03	1-09	1-15	1-19	1-22	1-25	1-26	1-27
	F	5-37	2-72	2-1	1-76	1-61	1-5	1-44	1-39	1-36	1-34	1-33
1-5	N	0-82	0-94	1-05	1-15	1-23	1-3	1-35	1-39	1-42	1-44	1-46
	F	18-7	3-82	2-69	2-16	1-93	1-78	1-69	1-63	1-59	1-56	1-54
1-7	N	0-87	1-02	1-14	1-27	1-36	1-45	1-51	1-56	1-59	1-63	1-65
	F	Inf	5-54	3-43	2-60	2-27	2-07	1-95	1-86	1-83	1-77	1-75
2-0	N	0-94	1-11	1-26	1-42	1-54	1-66	1-74	1-81	1-8	1-91	1-93
	F	Inf	11-2	4-98	3-4	2-86	2-53	2-35	2-23	2-15	2-10	2-07
2-5	N	1-03	1-25	1-44	1-66	1-82	1-98	2-11	2-21	2-29	2-35	2-39
	F	Inf	Inf	10-2	5-20	4-02	3-40	3-08	2-88	2-75	2-67	2-62
3-0	N	1-07	1-36	1-59	1-86	2-07	2-28	2-24	2-59	2-71	2-79	2-85
	F	Inf	Inf	33-4	8-03	5-51	4-41	3-89	3-57	3-37	3-25	3-17
5-0	N	1-24	1-65	2-0	2-45	2-84	3-26	3-62	3-94	4-22	4-43	4-58
	F	Inf	Inf	Inf	Inf	21-6	10-8	8-12	6-85	6-15	5-75	5-51
8-0	N	1-36	1-87	2-35	3-0	3-6	4-3	4-95	5-59	6-15	6-15	6-95
	F	Inf	Inf	Inf	Inf	Inf	60-0	21-0	14-1	11-5	10-1	9-42
17-0	N	1-147	2-1	2-71	3-62	4-54	5-73	6-95	8-28	9-56	10-7	11-7
	F	Inf	Inf	Inf	Inf	Inf	Inf	Inf	82-0	35-1	25-0	21-0
Inf	N	1-62	2-42	3-29	4-74	6-48	9-22	12-9	18-4	26-0	37-1	52-0

35mm Type Zoom Lenses

Focus	N/F											
1-5	N	0-97	1-08	1-16	1-24	1-3	1-35	1-39	1-42	1-44	1-46	1-47
	F	5-55	2-86	2-27	1-95	1-8	1-69	1-63	1-59	1-56	1-54	1-53
1-7	N	1-03	1-16	1-26	1-36	1-44	1-51	1-55	1-6	1-62	1-64	1-66
	F	13-0	3-94	2-86	2-35	2-11	1-96	1-88	1-82	1-79	1-76	1-74
2-0	N	1-1	1-27	1-39	1-53	1-63	1-73	1-79	1-85	1-89	1-92	1-94
	F	Inf	6-87	4-05	3-04	2-64	2-4	2-27	2-18	2-13	2-09	2-06
3-0	N	1-28	1-53	1-74	1-98	2-18	2-38	2-52	2-64	2-73	2-81	2-86
	F	Inf	Inf	18-9	6-97	5-03	4-12	3-75	3-48	3-33	3-22	3-16
5-0	N	1-47	1-84	2-18	2-61	2-99	3-41	3-72	4-03	4-26	4-46	4-59
	F	Inf	Inf	Inf	Inf	18-3	9-79	7-78	6-64	6-07	5-69	5-49
10-0	N	1-66	2-17	2-68	3-4	4-14	5-05	5-79	6-64	7-32	7-99	8-44
	F	Inf	Inf	Inf	Inf	Inf	Inf	40-4	20-8	15-9	13-4	12-29
20-0	N	1-77	2-38	3-03	4-02	5-12	6-64	8-03	9-8	11-4	13-2	14-51
	F	Inf	Inf	Inf	Inf	Inf	Inf	Inf	Inf	85-2	41-64	32-33
Inf	N	1-89	2-63	3-49	4-99	6-7	9-69	13-1	18-8	26-0	38-0	52-0

HYPERFOCAL DISTANCE TABLE

I f the lens is focused at the hyperfocal distance, everything from half that distance to infinity should be in acceptably good focus. See Chapter 4 for limitations on the use of hyperfocal distance and depth of field tables.

To use this table: (1) Find the lens aperture you are using (expressed as an *f*-stop) in the column at left. Read across that row to the right until you locate the lens focal length at which you are filming. This is the column in which the hyperfocal distance is indicated. (2) Find the circle of confusion you are using on the lower left side of the chart. Read across that row to the right until you come to the column you located in (1). This is the hyperfocal distance for the focal length/aperture combination you are using.

See Appendix C for suggestions on choosing a circle of confusion.

Hyperfocal Distance

Lens Focal Lengths (mm)

f-stop														
1					9	11	12.5	15	17.5	21	25	30	35	42
1.4				9	11	12.5	15	17.5	21	25	30	35	42	50
2			9	11	12.5	15	17.5	21	25	30	35	42	50	60
2.8		9	11	12.5	15	17.5	21	25	30	35	42	50	60	70
4	9	11	12.5	15	17.5	21	25	30	35	42	50	60	70	84
5.6	11	12.5	15	17.5	21	25	30	35	42	50	60	70	84	100
8	12.5	15	17.5	21	25	30	35	42	50	60	70	84	100	120
11	15	17.5	21	25	30	35	42	50	60	70	84	100	120	140
16	17.5	21	25	30	35	42	50	60	70	84	100	120	140	170
22	21	25	30	35	42	50	60	70	84	100	120	140	170	200

Circles of Confusion

Hyperfocal Distances

Circle of Confusion														
0.001in	2ft 6½in	3ft 7in	5ft 3in	7ft 3in	10ft 6in	14ft 9in	20ft 6in	29ft 6in	41ft	59ft	82ft	118ft	164ft	236ft
0.002in	1ft 3in	1ft 9½in	2ft 7in	3ft 7½in	5ft 3in	7ft 4in	10ft 6in	14ft 9in	20ft 6in	29ft 6in	41ft	59ft	82ft	118ft
0.025mm	0.8m	1.1m	1.6m	2.2m	3.2m	4.5m	6.3m	9m	12.5m	18m	25m	36m	50m	72m
0.05mm	0.4m	0.56m	0.8m	1.1m	1.6m	2.2m	3.2m	4.5m	6.3m	9m	12.5m	18m	25m	36m

ANGLE OF VIEW IN DIFFERENT FORMATS

This chart shows the horizontal angle of view (also called field of view) in different formats, as well as crop factors that help compare one format to another. To get a feel for the different sensor sizes, see Figure 2-7. To see the relationship between angle of view and sensor size, see Figures 4-6 and 4-7.

The first column in the table shows the focal length lens you'd need to get a shot with a 40-degree angle of view using cameras of different sensor sizes (all measured in 16:9 mode). For example, with a full-frame 35mm DSLR still camera, a 40-degree horizontal angle of view can be captured with a 50mm lens. If we now look at, say, the Four Thirds sensor, we can see that we'd need a 24mm lens to get the same shot with the smaller-sensor camera.

The full-frame 35mm still format is sometimes used as a benchmark by manufacturers when describing lenses intended for other formats.[1] You can use the crop factor shown in the second column to find the equivalent focal length in another format. To use the above example of the Four Thirds sensor, we can see that if we multiply the 50mm lens on the full-frame camera times the 0.5x crop factor we get roughly 24mm.

Similarly, you can use the crop factors in the fourth column to translate lenses you're familiar with to their full-frame 35mm equivalent. Say you've been shooting with a camcorder with a ½-inch sensor and you like the angle of view you get with a 5mm lens. Multiply that by the 5.2x crop factor to find that you'd need a 26mm lens when shooting with a full-frame 35mm sensor camera.

Crop factors (also called focal length multipliers) are a handy way to remember how one format relates to another, and you can easily determine how to translate directly between any two formats. For example, when translating a Four Thirds sensor to a Super 35 sensor, we can divide the focal lengths in the first column (33mm/24mm) to get a multiplier of a little more than 1.3 (put the sensor you're starting with in the denominator). So a 100mm lens on a camera with a Four Thirds sensor will have roughly the same field of view as a 130mm lens on a camera with a

---

1. This is for convenience and assumes that consumers have experience shooting stills in the full-frame 35mm format, which is a different aspect ratio and size from all conventional filmmaking formats. These days, the Super 35 digital format would make a better benchmark when comparing lenses for filmmaking. As described above, you can easily make this comparison yourself.

Super 35 sensor (100 x 1.3 = 130). If you start with the Super 35 sensor, the crop factor is 0.7x (24mm/33mm). So a 100mm lens on a Super 35 camera would have roughly the angle of view of a 70mm lens on the Four Thirds sensor.

For an excellent online tool with images showing the angle of view with different lenses and different formats, see the Field of View Comparator at www.abelcine. com. Also check out the MatchLens iPhone app, which helps you find equivalent lenses on specific cameras.

ANGLE OF VIEW IN DIFFERENT FORMATS

Sensor	Focal length needed to shoot 40-degree angle of view	Crop factor from full-frame 35mm DSLR to this format	Crop factor from this format to full-frame 35mm DSLR	Cameras (as of this writing)
Full-frame 35mm still camera (SLR & DSLR)	50mm	1.0x	1.0x	Canon 5D Mark II and EOS-1D X; Nikon D3s
RED Mysterium-X (16:9, 5K)	36mm	0.7x	1.4x	RED Epic
Super 35 (motion picture film)	34.5mm	0.7x	1.4x	Panavision, ARRI, Aaton film cameras
Super 35 (digital)	33mm	0.7x	1.5x	Panavision Genesis; ARRI D-21 and Alexa; Aaton Delta-Penelope; P+S Technik X35; Phantom Gold; Sony F3, F35, FS100, and FS700; Canon C300 and C500
APS-C	32mm	0.6x	1.5x	Canon 7D and 60D; Nikon D3100; Sony NEX-VG10E
RED Mysterium-X (16:9, 4K)	30.8mm	0.6x	1.6x	RED One
Four Thirds	24mm	0.5x	2.1x	Panasonic AG-AF100 and Lumix GH2
Super 16 film (16:9)	16.6mm	0.3x	3x	ARRI, Aaton, Bolex film cameras
Regular 16mm film (1.33:1)	13mm	0.3x	3.8x	ARRI, Aaton, Bolex film cameras
⅔ inch (16:9)	13.3mm	0.3x	3.8x	Silicon Imaging SI-2K; Panasonic VariCam series; Sony HDCAM and F23; most traditional newsgathering camcorders
½ inch (16:9)	9.7mm	0.2x	5.2x	Sony EX1 and EX3
⅓ inch (16:9)	7.3mm	0.1x	6.9x	Sony Z1, Z5, Z7, and NX5; Panasonic HPX170, HPX250, and HMC150; Canon XH A1, XA10, and XF series; JVC shoulder-mount camcorders (HD100 to GY-HM700)
¼ inch (16:9)	4.8mm	0.1x	10.3x	Sony V1; Panasonic HMC40; JVC GY-HM100

BIBLIOGRAPHY

Production, Business and Legal

Aufderheide, Patricia, and Peter Jaszi. *Reclaiming Fair Use*. Chicago: University of Chicago Press, 2011. Excellent resource on fair use history and current practices for filmmakers.

Donaldson, Michael C. *Clearance and Copyright*, 3rd ed. Beverly Hills: Silman-James Press, 2008. As the cover says: everything the independent filmmaker needs to know. Excellent resource, particularly for feature films.

Goodell, Gregory. *Independent Feature Film Production*. New York: St. Martin's Press, 1998. Manual on independent feature film production. Good on unions, casting agencies, budgeting, and distribution.

Honthaner, Eve Light. *The Complete Film Production Handbook*, 4th ed. Burlington, MA: Focal Press, 2010. Comprehensive guide to production management, including setting up a production office, hiring talent and crews, and dealing with unions and releases. Includes specific forms needed for all the business aspects of shooting a feature or TV show.

Players Directory (www.playersdirectory.com). Photographs of actors with agent listings. Regularly updated.

Ryan, Maureen. *Producer to Producer*. Studio City, CA: Michael Wiese Productions, 2010. Excellent, detailed, practical guide for producers of low-budget indie films.

Simens, Dov S-S. *From Reel to Deal: Everything You Need to Create a Successful Independent Film*. New York: Warner Books, 2003. Practical, useful, down-to-earth advice about producing your first feature.

Simon, Deke. *Film and Video Budgets*, 5th ed. Studio City, CA: Michael Wiese Productions, 2010. Sample budgets with detailed explanations of line items.

Direction and Writing

Bernard, Sheila Curran. *Documentary Storytelling:Creative Nonfiction on Screen*, 3rd ed. Burlington, MA: Focal Press, 2010. Insights on story, structure, research, and narration, including interviews with filmmakers.

Field, Syd. *Screenplay: The Foundations of Screenwriting*. New York: Dell Publishing, 2005. Oft-cited guide to screenwriting.

Goldman, William. *Adventures in the Screen Trade*. New York: Warner Books, 1983. Wry observations of a master screenwriter.

Katz, Steven D. *Cinematic Motion*, 2nd ed. Studio City, CA: Michael Wiese Productions, 2004. Guide to blocking the camera and actors in different types of scenes.

———. *Film Directing Shot by Shot: Visualizing from Concept to Screen*. Studio City, CA: Michael Wiese Productions, 1991. Guide to production design, composition, storyboarding, and other aspects of planning the visual treatment.

Kenworthy, Christopher. *Master Shots*. Studio City, CA: Michael Wiese Productions, 2009. Guide to blocking the camera and actors in different types of scenes.

McKee, Robert. *Story: Substance, Structure, Style, and the Principles of Screenwriting*. New York: HarperCollins, 1997. A distillation of McKee's popular screenwriting seminars, with useful insights on creating story, characters, and dialogue.

Proferes, Nicholas. *Film Directing Fundamentals: See Your Film Before Shooting*, 3rd ed. Burlington, MA: Focal Press, 2008. Analyzing scripts and films for keys to direction.

Trottier, David. *The Screenwriter's Bible: A Complete Guide to Writing, Formatting, and Selling Your Script*. Los Angeles: Silman-James Press, 2010. Writing the script and getting it out there.

Weston, Judith. *Directing Actors: Creating Memorable Performances for Film and Television*. Studio City, CA: Michael Wiese Productions, 1999. Advice on working with actors.

Cameras, Lenses, and Lighting

American Cinematographer (www.theasc.com). A monthly magazine devoted to camera and lighting techniques. Although it has a bias toward large-crew production, there are numerous articles on low-budget film and video.

Bergery, Benjamin. *Reflections: Twenty-one Cinematographers at Work*. Los Angeles: ASC Holding Company, 2002. Interviews, stills, and light setups.

Box, Harry C. *Set Lighting Technician's Handbook*. Burlington, MA: Focal Press, 2010. Thorough guide to professional lighting gear and techniques. A must for someone seeking employment as gaffer or lighting assistant.

Brown, Blain. *Cinematography: Theory and Practice*, 2nd ed. Burlington, MA: Focal Press, 2012. Wide ranging guide to shooting and lighting.

Burum, Stephen, ed. *American Cinematographer Manual*. Hollywood: American Society of Cinematographers Press, 2007. Camera threading diagrams, 35mm formats, and many useful charts. A standard manual for professional cinematographers.

Hart, Douglas C. *The Camera Assistant: A Complete Professional Handbook*. Boston: Focal Press, 1997. Thorough guide to professional film camera equipment and the duties of a camera assistant. A must for people seeking crew work as an assistant.

Malkiewicz, Kris. *Film Lighting*. New York: Prentice Hall Press, 1986. Examines lighting technique through direct instruction and interviews with cinematographers. A good resource for people with basic knowledge looking to improve their technique.

Malkiewicz, Kris, and M. David Mullen. *Cinematography: The Classic Guide to Filmmaking*, 3rd ed. New York: Fireside, 2005. Covers most technical aspects of motion picture production. Well written and illustrated. Includes an excellent section on cutting your own negative.

Millerson, Gerald, and Jim Owens. *Television Production*, 14th ed. Burlington, MA: Focal Press, 2009. Comprehensive guide to television production techniques. Particularly useful for studio and multicamera productions.

Samuelson, David W. *Hands-On Manual for Cinematographers*, 3rd ed. Burlington, MA: Focal

Press, 2011. Excellent resource for camera threading, lenses, special effects, and other aspects. Many useful charts and formulas for optical and film calculations.

Sound

Huber, David Miles, and Robert Runstein. *Modern Recording Techniques*, 7th ed. Burlington, MA: Focal Press, 2009. Thorough. Specializes in DAWs and concerns of studio music recording.

Rose, Jay. *Producing Great Sound for Digital Video*. San Francisco: CMP Books, 2003. For people who want to really understand digital audio and the recording arts. Lots of practical advice on microphones, camera settings, post tricks, and meters.

Woodhall, Woody. *Audio Production and Postproduction*. Sudbury, MA: Jones & Bartlett Learning, 2011. Recording, sound editing, sound design, and mixing.

Postproduction and Editing

Association of Cinema and Video Laboratories. *Handbook: Recommended Procedures for Motion Picture and Video Laboratory Services*. Bethesda: ACVL (www.acvl.org), 2011. Leader preparation and lab services.

Case, Dominic. *Film Technology in Post Production*. Oxford: Focal Press, 2001. Comprehensive guide to film and laboratory services.

Harrington, Richard. *Photoshop for Video*. Burlington, MA: Focal Press, 2007. Tips and tricks for preparing graphics for video.

Hirschfeld, Gerald. *Image Control: Motion Picture and Video Camera Filters and Lab Techniques*. Los Angeles: ASC Press, 2005. Thoroughly illustrated manual showing the effects of different filters, exposures, and processing on the image. Written by an experienced cinematographer.

Hollyn, Norman. *The Film Editing Room Handbook*, 4th ed. Berkeley: Peachpit Press, 2010. A guide to the skills needed to be a professional assistant editor. Particularly useful for those seeking employment in feature films.

Kauffmann, Sam. *Avid Editing: A Guide for Beginning and Intermediate Users*, 4th ed. Burlington, MA: Focal Press, 2009. An easy-to-read textbook about Avid editing that includes information on HD and script integration.

Murch, Walter. *In the Blink of an Eye*, 2nd rev. ed. Beverly Hills: Silman-James Press, 2001. Insightful views on editing, from the editor of *Apocalypse Now* and *The Unbearable Lightness of Being*.

Oldham, Gabriella. *First Cut: Conversations with Film Editors*. Los Angeles: University of California Press, 1995.

Poynton, Charles. *Digital Video and HD: Algorithms and Interfaces*, 2nd ed. Burlington, MA: Elsevier, 2012. Very technical and thorough engineering guide to digital video. Authoritative resource.

Van Hurkman, Alexis. *Color Correction Handbook: Professional Techniques for Video and Cinema*. Berkeley: Peachpit Press, 2011. In-depth guide for editors and colorists.

WEBSITES

General

American Film Institute. www.afi.com. Wide-ranging resource.

Foundation Center. www.foundationcenter.org. Database of funders and grants.

Independent Feature Project. www.ifp.org. Organization for filmmakers, festival programmers, and distributors. Hosts annual market in New York.

International Documentary Association. www.documentary.org. Organization for documentary makers. Lists resources and screening programs and publishes *Documentary* magazine.

Motion Picture, TV and Theatre Directory. www.mpe.net. Useful lists by category of suppliers of production and postproduction services and equipment.

Industry News and Magazines

Creative Planet Network. www.creativeplanetnetwork.com. Articles and reviews of the latest gear and techniques. Includes many magazines and sites including Digital Content Producer, DV magazine, and Millimeter.

Deadline Hollywood. www.deadline.com. News on film and TV deals and developments.

Filmmaker magazine. www.filmmakermagazine.com. Resource on indie filmmaking.

Indiewire. www.indiewire.com. News on independent filmmakers, festivals, and releases.

National Alliance for Media Arts and Culture. www.namac.org. Online support for independent media artists.

TV Technology. www.tvtechnology.com. New technology and practices for the broadcast industry.

Employment and Professional Directories

Craigslist. www.craigslist.org. Listing of freelance and full-time work by region.

Crew Net Entertainment Jobs. www.crew-net.com.

KFTV (www.kftv.com) and Mandy.com (www.mandy.com) are both databases of film and television producers, technicians, and facilities around the world, with listings of job openings.

Film and Festival Databases

Filmfestivals.com. www.filmfestivals.com. Listings and news of festivals worldwide.

Internet Movie Database (IMDb.com). www.imdb.com. Comprehensive listing of films and credits.

Rotten Tomatoes. www.rottentomatoes.com. Collects reviews from many sources for hundreds of films. Filmmakers check for their "Tomatometer" rating.

Withoutabox. www.withoutabox.com. Comprehensive listing of festivals, with convenient online submission tool and ability to post images and trailers.

Technical and Other

Cambridge in Colour. www.cambridgeincolour.com. Great tutorials and illustrations of photographic and digital principles. Geared toward still photography, but many articles apply to video as well.

Creative COW. www.creativecow.net. Hosted forums and articles on a wide range of cameras, editing systems, and software. A fabulous resource and place to find solutions and post questions.

DCinema Today. www.dcinematoday.com. Info and news about digital cinema developments.

Digital Cinema Initiatives. www.dcimovies.com. Specifications for making DCPs.

The Digital Video Information Network. www.dvinfo.net. Technical and creative resource, with a forum for posting questions and getting answers.

DMN Forums. www.dmnforums.com. Another technical resource with forums for specific advice.

Ken Stone's Final Cut Pro. www.kenstone.net. Collected articles and how-tos on various topics, including Final Cut Pro.

Media Lawyer. www.medialawyer.com. Legal resource, with information on entertainment, multimedia, and property law and links to legal providers.

No Film School. www.nofilmschool.com. Updates on new equipment and techniques.

StudioDaily. www.studiodaily.com. Technical reviews, articles, case studies, industry news.

Manufacturers and Products

AbelCine. www.abelcine.com. Film and video cameras. Sales, rental, service. Website has useful tools and a great blog about new gear and techniques.

Adobe. www.adobe.com. Software and products, including Premiere Pro and After Effects.

Apple. www.apple.com. Software and products, including Final Cut Pro.

Avid Technology. www.avid.com. Nonlinear editing systems and other digital products.

B & H Foto and Electronics. www.bhphotovideo.com. Just about any kind of equipment you need.

Canon. www.usa.canon.com. Professional and consumer camcorders and DSLRs.

Coffey Sound. www.coffeysound.com. Professional audio products and links to other audio sites.

Eastman Kodak. www.kodak.com/go/motion. Professional motion picture films and articles on their use.

Fletcher Camera and Lenses. www.fletch.com. Wide range of video and audio equipment, sales and rentals.

Fujifilm. www.fujifilmusa.com. Professional motion picture film, video, and digital.

JVC. http://pro.jvc.com. Professional video equipment.

Panasonic. www.panasonic.com/business/provideo/. Professional video equipment.

Sony. http://pro.sony.com. Professional video and audio equipment.

iPhone Apps

The following are a few useful apps for the iPhone and iPad. Some may also be available for Android.

AJA DataCalc and KataData. Calculate how much memory you'll need to store any format, or the recording time you'll get with the storage you have.

Artemis Director's Viewfinder. See Fig. 9-28.

doddle Premium. Production resources and personnel guide. Allows you to create online call sheets for the entire crew with directions, weather, etc.

DOFMaster and pCAM. Calculates depth of field, field of view, split focus. PCAM also helps with exposure compensation, HMI safe shutter speeds, and a host of other information.

DSLR Camera Remote Professional Edition. Control the camera's functions and see camera's image remotely. Requires camera connection to Wi-Fi–enabled computer.

Helios Sun Position Calculator. Determine the position of the sun at a particular location and date.

Hitchcock. Storyboarding app. Take a picture and add markings for camera moves. Record dialogue. Plays back previsualization like a slide show. Experiment with pacing and flow.

JumpStart LTC. Generates longitudinal timecode that can be used to jam slates, cameras, and audio gear.

MatchLens. You put in a lens/camera combination and it gives you the lens to use on another camera if you want to match the same framing.

MovieSlate. See Fig. 9-30.

Photo fx. Preview Tiffen filter effects by applying them over iPhone photos.

PocketLD. Calculator and reference on professional lighting gear.

Release Pro. Create an appearance, location, or materials release; take a picture; and get signature on your phone. PDF is emailed to production company.

setLighting. Info on professional lighting equipment.

Shot Lister and Pocket Call Sheet. Create shot lists and call sheets, update them as needed, and share with the crew.

theGripApp. Dolly and grip equipment and instructions for setup.

INDEX